EIGHTH EDITION

Teaching Secondary Mathematics

Techniques and Enrichment Units

Alfred S. Posamentier
The City College
The City University of New York

Beverly S. Smith
The City College
The City University of New York

Jay Stepelman

Allyn & Bacon

Boston New York San Francisco
Mexico City Montreal Toronto London Madrid Munich Paris
Hong Kong Singapore Tokyo Cape Town Sydney

Series Editor: *Kelly Villella Canton*
Editorial Assistant: *Annalea Manalili*
Marketing Manager: *Darcy Betts*
Production Supervisor: *Gregory Erb*
Production Management and Composition: *Progressive Publishing Alternatives*
Composition Buyer: *Linda Cox*
Manufacturing Buyer: *Megan Cochran*
Interior Design: *Progressive Publishing Alternatives*
Cover Designer: *Elena Sidorova*

For related titles and support materials, visit our online catalog at www.pearsonhighered.com

Between the time website information is gathered and then published, it is not unusual for some sites to have closed. Also, the transcription of URLs can result in typographical errors. The publisher would appreciate notification where these errors occur so that they may be corrected in subsequent editions.

Library of Congress Cataloging-in-Publication Data

Posamentier, Alfred S.
Teaching secondary mathematics : techniques and enrichment units / Alfred S. Posamentier, Jay Stepelman.—8th ed. / Beverly S. Smith.
p. cm.
Includes bibliographical references and index.
ISBN-13: 978-0-13-500003-8 (alk. paper)
ISBN-10: 0-13-500003-3 (alk. paper)
1. Mathematics—Study and teaching (Secondary) I. Smith, Beverly S. II. Stepelman, Jay. III. Title.

QA11.2.P67 2010
510.71'2—dc22 2008046443

Printed in the United States of America

10 9 8 7 6 5 4 3 2 1 BRG 13 12 11 10 09

Allyn & Bacon
is an imprint of

www.pearsonhighered.com

ISBN 10: 0-13-500003-3
ISBN 13: 978-0-13-500003-8

 About the Authors

Alfred S. Posamentier is Dean of the School of Education and Professor of Mathematics Education of The City College of the City University of New York. He is the author and co-author of more than 40 mathematics books for teachers, secondary school students, and the general readership. Dr. Posamentier is also a frequent commentator in newspapers on topics relating to education.

After completing his B.A. degree in mathematics at Hunter College of the City University of New York, he took a position as a teacher of mathematics at Theodore Roosevelt High School in the Bronx (New York), where he focused his attention on improving the students' problem-solving skills and at the same time enriching their instruction far beyond what the traditional textbooks offered. He also developed the school's first mathematics teams (both at the junior and senior level). He is currently involved in working with mathematics teachers, nationally and internationally, to help them maximize their effectiveness.

Immediately upon joining the faculty of The City College (after having received his masters' degree there), he began to develop in-service courses for secondary school mathematics teachers, including such special areas as recreational mathematics and problem solving in mathematics.

Dr. Posamentier received his Ph.D. from Fordham University (New York) in mathematics education and has since extended his reputation in mathematics education to Europe. He has been visiting professor at several European universities in Austria, England, Germany, and Poland, most recently at the University of Vienna (Fulbright Professor in 1990) and at the Technical University of Vienna.

In 1989 he was awarded an *Honorary Fellow* at the South Bank University (London, England). In recognition of his outstanding teaching, The City College Alumni Association named him *Educator of the Year* in 1994, and New York City had the day, May 1, 1994, named in his honor by the President of the New York City Council. In 1994, he was also awarded the *Grand Medal of Honor* from the Federal Republic of Austria. In 1999 upon approval of Parliament, the President of the Federal Republic of Austria awarded him the title of *University Professor of Austria,* in 2003 he was awarded the title of *Ehrenbürger* (Honorary Fellow) of the Vienna University of Technology, and he was recently (June 2004) awarded the *Austrian Cross of Honor for Arts and Science, First Class* from the President of the Federal Republic of Austria. In 2005 Dr. Posamentier was elected to Hall of Fame of the Hunter College Alumni Association, and in 2006 awarded the Townsend Harris Medal from the City College Alumni Association.

He has taken on numerous important leadership positions in mathematics education locally. He was a member of the New York State Education Commissioner's Blue Ribbon Panel on the Math A Regents Exams. He was on the Commissioner's Mathematics Standards Committee, which was charged with redefining the Standards for New York State, and he is on the New York City Chancellor's Math Advisory Panel.

Now in his 39th year on the faculty of The City College, he is still a leading commentator on educational issues and continues his long-time passion of seeking ways to make mathematics interesting to teachers (See *Math Wonders: To Inspire Teachers and Students,* ASCD 2003), students, and the general public—as can be seen from his latest four books, *Math Charmers: Tantalizing Tidbits for the Mind* (Prometheus Books, 2003), *π, A Biography of the World's Most Mysterious Number* (Prometheus Books, 2004), *The Fabulous Fibonacci Numbers* (Prometheus 2008), and *Mathematics: Amazements and Surprise,* (Prometheus, 2009).

Dr. Beverly Smith is an associate professor and the Program Head of Mathematics Education at The City College of New York. Believing that quality mathematics teachers must first be quality mathematicians, Dr. Smith mentors teacher candidates as they prepare to enter the teaching world. She also serves on the faculty of the Center for Teaching in America's Cities, and is a member of the Petrie Institute for Professional Development of Supervisors/Coaches of High School Mathematics Advisory Board, two organizations dedicated to improving the quality of mathematics education.

Throughout her career, Dr. Smith has been a tireless champion of equity in education. Her early college teaching experience involved working under a federally funded Special Services grant to create a developmental mathematics program designed to support at-risk inner-city students as they transitioned to college. While working toward her doctoral degree, she accepted a position at the State University of New York at Potsdam in the School of Education and worked with the Great Lake Collaborative to develop an integrated mathematics, science, and technology program for diverse K–12 schools from the Akwesasne Mohawk Nation all the way to the larger Syracuse City Schools.

It is Dr. Smith's philosophy that every student in a classroom should be inspired to the highest quality and level of mathematics education. She envisions the day when the mathematics classroom will represent a welcome destination for students. To that end, she encourages her teacher candidates to reflect on how to reach all students while planning their lessons by incorporating technology, mathematical tools, and rich tasks. Perhaps just as important, Dr. Smith impresses on her students the importance of mathematics literacy as an area of focus where students are taught to read, write, and think in mathematics.

Dr. Smith received an M.A. and her Doctorate in Mathematics Education from the Teachers College at Columbia University. In addition, she holds a B.S. in Mathematics Education from the State University of New York at Plattsburgh, and an M.S. in Computer Science from Union College. Dr. Smith has taught mathematics and science at the middle and secondary school levels in Watertown, New York. She has also taught computer science and mathematics as a faculty member at several northeastern colleges.

Now in her seventh year on the faculty at The City College of New York, she continues to focus her research on issues related to teacher development and issues of assessment in mathematics education.

Contents

Preface

Teaching Mathematics: An Art or a Science?

Is teaching mathematics an art or a science? If mathematics teaching is an art, then only highly talented people will be successful teachers of mathematics for an art is largely dependent on creativity and can be learned only to a limited extent. The rest must come intuitively. If mathematics teaching is a science, then anyone capable of learning to teach mathematics, regardless of talent, should be able to do it.

We consider the teaching of mathematics both an art and a science. One needs a certain amount of innate ability to teach successfully. With the rarest exceptions, this ability needs to be buttressed in varying amounts with sociological, psychological, philosophical, and commonsense principles. In this book, we provide both prospective and in-service teachers of mathematics a plethora of ideas covering all aspects of the profession—ideas that we believe will support the artist in everyone. In many cases we provide solid, experience-tested suggestions. We could have called this book Everything You Wanted to Know About Teaching Mathematics but Didn't Know Whom to Ask.

Techniques for Teaching Secondary Mathematics

The first part of the book discusses methods of teaching mathematics, considering all aspects and responsibilities of the job. We begin with an overview of the history of mathematics education so that the teacher of mathematics today understands how the teaching of mathematics has evolved. Next, we spend considerable time addressing how to craft rich and effective daily lesson plans, which can often be a daunting task for teachers, especially those entering the classroom for the first time. Moving on from lesson plans, we discuss a variety of instructional tools and strategies designed to help teachers raise the bar for and reach all of the students in their classrooms.

Since one of the most important aspects of mathematics instruction is the students' ability to solve problems both inside and outside the classroom, we have devoted an entire chapter to this topic. We approach problem solving in a variety of ways: from its instructional underpinnings to its recreational and motivational aspects. One emerging issue is the rapidly changing world of technology. In this edition we have revised and expanded the chapter dedicated to technology. However, there are two problems. First, no sooner will this book be printed than there will likely be changes in the technology available to the mathematics instructional program. At the same time, there are many schools in the United States that are less fortunate than others and may not yet have the technology to do all that is suggested in the book. Yet, we have attempted to address the current issues and situations to cover the majority of today's schools.

Mathematics teachers have additional responsibilities beyond the regular instructional program. They must concern themselves with enriching instruction for all of their students, and they ought to provide their more motivated students with extracurricular activities to further stretch their interest in mathematics. We conclude the first part of the book with a discussion of the professional responsibilities of mathematics teachers.

We make a conscious effort not to tell the teacher how to deal with every situation. Rather we attempt, as much as possible, to provide alternatives to allow the teachers to make professional judgments about their teaching performance. This is as it should be; no one method of teaching is suitable for all teachers. Personality differences among teachers dictate varying methods of instruction, and what works for one teacher may not work for another.

Enrichment Units

The second part of the book provides mathematics teachers with a collection of enrichment units appropriate for the entire secondary school curriculum spectrum. Each unit states its objective(s), provides a means for preassessment, and then provides an in-depth description of the subject so that a reader unfamiliar with the topic can easily learn it. This development is accompanied by suggestions for teaching the topic to a secondary school class. A postassessment is provided to help determine the level of learning (mastery) of the topic taught. A subject matter cross-index is provided at the beginning of the section to enable teachers to select units by topic and grade level.

NCTM and Technology

The National Council of Teachers of Mathematics (2000) Principles and Standards for School Mathematics (Standards) is referred to throughout the book. No one knows where the future emphases in teaching mathematics will be. Currently, the Standards are determining the agenda. Clearly, the significant technological advances we are seeing today, coupled with a decline in the cost of computers and calculators, will have a major impact on how mathematics is taught in the future. However, in many parts of the United States there is still uncertainty about the direction that mathematics education should take. We have therefore taken a forward-looking, yet cautious, approach to the teaching of mathematics, relying, when in doubt, on time-tested methods and ideas.

Intended Audience

The book is intended primarily for two audiences: for preservice teachers of mathematics who need training for the secondary schools, and for in-service teachers of mathematics who are seeking to improve their teaching skills and increase their resources through formal coursework. The book should also be available to mathematics teachers who simply want to have a comprehensive resource as ready reference. This will provide them an opportunity to review their teaching performance and refer to the second part of the book to find ideas with which to enrich their instructional program.

What's New in This Edition?

This edition of the book contains major revisions. The changes were made with the intent of keeping up-to-date with the ever-increasing advancements in technology and to reflect the most current thinking and research of a wide variety of groups with an interest in mathematics education.

When the first edition of this book appeared on the market in 1980, it was extremely well received because it seemed to be the first time that a methods book stressed practical aspects of teaching mathematics without the "burden" of the theoretical underpinnings for these practical aspects. With each subsequent edition, it was painful to make replacements to the previous edition, and so, in the course of time, the changes in the book merely reflect the changes in teaching practice between the four-year periods of publication.

The first change is one that would be expected of any new edition, namely, updating all time-sensitive aspects in the book and updating, with additional references, the various bibliographies throughout the book. Beyond the overall "cleaning" of the book, three chapters had significant changes reflecting changes in teaching practice.

Chapter 2 enhances the section on differentiated instruction and the discussion on "tiered-lessons" in an effort to assist teachers to meet the abilities of varying levels of students in their classes.

Chapter 6 introduces data-driven instruction to allow teachers to readily meet the demands of the federal law, No Child Left Behind.

Chapter 5 must, with every edition, be upgraded since technology changes and, consequently, its applications are seen in different ways as more teachers become accustomed to this valuable tool. So there are the necessary "modernizations" in this chapter.

Features of the Text

Differentiating Instruction. Recent reports show that today's classrooms are more diverse than in any other time in recent history. Students from varied backgrounds and ability levels work alongside each other to meet the rigorous learning standards set for all high school graduates. Therefore, to be successful in the modern classroom, teachers must diversify their instruction, and we illustrate how differentiated instruction can be infused into mathematics lessons on a regular basis.

Choosing Higher-Level Mathematical Tasks. Current research points out that an underestimated area of lesson planning where teachers can have a significant impact on student achievement is in their choice of mathematical tasks. Although it is important that students can complete tasks at all levels, too often students are only presented with lower level tasks instead of richer tasks that motivate higher learning. We will discuss how to analyze a task's level while planning lessons, as it is crucial to consider the cognitive level of the tasks used and raise the bar whenever possible.

Addressing Literacy in Mathematics. In the past, when it came to the language of mathematics, literacy has been associated with the ability to manipulate numbers and symbols using the principles of mathematics and their related algorithms. All too few teachers considered a student's reading and writing skills. Yet, many teachers find that students are unsuccessful in mathematics because of their inability to read and comprehend what is written about the mathematics. In this edition, we have included specific examples of how to improve students' mathematics vocabulary, reading comprehension of mathematics problems, and overall understanding of mathematical concepts.

Updating the Use of Technology. As mentioned above, keeping up with the latest technology is sometimes a Herculean task. We have addressed current trends in technology and tried to anticipate future ones. Although there are still several excellent examples of how to use the graphing calculator and the Geometer's Sketchpad, Chapter 5, Using Technology to Enhance Mathematics Instruction, now includes ways to use spreadsheet software to solve problems and enhance understanding of functions. Furthermore, we offer an overview of additional instructional support software such as Fathom, Equation Editor, and course management software such as BlackBoard. We have also cross-referenced the Enrichment Section with potential applications of technology.

Framing Purposes for Mathematics Assessment. Lastly, the assessment chapter is now framed by the four purposes of assessment as defined by the NCTM Assessment Standards for School Mathematics (1995). The key to these standards is that assessment should cease to separate or rank students as examinations often do. Teacher candidates are challenged to think of assessment as a tool for improving instruction as well as reporting the results of their actions.

Ensuring Equity in Mathematics Classrooms. In addition to what has been highlighted above, many of the lesson plans and word problems have been updated to reflect what is a central theme of modern-day education and this edition of the book, equity in the classroom. The goal of every teacher, from teacher candidate to twenty-year veteran, is to ensure that all of the students in the classroom reach their potential.

Acknowledgments

A book of this scope requires input from a wide variety of professionals. To ensure appropriateness, many secondary school teachers participated in the preparation of the enrichment units, a majority of which were originally published by Croft-NEI Publications (Waterford, Connecticut). We extend our sincere gratitude to these teachers: Renee E. Baxter, Peter Catranides, Beatrice F. Cohen, Steven Colello, Joyce A. Dato, James DeMetro, Benito Gomez, Adele Hayda, Cynthia Horvath, Howard Kale, Gladys Kornfield, Arlene Kuperberg, Susan Loeb, David Martinez, Robert Parisi, Patricia Pearson, Steven Pottash, Soraida Rivera, Amelia O. Roges, Howard Sardis, Vema Segarra, Max Sharf, Malcolm Singer, Joseph Skittone, Jon Sontz, Daniel Stolnitz, Richard A. Vitulli, Stanley Weinstein, Barbara Winters, and Betty York. Professor Evan Maletsky deserves particular thanks for his contributions to the Enrichment Unit section.

We thank Dr. Alice F. Artzt, Professor of Mathematics Education at Queens College (CUNY) who provided helpful input into previous editions of the book.

We also wish to thank Professor Alfred Weiss, formerly of The City College of the City University of New York, who contributed "A Psychological View of Problem Solving" as well as the section on "Creativity in Problem Solving" in Chapter 4.

We received an expert contribution for Chapter 5 on technology from Dr. Peter Brouwer, SUNY-Potsdam and for the current edition an updating of this contribution from-David Linker of The City College of the City University of New York. Special thanks are also extended to Dr. William Farber of The City College for his invaluable assistance with Chapter 1.

Meticulous reading of the manuscript for each edition was done by Jacob Cohen, former Assistant Principal in Charge of Mathematics at Theodore Roosevelt High School (New York City), who offered very insightful comments throughout.

For particular help in preparing the manuscript for this eighth edition we thank Peter Poole, who did much of the first-phase editing and made valued contributions along the way.

We appreciate permission granted by the National Council of Teachers of Mathematics to reproduce figures from Mathematics Teaching in the Middle School and Assessment Standards for School Mathematics. In addition we would like to acknowledge Mid-continent Research for Education and Learning for allowing us to adapt items from *Teaching Reading in Mathematics.*

We are also grateful to our editor Kelly Villella Canton for providing valuable support services and generally allowing us to work in a pressure-free atmosphere. Finally, we would like to thank the reviewers of our manuscript for their comments and suggestions: Mary Anderson, University of Illinois at Chicago; Yolanda De La Cruz, Arizona State University; Joan Cohen Jones, Eastern Michigan University; Terrie T. Poehl, Louisiana State University; Steven W. Ziebarth, Western Michigan University.

We thank Barbara and Howard for their patience and constant encouragement and we hope the ideas of this book will help provide a better future for Lisa, David, Danny, Andy, Alison, Max, Samuel and Jack.

Alfred S. Posamentier
Beverly S. Smith
Jay Stepelman

Chapter 1

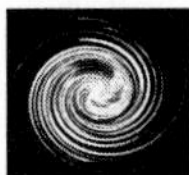 The Challenge of Teaching

The demands, challenges, and responsibilities of today's secondary school mathematics teachers are enormous. Mathematics teachers not only have to be specialists in the content area and pedagogical skills, but also must respond to the needs of an ever-changing technological society. Teaching secondary school mathematics is an active, cultural intervention that continually develops and advances as a function of the needs of society. Subsequently, the growth of technology, particularly the effects of computer applications and hand-held devices, along with further developments of pure and applied mathematics, has collectively broadened the breadth and knowledge of mathematics as a science.

These societal influences have altered the role of school mathematics; teaching methodologies must reflect these influences if we are to help empower students and better equip them for tomorrow's world. According to the vision and intent of the National Council of Teachers of Mathematics document *Principles and Standards for School Mathematics* (NCTM, 2000), all students should have the opportunity to learn, appreciate, and apply important mathematical skills, concepts, and principles both in and out of school. Moreover, the document supports a mathematics framework/curriculum that is conceptually based and promotes an active learning environment where students can develop mathematical thinking and reasoning abilities on an ongoing basis.

Above all, mathematics teachers must be ambassadors—constantly informing the general public about the power and beauty of mathematics. This promotion begins in the classroom, but does not end there. Mathematics teachers must ensure that the next generation appreciates the subject and uses it proudly to their advantage rather than accepting failure with misdirected pride.

Today's Students, Mathematics, and Society's Need

Nowadays secondary school students must prepare to live in a society that requires a significant understanding and appreciation of mathematics. Managing in the real world would be difficult if not impossible without the necessary knowledge, skills, and applications of mathematics. The demands of society require much more of secondary school mathematics students than merely being able to compute the total of a grocery bill or determine whether a personal checkbook is balanced. Students must be able to apply mathematical skills to real-life problem-solving situations.

For example, important principles in probability and statistics may be connected to the physical world, which may require individuals to collect, record, interpret, analyze, communicate, and represent data sets crucial to their decision-making processes. The interpretation of a graph as part of a medical diagnosis may influence a vital decision involving the health and well-being of an individual. Key concepts in numeration and algebra may help facilitate important personal financial decisions. The use of mathematical design enables the ongoing growth of computer technology, including the continued research and development of hardware, software, and further advancement of the Internet and telecommunication services. Careers and occupations in computer technology, business, the sciences, and engineering necessitate a more intense and multifaceted mathematical knowledge base than in the past. According to John Glenn, former astronaut and U.S. Senator, mathematics and science will also supply the core of knowledge that the next generation of innovators, producers, and workers in every country will need if they are to solve the unforeseen problems and dream the dreams that will define America's future (U.S. Department of Education, 2000). This continues to ring true today.

Crisis in Math Education

By the late 1980s, the shortcomings of traditional mathematics teaching reached epic proportions in America. This weakness was illuminated in the results of the National Assessment of Educational Progress (NAEP) and the Trends in International Mathematics and Science Study (TIMSS, formerly known as the Third International Mathematics and Science Study). Both of these assessments painted a troubling portrait of the average mathematics student in American schools. The NAEP reported that only half of our nation's 17-year-olds were able to successfully solve mathematics problems on the middle school level. Even of more concern was the TIMSS statistic that 1.5 million high school juniors and seniors were unable to perform the basic mathematical operations necessary for daily living let alone for so many of today's technologically influenced occupations. Thus, in comparison to its overseas neighbors and major economic competitors, America found itself woefully behind in producing a new generation of mathematically proficient youngsters. An even greater disparity was found on the home front between low-income and minority students from inner-city school districts and the more economically advantaged students in nonurban areas. These discouraging assessments presented an unprecedented challenge for our nation's mathematics teachers. Nationwide, a severe mathematics teacher shortage meant a dearth of qualified mathematics teachers, and the damage done to the school system was evident.

Steps were taken in the 1990s to remedy the situation and some progress was made. However, the performance gap separating Caucasian students from African-American and Hispanic students remained. The mathematics teacher shortage continued as well, forcing schools to hire uncertified, and sometimes unqualified, mathematics teachers to fill the void. These stopgap methods were implemented most often in low-income areas of the country, thus producing a recursive malaise. Given the societal change of providing all students a proper academic education, it was time to reevaluate the problem and revolutionize the way mathematics was taught in the public school system.

A fresh light on the problem began to shine in 2000 with analytical reports issued by the National Council of Teachers of Mathematics (NCTM). The crux of the NCTM's message was that the mathematics difficulties facing America's public school students could only be solved with a collaborative effort among teachers, parents/guardians, and students. The NCTM also called for raising the expectations to lower the achievement gap and reverse the defeatist attitude that American students could not compete on an international level when it came to mathematics.

These days, there is legitimate room for optimism. Besides having a solid, national plan in place that seeks to remedy the problem from the ground up, the latest assessment results have seen positive spikes in scores. In 2008, mathematics-assessment scores have risen across the board and the achievement gap between Caucasian and minority students narrowed. With the NCTM's 2006 publication, *Curriculum Focal Points for Kindergarten Through Grade 8 Mathematics: A Quest for Coherence*, the attention in mathematics education was drawn to the lower grades K–8. The purpose of these curriculum focal points was to highlight the key areas of emphasis for math instruction so as to begin dispelling the notion that American mathematics instruction was an inch high and a mile wide. In the spring of 2008, the President's commission on school mathematics issued a report further hoping to strengthen these pre-high school grades, indicating the importance of providing students with a firm foundation in algebra as they enter the high school curriculum. By all measures, much work is left to be done, but the national attitude adjustment vis-à-vis mathematics is in its infancy and the future looks far brighter than it did just a decade ago. The rest of this section will delve a bit deeper into the circumstances leading up to the troubles of the 1980s and 1990s as well as how the current plan for remedying the situation was formulated.

The Teacher Shortage

School systems across the United States are facing a severe shortage of secondary school teachers, particularly in mathematics and science. With the majority of experienced teachers having retired or approaching retirement age, mandated reduction of class size, an increase in the number of immigrant children, and higher expectations set for all students, American schools are in critical need of fully qualified mathematics teachers. To be fully qualified a teacher must have a college major in mathematics that includes appropriate content knowledge for teaching middle and high school mathematics, understand how adolescents develop and learn, understand diverse communities and cultures, be able to use a variety of teaching strategies, and be able to create classrooms environments were all students feel safe and can learn.

To better understand this quandary, we should consider the underlying historical and political reasons school districts across the nation are experiencing these teacher shortages. During the Great Depression of the 1930s, high-quality scientists with few alternatives for finding work were attracted to the teaching profession. Moreover, it was one of the few professions open to females and minorities before the Civil Rights Act of 1964. These early waves of professionals sustained the school system through the early 1960s until another national crisis, the Vietnam War, again channeled high-quality personnel into the teaching profession, this time through draft deferments issued to those teaching in hard-to-staff schools and in critical areas such as mathematics and science. After 1968, job opportunities for females increased significantly, providing them with viable alternatives to the teaching profession, which heretofore was their profession of choice. Similarly, minorities who once would have chosen teaching as their profession, are now being actively recruited into the business sector. Teacher shortages are at crisis proportions today because we are not adequately competing with the economic pull of the private sector. In fact, between 2 million and 2.5 million—an average of more than 200,000 teachers annually—will be needed during the next decade, according to the National Commission on Teaching and America's Future (NCTAF). Approximately one half of those teachers will be individuals barely prepared for the profession, and the remainder will be returnees from the emergency supply of teachers. However, many who left the teaching profession will not return. In most instances, those individuals believe their present salaries, working environment, and advancement opportunities are more favorable than are those of colleagues who remained in teaching.

In the past many school districts filled this need with uncertified or out of license teachers. However the federal No Child Left Behind Act (NCLB), passed in 2001, requires that all teachers be "highly qualified." Because it was left to each State to establish the criteria used to determine who was "highly qualified", many states have developed alternative certification programs that allow teachers with limited training and / or content knowledge to be identified as having met the "highly qualified" standard set for NCLB. At the same time the need for fully qualified teachers has increased because most States have raised graduation standards and now require all students to have a basic understanding of algebra, geometry and statistics prior to high school graduation. The lack of fully qualified teachers is most problematic in urban areas of the country where the student population is exceedingly large and there are a significant number of buildings to staff. In addition, many teachers are reluctant to teach in an urban school because of the greater social and educational problems that exist. As a result, school districts nationwide are having tremendous difficulty in attracting mathematics majors to relatively low-wage teaching positions in today's competitive and technologically driven job market.

Possible Solutions to the Teacher Shortage Problem

Although a comprehensive and substantive solution to the teacher shortage problem may not be readily available, there are worthwhile programs and strategies to consider in order to help alleviate the problem. Many of the following strategies and suggested programs are temporary, but may lead to a more far-reaching resolution of the problem.

- Import foreign teachers to fill immediate vacancies until permanent replacements can be found. For example, the Austrian Mathematics and Science Teacher Program, initiated by the City College of the City University of New York, is now in its tenth year, and includes teachers who wish to stay on longer than the initial 2- or 3-year period. This concept for meeting immediate shortages has now been replicated in many American cities, such as Philadelphia and with numerous other countries throughout the world.
- Introduce a project such as the New York City Teaching Fellows Program, which might meet the most severe shortages in mathematics teaching. For example, a survey of the 2,200 applicants accepted into this program during the past year might be used to determine which of these candidates has some interest, penchant, or experience in mathematics. Followed up with an aptitude test, a selection can be made of potential mathematics teachers for the middle school level. These candidates could then be given a series of mathematics courses to supplement their background and build a knowledge of the underlying mathematics concepts of the middle school curriculum. Coupled with preparation in appropriate pedagogy and in methods of teaching mathematics, this program could convert these Fellows into reasonably well-trained mathematics teachers.
- Offer incentives to qualified teachers who can teach in critical content areas such as mathematics.
- Offer competitive salaries and working conditions and recruit qualified people from industry.
- Allow some competent retired teachers to earn tax-levy money on top of their pensions for part-time teaching (for example, a 3/5 program). Provide incentives to qualified teachers in properly staffed subjects to retrain for teaching in areas of critical need.
- Conduct a much more aggressive recruitment program, with appropriate incentives, such as housing allowances,

moving-expense reimbursements, and even a recognition of (and reward for) excellent performance to current college majors in the areas of need (e.g., math/science).

- Create a new teacher–mentor program to help support teachers through their first few turbulent years of teaching.
- Create a state-wide or national "Teacher Search" database to better match teachers to job openings.
- Enable school systems to advertise for jobs earlier in the school year for the succeeding year. Many districts wait until late spring or summer to recruit teachers.

Goals and Challenges for Secondary Math Teachers Today

Making Math Accessible

According to the National Council of Teachers of Mathematics, educational equity in mathematics is a core element of the vision and intent of the *Principles and Standards for School Mathematics* (NCTM, 2000). Although the common thread is mathematics, our society must recognize and be sensitive to the issue of equity regarding mathematics education. The mathematics curriculum must reflect the understanding that all students are not the same. Students learn and assimilate knowledge in different ways and have diverse learning styles.

A multitude of exemplary programs that embody the NCTM Standards are being created, customized, revised, piloted, and implemented in classrooms throughout the United States. Despite the importance of these changes, there is no guarantee that any of these curriculum models will be comprehensive, supportive, or integrated with relation to equitable access for all students. Even if the mathematics curriculum is changed to cover the full range of mathematical content and methods, this change is insufficient. Students today are still not participating equally in the education process.

Research documents that students do not receive adequate amounts of teacher attention, that they are less likely to view the materials they study as functionally relevant to their lives, and that they are usually not expected or encouraged to pursue higher level mathematics (Council of Educational Development and Research, 1990). Therefore, all students must be encouraged to realize that mathematics and the sciences are vital and relevant to their lives, despite internal and external conflicts and pressures that may discourage them from continuing in mathematics. The implications are clear—the way in which mathematics is taught must change. The responsibilities of the teacher are essential to advancing systemic changes in the way mathematics instruction is imparted to students. If the teaching and learning of mathematics is to engage students, then teachers need to create an equitable classroom environment that encourages the mathematical development of all students.

Equity

The Equity Principle (NCTM, 2000) in mathematics education supports the belief that all students are capable of learning mathematics. Moreover, this principle requires high expectations for all mathematics learners. Often, teachers and administrators settle for lower expectations for students who may live in poverty, students who are categorized English language learners or ESL (English as a Second Language), students with special needs, female students, and minority students. However, expectations must be raised for these students as well, in order to promote mathematical equity. Teacher expectation could be the single most significant factor in student achievement and therefore requires serious attention.

High expectations must be conveyed by the teacher both verbally and nonverbally to all students during the course of the academic year. Teachers can communicate these expectations through remarks, notes, and observations made on students' reports, tests, or quizzes; when assigning students to cooperative learning groups; when having one-to-one communication with the student; and in their interactions at home with significant adults in the student's life. High expectations can be realized in part through educational programs that motivate students and encourage them to appreciate the significance and usefulness of sustained mathematical learning for their own expectations and opportunities.

Higher expectations are essential, but they are not enough to achieve the goals and objectives of a well-rounded school environment that supports and promotes equity for all students in mathematics education.

Every student should experience a comprehensive mathematics program/curriculum that supports his or her curiosity, interests, and learning. The program should also correspond to previous educational experiences, academic strengths, and real-life interests.

Some students may require additional support to meet high expectations in mathematics. For example, students who are classified as English language learners (ELL) may require additional help in meeting the goal of mathematical literacy. Some of these students may require translated versions of assessment instruments to accommodate their needs (i.e., if their knowledge of mathematics is graded in English only, their mathematical abilities and skills may not be accurately assessed). Some students with disabilities may need increased time to complete assignments, or may need more visual stimuli, such as charts, handouts, or presentations using an overhead projector. These students may also require auditory methods rather than a written approach to learning. Supplementary resources may be necessary to assist these students as well, such as extracurricular programs, additional advisement, peer coaching, or extra tutoring. Similarly, gifted and talented mathematics students may need enrichment programs or additional resources to challenge and engage them. For instance, a mathematics club can give these and other students the opportunity to explore mathematical topics that are not ordinarily discussed in class.

Equity in mathematics can also be achieved through the effective use of technology. For example, computers and calculators can offer all students the chance to investigate a multitude of mathematical problems and situations. In addition, specific computer tutorials can be designed to help students master skills and reinforce mathematical instruction.

Computer adaptive learning such as augmentative and alternative communication (AAC) devices can be extremely powerful tools for students with speech/language disorders. Assistive listening devices (ALD) can help students with severe hearing impairments. Also, computer screen magnification, descriptive video services, and screen readers can help students who are visually impaired. Additionally, voice recognition/creation software can give teachers the ability to assess students' mathematical thinking, without which they may be unable to share their thinking in a traditional mathematical setting. Technology can be useful in engaging students who are generally not motivated by a traditional teaching/learning approach to mathematics. Technology must be accessible to all students, and teachers must give students the opportunities to explore, investigate, and discover interesting and important mathematical ideas through technology.

Math Anxiety

Many people in our highly technological society experience a feeling of intimidation and fear when confronted with mathematics. Whether we classify this phenomenon as math avoidance, math phobia, or what is popularly known as *math anxiety*, it is a sobering reality that millions of people suffer from this condition. According to Dr. Sheila Tobias, math anxiety is a failure of nerve in the face of having to do a computation or an analysis of a problem involving numbers, geometry, or mathematical concepts. Math anxiety is a response, over time, to stress in the math classroom where tests are frequently given under time pressure, in the home where there is competition with siblings, or at the workplace.

Teachers need to recognize some of the traits, symptoms, and indicators of math anxiety in their students. For example, students may experience an inability and anxiety toward solving verbal problems. Moreover, students may freeze during a quiz or test. The notion that incorrect answers are perceived as "bad" answers and correct answers are perceived as "good" answers must change. The emphasis must be placed on the process rather than the product. With encouragement from the teacher, a nurturing environment, and permission to proceed at one's own pace, math anxious students can be helped to eventually eliminate math anxiety from their lives.

It was once thought that math anxiety had a greater effect on females than males. However, in 2001, researchers from the University of North Carolina at Charlotte studied the math scores of 20,000 students, ages 4 to 18, and found no discernible performance differential between males and females. Further, a study of 3 million SAT scores showed a virtual tie in gender performance on the mathematics portion (as cited in Barnett & Rivers, 2004). Yet, when these students advance to college, far more male students elect to take mathematics courses.

Today, women make up only 25 percent of the science, engineering, and technology workforce. Perhaps the reason for this disparity is the persistence of old stereotypes or maybe female students simply choose other avenues of study. Whatever the reasons for this disparity, mathematics teachers, acting as ambassadors, should try to encourage and embolden their female students to explore the subject on a more advanced level. Many of the future's high-paying jobs will require proficiency in mathematics, and women should have equal opportunities to pursue those jobs. Additionally, and aside from any gender issue, outreach and encouragement from mathematics teachers make sense on a practical level; these female students represent an untapped national resource.

Teaching for Understanding

Many mathematics education researchers (Midwest Consortium for Mathematics and Science Education), support the view that too much stress placed on mechanics and procedural mathematics hampers meaningful learning. This may lead to a widespread misconception about the power/limitations of mathematical teaching methods.

When students are given the opportunity to become actively involved in the learning process, they become more apt to develop their own meanings of mathematical ideas and concepts. Students will then gain a sense of ownership of the mathematical concept or topic. In turn, this will empower the student. The teachers who incorporate these learning strategies can function not only as teachers but as a facilitators as well. The major difference between the role of the teacher and the role of the facilitator is that the teacher disseminates information to students through informing, explaining, telling, and trying to make information as clear as possible to the student, whereas the facilitator guides, leads, and advises the students, who may eventually arrive at their own conjecture, proof, or conclusion.

The teaching of mathematics seeks not merely to dispense rules, definitions, and procedures for students to memorize, but to engage students as active participants in the learning process. Some of the recommended instructional strategies that support an active learning environment in the mathematics classroom are the use of concrete materials, encouraging student discussions of mathematical ideas, student writing (which may include learning journals), and cooperative learning groups for the sharing of experiences and ideas. Active participation of the student has the potential to expand the student's understanding of mathematical concepts. Other advantages of cooperative learning include the development of reasoning skills, increased self-esteem, improvement of attitudes and understanding toward minorities and other cultures, and acceptance of mainstreamed students.

Cooperative learning models have been proven effective in heterogeneous classes. An important difference exists between small group work and cooperative learning. The major theme of the cooperative learning model is that each student in the cooperative group is accountable for the final result of the group and the students must work together as a team to succeed. However, in small group work, although students may be physically arranged together, each student is accountable for himself or herself. Subsequently, members of the small group may be supportive of each other and confer with one another, but there are only individual results and no common goals.

Mathematics instruction that makes use of a wide variety of applications and multiple representations helps to develop student growth in both affective and cognitive domains. In general, mathematics focuses on the representation and communication of numerical, spatial, and data-related ideas and relationships. A multitude of educational activities support this theme. For instance, students may interpret their conceptual thoughts into symbolic forms and, hence, offer a verbal depiction of a similar situation. Other activities may consist of choosing the best model to physically clarify a relationship, using computers/calculators in unique ways to investigate a problem, and writing journal entries, annotations, or conjectures to explain observations in mathematics.

Teachers must customize instruction so that it is developmentally appropriate for students' learning. Students generally gain increased understanding of mathematics when they are given the opportunity to develop their own mathematical knowledge through direct experiences, reasoning, problem solving, exploring, and communicating. This type of instruction encourages student interaction, which furthers cognitive growth, self-esteem, and mathematical power. Moreover, this type of teaching does not necessarily require and limit students to simply record and store material that is beyond their scope of understanding.

Through the effective use of actual models and situations using concrete materials, cooperative learning, problem exploration, and classroom discussions, students are able to conceptualize and appreciate the usefulness and beauty of mathematics, which will contribute to the development of their cognitive growth.

In summary, learning environments that are functionally relevant to real-world situations engage students in realistic problems, require ingenuity and resourcefulness, and show the uses of mathematics in everyday life.

ROLE OF HANDS-ON MATERIALS Hands-on materials or manipulatives are tangible objects that students can explore, arrange, move around, group, sort, and use to measure as they model mathematical concepts and problems. For example, the use of algebra tiles may help students understand a variety of algebraic concepts, including the Pythagorean theorem. The use of geoboards may give students the opportunity to explore a variety of two-dimensional geometric shapes. An educational environment that supports the effective use of manipulatives may improve student understanding and achievement, if the manipulative materials used are clearly connected to the specific mathematical concepts and procedures they symbolize. Teachers need to help students make the transition from the concrete experience to abstract mathematical symbols. The transition between the concrete and the abstract is a continuum (i.e., from the concrete or hands-on model to the semiconcrete or diagrammatic, to the semiabstract or symbols that do not resemble the manipulatives they represent, to the abstract, which may represent a mathematical formula, equation, or proof).

Although manipulatives are commonly used in early grades, the effective use of concrete materials can play an important role in middle and high school instruction as well. Often, secondary school mathematics teachers impart information through a traditional, abstract model of instruction without ever considering a concretized experience. To meet the educational and mathematical needs of all students, teachers need to be flexible and consider the variety of learning styles of all students, which may include the use of manipulative materials.

Widespread research has shown that the proper use of technology helps to develop a student's conceptual understanding of mathematics and problem-solving skills. Therefore, the effective use of computers and calculators is essential in the mathematics classroom. Many worthwhile computer programs use the capabilities of the computer to simulate real-world mathematical applications and modeling. For example, dynamic computer programs such as the Geometer's Sketchpad and Fathom (both from Key Curriculum Press), Maple, and Mathematica can help students conceptualize abstract geometric and algebraic concepts through a combination of "hands-on" and "minds-on" modality. In addition, scientific and graphing calculators have built-in algebra logic systems that can give students the opportunity to appreciate mathematics through visual learning. In fact, many mathematics assessment instruments, such as the Scholastic Aptitude Test (SAT), require the use of a graphing or scientific calculator. New technology is constantly being researched and developed and much of this technology is having a profound effect on the teaching and learning of mathematics, and will continue to do so for generations to come.

The Standards

The Old Standards

In 1989, the NCTM, in order to effect change and advance systemic reform in mathematics education, published a trilogy of standards documents that detailed national goals for curriculum, teaching, and assessment in school mathematics K–12. These groundbreaking documents, known as the NCTM Standards, consisted of the following: *Curriculum and Evaluation Standards for School Mathematics* (1989), *Professional Standards for Teaching Mathematics* (1991), and *Assessment Standards for School Mathematics* (1995). These three documents have served as the impetus and framework to further develop city, state, and national efforts to improve school mathematics in the United States. More specifically, they offered a vision of what the teaching and learning of mathematics should be, delineated specific goals, and helped influence changes in mathematics teaching in classrooms throughout the United States. In general, the Standards were not meant to be a recipe guide for teaching mathematics. The purpose of the Standards was to present a vision consisting of goals with which mathematics curricula, teaching, and assessment practices could be examined. Each of the three documents was written by a team of professional mathematics educators, which included teachers, supervisors, researchers, mathematicians, and university professors of mathematics and mathematics education.

The first Standards document, *Curriculum and Evaluation Standards for School Mathematics* (1989), describes the essential topics in mathematics that students should conceptualize and apply. In addition, the Standards emphasize the importance of process-oriented skills, such as problem solving, reasoning skills, communication in mathematics, and making connections. The format of the Standards is segmented into grade-level categories (i.e., kindergarten through grade 4, grade 5 through grade 8, and grade 9 through grade 12), each containing 12 to 14 Standards. The Standards for secondary school mathematics are listed as problem solving, communication, reasoning, connections, numbers and relationships, number systems and number theory, computation and estimation, patterns and functions, algebra, statistics, probability, geometry, and measurement.

The second Standards document, *The Professional Standards for Teaching Mathematics* (1991), describes ways that educators can present mathematical activities that are congruous to the spirit, vision, and intent of the *Curriculum and Evaluation Standards.* Furthermore, these Standards are structured according to the basic choices educators make, such as selecting meaningful mathematical activities, initiating and encouraging verbal discourse connected to these activities, and maintaining a student-centered environment for learning. In addition, the Standards supports teacher training, professional development, and ongoing evaluation of mathematics teaching methodologies.

The third Standards document, *Assessment Standards for School Mathematics* (1995), describes a philosophy of recommended assessment practices that mathematics educators should consider in order to support the development of mathematical power for all students (NCTM, 1997). For mathematics assessment, tests and quizzes are not enough. These Assessment Standards emphasize and support the use of multiple assessment models to determine what students are learning. For example, there are numerous alternative indicators that can help teachers ascertain their students' abilities, progress, and achievement. Assessment instruments may include ways students solve problems in their homework, one-on-one student discussions, mathematics learning journals that reflect the students' written work, and videotaping, which may offer teachers new insights into students' thinking abilities and levels of understanding. Moreover, performance assessment in mathematics gives students the opportunity to show and display their thinking on paper. As a result, teachers can gain insight into the students' styles of learning and will be able to evaluate the students' progress on a more holistic basis.

The Assessment Standards also promote educational equity (i.e., high expectation for all students). Teachers must recognize students' diverse learning styles and range of abilities and seek to promote the active participation of all students in the mathematics learning experience. Assessment must provide for every student, including special learners, gifted and talented, the chance to express his or her understanding of a topic in a variety of ways. Assessment outcomes should be used to provide each student with the opportunity and necessary support to achieve the greatest levels of success.

During and shortly after the three Standards documents were published, NCTM decided to supplement the Standards with a series of booklets that offer specific examples and detailed suggestions of how to implement each Standard in the classroom. This series, entitled the *Addenda Series,* features several possible curriculum and mathematical models for organizing the mathematics content recommended in the *Curriculum and Evaluation Standards*. In addition, the *Addenda Series* offers sample curricula, lessons, and activities that help augment the Standards documents. There are 22 books in the complete *Addenda Series* set; 6 of those booklets are designed for middle school (Grades 5–8), and 5 booklets are designed for high school. These booklets serve as valuable teacher resources for presenting activities and lessons appropriate for secondary school students.

The Principles and Standards for School Mathematics

In a constant effort to meet the ever-changing demands of a technological society, and to continue to advance systemic change in mathematics education, NCTM published *Principles and Standards for School Mathematics* in April 2000. The purpose of this document was to revise, integrate, modify, and amend the goals of the original NCTM Standards of 1989. *Principles and Standards for School Mathematics* offers a direction and vision while allowing local school districts and schools to make important decisions regarding curriculum issues.

The NCTM *Principles and Standards for School Mathematics* introduces a comprehensive set of goals for mathematics that is designed for all students (K–12). The goals are intended to shape curricular, teaching, and assessment efforts for the future; to offer a valuable tool and resource for teachers, administrators, and policy makers for exploring and enhancing the quality of mathematical instructional programs; to guide the progress and upgrading of curriculum frameworks, assessments, and teaching materials; and to encourage ideas and continued dialogue on a national, state, and local level.

Secondary mathematics teachers must develop a global perspective of the teaching and learning of mathematics. For example, high school teachers should consider not only the scope and sequence of topics they are addressing in their present classrooms, but also the mathematics that was taught previously to students in both elementary and middle school, and the mathematics that students will study in subsequent grade levels in high school and eventually in higher education. This will enable teachers to treat the mathematics that they are teaching in a more global perspective. In addition, teachers will gain an increased level of sensitivity to the mathematical needs and learning styles of their students. Because the *Principles and Standards for School Mathematics* is organized using four grade bands (pre-kindergarten through grade 2, grade 3 through grade 5, grade 6 through grade 8, and grade 9 through grade 12), teachers will be able to conduct informal research of mathematical topics in earlier grades, and can subsequently organize their instruction to meet the specific needs of their students. For each grade band, a clear set of expectations is established for each of the content standards and also for the process goals from the teacher.

Standards are descriptions of what mathematics instruction should enable students to know and do—statements of what is valued for school mathematics education (NCTM, 2000). The *Principles and Standards for School Mathematics* describes and develops two types of Standards: content standards for learning specific mathematical topics, and process standards for pedagogy and methods of teaching. Standards 1 through 5 illustrate the *content* goals of mathematics for grades 6 through 12. These goals include number and operations, algebra, geometry, measurement, and data analysis and probability. Standards 6 through 10 represent the *process* goals of teaching mathematics for grades 6 through 12. These goals include problem solving, reasoning and proof, communication, connections, and representations. The content and process goals are not mutually exclusive of one another. They are naturally connected to each other. For example, it requires content knowledge in data analysis and probability to make clear connections/representations between the two content areas. Moreover, it would be very difficult to make logical conjectures in geometry without reasoning and proof. Also, it would be virtually impossible to plot accurate visual representations without knowledge of algebra and functions.

As an addendum to the *Principles and Standards for School Mathematics*, NCTM has published a series of booklets, entitled *The Navigation Series*. Similar to the NCTM's *Addenda Series*, the *Navigation Series* focuses on an in-depth look at various mathematical concepts. Each booklet focuses on a different grade band (pre-K–2, 3–5, 6–8, and 9–12).

The following chart summarizes the key topics of NCTM's *Principles and Standards for School Mathematics*. The first part of the chart presents the content standards and the second part of the chart describes the process standards.

In the fall of 2006, in order to provide further clarity to the NCTM's position and assist in the implementation of the standards, a document, *Curriculum Focal Points for Kindergarten Through Grade 8 Mathematics: A Quest for Coherence* was published. The curriculum focal points highlight the key areas in the mathematics curriculum that need to be stressed at each grade level. NCTM president Frances (Skip) Fennell said, "The focal points are compatible with the original Standards and represent the next step in realizing the visions set forth in *Principles and Standards for School Mathematics* in 2000. The focal points are intended for use by mathematics leaders as they examine their state and local mathematics expectations and seriously consider what is important at each grade level. This discussion, dialogue, or perhaps debate is designed to influence the next generation of curriculum frameworks, textbooks, and assessments."

CONTENT STANDARDS FOR SCHOOL MATHEMATICS

Number and Operations Standard	Instructional programs from pre-kindergarten through grade 12 should enable all students to ▶ Understand numbers, ways of representing numbers, relationships among numbers, and number systems; ▶ Understand meanings of operations and how they relate to one another; ▶ Compute fluently and make reasonable estimates.
Algebra Standard	Instructional programs from pre-kindergarten through grade 12 should enable all students to ▶ Understand patterns, relationships, and functions; ▶ Represent and analyze mathematical situations and structures using algebraic symbols; ▶ Use mathematical models to represent and understand quantitative relationships; ▶ Analyze change in various contexts.
Geometry Standard	Instructional programs from pre-kindergarten through grade 12 should enable all students to ▶ Analyze characteristics and properties of two- and three-dimensional geometric shapes and develop mathematical arguments about geometric relationships; ▶ Specify locations and describe spatial relationships using coordinate geometry and other representational systems; ▶ Apply transformations and use symmetry to analyze mathematical situations; ▶ Use visualization, spatial reasoning, and geometric modeling to solve problems.
Measurement Standard	Instructional programs from pre-kindergarten through grade 12 should enable all students to ▶ Understand measurable attributes of objects and the units, systems, and processes of measurement; ▶ Apply appropriate techniques, tools, and formulas to describe measurements.
Data Analysis and Probability Standard	Instructional programs from pre-kindergarten through grade 12 should enable all students to ▶ Formulate questions that can be addressed with data and collect, organize, and display relevant data to answer them; ▶ Select and use appropriate statistical methods to analyze data; ▶ Develop and evaluate inferences and predictions that are based on data; ▶ Understand and apply basic concepts of probability.

PROCESS STANDARDS FOR SCHOOL MATHEMATICS

Problem Solving Standard	Instructional programs from pre-kindergarten through grade 12 should enable all students to ▶ Build new mathematical knowledge through problem solving; ▶ Solve problems that arise in other contexts; ▶ Apply and adapt a variety of appropriate strategies to solve problems; ▶ Monitor and reflect on the process of mathematical problem solving.
Reasoning and Proof Standard	Instructional programs from pre-kindergarten through grade 12 should enable all students to ▶ Recognize reasoning and proof as fundamental aspects of mathematics; ▶ Make and investigate mathematical conjectures; ▶ Develop and evaluate mathematical arguments and proofs; ▶ Select and use various types of reasoning and methods of proof.
Communication Standard	Instructional programs from pre-kindergarten through grade 12 should enable students to ▶ Organize and consolidate their mathematical thinking through communication; ▶ Communicate their mathematical thinking coherently and clearly to peers, teachers, and others; ▶ Analyze and evaluate mathematical thinking and strategies of others; ▶ Use the language of mathematics to express mathematical ideas precisely.
Connections Standard	Instructional programs from pre-kindergarten through grade 12 should enable students to ▶ Recognize and use connections among mathematical ideas; ▶ Understand how mathematical ideas interconnect and build on one another to produce a coherent whole; ▶ Recognize and apply mathematics in contexts outside of mathematics.
Representation Standard	Instructional programs from pre-kindergarten through grade 12 should enable students to ▶ Create and use representations to organize, record, and communicate mathematical ideas; ▶ Select, apply, and translate among mathematical representations to solve problems; ▶ Use representations to model and interpret physical, social, and mathematical phenomena.

PRINCIPLES FOR SCHOOL MATHEMATICS

Equity	Excellence in mathematics education requires equity: high expectations and strong support for all students.
Curriculum	A curriculum is more than a collection of activities; it must be coherent, focused on important mathematics, and well articulated across the grades.
Teaching	Effective mathematics teaching requires understanding what students know and need to learn and then challenging and supporting them to learn it well.
Learning	Students must learn mathematics with understanding, actively building new knowledge from experience and prior knowledge.
Assessment	Assessment should support the learning of important mathematics and furnish useful information to both teachers and students.
Technology	Technology is essential in teaching and learning mathematics; it influences the mathematics that is taught and enhances students' learning.

Professional Development: A Teacher's Resource

Professional development is one of the most important resources in helping to advance effective teaching skills and techniques for the mathematics teacher. Mathematics education is continually undergoing growth and modification. Like the medical profession, where physicians, nurses, and other medical professionals regularly attend conferences and training sessions pertaining to new developments and innovations in their field, mathematics teaching professionals must also participate in ongoing professional development initiatives to further their knowledge, skills, and abilities as classroom teachers.

The term *professional development* is often used interchangeably with other terms such as teacher training, staff development, and in-service training. These activities must be well-organized, regularly scheduled, and carefully designed to augment, enrich, and improve the mathematical and teaching skills, knowledge, and abilities of educators.

The ultimate goal of professional development is the improvement of student learning. However, additional objectives of professional development initiatives may include the following:

1. To offer educators the opportunity for self-evaluation for professional growth

2. To help educators apply new concepts and principles in the teaching/learning process cognizant of technological advances
3. To assist educators to expand their mathematical horizons
4. To help educators in their personal and professional growth
5. To help support educators in developing methodologies and techniques that are significant and mathematically precise and that inspire, motivate, and empower students to appreciate and apply mathematics
6. To continue a high standard of excellence within the current mathematics program/curriculum
7. To allow for reaction to curricular or instructional problems
8. To apply innovative teaching and learning practices

Types of Professional Development

A variety of professional development activities can be offered to both small and large groups of teachers. These may include single workshops or a series of workshops, which are usually conducted by colleagues, mathematics teacher trainers, or consultants. Workshops can be offered in a variety of settings and formats and can be customized to meet the specific needs of the school or district during and after school hours or on weekends, if requested.

Schools and districts can request a single workshop, which can focus on a requested topic, or a series of workshops, which can have a common theme. Workshops can also be conducted as part of a conference, retreat, or institute. Workshops for new or novice teachers can help new teacher participants to acquire experiences that will sensitize them to the educational and psychological needs as well as the mathematical content needs of their students. These experiences can foster a better understanding of how secondary students think and learn. Workshops can also be designed for experienced teachers to further develop their skills in the teaching of their particular areas. Moreover, workshops can also be provided for staff developers and supervisors in order to further support within their particular school or district. Workshop emphasis should be placed on activities congruous to the needs of students, which involve implementation of local, state, and national standards.

Other effective modalities of professional development may include conferences, retreats, institutes, and university inservice courses. Conferences can provide for a large group plenary session and can feature various keynote speakers. Conferences may also consist of breakout workshops/seminars, which can accommodate smaller groups. In addition, guest speakers, including nationally and internationally renowned mathematics educators, can conduct interactive presentations through simulcast video broadcasting, which can reach a multitude of audiences both nationally and internationally. Conferences may be half-day or whole-day events.

Professional development retreats can provide for large group and small group breakout sessions. A retreat is an indepth approach to relevant topics in mathematics education. Retreats are usually 2-day or 3-day events and may include a theme/conference each day.

Professional development institutes can provide activities appropriate for large group settings. Institutes offer an intensive, long-term treatment of a topic or several topics. Professional development institutes may be 1-week, 2-week, or 3-week long activities that provide participants with the continuity that is much needed. Usually, institutes are conducted during the summer or during a mid-winter break, depending on the needs of the school or district.

Graduate courses can be offered in mathematics education, mathematics content, educational technology, and mathematics supervision, depending on the specific needs of the school or district. These courses can be offered through a cooperative program with a university. Moreover, graduate courses can be customized to reflect the needs of the school or district.

A multitude of other professional development opportunities are offered, either through mathematics education organizations on a local, state, or national level or in the form of teacher training activities conducted in local schools and school districts. Professional development initiatives can be customized and presented to teachers, supervisors, parents, and auxiliary staff, and should be consistent with local, state, and national standards. The following are examples of additional professional development initiatives:

- National or regional mathematics education conventions
- Teacher observations
- Teacher-mentors
- Curriculum development seminars
- School inter-visitations
- Teacher resource centers
- Private sector partnerships
- Foreign exchange programs
- Demonstration lessons
- Action research
- Textbook/software evaluation
- In-service courses
- Sabbaticals used for professional enhancement
- School-based support teams
- Mathematics working groups
- Peer advisement
- Technology resources and evaluation programs
- Teacher evaluations

In conclusion, professional development initiatives for teachers of mathematics must include a combination of mathematical content and appropriate teaching methodologies; the active participation of teachers; an understanding of the daily problems, teaching routines, and situations that arise in the classroom; a balance of both theoretical and practical applications; a clear statement of goals and objectives to participants; a chance for teachers to incorporate newly acquired skills and methods in their classrooms; and the continuation of ongoing support and supplementary activities.

Resources for Teachers

A multitude of accessible resources are available to aid mathematics teachers and help them grow and improve as professionals. These resources may be accessed either locally through the schools or school districts or through outside sources.

Schools and school districts can offer teacher training through in-service courses, tutorials, discussion groups, colloquia, committees, workshops, seminars, and other professional development initiatives. Many of these initiatives can be customized to meet the specific needs of teachers. In addition, specialized teacher/mathematics resource centers having the latest curriculum materials, textbooks, publisher samples, professional journals, manipulative materials, and audiovisual resources, such as CD-ROMS, computer software, videotapes, and audiotapes, can help improve a teacher's mathematical and pedagogical expertise.

Advice, counseling, and guidance may be obtained through a school-based professional, such as the department chairperson, mathematics coordinator, teacher trainer, or grade supervisor. These individuals can make key suggestions regarding curriculum implementation, classroom management, pedagogical skills, and the management of materials. In addition, they can conduct demonstration lessons on particular mathematical topics, modeling various types of teaching techniques.

A number of external resources are also available to mathematics teachers. Institutions of higher learing such as colleges and universities offer many teaching/learning opportunities for teachers. These opportunities include certification programs for pre- and in-service teachers. University resources include a campus library, which can provide pertinent books, academic journals, audiovisual materials, and other resources pertaining to teaching and learning; university faculty, who can offer assistance and expertise in specified areas of interest and research; mathematics and mathematics education coursework, conferences, workshops, and seminars; and special internships and partnership programs that capitalize on the educational alliance of the school-university connection.

Each state has a department of education that serves as a valuable resource to mathematics teachers. The services that the state provides include information on teacher certification, names and addresses of local schools, testing and evaluation policies, grant proposals/awards, and curriculum development.

Professional Organizations

One of the key organizations that assists mathematics teachers in all aspects of mathematics and mathematics education is the National Council of Teachers of Mathematics (NCTM). The NCTM provides professional mathematics education publications, which include *Teaching Children Mathematics, Teaching Mathematics in the Middle School, the Mathematics Teacher, the Journal of Research in Mathematics Education*, various NCTM newsletters, yearbooks, and a multitude of other publications that concentrate on significant topics in mathematics education. In addition, NCTM sponsors national and local conferences throughout the academic year. These conferences give mathematics teachers the opportunity to take part as workshop presenters or participants on a national or regional level.

Another important organizational resource for the mathematics teacher is the Mathematical Association of America (MAA). The MAA addresses content area mathematics, usually on a college level.

Funding and Other Support

In addition to mathematical and educational organizations, a number of resources are located in the private sector. Many corporations and businesses are very supportive of initiatives in mathematics education. In fact, many of these corporations have formed educational partnerships with local school districts and provide them with resources such as financial support through grant awards; school-, business-, and community-based projects; speakers and workshop leaders; cooperative educational and exchange programs; action research; and equipment donations.

Community Resources

Many valuable resources can be found right in the local community. For example, parents may have a particular skill, vocation, or expertise in a certain area of mathematics. These parents can visit schools and address students and teachers. Moreover, people representing the business and technology community (e.g., banking, insurance, sales, and computer technology) can serve as mentors and educational partners. Other community resources, such as federal agencies, museums, public parks, airports, and utility companies, can supply brochures, accommodate student trips, and conduct relevant presentations pertaining to the use of mathematics in the real world. Finally, many valuable resources are available through various publishing agencies. Publishers can provide textbooks, commercial materials, and training sessions for recently adopted textbooks.

Foundations

A large number of foundations support mathematics education on a national level, such as the National Science Foundation (NSF) or the U.S. Department of Education. However, a multitude of private foundations also support local initiatives. In fact, there is an entire library dedicated to foundations in the United States.

A Mathematics Debate

There exists a complex debate within the mathematics community regarding how mathematics should be taught in our schools. Representatives from school districts, individual schools, universities, and the private sector are organizing open forums, focus groups, and discussions regarding the efficacy of mathematics education. The traditional viewpoint supports procedural approaches, which may include memorization, drill, and practice of rules and definitions as the optimum way to teach and learn mathematics. On the other hand, nontraditional approaches, such as the constructivist point of view, suggest that students should utilize their innate abilities to formulate their own algorithms in order to gain ownership of the specified mathematical topic.

Mathematics educators have argued these and similar concerns for many years. In addition, these debates have been spurred by the results of the Third International Math and Science Study (TIMSS), where American eighth graders were average and twelfth graders' scores were deficient when compared with similar age groups in other countries.

The National Council of Teachers of Mathematics (NCTM) has continually supported the idea that mathematics should be conceptually taught (i.e., teachers should teach mathematics for understanding and should make mathematics more functionally relevant to the student's life). However, even NCTM has encountered resistance from educators who support more traditional approaches.

The NCTM Standards 2000 document presents a vision that includes a framework of ideas that may contribute to the future landscape of mathematics education in the next several decades. However, whether the NCTM Standards are embraced or not, professional discussion and debate must continue. Curriculum committees, local school boards, professional forums, working groups, and parent-teacher teams must have ongoing dialogue and develop the habit of reflective practice.

The methodologies for teaching and learning secondary school mathematics are an ever-changing process based on scientific advances and societal needs. Therefore, developing the habit of reflection can provide insight and guidance, and help facilitate positive systemic change in mathematics education and the mathematics classroom.

EXERCISES

1. From a secondary school perspective, describe the basic differences between *process* standards and *content* standards, as outlined by the NCTM *Principles and Standards for School Mathematics*.
2. Explain how societal influences have altered the role of school mathematics.
3. Describe how you, as a mathematics teacher, can empower students and better equip them for tomorrow's world.
4. Choose a mathematical topic and grade level and write an outline of a lesson plan that is representative of both NCTM process and content standards.
5. TIMSS compared the mathematics abilities of students in America with their international peers in 1995, 1999, 2003 and 2007. Compare the 2007 results with those reported in the earlier studies. Do you feel that American students are closing the achievement gap when compared to students in other countries? Justify your answer.
6. Describe three critical issues facing mathematics teachers today.
7. Too often, even the strongest female mathematics students choose not to continue to exceed the required number of mathematics courses in high school or college. How can high school teachers encourage female students to pursue the study of mathematics and/or related fields?
8. Describe how a mathematics program/curriculum can support high expectations for all students.
9. As a mathematics teacher, how would you address the problem of student math anxiety?
10. There are students who may require additional mathematical support. As a mathematics teacher, describe how you would accommodate these students so they can reach their full potential.
11. Briefly describe and justify five types of professional development activities that can enhance high school mathematics teachers' skills and techniques in the classroom.
12. List and describe five community resources that can enhance your mathematics curriculum.
13. The debate in mathematics education includes two basic perspectives: the traditional viewpoint, which supports procedural approaches including memorization, drill, and practice of rules and definitions, and the nontraditional approaches, such as the constructivist point of view, supporting the belief that students should utilize their innate abilities to formulate their own algorithms.
    a. As a high school teacher, describe your teaching approaches and include justification.
    b. Describe and outline a mathematics lesson that balances both perspectives.
14. Write a letter to your students' parents/guardians explaining why success in mathematics is important for their child and how they can be a part of the team working to ensure that success.

Chapter 2

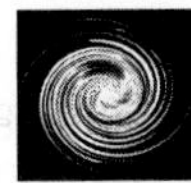

Long-Range and Short-Range Planning

> Teaching mathematics is a complex endeavor.... To be effective, teachers must know and understand deeply the mathematics they are teaching and be able to draw on that knowledge with flexibility in their teaching tasks. They need to understand and be committed to their students as learners of mathematics and as human beings and be skillful in choosing from and using a variety of pedagogical and assessment strategies. (NCTM, 2000, p. 17)

Today, teachers should see themselves as one of a team of educational guides along a student's journey toward mathematical proficiency. As such, teachers must design a plan to ensure that each student reaches predesigned goals by journey's end. Developing such a plan requires teachers to consider the stage in the journey for which they are responsible, where along the continuum each student begins this stage, and how to best facilitate student progress toward the next stage on the journey.

In a perfect world, each student would travel at an equal pace. However, in reality some students may move along the path more quickly than others. Should these students take side trips—perhaps over more difficult terrain—or should they advance to the next stage of the journey before expected? Teachers must decide how to enrich the learning experience for these quicker students.

What of those students who start a leg of the journey behind their peers? The teacher needs to determine how to help these students maintain reasonable progress. Maybe they missed a sign along the way and are lost, or perhaps they would prefer a different path. These students may not even see the relevance of the journey and thus need more motivation to proceed. In either case, plans for this journey entail first considering the long-term goals and then creating a series of short-term plans or "day trips" that will provide valuable learning experiences for all.

Each course you teach is part of a long-range plan for your students. Most likely, this long-range plan is in the form of a curriculum that must adhere to state and/or local standards. You need to determine what parts of the curriculum you are responsible for and how much time you have to meet those responsibilities. You will then divide your curriculum into a series of unit plans that you will, in turn, further refine into daily lessons. In this chapter and the next, we present an overview of long-term and short-term planning, including sample unit and daily plans.

Planning for Instruction

There are many facets to this endeavor of teaching. Beginning teachers can be overwhelmed by questions in the planning stages: What to teach, when to teach it, how to teach it, how to recognize if the students are learning, and how to represent student learning to others.

The quality of instruction is influenced by many teacher-related factors. These include a strong knowledge of mathematics, an ability to provide appropriate learning experiences, and an understanding of student learning and development. Teachers must also be aware of factors that they do not fully control such as the contexts in which their instruction takes place. By contexts we mean a school's organizational structures, assessment policies, and leadership. Additionally, contexts could mean external social systems including families, communities, and regulatory agencies. In any case, the quality of instruction depends largely on continual strengthening of teacher-related factors and consideration of external ones.

This chapter will focus on planning for quality instruction. It will start with what to teach and when to teach it. It will then discuss developing a grasp of concepts and skills through the use of appropriate mathematical tasks organized around individual lessons. Contextual concerns will also be addressed throughout the planning phase.

Long-Range Planning of the Curriculum

What is a mathematics curriculum? Reduced to its simplest form, a mathematics curriculum answers the question, "What do I teach?" The *Handbook of Research on Curriculum* provides a broader definition of it as an "operational plan for instruction that details what mathematics students need to know, how students are to achieve the identified curricular goals, what teachers are to do to help students develop their mathematical knowledge, and the context in which learning and teaching occur" (Romberg, 1992, p. 749)

In some countries, the curriculum is developed nationally, whereas in the United States, the responsibility for curricula resides at the state level. The standards movement has resulted in most states having defined curriculum standards—often outlined in a curriculum framework—that all students are expected to meet. School districts use their state's framework as a resource to design, implement, and assess their content area curricula. Statewide assessments are based on the standards outlined in these frameworks, so teachers must be familiar with their state standards and assessments as well as the school district's curriculum plan.

As a new teacher, you should read your state's standards and your school's mathematics curriculum, paying particular attention to the items pertaining to the grade level or course of study you are teaching. However, as part of a team of educational guides, make sure to familiarize yourself with the entire curriculum so that you are aware of what has come before your course and what is to follow in the students' journey.

The mathematics curriculum should also be reflected in the textbook and supplementary materials provided by the school. The depth of this reflection varies according to each book. In some cases, it is merely a reiteration of the list of topics such as a table of contents. Yet, in other cases, it may include a robust set of materials describing the daily lesson in detail along with a suggested script for the teacher to follow. Although planning is a key element of quality instruction in either case, the teacher who is given only a bare-bones topic list will need to invest far more time in long-range planning.

Scope and Sequence

Teachers need to develop a semester or yearlong scope, sequence, and pacing chart to ensure that students have the opportunity to learn all of the expected concepts and skills. This chart may be provided by the school district. Scope indicates what is to be taught, and at what level, whereas sequence indicates the order in which curricular elements are represented. The pacing chart adds a more restrictive overlay to the scope and sequence by providing guidance on a weekly or daily basis regarding the content of each lesson.

Developing an appropriate scope, sequence, and pacing chart is a difficult task, even for veteran teachers. It is therefore highly recommended that the new teacher work with more experienced ones at the school or district level to create these documents. Many schools have mathematics department chairpersons or lead teachers to help support new teachers with planning, and some school districts can provide support through their curriculum administrator. New teachers assigned to smaller schools may need to seek advice from outside the school by working with district-level personnel or teachers in other districts. Most textbooks include supplementary teaching materials to facilitate planning and instruction. Although these suggested lessons may need to be adapted for schools with double periods or semester-long courses, they can serve as a useful starting point for developing your long-term plan. However, you need to determine the alignment between the mandated curriculum and the textbook. You may find that your textbook does not include all the topics your course needs to address. Conversely, it may contain topics outside the scope of the curriculum. In either case, you will need to make modifications to ensure that students have the opportunity to learn the required curriculum. Opportunity to learn the curriculum has been identified as one of the most important variables in improving student achievement (Growes, 2004).

The following is the most basic scope, sequence, and pacing chart for an introductory algebra course. Note that this scope and sequence is aligned with the NCTM Standards for grades 9–12. You will see that we continually refer back to a set of standards as we plan. In your case you should continually align your instructional plans with your state or local standards.

SAMPLE SCOPE, SEQUENCE, AND PACING CHART FOR A 20-WEEK SEMESTER—INTRODUCTORY ALGEBRA

Sequence	Topic	NCTM Standard*
Week 1	Problem Solving	Problem Solving 9–12
Weeks 2–3	Algebraic Concepts and Basic Equations	Algebra 9–12: Represent and analyze mathematical situations and structures using algebraic symbols
Week 4	Functions and Their Graphs	Algebra 9–12: Understand patterns, relations, and functions
Weeks 5–6	Equations and Inequalities	Algebra 9–12: Understand patterns, relations, and functions
Weeks 7–8	Linear Equations	Algebra 9–12: Understand patterns, relations, and functions
Weeks 9–10	Systems of Equations and Inequalities	Algebra 9–12: Understand patterns, relations, and functions Algebra 9–12: Use mathematical models to represent and understand quantitative relationships
Weeks 11–12	Quadratic Equations and Functions	Algebra 9–12: Understand patterns, relations, and functions Algebra 9–12: Use mathematical models to represent and understand quantitative relationships
Weeks 13–14	Exponents and Exponential Functions	Algebra 9–12: Understand patterns, relations, and functions Algebra 9–12: Use mathematical models to represent and understand quantitative relationships
Week 15	Radical Expressions	Algebra 9–12: Represent and analyze mathematical situations and structures using algebraic symbols
Weeks 16–17	Polynomials	Algebra 9–12: Represent and analyze mathematical situations and structures using algebraic symbols
Weeks 18–19	Rational Expressions and Functions	Algebra 9–12: Understand patterns, relations, and functions Algebra 9–12: Use mathematical models to represent and understand quantitative relationships
Week 20	Review and Final Exam	

*For the purposes of this textbook, we have used NCTM Standards. Your scope and sequence should be aligned with local standards if they are available.

Unit Plans

Having established the scope, sequence, and pace of the course, you are ready to begin planning. Before you consider your daily lesson plans, you should think about each major content area as a whole unit. What follows is a breakdown of a unit plan supported by examples from a grade-9 algebra course.

Unit Planning Model

Unit Rationale

In broad terms, identify why this unit is important. In your rationale you might address the commonly asked question, "Why do I need to learn this stuff?"

EXAMPLE ▪ Introduction to Algebra Unit I: Problem Solving

Problem solving is something that must be infused throughout this course. Thus, a review unit will allow students to revisit many of the problem-solving strategies they have developed during prior years of mathematics instruction. Additionally, beginning the course with this unit provides for a variety of whole class and individual activities, as well as small group activities, designed to help build a classroom environment for cooperative learning. In this fashion, teachers may informally assess the students' problem-solving abilities, literacy skills, and ability to work in groups before the introduction of any new content. As a bonus this review unit can be used to set a tone from the beginning by introducing students to the classroom routines and rules a teacher wishes to implement throughout the school year.

Standards Addressed

Refer to your state or local standards document to identify the standards addressed in your unit. You might present this material in a table as we did with our scope and sequence. In addition, indicate whether you are introducing the standards, mastering the standard, or applying a previously met standard. Good unit plans ask students to continually apply previously learned concepts and skills.

Unit Goals

Here is where you identify the knowledge, skills, and dispositions you expect students to develop over the course of the unit. Your unit goals tend to be broader and more abstract than the specific objectives for the lesson plans you will create. Remember, writing down your goals is not merely an exercise of good teaching; it also serves to keep you on track and properly focused throughout the planning cycle.

Below you will find two goals for an introductory grade 9 unit on problem solving. These goals are very closely aligned with the NCTM Problem-Solving Standard for Grades 9–12 found on page 334 in the *Principles and Standards for School Mathematics* (NCTM, 2000).

EXAMPLES

Students will solve a variety of problems by applying or adapting one or more of the following strategies:

- working backwards,
- finding a pattern to generalize a rule,
- adopting a different point of view,
- solving a simpler problem,
- considering extreme cases,
- making a drawing,
- guessing and testing,
- accounting for all possibilities,
- organizing data,
- using logical reasoning.

Students will develop habits of mind to monitor and reflect on their own problem-solving practice.

Unit Content and Methods

In this section you begin to design the learning objectives for the unit. The first step is to create a list of objectives, grouped in a local order, based on the unit goals. Some teachers opt to include methodology within this list, whereas others leave teaching methods for the lesson planning stage.

As you consider the content of the unit, you should first identify the prior knowledge you expect students have; a school curriculum guide can be helpful for this task. Identifying and reinforcing prerequisite skills greatly increases the probability of your students meeting the unit goals. Too often, teachers reteach material as if their students have never seen it before, a method that often bores students. On the other hand, prior knowledge activities challenge students to recall concepts and skills acquired in previous courses.

Once you have tackled the prerequisite knowledge and skills needed and activation strategies, you are now ready to address the new content of the unit. After reviewing your unit goals, identify specific study topics that will enable all students to meet those goals. Be mindful of your district's curriculum guide as well as the scope and sequence developed earlier.

Our examples below provide one possible way to do this for our introductory problem-solving unit.

EXAMPLE

Lesson 1: 1 Day

Students will be placed in teams to complete teambuilding activities. Teachers will discuss the classroom rules and responsibilities.

Lesson 2: 1 Day

Using a brainstorming activity, students will identify their favorite problems and the strategies they have used to solve problems in the past. Students will then create a semantic map with words and phrases compiled through free association on problem solving. (See Chapter 3 for description of the semantic map.)

Lesson 3: 3 Days

Working in groups, students will solve three out of a set of various problems. They will then create solution posters to be placed around the classroom. These posters will be used as visual aids as students present their solutions to the class. After the student presentations, the class will revisit the semantic map created in the second lesson and suggest additions, deletions, and modifications.

You are now ready to develop the assessment plan if you so choose. However, some teachers prefer to develop full lesson plans at this point from which the assessments can be derived. We recommend that you use whatever method best fits with your planning style.

Unit Assessment

Experienced teachers continually assess their students' progress toward meeting the goals of the unit. These assessments can be informal, such as asking students questions during the lesson, or formal, such as requiring students to complete a test at the end of the unit. Because unit goals tend to be general and abstract, the unit assessment plan is more likely to outline more formal assessments such as quizzes, tests, and projects. Unit assessments must fit into the overall course assessment plan and also be aligned with state and local standards.

EXAMPLES

Create a rubric to assess problem-solving skills.

Analyze semantic map to assess progress in problem solving.

(Assessment will be discussed in Chapter 6.)

Materials and Other Special Considerations

As you develop your unit plan, you should identify materials and other special considerations that will be needed to support your unit. If you plan to use a computer lab or laptop cart for one of your lessons, keep in mind that most schools require a reservation for equipment ahead of time.

Most important, do not count on being able to make copies or borrow materials the morning of your lesson. Resources are scant at some schools and there is often a waiting line at the copy machine; being prepared and well organized are some of the major keys to success during your first year of teaching.

Final Thoughts on Unit Plans

You will find that many of the components of your unit plan will be used in your lesson plans. A well-defined unit plan makes lesson planning much easier. You will also find in drafting your lesson plans that you may need to go back and revise your unit plan and possibly your scope and sequence. When doing so, be sure to keep the whole course curriculum in mind. Too often the "taught curriculum" is not aligned with the "official curriculum" on which high-stakes assessments are based. When students do not have the opportunity to learn concepts and skills identified in the official curriculum, they are put at an unfair disadvantage when tested on that curriculum.

Interdisciplinary Planning

Some schools, especially middle schools, encourage interdisciplinary planning. Interdisciplinary planning involves teams of teachers across the disciplines working together to develop units based on a common theme. For the novice teacher this can seem like a daunting task. However, mathematics, like literacy, can fit into almost any topic.

Most teachers find working on interdisciplinary teams to be an enriching experience. Sharing ideas across disciplines helps teachers see connections that will enhance their own teaching. Care should be taken to ensure that the mathematics included in the interdisciplinary unit is aligned with local and state standards and allows for the use of rich mathematical tasks as part of the instructional model.

Planning From a Fully Developed Curriculum

Many mathematics teachers today have the opportunity to teach from a fully developed curriculum. Most textbook publishers provide teachers' editions and supplementary materials for teachers that include a recommended scope and sequence, pacing calendar, unit plans, lesson plans, assessments, and sometimes lesson scripts. Although it may seem that teaching with these types of materials eliminates the need to plan, this is not the case. Teachers must ensure that the program used is aligned with their school's curriculum. Some topics may need to be added, whereas others may need to be eliminated if time does not allow for appropriate attention to required topics.

To ensure that these commercially prepared materials are aligned with the required curriculum and appropriate for the intended student population, teachers should carefully read through the unit they are teaching and consider the following: Are the vocabulary and notation consistent with that used in the local standards and assessments? Is the suggested pacing reasonable for the students and teaching schedule? Could the context of the focus questions be made more relevant to the student population? Should practice modules be developed for students who need review of prerequisite skills? Should enrichment modules be available for students who have met the standards on which the unit was based? Does this topic connect to coursework in other classes?

Before each lesson, teachers should complete the in-class activities and homework assignments. This helps them avoid careless mistakes, consider additional questions, and assess the time needed for each activity. In addition, teachers need to identify and organize necessary materials prior to class in order to facilitate their use during the lesson.

Teachers may also want to supplement the lesson with more writing assignments, systematic reviews, use of technology, or relevant applications. Many curriculum materials include suggested activities for adding these supplemental elements.

Although, for many experienced teachers, the creative outlet of planning for instruction is a rewarding experience, new teachers are often overwhelmed by all that teachers are expected to do. If chosen carefully, a fully developed curriculum can provide new teachers much needed support while ensuring that their students are learning the appropriate material using research-based instructional strategies and assessment.

Sources to Assist in Long-Range Planning

If you become aware as much as a year or a full semester in advance that you will be teaching a particular course, some or all of the following steps are recommended to help you begin preparing yourself. If, however, you are aware of the situation for only a few days to a few weeks, modifications of the listed suggestions can be made. These modifications will vary, depending on the amount of preparation time available as well as on your own enthusiasm, experience, and expectations of student performance.

Observe an Experienced Teacher

No step you can take is more useful, practical, or helpful than your daily observation of an experienced, competent teacher who is presently teaching the course you expect to teach. First, obtain the teacher's consent to observe his or her teaching. If the teacher agrees, observe regularly and take careful notes on what you see and hear. Copy the questions, the remarks, even the jokes for possible future use. Note the handling of homework, testing procedures, and classroom management. Especially note motivational techniques and clever ways of developing a topic. Even if you ultimately decide to "improve" on his or her style, at least you have a basis for your judgment.

It will be helpful if the teacher you are observing can meet with you regularly to discuss the course and the reasons for using certain teaching techniques.

Obtain Several Course Outlines

Your supervisor may have given you the official school outline, course of study, or appropriate state curriculum. You can and should secure similar outlines from other schools or state education departments by sending away for them. Some may be available online. In addition to providing you with a suggested order of topics in the course, a good course outline will provide you with guidance regarding the approximate amount of time to be devoted to each topic in the course.

Some state or local curriculum guides even offer a series of lesson plans for use in regular (standard) courses. These should be consulted, but used sparingly so your style is not "cramped" by plans written by someone else and not necessarily designed for your needs. What is important is that you gather as much curriculum information as possible about the course you are about to teach.

Examine Various Textbooks

Before you begin any unit planning, consult several textbooks that cover the concepts you want to teach. Textbooks often provide various approaches to certain topics and a large source of problems from which to draw. College resource libraries or your school mathematics department should have an assortment of student editions or teacher editions of textbooks. If you are already teaching, publishers are generally pleased to provide you with copies of textbooks, hoping you will recommend the adoption of them for your classes.

Once you obtain a teacher's edition of a textbook, review the introductory material to determine the philosophical approach and viewpoint of the author. Note the order in which topics are presented, because that is likely to influence your own lesson presentation throughout a school year. Naturally, there will be some topics you will develop independent of the textbook's order, so you should avoid choosing a textbook that differs vastly from your own sense of appropriate topic presentation. Most important, you should select textbooks that offer instructional strategies that will best fit the learning styles of your students and that meet local or state course guidelines.

Familiarize Yourself with the School Library and Media Center

Your school or department library/media center may have books and Internet resources that your students will find useful. These resources may include a wide range of materials for students of all levels and abilities. Both you and your students should also launch your own personal mathematics collections. In addition to the seemingly limitless amount of commercial products, the NCTM publishes and makes available many aids.

Study Old Lesson Plans

Remember, an old lesson may have been taught by a master teacher. Even though teaching techniques have evolved over time, earlier lesson plans may still be informative with regard to style, methodology, strategy, questioning, knowledge, and more.

Find Ideas Online

The World Wide Web is an outstanding resource for teaching ideas and lesson plans that could be incorporated into unit plans. The number of sites and links is virtually limitless. You can find information on the latest educational theory, model lesson plans, ongoing research, new creative approaches to old topics, chat rooms on mathematics education, and much more by going online. Ideas for student projects, different kinds of lessons, and multimedia resources are just a click away.

Following are a few URLs for Web sites, providing an abundance of helpful information for teachers of all degrees of experience and backgrounds, as well as links to other useful sites. Bookmark these and any valuable sites you find yourself while surfing the Internet.

www.nctm.org
www.pbs.org/teachers/math
www.mathforamerica.org
www.powertolearn.com

Learn Students' Backgrounds

What types of young people will you be teaching? Some students will be keen on mathematics and excel in your classroom. Many students, however, will find mathematics challenging and intimidating. To help determine how to meet the individual needs of your students, you may wish to ask students to complete an interest/attitude survey at the beginning of the year. Provide students with a series of questions and a Likert-type scale (see Figure 2.1) to ascertain their motivation, or lack thereof, for participating in mathematics class. Be sure to ask students if they consider themselves weak or strong in particular areas of mathematics. Question students' prior successes and failures in mathematics courses or concepts. Getting some sense of how students view themselves as mathematicians may identify which students will need more support and more opportunities to work with concrete manipulatives or otherwise improve on mathematical understandings and thus avoid more mathematics failures.

Some students may be identified as having special learning needs. According to special education law, all students are to be educated to the maximum extent feasible and in the least restrictive way possible. If one or more of your students have been identified as having special learning needs, Individual Educational Plans or IEPs (sometimes referred to as 504s) will have been created for those students. These educational plans, developed by a team of specialists including special education professionals, school psychologists, and parents, should be made available to you. Read the plans carefully and work with your special education support personnel to ensure that you are ready to make the appropriate accommodations for these students.

Obtain Supplies

Besides the usual tools of the teaching profession, a mathematics teacher generally needs some special teaching resources. These might include board compasses and protractor, graph

FIGURE 2.1 Sample Questions for Mathematics Attitude Survey

	Strongly Agree	Agree	Uncertain	Disagree	Strongly Disagree
1. I find doing mathematics very enjoyable.					
2. Solving mathematics problems makes me uncomfortable.					
3. After I finish school, would like to work in a field that uses mathematics.					
4. I don't feel comfortable with geometric concepts.					
5. I enjoy finding applications of probability and statistics in the daily newspaper.					
6. I get very nervous when I have to take a mathematics test.					
7. I enjoy helping other people solve mathematics problems.					
8. I feel insecure when I have to solve a verbal mathematics problem algebraically.					
9. I feel mathematics is one of the important subjects I am studying.					
10. Reasoning skills are enhanced by studying mathematics.					

Notice that some statements are positive and others negative. This prevents a respondent from simply giving one type of response for all questions.

charts, graphing paper, geometric models, "flexible" quadrilaterals and other polygons and concrete manipulatives, two-dimensional manipulatives that can be projected onto overhead projectors, calculators (including graphing calculators), computers, and software (chief among these for teaching geometry is Geometer's Sketchpad and Fathom for teaching statistics). Ask about the availability of these kinds of resources when you first get a classroom assignment. If school funds are limited, you likely can find civic groups that will help make purchases of these items to fill your classroom needs.

Classroom Management

For many beginning teachers, the ability to manage a classroom is the major factor determining success. If their students are not engaged in the lesson, little learning will take place. Whether students are distracting others, being distracted, or just not paying attention, the time on task will be lost.

Most schools have discipline policies that are communicated through a student handbook. These policies should be the basis for your classroom policies. If, for example, your school does not allow students to wear hats, then you need to enforce that policy. Consistency is the key to successful classroom management; a policy is more likely to have success if every teacher enforces it.

Once you have considered the school's policies, it is time to build a set of rules to help manage your classroom. This set of rules, which should include good classroom citizenship and procedures for classroom transitions, must be precise and communicated to your students on the first day of class. You should also discuss your disciplinary plan with your mentor teacher or supervisor before the school year begins to ensure that you are in compliance with the school district's regulations. Remember, above all, the most effective way to maintain good discipline in class is to teach an engaging lesson where students are motivated to learn and are therefore enthusiastic about being in class.

Short-Range Planning

Now that the long-term plans have been drafted, it is time to focus on short-term instructional plans. Such plans, called lesson plans, often describe what is to be accomplished each day, but can also be developed for 2- or 3-day periods. Based on the learning goals and instructional practices outlined in the unit plan, lesson plans should provide specific details on the content, instructional tasks, questions, practice, and assessments taking place during the lesson.

Rationale for Planning Model

One of the most difficult tasks for teachers, especially new teachers, is obtaining and maintaining student engagement in the lesson. Today, students are programmed to focus for only short periods of time and are in the habit of controlling their own environment. As a mathematics teacher, your goal is to navigate students through a series of challenging and stimulating experiences. Any travel guide will tell you that when planning a journey the most challenging routes are often the most rewarding. However, travelers, like your students, must be given proper support and encouragement to continue the trek.

A summary of the research on effective teaching (Protheroe, Shellard, & Turner, 2003) found that the classrooms of highly effective teachers are likely to have the following characteristics:

Time on task is high and focused on academic content.

Learning goals are clear.

Instruction encourages students to be active learners.

Individualized instruction is provided in recognition of individual differences.

Skill-based instruction is balanced with higher level instruction, often teaching the skills in context.

The classroom climate is supportive and collaborative.

Lessons should be designed with these ideas in mind.

Daily Lesson Planning

Daily lessons are designed to engage students in tasks that will move them toward meeting the goals outlined in your unit plan. Every detail of classroom activities should be planned and relevant to those goals. The amount of detail you put into a written lesson plan compared with the detail you commit to memory will vary depending on your teaching experience and familiarity with a particular course. To infuse yourself with confidence and to ensure that you are covering topics carefully, begin planning daily lessons using the guidelines that follow.

Using your unit plan as a guide, carefully review your curriculum standards and the textbook the school system has selected. Reread the sections related to your unit. Identify terms and examples that you want to reinforce in your lesson while using terminology that is consistent with your textbook. Literacy is a key factor in students becoming mathematically proficient. Therefore, helping students use the textbook effectively will facilitate their ability to read and comprehend mathematics. Literacy issues will be presented in more detail in Chapter 3.

Review your student class list. Are there students in need of accommodations due to physical or learning disabilities? These students might already have Individual Educational Plans (IEPs) or 504 Plans that outline requirements for meeting their needs. If so, what support will be provided for you? Speak to your supervisor about resource or inclusion teachers who can help you adapt your lessons to accommodate students with disabilities.

Find out what schoolwide assessments will be given each year and when they will be administered. Ascertain, if possible, what portions of these assessments are directly related to the concepts you will be responsible for teaching. You may want to infuse questions similar to those asked on local and statewide assessments into the lesson. If you find that there will be items on the assessment that cover previously taught material, then you may want to review these items during the term by infusing them subtly into the homework or lessons.

Decide how you want to use your textbook for each lesson and how you will encourage students to read it. What supporting materials and ideas will you use? How will you supplement lessons to meet the needs of gifted and talented learners? How will you go about breaking concepts down into smaller, more manageable segments to accommodate struggling learners? Is there enough opportunity built into the lesson for students to practice what they have learned? We will help you provide answers to these questions as you continue to read through this book.

Lesson Plan Template

A detailed daily lesson plan includes what you are going to do and what you expect your students to do throughout a given classroom period. To create daily lesson plans, think through the format of the lesson, the relevant tasks in which students will be engaged, and any difficulties your students might encounter. When starting out, you should make your lesson plans quite detailed with the precise wording you intend to use for each facet of the lesson. This practice will help ensure that the steps in your plan are presented in a logical order. Additionally, including such detail forces you to go through a "mental dry run" that crystallizes your thoughts and anticipates possible pitfalls in the actual lesson.

Many teachers are given a plan book with small boxes in which to write their lesson plans. While these boxes are insufficient for recording the actual lesson, they can be used to record the pacing, objectives, and anecdotal records (short teacher observations) of the day's progress. This book can serve as a future guide for you, a record for supervisors or parents, and an aid to a substitute teacher. Yet it is advisable to write new plans every time you teach a course. This "recreation" ensures that you tailor each lesson to the specific needs of each new class. Writing new plans (rather than reusing old ones) also allows you to grow as a teacher; repeating the same lesson approach year in and year out can easily lead to teacher burnout.

There are many suggested formats for lesson plans. Check with your school administrators to see if they have a required format. If they do not, here are some basic features each lesson should include.

Every lesson plan should include what you want your students to show, create, compare, contrast, classify, prove, or any one of the many action words that identify how your students will be engaged in the lesson. Once you have collected appropriate action words, you should compose statements to describe these actions. These statements become the lesson objectives. Next, you need to determine how you will involve your students in activities that allow the class to meet those objectives. This is the instructional part of the lesson. Finally, the plan must indicate how the teacher will know if the students have met the lesson objectives. This is the assessment part of the lesson. Each of the three parts can include one or more subparts as described below.

The basic lesson plan format found below includes the following components: Topic, Grade Level Objectives, Instructional Activities, Assessment, Materials/Equipment, Vocabulary, and Homework. This planning model was used to develop a lesson titled "Introduction to Similar Figures." The goal of the lesson is for students to state and apply the mathematical definition of similar figures.

SAMPLE LESSON PLAN 1

TOPIC: INTRODUCTION TO SIMILAR FIGURES

GRADE LEVEL: 8

OBJECTIVES:

Given 12 shapes, made up of 4 sets of similar shapes, students—working in groups—will classify the shapes and describe their classifications orally and in writing.

Working in groups, students will identify and describe in writing the properties of similar shapes by measuring sides and angles of given similar shapes and determine which properties are consistent among all similar shapes.

Students will state the definition of similar figures or objects.

Students will create figures similar to given figures and use the definition of similar figures to justify their results.

Students will design a class logo and create two similar logos using different scaling factors.

INSTRUCTIONAL ACTIVITIES:

1. Start-up: Give working groups envelopes containing 12 shapes (4 sets of similar figures). Ask each group to classify the shapes and explain their classifications in writing.

2. Motivation: Present your students with a famous company logo and see if they can identify the company that uses the logo (e.g., Nike Swoosh, McDonald's Golden Arches). Show one of the logos in different sizes. Ask the students how the shapes are alike and how they are different. Informally introduce the word *similar*. Then ask why we might want the logos in different sizes. Tell them that we will design our own class logo later in the lesson.

3. Whole class instruction: Ask students how they classified the figures given out in the start-up activity. If one or more of the classification schemes uses similar shapes, save for last. If not, introduce it as a possible classification after students have presented their alternative schemes. Have all students reclassify the shapes using the informal definition of similar figures. Ask the students to predict
   a. how the corresponding sides of the shapes are related.
   b. how the corresponding angles are related.

Note: You may need to review the meaning of "corresponding" sides and angles.

4. Small group activity: Give students chart paper with tabular headings as indicated on page 25. They are to measure the sides and angles of the identified shapes, determine the ratio of the corresponding sides, and then answer the following questions:
   a. What is the relationship between the corresponding angles of similar figures?
   b. What is the relationship between the corresponding sides of similar figures?

Note: The figures represented in the chart are from the sets that were given out as part of the start-up activity. They should be numbered and have their sides and angles labeled.

5. Whole class instruction: Let the students post their charts and then have one or two groups present their results. Discuss the mathematical meaning of the word *similar* and have the students enter the definition in their notebooks. Also place this word on the "word wall."

Definition: In mathematics, figures are said to be similar if their corresponding sides are proportional and the measures of their corresponding angles are equal.

(continued)

SAMPLE LESSON PLAN 1 (*continued*)

6. Small group or individual activity:
   Instructions: Create two figures similar to the object given below. One figure should be three times as large and one figure should be half as large. Note: The three and the one-half are called scaling factors. As you are creating the similar figures describe, in writing, the steps you took to create the two new figures. Also indicate the relationships between the corresponding sides and angles.

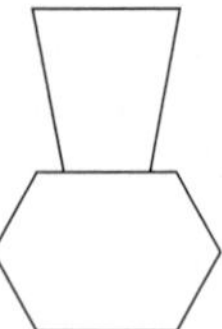

Optional: (Challenge) If you were given two shapes, how would you determine if they were similar? Describe your solution in writing.

7. Small group activity: Create a logo for our class.
   Instructions: We want to use the logo on the invitation to Math Night we are sending home to your parents, the sign on our door, and the Math Night Banner. The logo must use two different geometric shapes. The original logo should fit into a 10 by 10 cm square. The smaller logo must fit into a 4 by 4 cm square, and the largest logo must fit into a 30 by 30 cm square. Describe the design you have chosen and how to scale it up to 30 by 30 cm and down to 4 by 4 cm. If you use additional items in your logo, you must draw them to scale as well. You must write very specific measurements and instructions so that, if chosen, your logo can be re-created by others. When you have finished your design, think about where you would add our class name, Math 435, to the logo. Each design will be presented to the class and then posted along with the instructions for its creation. The class will review the designs over the next 2 days and vote for their favorite logo.

8. Summary: Close the lesson by asking the following questions:
   a. How would you create one shape that is similar to another with sides that are 1.5 times as large?
   b. What shapes in the room are similar but not congruent?

If you were given two shapes, how would you determine if they were similar?

ASSESSMENT:

Students will identify the properties of similar shapes by measuring sides and angles of given similar shapes and determining which properties are consistent among all of them. Assessed by written responses and discussion in activity 4 and homework.

Students will create figures similar to given figures. Assessed by products from activities 6 and 7, the discussion in activity 8, and homework.

Students will design a class logo and create two similarly shaped logos using different scaling factors. Assessed through products in activity 7.

MATERIALS/EQUIPMENT:

Similar shapes with sides and angles labeled, chart paper with tables created, rulers, protractors, markers, colored paper, and calculators.

VOCABULARY:

Similar, congruent, corresponding, scaling factor, and proportional

HOMEWORK:

Create a VVWA for the word *similar*. (*Note*: See Chapter 3 for information on the VVWA.)

Lesson Analysis

In the above lesson, the students move from whole class to small group to independent learning activities throughout the lesson. The tasks chosen allow students with different skill levels and interests to participate in the activities. Some students will measure sides and angles, and others will fill in the chart and calculate the ratio of corresponding sides. During the group activities, all students should be involved in discussing the questions, but one person per group will write up the answers to those questions. Each group member should be able to present the results to the class. The last activity in the lesson is an application of finding similar figures. It reinforces the concepts learned earlier while allowing the more creative students to contribute their artistic talents. This model of instruction allows all students to contribute and holds everyone accountable for understanding the material.

The lesson is designed for a class period that lasts at least 90 minutes. It can be adapted for a 2- or 3-day lesson depending on the time available and ability level of the class.

Lesson Components

TOPIC Stating the topic at the beginning of each lesson plan is a useful tool for improving your focus on the lesson as well as for filing the plan away for future use. Furthermore, adding a qualifying word to the topic will allow you to quickly identify the level for which the lesson is intended. In the similar figures lesson, the word *introduction* indicates that the lesson is appropriate for students who have no prior knowledge of the topic.

OBJECTIVES Objectives identify the purpose or aim of each lesson using specific student action words. They are related to, but more specific than unit goals. Writing the lesson objectives helps the teacher identify appropriate instructional and assessment activities for the topic. Formally written objectives (1) describe the instructional activity in which students will engage, and (2) identify the important conditions under which students will complete the activity. A third component commonly found in a lesson objective is used to indicate the level of completion you find acceptable. In our case we expect the students to successfully complete the task indicated and thus have left out this third component.

In the similar figure lesson the second objective is: "Working in groups, students will identify and describe in writing the properties of similar shapes by measuring sides and angles of given similar shapes and determining which properties are consistent among all similar shapes." In this objective the student action we seek is that they identify common properties among similar shapes. They will make this identification by measuring sides and angles of shapes and determining which properties are consistent among the similar shapes while working in groups. These are the conditions under which the action will take place. Because we expect each group to successfully complete the task, our criterion component is left out.

Let's see how this objective may have been developed. Remember first we would consider the standards related to our grade level and topic. For our purposes we used the NCTM Geometry Standard for grades 6 through 8. The following are two expectations listed in that standard:

- describe, classify, and understand relationships among types of two- and three-dimensional objects using their defining properties;
- understand relationships among the angles, side lengths, perimeters, areas, and volumes of similar objects. (NCTM, 2000, p. 232)

The unit plan goal aligned with this standard, and the topic for the similar figures lesson could be stated as follows:

> In this unit students will classify congruent and similar shapes based on properties related to the lengths of their sides and the measures of their angles. They will identify and describe the defining properties of congruent and similar objects and apply these properties to solve problems related to similar and congruent objects.

You can see that the goal, while more specific than the standard, is still too general to determine if it has been met by an individual student. Thus, we need to further define our goals by writing objectives.

To write the objective, we briefly describe the instructional activity in which students will engage. Here is where we will use specific action words such as *compare, draw, state*, or *measure* to identify what students will do during the activity or as a result of the activity. The second objective listed in the similar figures lesson states that ". . . students will identify and describe in writing the properties of similar shapes. . . ." The students' ability to identify and describe those properties becomes the actions we will assess.

Next we must indicate the important conditions under which students will complete the activity. We know that this age group is social and many learn best through active engagement. Thus we choose a structured group activity that will allow students to practice their measuring skills, use a chart to organize data, and draw conclusions from the data collected. These become the important conditions under which the activity will take place.

One of the keys to writing objectives is choosing words to identify observable outcomes or products. You may want to use the same action words found in the standard or goal, as we did in the objective listed above. One of the words used in the standard, goal, and objective was *describe*. We made the action more specific in the objective by stating the students would describe in writing. However, in some cases the "action" listed in the standard or goal is too general to be meaningful.

Let's consider another word in the standard that would not make a good action word in the objectives: *understand*. What if we asked students if they understand the relationships among similar figures? They might simply reply with a terse "yes" leaving us with no evidence to support their comprehension. Although we want students to understand the relationships among similar figures, *understand* is too vague to measure. We need to indicate how we would have the students demonstrate their understanding of the concept of similar figures. This is why we choose to have the students *identify and describe* the properties.

Writing good instructional objectives takes practice. Doing so allows you to think through the lesson and its assessment tasks while ensuring the lesson's alignment with state and local standards.

INSTRUCTIONAL ACTIVITIES In the instructional part of the lesson, you describe what your students will do throughout the classroom period. These activities should be aligned with your objectives and provide significant opportunities for your students to develop the proficiencies and conceptual understandings outlined in those objectives. New teachers should provide as much detail as possible in the instructional part of the lesson. The instructional part of our lesson is divided into four parts: start-up, motivation, sequenced mathematical tasks, summary.

START-UP The lesson start-up is a task that students complete as soon as they enter the classroom. It is usually posted in the same place everyday so that students can easily find the assignment. This activity gives the teacher time to take care of administrative tasks such as clearing the halls and taking attendance while the students are settling into their seats and transitioning to math class. A good teacher will also walk about the classroom, observing students at work. Start-ups can be used to review prior knowledge or bridge a past lesson to the day's topic. They should be short and accessible to each student. In the similar figures lesson, students used the figures in the start-up classification activity as objects to investigate further during the actual lesson.

MOTIVATION The lesson motivation is a short activity that piques the learner's curiosity at the beginning of the lesson. It can be a challenge problem or a question resulting from an interesting story. Teachers often use a typical math problem formulated in a context that is of interest to the age group of their audience. Using the name of the current favorite rap artist, sports figure, or pop icon can gain your students' attention—at least initially. In the similar figures lesson, the students are asked to identify common corporate logos. This activity is a bridge to introducing logos of different sizes and, then, to similar figures. Further discussion of motivational techniques can be found in Chapter 3.

SEQUENCED MATHEMATICAL TASKS Following the motivation is a carefully sequenced set of mathematical tasks. These tasks should allow the student to explore and apply new concepts and skills as well as reinforce previously learned material. When new concepts are introduced, as in the similar figures lesson, students should start by exploring the ideas related to the concept. Exploration of ideas will occur when you initiate open-ended, stimulating comments that cause students to think and talk, agree and disagree, thirst for more knowledge, and make conjectures. Here, the teacher should create an effective learning environment by using diagrams, graphs, sketches, physical models, and analogies to develop appropriate exploratory tasks. Further exploration of ideas will occur when you provide students with opportunities to record their mathematical thoughts in logs and journals.

In our lesson, students explore the shapes used in the start-up activity by measuring angles and sides, and recording their findings in a prepared chart. Such an activity enables students to use measuring devices such as rulers and protractors, record information in a chart, find ratios, and draw conclusions related to similar figures. Even though this activity will take more time than simply reteaching the material explicitly, it allows students to apply previously learned skills. Often, because students are working in groups, peers can help others to recall the prior knowledge. This reactivation and use of prior knowledge/skills should be built into each of your lesson plans. However, if your informal assessment indicates that most of the students have forgotten the material, you may want to call the class back to a whole group session and review the concept or skill in question.

After the exploration part of the lesson, you may want to move to a whole class instructional activity to share findings and ensure that all are ready to proceed with the next activities. In our lesson, we used this whole class time to give a formal definition of similar figures. We wanted to make sure that everyone used the same definition and that we had added it to the vocabulary list. This is especially important, because the word *similar* occurs in our normal conversation with a less specific definition. This is sometimes called the "explain" part of the lesson.

Following the explain part of the lesson, you will want to provide students with the opportunity to apply what they learned. Sometimes referred to as "practice," these activities reinforce the concepts and skills developed earlier in the lesson. The practice part of the lesson also allows the teacher to circulate among the class to informally assess understanding and provide support for those who need it.

In our similar figures lesson, the first practice problems include very specific tasks that are clearly aligned with the goals and objectives of the class. Our last problem, the open-ended logo design problem draws on the different strengths and interests of the students while they continue to develop their understanding of the properties of similar figures.

The teacher may want to bring the class back together as the students move through practice problems to discuss solutions, or the teacher may want to identify students who need more support and let the others proceed with the activities. These are decisions you should think about as you plan.

SUMMARY Providing time to summarize your lesson is important. This is a time when the teacher ties together all parts of the lesson. Sometimes a simple question to the class such as the following will elicit a summary: "Suppose your classmate was absent and called you on the phone to ask what today's lesson was about. What would you say about the lesson so that your classmate would get a clear idea of the topics missed?" You could ask more pointed questions that are aligned with your objectives. This is the approach taken in the similar figures lesson. If time is short, the teacher can summarize, although this is not recommended, as students are usually focused on copying down the homework assignment or meeting their friends before the next class.

ASSESSMENT Assessment is the third major component of our lesson plan. The objectives identify what we want the students to learn, the instructional part of the lesson describes how the students will be engaged in learning, and the assessment section describes how you will know if the students have met your objectives.

Most veteran teachers will tell you that they assess student understanding throughout the lesson. In our planning model we ask new teachers to explicitly identify when and how they are assessing student understanding. Too often, new teachers present a lesson and assume that students are learning. By the same token, students listen and assume they are learning as well. It is not until the tests are graded that both teachers and students realize that insufficient learning may have taken place.

After you have written your objectives and instructional activities, you should review for assessment opportunities. Did you list key questions and sample problems in the plan? A teacher should not depend on plucking effective sample problems and questions out of their hats during the lesson. Did you provide time for students to work independently or in small groups to check their own understanding? Again, teachers should not accept nods or a quiet classroom as indications of student comprehension.

After completing this lesson review, write a brief paragraph describing your assessment plan for the lesson. Also indicate any formal evaluations that will be recorded toward the grade for the course. This evaluation should fit into your overall assessment plan.

In the similar figures lesson, assessment opportunities are integrated throughout. Informal assessments take place through observation of the small group and individual work and during the whole class discussions. In addition there can be more formal assessment of the products produced during the lesson activities or through evaluation of the homework.

MATERIALS/EQUIPMENT Materials and equipment used during a lesson should be listed in the lesson plan. These include items such as board compasses, a graph chart, geometric models, an overhead projector, computers/calculators, and display units for these. This list will remind you of what you must reserve or order prior to the lesson. You will also need to build in time for dissemination and collection of materials and equipment during the lesson. In the similar figures lesson, you ask students to use rulers and protractors to measure sides and angles. You want to make sure that your students know how to use these measuring devices prior to the lesson or build time to review their use into the lesson.

A second item listed in the similar figures lesson is the prepared chart paper. You want to make sure that you have created the charts found in the "Charts for Introduction to Similar Figures Lesson" prior to class. Rather than have students invest their valuable instructional time in creating the charts, the teacher has created them ahead of time.

VOCABULARY Because understanding the language of mathematics is key to becoming a successful student of the discipline, we have added a plan component specifically for

Chart Paper

Shape	1	2	Ratio of Sides
Side a			a_1/a_2=
Side b			
Side c			
Side d			
Angle A			
Angle B			
Angle C			
Angle D			

Chart Paper

Shape	1	2	Ratio of Sides
Side a			
Side b			
Side c			
Angle A			
Angle B			
Angle C			

Charts for Introduction to Similar Figures Lesson

vocabulary. Mathematics teachers use a variety of vocabulary development strategies found in the literacy research. These techniques will be more thoroughly explored in Chapter 3.

HOMEWORK It is advisable that the homework assignment be carefully planned and included in the lesson plan. The assignment should be designed to help students refine their newly acquired skills, to promote independence, and to develop reflection and creative thinking skills. As means to those ends, each assignment completed by students is expected to be neat, organized, accurate, and as complete as possible.

Beginning teachers may have difficulty with assigning, reviewing, and grading homework. Therefore, we have provided a comprehensive look at homework assignments in the next section.

Assigning Homework

Most mathematics lessons require student follow-up to refine and sharpen their newly acquired skills. Therefore, you should carefully plan the homework assignment and include it within your lesson plan. An equally important reason for assigning homework is that student work done outside of the classroom helps to develop independent thought and creative thinking skills.

Homework should be discussed in class the day after it was given and usually reviewed as part of a small or large group activity. It might even occasionally be collected for the teacher's perusal and analysis. Small group or whole class analyses are appropriate for different types of assignments, and the teacher must make that determination—there is no formula for a best strategy. The remainder of this section is devoted to the nature of homework assignments.

What Should Be Involved in Preparing the Homework Assignment?

It is helpful for both the teacher and the students to anticipate the homework assignment. The teacher, as part of the preparation of the lesson and homework assignment, should work out all the exercises being assigned to the students for homework. This will not only be useful in more accurately determining the time required for a student to complete the assignment, but also enable the teacher to alert students about potential trouble spots in the homework assignment before they encounter them at home. By telling the students beforehand what is expected of them with regard to the homework assignment, the teacher makes the assignment a more meaningful part of the total learning process.

What Should Be the Nature of the Homework Assignment?

Many types of homework assignments are possible in a mathematics class. No one is necessarily better than another. The content of the lesson and the nature of the class should determine the type of homework. Perhaps the key concept to keep in mind when preparing a homework assignment is *variety*. Monotony is likely to be the chief factor influencing students to abandon their homework assignment.

Teachers should try to provide different kinds of exercises. For example, some of the types of exercises from which to choose would include drill exercises, verbal problems, proofs, construction exercises, thought questions, applications of newly taught principles, and reading assignments. Particularly in a mathematics class, a reading assignment needs a lot of student motivation, because a nonwritten assignment is likely to be omitted, being deemed unnecessary by the students.

In addition to varying the types of exercises offered, assignments may also vary in nature. For example, one assignment may be intended entirely for review of previously studied material, whereas another may include some discovery questions. Included in a review assignment may be a variety of different kinds of exercises. The assignment may simply offer exercises that review the previous lesson's work, or it may provide exercises that will assist the student to review for a test on an entire unit's work.

Another type of homework assignment may involve a discovery approach. Here the student is given a series of exercises that foreshadow the ensuing lesson. The questions are usually arranged in an order that will permit the student to discover a new idea after completing the sequence of questions. A few examples of this type of exercise follow.

EXAMPLE

The homework assignment just prior to a discussion on the slope relationship between two parallel and two perpendicular lines might include the following.

1. Use the slope-intercept form of the equation of a straight line to determine the slope of each line, and then use a graphing calculator to graph each pair of functions:

   a. $y = 2x + 1$ and $y = -\frac{1}{2}x + 3$

   b. $y = \frac{3}{5}x + 2$ and $y = \frac{3}{5}x - 2$

   c. $y = -\frac{5}{3}x + 2$ and $y = \frac{3}{5}x + 1$

   d. $5x + 3y = 5$ and $5x + 3y = 15$

2. Which lines appear perpendicular? What is the relationship of their slopes?
3. Which lines appear parallel? What is the relationship of their slopes?
4. Make a generalized statement regarding the slopes of parallel or perpendicular lines (based on the foregoing exercises).

This set of exercises provides review of a skill learned earlier, then requires the student to make some simple generalizations from the specifics presented.

EXAMPLE

The homework assignment the day before introducing the Pythagorean identity to a trigonometry class might include the following:

Use a scientific calculator to complete the following chart. Use the radical relationships when possible.

θ	$\sin\theta$	$\cos\theta$	$\sin^2\theta$	$\cos^2\theta$	$\sin^2\theta + \cos^2\theta$
30					
45					
60					
50					

What generalization seems to be true about $\sin^2\theta + \cos^2\theta$?

Although completing the chart ought to be relatively simple for students, it should lead them to discover an interesting relationship.

One of the more popular types of homework assignment is often called a *spiraled* assignment, because it spirals back over previously learned material. Perhaps it owes its popularity to its ability to satisfy two homework assignment functions. In addition to enabling students to reinforce the current classroom instruction, a spiraled assignment provides review of previously taught topics. For example, suppose you are assigning homework after a lesson on "angle measurement with a circle" in high school geometry. As part of this assignment, you might include one exercise reviewing similarity, one proof involving a parallelogram, and one construction. Regardless of which previous topics are selected for inclusion in a particular assignment, the selection ought to be done in an organized and orderly fashion.

One convenient method for spiraling the homework assignments is to mark dates of assignment in the margin next to the exercises in the teacher's copy of the textbook. This will assist in keeping a record of which items have or have not been assigned. The extent and degree of the spiral depends on each individual class's needs. This further reinforces the idea that lesson plans (including homework assignments) should not be used from one year to the next without making substantial adjustments for each class.

Many other types of homework assignments may be used for a mathematics class. These may include home experiments of some mathematical principle (e.g., coin tossing to compute probabilities empirically); short essays on famous mathematicians or some other vignette out of the history of mathematics (e.g., how Eratosthenes measured the circumference of the earth); library assignments (e.g., to find the origin of the $\sqrt{\ }$ symbol or the first use of the Greek letter π to represent the ratio of the circumference of a circle to its diameter); and brief papers on some topics related to, but not included in, the curriculum (e.g., a paper on applications of parabolas and parabolic surfaces).

Whichever assignment a teacher chooses to use for a particular situation, the key to success is variety. Also, the types of assignments should be dictated by the subject matter and therefore should change as needed. Although some teachers assign homework that consists of mixtures of the types of assignments described here, others exhibit no creativity in their homework assignments. Such teachers' assignments simply read, "Do page 353, ex. 1–29, odd numbers only." It does not take long for students to react in kind to this type of homework assignment. The result is a lost opportunity to achieve meaningful learning in mathematics outside the classroom. Remember, the needs of the class determine the type of homework to be assigned.

How Much Work Should Each Assignment Require?

The answer to this question must vary with each intended audience. We can answer this question only by providing guidelines for setting the proper assignment length for a particular class.

Each homework assignment will have specific objectives based on the needs of the class. The knack for preparing an appropriate assignment is to accomplish the objectives with the least amount of student work time. Unnecessary repetition should be eliminated, or at least minimized. The exercises should be carefully selected so that each one is highly effective in meeting the objectives of the particular homework assignment.

Students are quick to realize when an assignment is time-efficient and when it is loaded with superfluous material. When the exercises are largely repetitive, students can easily get bored and distracted. As a result, either they may do the work "just to get it done" or they may copy the work from a classmate and submit that. Naturally this results in a waste of student time, with little or no learning being accomplished. Therefore, the homework assignments should be succinct, properly covering the intended content in the minimum time.

It is difficult to specify a time limit to a mathematics homework assignment. The mathematics teacher obviously would prefer giving the class a longer homework assignment just to make sure everything is thoroughly covered. But she or he must remember that mathematics is only one of several courses each student must take. Therefore, the time allotted to mathematics homework should generally be kept to at most about one-half hour per assignment. (This is merely a guide and can vary with individual circumstances.)

Should All Students Be Assigned the Same Work?

Once again (and at the risk of repetition) the answer to this question depends on the type of class for which the homework assignment is intended. If the class is homogeneous with respect to student mathematical ability and achievement, then perhaps a uniform homework assignment for the entire class is appropriate. In reality, classes generally do not have this sort of uniform composition. Therefore an alternative to uniform assignments may be sought.

The best instruction is tailored to each student's individual needs. Unfortunately, it is not always practicable to satisfy such a desirable objective in the regular secondary school classroom. Perhaps one of the few ways of approaching such a goal is through the homework assignment. The homework assignment provides a useful means for adjusting class instruction to meet students' individual needs.

Special enrichment assignments can be provided for the more able students, who can then be excused from some of the drill or review exercises. On the other hand, students needing more drill and review of certain necessary skills can be given exercises designed for this purpose. The mathematics teacher should not neglect this fine opportunity to individualize at least a part of the learning process.

When Should Teachers Prepare Homework Assignments?

Those who favor assigning homework on a daily basis would probably argue that this is the only way in which the homework can be regularly tailored to instructional needs. Each day a new lesson is planned (based on the experience of the previous lesson), a homework assignment is prepared based on the immediate needs of the students. Such precisely fitted assignments are far more difficult (if at all possible) to achieve when assignments are given a week at a time. For one thing, teachers who have planned a week's assignments and have given them to the students may find altering them inconvenient and may therefore not only be reluctant to make changes based on instructional needs but also try to pace their lessons (to a degree) to this predetermined plan. Consider the case in which a teacher finds that, midway through a week's assignments, a class needs some drill on a particular skill. The class may be resentful of a last-minute augmentation of the assignments. This negative student attitude could adversely affect the educational benefits that were intended by this additional work. Even if some previously assigned work is deleted from the assignment to accommodate the additional work, the resulting assignment may still not be as effective as if it had been planned on a daily basis to meet the ongoing needs of the class. Thus, a daily planned assignment has as its chief advantage the ability to meet the regularly assessed needs of the students based on classroom experiences and previous homework performance.

Seemingly equally convincing arguments support weekly planned homework assignments. Here teachers will argue that by assigning homework a week (or more) at a time, they can better plan and spiral their homework assignments. They would also point out that by making the assignments only once every several days, they save classroom time otherwise taken up giving out new assignments. In addition, proponents of weekly homework assignments would indicate that by having a week's assignments in their possession, students who are absent from school could without much inconvenience try to keep up with the rest of the class.

The weekly assignment also enables a student to accelerate his homework by going ahead of the class (if he is able to). This has both advantages and disadvantages. For example, if a student finds that, say, on a Wednesday he will not have time to do his homework assignment, he might complete this assignment (if able to) on Tuesday. Although this is not an ideal practice, it is better than coming in to his Thursday class unprepared. The disadvantage to knowing future assignments is that the surprise factor is gone. There is some motivational advantage to having students discover new concepts. By knowing what future assignments are planned, students also know which topics are going to be studied and when. The removal of this element of discovery could be a weakness for the instructional plan.

The question of frequency of assignments, like many others in this chapter, is one that can be answered only by the individual teacher. We present the chief arguments for the various positions and leave the choice to the reader. Whatever the choice, substantial justification should be consistent with a teacher's personality, teaching style, and educational philosophy and with the nature of the class.

When Should Homework Be Assigned?

Perhaps an ideal time to give a homework assignment is at the point in the lesson that leads naturally to the work to be assigned. For example, a teacher may say, "Now that you know how to solve a quadratic equation, try the following for homework." It can be argued, however, that this approach breaks the continuity of the lesson and for this reason should be avoided.

Once again, for the teacher who elects to assign homework daily, there is probably no single "right time" to assign the homework. Those who argue for assigning the homework at the beginning of the lesson may say that asking students to write their assignment when they enter the room ensures that they are occupied as soon as they enter and that they will not forget to write down their assignment.

Others may argue that by assigning the homework at the beginning of the lesson, the teacher may reveal the topic of the ensuing lesson and thereby eliminate the effect or impact of a discovery approach. It is also possible that when an assignment is given out at the beginning of the lesson, some students may begin to work on it *during* the lesson just to "get it over with early" and as a result miss the new work presented during the lesson. This should certainly be discouraged.

Opponents may respond that a teacher could become so involved in the lesson that she might forget to assign the homework or possibly give it to the students when the period-ending bell sounds and students are in the process of leaving the room. This would not give the teacher an opportunity to explain the homework assignment to the class. In addition, some students might miss receiving the assignment by exiting too quickly. At any rate, a rushed assignment is not desirable.

In response, the proponents of the end-of-lesson assignment would argue that by assigning homework at the end of the lesson, the teacher would be able to make adjustments in the originally planned assignment based on the class performance during the lesson without the class's knowing it. This way no ill feeling on the part of the class can result.

Many more arguments can be offered for the "best time" to assign homework. We have simply presented a sample of the options available so that the reader can make a decision.

Whichever time the teacher finds best suited for both herself and the class, she must carefully review the assignment with the class. Ambiguous parts should be clearly explained and potential tough spots anticipated. This should also make students aware of the purpose of the particular homework assignment.

How Should the Assignment Be Made?

This will depend on the way in which the homework is being assigned. If the homework is being assigned on a weekly basis, then the assignments ought to be written and duplicated and passed out to the class. A typical assignment sheet might include the assignment number, the topic of the lesson, the date, the actual assignment, and some of the highlights of the lesson that ought to be studied. One possible arrangement is shown in the sample Weekly Homework Assignment Sheet.

For the student, such a homework assignment sheet can also serve the function of reinforcing the objectives of the lesson. In addition, this sheet can serve as an ongoing form of communication with the parents. It will allow them to be aware of the direction of the course and where possible offer some assistance to their children. The direction of the course will also become more clearly focused for the students as a result of using these homework assignment sheets.

A small, but potentially important, benefit of using homework assignment sheets is that it avoids the possibility of students accidentally writing a wrong assignment. Such can be the case if they must copy it from the chalkboard or from teacher dictation.

Homework assignment sheets may also be used by a teacher giving out the assignments on a daily basis, in which case the sheets will probably be cut into individual assignments or run off daily. A difficulty with using any assignment sheet for daily assignments is that any adjustments in the assignment must involve the class in making the change. This procedure could have a negative effect among the students, although if handled properly the negative effect could be minimized or even eliminated.

A popular way of giving out homework in the mathematics class is via the board. Teachers fortunate enough to have their own classroom may write the assignments for all their classes on the board; when each class enters the room, the students may simply copy the assignment into their notebooks.

Assignments may also be given orally, but this is usually not the most effective way. A student can miss hearing a portion of the assignment or possibly hear a part of the assignment incorrectly. The result may have negative effects on the learning process. Giving a homework assignment orally could require several repetitions and still cause confusion. When handled improperly, the oral assignment could leave students with the impression that the assignment is either optional or not too important.

Regardless of the manner in which the homework is assigned, the teacher should make every effort to be certain that there are no ambiguities. For example, if there are similarly numbered exercises at the top and bottom of a given textbook page, the location, top or bottom, should be specified in the assignment. Each assignment should be properly identified by class, date, and topic, as well as by any other relevant information. Above all, the manner in which the homework assignments are presented should be consistent with the teacher's instructional style and properly suited for the type of class. Some teachers feel that a weaker mathematics class is more apt to require homework assignments presented on sheets because they may copy their assignment incorrectly or simply forget to copy them. Thus, the type of class may well be an important consideration in selecting the best format in which to present the homework assignment.

How Should Long-Term Assignments Be Given?

Occasionally a long-term assignment may be appropriate for a mathematics class. A teacher may decide to assign a report on a famous mathematician, or students may be assigned a geometric construction project or a statistical experiment. For any of these long-term assignments, the manner in which the assignment is presented to the class is important.

The possibility of a long-term assignment should be announced to the class at the beginning of the course. When the teacher is ready to assign this project formally to the class, he or she must be sure to include the following:

- The extent of the work that will be required (specific topics should be listed)
- The specific guidelines for choosing a topic (if a choice is called for)
- The scope and limitations of the project
- The format for submission of the work
- The timetable for the assignment
- Available resources (e.g., school, department, public library, computers)

After a reasonable period of time, the teacher should monitor the students' progress. Those students who are floundering should be assisted and encouraged; those students who are working in the wrong direction should be redirected. At this time the teacher can discuss with the class difficulties some students may have encountered in the process of working on the assignment, possibly helping others facing similar problems.

Midway through the project, the assignment format should be reviewed with the class. Students should be reminded about resources available (e.g., mathematics department library or school library).

To make a long-term assignment as meaningful as possible, students should be scheduled for individual conferences with the teacher to get ongoing assistance. This provides not only a necessary input for direction but also a usually much-needed stimulus for further work.

Unlike the regular homework assignment, the long-term assignment requires continuous monitoring, guidance, assistance, and assessment. Unless special care is taken to prepare and assist students in these endeavors, such an assignment is likely to be ineffective.

Weekly Homework Assignment Sheet

____
(Class)

(Assignment No.)	(Topic)	(Date)

Book / Page / Exercises
" " "
" " "

Concepts and Relationships to Remember:

(Assignment No.)	(Topic)	(Date)

Book / Page / Exercises
" " "
" " "

Concepts and Relationships to Remember:

(Assignment No.)	(Topic)	(Date)

Book / Page / Exercises
" " "
" " "

Concepts and Relationships to Remember:

(Assignment No.)	(Topic)	(Date)

Book / Page / Exercises
" " "
" " "

Concepts and Relationships to Remember:

(Assignment No.)	(Topic)	(Date)

Book / Page / Exercises
" " "
" " "

Concepts and Relationships to Remember:

Format of the Homework Assignment

Much to the amazement of the beginning teacher, students seek out direction from the teacher in almost every aspect of schoolwork. This certainly includes direction regarding the format of the homework assignment. Two basic questions come up in this respect: How should it be arranged? Where should it be written? Although the responses to these two questions are closely related, we discuss them separately.

Questions About Arrangement of Homework

The format of the homework, if uniform among the students, is useful to the teacher when reading individual assignments. Endless options exist for selecting a convenient format for students to follow when writing their homework. We indicate some, with the hope that this discussion will generate other, perhaps more useful ideas for the reader. In deciding on a format to have your students follow, you ought to consider *your* work with these homework assignments as well as the students' eventual use for them.

IDENTIFYING INFORMATION? The teacher should specify what information should be written on the homework paper. In addition to the student's name, should the subject class, homework assignment number, the date, etc. be included? Should each assignment be numbered in a particular way? Whatever information the teacher chooses to require should be uniform throughout the class.

WRITING THE QUESTIONS? Another issue the teacher must decide is whether students should copy a homework question before answering it. Many teachers consider this a poor use of a student's time; others believe that if students have the questions before them, the homework assignment papers become a better source from which to study.

MARGINS? Any teacher who has received a homework assignment paper from a student who left no margins on the paper will appreciate having students leave sufficient margins for teacher comments. Students may also like to use this space to make necessary corrections after listening to a class review of the homework assignment.

FRAMING ANSWERS? Some teachers require students to frame in (with a rectangle) their answers to a question to separate them from the rest of the work. This makes the teacher's work easier when reading many papers. An extra benefit derived from this practice is that it requires students to identify the answer to a question, a skill often taken for granted but sometimes not so trivial. After working a problem, students sometimes lose sight of what exactly was being asked and, having worked the problem correctly, do not submit the proper answer.

FORMAT OF THE PAPER? For some short problems in algebra or arithmetic, a teacher might want the students to fold a sheet of paper into a specific number of rectangles. This not only may result in a neater paper but also allows the student to get more work onto a sheet of paper. A similar effect can be obtained by ruling lines on the paper instead of folding it.

Teachers often insist on a format for working particular types of problems. For example, for solving equations it is desirable to have students line up the equal signs vertically. Students may simplify radicals by working horizontally. Special directions may be given when the homework assignment involves graphing functions or proving geometric theorems. Since both of these latter types of exercises usually require using a full page for each problem, a more efficient format would involve folding a piece of $8\frac{1}{2}'' \times 11''$ paper in half to form a "booklet" ($5\frac{1}{2}'' \times 8\frac{1}{2}''$) of four pages, each of which can accommodate one problem (see the figure below). This format allows a student to place four, instead of two, longer problems (such as a geometry proof or a graph of a function) on a sheet of paper. Teacher handling of the paper also should be easier.

Regardless of which format a teacher chooses to use, uniformity among the students serves two useful functions: it gives the students the direction they desire, and it makes the teacher's job of reading the papers much easier.

WHERE SHOULD THE HOMEWORK BE WRITTEN? Depending on the type of class involved and the subject matter being taught, a uniform arrangement should be worked out for the class. For example, for high school geometry, the teacher may require a loose-leaf or spiral notebook ($8\frac{1}{2}'' \times 11''$) with a clip or large envelope fastened to the inside back cover. This will enable the students to keep their notes and their homework together in folded booklets.

Teachers may instead ask students to keep a separate homework section in their loose-leaf notebook (of a specified size) so that after it is collected by the teacher it can be reinserted in the notebook or placed in the students' portfolio.

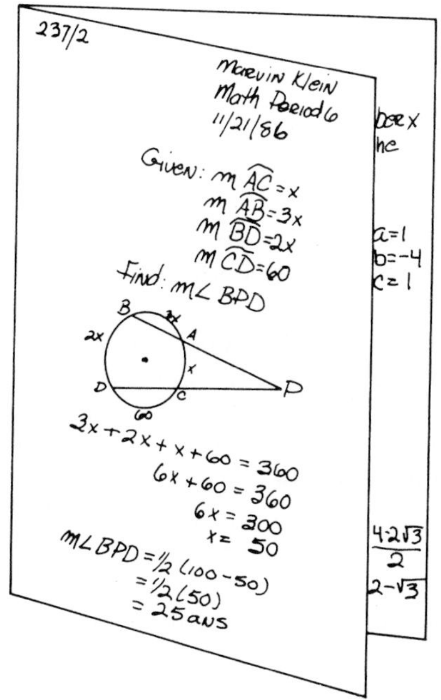

There are many useful ways to have students keep their homework. The exact manner should be determined by the teacher and may vary with each class, considering such things as subject matter, class discipline, and student work habits.

Reviewing the Homework Assignment

A teacher must answer several questions about the review of homework. The teacher must decide when and how to review the homework, whether to go over the homework with the class, and how much of it to discuss. That is, should every exercise be reviewed before the whole class or only a representative few? We discuss these questions in this section.

Questions About Reviewing Homework Assignments

When Should the Homework Assignment Be Reviewed? There is probably no "best time" during a lesson for discussing the previous night's homework. Some teachers hold that every lesson must begin with a review of the previous lesson's homework assignment. They argue that new work should not be presented until the previous work (in the form of the homework assignment) has first been mastered.

Other teachers review the previous lesson's homework at the end of the lesson so as to allow the new lesson to get off to a crisp and motivating start. These teachers prefer to begin the lesson with a motivating activity leading into the development of the lesson. Only after the new topic has been completely discussed do they want to go over the past homework assignment.

A teacher certainly could adopt both systems and even include one that calls for a review of the previous homework assignment at a point in the class period at which it most naturally fits! In the case of a "discovery-type" homework assignment, it might be appropriate to discuss the homework just before introducing a concept or relationship that might come up in the middle of the lesson. Here the homework would be useful to elicit from students the desired mathematical relationship. When used in this way, various parts of the homework might well be reviewed at different times throughout the class period. Although this variety is nice, the final determination should be based on the individual class's needs and the appropriateness for the lesson.

How Should a Whole-Class Homework Assignment Be Reviewed? Different kinds of homework exercises require different methods of review with the class. Some homework exercises can be gone over orally—for example, exercises that call for single-word (or short-phrase) answers.

Using the board is one of the most popular methods of reviewing homework in a mathematics class. The board can be used in a number of different ways. The teacher may write correct solutions or students may be assigned to write particular problems from the homework on the board. One popular way to review homework at the board is to assign students to write the solution to a particular homework problem at the side board when they enter the room. It is usually better to make these board assignments as students walk in rather than when the homework is first assigned so that, while doing their homework, students do not concentrate only on the assigned problem at the expense of the rest. At the appropriate time in the lesson, these students should explain their work to the rest of the class and answer any questions their classmates might have. Occasionally it may suffice simply to have the class read the work and ask the writer questions if something is not clear. This should not be done on a regular basis unless the teacher feels sure that no student lets a problem's solution go by without question when it is still unclear to him or her. Oftentimes, some teacher questions regarding the homework exercises will help determine the extent to which students understand the work. Only in special circumstances, such as when there is little time remaining in a lesson, should the teacher explain the students' work. Students may at first show reluctance at having to explain their own work to the rest of the class, but after a while they will begin to enjoy it, taking pride in their own work. This sort of procedure goes far to promote an active learning environment for the class.

Another way of reviewing homework is to have the specially selected students write their work on overhead projector transparencies. Then when the teacher is ready to have the class review the previous day's homework, these specially selected students simply exhibit their work on an overhead projector. For this system, each student in the class has a supply of reusable acetate transparencies so that when assigned specific problems from the homework for the next day's review, these students merely copy the solutions to the selected problems on the transparencies after they have completed their entire homework assignment. This method includes many of the desirable features of the other methods described and in a rather efficient manner. The only difficulty with this method is the continuous need for an overhead projector and the comparatively short time that the class sees the work flashed on the screen.

Of course in a technologically rich classroom, students could prepare their assigned work using software such as MathType, Geometer's SketchPad, or SmartBoard Notebook and email it, post it in a dropbox, or have it available on a disk. Then at the beginning of class, instead of copying homework on the board, students could load their solutions so that they might be displayed electronically. See Chapter 5 for more information about the use of technology in the mathematics classroom.

Small Group Homework Assignments

Part of every homework assignment should be a determination by the teacher of whether it is a small group or a whole class assignment. Review and drill assignments may best be accomplished in small groups; assignments in preparation for introductory lessons are best done in large groups.

Reviewing homework in small groups is an effective way to accomplish the goal of assigning responsibility to do homework. It becomes the group's responsibility to ensure mastery of the assignment by each member of that group. Students know that in the event someone who is unsure about a problem is selected to represent the group when it reports back to the entire class, it becomes a poor reflection on all. An advantage of this approach is subtle peer pressure to master the material adequately. In addition, explanations by one's peers in small group settings may offer insights that were overlooked in the teacher's original presentation. The teacher can clarify what may still be unclear after each group's report is presented.

This technique is also time efficient, allowing the focus of reviewing homework to be concentrated on the problem or problems of particular students. Thus, the remainder of the class is not burdened or bored with a repetition of material they may have already mastered.

The problem of copying homework for fear of being "caught" without it is eliminated, since homework has now become a group responsibility. Another situation reduced in significance is that of collecting and grading large numbers of individual homework assignments. Papers may still be collected, but they become the *group's* responsibility as to accuracy and completeness.

Absent pupils will also find value in the peer-directed explanations of small groups. Reviewing missed material for absent pupils in front of the entire class is unfair to the class, for it may be repetitive and not an efficient use of time. Thus, small group assignments are ideal.

HOW MUCH OF THE HOMEWORK ASSIGNMENT SHOULD BE REVIEWED? Teacher judgment is probably the only way to determine how much of the homework assignment should be reviewed. The teacher must consider the subject matter involved, the class level and their ability to learn the particular topic, the type of students, and their achievement. If the class is a high-ability mathematics class, then perhaps only a representative sample of the homework needs to be reviewed. If the teacher can ascertain that no one in the class had any difficulty with the assignment, then perhaps no review may be necessary, although in this case the teacher might just spot-check with some pointed questions to see if, in fact, the entire class really did have no difficulty with the homework.

On the other hand, a low-ability mathematics class could very likely require a complete review of the homework assignment, possibly in small groups. Many of the students might have missed some of the homework questions and would greatly benefit from a comprehensive review of the homework.

HOW FREQUENTLY SHOULD THE HOMEWORK ASSIGNMENT BE REVIEWED? In most cases, the homework assignment should be gone over with the class during the lesson following the assignment. Naturally, there are exceptions to this. For example, if a homework assignment has nothing to do with the succeeding lesson but does relate to a lesson a few days in the future, it might be more advisable to defer a discussion of this homework assignment until the later lesson.

The ability level (or achievement level) of a class can also be a determining factor in the frequency of a homework review. A gifted class may not require a daily review; here it might be done only on request. A teacher should be cautious about not reviewing homework daily. Students could give a teacher a false sense of security, saying they do not need to discuss the homework when, in fact, such a review might help them.

Generally, it is best to review a homework assignment immediately after it has been done by the students, for this ensures that it is still fresh in their minds and remains part of the total learning process.

Checking Homework Assignments

Once the homework has been assigned and completed according to a prescribed format, the teacher should direct a review of this work. At the same time, the teacher must grapple with the issue of collecting and checking each individual's homework. The following questions arise: Should the homework be collected? From whom? How regularly? Should it be graded? Aside from reading a student's homework, how can the teacher determine the level of student mastery of the homework? We now consider these and other questions about checking homework assignments.

Questions on Checking Homework Assignments

SHOULD HOMEWORK BE COLLECTED? Although some teachers collect homework daily, it is quite a chore for the teacher carrying a full teaching load to read so many papers. Suppose a teacher has five classes, each consisting of 30 students. If this teacher were to collect every student's paper daily, she would have to read 750 papers per week! If she spent just one minute on each paper (far too little time to offer meaningful comments), she would be spending $12\frac{1}{2}$ hours per week reading homework assignments. This is an inordinate amount of work, especially when coupled with the chores of planning lessons, preparing tests, and caring for other schoolrelated matters. Unless a teacher is willing to devote these vast amounts of time to reading students' homework papers, it is probably better to collect fewer papers but to read them more carefully.

If the homework is important enough to assign, then it is important enough to check. Therefore, whatever homework is assigned should also be checked. Since there is a gargantuan chore involved in reading and making meaningful comments on each student's homework paper every day, it would be advisable to collect only a small portion of the class's homework daily and enter these into the students' portfolio for future reference. By reading a different sample of student homework papers each day, the teacher ought to get a reasonably good feeling for the progress of all the students in the class.

For some classes, it may not be necessary to collect homework papers for some topics. The teacher may walk about the room during the lesson, when students are working on a classwork problem, and quickly check some of the students' homework papers. This sort of homework reading might be possible when the assignment involves graphing some functions, which can be checked quickly by inspection.

Constructive criticism as well as complimentary remarks should be made to the students on the papers that are looked over. Remember, this is part of the learning process.

The following discussions may appear to be about somewhat punitive methods but should still be brought to the attention of the teacher.

HOW SHOULD THE HOMEWORK ASSIGNMENT BE COLLECTED? Students should not be able to predict when their homework papers will be collected by the teacher. Otherwise they may avoid doing their homework on days when they feel reasonably sure their homework papers will not be collected. The teacher should set up a random selection, noting in his record book when each student's work was read.

The teacher might collect one row's homework on one day, then a diagonal the next day, then perhaps a column of students the following day. Such a system would allow the teacher to collect the homework from one particular student in need of extra help on two or three consecutive days without embarrassment before the class. This would be the student who could be made to be at the intersection of a row, column, and diagonal of students in the room. The student might just view his multiple collections as "bad luck" when, in fact, it was deliberately planned. The teacher then has the opportunity to give this student extra help with the homework.

WHAT SHOULD BE DONE WITH THE COLLECTED HOMEWORK ASSIGNMENTS? There is a wide range of choices about what might be done with collected homework assignments. One option is for a teacher to do nothing with the collected work; another is to do an in-depth evaluation of every homework paper, with comments and a grade. Neither extreme is advisable. Doing nothing with the homework collected is dishonest to the students. If homework is collected, the student expects that it will at least be looked at, and rightly so.

The other extreme is ill-advised from the point of view of the workload consideration discussed earlier. In addition, this extreme also introduces the question of grading homework papers. This is generally a bad practice to follow, since it brings a potentially punitive aspect to the homework assignment. When homework papers are graded, students are likely to go out of their way to get the right answers. They may go to classmates, parents, friends, or even other teachers and have these people do the homework assignment for them. Although this sometimes has educational value (such as when students actually learn the material as a result of seeing it done correctly by others), the concern usually lies with getting the correct answer down on paper to show to the teacher rather than learning how to solve the problem correctly.

Those homework papers that have been collected should be read for completeness and accuracy. Where appropriate, detailed comments should be made and complimentary remarks should be offered for encouragement. Having read some sample homework assignments, the teacher is far better equipped to teach the class, for she will now know more precisely the weaknesses and strengths of the students. Such information can improve the learning process significantly.

There may be situations when the teacher wishes to check a class's homework in detail. She may want to determine whether a particularly difficult point was properly mastered, or whether the students are properly preparing themselves for an upcoming examination (such as the Advanced Placement Examination given by the Educational Testing Service).

Remember, the primary value of a homework assignment is the students' work on it. The teacher's checking of the homework can serve as motivation for the student for the next lesson. This ought to be kept clearly in mind when offering comments on the students' papers.

HOW SHOULD THE TEACHER DEAL WITH STUDENTS WHO COPY HOMEWORK FROM OTHERS? Traditionally the student who copied homework (if this can be proved) is penalized in some manner. If desperate, the student may try again at some future date, taking a chance at copying it from a classmate's work rather than be penalized for not having done the homework assignment. An effective way to deal with this problem is to "dry up the source." Penalizing the student who *gave* the homework assignment to the other student to copy will make the giver far more reluctant to repeat this incident. Thus, attacking the source may eliminate the problem of copied assignments.

Another effective way to handle this problem is to speak to both students involved. Confront them with the "evidence" and discuss the virtues of honesty. After a second occurrence, parents of the copier should be notified. A warning to the class of this plan at the beginning of the course could prevent the problem entirely.

SHOULD QUIZZES BE USED TO CHECK IF HOMEWORK ASSIGNMENTS HAVE BEEN MASTERED? As long as a quiz is not given for primarily punitive reasons, it may be used sparingly to determine the true level of mastery of the class on a particular homework assignment. The quiz should be brief and should consist of material covered in the homework (if that is the area of concern). The questions on the quiz should be stated simply and with no complications so as to avoid confusion. The extrinsic motivation presented by the expectation of a quiz could also be a useful factor in the total learning process.

Another Sample Lesson Plan

In our first sample lesson, students investigated similar figures and discovered properties of these objects. Our next lesson also uses investigation as an instructional strategy. In this case students will develop a procedure for factoring trinomials.

Too often teachers, in their attempts to make mathematics clear and understandable by all, allow the subject to become a set of rules and procedures instructed by the teacher and practiced by the students. When students learn mathematics solely in this manner, they risk never learning to think mathematically and never becoming confident in their ability to do mathematics. Even if they are able to solve problems that are exactly like those taught in class, they are often unable to tackle variations of those problems. On the other hand, learning mathematics through investigation allows students to see that they can discover many of the rules and procedures of mathematics on their own. Thus, if they forget a rule or procedure, they can rediscover it.

Clearly students would not have enough time to rediscover all of high school mathematics. Yet, there are many concepts and procedures that students can easily be guided toward discovering. The following lesson shows how students can work in small groups to discover strategies for factoring trinomials of the form $ax^2 + bx + c$ into the product of two binomials.

SAMPLE LESSON PLAN 2

TOPIC: INTRODUCTION TO FACTORING TRINOMIALS

Comments

Introductory lesson on factoring a trinomial of the form $ax^2 + bx + c$ into a product of two binomials.

OBJECTIVES:

Students will evaluate multiplication of binomial problems and determine a pattern in the resulting trinomials.

Using the discovered pattern, students will factor trinomials into binomials when possible.

INSTRUCTIONAL ACTIVITIES:

1. Start-up: Write the following numbers as a product of two integer factors. Create as many solutions as possible.

   a. 6, b. −12, c. −36, d. 9, e. −120

   Find the two factors of 6 whose sum is +5.
   Find the two factors of −12 whose sum is −1.
   Find the two factors of 9 whose sum is −6.

Review the answers before the beginning of the lesson. Review the word factor.

2. Motivation: In groups of four, the group leader will assign each group member a set of "product of binomial problems" from the list below. Each group member will compare his or her set to the other sets and discuss how they are alike and how they are different. Then as a group the students will predict how the products of their set will be alike and how they will be different from the others. The group recorder should note the comparisons and the predictions.

Set 1	Set 2	Set 3	Set 4
$(x + 3)(x + 2)$	$(x + 3)(x - 2)$	$(x - 3)(x + 2)$	$(x - 3)(x - 2)$
$(x + 1)(x + 7)$	$(x - 1)(x + 7)$	$(x + 1)(x - 7)$	$(x - 1)(x - 7)$
$(x + 4)(x + 3)$	$(x + 4)(x - 3)$	$(x - 4)(x + 3)$	$(x - 4)(x - 3)$
$(x + 2)(x + 5)$	$(x - 2)(x + 5)$	$(x + 2)(x - 5)$	$(x - 2)(x - 5)$
$(x + 6)(x + 6)$	$(x + 6)(x - 6)$	$(x - 6)(x + 6)$	$(x - 6)(x - 6)$

Now each student is to multiply the pairs of binomials in his or her set and compare his or her answers to the others in the group. Did the results support their predictions? What patterns do they see in their answers? What do they notice about the signs of the coefficients in the trinomial? What do they notice about the terms in the trinomial? Make up another multiplication of binomials problem and test it. Does the pattern hold?

This activity encourages students to inspect the product of binomial problems prior to solving them. Because the students have multiplied binomials prior to the lesson, they may have noticed some patterns related to the different sets. The teacher expects the students to say that the sets are alike because they are all products of binomials and the numbers are the same in each row. Within each set the operation in the binomial terms are the same. Across each set the operations in the binomial terms are different.

Asking students to make predictions prior to solving a problem gives the students a stake in the answer. It also helps develop the students' ability to estimate, calculate mentally, and look for patterns in their work. In addition, if students are asked to explain how they made their predictions, it can foster good communication skills and develop mathematical thinking. Listening to the predictions and the explanation provides the teacher with an opportunity to informally assess student thinking. Because this is a prediction, there is no right or wrong answer—just better predictions. You can expect students to predict that multiplying the two binomials will result in a trinomial with an x^2 term. Some will remember that if the binomial terms are alike except for the signs, their product will result in a binomial because the coefficient of the middle term in the trinomial is 0. You also want to elicit predictions about the signs within the trinomial. For example, they might say that all of the signs in Set 1 will be positive and all of the signs in Set 4 will be negative. They should recognize that the last term is the product of the two numbers in the binomial and the coefficient of the middle term is the sum of the two numbers in the binomial.

3. Whole class instruction: Return to the whole class and ask each group reporter to discuss the findings. Give an additional example $(x + 8)(x + 5)$ and its related terms. Have the students predict the format and signs of the product. x^2_____ x _____.

This is an opportunity to clarify misunderstandings before the next part of the lesson. It also allows students to present their thinking and respond to questions from the class.

(continued)

SAMPLE LESSON PLAN 2 (*continued*)

4. Small group activity: Pass out envelopes with the following 15 trinomials and binomials on individual slips of paper.

a. $x^2 + 7x + 10$	f. $x^2 - x - 20$	k. $x^2 - 81$
b. $x^2 - 5x + 6$	g. $x^2 + 3x - 40$	l. $49 - x^2$
c. $x^2 - 7x + 6$	h. $x^2 - 6x + 9$	m. $x^2 - \frac{25}{36}$
d. $x^2 - 2x - 15$	i. $x^2 - 64$	n. $x^2 + 2x + 4$
e. $x^2 + 5x - 14$	j. $x^2 + 4x - 12$	o. $x^2 - 10x + 16$

Inform the class that you have created each of the polynomials by multiplying two binomials. Ask each group to sort the 15 polynomials into sets based on some classification scheme and to describe that scheme. As a hint, ask them to think about the classification scheme that was used for the provided sets in the earlier activity. The goal is to choose a scheme that will help them find the binomial factors of the polynomial.

Then, for each set, have the students determine the two binomial factors you multiplied to create the given trinomial or binomial. To generalize this task, ask each group to describe in writing a process for determining the binomial factors of any given polynomial if those factors exists.

Comments

If you feel that this activity will be too difficult for your students, you can give them the list already classified as you did above. However, don't underestimate your students. You should make the problem challenging and then provide hints where necessary.

5. Summary: Have each group review their results and explain their procedure. If the students have not already named the procedure, tell them that it is commonly referred to as factoring trinomials into the product of two binomials. Practice an additional problem using the procedure.

When students present, encourage them to use the words factor, trinomial, binomial coefficient, term, *and* constant. *Make sure that these terms are on your "word wall."*

ASSESSMENT:

Students will evaluate multiplication of binomial problems and determine a pattern in the resulting trinomials. Assessed in activities 2 and 3.

Using the discovered pattern, students will factor trinomials into binomials when possible. Assessed in activities 4, 5, and homework.

VOCABULARY:

factor, binomial, trinomial, coefficient, term, constant

MATERIALS/EQUIPMENT:

Sets of products of binomials and envelopes with 15 trinomials and binomials.

HOMEWORK:

Distribute additional sheets of practice exercises for all students. Discuss the homework solutions in small groups in class the next day. Continue to assign daily additional homework on the same topic, including expansions to include trinomials with initial coefficient other than 1.

Lesson Analysis

The lesson described above is frequently taught as a direct instruction lesson. In the direct instruction lesson, the teacher gives the rules for factoring trinomials and the students practice the rules. With a few simple revisions, this lesson becomes more challenging and allows for more student engagement at a higher level. At the end of the investigation lesson, students are more likely to understand that the "rules" for factoring trinomials simply make it easier to find the factors and can be discovered if one forgets them. Learning mathematics in this manner gives students more confidence in their ability to do mathematics. Although the lesson may take longer than the direct instruction version, the benefits gained from involving students in this type of task far outweigh the disadvantages.

Investigations will promote better understanding of new concepts, skills, knowledge, and positive attitudes among your students. Suggestions from other teachers, a variety of textbooks, and the NCTM journals—*The Mathematics Teacher, Mathematics Teaching in the Middle School*, and *Teaching Children Mathematics* (formerly *The Arithmetic Teacher*)—will all be invaluable in helping you create appropriate class activities. In addition, a sense of excitement and challenge will set the tone for your own performance and the positive results you hope to attain in the years ahead.

Spiraling Content

The Equity Principle outlined in the NCTM *Principles and Standards for School Mathematics* (2000) states that "Excellence in mathematics education requires equity—high expectation and strong support for all students" (p. 12). This view is supported in the No Child Left Behind Act requiring that all children—including the disadvantaged—become "academically proficient" in reading and mathematics. Today students complete several years of required mathematical study that demonstrates variations in depth and breadth of the treatment of topics and applications. Accordingly, all students, regardless of ability level, will experience the entire range of mathematics topics in the curriculum. Thus, students who might previously have been selected for a general or a business track, with its own specialized curriculum, will now be exposed to the same subject matter as the college bound. The following core lessons illustrate how the same content may be presented at different levels of abstraction, even though teaching strategies will vary in accordance with students' levels of interest, skills, and goals.

First Sample Core Lesson

Consider the graph of the parabola $y = x^2 + x - 6$.

FIRST LEVEL Students should already have developed skills in evaluating algebraic expressions containing exponents for both positive and negative values of x. They should also be prepared to plot points in a rectangular coordinate system. All students should complete the following table, plot the points on a coordinate grid, and connect them with a smoothly drawn continuous curve (Figure 2.2).

x	y
−4	6
−3	0
−2	−4
−1	−6
0	−6
1	−4
2	0
3	6

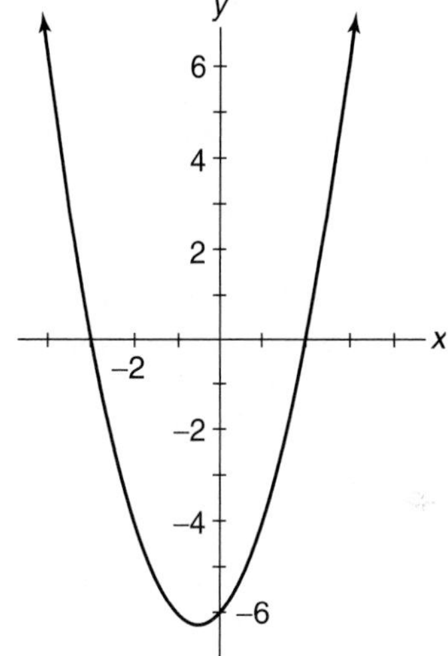

FIGURE 2.2 $y = x^2 + x - 6$.

The reflective properties of a parabola (Figure 2.3) should be mentioned, including its uses in antennae and headlights.

SECOND LEVEL Students will use a graphing calculator to graph $y = x^2 + x - 6$ and to determine its zeros. The parabola will appear as in Figure 1, and its zeros will be the intersections with the x-axis, at -3 and 2.

THIRD LEVEL Students will draw a line of symmetry in the graph developed for levels 1 and 2. They will realize that this line of symmetry, which is also known as the *axis of symmetry*, falls midway between the zeros of the function, -3 and 2. They will then generalize that the axis of symmetry passes through the midpoint of the segment on the x-axis that joints the two zeros. For this example, the equation of the axis of symmetry is seen to be $x = -\frac{1}{2}$. They will further generalize when they realize that the midpoint is the mean value between the two zeros. From a previously learned formula for the sum of the roots of a quadratic equation, sum $= \frac{-b}{a}$, the equation of the axis of symmetry for the general function $y = ax^2 + bx + c$ must therefore be $x = \frac{-b}{2a}$. Students can then easily generate symmetrically arranged tables that will yield "symmetric" parabolas, beginning with the axis of symmetry and then selecting the same number of points on both sides.

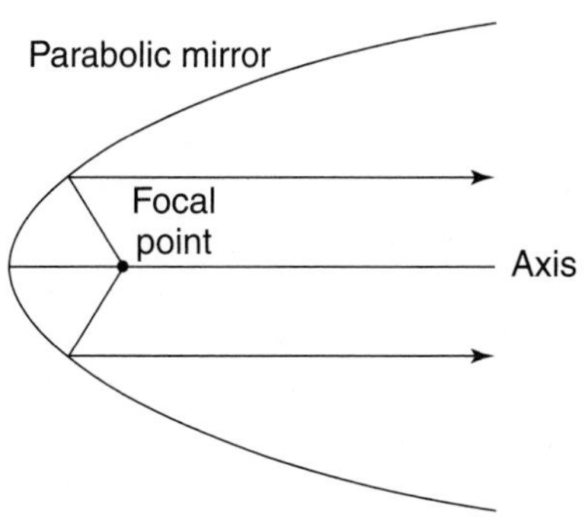

FIGURE 2.3 A parabolic mirror.

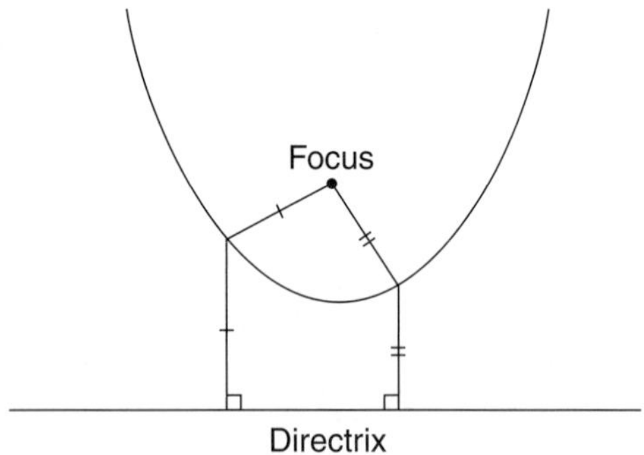

FIGURE 2.4 The parabola as a locus.

FOURTH LEVEL After completing the first three levels, students will use the locus approach to sketch a parabola. This locus definition of a parabola should be introduced: *A parabola is the set of all points in a plane equidistant from a fixed line (the directrix) and a fixed point (the focus) not on the fixed line.* A general drawing should then be made illustrating this locus definition, together with specific examples of parabolas of the form $y = ax^2$ or $x = ay^2$. Students should be asked to determine the coordinates of the focus and the equation of its associated directrix. A manipulative consisting of a fixed point (nail) and a piece of string may be used to demonstrate the definition (Figure 2.4).

Figure 2.5 describes the parabola formed from the envelope created by tangent folds of a piece of waxed paper. (The basis of this construction is the definition of the parabola given earlier. This rather clever paper-folding technique is done as follows: Take a large piece of waxed paper, mark a point on it for the focus, and draw a line for the directrix. Fold the waxed paper several times so as to place the focus on the directrix each time, and crease each fold. The creases will form an envelope for the parabola.) Envelopes for the remaining conic sections may now be demonstrated, with an introduction to "string" art. The string art may be appropriate at other levels also (see Chapter 3 for reference to string art constructions).

Practice exercises may involve parabolas symmetric with respect to the y- or x-axes, or with axes that are rotated through any angle.

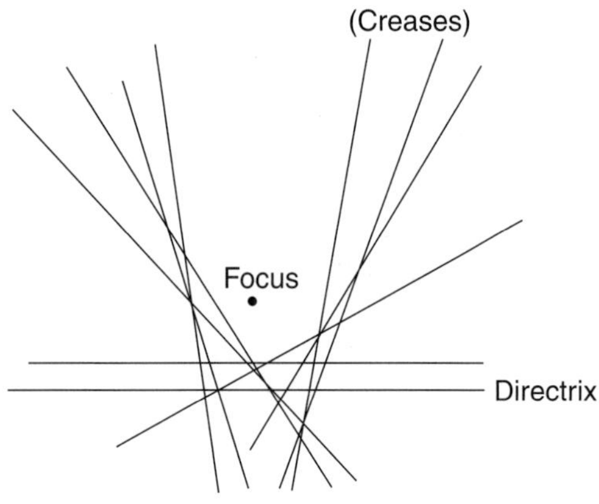

FIGURE 2.5 Parabolic envelope.

FIFTH LEVEL At this level, college-bound students will learn that a parabola is a section of a cone formed from a "slice" that is parallel to one of its elements. This model will then be expanded to include proofs that "slicing" a cone in other directions will produce a circle, if it is a circular cone, or an ellipse, a hyperbola, or even two intersecting lines (Figure 2.6).

A challenging enrichment exercise for the fifth level might be to prove the following: A uniform cable that hangs freely under its own weight takes the shape of a catenary. However, it will hang in the shape of a parabola when it is weighted in such a way that the net weight per horizontal foot is constant. College-bound students with superior mathematical ability will be able to use vector geometry to prove these facts.

Second Sample Core Lesson

In postulational geometry, consider this definition: *The area of any plane surface is the number of square units it contains.*

FIRST LEVEL Working in groups the students will define and illustrate the important words in the following four statements. They will then provide concrete examples to illustrate the statements. (Arithmetic numbers used to represent dimensions may be whole, fractional, or decimal, as appropriate for the class.) More advanced students may be asked to generalize their statements by representing the dimensions with algebraic expressions instead of arithmetic numbers.

1. The area of a rectangle is equal to the product of the lengths of its base and altitude.
2. The area of a parallelogram is equal to the product of the lengths of one side and the altitude drawn to that side.
3. The area of a triangle is equal to one-half the product of the lengths of a side and the altitude drawn to that side.
4. The area of a trapezoid is equal to one-half the product of the length of the altitude and the sum of the lengths of the bases.

SECOND LEVEL The teacher will postulate the first statement and follow with geometric proofs of the following sequence of theorems, where each proof is based on preceding theorems:

$$(2) \rightarrow (3) \rightarrow (4)$$

Note: Numbers used to represent the dimensions of the figures may be rational or irrational.

THIRD LEVEL Students will gain a historical perspective of the development of postulational systems by referring to Euclid's *Elements* and his five postulates of geometry. A discussion of

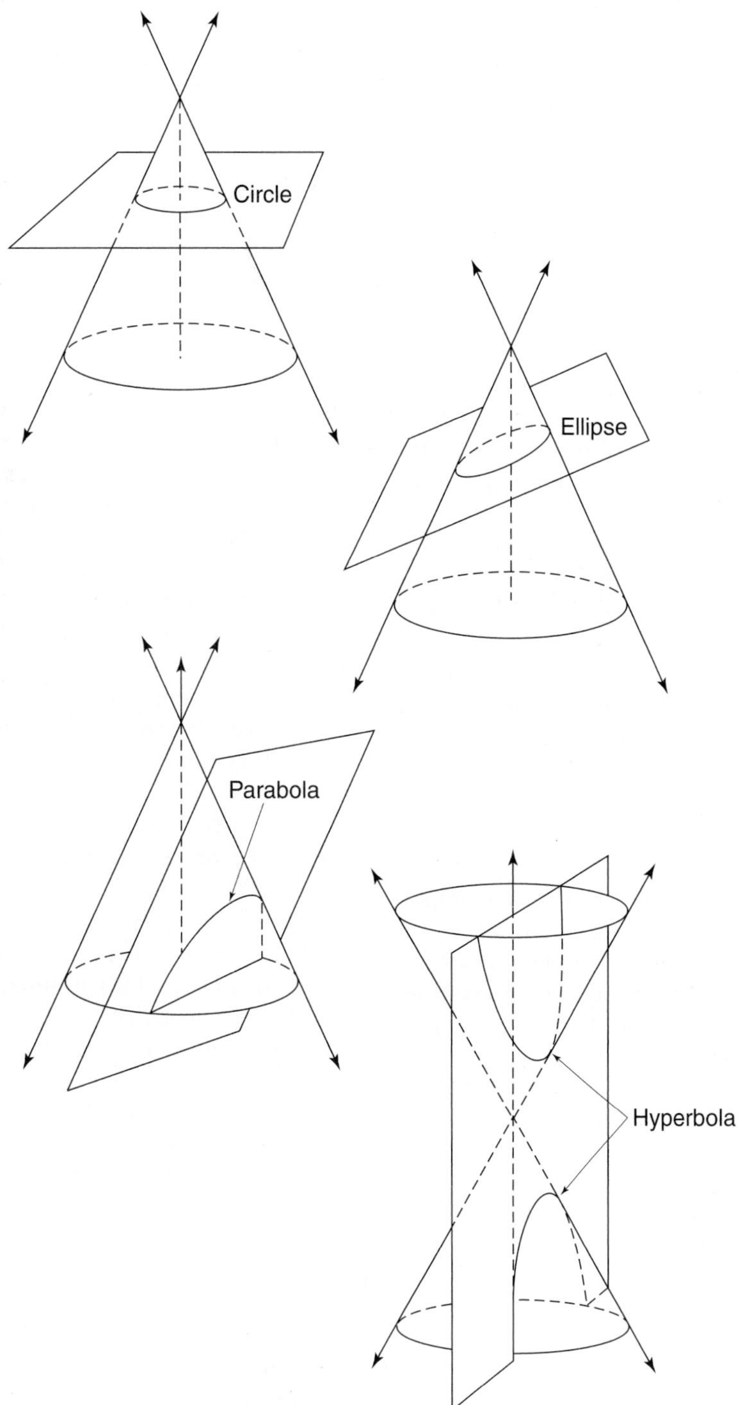

FIGURE 2.6 The conic sections.

Euclid's fifth postulate, Playfair's postulate, and the Saccheri quadrilateral are additional extensions that led to the development of non-Euclidean geometry, a significant breakthrough in the history of mathematics.

Recommended enrichment includes studying the spherical, elliptic, and hyperbolic non-Euclidean geometries. Compass and straightedge constructions, constructions with other tools, trisecting an angle, and "duplicating the cube" may be discussed as well, leading to a discussion of Galois and the theory of groups.

FOURTH LEVEL Students will be asked to create their own minipostulational systems from any other area of mathematics or from any real-life situation. The study of symbolic logic, syllogisms, and truth tables will assist students in their efforts to create consistent systems.

Third Sample Core Lesson

Pythagoras' well-known theorem for right triangle ABC, $a^2 + b^2 = c^2$, is the foundation of linear measurement in geometry. In both two- and three-dimensional geometric situations, the impact of the Pythagorean theorem has been major. But linear measure is certainly not the only significance of the Pythagorean theorem. A generalization of this theorem, known as Fermat's last theorem, has also left an indelible mark on the theory of numbers.

FIRST LEVEL The teacher will display a manipulative model of a 3-4-5 right triangle with plastic square units that can be arranged to form a square on each side to demonstrate that the sum of the areas of the squares on the legs is equal to the area of the square on the hypotenuse (Figure 2.7).

The more well-known Pythagorean triples, besides 3-4-5, are 5-12-13, 8-15-17, and 7-24-25, as well as multiples and fractional parts of these. They will be used in real-life practical problem situations.

Students will learn algebraic techniques for determining the third side of any right triangle given the dimensions of the other two sides. Students will, in effect, be learning to solve equations of the form $x^2 = k$. This will involve the use of calculators, rational and irrational numbers, extraneous answers, rounding, and estimating.

SECOND LEVEL After developing the three mean proportional theorems that result from drawing an altitude to the hypotenuse of a right triangle, students will be prepared to fill in the blank spaces on their duplicated worksheets to answer the seven questions in the model lesson plan shown nearby.

Seven practice and challenge questions would follow. It would be advisable for these to be solved as part of a small group discussion. After the class reassembles as a large group, students may be asked to discuss the final summary questions. At this point homework should be assigned. If desirable, the indicated challenge problem may be added to the homework assignment. Both the assignment and the challenge may be discussed in small groups the following day.

Right triangle trigonometry may be introduced here, with calculators being used to determine the values of trigonometric functions of any acute angle.

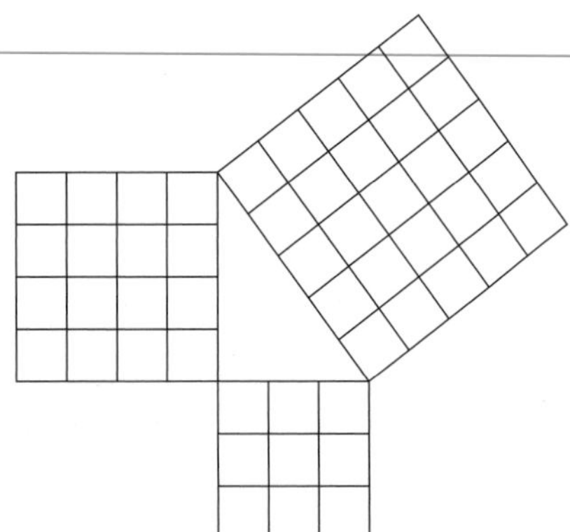

FIGURE 2.7 Plastic 3-4-5 Pythagorean triple model.

THIRD LEVEL Students will use coordinate geometry to plot points that form various right triangles in a variety of plane figures. They will derive the distance formula for two- and three-dimensional figures. Applications in plane or coordinate geometry are also appropriate, such as finding the diagonal of a cube of side 2 or of a rectangular prism with dimensions 2, 3, and 4. Also appropriate for this level is a discussion of indirect proofs in mathematics, such as that for proving the converse of the Pythagorean theorem.

The law of cosines and the law of sines for any triangle may also be developed in both synthetic and coordinate geometry formats at this level. Extensive problem-solving applications, using calculators, as they relate to the solution of triangles are appropriate here. Solutions of these problems will lead to the development of definitions of inverse trigonometric functions.

FOURTH LEVEL Students will now be prepared to understand spherical geometry and to define right angles on a sphere. An introductory lesson in non-Euclidean geometry will result in an informative diversion into the history of geometry, specifically, the consequences and implications of considering variations of Euclid's fifth postulate. Topological properties of non-Euclidean models, such as the sphere and hyperbolic paraboloid, may be presented, alongside the transformations of rubber-sheet geometry.

On the heels of the Pythagorean theorem comes what is known as Fermat's last theorem. In the margin of one of the books in his library, Fermat wrote that the equation $x^n + y^n = z^n$ cannot be solved in positive integers x, y, z, for $n = 3,4,5,\ldots$

Fruitless attempts to prove this conjecture produced much good mathematics for a period of more than 350 years, but no proof that was able to stand up to scrutiny by the mathematics community. The search for a valid proof culminated with a proof by Dr. Andrew Wiles of Princeton University in June 1993 (with a correction by him a year later).

Further analysis of Fermat's theorem should evolve into discussions of finding solutions of Diophantine equations, especially of the first degree (i.e., of finding all pairs of integers x, y that satisfy the equation $ax + by = n$, where a, b, and n are given integers).

Students at this level will learn the meaning of "relatively prime" and may be led to discover a method for generating primitive Pythagorean triples.

MODEL LESSON PLAN

TOPIC: REVISITING THE PYTHAGOREAN THEOREM—A PROOF AND APPLICATIONS

Comments

For the high school geometry course.

OBJECTIVES:

Given an incomplete proof of the Pythagorean theorem, students will fill in the missing information and provide justifications for their statements to complete the proof.

Given the lengths of two sides of a right triangle, students will use the Pythagorean theorem to determine the length of the third side.

Students will use the Pythagorean theorem to solve problems.

Use action words to describe how the students will be involved in the lesson. These actions and outcomes should be assessed throughout the lesson.

INSTRUCTIONAL ACTIVITIES:

1. Start-up: In the figure, $\overline{CD}$ is an altitude of right $\triangle ABC$, right angle at C. The lengths of the segments are marked. Referring to the figure, complete each of the following:

This set of exercises will be duplicated and distributed to the class.

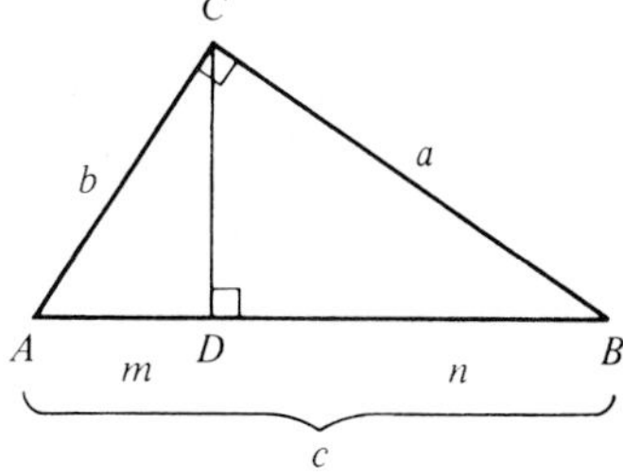

a. AC is the mean proportional between $\textcircled{AB}$ and $\textcircled{AD}$.

b. Therefore $\frac{c}{\textcircled{b}} = \frac{b}{\textcircled{m}}$, or $b^2 = \textcircled{cm}$. Why?

c. $\textcircled{BC}$ is the mean proportional between AB and BD.

d. Therefore $\frac{\textcircled{c}}{a} = \frac{\textcircled{a}}{n}$; or $a^2 = \textcircled{cn}$. Why?

e. Adding the results of items 2 and 4, we get $a^2 + b^2 = \textcircled{cm} + \textcircled{cn} = \textcircled{c}(m + n)$.

f. But $m + n = \textcircled{c}$.

g. Therefore $a^2 + \textcircled{b^2} = \textcircled{c^2}$.

N.B. Circles indicate correct answers to be supplied by students, and which are obviously not included on actual answer sheets.

Notice also that these exercises review the mean proportional theorems while at the same time permitting the student actually to prove the Pythagorean theorem. Although students may not realize this at first, they will be led to see this during the development of the lesson.

2. Motivation: Ask the students (make up a story) whether they can get a 10-ft-diameter circular tabletop through a door that is only 8 ft high and 6 ft wide. Have the students work in groups and develop a poster justifying their answer. Choose some solutions to present to the class.

Do not rush through your story in an effort to get to the "meat" of the lesson. That will diminish the effectiveness of this approach.

3. Whole class instruction:

   a. Use the prepared overhead transparency to review the "motivational activity" exercise with the class.

   This prepared transparency should be just like the copy of the exercise given to the class.

   b. Indicate to the class the significance of this exercise. That is, *they* have just *proved* the Pythagorean theorem.

   This must be carefully presented so as to reap the full impact intended from these exercises. You may want to ask the students if they see the significance in this exercise.

   c. Ask the class what Euclid and President James A. Garfield had in common. Now give the class some historical notes about the Pythagorean theorem (such as the Egyptian "rope stretchers" over 400 proofs). (See E.S. Loomis, *The Pythagorean Proposition,* Washington DC: NCTM, 1968.)

   Both proved the Pythagorean theorem!

   This brief discussion should generate some extra interest in this topic.

   d. Discuss an application of the Pythagorean theorem with the class.

(continued)

MODEL LESSON PLAN (*continued*)

4. Small group activities:
   a. Find the length of the hypotenuse of the following right triangle:

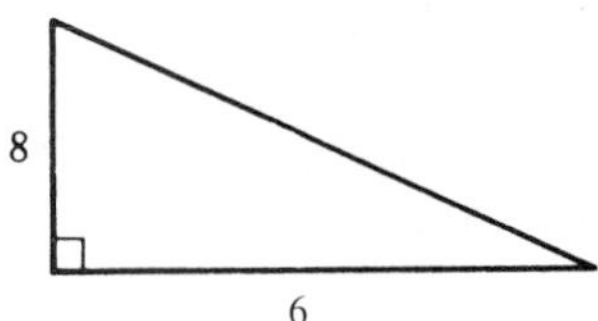

Visual aids would be quite helpful here.

This is a very simple application and should be done together with the class.

   b. Find x in each of the following:

These are simple exercises that apply only the Pythagorean theorem and require no other prior knowledge.

1.

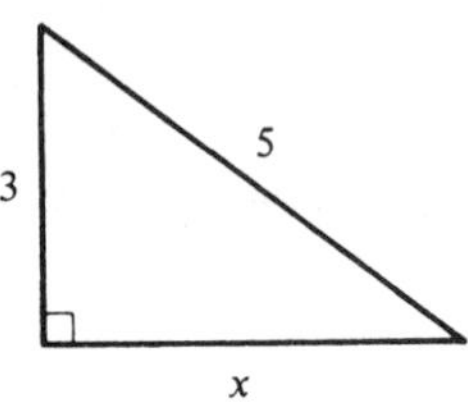

2.

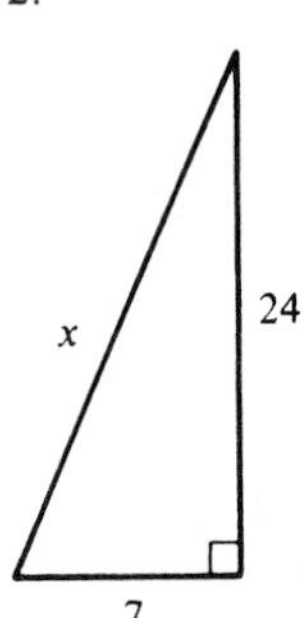

3.

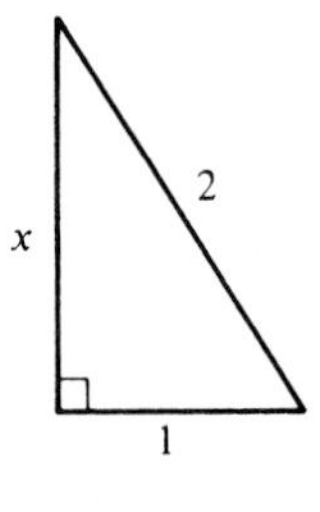

Students will be asked to present their correct solutions to the class. These correct solutions will be detected by the teacher during his or her walk throughout the classroom while the students are working on these exercises.

5. Whole class instruction (check for understanding):
   a. Report results back to class.
   b. State the Pythagorean theorem.
   c. For what can we use the Pythagorean theorem?
   d. Can the Pythagorean theorem be applied to any triangle for which the lengths of two sides are given? How do you know this?

These questions should elicit the key points of the previous part of the lesson and thus serve as a summary up to this point in the lesson.

6. Small group or individual activity:

   Find x in each of the following:

You might ask students to do their original work in front of the whole class as a "Think Aloud," rather than first working the problems at their seats. Listening to one's classmates think through a problem, even when missteps are introduced, can be a powerful learning experience.

a.

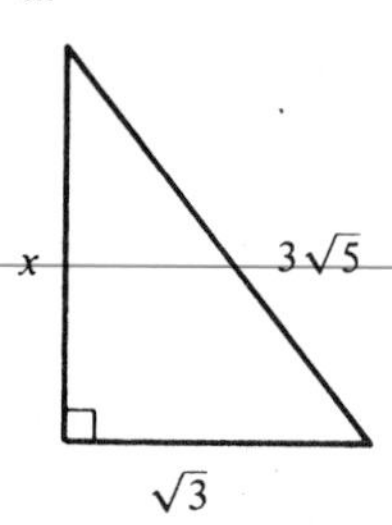

b.

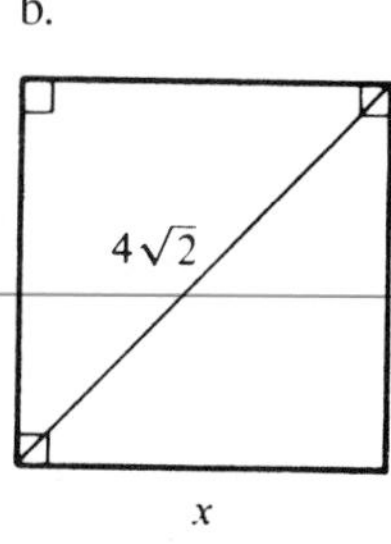

c.

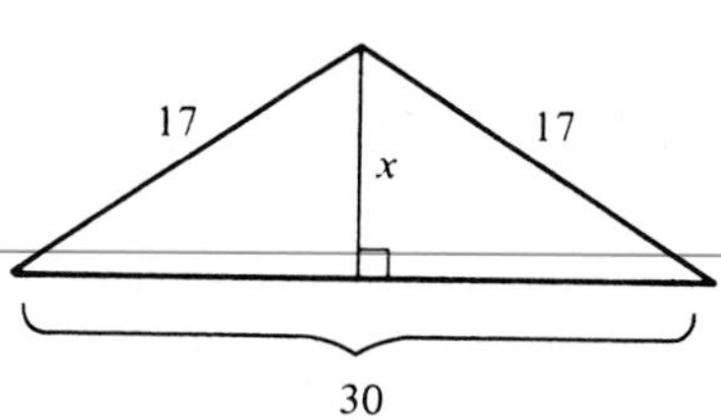

   d. Given: $\overline{PS}$ is an altitude of ΔPQR.
   Prove: $PQ^2 - RP^2 = QS^2 - SR^2$

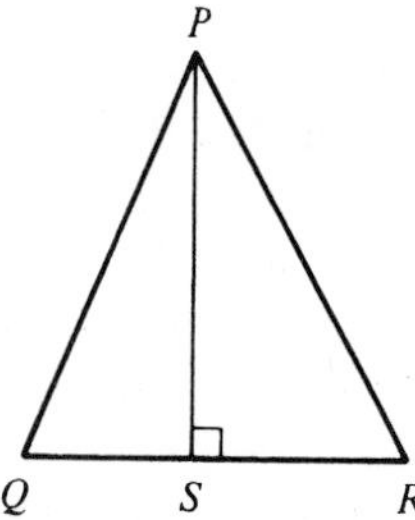

MODEL LESSON PLAN (*continued*)

Comments

This assessment is designed to review the topic of this lesson and allow students to show that they really understand what it is and how it can be used. Questions 3-5 foreshadow the next lesson on the converse of the Pythagorean theorem.

ASSESSMENT (ASK THE FOLLOWING QUESTIONS):

1. State in words the Pythagorean theorem.
2. How can the Pythagorean theorem help us find the length of a diagonal of a rectangle when we are given the lengths of the sides of the rectangle?
3. Can the Pythagorean theorem be applied to any triangle for which the lengths of two sides are given?
4. What would you guess to be true about a triangle whose sides have lengths 3, 4, and 5?
5. Have we proved your conjecture to question 3?

This homework assignment is a spiraled assignment that reviews previously learned material as well as the newly presented topic. (See the discussion on homework assignments earlier in this chapter.)

HOMEWORK ASSIGNMENT:

1. Four exercises similar to those in the application section of the lesson plan
2. One proof involving the Pythagorean theorem
3. One exercise using the mean proportional theorems
4. One exercise on similar triangles

This problem involves numerous applications of the Pythagorean theorem. It is a departure from the previous simpler applications.

SPECIAL PROJECT (DISCUSS THE FOLLOWING CHALLENGE PROBLEM WITH THE CLASS):

In the figure $\overline{PC} \perp \overline{BD}$ at C and $\overline{PB} \perp \overline{AB}$, $AP = 17$, $AB = 8$, $BC = 9$, and $CD = 3\frac{1}{2}$. Find PD.

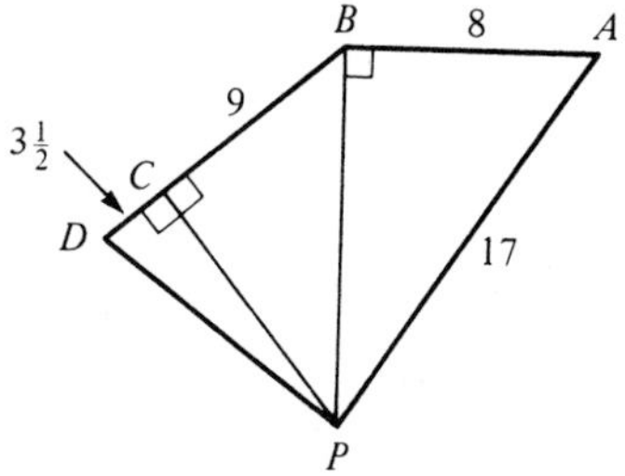

MATERIALS/EQUIPMENT:

Copies of the Motivational Activity as well as a transparency of it, an overhead projector, colored chalk, and ruler (or some sort of chalkboard straightedge)

VOCABULARY:

Pythagorean theorem, hypotenuse, altitude, and mean proportional.

Reflecting on Your Lesson

Lesson reflection is an important part of the planning process. As soon as possible after the lesson has concluded, teachers should, in writing, identify what worked well and what should be changed. Maybe the pacing was off or the lesson was too easy. Perhaps there was a misunderstanding of the directions that could have been avoided by adding a few more instructions. More important, teachers should think about the tasks they chose and the questions they asked. Did the chosen tasks and related questions help their students engage in meaningful learning of mathematics? Were there unexpected solutions or questions that should be identified for future reference? Did the tasks engage all students or should a broader range of activities be provided? Making note of your reflections at the end of the class or end of the day can provide a valuable resource for you should the opportunity arise to teach the lesson again at a future date.

Differentiated Instruction

Today's classrooms are rich with diversity. Students from varied backgrounds and ability levels work alongside each other to meet the rigorous learning standards set for all high school graduates. To be successful in the modern classroom, teachers must diversify their instruction.

Differentiated instruction is based on the philosophy that teachers should adapt instruction to student differences. Some students learn best by reading and reflecting on an individual basis, whereas others prefer to investigate a concept and engage in discussions with their peers to clarify their ideas. Struggling learners may need additional time on task and substantial support to absorb new concepts, whereas more advanced learners are quick to understand and seek more challenging experiences. Some students do not possess English skills at a level necessary to understand the teacher or the textbook, and those students may need additional visual prompts. Although meeting the needs of each individual student all of the time may be impossible, differentiating instruction through careful planning can aid in consistent support of all students.

Tiered Lessons

Creating tiered lessons is one planning strategy teachers use to meet the diverse academic needs of their students. The following steps show how to create a tiered lesson based on learning levels. It is designed to help students understand and become proficient in simplifying exponential algebraic expressions with zero and negative exponents.

Step 1: Connect to the Standards.

The first step in constructing a tiered lesson is to identify the targeted standards or performance indicators. To provide a context for the lesson, the relevant unit goals are also given below.

Unit goals:

Students will expand their understanding of algebraic expressions with exponents to include zero and negative exponents.

Students will discover properties of exponents and generalize those properties to algebraic expressions.

Students will explore exponential functions and graph those functions. They will compare and contrast exponential, linear, and quadratic functions and apply their knowledge of exponents and exponential functions to solve problems related to exponential growth and decay.

The objectives for this lesson are:

Given ordered lists of numbers written in exponential form, students will write the simplified form of each number. They will use their results to conjecture a rule for operating with zero and negative exponents.

Students will formalize their rules for operating with zero and negative exponents by stating and refining their definitions for operating with zero and negative exponents.

Given a set of numeric and algebraic expressions with negative and zero exponents, students will apply their definitions of zero and negative exponents to simplify those expressions.

Step 2: Determine Prerequisite Knowledge.

Teachers must think about the prerequisite knowledge needed for the lesson. In this lesson, students should know how to evaluate positive exponential expressions using both integers and rational numbers. *At-level* students can simplify and evaluate positive algebraic exponential expressions. Through the use of prior assessments such as unit tests, homework, or even the lesson "Start-up," the teacher should know where along the continuum toward mastery of the unit objectives each student lies.

In this lesson, the teacher knows that five students have not mastered how to simplify expressions with positive exponents. We will call this the *below-level group*. She also knows that two students already have some proficiency in applying the zero and negative exponent properties to simplify numeric and algebraic expressions with one variable. We will call these students *above level*. The remaining 21 students, or the *at-level* group, have the prerequisite skills and are ready to engage in the basic lesson. The teacher's goal is to develop a tiered lesson that addresses the needs of all three groups of students.

Step 3: Develop the At-Level Lesson.

When developing the tiered lesson, it is best to draft the at-level lesson first. In this sample lesson, students complete the table below to review their knowledge of expressions with positive exponents and then look for a pattern to conjecture a rule they can apply to expressions with zero and negative exponents.

TIER I: AT-LEVEL ACTIVITY

1. In the table below, evaluate each exponential expression and write the value in the appropriate column. If needed, you may use a calculator to evaluate expressions with exponents greater than 3.

2^x	4^x	5^x	10^x
2^4	4^6	5^5	10^4
2^3	4^5	5^4	10^3
2^2	4^4	5^3	10^2
2^1	4^3	5^2	10^1

2. Now look at each column in the table and describe a pattern you observe. Be sure to describe a pattern that can

be applied to all four columns. You may want to use the words *base* and *exponent* to generalize the description of your pattern.

3. Use the pattern you described in item 2 above to complete the table below. This time do not use a calculator. Write values less than 1 in standard fraction form.

2^x	4^x	5^x	10^x
2^1	4^3	5^2	10^1
2^0	4^2	5^1	10^0
2^{-1}	4^1	5^0	10^{-1}
2^{-2}	4^0	5^{-1}	10^{-2}

4. What do you notice about expressions with an exponent of zero? Write a rule or definition of zero exponents.
5. What do you notice about expressions with an exponent of -1? Write a rule or definition for simplifying expressions with exponents of -1.
6. Generalize the rule to define all negative exponents. Explain in writing why you think this definition is correct.
7. Apply your definitions to the following:
   a. 4^{-3} b. 5^{-2} c. 7^0 d. 6^{-1}
8. How do you think you would write the following in simplest form?
   a. m^{-3} b. x^{-2} c. y^0 d. c^{-4}
9. Vanessa thinks that $5m^{-3} = \frac{1}{5m^3}$. Do you agree or disagree? Explain.

Below you will find Tier II and III activities that expand on the Tier I lesson. In the Tier II activity for below-level students, the learners will be given time to review expressions with positive exponents before filling in the table. They will not be asked to complete the more abstract questions at the end of the lesson. Also note how the questions asked are more specific, use different language, and provide more detail. This is an example of scaffolding the lesson to support learners who need very specific instructions. It should be noted that sometimes students are below level because they have trouble reading. Therefore the teacher should plan to be readily available to this group as they begin the activity.

Tier II: Below-Level Activity

1. Mathematicians try to write expressions in a simplified form to save time and reduce the potential for errors. One commonly used shortcut for repeated addition is multiplication. For example, 8 + 8 + 8 + 8 + 8 can be written as 5 × 8. Recently you learned to use exponential notation to represent repeated multiplication expressions. Write the following using exponential notation.
   a. 3 × 3 × 3 × 3 × 3 × 3 ____________
   b. 5 × 5 × 5 × 5 ____________
2. For each problem in item 1, identify the base and the exponent.
   a. Base ________ Exponent ________
   b. Base ________ Exponent ________
3. Write the following in exponential expression form. Identify the base and the exponent.
   a. 6 × 6 × 6 × 6 × 6 b. $\left(\frac{3}{4}\right)\left(\frac{3}{4}\right)$ c. $-2 \times -2 \times -2 \times -2 \times -2$
4. Evaluate the following by expanding the expression and then simplifying the answer.
   a. 2^4 b. 4^5 c. 10^1 d. $\left(\frac{2}{3}\right)^3$ e. -10^4 f. a^3
5. In the table below evaluate each exponential expression by first expanding the expression and then writing the product. The first problem has been completed for you. If needed, you may use a calculator to evaluate expressions with exponents greater than 3.

2^x	4^x	10^x
$2^4 = 2 \times 2 \times 2 \times 2 = 16$	4^4	10^4
2^3	4^3	10^3
2^2	4^2	10^2
2^1	4^1	10^1

6. The heading of the first column is 2^x. This means that each number in the column has a base of 2. Why do you think the exponent is represented with an "x" in the column heading?
   Now look at each column in the table. What happens to the simplified value for each expression as you move down the column? Describe a pattern that you observe each time the exponent is decreased by 1. Be sure to describe the pattern that is be found in all three columns. You should use the words *base* and *exponent* to describe your pattern.
7. Use the pattern you found in the table above to simplify the expressions listed below. This time do not use a calculator. Write values less than 1 in standard fraction form.

2^x	4^x	5^x	10^x
2^1	4^1	5^1	10^1
2^0	4^0	5^0	10^0
2^{-1}	4^{-1}	5^{-1}	10^{-1}
2^{-2}	4^{-2}	5^{-2}	10^{-2}

8. What do you notice about expressions with an exponent of 1? Write a rule or definition for simplifying expressions with an exponent of 1.
9. What do you notice about expressions with an exponent of zero? Write a rule or definition for simplifying expressions with zero exponents.

10. What do you notice about expressions with an exponent of -1? Write a rule or definition for simplifying expressions with exponents of -1.
11. Generalize the rule to define all negative exponents. Explain in writing why you think this definition is correct.
12. Apply your definitions to the following:
 a. 4^{-3} b. 5^{-2} c. 7^0 d. 6^{-2}
13. How do you think you would write the following in simplest form?
 a. m^{-3} b. x^1 c. y^0 d. c^{-4}

The Tier III activity is for students who have some familiarity with the negative and zero exponent properties. While they complete the same task as the at-level students, they do so with less support. In addition, they are asked to go beyond the at-level lesson by researching a higher-level concept related to the use of exponential notation.

TIER III: ABOVE-LEVEL ACTIVITY

1. In the table below, evaluate each exponential expression and write the value in the appropriate column. If needed, you may use a calculator to evaluate expressions with exponents greater than 3.

2^x	4^x	5^x	10^x
2^4	4^6	5^5	10^4
2^3	4^5	5^4	10^3
2^2	4^4	5^3	10^2
2^1	4^3	5^2	10^1

2. Now look at each column in the table and describe a pattern you observe. Be sure to describe a pattern that can be applied to all four columns. Make sure you use appropriate mathematical language to generalize the pattern.
3. Use the pattern you described in item 2 above to complete the table below. This time do not use a calculator. Write values less than 1 in standard fraction form.

2^x	4^x	5^x	10^x
2^1	4^3	5^2	10^1
2^0	4^2	5^1	10^0
2^{-1}	4^1	5^0	10^{-1}
2^{-2}	4^0	5^{-1}	10^{-2}

4. Based on the pattern you see, define the zero exponent property.
5. Based on the pattern you see, define the negative exponent property.
6. Apply your definitions to the following:
 a. 6^{-2} b. x^{-2} c. -3^0 d. y^0
7. Express the following using a zero or negative exponent.
 a. 1 b. $\frac{1}{4}$ c. $\frac{1}{r^3}$ d. $\frac{1}{100{,}000}$
8. Vanessa thinks that $5m^{-3} = \frac{1}{5m^3}$. Do you agree or disagree? Explain.
9. Your textbook states that zero cannot be used as a base in an exponential expression. Read the explanation for this found in your book. Then research this question using three other sources. You may use approved sources from the Internet and the class mathematics library. Prepare a 5-minute presentation to help your classmates understand why zero cannot be used as a base in an exponential expression.

Step 4: Implement the Plan.

Teachers need to be very organized to implement a tiered lesson. Appropriate groups must be formed as the students enter the classroom. Readily accessible materials and resources is a key element to the success or failure of such a lesson. The teacher may need to provide direct instruction for some groups and become a facilitator for others. She should set up the tiers so that different groups can work independently at different times. This allows her to be accessible to students when they most need her.

Step 5: Assign Homework.

Tiered lessons should be followed by tiered homework. Some students will need practice to automate skills. Others learn best by limited practice and more time to investigate the big ideas related to the topic.

Step 6: Assessment.

Ongoing assessment is a critical element of any lesson. The teacher is now measuring progress at three positions along the continuum toward meeting the goals of the unit. Chapter 6 will address a variety of assessment strategies for formative lesson assessment.

Final Thoughts on Tiered Lessons

Clearly developing tiered lessons adds to a teacher's planning time. This burden is made easier because many textbooks include suggestions for differentiating instruction based on learning levels, learning styles, and student interests. New teachers are advised to start by designing lessons with two levels. These lessons might include a whole class introduction, followed by tiered group work. As you learn more about your students and the curriculum, developing tiered lessons will become a standard stage of the planning process.

Additional Differentiation Strategies

While not as explicitly differentiated, the lessons presented earlier in this chapter provide additional strategies addressing the needs of all students. In Sample Lesson Plan 1, Introduction to Similar Figures, students are asked to classify the shapes given. This is an opportunity for students of all levels to contribute. Some students may see characteristics such as number of sides and thus classify the figures as four-sided or three-sided, whereas the more sophisticated thinkers may focus on types of angles.

This lesson also includes an activity that involves measuring the sides and angles of the figures. Students will break into groups to measure, record the results, find the ratio of the sides, and, with the highest-level task, summarize the results in writing. The teacher might assign these tasks based on the strengths and weaknesses of each student. In any case, the whole group should agree on this summary because any one member may have to represent it to the class. Such an assignment also allows the teacher to circulate among the students and provide support on an individual or small group basis.

This is also a time when students who are not otherwise engaged may begin to disrupt the class. To counteract any distractions, the teacher should provide additional or bonus questions for groups that finish early. In the similar figures lesson, an additional challenge was added asking students to explain how they would determine whether two given figures were similar. This question extends beyond the expected lesson objectives but is closely related to the lesson. Along with stimulating the more gifted students, bonus activities allow the teacher precious time to work with those students who need additional support.

Another way to differentiate instruction is to physically arrange your classroom so that students can easily move from whole class to small groups, and from groups to individual instruction. You might sit students in pairs that can be quickly turned into groups of four. Even in whole class situations, students should be encouraged to confer with a neighbor before responding back to the class; a teaming called Think-Pair-Share. This type of questioning technique gives everyone a stake in the answer and allows those less inclined to volunteer to feel more confident to take the risk of answering a question.

Think-Pair-Share also works well for students who are English language learners (ELL). By pairing a student who has limited English abilities with one who is bilingual, the ELL student is more apt to share an answer with the class. If a bilingual student is not available, pairing ELL students of the same native language and encouraging them to discuss the task in their mother tongue might give them more confidence when trying to explain their answer in English.

No matter the composition, encouraging students to work in groups allows those who have developed an understanding of a concept to explain it to someone else. Such a process helps clarify the understanding of the former while improving that of the latter. More specific discussion about using formal cooperative groups is given later in the chapter.

Additionally, teachers can differentiate instruction by allowing students to choose a topic for graded projects or long-term assignments. Whether running a survey on favorite cafeteria food or modeling growth using an exponential function, students can develop a better understanding of mathematics through real-world applications. To further engage the students in such applications, the teacher could allow the students to choose from topics related to sports, finance, science, or social science. Providing students a choice in the topic gives them more of a stake in the outcome of the project.

Students should be allowed to demonstrate their understanding though a variety of methods. Tests, projects, and oral presentations all draw on different strengths. Thus, your assessment plan should include diverse ways to show mastery of the topic. However, in these days of high-stakes testing, students must be familiar with the types of questions asked on required tests and how their answers will be evaluated. Good tests ask for different types of answers. Even exceptional mathematics students sometimes encounter trouble when a test asks for a written explanation or graphic representation. Thus, students may need explicit instruction on the type of answer expected and access to the scoring guide.

The traditional mathematics classroom found the teacher first reviewing homework, and then showing students a new concept or procedure, followed up by providing time for practice of that procedure. Even though this type of instruction worked well for some people, it left behind many others who feel that they "just can't do mathematics." In today's information and technological world, all of our citizens must be mathematically literate. It is the responsibility of the mathematics teacher to use a variety of instructional strategies and formats to provide meaningful learning experiences for all. This is a special challenge for new teachers, but in the long run will make their teaching experience much more rewarding. (Additional information about differentiating instruction can be found in the resources listed at the end of this book.)

Cooperative Learning

Collaboration and social interaction among groups of students encourage the students to support the learning of one another. Students in well-planned cooperative group activities will verbalize and listen to one another's mathematics ideas, check for understanding, assist each other in staying on task, and offer support for naïve understandings or a lack of understanding. Further, cooperative grouping succeeds in promoting social skills and the acceptance of diversity in exceptionalities, achievement, ethnicity, and gender.

What Is Cooperative Learning?

Cooperative learning goes beyond merely putting students together in small groups and giving them an assignment. Certain elements are necessary to ensure that when students *do* work in groups, they work cooperatively. First, the members of a group must perceive that they are part of a team and that they all have a common goal. Second, group members must realize that the problem they are to solve is a group problem and that the success or failure of the group will be shared by all the members of the group. Third, to accomplish the group's goal, all students must talk with one another—engage in discussion of all problems. Finally, it must be clear that each member's individual work has a direct effect on the group's success. Teamwork is of utmost importance.

It is *not* a cooperative environment if students sit together in groups and work on problems individually or let one person do all the work. True cooperation in the learning process requires the guidance of a teacher who can help students understand group dynamics, develop the cooperative skills they need, and learn mathematics by working in groups.

True cooperative learning capitalizes on the presence of student peers, encourages student-to-student interaction, and establishes a symbiotic relationship among team members. Students in effective groups learn to listen to others' ideas, to discuss and disagree, to offer and accept constructive criticism from their peers, and to be comfortable about making mistakes.

How to Structure Small Learning Groups

Small learning groups can be structured in many ways. The literature sets forth many techniques that researchers and teachers have developed and studied. Each of these methods is designed to ensure that within each group there is positive interdependence, individual accountability, face-to-face verbal communication, and positive social interaction. The techniques address four essential areas: group formation, cooperative learning task designs, reward structures, and group processing.

Group Formation

Those who are experienced in the field of small learning groups recognize that group formation is critical to its effectiveness—to maximize the benefits of small learning groups, the membership should be heterogeneous in ability and personal characteristics. The group must stay together long enough for cohesiveness to develop. A successful group will be small enough for everyone to be needed but large enough to permit a diversity of ideas and skills.

The most effective way of ensuring heterogeneity is for the teacher to organize the groups. Teachers know their own students best and can see to it that they place readers with nonreaders, task-oriented students with non-task-oriented students, high-ability students with medium- and low-ability students, minority students with majority students, non-English-speaking students with those who speak English, students who have disabilities with nondisabled students, and females with males. Students can be asked to indicate with which peers they would like to work, and the teacher can consider their wishes when groups are being formed. It is important that students be happy in their groups, if they are to work well.

One of the criteria for group success is the durability of the group. It takes time for group cohesiveness to develop. When students know that their group will be together for some time, they realize that they must improve their interpersonal skills so that they can function effectively. Small learning groups may stay together during a unit of work, a semester, or a year. Although it is important that groups stay together and learn how to work productively and harmoniously, if some groups are not working out well, changes should be made. When students are dissatisfied with fellow group members, they are not likely to engage in the free expression and exploration of ideas. Therefore, the teacher must stay informed about the attitudes and behavior of each group member. One way teachers do this is by observing how students interact with one another within the group. A group may seem to be functioning well, but sometimes observations are deceiving. Students can be asked to use journals to communicate their feelings about their groups and the way that they function within the group. They should comment on the help they have given or received within the group. Together, the students and the teacher should decide when and if group arrangements should be changed.

The size of a group affects its ability to be productive. Experience has shown that groups of three to five students work well. If a learning group has too many students, it may have difficulty functioning effectively. The most vocal students tend to take over, and the quiet ones recede into the background. Furthermore, it is difficult for a large group to get organized, to coordinate the work of its members, and to reach agreement.

To add to the feeling of camaraderie, each group might agree on a name for itself. In cases in which the groups have stabilized, the teacher may wish to take photographs of the groups, have the students mount them on group-designed construction paper, and then post them on the bulletin board. This can add to the warmth and enjoyment of being part of a learning group.

Cooperative Learning Task Designs

For small group learning to succeed, the students must perceive themselves as being dependent on one another, they must communicate with one another, and they must be individually accountable for the work. To maximize the chances for these conditions to exist, group tasks must be designed thoughtfully.

Responsibility for each person's learning is shared by other group members. Group members are expected to help and encourage one another. The emphasis is on working and learning together. Nevertheless, individual students are held accountable for their own learning and for their individual contributions to the group. Thus, each member of the group is responsible for mastering the material. Members are individually accountable and are expected to learn and to participate in the group's work.

One way to ensure that each student participates in the group assignment is to divide tasks in such a way that each student is responsible for doing one part of the work. In the similar figures lesson presented earlier in this chapter, student roles could include group manager, data collectors (measurers), and recorder. The manager is responsible for gathering materials before and after the lesson and seeing that the task is completed. The data collectors ensure that the measurements and calculations are correct, and the recorder writes the data on the chart and summarizes the group response to the questions asked. Group roles should not suggest that some students can sit back when their task is complete. All students must be invested in answering the questions and be responsible for those answers.

To achieve the group's goal or to complete the group's task, each member of the group needs to hold the others accountable for learning concepts and skills. Cooperative group tasks should be designed to serve as a scaffold for learning. Processes and procedures should be clearly understood by some members of each group so they can help others learn. Group members also need opportunities to practice what they learn.

Cooperation is based on reciprocity. Maintaining effective working relationships among group members requires each student to appreciate the value of reciprocation. Each student must be prepared to give as well as receive.

Reward Structures

A well-designed reward structure gives added incentives for small group learning behavior among students. For example, after the groups have submitted assignments, each group's products are evaluated by both the teacher and the students, and each group's score is recorded on a chart that is accessible to all students. To ensure individual accountability, a group gets full credit for its results only if a randomly selected student in the group can adequately explain the solutions. There are many ways to score group products, depending on the nature of the assignments. Scoring may involve counting the number of correct solutions, quantitatively evaluating a solution strategy with a letter grade, or ranking the work from each group. Groups may compete with one another or strive to meet certain preestablished criteria. Care must be taken that this competition does not drive the weaker members into passive "backseat" roles. Rather, they must be as active as the more involved students.

Students working within such a reward structure are eager to check with one another to be sure that each person in the group understands the material, agrees with the results or conclusions, and is able to represent the group as spokesperson. Students ask one another for help or clarification, they ask questions, and they answer questions. The quality of the verbal interaction is an important factor in the group's success.

Another motivating strategy is Student Teams-Achievement Divisions (STAD). The teacher presents a lesson, and then the students meet in teams of four or five to complete a set of worksheets on the lesson. Each student then takes an exam on the material, and the scores the students contribute to their teams are based on the degree to which they have improved over their individual past averages. Another method, Teams-Games-Tournament (TGT), is similar to STAD, but instead of taking quizzes, the students play mathematics games as representatives of their teams. They compete with other students having similar achievement levels.

With these types of reward structures, students are encouraged to be concerned not only about themselves, but also about the other members of the group. Students engage in peer teaching because they acknowledge that each group member must understand the material. Each student recognizes that the group expects each member to complete the assigned work and to make a contribution to the group. Students help one another. One student explains a difficult concept to another in his or her own words. Group members share resources, act as resources for one another, and encourage one another to participate. Even those who are usually silent are made to feel that the group relies on them to participate in the group's activities. It is "all for one and one for all" because that is what makes group success possible.

Sample Lesson for Cooperative Group Work: Solving Radical Equations

Nearly any lesson can be taught in a group setting. As discussed earlier, the reasons for offering a cooperative learning lesson are many and varied. Here we take a lesson on radicals and propose using cooperative learning. For this activity on solving radical equations, we suggest groups of approximately five students each. Heterogeneous grouping of the class should allow for an exchange of varied insights without necessarily relying on the class leaders to the exclusion of others.

After organizing the class into heterogeneous groups, distribute one copy of the following worksheet to each group recorder. The problems are ordered so as to enable students to discover the procedures for solving radical equations. For each, *solve, check*, and *state solution set*. Show each step.

1. $\sqrt{x} = 5$
2. $\sqrt{x+1} = 5$
3. $\sqrt{x+1} = -5$
4. $\sqrt{x+1} - 1 = 5$
5. $\sqrt{x+1} + 5 = 1$
6. $x = 1 + \sqrt{x+5}$
7. $\sqrt{3x-1} = 2\sqrt{8-2x}$
8. $\sqrt[3]{4x+5} = 3$

HINTS: For #4, #5, and #6: Isolate the radical

QUESTIONS:

Which equations yielded extraneous roots?
Explain why the roots are extraneous.

CHALLENGE:

$$\sqrt{x+1} = 1 - \sqrt{2x}$$

In addition to the intrinsic rewards experienced by members of successful cooperative groups, additional incentives may be offered. Members of successful groups may be presented with certificates. Names of successful groups for the month may be listed on the bulletin board. Students are always motivated to improve their grades, but rewarding students in this way must be done very carefully. One valid technique is to count "cooperation" as a percentage of their final grade. Members of successful teams may then be given extra "cooperation" points.

Group Processing

The teacher must help students realize that for a group to interact well, members must feel free to express their ideas, ask questions, and clarify differences. Thus, each person must be patient and exert self-control. Once all ideas have been discussed, group members must be willing to compromise—to integrate different perspectives into a single group solution that is acceptable to all. Agreement may be difficult and not always achievable because of the students' prior educational experiences.

It is not unusual for differences and disagreements to arise even though the group is working cooperatively. Group members need the skills to manage such controversies. Teachers must help students realize that group members should be critical of ideas but not of people. They should understand that controversy strengthens understanding and helps the group reach consensus. They must learn how important it is to listen carefully to what other group members are saying and to try to understand ideas with which they disagree. Such skills of conflict management are essential to any group's functioning.

Teachers must monitor the groups while they are in progress and provide assistance as it is needed. When a group is functioning poorly, the teacher will want to intervene to help students with the skills they need. Once these skills have been identified and discussed, the teacher will want to see how well the group is practicing them and whether it is functioning more effectively. The teacher should provide feedback so that students know how well they are doing. The teacher may ask the groups to monitor their own performance by answering questions about the group's behavior and functioning. Is each person participating? Are students helping one another? Are they handling conflicts well?

The Teacher's Role in Managing Small Group Learning

The teacher plays a vital role in the implementation of effective small group learning. First, students need to learn how to work cooperatively. Team-building activities must be taught and practiced on a regular basis. Suggestions for such activities can be found in the materials listed in the Suggested Readings for this chapter. In addition, at the beginning of any group activity, the teacher must give an explanation of the assignment, the time allowed for the activity, the academic expectations for the group, the expected collaborative behaviors, the procedures to follow, and the definition of group success.

The teacher, as class manager, must organize the room in such a way that the members of a group are close enough to one another to work together comfortably and talk with one another quietly. The groups must be separated so that they do not interfere with one another.

During group work it is often difficult to get the attention of students. An effective technique that does not entail raising one's voice is for the teacher simply to raise a hand and require that each student who sees the hand raised do the same and stop talking. Then each student who sees another student's hand raised must do the same. This chain reaction stops when everyone raises a hand and the class is quiet and ready to pay attention to the teacher. This procedure must be implemented with care and forethought so that it may not appear too childish for the higher secondary grades.

As teachers become comfortable with the small group learning approach, they will decide for themselves how best to facilitate the process. Several of the lessons plans described in this chapter provide ideas for incorporating easily implemented cooperative learning activities. A few additional suggestions follow for simple ways of getting started.

Test Preview/Review

The group structure makes it convenient for students to help one another in preparing for a test. A sample test can be assigned for homework. The students then meet in groups to discuss the sample test and to deepen their understanding of the concepts and techniques that will be tested. By working on the sample test individually, each student comes to the group discussion with an accurate picture of his or her understanding. Students are able to prepare themselves and other group members for the forthcoming test. Once again, each group agrees on the solutions to the problems and hands in one group paper. The teacher allows time for the whole class to discuss those areas that need clarification.

Learning must also take place after a test has been returned! Members of a group can help one another understand and correct their errors. Students might even be given the opportunity to resubmit the problems they got wrong, provided that they do each problem correctly, explain why their original solution was incorrect, and justify their new solution by giving a written explanation of the thought processes they used. This procedure can counterbalance the natural reaction of many students, which is to accept past failure, only to move on to the next task, where a "clean slate" awaits them. The tests can then be regraded and a final grade can be formed by taking a weighted average of the first and second test grades, perhaps using the first test as one-third of the grade and the second test as two-thirds of the grade.

Enrichment

Group work is an excellent way of incorporating enrichment experiences in the mathematics class. To spark student interest in a new topic, small learning groups can investigate the historical development of the topic. The members of the group should divide the work among themselves. For example, one student may look up the dateline in the development of the

EXERCISES

1. A teacher notices that in some of the cooperative learning groups in class, the brightest students are doing all the work. What are some techniques that the teacher can use to keep this from happening?
2. You receive a phone call from an angry parent of one of the brightest students in your class. The parent complains that his child is being held back by having to help the weaker students in his group. How would you respond to this parent?
3. The teacher notices that one of the lower ability students is not participating in her group. How should the teacher handle this situation?
4. Design a cooperative learning exploration lesson that will enable students to make a conjecture regarding the relationship of the three angles of a triangle.
5. A teacher realizes that many of the cooperative groups in his class are not functioning effectively, so he decides to change the group formations at the end of the unit. What procedures can he use to rearrange the groups in the best possible manner?
6. Describe three student characteristics that a teacher should consider when forming heterogeneous groups.
7. Why are conflict management skills needed by members of an effective cooperative learning group?
8. A student reports that her group is operating very well; there are no conflicts or disagreements. Yet the achievement is not what it ought to be. How would you handle this situation?
9. Describe some ways that a teacher can monitor the progress of cooperative learning groups.
10. Design a lesson that will enable members of cooperative learning groups to discover that the sum of the roots of an equation of the form $ax^2 + bx + c = 0$ is $-b/a$ and that the product of the roots is c/a. Assume that students can solve such a quadratic equation by factoring or by formula.

topic and another student may be responsible for uncovering the mathematicians who were instrumental in the development of the topic. The group also may want to have a person look for anecdotes and events related to the topic. Finally, it will be of interest for a group member to investigate how knowledge of this topic has affected the world as it is today. This group project might culminate in a bulletin board display or a report.

Small learning groups can engage in recreational mathematics that challenge the students to do creative problem solving (see Chapter 4 for problem solving). For example, the work can be organized in different ways, or the groups can be given a problem that is to be solved by the end of the week. At the end of the week, those groups that claim to have solved the problem present their solutions. The teacher chooses a spokesperson for each group. The spokesperson must present the group's solution satisfactorily before the group can get credit for having solved the problem.

Group problem solving has many advantages. Members of the group engage in brainstorming, an activity that enables all members to participate in a free flow of ideas. The student who is poor at solving problems has the opportunity to engage in the problem-solving process along with peers who are more able. All students not only learn how to solve problems, but also share in the excitement the group experiences when the problem has been solved.

Mathematical Tasks

Teachers can have a significant impact on student achievement through their choice of mathematical tasks. In 2000, the NCTM *Principles and Standards for School Mathematics* indicated that effective teachers use well-chosen mathematical tasks to "introduce important mathematical ideas and engage and challenge students intellectually" (NCTM, 2000, p. 18).

How do teachers choose appropriate tasks to maximize student learning? To make such choices teachers must be able to classify tasks in a number of ways. One way is to identify the concept or skill the task is designed to develop. This type of classification ensures that tasks are aligned with the course's learning objectives.

Another important type of classification is the level of cognitive demand. Research indicates that mathematical learning is enhanced when instruction emphasizes student engagement with tasks that are both meaningful and challenging (Stein & Lane, 1996). Such engagement helps develop the higher order thinking students need for a truer understanding of mathematics.

To help teachers decide how to choose challenging mathematical tasks, Smith and Stein (1998) provided a framework for task classification based on levels of cognitive demand. Listed from the least to most demanding, they are memorization, using procedures without connections to concepts or meaning, using procedures with connections to concepts and meaning, and doing mathematics. A more detailed description of these levels of cognitive demand can be found in Figure 2.8.

To better understand these cognitive levels, we will classify the following mathematical tasks:

Task A: State the quadratic formula.

Task B: Find all solutions for x using the quadratic formula.

$$0 = 3x^2 - 12x + 4$$

FIGURE 2.8 Characteristics of Mathematical Instructional Tasks

Levels of Demands

Lower-Level Demands (Memorization)

- Involve either reproducing previously learned facts, rules, formulas, or definitions or committing facts, rules, formulas, or definitions to memory.
- Cannot be solved using procedures because a procedure does not exist or because the time frame in which the task is being completed is too short to use a procedure.
- Are not ambiguous. Such tasks involve the exact reproduction of previously seen material, and what is to be reproduced is clearly and directly stated.
- Have no connection to the concepts or meaning that underlie the facts, rules, formulas, or definitions being learned or reproduced.

Lower-Level Demands (Procedures without Connections)

- Are algorithmic. Use of the procedure either is specifically called for or is evident from prior instruction, experience, or placement of the task.
- Require limited cognitive demand for successful completion. Little ambiguity exists about what needs to be done and how to do it.
- Have no connection to the concepts or meaning that underlie the procedure being used.
- Are focused on producing correct answers instead of on developing mathematical understanding.
- Require no explanations or explanations that focus solely on describing the procedure that was used.

Higher-Level Demands (Procedures with Connections)

- Focus students' attention on the use of procedures for the purpose of developing deeper levels of understanding of mathematical concepts and ideas.
- Suggest explicitly or implicitly pathways to follow that are broad general procedures that have close connections to underlying conceptual ideas as opposed to narrow algorithms that are opaque with respect to underlying concepts.
- Usually are represented in multiple ways, such as visual diagrams, manipulatives, symbols, and problem situations. Making connections among multiple representations helps develop meaning.
- Require some degree of cognitive effort. Although general procedures may be followed, they cannot be followed mindlessly. Students need to engage with conceptual ideas that underlie the procedures to complete the task successfully and to develop understanding.

Higher-Level Demands (Doing Mathematics)

- Require complex and non-algorithmic thinking—a predictable, well-rehearsed approach or pathway is not explicitly suggested by the task, task instructions, or a worked-out example.
- Require students to explore and understand the nature of mathematical concepts, processes, or relationships.
- Demand self-monitoring or self-regulation of one's own cognitive processes.
- Require students to access relevant knowledge and experiences and make appropriate use of them in working through the task.
- Require students to analyze the task and actively examine task constraints that may limit possible solution strategies and solutions.
- Require considerable cognitive effort and may involve some level of anxiety for the student because of the unpredictable nature of the solution process required.

These characteristics are derived from the work of Doyle on academic tasks (1988) and Resnick on high-level-thinking skills (1987), the Professional Standards for Teaching Mathematics (NCTM 1991), and the examination and categorization of hundreds of tasks used in QUASAR classrooms (Stein, Grover, and Henningsen 1996; Stein, Lane, and Silver 1996).

Task C: The following data shows the payroll of a baseball team.

Pitcher	$432,500
Second baseman	$480,000
Designated hitter	$750,000
Second baseman	$308,000
Outfielder	$7,000,000
First baseman	$400,000
Pitcher	$200,000
Pitcher	$3,000,000
Pitcher	$3,800,000
Pitcher	$301,500
Shortstop	$12,500,000
Outfielder	$750,000
Pitcher	$3,425,000
Pitcher	$4,500,000
Pitcher	$18,500,000
Outfielder	$500,000
Pitcher	$3,600,000
First baseman	$3,200,000
Catcher	$820,000
Third baseman	$2,100,000
Outfielder	$4,500,000
First baseman	$4,587,500
Outfielder	$23,500,000
Second baseman	$1,000,000
Pitcher	$12,000,000
Pitcher	$303,000
Pitcher	$2,500,000
Catcher	$6,800,000
Pitcher	$4,350,000
Pitcher	$3,100,000

1. Create a histogram using the baseball payroll data.
2. Using the histogram, estimate the mean, median, and mode of those salaries. Then calculate the three statistical summaries. Which of these three measures of central tendency best describes the salary of players on this team? Explain why you think your choice best represents the salary data for the team.
3. If you were asked to summarize the data for a report, what additional information might you provide? Why do you think that information would help the reader better understand the data?

Task D: Given a piece of paper, 14 by 8.5 inches, form a box by cutting out the same-size squares from each corner. What size squares should you cut if you want to create a box with the largest volume possible? (Note: You are to create a rectangular box with no top. See figures below.) Explore possible solutions to this problem and write about your findings.

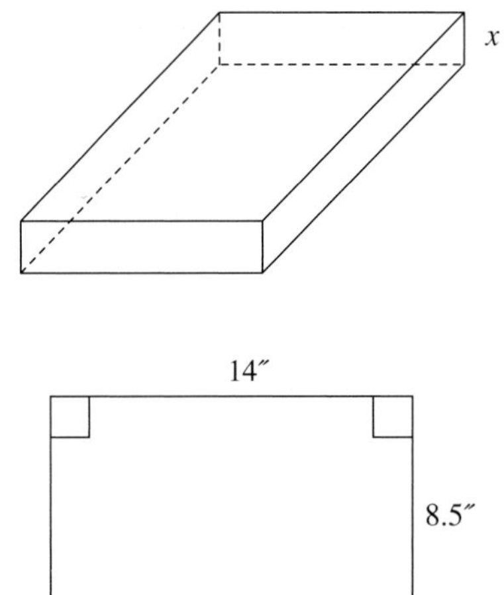

The tasks listed above would be classified as follows:

Task A is clearly memorization. It has no connections to the use of the quadratic formula and does not require that students use the formula.

Task B is a procedure without connections. The algebraic procedures of substituting in values and then solving an equation are applied, but there is no connection to meaning.

Task C is an example of procedures with connections. Although students are asked to create a specific graph and find specific measures of central tendency, they are also asked to choose the most appropriate measure of central tendency for this data set and explain that choice. In addition, they are asked to further describe the data. Thus, the task focuses on using the procedures to build deeper understanding of the topic.

Task D suggests no pathway to the solution of the task. The students need to access relevant knowledge and experiences in order to solve the problem.

Although students must be able to complete tasks at all levels, too often students are only presented with lower level tasks. Research has shown that the most gains in student achievement occur when students routinely participate in higher level tasks (Growes, 2004). Therefore, while planning your lessons, you should consider the cognitive level of your tasks and raise the bar whenever possible.

Another major aspect of tasks to consider is how you will present them to the class. Sometimes, even the most carefully prepared and challenging tasks are reduced to a low-level activity when students are not given the appropriate scaffolding or support. At times, such support requires the teacher to perform a balancing act. Looking at Figure 2.9, you will find subtle differences between maintaining the cognitive demands of a high-level task and allowing it to slip into a lower level. Balancing the students' need for guidance during the problem-solving process with a teacher's temptation to fill in the blanks requires a deft touch. Try to keep in mind that the teacher as tour guide is just that, a guide whose presence provides the group of travelers with the confidence to explore new terrain.

FIGURE 2.9 Factors Associated with Maintenance and Decline of High-Level Cognitive Demands

Factors Associated with the Maintenance of High-Level Cognitive Demands

1. Scaffolding of student thinking and reasoning is provided.
2. Students are given the means to monitor their own progress.
3. Teacher or capable students model high-level performance.
4. Teacher presses for justifications, explanations, and meaning through questioning, comments, and feedback.
5. Tasks build on students' prior knowledge.
6. Teacher draws frequent conceptual connections.
7. Sufficient time is allowed for exploration—not too little, not too much.

Factors Associated with the Decline of High-Level Cognitive Demands

1. Problematic aspects of the task become rote (e.g., students press the teacher to reduce the complexity of the task by specifying explicit procedures or steps to perform; the teacher "takes over" the thinking and reasoning and tells students how to do the problem).
2. The teacher shifts the emphasis from meaning, concepts, or understanding to the correctness or completeness of the answer.
3. Not enough time is provided to wrestle with the demanding aspects of the task, or too much time is allowed and students drift into off-task behavior.
4. Classroom-management problems prevent sustained engagement in high-level cognitive activities.
5. Task is inappropriate for a given group of students (e.g., students do not engage in high-level cognitive activities because of lack of interest, motivation, or prior knowledge needed to perform; task expectations are not clear enough to put students in the right cognitive space).
6. Students are not held accountable for high-level products or processes (e.g., although asked to explain their thinking, unclear or incorrect student explanations are accepted; students are given the impression that their work will not "count" toward a grade).

EXERCISES: SAMPLE LESSONS

The plans that follow describe lessons from different teachers' records. Some lessons are very traditional in nature, whereas others attempt to incorporate ideas promoted by the NCTM Standards. If you analyze and discuss these lessons, you will find strengths and weaknesses in each.

Using what you have learned from this chapter, redesign the lessons with the following criteria in mind:

1. Rewrite (if necessary) the instructional objectives so that the student actions are clearly stated and the conditions under which those actions take place are clearly specified.
2. Identify the curriculum standards addressed in each lesson plan.
3. Indicate how the lesson could be differentiated to meet the needs of lower and higher achieving students.
4. Using the framework provided in Figure 2.8, identify a level one or two task. Indicate how you might modify this task so that students are engaged in a level three or four activity.
5. Identify key vocabulary words used in the lesson.
6. How could calculators and computers play a more significant role in this lesson?
7. To what extent could a small group activity be a useful strategy for this lesson? Where is whole class instruction most appropriate?
8. Where would manipulatives or technology be useful or needed?
9. To what extent are questions provocative? Open-ended?
10. What assessment strategies would you employ during the course of the lesson? At the conclusion of the lesson?

Remember, old lessons may have been taught by master teachers. Even though teacher roles have changed, their plans may still be informative with regard to style, technique, strategy, questioning, knowledge, and more. Note that the comments section is included to assist you in reviewing the teacher's rationale for lesson components. You do *not* need to include lesson comments of your own. Rather this section could be reserved for feedback from your peers.

Lesson Plan 3 is specifically for middle school or junior high school students.

Final Thoughts on Lesson Planning

Just as no hiker wants to climb the same trail day in and day out, so no student enjoys sitting for the same type of lesson every day. It ruins initiative and dulls the imagination. It might also affect a teacher who, for example, uses the small group instructional format every day. Variety is what makes the learning process, as well as the teaching aspect of that process, a pleasant one. Thus, whole class discussions, peer instruction, individual exploration, guest lecturers, and video presentations must all become part of the mathematics teacher's repertoire.

Every lesson, however, ought to contain at least some task-oriented features, such as challenging activities, use of calculators, computers, or manipulatives whenever appropriate, and stimulating, open-ended type of questions *always*.

Whenever you plan a unit of work, a daily lesson, or an assessment strategy, do so carefully and imaginatively. You have a wide range of options to choose from, so choose wisely and try to use as many approaches as possible throughout the semester.

LESSON PLAN 1

Comments

OBJECTIVE:

Given a quadratic equation, students, will solve by factoring when possible. Given a factorable quadratic equation, students will justify the procedure of setting each factor equal to zero.

DO-NOW:

When a number is multiplied by 3 more than itself, the result is 0. Find the number.

These are the answers the teacher expects to elicit when reviewing the do-now.

$$x = \text{number}$$
$$x + 3 = 3 \text{ more that the number}$$
$$x(x + 3) = 0$$

Let's stop for a moment and see whether we can discover something that will help us solve this equation.
Everybody, think of two numbers whose product is 0. (Write answers on board.)
What do you notice about each pair of numbers?
Who can say in words what we just noticed? (Write on board: If $ab = 0$, then $a = 0$ or $b = 0$.)
Now, let's use this fact to solve our equation:

These are the major questions and comments, written in the same order they were asked by the teacher.

x	$(x + 3)$
$x = 0$	$x + 3 = 0$ $x = -3$

How would you use this same fact to solve $x(x + 4) = 0$?
How would you solve $x^2 + 4x = 0$? (Elicit "factoring.")
What about this one: $x^2 + 5x + 6 = 0$?
How would you solve $x^2 - 4 = 0$?

This question was not asked because the teacher saw that the lesson was running too long and wanted to begin to cut out some parts of the prepared lesson.

Looking back at the equations we've just solved, who can tell us the steps we used?
(Elicit the following.)
(Write on board.)

Developing steps used in solving a quadratic serves as a medial summary.

1. Factor.
2. Set each factor $= 0$.
3. Solve each linear equation.

   Now use these steps to solve the following:

   a. $x^2 + 5x = 0$ b. $x^2 + 6x + 8 = 0$ c. $x^2 - 16 = 0$

   (Go over solutions.)

Example (c) was cut out of the class presentation to save time.

(continued)

LESSON PLAN 1 (*continued*)

Comments

How are these equations different from the ones you've learned to solve before today? ("degree 2," "two answers," etc.)

A pivotal question comparing students' new knowledge with previous knowledge.

These equations are called QUADRATIC EQUATIONS.
Which of the following are quadratic equations?

The teacher wrote on the board the aim of the lesson: How to solve quadratic equations.

a. $x^2 + 7x + 12 = 0$ b. $x^2 - 2x = 0$ c. $x^2 = 2x$
d. $x^2 + 7x = -12$ e. $x + 3 = 0$

Compare (a) and (d); (b) and (c).
Who can summarize for us how we go about solving quadratic equations?

(Note: Extra step of gathering all terms on one side in descending powers.)

HOMEWORK ASSIGNMENT:
Study pages 157 and 158.
Do examples 3, 5, 7, 11, 13, 17, 19.

Students were asked to read the text explanation of the same topic and to do practice examples. NOTE 1: The homework assignment was not spiral. NOTE 2: Although the assignment was written last in the plan, it was written on the board FIRST by the teacher. At the end of the period, the teacher changed the assignment by eliminating the types of examples that were not discussed.

Go over homework today. Page 140/ 2, 3, 4, 6.

This was not done in class because of insufficient time.

IF TIME:
Solve each quadratic equation:

This also was not done in class.

a. $x^2 + 8x + 15 = 0$ b. $x^2 - 64 = 0$ c. $a^2 = 7a$ d. $b^2 + 6b = -8$

Boardwork (front):

The classroom has three front board panels, and the teacher planned where everything was to be written.

Panel I	Panel II	Panel III
DN	1. If $ab = 0$, $a = 0$ or $b = 0$	Solve: $x^2 + 5x = 0$
$x(x + 3) = 0$	2. Steps to solve (quadratics)	$x^2 + 6x + 8 = 0$
$x(x + 4) = 0$	a. Collect terms on one side.	$x^2 - 16 = 0$
$x^2 + 4x = 0$	Set = 0.	Which are quadratics?
$x^2 + 5x + 6 = 0$	b. Factor.	$x^2 + 7x + 12 = 0$
$x^2 - 4 = 0$	c. Set each factor = 0.	$x^2 - 2x = 0$
	d. Solve linear equations.	$x^2 = 2x$
	3. Facts about equations:	$x^2 + 7x = -12$
	a. degree 2	$x + 3 = 0$
	b. two answers	

(Note: Homework on side boards.)

LESSON PLAN 2

TOPIC: INTRODUCTORY LESSON ON PROPERTIES OF THE PARALLELOGRAM

OBJECTIVES:

Students will discover and prove the following properties of parallelograms.

a. Consecutive angles of a parallelogram are supplementary.
b. Opposite angles of a parallelogram are congruent.
c. Each diagonal of a parallelogram divides it into two congruent triangles.
d. Opposite sides of a parallelogram are congruent.
e. Diagonals of a parallelogram bisect each other.

Students will solve problems by applying the properties of parallelograms stated above.

PREVIOUSLY LEARNED:

a. Properties of angles formed when parallel lines are cut by a transversal
b. Methods of proving triangles congruent
c. Definitions of quadrilateral and diagonal

DO-NOW:

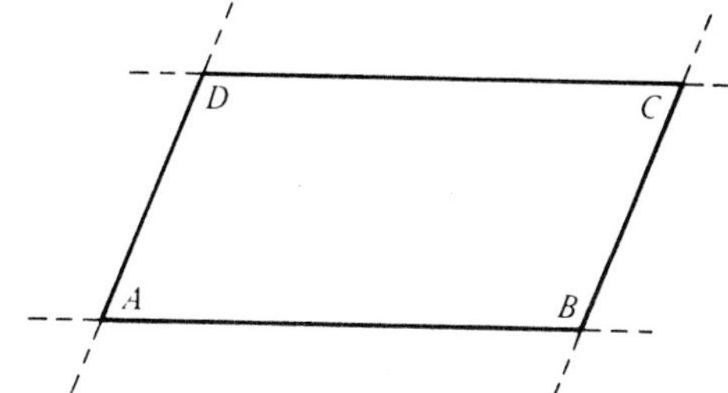

Given: Quadrilateral *ABCD*
$\overline{AB} \parallel \overline{CD}$; $\overline{AD} \parallel \overline{BC}$
Question: What relationship exists between $\angle A$ and $\angle B$? Why?

DEVELOPMENT AND METHODS:

(Students are not to write in their notebooks until told to do so by the teacher. All proofs of theorems that are elicited from the class will be done orally. Record all responses in tabular form as shown at the end of the plan.)

1. Define "parallelogram." (Head the table "In a parallelogram:" and elicit the aim of the lesson.)

2. Discuss the do-now. (Elicit: "Consecutive angles are supplementary," and prove.)

3. Question: What must be true about $\angle A$ and $\angle C$? Why? (Elicit and prove: "Opposite angles are congruent.")

4. Draw $\overline{BD}$.

5. Question: What new things can you see in the diagram as a result of having drawn $\overline{BD}$? (Elicit and prove: "Two congruent triangles are formed, and opposite sides are congruent.")

6. Erase $\overline{BD}$; draw $\overline{AC}$.

7. Question: Does drawing $\overline{AC}$ yield anything new that we can prove?

8. Medial Summary: Have students read and explain the list developed so far and copy it into their notebooks.

(continued)

LESSON PLAN 2 (*continued*)

PRACTICE:

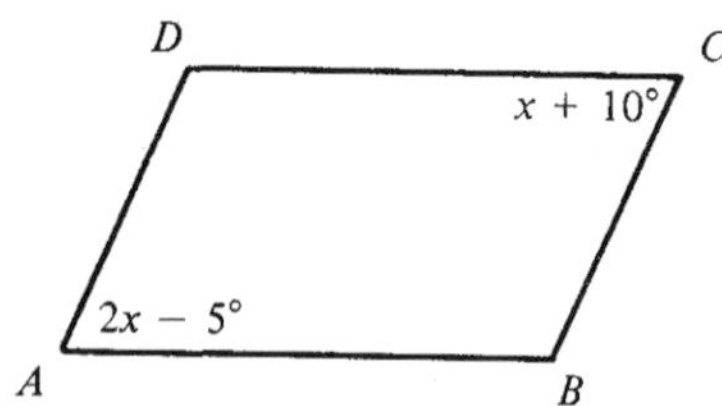

ABCD is a parallelogram. Find *x*. (Reason?)

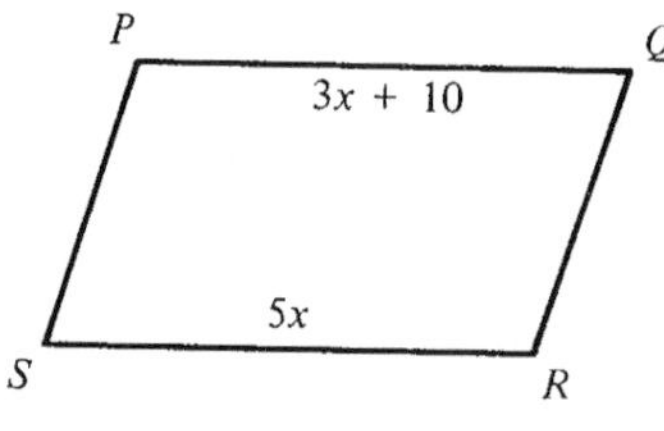

PQRS is a parallelogram. Find *x*. (Reason?)

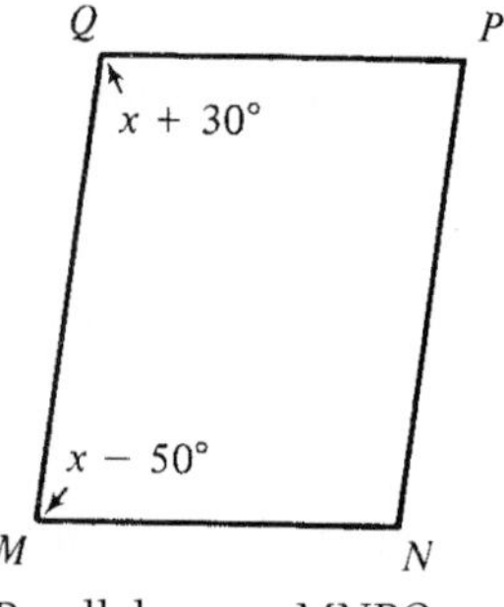

Parallelogram *MNPQ*. Find $m\angle P$.

DEVELOPMENT (CONTINUED):

9. Draw both diagonals.

10. Question: State and prove a conclusion you might reach about the two diagonals that appear together in the diagram. (Answer: "Diagonals bisect each other.")

PRACTICE:

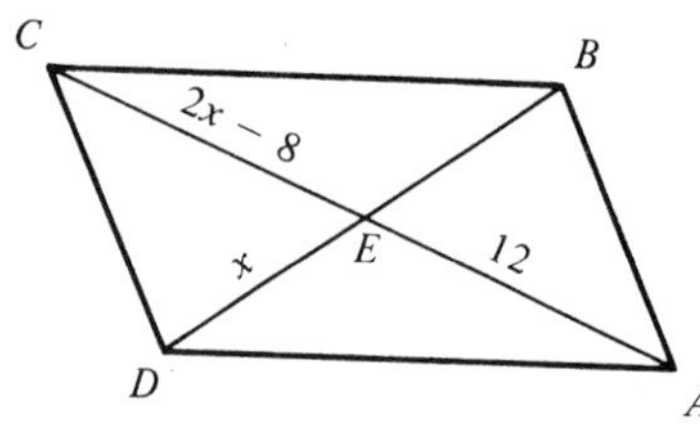

ABCD is a parallelogram. Find *DE*.

SUMMARY:
Erase the table from the board and ask, "List in your own words the properties of a parallelogram that we discussed earlier."

HOMEWORK:

a. Six examples in textbook, similar to practice that was done in class
b. Several other examples from a previous topic

IF TIME:
As many examples on the same topic as time permits. (Specific examples should be listed here.)

Table (on side of front board):

IN A PARALLELOGRAM:

(Definition)	1. Opposite sides are parallel.
(Theorem)	2. Consecutive angles are supplementary.
(Theorem)	3. Opposite angles are congruent.
(Theorem)	4. Diagonal divides it into two congruent triangles.
(Theorem)	5. Opposite sides are congruent.
(Theorem)	6. Diagonals bisect each other.

LESSON PLAN 3

TOPIC: ADDITION OF SIMPLE ARITHMETIC FRACTIONS

PRIOR KNOWLEDGE:

1. Students are familiar with the basic concepts of fractions.
2. Students have studied multiplication and simplification of simple fractions.

DO-NOW:

Use this diagram:

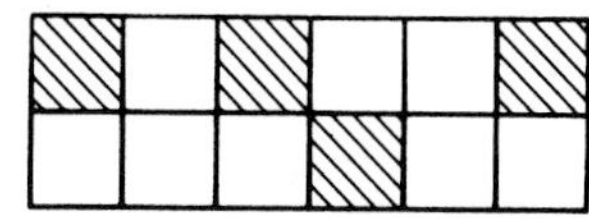

How many parts are shaded? (4)
Not shaded? (8)
What are the total number of parts? (12)

Write the following fractions:

$\frac{\text{shaded}}{\text{total}} = \frac{4}{12}$

$\frac{\text{not shaded}}{\text{total}} = \frac{8}{12}$

Reduce each fraction to lowest terms:

$\frac{4}{12} = \frac{1}{3}$

$\frac{8}{12} = \frac{2}{3}$

Review procedure for simplifying fractions:

$$\frac{4}{12} = \frac{\cancel{2} \times \cancel{2}}{\cancel{2} \times \cancel{2} \times 3} = \frac{1}{3}$$

$$\frac{8}{12} = \frac{\cancel{2} \times \cancel{2} \times 2}{\cancel{2} \times \cancel{2} \times 3} = \frac{2}{3}$$

CHALLENGE:

What must $\frac{4}{12} + \frac{8}{12} =$? Why?

Use diagram to illustrate answer.

What must $\frac{1}{3} + \frac{2}{3} =$? Why?

Look at next diagram:

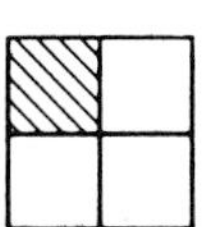

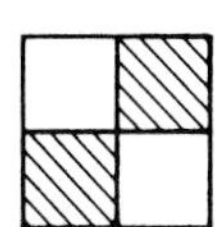

Name the fraction in each diagram:

$\frac{\text{shaded}}{\text{total}} = \frac{1}{4}$

$\frac{1}{4} + \frac{2}{4} = \frac{3}{4}$

$\frac{2}{4}$

Simplfy $\frac{2}{4}$ $\frac{1}{2}$

$\frac{1}{4} + \frac{1}{2} = \frac{3}{4}$

What topic will we learn today?
Write: Addition of Fractions on board.

Comments

This refers to previously learned material relevant to this lesson. It is usually one of those details kept in back of the teacher's mind rather than recorded in the plan.

The expected answers are circled.

The aim of the lesson is elicited here. It was written on the board well into the lesson.

(continued)

LESSON PLAN 3 (*continued*)

Comments

CHALLENGE:

(1). 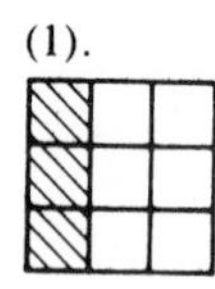

(2). 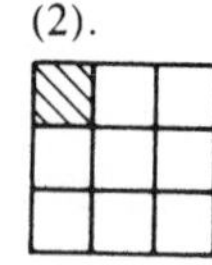

Name the fraction in each diagram.

$\frac{3}{9}$ and $\frac{1}{9}$

Simplify $\frac{3}{9}$ $\frac{1}{3}$

$\frac{3}{9} + \frac{1}{9} = ?$ $\frac{4}{9}$

$\frac{1}{3} + \frac{1}{9} = \frac{4}{9}$

Look at the two examples:

$$\frac{1}{4} + \frac{1}{2} = \frac{3}{4} \Leftrightarrow \frac{1}{4} + \frac{2}{4} = \frac{3}{4}$$
$$\frac{1}{3} + \frac{1}{9} = \frac{4}{9} \Leftrightarrow \frac{3}{9} + \frac{1}{9} = \frac{4}{9}$$

What must be true about the denominators of fractions when we add? (Same)

PRACTICE:

$\frac{3}{5} + \frac{1}{10}$ Are the denominators the same or different?

Name the common denominator: (10)

The teacher demonstrated the addition in a vertical as well as in a horizontal arrangement.

$\frac{3}{5} = \frac{6}{10}$ Why? $\frac{3 \times 2}{5 \times 2} = \frac{6}{10}$

$$\frac{6}{10} + \frac{1}{10} = \frac{7}{10}$$

MORE PRACTICE:

$$\frac{4}{7} + \frac{1}{21} = ?$$

CHALLENGE QUESTIONS:

These are really "if time" questions, and in fact only the first was done.

$\frac{3}{5} + \frac{2}{3}$ What is the common denominator?

$\frac{1}{2} + \frac{2}{3} + \frac{5}{6}$

$\frac{2}{5} + \frac{1}{2} + \frac{2}{3}$

FINAL SUMMARY:
What have we learned today?

HOMEWORK:
Page 157, exs. 2, 3, 5, 7, 9, 11, 12, 13, 15, 18.

Chapter 3

Teaching More Effective Lessons

Every teacher is a resource person who determines which classroom teaching strategies will be most effective. The good teacher strives to make the classroom a place where students will enjoy the learning process. Active student learning is usually a concomitant goal. Certainly, the manner in which new material is presented to a class will determine the true learning atmosphere. If students are *told* all the information they are required to know about a topic, they will inevitably become bored, lose interest, and ultimately "tune out." Thus, the teacher must constantly try to promote an exciting learning atmosphere in the classroom. One way of keeping students' interest is to provide mental stimulation throughout the lesson. You can stimulate students by regularly offering moderate mental challenges (in either small or large group settings). In this chapter refined techniques and strategies are designed to help you motivate, question, and otherwise stimulate student thinking, providing you with more effective ways to teach.

Motivational Techniques

One of the more difficult tasks teachers of mathematics face is that of motivating students for a particular lesson. Planning motivation requires creativity and imagination. The needs and interests of students must be carefully considered. This will naturally vary with the many student characteristics found in today's schools.

It would appear that geometry, because of its visual nature, would readily generate interest among students. Unfortunately, this is not always the case. Much of the course deals with proving theorems and then applying these theorems to artificial problems. Interested mathematics students will be excited by this, as they will be by almost any other mathematical activity. The teacher must focus attention on less interested students, however, in planning appropriate motivation, since they will not be enchanted with such concepts as the postulational nature of geometry.

To motivate students is to channel their interests to the specific topic to be learned. In this chapter we consider some techniques that can be used to motivate secondary school students in mathematics. Specifically, ten different techniques are presented, and a number of examples from algebra and geometry are provided for each. (Note that the technique is the important part to remember. The examples are provided merely to help understand the techniques.)

What Is Motivation?

How to motivate students to learn is at the crux of one's concerns when preparing to teach a lesson, for if students can be made to be delightfully receptive learners, then the rest of the teaching process becomes significantly easier and profoundly more effective.

Naturally, when thinking of how to "make a student want to learn" what you are about to teach, certain *extrinsic* methods of motivation may come to mind. These may include token economic rewards for good performance, peer acceptance of good performance, avoidance of "punishment" by performing well, praise for good work, and so on. Extrinsic methods are effective for students in varying forms. Students' earlier rearing and environment have much to do with their adaptation of commonly accepted extrinsic motivators. However, many students demonstrate intrinsic goals in their desire to understand a topic or concept (task-related), to outperform others (ego-related), or to impress others (social-related). The last goal straddles the fence between being an intrinsic and an extrinsic goal.

In a more structured form, *intrinsic motivators* tend to conform to the following basic types:

THE LEARNER WANTS TO DEVELOP COMPETENCIES Students are often much more eager to do a challenging problem than one that is routine. It is not uncommon to see students beginning their homework assignment with the "challenge for experts" problem, even if the time spent on this prevents them from completing their routine work.

THE LEARNER IS CURIOUS ABOUT NOVEL EVENTS AND ACTIVITIES It is a natural human trait to seek out unusual situations or challenges that can be conquered by existing skills and knowledge and thereby provide a feeling of competence. When the learner's curiosity about unusual stimuli is piqued, it becomes a form of motivation.

THE LEARNER HAS A NEED TO FEEL AUTONOMOUS The desire to act on something as a result of one's own volition is often a motivating factor in the general learning process. To determine for oneself what is to be learned, rather than to feel learning is being done to satisfy someone else or to get some sort of extrinsic reward is another basic human need.

THE LEARNER REACTS WITH SOME INTERNALIZED SOCIAL VALUES Not to be overlooked when trying to simplify (and catalog) human needs and motives is the notion that all learners have certain moral values that have been internalized through years of social reinforcement—most often in the home environment. For example, if a parent constantly tells a child that hard work is good, then that value is manifested in the child and becomes a part of the motives that make the child function.

The teacher's task is to understand the basic motives already present in the learners and to capitalize on these. The teacher can then manipulate this knowledge of students' motives to maximize the effectiveness of the teaching process. Often, this manipulation can result in some rather artificial situations, contrived specifically to exploit a learner's motives in order to generate a genuine interest in a topic. This is eminently fair and highly desirable!

With these basic concepts in mind, we now explore how they can be used to motivate mathematics instruction. Naturally these specific techniques should be expanded, embellished, adapted to the teacher's personality, and, above all, made appropriate for the learner's level of ability and environment.

Motivating Students: Ten Techniques

Indicate a Void in Students' Knowledge

Students usually have a natural desire to complete their knowledge of a topic. This motivational technique involves making students aware of a void in their knowledge and capitalizes on their desire to learn more. For instance, you may present a few simple exercises involving familiar situations followed by exercises involving unfamiliar situations on the same topic. Or you may mention (or demonstrate) to your class how the topic to be presented will complete their knowledge about a particular part of mathematics. The more dramatically you do this, the more effective the motivation. Often, guiding students to discover this void in their knowledge is effective. Following are some examples of how this technique may be used.

EXAMPLE

(Introducing the general angle—second-year algebra.) Present the following questions to your students:

Find the value of each without the aid of a scientific or graphing calculator:

1. $\sin 30° = ?$
2. $\cos 60° = ?$
3. $\cos 120° = ?$

Students familiar with the 30-60-90 triangle ought to be able to answer the first two questions easily. The third question will cause students some discomfort, since students are unfamiliar with trigonometric functions of angles whose measures are greater than 90°. You should now have students realizing that there is a void in their knowledge. They are now motivated to learn how to find the values of trigonometric functions of angles greater than 90°.

EXAMPLE

(Introducing the measures of angles with their vertices outside a given circle—geometry.) Suppose students have learned the relationships between the measures of arcs of a circle and the measures of angles (whose rays subtend these arcs) with their vertices *in* or *on* the circle but not *outside* the circle. A possible set of exercises is shown below.

Find the value of *x* in each of the following:

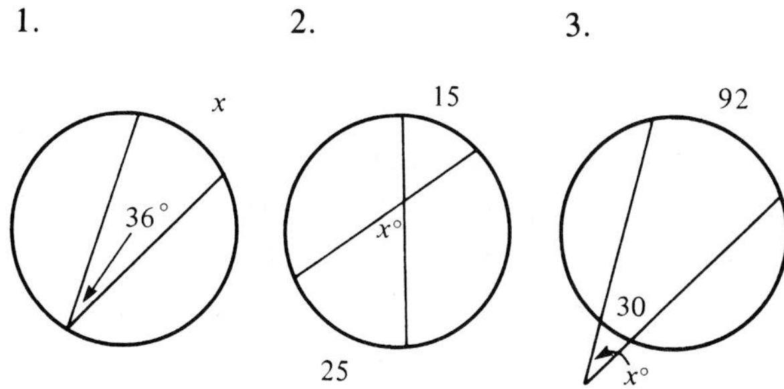

After completing the first two exercises, students should *want* to learn the relationship exhibited in the third exercise. This should serve as a good springboard into the lesson. (For an interesting alternative to teaching this unit, see Enrichment Unit 56, "Angle Measurement with a Circle.")

Discover a Pattern

Setting up a contrived situation that leads students to discovering a pattern can often be quite motivating, as students take pleasure in finding and then "owning" an idea. Consider the following examples of pattern discovery.

In mathematics, the desire to maintain patterns can provide the motivation for expanding and creating new mathematics, as illustrated in obtaining the rules for multiplying signed numbers.

Before beginning this topic, students must be familiar with the number line. They must also be aware that positive numbers can be written both with and without signs.

Have students study the pattern in the following chart and replace each "?" with a number:

Factor 1	×	Factor 2	=	Product
3	×	3	=	9
3	×	2	=	6
3	×	1	=	3
3	×	0	=	0
3	×	−1	=	?
3	×	−2	=	?
3	×	−3	=	?

Another example of how pattern recognition can serve to motivate students is shown below:

Have students study the pattern in this chart and replace each "?" with a number:

$2^5 = 32$	$3^5 = 243$	$4^5 = 1024$
$2^4 = 16$	$3^4 = 81$	$4^4 = ?$
$2^3 = 8$	$3^3 = ?$	$4^3 = ?$
$2^2 = 4$	$3^2 = ?$	$4^2 = ?$
$2^1 = 2$	$3^1 = ?$	$4^1 = ?$

The chart should be extended up a bit. When students attempt to extend it down to include the question marks, they will realize that each number is one-half, one-third, one-fourth, etc., of the number above it, depending on the column.

By following this pattern they will conclude:

$$2^0 = 1 \qquad 3^0 = 1 \qquad 4^0 = 1$$

Continuing to work down with the pattern, students will extend the chart until it looks like this:

$2^{-1} = \frac{1}{2}$	$3^{-1} = \frac{1}{3}$	$4^{-1} = \frac{1}{4}$
$2^{-2} = \frac{1}{4} = \frac{1}{2^2}$	$3^{-2} = \frac{1}{9} = \frac{1}{3^2}$	$4^{-2} = ?$
$2^{-3} = \frac{1}{8} = \frac{1}{2^3}$	$3^{-3} = ?$	$4^{-3} = ?$
$2^{-4} = \frac{1}{16} = \frac{1}{2^4}$	$3^{-4} = ?$	$4^{-4} = ?$

Students can now generalize and establish these rules:

$$\text{If } x \neq 0, \text{ then } x^0 = 1 \qquad \text{and} \qquad x^{-m} = \frac{1}{x^m}$$

A word of caution must be made here. There are patterns that appear to go in one way and need not necessarily follow the anticipated direction. Teachers must be careful to select those that will not lead the class through an ambiguous situation. One example of that is the sequence: 1, 2, 4, 8, 16, . . . , which can follow at least two perfectly correct mathematical patterns:

$$1, 2, 4, 8, 16, 32, 64, 128, \ldots$$

or

$$1, 2, 4, 8, 16, 31, 57, 99, \ldots$$

To find out more about this second variation see: *101 plus Great Ideas for Introducing Key Concepts in Mathematics* by Alfred S. Posamentier and Herbert A. Hauptman (Thousand Oaks, CA: Corwin Press, 2006).

Show a Sequential Achievement

Another technique is that of having students appreciate a logical sequence of concepts. This differs from the first technique in that it depends on students' desire to increase, but not complete, their knowledge. A chart may be useful in applying this method of motivation.

EXAMPLE

(Quadrilaterals—geometry.) In the development of the properties of quadrilaterals, a chart such as the one below may be developed:

Students could be led to want to reach, sequentially, various levels of this diagrammed development. The chart must be developed carefully, with its intended purpose clearly in focus.

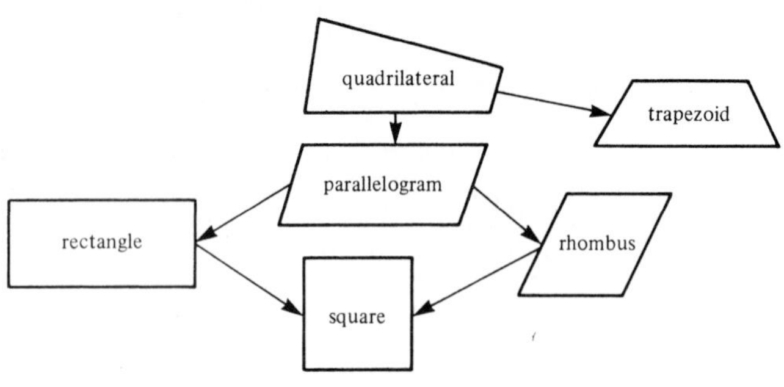

Present a Challenge

When students are challenged intellectually, they react with enthusiasm. Great care must be taken in selecting the challenge. The problem (if that is the type of challenge used) must not only definitely lead into the lesson, but also be within reach of the students' ability. A challenge should be short and not complex. It should not be so engrossing that it may detract from the intended lesson. This would certainly defeat the purpose for which this challenge was intended. Thus, challenges providing motivation for one class may not do so for another. Teacher judgment is most important here.

EXAMPLE

(Properties of tangents—geometry.) Suppose you wish to motivate your students to learn a lesson on tangents to a circle. Have students consider the following problem:

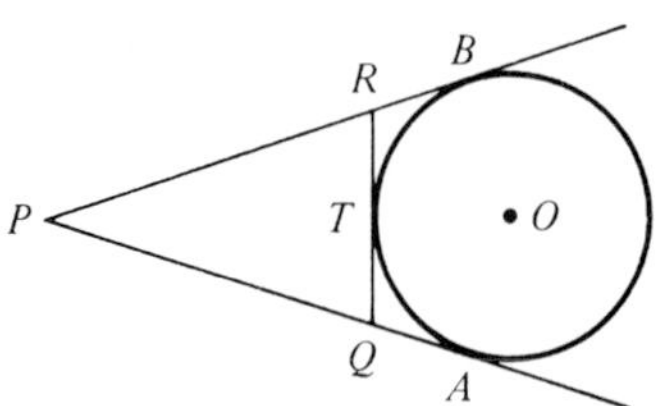

Given: $\overline{AQP}$, $\overline{BRP}$, and $\overline{QTR}$ tangent to circle O at A, B, and T, respectively. $AP = 18$.
Find: The perimeter of ΔPQR.

Students may feel that insufficient information was supplied. To solve this problem, they need to know only the relationship between the lengths of two tangent segments to a circle from a common external point. Once the need for this theorem has been established (via this little challenge), students ought to be able to solve the problem by noting the equalities $AP = BP, AQ = TQ$, and $BR = TR$. That is, the perimeter of $\Delta PQR = PR + PQ + TR + TQ = PR + PQ + BR + AQ$. Also, $AQ + PQ = AP = 18$, and $BR + PR = BP = 18$. Therefore the perimeter of $\Delta PQR = 36$.

EXAMPLE

(Concurrency of angle bisectors of a triangle—geometry.) Another possible challenge may be used when introducing the idea of concurrency of the angle bisectors of a triangle. The student is asked to determine (or draw) the angle bisector of an angle whose vertex is located within an inaccessible area. Students should be familiar with constructions that require the use of straightedge and compasses.

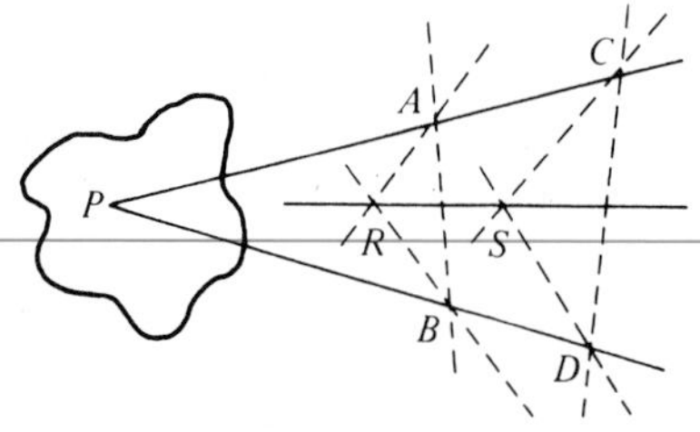

One desired solution requires drawing any lines $\overleftrightarrow{AB}$ and $\overleftrightarrow{CD}$ intersecting the rays of the angle, whose vertex is inaccessibly located at P. Angle bisectors of the four angles (as shown) are drawn, and points R and S determine the desired angle bisector. Students should notice that because the bisectors of the angles of a triangle are concurrent (here considering ΔAPB and ΔCPD separately), both points R and S *must* be contained in the bisector of the inaccessible angle. After witnessing this solution, students should want to prove the concurrency of the angle bisectors of a triangle. (For a more in-depth consideration of this problem, see Enrichment Unit 37, "The Inaccessible Angle.")

EXAMPLE

(Introducing the sum of a geometric series—second-year algebra.) Present the following challenge to your students:

Which of the following would you rather have?

a. $100,000 per day for 31 days

or

b. 1¢ the first day
   2¢ the second day
   4¢ the third day
   8¢ the fourth day
   16¢ the fifth day
   and so on for 31 days

Most students will opt for choice (a) because that seems like a lot of money; after 31 days, $3,100,000 will have been attained. The job of adding the 31 terms in (b) will be somewhat exhausting. Students should now be motivated to find a shortcut for this addition. After they have developed the formula for the sum of a geometric series, the students can apply it to this problem. They may be surprised to discover the large number resulting: $21,474,836.47.

Entice the Class with a "Gee-Whiz" Amazing Mathematical Result

To motivate basic belief in probability, a very effective motivation is to discuss with the class the famous "Birthday Problem." It's amazing (and we dare say, unbelievable) result will have the class in awe. Consider the following:

It is best that you present this motivational activity to your class with as much "drama" as you can, as it will win you converts to the study of probability as no other example can, because it combats the students' intuition quite dramatically.

EXAMPLE

Let us suppose you have a class with about 35 students. Begin by asking the class what they think the chances (or probability) are of two classmates having the same birth date (month and day, only) in their class of about 30+ students. Students usually begin to think about the likelihood of 2 people having the same date out of a selection of 365 days (assuming no leap year). Perhaps 2 out of 365?

Ask them to consider the "randomly" selected group of the first 35 presidents of the United States. They may be astonished that there are two with the same birth date:

The 11th president, James K. Polk (November 2, 1795), and
The 29th president, Warren G. Harding (November 2, 1865).

The class will probably be surprised to learn that for a group of 35, the probability that two members will have the same birth date is greater than 8 out of 10, or $\frac{8}{10}$.

Students may wish to try their own experiment by visiting 10 nearby classrooms to check on date matches. For groups of 30, the probability that there will be a match is greater than 7 out of 10, or in 7 of these 10 rooms there ought to be a match of birth dates. What causes this incredible and unanticipated result? Can this be true? It seems to go against our intuition.

To relieve students of their curiosity guide them as follows:

First ask what the probability is that one selected student matches his own birth date? Clearly *certainty*, or 1.

This can be written as $\frac{365}{365}$.

The probability that another student does *not* match the first student is $\frac{365-1}{365} = \frac{364}{365}$.

The probability that a third student does *not* match the first and second students is $\frac{365-2}{365} = \frac{363}{365}$.

The probability of all 35 students *not* having the same birth date is the product of these probabilities:

$$p = \frac{365}{365} \cdot \frac{365-1}{365} \cdot \frac{365-2}{365} \cdot \ldots \cdot \frac{365-34}{365}.$$

Because the probability (q) that two students in the group *have* the same birth date and the probability (p) that two students in the group do *not* have the same birth date is a certainty, the sum of those probabilities must be 1. Thus, $p + q = 1$.

In this case,

$$q = 1 - \frac{365}{365} \cdot \frac{365-1}{365} \cdot \frac{365-2}{365} \cdot \ldots \cdot \frac{365-33}{365} \cdot \frac{365-34}{365} \approx .8143832388747152.$$

In other words, the probability that there will be a birth date match in a randomly selected group of 35 people is somewhat greater than $\frac{8}{10}$. This is quite unexpected when one considers there were 365 dates from which to choose.

Students may want to investigate the nature of the probability function. Here are a few values to serve as a guide:

Number of People in Group	Probability of a Birth Date Match
10	.1169481777110776
15	.2529013197636863
20	.4114383835805799
25	.5686997039694639
30	.7063162427192686
35	.8143832388747152
40	.891231809817949
45	.9409758994657749
50	.9703735795779884
55	.9862622888164461
60	.994122660865348
65	.9976831073124921
70	.9991595759651571

Students should notice how quickly almost-certainty is reached. With about 60 students in a room the table indicates that it is almost certain (.99) that two students will have the same birth date.

Were one to do this with the death dates of the first 35 presidents, one would notice that two died on March 8th (Millard Fillmore in 1874 and William H. Taft in 1930) and three presidents died on July 4th (John Adams and Thomas Jefferson in 1826, and James Monroe in 1831).

Above all, this astonishing demonstration should serve as an eye-opener about the inadvisability of relying entirely on intuition.

Indicate the Usefulness of a Topic

Here a practical application is introduced at the beginning of a lesson. The applications selected should be of genuine interest to the class. Once again the applications chosen should be brief and not too complicated so that they motivate the lesson rather than detract from it. Student interest must be considered carefully when selecting an application. Remember, *usefulness* is appropriate only when a student has a prior knowledge of the topic involving the application. The following examples are offered to illustrate this technique.

EXAMPLE

(Properties of a line perpendicular to a plane—geometry.)

In erecting a flagpole, students will be interested in knowing how to ensure perpendicularity—hence, a natural motivation for the theorem: "If a line is perpendicular to each of two intersecting lines at their point of intersection, then the line is perpendicular to the plane determined by them." Further elaboration on the flagpole problem depends on the ability level and interest level of the class. (This is true with all methods of motivation presented here.)

EXAMPLE

(Relationship between the segments of two intersecting chords of a circle—geometry.)

Finding the size of a cracked plate in which the largest remaining piece is a small segment of the original circle is an application in which students are required to find the diameter of the circle of which ACB is a minor arc. Perhaps couching this problem in a story might be even more motivating.

Draw any chord $\overline{AB}$ of the arc and the perpendicular bisector $\overline{CDE}$ of that chord (where C is on the arc). Measure $\overline{AD}$ and $\overline{CD}$. Then use similarity to establish the proportion $DE/AD = BD/CD$. Thus DE and then CE, the desired diameter, may be found easily. This problem can serve as motivation for the theorem that states, "If two chords intersect in the interior of a circle, thus determining two segments in each chord, the product of the lengths of the segments of one chord equals the product of the lengths of the segments of the other chord." Although students may be able to solve the problem in the manner shown here, they would welcome a shorter method. Hence, the problem has created a need for establishing the relationship $AD \cdot BD = DE \cdot CD$. The proof of the theorem is embedded in the solution just given.

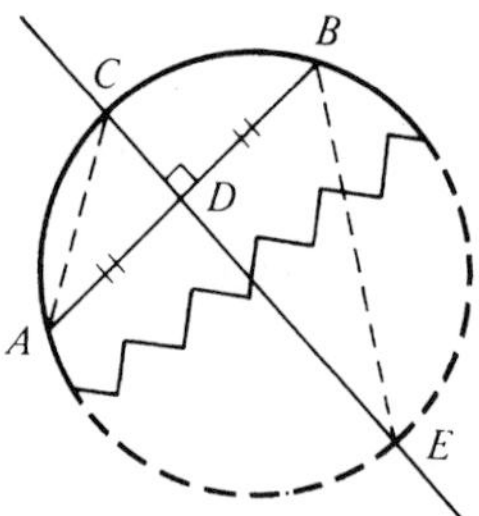

EXAMPLE

(Properties of similar triangles—geometry.)

When introducing properties of similar triangles, ask the class how the "cross-legs" of an airplane service truck have to be positioned so that the plane of the box will be parallel to the plane of the truck.

As the cross-legs shift position, it should be noticed that the legs must always partition each other proportionally if the plane of the box is to remain parallel to the plane of the truck. This ought to motivate students to prove this fact.

There are also times when the usefulness of a topic is intrinsic to mathematics alone. For example, when introducing the technique of rationalizing a denominator of a fraction, many students may wonder why we must go through this extra procedure. A "dramatic" illustration—which shows how useful this procedure can be—would be advantageous. Consider the following problem:

Evaluate the series sum:

$$\frac{1}{1+\sqrt{2}}+\frac{1}{\sqrt{2}+\sqrt{3}}+\frac{1}{\sqrt{3}+\sqrt{4}}+\cdots+\frac{1}{\sqrt{1999}+\sqrt{2000}}$$

To start, the solution of this problem can be quite difficult if one is not accustomed to expressing denominators in terms of rational numbers. This procedure should be discussed and taught at this point before the above problem is revisited.

When the process of rationalizing a denominator of a fraction has been mastered, the problem stated above can be approached by considering the general term:

$$\frac{1}{\sqrt{k}+\sqrt{k+1}}$$

Rationalizing this denominator yields:

$$\frac{1}{\sqrt{k}+\sqrt{k+1}}\cdot\frac{\sqrt{k}-\sqrt{k+1}}{\sqrt{k}-\sqrt{k+1}}=\sqrt{k+1}-\sqrt{k}.$$

This will allow us to rewrite the series as:

$$\left(\sqrt{2}-\sqrt{1}\right)+\left(\sqrt{3}-\sqrt{2}\right)+\left(\sqrt{4}-\sqrt{3}\right)+\cdots+\left(\sqrt{1999}-\sqrt{1998}\right)+\left(\sqrt{2000}-\sqrt{1999}\right)$$

which equals

$$\sqrt{2000}-\sqrt{1}=20\sqrt{5}-1\approx 43.7213596.$$

By showing how the process of rationalizing the denominator of a fraction makes the fraction much more workable, the procedure will become a welcome tool in the arsenal of techniques taught in algebra.

Use Recreational Mathematics

Recreational motivation consists of puzzles, games, or paradoxes. In addition to being selected for their specific motivational gain, these devices must be brief and simple. A student should realize the "recreation" without much effort in order for this technique to be effective.

EXAMPLE

(Area of a circle—geometry.)

When beginning the study of the area of a circle, students may be presented with five concentric circles (the smallest has a radius of 1 unit) whose radii differ by 1 unit, respectively, and asked to compare *intuitively* the areas of the two shaded regions (see diagram).

Most students conclude that the "inner region" has a greater area than the region of the "outer ring." Consideration of the area of a circle yields the true relationship. Students are generally astonished to find that the two regions have equal areas.

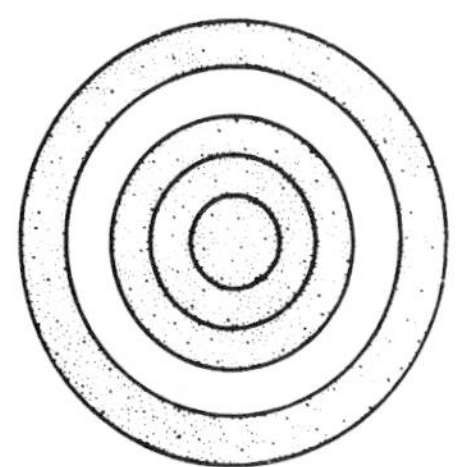

EXAMPLE

(General.)

Such topics as division by zero, betweenness, definitions such as $\sqrt{ab}=\sqrt{a}\cdot\sqrt{b}$ when a and b are nonnegative, and the existence of reflex angles are often dramatically presented via mathematical fallacies. Many books describe fallacies that involve these topics as well as many others. Some of these are:

Ball, W. W. Rouse. *Mathematical Recreations and Essays*. Revised by H. S. M. Coxeter. New York: Macmillan, 1960.

Barbeau, Edward J. *Mathematical Fallacies, Flaws, and Flimflam*. Washington, DC: Mathematical Association of America, 2000.

Cipra, Barry. *Misteaks and How to Find Them Before the Teacher Does*. San Diego, CA: Academic Press, 1989.

Dubnov, Ya. S. *Mistakes in Geometric Proofs*. Translated by A. K. Henn and O. A. Titelbaum. Boston: Heath, 1963.

Eastway, Rob and Jeremy Wyndham. *Why Do Busses Come in Threes?* New York: John Wiley & Sons, 1998.

Maxwell, E. A. *Fallacies in Mathematics*. London, England: Cambridge University Press, 1959.

Northrup, E. P. *Riddles in Mathematics*. Princeton: Van Nostrand, 1944.

EXAMPLE

(Introduction to digit problems—algebra.)

Begin your presentation by asking your students to select any three-digit number in which the hundreds digit and units digit are unequal. Then have them write the number whose digits are in the reverse order from the selected number. Now tell them to subtract the smaller number from the larger one. Once again, tell them to take this difference, reverse its digits and add the "new" number to the *original difference*. They *all* should end up with 1089.

For example, suppose a student selected the number 934. The number with the digits reversed is 439. Her computation would appear as:

934	
439	
495	(difference)
594	(reversed digits)
1089	(sum)

When students compare results they will be amazed to discover the uniformity in their answers. At this point they should be quite eager to find out *why* they all came up with the same result. A detailed discussion of this unusual number property is presented in Enrichment Unit 75, "Digit Problems Revisited."

Tell a Pertinent Story

A story of a historical event or of a contrived situation can motivate students. All too often teachers, already knowing the story they are about to tell and eager to get into the "meat" of the lesson, rush through the story. Such a hurried presentation minimizes the potential effectiveness the story may have as a motivational device. Thus, a carefully prepared method of presentation of a story for motivating a lesson is almost as important as the content of the story itself.

EXAMPLE

(Introducing the sum of an arithmetic series—algebra.)

Tell your students about young Carl Friedrich Gauss, who at age 10 was in a class that was asked by its instructor to add the numbers from 1 to 100. Much to the astonishment of the instructor, young Gauss produced the correct answer immediately. When asked how he arrived at the answer so quickly, he explained that

$$1 + 100 = 101$$
$$2 + 99 = 101$$
$$3 + 98 = 101$$

and so on. Because there are 50 such pairs, the answer is $50 \times 101 = 5050$.

This scheme can be used to develop the formula for the sum of an arithmetic series.

EXAMPLE

(Various topics—geometry.)

For the study of parallel lines, the story of Eratosthenes measuring the circumference of Earth might be appropriate.

Measuring Earth today is not terribly difficult, but thousands of years ago this was no mean feat. Remember the word *geometry* is derived from "earth measurement." Therefore it is appropriate to consider this issue in one of its earliest forms. One of these measurements of the circumference of the earth was made around 230 B.C. by the Greek mathematician Eratosthenes. His measurement was remarkably accurate, having less than a 2 percent error. To make this measurement, Eratosthenes used the relationship of alternate-interior angles of parallel lines.

As librarian of Alexandria, Eratosthenes had access to records of calendar events. He discovered that at noon on a certain day of the year, in a town on the Nile called Syene (now called Aswan), the sun was directly overhead. As a result the bottom of a deep well was entirely lit and a vertical pole, being parallel to the rays hitting it, cast no shadow.

At the same time, however, a vertical pole in the city of Alexandria did cast a shadow. When that day arrived again, Eratosthenes measured the angle ($\angle 1$ in the figure below) formed by such a pole and the ray of light from the sun going past the top of the pole to the far end of the shadow. He found it to be about 7°12′, or $\frac{1}{50}$ of 360°.

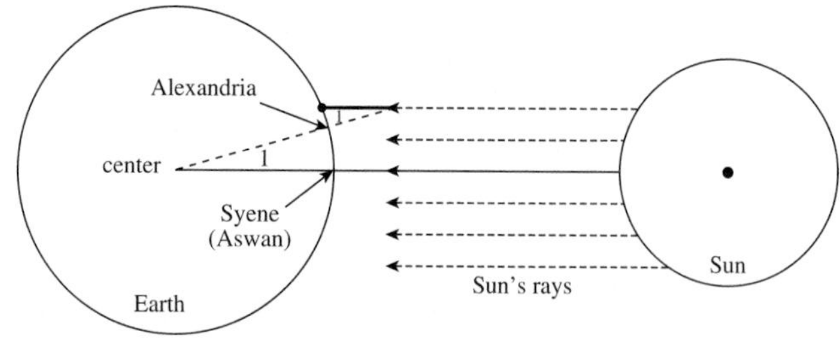

Assuming the rays of the sun to be parallel, he knew that the angle at the center of the earth must be congruent to $\angle 1$, and hence must also measure approximately $\frac{1}{50}$ of 360°. Because Syene and Alexandria were almost on the same meridian, Syene must be located on the radius of the circle, which was parallel to the rays of the Sun. Eratosthenes thus deduced that the distance between Syene and Alexandria was $\frac{1}{50}$ of the circumference of Earth. The distance from Syene to Alexandria was believed to be about 5,000 Greek *stadia*. A *stadium* was a unit of measurement equal to the length of an Olympic or Egyptian stadium. Therefore Eratosthenes concluded that the circumference of Earth was about 250,000 Greek stadia, or about 24,660 miles. This is very close to modern calculations. So how's that for some *real* geometry! Your students should be able to appreciate this ancient use of geometry.

Other Story Ideas

An endless number of stories, historical and otherwise, can be used for motivational purposes. Before proving that the base angles of an isosceles triangle are congruent, the teacher may find a brief discussion of *Pons Asinorum* appropriate. Telling students that during the Middle Ages this proof separated weak students from better students should provoke attempts toward solution by all students. Other useful stories include the following topics (after each we offer references). Many other references can be found in *A Bibliography of Recreational Mathematics* (4 vols.) by William L. Schaaf (Washington, DC: National Council of Teachers of Mathematics, 1970(2), 1973, 1978).

1. The origin of certain symbols or terms to be introduced

Cajori, Florian. *A History of Mathematical Notations* (2 vols.). La Salle, IL: Open Court, 1952.

Schwartzman, Steven. *The Words of Mathematics*. Washington, DC: Mathematical Association of America, 1994.

2. The history of π

Beckmann, Petr. *A History of* π. New York: St. Martin's Press, 1971.

Berggren, Lennart, J. Borwein, P. Borwein. *Pi: A Source Book*. New York: Springer-Verlag, 1997.

Posamentier, Alfred S., and Ingmar Lehmann. *π: A Biography of the World's Most Mysterious Number*. Amherst, NY: Prometheus Books, 2004.

3. The Golden Rectangle

Dunlap, Richard A. *The Golden Ratio and Fibonacci Numbers*. River Edge, NJ: World Scientific Publishing, 1997.

Herz-Fischler, Roger. *A Mathematical History of the Golden Number.* New York: Dover, 1998.

Huntley, H. E. *The Divine Proportion*. New York: Dover, 1970.

Livio, Mario. *The Golden Ratio: The Story of Phi, The World's Most Astonishing Number*. New York, NY: Broadway Books, 2002.

Posamentier, Alfred S. *Advanced Euclidean Geometry: Excursions for Secondary Teachers and Students.* New York, NY: John Wiley Publishing, 2002.

Runion, Garth E. *The Golden Section and Related Curiosa.* Glenview, IL: Scott, Foresman, 1972.

Walser, Hans. *The Golden Section*. Washington, DC: Mathematical Association of America, 2001.

4. Ancient measuring devices

Kline, Morris. *Mathematics: A Cultural Approach*. Reading, MA: Addison-Wesley, 1962.

Martzloff, Jean-Claude. *The History of Chinese Mathematics*. New York: Springer-Verlag, 1997.

Polya, George. *Mathematical Methods in Science*. Washington, DC: Mathematical Association of America, 1977.

5. Major breakthroughs in mathematics

Bunt, L., P. Jones, and J. Bedient. *The Historical Roots of Elementary Mathematics*. Englewood Cliffs, NJ: Prentice-Hall, 1976.

Smith, David E. *A Source Book in Mathematics*. New York: McGraw-Hill, 1929.

Newman, James R. *The World of Mathematics* (4 vols.). New York: Simon & Schuster, 1956.

Struik, D. J. (Ed.). *A Source Book in Mathematics, 1200–1800.* Princeton, NJ: Princeton University Press, 1986.

6. Pertinent biographical notes

Bell, E. T. *Men of Mathematics*. New York: Simon & Schuster, 1937.

Biographical Dictionary of Mathematicians. Volumes 1–4. New York: Charles Scribner's Sons, 1991.

Coolidge, Julian L. *The Mathematics of Great Amateurs*. New York: Dover, 1963.

Gindikin, S. G. *Tales of Physicists and Mathematicians*. Boston: Birkhaüser, 1988.

James, Ioan. *Remarkable Mathematicians: From Euler to von Neumann*. Washington, DC: Mathematical Association of America, 2002.

Perl, Teri. *Math Equals Biographies of Women Mathematicians and Related Activities*. Menlo Park, CA: Addison-Wesley, 1978.

Schmalz, Rosemary. *Out of the Mouths of Mathematicians*. Washington, DC: Mathematical Association of America, 1993.

Turnbull, Herbert W. *The Great Mathematicians*. New York: New York University Press, 1961.

7. Pertinent anecdotes

Aaboe, Asger. *Episodes from the Early History of Mathematics*. Washington, DC: Mathematical Association of America, 1964.

Anderson, Marlow, Victor Katz, and Robin Wilson (Eds.). *Sherlock Holmes in Babylon and Other Tales of Mathematical History*. Washington, DC: Mathematical Association of America, 2004.

Devlin, Keith. *All the Math That's Fit to Print*. Washington, DC: Mathematical Association of America, 1994.

Dunham, William. *Journey Through Genius: The Great Theorems of Mathematics*. New York: John Wiley and Sons, 1990.

Eves, Howard. *In Mathematical Circles* (2 vols.). Boston: Prindle Weber and Schmidt, 1969.

Eves, Howard. *Mathematical Circles Revisited.* Boston: Prindle Weber and Schmidt, 1971.

Kaplan, Robert. *The Nothing That Is, A Natural History of Zero*. New York: Oxford University Press, 1999.

Katz, Victor J. *Using History to Teach Mathematics*. Washington, DC: Mathematical Association of America, 2000.

EXAMPLE

A pertinent story can also be something that enables students to concretize their understanding of a new concept, such as the notion of a function. Consider the following:

> In mathematics, finding concrete analogues to represent abstract concepts is not always easy. One example where a physical model can be used to explain an abstract concept is in the development of the notion of a function.
>
> We will use the model of a bow shooting arrows at a target. The arrows will represent the *domain* and the target represents the *range*. The bow (and its aiming) is the *function*. Because an arrow can only be used once* we know that the elements in the domain can be used only once. The bow can hit the same point on the target more than once. Therefore, points in the range can be used more than once. This is the definition of a function: a *mapping* of all elements of one set onto another, with the elements of the first set used exactly once. Some points on the target may never be hit by an arrow. Yet, all the arrows must be used. Analogously, some elements in the range may not be used, but all elements in the domain must be used. Or conversely, through a mapping (or a "pairing") of all elements in the domain, some elements in the range may not be used.
>
> When all points on the target (the range) are hit,** then the function (or mapping) is called an *onto function*.
>
> When each point on the target is used only once, then the function is called a *one-to-one function*.
>
> When each point on the target is used exactly once (i.e., once and only once), then the function is called a *one-to-one onto function*, or may be called a *one-to-one correspondence*.

Using the bow-shooting-arrows-to-a-target analogy to represent the concept of a function enables the learner to

*Actually a gun and bullets would be a better analogue than the bow and arrow, because there the bullet can *really* be used only once. For this illustration, make it clear that the arrow, once shot, cannot be used again.

**Obviously, in reality an infinite number of arrows would be required, so it must be appropriately simulated.

conceptualize this abstract notion in a way that should instill permanent understanding of the concept of a function.

Get Students Actively Involved in Justifying Mathematical Curiosities

One of the more effective techniques for motivating students is to attempt actively to justify a pertinent mathematical curiosity. The students should be comfortably familiar with the mathematical curiosity before you "challenge" them to justify it. Although this could consume more time than may be normally allotted for a motivational activity, to proceed with a justification before sufficient exposure has been achieved would be counterproductive.

EXAMPLE

(Introducing the line joining the midpoints of two sides of a triangle (the midline)—geometry.)

Suppose students are about to study the properties of a midline of a triangle. As motivation, they may be asked to draw any five quadrilaterals and then in each quadrilateral to join the midpoints of the adjacent sides with line segments. Much to their amazement, they will find that they have drawn five parallelograms.

A request for a proof of this can be expected from the class. One of the more elegant proofs is based on the properties of a midline of a triangle. Thus, the teacher has an excellent opportunity to introduce the midline and its properties.

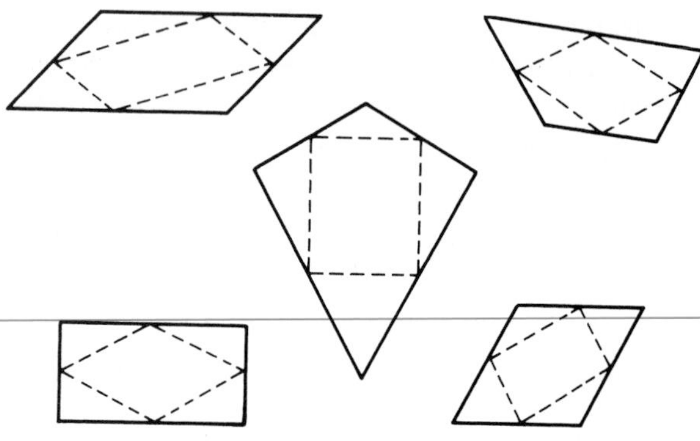

EXAMPLE

(Similarity—geometry.)

Another geometric curiosity is the *pantograph*, an instrument used for drawing similar plane figures. Students can construct this instrument at home. At the beginning of the lesson in which similarity is to be considered, the operation of the pantograph can be justified.

The pantograph consists of four bars hinged at points A, B, C, and D. Point P is fixed, and pencils are inserted in holes at D and Q. Various holes may be provided on the bars for other ratios of similitude, BC/BQ.

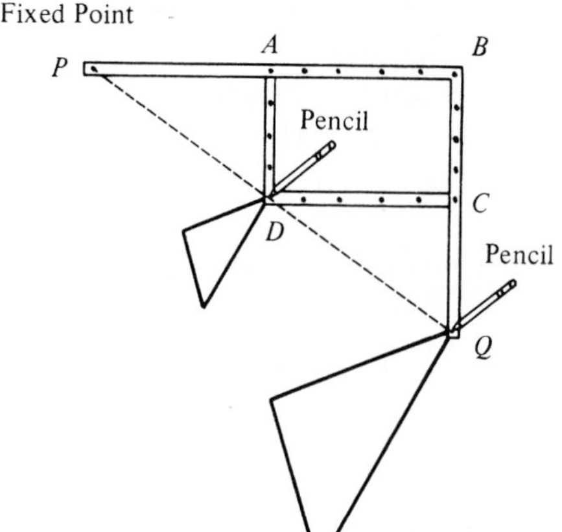

Here is a fun activity that can be presented in a number of different ways. The best-suited method should be selected by the classroom teacher. The justification uses simple algebra, but the fun is in the oddity. Have your students consider this very unusual relationship.

Any two-digit number ending in 9 can be expressed as the sum of the product of the digits and sum of the digits.

More simply stated:

Any two-digit number ending in 9 = [product of digits] + [sum of digits]

One of the real advantages of algebra is the facility with which, through its use, we can justify many mathematical applications. Why is it possible to represent a number ending in a 9 in the following way?

$$
\begin{aligned}
19 &= (1 \cdot 9) + (1 + 9) \\
29 &= (2 \cdot 9) + (2 + 9) \\
39 &= (3 \cdot 9) + (3 + 9) \\
49 &= (4 \cdot 9) + (4 + 9) \\
59 &= (5 \cdot 9) + (5 + 9) \\
69 &= (6 \cdot 9) + (6 + 9) \\
79 &= (7 \cdot 9) + (7 + 9) \\
89 &= (8 \cdot 9) + (8 + 9) \\
99 &= (9 \cdot 9) + (9 + 9)
\end{aligned}
$$

Students will certainly be turned on by this neat pattern of calculation. You must be careful not to allow this pattern to be an end in itself, but rather a means to an end, namely, a consideration of why this actually works.

Let's use algebra to clear up this very strange result, established above by example. Point out to students that we will be using algebra to help us understand this mathematical quirk.

We typically represent a two-digit number as $10t + u$, where t represents the tens digit and u represents the units digit. Then the sum of the digits is $t + u$ and the product of the digits is tu.

The number meeting the above conditions is

$$
\begin{aligned}
10t + u &= (tu) + (t + u) \\
10t &= tu + t \\
9t &= tu \\
u &= 9 \text{ (for } t \neq 0)
\end{aligned}
$$

This discussion should evoke a curiosity among students about numbers with more than two digits. For example:

$$109 = (10 \cdot 9) + (10 + 9)$$
$$119 = (11 \cdot 9) + (11 + 9)$$
$$129 = (12 \cdot 9) + (12 + 9)$$

Here the digits to the left of the 9 are considered as a number and treated just as we treated the tens digit above. The results are the same.

This can be extended to any number of digits as long as the units digit is a 9.

A plentiful source for other such mathematical curiosities is *Math Wonders to Inspire Teachers and Students*, by Alfred S. Posamentier (Alexandria, VA: Association for Supervision and Curriculum Development, 2003).

Use Teacher-Made or Commercially Prepared Materials

Here motivation can be achieved by presenting the class with concrete material of an unusual nature. This may include teacher-made materials, such as models of geometric shapes, geo strips, or specifically prepared overhead transparencies, or practical "tools" that illustrate a specific geometric principle. Some fine commercially prepared materials are available, ranging from geometric models to CD-ROMS of various kinds. Materials selected should be reviewed carefully and their presentation carefully planned so as to motivate students for the lesson and not to detract attention from it.

Summary

Remembering a few general rules for using these ten motivational techniques will make them more effective.

1. The motivation should be brief.
2. The motivation should not be overemphasized. It should be a means to an end, not an end in itself.
3. The motivation should elicit the aim of the lesson from the class. This is a fine way of determining how effective the motivation actually is.
4. The motivation should be appropriate for the class's level of ability and interest.
5. The motivation should draw on motives actually present in the learner.

Although planning the motivation for a lesson is challenging, and at times difficult, the rewards are immeasurable. The higher degree of student learning resulting from a well-planned and well-executed activity will make this additional work worthwhile.

EXERCISES

1. How can you determine whether your motivational activity was successful?
2. For each of the following topics, prepare a motivational activity using one of the techniques presented in this chapter.
   a. The introductory lesson on area (geometry).
   b. The introductory lesson on solving factorable quadratic equations.
   c. The introductory lesson on reducing fractions (arithmetic).
   d. The introductory lesson on multiplication of signed numbers.
   e. The introductory lesson on mathematical induction.
   f. The introductory lesson on solving simultaneous equations algebraically (addition method).
   g. The introductory lesson on locus.
   h. The introductory lesson on truth tables (tautologies).
   i. The introductory lesson on parallelograms.
   j. The introductory lesson on proving trigonometric identities.
   k. The introductory lesson to bases other than 10.
   l. The introductory lesson to the metric system.
3. Prepare a second motivational activity for each of the topics in Exercise 2.
4. Suppose you prepared a motivational activity that so captured the class interest that they did not want to leave the topic. What would you do to make this activity serve its intended purpose, that is, to excite students about the topic of the lesson? Justify your answer.
5. Select a topic in the secondary school mathematics curriculum and prepare two different motivational activities using the techniques presented in this chapter.
6. Repeat Exercise 5 using another topic from the secondary school mathematics curriculum.
7. Prepare three motivational activities for the same topic in the secondary school mathematics curriculum. After incorporating these motivational activities into the same lesson plan, teach this lesson (each, of course, with a different motivational activity at the beginning) to three different classes. If you cannot videotape these three lessons, have an experienced mathematics teacher observe the three classes. At the completion of this activity, analyze the three lessons with an experienced mathematics teacher and determine which of the three motivational devices worked best and why it worked best. Such factors as the appropriateness of the technique, the type of class with which it was used, and the personality of the teacher using the technique should be addressed in the analysis.
8. Repeat Exercise 7. This time the teacher of the three lessons should be a volunteer, an experienced teacher of mathematics. However, the planning of the motivational devices can be done cooperatively.

Classroom Questioning

By asking a class well-constructed questions, the teacher encourages active learning on the part of the students. What should be the goal of such questioning? Classroom questioning should elicit student responses consisting of information that would otherwise have been presented by the teacher. (Sometimes some valuable "original" comments are also received!) Although this is, in fact, quite difficult to achieve fully, it is a goal toward which to strive.

Consideration must be given to the construction of good questions that are not gender or culturally biased. Good questioning is an art and is one of the most important elements of good teaching. As a result, it is either a great strength or a serious weakness in classroom work. Questions must be conscientiously prepared and patiently practiced. There are a number of pitfalls to avoid in asking classroom questions. We shall consider these pitfalls later.

Classroom Questioning Features to Develop

Teachers must consciously develop habits of questioning that will strengthen their teaching performance. Each of the following suggestions for developing an effective style of classroom questioning should be practiced carefully, for their benefits extend beyond classroom questioning and can have a substantial impact on the teaching-learning process.

Direct and Simple Language

Classroom questions should be direct and simple in language. Student focus should be on a question's content, not on the language used in its delivery. That is, if the language distracts students from the content, by being either too complex or perhaps too humorous, the potential effectiveness of a question may be lost. By using direct and simple language (i.e., appropriate for the level of the intended class), a teacher can employ classroom questions to fulfill their desired function.

Definite and Clear Meaning

Classroom questions should be definite and clear in meaning. If a question lends itself to various interpretations, students may be reluctant to respond. To maximize the number of volunteer respondents, ambiguities should be avoided. Often, shorter questions are less confusing.

A question should call for only one or two points in a line of reasoning. A teacher should ask more questions rather than try to limit the number of questions and lengthen each one. By trying to ask too much in a single question, the teacher may become prone to asking multiple or overlaid questions (see page 75).

Logical Sequence

Questioning should develop a train of thought in logical sequence. An inexperienced teacher's impatience with the developmental process may cause him to rush to the pivotal (or prime) question of a lesson without spending enough time leading up to it with shorter preparatory questions. This impatience often diminishes the ultimate effectiveness of the pivotal question. Because the pivotal question generally elicits a highlight of the lesson, its effectiveness should not be weakened. Thus, teachers should give special attention to all parts of a line of questioning that develops a train of thought in logical sequence. This means that the same care should be given to the early, perhaps almost trivial (or review) questions as is given to the pivotal and culminating questions. Remember, the pivotal question is rarely effective if it is not properly built up through a carefully developed sequence of subordinate questions in predetermined order.

Questions Keyed to Class Ability

The level of ability of a class should determine the language and complexity of the classroom questions used. It is easy for a teacher to use the same questions during two consecutive class periods, especially when the same lesson is involved. Yet if the ability levels of the two classes are different, this practice should be consciously avoided. For the slower or perhaps less sophisticated class, simpler language might be used than with a class comprising more able students. Teachers should be careful not to use condescending language, but at the same time they should not conduct the class with language beyond the students' ability to grasp the content comfortably. By asking questions properly suited for the intended audience, teachers will improve communication with classes at all levels.

Questions That Stimulate Effort

Questions should arouse an effort. While gearing the phrasing of a question to the appropriate level for a class, teachers must make a special effort to prepare questions that are sufficiently difficult to arouse an effort yet not too difficult to stifle the class. Good classroom questioning should create a moderately challenging atmosphere throughout the lesson. Classroom questions should be short and crisp, and arranged in a logical sequence that builds to the desired point. A sequence of questions might well consist of a blend of factual and thought questions, with a majority of the latter kind. Included would be a balanced mixture of some short yet challenging questions along with other review or connecting questions. Such a blend should go far to stimulate active learning.

Open-Ended Questions

Open-ended questions allow students to reach conclusions and make mathematical decisions consistent with their understanding and development. On a class examination, students can demonstrate the kind of depth that is impossible to determine on the basis of choosing one of several multiple-choice items or writing a single-number response. Open-ended questions also permit pupils to arrive at many possible "correct" answers.

EXAMPLE

Discuss whether it is possible to have a triangle with the dimensions as shown on the next page.

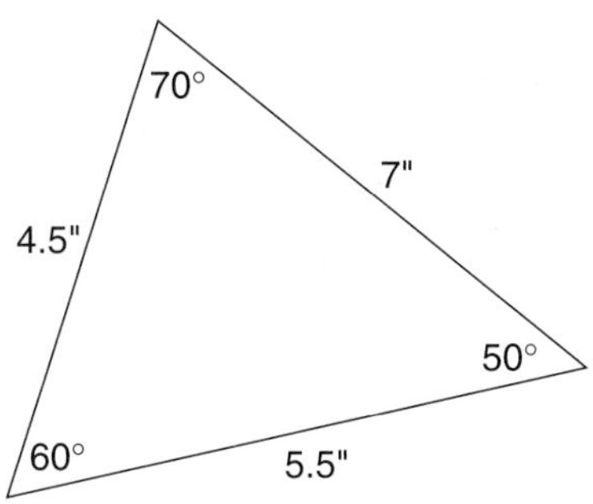

EXAMPLE

Your friend shows you the following examples:

$\frac{16}{64} = \frac{1}{4}$ by canceling the 6s,

$\frac{26}{65} = \frac{2}{5}$ also by canceling the 6s,

$\frac{19}{95} = \frac{1}{5}$ by canceling the 9s,

$\frac{49}{98} = \frac{1}{2}$ also by canceling the 9s.

By the same logic, he claims, the following must also be valid. Explain why his reasoning is incorrect.

$\frac{12}{23} = \frac{1}{3}$ (cancel the 2s)

$\frac{15}{55} = \frac{1}{5}$ (cancel the 5s)

$\frac{28}{81} = \frac{2}{1}$ (cancel the 8s)

Maintaining Student Interest

Classroom questioning should hold student interest throughout a lesson. A few important points should be included regularly.

Every effort should be made to call on as many different students throughout a lesson as possible and to try to avoid predictability in calling on students. Mixing calling on nonvolunteers with calling on volunteers will keep everyone attentive. Beginning a course by requiring students to give complete answers to classroom questions will help to ensure that such a practice will eventually become habitual in the class.

It is a good habit to praise students (with tact) for correctly answering a question. It is equally important, however, for a teacher to handle incorrect answers properly.

The best treatment for an incorrect answer depends on the type of class and the time available in the lesson. Under no circumstances should the teacher be abrupt or scold a student for giving an incorrect answer. This would likely have an adverse effect on the student's learning and inhibit future willingness to respond to the teacher's questions.

With classroom time permitting, the teacher may guide the student to realize an error through a series of questions specially tailored to this discovery. Alternatively, the teacher may choose to refer the question to the rest of the class.

Student questions may also be answered by other students. The teacher should not feel that only she should provide the answers. Peer interaction can produce interesting results. For example, by answering another student's question, the first student can learn better the concepts under consideration. Teaching usually allows the teacher to understand better the subtleties of subject matter being taught. The same can be true when one student explains a concept to a classmate.

When students are expected to respond to one another's questions, there is a greater degree of alertness throughout the classroom, because students cannot predict precisely when they will be called on to correct or answer another student. This alertness should go far to enliven the class.

Some Precautionary Considerations for Improving Classroom Questioning

Avoiding Repetition

The teacher's question should generally not be repeated. Naturally, if for some unusual reason the question was inaudible, then repetition may be necessary. Variety can be provided by having a student repeat a question when it was not heard by some students. Habitually repeating a question can make the class inattentive, because they can rely on the question being repeated. Students also may continually call for the repetition of a question to waste class time, but if they know that the repetition of a question is not easily obtained, this scheme will not work. The result will be an attentive class, with no time wasted.

Sometimes a teacher, having asked a question of the class, may repeat the question in perhaps a rephrased form before the class has even had a chance to respond to the question. An uncertainty on the part of the teacher about the clarity of the question will provoke this immediate repetition of the question. Very often only the teacher finds the question unclear. The class may have been ready to respond to the original question, but after hearing the rephrased question may be somewhat confused. The teacher should let the original question stand, give students sufficient time to respond, and rephrase the question only if no correct response is forthcoming. Students often have an unsuspected ability to interpret a teacher's question properly, even if it is a bit unclear. At such times teachers should not be overly critical of their own questions. Proper questioning preparation could prevent this entire situation.

Avoiding Repetition of Student Answers

The teacher should not repeat student responses, for reasons similar to those just discussed. If students can rely on the teacher to repeat most of the more important student responses to teacher questions, they may eventually not even listen to their classmates. This will greatly inhibit active student interaction throughout a lesson. If, in the teacher's judgment, a student's response is inaudible, then the teacher should have the student or another student repeat the response. Consistency with this procedure will eventually cause students automatically to speak loudly and clearly just to avoid having to repeat their responses (or hear other students do so).

Some teachers have a habit of "mentally processing" a student's response aloud. This results in a repetition of the student's response. Most teachers, when made aware of this habit, can curtail it. Tape recording a teacher's lesson will be helpful in demonstrating this flaw in a teacher's performance. A teacher who cannot avoid such repetitions, however, should at least try to incorporate this repetition into the next statement or question. This way it may not appear as a simple repetition of what has already been said.

Teacher repetitions of student responses are also caused by the teacher's fear that unless a substantive statement is made by the teacher, the class will not note it properly. This, too, will only be so if the teacher allows it to happen. The teacher sets the class tone and routines and the manner in which classroom questioning and the resulting student responses are handled.

Calling on Students

Another way to generate constant student attention is to call on a particular student for a response after a pause at the end of a question.

EXAMPLE

Why is $\overline{AB}$ the perpendicular bisector of $\overline{CD}$ (pause), David?

If the class is accustomed to having the teacher call on a student to respond to a question after it has been asked, each student will be attentive just in case he or she is the one selected by the teacher to respond. On the other hand, if a teacher addresses David before asking the question, perhaps only David will be attentive, because the rest of the class will know they are not being asked the question. This latter situation does not promote an active involvement in the learning process. Thus, the teacher should address particular students at the end of the question and thereby ensure student attention throughout the lesson.

It is sometimes helpful to discover which students in the class are trying to avoid being called on. There are times when it may be wise to call on them or simply meet with these students after class to discuss their apparent avoidance. The question is, "How can the teacher discover which students are trying to avoid being called upon?" Experience has shown that if after the teacher asks a question of the class and pauses to look around for a student to call on for a response, a student appears to make a conscious effort to avoid eye contact with the teacher, then the teacher can assume that student does not want to be called upon. This avoidance sometimes manifests itself in the student's appearing to be very "busy" so that the teacher's calling on him would be seen as interfering with his "concentration." Sometimes the teacher can discourage this by making a general statement to the class about this type of avoidance. Done properly, the class may find this humorous (because many of the students may have been guilty of this type of behavior at one time or another) and realize that this teacher must be very clever and not easily fooled. However, the teacher then must be watchful for other, perhaps more creative, techniques that some students may use to avoid questions (especially when they feel they cannot answer them properly).

Wait-Time After Asking a Question

Allowing students sufficient time to think about a teacher-posed question is a very important aspect of classroom questioning. One of the leading researchers in the questioning behavior of teachers is Mary Budd Rowe. Her findings over the years have had a significant impact on teacher performance in the classroom. In her extensive analysis of classroom performances, she has found that most teachers, on average, wait less than one second for students to respond to their questions. On the other hand, some teachers wait an average of three seconds for students to reply. When she compared student responses with different wait-times, she found that the longer wait-times (three seconds or more) produced more thoughtful responses, increased classroom discussion, and enabled students to analyze a situation more critically than did the shorter wait-times following the teacher's questions. Dr. Rowe also found that teachers who waited an average of more than three seconds before calling for a response enjoyed the following results:

- the length of student responses increased 400%–800%
- the number of voluntary, yet appropriate, responses increased
- failure to respond decreased
- student confidence increased
- students asked more unsolicited questions
- weaker students contributed more (increases ranged from 1.5% to 37% more)
- there was a greater variety of student responses—creative thinking increased!
- discipline problems decreased

One effective technique to determine the wait-time following your class questions is to make a tape-recording of your lesson and then, during the playback, to time the periods of pause following each question. Try increasing your wait-time if it is too short and again tape the lesson to inspect for an increase of wait-time. Such an exercise ought to produce favorable results.

Once you have succeeded in increasing the wait-time following your classroom questions, you might try to pause briefly after a student has responded, to allow for reflection or to permit a student to add more information to his first response. This second type of wait-time has similar effects on the learning environment as the first type of wait-time. This has been shown by an analysis conducted by Dr. Rowe of more than 800 tape recordings of lessons in urban, suburban, and rural schools.

Variety in Questioning

Perhaps one of the most important elements in good classroom questioning, as in most aspects of good teaching, is variety. Variety can refer to the types of questions asked, to the manner in which questions are asked, to the way students (volunteers and nonvolunteers) are called on to respond to questions, and to the procedure by which responses are handled. Variety reduces predictability, which in turn ought to promote continuous stimulation. When teachers vary the types of questions asked, students are required to be alert to more than simply the content of the questions. This additional alertness should have a refreshing spin-off toward improved learning. In addition to providing students with a more interesting experience, teachers also are more apt to be energized by the challenge of creating continuous variety in their questioning.

Ten Types of Questions to Avoid

In any sequence of questioning a few weak questions may be asked without harm, but many poor questions will weaken a lesson. Following are ten types of questions a teacher should consciously avoid, for they may be counterproductive.

Overlaid Question

Often teachers, in the midst of asking their classes a question, find that the question is not specific enough to elicit the desired response. Rather than let the original question ride on its merits and give students a chance to answer it, teachers may augment the question before students have even had a chance to answer the original question. When this happens, students who may have understood the original question may now hesitate to answer, because they are uncertain about their understanding of the entire question. Thus, by elaborating on a question they felt was unclear, teachers may have caused confusion by tagging on an additional thought.

EXAMPLE

What method shall we use to solve this problem, and that will make our solution elegant?

Even if a student knows which method to use to solve the problem in question, he may avoid answering the question because of uncertainty about the second part of the question, namely, whether his method will produce an "elegant solution." An improved way to ask this question is: "What method shall we use to solve this problem (pause), Barbara?" "What would be a good first step in this solution, Max?"

EXAMPLE

Which two triangles are congruent and also share a common angle?

Students might be ready to answer the first part of the question but then may hesitate on hearing the second part, for an inspection of the "common angle" would require further thought. Furthermore, some students may simply be overwhelmed by the question and shy away from it. This question may be asked as: "Which two triangles sharing a common angle are congruent (pause), Joan?" You may also choose to ask the question as two separate questions.

In each of the two examples of an overlaid question, an elaboration of an original question was tagged on. This had exactly the opposite effect of what was intended.

Multiple Question

A multiple question is formed by asking two related questions in sequence without allowing for a student response until both parts of the question have been asked.

EXAMPLE

Which triangles should we prove congruent, and how will they help us prove $\overline{AB}$ parallel to $\overline{CD}$?

Although a student may know which triangles need to be proved congruent, he may not know how congruent triangles will help prove $\overline{AB} \| \overline{CD}$. This student will probably not answer the question. However, if the question is asked in two parts, allowing for an answer to the first part before the second part is asked, then more students will be likely to respond. This may be done as follows: "Which triangles should we prove congruent (pause), Andy?" "How will these congruent triangles enable us to prove $\overline{AB} \| \overline{CD}$ (pause), Alison?"

This type of question is similar to the overlaid question in that it also has two parts. It differs from the overlaid question by being two questions that could actually stand separately. Teachers often resort to multiple questions when they feel that the time remaining for a lesson is too short, or when they get somewhat impatient and want the lesson to move along more rapidly. As before, students can easily be discouraged from answering this type of question. To provide a correct response, a student must be able to answer correctly *both* parts of the question. Thus, a student who can correctly answer only one part of the question will not volunteer to respond. By reducing the pool of students who will respond to questions, the teacher diminishes active learning throughout the class.

EXAMPLE

What is the discriminant of this equation (pointing to a quadratic equation), and what type of roots does it have?

This multiple question could stand as separate questions, but in its present format it will most likely discourage students from responding. The same information can be elicited by asking: "What is the discriminant of this equation (pointing to a quadratic equation) (pause), Carla?" and "Based on the value of the discriminant, what type of roots does this equation have (pause), Samuel?"

By stifling student responses, multiple questions reduce the effectiveness of a lesson and should therefore be avoided.

Factual Questions

There is certainly nothing wrong with asking a question that has a simple factual response if the question is part of a buildup of a series of sequential facts necessary for the solution to the problem under consideration. Otherwise, however, isolated factual questions do little to stimulate student thinking.

EXAMPLE

What is the Pythagorean theorem?

Not much thought is required to respond to this question. A student either knows the answer or does not know it.

If we agree with our original premise regarding classroom questioning, then aside from being a part of a sequence of questions, factual questions contribute little to an active learning environment in the classroom.

Elliptical Questions

Questions that are unclear because the teacher has omitted specifics offer nothing to a lesson. Although not particularly harmful to a lesson, an elliptical question is simply an unnecessary waste of time.

EXAMPLE

How about these two angles?

Teachers frequently have a habit of thinking aloud. They may be looking at a pair of angles and thinking of what to ask about them, such as "What is their relationship" or "Which angle has the greater measure?" In either case, the teacher may instead first voice the thought: "How about these two angles?" Verbalizing this thought into a question that has no answer wastes classroom time. The teacher might have asked, "What is the relationship between these two angles (pause), Jamal?", where a definite answer was required.

Had the teacher wanted to say something (so as to avoid a lull in the lesson) when he was thinking about the two angles, he could have said, "Consider these two angles." This would have served the intended purpose and not wasted classroom time with possible student wisecrack answers such as "How about them!"

EXAMPLE

What about these two parallel lines?

As before, this elliptical question asks for either nothing or more than most students are prepared to offer. At any rate, because of the omission of specifics, it leaves itself open to wisecrack responses. The teacher may wish to say something like "Which angles can we prove congruent using these parallel lines (pause), Lisa?"

The teacher does not have to overreact to avoid lulls. Instead, she should stop and give some thought to a question rather than ask it in a form that has no clear response.

Yes-No or Guessing Questions

For the most part yes-no or guessing questions have little value. With few exceptions a yes-no question can easily be transformed into a good thought question.

EXAMPLE

Is $\overline{AB}$ perpendicular to $\overline{CD}$?

A student attempting to answer this question takes a very small risk. His chances of being correct are actually better than 50 percent. The teacher asking the question more often than not is seeking a positive response. In addition, the diagram to which this question relates should also offer assistance. Thus, the question becomes somewhat rhetorical. This question might be transformed to read, "What is the relationship between $\overline{AB}$ and $\overline{CD}$ (pause), Eric?" This would require the student to explore the possible relationships that two line segments may have and then choose the one he feels is appropriate. In its transformed state, the question provokes active learning among the students.

EXAMPLE

Is triangle ABC isosceles?

Why would a teacher ask this question if the triangle were, in fact, not isosceles? Unless the teacher were set to trick the class, students would be correct in assuming that the teacher is simply seeking an affirmative response. Why then ask the question? The question will be far more productive when asked as "What type of triangle is ΔABC (pause), José?" It is therefore a good practice to avoid yes-no or guessing questions whenever possible.

Ambiguous Questions

Occasionally, a teacher may seek a response that requires a specific interpretation of a situation. Here the questioner, trying to get the desired response with one question, may likely ask an ambiguous question, one that can have a variety of different, yet correct, answers. The desired response would be more easily attained by asking a series of short sequential questions.

EXAMPLE

How does the law of sines differ from the law of cosines?

Many different correct answers to this question can be given. Certainly the context in which this question is asked will help narrow the choices among the correct responses. Students will tend to shy away from responding to this question, however, out of obvious confusion caused by its ambiguity. Students may wonder if the question refers to the difference in appearance of the two laws, the difference in application, the difference in derivation, and so on. One possible form in which this question may be asked is "Under what different circumstances are the laws of sines and cosines used (pause), Aaliyah?"

Because such confusion is obviously counterproductive, ambiguous questions should be consciously avoided in classroom questioning.

EXAMPLE

What is the relationship between the area of a circle and the circumference of a circle?

Once again this question has many correct answers. Is the questioner concerned about the numerical relationship, the physical relationship, the dimensional relationship, or some other, less obvious relationship? Although the context in which the question is asked will assist students in responding to the question, confusion is rarely avoided when an ambiguous question is asked. One specific way of asking this question is "What is the ratio between the area and circumference of a circle (pause), Gabriella?"

Note: It is not necessarily a bad or undesirable feature to pose questions having several correct answers. We are considering the "ambiguous question" here rather than this type of question. Before asking a question that is likely to be ambiguous, set the specifics about the situation, then ask short, simple questions to elicit the desired response.

Chorus Response Questions

Although a question calling for a chorus response may be good, the chorus response often provides little value to the lesson. When a class responds in chorus to a question, the teacher usually cannot determine which students are answering incorrectly and which students are not responding at all. Furthermore, a chorus response can become too unclear for students eager to learn from the answer to hear the answer correctly. By missing the answer to a question, a student could be missing an important link in a chain of reasoning, resulting in damage to the learning process for this student.

EXAMPLE

What type of quadrilateral is *ABCD*, class?

If we assume that not everyone in the class knows the correct answer to the question, some students will be shouting an incorrect answer while others will be answering correctly. Should one student not respond but instead listen for the correct answer, he may hear an incorrect answer (because a wrong response may have come from someone close by) and then try to learn a concept with an incorrect piece of information. The time lost in correcting this error is certainly undesirable.

A preponderance of chorus response questions will allow some students to glide through the lesson without actually learning the subject matter presented. The teacher in this situation will be unable to detect individual difficulties, because they are likely to be clouded by the chorus responses. This gives further reason to avoid the chorus response question as much as possible.

But an occasional use of this type of question may be acceptable if the response is not too crucial to a development and if it is necessary to involve the entire class, even for the sake of variety. A change of style, offering variety to the lesson, may be a healthy feature. Even when serving this purpose, however, the chorus response question should be used sparingly.

Whiplash Questions

A whiplash question usually is not planned by the teacher. It comes about when a teacher decides to make a question out of a statement midway through it.

EXAMPLE

The slope of this line is, what?

Aside from possibly frustrating students, little harm is caused by this type of question. Perhaps its greatest flaw is its uselessness. Not expecting a question, the students are caught off guard. They must first mentally rephrase the question before attempting an answer. Under normal circumstances the beginning key word of a question (e.g., why, when, what, how) puts the students in a psychological set, ready to receive and process a question. The whiplash question does not provide this readying process and thereby wastes time and loses much of the student audience. A more productive way to ask this question would be: "What is the slope of this line (pause), Wei?"

EXAMPLE

We now have $\overline{AB}$ parallel to $\overline{CD}$ because of which theorem?

This question would have been much more effective had the key word announcing a question been at the beginning of the question. It would then read, "Which theorem justifies the fact that $\overline{AB}$ is parallel to $\overline{CD}$(pause), Simone?" In this form, the students know from the first word that a question is being asked. The second word has them focus on the various theorems learned while they listen to the remainder of the question. At the completion of the question they are ready to respond without wasting time to rephrase the question. This latter form of the question is clearly more efficient than the whiplash format, and a teacher need not turn every statement into a question just for the sake of producing student participation. Such an attempt at increasing student participation could easily become counterproductive.

Leading Questions

A leading question is one that tugs the desired response from the student. This type of question serves no reasonable function.

EXAMPLE

Wouldn't you say that ΔABC is equilateral?

Most students would be quite reluctant not to agree with the teacher asking such a question. Thus, the question does not provoke much thought, because the student is more than likely simply to respond in the affirmative.

EXAMPLE

Seven is a factor of 35, isn't it?

Again, there is no need to turn the statement "Seven is a factor of 35" into a question. The teacher would be better served either by leaving the statement stand as is or by asking a question such as "What are the factors of 35 (pause), Antonio?" or "By what number must 7 be multiplied to yield 35 (pause), Miguel?" Each of these questions requires some thought on the part of the students before they answer. In addition to replacing a time-wasting question, each induces active learning.

Teacher-Centered Questions

It is generally desirable to have students consider the teacher as part of the class. Although students are well aware of the different roles of the teacher and the student, when addressing the class it is more effective for the teacher to use the first person plural (i.e., *we* and *us*) when appropriate. For example, saying "Let us consider the following . . ." rather than "I have the following . . ." would make the class feel that they are all part of one group working together on a common problem. They do not need a constant reminder that they are the students and the teacher is distinct from them. Regular use of the first person singular (i.e., *I* and *me*) could create an invisible barrier between the teacher and the class, a possible detriment to a healthy, active learning environment.

EXAMPLE

Give me the solution set of $3x - 5 = 2$.

A better way to ask this is: "Give us the solution set of $3x - 5 = 2$ (pause), Sam."

EXAMPLE

What must I do next to solve this problem?

This question ought to be asked as: "What must we do next in solving this problem (pause), Jack?"

Each of the preceding examples illustrates the sort of teacher comment that seeks to set apart (albeit subconsciously) the teacher from the students, which is not particularly conducive to a good classroom learning environment.

Classroom Questioning as a Means to Generate Higher Order Thinking

Questioning in an optimally interactive classroom is used by the teacher to help students gain understanding and by students to obtain guidance that will assist them to clarify ambiguities and resolve confusion. Traditional guidelines for questioning deal exclusively with the teacher's questions, setting down formal guidelines for what is acceptable and what is not. Those guidelines are valuable today.

Several issues must be raised based on student psychology as it is now understood. For example, not all ambiguity is bad. We will explore ways in which ambiguity might be employed consciously, on occasion, to assist students in acquiring a deeper understanding of familiar material. Some new formats for traditional questions are likely to reduce student anxiety without in any way lessening the quality of learning. Other new techniques are powerful in their own right.

Accepting new ideas authenticates older practices. It builds on the body of new knowledge about students, the way the brain works, and the routes by which skills and understanding are incorporated into long-term memory. It recognizes pedagogy as a living art and science.

Explain Your Thinking

The value of questions that probe the rationale for a student's answer is clear. Every student should have a reason for each response given; the accessibility of rationale assists the student in reconstructing correct answers and storing new information in long-term memory. Unfortunately, many people, young and old, find "why" questions threatening.

A student has correctly answered the challenge to compute -5×-4 with the answer $+20$. The teacher asks, "Why is positive 20 the correct answer?" The student panics and responds, "The rule says that when you multiply two signed numbers with the same sign, the answer must be positive." Is that what the teacher wants to hear? If so, the teacher is encouraging rote learning. If not, exactly what does the teacher now say to correct the student's correct but undesired response?

Superior psychological and pedagogical technique would be to follow up with the challenge to "Explain your thinking." To the student response noted in the previous paragraph the teacher might say, "That is not your own thinking. Explain why *you* think the product of two negative numbers must be positive."

A second advantage of asking students to explain their thinking is that most people find it far less threatening to talk about what *they* think than to try to explain what *someone else* thinks.

A third advantage to "Explain your thinking" is that it pinpoints the best route to long-term memory, namely, the reconstruction of knowledge resulting from the student's own thought processes.

Compare and Contrast

An earlier section cautions against ambiguous questions like "What is the relationship between the arc of a circle and the circumference of a circle?" The student may become confused because this question, as previously noted, has many answers. The value of the question can be preserved and heightened by using the unambiguous *compare and contrast* format.

EXAMPLE

Compare and contrast the circumference and the area of a circle.

All of the student's insights are called for. The student might compare circumference to area by citing that both measures are associated with the circle, involve the number π, depend on the radius of the circle, etc. The student might contrast circumference and area by noting that circumference is a measure of (arc) length, whereas area is a measure of the extent of a region, or by noting that the area can be deduced from the circumference by extending the formula for the area of a regular polygon, $A = \frac{1}{2}ap$ (where a = apothem and p = perimeter), or by noting that for a circle, $A = \frac{1}{2} \times r \times 2\pi r = \pi r^2$.

EXAMPLE

Compare and contrast the ways you think about adding fractions and multiplying fractions.

Students would be able to both cite the algorithms *and* discuss the rationale behind the algorithms. Students might be led to consider the problem of adding and subtracting any expressions involving units (because, after all, a denominator is a unit). A student who could insightfully compare and contrast the rationale or impossibility behind adding 5 pounds to 4 feet, multiplying 5 pounds by 4 feet, adding 5 inches to 4 feet, and multiplying 5 inches by 4 feet is well on the way to understanding both mathematics and science more fully.

Prove or Disprove

Students will benefit from being exposed to the *prove or disprove* format early in their introduction to proof. The direction to *prove* tells them that the statement they are given holds in general. To be truly adept at proof, students must realize that most statements they formulate themselves will not be provable. The *prove or disprove* format encourages students to try to find a counter-example to an unknown assertion *before* trying to find a proof.

EXAMPLE

Prove or disprove that any quadrilateral with diagonals that are both perpendicular and equal in length is a square.

A simple diagram of a kite would serve as an adequate disproof.

EXAMPLE

Prove or disprove that fractions can always be added by adding numerators and denominators.

A disproof accessible to almost any student is $\frac{1}{2} + \frac{1}{2} = \frac{2}{4}$ because the sum is actually 1, whereas $\frac{2}{4} = \frac{1}{2}$.

As long as many *prove or disprove* items encountered by a student end up as proofs while at least one of three end up as disproofs, the student will learn to think about conjectures in the way that many mathematicians think: skeptically.

Teaching Students to Pose Questions

People remember their own questions more easily than they remember questions posed by others. Furthermore, the very process of formulating your own question helps you to clarify perplexing issues. Far too little time is spent in helping students to improve their own questioning skills. Students do not learn to ask good questions simply by hearing the teacher ask good questions. They learn to ask good questions by actually formulating good questions.

Question Template One method that works is to provide students with a template for questions and by daily discussing the value of each question as the teacher models them in the classroom. Students might be asked to write and answer one question each based on the day's work as part of their homework. They could each be called on to ask their question the next day and to call on classmates. A bulletin board could be used to highlight the best student question of the week. Each test might include one excellent question created by a student during the previous weeks.

The following list gives a starting point for a student question template. It could be copied on a single page and distributed to all students to be inserted as the first page of their notebooks. It might also be available on their computers so that they can block, cut, and paste the questions they want to use.

What are [or accounts for] the similarities between ______ and ______?

What are [or accounts for] the differences between ______ and ______?

Give an example of [something] that is ______ but not ______.

Under what conditions are we allowed to ______?

Why is it so much more difficult to ______ than to ______?

What is the connection between [something learned earlier] and [new skill, procedure, or concept]?

When should I use [new skill, procedure, or concept] instead of [old skill, procedure, or concept]?

If [some condition or number in a given problem] is changed to ______, how would the method we used have to change?

Examine the conjecture ______ in the extreme case where ______.

How do I decide which of the following figures is best for consideration of the [problem, conjecture, data] ______?

How would I know to ______ instead of ______ at this point in the [problem, proof, argument]?

How do I decide what to do first when trying to [solve, prove] ______?

EXAMPLES

How would I know to set a quadratic equation equal to zero instead of gathering all variables on one side of the equal sign and all constants on the other side [as I do with linear equations]?

What accounts for the differences in the rules for adding signed numbers and for multiplying signed numbers?

How do I decide what to do first when trying to prove that if two medians of a triangle are equal in length, then the triangle is isosceles?

Under what conditions are we allowed to cancel like quantities in the numerator and denominator of a fraction?

The very formulation of some of these questions would be a major step to quality understanding of major mathematical concepts.

The Question Box

One way to help students follow up on their own questions while improving their ability to write questions and to organize their thinking is to encourage them to keep a *question box.* They keep an index card box at home in which they file their own daily questions about school and learning. Each week they review the questions entered that week and write on the back of the index card any answers they can now add. They also may sharpen unanswered questions or break unanswered questions into several simple ones. Each vacation break they go through the question box answering any old questions they can now successfully address and removing index cards containing answered questions they now fully understand. Over the years, the question box serves as a review and as a source for research projects. The question box helps students to reinforce learning, to think about what they need to know and what they need to review, and to develop areas for future investigation. It helps youngsters to assume responsibility for their own education.

Summary

Remember, when asking a classroom question, *listen to your own question* with a critical ear. You may be one of your own best critics. Should more careful self-analysis be desired, a videotape recording would be helpful. Constant self-assessment of your teaching performance should produce rewarding results.

EXERCISES

1. State whether or not each of the following is a good classroom question; if it is not, explain why.
   a. "What is the solution set for the equation $3x - 5 = 8$, and how will it help us solve the problem (discussed earlier with the class), Lisa?"
   b. "How about this set of numbers (pause), Daniel?"
   c. "Why is ΔABC isosceles, David?"
   d. "Yolanda, wouldn't you say these triangles are congruent?"
   e. "Class, is this curve a parabola?"
   f. "The discriminant of this equation is what?"
   g. "What is my next step in solving this problem?"
   h. "What is the greatest common factor of these two numbers, and how can we be sure that there is no greater common factor, Joshua?"
   i. "How can we change the equation $\frac{x}{3} + \frac{5x}{7} = 2$ to one without fractions, Henry?"
   j. "For what conditions will the roots of this equation (pointing at the chalkboard) be imaginary, and how will this help solve our problem, Evelyn?"
   k. "Who can tell me what the solution to this equation (pointing to the chalkboard) is?"
   l. "Which is the longest side of this triangle (pointing to right ΔABC), class?"
   m. "How does solving a linear equation differ from solving a quadratic equation, Christa?"
   n. "Am I correct in dividing both sides of this equation (at chalkboard) by 5 (pause), Noelle?"
   o. "What is $\sqrt{196}$, class?"
   p. "If we apply the Pythagorean theorem to this triangle, we find *AB* equals what, Alice?"
   q. "Why is there only one acceptable answer to this problem, Omar?"
2. Rephrase each question in Exercise 1 that is not a good classroom question.
3. Explain why it is more desirable to call on a student after a question has been asked rather than before.
4. How would you react to the following student responses to your question?
   a. "I didn't hear the question."
   b. "I was absent yesterday."
   c. "I don't know."
   d. Silence
5. Choose a short topic from the secondary school mathematics curriculum. Prepare a series of questions you might use to develop this topic (through "guided discovery") with your class.

Strategies For Teaching More Effective Lessons

Effective teachers have available to them a broad range of specific teaching strategies, especially for pivotal lessons. Determining the best strategies for your lessons is an important aspect of your creative role in the classroom. Many of the strategies explained in the following pages will work equally well with examples other than those described. Furthermore, the illustrations shown certainly do not constitute an exhaustive set of either examples or strategies, for the number of strategies used by the creative teacher is endless.

Using Tree Diagrams, or Branching

Tree diagrams, or branching, are often useful when a pupil faces a variety of choices and alternatives. They may provide insight into the overall view of a problem in question and may even offer direction as to decisions that must be considered in its solution. This strategy can arise in virtually any branch of mathematics, though not necessarily for every topic. Illustrations shown here represent topics in algebra, probability, permutations, set theory, and geometry.

EXAMPLE 1

(Algebra): *Prime Factorization of Whole Numbers*

A. Begin the lesson by defining and illustrating these three terms:

1. A *factor* of a given number is one of two or more numbers whose product is the given number. Thus, since the product of 2, 3, and 4 is 24, it follows that 2, 3, and 4 are factors of 24, i.e.,

$$24 = 2 \times 3 \times 4$$

Ask students to write 15 as the product of two factors. They will probably answer,

$$15 = 3 \times 5$$

However, they might answer $15 = 1 \times 15$. But you should point out that "1" is a special case because we could write *any* product with a whole string of 1s as factors, and that would not be very meaningful.

2. A *prime number* is a number whose *only* factors are 1 and itself. Thus, the only factors of 7 are 1 and 7, so $7 = 1 \times 7$.

   Although it is true that $15 = 1 \times 15$, 1 and 15 are not the *only* factors, since it is also true that $15 = 3 \times 5$. So we see that 15 is *not* a prime number, whereas 7 *is* a prime number.
3. A number that is not prime is called *composite*.

B. Point out that "2" is considered the smallest prime number. Ask students to list all numbers from 2 through 50 and to circle the primes.

Answer: The circled numbers will be 2, 3, 5, 7, 11, 13, 17, 19, 23, 29, 31, 37, 41, 43, and 47. The remaining numbers are composite.

C. Now, mention to the class that it is sometimes desirable to find only the *prime factors* of a number, for example, when you need to determine the least common denominator of several fractions. One strategy for finding prime factors is to use the *branching* method shown next. Whenever a prime number appears at the end of a branch, put a circle around it.

   Students should now be shown how to use the branching method to express 12, 18, and 144 as the product of prime factors.

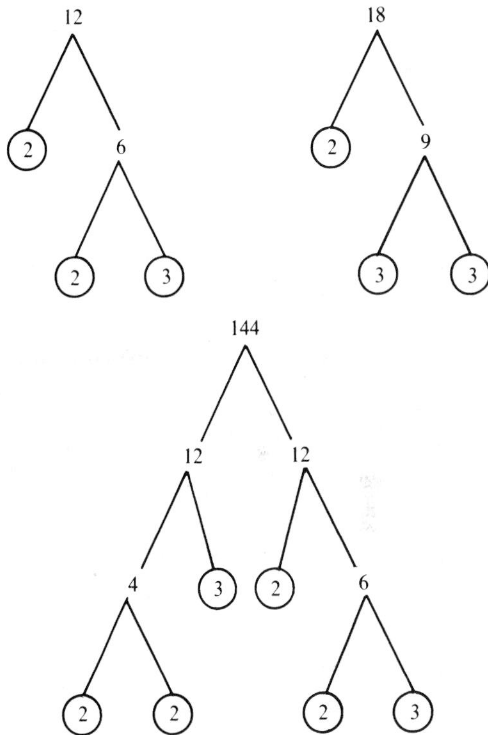

Here are the answers:

$12 = 2 \times 2 \times 3$	$18 = 2 \times 3 \times 3$
or	or
$12 = 2^2 \times 3$	$18 = 2 \times 3^2$

$$144 = 2 \times 2 \times 2 \times 2 \times 3 \times 3$$

or

$$144 = 2^4 \times 3^2$$

For practice, ask the class to use the branching method to express these numbers as the product of prime factors: 48; 36; 108; 72; 400; 125; 1024; 1215.

EXAMPLE 2

(Probability): *Permutations*

Define a *permutation of a set of objects* as an ordered arrangement of all or some of the objects.

Ask the class: How many three-digit numbers can be formed with three discs marked, respectively, 1, 2, and 3? After listing their answers on the chalkboard in a random manner, show how to *organize* the arrangements of numbers with this tree diagram:

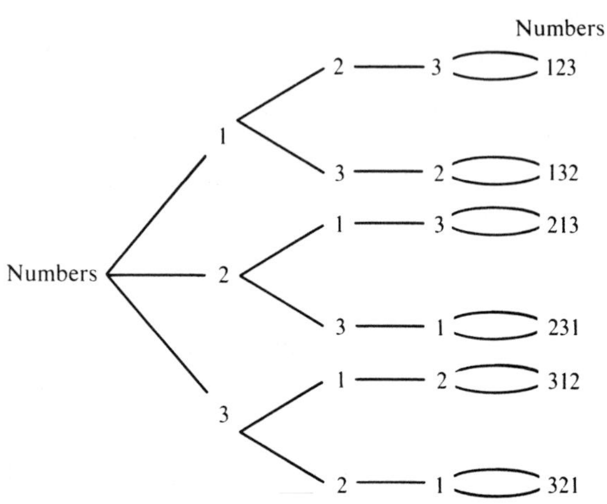

The equation $3 \times 2 \times 1 = 6$ suggests a rule for finding the number of permutations without drawing the tree.

As a second illustration, use a tree diagram to show that there are 24 ($4 \times 3 \times 2 \times 1$) permutations, or arrangements, of the letters of the word *five*.

For practice, ask the class to exhibit a tree arrangement to illustrate the permutations of 5 or 6 objects. Note that the numbers become quite large, so introduce factorial notation:

$$n! = 1 \times 2 \times 3 \times 4 \times 5 \times \cdots \times (n-1) \times n$$

Using Paper Folding or Cutting

Paper folding and cutting is a strategy often used in middle and junior high schools. It serves to demonstrate concepts or theorems that require a higher level of mathematical maturity than students of that age can be expected to have achieved. Nevertheless, a clever teacher will be alert to any situation, at any level of school, where cutting or folding paper may serve to enlighten, to clarify, to motivate. The following illustrations demonstrate these points.

EXAMPLE 1

(Geometry): *Demonstrate the theorem "The sum of the measures of the angles of a triangle is 180°."*

1. Cut out a cardboard triangle *ABC*.

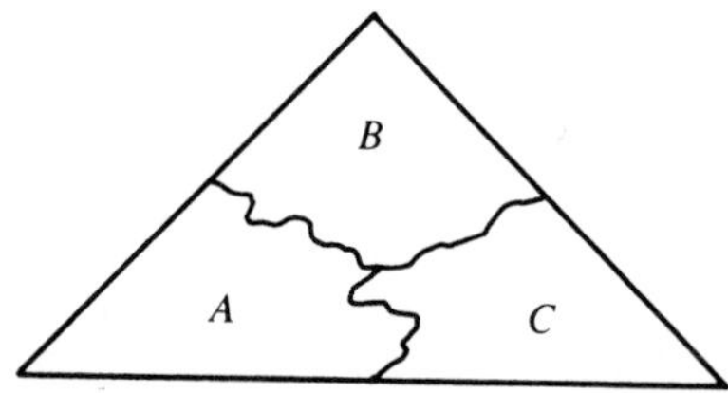

2. Cut off the three angles and rearrange them along a straight line:

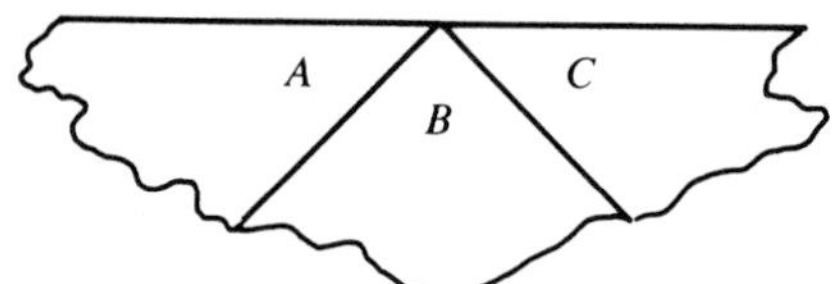

3. Remind students that the sum of measures of angles along a straight line is 180°, because a straight angle is formed by a straight line. This completes the demonstration.

EXAMPLE 2

(Geometry): *Prove the theorem "If two sides of a triangle are congruent, the angles opposite these sides are congruent" (also known as "Base angles of an isosceles triangle are congruent").*

This is usually the first lesson in which students are asked to write a formal proof from a verbal statement. Begin by reviewing the if-then form of a statement, with the phrase following the "then" known as the *conclusion*. Thus, the hypothesis in this example is "two sides of a triangle are congruent," and the conclusion is "the angles opposite these sides are congruent."

Draw and label a diagram and list what is "given" and what is "to be proved" based on the letters in the diagram (see illustration):

Given: ΔABC
$\overline{AC} \cong \overline{BC}$
Prove: $\angle A \cong \angle B$

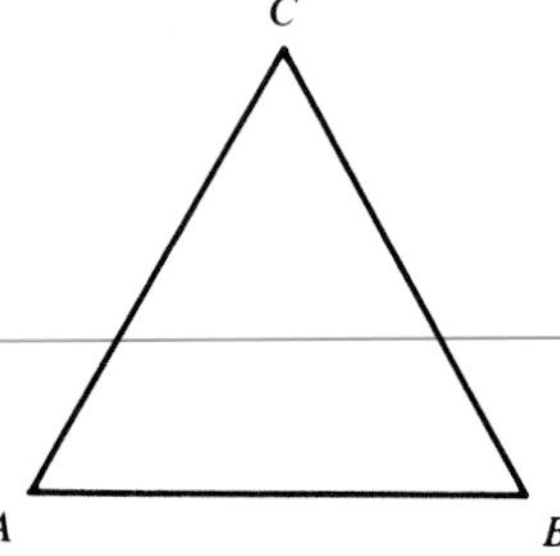

Guide pupils to the need for using an auxiliary line in developing the formal proof as follows:

1. Cut out the isosceles triangle.
2. Hold the congruent sides together and fold down with a crease partway down, starting at the vertex (see Figure (a)). (Note that the crease is in reality an angle bisector of the vertex angle.)
3. Extend the crease (angle bisector) until it hits the opposite side, forming two triangles (Figure (b)).
4. Prove the two triangles congruent by SAS, as illustrated (Figure (b)).
5. The two base angles are now congruent, which was to be proved.

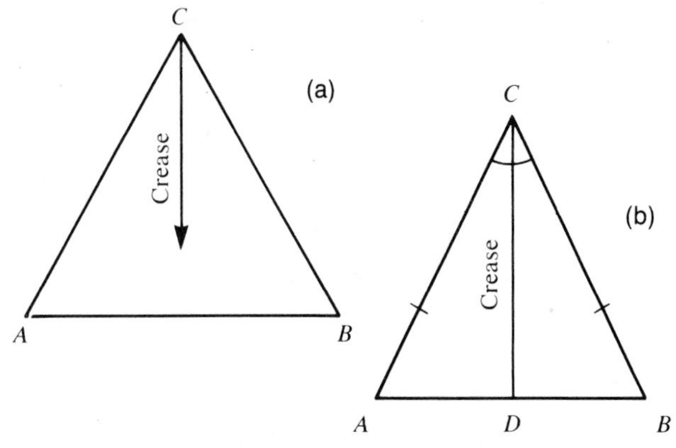

A Picture Is Worth a Thousand Words

This strategy is probably the most universally accepted by mathematicians at every level of achievement and sophistication. It guides students' thinking by suggesting insights toward solutions of problems, as well as toward generalizations of these problems. These ideas are represented here on a simple level with illustrations from mixture problems in algebra, probability, and Venn diagrams.

The value of "pictures," or diagrams, in geometry is well known. Expanding these pictures from two to three dimensions has even allowed mathematicians to dare to think in terms of dimensions of higher order.

EXAMPLE 1

(Algebra): *Mixture Problem*

A 3-gallon, 20% alcohol-water mixture is to be upgraded by adding to it a certain amount of a 70% alcohol-water mixture. How many gallons of the 70% mixture must be added to make the new, enriched mixture a 40% alcohol-water mix?

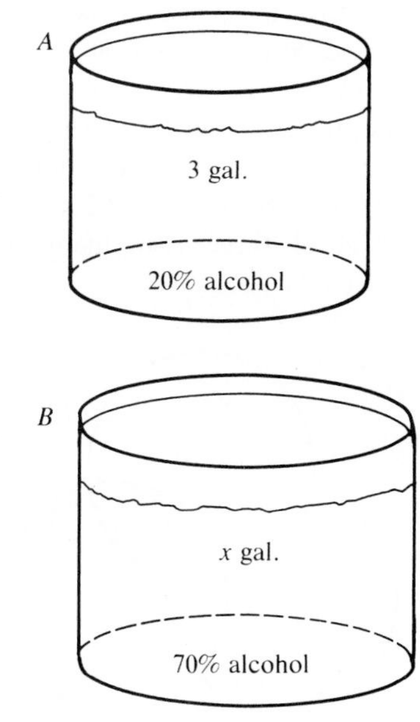

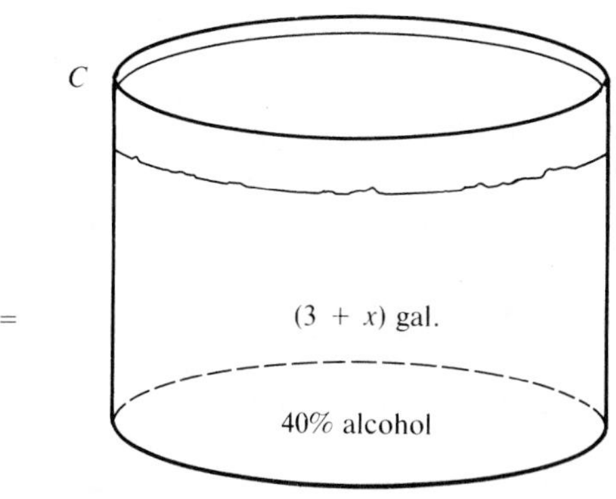

SOLUTION

Picturing the containers that hold the mixture is a great aid and makes for a more real situation. Begin by drawing a diagram of the three containers. The amount of alcohol in each container can now be easily obtained:

$$A\text{: } (0.20)(3) \quad B\text{: } (0.70)(x) \quad C\text{: } (0.40)(3 + x)$$

Similarly, the amount of water in each container is

$$A\text{: } (0.80)(3) \quad B\text{: } (0.30)(x) \quad C\text{: } (0.60)(3 + x)$$

Because the amount of alcohol in container C is equal to the sum of the alcohol amounts in containers A and B, we get a

PURE ALCOHOL equation:

$$(0.20)(3) + (0.70)(x) = (0.40)(3 + x)$$

Also, because the amount of water in container C is equal to the sum of the water amounts in A and B, we get a

PURE WATER equation:

$$(0.80)(3) + (0.30)(x) = (0.60)(3 + x)$$

In either of these equations we get $x = 2$.

EXAMPLE 2

(Algebra): *Visualization*

Although the following problem is not a typical probability exercise, its solution involves a visualization principle that may be applicable to many areas in mathematics, such as coordinate geometry, statistics, topology, logic, and number theory as well as probability:

> A pair of dice (one red and one green) are rolled. What is the probability that the difference of the numbers coming up is less than or equal to 1?

The figure shows the entire set of 36 possible outcomes. The dot with coordinates (5, 4) corresponds to the outcome: red die shows 5 while the green die shows 4. The favorable outcomes are indicated in the enclosed region and consist of a total of 16 events.

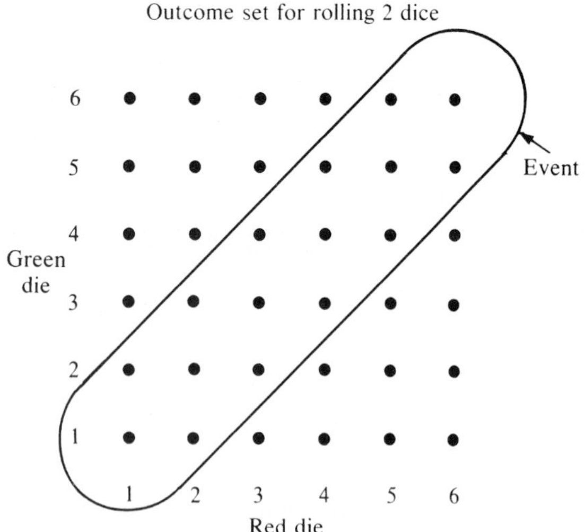

Because all 36 outcomes are equally likely, each is given a probability of 1/36. The event has 16 outcomes, so its probability is 16(1/36) = 16/36, or 4/9.

For this problem we could also have used the rule

$$\frac{\text{number of favorable outcomes}}{\text{total number of possible outcomes}} = \frac{16}{36} = \frac{4}{9}$$

because all the outcomes are equally likely.

EXAMPLE 3

(Algebra): *Venn Diagrams*

Certain types of problems involving sets of elements and logical reasoning can best be solved with Venn diagrams, which are simply sets of overlapping circles. The *intersection set* is the smallest set of all common elements, and the *union set* is the smallest set of all different elements. Thus, in the diagram, if A and B are sets, $A \cap B$ represents the intersection set and $A \cup B$ the union:

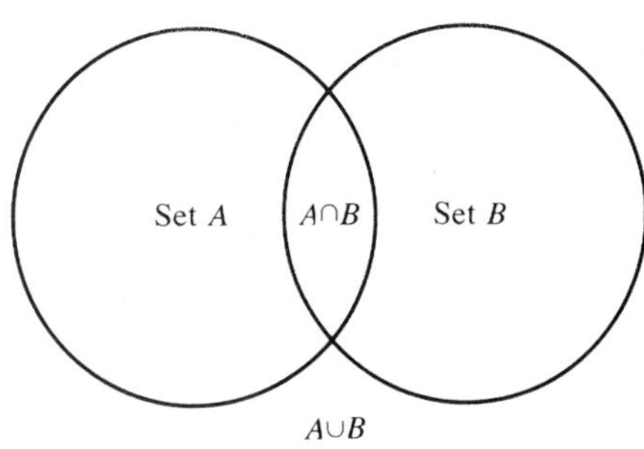

Illustration: Two sets are $\{a, b, c, d\}$ and $\{e, b, c, f\}$. Draw a Venn diagram for the two sets and indicate the union and intersection sets.

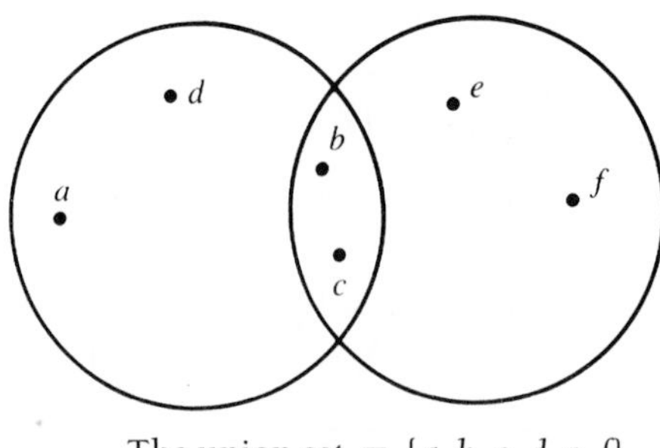

The union set = $\{a, b, c, d, e, f\}$
The intersection set = $\{b, c\}$

Now you can show your classes how to solve with relative ease "counting" problems like the following.

PROBLEM

A student was paid 50 cents per person to ask how many liked Republican policies and how many Democratic. He reported that 27 liked Republican, 31 liked Democrat, and 18 liked both. How much money did he earn?

SOLUTION

The Venn diagram shows that there were only 13 + 18 + 9 = 40 elements in the union set, giving him $20.00.

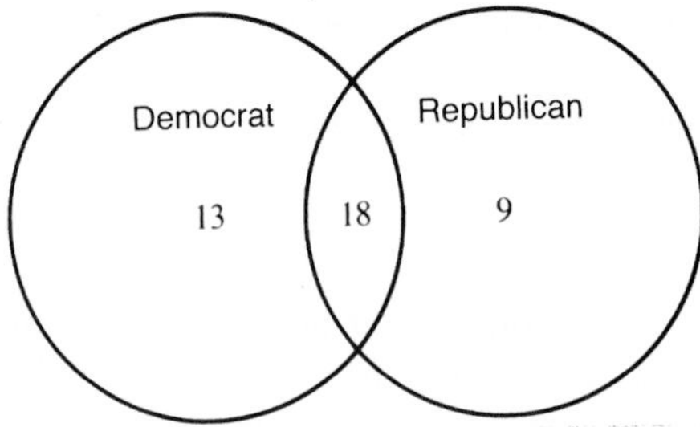

Here are some additional practice problems:

1. In a school newspaper poll, 110 students voted that they liked English, 150 voted that they liked mathematics, and 50 said they liked both. If everyone who was interviewed voted, how many students were actually interviewed?
2. An automobile survey showed that 19 people liked model X, 18 liked model Y, and 20 liked model Z. Five of these people liked X and Y, 8 liked Y and Z, and 7 liked X and Z. Two people liked all three. How many people were surveyed? *Hint:* Use this diagram:

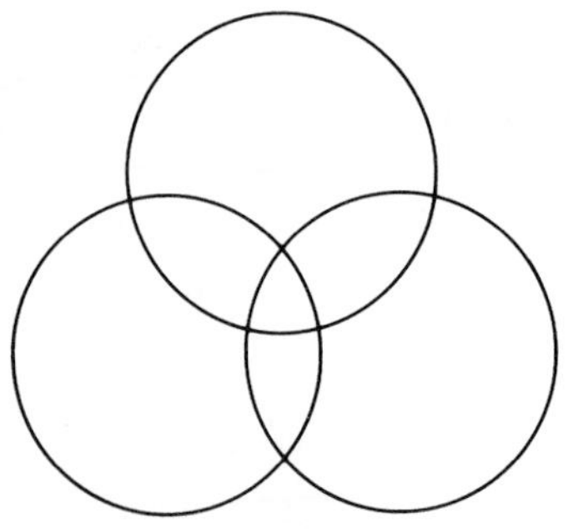

EXAMPLE 4

(Algebra): *Multiplying Binomials*

The visual demonstration that $(a + b)(a + b) = a^2 + 2ab + b^2$ starkly contrasts with the traditional proof that uses the distributive property. The demonstration follows.

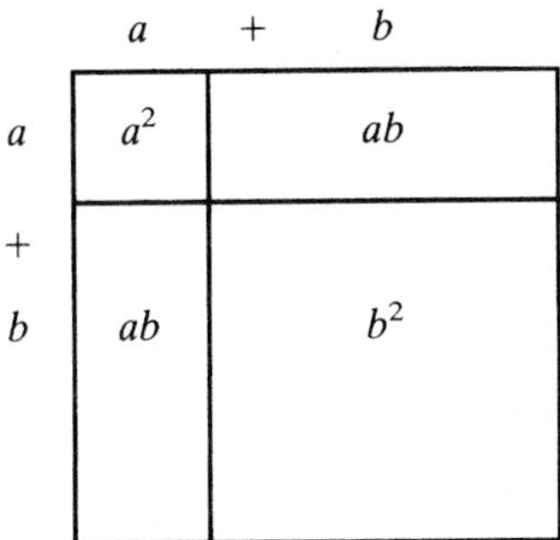

Because the area of the square is both $(a + b) \cdot (a + b)$ *and* the sum of the areas of the four sections, $a^2 + ab + ab + b^2$, we have $(a + b)^2 = a^2 + 2ab + b^2$.

Recognizing Patterns

Recognizing and maintaining patterns is a powerful force in human behavior. It establishes the stability and routine that many people, especially youngsters, need. For the mathematician, it offers clues to the extension of ideas into new domains. The illustrations presented here appear simple and perhaps even trivial, yet their real purpose is to help germinate ideas for the teacher in order for him or her to think and plan along the lines suggested.

EXAMPLE 1

(Geometry): *The Sum of the Angles of a Polygon*

Have the class consider the question "What is the sum of the measures of the angles of a polygon of any number of sides?"

By dividing the polygons into triangles, you can establish a pattern that will guide the class to the answer. The class should, of course, be aware that a straight angle has the measure 180°.

- The sum of the angles of a polygon of 4 sides is 2 straight angles = 360 degrees.
- The sum of the angles of a polygon of 5 sides is 3 straight angles = ? degrees.
- The sum of the angles of a polygon of 6 sides is ? straight angles = ? degrees.

To find the sum of the angles of a polygon of 16 sides, we note that there will be 14 triangles. Hence, the sum of its angles is ? straight angles.

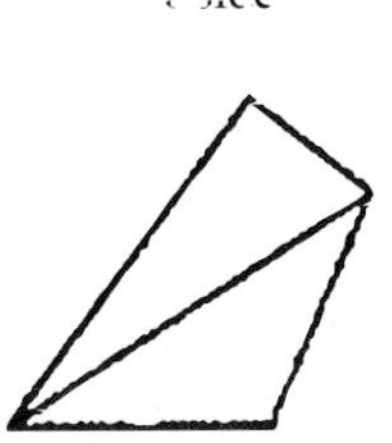

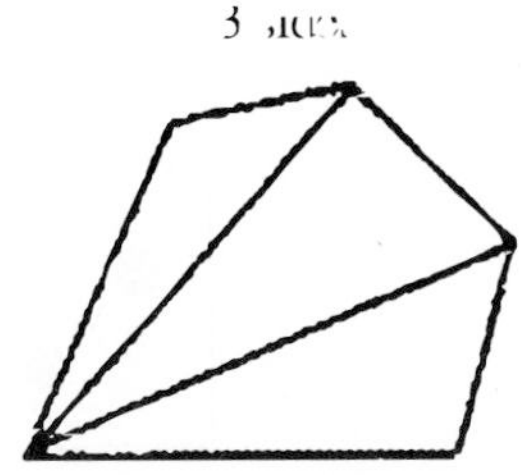

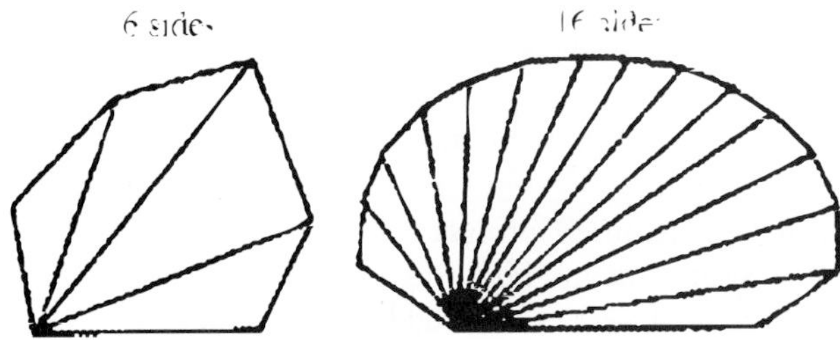

Students should be able to conclude that a polygon of n sides can be divided into $n - 2$ triangles, so the sum of the measures of its angles is $n - 2$ straight angles, or $(n - 2)180$ degrees.

EXAMPLE 2

(Algebra): *Sum of an Arithmetic Progression*

When Carl Friedrich Gauss was a young boy, his propensity for mathematics became evident in a classroom incident that has since become a classic tale of budding genius. When his teacher asked the class to find the sum of all integers from 1 through 100, the class was struggling with their slates and writing implements while young Carl observed a pattern that could produce the answer rather simply and quickly.

Carl observed that if he paired the terms of the sequence of numbers from 1 through 100 as shown below, and added them, he would get 50 pairs of 101. The sum would thus be $50 \times 101 = 5050$.

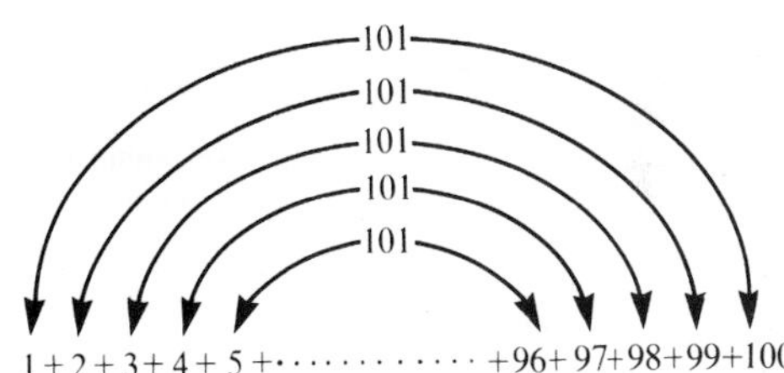

Now generalize the technique Gauss used to determine a formula for the sum of the first n terms of an arithmetic progression. Let a be the first term and d be the common difference between terms. Thus, the sum of these n terms is

$$a + [a + d] + [a + 2d] + [a + 3d] + \cdots + [a + (n - 2)d] + [a + (n - 1)d]$$

Adding the first and nth terms gives

$$a + [a + (n - 1)d] = 2a + (n - 1)d$$

and adding the second and $(n - 1)$th terms gives

$$[a + d] + [a + (n - 2)d] = 2a + (n - 1)d$$

and adding the third and $(n - 2)$th terms gives

$$[a + 2d] + [a + (n - 3)d] = 2a + (n - 1)d$$

Continue this process until all pairs have been added. If there are $n/2$ such pairs, the sum of the terms is

$$S = \frac{n}{2}[2a + (n - 1)d]$$

which is the required formula.

Ask your students how this procedure accounts for the middle term of a series of an odd number of terms.

EXAMPLE 3

(Geometry): *Polyhedra*

Leonhard Euler (1707–1783) discovered an interesting relationship among the vertices, faces, and edges of ordinary polyhedra. He said that if you take regular or nonregular polyhedra and let

V = number of vertices
E = number of edges
F = number of faces

then for every such solid, $V - E + F$ = a constant.

FIVE REGULAR POLYHEDRA

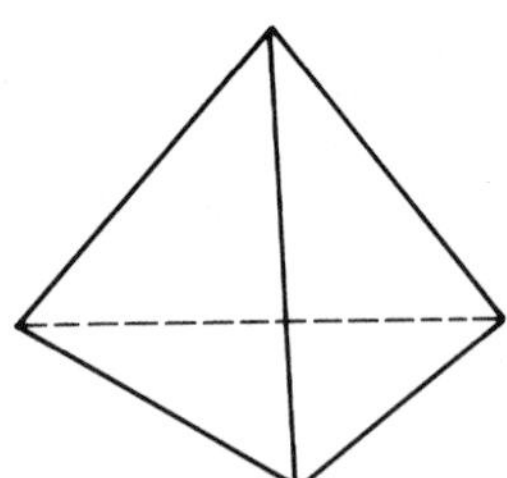

Tetrahedron
(4 equilateral triangles)

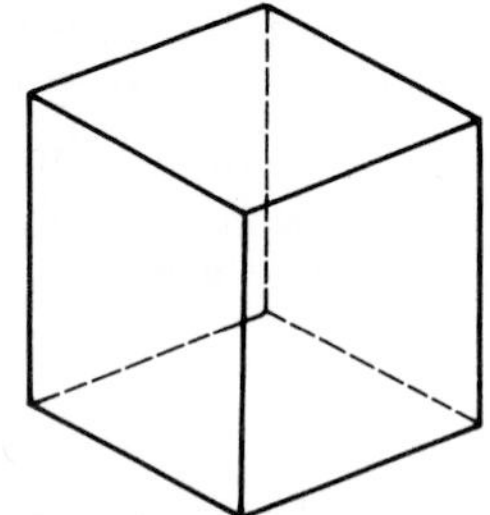

Hexahedron or Cube
(6 squares)

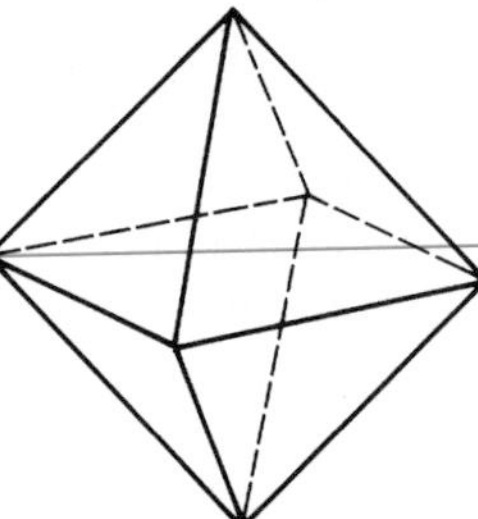

Octahedron
(8 equilateral triangles)

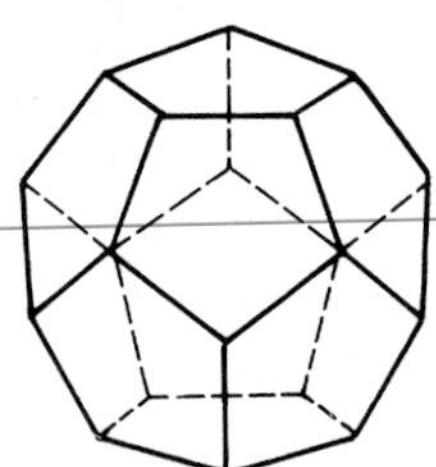

Dodecahedron
(12 regular pentagons)

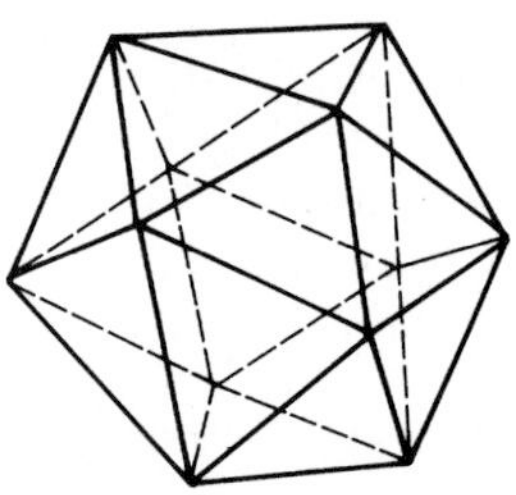

Icosahedron
(20 equilateral triangles)

Use the above figures to help you visualize patterns among these quantities for the five regular polyhedra and verify the formula $V - E + F = 2$ for each case.

V	E	F	Name
		4	Tetrahedron
		6	Cube
		8	Octahedron
		12	Dodecahedron
		20	Icosahedron

Using Mathematical Models and Manipulatives

Mathematicians and artists continue their attempts to produce physical models that simulate the abstract models that come from the mind. Students and teachers can also try their hand at homemade models, such as the five regular polyhedra, string art, roulette wheels, transits, and whatever else the imagination conjures up. Even routinely used items such as rulers, compasses, and protractors are examples of mathematical models.

EXAMPLE 1

(Probability, Algebra): *Probability Models*

Among the models commonly used to demonstrate the concept of probability are dice, spinners, playing cards, coins, and a jar filled with marbles of different colors. All are relatively easy to obtain for classroom demonstration purposes.

Although the concept "the probability that an event will occur" appears to be intuitive among many youngsters, this would seem to be not universal and so must be formally defined at the outset.

The probability P that an event will occur is

$$P = \frac{\text{number of favorable ways}}{\text{total number of possible ways}}$$

The teacher can use the models mentioned earlier to illustrate and amplify the definition.

A *die* is well known as a six-sided solid object, called a *cube*. Each side or face of the cube is a *square*. The sides are numbered 1, 2, 3, 4, 5, 6 with dots, as shown. The plural of *die* is *dice*.

Find the probability of getting a 5 when rolling a die.

ANSWER

$P(5) = 1/6$

A spinner is a simulated roulette wheel. It might contain, for example, eight regions, all of equal size, numbered 1 through 8. The arrow has an equally likely chance of landing on any of the eight regions. Assuming the arrow does not land on a line, what is the probability that it will land on 3?

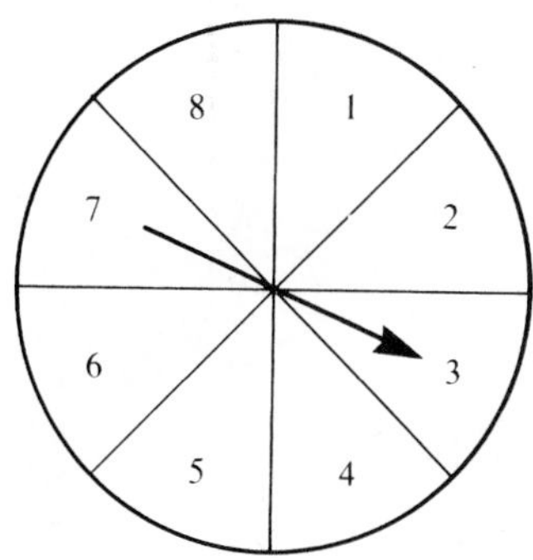

ANSWER

$P(3) = 1/8$

A standard deck of playing cards contains 52 cards. There are 4 suits: spades, diamonds, hearts, and clubs. Each suit contains 13 cards: 2, 3, 4, 5, 6, 7, 8, 9, 10, jack, queen, king, ace. Spades and clubs are black, diamonds and hearts are red.

In picking a card at random, explain why the probability of drawing (a) the two of diamonds, (b) a two, or (c) a diamond is

ANSWER

a. $P(\text{two of diamonds}) = 1/52$
b. $P(\text{two}) = 4/52 = 1/13$
c. $P(\text{diamond}) = 13/52 = 1/4$

A jar contains 8 marbles: 3 are red and 5 are white. A marble is selected at random. What is the probability that it is red?

ANSWER

$P(\text{red}) = 3/8$

Note that many variations and extensions of these problems can be developed with classes at many levels—from junior to senior high school and from basic math classes to advanced ones. Each class will, of course, have its own level of sophistication.

EXAMPLE 2

(Geometry): *Linkages*

Commercially produced models of high-quality metal or transparent plastic are commonly available and can be used by the classroom teacher with or without an overhead projector to demonstrate the following theorems:

- Alternate interior angles of two parallel lines cut by a transversal are congruent.
- Opposite sides of a parallelogram are parallel and congruent to each other.

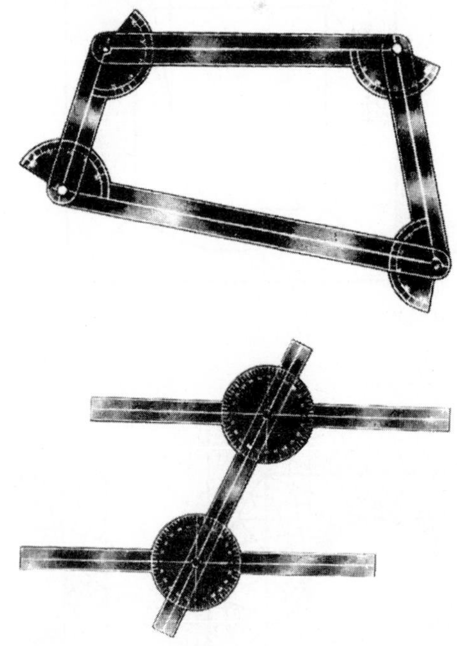

- Diagonals of a parallelogram bisect each other.
- Opposite angles of a parallelogram are congruent to each other.
- Consecutive angles of a parallelogram are supplementary.

The quadrilateral is also known as a "flexible quadrilateral" and provides a beautiful, clear, dramatic model that the teacher can hold up in front of a class, moving sides in and out while at the same time changing angle size. Students can propose a list of properties of parallelograms based on the manipulative. It is clear from manipulating the quadrilateral that diagonals of all parallelograms bisect each other but are not necessarily congruent. The Geometer's Sketchpad can serve a similar function.

EXAMPLE 3

(Geometry): *String Designs*

The straight-line segments that appear in the following diagrams suggest curves known as "envelopes." An *envelope* is a curve that is tangent to every member of a family of straight lines. Strings of several colors can be used to represent the straight lines, and these can create a variety of envelope patterns that are both colorful and beautiful. These could serve as enrichment or motivation to study geometry, especially at the junior high school level—grades 7 and 8. Class projects could be proposed that might encompass a unit in geometric designs for a mathematics class. The following vocabulary and concepts are just some of the items that might be discussed and illustrated: circle, tangent, pentagon, hexagon, rhombus, and parabolic curve.

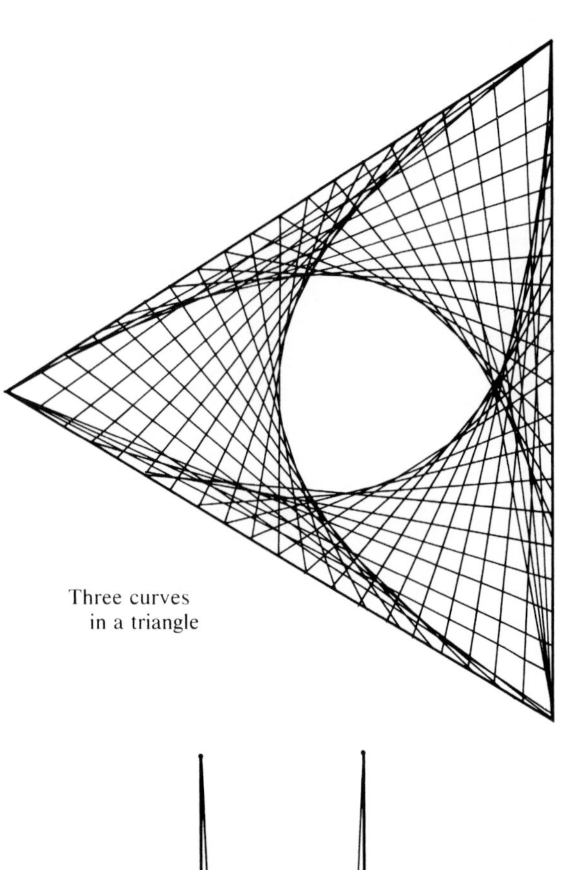

Three curves in a triangle

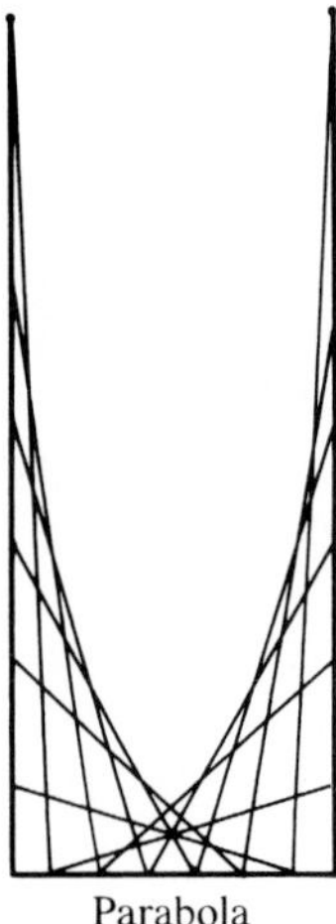

Parabola

Circle in a sqaure

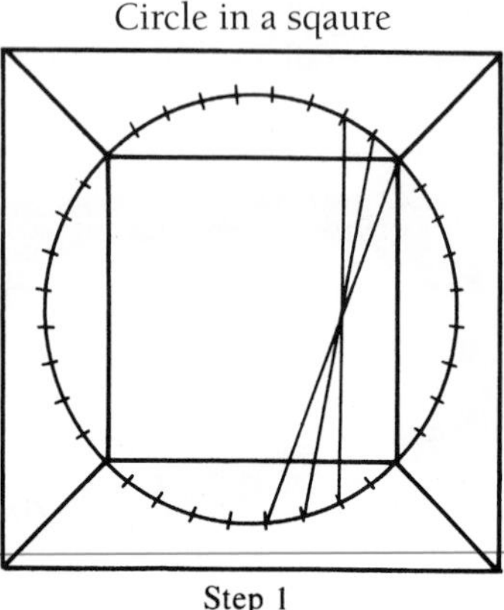

Step 1

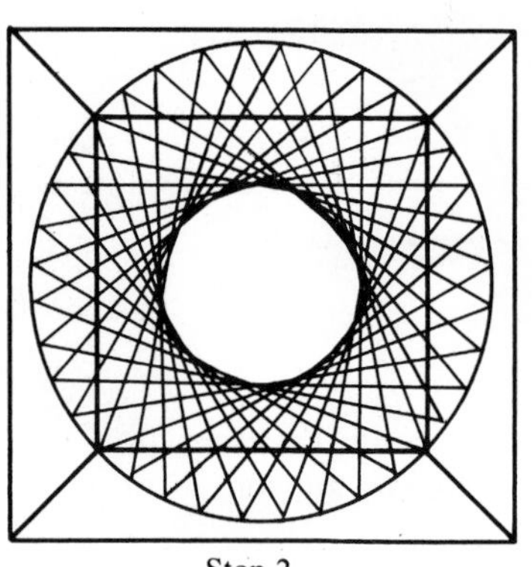

Step 2

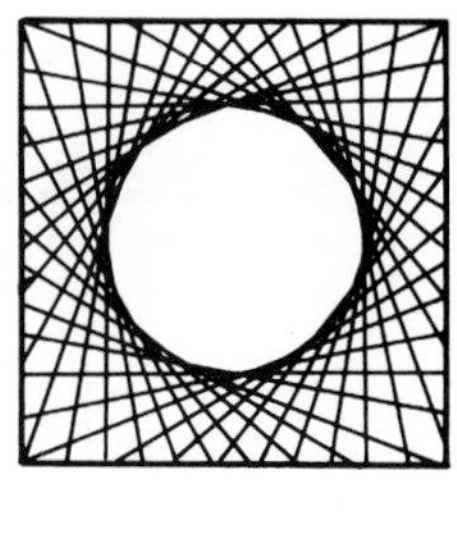

Step 3

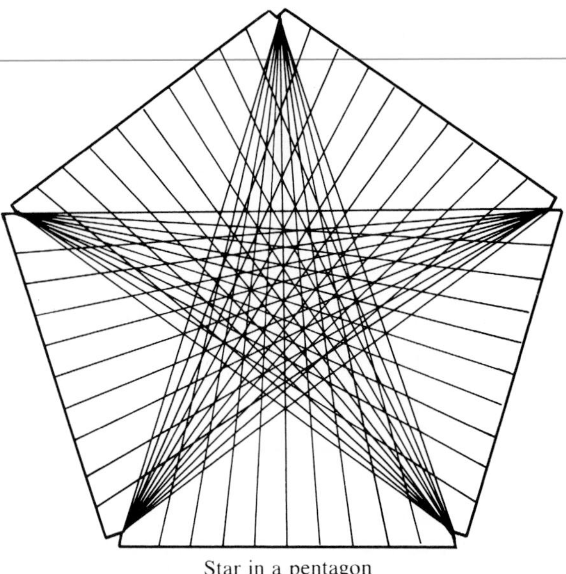

Star in a pentagon

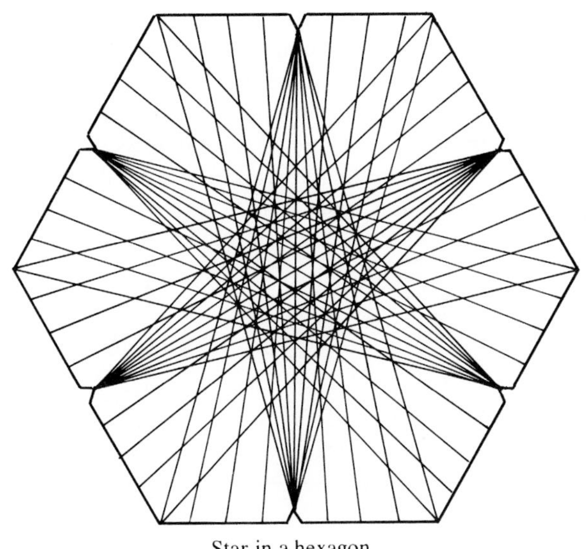
Star in a hexagon

How to Enrich Geometry Using String Diagrams by Victoria Pohl (NCTM, 1986) contains a variety of two- and three-dimensional string diagram instructions with illustrations.

As part of any project, you might also want to involve an art or computer teacher to assist in technical matters as well as an English teacher to guide the students in reading and following very detailed directions about the design constructions.

EXAMPLE 4

(Geometry): *Find the relationship between the measure of an angle and the arcs it intercepts on a circle.*

It is assumed that students have already learned that the measure of an inscribed angle of a circle is one-half the measure of its intercepted arc.

Begin by cutting out an appropriately large rectangular piece of cardboard and a cardboard circle. Staple two pieces of string to the rectangular cardboard, forming a convenient angle near the middle, and draw an angle of the same measure (as the angle formed by the two pieces of string) as an inscribed angle of the circle.

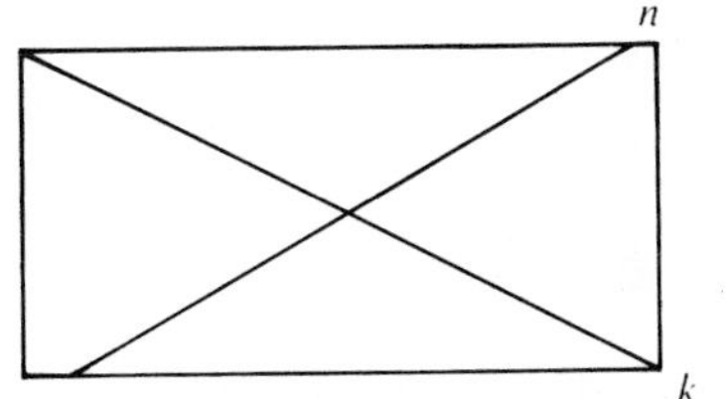

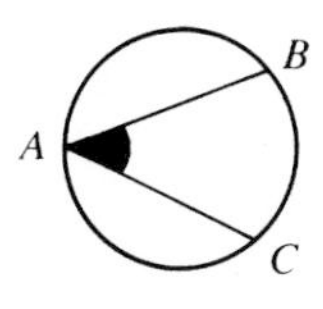

By moving the circle into various positions relative to the rectangle, all the theorems relating the circle to the different types of angles can be easily developed (and proved!).

1. An angle formed by two chords intersecting inside the circle has a measure equal to one-half the sum of the intercepted arcs.

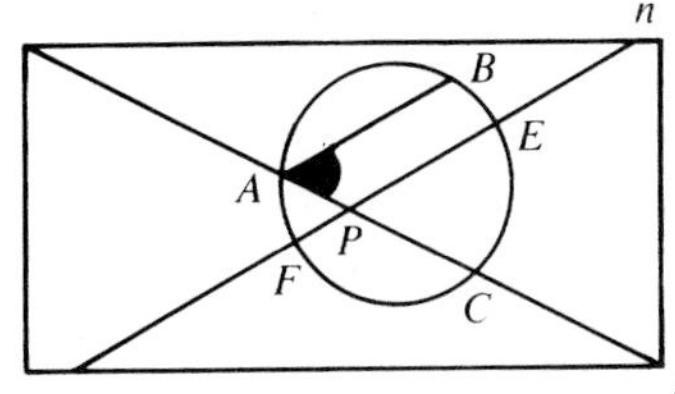

Place the circle so that $\overline{AB} \parallel n$ and $\overline{AC}$ is on k, as in the preceding figure.

$$m\angle A = \tfrac{1}{2}\, m\widehat{BEC}$$
$$m\angle A = m\angle P$$

Therefore, $m\angle P = \frac{1}{2}m\widehat{BEC} = \frac{1}{2}(m\widehat{BE} + m\widehat{EC})$. But $m\widehat{BE} = m\widehat{AF}$, therefore,

$$m\angle P = \tfrac{1}{2}(m\widehat{AF} + m\widehat{EC})$$

2. An angle formed by two secants intersecting outside the circle has a measure equal to one-half the difference of the intercepted arcs.

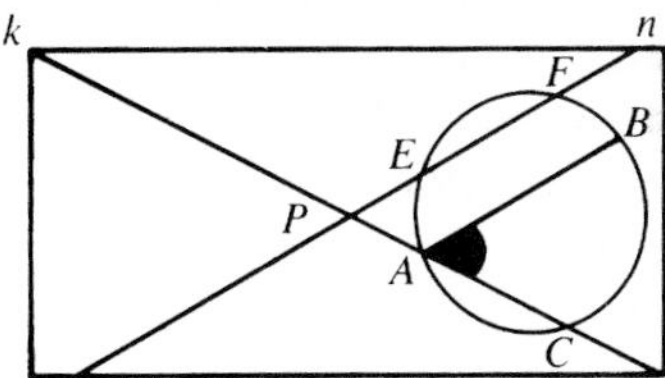

Place the circle so that $\overline{AB} \parallel n$ and $\overline{AC}$ is on k, as in the preceding figure.

$$m\angle A = \tfrac{1}{2}\widehat{BC}$$
$$m\angle A = m\angle P$$

Therefore, $m\angle P = \frac{1}{2}m\widehat{BC} = \frac{1}{2}(m\widehat{FBC} - m\widehat{FB})$. But $m\widehat{FB} = m\widehat{AE}$, therefore,

$$m\angle P = \tfrac{1}{2}(m\widehat{FBC} - m\widehat{AE})$$

A similar argument can be made for the following.

3. An angle formed by two tangents:

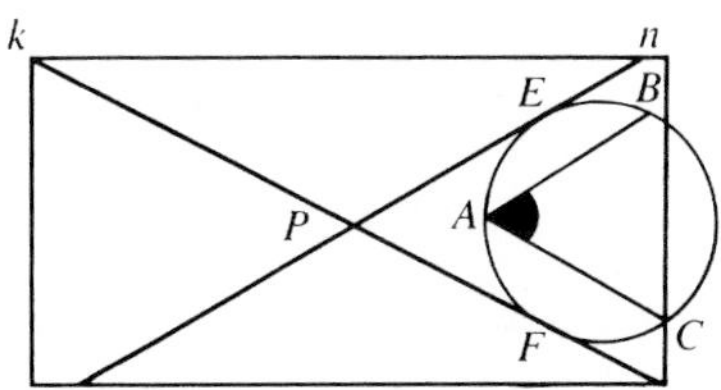

4. An angle formed by a tangent and a secant:

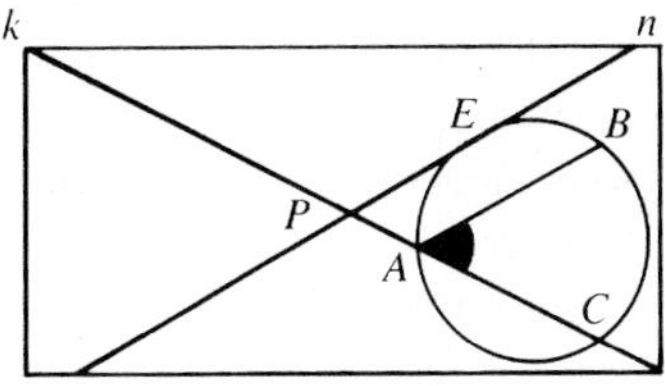

5. An angle formed by a tangent and a chord:

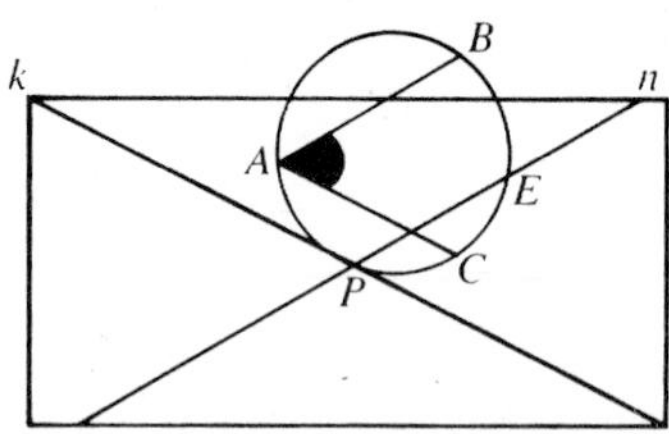

The development of each of these is very similar and allows fast proofs of all these theorems in the same lesson! An important part of this type of development is to let students anticipate each succeeding circle placement and consequent argument.

EXAMPLE 5

(Trigonometry): *Angles of Elevation and Depression*

Before beginning this lesson, pupils should be made aware of the definition of *angle of elevation* and *angle of depression*.

Definition: If an object *A* is observed from point *O*, the angle of elevation or depression is the angle that the line segment $\overline{OA}$ from the eye of the observer to the object makes with a horizontal line in the same plane.

If the object lies higher than the observer, the angle is an angle of elevation; if lower, it is an angle of depression, as in the illustrations.

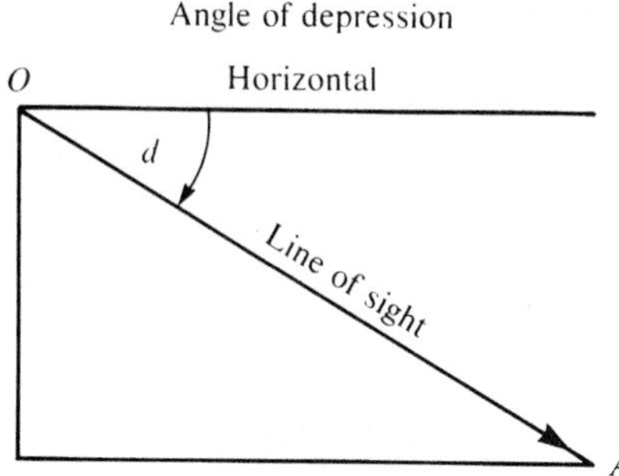

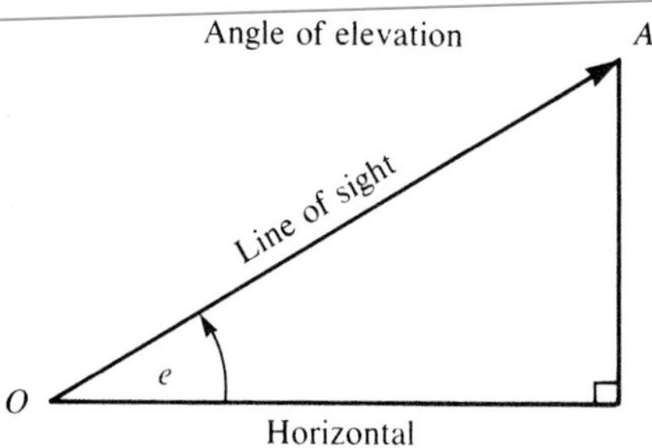

A *transit* is a device used by many engineers for measuring angles of elevation and depression. It can be acquired for use in trigonometry lessons but is rather expensive. Students can learn to construct an alternate means of determining either of these angles with only a standard student's protractor, a piece of string, and some chalk to provide weight at the end of the string.

Guide students to prove that the angle of elevation *e* of an object may be measured as follows:

Fix a protractor in a vertical position as shown in the diagram below so that the prolongation of $\overline{BO}$ passes through *A*. Your eye must guide you here as accurately as possible. You might try gluing an ordinary drinking straw along $\overline{BO}$ and looking through it as a "sight."

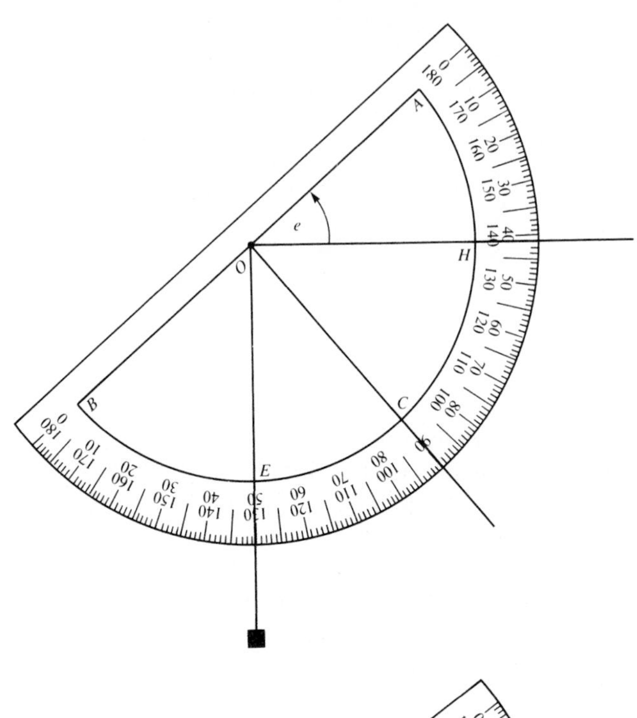

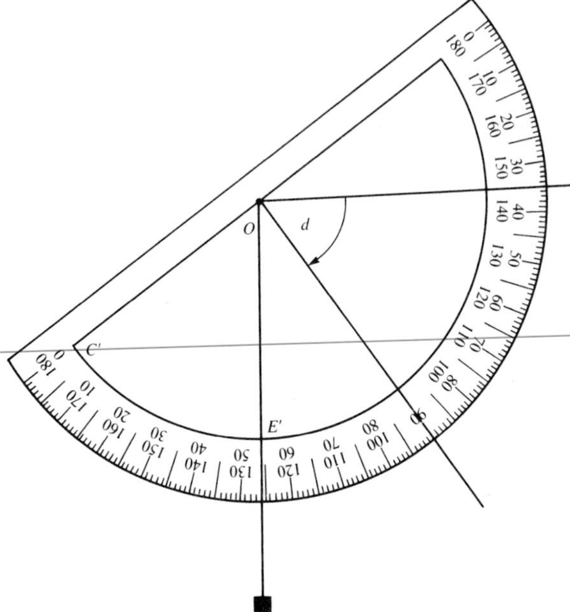

A plumb bob (string with a weight attached to one end), held by a tack or nail at point *O*, intersects arc *BC* at *E*. The angle of elevation is measured by arc *EC* on the protractor.

Similarly, arc *C′E′* measures the angle of depression *d*. Also, develop a proof for the angle of depression.

In both proofs, you must use the theorem "Complements of the same angle are congruent." Students will have no difficulty "seeing" the proofs.

EXAMPLE 6

(Intuitive Geometry): *Volumes*

Remind students that just as surface area is measured in square units, volume is measured in cubic units, such as cubic centimeters and cubic inches. Thus, if the dimensions of this box (rectangular prism) are $2 \times 3 \times 4$ centimeters, the box contains 24 cubic centimeters, as shown in the diagram.

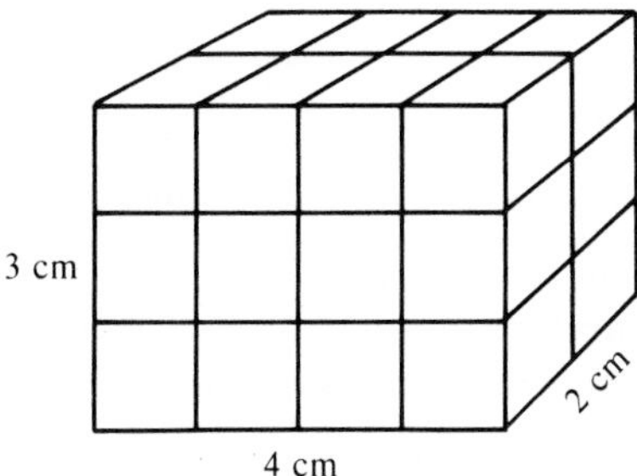

Students will readily agree that practical experience as well as some physical models will lead to the reasonable conclusion that for a rectangular solid, the volume is equal to the product of its three dimensions ($V = lwh$), or the volume is equal to the product of the area of its base and its altitude ($V = Bh$).

Another volume relationship can be demonstrated with the solids shown in the figure below. The pyramid and the prism have equal bases and equal heights. When the pyramid is filled with liquid and emptied into the prism, the prism fills up just one-third of the way.

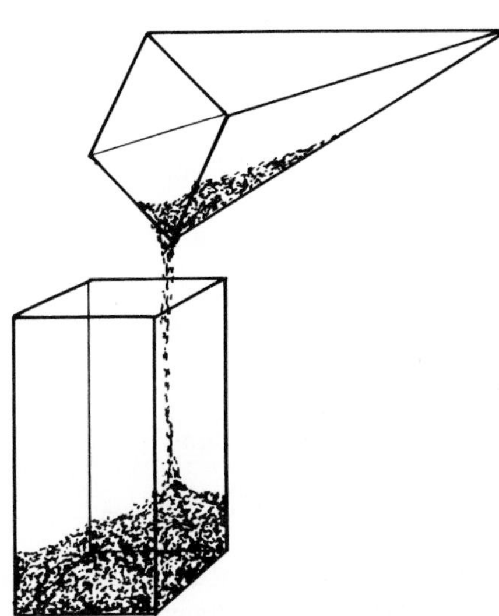

Here, too, students will agree, after some additional experimentation, that the volume of a prism is equal to the product of the area of its base and its altitude ($V = Bh$).

They will also agree that the volume of a pyramid is equal to one-third the product of the area of its base and its altitude ($V = \frac{1}{3}Bh$).

The preceding formulas are valid even when the pyramids and prisms are oblique, as shown below.

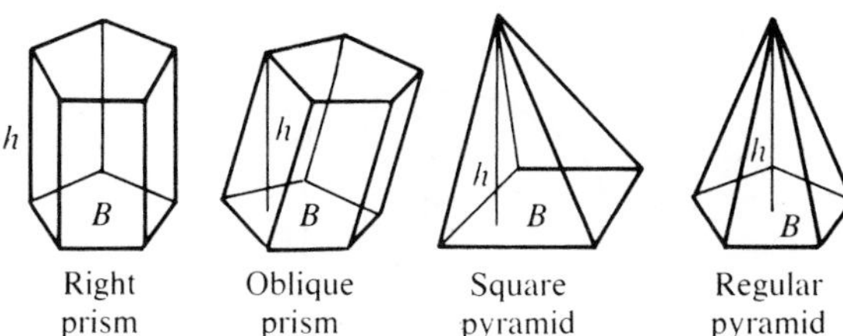

In fact, they are valid even if the base is not a polygon but curved, such as a circle. Thus, in addition to the prism we can also discuss the right circular cylinder and cone. The same formulas apply. These can, however, be adjusted by using the formula $B = \pi r^2$. In these cases the volume of a right

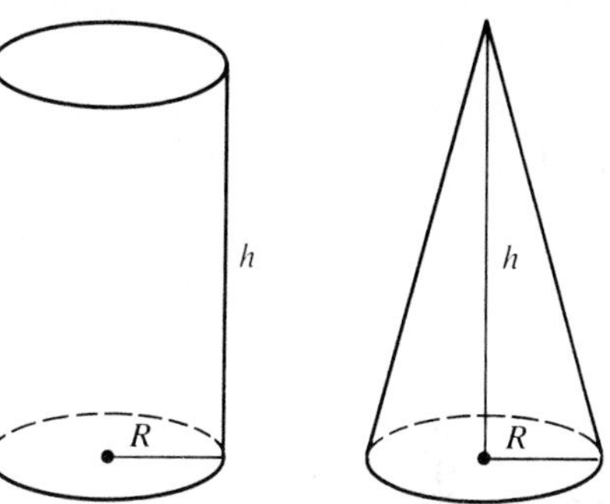

circular cylinder is $V = \pi r^2 h$ and for a right circular cone it is $V = \frac{1}{3}\pi r^2 h$. See the diagrams.

Extending Familiar Concepts

EXAMPLE 1

(Trigonometry): *Functions of an Obtuse Angle*

Before beginning this lesson, students must be familiar with the three basic trigonometric functions of an acute angle in a right triangle. These functions will be extended to an obtuse angle.

Students must also be familiar with the properties of the 30-60-90 and 45-45-90 triangles.

Consider an angle in "standard position," where the initial ray is on the x-axis and the vertex is at the origin. Let the intersection of the terminal ray and a circle of radius r centered at the origin be the point (x, y) (see the following diagram). Using the traditional definitions for the functions of an acute angle:

$$\sin\theta = \frac{\text{opposite leg}}{\text{hypotenuse}} = \frac{y}{r}$$

$$\cos\theta = \frac{\text{adjacent leg}}{\text{hypotenuse}} = \frac{x}{r}$$

$$\tan\theta = \frac{\text{opposite leg}}{\text{adjacent leg}} = \frac{y}{x}$$

Note that r is always considered to be positive.

These definitions were based on the definitions for functions of an acute angle of a right triangle. If, however, we allow the terminal side to rotate in a direction such that the angle θ

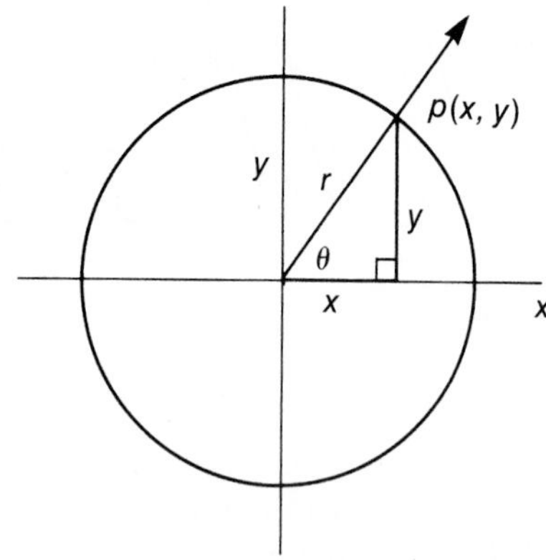

becomes right, obtuse, straight, or even negative, and if we further agree to *extend* the same definitions to these new angles, we will arrive at some very "unusual" results.

After studying the following diagrams, students should easily see that:

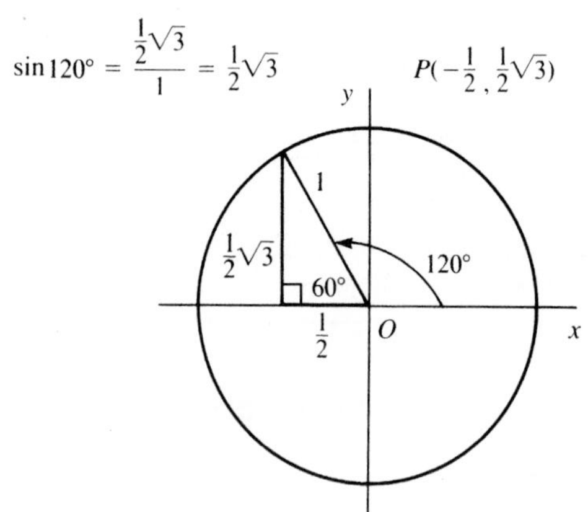

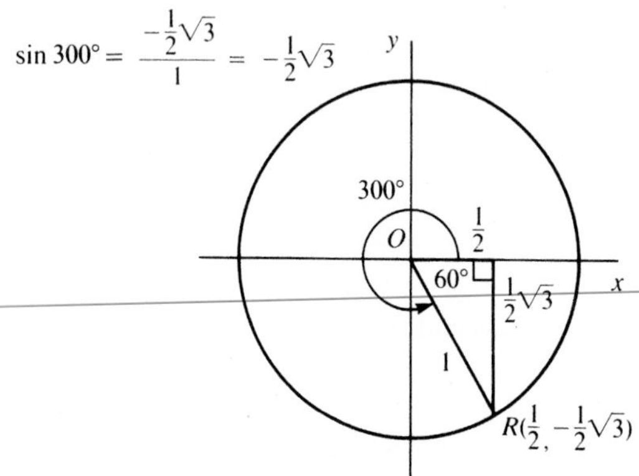

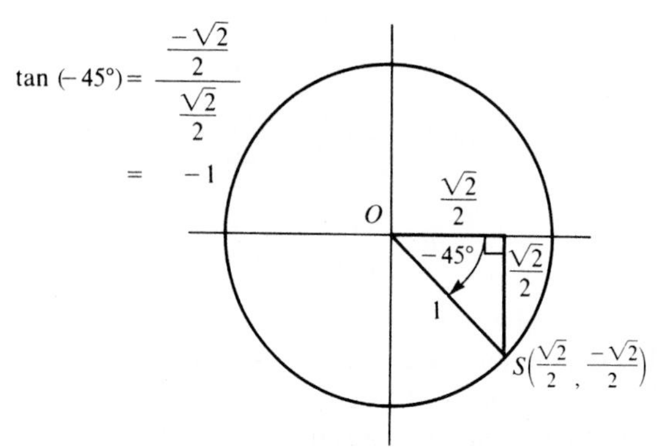

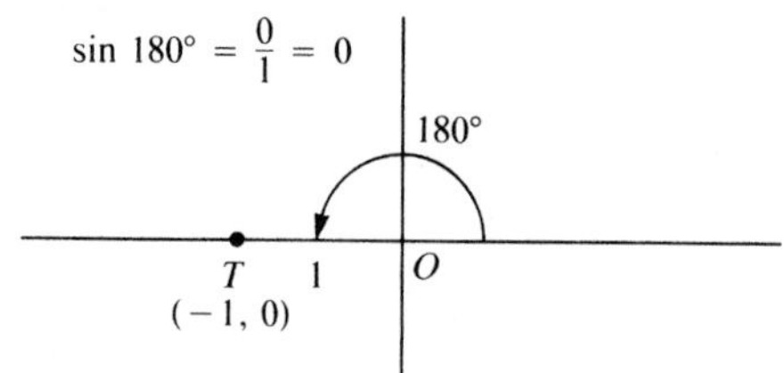

Additional practice examples must be given to reinforce these concepts.

EXAMPLE 2

(Trigonometry, Geometry): *Law of Cosines*

A traditional and simple method for introducing the law of cosines is a direct extension of the Pythagorean theorem.

Consider the acute ΔABC (with altitude $\overline{CD}$):

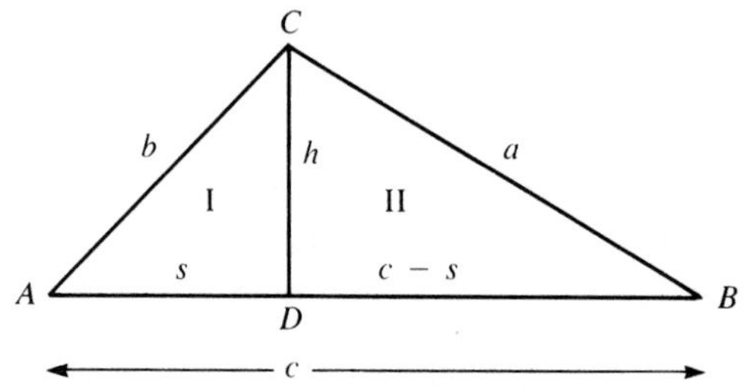

Using the Pythagorean theorem in ΔII we get

$$a^2 = h^2 + (c - s)^2$$

Then

$$a^2 = h^2 + c^2 - 2cs + s^2$$

$$a^2 = (h^2 + s^2) + c^2 - 2cs \quad [1]$$

However, using the Pythagorean theorem again, in ΔI, we get

$$h^2 + s^2 = b^2 \quad [2]$$

Also,

$$\frac{s}{b} = \cos A \quad \text{or} \quad s = b \cos A \quad [3]$$

Substituting Eqs. [2] and [3] into Eq. [1] we get

$$a^2 = b^2 + c^2 - 2bc \cos A$$

This is the law of cosines for an acute triangle.

Continue this extension by drawing an obtuse triangle, obtuse angle *C*.

EXAMPLE 3

(Algebra): *Distributivity*

In this lesson, students will extend their familiarity with arithmetic to conclude that multiplication and division are distributed over addition and subtraction and that powers and roots may be distributed over multiplication and division.

The conclusions will be arrived at as conjectures after the teacher reviews the order of operations and symbols of grouping, followed by these arithmetic illustrations:

(I) $$3(4 + 5) = 3 \cdot 4 + 3 \cdot 5?$$

Answer: YES (Multiplication may be distributed over addition.)

$$5(3 - 2) \stackrel{?}{=} 5 \cdot 3 - 5 \cdot 2$$

Answer: YES (Multiplication may be distributed over subtraction.)

(II) $$\frac{36 - 4}{4} \stackrel{?}{=} \frac{36}{4} - \frac{4}{4}$$

Answer: YES (Division may be distributed over subtraction.)

$$\frac{40 + 15}{5} = \frac{40}{5} + \frac{15}{5}?$$

Answer: YES (Division may be distributed over addition.)

(III) $$(2 + 3)^2 = 2^2 + 3^2?$$

Answer: NO (Powers are *not* distributed over addition.)

$$(2 \cdot 3)^2 = 2^2 \cdot 3^2?$$

Answer: YES (Powers may be distributed over multiplication.)

(IV) $$\sqrt{4 + 9} = 2 + 3?$$

Answer: NO (Roots are *not* distributed over addition.)

$$\sqrt{4 \cdot 9} = 2 \cdot 3?$$

Answer: YES (Roots may be distributed over multiplication.)

$$\sqrt{\frac{4}{9}} = \frac{2}{3}?$$

Answer: YES (Roots may be distributed over division.)

(V) Challenge: $$\frac{3 \cdot 5 + 2}{3} \stackrel{?}{=} 5 + 2$$

Answer: NO

The teacher should illustrate amply with examples and counter-examples, such as $2(3 \times 4)$ is *not* equal to 2×3 times 2×4. Likewise, when multiplying $0.03(2000 - x)$ by 100, only one of the factors is multiplied by 100, *not* both.

EXAMPLE 4

(Algebra): *Dividing Polynomials*

To divide one polynomial by another, we first recall how to divide two numbers in arithmetic. When we divide 806 by 26, we are really discovering how many times 26 is contained in 806 by using repeated subtraction. Using the same procedure and the same reasoning, when $x^2 + 5x + 6$ is divided by $x + 3$, we find by repeated subtraction that $x + 3$ is a factor in $x^2 + 5x + 6$, $x + 2$ times. We can thus extend the familiar arithmetic division algorithm to the algebraic division of polynomials.

A side-by-side comparison will be helpful for students. Students should be familiar with the terms *dividend, divisor*, and *quotient*.

Step	Arithmetic	Algebra
1. Usual long division:	$26\overline{)806}$	$x + 3\overline{)x^2 + 5x + 6}$
2. Divide left number of dividend by left number of divisor to get digit of the quotient.	3 $26\overline{)806}$	x $x + 3\overline{)x^2 + 5x + 6}$
3. Multiply entire divisor by first digit of quotient.	3 $26\overline{)806}$ 78	x $x + 3\overline{)x^2 + 5x + 6}$ $x^2 + 3x$
4. Subtract this answer from dividend. Bring down next number of dividend to get new dividend.	3 $26\overline{)806}$ 78 26	x $x + 3\overline{)x^2 + 5x + 6}$ $x^2 + 3x$ $2x + 6$
5. Divide left digit of new dividend by left digit of divisor. Get next number of quotient.	31 $26\overline{)806}$ 78 26	$x + 2$ $x + 3\overline{)x^2 + 5x + 6}$ $x^2 + 3x$ $2x + 6$
6. Repeat steps 3 and 4 by multiplying whole divisor by second digit of quotient. Subtract result from new dividend. Last remainder in this case is zero.	31 $26\overline{)806}$ 78 26 26 0	$x + 2$ $x + 3\overline{)x^2 + 5x + 6}$ $x^2 + 3x$ $2x + 6$ $2x + 6$ 0
	Answer: 31	*Answer:* $x + 2$

The division process for arithmetic comes to an end when the remainder is zero; for algebra it ends when the remainder is less than the divisor.

EXAMPLE 5

(Algebra): Solving Digit Problems

Students must be reminded of the meaning of hundreds (h), tens (t), and units (u) digits and should then be shown how to express two- and three-digit numbers in terms of these letters. Assign drill and practice.

Ask students to select any three-digit number with all digits different. Let us select 365. Have students write all possible two-digit numbers using the digits 3, 6, and 5. Now find the sum of these numbers:

$$\begin{array}{r} 36 \\ 35 \\ 63 \\ 53 \\ 65 \\ \underline{56} \\ 308 \end{array}$$

Now divide this sum by the sum of these digits, $3 + 6 + 5 = 14$;

$$\frac{308}{14} = 22$$

Students will wonder why everyone gets 22 as the answer regardless of which number was selected at the start. The justification for this can lead to a discussion of what are traditionally known as "digit problems."

Justification: Let the three-digit number be represented by $100h + 10t + u$. The six possible numbers are:

$$\begin{array}{l} 10h + t \\ 10t + h \\ 10h + u \\ 10u + h \\ 10t + u \\ 10u + t \end{array}$$

The sum is $20(h + t + u) + 2(h + t + u) = 22 \times (h + t + u)$. Now we are asked to divide by the sum of the digits, $(h + t + u)$, so $22(h + t + u)/(h + t + u) = 22$.

When using this type of development, you must keep a clear focus on the purpose of this "trick."

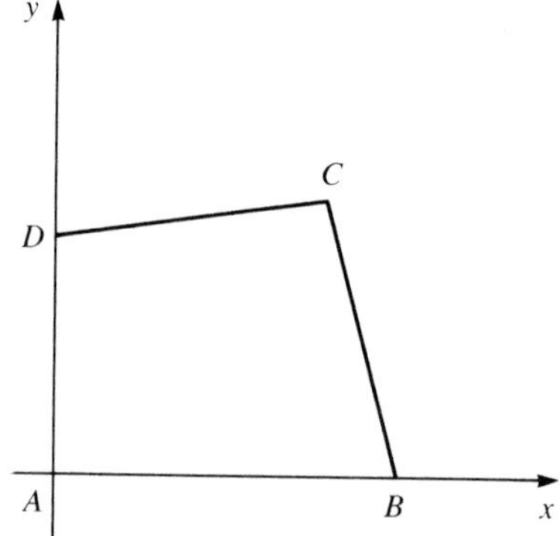

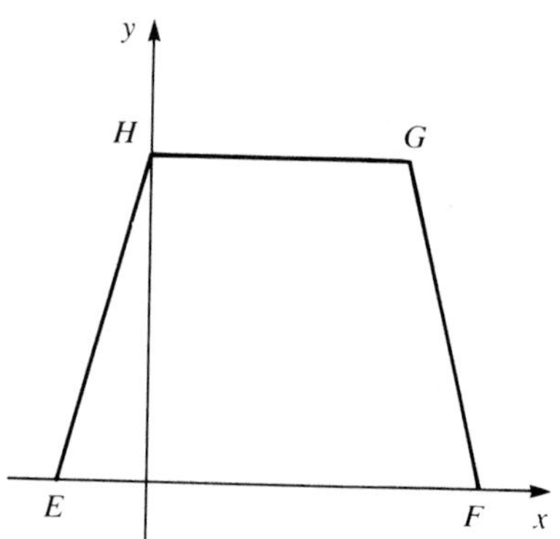

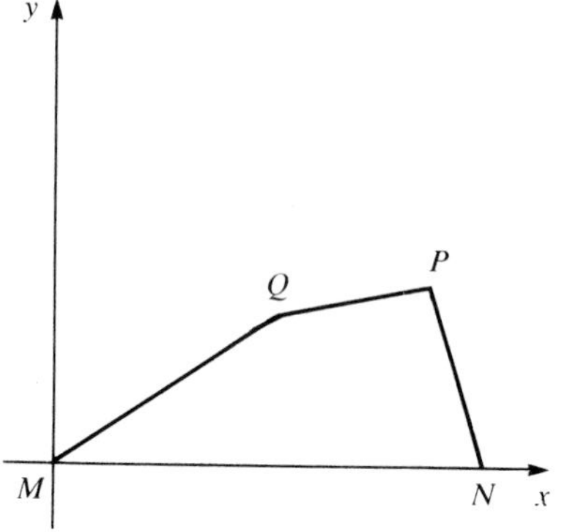

EXAMPLE 6

(Geometry): *Use methods of coordinate geometry to prove that the diagonals of a parallelogram bisect each other.*

Many exercises of plane geometry can be proved more easily by methods of coordinate geometry than by those of Euclidean plane geometry.

When solving an exercise by means of coordinate geometry, half the battle in finding a proof is often won by setting it up well. It is frequently helpful to use the origin and one of the axes as vertex and side, respectively. (Below are some sample useful placements of quadrilaterals.)

For this exercise, students must be familiar with simple coordinate geometry principles such as plotting points on a coordinate plane, midpoint formula, and definition and properties of a parallelogram.

SOLUTION

Place vertex A of parallelogram $ABCD$ on the origin and one side along the x-axis. Use $(a, 0)$ as the coordinates of B, and (c, b) for C. The coordinates of D will be $(c - a, b)$. From the midpoint formula, the midpoint of $\overline{AC}$ is $\left(\frac{c}{2}, \frac{b}{2}\right)$, and the midpoint of $\overline{BD}$ is

$$\left(\frac{a + c - a}{2}, \frac{b}{2}\right) = \left(\frac{c}{2}, \frac{b}{2}\right)$$

Since the diagonals have the same midpoint, they bisect each other.

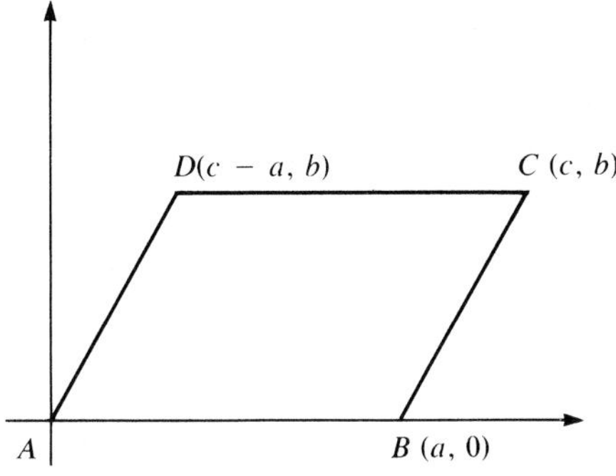

EXAMPLE 7

(Calculus): *Use a graphing calculator to investigate the number of relative maximum and minimum points in a polynomial function of order n.*

Before beginning the investigation, students should draw the graph of a straight line, $y = ax + b$. They should know that this is a function of the first degree, which may look something like this:

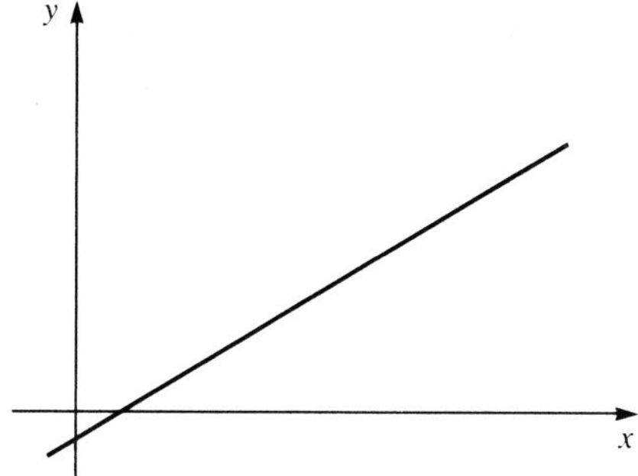

Next, draw a function of the second degree. The equation has the general form

$$y = ax^2 + bx + c$$

and looks something like this (a parabola) (note the possible positions):

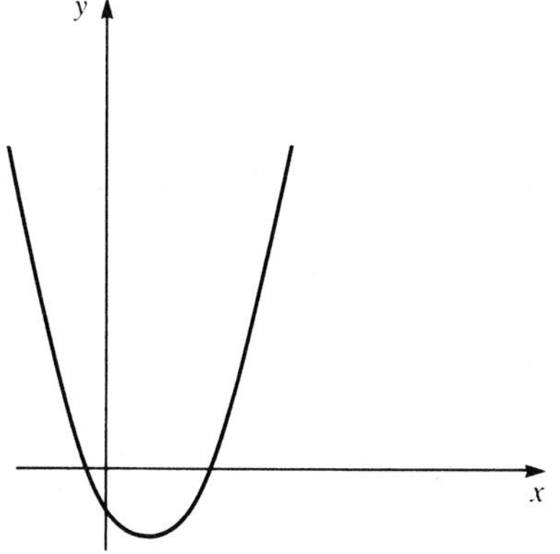

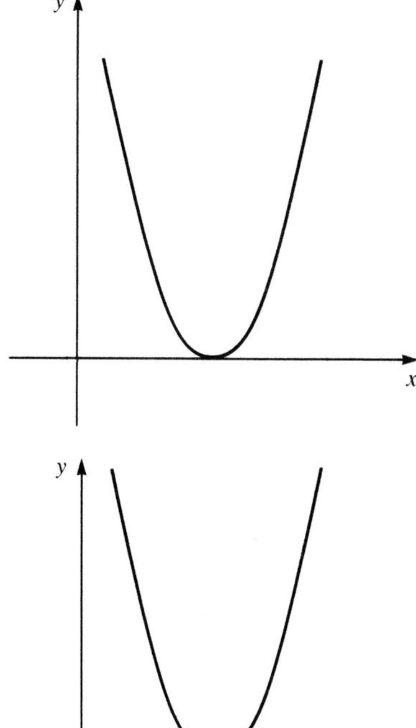

Next, obtain a picture of a third-degree polynomial function (a cubic function):

$$y = ax^3 + bx^2 + cx + d$$

(Note the possible positions.)

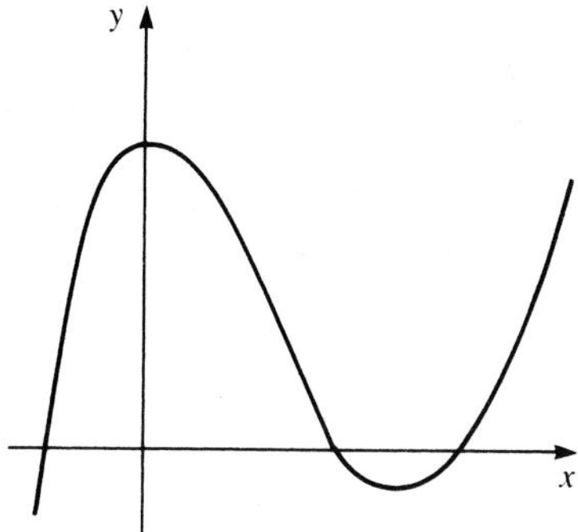

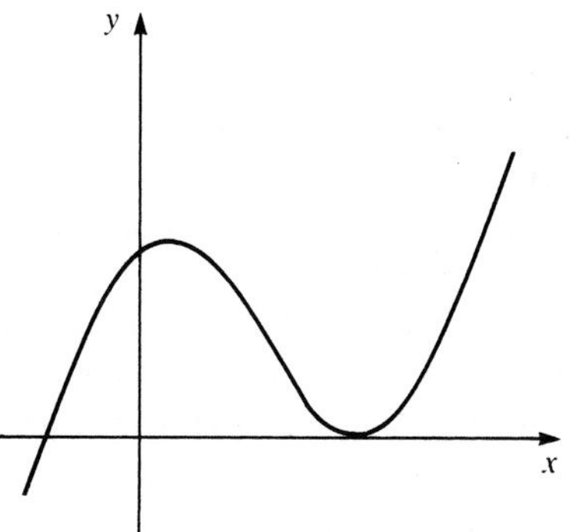

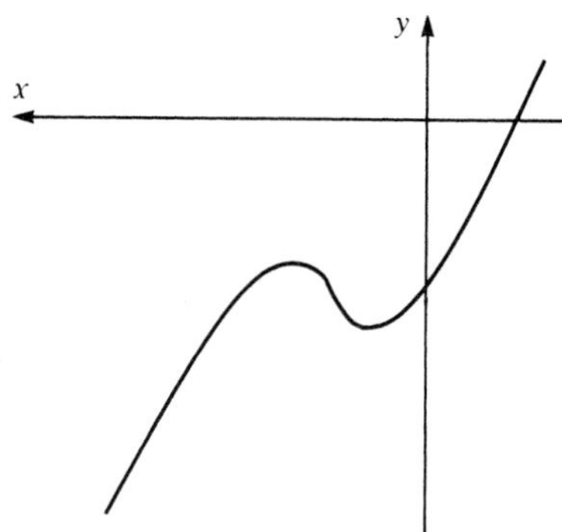

Finally, a picture of a fourth-degree polynomial function (a quartic function):

$$y = ax^4 + bx^3 + cx^2 + dx + e$$

(Note the possible positions.)

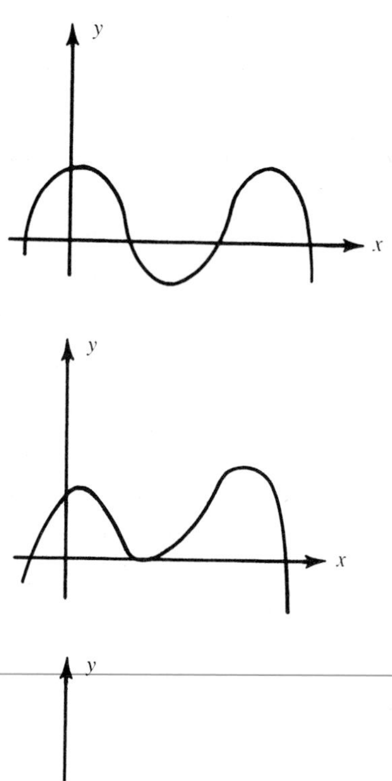

Study all the diagrams to conclude as follows:

- A first-degree function has 0 relative maximum or minimum points.
- A second-degree function has 1 relative maximum or minimum point.
- A third-degree function has at most 2 maximum or minimum points.
- A fourth-degree function has at most 3 maximum or minimum points.

Students should now be able to generalize, on an informal level only, the maximum number of relative maximum and minimum points for a polynomial function of order n.

Further analysis with calculus would be in order at this time.

Using a Graphing Calculator

EXAMPLE 1

(Calculus): *Use a graphing calculator to find the real positive root of the equation* $x^3 - 2x - 5 = 0$ *correct to three decimal places.*

After the graph appears on the screen, the root of the equation (i.e., the zero of the function) is obtained by finding its intersection with the x-axis. The zero may be determined to any reasonable degree of precision by placing the cursor as near as possible to the intersection with the x-axis and then repeating the process on a magnification of the graph until desired accuracy is achieved. The approximate value of the root, 2.095, will appear on the screen (see figure below).

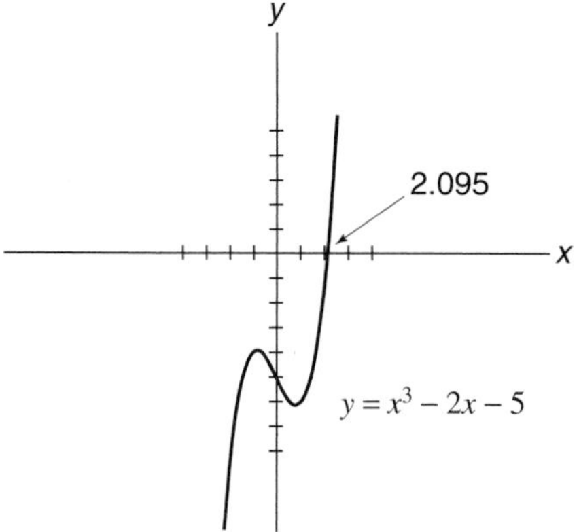

Summary

In a past era, a chalkboard and a piece of chalk were the only tools a teacher needed to present a good lesson. This is not true any longer, especially because we are all accustomed to viewing "perfect" performances on our television and movie screens.

If teachers hope to attract students' attention, they must compete with the image of the professional, highly paid actor or actress. Thus, a teacher now needs those tools and skills that may be used in each "performance." Among these are the ability to respond on the spot to clear up a youngster's confusion about difficult mathematics concepts when noticing confusion in a student's eyes, being a skilled mathematician who is at ease with mathematics and its history, and the ability to respond to any related questions. The creative teacher can also design and produce overhead projector acetates, string art, models, and appropriate graphics problems. This chapter illustrated some strategies and tools teachers can use to produce more effective lessons.

The interaction among students sitting together in a small or large room, under a teacher's guidance, also produces mental stimulation and challenge not produced by sitting alone in front of a screen.

EXERCISES

1. Write a lesson using number patterns and Pascal's triangle for
   a. 8th grade
   b. 12th grade
2. Write a lesson on the properties of a rhombus.
3. Write a lesson on probability with and without replacement that asks students to engage in higher order thinking. Defend your ideas.

4a. Prepare a lesson with three word problems to be solved in a first-year algebra class. (*Suggestion:* Use an overhead projector and a graphing calculator.)

b. Ask students to use your word problems as a basis for creating five new, similar problems.

5. Prepare a lesson on "The sum of the angles of a triangle, quadrilateral, pentagon, etc., is constant (for each type of polygon)" using paper folding and/or physical models.
6. Develop a geometry lesson that uses geoboards.
7. Write a whole class trigonometry lesson that introduces graphs of trigonometric functions. (*Suggestion:* Use a graphing calculator.)

Literacy in Mathematics

Literacy in any language is usually associated with the ability to read, write, and reason. However, when it comes to the language of mathematics, literacy is often associated with the ability to manipulate numbers and symbols using the principles of mathematics and their related algorithms; all too few teachers consider a student's reading and writing skills while formulating a mathematics lesson. Such a traditional concept of literacy in mathematics is no longer in line with contemporary curricula and assessments. To be mathematically literate in today's classroom, a student must be comfortable with the rich and diverse language that is mathematics.

Language Acquisition

Just as teachers in a language course, mathematics teachers must guide their students toward developing a sound vocabulary. One way to accomplish this is to point out the use of mathematical terms outside of mathematics. For example, from where does the term *acute angle* come? It comes from the fact that an angle whose measure is less than 90° may be considered a "sharp" point if it is used as an arrowhead. Acute means sharp, as in "an acute pain." Similarly, an obtuse angle used in this way would be seen as "dull" or "blunt." A person described as obtuse is not a particularly sharp or bright person. To learn the meanings of the most frequently used mathematical terms without connecting them back to their common English usage deprives students of getting a genuine understanding of the terms involved and keeps them from appreciating the richness and logical use of the English language.

Additional strategies for vocabulary development are outlined in resources such as *The Teaching of Reading in Mathematics* by M. Barton and C. Heidema (2002). One strategy, titled "Verbal and Visual Word Association (VVWA)," places a vocabulary word into one section of a four-by-four graphic. The remaining three sections are filled with a visual representation of the word, a definition and/or equation, and, finally, a personal association.

For example, the VVWA for the word *slope* might look something like this:

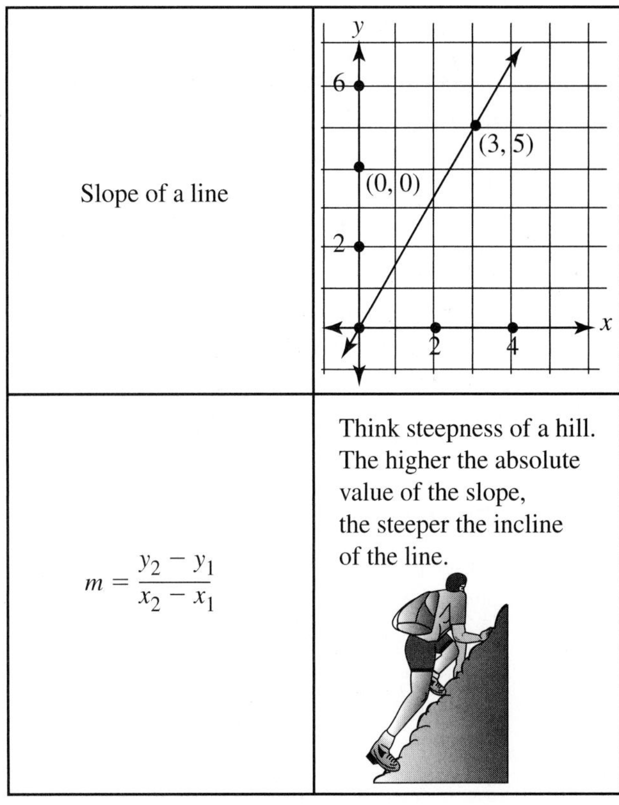

Adapted from *Teaching Reading in Mathematics, 2/e* (p. 85), by M. L. Barton and C. Heidema, 2002, Aurora, CO: Mid-Continental Research for Education and Learning.

Familiarizing students with new words is not the only vocabulary task for mathematics teachers. In fact, sometimes an already familiar word in Standard English has a much more precise and, at times, somewhat different meaning in mathematics. Examples of such words are *simplify*, *similar*, *factor*, *rational*, *irrational*, *radical*, and *odd*.

For example, 5 is an "odd" number, but 1,000,504 is not.

In the figures below, A and C are similar but B is similar to neither A nor C.

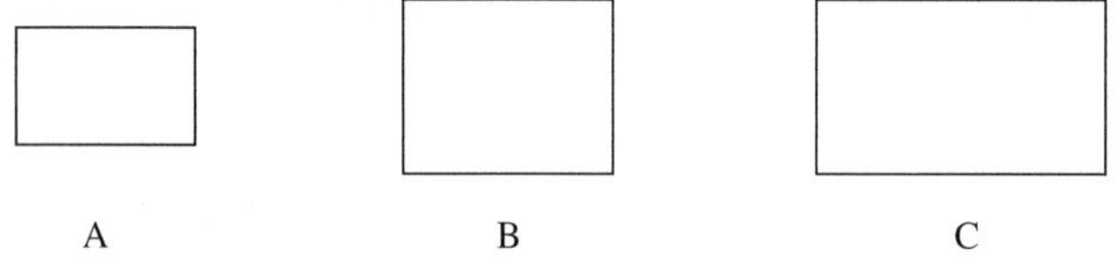

A B C

Whether introducing students to new words or revisiting familiar ones, a mathematics teacher must lay the groundwork for a solid mathematics vocabulary. As students develop so should their vocabulary, and precision in word choice is the next step in the language acquisition process. Students should be encouraged to use appropriate language such as substituting "numerator" for "top number" or "invert the divisor" instead of "flip the second number." For only through the use of appropriate language can one become proficient.

The use of compare and contrast activities is another way to deepen the understanding of mathematical concepts. For example, asking students to compare and contrast terms such as *congruent* and *similar* leads them to a deeper understanding of these commonly used mathematical terms. A Characteristic Table (see below) is an especially potent tool for guiding students in this kind of critical analysis. In our example Characteristic Table, students are asked to choose which characteristics of similar and congruent polygons are always true. The teacher has already chosen the characteristics for the students to consider. However, depending on the level of the class, the teacher might allow the students to come up with the characteristics themselves, making the exercise all the more challenging. Students should investigate polygons that they have classified as similar and congruent before completing the table. After completing the table, they should describe in their own words how such objects are alike and how they are different.

CHARACTERISTICS TABLE

In the table below, identify the characteristics of similar and congruent polygons that are always true.

Relation	Measures of corresponding sides are equal	Measures of corresponding sides are proportional	Measures of corresponding angles are equal
Similar Polygons		X	X
Congruent Polygons	X	X	X

Both the VVWA four-by-four graphic and the Characteristic Table are examples of graphic organizers. These pedagogical tools, whether they are tables, charts, or diagrams, help teachers and students organize information in a visual format. In this manner, graphic organizers facilitate the student's ability to see the connections between the vocabulary word and its use in real-world mathematics.

In concert with developing their students' vocabulary, today's mathematics teachers must focus on bolstering reading comprehension skills in the classroom.

Comprehension

At one time early reading comprehension strategies for mathematics centered on looking for *key words*. However, this only worked well for problems that were written specifically for such words. Today's assessments no longer comprise low-level cognitive tasks and specially constructed word problems. They instead comprise word problems that test students' ability to first understand the problem and, only then, to solve it. For example, students who were taught to read a problem and look for key words to identify the appropriate operation used in its solution might find the following problem especially confusing.

> Samantha was given a bag of candy for her birthday. She suspects her little brother, Manny, may have eaten some of the candy. Samantha tries to determine how many pieces of candy her brother has eaten. The information on the package says that the total weight of the candy is 210 grams. Samantha's bag now weighs 144 grams, much less than the amount indicated on the package. She finds that, on average, one piece of candy weighs about 6 grams. Approximately how many pieces of candy are missing from the bag?

Although the key words *total*, *less than*, and *average* may be clues in how to solve this problem, the reader must understand the context of the problem and how the information provided is related in order to find a reasonable answer. Therefore, students who have relied on the key-word approach to problem solving may need help as they transition to more complex problem-solving situations.

To ease this transition, mathematics teachers should encourage their students to reflect on the problem-solving process itself. In fact, the key to today's method of teaching mathematics is motivating students to reason and express themselves in the language of mathematics when tackling a word problem.

Some motivational strategies for guiding students to solutions of word problems are:

- Have the student read the problem and identify what information is given and what the problem is asking them to find. (*Note*: Some students will benefit from the use of colored highlighters to identify parts of the text that include this information.)
- Have the student read the problem and explain it to a friend.
- Have the student read the problem and produce a visual representation.
- Have the student read the problem and write down in prose how they might approach the solution.

Each of the options listed above can be expanded into problem-solving exercises called "think alouds." These exercises encourage students to play to their individual strengths and preferences when it comes to attacking a word problem. During the think alouds, individual students discuss each step of the thought process as opposed to merely going up to the board and solving the problem. In other words, if students choose to produce a visual representation, they will expain what pieces of information from the problem went into the picture. Such exercises will free students from the frustration of not understanding how a problem is initially attacked, a common reason for students throwing their arms up in defeat.

Discussing missteps or unsuccessful strategies that were tried and discarded is also helpful. This shows the class that even top mathematics students have been known to begin solving a problem with faulty strategies. In addition to providing students with self-confidence, such an exercise reinforces the importance of constant self-reflection in problem solving. Mathematics teachers should encourage all of their students to constantly monitor their strategies and thinking as they work through a task.

Semantic Mapping

The journey toward mathematical literacy is a long one, and students should not forget past paths when heading into new territory. A semantic map is an especially useful tool for teachers and students alike to evoke prior knowledge and experiences. To begin a semantic map, students are presented with a term and then asked to compile a list of words or phrases they associate with this term. After the brainstorming activity, students present and classify their lists to create the semantic map as a whole-group activity. The figure below shows a possible result of this activity using the term *problem solving*. The semantic map allows the teacher to informally assess prior student knowledge and determine where to begin the discussion. For example, the semantic map below shows that these students have had significant experience with problem solving and developed differing dispositions toward the topic. However, they only recalled five of the ten problem-solving strategies outlined in this textbook (see Chapter 4). Thus, the teacher might want to begin with problems that can be solved using the other five strategies: adopting a different point of view, considering extreme cases, intelligent guessing and testing, accounting for all possibilities, or logical reasoning.

Guided Reading

One of the most underutilized tools available to support student literacy is the mathematics textbook. Today's textbooks are written with diverse learners in mind and can be used to support the vocabulary building and problem-solving skills we have been discussing. Mathematics teachers can encourage students to read the textbook by making it part of a homework assignment that includes a guided reading outline in addition to assigning problems. The guided reading portion of the assignment should included reading comprehension questions and vocabulary building activities that use graphic organizers such as the VVWA and the compare and contrast tables discussed earlier in this section. In addition, students could be asked to copy solved problems and justify each step of the solution in the students' own words.

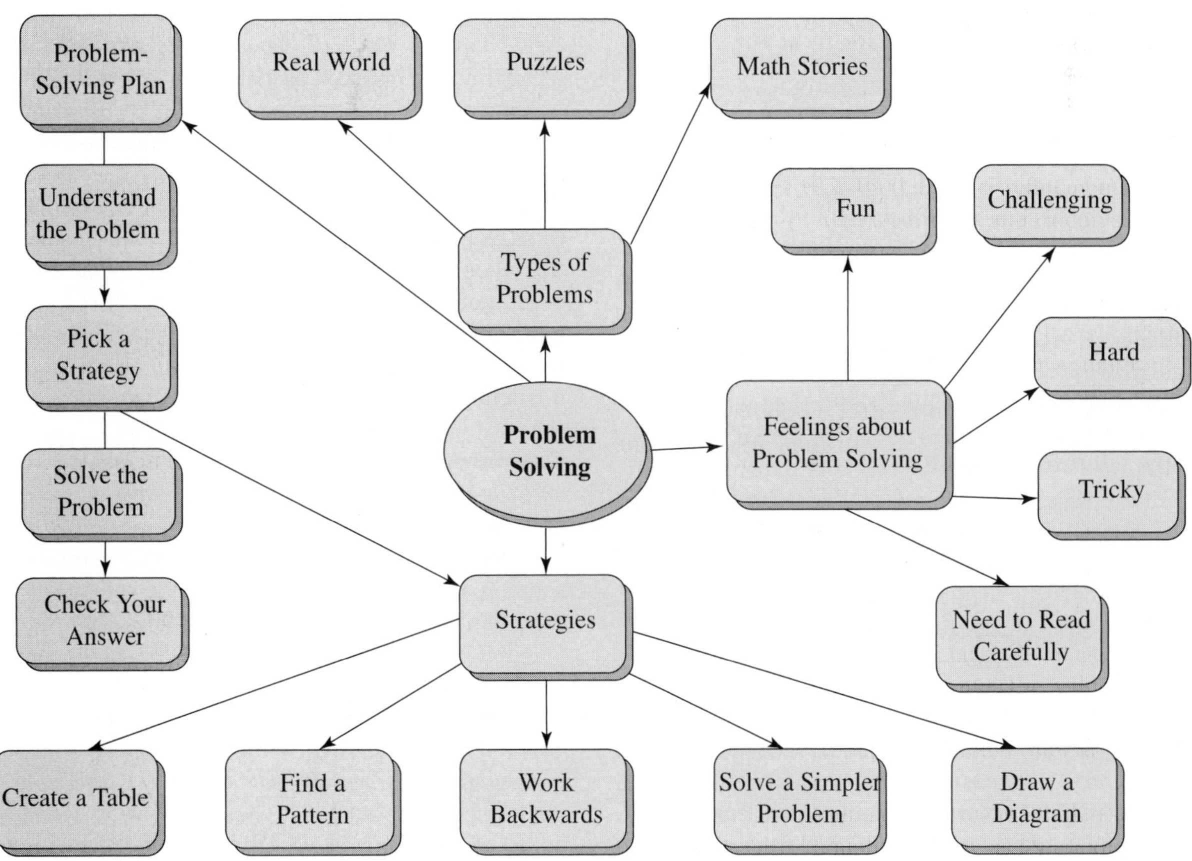

Rich Mathematical Literacy Environment

Literacy in mathematics can be bolstered in the classroom itself. Mathematics teachers should use their physical spaces to foster literacy. For example, one classroom wall can be designated the "word wall." This wall can be used in conjunction with a student-maintained glossary to improve vocabulary. Thus, whenever a student encounters an unfamiliar word, the teacher should place it on the word wall and then have the students place the definition into their glossaries. The classroom's other walls can be covered with student-generated VVWAs and problem-solving posters. Teachers might even use part of their materials budget to put up bookshelves for mathematical-related readings. Age-appropriate books on the history of mathematics, interesting problems and puzzles, and interdisciplinary applications of mathematics can support enrichment activities or engage students who finish tests early. In short, the mathematics classroom can be made an even more colorful and stimulating environment that lends itself to literacy in mathematics.

Writing

The average mathematics teacher usually responds to the suggestion of incorporating writing assignments into the classroom with astonishment, claiming that there is hardly enough time to do the mathematics, let alone additional work with writing. The advantage of writing is that it allows students to reflect on the ideas of the class, because the process requires a slower form of thinking than does oral expression.

Much psychological literature indicates that students who verbalize their learning have a far better recall of that learning, and students who write these newly learned concepts have a far more precise recall of that learning than students who do neither. Therefore, writing would appear to be a strengthening factor in the learning process. This section explores a variety of ways in which writing can be incorporated into the mathematics classroom. Illustrative examples provide further clarification of these suggestions.

There are various formats in which writing can be used in the mathematics classroom. One such format is the *student log*. Such logs summarize either a class activity (usually done on a regular basis) or students' experiences when working on their homework assignments. A second type of writing is the *student journal*. A journal differs from a log in that the journal is more informal and includes perceptions and student opinions about the material that has been covered, whereas a log is merely a report of material covered. A rather broad form of writing is *exposition*, in which students write about assigned mathematical topics or themes. This activity can include explorations as well as merely reporting.

Student Logs

A student log, the more formal reporting of a learning activity, can be a highly structured instrument, with several subtitles for easy entry. Students might be given sheets listing categories such as date, title, new relationships learned, new definitions, how to do something new, and important things to remember, and all they need do is respond to each category. In all writing assignments, students should be urged to write complete sentences rather than just key words. These writing assignments force them to verbalize, thereby further strengthening their understanding.

Student Journals

A journal can become the students' most direct form of communication with the teacher. It may be a daily, less formal form of reporting than the log. Students are urged to write about what they have just learned, to note any important facts, and to comment on this recent learning experience.

It is desirable for teachers to read the journals daily and to respond to students, also in writing, about what they read. Besides benefiting the students, who are allowed to less formally verbalize their understanding of the new mathematics presented, the journal writing assignments also provide the teacher with an excellent opportunity to assess the students' understanding of the concepts being presented to them. Students will find their own learning enhanced, and they will have a complete record of what they have learned. The students may begin to realize that they are now involved in a direct daily communication with the teacher. The extra work that journal writing requires is more than offset by the insights that it gives the teacher into the students and their learning habits.

Exposition

Expository writing is an activity used to explore further the material presented in the classroom, to help the students understand better the material presented in the classroom, or to expand or extend the material considered in the classroom (see Chapter 7 on "Enriching Mathematics Instruction" for the distinction between "expand" and "extend").

Some examples of the ways in which expository writing may be used in the context of mathematics instruction follow.

EXPLAINING A CONCEPT Students might be asked to explain a concept in their own words, such as "In what instances is multiplication used in calculating probability, and in what instances is addition used in calculating probability?" Another possible topic for an expository writing assignment might be "Connect the concept of locus with its use in everyday life," or "Explain the significance of the Pythagorean theorem in trigonometry."

EXPLAINING AN ALGORITHM (OR DESCRIBING A PROCESS) Students might be asked to present a written explanation of how an arithmetic operation, such as division of fractions, is performed or how a particular algebraic expression can be simplified. This type of activity entices students to inventory their thinking and formulate it in a logical way to make it intelligible to someone else.

EXPLAINING A THEOREM Here students would be asked not only to explain a particular theorem but also to justify it and thereby give a paragraph proof. It could be a simple theorem or a complex one, such as "The line segment joining the midpoints of two sides of a triangle is parallel to and one-half the length of the third side." The students should be encouraged to explain the theorem in their own words, not merely to paraphrase it.

DESCRIBING OR INTERPRETING A GRAPH The students might be given a mathematical curve and asked to try to explain curve inflection, turning point(s), slope, or any other features that can be described about it. Alternatively, students might be shown a descriptive graph, such as a statistical one from a newspaper, and be asked to explain what the graph tells the reader. Not only should the students read the graph and explain directly what they see, but they should also be encouraged to interpret what is being presented. A graphing calculator might be helpful for interpreting the graph of a polynomial or transcendental function.

DISCUSSING THE SOLUTION TO A PROBLEM After having solved a problem, students might be asked to write an explanation of the solution. Not only does this activity give them, or their group, a chance to bask in the success of having solved the problem, but it also forces them to reinforce that success by verbalizing it! This verbalization will help reinforce further their understanding of the solution.

WRITING A PROBLEM Composing a problem, particularly a word problem, can be a very challenging activity for most students; however, they should be encouraged to do that and, of course, to provide a solution. The problem can be on something very simple, drawing on examples in everyday life, or it can cover topics previously presented in the classroom. Students should be encouraged not merely to change numbers and repeat a textbook problem, but rather to pull a problem out of their everyday experiences that relates to the techniques learned in the mathematics classroom.

CONNECTING THE MATHEMATICAL SIGNIFICANCE WITH A PARTICULAR NEWSPAPER ARTICLE Either the students might be asked to find an article that uses some mathematics to describe a situation or the teacher might select a few representative articles from local newspapers and have the students write about the mathematics in them. There are advantages to both tasks. Students should be encouraged to feel free about their interpretations and about where they see mathematics applied. Thus, their work is open ended, which makes the assignment that much more exciting.

REWRITING AN "UNCLEAR" TEXTBOOK EXPLANATION It can happen that a textbook explanation of a concept is not particularly clear to a student using the book. When a teacher senses that that may be the case, he might suggest to the students that they rewrite that explanation in their own words and in a way that will benefit the next class using the textbook. Thus, the students not only have to make sure they understand the concept but also have the opportunity to verbalize it, thereby further strengthening their understanding.

DESCRIBING A GEOMETRIC FIGURE Perhaps the best way to develop a writing assignment describing a geometric figure is to have the students imagine that they are about to describe that figure to a friend on the telephone. They should then be asked to verbalize their descriptions of the geometric figure. This activity requires students to think logically and thoroughly and sorts out a lot of untidy thinking.

GENERALIZING A CONCEPT Very often, a concept is presented and kept in a concise form. Frequently, generalizations are limited because of classroom time constraints. A teacher might challenge the class to consider the day's topic (e.g., the factoring of a trinomial) by asking students to generalize the topic (e.g., factoring). Students might be asked to consider the Pythagorean theorem and see if it can be generalized to a power higher than 2 (Fermat's last theorem), or whether a consideration of three dimensions might prove enlightening, or whether it can be generalized to triangles other than right triangles (law of cosines). In any case, the challenge should be an open-ended one, and the generalizations should be the students' personal choice. Some generalizations may be correct and some incorrect. Occasionally, students' generalizations will be unanticipated by the teacher (and yet prove to be pleasantly surprising for the teacher). These kinds of open-ended assignments have led to some very interesting student investigations that provided entire classes with the benefit of an individual student's imagination.

THE MATHEMATICS REPORT There are a host of activities that can be reported on. Students might discuss topics from the history of mathematics, such as the development of a particular branch of mathematics (e.g., coordinate geometry or non-Euclidean geometry), or trace the history of the refinement of a value such as π. Students might also investigate the history of mathematical notation. There are nice surprises embedded in this topic, which makes it appealing.

One natural topic in the history of mathematics is the presentation of a brief study of the life of a famous mathematician. Biographical sketches can include some mathematics as well as a life story. Students might discuss controversies that occurred in the development of mathematics. For example, a number of theorems are named for people who did not invent them—Simson's theorem in geometry was actually not known to Robert Simson, an important geometer of the seventeenth century, but rather was developed by William Wallace in 1797, long after Simson's death. Another colorful controversy centers on the true developer of a solution to a nonfactorable cubic equation: Cardano or Tartaglia? Students might also report on new findings in mathematics, such as the recent solution of the Four Color Map Problem or the proof of Fermat's last theorem.

The history of mathematics offers perhaps one of the richest areas for exploration and for expository writing, and should be used for that purpose.

Criteria for Evaluating Student Writing Samples

1. Students may be a bit too brief, and in their brevity be either ambiguous or imprecise. Students' brevity is caused

by a concern that too much detail will insult the reader who already knows the material anyway.

2. Students may not realize the difference between necessary and sufficient conditions in describing something.
3. Students may take an implication for granted without proper justification.
4. Students may be unaware of what actually constitutes a proper proof.
5. Students may make inaccurate diagrams that are too small to work with or that are inappropriately or incompletely labeled.

The foregoing are merely some of the things to look for in student writing. There are many other potential shortcomings in beginning written assignments. Teachers must assist the student in writing as soon as they detect weaknesses.

The question of whether writing should be assessed from a grammatical standpoint is an open one. For years, school classrooms exhibited the sign *Every Class Is an English Class*, and there are many teachers who still subscribe to that philosophy. There are others in the mathematics teacher community who feel that their concern with grammar would distract students from the content, and so they ignore any grammatical, style, or form weaknesses in the students' writing. If the latter is the case, the teacher should make it very clear that a lack of comments about grammar, style, and form does not imply that they are correct but that these factors were intentionally overlooked in order to concentrate comments solely on the content.

Benefits of Writing Activities in the Mathematics Classroom

Writing can be a catalyst for generating classroom discourse that might otherwise not take place. Consistent with the NCTM's *Standards*, writing assignments can be the kickoff for this kind of activity. The mathematics classroom environment could become less formal and, with the increased communication between students and teacher, far better tuned to the needs of the students. Thus, the students could enjoy a much more closely tailored mathematics presentation, and the instructor would be more aware of the students' learning, their needs and personalities, and their perceptions. Review of previously taught material can be handled far better in an atmosphere where writing activities in the form of logs or journals have been used, thus keeping current the review of concepts taught.

Peer evaluation may also be used when written assignments, whether they be expository or logs, are exchanged among students. Although this activity may create another level of anxiety (typical for teenagers), if handled properly it can also establish a rather refreshingly enlightened classroom.

Mathematics teachers are probably the most difficult group to convince of the value of writing in the mathematics class. After all, isn't the mathematics curriculum already overstuffed with topics that are mandated to be taught under state education requirements? All teachers continually assess every student's progress during the daily classroom experiences. Student portfolios, logs, reports, and other written reactions already reflect their comprehension, creativity, and achievement in that class.

The following sample written responses to a first-day classwork assignment in a geometry class provide some caveats for all teachers, both experienced and new.

Question: What do you expect from your teacher this term, and what can your teacher expect from you?

Replies:

Juan—I expect to learn new things and how to solve problems. I expect to go on some trips. I also expect that if I do good in class you will tell my parents.

Patricia—In class I expect my teacher to be open-minded to our way of solving problems, not just by teaching one method and having the class become familiar with only that one method. You should be aware not to give us too much homework but enough that we can go home and keep in mind what we learned in class that day. Tests should be given every few weeks, not too often.

Jaime—What my teachers should expect from me is respect, to hand my homework in on time, to be kind to my classmates, to come prepared to class always, and to listen when she is talking.

Vincent—What you should expect from me is dedication and hard work, to participate in class, and if I need help I will definitely tell you.

The following are sample excerpts from students' journals:

Student One. I learned how to solve radical equations today. A radical in an equation means only the positive square root. An equation that has a radical in it is called a radical equation. For example, $\sqrt{x} = 7$. A regular equation is solved by adding or subtracting from both sides. But radical equations must be checked because answers don't always work.

1. The teacher showed these examples:

$$\begin{aligned} \sqrt{2x-5} &= 7 \\ \left(\sqrt{2x-5}\right)^2 &= 7^2 \\ 2x-5 &= 49 \\ 2x &= 54 \\ x &= 27 \qquad \text{Answer} \end{aligned}$$

Check:

$$\begin{aligned} \sqrt{2x-5} &= 7 \\ \left(\sqrt{2(27)-5}\right) &\overset{?}{=} 7 \\ \left(\sqrt{54-5}\right) &\overset{?}{=} 7 \\ \sqrt{49} &\overset{?}{=} 7 \\ 7 &= 7 \end{aligned}$$

2. Then the teacher showed us another example. But this time one of the answers didn't check.

$$\begin{aligned} \sqrt{4x-3} &= -4 \\ \left(\sqrt{4x-3}\right)^2 &= -4^2 \end{aligned}$$

$$4x - 3 = 16$$
$$4x = 19$$
$$x = \frac{19}{4}$$

Check:

$$\sqrt{4x - 3} = -4$$
$$(\sqrt{4(^{19}/_{4}) - 3}) \stackrel{?}{=} -4$$
$$(\sqrt{19 - 3}) \stackrel{?}{=} -4$$
$$\sqrt{16} \stackrel{?}{=} -4$$
$$4 = -4 \quad \underline{\text{No!}}$$

I wonder why that happens.

Student Two. We learned today about two special triangles called the 45-45-90 and the 30-60-90 triangle. These are the rules they follow.

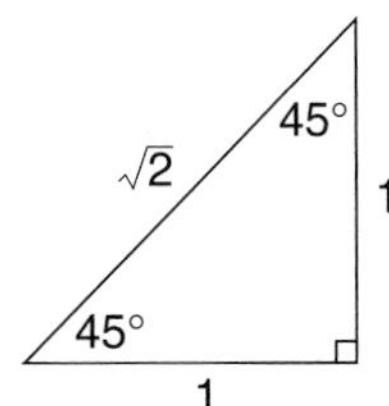

This triangle on top is called the 45-45-90 triangle because it's like half of a square.

This is called a 30-60-90 triangle because it's like half of an equilateral triangle. The teacher explained about half of the square and half of the equilateral, but I didn't catch it.

Then she showed two examples that I did follow, the side opposite the 30° angle is half of the hypotenuse, and

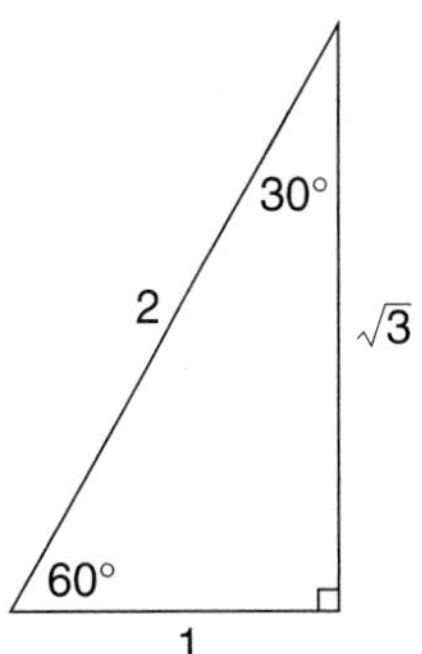

the side opposite the 60° angle is half of the hypotenuse times $\sqrt{3}$.

I like geometry because it uses diagrams so you can see what you are doing.

Student Three. In today's lesson I learned how to find the area of a regular polygon with the formal $A = \frac{1}{2}$ (apothem) · (perimeter). The teacher showed us how to derive the formula by using a picture of a regular polygon and then breaking it up into isosceles triangles that had congruent bases and altitudes. Since each triangle had its area = $\frac{1}{2}$ base × altitude, the sum of all the little areas was the area of the whole polygon.

Summary

Writing in the mathematics classroom has been gaining popularity in recent years. Furthermore, a not-to-be-neglected asset of the writing process in the classroom is the feedback the teachers get from students. Teachers have a marvelous opportunity here to generate a regular form of communication with their students.

EXERCISES

1. Create a VVWA for the following:
   a. Angle
   b. Relation
   c. Distributive property
   d. Equation
   e. Variable
2. Create a compare and contrast activity for two related concepts from the following areas of study:
   a. Linear equations and inequalities
   b. Transformations
   c. Functions
3. Create a semantic map for the following:
   a. Fractions
   b. Geometry of a circle
   c. Logic
4. Review a statewide mandated mathematics test for mathematics vocabulary. For each question identify terms and phrases that students would most likely not encounter outside of mathematics class. Identify words and phases that may have a different meaning when used in a nonmathematical context.
5. How would you respond to the following comment made by a student in one of your mathematics classes: "We don't do any math in my English class. Why do we have to do writing in our math class?"
6. Select a topic that you presented while teaching one of your mathematics classes. Compare and contrast the

(Continued)

entry a student might make in a log with one he might make in a journal on this topic.

7. One of your students asks for help in planning a piece of expository writing on either the Fibonacci sequence or Pascal's triangle. She hopes to submit her paper to the school's mathematics journal for possible publication. What suggestions might you offer?
8. You have assigned the writing of an expository paper in one of your mathematics classes, consisting of average-to-better students. Some of the papers submitted are very poor, written in a perfunctory fashion and clearly showing a lack of sincere effort. What action would you take?
9. A student whose native language is not English submits an expository paper whose content is of high quality but that contains numerous errors in grammar, spelling, syntax, and the like. Would you correct his English? Why?
10. Select a difficult portion of any chapter from a textbook your students are using, and ask them to rewrite it in a way they think will be clearer to the reader. Have all students discuss their rewritten portions in small groups, and have each group try to conclude which is the clearest.

Chapter 4

The Role of Problem Solving

Over the years problem solving has emerged as one of the major concerns at all levels of school mathematics. The National Council of Supervisors of Mathematics (NCSM) points out that "learning to solve problems is the principal reason for studying mathematics" (NCSM, *Position Paper on Basic Mathematical Skills*, 1977). This premise has not changed much in recent years, and has even become a stronger issue. The National Council of Teachers of Mathematics (NCTM) states rather boldly in *Principles and Standards for School Mathematics* (NCTM, 2000) that "Problem solving is not only a goal of learning mathematics but also a major means for doing so." The Council goes on to say that problem-solving "strategies are learned over time, applied in particular contexts, and become more refined, elaborate, and flexible as they are used in increasingly complex problem situations." We are in complete agreement! In fact, we would go one step further: We feel that problem solving is not only a skill to be taught and used in mathematics but also one that will be carried over to everyday "problems" or decision-making situations, thus serving a person well throughout life. It is precisely this notion that is our overriding theme in this chapter.

In many cases, students seem to feel (perhaps because of earlier experiences) that a problem can only be solved in a single way, specific to the "type" of problem being taught (i.e., motion problems, age problems, mixture problems, and so on). Students often feel that an algebraic approach is the only procedure that will "work." In recent years, with the everexpanding technological advances enhancing our view of mathematics, this notion has become antiquated. Many state curriculum guides are now encouraging students to "think out of the box." Under these circumstances an algebraic solution to a problem is not the only acceptable procedure; nor is a solution that uses a recognized pattern or one that evolves from a diagram (where one was not called for in the problem). This chapter presents illustrations of multiple solutions.

Sometimes teachers are not aware of the numerous problem-solving strategies that can be used to provide efficient and elegant solutions to many problems. They may unintentionally convey to their students the notion that problems can only be solved using a particular algebraic approach. While we would agree that algebra is a most powerful tool, it is still only one of the many approaches students should consider when it comes to searching for the solution of a problem. This chapter is designed for the in-service or preservice classroom teacher who has a sincere desire to help students succeed as problem solvers both in mathematics and beyond.

We will examine ten strategies, which are widely used in problem solving both in mathematics and in real-life decision-making or problem-solving situations. In the mathematics classroom, these strategies provide an alternate plan for resolving many problem situations that arise within the curriculum. We have selected problems to illustrate these strategies, anticipating that teachers will enjoy the illustrative examples, then begin applying these strategies to their regular instructional program. To do this, we recommend a careful review and study of the examples provided for each strategy so that the strategy becomes a genuine part of the teacher's thinking processes or, one might say, a part of their arsenal of problem-solving tools. As the NCTM in their *Principles and Standards for School Mathematics* (2000) states, "By the time students reach the middle grades, they should be skilled at recognizing when various strategies are appropriate to use and should be capable of deciding when and how to use them. By high school, students should have access to a wide range of strategies, be able to decide which one to use, and be able to adapt and invent strategies." How to reach these objectives is the goal of this chapter.

Although most of the problems can be solved using the tried-and-true techniques of algebra and geometry (and we *do* show these solutions as well), the purely "mechanical" approach often masks some of the efficiency, beauty, and elegance of the mathematics. In many cases, the problem-solving strategies presented here as alternative methods make the solution of a problem much easier, much neater, and much more understandable and, thereby, enjoyable!

Throughout the chapter we try to show how each of these strategies occurs and ought to be consciously used in real-life situations. Many people already make use of these strategies in normal decision making without realizing it. This carryover into life-outside-of-the-school adds importance to the mathematics our students study, and will ultimately improve their everyday performances.

Understand that problem solving must be the cornerstone of any successful mathematics program, then try to infuse an enthusiastic feeling and attitude about it into your daily teaching. This concentrated effort will make you a better problem solver and, in turn, will help your students to also become better problem solvers. Not only will their attitude toward mathematics improve, but so will their skills and abilities. That should be your ultimate goal.

One should not lose sight of the importance of the topics being taught. Building a solid foundation in the understanding of mathematics—clearly the task of all mathematics teachers—is still the primary objective. We see the thematic approach to teaching mathematics nicely complemented by the emphasis on problem solving throughout the instructional program. It is in that spirit that problem solving is being presented here.

There are many aspects to problem solving. One such is the psychological view of problem solving. How one might approach a problem situation, and how one's psychological set might affect his or her approach to and success with a problem, contributes to the process of problem solving. We will explore these factors affecting problem solving so that the teacher cognizant of them can anticipate difficulties students may have and provide appropriate remedies.

Problem solving is an excellent source and vehicle for enrichment in mathematics. Challenging problems, oftentimes those "off the beaten path," can lead to some very interesting investigations of mathematics outside of the regular curriculum. They also serve as a wonderful opportunity to stretch the mind. Mathematics teachers must always be prepared to provide some appropriate material for the more gifted students, while not neglecting the less-gifted students, who also benefit from appropriately challenging problems. In this chapter we offer some ideas in this direction along with examples.

The Nature of Problem Solving

The characteristics of concrete operational and formal operational thought are observable in the thinking involved in mathematics problem solving. The *concrete operational* student can order and organize that which is immediately present, but does not recognize and evaluate the possible. Such a student is unable to distinguish the setting of a problem situation from its structure. The concrete operational student is unable to reason from a hypothesis that is not attached to reality.

Formal operational students are capable of hypothetical thought and logical reasoning from a proposition. They are capable of forming all combinations of objects and isolating variables in the analysis of a problem situation. Formal operational students generally use more efficient strategies than concrete operational students and consequently are better problem solvers. They tend to use a greater number and variety of processes directed toward the goal than do concrete operational students. Formal operational students are able to draw diagrams, set up equations, establish key relationships, and recall facts, all of which are mental skills effective in producing a solution.

Formal operational students use a greater variety of processes and do more deductive thinking and subsequent evaluation, whereas concrete operational students make more effort and find even problems of simple structure to be difficult. Formal operational students perform significantly better on simple rather than complex problems.

Although there has not been a great deal of research on the effects of developmental level on problem-solving performance, a few inferences can be made. As students mature, they seem better able to organize their thinking so that more than one variable can be considered. Systematic deduction and successive approximation are strategies exhibited more often as students develop cognitively. These characteristics have some implications for approaches to instruction in problem solving. A few suggestions can be made for a problem-solving curriculum that may help students develop their abilities.

It is important for teachers to build problem-solving skills in all of their students, whether they be concrete operational or formal operational individuals. Teachers have to build on the capabilities possessed by concrete operational students and recognize their inability to organize, systemize, and efficiently carry out the solutions, especially when several variables or relationships are involved. The approaches needed to bridge the gap between intuition and formal processes are those that help to organize data and relationships for systematic processing. In addition, students should be encouraged to use intelligent guessing and testing, or try any other strategy they wish to use. In this way, more organized and efficient strategies can be assimilated naturally, built on the intuitive understanding and planning processes that the students can already use effectively. Later in this chapter you will have an opportunity to inspect and play with problem-solving strategies of a wide variety.

Two approaches are possible for the selection of problems and for instruction in problem solving. The first approach is to select tasks that require the use and practice of specific methods. The second approach is to select tasks that can elicit creative and insightful thought and consequently develop general problem-solving abilities. There are many examples of mathematics problems in the normal secondary school coursework; these can be used to develop creativity and insight.

The majority of the normal secondary school mathematics content can be taught with a problem-solving approach. To many teachers this would be a rather new experience and would require much effort and additional planning. Teachers may begin by having students work with problems whose solution leads to further investigations in the direction in which the course is aimed. This aroused curiosity then serves as a motivator for further study.

Teachers who are inclined to pursue problem solving for its own sake should allow students to work with pairs of problems that are similar in structure and that involve similar tasks. It is helpful for students to develop a good memory for problems and have experience with a variety of problem structures. Some useful activities could include the following:

1. Have students select from a second pair of problems the one that is similar to the first pair.
2. Ask students to write a problem having the same structural relationships as the first pair.
3. Generalize the data and solution of the pair.

Such exercises with problem recognition and ordering allow students to inspect the entire problem-solving process so a form of metacognition can help develop a problem-solving sensitivity. This metacognition simply adds to the awareness of the need for and importance of problem-solving skills.

In this chapter we also consider the topic of problem solving from the psychological point of view, with an aim to develop specific, and then easily recallable, problem-solving strategies. We also inspect some example problems that contain interesting messages for further problem solving and for a deeper understanding of mathematical concepts.

A Psychological View of Problem Solving

All problem solving involves some form of information (perceptual, physiological, sensory) and the use of that information to reach a solution. Given the individual differences we find in development as well as the varieties of content and levels of complexity of problem situations, a single, simple approach to problem solving would be difficult to discover (let alone implement).

As far back as 1910, John Dewey, in his book *How We Think* (Boston: D. C. Heath), outlined five steps for problem solving. They were presented in the following order.

1. Recognizing that a problem exists—an awareness of a difficulty, a sense of frustration, wondering, or doubt.
2. Identifying the problem—clarification and definition, including designation of the goal to be sought, as defined by the situation that poses the problem.
3. Employing previous experiences, such as relevant information, former solutions, or ideas to formulate hypotheses and problem-solving propositions.
4. Testing, successively, hypotheses or possible solutions. If necessary, the problem may be reformulated.
5. Evaluating the solutions and drawing a conclusion based on the evidence. This involves incorporating the successful solution into one's existing understanding and applying it to other instances of the same problem.

Although not all problem solving will necessarily follow this order, Dewey's analysis of the thinking process in problem solving has not been improved on yet. Note that it involves both the intake or reception of information and discovery learning in an interrelated process—one in which the learner is an active participant in his own learning.

In terms of mathematics, the work of George Polya in *How to Solve It* (Princeton University Press, 1945) presents techniques for problem solving that not only are interesting but are also meant to ensure that principles learned in mathematics will transfer as widely as possible. His techniques are called *heuristics* (serving to discover), strategies that aid in solving problems. He says that there is a "grain of discovery" in the solution of any problem. "Your problem may be modest; but if it challenges your curiosity and brings into play your inventive facilities, and if you solve it by your own means, you may experience the tension and enjoy the triumph of discovery."

He suggests the following heuristic methods.

1. Understand the problem. What is the unknown? What are the data? What is the condition? Draw a figure, introduce suitable notation. Separate the various parts of the condition.
2. Devise a plan. Find the connection between the data and the unknown. Have you seen it before? Do you know a related problem?
3. Carry out the plan. Check each step. Can you see that each step is correct? Can you prove that it is correct?
4. Look back. Examine the solution obtained. Can you check the result? Can you check the argument? Can you derive the result differently? Can you see it at a glance? Can you use the result, or method, for some other problem?

In 1974, a study revealed that teachers asked for rote responses in all but 5 percent of classrooms observed. Such teaching methods tend to promote habitual, rigid thinking. Such "set" thinking interferes with more effective problem-solving techniques.

As an example, examine this series of problems presented by Luchins and Luchins in their book *Rigidity of Behavior* (University of Oregon Press, 1959). Students were given the following chart and asked to solve each problem regarding water jars. Given three jars with listed capacities, they were asked to measure the amount of water requested in a fourth column. (Only three of the seven problems will be listed here.)

Problem Number	Jar Capacity (quarts)			Quarts Needed
	A	*B*	*C*	
1	29	3	0	20
4	18	43	10	5
7	23	49	3	20

In each of the first six cases, the largest jar is filled first and emptied into the smaller jars until the required amount is obtained. Most students attempt to solve the seventh problem in the same way, even when they are cautioned to "look carefully."

Polya presents many aspects of mathematical problem solving—from induction to working backward. Let us illustrate his approach with a problem similar to the one just given that he presents to illustrate working backward.

1. Let us try to find an answer to the following tricky question: *How can you bring up from the river exactly six quarts of water when you have only two containers, a four-quart pail and a nine-quart pail, with which to measure?* [He proceeds immediately to visualize the pails with no scale markings (what is given).]

[Then] we do not know yet how to measure exactly six quarts, but could we measure something else? (If you cannot solve the proposed problem, try to solve first some related problem. Could you derive something useful from the data?) [He notes that most people, when confronted with a puzzle, work forward, trying this or that, and goes on to say:]

2. But exceptionally able people, or people who had the chance to learn in their mathematics classes something

more than mere routine operations, do not spend too much time in such trials but turn around and start working backward. [Polya notes that the Greek mathematician Pappus gave an important description of this method. See Enrichment Unit 93, "Problem Solving—A Reverse Strategy."]

What are we required to do? What is the unknown? Let us visualize the final solution as clearly as possible. Let us imagine that we have here before us exactly six quarts in the larger container and the smaller container is empty. (Let us start from what is required and assume what is sought as already found, says Pappus) [Polya, pp. 198–199].

Polya goes on to demonstrate the subsequent steps in solving the problem. He asks, "From what antecedent could the desired result be derived?", and says that if the larger container were filled and exactly three quarts poured out, we would achieve the result. How to do that? Well, if only one quart were left in the smaller container, then we would pour out exactly three ("let us inquire into what could be the antecedent of the antecedent"). He notes that this may be encountered accidentally, possibly seen before. Certainly by pouring four quarts from the larger container twice in succession "we come eventually upon something already known (these are Pappus's words) and following the method of analysis, working backward, we have discovered the appropriate sequence of operations."

As the fine teacher he was, Polya used problemsolving techniques that include both associative and insightful learning. He added an ingredient of personal enthusiasm for his subject and a respect for the capacities of his students. One could ask little more of a teacher in any subject—that he be informed, use his information in a skillful manner in sharing with students, and provide them an opportunity to explore, analyze, and demonstrate their own skills.

Problem-Solving Preliminaries

As we begin our discussion of problem solving in the classroom, we need to consider some basic ground rules.

Students often form a psychological set when they approach a problem. For one thing they expect numerical answers to a problem to be simple; and when something complex emerges as a possible answer, students doubt their work and try again. A student's psychological set can also manifest itself in a more dramatic way. Consider the following examples.

PROBLEM

As quickly as you can, point to each of the numbers on the following chart in consecutive order beginning with 1.*

15	13 / 28	26 | 34	11 / 16 | 9	23	38 / 2
4 / 17	30	39	22 / 36	3	18
6 | 32	24	8 | 37	20 | 7 / 29 | 1	33 | 25	5
10	19 / 21	35	31 / 27	14	40 | 12

As students take on this seemingly easy challenge, they find frustration setting in very early. It is not as easy as expected to move along quickly because a psychological set develops that has students looking for each successor number to be of the same size as its predecessor. Only after students become aware of this psychological set and consciously avoid looking for numbers of the same size can they count the numbers more rapidly.

A similar syndrome is established with the following problem.

PROBLEM

Using only four straight lines, connect the following nine dots, without lifting your pencil off the paper and without retracing a line.

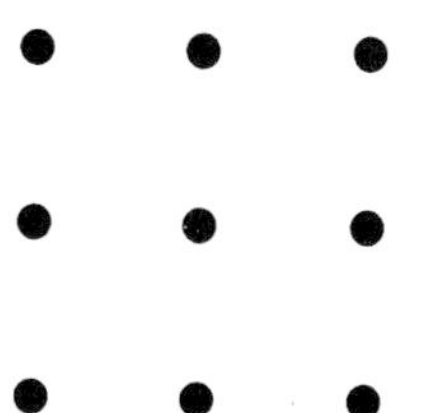

Most students will begin with one of the following attempts:

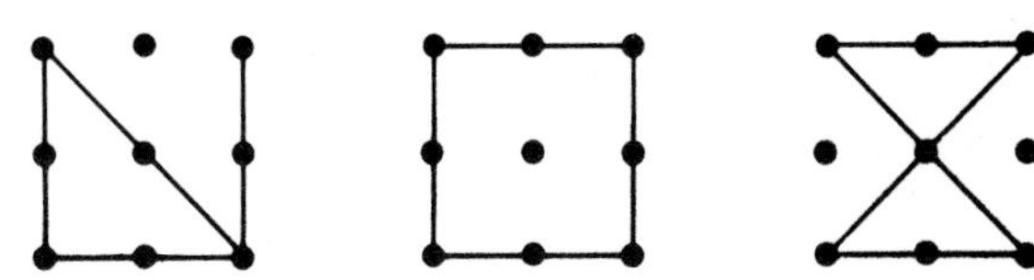

Other similar tries usually will be equally unsuccessful. To break this psychological set, students should be encouraged to *negate unsuccessful attempts.*

They see that beginning at one dot and staying within the matrix of nine dots does not work. To *negate* this psychological set say, "Do *not* be restricted by the matrix; instead consider a straight line segment that is partially *outside* the matrix." This will lead to a solution such as the one below.

*This problem was contributed by Professor Brigitte Rollett of the University of Vienna (Austria).

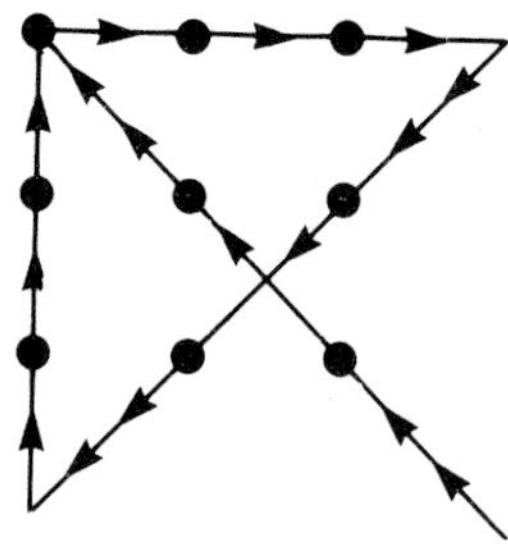

Another problem that dramatizes the problem-solving technique of negating an unsuccessful attempt follows.

PROBLEM

Given four separate pieces of chain (each three links long), show how to join these four pieces into a single circle by opening and closing *at most* three links.

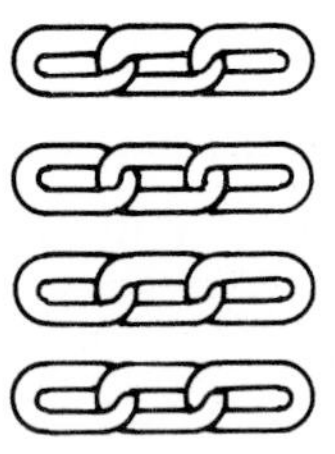

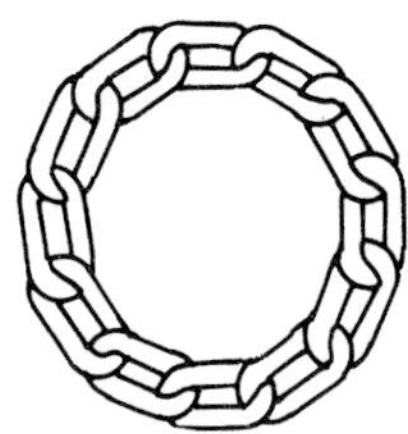

A typical first attempt is to cut an end link of each of the first three pieces. Negate this psychological set by saying "do *not* cut one link in each piece," or "cut *all* links in *one* piece." This leads to a solution directly, since the three cut links can be used to join the remaining pieces of chain to form the desired circle.

Another basic tenet of problem solving is to have students list all the information given (or implied) by the problem. Consider the following problem.

PROBLEM

Given a checkerboard and 32 dominoes (each of which covers exactly two squares of the checkerboard), show how 31 of these dominoes can cover the checkerboard with a pair of opposite corner squares deleted.

Experience shows that most students will immediately begin to shade pairs of squares in order to establish a pattern for the solution of the problem. This will not work. Furthermore, it will result in a rather messy situation, especially if a student uses ink, rather than pencil, to do mathematics. Students should be encouraged to list all the facts they are given:

- There are 64 squares on the checkerboard.
- There are 32 dominoes, each the size of exactly 2 squares.
- Two white squares are deleted.
- There are only 62 squares remaining on the truncated checkerboard.
- There are 32 black and 30 white squares.
- The number of black squares is not equal to the number of white squares.
- Each domino must cover a black and a white square.

Therefore, since the numbers of black squares and white squares are not the same, it is *impossible* to cover the truncated checkerboard with the 31 dominoes as requested, and the problem *is solved*. Teachers should stress the importance of recognizing that this is now a solved problem, even though what was requested in the problem led to a disappointing solution.

An analogous situation in the history of mathematics is Leonhard Euler's solution of the famous "trisection problem." He proved that trisecting any angle with straightedge and compasses *cannot* be done; this is *not* to say we don't know *how* to do it. The discussion of such a solution is a worthwhile investment of time.

Perhaps the best way to prepare students to be effective problem solvers is to provide them with many examples covering a variety of problem-solving techniques. Naturally it is helpful at the beginning to classify the techniques shown, although over time it is wise to have students discover the appropriate technique (of course, not problem specific) for the solution to a particular problem, since that is an important part of the problem-solving process.

Self-awareness, especially with regard to learning habits, is helpful to the learning process. *Metacognition*, which refers to a knowledge of (and belief in) the cognitive process, leads to an eventual control of the regulation and control of the cognitive actions.

When a problem situation is presented, the raw information must be processed and refined to an acceptable answer. The processing is usually a multistep operation in which each step feeds off the results of the preceding one, using whatever available equipment is stored in the problem solver's arsenal of skills and knowledge. The planning step is the development of a processing schedule, designed for the specific problem being considered.

Successful conception of a good plan is the primary achievement in the problem-solving process. It is also the most difficult part of the process to teach. In his article "Metacognitive Aspects of Problem Solving" (in *The Nature of Intelligence*, Erlbaum, 1976), John Flavell states that metacognition is an essential element in a student's development of a solution plan. According to Flavell, "Metacognition refers to one's own cognitive processes or anything related to them. It refers not only to one's awareness of cognitive processes but also to the self-monitoring, regulation, evaluation, and direction of cognitive activity."

These metacognitive activities involve making connections between the problem statement, broken down into its intelligible parts, and the students' previous knowledge and experiences. This process continues until the problem can be classified into some already familiar group ready for solution. The ability to classify and to have groups of problem types available is crucial to the process. Sometimes this may require breaking down a problem into smaller parts that are simpler to classify. Monitoring this process by the problem solver is essential. This self-awareness produces *control* of the processing.

The key to successful problem solving is to be in *control* of the process. It is perfectly normal, even desirable, to talk to yourself (subvocally) when working on a mathematics problem. This is a way of trying to control the problem-solving process. To be in control is to have a mastery of the necessary heuristics so you can select and pursue the correct approach for the solution. By talking to yourself, you are monitoring the problem-solving process, which is key to enabling control.

There are a number of possible control decisions that ought to be considered:

- **Thoughtless decisions** move the process in scattered directions and do not build on any previous experiences or knowledge.
- **Impatient decisions** either stop the process entirely or keep the problem solver moving directionless in quest of a solution without even seeing a path to a conclusion, either successful or unsuccessful.
- **Constructive decisions** involve carefully monitoring control while employing knowledge and skills in a meaningful way, using proper solution paths and abandoning unsuccessful ones.
- **Immediate procedure decisions** require no control, since they simply access the appropriate solution path stored in long-term memory.
- **Nondecision** results when the statement of the problem is so perplexing that no knowledge or prior experience is helpful in the solution and the problem solver gives up.

An awareness of the problem-solving process is the first step for attaining control. This control enables the learner to find a proper solution path.

An Introduction to Problem-Solving Strategies

Before we can discuss what problem solving is, we must first come to grips with what is meant by a problem. In essence, a problem is a situation that confronts a person that requires resolution and for which the path to the solution is not immediately known. In everyday life, a problem can manifest itself as anything from a simple personal problem such as the best strategy for crossing the street (usually done without much thinking) to a more complex problem such as how to assemble a new bicycle. Of course, crossing the street may not be a simple problem in some situations. For example, Americans become radically aware of what is usually a subconscious behavior pattern while visiting a country such as England where their usual strategy for safely crossing the street just will not work. The reverse is also true; the British experience similar feelings when visiting the European continent where traffic is oriented differently from that in Britain. These everyday situations are typically resolved subconsciously without our taking formal note of the procedures by which we found the solution. A consciousness of everyday problem-solving methods and strategies usually becomes more evident when one travels outside of her daily cultural surroundings. There the normal way of life and habitual behaviors may not fit or may not work. One may have to consciously adapt other methods in order to achieve one's goals.

Much of what we do is based on our prior experiences. As a result, the level of sophistication with which we attack problems will vary. Whether the problems we face in everyday life involve selecting a daily wardrobe, relating to friends or acquaintances, or dealing with professional issues or personal finances, we pretty much function automatically, without considering the method or strategy that would best suit the situation. We go about addressing life's challenges with an algorithmic-like approach, and can easily become a bit frustrated if that approach suddenly doesn't fit. In these situations we are required to find a solution to the problem. That is, we must search our previous experiences to find a way we solved an analogous problem in the past. (This is a notion very eloquently put forward by George Polya, 1957.) We could also reach into our bag of problem-solving tools and see what works.

When students encounter problems in their everyday school lives, their approach is not much different. They tend to tackle problems based on their previous experiences. These experiences can range from recognizing a problem as one very similar to one previously solved, to taking on a homework exercise similar to those presented in class that day. The student is not doing any problem solving, but rather is merely mimicking (or practicing) the earlier encountered situations. This is the behavior seen in a vast majority of classrooms. Repetition of a skill is useful in attaining the skill. This holds true for attaining problem-solving skills.

Using familiar approaches to deal with what are often seen as artificial situations created especially for the mathematics class does not directly address the idea of problem solving as a process to be studied for its own sake, and not merely as a facilitator. People do not solve "age problems," "motion problems," "mixture problems," and so on in their real lives. Historically, the study of mathematics has been considered topically. Without a conscious effort by educators, this will clearly continue to be the case. Teachers might rearrange the topics in the syllabus in various orders, but it will still be the topics themselves that will link the courses together rather than the mathematical procedures involved. And this is not the way that most people think! Reasoning involves a broad spectrum of thinking.

Students in a mathematics class who learn to consider problem solving as an end in itself and not merely as a means to an end will benefit greatly in class as well as in their everyday lives. Problem solving can be the vehicle used to introduce students to the beauty that is inherent in mathematics. It can also be the unifying thread that ties their mathematics experiences together into a meaningful whole. One immediate goal would be to have students become familiar with numerous problem-solving strategies and to practice using them. This procedure would begin to show itself in the way they approach problems and ultimately solve them. Enough practice of this kind should make a longer-range goal attainable, namely, that students would come to use these same problem-solving strategies in solving not only mathematical problems but also in resolving problems in everyday life. This transfer of learning (back and forth) can be best realized by introducing problem-solving strategies in both mathematical and real-life situations concomitantly. Changing an instructional program by relinquishing some of its time-honored emphasis on isolated topics and concepts, and devoting the time to a procedural approach, will require teacher support to succeed. Teachers must realize that the end results will prepare more capable students for this era, where the ability to think is becoming more and more important as sophisticated technology continues to be developed and used.

When one studies the history of mathematics, one finds breakthroughs, which although simple to understand, often are reacted to with: "Oh, I would never have thought about that approach." Similarly, when clever solutions are found to certain problems and presented as "tricks," they have the same self-disparaging effect as the great breakthroughs in the history of mathematics. Teachers must help students avoid this mindset and learn to make clever solutions part of an attainable problem-solving strategy knowledge base, which is constantly reinforced throughout the regular instructional program.

One should be cautioned that in the last few decades there has been much talk about problem solving. The National Council of Teachers of Mathematics' *Agenda for Action* (1980), the widely accepted and innovative *Curriculum and Evaluation Standards for School Mathematics* (1989), and most recently the *Principles and Standards for School Mathematics* (2000) have played major roles in generating the general acceptance of problem solving as a major curricular thrust. Everyone seems to agree that problem solving and reasoning are, and must be, an integral part of any good instructional program. Then why has this not come to pass? The major impediment to a successful problem-solving component in regular school curriculum is the weak training that teachers receive in problem solving, as well as the lack of attention paid to the ways in which these skills can be smoothly incorporated into a regular teaching program. Teachers need to focus their attention on what problem solving is, how they should utilize problem solving, and how it should be presented to their students. They must understand that problem solving can be thought of in three different ways:

1. Problem solving is a subject for study in and of itself.
2. Problem solving is a way to approach a particular problem.
3. Problem solving is a way of teaching.

Although all of these ways are correct, the third concept is the overriding one for mathematics teachers to consider. Problem solving should become an integral part of their teaching process. This section presents ten problem-solving strategies that might become the basis for such a teaching approach. Teachers must initially focus their attention on their own ability to become problem solvers. They must learn what problem-solving strategies are available to them, what they entail, and when and how they can be used. They must then learn to apply these strategies, not only to mathematical situations but also to everyday life experiences. Often simple problems can be used in clever ways to demonstrate these strategies. Naturally, some more challenging problems will show the power of the problem-solving strategies. By learning the strategies, beginning with simple applications of them and then progressively moving toward solving more challenging and complex problems, students will have opportunities to grow in the everyday use of their problem-solving skills. Patience must be used with students as they embark on, what is for most of them, this new adventure in mathematics. Only after teachers have had the proper immersion in this alternate approach to mathematics in general and to problem solving in particular, and after they have developed sensitivity toward the learning needs and peculiarities of students, then, and only then, can teachers expect to see some genuine, positive change in their students' mathematics performance.

It is rare that a problem can be solved using all of the ten strategies presented here. Similarly, it is equally rare that a single strategy can be used to solve a given problem. Rather, a combination of strategies is the most likely occurrence when solving a problem. Thus, it is best to become familiar with all the strategies and to develop facility in using them when appropriate. The strategies selected here are not the only ones available, but represent those most applicable to mathematics instruction in the schools. The user will, for the most part, determine appropriateness of a strategy in a particular problem. Determining the appropriate strategy is analogous to a repairman, who, when called upon to fix a problem, must decide which tool to use. The more tools he has available, and the better he knows how to use them, the better we would expect his results to be. However, just as not every task the repairman has to do will be possible using the tools in his toolbox, so, too, not every mathematics problem will be solvable using the strategies presented here. In both cases experience and judgment play an important role.

Every teacher, in order to help students learn and use the strategies of problem solving, must have a collection from which to draw examples. Strategies are labeled so they can be used and called on quickly as they are needed. The repairman, in deciding which tool to use in repairing something, will usually refer to it by name (i.e., a label). Having a label (or name) attached to a strategy will make it more likely for the problem solver to recall it for use in the process.

All of the strategies presented can, and ought to, be regularly applied to everyday-life decision-making processes (or problem solving in real-life situations). This practice should solidify their use and understanding and make their application to a mathematical context more natural.

For you to better understand the strategies presented here, we shall introduce each with a description, apply it to an everyday problem situation, and then present an example of how it can be applied in mathematics. In each case, the illustrations are not necessarily meant to be typical, but are presented merely to best illustrate the use of the particular strategy under discussion. Following are the strategies that will be considered in this book:

1. Working backwards
2. Finding a pattern
3. Adopting a different point of view
4. Solving a simpler analogous problem (specification without loss of generality)
5. Considering extreme cases
6. Making a drawing (visual representation)
7. Intelligent guessing and testing (including approximation)
8. Accounting for all possibilities (exhaustive listing)
9. Organizing data
10. Logical reasoning

As already mentioned, there is hardly ever a unique way to solve a problem. Some problems lend themselves to a wide variety of solution methods. As a rule, students should be encouraged to consider alternative solutions to a problem, such as by considering classmates' solutions and comparing them to the "standard" solution (that is, one given in the textbook or supplied by the teacher). Remember, many problems may require more than a single strategy for solution. The data given in the problem statement, rather than merely the nature of the problem, can determine the best strategy to be used in solving the problem. All aspects of a particular problem must be carefully inspected before embarking on a particular strategy.

Let's consider a problem which most people can resolve by an intuitive (or random) trial and error method, but which might take a considerable amount of time to reach the answer. To give you a feel for the use of these problem-solving strategies before we look at them individually, we shall approach the problem employing several of the strategies listed.

PROBLEM

Place the numbers from 1 through 9 into the grid below so that the sum of each row, column, and diagonal is the same. (This is often referred to as a "magic square.")

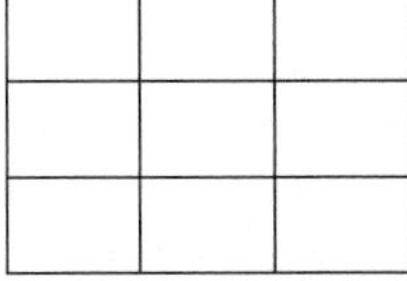

SOLUTION

A first step to a solution would be to use *logical reasoning*. The sum of the numbers in all 9 cells would be $1 + 2 + 3 + \cdots + 7 + 8 + 9 = 45$. If each row has to have the same sum, then each row must have a sum of $\frac{45}{3}$ or 15.

The next step might be to determine which number should be placed in the center cell. Using *intelligent guessing and testing* along with some additional *logical reasoning*, we can begin by trying some *extreme cases*. Can 9 occupy the center cell? If it did, then 8 would be in some row, column, or diagonal along with the 9, making a sum greater than 15. Therefore, 9 cannot be in the center cell. Similarly, 6, 7, or 8 cannot occupy the center cell, for then they would be in the same row, column, or diagonal with 9 and would not permit a three-number sum of 15. Consider now the other extreme. Could 1 occupy the center cell? If it did, then it would be in some row, column, or diagonal with 2, thus requiring a 12 to obtain a sum of 15. Similarly, 2, 3, or 4 cannot occupy the center cell. Having *accounted for all the possibilities*, this leaves only the 5 to occupy the center cell.

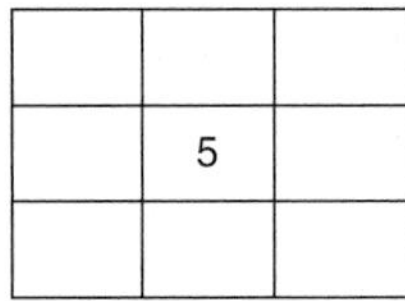

Now, using *intelligent guessing and testing*, we can try to put the 1 in a corner cell. Because of symmetry, it does not matter which corner cell we use for this guess. In any case, this forces us to place the 9 in the opposite corner, if we are to obtain a diagonal sum of 15.

1		
	5	
		9

With a 9 in one corner, the remaining two numbers in the row with the 9 must total 6; that is, 2 and 4. One of those numbers (the 2 or the 4) would then also be in a row or a column with the 1, making a sum of 15 impossible in that row or column. Thus 1 cannot occupy a corner. Placing it in a middle cell of one outside row or column forces the 9 into the opposite cell so as to get a sum of 15.

	1	
	5	
	9	

The 7 cannot be in the same row or column with the 1, for it would then require a second 7 to obtain a sum of 15.

7	1	?
	5	
	9	

In this way, we can see that the 8 and 6 must be in the same row or column (and at the corner positions, of course) with the 1.

8	1	6
	5	
	9	

This then determines the remaining two corner cells (4 and 2) to allow the diagonals to have a sum of 15.

8	1	6
	5	
4	9	2

To complete the magic square, we simply place the remaining two numbers, 3 and 7, into the two remaining cells to get sums of 15 in the first and third columns.

8	1	6
3	5	7
4	9	2

What is to be observed in this solution to the problem is how the various strategies were used for each step of the solution.

Problems can (and should) be solved in more than one way. Let's examine an alternative approach to solving this same problem. Picking up the solution from the point where we had established that the sum of every row, column or diagonal is 15, we list all the possibilities of 3 numbers from this set of nine that have a sum of 15 (*accounting for all the possibilities*). By *organizing the data* in this way, the answer comes rather quickly.

1, 5, 9	2, 6, 7
1, 6, 8	3, 4, 8
2, 4, 9	3, 5, 7
2, 5, 8	4, 5, 6

We shall now *adopt a different point of view* and consider the position of a cell and the number of times it is counted into a sum of 15 (*logical reasoning*). The center square must be counted four times: twice in the diagonals and once each for a row and a column. The only number that appears four times in the triples we have listed above is 5. Therefore, it must belong in the center cell.

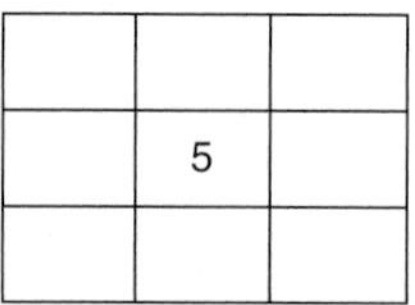

The corner cells are each used three times; therefore, we place the numbers used three times (the even numbers 2, 4, 6, and 8) in the corners.

8		6
	5	
4		2

The remaining numbers (the odd numbers) are each used twice in the above sums and therefore are to be placed in the peripheral center cells (where they are only used by two sums) to complete our magic square.

8	1	6
3	5	7
4	9	2

This *logical reasoning* was made considerably simpler by using a *visual representation* of the problem. It is important to have students realize that we have solved the same problem in two very different ways. They should try to develop other alternatives to these, and they might also consider using consecutive numbers other than 1 to 9. An ambitious student might also consider the construction of a 4×4 or a 5×5 magic square.

As we have stated before, it is extremely rare to encounter a problem that can be efficiently solved using each of the ten problem-solving strategies we have listed. However, there are times when more than one strategy can be used, either alone or in combination, with varying degrees of efficiency. Of course, the level of efficiency of each method may vary with the user. Let's take a look at one such problem. It's a problem that is well known, and you may have seen it before. However, we intend to approach its solution with a variety of different strategies.

PROBLEM

In a room with 10 people, everyone shakes hands with everybody else exactly once. How many handshakes are there?

SOLUTION 1

Let's use our *visual representation* strategy by drawing a diagram. The 10 points, no 3 of which are colinear, represent the 10 people. Begin with the person represented by point *A*.

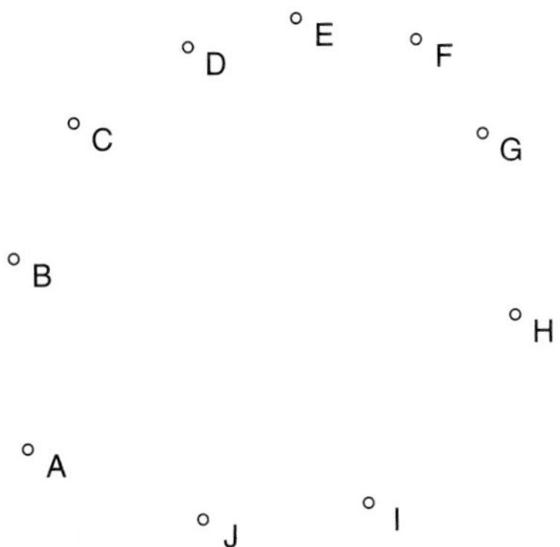

We join A to each of the other nine points, indicating the first 9 handshakes that take place.

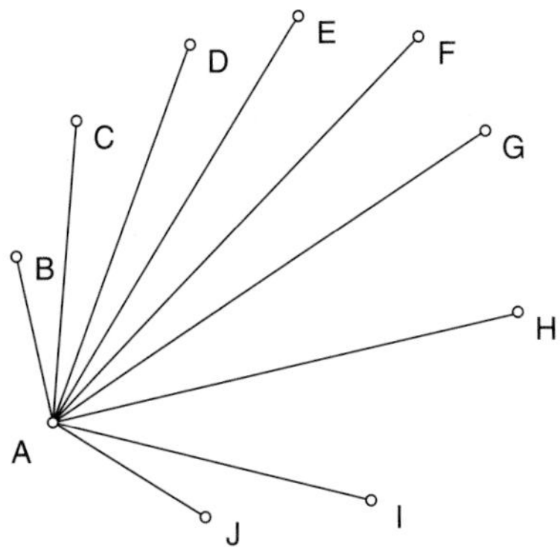

Now, from B there are 8 additional handshakes (since A has already shaken hands with B, and $\overline{AB}$ is already drawn). Similarly, from C there will be 7 lines drawn to the other points ($\overline{AC}$ and $\overline{BC}$ are already drawn), from D there will be 6 additional line segments or handshakes, and so on. When we reach point I, there is only one remaining handshake to be made, namely, I with J, since I has already shaken hands with A, B, C, D, E, F, G, and H. Thus the sum of the handshakes equals $9 + 8 + 7 + 6 + 5 + 4 + 3 + 2 + 1 = 45$. In general, this is the same as using the formula for the sum of the first n natural numbers, $\frac{n(n+1)}{2}$, where $n \geq 1$.

(Notice that the final drawing will be a decagon with all of its diagonals shown.)

SOLUTION 2

We can approach the problem by *accounting for all the possibilities*. Consider the grid shown, which indicates persons $A, B, C, \ldots, H, I, J$ shaking hands with one another. The diagonal with the X's indicates that people cannot shake hands with themselves.

The remaining cells indicate doubly all the other handshakes (i.e., A shakes hands with B and B shakes hands with A). Thus we take the total number of cells (10^2), minus those on the diagonal (10), and divide the result by 2.

In this case, we have $\frac{100 - 10}{2} = 45$.

	A	B	C	D	E	F	G	H	I	J
A	X									
B		X								
C			X							
D				X						
E					X					
F						X				
G							X			
H								X		
I									X	
J										X

In a general case for the $n \times n$ grid, the number would be $\frac{n^2 - n}{2}$.

SOLUTION 3

Let's now examine the problem by *adopting a different point of view*. Consider the room with 10 people, each of whom will shake 9 other people's hands. This seems to indicate that there are 10×9 or 90 handshakes. But we must divide by 2 to eliminate the duplication (since, when A shakes hands with B, B is shaking hands with A): $\frac{90}{2} = 45$.

SOLUTION 4

Let's try to solve the problem by *looking for a pattern*. In the table shown below, we list the number of handshakes occurring in a room as the number of people increases.

Number of People in Room	Number of Handshakes for Additional Person	Total Number of Handshakes in Room
1	0	0
2	1	1
3	2	3
4	3	6
5	4	10
6	5	15
7	6	21
8	7	28
9	8	36
10	9	45

The third column, which is the total number of handshakes, gives a sequence of numbers known as the *triangular numbers*, whose successive differences increase by 1 each time. It is therefore possible to simply continue the table until we reach the corresponding sum for the 10 people, or else we note that the pattern at each entry is one-half the product of the number of people on that line and the number of people on the previous line.

SOLUTION 5

We can approach the problem by a careful use of the *organizing data* strategy. The chart shown below shows each of the people in the room and the number of hands they have to shake each time, given that they have already shaken the hands of their predecessors and don't shake their own hands. Thus person number 10 shakes 9 hands, person number 9 shakes 8 hands, and so on, until we reach person number 2, who only has one person's hand left to shake, and person number 1 has no hands to shake because everyone already shook his hand. Again the sum is 45.

Organized Data

Person number	10	9	8	7	6	5	4	3	2	1
Number of handshakes	9	8	7	6	5	4	3	2	1	0

SOLUTION 6

We may also combine *solving a simpler problem* with *visual representation* (drawing a picture), *organizing the data*, and *looking for a pattern*. Begin by considering a figure with one person, represented by a single point. Obviously, there will be 0 handshakes. Now, expand the number of people to 2, represented by 2 dots. There will be 1 handshake. Again, let's expand the number of people to 3. Now, there will be 3 handshakes needed. Continue with 4 people, 5 people, and so on.

The problem has now become a geometry problem, where the answer is the number of sides and diagonals of an "n-gon." Thus, for 10 people we have a decagon, and the number of sides $n = 10$. For the number of diagonals, we may use the formula

$$d = \frac{n(n-3)}{2}, \text{ where } n > 3.$$

$$d = \frac{(10)(7)}{2} = 35$$

Thus the number of handshakes $= 10 + 35 = 45$.

Number of People	Number of Handshakes	Visual Representation
1	0	•A
2	1	A, B
3	3	A, B, C
4	6	A, B, C, D
5	10	A, B, C, D, E

SOLUTION 7

Of course, some students might simply recognize that this problem could easily be resolved by applying the combinations formula of 10 things taken 2 at a time.

$${}_{10}C_2 = \frac{10 \cdot 9}{1 \cdot 2} = 45$$

This solution, however, while quite efficient, brief, and correct, hardly utilizes any mathematical thought (other than application of a formula) and avoids the entire problem-solving approach. Although it is a solution that should be discussed, we must call the other solutions to the students' attention.

You should become familiar with all of the strategies, practice them until you have mastered them, and only then begin to present them to your students. In this way, you and they can develop facility with the basic tools of problem solving. You can present the tools by formatting more and more of your teaching in a problem-solving mode. That is, encourage your students to be creative in their approach to problems, encourage them to solve problems in a variety of ways, and encourage them to look for more than one answer to a problem. Have your students work together in small groups solving problems and communicating their ideas and work to others. The more students talk about problems and problem solving the better they will become in this vital skill. Referring to the various problem-solving methods or strategies by name will ensure better and more efficient recollection of them when they are needed. Remember that the concept of metacognition (that is, being aware of one's own thought processes) is an important factor in problem solving. Encouraging students to talk to themselves when tackling a problem is another way of having the students become aware of their problem-solving success.

The Ten Problem-Solving Strategies

Working Backwards

Although we use this problem-solving strategy quite often in everyday-life decision-making situations, it is not a natural method to call on when tackling a mathematics problem. We use this method when developing a schedule for various tasks that must be completed by a certain time. We often start with what has to be done, the time at which all the work must be completed, and how long each task should take. We then work backwards to assign time slots to each task, and thus to arrive at the appropriate time to begin the work.

The working-backwards strategy is also widely used every day in traffic investigations. When the police investigate an automobile accident, they must begin to work backwards from the time of the accident to see what were the causes, which car swerved immediately before the collision, who hit whom, which driver was at fault, what were the weather conditions at the time of the accident, and so on, as they attempt to reconstruct the accident.

When we look at the procedures which students are shown in many of their typical textbook exercises, we sometimes see very useful techniques presented. Unfortunately, these are often taken for granted and not called to the students' attention. Students may be required to reason in the reverse order, even though they have not been told to do so. An obvious example is the procedure students should use when writing proofs in a high school geometry course. They should begin by examining what they are trying to prove before doing anything else. Thus, an attempt to prove line segments congruent might stem from proving a pair of triangles congruent. This, in turn, should suggest that the students look for the parts necessary to reach this triangle congruence. Continuing in this manner, the students will be led to examine the given information. They are, in essence, *working backwards*. When the goal is unique but there are many possible starting points, a clever problem solver begins to work backwards from the desired conclusion to a point where the given information is reached.

When there is a unique end point (that which is to be proved) and a variety of paths to get to the starting point, the working backwards strategy may be desirable. However, the *working-forward* method is still the most natural method for solving the problem. In fact, working in the forward direction is used to solve *most* problems. We are not saying that all problems should be attempted by the working-backwards strategy. Rather, after a natural approach (usually *forward*) has been examined, a backwards strategy might be tried to see if this provides a more efficient, more interesting, or more satisfying solution to the problem.

A theorem that very dramatically demonstrates the value of reasoning backwards uses only the most elementary geometric knowledge. It states that *the segments joining each vertex of a given triangle (of any shape) with the remote vertex of the equilateral triangle (drawn externally on the opposite side of the given triangle) are congruent.*

That is, $\overline{AE}$, $\overline{BD}$, and $\overline{CF}$ are congruent to one another. Your students should take note of the unusual nature of this situation, because we started with *any* triangle and still this relationship holds true. If each of your students were to draw their own original triangle, they all will come up with the same conclusion. Either straightedge and compasses or *Geometer's Sketchpad* would be fine for this; however, the latter would be better.

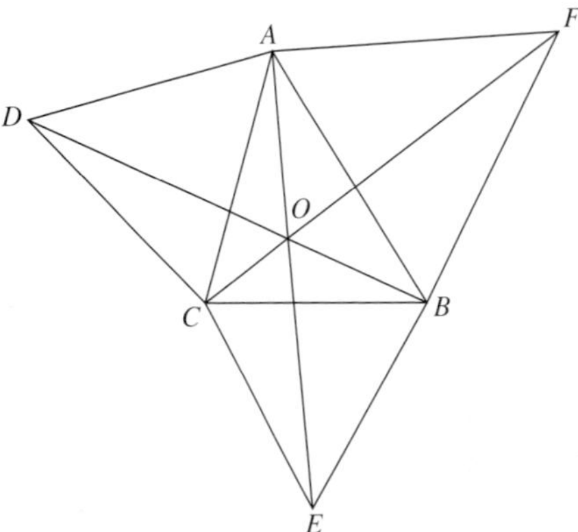

You may want to give your students a hint as to how to prove this theorem. They should be conditioned to working backwards when doing such a proof. That will involve them identifying the proper triangles to prove congruent. They are not easy to identify. Remember, the triangles chosen should have $\overline{AE}$, $\overline{BD}$, and $\overline{CF}$ as one of their sides.

One pair of these triangles is shown below. These two triangles can be proved congruent by showing that two pairs of sides are also sides of two equilateral triangles and the included angles are congruent because you are adding a 60° angle to the common angle *ACB*. This triangle congruence will establish the congruence of $\overline{AE}$ and $\overline{BD}$. The other segments can be proved congruent in a similar way with another pair of congruent triangles.

The key idea here is that by working backwards the proof became manageable.

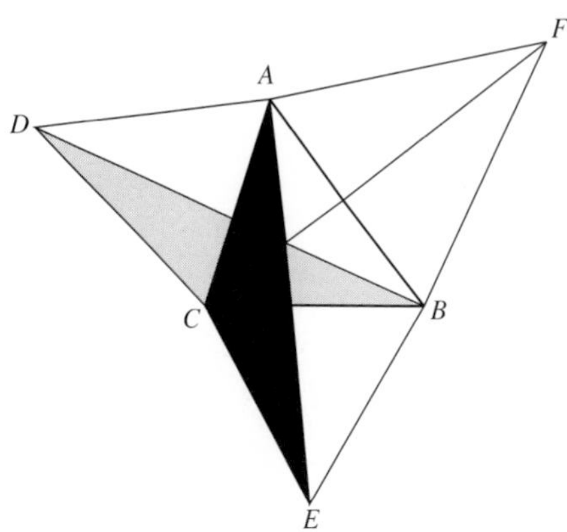

Another example of a proof that would be otherwise very difficult to do without reasoning backwards follows:

PROBLEM

Consider a scalene triangle with a 120° angle and all three of its angle bisectors drawn as seen in the figure at top right. We must prove that the segments joining the feet of the angle bisectors $\overline{FE}$ and $\overline{DE}$ are perpendicular.

SOLUTION

You might try tackling this one before reading on. It is quite difficult unless you use the following backward reasoning.

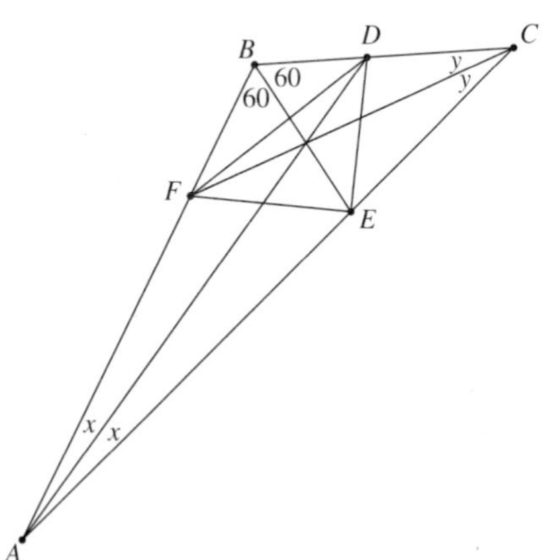

The segments $\overline{FE}$ and $\overline{DE}$ would be perpendicular if they each would bisect the two supplementary angles $\angle AEB$ and $\angle CEB$. But how can we show that either one is an angle bisector? Could we show that a point say, F, is equidistant from the sides of the angle? Let's pursue this tack.

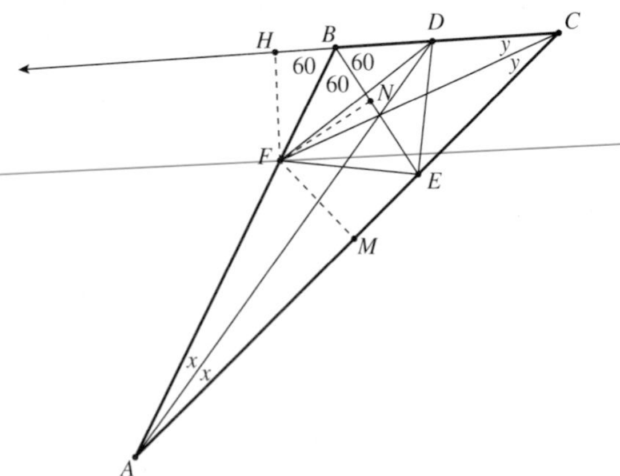

We extend $\overline{CB}$ to point H where $\overline{FH} \perp \overline{CH}$. Because of the angle bisector property,

$$FH = FN, (\overline{FN} \perp \overline{BE}).$$

Since $\overline{FM} \perp \overline{AC}$, and since $\overline{FC}$ is an angle bisector, $FM = FH$.

Therefore, $FM = FN$.

Thus, $\overline{FE}$ is also an angle bisector.

Similarly, $\overline{DE}$ is an angle bisector. It then follows that $\angle FED$ is a right angle.

A rather nifty, yet very elementary proof, if you use backward reasoning.

Although many problems may require some reverse reasoning (even if only to a small extent), there are some problems whose solution is dramatically facilitated by working backwards. Consider the following problem; beware that it is not typical of the school curriculum, but rather a dramatic illustration of the power of working backwards.

PROBLEM

The sum of two numbers is 12 and the product of the same two numbers is 4. Find the sum of the reciprocals of the two numbers.

SOLUTION

Most students will immediately generate two equations: $x + y = 12$ and $xy = 4$, where x and y represent the two numbers. They have been taught to solve this pair of equations simultaneously by substitution. If, in this complicated example, the students do not make any algebraic errors, they will arrive at a pair of rather unpleasant looking values for x and y, that is, $x = 6 \pm 4\sqrt{2}$ and $y = 6 \pm 4\sqrt{2}$. They must then find the reciprocals of these numbers and finally their sum. Can this problem be solved in this manner? Yes, of course! However, this rather complicated solution process can be made much simpler by starting from the end of the problem, namely what we wish to find, $\frac{1}{x} + \frac{1}{y}$.

The students might now ask themselves: "What do we usually do when we see two fractions to be added? How do we add them?" If we compute the sum in the usual way, we obtain $\frac{x + y}{xy}$.

However, since $x + y$ was given as 12 and xy was given as 4, this fraction becomes $\frac{12}{4} = 3$. (Notice that students were never asked to find the specific values of x and y; rather, they were asked for the sum of their reciprocals.)

Special care must be taken to avoid having students, discouraged by their frustrations, take the attitude that "I would never have been able to come up with that trick solution." Instead encourage them to see that this valuable and unusual problem-solving strategy is one with which they should become familiar, and its use is indeed attainable by them with some additional practice.

Finding a Pattern

One of the inherent beauties of mathematics is the logic and order that it exudes. This logic can also be seen "physically" as a pattern, or as a series of patterns. The nonmathematician often appreciates geometry for the patterns it provides. The mathematician uses patterns as an aid to solving problems not only in geometry, but in many other fields as well. We see mathematics problems in the secondary school curriculum that clearly require pattern recognition for their solution. For example, to find the next two numbers in the sequence 1, 3, 4, 7, 11, 18, ___, ___, we must first search for and then recognize a pattern. One possible pattern has each number after the first two as the sum of the two preceding numbers. Recognizing that this is an example of a Fibonacci-type sequence (known as the Lucas numbers) leads to the next two numbers, namely 29 and 47. It is true that there may be more sophisticated (and more cumbersome) ways to find the immediate successors of 18 in the given sequence. However, consider finding the next two terms of the sequence 1, 10, 2, 7, 3, 4, 4, ___, ___. It is very unlikely that this can be resolved in any way other than by recognizing that this sequence is actually two separate sequences interwoven. One sequence is from the numbers in the odd positions: 1, 2, 3, and 4 (a difference of +1). The other is formed by the numbers in the even positions: 10, 7, 4 (a difference of −3). Thus the next two terms would be 1, 5.

These are problems whose resolutions are, by their very nature, one of pattern recognition. In these cases, the use of pattern seeking was announced by the very type of problem. We will consider problems where pattern recognition is not expected, yet proves to be an invaluable aid to solving the given problem more simply than the traditional or common solution method.

In everyday-life situations we (sometimes subconsciously) use pattern recognition to deal with a problem. For example, when you are looking for an even-numbered address on a street, you will look to the side where the even numbers are and you will search for it in numerical order. Pattern recognition is found in a variety of situations. The police often make use of the finding a pattern strategy in other ways, too. For example, when the police are confronted by a series of crimes (say robberies), they often try to find a pattern in the crimes as they look for a modus operandi that might lead them to a particular criminal. Scientists involved in medical research often utilize the finding a pattern strategy to permit them to locate and isolate similar variables, and thus draw conclusions about the particular virus or bacteria they are examining.

To look for a pattern in a mathematics problem that calls for finding a pattern is not what this problem-solving technique is all about. The technique of finding a pattern is most useful when the problem does not call for a pattern to be found. Consider the following problem.

PROBLEM

Find the sum of the first 20 odd numbers.

SOLUTION

The problem calls for a simple addition. With the help of a calculator this is a trivial, although time-consuming, task. The 20th odd number is 39. Thus, we wish to find the sum of $1 + 3 + 5 + 7 + \cdots + 33 + 35 + 37 + 39$. Of course, some students may decide to solve this problem by simply writing out all of the odd numbers from 1 through 39 and actually adding them. Some might apply the *looking for a pattern* strategy in a manner similar to the way we believe young Carl Friedrich Gauss did when he was in elementary school. This would involve listing the 20 odd numbers as 1, 3, 5, 7, 9, . . ., 33, 35, 37, 39. Now, notice that the sum of the 1st and 20th number is $1 + 39 = 40$, the sum of the 2nd and 19th number is also 40, $(3 + 37)$, and so on. This then requires determining how many 40s to add. Since there were 20 numbers under consideration, we have 10 pairs, and we multiply $10 \times 40 = 400$ to get the answer.

We can examine this problem by *looking for a pattern*, but in a different manner.

Addends	Number of Addends	Sum
1	1	1
1 + 3	2	4
1 + 3 + 5	3	9
1 + 3 + 5 + 7	4	16
1 + 3 + 5 + 7 + 9	5	25
1 + 3 + 5 + 7 + 9 + 11	6	36

The table reveals quite clearly that the sum of the first n odd numbers is n^2. Thus the answer to our problem is simply $20^2 = 400$. Once again, detecting a pattern (of course, when one exists) can be quite helpful in solving the problem.

Adopting a Different Point of View

This strategy is a very useful method that requires "forcing" yourself to attempt to solve a problem by thinking about it in a different way. Consider the problem of a 25-team league trying to find the number of games that must be played to determine a champion in a single-elimination tournament. Most students faced with this problem will probably try to simulate the situation and begin with 12 teams eliminated after the first round (requiring 12 games played), and then continue considering only the winners, leaving the losers eliminated. This approach should lead to a correct answer, although it is a bit tedious. By adopting a different point of view, one might consider counting the losers. How many losers must there be? There must be 24 losers to get a champion. The number of games played to get 24 losers is 24. So the problem has been simply solved just by taking a different point of view.

In an everyday-life discussion with a friend it sometimes helps to consider the friend's point of view as a way to resolving an issue. In a debate this is a particularly useful strategy. Another illustration of how this technique can be useful is in taking attendance in a class. Rather than to call out the names of those present, consider adopting another point of view and count the absentees. The rest are then present. Another illustration will help you to appreciate this technique.

Consider the following problem.

PROBLEM

A cat chases a mouse, which has a 160-meter head start. For every 7 meters the mouse runs, the cat runs 9 meters. How far must the cat run to catch the mouse?

SOLUTION

This typical uniform motion problem has one disconcerting aspect: it doesn't give the speeds in the usual form, as "meters per minute" or "meters per second," etc. Thus, a usual textbook solution is not immediately forthcoming. However, students should see that the relative speeds are, in fact, given since for any time interval, seconds, minutes, or hours, the speeds can be called (for example) $9x$ and $7x$ meters per minute (or any other time interval).

Once this complication has been settled, the rest of the problem can be solved in the usual way. That is, if the distance the mouse runs is d, then the distance the cat runs is $d + 160$. Therefore, the time the mouse runs is $\frac{d}{7x}$ and the time the cat runs is $\frac{d + 160}{9x}$. Because both times are the same $\frac{d}{7x} = \frac{d + 160}{9x}$ and $d = 560$, the cat runs $560 + 160 = 720$ meters.

We can look at this problem from *another point of view*. The cat gains $9 - 7 = 2$ meters for each 9-meter interval it runs. To make up the mouse's 160-meter head start, the cat must run $\frac{160}{2} = 80$ intervals. But, each interval for the cat is 9 meters so the cat runs $(80)(9) = 720$ meters.

The better method to use to solve a problem is the one that the individual learner feels comfortable with and can genuinely understand. Some students may not be able to exercise a sufficient level of abstraction to understand the method using the *considering a different point of view* strategy. These students may feel more comfortable using a more "automatic," more "mechanical" procedure. For students who can appreciate the second (perhaps more elegant) method, the teacher has an obligation to demonstrate and explain that method. The more solutions a teacher shows the class, the more the teacher can reach to the individual learner, and the broader the instructional program will be. This instructional broadening is a desirable form of enrichment.

Solving a Simpler Analogous Problem

One method that sometimes turns out to be most revealing is to change the given problem into one which may be easier to solve, and, by solving this ancillary problem, gain the insight needed to solve the original problem. This particular strategy, *solving a simpler analogous problem*, can be referred to as specification without loss of generality. That is, if no restrictions are given in the problem, we may select a special case of the given situation to examine.

Although the following example seems to skirt the issue of exactness, it is a practical way of dealing with an everyday problem that does not require an exact answer.

When Americans travel abroad, they find that daily temperatures are usually given in degrees Celsius. Thus, they must convert Celsius temperatures to the more common (to them) Fahrenheit scale. Rather than use the formula $F = \frac{9}{5}C + 32$, they can approximate by doubling the given Celsius temperature and adding 30°. Although the Fahrenheit temperature is merely an approximation, it is generally adequate for everyday purposes. We see here, however, that by solving a somewhat simpler problem, we have essentially arrived at a useful answer.

Oftentimes, this strategy may be used to make a problem easier to grasp by replacing some numbers or variables with easier ones and then reverting back to the original problem. For example, sometimes a problem can appear to be unusually overwhelming. Yet by considering a simpler case of the situation presented, the problem can become much more manageable. Take for example the following problem.

PROBLEM

If ${}_xP_y = \frac{((25!)!)!}{((3!)!)!}$, what is the value of $x - y$?

SOLUTION

At first glance the nest of factorials can be a bit upsetting. Considering a *simpler analogous problem* where, say, ${}_7P_3 = \frac{7!}{(7-3)!}$, we notice that only the denominator plays a role in the determination of $x - y$. Thus we must only evaluate $(3!)! = 720$ to get the answer. The inspection of a simpler analogous problem gave us the necessary key to the solution, namely, the numerator did not play a role in answering the question.

The following problem is another example of solving a simpler analogous problem.

PROBLEM

Given that the angle sum of all pentagrams (i.e., five-cornered stars) is constant, determine that angle sum. (One such is shown in Figure 1.)

SOLUTION

Since the type of pentagram was not specified, we can assume the pentagram is either regular or one that is merely inscribable in a circle (i.e., all the vertices lie on a circle) (Figure 2). In the latter case, we notice that each of the angles is now an

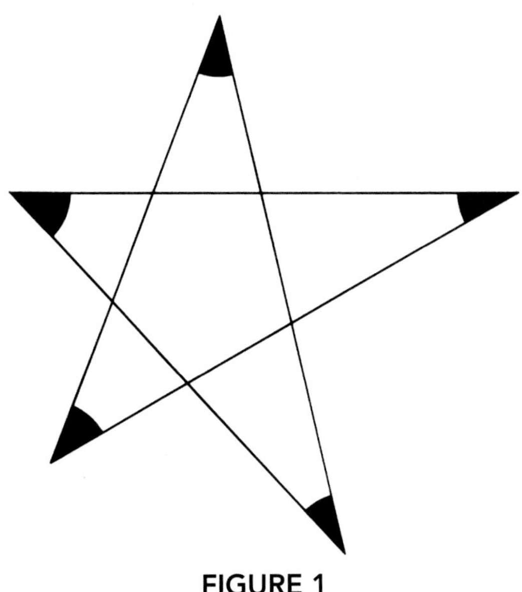

FIGURE 1

inscribed angle of the circle and so has half the measure of the intercepted arc. Consequently we get the following:

$$m\angle A = \frac{1}{2}\overset{\frown}{CD}, \quad m\angle B = \frac{1}{2}\overset{\frown}{ED}, \quad m\angle C = \frac{1}{2}\overset{\frown}{AE},$$

$$m\angle D = \frac{1}{2}\overset{\frown}{AB}, \quad m\angle E = \frac{1}{2}\overset{\frown}{BC},$$

$$m\angle A + m\angle B + m\angle C + m\angle D + m\angle E$$
$$= \frac{1}{2}\left(m\overset{\frown}{CD} + m\overset{\frown}{ED} + m\overset{\frown}{AE} + m\overset{\frown}{AB} + m\overset{\frown}{BC}\right)$$

That is, the sum of the measure of the angles of the vertices is one-half the degree measure of the circumference of the circle, or 180°. Again, there was no loss of generality by allowing the nonspecified pentagram to assume a more useful configuration. Yet this change made the problem much more manageable (and solvable). Adopting a different point of view gave us a simpler and yet analogous problem to solve, one that led to the immediate solution of the original problem.

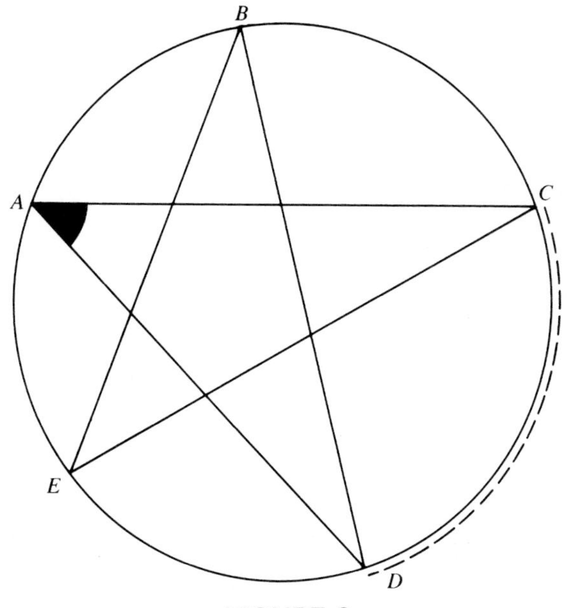

FIGURE 2

Another special case that could be used to demonstrate this strategy would be to assume the pentagram is a regular one and then find the angle sum (where each of the angles has the same measure).

PROBLEM

In the figure shown below, point E lies on $\overline{AB}$ and point C lies on $\overline{FG}$.

The area of parallelogram $ABCD$ = 20 square units. Find the area of parallelogram $EFGD$.

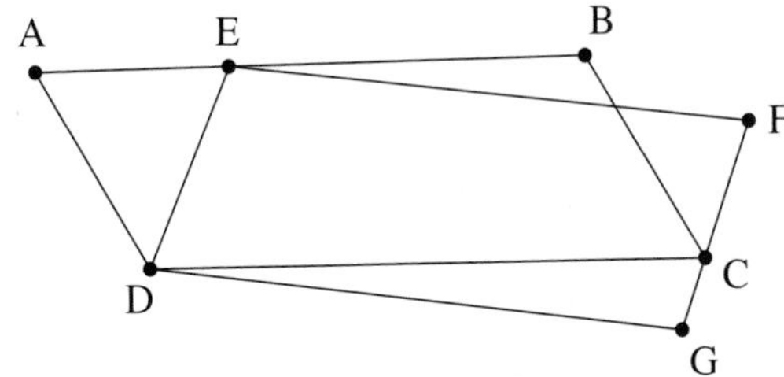

SOLUTION

Although the solution is not one that would occur to many people at first thought, the problem can be readily solved using only the tools found in a high school geometry course. Begin by drawing $\overline{EC}$.

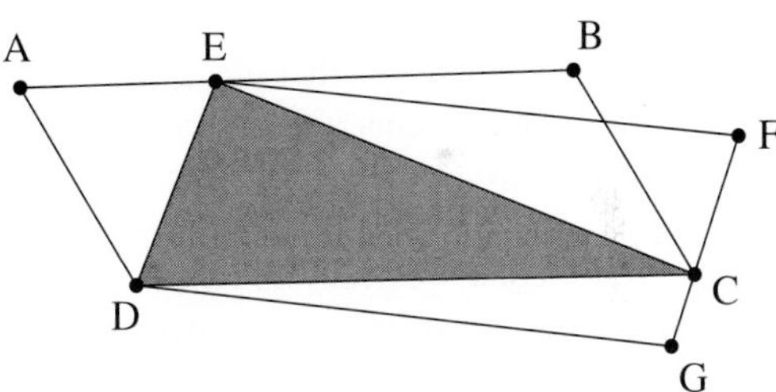

Since triangle EDC and parallelogram $ABCD$ share a common base ($\overline{DC}$) and a common altitude (a perpendicular from E to $\overline{DC}$), the area of triangle EDC is equal to one-half the area of parallelogram $ABCD$.

Similarly, triangle EDC and parallelogram $EFGD$ share the same base ($\overline{ED}$), and the same altitude to that base (a perpendicular from C to $\overline{ED}$), so the area of triangle EDC equals one-half the area of parallelogram $EFGD$.

Now, since the area of parallelogram $ABCD$ and the area of parallelogram $EFGD$ are both equal to the same area (twice the area of triangle EDC), the area of the two parallelograms must be equal. Thus, the area of parallelogram $EFGD$ is 20 square units.

Although the solution method, which we have just shown, is not often used, it is effective and efficient. Nevertheless, this problem can be solved quite elegantly by *solving a simpler, analogous problem* (without loss of generality). Recall that the original given conditions were that the two parallelograms had to have a common vertex (D), and a vertex of one had to be on the side of the other as shown with points E and C. Now, let us suppose that C coincided with G, and E coincided with A. This satisfies the given condition of the original problem and makes the two parallelograms coincide. Thus the area of parallelogram $EFGD$ is 20 square units.

We could also look at this last solution as one of *using extremes* (our next strategy). That is, we might consider point E on $\overline{AB}$, yet placed at an extreme, such as on point A. Similarly, we could place C on G and satisfy all the conditions of the original problem. Thus the problem is trivial, in that the two parallelograms overlap.

Considering Extreme Cases

To analyze some situations, whether in a mathematical setting or not, it can be helpful to look at extreme cases. Holding some variables constant, while others vary to extremes, sometimes yields some useful insights into a given situation. Some problems can be solved much more easily by considering extreme cases of the given situation. By considering extremes, we may be changing variables in the problem, but only those that do not affect the actual problem situation. Here, one must be careful only to consider extremes that do not change the nature of the crucial variables of the problem. In addition, we must be careful not to change a variable that affects other variables.

Used properly, considering extreme cases can be one of the most useful strategies for solving mathematical problems as well as those in everyday life. We frequently use this sort of reasoning when we are about to confront someone in a negotiation situation. Suppose you feel that your position is a right one, but you are concerned that pushing your point too far could cause other problems. Often, we examine such a situation in the context of what the worst-case scenario would be. That is, what is the worst that can happen if our argument goes awry? Then we proceed. Anticipating a worst-case scenario is a form of extreme case consideration. We use it frequently in everyday life when budgeting time, budgeting finances, and so on. To best grasp the value of this technique consider the following problem.

PROBLEM

Two concentric circles are 10 units apart as shown in the figure below. What is the difference between the circumferences of the circles?

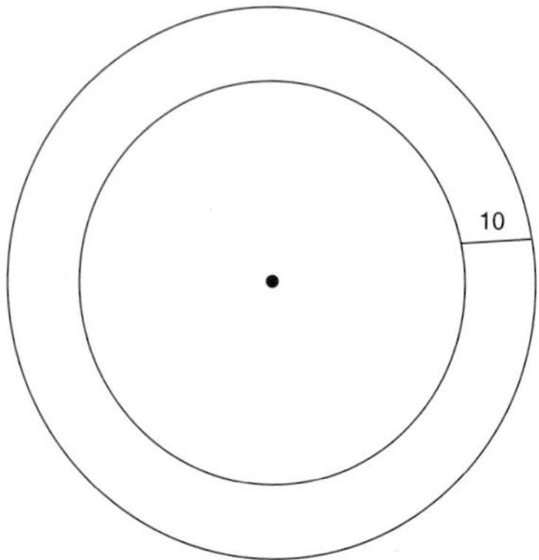

SOLUTION

The traditional straightforward method for solving this problem is to find the diameters of the two circles, find the circumference of each circle, and then find their difference. Since the lengths of the diameters are not given, the problem is a bit more complicated than usual. Let d represent the diameter of the smaller circle, then $d + 20$ is the diameter of the larger circle. The circumferences of the two circles will then be πd and $\pi(d + 20)$, respectively. Their difference is $\pi(d + 20) - \pi d = 20\pi$.

A more elegant procedure would be to *use an extreme case*. Let the smaller of the two circles become smaller and smaller until it reaches an "extreme" and becomes a "point-circle." In this case, it would become the center of the larger circle. The distance between the two circles now becomes the radius of the larger circle. The difference between the lengths of the circumferences of the two circles at the start is now merely the circumference of the larger circle, or 20π.

Although both procedures yield the same answer, notice how much more work is used for the traditional solution by actually taking the difference of the lengths of the circumferences of the two circles.

Making a Drawing (Visual Representation)

To make a drawing to solve a geometric problem is expected; not to do so is foolhardy! However, in this section, we are considering the use of a drawing to solve a problem where a visual representation is not the usual approach based on the nature of the problem. In real life, many decisions are made based on the visual presentation of data and relationships, where a visual representation acts more as a facilitator than as an expected element of the situation. In sociology, for example, there are sociograms, which show visually the interrelationships of a group. Graph theory enables the inspection of geometric relationships, which depend on location and interdependence rather than on size or shape. The famous "Bridges of Königsberg" problem can easily be resolved or explained by setting up a network diagram as a visual representation of the situation (see Enrichment Unit 96).

We use diagrams or drawings frequently in everyday life. We use a map to determine how to reach a specific destination. We sometimes sketch our own maps to explain a route to another person, when we could explain the travel instructions verbally. Drawing a picture makes the description clearer and easier to follow. After all, it has been said many times that one picture is worth 1,000 words!

Consider the following problem, one in which it is not expected that a diagram should be drawn.

PROBLEM

At 5:00 o'clock, a clock strikes 5 chimes in 5 seconds. How long will it take the same clock at the same rate to strike 10 chimes at 10:00? (Assume that the chime itself takes no time.)

SOLUTION

The answer is *not* 10 seconds! The nature of this problem does not lead us to think that a drawing should be made. However, let us use a drawing of the situation to see exactly what is taking place. In the drawing, each dot represents a chime. Thus, in the figure below, the total time is 5 seconds and there are 4 intervals between chimes.

Therefore, each interval must take $\frac{5}{4}$ seconds. Now let's examine the second case:

Here, we can see from the diagram that the 10 chimes give us 9 intervals. Because each interval takes $\frac{5}{4}$ seconds, the entire clock striking at 10:00 o'clock will take $9 \times \frac{5}{4}$, or $11\frac{1}{4}$ seconds.

Intelligent Guessing and Testing (Including Approximation)

This technique is often referred to as the method of "trial-and-error." But that name is an oversimplification, for this problem-solving strategy is, in its own right, quite sophisticated. *Intelligent guessing and testing* is particularly useful when we need to limit the values for a variable to make the solution more manageable. It is also helpful when the general case may be far more complicated than a specific case. By approximating we can try to narrow down the options in an effort to focus on the correct answer. In using this strategy, we make a guess, then test it against the conditions of the problem. Each succeeding guess is based on information obtained from testing the previous guess. Keep in mind that there is a great deal of difference between a "guess" and an "intelligent guess."

Solving an equation is really only a variation of intelligent guessing and testing. What we are doing in the solve part is putting forth a guess, arrived at intelligently by some careful mathematical manipulations. It is in the check or verification part that we are testing our guess to show that it is, indeed, correct.

In everyday life situations this strategy is used constantly. A common use for this procedure is the test poke that we make when cooking a roast to see if it is ready to be served. We poke a thermometer into the center of the meat, rather than cut the roast prematurely. We can read the temperature inside the meat to verify our guess, enabling us to more accurately determine its state of readiness. We are guessing and testing. If our initial guess that the roast was done proves incorrect when we test the guess with the thermometer, we continue cooking the meat for another few minutes until we are ready to guess again.

This same procedure is also used by a carpenter who cannot get the precise measurements of an odd-shaped piece of wood to fit a specific place. He, too, estimates the size and shape of the piece of wood and then, by continuously testing its fit and reshaping it, solves his construction problem.

Were someone to get the question "Find three consecutive numbers whose product is 24," the algebraic solution would be quite challenging. The equation would look like this: $(x)(x + 1)(x + 2) = 24$, which is a cubic equation and not too easily solved. However, using the *intelligent guessing and testing* strategy, we can find the three numbers easily: 2, 3, and 4. Another more realistic example of this strategy is found in the solution of the following problem.

PROBLEM

Find the two positive integers that differ by 5 and the sum of whose square roots is also 5.

SOLUTION

The traditional approach is to set up a system of equations as follows:
Let x = the first integer
Let x = the second integer
Then,

$$y = x + 5$$
$$\sqrt{x} + \sqrt{y} = 5$$
$$\sqrt{x} + \sqrt{x + 5} = 5$$

Squaring both sides,

$$x + x + 5 + 2\sqrt{x(x + 5)} = 25$$

Simplifying,

$$2\sqrt{x(x + 5)} = -2x + 20$$

Squaring again,

$$4x^2 + 20x = 4x^2 - 80x + 400$$
$$100x = 400$$
$$x = 4$$
$$y = 9$$

The two integers are 4 and 9.

Obviously, this procedure requires a knowledge of equations with radicals as well as careful algebraic manipulation. As an alternative, let us make use of our *intelligent guessing and testing* strategy to solve this problem. Since the sum of the square roots of the two integers is 5, the individual square roots must be 4 and 1, or 3 and 2. Thus, the integers must be 16 and 1, or 9 and 4. However, only 9 and 4 have a difference of 5, and must therefore be the correct answer.

Accounting for All Possibilities

Considering all the options can be an effective way to solve a problem. Although there may be instances where this strategy is not the most sophisticated procedure, it may be the simplest to use, since it is typically not very abstract. However, the issue of accounting for *all* the possibilities is crucial in the use of this strategy. If one does not have an organized procedure for accounting for all the possibilities, the strategy often goes awry.

We often use this problem-solving strategy in everyday life without being aware that it is even being employed. Suppose you are asked to attend a meeting in a hotel about 150 miles away. The way most people would decide on the best way to travel to the meeting is to list all the possible modes of transportation (e.g., train, plane, car, bus, helicopter, etc.), either in writing or mentally, and then by elimination or direct selection (due to time, cost, etc.), select the most efficient mode. When a computer program malfunctions and we have to determine the cause, we usually begin by listing (again, perhaps mentally) the various possible reasons for the malfunction. Then, one by one, we inspect the potential trouble spots on the list until we find the one causing the malfunction. A similar approach is used when we try to determine why a lamp is not working. We list the possible causes of the malfunction (e.g., bad wire, burned-out bulb, dead outlet, etc.) and then, one by one, eliminate the ones that are functioning until the culprit cause is discovered. When people are first seated in a restaurant, they are usually handed a menu with a large selection of appetizers, salads, entrees, and desserts. From the menu, they are expected to select those dishes that will provide them with a complete meal. The usual procedure for most people is to read the entire menu through, and then place an order providing them with a balanced, satisfying meal. Even though they usually do not consciously realize it, they are using the *accounting for all the possibilities* strategy in selecting their dinner.

In mathematics there are many examples where the preferred strategy would be to account for all possibilities. We consider one such here.

Consider the following problem.

PROBLEM

If four coins are tossed, what is the probability that at least two heads will be showing?

SOLUTION

Naturally, we can use methods of probability calculation to obtain this answer quite quickly—if we recognize the appropriate formula to use. However, it is quite simple to list all the possibilities (the sample space) and then to highlight those that fit the requirements of being at least two heads. Here is the entire list of all possibilities:

HHHH	HHHT	HHTH	HTHH
THHH	HHTT	HTHT	THHT
HTTH	THTH	TTHH	HTTT
THTT	TTHT	TTTH	TTTT

The bold events are those that have two or more Hs and satisfy the given conditions. There are 11 of these; thus, the required probability is $\frac{11}{16}$.

Another illustration of where this strategy is most useful can be seen in the solution to the following problem.

PROBLEM

In triangle *ABC*, $\cos\angle A \cdot \cos\angle B \cdot \cos\angle C > 0$.
What kind of triangle is triangle *ABC*?

SOLUTION

Some students will attempt to substitute values for angles *A*, *B*, and *C* and try to resolve the problem. This approach usually leads to difficulties. We shall solve the problem by *considering all possibilities* of types of triangles.

1. *Triangle ABC is a right triangle.* If triangle *ABC* is a right triangle, then one of its angles must measure 90°, and $\cos 90° = 0$.Then $\cos\angle A \cdot \cos\angle B \cdot \cos\angle C = 0$, which contradicts the given.
2. *Triangle ABC is an obtuse triangle.* If triangle *ABC* is an obtuse triangle, then one of its angles (let us assume it is angle *B*) must have measure greater than 90° while angle *A* and angle *C* must both be acute. Then $\cos\angle B < 0$, while $\cos\angle A > 0$ and $\cos\angle C > 0$. Here, $\cos\angle A \cdot \cos\angle B \cdot \cos\angle C < 0$. Again, this is a contradiction of the given.
3. *Triangle ABC is an acute triangle.* If triangle *ABC* is acute, then all of its three angles must be acute. Thus, $\cos\angle A > 0, \cos\angle B > 0$, and $\cos\angle C > 0$. This makes $\cos\angle A \cdot \cos\angle B \cdot \cos\angle C > 0$. Thus our triangle is an acute triangle.

Organizing Data

It is not uncommon to find a student, who, a bit baffled by a problem, emerges from this state of confusion by organizing given data from the problem situation in a way different from the way it was presented. This reorganization may be visual or it may simply be an alternate way to look at the situation.

This problem-solving strategy manifests itself frequently in our everyday planning processes. We visually organize data when we do home budgeting and arrange bills according to category. Also, when faced with several tasks and the problem of how best to approach them, we tend to organize the tasks by time, place, difficulty, or some other important criterion. For example, we use the *organizing data* strategy when we want to make the best use of the time available on a shopping trip. We list the items to be purchased and then organize them in the order which makes the most sense in avoiding crowds of people, or minimizing the travel time to and between stores. Similarly, a tourist wanting to make her sightseeing most efficient would organize the sights by location. When we gather together the information needed to prepare our annual taxes, the way in which we organize our receipts, checks, W-2 forms, 1099 forms, etc., becomes critical. If these papers are not organized, it becomes impossible to fill out the tax forms efficiently or properly. The problem of passing a history test is sometimes dependent on one's ability to organize data. Organizing data can help one analyze concepts, or establish common issues in history, which can lead to determining a policy or principle. Just such a question could appear on a test, so that the student who has the ability to first organize data and ideas and then analyze them is at a distinct advantage.

Organizing data in the solution to a mathematics problem can manifest itself in various ways. One such can be seen in the following problem's solution.

PROBLEM

Find the greatest possible product of two natural numbers whose sum is 41.

SOLUTION

Students can set up the equation $y = x(41 - x)$ where x is one of the numbers, $(41 - x)$ is the other, and y is the product. By drawing the graph, they can obtain a parabola. They can then determine the maximum point of the parabola in order to find the value required.

However, we can easily solve the problem by *organizing the data* in tabular form:

Numbers		Product
1	40	40
2	39	78
3	38	114
:	:	:
15	26	390
16	25	400
17	24	408
18	23	414
19	22	418
20	21	420

The greatest possible product is 420.

Another form of *organizing the data* can be seen with the solution to the next problem.

PROBLEM

If A apples cost D dollars, what is the cost in cents of B apples at the same rate?

SOLUTION

There are several ways that students tackle this problem. Most often, they will use numbers in place of the letters, and then try to reinsert the letters to find the answer. This method can easily lead to confusion and, unfortunately, to an incorrect answer. Some students have been taught to look for unit costs and proceed from there. Again, this, too, may lead to confusion.

As a general rule, a problem like this one can best be solved by *organizing the data* in some meaningful manner. Here, we will use proportionality together with some common sense. The proportionality is obtained by setting up the proportion with the same units of measure in each fraction.

$$\frac{A}{B} = \frac{\text{cost of A apples}}{\text{cost of B apples}} = \frac{100D}{x}$$

Notice that we have used common sense in obtaining the last fraction. Because the problem called for the answer in cents, we use a fraction with cents as the unit rather than dollars. Thus, when we find x, we have found the answer. The rest is simple.

$$\frac{A}{B} = \frac{100D}{x}$$

$$x = \frac{100BD}{A}$$

Logical Reasoning

When dealing with friends and colleagues, we find that what we say will often evoke a certain response. That response can then lead to another, and so on. When we try to predict a conversation scenario, or a potential discussion/argument, we are, in effect, using *logical reasoning*. For example, if you say A, then you expect the response will be B, which will lead to statement C, which will likely be responded to with statement D. Logical reasoning, done effectively, can improve interpersonal relationships by helping solve (or perhaps avoid) problems before they arise. We often analyze a situation without being aware of the actual process. However, in mathematics, we make our students aware of this thinking process. We try to guide them, or train them, to think logically. Since inductive thinking (i.e., going from several specific examples to a generalization) may be more natural, the logical form of reasoning requires some practice.

In everyday-life situations, we typically rely on logical reasoning to plan a strategy for a work plan, or we may use it to argue a point with a colleague or boss. The strength of an argument often depends on the validity of the logical reasoning used. Validity can mean the difference between success and failure of an argument. How an argument is posed can affect success or advancement on the job, as well as status. In addition, the success or failure of a business deal can depend on one's facility with logical reasoning. Almost every mathematics problem we tackle involves a degree of logical reasoning, even the selection of the most efficient problem-solving strategy.

Formal logic is fundamental to pure mathematics and to proofs. Often, logical reasoning that does not seem to be a proof will enable analysis of a problem. When it is appropriate for students to do proofs, it is suggested that they be given "prove-or-disprove" problems often enough for them to develop the habit of trying out a conjecture before attempting to prove it. This approach is second nature to mathematicians confronting unfamiliar conjectures. Needless to say, some of the problems given in the "prove-or-disprove" mode should end up having to be disproved.

PROBLEM

Prove that it is impossible to cover a checkerboard with fifteen 3×1 L-shaped quadrominoes (an extension of the word *domino* that refers to figures consisting of four connected squares in which adjoining squares share an edge) and one 2×2 square quadromino.

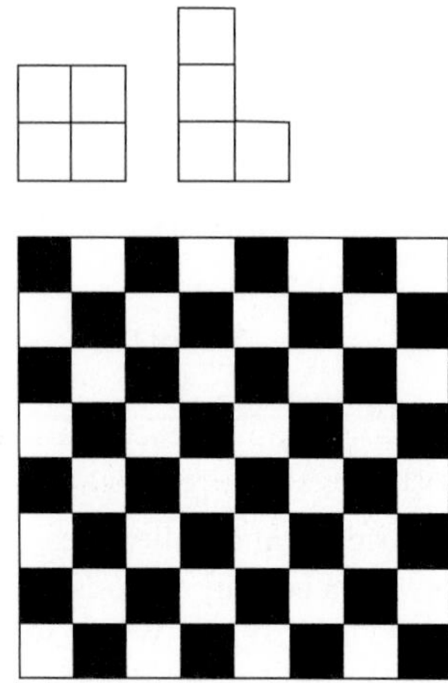

SOLUTION

This problem is a delightful adjunct to the problem presented earlier concerning 31 dominoes and the checkerboard with two diagonally opposite squares deleted (p. 110). To examine the color patterning of the standard checkerboard will yield no insight into the current problem, because both types of figures involved in the new problem cover two white squares and two black squares. Logic dictates a color patterning that *distinguishes* between the two types of quadrominoes in the problem. The simplest such color patterning is the striping of the checkerboard (so that, for example, each row has the opposite color of the adjoining row[s]). Now, each L shape must cover *three* squares of one color and *one* square of the other color no matter how it is placed. The square must cover two squares of each color. Since odd × odd must yield an odd result, the fifteen L shapes must cover an odd total of white squares and an odd total of black squares. Since odd + even must yield an odd result, the total number of black squares covered by the sixteen quadrominoes must be odd, and the total number of white squares covered by the sixteen quadrominoes must be odd. But the striping yields thirty-two white squares and thirty-two black squares, so the covering under consideration is impossible.

PROBLEM

Prove or disprove that a quadrilateral that has perpendicular diagonals of equal length and that has at least one diagonal that bisects the other must be a square.

SOLUTION

The disproof (by counterexample) might consist of simply drawing a horizontally symmetrical kite that is not vertically symmetrical and in which the length of the crossbeam equals that of the vertical beam.

Reasoning logically can often save considerable work in solving some problems. Before plunging into a typical algebraic solution one ought to consider trying to "reason out the answer." The following two illustrations show dramatically how this may be done.

PROBLEM

The four-digit number $x56y$, where x and y are the first and last digits respectively, is divisible by 9. What is the value of $x + y$? $(x \neq y)$

SOLUTION

Typically, a student will simply try various values for x and y to see which enable divisibility by 9. Although this is a form of guessing and testing, it is not sufficient. It must be combined with *logical reasoning* from the given information.

Recall that, in order for a number to be divisible by 9, the sum of the digits of the number must be a multiple of 9. Therefore, $x + 5 + 6 + y = 9M$, or $x + y + 11 = 9M$. The largest $x + y$ can be is $9 + 8 = 17$. But $17 + 11 = 28$, and 28 is not a multiple of 9. Can we obtain 27? $x + y$ would then have to be 16, and $7 + 9 = 16$. The next smaller multiple of 9 counting back from 27 would be 18. Then $x + y = 7$. A lower multiple of 9 would be too small to work. There are no others. Thus, $x + y = 16$ or 7.

PROBLEM

Find all pairs of prime numbers whose sum equals 999.

SOLUTION

Many students will begin by taking a list of prime numbers and trying various pairs to see if they obtain 999 for a sum. This is obviously very tedious as well as time consuming, and students would never be quite certain that they had considered all the prime number pairs.

Let's use our *logical reasoning* strategy to solve this problem. To obtain an odd sum for two numbers (prime or otherwise), exactly one of the numbers must be even. Since there is only one even prime, namely 2, there must be only one pair of primes whose sum is 999, and that pair is 2 and 997.

These 10 problem-solving strategies must be practiced with motivating problems that show the power of the strategies. The names of the strategies should be used whenever they are used, for research shows repetition improves retention of the strategy. We suggest referring to the following book for the reinforcement necessary to become more facile with these techniques.

Posamentier, A. S., and S. Krulik. *Problem-Solving Strategies for Efficient and Elegant Solutions: A Resource for the Mathematics Teacher*. Thousand Oaks, CA: Corwin Press, 2008.

Once familiar with the strategies, try to find ways to apply them to textbook problems and exercises, thereby reinforcing their use. Also use the strategies to find alternative methods of solution, but don't simply be satisfied to have gotten the solution. How one gets to a solution is often as important as getting the solution. Remember, there is usually a "poet's way" and a "peasant's way" of getting a solution. We would like all our students to eventually use the poet's way.

Creating Mathematical Problems

The changes made in two of Euclid's five postulates (the Parallel Postulate and the Infinitude of a Line) led to a revolution in mathematics—the development of non-Euclidean geometries. The technique of making minor or major adjustments in the given conditions of a mathematics problem "just for the fun of it" has a long tradition among mathematicians and students of mathematics. The results have, on occasion, proved startling, to say the least—as evidenced by the example just cited. Another example is an extension of the fact that there exist Pythagorean triples (x, y, z) that satisfy $x^2 + y^2 = z^2$. However, one would not have such an easy time trying to find integers x, y, and z that satisfy $x^n + y^n = z^n$ for integral $n > 2$. In fact this leads to the well-known "Fermat's last theorem" (proved by A. Wiles in June 1993 and corrected in October 1994).

Students can be trained to develop and solve their own, self-made problems by making changes, even simple changes, in existing ones. When students are developing their own problems, they may occasionally create problems that are beyond their ability or capacity to solve, however. Some may even be unsolvable.

Every problem that is posed can have some conditions changed to produce a new problem or variation of the original problem. Thus, the teacher should determine some alternative assessment scheme for giving credit to students not only for solving problems correctly, as is traditionally the case, but also for creating problems. Through this creative effort students really begin to understand what problems are all about.

As an aid to teachers and prospective teachers, we offer some suggestions on how specific problems can be changed to produce new ones. These can be used to demonstrate to students the types of variations that might be made. The real creativity, however, will come from students' own variations of problems.

PROBLEM

David has 45 coins, consisting of nickels and dimes. The total value is $3.50. How many coins of each kind does he have?

POSSIBLE VARIATIONS

1. What is the largest number of nickels and dimes he could have that would total $3.50?
2. What is the smallest number?
3. How would the problem change if it included quarters as well as nickels and dimes?
4. Is it possible to have only dimes and quarters instead of nickels and dimes?
5. In how many ways could $3.50 be represented in nickels and dimes?

PROBLEM

By construction (using straightedge and compasses), locate the midpoint of segment AB:

POSSIBLE VARIATIONS

1. Are there any ways of locating the midpoint of a segment?
2. Suppose a student forgot to bring a straightedge to school. Is it possible to locate the midpoint with compasses alone?
3. With straightedge alone?
4. Suppose a student had a pair of compasses that were rusted and could not be adjusted. Can the segment $\overline{AB}$ be bisected with unadjustable compasses?

PROBLEM

At a point on level ground 100 feet from the foot of a flagpole, the angle of elevation of the top of the pole measures 31°. Find the height of the flagpole to the nearest foot.

POSSIBLE VARIATIONS

1. Suppose the same pole had a 15° tilt. How would you then compute the length of the pole?
2. Suppose the original flagpole is standing vertically on a hill that has a 15° rise. How would you compute the height of the pole?

PROBLEM

Prove that in a circle, chords are congruent if they are equidistant from the center.

POSSIBLE VARIATIONS

1. State and prove the inverse of the problem.
2. State and prove the converse of the problem.
3. State and prove the contrapositive of the problem.
4. Are there any other variations?

Creativity in Problem Solving

If there is difficulty in teaching effective ways of using the techniques of problem solving, there is, perhaps, greater difficulty in teaching "creativity." One of the major difficulties is in defining the term itself. At one time, it was thought that creativity was a genetic capacity granted to the fortunate few; but now a number of psychologists have attempted to demonstrate that processes associated with creativity are teachable (or, at least, encourageable). For our purposes, we may define creativity as the ability to evolve unusual, highly useful, or unique solutions to problems. (Remember that such solutions do not necessarily occur quickly. It took Johannes Kepler almost 20 years to develop his three laws of planetary motion—one of the most creative performances in scientific history.)

Although there is continuing investigation into the relationship between creativity and intelligence, preliminary findings indicate that the domains are not identical. Highly creative students are not necessarily those with the highest I.Q. Different tests of creativity may, of course, be responsible for some of the differences in findings, but some psychologists seem to agree that intelligence tests do not measure the same operations as found in creativity.

Following are some suggestions for encouraging creativity in the classroom.

1. Provide a classroom atmosphere that encourages freedom of expression.
2. Respect unusual questions, and set an example by your own inquiry and creativity.
3. Respect and reward unusual ideas.
4. Provide opportunities for learning that involve searching for students' own solutions without being graded.
5. Do not discourage controversy.
6. Encourage students to value their own ideas and to record them in concrete form whenever possible.
7. Share examples of the efforts of famous creative people—and their difficulties.
8. Encourage the acquisition of knowledge in a variety of fields.
9. When giving assignments, provide opportunities for originality and exploration.
10. Encourage cooperative learning efforts in developing creative problems.

Summary

The one statement that best summarizes this chapter is: "We learn best how to solve problems by solving them." This is the case whether the problems are of the standard varieties found in algebra or geometry textbooks, or any of the challenging types one finds in some textbooks as well as special puzzle or problem books (see list in the References Section). It is impossible to include in any chapter on the subject a sampling of every solution type. Rather, we have tried to impart a feeling or sensitivity toward the whole area of problem solving that establishes it as an interesting, challenging, and fruitful branch of mathematics, as well as one that can be very helpful in real-life decision making.

Problem solving, perhaps more than any other aspect of mathematics, sharpens a student's analytical and critical powers. At the same time, it may help develop a sense of accomplishment and achievement in students. As a matter of fact, the discovery (or development) of many areas of mathematics is a direct result of problem solving. Much of probability theory results from the solution of posed problems and challenges.

Whatever one can say about the achievement of mathematical power through problem solving applies to both the college-bound and the non-college-bound student. Teaching the fine art of problem solving to all students is indeed a challenge—to students and teachers alike.

EXERCISES

1. Write lesson plans for small groups to create and solve problems dealing with uniform motion, coins, mixture, and investment.
   a. Recommend the incorporation of calculators, computers, diagrams, and tables.
   b. Suggest presentation of each group's results to the entire class by a group representative.
2. Prepare a lesson on how you would teach students to create new problems by changing part of the hypothesis or given conditions for
   a. algebraic problems.
   b. geometric problems.
3. Write any two verbal problems in algebra and one geometric "proof" that have
   a. insufficient data.
   b. excessive data.

   Write a lesson plan indicating how you would introduce this type of problem to an algebra (or geometry) class.
4. Look in some of the books listed in the references at book's end, and select five challenging problems and their solutions that are appropriate for a middle school or high school mathematics class (you select the level). Indicate how you would use these problems in your classes.
5. List five activities that can be described as problem solving for a ninth grade algebra class.
6. Consider the following challenging problems. In which types of classes would you present them? Indicate the benefits you think your students could derive from these problems.

a. One method of obtaining the product of two numbers, say, 43 and 75, is illustrated by the following:

43	75
21	150
(10)	(300)
5	600
(2)	(1200)
1	2400

from which

$$43 \times 75 = 75 + 150 + 600 + 2400 = 3225$$

i. Use this method to multiply 73×120.

ii. Explain why the method is valid.

b. Find, to the nearest hundredth, the value of

$$1 + \cfrac{1}{1 + \cfrac{1}{1 + \cfrac{1}{1 + \cfrac{1}{1 + \cdots}}}}$$

c. Solve:

$$x + y = 5xy$$
$$y + z = 7yz$$
$$z + x = 6xz$$

d. If $3^{2x} + 9 = 10(3^x)$, solve for x.

e. Determine which is larger: $\sqrt[9]{9!}$ or $\sqrt[10]{10!}$

f. How many positive integers less than or equal to 1 million are squares or cubes of integers?

7. Read *How to Solve It* by George Polya (Princeton University Press, 1945 and later), then discuss how some of Polya's heuristic strategies can be applied to the secondary school mathematics curriculum. Consider at least three strategies in your response to this exercise.

8. Read *How to Solve Problems* by Wayne A. Wickelgren (W. H. Freeman & Co., 1974), then discuss how Wickelgren's heuristic strategies can be applied to the secondary school mathematics curriculum. Consider at least three strategies in your response.

9. Read the 1980 Yearbook of the National Council of Teachers of Mathematics, *Problem Solving in School Mathematics*, then prepare a report on Chapter 3, "Heuristics in the Classroom," by Alan R. Schoenfeld.

10. Select one of the challenging problems from *Mathematics As Problem Solving* by Alexander Soifer (Center for Excellence in Mathematics Education, 1987), and then take the problem you have selected and show how the unusual nature of the problem or the solutions given by the author can serve to model skills students ought to incorporate into their problem-solving activities. Repeat this exercise for two other problems in the book.

11. The book *The Art of Problem Solving: A Resource for the Mathematics Teacher* by Alfred S. Posamentier and Wolfgang Schultz (eds.) (Corwin Press, 1996) has 20 chapters, each written by an author who exhibits a specialty in the field of mathematics problem solving. Select one of the chapters and prepare a short report on how the material in that chapter can be useful in teaching one of the secondary school mathematics topics or areas.

12. Read *Problem Solving Strategies for Efficient and Elegant Solutions: A Resource for the Mathematics Teacher* by A. S. Posamentier and S. Krulik (Corwin Press, 2008). For each of the 10 problem-solving strategies presented with motivating problems, find *another* problem that illustrates that strategy.

13. Use a typical high school mathematics textbook and select five exercises. For each, show how one or more of the 10 problem-solving strategies may be used to do the exercise.

Chapter 5

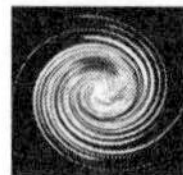

Using Technology to Enhance Mathematics Instruction

In the 2000 revision of *Principles and Standards for School Mathematics*, the National Council of Teachers of Mathematics wrote its "Technology Principle." It states that "technology is essential in teaching and learning mathematics; it influences the mathematics that is taught and enhances students' learning." The National Council of Teachers of Mathematics also concludes that technology is not a panacea. The teacher's use of technology can enhance students' learning experiences by taking advantage of what technology does efficiently and well—graphing, visualizing, and computing. Technology does not *replace* mathematics teachers, but gives teachers additional tools to help them teach and to help students learn mathematics.

The handheld calculator first became available in the early 1970s. The very first calculator on the market, the "Bowmar Brain," cost more than seven hundred dollars. It was a four-function calculator, had very little memory, and was quite bulky, although it could fit in a large shirt pocket. In 1976, the price barrier was finally broken when the cost of scientific calculators came down to a little more than one hundred dollars. They quickly replaced the slide rule, a mechanical device that was quite popular among scientists and engineers. A controversy as to whether or not calculator use should be permitted quickly arose. Students started using calculators at home and in school as critics claimed that students would not use their brains, but would rather let calculators do all the work for them. More than 30 years later, we have seen that this line of reasoning was incorrect. Studies have shown that those who grew up using calculators do at least as well as those who did not use calculators. In fact, in many cases, scientific and graphing calculators have become a necessity. Years ago, for example, tables of values of trigonometric and logarithmic functions had to be used. Nowadays, they are not even published because calculators produce needed trigonometric and logarithmic values instantaneously. In fact, the use of calculators has made dealing with these subjects a lot more pleasant, because many of the tables were not easy to use and students had to use "numerical interpolation" to get the most accurate results. This ponderous task has virtually been eliminated.

In 1986, the first graphing calculators became available. These machines had all the power of scientific calculators as well as the ability to draw graphs. At first their use in the classroom was minimal. In the early 1990s the Educational Testing Service announced that starting with the 1995 Advanced Placement Calculus Examinations, students would be required to use graphing calculators. As a result, high school students had to learn to use these machines in Advanced Placement Calculus. Most schools realized that to do a calculus course justice, students would have to be quite adept with the use of graphing calculators *before* studying calculus. The use of these machines has since filtered down to lower grades, and it is not unusual to see their use in middle schools. It has been shown

The authors gratefully acknowledge the contributions to this chapter made by Dr. Peter Brouwer, SUNY-Potsdam.

that students can experiment with calculators to discover many mathematical ideas. Such activities can help students become very creative. Although Texas Instruments' graphing calculators are the most widely used, there are also excellent graphing calculators made by Casio, Sharp, and Hewlett Packard, to name a few. In this chapter, we will explore some graphing calculator activities that can be used in your classroom to enrich the learning of mathematics at several levels of secondary mathematics.

In the 1980s, as personal computers (PCs) became widely used, much general-purpose and educational software was written. Spreadsheets were one of the first general computer applications programmed for PCs and one of the most successful. Their ease of use and flexibility made them useful for a range of business applications. Over time, educators began to see the value of spreadsheets in mathematics education. Such software is particularly valuable for solving problems that are iterative, recursive, or tabular in nature. Spreadsheets also support the investigation of the important "what if?" types of questions that arise in mathematical explorations. In this chapter, we will explore some of the power of spreadsheets for enhancing mathematics instruction.

In 1985, Judah Schwartz and Michal Yerushalmy of the Education Development Center developed a revolutionary set of programs to be used in the secondary classroom called Geometric Supposers. These programs allowed the user to draw various shapes, make measurements, and draw conclusions. Early in the 1990s, two more sophisticated geometry programs, Cabri Geometry and The Geometer's Sketchpad, became available. These programs allowed the user to construct geometric objects and to manipulate them so that the user could more easily explore geometric concepts and arrive at his or her own conclusions. In this chapter, we will explore The Geometer's Sketchpad in detail and see how it can become a useful tool for the mathematics classroom.

Most people using this book should have had some experience using technology. It is our aim here to show how to enrich your classroom using the latest technology by providing alternate approaches to teaching some traditional ideas.

Calculators

By experimenting with calculators, students can see various relationships between numbers evolve. For example, they can discover what type of divisors will generate repeating or terminating decimals. They can discover ways of detecting prime numbers. They may discover unusual number patterns. They can dissect the common arithmetic computational algorithms and perhaps devise others. All these activities can lead to creative work. Yet, most important is proper teacher guidance, for without this, the student could end up losing the educational benefits of this attractive and useful device.

Appropriate Use of Calculators in the Mathematics Classroom

A diversity of opinion has existed in the mathematics education community about what the appropriate role of calculators is in mathematics instruction. The emergence of low-cost but powerful calculators that can perform much of the mathematical procedures of the school curriculum has raised important questions about the role of this technology in school mathematics. These questions cut to the core of our beliefs about and practice of mathematics teaching:

- To what extent should children learn and perform arithmetic procedures before using the calculator?
- What type of understanding does one obtain through repeated applications of algorithms, particularly ones that the calculator can perform more efficiently and precisely?
- How important are speed and accuracy with paper-and-pencil techniques when a calculator is usually faster and more accurate?
- What new understandings may be gained from calculator use? What may be lost?
- What mathematical topics or procedures no longer need to be taught because of the use of calculators?

The NCTM, as well as the majority of mathematics educators, has taken the stance that the use of calculators is here to stay, and that appropriate use of this technology in the school mathematics classroom should be embraced. The NCTM position statement "Calculators and the Education of Youth" (www.nctm.org/about/position_statements) recommends "the integration of calculators into the school mathematics program at all grade levels." Teachers should incorporate appropriate instruction that includes calculators in such a way as to "extend students' understanding of mathematics" and "allow all students access to rich problem-solving experiences." Teachers need to develop students' ability to know how and when to use a calculator in appropriate ways and emphasize skill in estimation as a way to determine whether a technology-based solution is a reasonable one. (For more information on this debate, see the NCTM's May/June 1999 issue of *Mathematics Education Dialogues* entitled "Calculators—What Is Their Place in Mathematics Classrooms?" available at www.nctm.org/dialogues/index.htm.)

Most mathematics educators do believe that children should learn and become proficient in the standard arithmetic procedures and learn basic number facts for the development of number sense. However, the question of how far to continue with these procedures is under debate. A good case in point is the question of whether the long division algorithm should be taught in school or whether teaching the procedure is obsolete. Some say that teaching the process of long division is important, because it can reinforce important elementary mathematics concepts and lead the way to advanced mathematics, such as the division of polynomials or in using Euclid's greatest common factor method. Others argue that long division is not a procedure most people will ever use again and, given the standard way of teaching it, the procedure is difficult for most students to grasp and leads students to seeing mathematics not as something they can figure out, but rather as something they need to memorize. Most would agree that if it is to be taught, it should not be taught mechanically, but rather in a constructive fashion, with student understanding as a goal. (See the NCTM's March 1998 issue of *Mathematics Education dialogues* entitled "Is Mathematics Obsolete? Is Long Division Obsolete?")

Calculators as an Aid to Problem Solving

A common complaint among teachers is that students have great difficulty with computation and, what is worse, they are very weak in problem solving. Unfortunately this complaint is a self-perpetuating ill. Students who cannot succeed with arithmetic computation are constantly told to drill these skills and are rarely allowed to practice any problem-solving skills. Those who do go on to working on some elementary problems often do not get near an answer because of computational deficiencies. Their only exposure to problem solving is one of frustration, and they rarely realize success because of computational obstacles. Here the calculator can be of significant assistance. Selective use of the calculator to bypass potential computational barriers will allow students to concentrate on problem-solving skills without fear of meeting frustration previously caused by their computational deficiencies. Such activities should be carefully designed and monitored to be effective. After realizing success in problem solving, students should then be intrinsically motivated to conquer their computational deficiencies.

Although continuously nurtured on typical textbook problems, students usually find them boring and unrealistic. Traditionally, textbook authors design the problems in a way that will make the arithmetic computations as simple as possible so as not to detract from the problem. Real-life situations frequently are quite different. The numbers used are generally not simple. With the aid of a calculator, a teacher can provide realistic situations for problem solving and not worry about computational distractions. A uniform-motion problem, for example, can involve fractional quantities and yield an answer that is not an integer and still cause no displeasure for the student who has a calculator available. Furthermore, students using a calculator can be encouraged to create problems based on their own experiences (e.g., calculating their average speed walking to school). New vistas are opened up when a calculator is used to assist in problem solving bypassing arithmetic.

Problems in advanced secondary school mathematics courses can often involve extensive calculations. Not many years ago the slide rule or logarithms were used to solve such problems. Even Napier's rods and the abacus played a role at one point in the history of people's attempts to be free of the burden of onerous manual calculations. The abacus is still used in some parts of the less technologically advanced world. Today, the logical method of computation at this level is the calculator. A scientific calculator (i.e., one that, among other features, includes trigonometric functions) and a graphing calculator are very useful aids to instruction, but by no means replace instruction.

Examples of Calculator Activities

Explorations

Calculators can become wonderful tools for students to experiment with, look for patterns in, and construct their own conclusions about mathematical ideas. Exploration activities can occur at all grade levels of instruction. The following problems can be assigned anywhere from grade five on. For example, in the earlier grades, students can explore the following problem quite easily after learning about repeating decimals.

PROBLEM

What are the decimal equivalents of $\frac{1}{11}, \frac{2}{11}, \frac{3}{11}, \frac{4}{11}, \ldots$? Can you predict the decimal equivalent of $\frac{9}{11}$ without using your calculator?

SOLUTION

Although this problem can be explored using any calculator, the large-screen display of a graphing calculator allows students to see more information and to draw conclusions more easily.

```
1/11
          .0909090909
2/11
          .1818181818
3/11
          .2727272727
■
```

The screens on the left were generated using a Texas Instruments TI-83 Plus graphing calculator. Students should be able to discover the following from these screens:

- The decimal equivalents generated are repeating decimals. While 10 decimal places are shown, we can surmise that this is only because of calculator limitations.

```
        .1818181818
3/11
        .2727272727
4/11
        .3636363636
5/11
        .4545454545
```

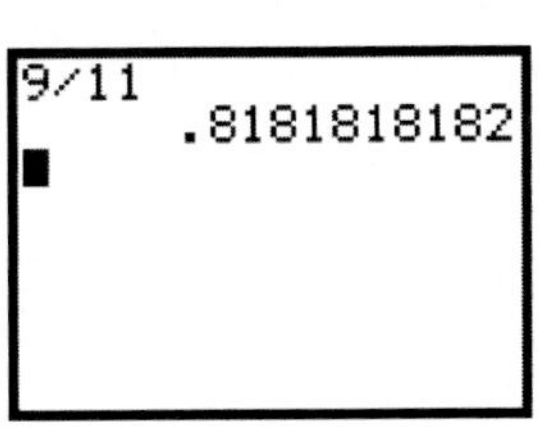

▶ The repetends (09, 18, 27, 36, . . .) are multiples of 9.

▶ Should this pattern continue, the decimal equivalent of $\frac{9}{11}$ should be 0.81818181. . . .

Of course, when entering $\frac{9}{11}$, students will see that their conjecture holds, except for the last decimal place shown on the calculator. This unexpected digit can lead to a discussion of the rounding nature of calculators and motivate the students to more accurately predict the decimal equivalents of $\frac{6}{11}$, $\frac{7}{11}$, and $\frac{8}{11}$.

The power of this problem is that without using a calculator the data would be more difficult to generate. Students working by hand may make errors, and most would not be motivated to look for a pattern after doing the long divisions. The opportunity to discuss rounding may not arise as naturally as it did here. Follow-ups to this problem include exploring patterns for fractions with denominators such as 9, 90, 110, and 7.

PROBLEM

Pablo invests \$5000 in an account that pays 6% interest compounded annually. How much money will be in the account at the end of 10 years?

Before the use of technology in the schools, there were two basic approaches to solving this problem.

SOLUTION 1

By hand, students could do the following calculations:

At the End of Year #	Amount
1	\$5000 + .06(\$5000) = \$5300
2	\$5300 + .06(\$5300) = \$5618
3	\$5618 + .06(\$5618) = \$5955.08
•	•
•	•
•	•
10	\$8954.24

Doing the calculations without the aid of a calculator would be quite brutal for even the best of students. The computations would discourage anyone attempting the problem.

SOLUTION 2

Students in a higher-level course could generalize the above calculations using the formula $A = P(1 + r)^n$ so that they realize they need to compute the value of $\$5000(1.06)^{10}$. Without technology, this problem was traditionally done by using logarithms. Students would do the following:

$$A = 5000(1.06)^{10}$$
$$\log A = \log 5000(1.06)^{10}$$
$$\log A = \log 5000 + 10 \log 1.06$$
$$\log A = 3.6990 + 10(.0253)$$
$$\log A = 3.9520$$
$$A = 8953.65$$

Note that the use of a logarithm table, which has some rounding errors built in, leaves a \$0.59 error. Before calculators were used to do computations, logarithms were the chief means to simplify calculations. Less attention was paid to studying the properties and graphs of the logarithm function.

Let us look at a few other solutions that take advantage of technology.

SOLUTION 3

Enter \$5000(1.06)^10 on a scientific or graphing calculator set to two decimal places to get \$8954.24. This solution is somewhat trivialized by the calculator.

SOLUTION 4

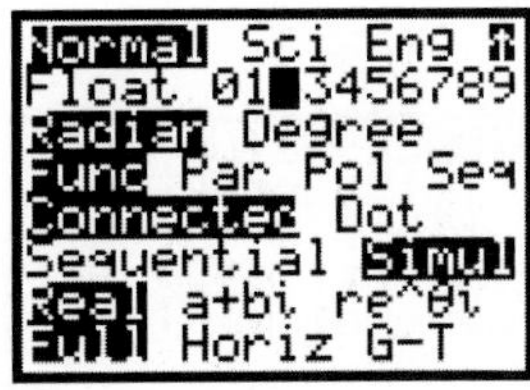

Even in lower grades, the recursive power of a graphing calculator can make this problem more interesting. Since the problem deals with dollars and cents, the calculator's mode should be set to two decimal places. The second line of the diagram on the left indicates that this had been done on a TI-83 calculator.

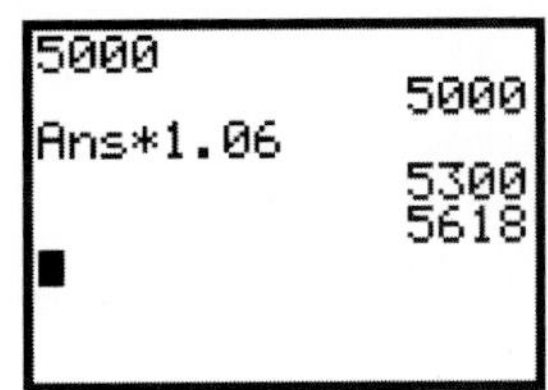

Type in 5000, followed by the ENTER button. By pressing Ans* 1.06, the calculator finds 5000(1.06), or the principal after one year (\$5300). At this point, pressing ENTER tells the calculator to repeat the last instruction (Ans * 1.06), which gives the principal at the end of two years (\$5618).

Pressing ENTER eight more times, as shown below, gives the result we seek.

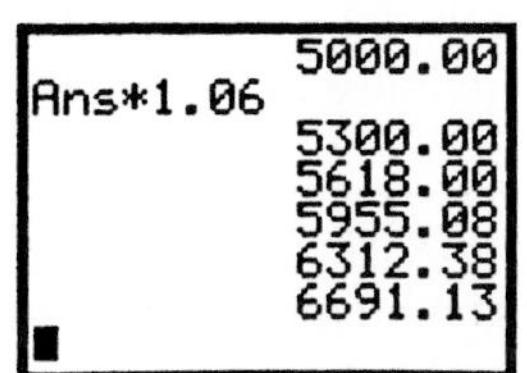

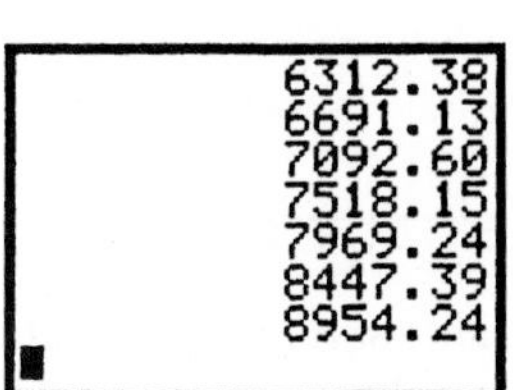

The exciting feature of this solution is that it gives the answer very quickly. As a result, it enables us to extend the problem to consider interesting related questions such as:

- How long (i.e., how many years) will it take for Pablo's money to double? To triple?
- Change the interest rate to 4% and
  a. compare his final principal after 10 years with the result for 6%.
  b. compare the time it takes for the money to double at the 4% interest rate with the time it took to double when the interest rate was 6%.
  c. compare the time it takes to triple the sum at the 4% interest rate with the tripling time for 6%.
- Suppose the compounding were semiannual. How will Pablo's final principal compare with the final principal he received under annual compounding?
- Suppose the compounding were monthly. How will Pablo's final principal compare with the final principal he received under annual or semiannual compounding?

SOLUTION 5

The major difficulty with Solution 4 is that we must mentally keep track of how many times the ENTER button has been pressed. If you lose count, you must begin again. Keeping a count can confuse many students. Another solution, using the TABLE feature of many graphing calculators, avoids this problem.

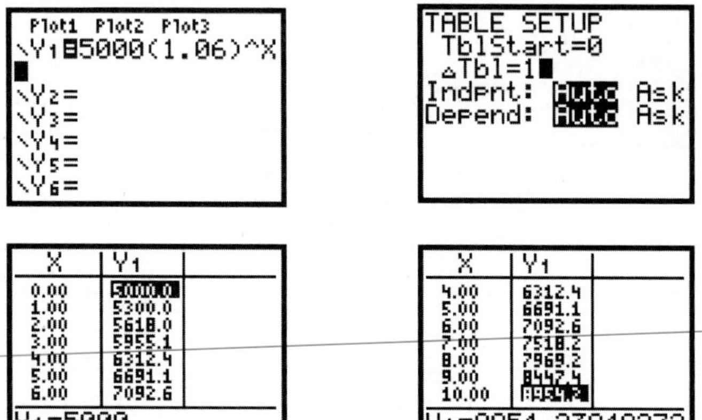

Turn on the graphing menu by pressing the (Y1=) button, then enter the function Y1 = 5000(1.06)^X, as shown in the first graphic above. Have the graphing calculator produce a table by first pressing the (TBLSET) ((2nd)(WINDOW)) button and entering the starting value of X to be 0 and the Δ table to be 1. Now press (TABLE) ((2nd) (GRAPH)) and scroll down until you get to the results after 10 years, shown in the fourth graphic below. The result at the bottom must be rounded to $8954.24.

SOLUTION 6

This solution takes advantage of the graphing capabilities of graphing calculators. As in Solution 5, the function must be entered into the calculator. Before graphing, we must make sure that the window for graphing is reasonable and friendly. If the domain and range are not reasonable, you may not get integer values for X when tracing the graph. Below is an example of such a friendly window. Pressing (GRAPH) produces the graph as shown in the third graphic below. Press (TRACE) and move the cursor until the value of X is 10. This diagram shows the same results as the previous solutions, without the proper rounding.

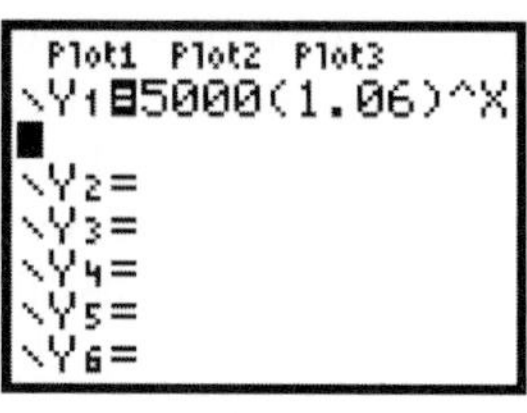

Enter the function.

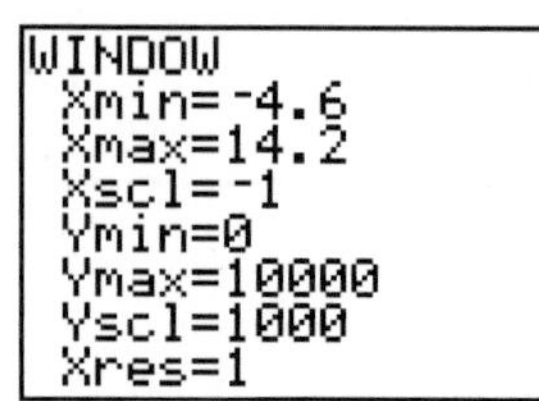

Enter the window for graphing.

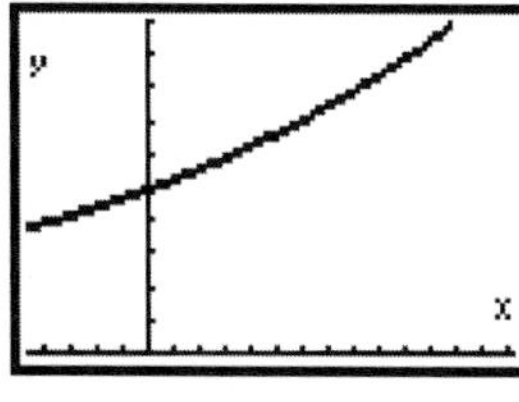
Graph.

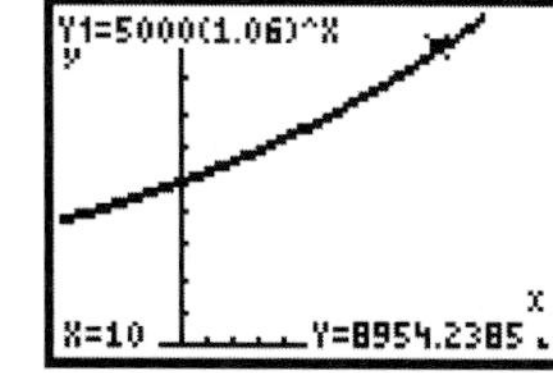

Trace until the value of X is 10.

Often, a graphing calculator can be used to solve problems that would be practically impossible to solve by more traditional approaches. Consider the following problem.

PROBLEM

Find the coordinates of all points of intersection of the graphs of the curves whose equations are $y = 2^x$ and $y = x^2$.

SOLUTION

The solution may seem obvious at first because inspection of the equations gives the coordinates of two points of intersection to be (2,4) and (4,16). However, a well-drawn graph, such as the one on the following page, shows that there are *three* points of intersection, the two listed above and another point in Quadrant II. One may try to find the coordinates of the points of intersection by using the techniques we use in secondary school mathematics. These techniques will not be very helpful. For example, one may try to use logarithms:

$$x^2 = 2^x$$

$$2 \log x = x \log 2$$

This approach is not applicable for finding solutions of $x < 0$, because $\log x$ is not defined unless $x > 0$.

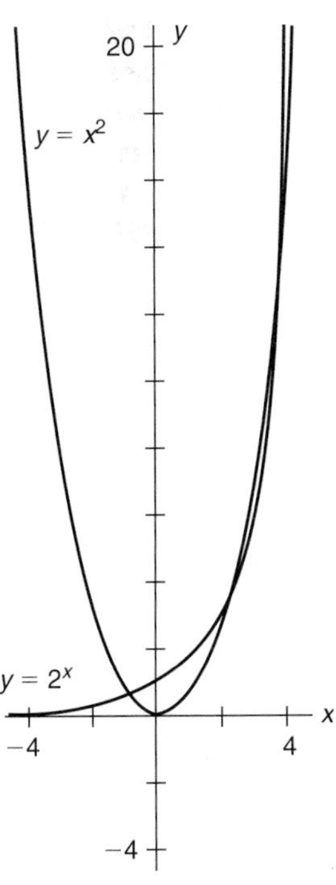

A graphing calculator can be used to find each of the three solutions. The solution for finding the third intersection is shown in the following steps.

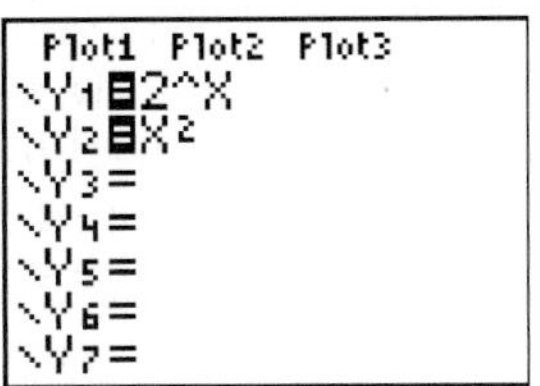

Enter the functions.

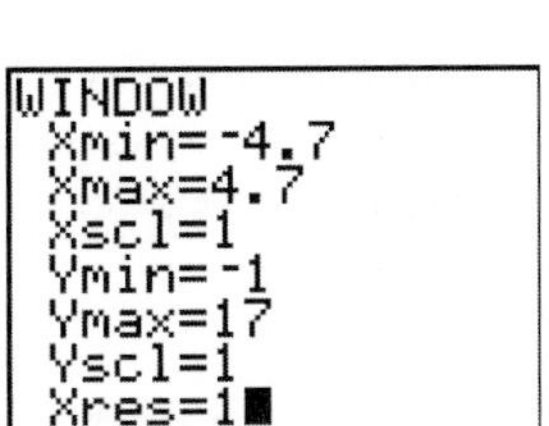

Enter the window for graphing.

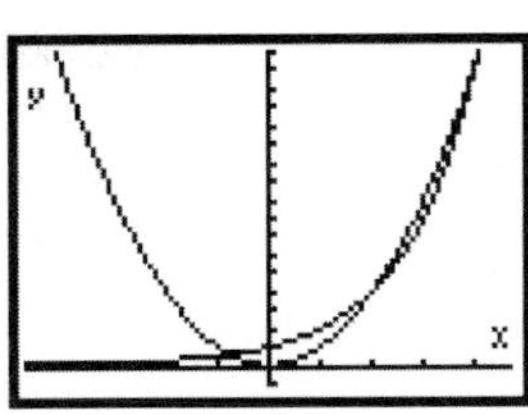

Graph.

Choose the option to calculate point of intersection.

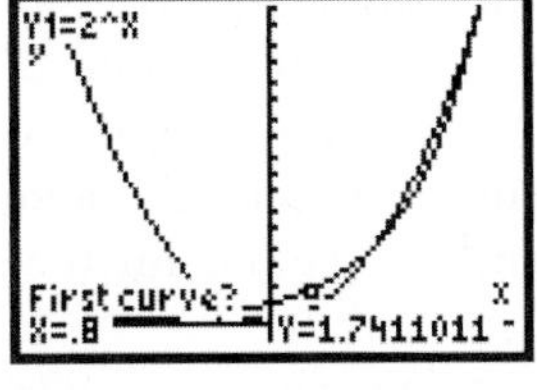

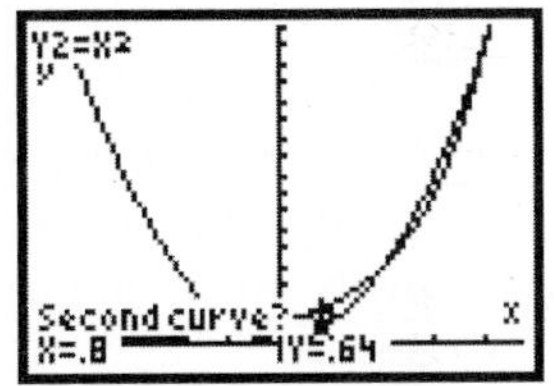

Select the two curves.

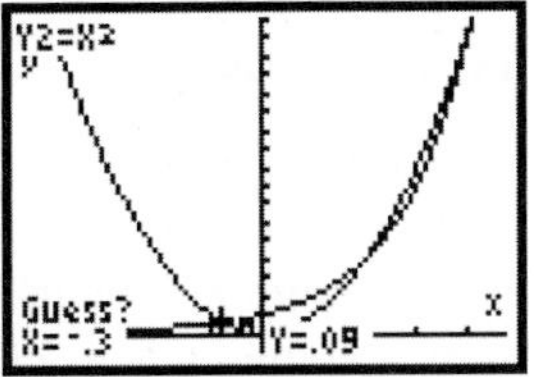

Choose a point near the desired intersection.

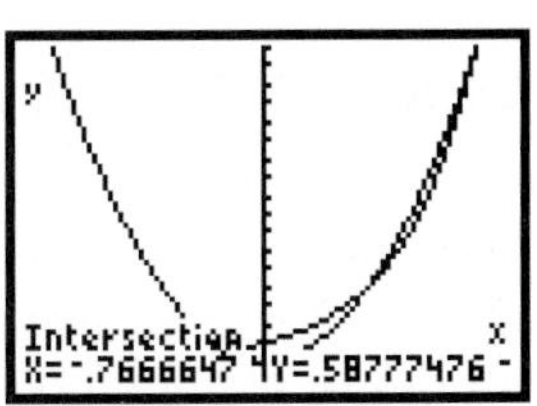

Read the answer.

The answer for the third point, correct to the decimal accuracy of the calculator, is $(-.7666647, .58777476)$.

Simulations

A major strength of graphing calculators is their ability to use mathematical ideas to perform simulations. Consider the following traditional algebra problem.

PROBLEM

New York and Chicago are 850 miles apart. At 9:00 one day, a local train leaves Chicago for New York, traveling at a uniform speed of 50 miles per hour. An hour later, an express train leaves Chicago and follows the same route, traveling at a uniform speed of 55 miles per hour. At what time will the express train catch up to the local?

TRADITIONAL SOLUTION

Let t = the number of hours the local train was traveling

$t - 1$ = the number of hours the express train was traveling

After 1 hour, the local has gone 50 miles, the express train has gone none.

After 2 hours, the local has gone 100 miles, the express train has gone 55 miles.

After 3 hours, the local has gone 150 miles, the express train has gone 110 miles.

•
•
•

After t hours, the local has gone $50t$ miles, the express has gone $55(t - 1)$ miles.

When the express has caught up to the local, each of the trains has traveled the *same* distance, represented by the equation $50t = 55(t - 1)$, which yields $t = 11$. Because the local left at 9:00 AM, 11 hours later, at 8:00 PM, the express will catch up to the local.

GRAPHING CALCULATOR SOLUTION

Students in the new millennium have grown up in the computer age, where graphics and visuals are commonplace and expected. Graphic and visual functions of a graphing calculator can be used to make the problem on the previous page, and its solution, more interesting and meaningful than the traditional solution for many students.

First we must imagine two trains traveling across the calculator screen. One such representation follows.

Placing this representation on a coordinate system enables us to set the simulation up in the following way:

The y-coordinate of the local train is always constant. Let it be $y = 1$.

The y-coordinate of the express train is also a constant. Let it be $y = 2$.

We can consider these y values to be track numbers. Thus, the local train is on track number 1 at all times, and the express train is on track number 2 at all times. These track numbers are entirely arbitrary; however, we should make sure that they are different for the two trains.

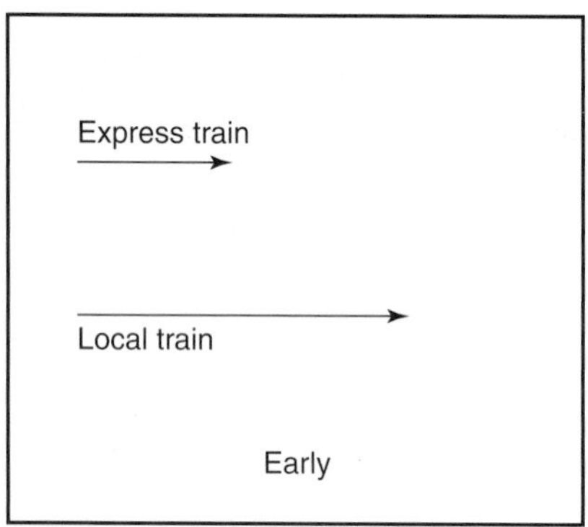

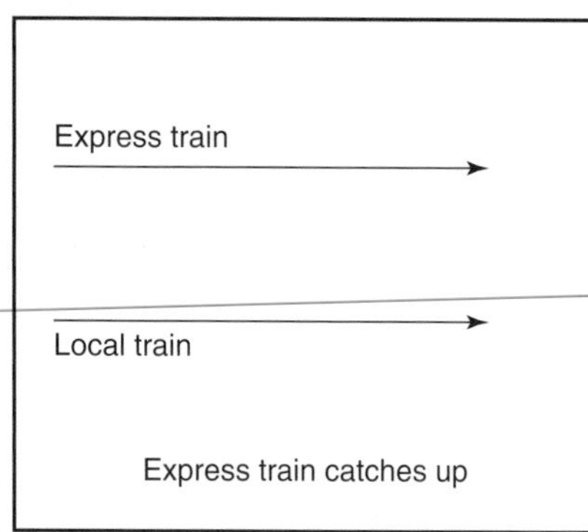

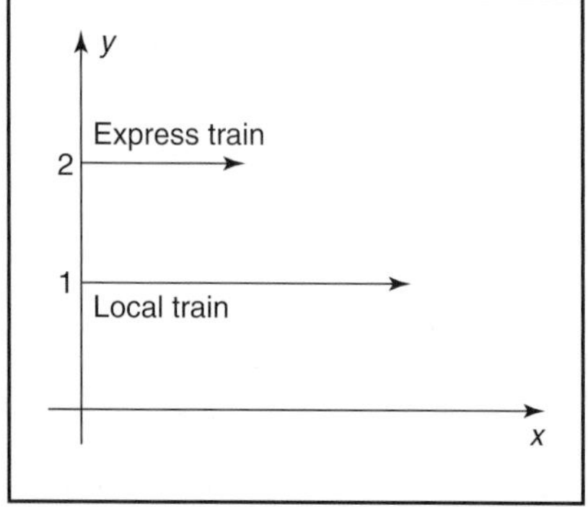

The x-coordinates of the trains represent the distance from Chicago. For example, at 11:00 AM, 2 hours after the local left, the x-coordinate of the local is 100 and the x-coordinate for the express is 55. The x-coordinates of both trains depend on the time that has elapsed. The x-coordinate of the local after t hours is $50t$. The x-coordinate of the express after t hours is $55(t - 1)$.

The equations that describe the motion for the local train are $x = 50t$ and $y = 1$.

The equations that describe the motion for the express train are $x = 55(t - 1)$ and $y = 2$.

A situation such as this, in which two variables (x and y) depend on a third variable (t), is an example in which parametric equations are needed. In fact, in most computer or calculator simulations, the mode for the solution is parametric, given that variables are a function of time.

With this in mind, we can set up the calculator simulation quite easily. The following steps were set up on a TI-83 Plus calculator, although the setup is similar for other calculators as well.

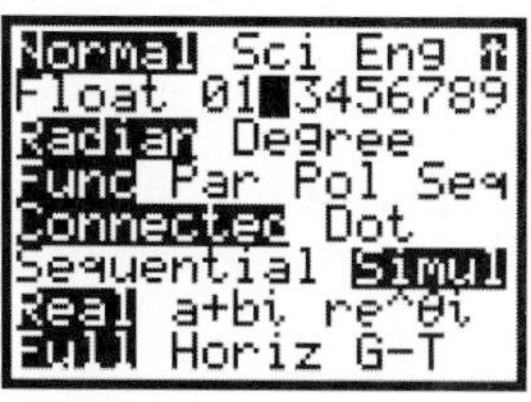

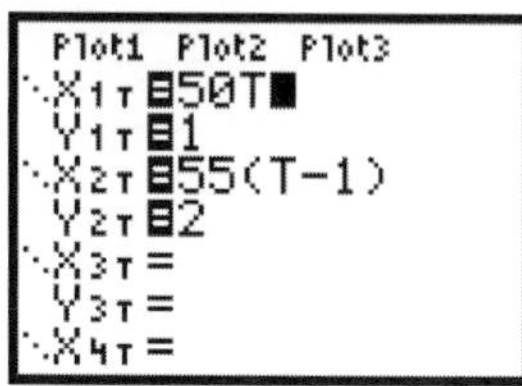

1. Select the MODE button and choose the options as shown on the left. (The settings should be on Par for parametric and Simul so that we see the trains moving simultaneously.)
2. To enter the equations, select the Y= button as you did in previous situations. Since the mode is set for parametric, the equations to be entered are set up in pairs. The use of subscripts in the calculator allows for sets of equations to be entered.
3. It is essential that the window be set up in advance to allow an adequate viewing of the trains. There are three stages for setting up the appropriate window:
   a. *For time:* T is the number of hours the local train is traveling. It is traveling at 50 miles per hour, so it would take $\frac{850}{50} = 17$ hours for the local to reach New York from Chicago. Thus, we set the minimum and maximum time settings as $T_{min} = 0$ and $T_{max} = 17$(hours). The setting T_{step} controls how the value of T is to change for graphing purposes. If T_{step} is set to be 1 (hour), the calculator will display the position of the trains at the end of each hour, providing very rapid movement. By using a smaller value of T_{step}, say 0.1, we will see the motion of the trains at every 0.1 hours, or every 6 minutes. This is one value with which you can experiment and see the different results.
   b. *The x values:* Since the trains are traveling 850 miles from Chicago to New York, we set $X_{min} = 0$ and

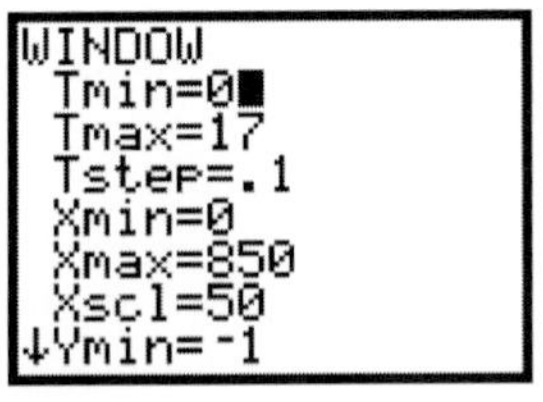

$X_{max} = 850$. The value of X_{scl} (x scale) is the distance between ticks on the x-axis. Thus, if $X_{scl} = 50$, there will be ticks at $x = 50, 100, 150, 200, \ldots, 850$.

c. *The y values:* Since the y value represents the track number in this setup, setting $Y_{min} = -1$, $Y_{max} = 3$, and $Y_{scl} = 1$ will be sufficient. By using $Y_{min} = -1$, the viewer will be able to see the x-axis with its ticks quite easily.

The above graphics on the left show the information that needs to be entered after pressing the (WINDOW) button for the simulation. At this point, the user can press the (GRAPH) button and watch the trains go across the screen. To clear the screen and view the trains a second time, press (2nd) and then (PRGM) (the DRAW function, then enter 1 for Clear Draw).

The following are snapshots of the screen capturing the motion of the trains.

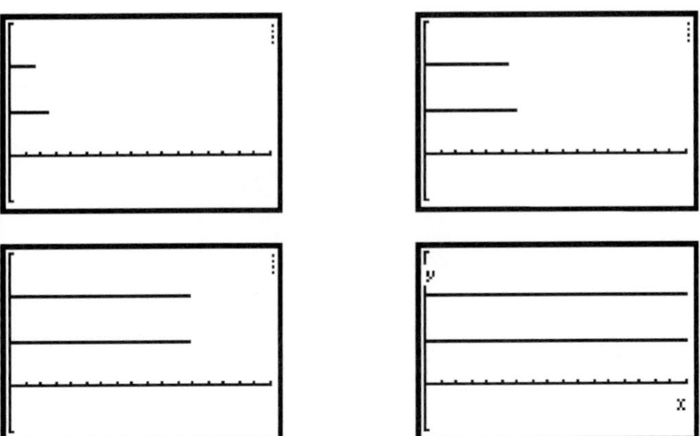

To slow the trains up in the simulation, change T_{step} in the window. A more reasonable choice, $T_{step} = 0.05$, shows the position of each train at 3-minute intervals.

At this point, however, we have not yet solved the original problem. To find the moment the express train catches up to the local, all we need do is press the (TRACE) button. The following graphics show the screens as you press the right arrow button.

The first window shows the initial values.

Move the cursor to the right and see the values for a greater value of T.

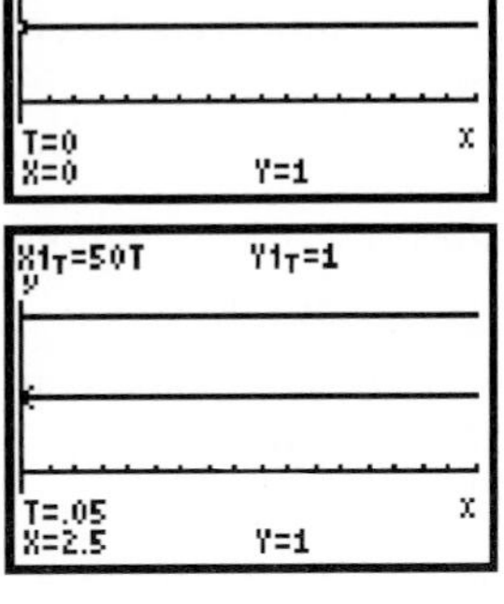

In each case the values of T, X, and Y are shown. As you can see, every time you press the right arrow, the value of T is increased by 0.5, because we set T_{step} that way.

Continue moving the cursor until T = 5.

Pressing the up arrow enables you to switch between the two trains.

Continue tracing until T = 10.

Notice that the trains are 500 and 495 miles from Chicago.

Continue tracing until T = 10.95.

The two trains are only $\frac{1}{4}$ mile apart.

Continue tracing until T = 11.

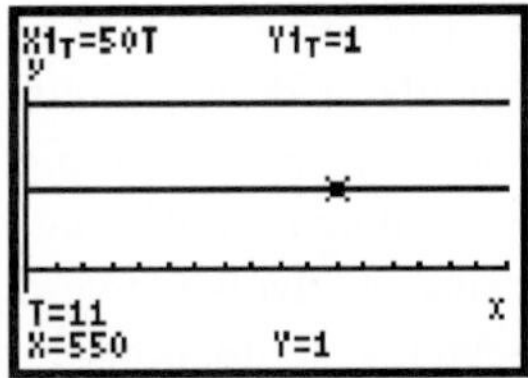

The two trains are 550 miles from Chicago. The express has caught up to the local.

As a result of tracing, students can see that both trains are 550 miles from Chicago when T = 11, or 8:00 PM.

Teachers have made these observations when using simulations to teach this type of problem:

- The motivational level of the students is very high. Most students are involved in the problem and its solution.
- Students observe certain patterns that they may not have noticed using more traditional approaches. For example, as they trace, students often notice that the express train is gaining five miles on the local each hour. For example,

When T = 5	$X_{1T} = 250$	$X_{2T} = 220$
When T = 6	$X_{1T} = 300$	$X_{2T} = 275$
When T = 7	$X_{1T} = 350$	$X_{2T} = 330$

(At this point, students may notice that because there are 20 miles for the express train to catch up, it will need an additional 4 hours, giving the solution T = 11.)

- Students become creative. For example, they may put the two trains on the same track, or suggest redoing the problem with the trains leaving from opposite directions and eventually passing each other.
- Problems of this type naturally lead to algebraic solutions.

Simulations to consider include traditional uniform motion problems: dropping a ball from a rooftop, throwing an object vertically into the air, throwing an object diagonally, etc. All of these, with some care, can be treated in the secondary school curriculum.

Solving Equations Using Matrices

PROBLEM

Use the graphing calculator to solve each of the following systems of equations:

a. $3x + 5y = 2$
   $7x + 4y = 6$

b. $2A - 3B + 2C - 4D + 2E = 8$
   $3A + 2B - 3C + 3D - 3E = -5$
   $5A - 7B + 5C - 5D + 7E = 9$
   $11A - 5B + 4C + 3D + 5E = 2$
   $7A - 9B - 7C - 13D - 7E = 1$

The first system of equations can be solved by having the calculator draw the graphs of the equations and by finding the coordinates of the point of intersection of the lines. The second system of equations cannot be solved graphically because it involves five dimensions. A useful way of solving systems of equations such as these is to use the matrix capabilities of graphing calculators.

SOLUTION

In (a)

Let matrix $A = \begin{pmatrix} 3 & 5 \\ 7 & 4 \end{pmatrix}$. This is the coefficient matrix for the given system of equations.

Let Let $X = \begin{pmatrix} x \\ y \end{pmatrix}$. This is the variable matrix for the given system of equations.

Let $B = \begin{pmatrix} 2 \\ 6 \end{pmatrix}$. This is the constant matrix for the system of equations.

If we multiply matrices A and X, we get $\begin{pmatrix} 3x + 5y \\ 7x + 4y \end{pmatrix}$, which is equal to $\begin{pmatrix} 2 \\ 6 \end{pmatrix}$. according to the given system of equations. This result can be rewritten as the matrix equation $AX = B$. Assuming there is a solution and that matrix A has an inverse, we can write that $X = A^{-1}B$. Note that it must be written in this order, as matrix multiplication is not commutative. The equation provides us with a simplified way of solving such a system using a graphing calculator. We merely need to enter the coefficients of matrix A and matrix B into the calculator as follows.

Press the Matrix button marked MATRIX.
(2nd x^{-1}).

NAMES MATH EDIT
1:[A] 1×1
2:[B]
3:[C]
4:[D]
5:[E]
6:[F]
7↓[G]

Choose EDIT and select matrix A.

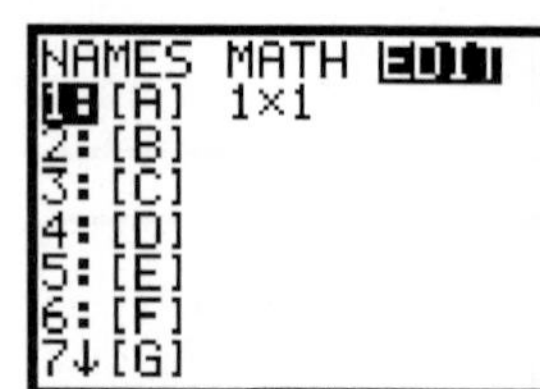

Enter the dimensions of matrix A (2 by 2).
Note how the calculator will automatically set up a new 2 × 2 matrix whose entries are all zero.

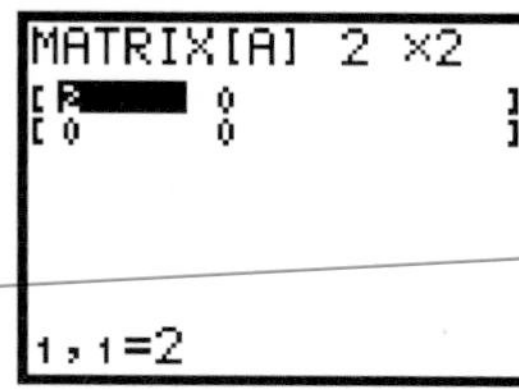

The coefficients of matrix A should be entered entry by entry. Press
QUIT
(2nd MODE).
We are now ready to enter matrix B.

Press the Matrix button
MATRIX
(2nd x^{-1}) and edit matrix B to be a 2 by 1 matrix.

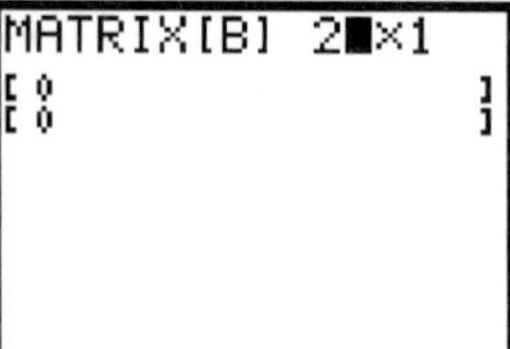

Enter the coefficients of matrix B. Press QUIT (2nd MODE).

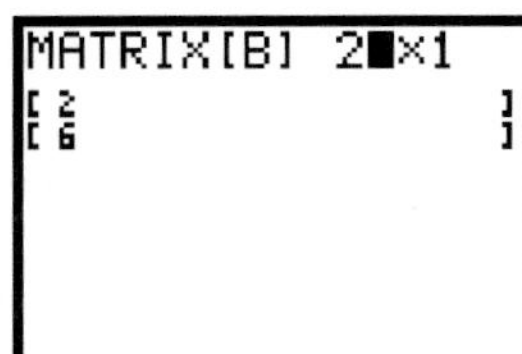

We can now have the calculator compute $A^{-1}B$. To do this, press MATRIX (2nd x^{-1}) and select A.

Now press x^{-1} (so that the inverse will be taken), 2nd MATRIX (x^{-1}), and select B.

This screen should appear:

Now pressing ENTER will yield the solution:

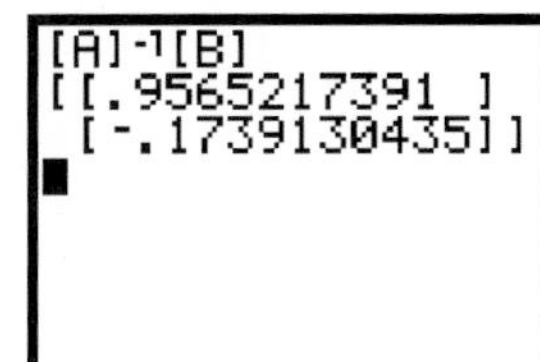

At first sight, you may believe this result to be in error. Press MATH and you will see this screen:

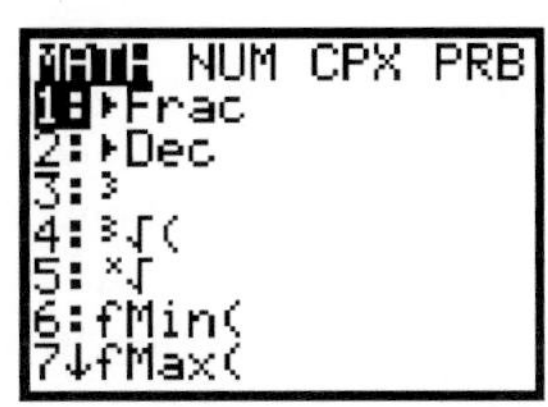

Choose option 1 to change the results to fractions so the solution will appear in fractional form.

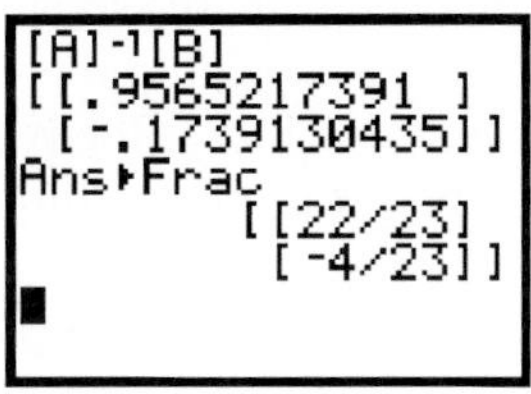

This solution checks both equations. The matrix method is especially powerful since it involves entering coefficients into matrix A and matrix B. It does not matter whether there are 2 equations in 2 variables or 15 equations in 15 variables!

We now show that the solution for system (b) is found essentially the same way.

Press the Matrix button MATRIX (2nd x^{-1}).

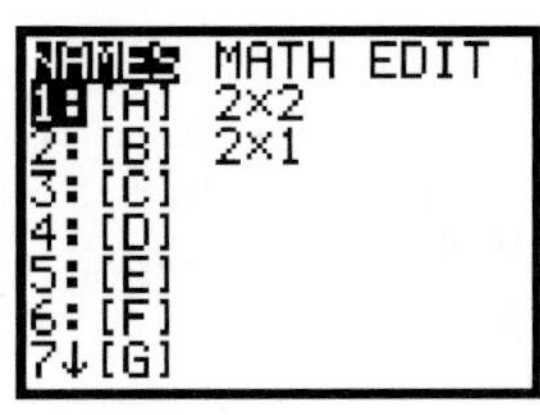

Choose EDIT and select matrix A.

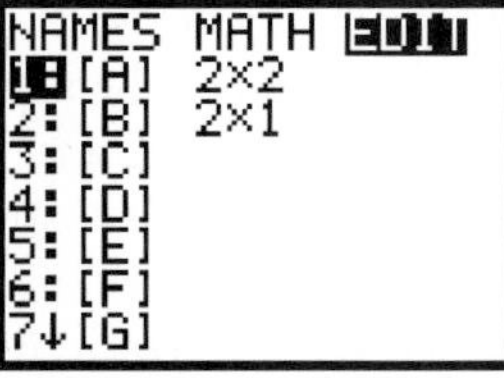

Change the dimensions of matrix A to 5 by 5.
Note how the calculator will automatically set up a new 5 × 5 matrix. Some entries remain from the previous matrix A.

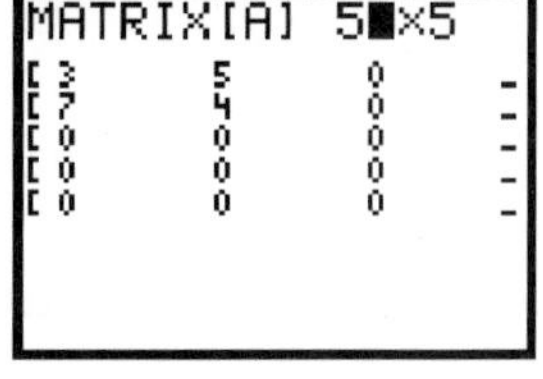

The coefficients of matrix A should be entered entry by entry. Press QUIT (2nd MODE).

Now change matrix B to be a 5 by 1 matrix and enter its coefficients. Entering $A^{-1}B$ the same way as was done before yields the solution.

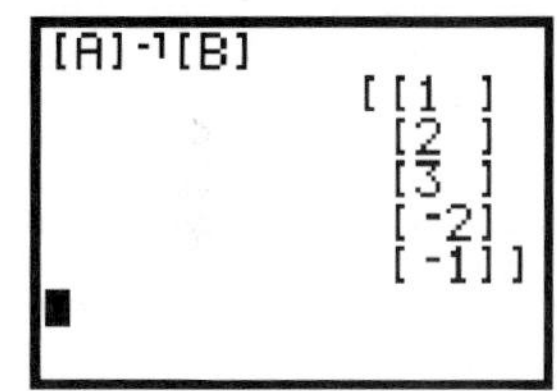

This solution tells us that the solution to the original system is $A = 1, B = 2, C = 3, D = -2$, and $E = -1$. Interestingly, using matrices to find the solution to a system of *five* equations in *five* variables is no more difficult than finding the solution to a system of *two* equations in *two* variables, with the exception of having to enter more data.

Another nice way to solve a system of $n \times n$ independent linear equations is to use the rref (reduced row-echelon form) in matrices. To solve the previous problem (a), we can do the following:

Press the MATRIX button.

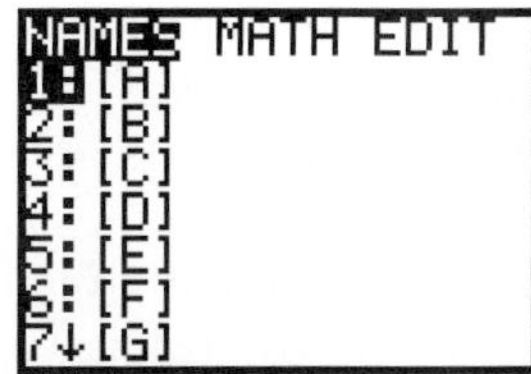

Choose EDIT and select matrix A.

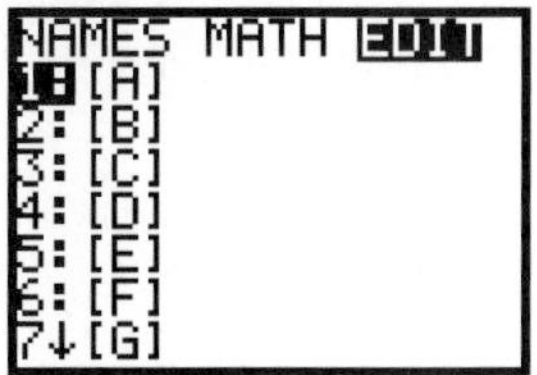

Enter a 2 × 3 matrix of the coefficients and the constants of the equation.

Return to the Home Screen and press MATRIX, then the MATH column, and then select B (rref). To make sure that we see the answer as a fraction, if it is possible, press MATH, 1. You should see the following: (Note that this means for $1x$ and $0y$, the answer is $22/23(x = 22/23)$ and for $0x$ and $1y$, the answer is $-4/23(y = -4/23)$.)

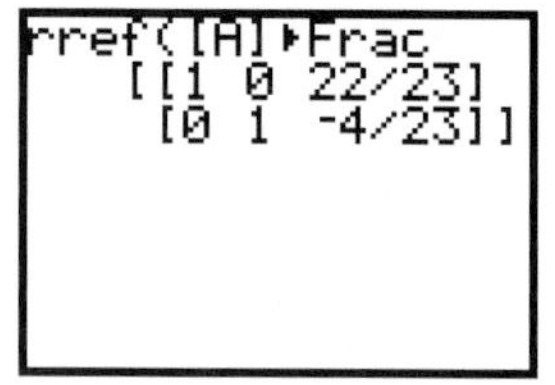

Calculus Applications

Derivatives

One of the most interesting options built into graphing calculators is the ability to find a numerical derivative. For example, suppose we wanted to find $f'(1.5)$ if $f(x) = x^3 - 4x$. One way to accomplish this is by having the calculator draw the graph of $y = x^3 - 4x$ and then have it draw a tangent at the specified point. The sequence below shows this process in a TI-83 Plus calculator.

On the right is shown the graph of $y = x^3 - 4x$.

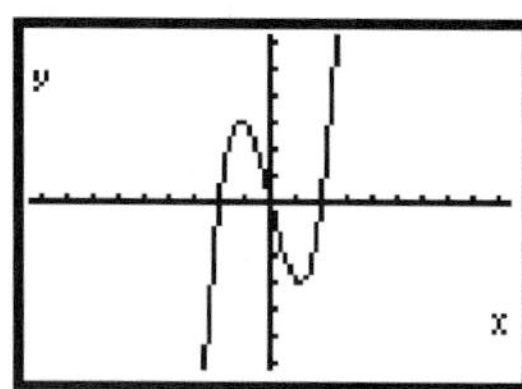

DRAW

Choose (2nd)(PRGM), then option 5 for drawing a tangent.

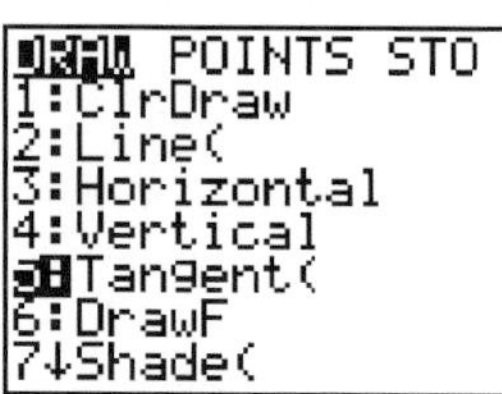

Either type in 1.5 for X, or move the cursor until it reaches $X = 1.5$ and press (MATH). The calculator draws the tangent to the function and gives its equation. The given slope, 2.750001, is a very accurate approximation for the actual slope, 2.75.

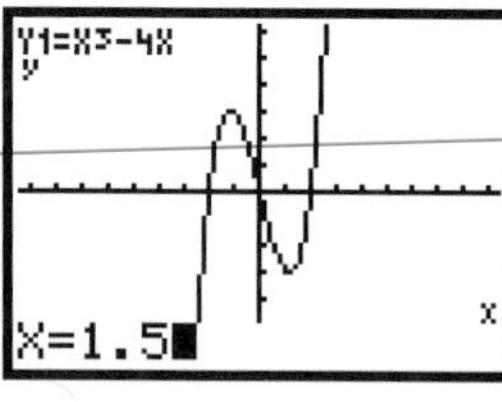

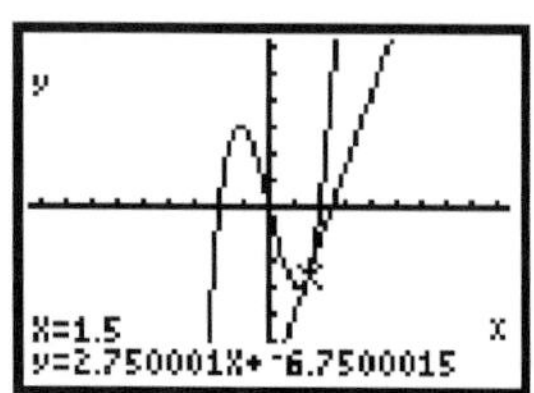

Another way of finding the numerical derivative of a function at a point is to use the NDERIV (or NDER) function built into most graphing calculators. This method does not depend on having the graph drawn. For the above example, the sequence is shown using a TI-83 Plus calculator.

Press the button marked (MATH). Choose the option for the NDERIV function. Enter the function (either explicitly or by going to the (VARS) option and finding the list of y-variables and choosing Y_1). The second parameter is the name of the independent variable, in this case X. Lastly, enter the x value of the point at which you want the derivative and then press (ENTER).

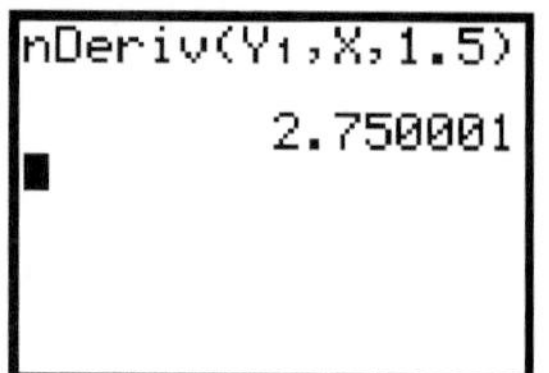

At this point, two questions should come up naturally: How does the calculator find the numerical derivative? And why is the result slightly inaccurate in this case?

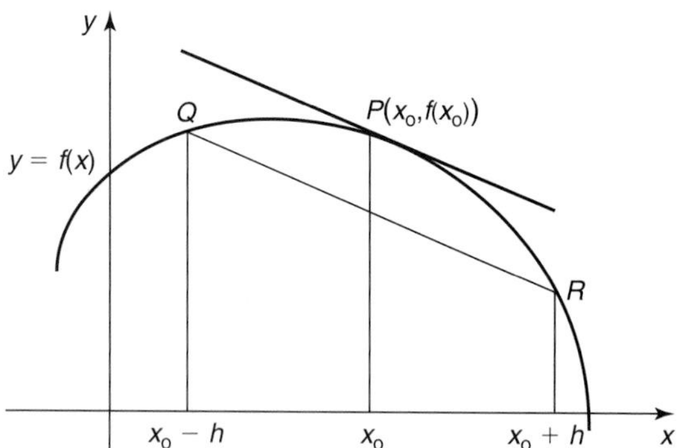

The diagram above shows a general "well-behaved" function, $y = f(x)$, and the tangent drawn at the point $P(x_o, f(x_o))$. If we move a small amount (h) away from x_o in *both* directions on the x-axis, we end up at two points, with values $x_o - h$ and $x_o + h$. On the curve corresponding to these two points are $Q(x_o - h, f(x_o - h))$ and $R(x_o + h, f(x_o + h))$. If h is small enough, the secant through points Q and R will practically be parallel to the tangent through point P. Calculating the slope of $\overline{QR}$ will give a very accurate approximation of the slope of the tangent through P.

$$\text{The slope of } \overline{QR} = \frac{f(x_o + h) - f(x_o - h)}{2h}$$

This value is called the numerical derivative of the function $y = f(x)$ at $x = x_o$. It is the method used by graphing calculators for finding the value of a derivative of a function at a given point. The value of the numerical derivative depends on the value of h used. The default value of h on many graphing calculators is 0.001. This result generally gives surprisingly accurate results.

```
nDeriv(Y1,X,1.5)
                2.750001
nDeriv(Y1,X,1.5,
0.001)
                2.750001
```

Earlier when we found NDERIV (shown on the right), the calculator automatically used a value of $h = 0.001$. To control the value of h, add a fourth entry to the NDERIV function, entering

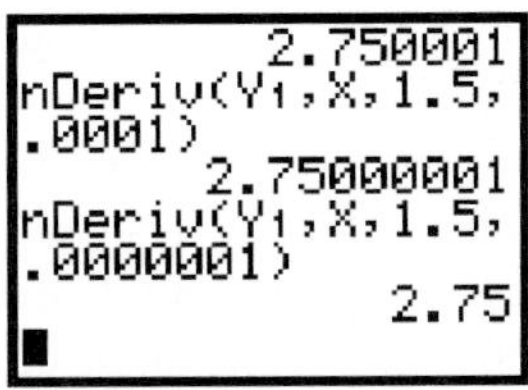

the value of h at the end, as shown on the right. When using a very small value of h, the numerical derivative actually equals the derivative.

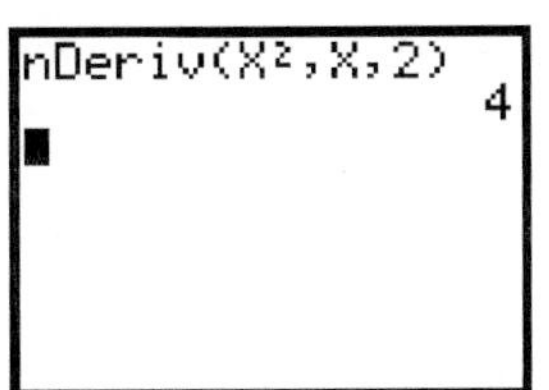

Depending on the function and the point used, the default value of $h = 0.001$ may produce the derivative exactly, as shown on the right.

Definite Integrals

We reproduce the graph of $y = x^3 - 4x$ on the next page. The graphing calculator can be used to approximate definite integrals. For example, in this case, suppose we wanted to approximate

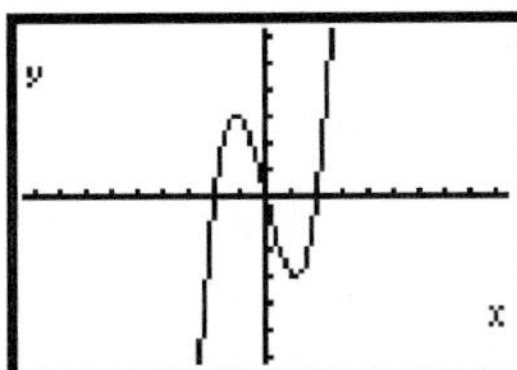

$$\int_0^2 (x^3 - 4x)dx.$$

CALC

Press (2nd) (TRACE) to produce the screen on the left. Choosing the last option will set up the numerical integration feature. The following sequence of choices will appear on the screen. Moving the cursor to the desired lower and upper limits and pressing (ENTER) will yield the desired results, as shown in the last graphic.

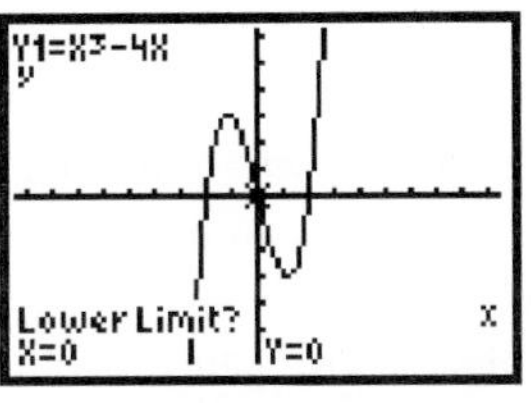

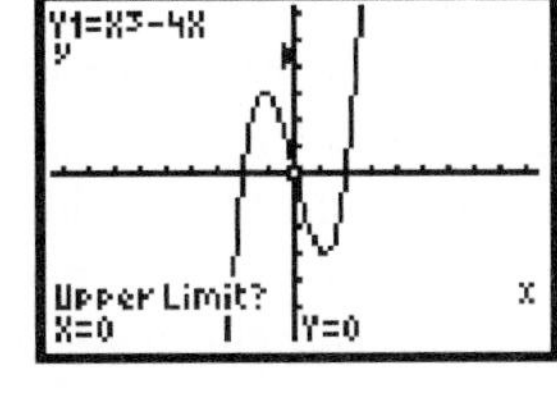

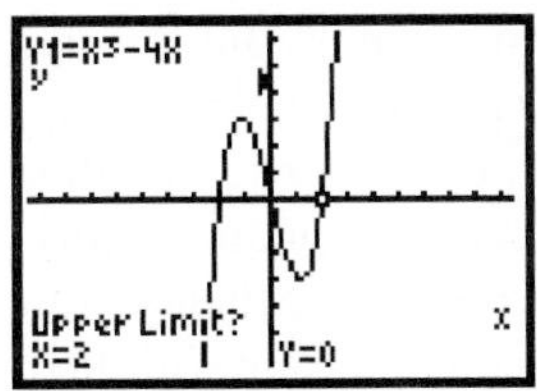

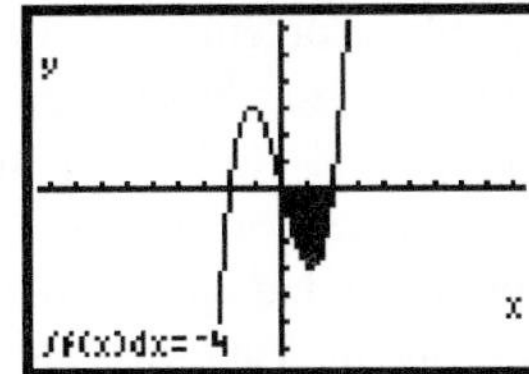

From a pedagogical point of view, this last screen stresses two results we try to emphasize in calculus:

1. The geometric interpretation of a definite integral is an area (represented by the shading).
2. When the curve is below the x-axis, the definite integral is negative.

An alternate way of finding a definite integral does not depend on having the graph drawn.

Press the button marked (MATH). Choose the option for finding the definite integral, "fnInt(." Enter the function, either explicitly or by going to the (VARS) option and finding the list of y-variables and

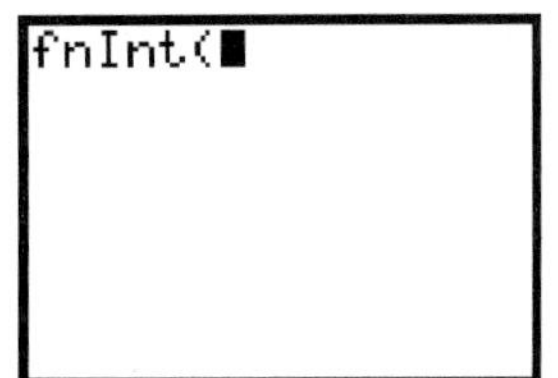

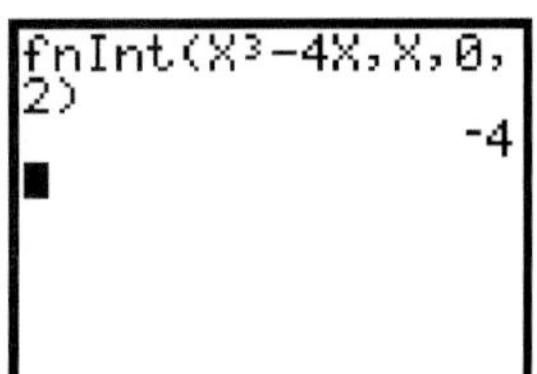

choosing Y_1. As with the numerical derivative, enter the name of the independent variable (X) and then the limits of integration. Note that accuracy of the result is dependent on the nature of the function on the specified interval.

Computers

In the 1960s, many schools started to use computers in the curriculum. In most schools, the first department to use computers was the mathematics department, because in those days the only use of computers was for programming. Students learned to use a programming language like FORTRAN, COBOL, or BASIC, and then PASCAL or C, and more recently Visual Basic, C++, or Java. They were given mathematical problems to solve using these languages. Courses were designed largely for the most talented students. As a result, many students did not take computer programming.

In the 1980s and 1990s, with the advent of the personal computer, there was a shift from computer programming to using application software. Other departments began using word processing programs and spreadsheet programs. Consequently, there was a great increase in the number of students using computers in secondary schools.

Appropriate Use of Computer Technology in the Mathematics Classroom

Let us consider various aspects of using the computer in the instructional program.

Computer-Based Tutorial Programs

Computer programs that provide students additional practice with selected topics in the secondary school curriculum can be developed or purchased. With these programs, the computer can drill students in algebra, geometry, and trigonometry as well as in arithmetic. Moreover, the computer can do more than just acknowledge a correct answer and generate another problem (or indicate "error" and repeat the same problem). The software can indicate where an error was made or offer suggestions for reaching a correct answer based specifically on the student's incorrect answer.

Computers can be used for tutorial, drill, and practice in a number of ways. The software should be adjustable in terms of level of difficulty, number of problems, and mastery level. The software should be intelligent; it should sense when a student is having difficulty with a particular operation or concept and automatically branch to a tutorial with another set of problems. Software that includes a classroom management component and a record-keeping facility is helpful in planning lessons and tracking students' progress.

One of the major problems for a teacher of a large class is not being able to provide adequate individual instruction, even with an aide or teacher's assistant. Weaker students often require considerable attention. A computer with appropriate software can help these students work on their deficiencies, of which they usually are acutely aware, without taking up significant teacher or class time. The argument that computers are nonthreatening, noncritical, and nonjudgmental is certainly valid, especially if the software includes positive reinforcers or if the mathematics is presented in the context of a game or a challenge.

Computers as a Source for Recreational Activities

Many programs are available that allow students to play games with the computer. Carefully selected games can be effective in furthering the development of a student's skills in logic. The level and sophistication of the game must be selected by the teacher with the specific student user clearly in mind. A game that is not challenging enough may either bore the student or make for a silly experience. On the other hand, a program that generates a game beyond the level of the intended student user may cause frustration and eventually turn the student away from computers. Teachers are cautioned to evaluate games for undue violence or sexual bias before using them in the classroom. Students who are properly motivated might create their own games. This activity would then be a worthwhile experience.

Classroom Management with Computers

When called on to teach a class with computers, you will be faced with classroom management decisions that differ from those of the traditional mathematics classroom. Some of the things you will need to consider include:

1. How to assign hands-on time for each student.
2. How to provide access to software in a legal fashion.
3. What to do with students not working on the computer.
4. What to do with the early finishers.
5. How to minimize improper copying of files.
6. How to manage password protection.
7. How to ensure printer access for each student.
8. How to avoid damage to hardware, software, and data.

Optimally, the ratio of students to computers should be 1:1. But most of us are not teaching in Utopia, so we must solve the problems of handling more students than there are computers in the classroom. Many teachers have found that having students work in groups of two is manageable and can be educationally constructive.

Students can learn a great deal from their peers by watching them work on the computer for several minutes. They can learn what to do and what not to do. It will be helpful if you have a kitchen-type timer at your desk. Divide the hands-on part of the period into a number of equal parts, with enough time for each student to get one or two turns on the computer, depending on your particular situation and the particular day. Set the timer to help you keep track of "save and switch" time. You will be so busy helping students with problems, that without a timer, it will be extremely difficult for you to keep accurate track of the time elapsed for each turn. The students not actually working on the computer either may be allowed to do preparatory work for their upcoming turns or may be asked to watch their partners to distinguish between the positive and negative aspects of their work.

Some Examples of Using the Computer to Enhance Instruction

In 1989, the National Council of Teachers of Mathematics (NCTM) published *Curriculum and Evaluation Standards for School Mathematics*, which called for significant changes in the way mathematics is taught. For example, in the teaching of geometry, the *Standards* called for decreased emphasis on the presentation of geometry as a complete deductive system as well as decreased emphasis on two-column proofs. The *Standards* called for an increase in open exploration and conjecturing and increased attention to topics in transformational geometry. In its call for change, the *Standards* recognize the impact that technology tools can have on the way mathematics is taught. The *Standards* describes good uses of technology as those that free students from time-consuming, mundane tasks and allow them the time and means to see and explore interesting relationships and engage in real-world applications.

Internet Resources and Activities

The Internet makes it possible for people anywhere to share information. The World Wide Web (WWW) is an innovative application of this technology. Web pages (or interactive course management systems such as Blackboard) can serve entire populations, including teachers as well as students with specific problems, not bound by spatial proximity. Information of interest to a broad group, or a very specific population, may be "posted" to a Web site. Teachers can share information and suggestions on how to teach a certain topic most effectively or what approach ought to be considered when solving a problem. Via e-mail, students can communicate with their teachers and other students. There are now schools that are providing textbooks online as opposed to each student having his or her own.

The Internet has opened up a plethora of possibilities for use of the computer. It provides access to a rich set of resources, including mathematics history and content; collections of problems; data for exploration; simulations; teaching ideas, lessons and resources; and professional resources. The opportunities for enhancing instruction and ensuring a deeper understanding of mathematical concepts using the Internet are only limited by a teacher's creativity.

"A listing of mathematics Web sites could fill the pages of a book. They are available for all levels of mathematics. Some are interactive, while others are meant for reference work. Below we list a brief sampling of some of the sites that have proved valuable to students in various stages of their mathematics development. Most universities also list sites that have been developed by their students.

http://en.wikipedia.org/wiki/Mathematics
http://mathworld.wolfram.com
http://dir.yahoo.com/Science/Mathematics
http://math.about.com
www.sciencedaily.com/news/computers_math/mathematics
www.homeschoolmath.net/math_resources_4.php
www.highschoolace.com
http://mathforum.org/students/high
www.awesomelibrary.org/Classroom/Mathematics/Middle-High_School_Math/Middle-High_School_Math.html
www.eduref.org/cgi-bin/lessons.cgi/Mathematics

Spreadsheets

Spreadsheets are a widely available computer-based computational environment (e.g., Microsoft Excel is included in the Microsoft Office suite). They are used extensively in the business world. The spreadsheet environment has also proven useful for modeling a wide variety of mathematical problems and situations. Some of the advantages of using spreadsheets are that they:

- are readily available for problems that are iterative, recursive, or tabular in nature;
- enable teachers and students to "tinker" with the values of variables and explore "what-if" questions;
- free students from being hampered by laborious manipulation of numbers and allow them to concentrate on the problem at hand; and
- allow the user to see a progression of calculations and permit the changing of one variable at a time to see the effect on the overall pattern (Masalski, 1999).

Spreadsheets can be used at all levels of the school mathematics curriculum. In the elementary and middle grades, spreadsheets can be a valuable tool for data collection, analysis, and presentation. Using data collected in real-life, relevant problem situations, students can use the spreadsheet to display attractive bar graphs or pie charts of their data. At the middle school level, algebraic thinking can be enhanced by exploring patterns with the aid of a spreadsheet. In particular, the concept of slope can be developed fruitfully by investigating patterns with linear functions. The examples that follow are primarily aimed at the secondary level.

A spreadsheet is a large rectangular array (matrix) of cells, each with a unique address. In each cell, one can place text, a value, or a formula. The power of a spreadsheet comes from the fact that each cell can contain either a numerical value or a formula that uses information from other cells in the spreadsheet. In the latter case, the cell formula will dynamically recalculate the cell's value as the cells it refers to change. Coupled with the spreadsheet's ability to use relative addressing, this feature provides a powerful, dynamic environment for modeling mathematical situations, as many mathematical situations consist of a process that depends on a variable (or set of variables) either directly or recursively.

Each cell in the spreadsheet contains a unique address, typically a letter to indicate the column in which the cell is located and a number to indicate the row. For example, to refer to the cell containing the value 100 in the figure below, the address A1 is used to indicate the cell is located in column A, row 1. If a cell contains a value, it will be displayed in the cell.

File Edit View Insert Format Tools Data Window Help

Geneva 9 B I U $ %

B2 = =A1^2

	A	B	C
1	100		
2		10000	
3			
4			
5			
6			

Cells can also contain formulas, but the formulas are not displayed in the spreadsheet directly. If you click on a cell that contains a formula, you can see the formula in the formula bar. In the spreadsheet above, Cell B2 contains a formula "= A1^2". The value 10000 that is displayed in cell B2 was calculated from the square of the value in cell A1. If the value in cell A1 is changed to 50, the value displayed in cell B2 automatically changes to 2500 as shown below.

Spd figure 2

	A	B	C	D
1	50			
2		2500		
3				
4				
5				
6				
7				

Let us now consider a set of problems that are recursive and iterative in nature, types that a spreadsheet is ideally suited to model.

To start, we return to Pablo's investment problem, first posed in the calculator section (p. 138). To summarize, Pablo wants to invest $5000 and consider the effect of various interest rates on doubling and tripling periods. The formula can be stated:

$$A_1 = 5000$$

$A_n = (1 + r)A_{n-1}$, where n is the number of years, r is the interest rate, and A_n is the amount compounded annually for n years

Given the tabular nature of this problem, it can be naturally modeled by a spreadsheet developed as follows.

First, start by adding the text labels "Year," "Amount (6%)," and "Amount (4%)" to cells A1, B1, and C1, respectively, in a new spreadsheet. Next, let's establish the column of years in the first column. Enter the number 0 in cell A2. Once this is in place, we can easily generate the rest of the column by clicking on cell A2. We will see a small handle appear in the lower right corner of the cell. Now grab the handle with the left mouse cursor, and hold down the Ctrl key on the keyboard. Drag this down through cell A31. A column of years from 1 to 29 is generated.

Next, we need to enter the initial account balance and the formula for successive years. Enter 5000 into cell B2. Then enter the formula "= 1.06*B2" into cell B3. Notice that the account balance of $5300 is generated. Now copy the formula in B3 down through the rest of the column as we did with the years. The unfolding of account balances over time should appear. Now repeat this same process in column C to obtain results for a 4% interest rate (use 1.04*C2 as the formula in cell C3). The remaining spreadsheet should appear as shown below.

	A	B	C	D
1	Year	Amount (6%)	Amount (4%)	
2	0	5000.00	5000.00	
3	1	5300.00	5200.00	
4	2	5618.00	5408.00	
5	3	5955.08	5624.32	
6	4	6312.38	5849.29	
7	5	6691.13	6083.26	
8	6	7092.60	6326.60	
9	7	7518.15	6579.66	
10	8	7969.24	6842.85	
11	9	8447.39	7116.56	
12	10	8954.24	7401.22	
13	11	9491.49	7697.27	
14	12	10060.98	8005.16	
15	13	10664.64	8325.37	
16	14	11304.52	8658.38	
17	15	11982.79	9004.72	
18	16	12701.76	9364.91	
19	17	13463.86	9739.50	
20	18	14271.70	10129.08	
21	19	15128.00	10534.25	
22	20	16035.68	10955.62	
23	21	16997.82	11393.84	
24	22	18017.69	11849.59	
25	23	19098.75	12323.58	
26	24	20244.67	12816.52	
27	25	21459.35	13329.18	
28	26	22746.91	13862.35	
29	27	24111.73	14416.84	
30	28	25558.43	14993.52	
31	29	27091.94	15593.26	
32				
33				
34				

At 6% interest (compounded annually), it takes about 12 years for the original investment to double and about 19 years to triple, whereas at 4% interest it takes about 18 years and 29 years, respectively. Once the spreadsheet is developed, a variety of questions can be posed and investigated. One can easily "tinker" with the spreadsheet to explore the effect of changing the starting investment amount or interest rates. For example, students could explore the mathematical validity of the investment rule-of-thumb: "You will double your money when the product of your interest rate as an integer, and the number of years at this rate, is approximately 72 (The Rule of 72)".[1]

Next, let's examine a classic recursive problem.

PROBLEM

Determine the 15th value in the Fibonacci sequence given by the recursive relation defined below:

$$F_1 = 1$$
$$F_2 = 1$$
$$F_n = F_{n-1} + F_{n-2}$$

Explore the ratio between consecutive terms in the Fibonacci sequence, i.e., F_{n+1}/F_n.

SOLUTION

Constructing this spreadsheet is relatively straightforward for this recursive problem. One can use column A for the index variable n. Enter 1 in cell A2, and as previously shown, fill A3 to A16 with 2 to 15. To develop the column representing the Fibonacci numbers, one should first enter the value 1 into cells B2 and B3 (representing the base cases $F_1 = F_2 = 1$). Cell B4 should contain the formula "= B2 + B3" (to represent $F_n = F_{n-1} + F_{n-2}$), and then this formula should be copied down the column through cell B16. Each of the cells B4 through B16 then contains the sum

	A	B	C
1	n	F(n)	F(n+1)/F(n)
2	1	1	
3	2	1	1.000000
4	3	2	2.000000
5	4	3	1.500000
6	5	5	1.666667
7	6	8	1.600000
8	7	13	1.625000
9	8	21	1.615385
10	9	34	1.619048
11	10	55	1.617647
12	11	89	1.618182
13	12	144	1.617978
14	13	233	1.618056
15	14	377	1.618026
16	15	610	1.618037
17			

[1]For a more detailed discussion of the number of years required for compound interest to double money, see *101 Great Ideas for Introducing Key Concepts in Mathematics*, A.S. Posamentier, and H. Hauptman.

of the contents of the previous two cells (relative to each cell), thus, in effect, calculating the terms of the sequence (see accompanying figure).

Finally, column C is set up to allow us to examine the ratio of successive terms of the Fibonacci sequence. Cell C3 contains the formula "$= B3/B2$" and this formula is copied down through cell C16. Students may note that the ratios seem to converge. In fact, they do converge to a number, call *Phi*, sometimes referred to as the *golden ratio*. See Enrichment Units 30 and 85 for more detail on the golden ratio and the Fibonacci sequence.

Now, consider the following iterative problem from the NCTM *Principles and Standards for School Mathematics* (2000).

PROBLEM

A student sprained her knee in an intramural volleyball game, and her doctor prescribed an anti-inflammatory drug to reduce the swelling. She is to take two 220-milligram tablets every 8 hours for 10 days. If her kidneys filtered 60% of this drug from her body every 8 hours, how much was in her system after 10 days? How much of the drug would have been in her system if she had continued to take the drug for a year?

SOLUTION

Students might begin by calculating the first few values of the drug concentration over time and looking for a pattern. They may soon realize that the problem can be represented informally as

$$\text{NEW} = 0.4(\text{PREV}) + 440, \text{start at } 440,$$

or more formally as

$$A_n = 0.4A_{n-1} + 440 \text{ for } 1 \leq n \leq 31, \text{and } A_1 = 440$$

where n represents the dose number (dose 31 would be taken at 10 days or 240 hours) and A_n represents the amount of the drug in the bloodstream just after the nth dose. Once the iterative nature of this problem is understood, it can be readily modeled by the spreadsheet (see figure below). Note that

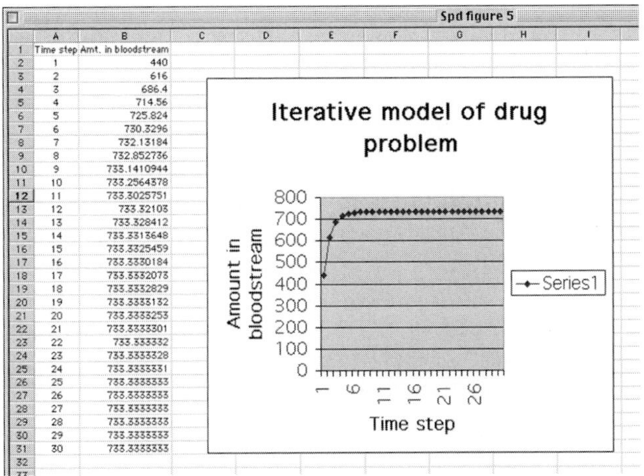

Time step	Amt. in bloodstream
1	440
2	616
3	686.4
4	714.56
5	725.824
6	730.3296
7	732.13184
8	732.852736
9	733.1410944
10	733.2564378
11	733.3025751
12	733.32103
13	733.328412
14	733.3313648
15	733.3325459
16	733.3330184
17	733.3332073
18	733.3332829
19	733.3333132
20	733.3333253
21	733.3333301
22	733.333332
23	733.3333328
24	733.3333331
25	733.3333333
26	733.3333333
27	733.3333333
28	733.3333333
29	733.3333333
30	733.3333333

spreadsheets have the ability to graph relationships among variables as well. Students should realize that, over time, the amount of drug in the bloodstream comes to an equilibrium value of about 733 1/3 milligrams.

Once this model has been constructed, a number of investigations can be carried out by modifying key values or formulas in the spreadsheet:

- What happens to the equilibrium value if the initial dose is different?
- What happens to the equilibrium value if the regular ongoing dosage is altered?
- If the athlete stops taking the medication after 10 days, how long would it take her system to eliminate the drug?
- How could you determine a dosage that would result in a targeted after-dosage equilibrium level of 500 milligrams?

These investigations can open the door to explorations of finite and infinite sequences and series and to the informal consideration of limits.

This brief introduction to spreadsheets illustrates their power for exploring mathematical situations that are recursive, iterative, or tabular in nature and enriching the mathematics classroom.

Introduction to Dynamic Geometry and The Geometer's Sketchpad

Of the countless mathematical software programs written, some of the most interesting are in geometry. Traditionally, geometry has been one of the most difficult subjects to teach; however, software has greatly eased the burden and increased the joy of teaching geometry. We will explore one of these programs, The Geometer's Sketchpad, and see how it can enhance the teaching of geometry.

The Geometer's Sketchpad, first released in 1991, built on the idea that students should use computers as learning tools. By enabling students to put their constructions in motion, Sketchpad eliminated the need to repeat an experiment again and again before making a generalization. Perhaps most important, Sketchpad made the process of geometric exploration more interactive and engaging.

The approach of The Geometer's Sketchpad is consistent with research done by the Dutch mathematics educators Pierre van Hiele and Dina van Hiele-Geldof. From classroom observations, the van Hieles learned that students pass through a series of levels of geometric thinking: visualization, analysis, informal deduction, formal deduction, and rigor. Standard geometry texts expect students to employ formal deduction from the beginning. Little is done to enable students to visualize or to encourage them to make conjectures. A main goal of The Geometer's Sketchpad is to bring students through the first three levels of learning, encouraging a process of discovery that more closely reflects how mathematics is invented: a mathematician first visualizes and analyzes a problem, making conjectures before attempting a proof.

The Geometer's Sketchpad was developed as part of the Visual Geometry Project (VGP), a project funded by the National Science Foundation under the direction of Eugene

Klotz at Swarthmore College and Doris Schattschneider at Moravian College in Pennsylvania. Sketchpad creator and programmer Nicholas Jackiw joined VGP in the summer of 1987 and later joined Key Curriculum Press in 1990. Sketchpad was developed in an open, academic environment in which many teachers and other users experimented with early versions of the program and provided input into its design. The openness with which Sketchpad was developed generated incredible enthusiasm for the program. By the time of its release in 1991, it had been used by hundreds of teachers, students, and other geometry lovers and was already the most talked-about and most-awaited piece of school mathematics software in recent memory.

From the time teachers and students first used Sketchpad, Key Curriculum Press solicited feedback on the types of activities that could be used most effectively in the classroom. Funding from the National Science Foundation enabled curriculum developers to visit classrooms and interview teachers and students. In this way, they could observe directly the kinds of activities that work best. Two important messages came through in the research:

1. The instructional power of Sketchpad can be best taken advantage of if initial activities require only simple constructions. With experience, students can use Sketchpad to create figures of arbitrary complexity. But students who are beginners at using the program grasp concepts best when their thinking is directed toward relationships and *not* toward constructions.
2. Sketchpad can integrate different geometry topics in ways textbooks do not. For example, in a single Sketchpad triangle investigation, students might investigate line and angle relationships, area, transformations, and symmetry.

The Geometer's Sketchpad was designed primarily for use in high school geometry classes. Testing has shown, though, that its ease of use makes it possible for younger students to use Sketchpad successfully, and the power of its features has made it attractive to teachers of college-level mathematics and teacher education courses. Coordinate geometry features make Sketchpad an important tool for investigating many concepts in a first- or second-year algebra course.

Sketchpad can be used to investigate all of the geometry content of the secondary curriculum, with the exception of some three-dimensional topics such as volume. Courses using an inductive approach could use Sketchpad virtually every day to discover geometry properties. Students in courses taking a more deductive approach could use Sketchpad to discover theorems they would then prove, or to confirm and develop understanding of theorems after they prove them. Even in deductive courses, Sketchpad could become an everyday tool. But Sketchpad must be used in moderation. It is just one of a variety of different learning opportunities to which students should be exposed in learning mathematics. Any one type of learning experience can become routine and boring if it is used to the exclusion of other experiences.

Using The Geometer's Sketchpad

In the event that only a single computer is available in the classroom, the best approach might be to have small groups of students take turns using the computer. Each group can investigate or confirm conjectures they have made while working at their desks or tables using standard geometry tools such as compasses and straightedge. That way each group would have an opportunity during a class period to use the computer for a short time. Alternately, you can give each group a day on which to do an investigation on the computer while other groups are doing the same or different investigations at their desks. A single computer without an overhead projection device or large-screen monitor has limited use as a demonstration tool. Although preferences can be set in Sketchpad for any size or style of type font, a large class will have difficulty seeing a small computer screen.

Ideally, the math teacher will have access to a computer lab. Students can be guided through investigations that lead to the discovery of geometric properties or theorems. With a well-designed worksheet, students can go to the computer lab and work on computers, either individually or in small groups, at their own pace. By following a series of well-crafted directions, and being asked to respond to appropriate questions, students can be led to mathematical insights. Writing such worksheets is not easy and requires practice. A series of such activities is given later in the chapter.

The Geometer's Sketchpad was designed to work well with overhead projection display units. With an overhead projection display, you and your students can prepare demonstrations, or students can make presentations of findings that they made using the computer or other means. You or a student can lead an investigation, asking the class such questions as "What should we try next? Where should I construct a segment? What objects should I reflect? What do you notice as I move this point?" Sketchpad becomes a dynamic chalkboard on which you or your students can draw more precise, more complex figures that, best of all, can be distorted and transformed in an infinite variety of ways without

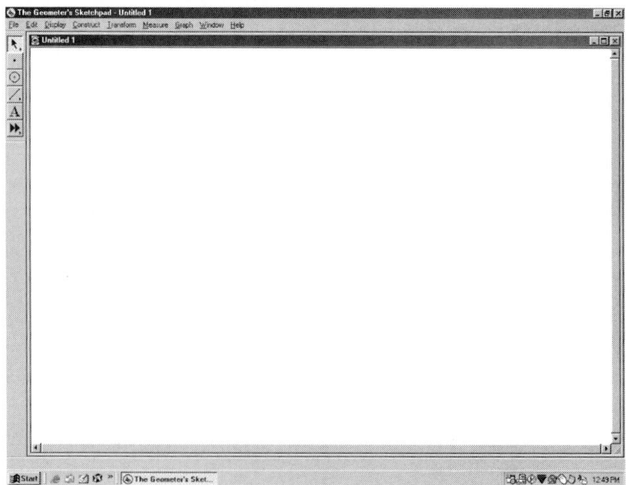

PC Version of The Geometer's Sketchpad

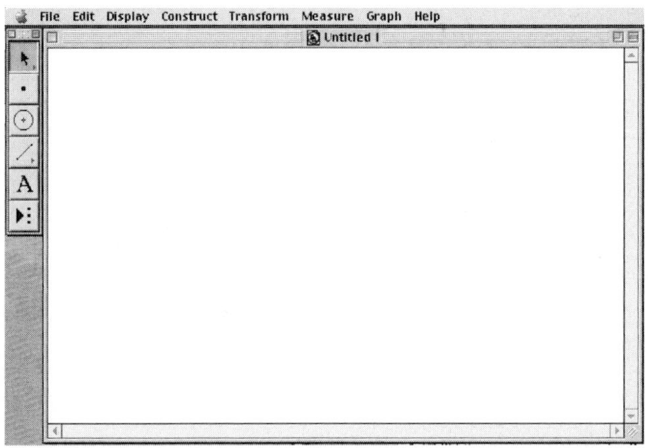

Macintosh Version of The Geometer's Sketchpad

having to erase or redraw. The best way to experience the marvels of Sketchpad is to actually try it. We shall show some applications of this program now.

If you have The Geometer's Sketchpad (version 4) installed on your computer, launch it and you will see a screen similar to either the PC-version or the Macintosh-version screen shown below. The software runs in an equivalent fashion on the two platforms.

A trial version of The Geometer's Sketchpad can be downloaded by the instructor at www.keypress.com; however, the 30-day trial version does not allow you to save a file or to print the sketch.

When Sketchpad comes up on the screen, you will see a selection of tools located on the left-hand side of the worksheet that can be used to construct geometrical figures.

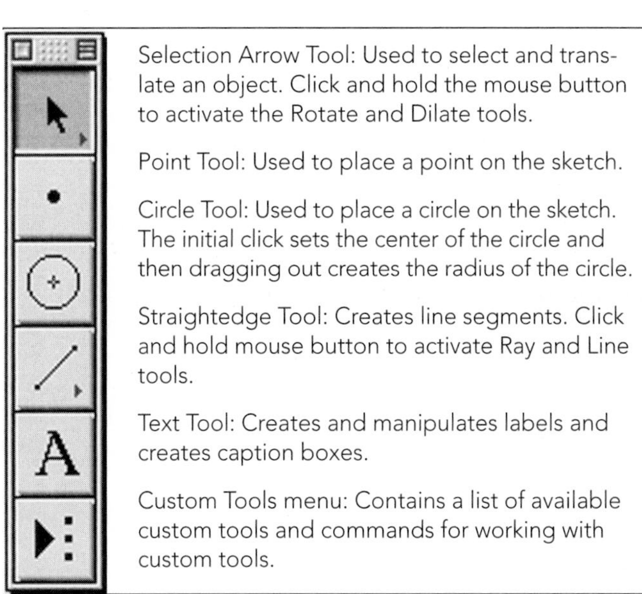

In the following diagram, notice that the Point Tool has been selected. You can tell this because the box indicating the Point Tool appears depressed. In addition, at the bottom of the screen, in the lower right corner, Sketchpad indicates which tool is in use. Refer to this to make sure Sketchpad is doing what you want it to do. The tools used most often are the Selection Arrow Tool and the Point Tool.

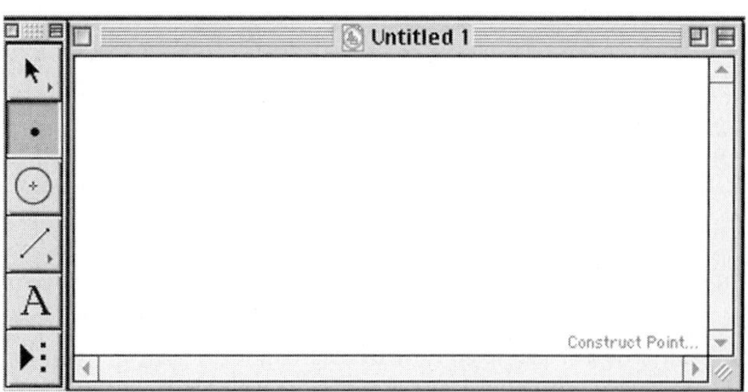

Try These Sketches

Before examining the dynamic features of Sketchpad, try drawing the following four sketches. If the points are not automatically labeled (the Preferences option under the Edit menu), you can label points by selecting the Text Tool and clicking on each of the three points. You may need to experiment by selecting certain objects and going to the Construct menu. Do not delete the sketches, as you will use them later.

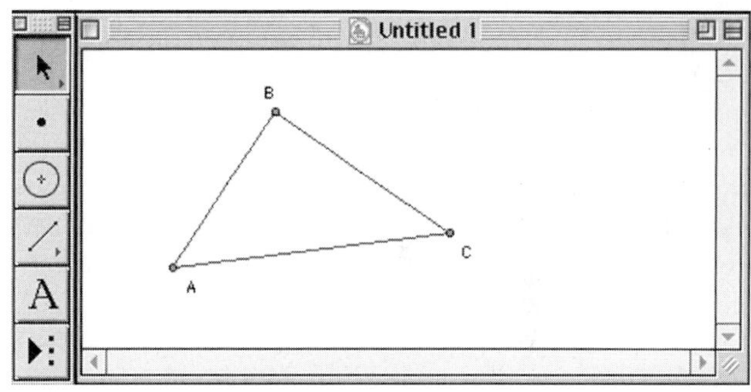

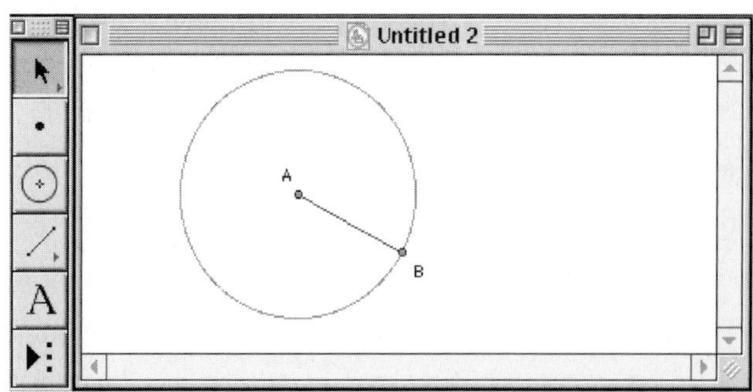

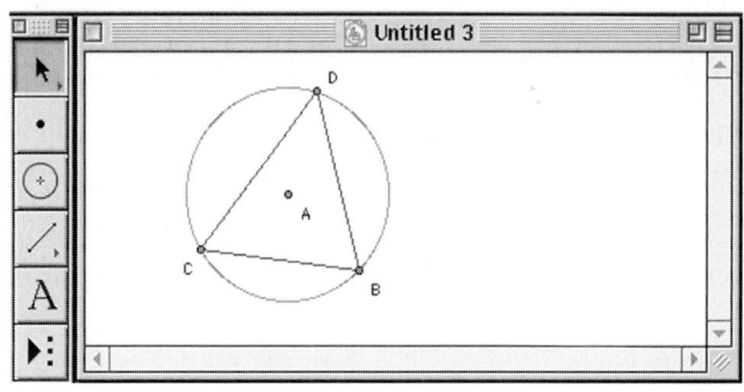

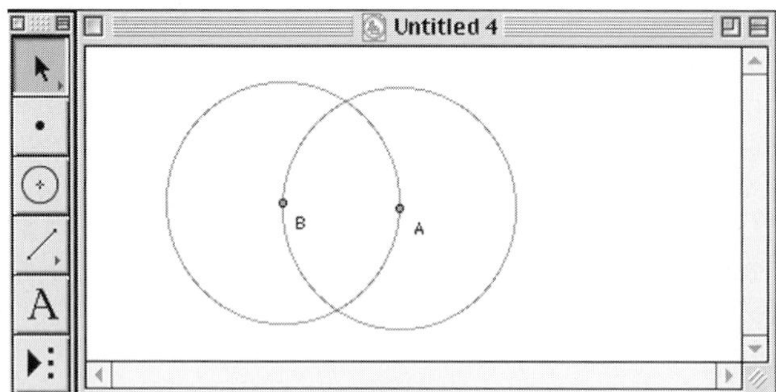

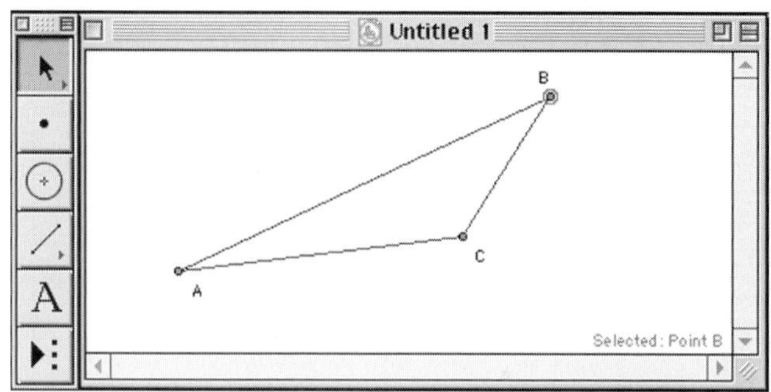

You can experience the dynamic aspects of Sketchpad by using the Selection Arrow Tool. Try it by going back to the sketch you made of a triangle in Untitled 1. Click on triangle vertex *B* and, with the mouse button held down, move the mouse to the right or the left. You will see the triangle change position, as shown in the following diagrams. In each sketch, $\overline{AC}$ has not changed length or location, whereas $\overline{AB}$ and $\overline{BC}$ have either been elongated or shortened.

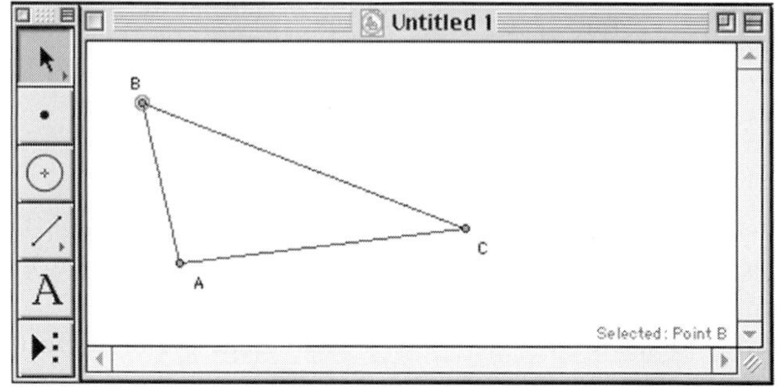

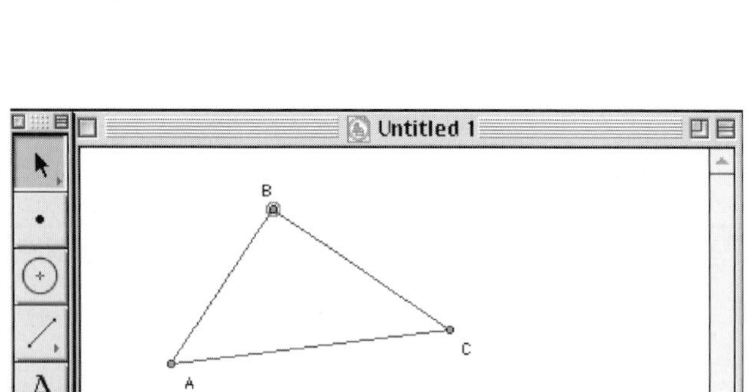

Another way to move geometric figures in Sketchpad is to drag a segment. Use the mouse to click on $\overline{AC}$ in ΔABC (note that the segment becomes highlighted, see figure below), then move the mouse around. When you release the mouse, $\overline{AC}$ will be in a new position (see figure, upper left, page 155). Its length has not changed, but the lengths of the other two sides and the measures of the angles have likely changed. The table below is a summary of the constructions that Sketchpad (version 4) supports.

To construct:	You must select:
Point On Object	1 or more paths (segments, rays, lines, circles, arcs, interiors, axes, function plots, or point loci)
Midpoint	1 or more segments
Intersection	2 straight objects (segments, rays, etc.), circles, or arcs
Segment, Ray, Line	2 or more points
Parallel Line, Perpendicular Line	1 point and 1 or more straight objects; or 1 straight object and 1 or more points
Angle Bisector	3 points (select vertex of angle to bisect second)
Circle By Center + Point	2 points (select center of circle first)
Circle By Center + Radius	1 point and 1 segment or distance measurement
Arc on Circle	1 circle and 2 points on circumference
Arc Through 3 Points	3 non-collinear points
Interior	3 or more points for **Polygon Interior**; 1 or more circles for **Circle Interior**; 1 or more arcs for **Arc Segment** or **Arc Sector Interior**
Locus	1 driver point (constructed on a path) and 1 driven object (point, segment, circle, etc.) whose position depends on driver point

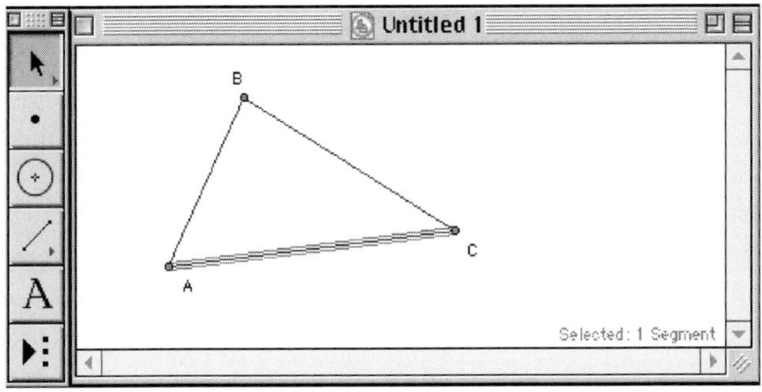

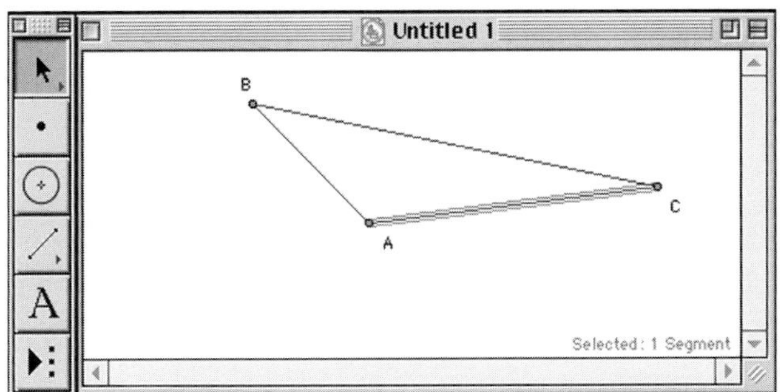

Before continuing, you may wish to practice using the dynamic features of Sketchpad. Here are some useful ways you can practice changing a geometric figure dynamically:

- Using your sketch of ΔABC Untitled 1, move the entire triangle *without* changing any of the side lengths or angles.
- Using your sketch of the first circle, Untitled 2, keeping the center point A in the same position, make radius $\overline{AB}$ longer (or shorter).
- Using your sketch of the first circle, Untitled 2, keeping the circle point B in the same position, make radius $\overline{AB}$ longer (or shorter).
- Using your sketch of the second circle, Untitled 3, *without* changing the radius of the circle, move point B so that ΔBCD becomes a right triangle.
- Using your sketch of the pair of circles, Untitled 4, move point A away from point B. What happens to the circles as A gets farther away from B? What happens when A gets closer to B?

Let us focus on some projects you may use with your middle or high school students using Sketchpad.

Project One: The Sum of the Measures of the Angles of any Triangle

Preliminary: Students must be able to draw an angle and be able to measure it.

Open a new sketch and use the Point Tool to place three points. Connect points A and B and points B and C with line segments (either manually construct the line segments with the Straightedge Tool, or preferably, with two points selected, Construct a Segment).

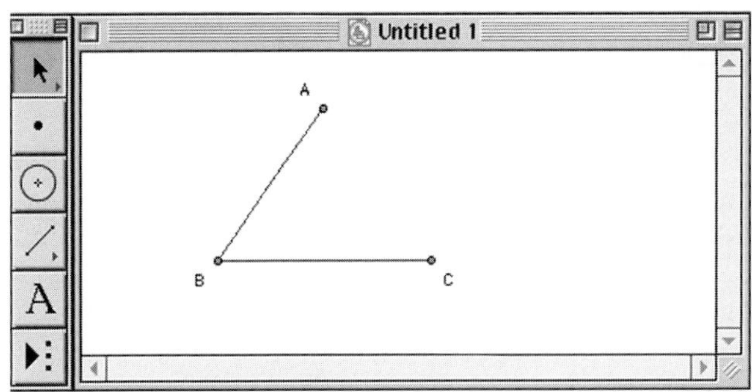

To measure an angle in Sketchpad, you need to specify the angle by its three-letter name. For instance, to select $\angle ABC$ for measurement, you must click on point A, then point B, and finally on point C. The second point selected serves as the vertex of the angle. Alternatively, you could select $\angle CBA$ by clicking on points C, then B, and then A. This is, of course, the same angle, with the vertex at B.

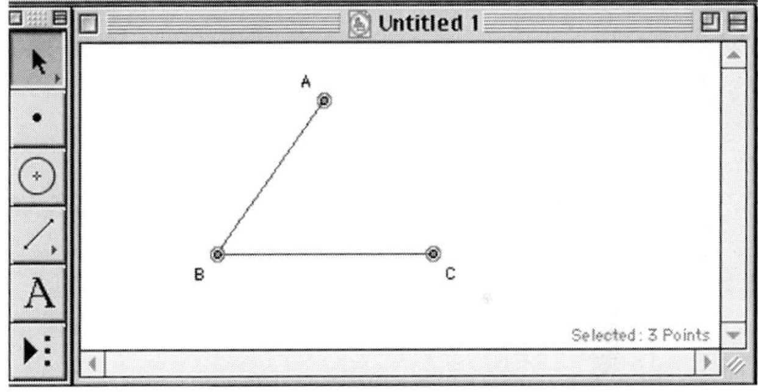

Click on the Measure menu and, with the mouse button held down, select Angle. The angle measure will appear as shown below.

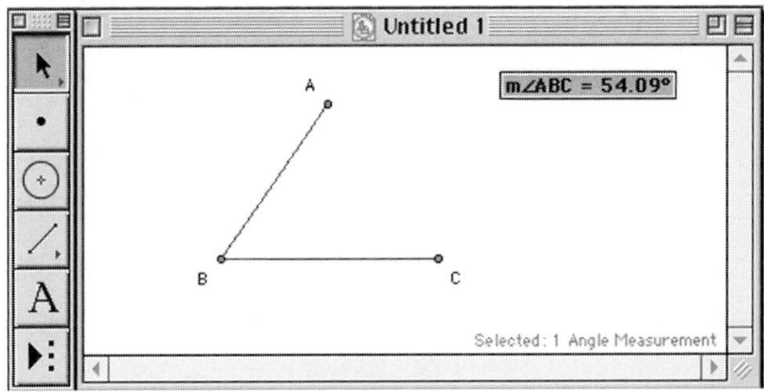

Moving one of the vertices will cause the measure to change. This is one reason why Sketchpad is said to support "dynamic geometry"—measures change as points or segments are moved.

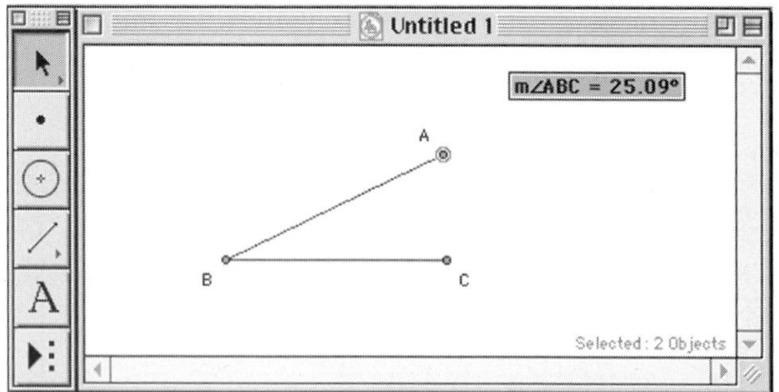

Now that you can use Sketchpad to find the measure of an angle, we will explore how it can be used to find the sum of the angle measures of any triangle. Construct the remaining side segment *AC* to form a triangle and measure the other two angles.

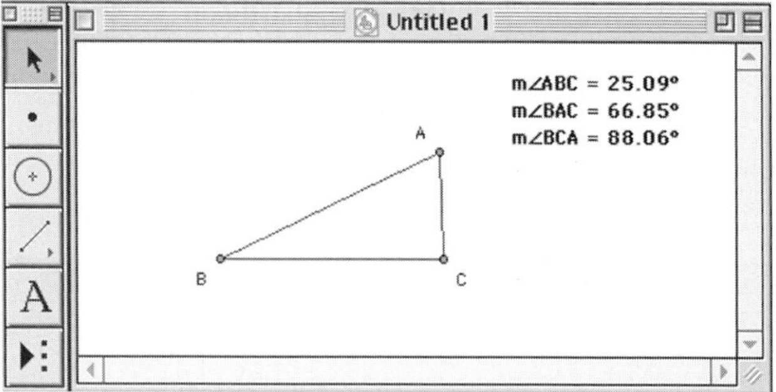

You can now have Sketchpad calculate the sum of the angle measures by taking the following steps. Go to the Measure menu option and select Calculate. A calculator will appear on your screen.

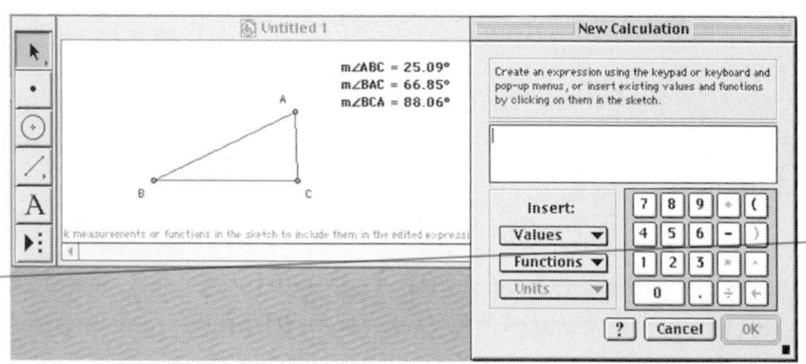

Click on the first angle measure in your sketch, then click the + button on the calculator. The measure of the angle will be displayed.

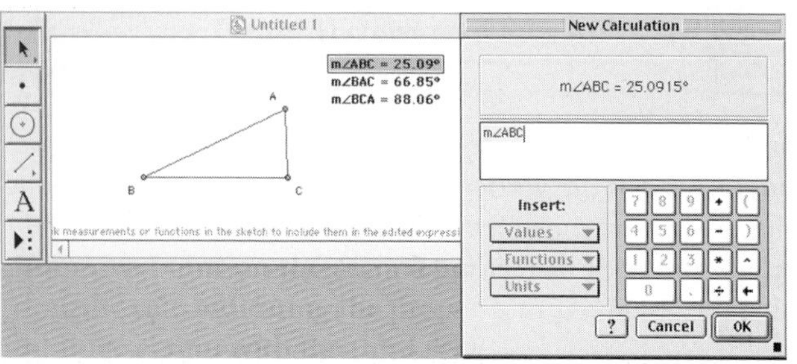

Next click on the second angle measure in your sketch, then +, and then the third angle measure. Now press the OK button on the calculator to calculate the sum of the three angles. Sketchpad will display the sum of the three angle measures. Note that the sum is 180°. Students may wonder if this is the case for this sketch only or if this is always true for any arbitrary triangle. Moving any of the vertices around should convince students that, although the angle measures change, their sum remains constant.

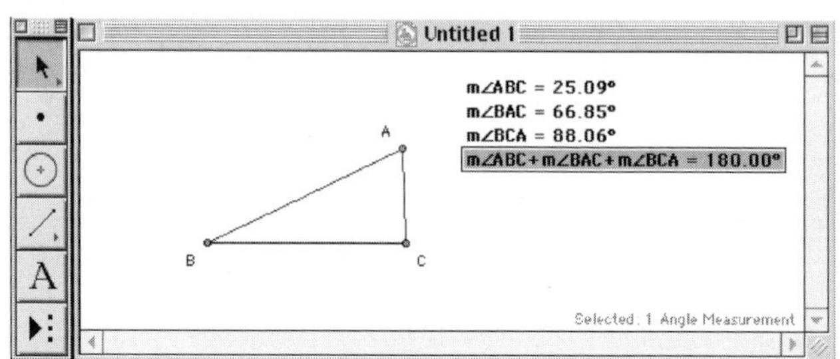

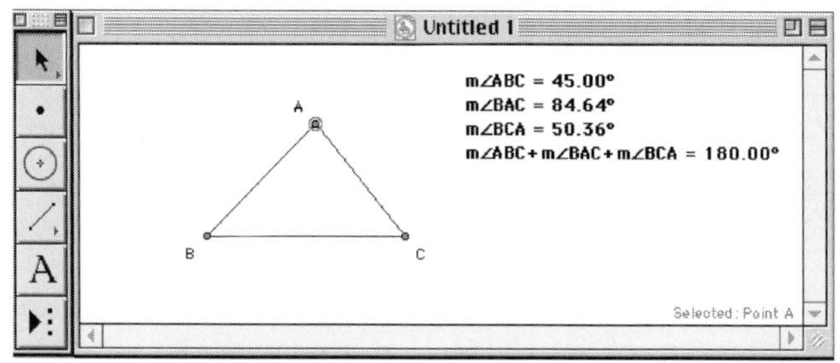

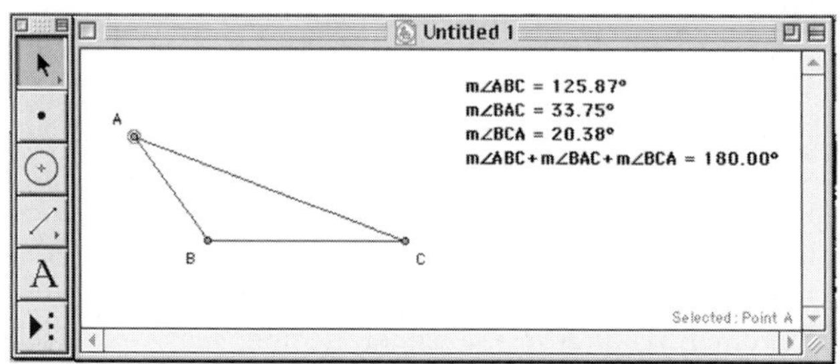

Project Two: The Three Medians in a Triangle

A median in a triangle connects a vertex with the midpoint of the opposite side. In this investigation, we will discover properties of medians in a triangle.

Construct a triangle ΔABC. Construct the three midpoints of the three sides (select each of the three sides and choose Midpoint under the Construct menu). You should have a triangle that looks as follows.

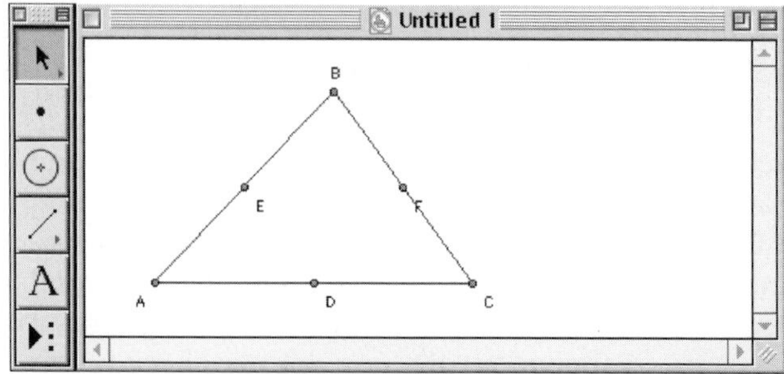

Construct two of the three medians, each connecting a vertex with the midpoint of the opposite side.

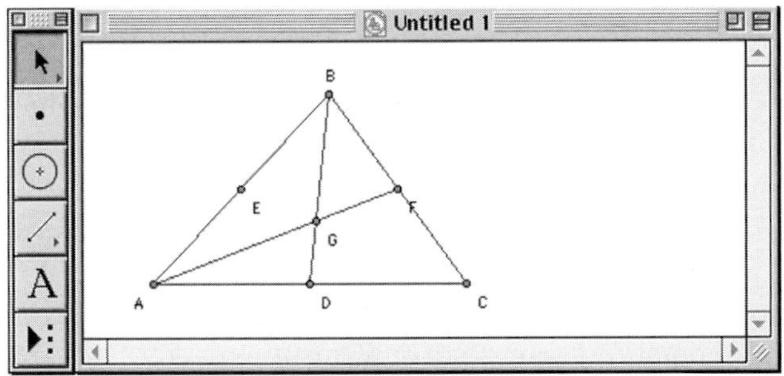

Construct the point of intersection of the two medians. If you've already constructed three medians, select two of them and then, in the Construct menu, choose Intersection.

Construct the third median. What do you notice about this third median? Drag a vertex of the triangle to confirm that your conjecture holds for any triangle.

The point where the medians intersect is called the *centroid*. Change its label to *Ce* as below. Note that if a label is not showing, use the text tool and click once on the object to show its label. Double-click on the object to change its label.

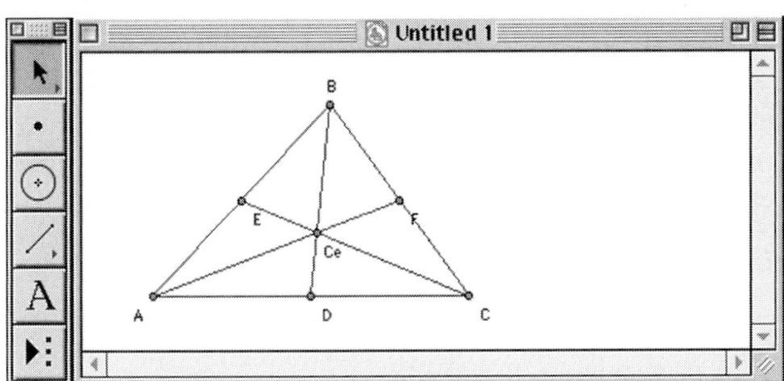

Now measure the distance from *B* to *Ce* and the distance from *Ce* to the midpoint *D*. Drag the vertices of ΔABC and look for a relationship between *BCe* and *CeD*. Note that before you measure a distance between two points, you must select the two points, and only have the two points selected.

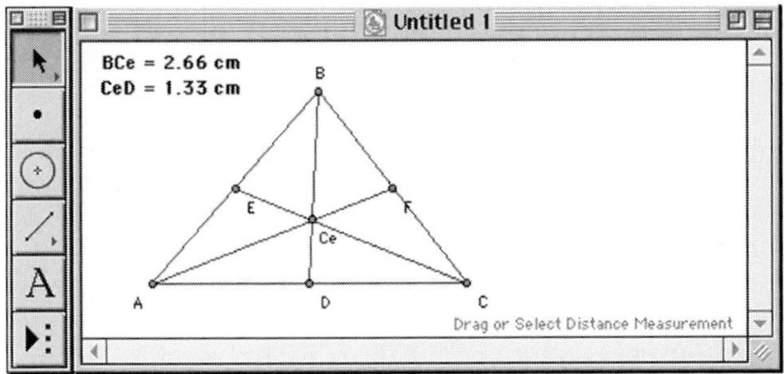

Make a table with these two measures. Select the two measurements; then, in the Graph menu, choose Tabulate. Then change the triangle and double-click on the table values to add another entry. Keep changing the triangle and adding entries to your table until you can see a relationship between the distances *BCe* and *CeD*.

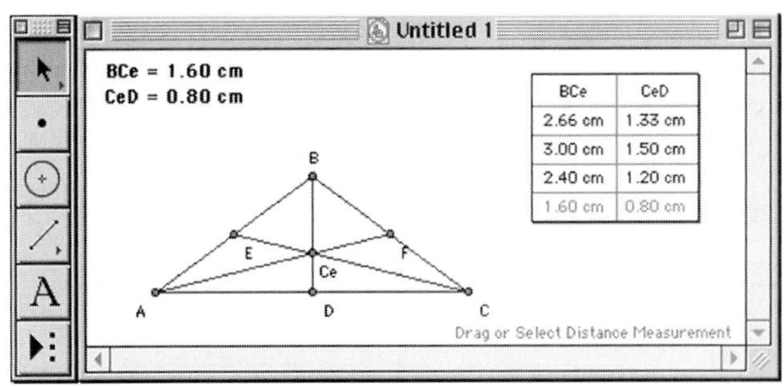

Based on what you see in the table entries, make a conjecture about the way the centroid divides each median in a triangle.

Plot the table data. To make a plot, select the table; then in the Graph menu, choose Plot Table Data. In the Plot Points dialog box, click Plot. Note that you don't want to change any of the data. You should get a graph with several collinear points. Construct a line through any two of the data points and measure its slope. Explain the significance of the slope of the line through the data points.

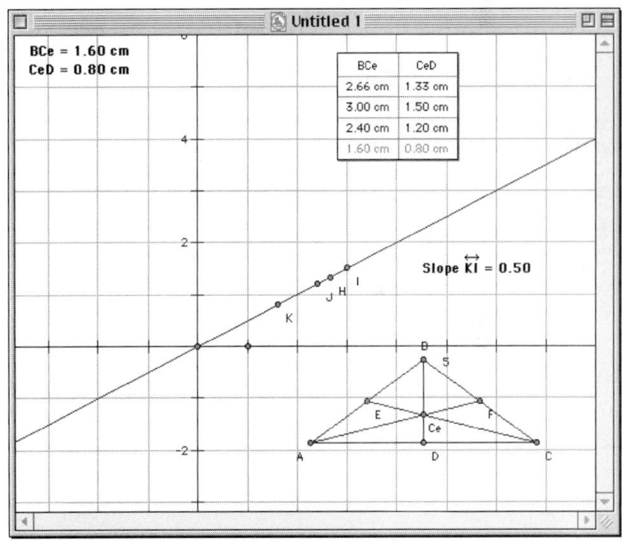

Project Three: Relation of the Median of a Triangle to the Area and Perimeter of the Triangle

Have the students draw a triangle ΔABC and construct the median $\overline{AM}$ (as in Project Two). Select points *A*, *B*, and *M*.

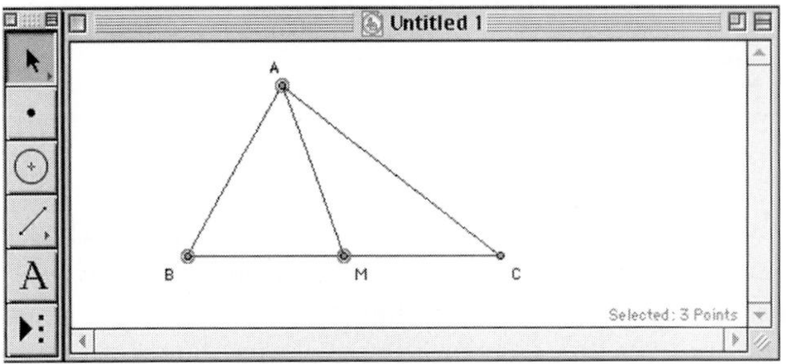

In the Construct menu, choose Triangle Interior. This option will shade in ΔABM. You may change the default color by going to the Display menu. The result should look like the sketch below.

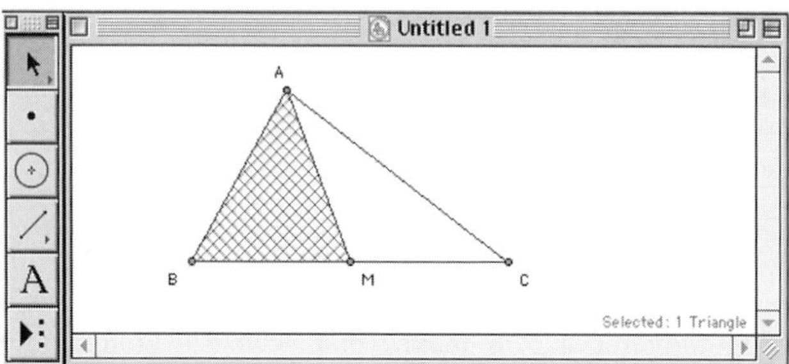

Repeat this process for ΔMAC and shade it a different color. The result is shown below.

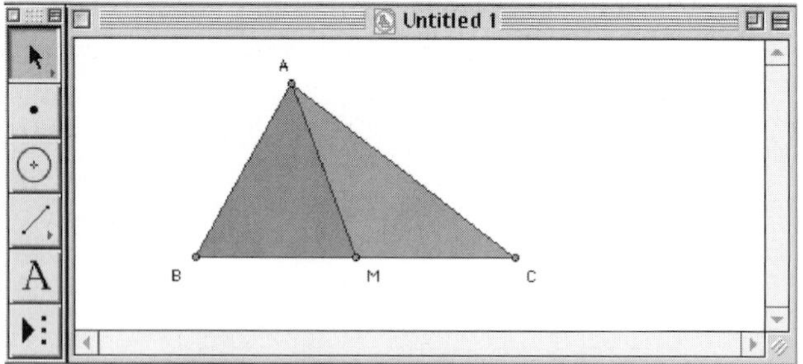

Now click anywhere in the interior of ΔABM to select it. If you go to the Measure menu, you see that Sketchpad can now calculate the area or perimeter of ΔABM. With ΔABM highlighted, first Measure the Area, then Measure the Perimeter. Sketchpad will calculate and display the area and perimeter of ΔABM. The window should look like the one below, with appropriate numbers for your triangle.

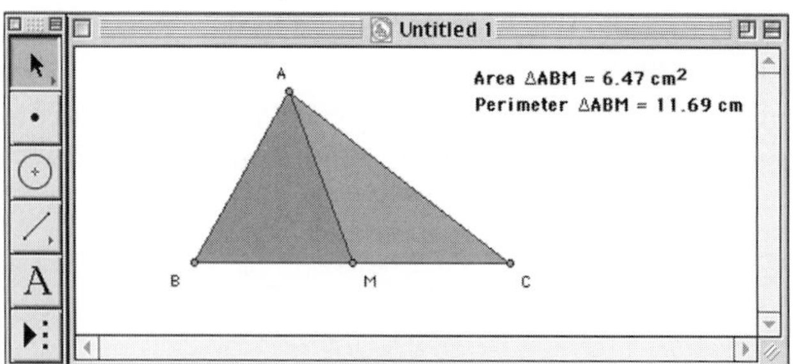

Now repeat the process after clicking inside ΔMAC. The area and perimeter of ΔMAC will be displayed. This reveals that the two triangles have the same area, but different perimeters. Students may wonder if this is always the case.

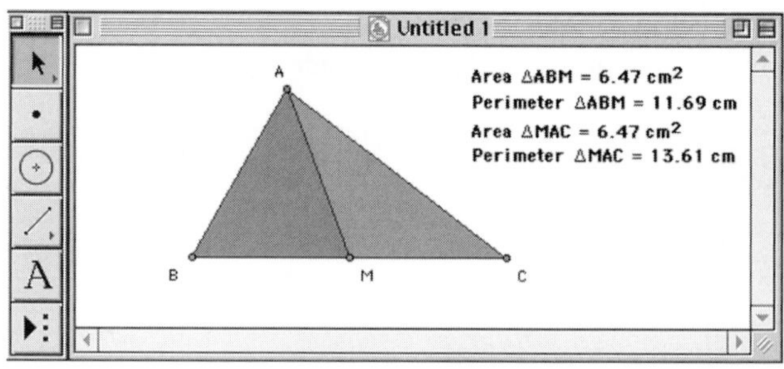

Investigate by dragging on point A. Students will clearly see that as point A (or any point or segment) is dragged, the areas of ΔABM and ΔMAC are always equal, but their perimeters are not.

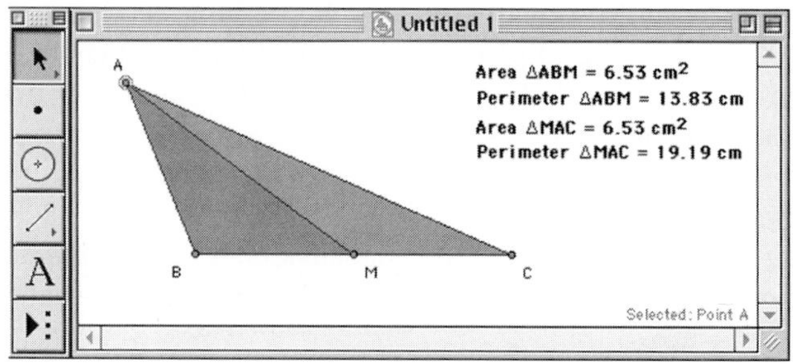

In a first-year algebra course, this example can lead to numerical and algebraic applications. In a geometry course, students could be asked to prove that when a median of a triangle is drawn, the areas of the two resulting triangles are equal.

Project Four: Midpoint Quadrilaterals

In this investigation, you'll discover something surprising about the quadrilateral formed by connecting the midpoints of the sides of another quadrilateral. This project models a guided-discovery worksheet that could be used with students.

Carry out the following steps and write a response where appropriate.

1. Construct quadrilateral $ABCD$.
2. Construct the midpoints of the sides. Note that if you select all four sides, you can construct all four midpoints at once.
3. Connect the midpoints to construct another quadrilateral, $EFGH$ (see sketch below).

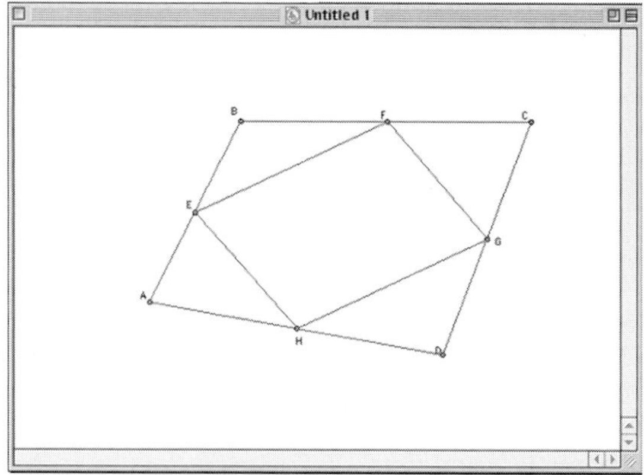

4. Drag vertices of the original quadrilateral *ABCD* and observe the midpoint quadrilateral.
5. Measure the four side lengths of this midpoint quadrilateral.
6. Measure the slopes of the four sides of the midpoint quadrilateral (see below).

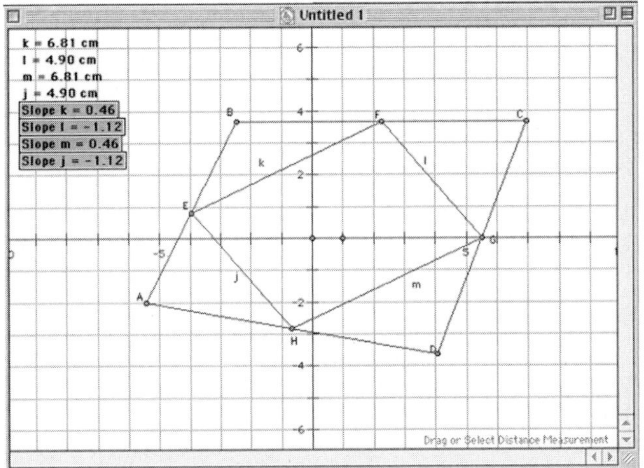

7. Consider what kind of quadrilateral the midpoint quadrilateral appears to be. How do the measurements you've made support that conjecture?
8. Construct a diagonal of the original quadrilateral.
9. Measure the length and slope of this diagonal (see below).

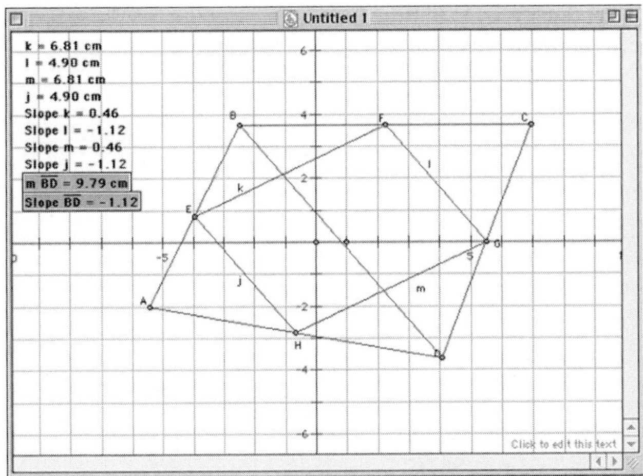

10. Drag the vertices of the original quadrilateral and observe how the length and slope of the diagonal are related to the lengths and slopes of the sides of the midpoint quadrilateral.

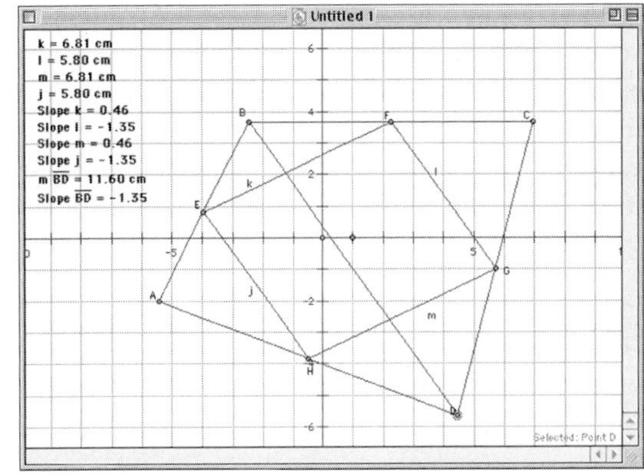

11. Note that the diagonal divides the original quadrilateral into two triangles. Each triangle has as a midsegment one of the sides of the midpoint quadrilateral. Use this fact and what you know about the slope and length of the diagonal to explain why the conjecture you made in question 7 is true.

Additional explorations:

1. Construct the midpoint quadrilateral of the midpoint quadrilateral. Then construct *its* midpoint quadrilateral. Repeat this two or three more times. Describe any patterns you see in the midpoint quadrilaterals.
2. Construct the polygon interiors of a quadrilateral and its midpoint quadrilateral. Measure their areas. Make a conjecture about these areas.
3. What's the midpoint quadrilateral of the trapezoid? An isosceles trapezoid? A parallelogram? A kite? A rhombus? A rectangle? A square? Organize and explain your findings.
4. Under what conditions is a midpoint quadrilateral a rectangle? A rhombus? A square? See if you can construct the most general quadrilateral whose midpoint quadrilateral is one of these.

Project Five: Drawing a Square with a Given Side

Draw a line segment $\overline{AB}$, as shown below. How would you construct a square with $\overline{AB}$ as a given side? Our solution to this challenge will serve as a tool in the next project.

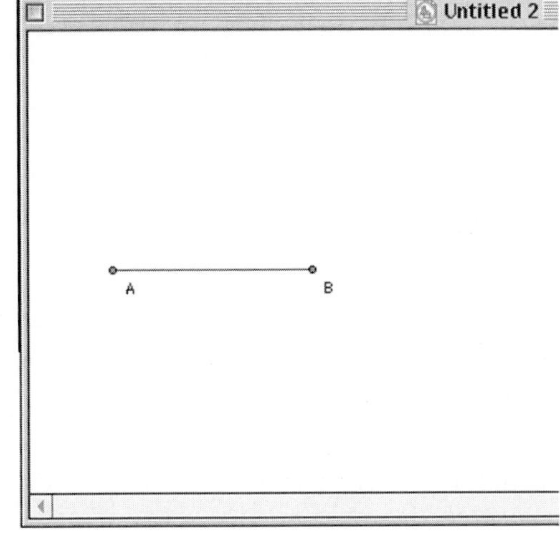

There are several approaches to constructing squares. In any of the approaches, the ability to construct perpendicular or parallel lines comes into play. Try the following approach. Select point *B* and then point *A*. Under the Construct menu, choose Circle By Center + Point. This will create a circle with center at *B* and radius of length *AB*, as shown in the upper right.

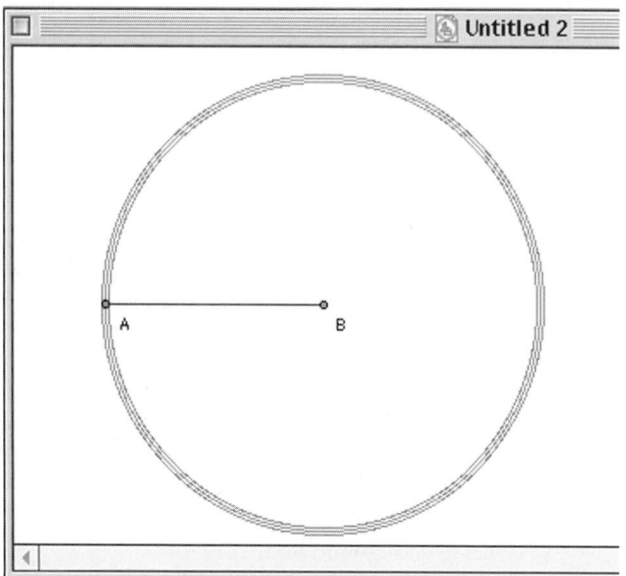

The goal is to construct perpendicular lines at points *A* and *B*, giving right angles. We can construct a line perpendicular to $\overline{AB}$ through point *A* by selecting both $\overline{AB}$ and *A* and then from the Construct menu choosing Perpendicular Line. Then select $\overline{AB}$ and *B* and repeat the construction. At this point, your sketch should look like the one below.

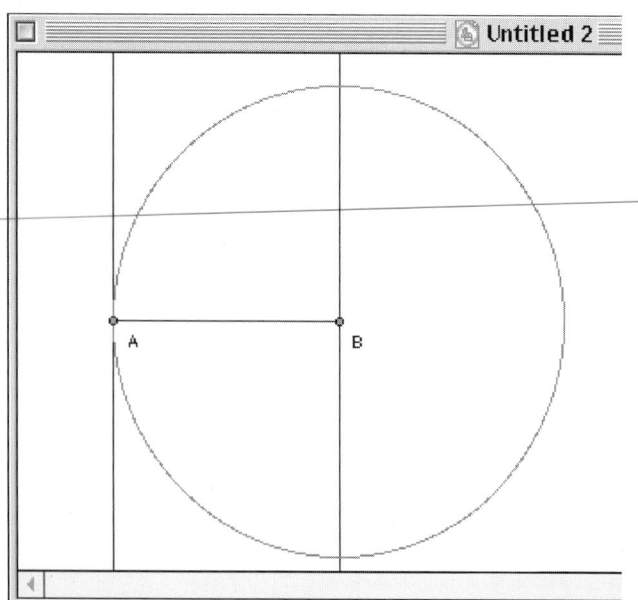

To continue, we need to place a point at the intersection of the perpendicular line through *B* and the circle. Place your mouse at the point of intersection and click. This will construct a new point at the intersection.

Now with this recently constructed point (*C*) selected, select line $\overleftrightarrow{BC}$ and have Sketchpad construct one more perpendicular line. Place a point (*D*) at the final intersection. This will complete the square, as shown below.

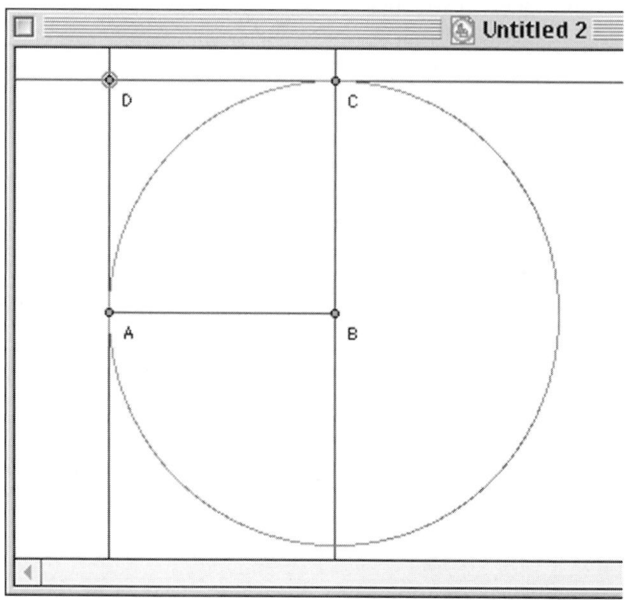

As the sketch shows, *ABCD* is the desired square. However, there are two difficulties at this point:

- There are *lines* instead of *segments* drawn to connect *A*, *B*, *C*, and *D*.
- We do not need to see the circle after the sketch has been completed.

To end up with just the square showing, select the circle as well as all of the lines and segments, and from the Display menu, select Hide Path Objects. You will now be left with only the four points *A*, *B*, *C*, and *D* showing, as below.

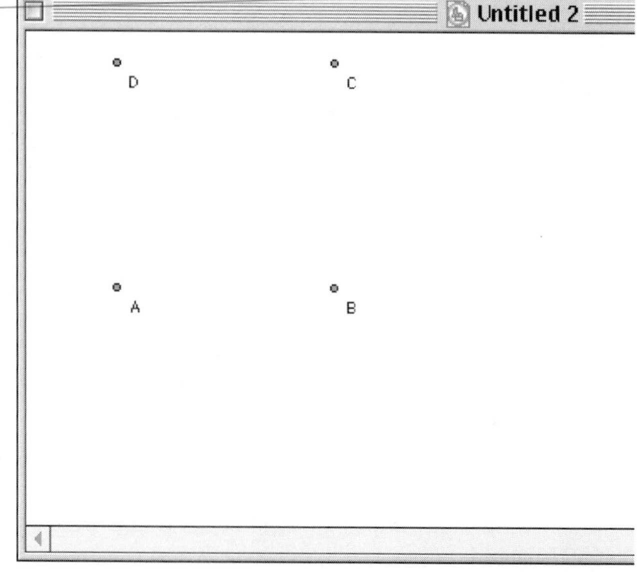

We now have Sketchpad create the square *ABCD* by selecting all four points (in order) and from the Construct menu, selecting Segments.

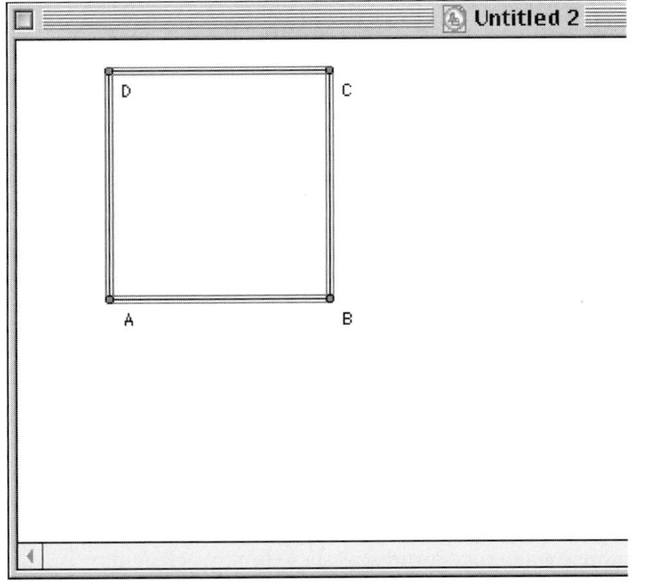

Because we will need Sketchpad to draw multiple squares for us in the next project, we can have it remember and reenact all of the directions we just instructed it to carry out. In the Edit menu, choose Select All. Next, click and hold on the Custom Tool button and select Create New Tool. Give your new tool a name, such as "Square Builder," and click OK. Save this sketch, but don't close it.

The Custom Tool function produces a program that automatically produces a square if the given conditions are met. On a new sketch, click on the Custom Tool button and find your custom tool to build a square. It is likely located under Other Documents, under the name of the sketch in which you created the tool. Notice that the cursor changes to having a little ball on the tip. This indicates that your custom tool is active. Click anywhere on the new sketch. Holding the mouse button down, drag out and you will see a square appear, as if by magic. Sketchpad is following the programmed directions and producing squares, at your command. Experiment with your tool by constructing squares of different sizes and orientations. Try building squares on squares and building larger objects out of square building blocks.

Project Six: Develop the Pythagorean Theorem

Note: We will be using the custom tool created in Project Five to create squares on demand. Have students open the sketch in which they created their square building tool. Then have them open a new sketch.

Ask students to draw a triangle ΔABC and find the lengths of its three sides as below:

Then, using the custom tool created in Project Five, draw a square on each of the sides of the triangle. Remember that when the square drawing custom tool is activated, the Selection Tool will change appearance.

Next have Sketchpad find the measure of $\angle ACB$ and the areas of the three squares. Remember that to measure the areas of the squares, you must choose the four vertices of each square, then choose Construct Quadrilateral Interior from the Construct menu, and then measure the area of each square by selecting its interior and choosing Area from the Measure menu. The result should be similar to the following picture.

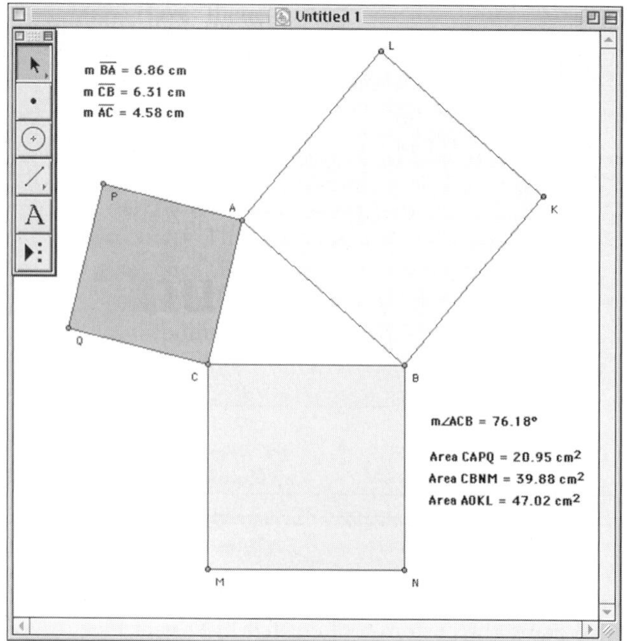

Have the students move point A or B so that the measure of $\angle ACB$ is 90°. Ask them if they notice anything interesting. Your students should have a sketch similar to the one below.

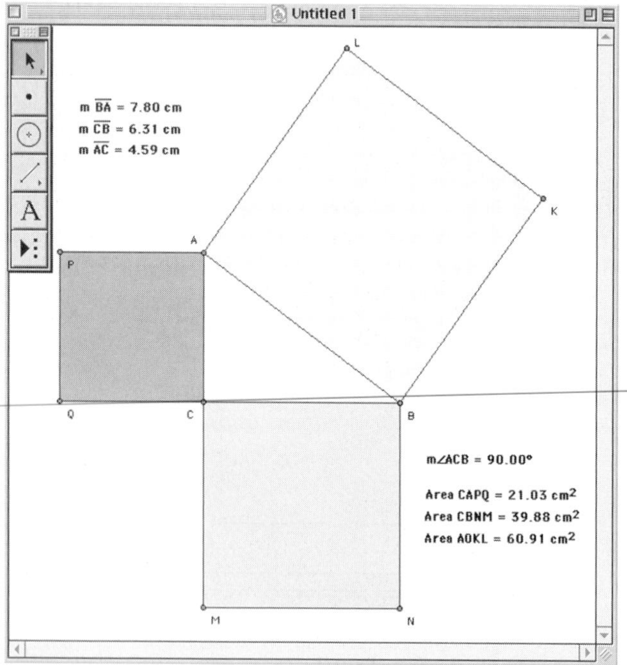

Lead them to the observation that when the original triangle is a right triangle, the sum of the areas of the two smaller drawn squares is equal to the area of the larger third square. (Note that in some cases, due to rounding error, this result might be off in the last decimal.)

This finding leads to the generalization that in a right triangle, the sum of the squares of the lengths of the legs is equal to the square of the length of the hypotenuse, $a^2 + b^2 = c^2$.

Where to Go from Here

If you've been successful with this quick start, and if you have The Geometer's Sketchpad and its documentation, there are a number of places you could go next.

- Try the sample activities in the *Teaching Mathematics With The Geometer's Sketchpad* booklet that comes in the binder with the Sketchpad documentation.
- Look at the sample sketches that come with Sketchpad. They contain many useful and instructive ideas.
- Select tours featured in the *Learning Guide* that involve parts of the program that especially interest you. For example, you may be interested in learning more about custom tools or analytic geometry.
- Experiment! Make sketches that interest you.

Dynamic Data Analysis and Fathom

Key Curriculum Press has also developed a program, called *Fathom*, which can serve as a learning environment for dynamic data analysis and statistics. It allows teachers and students to do data analysis and statistics with real data, and to illuminate statistical concepts in a visual way. For example, students can examine the effect of changing individual data points on measures of central tendency or variation.

Computer Algebra Systems

Recently, powerful handheld technology has emerged that contains the functionality of a computer-algebra system (CAS). Calculators such as the TI-92, TI-89, and Voyage 200 have a version of the CAS program Derive that allows powerful symbolic manipulation capability. These machines have the power to carry out most of the procedures of school mathematics, including those of calculus. In addition, the calculators support versions of *Sketchpad* or *Cabri* geometry. This will again raise the question of what mathematics needs to be taught in light of this emerging technology. In the meantime, teachers should consider how these sophisticated tools can be used for demonstration or investigation purposes in the classroom. Grants are often available if teachers would like to purchase a classroom set for student use.

Mathematical Equation Editors

A computer program that is essential to the daily work of mathematics teachers is a mathematical equation editor. Whether you are preparing overheads, student handouts, or an assessment, it is important to have a tool that allows you to compose and format mathematical notation properly within a word processing document. Most people have access to *Equation Editor*, a program that comes as part of the *Microsoft Word* program. However, depending on your version, it may not be installed with the standard installation. A more full-featured and robust version, called *MathType*, may also be purchased (see www.dessci.com).

Multimedia

Teachers may take advantage of a wide range of multimedia materials that are available to help mathematics "come alive" in the classroom. In addition, a number of multimedia programs have been developed that allow students to investigate realistic problem-solving situations that involve mathematics. A particular set of these programs has been developed around the theory of anchored instruction, and involves mathematical problem finding and solving in real-life contexts. One popular example is *The Adventures of Jasper Woodbury*. More information about this package can be found at http://peabody.vanderbilt.edu/projects/funded/jasper/Jasperhome.html.

Course Management Systems

Some teachers now have access to course management systems (such as BlackBoard or WebCT) that allow online access to course materials and support electronic submission of assignments. These systems also allow teachers to create threaded discussion lists and electronic grade books accessible over the Web. Given these course management tools, it may be possible to design courses that are distance learning in format or a hybrid mixture of face-to-face and online learning. One ongoing challenge associated with making mathematics available online is the difficulty of displaying mathematics notation.

Test Generating Programs

There are a number of programs available that can be used to generate tests and worksheets for students. This is a tremendous advantage to the teacher in many ways. For assessments, the teacher can generate different versions of the same test to prevent students from copying from each other. Answer keys are also generated for each different version. The program can do a statistical analysis of the assessment to generate a report which will help the teacher to note which of the problems or problem types were difficult and may need revisiting. Homework sheets may be easily generated. The teacher can choose between a number of problems on the same or similar topics, or a spiraled assignment that includes previous topics. Some noted programs are:

Exam View by Prentice Hall, available for all levels of middle school and high school math.

Examgen

Eduware

Gradebook Programs

Keeping proper records of attendance and grades is an important part of being a successful teacher. There are a number of programs available that set up templates to help the teacher to see at a glance how the students are doing. Many of these also generate reports that can be sent to parents to keep them aware of the progress of their child. Student averages can be tracked and all facets that go into education and evaluation can be weighted as per the guidelines of the school and the department. There are two basic types of these programs, those that can be used only by the teacher and those that have Internet capability. The ones with Internet capability allow the teacher to provide students and their parents with a password that allows access to different modules. The homework assignments may be posted online; the student's grades may be made available, the parents can be contacted through e-mail to inform them of problems, or to congratulate achieving students. Some of the programs that we have used successfully are:

Gradekeeper

PCGradebook

Gradebookpower

EZGrader

Mygradebook

Gradebookplus

Interactive White Boards

Many schools are installing Interactive White Boards (IWBs) in their classrooms. Two of the most popular of these are the SmartBoard, made by Smart Technologies (www.smarttech.com), and the Intelliboard, made by the Numonics Corporation (www.numonics.com). The boards allow teachers to prepare lessons in advance and to use them in class. The work can be added to in class by the students. The students love using the technology and are far more likely to volunteer to demonstrate their ideas. There are numerous templates, such as graphs of the Cartesian coordinate system that can be used. There are even virtual manipulatives included in the software. There is no chalk, and lesson files can be saved indefinitely for review by students or for use in other classes. Some teachers have now begun to save the files and post the student-annotated lessons on the Web each day for student review. Students and their parents can actually sit at home and see what was done in class. IWBs bring life and excitement into the classroom and are sure to be the wave of the future.

Summary

Teachers at every grade level should constantly watch for appropriate calculator and computer activities and projects. Every effort ought to be made to utilize technology in the classroom to provide additional enrichment and stimulation. Students may use calculators or computers to analyze or reinforce problem-solving techniques; play games of logic; sharpen geometric, algebraic, or arithmetic skills; or merely improve their computer or calculator operational abilities.

Texas Instrument's TI-83 Plus and TI-84 Plus calculators are particularly valuable in demonstrating useful algebraic, geometric, or graphics concepts to the seasoned or unseasoned user. Spreadsheets are valuable for exploring situations involving functions that can be viewed in an iterative or recursive fashion. The Geometer's Sketchpad offers in-depth insights into a dynamic investigation of the fundamentals of geometry.

More and more sophisticated mathematical programs can be found on handheld calculators. For instance, *Cabri Jr.* is dynamic geometry software available for the TI-83 (Plus and Silver Edition) and the TI-84 (Plus and Silver Edition). The Geometer's Sketchpad is available for the TI-89 and Voyage 200 calculators. All of the aforementioned calculators have an application called *Cell Sheet* that allows data sharing with *Microsoft Excel*.

In all of the foregoing activities, the hands-on approaches to solving problems with technology enable students to grasp and expand their understanding of mathematical concepts.

EXERCISES

1. Select a topic that is appropriate for demonstration on The Geometer's Sketchpad for each of the following:
   a. An average-ability eighth-grade mathematics class
   b. A gifted tenth-grade class
   c. A ninth-grade class that is in need of remedial services
   d. An average-ability eleventh-grade core class
   e. A gifted seventh-grade class
   f. A twelfth-grade class that is now studying statistics
2. The following questions are open ended and offer the student much flexibility in his or her response. Use a TI-83 calculator to develop a tenth-grade lesson on each of the following:
   a. Quadrilaterals
   b. Solving a system of linear equations
   c. Solving polynomial equations of any degree
   d. Solving quadratic inequalities
   e. Differentiation of trigonometric functions
   f. The slope of a straight line
3. Suppose you are approached by the parents of one of your better-achieving students, who ask that you accelerate their child's progress even more rapidly than the remainder of the class. How would you develop lessons if you find the student to be:
   a. Of only average ability in mathematics
   b. Quite talented in mathematics
4. Select an appropriate calculator to teach one of the enrichment topics at the end of this book and prepare the lesson.
5. Prepare a computer lesson for one of your mathematically needy classes. Obtain your teaching information from the World Wide Web.
6. Research your state's learning standards for mathematics.
   a. What do the standards say about the role of calculators in mathematics learning and their use on state assessments? How will this affect your approach as a mathematics teacher?
   b. What do the standards say about the role of computers in mathematics learning? How will this affect your approach as a mathematics teacher?
7. Locate a Web site related to school mathematics. Evaluate it along the following questions: What is its intended audience? For what grade levels would it be appropriate? What mathematics topics are addressed? What types of resources does it contain? Rate its ease of navigation, visual appeal, and level of interactivity.
8. Develop an Internet-based student activity page. There is a wealth of mathematics content resources available on the Internet. Develop a worksheet that guides students to and through a set of Web sites—choosing ones that will introduce them to appropriate mathematics content and engage them in a variety of mathematical activities.
9. Model a mathematical problem situation using a spreadsheet. What assumptions did you make? What does the model predict? Investigate how predictions based on the model change if you alter your assumptions (e.g., starting values).
10. Develop a student Geometer's Sketchpad worksheet that will guide students through a series of investigational activities that will result in them "discovering" an important geometrical property or theorem. Assume that students will be working individually (or in small groups) in a computer lab.

Chapter 6

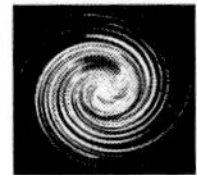

Assessment

New mathematics teachers might think of assessment as an examination designed to measure student progress and achievement. Although examinations, as well as other graded materials, are an important component of assessment, they are but a piece of a greater whole. The use of good assessment data from a variety of sources can not only record student achievement, but improve it as well, for every student.

In 1995, the NCTM released a document, *Assessment Standards for School Mathematics*, to help reform traditional thinking about assessment in mathematics. The document was written with the understanding that "all students are capable of learning mathematics," and highlighted six assessment standards: assessment should reflect the mathematics that all students need to know and be able to do, enhance mathematics learning, promote equity, be an open process, promote valid inferences about mathematics, and be a coherent process.

The key to these standards is that assessment be used not to separate or rank students as examinations often do, but as a tool to improve instruction as well as report the results of that instruction. To that end, the NCTM defined four purposes of assessment (see the ellipse in Figure 6.1): monitoring students' progress, making instructional decisions, evaluating students' achievement, and evaluating programs. The rest of this chapter is dedicated to expounding on these purposes in the hopes of bringing new teachers a broad perspective on assessment.

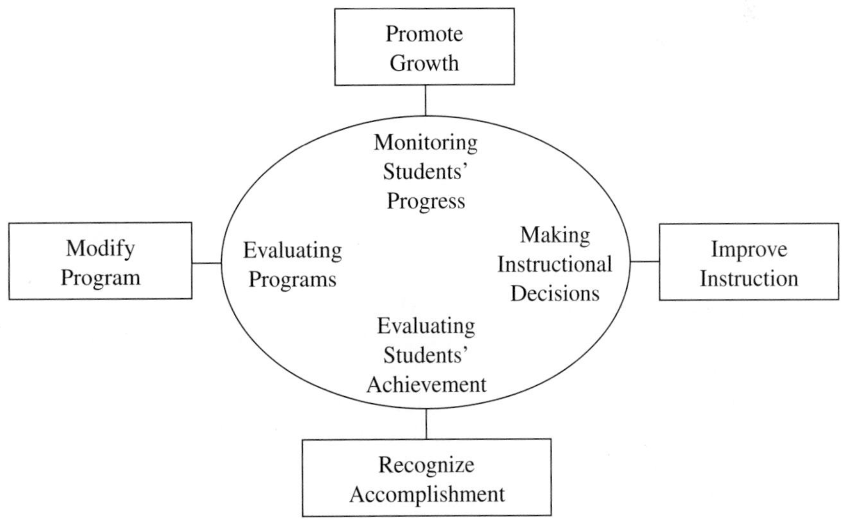

FIGURE 6.1 NCTM Purposes and Outcomes of Assessment

Assessment For Monitoring Student Progress

Student progress must be continually monitored by teachers, parent/guardians, and the students themselves. Many schools encourage or, in some cases, require teachers to complete progress reports and attend conferences with students and/or their parent/guardian on a regular basis. These checkups are designed to allow students, their parent/guardians, and teachers to discuss student progress without assigning a value to the progress.

Struggling students can express their concerns and seek alternative instructional opportunities. Other students may have mastered the material and need enrichment to continue their growth. In both cases the teachers can adjust instruction to better meet the needs of students before more formal assessments take place.

Bringing such struggles out into the open should serve to assuage the test-taking anxiety so many students face. Well-monitored students do not go into an examination dreading what weakness it will expose. They see instead the exam as a way to exhibit their hard work and newly found confidence. This should be the goal for the three-way partnership among teachers, students, and parent/guardians.

Such a partnership is formed and strengthened through conferences at the school. These conferences allow teachers to report students' educational status to the parent/guardians in the presence of the students. Discussing progress impediments such as missing homework assignments or poor class participation allows the parent/guardian to partner in finding the root of the problem and, from there, a remedy.

During the conference, or at home afterwards, students may express that they are genuinely making an effort but are unable to complete the assigned work without additional help or support. Based on this information, the teacher might recommend some study strategies or encourage students to attend a homework club or after-school program. Parents or guardians can be powerful teacher allies, and you should regularly include them in the progress-monitoring phase. Remember, home support is a crucial factor in student success. Another factor in student success is including the students themselves in the evaluation process.

Effective self-monitoring tools allow teachers and their students to work together to monitor progress. For example, students can keep daily journals allowing them to reflect on what they have learned and to record both their struggles and successes. Teachers may then collect these journals and get a sense of what material needs to be reviewed or approached differently. Similarly, as students reread their returned journals, they may see that what was once confusing or frustrating is now conquered or even trivial, empowering them next time they struggle to understand new concepts and acquire new skills.

Another self-monitoring tool involves having students create a portfolio of their progress. Portfolios are collections of student work over time along with reflections on that work. Often teachers set the criteria or standards for artifacts collected, but allow the students to choose the included artifacts. For example, one criterion may be to show improvement in student learning related to solving systems of equations. The student may choose two homework assignments or tests that show improvement in that area. The teacher would ask the student to include a written statement that explains why these two artifacts show growth in understanding of the topic specified. A second example could be demonstrating that the student can use a technology to solve an extended problem. The student may have used several different technologies to solve problems over the course of the year, but will choose one to meet this standard and reflect in writing on its choice.

Within this portfolio, students can chart their grades and absences just as the teacher does. The portfolio can be taken a step further and used as a reporting tool. For example, the teacher might ask students to assess their performance after 5 weeks and then map out an improvement plan for the 10-week mark. Having students regularly maintain their portfolio makes them more accountable for their actions. Students will learn that grades are not something the teacher assigns; they are earned as a result of student work.

Many publishers include software with their textbooks that can be used as an additional self-monitoring tool. With the use of computers, teachers can have their students take progress-monitoring tests with questions that are keyed to specific standards set for the course. The computer software analyzes what knowledge and skills the students have mastered as well as those still in need of development. These overall progress charts are immediately available for both the teacher and student.

Whichever progress-monitoring assessment you implement, the information it generates must be acted on for the time spent to be worthwhile. For students, using the information to identify areas in need of improvement is the first step. However, students need to be encouraged to utilize their school, teachers, peers, and parent/guardian to remedy these struggles. For teachers, the information gleaned from progress-monitoring assessments can be used to inform and improve their classroom instruction.

Assessment For Making Instructional Decisions

As indicated in Chapter 2 teachers should build ongoing instructional assessment into their daily lessons. This will allow teachers and students to check for understanding prior to leaving the classroom or advancing to the next topic. When teachers find that their students are unable to answer a question or complete an in-class assigned task, they need to make lesson adjustments either for the whole class or for small groups of students. Remember, the key goal is that every student meets the objectives set for the lesson. Such in-lesson assessments are referred to as formative assessment.

The purpose of formative assessment is to allow for alternative instructional activities prior to engaging in more formal or higher stakes assessments. The lesson examples in

Chapter 2 demonstrated several types of formative assessment. One example could be found in the "start-up" at the beginning of the lesson on factoring trinomials. This activity was designed to review the prerequisite skill of identifying factors of given integers. If the teacher had found that the students could not answer these basic factoring questions, review activities would then need to be provided before asking students to factor trinomials.

A second formative assessment took place during the lesson on similar figures (page 21). During the first small group activity, the teacher circulated among the students to determine whether they could measure the sides of the figures and could find the ratio of corresponding sides. If some students were unable to complete this part of the lesson, the teacher could work with them independently while setting the other students to a more challenging application.

Assigning, collecting, and reviewing homework is another way for teachers to provide formative assessment. The teacher must determine how many students are having problems with their homework. Occasionally, students attempt their homework outside of class and find that they cannot do it. Some think they have completed it only to find that their answers are wrong. This is a signal for change in both the student and the teacher's behavior.

For example, sometimes the teacher or gifted group members provide so much support during an in-class lesson that the other students are lulled into a false confidence that they grasp the concept. Yet, once these students attempt the homework on their own, they find themselves unable to complete the questions. If this is the case, chances are the student will also be unsuccessful when asked to answer similar questions on a test. Both students and teachers need to recognize this situation.

Students need to bring difficulties to the teacher's attention rather than stew in silent frustration. Teachers, for their part, need to build in supporting structures or "scaffolding" that will be gradually removed during the in-class lesson so that both teacher and student can make a fair assessment of skill development and understanding. Ongoing formative assessments are an essential part of any lesson. Teachers must use the information gained from responses to questions, group work results, and homework to improve instruction. Only then will they be able to provide effectively aimed lessons.

Data-Driven Instruction

While the informal formative assessment strategies just presented are essential components of the teaching and learning cycle, many school districts have created or purchased more formal assessment systems. These formative or "benchmark" assessments will help teachers determine what students have learned as they move through the school year and should provide support for reteaching or providing additional practice for those students who have not yet mastered key concepts or skills. A basic formative assessment system provides for regular diagnostic and predictive assessments during the school year to help teachers, students, administrators, and families understand what students know and what knowledge and skills they need to develop. Many such systems include standard-linked tutorials that can be assigned, completed, and evaluated electronically. The following excerpt of an assessment report is provided to show you how this information can be used in your classroom.

The table shows the results of a mid-year diagnostic assessment report for an eighth-grade Algebra 1 class. The focus of this assessment is student understanding of linear equations and solving equations with one variable. A, B, C, and D are possible responses to multiple-choice questions aligned with each indicator. The numbers in each column represent the percentage of students in this class who selected that option to answer the question, and the highlighted number indicates the correct response. You can see that 41% selected B, the correct answer, for the question aligned with performance indicator 8.A.38.

Using the Data to Inform Instruction

All teachers should be able to glean basic information about their class as a whole and about individual students from the information provided in the table. First, let's consider what the students know. It appears that most students correctly answered the questions related to solving simple equations (see indicators 8.A.40 and 8.A.41). The ability to solve simple equations is an essential skill for further study of algebra; thus teachers must plan to address this weakness immediately for those who answered incorrectly. However, it would

SAMPLE REPORT FROM A FORMATIVE ASSESSMENT

Performance Indicator	A	B	C	D
8.A.38 Determine the slope of a line, given the coordinates of two points.	14%	**41%**	17%	28%
8.A.39 Determine the equation of a line, given the slope and one point.	**48%**	7%	28%	17%
8.A.40 Determine the solution to a given equation : two steps using addition and subtraction.	3%	3%	**91%**	3%
8.A.41 Determine the solution to a given equation : two steps using addition, subtraction, multiplication, and division.	3%	10%	10%	**77%**
8.A.42 Determine and describe using a number line, the solution set for a simple inequality.	7%	**33%**	60%	0%

be inappropriate to reteach this topic to the whole class. For the few students who answered incorrectly, extra support should be provided, in the form of peer tutoring or outside-of-class instruction. If available, a computer tutorial may facilitate the individualization of instruction needed to support students struggling with these indicators.

Now let's consider what the class does not know. The majority of students had trouble answering questions related to slopes of linear equations (see indicators 8.A.38 and 8.A.39). In addition, one can see that the wrong answers to linear equation–related questions were distributed across the options of incorrect responses. Thus, there is no obvious misconception demonstrated among the incorrect answers. The teacher must re-address this topic and can do so in several ways. Some suggestions are listed below:

- The teacher could develop a tiered lesson with a focus on slopes of linear equations as one of the first levels.
- The teacher could create a lesson with two strands, one focusing on review of slopes of linear equations and the other a more advanced application of the topic.
- Students could engage in individualized tutorials, with struggling students participating in activities related to slopes of linear equations.

Whatever method is used, those students who have demonstrated mastery of the concepts should be provided an opportunity to grow mathematically while others are reviewing the concept.

The last performance indicator in the table indicates that the majority of students have the same misunderstanding of the concept or skill. For indicator 8.A.42, 60% selected C as the wrong answer. To decide how to respond to these results, we must look at the question itself. Since multiple-choice questions are designed so incorrect responses (or distracters) represent common misunderstandings about the questions, looking at the incorrect response provides the teacher with valuable information. In our case the question was:

Which graph represents the solution set of the inequality $3x - 9 \geq 24$?

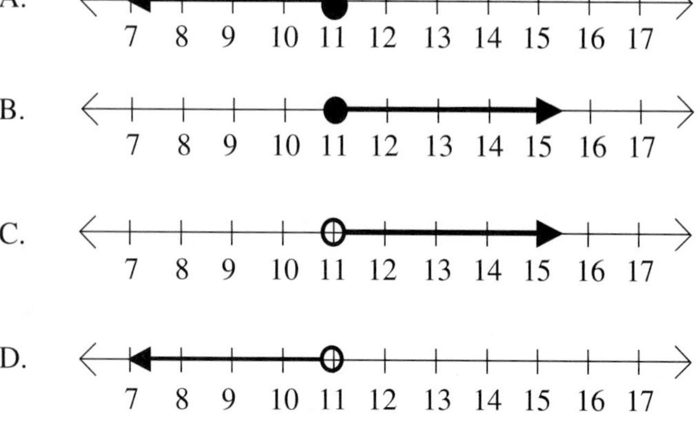

Upon review of the question, the teacher can see that students were able to correctly solve the inequality, but confused the open and closed circle on the graph. A quick review for the whole class would be appropriate here. The teacher could ask those students who selected the correct answer for suggestions to help their peers remember when to use the open circle and when to use the closed circle.

Final Thoughts on Data-Driven Instruction

Using data from carefully developed assessments can provide teachers with a wealth of information about their students. While teachers must continue to follow the pacing calendar, they also need to plan for reteaching, for providing more practice along the way, and for enriching lessons. Careful attention to assessment results will help teachers individualize instruction to maximize learning for all.

Evaluating Student Achievement

Eventually teachers must evaluate student learning in a manner that can be reported more formally, such as report card grades or final grades. These evaluations, called summative assessments, are used to make decisions regarding promotion and retention. They can affect a student's class rank, eligibility for participation in extracurricular activities, and access to special enrichment or remedial programs. Teachers must carefully plan for such assessments and inform their students and parent/guardians of this plan.

The most effective teachers make use of multiple assessment instruments as strategies for determining their students' mathematical growth, power, and achievement. A balance of multiple means of assessment promotes equity, which gives students the opportunity to display their varied abilities. Students who are assessed in various ways will learn to appreciate that mathematics is not a cluster of rules to learn by rote and follow, but a process that will empower them.

Multiple assessment instruments may include written tests, quizzes, classwork, written and verbal contributions to class discussions, small/large group work, projects, oral reports, student journals, open-ended question responses, portfolios, observations, student self-assessment/peer evaluation, homework, and evaluation of student notebooks' comprehensiveness and neatness. Additional assessment strategies may include take-home tests, standardized achievement tests, and the confidence and skill demonstrated by students in their use of calculators, computers, and other mathematical tools. Evaluation assessments should also reflect the diversity of a teacher's instructional style and the assessment philosophy and policies established by the school or district.

Each teacher's personal and ongoing experiences with different assessment techniques will be helpful in arriving at the best balance of strategies. We suggest alternatives that should be considered in the evaluative process. Assigning a numerical grade that becomes a weighted average to each category of assessment for evaluation purposes is a professional judgment that each teacher will make and justify to students, parents, supervisors, and colleagues. No predetermined formula is suitable for all teachers or students. Because the final grade is a sum of each of its parts, the teacher should feel confident that the resultant grade is a valid reflection of the students' performance with respect to the objectives and standards set for the course.

Assessment instruments that should be considered include:

- Class tests, quizzes, and performance assessments
- Mid-semester evaluation
- Final examination grade
- Standardized test results

Although the assessment instruments just listed may be assigned unambiguous numerical grades, the following more subjective categories may be ranked by the teacher using a predetermined set of criteria:

- Degree of student's acceptance by other group members
- Success rate of the group in which a student participated in completing assignments correctly
- Quality of the student's participation in large groups
- Oral reports
- Projects
- Written comments and evaluations as found in portfolios
- Attempts at solving enrichment exercises
- Completeness and overall quality of homework
- Scientific and graphing calculator skills
- Use of computer technology
- Applications of prepared/self-generated manipulatives

Using Performance Assessment Tasks

A performance assessment task (PAT) allows students the opportunity to apply their mathematical knowledge and skills to complete a high-level mathematical task. A PAT differs from an instructional task in that students are required to complete it with little intervention from the teacher. A PAT establishes what students understand and what they can do. The task should be significant, realistic, and have merit. A performance task:

- Should be correlated with the goals, objectives, and content of the curriculum.
- Should promote mathematics as a process allowing students to show their thinking and conceptual understanding of a mathematical problem.
- Should give an opportunity for an evaluation of the processes implicated in the tasks.
- Should be motivational, include critical thinking, and be related to a real-life situation.
- Should be connected to the goal being assessed so a student's performance can be discussed.
- Should emphasize conceptual understanding more than rote learning.
- Should be more open ended than strictly structured.
- Should be multifaceted and not have only one methodology.
- Should lead to other mathematical extensions and questions.

Performance assessment tasks lend themselves to conceptual understanding of mathematical concepts and principles. These tasks cannot generally be assessed using traditional quizzes and tests. Usually, performance assessment tasks are process oriented and open-ended items, and rarely yield a single answer. The evaluation of PATs involves the judgment of a trained professional educator based on predetermined criteria that are closely aligned with the goals and objectives set by the curriculum. Oftentimes mathematics problems, examples, or illustrations appearing in a textbook can be converted into a PAT by posing open-ended questions such as "What's the difference between ...?"; "Under what conditions will ...?"; "Explain why this fact is either true or false." Posing productive questions that facilitate conceptual understanding changes the thinking patterns from procedural thinking to critical thinking and therefore correlates meaningful questions with meaningful instructions.

Examples of Performance Assessment Tasks

- Create an itinerary for a 7-day trip with limits on cost, types of attractions you want to visit, and/or time.
- Monitor the growth of mold on a piece of bread over a 2-week period. Plot the growth and determine the function that best describes that growth.
- Analyze the amount of paper used by students in your math class. Create a spreadsheet to describe daily and weekly use. Predict yearly use. Also analyze how the paper is used. Based on your results, make some suggestions for reducing the waste of paper in your classroom.
- According to the History Channel, in a program titled *The Universe: Gravity*, if a straight-line tunnel, connecting any two locations on Earth, were built and you jumped in, it would take you 42 minutes to travel from one location to the other. This would be true if you traveled from Chicago to Baghdad or from Paris to Tokyo. Investigate this assertion and explain why you think it is or is not true.

Using Rubrics to Evaluate Student Work

Rubrics are detailed criteria or procedures used to assess the work of students. They explain what is being evaluated, show an achievement level, and assist the teacher in categorizing students' work on the appropriate level. Moreover, rubrics give students a better understanding of the expectations of the teacher. A rubric is made up of specific criteria for assessing student performance and contains a rating key for application of those criteria. A scoring rubric establishes the criteria for judging work on a particular performance. Teachers should help students understand rubrics when giving assignments, so that the students become familiar with and try to accomplish what is required of them.

EXAMPLE OF A MATHEMATICS RUBRIC FOR ASSESSING A PERFORMANCE TASK

Level	Conceptual Understanding	Mathematical Reasoning and Problem-Solving Strategies	Communication
Unsatisfactory	▶ No solution exists, or the solution is not connected to the test question. ▶ Skills and concepts used are inconsistent and do not apply to the test question.	▶ No evidence of a problem-solving strategy. ▶ No plan or use of a strategy, or uses a procedure that does not help solve the problem. ▶ No indication of mathematical reasoning. ▶ Too many mathematical errors so that the problem could not be solved.	▶ Solution is not explained, or the explanation is incomprehensible or not connected to the problem. ▶ No mathematical representations (e.g., figures, diagrams, graphs, tables, etc.) are used. ▶ Usage of mathematical terms is incorrect.
Approaching Satisfactory	▶ Incomplete solution, i.e., showing parts of the problem are not recognized.	▶ Uses a strategy that is somewhat useful, leading toward an incomplete solution. ▶ Some indication of mathematical strategies. ▶ Incomplete mathematical procedures.	▶ There is an incomplete and unclear explanation. ▶ There is minimal use of correct mathematical representation. ▶ There is minimal use of mathematical terminology and notation appropriate to the problem.
Satisfactory	▶ The solution indicates that the student has more than a basic comprehension of the problem and the main concepts necessary for its solution.	▶ Uses a sound strategy that leads to a solution of the problem. ▶ Uses mathematical reasoning correctly. ▶ Mathematical procedures are applied.	▶ The explanation is clear. ▶ Mathematical representation used is accurate and appropriate. ▶ Mathematical terminology and notation is used effectively.
Superior	▶ The solution shows a deep conceptual understanding of the problem, including the ability to apply the correct mathematical concepts and the necessary information for its solution.	▶ Uses a well-organized and high-level strategy that leads directly to a sound solution. ▶ Uses complex reasoning. ▶ Uses correct procedures to solve the problem and validate the solution.	▶ Explanation is clear and comprehensive. All details are represented to solve the problem. All steps and procedures are incorporated so that the explanation of the solution is understandable to the reader. ▶ Precise mathematical representation is used to communicate concepts related to the problem's solution. ▶ The use of precise mathematical language, terminology, and notation is applied throughout the solution of the problem.

Rubrics generally fall into one of two categories: analytic or holistic. Analytic rubrics break the task into specific assessment categories and evaluate each category separately. The rubric above titled "Example of a Mathematics Rubric for Assessing a Performance Task" will evaluate the performance task based on a student's conceptual understanding, mathematical reasoning and problem-solving strategies, and communication. A student could receive a "Satisfactory" rating in conceptual understanding but an "Unsatisfactory" in communication.

A holistic rubric considers the product as a whole. The rubrics found on pages 165 and 170, titled "Performance

Assessment: Geometric Proof" and "Performance Assessment Task in Geometry," respectively, are examples of holistic rubrics. Students receive one score based on various criteria.

The following problems are actual students' work. Each problem is graded using a 5-point rubric; i.e., 0 through 4; a grade of 0 indicates virtually no understanding of the problem, a grade of 1 or 2 indicates very little knowledge of the problem, a grade of 3 indicates a working knowledge of the problem, and a grade of 4 indicates complete knowledge and proficiency of the problem.

Performance Assessment: Geometric Proof

The following rubric serves as a general guideline and lists criteria to be used to assess the above performance-based geometric proof. There are a multitude of ways to approach this proof; however, for illustrative purposes, the proof will be approached from one vantage point. Moreover, the proof will be graded on a five-point scale as follows:

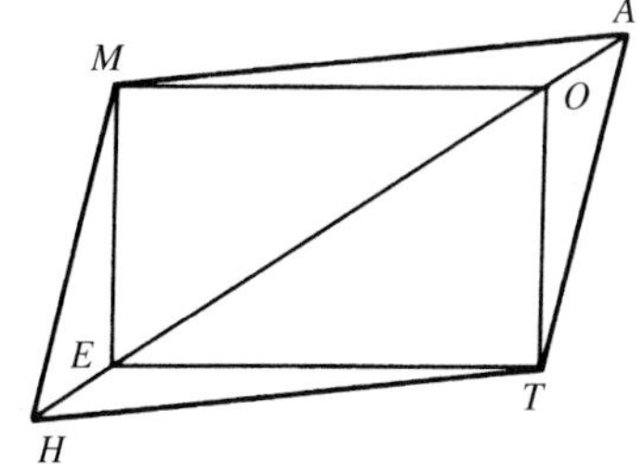

Given: parallelogram *MOTE*
$\overline{HO} \cong \overline{AE}$
Prove: *MATH* is a parallelogram.

④ The student demonstrates a series of comprehensive logical arguments based on a particular plan, which may include given information, accurate definitions, and appropriate postulates and theorems in order to draw the required valid conclusion of the proof. The student may list and number each step in the proof by putting a statement in one column and a corresponding reason in another column. The student may also offer a descriptive analysis of the proof in narrative form. All labels, symbols, and other mathematical notation must be consistent with the logical arguments involved with the proof.

③ The student follows a series of logical arguments based on a particular plan, but excludes one important definition, theorem, or postulate throughout the proof. Therefore, the student draws an invalid conclusion based on somewhat limited information.

② The student attempts to follow a series of logical arguments and reasons, but uses incorrect information and labeling to draw an invalid conclusion using invalid reasons.

① The student lists the given information, but there is no apparent plan or logical sequence of ideas to lead to a valid conclusion.

OR

A conclusion is drawn based on illogical arguments and reasons.

⓪ The answer is completely incorrect, unrelated, or illogical, or is a correct answer that was obtained by a noticeably invalid process.

Student 1

GRADE: ④

This work sample illustrates standard-setting performance. The student shows comprehensive logical arguments based on a particular plan using descriptive analysis of the proof in narrative form. The proof includes a series of accurate definitions, postulates, and theorems based on the given information and leads to the required valid conclusion of the proof.

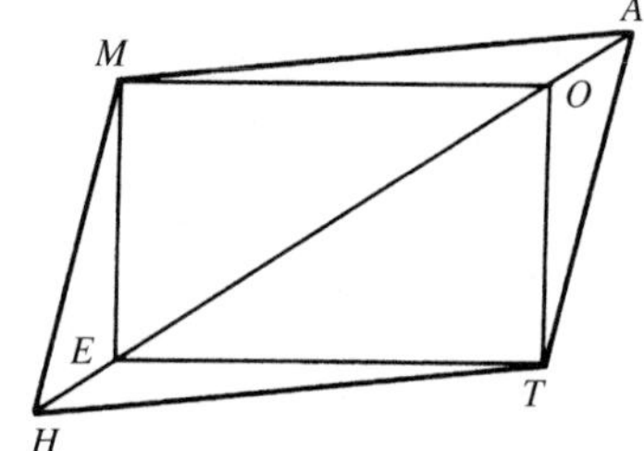

Given: parallelogram *MOTE*
$\overline{HO} \cong \overline{AE}$
Prove: *MATH* is a parallelogram.

Plan: my plan is to prove $\triangle HET \cong \triangle MOA$ by sas $\cong$ sas, and to prove $\overline{HT} \cong \overline{MA}$ + $\overline{HT} \parallel \overline{MA}$ therefore, if one pair of opposite sides of a quadrilateral is both congruent and parallel, the quadrilateral is a ▱.

It is given that MOTE is a ▱, then $\overline{MO} \cong \overline{ET}$* (SIDE) and $\overline{MO} \parallel \overline{ET}$ because opposite sides of a ▱ are congruent and parallel. It is also given that $\overline{HO} \cong \overline{AE}$. $\overline{EO} \cong \overline{EO}$ because of identity, and $\overline{HO} - \overline{EO} = \overline{AE} - \overline{EO}$ from the subtraction postulate, so $\overline{EH} \cong \overline{AO}$ * (SIDE)

$\angle OET \cong \angle MOE$ because alternate interior angles of $\parallel$ lines are $\cong$. Now, $\angle MOA \cong \angle HET$* (ANGLE) because supplements of $\cong$ $\angle$'s are $\cong$.

Then, $\triangle HET \cong \triangle MOA$ by sas $\cong$ sas. So $\overline{MA} \cong \overline{HT}$ and $\angle MOA \cong \angle THE$ because corresponding parts of $\cong$ $\triangle$'s are $\cong$.

Also $\overline{MA} \parallel \overline{HT}$ because if 2 coplaner lines are cut by a transversal, forming a pair of alt. int. $\angle$'s that are $\cong$, then the two lines are $\parallel$.

Therefore MATH is a ▱, because if one pair of opposite sides of a quadrilateral is $\cong$ and $\parallel$, the quadrilateral is a ▱.

Student 2

GRADE: ③

The student follows a series of logical arguments based on a particular plan but excludes one important theorem throughout the proof (i.e., omitting the fact that a quadrilateral is a parallelogram if one pair of sides is both congruent and parallel) and therefore draws an invalid conclusion based on somewhat limited information.

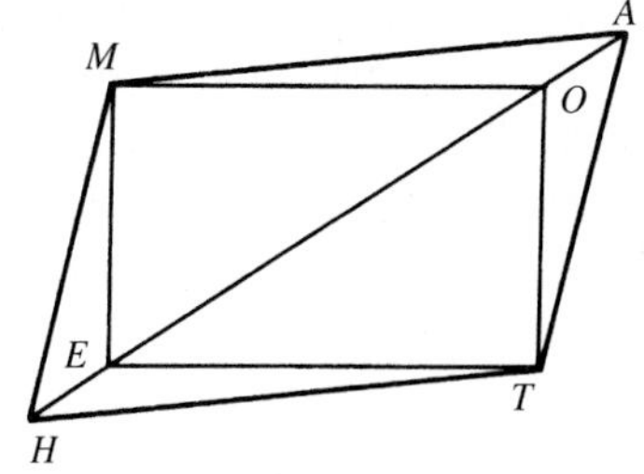

Given: parallelogram *MOTE*
$\overline{HO} \cong \overline{AE}$

Prove: *MATH* is a parallelogram.

Plan: My plan is to first prove that $\triangle HET \cong \triangle MOA$ by SAS, then prove $\overline{HT} \cong \overline{MA}$. This shows that if one pair of opposite sides of a quadrilateral is congruent, the quadrilateral is a parallelogram.

Statements	Reasons
1. MOTE is a parallelogram	1. Given
2. $\overline{MO} \cong \overline{ET}$	2. Opposite sides of a parallelogram are congruent.
3. $\overline{HO} \cong \overline{AE}$	3. Given
4. $\overline{EO} \cong \overline{EO}$	4. Identity
5. $\overline{HO} - \overline{EO} = \overline{AE} - \overline{EO}$	5. Subtraction postulate
6. $\angle OET \cong \angle MOE$	6. Alternate interior angles of parallel lines are congruent.
7. $\angle MOA \cong \angle HET$	7. Supplements of congruent angles are congruent.
8. $\triangle HET \cong MOA$	8. SAS ≅ SAS
9. $\overline{MA} \cong \overline{HT}$	9. Corresponding parts of congruent triangles are congruent.
10. MATH is a parallel	10. If one pair of opposite sides of a quadrilateral is congruent then the quadrilateral is a parallelogram.

Student 3

GRADE: ②

The student attempts to follow a series of logical arguments and reasons but uses incorrect information and labeling to draw an invalid conclusion using invalid reasons. For example, the student labels the given information incorrectly in statement 3. Also, the student indicates the congruence of two angles that are not situated inside the intended triangles in statement 4. Finally, the student's conclusion in reason 7 is limited.

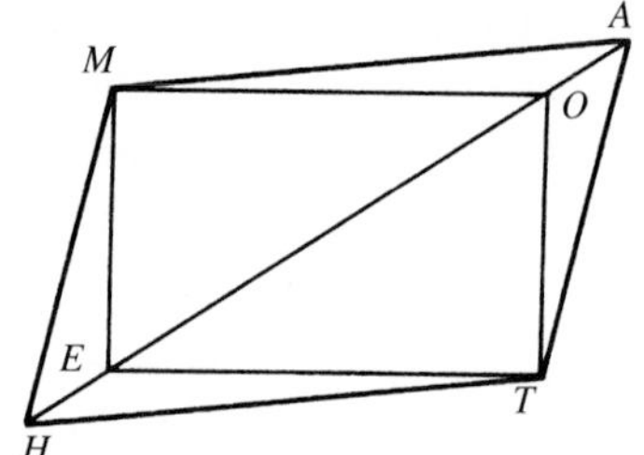

Given: parallelogram *MOTE*
$\overline{HO} \cong \overline{AE}$
Prove: *MATH* is a parallelogram.

STATEMENTS	REASONS
1- MOTE is a ▱	1- Given
2. $\overline{MO} \cong \overline{ET}$ (S) and $\overline{MO} \parallel \overline{ET}$	2 - opposite sides of a Parallelogram are congruent + parallel
3. $\overline{HE} \cong \overline{OA}$ (S)	3- Given
4- ∡OET ≅ ∡MOE (A)	4- alternate interior angles of parallel lines are congruent
5- ΔHET ≅ ΔMOA	5 - SAS ≅ SAS
6 - $\overline{MA} \cong \overline{HT}$	6 - Corresponding parts of congruent triangles are congruent.
7- MATH is a parallelogram	7- opposite sides of a parallelogram are congruent.

Student 4

GRADE: ①

The student lists the given information but there is no apparent plan or logical sequence of ideas to lead to a valid conclusion.

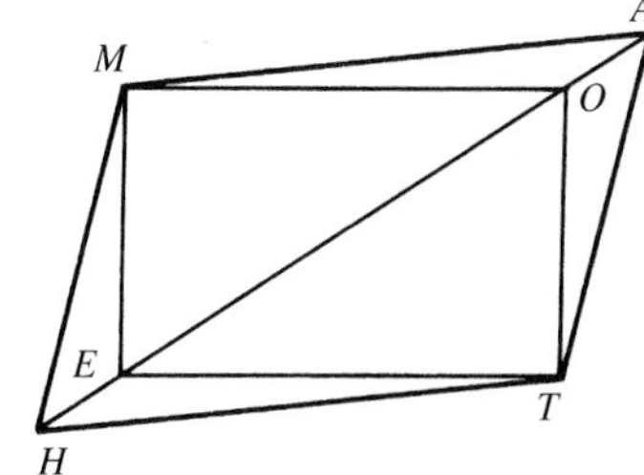

Given: parallelogram *MOTE*
$\overline{HO} \cong \overline{AE}$
Prove: *MATH* is a parallelogram.

MOTE is a ▱ is given, so $\overline{MO} = \overline{ET}$ (SIDE) and $\overline{ME} \cong \overline{OT}$ (SIDE) because opposite sides of a ▱ are ≅. $\overline{HO} \cong \overline{AE}$ (SIDE) is given. So, $\triangle HET \cong \triangle MOA$ by SSS.

Student 5

GRADE: ⓪

The answer is completely incorrect, unrelated, or illogical, or is a correct answer that was obtained by a noticeably invalid process.

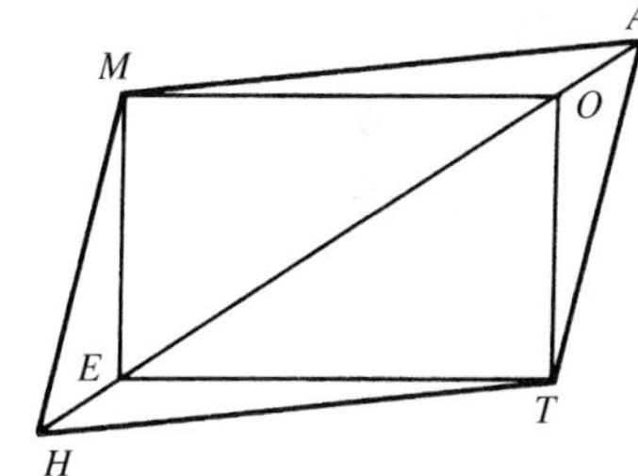

Given: parallelogram *MOTE*
$\overline{HO} \cong \overline{AE}$
Prove: *MATH* is a parallelogram.

Statements	Reasons
1- MOTE is a parallelogram	1- Given
2- $\overline{HO} \cong \overline{AE}$	2- Given

Student 2

GRADE: ③

The diagram and labels are accurate; however, makes one arithmetic error in calculating the measurement of the vertex angle of the isosceles triangle.

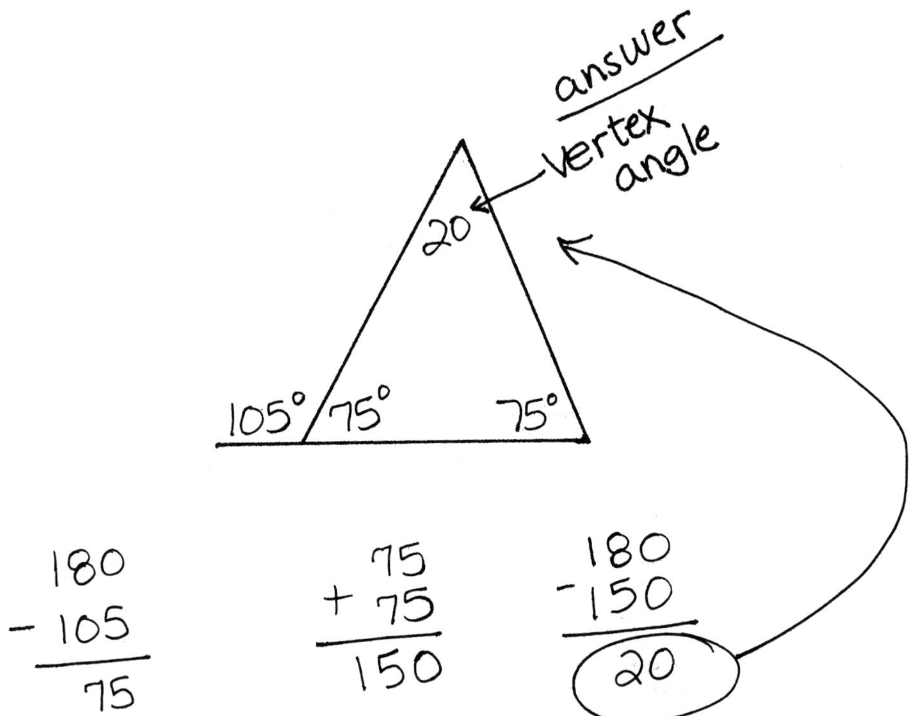

Student 3

GRADE: ②

Makes an arithmetic error calculating the measurement of the supplement of the exterior angle of 105° and therefore carries this error through and miscalculates the measurement of the vertex angle of the isosceles triangle.

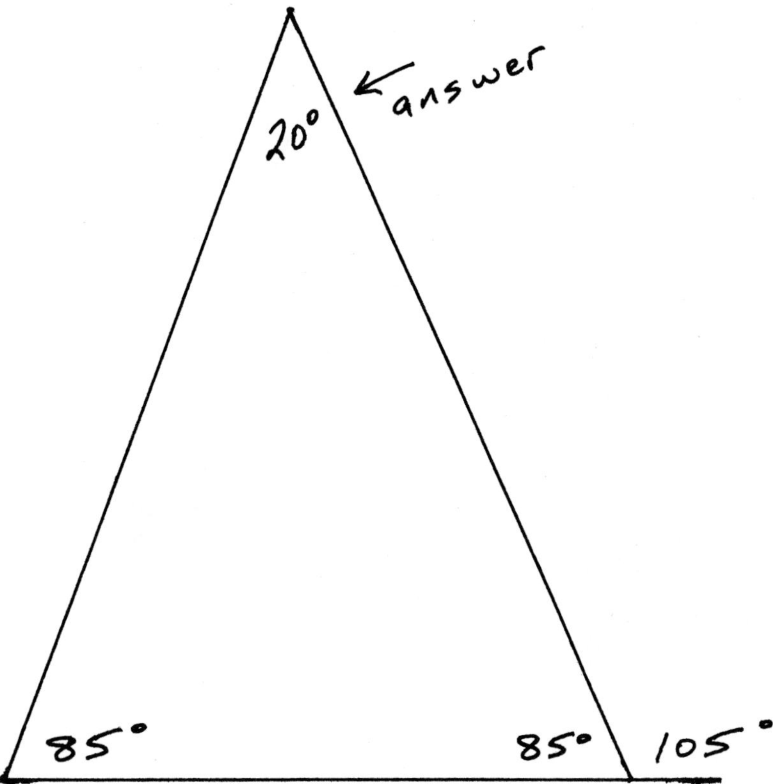

$$\begin{array}{r} 85 \\ +\,85 \\ \hline 170 \end{array} \qquad \begin{array}{r} 180 \\ -\,170 \\ \hline 20° \end{array} \qquad \begin{array}{r} 180\,- \\ 105 \\ \hline 85° \end{array}$$

Student 4

GRADE: ①

Finds the measurement of the supplement of the exterior angle of 105° only.

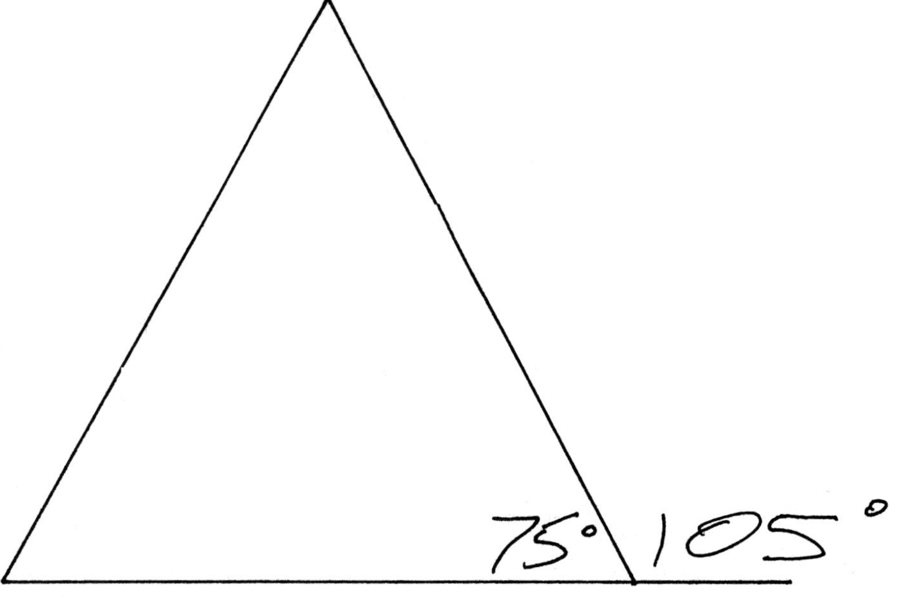

Student 5

GRADE: ⓪

The answer is completely incorrect, unrelated, or illogical, or is a correct answer that was obtained by a noticeably invalid process.

180 − 105

$$\begin{array}{r} 180 \\ -105 \\ \hline 85 \end{array}$$

answer 85

Constructing a Rubric

Most new teachers find the task of constructing a rubric difficult. As rubrics should be shared with students when assigning the task, teachers must create the rubric before they have an opportunity to use it. However, once used, teachers often find the rubric does not fit the students' work. The development of rubrics improves with experience, and there are several excellent resources that provide performance tasks with existing rubrics that new teachers should use before creating their own.

If a teacher plans to create a rubric for a performance task, the process is outlined in the following steps:

- Review the goals and objectives of the task and identify how students can demonstrate having met those goals and objectives. For example, in the analytic rubric on page 164, its author assessed students on their understanding of concepts, mathematical reasoning, and communication skills.
- Write statements describing levels of performance for each criterion. For example, under Communication, the author identified "Usage of mathematical terms is incorrect" as Unsatisfactory, and "Mathematical terminology and notation is used effectively" as Satisfactory.
- Organize your rubric into an analytic or holistic model. Teacher preference tends to dictate whether an analytic or a holistic model should be used. Teachers may want to create rubrics that reflect the model used in high stakes assessments to better prepare their students for success on those types of tests.

Test your rubric and revise it. One way to test your rubric is to create exemplars of student work at the low, medium, and high level anticipating common student errors, and then use the rubric to assess these exemplars. Another way to test your rubric is to give students a similar task for homework and use the rubric to informally evaluate this assignment.

It is important for teachers to be able to evaluate students' work diagnostically. This means that teachers must be able to determine students' errors and be able to correctly categorize those errors. With a performance assessment, a teacher may find that students are consistently losing credit because they fail to explain their reasoning. The teacher can provide scaffolding for this type of error by inserting blank lines on the assignment paper with the instructions "explain your reasoning." The rubrics must help the teacher and the student focus on the subskills of the assignment and identify—on an individual basis as well as a whole class basis—the types of errors being made in the assignment. This information is part of the feedback loop for informing instruction and helping students monitor their progress. Much practice is needed to be able to diagnose students' work accurately. In addition, teachers should be aware that some students "think outside the box," and rubrics should be developed accordingly.

Constructing a Class Test

The art of constructing a good class test is mastered over time and with help from as many sources as possible. Teachers should consult with their supervisors and their colleagues, especially those who have taught or are teaching the same courses as they are, and they should check files of old examinations for style, content, and format. Many department offices contain such files for reference, and the new teacher should not hesitate to consult them. Other members of the mathematics department often will be happy to share their experiences with new colleagues. Their suggestions on the preparation of class tests are frequently very helpful.

In addition, many textbook publishers provide teachers with support, such as test banks. These banks may include fully formed tests or multiple forms of questions stored electronically for test creation. The publisher's test questions have usually been piloted and reviewed for reliability. Using them may avoid some of the ambiguities found in questions created by inexperienced teachers. The new teacher should draw on all sources of help as much as possible, thus benefitting from other experienced teachers.

How to Begin

The first step in preparing a test, of course, is to determine what is to be tested. Every test has an objective, whether it is narrow or broad, and the teacher must have this purpose clearly in mind to prepare a test that is appropriate for the class.

A test may be very limited in scope, covering only one or two topics, and of short duration—perhaps 5 or 10 minutes. Such tests are usually referred to as quizzes, and they often contain only a single question or perhaps a few simple ones. Quizzes are often designed to measure student understanding of a topic taught the previous day. Or they may be given to determine whether the students in a particular class have done their assigned homework for the day, in which case the quiz question(s) will most likely be similar to the ones assigned the day before for homework. A quiz may not be announced in advance. You should, however, make known to the class early in the semester that unannounced quizzes will be given. In addition, students must be made aware whether they may use scientific or graphing calculators to solve any problem during regular classwork, homework, a quiz, or a test (unless directed by you to do otherwise). Samples 1–5 show some sample quizzes.

A more comprehensive examination would be designed to measure the extent of student mastery of several topics and would most likely be planned to require a full class period to complete. Such tests are generally administered on completion of a unit of work in the classroom. They should be announced several days in advance to enable students to prepare, through review of their text sections, notes, homework assignments, and class exercises. Topics should be listed on the board and typical test questions given the day before. Such tests carry much more weight in student evaluation than do single quizzes, and students may be expected to devote much effort to preparing for them. The scope of full-period tests is generally quite broad. Samples 6–8 are three sample tests; two are actual full-period tests and one is a double-period (midyear) examination. Study carefully their questions, point values, types of questions, use of extra credit, and so on. Note that collaboratively answered examinations will be most valuable as an instructional tool when the test contains topics suitable for small group discussions and when some members of each group are strong and others weak in their understanding of those topics. Collaboratively prepared answers may also serve as a review lesson on those topics appearing on the test and will be especially worthwhile for students who need the review most. Group responsibility for each student's understanding of every answer is reinforced when they are reminded that *any* student may be called on to explain *any* solution that appears on the group's collaboratively prepared answer sheets and that the collective grade for the examination belongs to each group member.

Sample 1. First-Year Algebra Quiz (10 Minutes)

Name:

Answers

SHOW ALL WORK

1. Express as a trinomial $(2a + 5)^2$. 1. ______
2. For which value of the variable is the fraction $\frac{x + 2}{3 - x}$ meaningless: 2. ______

   a. 3 b. 2 c. −3 d. −2
3. Express in lowest terms $\frac{x^2 - 4}{3x - 6}$. 3. ______
4. Factor completely $3ax + 6a$. 4. ______
5. The product of two factors is $2x^2 + x - 6$. One of the factors is $(x + 2)$. What is the other factor? 5. ______

Sample 2. Plane Geometry Quiz (5 Minutes)

The measure of an exterior angle at the base of an isosceles triangle is 105°. Find the measure of the vertex angle of the triangle. Show all work.

Sample 3. Second-Year Algebra Quiz (8 Minutes)

Given the equation $2x^2 - 3x - 7 = 0$:

1. Calculate the value of the discriminant.
2. Describe the nature of the roots of the equation.

Sample 4. Eighth-Grade Quiz (10 Minutes)

1. What is 20% of 40?
2. Express 7% as a decimal.
3. What percent is equivalent to 0.3?
4. Sierra bought two CDs and paid a total of $33.89. If each CD costs $15.98, then:

   a. How much sales tax did Sierra pay?

   b. What was the rate of the paid sales tax, rounded to the nearest whole percent?

Sample 5. Performance Assessment

THE LADDER PROBLEM

A ladder 13 feet long is leaning against a building and reaches the ledge of the first floor window (see Diagram A below). The foot of the ladder is 12 feet from the base of the building. For the ladder to reach the ledge of the second floor of the building, it is moved 6 feet closer to the base of the building (see Diagram B below).

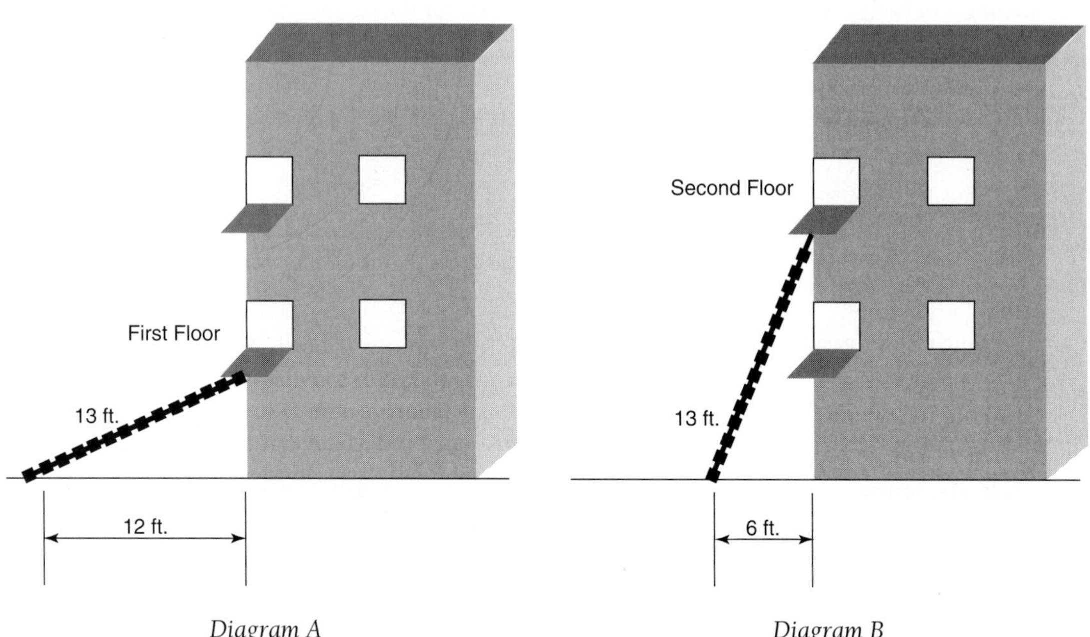

Diagram A *Diagram B*

Find, to the nearest foot, the distance the ladder moved up the side of the building from the first floor window ledge to the second floor window ledge. Show how you obtained your answer.

The following rubric serves as a general guideline and lists criteria to be used to assess the above performance-based problem, which will be graded on a four-point scale as follows:

④ Finds the height of 5 feet in Diagram A using the Pythagorean theorem or trigonometric functions.

Finds the height of 11.53 feet or 12 feet in Diagram B using either the Pythagorean theorem or trigonometric functions.

Subtracts 5 feet from 12 feet to obtain the correct answer of 7 feet.

③ All computations are accurate but the answer is not rounded to the nearest foot.

OR

Makes one error in calculating the altitudes and does not find the difference.

② Successfully finds 5 feet as the first height in Diagram A and makes an effort to use the Pythagorean theorem to find the height in Diagram B, however, makes an incorrect calculation/substitution.

OR

Calculates the two required heights using the Pythagorean theorem or trigonometric functions; however, uses wrong substitution.

① Finds 5 feet as the height in Diagram A only.

OR

Tries to use the Pythagorean theorem or trigonometric functions, but the substitution and answer are incorrect.

Sample 6. Plane or Collaborative Geometry Test—Parallelograms (full period)

Name: ______________________________

I. Place the answer in the space provided (5 points each).

1–5. Indicate whether Always, Sometimes, or Never True.

______________ 1. Diagonals of a rhombus bisect each other.

______________ 2. In a plane, if two lines are perpendicular to the same line, they are parallel.

______________ 3. An equilateral quadrilateral is equiangular.

______________ 4. If the diagonals of a quadrilateral are perpendicular, it is a rhombus.

______________ 5. Opposite angles of a parallelogram are supplementary.

6–9. Choose the best answer.

______________ 6. An exterior angle at the base of an isosceles triangle is

a. acute b. obtuse c. right d. dependent on the type of triangle.

______________ 7. If the measures of the angles of a triangle are represented by x, y, and $x + y$, the triangle is

a. acute b. obtuse c. right d. unknown—depends on x and y.

______________ 8. Which of the following is used to prove that the accompanying construction (of a line parallel to a given line through a given point) is correct: (a) Through a given outside point only one line can be constructed || to a given line. (b) If two lines are parallel, their corresponding angles are congruent. (c) Two lines are || if their corresponding angles are congruent.

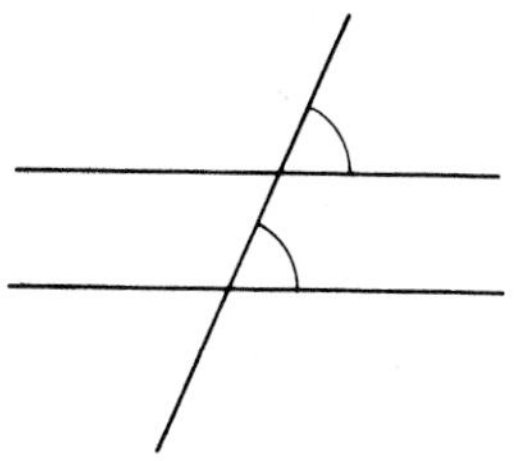

______________ 9. In ΔABC, $\overline{BC}$ is extended through C, forming $\angle x$. Which of the following must be true?

a. $m\angle x > m\angle BCA$ b. $m\angle x < m\angle BCA$ c. $m\angle x > m\angle B$ d. $m\angle x < m\angle B$

10–13. If always true write TRUE, otherwise write FALSE.

______________ 10. In a plane, two lines are either parallel or intersecting.

______________ 11. If a diagonal divides a quadrilateral into two congruent triangles, it is a parallelogram.

______________ 12. The bisectors of a pair of opposite angles of a parallelogram coincide.

______________ 13. If the diagonals of a quadrilateral are both congruent and perpendicular, then the quadrilateral is a square.

14–16. Numericals

______________ 14. Find the perimeter of a triangle formed by joining the midpoints of the sides of a triangle with sides of lengths 5, 12, 13.

______________ 15. Given rhombus $ABCD$, where $AB = 5$ and $m\angle ABC = 120°$, find BD.

______________ 16. Given parallelogram $ABCD$, where $m\angle A = 50°$, and $m\angle ABD = 75°$, find $m\angle CBD$.

(continued)

II. (20 points)

Statements **Reasons**

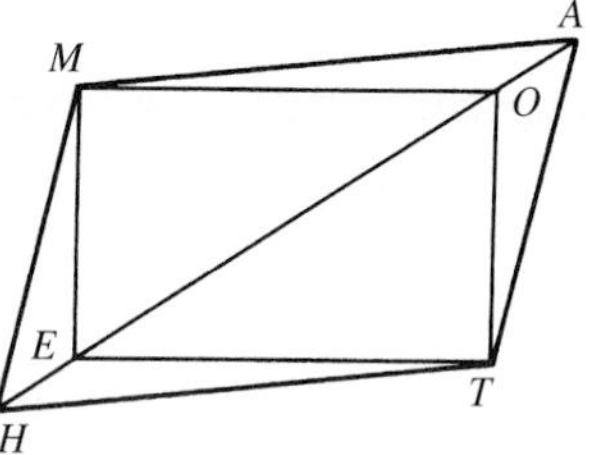

Given: parallelogram $MOTE$ $\overline{HO} \cong \overline{AE}$

Prove: $MATH$ is a parallelogram.

Fold here and continue proof on other side.

FOR EXTRA CREDIT (show work on other side):

Prove: If the diagonals of a trapezoid are congruent, it is isosceles.

Sample 7. Pre-Algebra Math Test—Fractions and Decimals (full period)

Name: ______________________ Date: ______________________

1. Find the area:

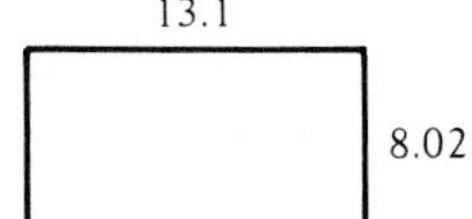

2. Find the perimeter:

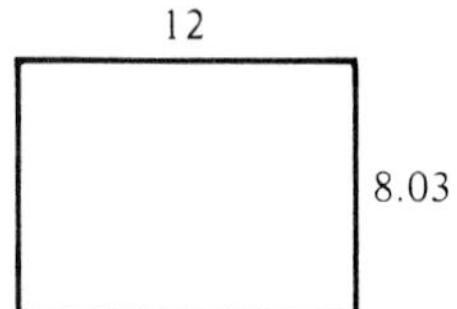

3. From 269 subtract 0.33.
4. Divide:
   a. $7\overline{)14.35}$ b. $.05\overline{)51.510}$
5. Draw a circle around the fractions equivalent to the first fraction in each of the following:
   a. $\frac{1}{2}$ $\frac{3}{5}, \frac{4}{8}, \frac{5}{10}, \frac{7}{15}, \frac{20}{40}$
   b. $\frac{2}{5}$ $\frac{4}{9}, \frac{3}{8}, \frac{8}{20}, \frac{7}{15}, \frac{14}{35}$
6. Simplify:
   a. $\frac{9}{24}$ b. $\frac{8}{56}$ c. $\frac{5}{45}$
7. Use the symbols $<$ and $>$ between the two given numbers:
   a. 8 3 ______
   b. $\frac{3}{5}$ $\frac{4}{7}$ ______
   c. $\frac{1}{2}$ $\frac{2}{5}$ ______
8. Draw a diagram to illustrate the fraction $\frac{2}{3}$.
9. List the following numbers in order, smallest to largest.
   $0.25, -\frac{3}{4}, \frac{2}{11}, -0.34, 1.5, \frac{8}{7}$
10. Find the missing number:
    a. $\frac{2}{3} = \frac{\quad}{12}$ b. $\frac{4}{5} = \frac{\quad}{100}$
11. Add (simplify your answers):
    a. $\frac{2}{3} + \frac{1}{3}$ b. $\frac{3}{10} + \frac{1}{10}$ c. $\frac{1}{2} + \frac{3}{2}$
12. Find the missing number:
    a. $\frac{13}{8} = 1\frac{?}{8}$ b. $\frac{13}{4} = ?\frac{1}{4}$
13. Add (simplify):
    a. $2\frac{3}{8} + 3\frac{3}{8}$ b. $5\frac{7}{10} + 4\frac{9}{10}$
14. Pablo is baking cookies and he wants to make half the recipe. If the original recipe calls for $2\frac{1}{2}$ cups of flour, how much flour does Pablo need to make half the recipe? Explain your answer.
15. Alexa divided 8 by $\frac{1}{4}$ and got an answer of 32. She does not think this could possibly be the right answer. Provide a written explanation for why the answer 32 is or is not correct.

Sample 8. Second-Year Algebra—Midyear Examination (80 Minutes)

DO NOT WRITE ON THIS PAPER. SHOW ALL WORK ON YOUR ANSWER PAPER. WRITE NEATLY.

Part I: Answer all questions (5 points each).

1. Express in terms of i the sum of $5i$ and $3\sqrt{-100}$.
2. a. If $93{,}000{,}000 = 9.3 \times 10^n$, find the value of n.

   b. If $0.0000286 = 2.86 \times 10^k$, find the value of k.
3. Simplify:

$$\frac{\frac{a}{b} - 2}{4 - \frac{a^2}{b^2}}$$

4. If $\log x = a$, $\log y = b$, and $\log z = c$, express $\log \frac{\sqrt{xy}}{z^3}$ in terms of a, b, and c.
5. Write the quadratic equation whose roots are $1 + i$ and $1 - i$.
6. Use a calculator to find x if $\log x = 8.4365 - 10$.
7. If $x = 7$, find the value of $3x^0 + (x + 2)^{1/2} - 49x^{-2}$.
8. If $R = \{(1, 2), (-1, 5), (6, 2), (3, -7)\}$, find R^{-1} and state whether R and R^{-1} are functions, and why.
9. Solve for x: $3^x = 9^{x-1}$.
10. Find the value of k such that the following equation will have equal roots: $x^2 - 4x + k = 0$.
11. If $f(x) = x^2 - 4x + 1$, find the value of $f(\frac{1}{2})$.

Part II: Answer all three (3) questions (15 points each).

12. Find the roots correct to the nearest tenth: $2x^2 - 3x - 1 = 0$
13. Solve the following for a, b, and c and check in all three equations:

    $a + 3b - 4c = -13$

    $2a - b + 2c = 4$

    $4a - 6b + c = -1$
14. Write an equation or system of equations that could be used to solve the following problems. In each case, state what the variable(s) represent. (*Solution of the equation(s) is not required.*)

    a. A motorboat travels 8 miles downstream in $\frac{1}{3}$ hour and then returns upstream to its starting point in $\frac{1}{2}$ hour. Find in miles per hour the rate of the boat in still water and the rate of the current.

    b. A two-digit number is 2 less than 5 times the sum of its digits. If the digits are reversed, the new number will be 9 more than the original number. Find the original number.

Whether the examination is a short quiz or a lengthy midyear examination, certain procedures should be followed. In selecting topics and questions, the teacher should try to include a number of questions similar to those done in class or as part of homework assignments. A test that is as important to most students as a full-period class test should not be filled with surprises (unexpected or novel questions). It should be designed so that a student who has done the work conscientiously and has a reasonably good grasp of the subject will have success.

A sample test might be presented and discussed the day before the actual test so students will be familiar with the test format and type of questions to be asked, thus allowing the students to focus on content and conceptual knowledge on test day.

Test papers should be marked promptly by the teacher. Teachers should grade the examinations to diagnose, recognize, and become sensitive to the types of errors students are making. Ideally, the examinations should be graded and returned to students the next day, while the test material is still fresh in their minds.

If the tests are returned at the beginning of the period, the teacher should be prepared to review the test for most of that period (except for quizzes that might already have been reviewed immediately after they were given). If papers are returned at the end of the period, students can be assigned to correct their papers at home and be prepared for the in-class review the next day. An advantage of returning papers at the end of the period is that the commotion caused by returning tests at the beginning is avoided, since students are often more interested in what grades their classmates earned on the test than on why they themselves got something wrong.

Selecting Priorities Among Topics and Concepts Taught

No test, no matter how broad its scope, can test everything. When we remember that most tests administered by teachers during the course of a school term or year are limited to single class periods, we realize that priorities must be established. The teacher must select from among all the topics that have been taught in class in a given interval of time and determine which to include and which to omit on a given test. This does not mean that the latter topics will never be tested. They may be tested on a future class test, especially one of a cumulative nature, and they may certainly appear on midyear or final examinations, whether teacher prepared or uniform throughout a department. The teacher also must decide whether to "spiral" back to topics taught earlier in the term on a given test. If possible, teachers should administer a test during a double period of class time. This way the test can be more comprehensive and students will not feel rushed.

Types of Tests

The type of test presented to a mathematics class depends, of course, on the purpose for which the test is being given. Most often, the teacher will be seeking to measure student achievement. Achievement tests may range in scope and length from brief quizzes to comprehensive midyear and final examinations. A quiz may be prepared to test student understanding of just one or two concepts, or it may be designed to achieve a prompt start of a lesson or to check student comprehension of a homework assignment or of the work taught the previous day. Administering multiple types of assessment can provide the teacher with additional grades and information in order to evaluate students' work and achievement accurately.

Comprehensive tests of student achievement include full-period class tests on work covered over an extended time, perhaps 2 weeks or longer, unit examinations, midyear examinations, and final examinations. Final examinations may be prepared by individual teachers for administration in their own classes, or they may be prepared by committees of department members for uniform usage. In any case, they must be constructed carefully to measure the objectives of the unit or course and the extent to which students have mastered the objectives.

Teachers of mathematics are sometimes called on to prepare other types of tests. Diagnostic tests are used to identify student strengths and weaknesses in a particular area of mathematics so that the teacher may build on the strengths and plan remedial activities to overcome the weaknesses. Although many such tests are commercially prepared for administration on computers, the teacher may wish to prepare his or her own test to measure some specific aspect of student background or to supplement the information provided by standardized tests. However, when teachers construct a test, they should provide a set of guidelines for assessing content validity and reliability of the test.

WHAT IS CONTENT VALIDITY? The fundamental criteria of a sound test is that it measures outcomes that are consistent with its objectives. Any assessment instrument that measures what we anticipate it to measure is said to have *content validity*. If an assessment instrument does not have a purpose or objective, it will be impossible to determine its content validity.

WHAT IS TEST RELIABILITY? The word *reliability* is used to indicate a test's accuracy. Reliability refers to the degree to which a test is consistent in measuring whatever it does measure—time after time and item after item. Consistency over time and items is basic to the concept of reliability.

Types of Questions

The types of questions to be included on any test are determined by a number of factors, including the ability level of the class, the nature of the material to be tested, and the time available for the test. The following are illustrations of some types of questions commonly found on mathematics tests:

- *True-false questions* may involve only a simple decision one way or the other, but must be carefully constructed. The teacher may require that an answer of "false" be accompanied by a correction of the statement offered.
- *Always-sometimes-never questions* are modifications of true-false questions since they require a determination as to whether a statement is always true (indicated by a response of "true" if in true-false form) or only sometimes true or never true (both of the latter require responses of "false" on true-false tests). A decision with two options now becomes a decision with three options.
- *Multiple-choice questions* require selection of a correct answer from four or five responses offered.
- *Enhanced multiple-choice questions* require students to make connections among several concepts before arriving at an answer that is the "best choice." They may find it necessary to use more than one strategy to solve the problem and will thus require perhaps two or three additional minutes to answer the question. Students must briefly supply the reasons for selecting the best choice.
- *Completion questions* reduce many aspects of guessing. They require a student to supply a correct response to an incomplete statement.
- *Matching questions* permit some guessing, but this can be minimized by providing more choices in the column from which selections are being made than in the other column.
- Numerical and algebraic exercises are *objective questions* that may be used to test understanding of principles, recall and application of formulas, and so on.
- *Discussion questions* ask students to discuss a topic and thereby explain a concept (whose content is being tested). This could include explaining a theorem, describing a relationship between topics, proving a theorem, etc.

Types of questions mentioned thus far (except for the last one) are essentially objective. Geometric proofs fall more into the subjective category (as the last in the list), corresponding to essay questions in other subject areas. Like an essay question, a proof can often be done in a variety of ways and still be correct (i.e., there may be more than one correct solution). They require recall of postulates, definitions, and theorems proved in earlier work. They also may call for some degree of memorization, since some theorems are of such major importance that, although their proofs are included in the textbook, their recall may be expected of students. Other theorems whose proofs are called for on examinations may measure the ability to reason sequentially and logically better than those that are often memorized.

Questions requiring sequential reasoning through several parts must be constructed carefully. If possible, the parts should be somewhat independent of each other. Otherwise, an early error in the work results in a string of errors and perhaps a situation in which it is impossible for a student to work subsequent parts of the question at all.

The first example below is a theorem whose proof is found in every textbook on plane geometry. The second example might be considered an original one. It challenges students to draw and label properly an appropriate diagram and to reason logically. It asks for further recall of properties of similar triangles and proportions, and reviews the concept of ratio of similitude. Finally, the question combines geometry, algebra, and arithmetic.

EXAMPLE

(Geometry)

1. Prove that the sum of the measures of the angles of a triangle is 180°.
2. In parallelogram $ABCD$, M is the midpoint of $\overline{AD}$ and $\overline{BM}$ intersects diagonal $\overline{AC}$ at E.

Prove: a. $\Delta BEC \sim \Delta MEA$
b. $(AE)(BE) = (ME)(CE)$
c. If $BE = 8$, what is the length of ME?

EXAMPLE

(Trigonometry)

A flagpole 40 feet high is anchored to the ground by a wire extending from the top of the pole to a point 30 feet from the base of the pole. The pole is perpendicular to the ground.

a. Find the measure of the angle made by the wire with the ground, to the nearest degree.
b. Find the length of the wire, to the nearest foot.

A student who uses the result of part (a) to answer part (b), using the sine or cosine function, gets a slightly different result from that obtained by the student who does part (b) independently using the Pythagorean theorem. As a matter of fact, the second student may wonder why the specification "to the nearest foot" is made when the answer is exactly 50. The first student accepts this specification as something to be expected, and rounds off the answer to 50 also, unless he or she has made an error in part (a), in which case there will be an error in part (b) also. This difficulty could easily have been avoided by reversing parts (a) and (b) and phrasing the new part (a) unambiguously: (a) Find the length of the wire.

Writing a Good Question and Arranging Questions

Writing a good test is indeed an art. The questions must be prepared carefully and arranged on the test paper to enable students to achieve to the best of their ability. Before actually constructing the exam, the teacher should list the topics and concepts to be tested, including all major facts, skills, concepts, and principles. Clear, concise, straightforward questions should then be prepared for each of these areas. Guidelines used in preparing good classroom questions apply in writing test questions as well. For example, test questions should be simple in structure and precisely phrased; if multiple concepts are involved in constructing particular questions, they should be included in separate parts of each question. Test items should test students' abilities to think critically as well as to merely recall information. Types of questions will vary with the content being tested and the ability of the class, but an effort should be made to include both objective questions and subjective ones, such as problems and proofs. Examinations may be filed for future use in the teacher's personal file or in files maintained in the mathematics department office. New teachers are advised to have their tests critiqued in advance by more experienced colleagues and/or by their supervisors. In this way, unanticipated pitfalls, inconsistencies in questions, and the like can be caught before they reach the students. The new teacher will soon learn how often a question that appears straightforward to the teacher may seem ambiguous or unclear to a student.

EXAMPLE

Find the slope of each of the lines whose equations follow:

a. $y = 3x - 5$
b. $2x + y = 3$
c. $y = -7$
d. $x = 2$

The question tests understanding and recognition of slopes of straight lines from their equations. But the line whose equation is given in part (d) has no slope. From the wording of the question, however, students may think that each of the lines given must have a slope and therefore may search fruitlessly or incorrectly for a number that does not exist for the slope of (d). Better wording of the question, which would avoid this problem, might be "Find the slope of each of the lines whose equations follow. If no slope, write 'none.'"

Test questions should proceed from the simple to the more complex. This arrangement helps to build student confidence and encourages poorer students to do their best because they encounter the simpler questions first. Teachers sometimes wonder whether it is wise to provide students with a choice of questions on a test. Choices are most often found on final examinations, especially if the examinations are uniform throughout a department. Choices provide students with some latitude to compensate for different depths of treatment of various topics by different teachers. In these cases choice of questions may be appropriate. For relatively short class tests (one period or less), however, providing a choice of questions is not recommended, since students often waste inordinate amounts of time browsing the questions, making poor starts and then abandoning questions, and losing valuable time and credit.

Assigning a Rubric with Point Values to Parts of the Test

Credit for each question should be determined by the teacher before the test is administered to a class. Students are always interested in knowing how much each question on a test is worth. Values serve as somewhat of a guide to them as to how to apportion their time. Credit values should be assigned in proportion to a number of factors, including the relative importance and difficulty of each question and the time expected to be required by an average student to work each question. For a single-period test, less challenging questions requiring little time (such as objective questions of a factual or simple computational nature, true-false questions, always-sometimes-never questions, and simple fill-ins) should generally be assigned the least amount of credit. More time-consuming problems, such as multistep word problems and proofs, should be assigned credit based on the number of steps, concepts used, and amount of time needed to solve the problems. These types of questions are usually graded using a rubric that indicates how the points should be assigned.

The teacher should take the test to check its time requirements before administering it to the class. A test designed to be done by a class in a 40-minute period should not take the teacher more than 10 minutes to complete.

Administering a Test

The primary concern of the teacher in administering a class test should be to provide optimum conditions, so that the students may have the best opportunity to demonstrate their knowledge. To achieve this objective, the teacher can follow a number of simple principles in presenting a class test.

Alternatives for Administration

Every test should begin promptly so that students have the full time promised to them for working on the questions presented. A late start, for whatever reason, both upsets students and deprives them of working time. Students must be told in advance of any special equipment they are expected to bring to the test, such as rulers, compasses, calculators, or graph paper. Make sure that all students have the equipment needed before starting the test to avoid disruptions later.

Alertness During Proctoring

Even the most experienced and skilled teacher sometimes encounters the problem of cheating, in spite of all precautions taken to prevent it. Teachers should make it clear at the beginning of the test period that the students are not to collaborate on the test. If necessary, teachers can make multiple forms of the test so that the answers are not the same for students sitting adjacent to each other.

In today's world, students have access to electronic devices that allow them to bring notes to class via their calculators or access their friends electronically while taking a test. Some teachers ask students to clear all programs from their calculators to alleviate the concern that these devices have been programmed with formulas or information that students have been required to memorize. The addition of text messaging adds a new dimension to students' access to information during an exam. Again, alertness during proctoring can help prevent inappropriate use of this technology.

Most teachers who observe attempts at cheating on a test usually speak quietly to the offender first. The student is warned, without making a scene that would disturb other students while they are trying to concentrate on their work, and perhaps the student's seat is changed. The teacher also may make a notation on the student's test paper to indicate at which point in the test the cheating occurred; presumably, work following that point may be considered the student's own (if no further attempts at cheating are observed). Penalties for cheating must be decided on by each teacher. New teachers should consult a supervisor on these matters. Experience will help the teacher to formulate his or her own consequences and practices with regard to this problem and to refine these as circumstances change.

Cheating discovered only after a test is over, during the course of grading papers, is a different and more difficult problem with which to deal. Identical errors on papers of students who were seated adjacent to each other during a test may suggest a lack of vigilance on the part of the teacher. Accusations at this point may accomplish little more than to build bad feelings; students will deny wrongdoing, and one student actually may be innocent! It is possible for one student to copy from another without the latter's knowledge. Some teachers may be tempted to retest the suspected parties, but many will prefer just to minimize the significance of these particular grades for the students involved and to make a mental note to themselves to be more alert next time. In effect, the teacher learns from experience as much as the students do, whether that experience is positive or not. However, the easiest way to avoid cheating is to help students see the value of accurate assessment of their academic process. When the students become part of a community of learners who respect each other and accept their role in the learning process, they are much less likely to cheat, even when someone is not watching them.

Early Finishers

A test should be so constructed as to require the time planned for its completion from almost all the students in a given class. If a great many students finish early, the test was too short. Some students in every class, however, will work faster than their classmates and will, accordingly, finish a given test before the time allotted. The teacher should be prepared to provide alternative work for these students. This work could include extra-credit problems, a list of challenging activities (perhaps of the students' choice), or reading literature related to mathematics. In any case, such activities should be carefully prepared and appropriate for the intended audience.

Absentees

The problem of dealing with students absent from a test is a perennial one that has no simple or entirely satisfactory solution. The best advice to the beginning teacher is to evaluate each case on its own merits and discuss the situation with the supervisor. The primary concern is to be fair to all students involved.

Grading a Test

Grading test papers is a time-consuming task, but it is a most important one for teachers. Not only do tests evaluate the work of students, but the teacher's own work as well. By studying students' techniques and diagnosing errors, the teacher can measure the success of his or her own teaching program. The teacher may be in for a number of surprises, including student misunderstandings, when grading a set of test papers.

Assigning Partial Credit

Partial rather than full credit should be given for a student's answer that indicates some, but not complete, understanding of how to arrive at that answer. Also, a student who makes an obviously careless error fully deserves most of the credit the problem is worth. Many questions, indeed, do not lend themselves to the assignment of partial credit. Included in this category are true-false questions, always-sometimes-never questions, and factual questions (e.g., write the quadratic formula). On the other hand, more lengthy problems that involve numerous calculations in sequence (any one of which a student might inadvertently perform incorrectly, leading to an incorrect final result) would certainly be deserving of partial credit. Geometric proofs done with a substantial degree of accuracy, and with only minor errors by the student, also deserve some recognition. Experience and consultation with others will help the beginning teacher to formulate policies on partial credit and to modify these as circumstances dictate.

Students often have much correct work in connection with a test exercise, but a blunder somewhere along the way leads to an incorrect final result. Conversely, students may have little, if any, correct work on a particular exercise, but they may have the correct final result. Consider the following examples.

EXAMPLE

(Elementary Algebra)

Reduce the fraction

$$\frac{x^2 - 25}{x - 5}$$

Correct procedure:

$$\frac{(x + 5)(x - 5)}{x - 5} = x + 5$$

Student's incorrect procedure:

$$\frac{\overset{x\ +\ 5}{\cancel{x^2} - \cancel{25}}}{\cancel{x} - \cancel{5}}$$

Here the student has obtained the correct answer by an outrageous procedure. Such a procedure, although it delivered the correct result, clearly shows no understanding of factoring of binomials or of reduction of algebraic fractions, and deserves no credit of any kind. In the normal course of grading, a teacher would see the answer, not the method, and give credit.

EXAMPLE

(Trigonometry)

Find the value of sin 75° in radical form.
Student response:

$$\begin{aligned}\sin 75^\circ &= \sin(45^\circ + 30^\circ)\\ &= \sin 45^\circ \cos 30^\circ + \cos 45^\circ \sin 30^\circ\\ &= \frac{\sqrt{3}}{2}\cdot\frac{1}{2} + \frac{\sqrt{3}}{2}\cdot\frac{\sqrt{2}}{2}\\ &= \frac{\sqrt{3} + \sqrt{6}}{4}\end{aligned}$$

Here a student clearly deserves some partial credit, although he has confused the radical forms of the values of the trigonometric functions. Credit is deserved for realizing that sin 75° can be written as the sine of the sum of 45° and 30°, for knowing the correct expansion of $\sin(A + B)$, and for knowing how to multiply and add fractions properly, albeit the wrong fractions. Thus, if the question were worth ten points, it might be given six points of credit.

In geometry, students are called on to write proofs of theorems on examinations. The teacher must first glance at the entire proof to see if it makes any sense at all. Many students make errors in some of the statements and/or reasons in these theorems. If the errors are so numerous and the reasoning so poor as to show little understanding on the part of the student, then perhaps no credit at all is deserved. However, when the student shows a good deal of knowledge but perhaps has minimal errors, or some of the student's steps are not properly sequenced, then partial credit certainly is deserved. Generally speaking, a minor mechanical error might be penalized to the extent of a 10 percent deduction, whereas a major error in theory might result in deductions ranging from 30 to 50 percent of the credit value of a given problem, depending on its weight. These are only general guidelines; beginning teachers will want to modify them as they gain experience.

Can a Wrong Answer Not Result in a Deduction?

Often a student will obtain an incorrect answer to a problem by using a correct procedure and making no mechanical errors. How is this possible? Quite simply, the student is working on a problem involving sequential reasoning and several steps, some of which make use of answers obtained in earlier steps. The student should be penalized for the original error(s) only. Deductions should not be made twice because of the initial error.

EXAMPLE

(Trigonometry)

In ΔABC, $\angle C$ is a right angle, $m\angle A = 37°$, and $BC = 6$. Find, to the nearest integer, AC and AB.
Student response:

$$\tan 37° = \frac{6}{x}$$

$$0.6018 = \frac{6}{x}$$

$x = 10$, to the nearest integer

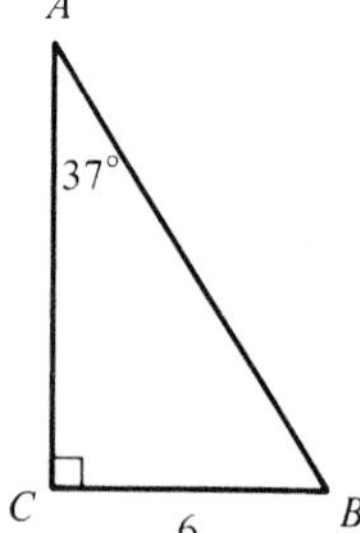

Error: The student pressed the calculator key incorrectly—sin 37° instead of tan 37°. The student thinks she has now found AC, but she has actually found AB. If she now tries to find AB by the Pythagorean theorem, obtaining an answer of 12, to the nearest integer, she has made what is called a "consistent error." There should be only one deduction, since there was only one error.

Rounding off answers in early parts of a problem can lead to numerous errors later on in the same problem. Problems should be formulated so as to minimize the effects of such procedures. Alternative approaches to some problems (e.g., using the Pythagorean theorem or using trigonometry of the right triangle to find the lengths of the legs or the hypotenuse of the triangle) may result in slightly different results; if these results are then to be used in subsequent parts of the same problem, difficulties may arise. The teacher must be aware of these possibilities.

What to Look for in Grading a Test

The teacher must make every effort to grade each test paper carefully and fairly. Students compare graded test papers with those of their peers and will be upset if they believe that they were not treated equitably. They also may compare their papers to tests they took earlier in the term to measure their own improvement.

Generally speaking, the teacher will examine test papers to determine students' depth of understanding of the concepts being tested, their ability to reason logically and sequentially and to solve problems, and their ability to carry out numerical calculations and algebraic procedures carefully and correctly. In grading papers, the teacher discovers the most common errors made by students and can then plan appropriate remedial or reteaching activities. These errors should be explored carefully with the class to minimize the likelihood that they will be repeated on the next test. In fact, the entire test should be reviewed with the class after it has been returned to them, corrected and graded. Reviews may be accomplished by having students place their solutions to individual problems on the board and then explaining their procedures to their classmates and answering questions posed by the latter. When time is an important factor, a review may also be accomplished by the teacher's distributing to all students copied or duplicated sheets containing correct and complete solutions to all test questions, and then answering student questions on these solutions after they have had some time to study them. Although this procedure does save some time, it also reduces student participation in the review (and the learning) process. A whole class review is most suitable.

Small groups are often more effective for review lessons than larger groups, since students will have a greater opportunity to discuss, consider, and correct their own errors in this type of setting, as opposed to a larger, whole class setting. In either case, the teacher should prepare an answer sheet to guide the groups in their review. Teachers should also be available to answer further questions or make additional comments, as needed.

Interpreting Test Results

After a test has been given to a class, graded, and reviewed with the students, the teacher should examine the test closely to interpret the results. The teacher can then plan the teaching of future units more carefully, plan for necessary remediation or complete reteaching of certain material, and plan for better construction of the next test if the present one contained surprises or caused unexpected problems (misunderstanding of questions by students, insufficient time to complete, etc.).

What the Test Results Indicate

Tests are measurement devices. As such, they indicate the degree to which students understand the material being tested. A test may measure the amount of attention students paid during lessons, the degree to which they grasped the concepts being taught, their ability to apply concepts to solving problems of various types, and whether they did the assigned homework.

Tests also provide information about a teacher and his or her teaching strategies. They often reflect the degree to which the teacher was understood. The new teacher who feels frustrated and concerned that students are not performing well enough is usually the one who ends up being a fine teacher, constantly seeking the means to improve teaching techniques so student learning improves.

Analyzing Individual Items or Parts of a Test

Analyzing a test that has been marked is a valuable technique for improving construction of tests. It helps the teacher to determine which questions are too simple, too difficult for the average student but perhaps suitable as honor or extra-credit questions, too difficult for almost all students, too short, too long, unclear, confusing, subject to misinterpretation because of the use of poor terminology or notation, or perhaps unfair as far as the assignment of appropriate credit is concerned. Test analysis can also help a teacher determine which topics were understood best by the class and which least.

Item analysis is a question-by-question analysis of student responses. It often leads to a conclusion concerning the significance or validity of a particular question on a test. A good question is an effective discriminator between the more and the less able students.

Multiple-Choice Tests

With the ever-increasing availability of computers in schools, short-response tests are being used where in earlier years they may have been avoided. The most popular test is the multiple-choice (or response) test. Computer use is most convenient here, since the respondent must give only one-letter answers. To make such an examination effective, care must be taken in preparing and interpreting these instruments.

When writing test items, the teacher must be careful (as always) to ensure against ambiguities. If one has the luxury of time, it is wise to write the test and set it aside for a few days. A second reading of the items (after a period of time) usually will reveal possible ambiguities.

The multiple-choice item is not a particularly easy item to write because part of its effectiveness rests on the writer's ability to construct good "distractors"—incorrect responses. The test constructor should try to anticipate the kinds of errors students might commit in each item and derive these distractors from these incorrect procedures.

Naturally, if one has time available, an item analysis ought to be done for each item before the test is administered. This procedure, however, requires administering the test to a representative student group and analyzing the effectiveness of each item as a discriminator between high-, average-, and low-achieving scorers. An item is deemed effective if the high scorers answer correctly and the low scorers do not. An item analysis is not usually practicable for regular classroom tests, since administering a test twice is usually not possible. For major schoolwide tests, such a procedure might be reasonable, especially if the test is to be used for more than one semester.

The question about how a multiple-choice test should be scored is sometimes controversial. Some educators claim that the number of items answered correctly should determine the test score, whereas others hold that a multiple-choice test should be "corrected for guessing." That is, the test score (or raw score) should be obtained from the formula

$$\text{raw score} = R - \frac{W}{n-1}$$

where R is the number of correct items, W is the number of incorrect items, and n is the number of choices provided for each item. The number of items omitted does not figure into the calculation directly.

Although multiple-choice tests are easier to score (especially with the help of a computer) when properly prepared, they are much more difficult to construct, since there is more to writing the item than just constructing a question. Creating good distractors can be quite time consuming.

Determining the Course Grade

One of the most difficult responsibilities for teachers, occurring at the end of each marking period, is the assignment of course grades. Many schools have their own grading policies; thus, new teachers should check with their supervisors regarding such policies before developing their own. New teachers should also be aware of the timing of grade reports and set aside time for this additional work in their schedules.

Course grades are a culmination of a process of evaluation and should measure student achievement with respect to a set of performance standards. While factors such as class participation, group work, and portfolio review may impact a student's course grade, clear criteria must be established and disseminated to the students and their parents/guardians prior to using these criteria to assign a course grade. Teachers should keep careful records and encourage their students to use portfolios to monitor their own progress.

No matter what procedure is used to summarize student progress, students should understand that grades are something they have earned, not something that the teacher has arbitrarily assigned. These grades should be assigned fairly, aligned with performance standards and based on criteria known to all stakeholders.

Evaluating Programs

The fourth purpose of assessment identified by the NCTM Assessment Standards is program evaluation. At regular intervals, teachers should work with department heads and curriculum coordinators to determine how well their school's mathematics program is meeting the needs of the students. Information provided by analyzing assessment data can help determine how well-aligned the curriculum is with state and local standards. It may also aid with textbook selection and provide focus for teachers' professional-development needs.

Summary

These four purposes of assessment clearly underline that assessment is not just an examination but an integral part of any teacher's planning cycle. Teachers need to think about assessment as they review the standards their students are expected to meet, and create assessment opportunities throughout the instructional process. Further, teachers must use the results of their assessments to improve instruction in the short-run and improve their school's mathematics program over time.

EXERCISES

1. Write a letter to your students and their parents/guardians outlining your assessment plan. Indicate what items (homework, quizzes, tests, projects, participation, etc.) will be used to determine a student's grades for the course. Explain why you think this assessment system will accurately represent student achievement in your course.
2. Create a performance assessment task (PAT) designed to help students explore exponential growth. Create a rubric for assessing that task.
3. Develop a 10-minute quiz for assessing the following objectives:
   a. Students will graph linear equations of the form $y = mx + b$ and $ax + by = c$.
   b. Students will determine the inverse of a given exponential function and graph the results.
4. Create a test to assess student understanding of systems of linear equations and inequalities. Using a curriculum guide, identify the objectives you would like to measure and then develop the questions to measure those objectives.
5. How do you see portfolios being used in the classroom? How would you determine the artifacts to be placed in a student's portfolio? Would you base part of a student's grade for the course on his or her portfolio? How would you evaluate the portfolio?
6. Design a rubric for the performance task outlined below. Create three exemplars (typical or representative examples) for this task. Exemplars should represent work at high, medium, and low levels. Use your rubric to assess the exemplars and reflect on the results. What do you think worked well? How would you change the task? How would you change the rubric?

Performance Task (for Exercise 6)

Task Overview

In 2004 the state of Colorado proposed that each presidential candidate receive the number of electoral votes equal to the percentage of the popular vote received (rounded to the nearest whole number). Using presidential election data found on the Internet, determine how this division of electoral votes would have affected earlier elections if all states apportioned electoral votes in this manner.

Research

a. Choose an election year.
b. Determine the states involved in the election that year and the number of electoral votes assigned to each state.
c. Identify the candidates running for president that year.
d. Identify the number of votes for each candidate in each state.

Investigation

a. Enter the information found above into a spreadsheet.
b. Calculate the percentage of the vote each candidate received per state.
c. Apply those percentages to each state's electoral votes for each candidate.
d. Determine who would have won the election based on your results.

Summary

a. Write a report that describes what you did and summarizes your findings.
b. Describe the pros and cons of changing the Electoral College system to apportion its votes in this manner.

Chapter 7

Enriching Mathematics Instruction

Consistent with all versions of *Standards* issued over the past few years is the notion that mathematics instruction should be enriched wherever possible and feasible. First it must be emphatically stated that mathematics enrichment is *not* reserved for gifted youngsters. Students of all ability levels should have their mathematics instruction enriched. In this chapter we shall explore ways in which one might enrich mathematics instruction for all students.

Enrichment of mathematics can manifest itself in at least three different ways. The easiest and least creative to implement is *acceleration*. This refers to the process of moving a better student along the mathematics path more rapidly. Acceleration has a few drawbacks. First, a student can be moved along so fast that he accelerates right out of mathematics. That is, the student may finish the coursework a high school has to offer and then be left with no further mathematics courses to take, while not having completed the rest of the high school coursework. In this situation, a student may work privately with a teacher who volunteers to be a mentor for the remainder of the student's high school career, or the student may enroll in a course at a nearby college (if that option exists), or the student "takes a vacation" from mathematics. The last would be an inexcusable shame, for a bright student might ultimately be lost to mathematics study later on.

Another reason for enriching a bright student in ways other than to accelerate him or her is that such enrichment can stimulate the student to pursue mathematics study more seriously later on, or it may simply motivate the student to improve his or her understanding of mathematical concepts and ideas. There are many topics for a student to investigate, topics which are not part of the regular school curriculum. A consideration of these many topics (some of which might be considered "off the beaten path") can be taken more seriously after reviewing some of the many ideas that are presented as Enrichment Units at the back of this book.

Another form of enrichment may be called *expansion*. This term refers to the resourcefulness of the mathematics teacher to delve into regular curriculum topics in greater than normally required detail. Presenting more details will spur on better students to investigate in greater depth topics regularly taught in the classroom.

Digression, another form of enrichment, refers to taking class time to consider a topic that is not in the regular curriculum but relates to one that is. Moving out of the confines of the syllabus to related topics and studying them in appropriate detail can open up new areas of interest for students. One must keep in mind that younger students on average do not have the very sophisticated ability to abstract as do older, more mature students.

As evidenced by the Enrichment Units in this book, we are committed to the notion of enriching the mathematics instruction in the secondary schools. The time taken away from syllabus topics to do enrichment activities is not to be seen as time lost from the regular instruction. Quite the contrary! The time used for enrichment activities is actually an investment of time. Students will become more active participants in the classroom and more efficient learners when their instructors spend time to motivate and interest them in mathematics. A "turned on" audience needs less time to learn new concepts.

Enriching Mathematics Instruction with a Historical Approach

It is a popular myth that a mathematics class is lifeless and dull. Unfortunately, that myth is too often true—though it need not be so! We frequently find ourselves concentrating on the teaching of mathematics to reach a deadline, such as giving a test or completing a course of study. The luxury of teaching what mathematics is all about seems to be beyond our grasp. But is it really? We can easily teach where mathematics comes from, who first thought of it, and who later developed and refined it. In short, we can use the history of the subject, including the lives, loves, successes, and failures of the people who created it, to breathe life into what might otherwise be rather dull. There are times when history should be integrated into the subject matter in a light and lively way.

The sections that follow provide a small sample of how such integration might be accomplished for certain topics in secondary school mathematics. A carefully selected bibliography appears at the end of the chapter that can help you develop the background needed to use the "historical" approach when teaching mathematics.

Geometry: In the Beginning

The original development of geometry in Egypt and Babylonia was a result of the desire of priests to construct temples and of kings to survey land for tax purposes. The techniques were crude and intuitive but sufficiently accurate for their needs. We have evidence of some of these techniques in the Ahmes Papyrus, which was written about 1650 B.C. and discovered in the 19th century. Portions of it are preserved in museums in London and New York. The papyrus contains formulas for calculating areas of rectangles, right triangles, and trapezoids that have one leg perpendicular to the bases, and for approximating the area of a circle. The Egyptians apparently developed these formulas from their experience with area of land.

The first mathematician who appeared to be dissatisfied with methods based solely on experience was Thales (ca. 640–546 B.C.). We honor him today as the man who always said, "Prove it!" And he frequently did. Among the better-known theorems first proved by Thales are:

The base angles of an isosceles triangle are congruent.
Vertical angles are congruent.
An angle inscribed in a semicircle is a right angle.

Pythagoras (ca. 582–507 B.C.) and his followers, the Order of the Pythagoreans, followed in the footsteps of Thales. They used his method of proof to develop not only the Pythagorean theorem, but also theorems concerning the sum of the measures of the angles of a polygon, the properties of parallel lines, the five regular solids, and incommensurable quantities.

It was Thales' work, however, that marked the beginning of an era of mathematical development in which deductive proof became the accepted method of logical reasoning. This method is used to derive theorems from postulates and, in this way, to develop a system of logically arranged statements. This era reached its apex with Euclid's *Elements*, 300 years after Thales.

In the *Elements*, Euclid unified the work of the scholars who had preceded him by presenting all the mathematics known in his day in a systematic manner—a truly stupendous achievement. Much of his work was also original, for by means of the deductive method he demonstrated the vast amount of knowledge that can be acquired through reasoning alone. Euclid included algebra and number theory as well as geometry in his writings.

The *Elements* turned out to be a work of major importance in the history of the civilized world. In later years it was translated from Greek to Arabic (ca. 800) and from Arabic to Latin (ca. 1120). The first printed edition appeared in Latin (1482), and many other editions followed. Next to the Bible, the *Elements* has been published in more editions and in more languages than any other book.

The original work was written in 13 separate parchment scrolls, or "books." The fifth theorem in Book I is the familiar "Base angles of an isosceles triangle are congruent." (*Isosceles* is derived from the Greek words *isos*, meaning equal, and *skelos*, meaning legs.) The method now most frequently used to prove this theorem requires the construction of an angle bisector through the vertex angle. This process has been disputed by "purists," since it prematurely introduces the angle bisector. Euclid, however, demonstrated it differently. A sketch of his proof follows:

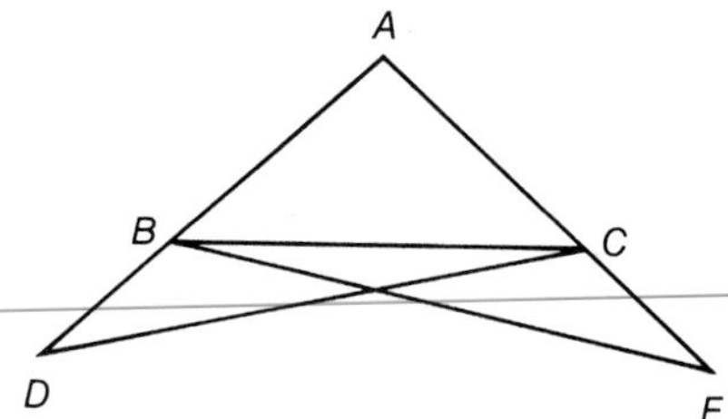

Given ΔABC with $\overline{AB} \cong \overline{AC}$. Extend $\overline{AB}$ and $\overline{AC}$ through B and C, respectively, to points D and E, so that $\overline{BD} \cong \overline{CE}$. Therefore, $\Delta ADC \cong \Delta AEB$, so $\angle D \cong \angle E$ and $\overline{DC} \cong \overline{EB}$. Then $\Delta BDC \cong \Delta CEB$, so $\angle DBC \cong \angle ECB$. Therefore, $\angle ABC \cong \angle ACB$. *Q.E.D.*[1]

The theorem just proved was known as the "pons asinorum," or "bridge of asses (fools)" in the Middle Ages. The implication was that certain students had difficulty "crossing"

[1]Q.E.D. is an abbreviation for *quod erat demonstrandum*, which means "that which was to be demonstrated." It is sometimes written after the conclusion of a proof in mathematics.

this bridge in order to proceed further in their study of geometry. Euclid proved the converse of this theorem by the indirect method (*reductio ad absurdum*):

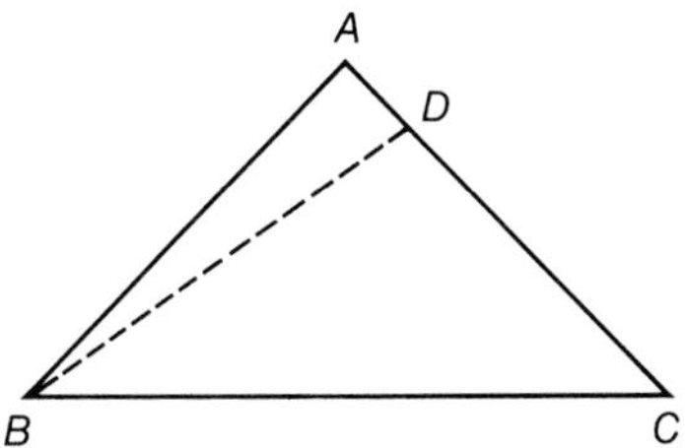

Given ΔABC, where $\angle B \cong \angle C$. If $\overline{AB} \not\cong \overline{AC}$, then assume $AC > AB$. Mark off point D in $\overline{AC}$ such that $\overline{DC} \cong \overline{AB}$. Then $\Delta DCB \cong \Delta ABC$. This is impossible, so $\overline{AB} \cong \overline{AC}$.

Throughout the course of history, but especially during the last four centuries, Euclid's *Elements* has endured unimaginable "torture." It has been simplified, complicated, projected, distorted, deformed, and sometimes changed beyond recognition. The result? Analytic geometry, projective geometry, topology, non-Euclidean geometry, logic, and even calculus and contemporary theoretical physics. The end is not yet in sight!

Constructions: Compasses and Straightedge

Whenever constructions are required in geometry, the tools to be used, unless otherwise noted, consist of the ordinary compasses and an unmarked straightedge only.[2] The justification for the employment of these instruments rests on the following three postulates mentioned at the beginning of Euclid's *Elements*:

Let it be granted

1. That a straight line may be drawn from any one point to any other point. [straightedge]
2. That a line segment may be extended to any length along a straight line. [straightedge]
3. That a circle may be drawn from any center at any distance from that center. [compasses]

Euclid worked with rather crude collapsible compasses. The ones we use today can be used only with the preceding postulates, and they have the advantage of making the constructions somewhat simpler than they were for Euclid.

Performing the familiar constructions of Euclidean geometry with compasses alone is possible. In 1797, Lorenzo Mascheroni, an Italian mathematician, wrote *The Geometry of Compasses*, in which he proved that all construction problems that can be solved by the use of straightedge and compasses can be solved by compasses alone.[3] These are known as *Mascheroni constructions*. Here is an example of a simple Mascheroni construction:

> Given a line segment $\overline{AB}$. Determine with compasses alone the midpoint, M, of $\overline{AB}$.

The following sequence of diagrams utilizes the popular compasses of today and demonstrates the solution to the problem just posed.

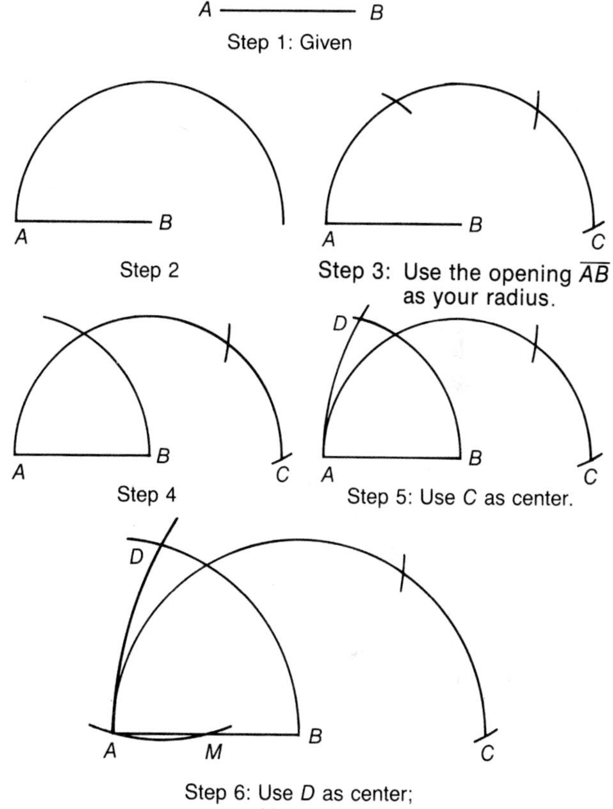

Here is another outline of the proof that the construction is correct.

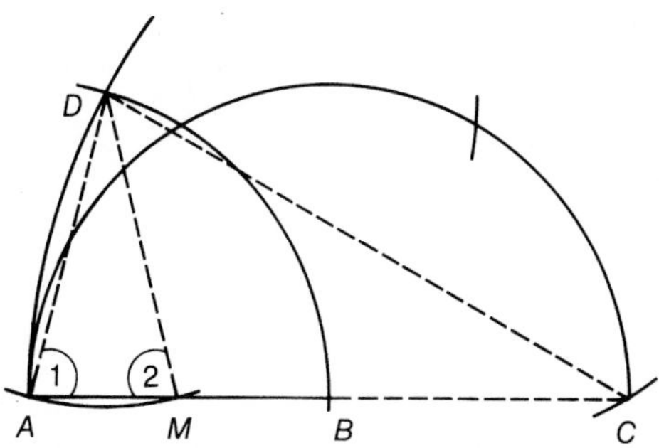

---

[2]The word *compasses* is a plural noun, as are the words *pants* and *scissors*, because each has two branches. Although the word *compass* is often used to denote "compasses," a compass is, strictly speaking, an instrument for determining direction.

[3]For a proof that the straightedge alone can replace the straightedge and compasses, see *Advanced Geometric Constructions* by A. S. Posamentier and W. Wernick (Palo Alto, CA: Dale Seymour, 1988).

Draw the construction lines as indicated. Note that $\overline{ABC}$ is a straight line.

1. Since ΔACD is isosceles, $\angle CDA \cong \angle 1$.
2. Since ΔDAM is isosceles, $\angle 1 \cong \angle 2$.
3. Therefore, $\Delta ACD \sim \Delta DAM$.
4. Therefore,

$$\frac{AM}{AD} = \frac{AD}{AC} \quad \text{or} \quad AM = \frac{(AD)^2}{AC}.$$

5. But $AD = AB$ and $AC = 2(AB)$.
6. Therefore,

$$AM = \frac{(AB)^2}{2(AB)} \qquad \text{or} \qquad AM = \frac{AB}{2}.$$

Bisecting a line segment or an angle with compasses and straightedge is a simple matter. Trisecting a line segment is a bit more complicated but clearly possible. Early Greek geometers must have been quite puzzled when they were unsuccessful in all attempts to trisect an angle with straightedge and compasses alone. (We are speaking here of a general angle, not the special ones like right angles, which can be trisected by constructing a 60° angle and then a 30° angle.)

One of the most productive techniques in mathematics is that of changing the regulations under which you operate, if these regulations tie your hands. Thus, if the restriction to use traditional construction tools leads to failure in seeking a solution for the trisection problem, perhaps other tools will do the trick. This means, of course, that Euclid's construction postulates must be altered.

Archimedes suggested that he could trisect an angle with compasses and a straightedge that had only two marks on it. Here is a description of Archimedes' construction. The proof follows:

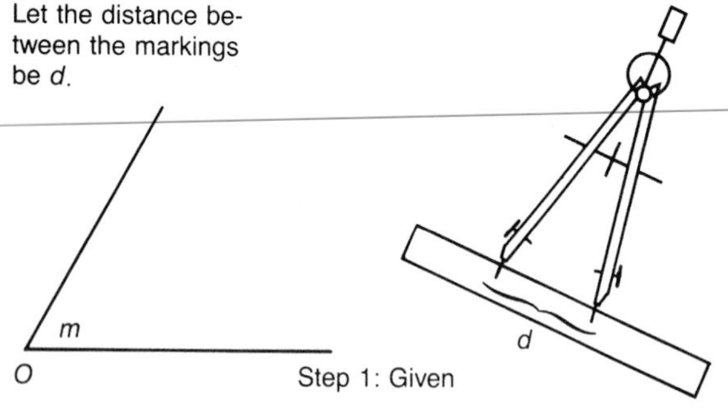

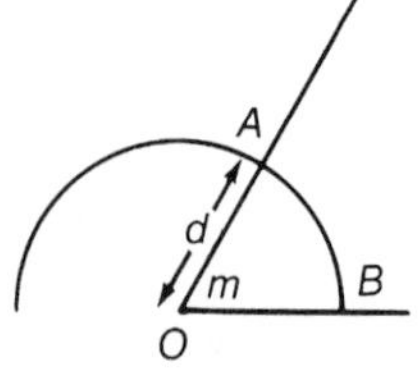

Step 3

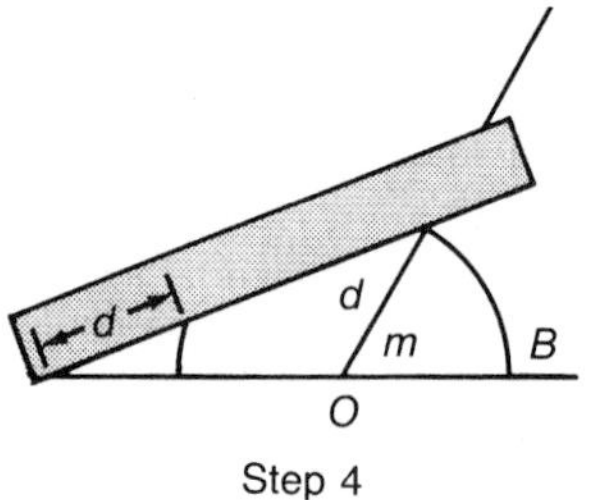

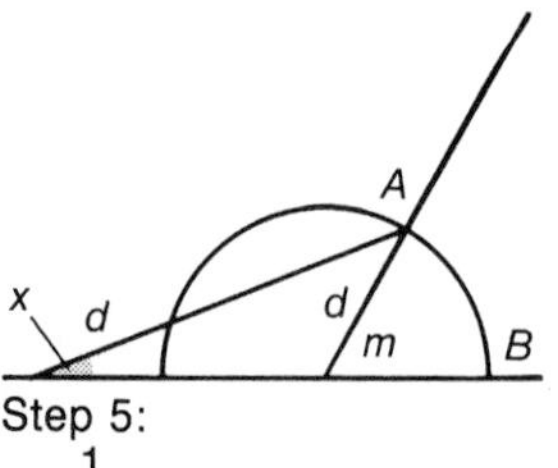

Proof

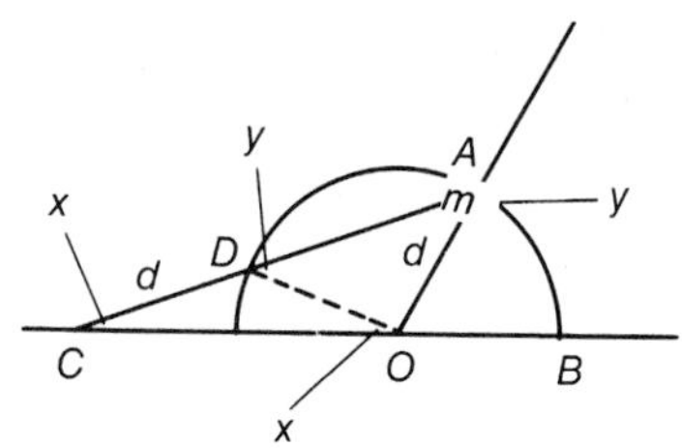

1. $\overline{OD}$ is drawn. $OD = d$.
2. Isosceles ΔDCO has congruent base angles. Isosceles ΔADO has congruent base angles.
3. In ΔDCO, $y = x + x = 2x$.
4. In ΔACO, $m = y + x$.
5. Therefore, $m = 2x + x$, or $x = m/3$.

This construction was made possible because the rules of the game (the postulates) were changed. Other mathematicians in ancient as well as contemporary times have changed the rules even more dramatically and have produced ingenious and elegant procedures for trisecting an angle.

The French mathematician Blaise Pascal invented an unusual instrument to trisect an angle. Here the rods represented by $\overline{PQ}$, $\overline{QO}$, and $\overline{OR}$ are equal in length. Q and O are movable pivots, and R moves a long the slot.

You can easily prove that:

$$x = \tfrac{1}{3} m\angle AOB$$

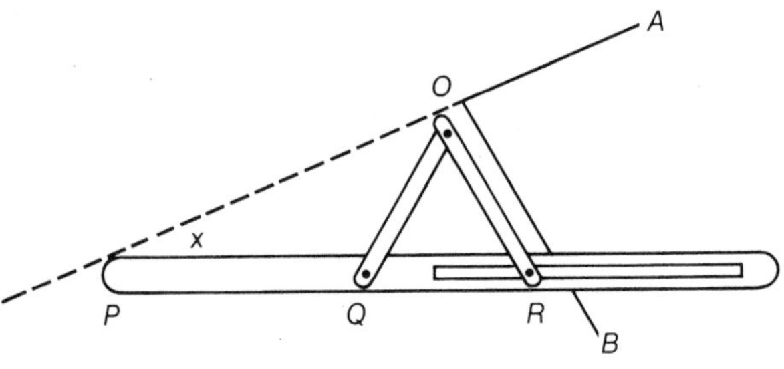

Still other constructions baffled the Greeks and later mathematicians for more than 2000 years. One of these, "squaring a circle," requires the construction of a square whose area is equal to that of a given circle. Another, "duplication of the cube" (doubling the volume), requires the construction of a cube whose volume is to be twice that of a given cube. These, like the trisection problem, were proved only in contemporary times to be incapable of construction with compasses and straightedge alone.[4]

Other constructions also eluded the capabilities of the best mathematicians for centuries. Although certain polygons could be constructed with ease using the traditional tools of geometry, others, such as the regular seven-sided polygon (heptagon, or 7-gon) or regular 17-gon, seemed to be beyond their reach. In 1796, a 19-year-old youth, Carl Friedrich Gauss, proved that it was possible to construct a regular 17-sided polygon with compasses and straightedge only and that certain others, such as the regular 7-gon, could not.

What Gauss proved is that a regular polygon with an odd number of sides can be constructed if either of the following conditions is satisfied:

CONDITION 1

The number of sides is equal to $2^{2^n} + 1$, where n is a whole number and $2^{2^n} + 1$ is a prime number. Examples can be found in the following chart.

n	$2^{2^n} + 1$	Can a polygon be constructed?	Number of sides
0	3	Yes	3
1	5	Yes	5
2	17	Yes	17
3	257	Yes	257
4	65537	Yes	65537
5	Not prime	No	—

CONDITION 2

The number of sides is the product of two or more different numbers obtained in Condition 1. (You can construct a regular polygon of, say, 15 sides, because $15 = 5 \times 3$, and 5 and 3 are numbers derived from the rule in Condition 1.)

The discovery of this remarkable theorem convinced Gauss to enter into the field of mathematics for his life's work, instead of linguistics, in which he also excelled. A monument erected to him in Brunswick, Germany, at the place of his birth consists merely of a regular 17-gon, the symbol of his great achievement.

Practical Trigonometry: The Original Sin

Although Euclid showed in his *Elements* that two triangles that agree with respect to two sides and an included angle are congruent (SAS), in other words, that the size of the triangle is fixed when the measures S, A, and S are given in that order, he did not indicate any particular concern about finding the specific measures of the remaining three parts of the triangles. Similarly for ASA and SSS. The Greek mathematician-philosophers of Euclid's day did not consider "practical" or "applied" geometry to be worthy of any serious consideration. This view slowed the development of that branch of mathematics known as trigonometry.[5]

Regardless of popular opinion against any serious study of the subject, trigonometry managed to get itself born among the Greeks. Its inventor, Hipparchus (ca. 140 B.C.), encountered the need for triangle measurements in connection with his work in astronomy and developed techniques for determining the measure of the dimensions of a fixed triangle. Menelaus (ca. A.D. 100) also contributed knowledge to this field by developing "spherical trigonometry," the measurement of triangles on a spherical surface, which he needed in connection with his work in astronomy. However, it remained for Ptolemy (ca. A.D. 150), the great astronomer and mathematician who lived in Alexandria, to produce the first major contribution in the field of trigonometry (also in connection with astronomy) in his book *The Almagest*. In this work, whose title means "the greatest," the first extensive trigonometric tables appeared.

Trigonometry remained a servant of astronomy until 1464, when the German mathematician Johann Müller (also known as Regiomontanus) wrote a book that treated trigonometry as a purely mathematical subject, an outgrowth of geometry, which stood on its own merits. Today trigonometry is an important tool in mathematics, because the nature of trigonometric functions is such that they are appropriate for use in analyzing physical phenomena that occur with periodic regularity, such as electricity, music, and light.

We say that "a triangle is solved" when the measures of its six dimensions (three angles and three sides) have been determined. The four major tools used to solve triangles are

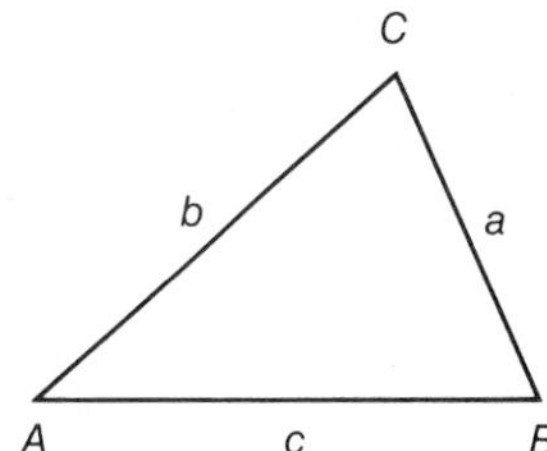

1. The Pythagorean theorem.
2. The sum of the measures of the angles of a triangle is 180°.
3. The law of sines:

   For any triangle ABC,

$$\frac{a}{\sin A} = \frac{b}{\sin B} = \frac{c}{\sin C}.$$

[4]For a proof of the impossibility of the angle trisection see Enrichment Unit 97.

[5]Trigonometry is derived from the Greek words *trigonon*, meaning "triangle," and *metria*, meaning "measurement."

4. The law of cosines:
For any triangle ABC,

$$c^2 = a^2 + b^2 - 2ab\cos C$$
or
$$b^2 = a^2 + c^2 - 2ac\cos B$$
or
$$a^2 = b^2 + c^2 - 2bc\cos A.$$

The trigonometric tables we use today to solve triangles had as their forerunner a table invented by Ptolemy. We now present a general idea of how the trigonometric table was developed by Ptolemy, except that we will use contemporary notation and symbols. (Ptolemy used the sexigesimal, base-60 number system.) First, we give some background.

I. Trigonometric functions may be represented as line segments.
In a unit circle, O,

$$\sin x = \frac{AD}{OD}; \quad \cos x = \frac{OA}{OD}; \quad \tan x = \frac{BC}{OB}.$$

Since $OD = OB = 1$, then

$$AD = \sin x,$$
$$OA = \cos x,$$
$$BC = \tan x.$$

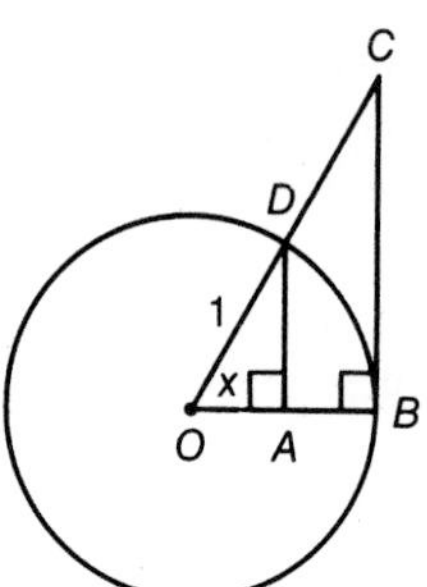

II. Derivation of the word *sine*: The segment $\overline{AD}$ in the diagram is a half-chord known as a *jiva* in Sanskrit. This word was first found in Hindu writings in the year 510. Translators mistakenly wrote this as *jaiv* in Arabic, meaning "pocket" or "cavity." This was eventually translated into the Latin word for "cavity"—*sinus*. Thus, the half-chord, *jiva*, became *sine*, or *sin* in abbreviated form.

III. Certain formulas used to develop the trigonometry table appeared in the *Almagest*. Several of these follow.

1. $\sin^2 x + \cos^2 x = 1$
2. $\sin(x - y) = \sin x \cos y - \cos x \sin y$
3. $\sin(x + y) = \sin x \cos y + \cos x \sin y$
4. $\sin 2x = 2\sin x \cos x$
5. $\sin \frac{1}{2}x = \sqrt{\frac{1 - \cos x}{2}}$
6. $\tan x = \frac{\sin x}{\cos x}$

The sixth formula, for tan x, was used by the Arab mathematician el-Hasib in the year 860 to produce the first table of tangents. (Derivations of these formulas can be found in any standard trigonometry textbook.)

IV. Ptolemy computed a table of lengths of chords for arcs from 0° to 180°, in steps of $\frac{1}{2}^\circ$, in a circle whose radius equals 60 units. Thus, his table gives the measure of chord $\overline{ED}$, which cuts off an arc of x°, for $0^\circ < x^\circ < 180^\circ$.

Part of the table, translated into notation we can follow easily, is reproduced here. The lengths of the chords are stated in sexigesimal notation. For example, 2, 5, 40 in sexigesimal becomes

$$2 + \frac{5}{60} + \frac{40}{60^2} = 0.0350 \text{ in decimal.}$$

Arcs	Chords
$\frac{1}{2}^\circ$	0, 31, 25
1°	1, 21, 50
$1\frac{1}{2}^\circ$	1, 34, 15
2°	2, 5, 50
$2\frac{1}{2}^\circ$	2, 37, 4
3°	3, 8, 28
$3\frac{1}{2}^\circ$	3, 39, 52

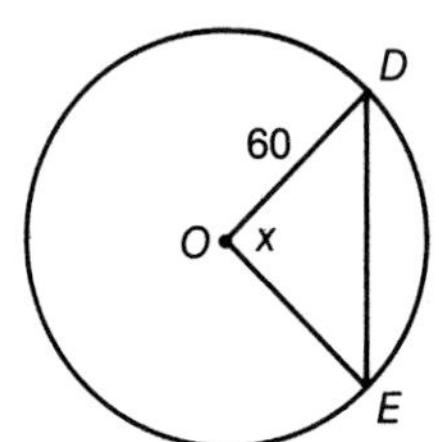

Contemporary trigonometric tables give the length of the half-chord $AD (= \sin y)$ for the corresponding angle $2y$ in the circle of unit radius.

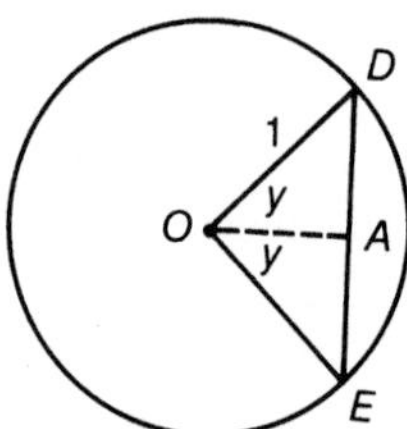

Thus, if you look up the value of sin 45° in your trigonometric table, you will find it to be .7071, whereas the corresponding notation in Ptolemy's table, after appropriate conversions, will tell you that an arc of 90° cuts off a chord of length 1.4142. In this way one can convert from Ptolemy's table of chords to the contemporary sine function.

The cosine and tangent can then be computed from the formulas

$$\sin^2 x + \cos^2 x = 1 \quad \text{and} \quad \tan x = \frac{\sin x}{\cos x}.$$

The following is an outline of a proof known as Ptolemy's theorem, from which Ptolemy derived many of the formulas he needed to construct tables such as $\sin(x - y)$ and $\sin(x + y)$.

THEOREM

If *ABCD* is a quadrilateral inscribed in a circle, then the sum of the products of the opposite sides equals the product of the diagonals.

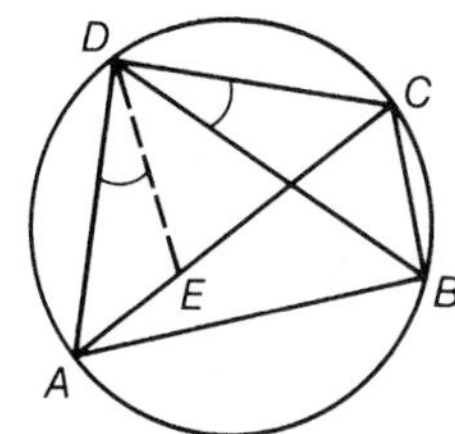

Given: Quadrilateral *ABCD* inscribed in a circle; diagonals $\overline{AC}$ and $\overline{BD}$.

Prove: $AB \times CD + BC \times AD = DB \times AC$.

1. Construct $\angle ADE \cong \angle BDC$.
2. $\angle CDE \cong \angle ADB$.
3. $\angle ACD \cong \angle ABD$.
4. $\therefore \Delta ADB \sim \Delta CDE$.
5. $\therefore \dfrac{CD}{DB} = \dfrac{CE}{AB}$ or $AB \times CD = CE \times DB$.
6. Show that $\Delta ADE \sim \Delta CDB$.
7. $\therefore \dfrac{AD}{DB} = \dfrac{AE}{BC}$ or $BC \times AD = DB \times AE$.
8. From steps 5 and 7:

$$\begin{aligned} AB \times CD + BC \times AD &= CE \times DB + DB \times AE \\ &= DB(CE + AE) \\ &= DB \times AC. \end{aligned}$$

Q.E.D.

EXERCISE

Use Ptolemy's theorem to derive the formula

$$\sin(x - y) = \sin x \cos y - \cos x \sin y.$$

An outline of the proof follows:

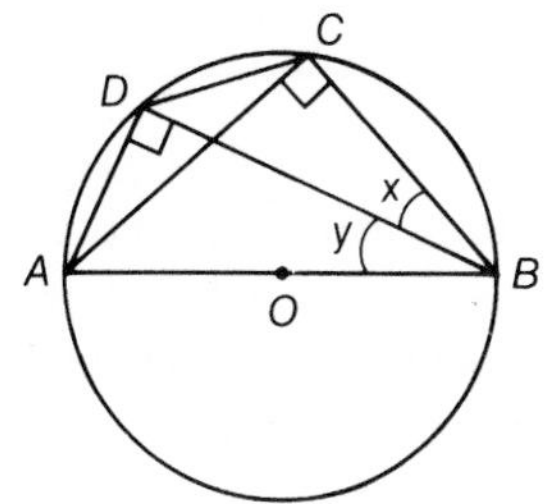

In a circle of unit diameter *AB*,

1. $AB \times CD + BC \times AD = DB \times AC$.
2. In right ΔBDA, $AD = \sin y$ and $DB = \cos y$.
3. In right ΔBCA, $BC = \cos x$ and $AC = \sin x$.
4. In ΔDCB, $\dfrac{CD}{\sin(x - y)} = \dfrac{BC}{\sin\angle CDB}$.
5. But since $\angle CDB = \angle CAB$, then

$$\sin\angle CDB = \sin\angle CAB = \frac{BC}{AB} = \frac{BC}{1} = BC.$$

6. From steps 4 and 5,

$$\frac{CD}{\sin(x - y)} = \frac{BC}{BC} = 1 \quad \text{or} \quad CD = \sin(x - y).$$

7. Now verify, by substituting the results of steps 2–6 into step 1, that $\sin(x - y) = \sin x \cos y - \cos x \sin y$.

Q.E.D.

EXERCISE

Use this diagram and Ptolemy's theorem to derive the formula

$$\sin(x + y) = \sin x \cos y + \cos x \sin y.$$

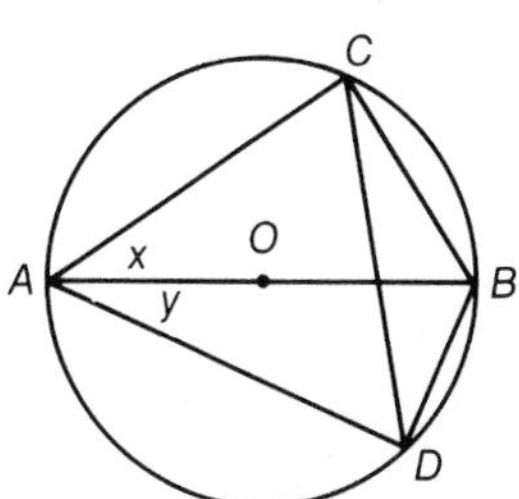

Most of the material needed to solve a triangle was developed prior to the year 1600. Further refinements came about as a result of work with logarithms and calculus.

DeMoivre's theorem (ca. 1722) demonstrated a relationship between the trigonometric functions and the imaginary *i* in the formula

$$(\cos A + i \sin A)^n = \cos nA + i \sin nA.$$

By the end of the 17th century the infinite series for $\sin x$ and $\cos x$ were known:

$$\sin x = x - \frac{x^3}{3!} + \frac{x^5}{5!} - \frac{x^7}{7!} + \cdots$$

$$\cos x = 1 - \frac{x^2}{2!} + \frac{x^4}{4!} - \frac{x^6}{6!} + \cdots$$

Today's scientific calculators take advantage of the convergence of these series to determine the values of sine and cosine of any angle whose measure is in radians. The number of displayed decimal places is limited only by the size of the calculator.

So, although trigonometry began as a tool to solve triangles in geometry, it is thought of today as a periodic relationship of complex numbers—quite different from its practical beginnings.

Algebra: Mathematical Shorthand

The algebra that is traditionally taught to our secondary school students came about as a result of independent developments by mathematicians of ancient Greece and the Hindu and Arab worlds.

The treatment of algebra by the Greeks was geometric. A large portion of Euclid's *Elements* is in fact devoted to finding solutions, geometrically, to what today we call algebraic equations. An illustration of this is shown later in this section. Thus, what we write as

$$(a + b)^2 = a^2 + 2ab + b^2$$

was thought of by the Greeks in terms of this diagram:

a + b

ab	b^2
a^2	ab

a + b

Much of the algebraic knowledge of the Greeks was brought together by Diophantus (ca. 275), a prominent mathematician whose work on integral solutions to certain types of equations is still studied today. Incidentally, the first woman mathematician we hear of in ancient times is Hypatia (ca. 410), who wrote commentaries on the work of Diophantus.

In another part of the world, Hindu mathematicians were also concerned with methods for solving equations, especially the quadratic. One of their more interesting contributions to the subject is that they enjoyed posing problems in a colorful way. Here is one example (many more can be found in books on the history of algebra that are listed in the bibliography at the end of this section):

> Of a collection of mango fruits, the king took $\frac{1}{6}$, the queen took $\frac{1}{5}$ of the remainder, and the three chief princes took $\frac{1}{4}$, $\frac{1}{3}$, and $\frac{1}{7}$ of that same remainder, and the youngest child took the remaining 3 mangoes. Oh, you who are clever in problems on fractions, give out the number of mangoes in that collection.

Arab writers dominated the scene of algebraists in ancient times for many centuries. The greatest Arab writer on algebra was Mohammed ibn Musa al-Khowarizmi (ca. 825), from whose book *Al-Jabr W'al Mukabala* the name *algebra* is derived. His major contribution was the introduction of the use of algorithms as a mathematical tool. Incidentally, the word *algorithm* is derived from the name *al-Khowarizmi*.

Al-Khowarizmi's work became known in Europe in the 12th century. By the 16th century, the symbols we now use in algebra had already been, for the most part, slowly and painstakingly developed. Here are two examples of how equations were written in the years indicated. Just imagine how cumbersome they were to work with. (The contemporary notation is given in parentheses.)

1545: cubus p 6 rebus aequalis 20. $(x^3 + 6x = 20)$

1631: $xxx + 3bbx = 2ccc$. $(x^3 + 3b^2x = 2c^3)$

The "=" sign was first introduced by Robert Recorde in his 1557 book *The Whetstone of Witte*.

In 1637, René Descartes introduced the exponent notation that we take for granted today.

Quadratic equations and their solutions played a special role in the history of algebra. The Babylonians first solved certain forms of quadratic equations 3600 years ago, as found in tablets that are now in a collection, YBC 6967, at Yale University. A translation of the problem on these tablets is equivalent to "Find the dimensions of a rectangle whose length exceeds its width by 7 and whose area is 60." The Babylonian solution uses no algebraic notation but serves as a prototype for similar problems. Thus, the solution to the Babylonian quadratic

$$x^2 + px = q, \quad q > 0$$

is shown in the tablet to be

$$x = \sqrt{\left(\frac{p}{2}\right)^2 + q} - \frac{p}{2}.$$

So for y = length and x = width, the equations $y = x + 7$ and $xy = 60$ reduce, after appropriate substitution, to the Babylonian type $x^2 + 7x = 60$. Thus, the solution to the problem posed is

$$x = \sqrt{\left(\frac{7}{2}\right)^2 + 60} - \frac{7}{2} = 5.$$

Compare this solution with the quadratic formula solution used today.

Another famous quadratic is solved geometrically by Euclid in position 11, Book 2 of *Elements*:

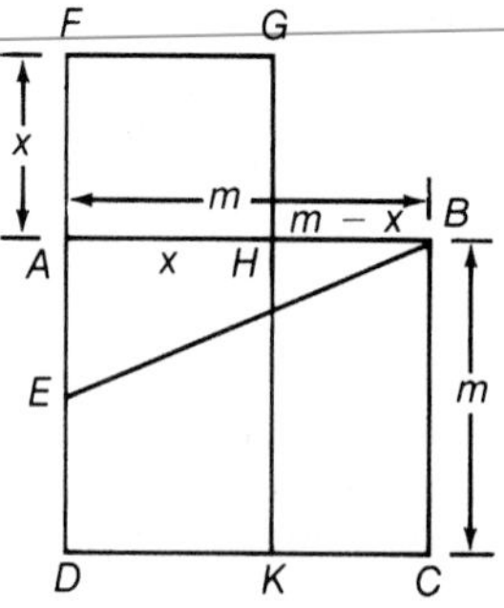

PROPOSITION

To divide a given straight line into two segments such that the rectangle contained by the whole line and one of its segments is equal to the square of the remaining segment [i.e., to divide a line ($AB = m$) into two parts x and $m - x$, such that $m(m - x) = x^2$].

SOLUTION

1. On $\overline{AB}$ construct a square $ABCD$.
2. Bisect $\overline{AD}$ at E and draw $\overline{EB}$.
3. Extend $\overline{AD}$ through A to F so that $\overline{EF} \cong \overline{EB}$.
4. On $\overline{AF}$ construct a square, $AFGH$.
5. Extend $\overline{GH}$ to intersect $\overline{DC}$ at K.
6. Therefore rectangle $HBCK$ equals, in area, the square $AHGF$.

PROOF

1. $\overline{AE} \cong \overline{ED}$ (because E is a midpoint).
2. Area of rectangle $FGKD = (EF + ED)(EF - ED)$.
3. Area of rectangle $FGKD = EF^2 - ED^2$.
4. Area of rectangle $FGKD = EF^2 - AE^2$.
5. $\therefore FGKD + AE^2 = EF^2$.
6. $AB^2 + AE^2 = EB^2 = EF^2$ (because $EF = EB$ and AEB is a right triangle).
7. $\therefore AB^2 + AE^2 = FGKD + AE^2$, or $AB^2 = FGKD$.
8. $\therefore AH^2 = HBCK$ (by subtracting $AHKD$ from both sides). Q.E.D.

What Euclid did here, translated into algebraic symbolism, is to show how to divide the given line segment AB into segments x and $m - x$ such that $m(m - x) = x^2$, and segment AH, or x, is the required number. We now know by the quadratic formula that

$$x = \frac{m(\sqrt{5} - 1)}{2}.$$

Those who delve beyond secondary school mathematics know that algebra has become a powerful tool to solve problems through group theory and linear algebra.

Historical Notes

The embellishment resulting from the inclusion of historical notes in a mathematics lesson may be considered enrichment. Students usually get a more complete appreciation of a topic if they can relate to its origin. Any book on the history of mathematics can provide useful ideas for enriching your instruction by the inclusion of short anecdotes from the history of mathematics. The following references are of particular value for this use.

Beckmann, Petr. *A History of π*. New York: St. Martin's Press, 1971.

Bell, E. T. *Mathematics, Queen and Servant of Science*. Washington, DC: Mathematical Association of America, 1979.

Bell, E. T. *Men of Mathematics*. New York: Simon & Schuster, 1937.

Boyer, Carl B. *A History of Mathematics*. New York: John Wiley, 1968.

Burton, David M. *The History of Mathematics, An Introduction*. Boston: Allyn and Bacon, 1985.

Campbell, Douglas M., and John C. Higgins, Eds. *Mathematics: People, Problems, Results*. Belmont, CA: Wadsworth, 1984.

Dunham, William. *Journey Through Genius*. New York: Wiley, 1990.

Eves, Howard W. *An Introduction to the History of Mathematics*. New York: Saunders College Publishing, 1983.

———. *The Other Side of the Equation*. Boston: Prindle, Weber, and Schmidt, 1971.

———. *Mathematical Circles Revisited*. Boston: Prindle, Weber, and Schmidt, 1971.

———. *In Mathematical Circles*, Vols. 1 and 2. Boston: Prindle, Weber, and Schmidt, 1969.

Gamon, George. *One, Two, Three . . . Infinity*. New York: Viking Press, 1947.

Gray, Shirley B., and C. Edward Sandifer. "The Sumario Compendioso: The New World's First Mathematics Book." *Mathematics Teacher* 94 (2001): 98–103.

Kaplan, Robert. *The Nothing That Is: A Natural History of Zero*. New York: Oxford University Press, 1999.

Kasner, E., and J. Newman. *Mathematics and the Imagination*. New York: Simon and Schuster, 1940.

Kelley, Loretta. "A Mathematical History Tour." *Mathematics Teacher* 93 (2000): 14–17.

Lee-Chua, Queena N. "Mathematics in Tribal Philippines and Other Societies in the South Pacific." *Mathematics Teacher* 94 (2001): 50–55.

Mathematics Teacher 98 (November 2000), the entire issue.

Moritz, R. E. *On Mathematics: A Collection of Witty, Profound, Amusing Passages about Mathematics and Mathematicians*. New York: Dover, 1958.

National Council of Teachers of Mathematics. *Historical Topics for the Mathematics Classroom*. 31st Yearbook. Reston, VA: NCTM, 1969.

Norwood, Rick. "A Star to Guide Us." *Mathematics Teacher* 92 (1999): 100–101.

Posamentier, Alfred S., and Noam Gordon. "An Astounding Revelation on the History of π." *Mathematics Teacher* 77 (1984): 52.

Posamentier, Alfred S., and Ingmar Lehmann. *π: A Biography of the World's Most Mysterious Number*. Amherst, NY: Prometheus Books, 2004.

Resnikoff, H. L., and R. O. Wells, Jr. *Mathematics in Civilization*. New York: Dover, 1984.

Schaaf, William L., ed. *Our Mathematical Heritage*. New York: Macmillan, 1963.

Stillwell, John. *Mathematics and Its History*. New York: Springer-Verlag, 1989.

Turnbull, H. W. *The Great Mathematicians*. New York: New York University Press, 1961.

Veljan, Darko. "The 2500-Year-Old Pythagorean Theorem." *Mathematics Magazine* 73 (2000): 259–272.

Willerding, Margaret. *Mathematical Concepts, A Historical Approach*. Boston: Prindle, Weber, and Schmidt, 1967.

Some of these books will lend themselves better to quick extraction of anecdotes for classroom use; others will require a somewhat more thorough reading. These books should provide you with ample resources for enrichment through historical anecdotes.

Enrichment Techniques for All Levels

The core curriculum of the *Standards* proposes that all students be exposed to the same mathematics, though differentiated by levels of abstraction of tasks and concepts.

Opportunities for enrichment of instruction exist at every level, particularly when integrated with real-life applications.

The teacher will determine the extent of movement from concrete to abstract for each student, the utilization of small or large groups of students, project work, or lectures. Flexibility is the key to productive enrichment.

When enrichment activities are reserved for small groups, each particular group can move at its own pace. Students will delve into ideas with classmates who may be interested in similar ideas. They will have an opportunity to look more deeply into and even beyond those ideas developed during regular class sessions. Thus, they will make more challenging explorations and broader connections within and outside of mathematics.

Relevant Applications

Realistic and relevant *applications* of the mathematics being studied generally can provide an excellent source for enrichment, as illustrated by the following examples.

TOPIC

Addition and multiplication of fractions

ENRICHMENT

Computing simple probabilities after developing some class-made probability games (e.g., selecting cards from a deck, tossing a coin or die). The teacher's creativity is very important in making this a success.

TOPIC

Percentage

ENRICHMENT

Computation of and verification of newspaper advertisements involving percentages (e.g., sales, bank advertisements). Handled properly, these investigations can be both motivating and revealing. Some astonishing results often appear.

TOPIC

Using formulas

ENRICHMENT

Have students compute the areas of real floor plans, or compute bank interest, or compute the volume of real but irregular shapes. When possible, these computations should take place in a realistic setting so as to take on more meaning for the students.

TOPIC

Reading tables

ENRICHMENT

Provide students with realistic problems using mileage charts, postal rate schedules, telephone rate schedules, bus schedules, income tax schedules, etc. Where possible, these should relate to local situations.

TOPIC

Basic concepts of geometry

ENRICHMENT

Direct and indirect measurement of local structures. Students should be asked to compute areas, volume, etc., from the data gathered.

Recreational Mathematics

Another form of enrichment is *recreational mathematics*. Anything "recreational" is generally of interest to students. Therefore, mathematics topics being studied can be reinforced enthusiastically under the guise of recreation.

TOPIC

Reducing fractions

ENRICHMENT

Introduce some divisibility rules for easier recognition of common factors (see Enrichment Unit 84).

TOPIC

Practice with addition

ENRICHMENT

Magic squares of various kinds (see Enrichment Units 1 and 2) can be used to reinforce addition facts through an unusual drill.

TOPIC

Miscellaneous computation drill

ENRICHMENT

Various games and puzzles that require students to do computations as part of the activity can enrich an otherwise boring topic. These may be competitive games or puzzles that are individual activities. Here the enrichment activity can be very instrumental in the class's ultimate success with the regular work, because a motivated student should perform better than a student "turned off" to mathematics.

TOPIC

Miscellaneous calculator activities

ENRICHMENT

Games and puzzles with a handheld calculator (see Enrichment Unit 11). These must be carefully selected (and planned).

It is easy to fall into a trap of letting the recreational aspects of a lesson dominate the session. When taken to this extreme, the introduction of recreational topics can become counterproductive; any attempt to return to the intended curriculum will be viewed by the students with displeasure. Remember, the recreational aspect of a lesson is designed merely to enrich, not to replace, the regular curriculum.

Field Trips

It is uncommon to think of field trips as a way to enhance the mathematical instructional program. Yet such activities are not reserved only for the social studies class. There are sites that can enhance the mathematics taught. For example, if probability is the topic studied, a trip to a nearby racetrack, where betting is supposedly based on the likelihood of a horse winning, would be interesting to visit. Classes have been known to visit the backstage areas to see how the betting odds are calculated.

The more usual sites to visit would be to see how mathematics is used in industry: actuarial work, engineering, architecture, business, computer programming, etc. In each case before a field trip is made, there should be a thorough preparation session for the class. The preparation session is sometimes almost as valuable as the trip. The teacher can spark students' interest by using a variety of audiovisual aids, including the Internet site of the place of visit.

A teacher may want to apply a mathematics principle, learned earlier in the classroom, by performing an experiment outdoors. For example, measuring a sports area, or determining the height of a flagpole atop a building, or finding the height of a nearby tower all can be appropriate applications of some elementary trigonometry. Such field trips will show the usefulness of the mathematics the class is learning to everyday situations.

Above all, it is of the utmost importance to preplan a field trip with the class. When students participate in the planning, they know precisely what the purpose of the trip is and what the expected outcomes are. Consequently, during the trip they will focus their time properly. Almost as important as planning is the post-visit session that reviews all that has been or should have been learned from the trip. Done properly, a field trip can enhance and make real the mathematics being taught.

The Internet

The Internet has boundless resources to enrich the instructional program. A listing of web sites, however, can quickly become outdated, for new sites appear daily and some older ones disappear. Local teacher organizations and the NCTM are good sources for current sites. Relevant Internet sites can:

- provide historical notes,
- share teaching ideas,
- offer exemplary lessons (enhanced by videoclips),
- list ideas for enrichment activities,
- provide challenging problems,
- suggest connections with classes in other parts of the country or in other countries with whom to share ideas,
- provide videoclips of applications of mathematics,
- suggest and guide gifted students through mathematics research activities,
- indicate connections between various areas and/or topics in mathematics, and
- many other ideas as boundless as your imagination!

The Gifted Student

Gifted students in mathematics are usually described as exhibiting ingenuity, intellectual curiosity, creative talent, an ability to assimilate and generalize, and a high level of mathematical achievement. Gifted students usually will participate in many extracurricular activities in mathematics. They are also more apt to read mathematics books, periodicals, and pamphlets. These independent activities may lead the more motivated among them to pursue a study of topics in mathematics that are either "off the beaten path" or are a part of some more advanced course (likely to be studied at a later date). Perhaps one of the more rewarding experiences for a teacher of gifted students is to observe a student making a discovery or developing an unusual approach to a topic or problem. This rare insight possessed by the gifted should be nurtured by the teacher through appropriately selected enrichment activities.

Enrichment activities for gifted students can be categorized into three types: *acceleration*, *expansion*, and *digression*.

Acceleration

Acceleration usually involves moving gifted students along at a faster than usual pace. This might mean starting the study of elementary algebra earlier and then enabling the student to reach calculus (and sometimes beyond) while still in high school. It could also mean that full-year courses would be covered in less time, making room for a study of more advanced topics earlier. Perhaps the main advantage of this practice is that it allows the gifted student to remain appropriately challenged and thereby prevents loss of interest resulting from an otherwise lockstep curriculum geared to the average-ability student.

But there are also possible dangers to watch for when accelerating gifted students. If the acceleration is too rapid, the student may be asked to work with too much abstraction too quickly or too soon, that is, before he or she is actually ready for it. This sort of experience could be counterproductive and have long-lasting effects. The teacher must not only look for student readiness, but also be heedful of the motivation that any student needs, regardless of ability. A student, after having been identified as gifted, should not merely be *pushed* along a predetermined track. If a proper balance between interest and ability is not achieved, there exists a likelihood that this gifted student could be turned off to mathematics.

Regardless of the form and degree of the acceleration, careful monitoring of the student both academically and socially is of paramount importance. The teacher must be sensitive to signs that may indicate that a student is perhaps mathematically overextended, generally overworked, or improperly placed socially. With this prescribed care, the acceleration process can be worthwhile; without such care it could be irreparably harmful.

Expansion

Expansion refers to that form of enrichment that allows students to delve more deeply into the topics being studied. Such expansion of the regular mathematics curriculum would take place primarily as part of the classroom mathematics instruction, but it might be a part of an extracurricular program as well. Let us look at some examples.

TOPIC

The Pythagorean theorem (high school geometry course)

ENRICHMENT

Expansion would allow the student to study any or all of the following.

1. Investigate a variety of proofs of the Pythagorean theorem.
2. Investigate the expansion of the Pythagorean theorem to acute and obtuse triangles (i.e., for acute triangles, $a^2 + b^2 > c^2$, and for obtuse triangles, $a^2 + b^2 < c^2$).
3. Study some of the properties of Pythagorean triples, beginning with the formulas for generating these triples:

$$\begin{aligned} a &= m^2 - n^2 \\ b &= 2mn \\ c &= m^2 + n^2, \quad \text{where } m > n \end{aligned}$$

4. Classify various types of Pythagorean triples, for example, by discovering the generating values of m and n that produce triples where $|a - b| = 1$ or where $|b - c| = 1$, and so on.
5. Consider the relationship of the Pythagorean theorem to other topics in mathematics (e.g., trigonometry, Ptolemy's theorem, and Diophantine equations).
6. Generalize the Pythagorean theorem to the law of cosines.

TOPIC

Factoring

ENRICHMENT

From the usual factoring techniques (such as factoring the difference of two squares) an expansion might have students consider some special factorings, such as

$$\begin{aligned} a^3 - b^3 &= (a - b)(a^2 + ab + b^2) \\ a^3 + b^3 &= (a + b)(a^2 - ab + b^2). \end{aligned}$$

For the very gifted students, the general cases might be very rewarding.

1. For *odd* n: $x^n + y^n = (x + y)(x^{n-1} - x^{n-2}y + x^{n-3}y^2 - \cdots + y^{n-1})$
2. For *all* n: $x^n - y^n = (x - y)(x^{n-1} + x^{n-2}y + x^{n-3}y^2 + \cdots + y^{n-1})$
3. For *even* n: $x^n - y^n = (x^{n/2} + y^{n/2})(x^{n/2} - y^{n/2})$

In addition, some more intricate factoring examples might be provided for students to work on, such as

$$y(y - 1)x^2 + (2y^2 - 1)x + y(y + 1).$$

which can be factored as

$$(xy + y + 1)(xy - x + y).$$

A good source for some of these more unusual factoring examples is

Hall, H. S., and S. R. Knight. Revised by F. L. Sevenoak. *Algebra for Colleges and Schools*. New York: Macmillan, 1941.

Other older algebra texts generally have similar material.

TOPIC

Trigonometry

ENRICHMENT

The trigonometry teacher might lead students to expand the law of sines to the law of tangents.

After the law of cosines has been developed, some more complicated triangle solution problems might be presented as an expansion of the usual problems found in current textbooks.

Once again, older textbooks provide an excellent source for expansion of a topic. One such book on trigonometry is

Kells, L. M., F. K. Willis, J. R. Bland, and J. B. Orleans. *Elements of Trigonometry*. New York: McGraw-Hill, 1943.

TOPIC

The geometry of the circle

ENRICHMENT

One possible expansion of this topic might involve a discussion of the definition and history of π, beginning with its reference in the Bible (I Kings 7:23)[6] and tracing its development to the modern computer methods of computation. A discussion of the calculation of π can lead to some very interesting investigations (e.g., see "Constructing π," Enrichment Unit 59).

TOPIC

Probability

ENRICHMENT

As easy as it is to state the Birthday Problem, that is how difficult it is to comprehend this unusual phenomenon. The

[6]For an interesting interpretation of this reference, see "An Astounding Revelation on the History of π" by A. S. Posamentier and N. Gordon. *The Mathematics Teacher* 77 (Reston, VA: National Council of Teachers of Mathematics. January, 1984, p. 52).

development of the various probabilities makes a nice expansion of elementary probability and can lead students to other related investigations (see "The Birthday Problem," Enrichment Unit 31).

TOPIC

Triangle constructions

ENRICHMENT

Usually the only geometric constructions (using straightedge and compasses) of triangles in high school geometry are those made from given measures of sides and angles. The expansion of the givens to include the measures of any three angle bisectors, medians, altitudes, and other triangle-related parts should lead students to a more genuine understanding of triangle properties. You can begin to acquaint yourself with this topic by reading "Triangle Constructions," Enrichment Unit 38. A far more extensive treatment of this very rich topic can be found in *Advanced Euclidean Geometry: Excursions for Secondary Students and Teachers* by A. S. Posamentier (New York, NY: John Wiley Publishing, 2002).

In each of the preceding examples of enrichment through the expansion of a topic in the regular curriculum, you will notice that the discussion was always confined to an embellishment of the original topic and not a digression to another topic. This latter situation is our last form of enrichment for the gifted student to be discussed.

Digression

A popular form of enrichment generally results when the teacher *digresses* from a topic in the regular curriculum to consider another topic that is related to and generally an outgrowth of the first topic. Since a gifted class can usually master a topic more quickly than an average class, more time is available for discussion of another related topic before continuing with the regular prescribed curriculum. These digressions are usually rewarding and can last from a portion of a class session to several sessions. As with other enrichment activities discussed, digressions should be used to enrich the regular curriculum, not detract from it. Often these enrichment activities can be glamorous, which by contrast can make the regular curriculum appear somewhat less appealing. Therefore, the teacher, conscious of this possibility, should try continually to relate a digression to the regular curriculum so that instead of detracting from it, the enrichment topic will in fact embellish it. The following examples should help provide a better understanding of what is meant by an enrichment activity that represents a digression from the regular curriculum.

TOPIC

Geometry (junior high or middle school)

ENRICHMENT

Treated appropriately, the topic of networks can be a worthwhile digression from the study of informal geometry. With the possible goal of investigating the Königsberg Bridge problem, the study of networks can be exciting and can lead to other related topological investigations (see "Networks," Enrichment Unit 96).

TOPIC

Trigonometry (high school level)

ENRICHMENT

After a student has a good working knowledge of the trigonometry included in the regular curriculum, an interesting digression might be one that allows the student to study spherical trigonometry. Of course, this presupposes some knowledge of spherical geometry. Yet, this sort of digression can lead to a more complete understanding of trigonometry.

TOPIC

Concurrency (high school geometry)

ENRICHMENT

Perhaps because the topics of concurrency and collinearity are often slighted in the high school geometry course, a digression to study these topics more fully might be worthwhile. Specifically, the development of the theorems of Giovanni Ceva (1647–1736) and Menelaus of Alexandria (ca. A.D. 100) can lead to many other interesting geometric phenomena. To begin to acquaint yourself with these topics, see "Proving Lines Concurrent," Enrichment Unit 53, and "Proving Points Collinear," Enrichment Unit 55. For further ideas you may wish to consult *Advanced Euclidean Geometry: Excursions for Secondary Students and Teachers* by A. S. Posamentier (Emeryville, CA: Key College Publishing, 2002).

TOPIC

Quadratic equations (algebra)

ENRICHMENT

After studying the various ways to solve quadratic equations, students may wish to learn how to solve other higher-degree equations. A consideration of some methods of solving cubic equations might be enlightening to gifted students. This sort of investigation will lead them to appreciate some of the work of the early mathematicians (e.g., Nicolo Tartaglia, 1506–1557). (See calculator section, of this chapter.)

TOPIC

Conic sections (advanced high school level)

ENRICHMENT

The resourceful teacher certainly will discuss some of the many physical applications of conic sections, yet rarely will a teacher digress to discuss how conics can be constructed. This discussion should lead to envelopes of the conic curves. An enjoyable offshoot of this investigation is the topic of curve stitching (see "Constructing Ellipses," Enrichment Unit 106, and "Constructing the Parabola," Enrichment Unit 107).

The only restriction on the topics that make appropriate digressions for enrichment is the teacher's judgment. There are many possible topics from which to choose. The selected digression should be related to the topic in the curriculum that is to serve as the takeoff point and should be properly planned so as to have a clear beginning, a logical conclusion, and, above all, a specific purpose.

Using Calculators to Enrich Instruction

Investigating Unusual Curiosities

With the aid of a calculator, many interesting (and often unquestioned) mathematical curiosities that appear in the average citizen's everyday experiences can serve as excellent applications of high school mathematics. For example, bank advertisements highlight the *effective annual yield* after stating their annual interest rate. An inspection of four such ads turned up the following effective annual yields for a $5\frac{1}{4}$% annual interest rate compounded daily: 5.35%, 5.38%, 5.39%, and 5.46%. Legally inserting a varying number of days (in a year), n, at different parts of the formula

$$I = \left(1 + \frac{r}{n}\right)^n - 1$$

creates a variety of answers. Availability of a calculator encourages this sort of investigation. Another possible investigation might involve determining the effect of tax-exempt income on individuals in various income tax brackets.

An example in the *Standards* illustrates how the same content can be presented at different levels even though teaching strategies will vary in accordance with levels of interest, skills, and goals. A brief description of the example follows.

EXAMPLE

Consider the problem of finding the amount of money that will be in a savings account at the end of 10 years given the amount of the original deposit ($100) and an interest rate compounded annually (6%).

At Level 1 in the core curriculum, students use calculators to solve the problem by determining the amount after each successive year. They might also use a computer spreadsheet. Students are encouraged to find an underlying pattern, for example:

$$\text{Amount at the end of 1 year} = 100(1.06)^1$$
$$\text{Amount at the end of 10 years} = 100(1.06)^{10}$$

At Level 2, students generalize this problem in stages, finally arriving at the formula $A_n = A_0(1 + r)^n$, where A_n is the amount after n years, A_0 is the amount of the original deposit, and r is the annual interest rate.

At Level 3, students further generalize the formula so that they can explore problems in which the rate is compounded semiannually, quarterly, monthly, or daily.

At Level 4, students should be able to solve the formula given by Level 2 for any of the variables.

Possible extensions of the topic include:

- Solving problems in which compound growth in biology and rate of decay in chemistry provide appropriate applications.
- Proving the results using mathematical induction.
- Making a connection between this topic and the irrational number e.

Many other real-life problems (such as loans, taxes, and installment purchases) can be investigated with the aid of a calculator. Such investigations can serve as excellent sources of applications for the regular secondary school curriculum. There are many ideas for problems in the NCTM's 1979 Yearbook, *Applications in School Mathematics*.

Classroom Calculator Activities

Teachers ought to take advantage of the fact that calculators can generate data accurately and rapidly. The student using a calculator is thus allowed the luxury of exploring mathematics and making observations and conjectures without being burdened with tedious and difficult calculations. A class can now have the opportunity to explore problems that would otherwise remain within the realm of the staggering or possibly even the discouraging. Problems that would *never* be considered are now candidates for solution by students with only marginal arithmetic ability. It is hoped that the result will be a sharpening of thinking and analytical skills.

Preliminary activities, such as gathering or estimating appropriate data, will make these problems far more realistic and enjoyable than the traditional ones with their plug-in solution techniques. Here are some examples of the types of problems that might be considered, depending on the grade level, ability, and maturity of the class.

1. How many drops of water are contained in an ordinary drinking glass?
2. How many hairs are on the heads of all students in the class?
3. What is the number of grains of sand in a box whose dimensions are 12 inches × 4 inches × 6 inches?
4. Estimate the area of a circle whose radius is 5 inches. Find the dimensions of a rectangle whose area is approximately that of the circle.

5. How many minutes, or hours, or days do you spend watching television each month? Each year? Compare this number with the amount of time you spend in school.
6. How many feet are there in the circumference of the earth? How many inches? How many meters?

There is an unlimited variety of problems that a creative teacher can encourage students both to *write* and to *solve* with a calculator. See Enrichment Unit 11, "Enrichment with a Handheld Calculator."

Following are six additional calculator activities that could serve as special challenges for students in grades 7–9.

CONJECTURING RULES Complete the chart:

List 50 random whole numbers	(1) Multiply by 2	(2) Multiply by 10	(3) Multiply by 100	(4) Multiply by 1000
1				
2				
17				
23				
107				
113				
.				
.				
.				

Now answer these questions:

1. What do you notice about the last digit of each number in column 1? Make a conjecture.
2. Compare columns 2, 3, and 4. What do you notice? Make a conjecture.
3. Complete the chart for 50 random decimals. Make some conjectures and test them. Can you prove your conjectures?
4. Complete the chart for 50 random decimals but divide in columns 2, 3, and 4. Make and test some conjectures. Can you prove them?

FOUR MAGIC DIGITS

1. Choose any four different digits, such as 2, 3, 4, and 5. Follow these steps:
   a. Form the largest number you can: 5 4 3 2
      Form the smallest number: −2 3 4 5
      Subtract: 3 0 8 7
   b. With the digits 3, 0, 7, and 8, from the difference, follow these steps:
      Form the largest number: 8 7 3 0
      Form the smallest number: − 3 7 8
      Subtract: 8 3 5 2
   c. With 8, 3, 5, and 2, follow these steps:
      Form the largest number: 8 5 3 2
      Form the smallest number: −2 3 5 8
      Subtract: 6 1 7 4

   After three subtractions you have a number with the magic digits 1, 4, 6, 7.

2. Repeat Exercise 1 with 1, 5, 6, and 8. You will find the magic digits 1, 4, 6, 7 in some order after three subtractions. Write your solution as in Exercise 1.
3. With four different digits, it is always possible to reach a four-digit number having 1, 4, 6, and 7 in some order. Start with the digits 9, 8, 7, and 6. See if you can reach 6174 after three subtractions.
4. Study your solution for Exercise 2. Starting with four digits obtain a number with 1, 4, 6, and 7 in it after these numbers of subtractions: 1, 2, 4, 5, 6.

MAGIC SQUARES

1. This magic square has four rows, four columns, and two diagonals. Find the sum of each. If the eight sums are not the same, check your work.

16	2	3	13
5	11	10	8
9	7	6	12
4	14	15	1

2. Find sets of four numbers in a pattern whose sum is 34. Here are 3 examples. Find 12 more examples. Draw 4-by-4 squares to show your solutions. (See Enrichment Units 1 and 2.)

16			13
4			1

	2		
5			
		12	
		15	

		10	8
9	7		

STRANGE PRODUCTS

1. Find each of the following products:
   a. 68 × 43   86 × 34
   b. 63 × 24   36 × 42
   c. 93 × 13   39 × 31
2. a. Are the two products in Exercise 1 equal in (a), (b), and (c)?
   b. Are the digits in the factors reversed in Exercise 1(a), 1(b), and 1(c)?

3. Find each of the following products:

a.	84 × 12	48 × 21	b.	64 × 23	46 × 32
c.	82 × 14	28 × 41	d.	56 × 21	65 × 12
e.	49 × 63	94 × 36	f.	75 × 68	57 × 86

4. a. Are the digits in Exercise 3 reversed in each factor?
   b. In which pairs of Exercise 3 are the products equal?
   c. Try to write examples such as Exercise 3(a) to 3(c) where the products are equal.
5. Check to make sure the products are equal in each of the following:

a.	96 × 23	69 × 32	b.	84 × 36	48 × 63
c.	93 × 26	39 × 62			

6. Make up some examples like those in Exercises 1 and 5.
7. Write the rule you used for making up the examples in Exercise 6.

SURPRISES

1. a. Choose a three-digit number, for example, 295.
   b. Make a six-digit number by repeating the 295. The number is now 295, 295.
   c. Divide 295, 295 by 13. The quotient is ________.
   d. Divide that quotient by 11. The quotient is ________.
   e. Divide that quotient by 7. The quotient is ________.
2. Repeat Exercise 1 with the numbers 347, 347, 921, 921, and 164, 164.

SOCIAL CHAINS Two numbers are amicable (or friendly) if each is the sum of the proper divisors of the other. For example:

- 284 and 220 are amicable.
- The proper factors of 220 are 1, 2, 4, 5, 10, 11, 20, 22, 44, 55, and 110. The sum is 284.
- The proper factors of 284 are 1, 2, 4, 71, 142. The sum is 220.

The amicable pair 220 and 284 was known to Pythagoras about 500 B.C. No new pair of amicable numbers was discovered until 1636, when the French number theorist Fermat announced 17, 296 and 18, 416 as another pair. In about 1760, after searching systematically, Euler discovered over 60 pairs. A small pair that he overlooked (1,184 and 1,210) was discovered by Nicolo Paganini, a 16-year-old boy, in 1886. Today, about 1,000 pairs of amicable numbers are known. The last pair was discovered in 1976. One number in this pair is 5, 070, 746, 263, 958, 274, 212, 545, 800,175, 616.

Here are some exercises exploring this concept:

1. Prove that 17,296 and 18,416 are amicable.
2. Prove that 1,184 and 1,210 are amicable.
3. Can you prove that the numbers must be both even or both odd?

Models and Manipulatives That Enrich Instruction

Explorations with models and manipulatives is an alternative instructional method that bears consideration for some students and for selected topics. Departing from traditional teacher-led discussions and demonstrations, small group and individual explorations of creative models or manipulatives can demonstrate underlying principles of algebraic processes or geometric relationships.

Today's software programs can replace (conceptually) many of yesterday's manipulatives. One such program is the Geometer's Sketchpad (Key Curriculum Press), which is a wonderful tool to explore geometric concepts, especially invariants. Take, for example, the theorem that the quadrilateral formed by joining the midpoints of the sides of any quadrilateral is a parallelogram. Drawing a quadrilateral with Geometer's Sketchpad, joining consecutive side midpoints with segments, then dragging the mouse to move any vertex of the larger quadrilateral to any position (thereby distorting the original quadrilateral), shows that the one joining the midpoints is always a parallelogram. Further experiments with this figure will reveal when this parallelogram is a rhombus, or a square, or a rectangle. Such modern manipulatives provide an incredibly useful view of mathematics not possible in prior years. Teachers should make use of these invaluable learning aids.

Regular Polyhedra (Platonic Solids) Activities

Historical perspectives may surface in the process of using mathematical models, such as for the regular polyhedra shown on the next page.

Arrange the class in groups of six students, working in pairs. Each group will make cardboard models of the regular polyhedra by constructing these patterns (see page 205), cutting them out, folding on the dotted lines, and using tape to hold the edges together. (Note: Make each edge = 2 units long.) Each group will report back to the entire class with the results of their investigations after they complete the chart and answer the questions.

QUESTIONS

1. Suggest a formula that relates the number of vertices (V), the number of edges (E), and the number of faces (F) for each of the polyhedra.
2. Choose a face of each polyhedron. How many of the remaining faces (a) are parallel to your chosen face? (b) intersect your chosen face?
3. Choose an edge of each polyhedron. How many of the remaining edges (a) are parallel to your chosen edge? (b) intersect your chosen edge? (c) are skew to your chosen edge?
4. Find the total surface area of each polyhedron. Recall the formulas for the areas of an equilateral triangle, a square, and a pentagon.

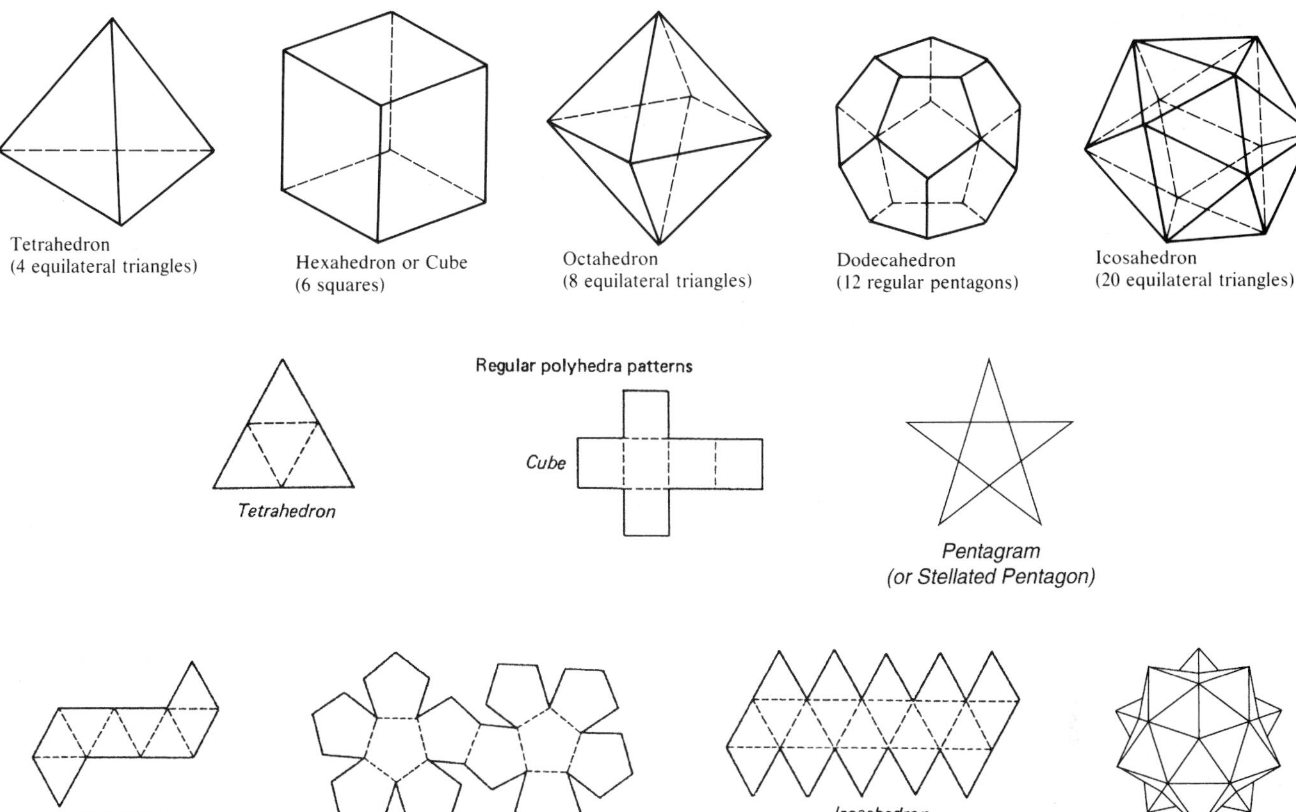

REGULAR POLYHEDRA

Exploration	Regular tetrahedron	Regular hexahedron	Regular octahedron	Regular dodecahedron	Regular icosahedron
Number of faces					
Number of vertices					
Number of edges					

5. Find the volume of the hexahedron, tetrahedron, and octahedron. Recall that the octahedron is composed of two pyramids, and the formula for the volume of a pyramid is $\frac{1}{3}$ (area of base) $\times$ (height).
6. Verify that the formula known as Euler's formula, $V - E + F = 2$, is valid for other than the regular solids, such as the parallelepiped, prism, and pyramid.
7. As a challenge exercise, prove Euler's formula.

HISTORICAL COMMENTS The regular polyhedra are also known as *Platonic bodies*, in honor of Plato, who associated them with the spherical layers of earth, water, air, and fire. These were believed to be the fundamental elements that surrounded the universe. Euclid reserved the study of the regular polyhedra for the concluding topic in his geometry text, the *Elements*, believing, apparently, that the last was the best. Knowledge about the properties of polyhedra has expanded since the times of the ancient Greeks. Johannes Kepler (1571–1630) discovered a new type of polyhedron. He first noted that if the sides of a regular polygon are extended, a new regular polygon may be formed. Thus, a regular pentagon became the stellated pentagon, or pentagram shown above. Generalizing this technique, he could also construct such solids as the stellated dodecahedron. For additional investigations, see *Mathematical Recreations and Essays* by W. W. R. Ball (New York: Macmillan, 1962).

Geoboard (Dot Paper) Activities

Pick's formula states that the area of a triangle whose vertices are all on pegs of a geoboard, or on the dots of dot paper, is

$$\frac{b}{2} + i - 1,$$

where b is the number of dots on the boundary of the triangle and i is the number of dots in the interior of the triangle. Thus, the area of ΔABC is 7 square units.

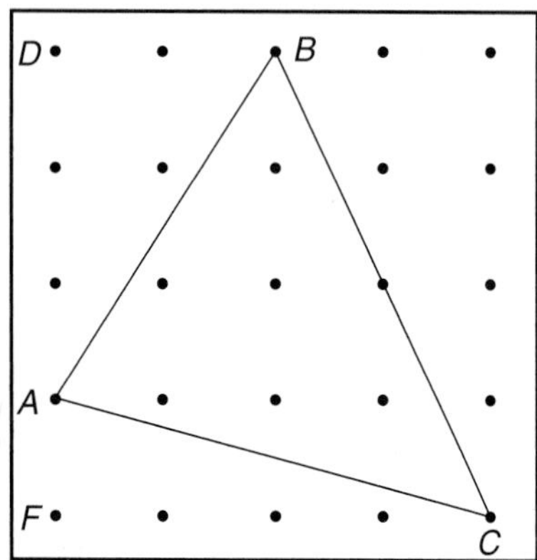

Exercises

1. Use 5-dot × 5-dot paper to construct a second triangle, RST, of area 7.
2. Circumscribe a square around triangle RST. If the distance between each pair of dots is 1 unit, find the number of square units in each right triangle in the picture of triangle RST. Add the areas of the right triangles and subtract the sum from the area of the square, 16, to verify the answer 7.
3. Use the Pythagorean theorem to find the length of $\overline{RS}$; of $\overline{ST}$; of $\overline{TR}$.
4. Use the formula of area $\frac{1}{2}$(base) × (height) to find the length of the altitude from R; from S; from T.
5. Construct a parallelogram on the geoboard and find its area; its sides; its altitudes.

Group Properties of Braids

The most useful models and manipulatives are often of the homemade variety. One such model uses braids to illustrate the properties of mathematical groups.

A braid of order 3 consists of two rods connected by three strands, as in Figure 1. The rods P and Q, holding the upper and lower strands, may be spread apart or moved together without changing the braid configuration. Thus, braids illustrated in Figures 1 and 2 are equivalent.

The *addition operation* occurs as follows: Place two braids, A and B, in the position indicated in Figure 3a, and after removing the rods Q and R, tie the corresponding strands together. The resulting braid is $A + B$ (Figure 3b).

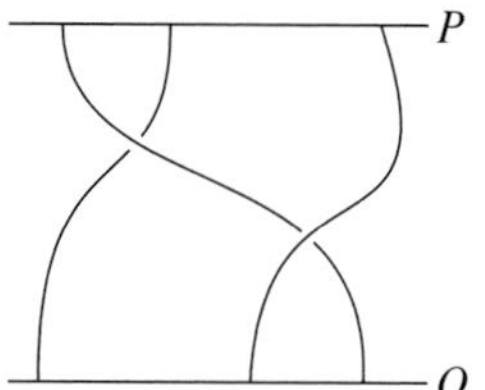

FIGURE 1

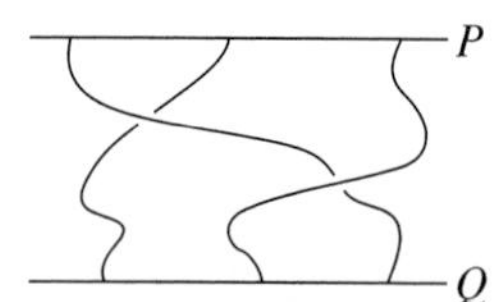

FIGURE 2

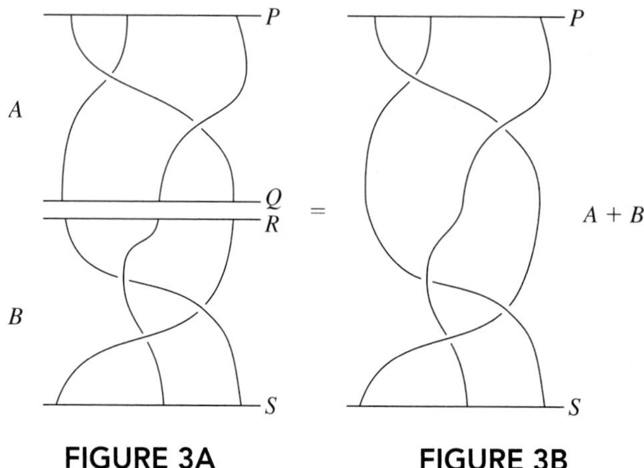

FIGURE 3A

FIGURE 3B

The *closure* condition is satisfied, since the sum of two braids of order 3 is still a braid of order 3 and must be in the group.

The *associative law* is satisfied, since for braids A, B, and C, the result of first removing the rods between A and B, and then between $A + B$ and C, is the same as of removing the rods between B and C first and then the rods between A and $B + C$. Thus, $(A + B) + C = A + (B + C)$.

Identity element: I (see Figure 4):

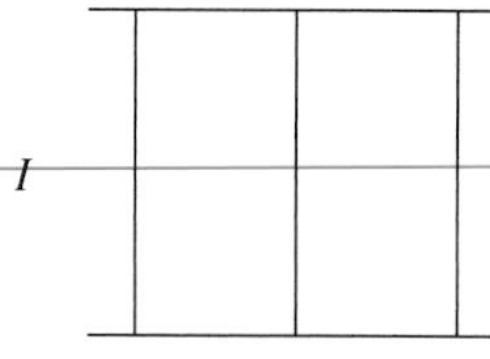

FIGURE 4

Clearly, $A + I = A$ (see Figure 5).

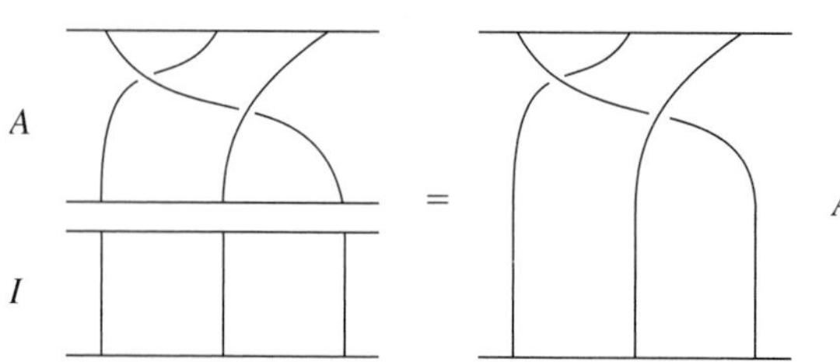

FIGURE 5

Inverse element of a braid, A, is its mirror image, $-A$. Thus, $A + (-A) = I$ (Figure 6).

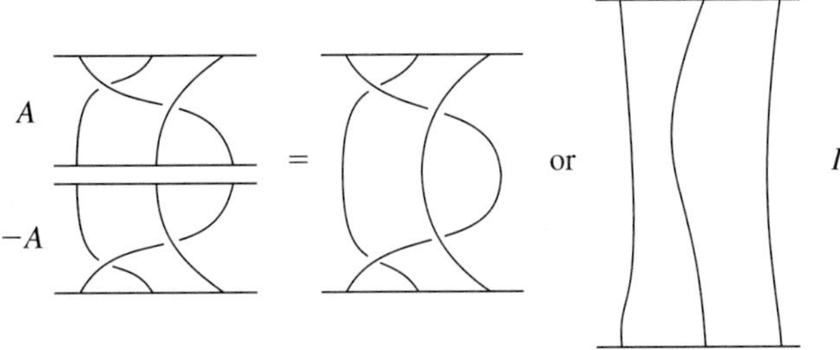

FIGURE 6

(*Note:* When the two braids are added, the result is obviously the identity braid, which is more easily recognized by spreading the upper and lower rods farther apart.)

The group is *not Abelian*, since, for any two braids A and B, $A + B$ is not necessarily equal to $B + A$.

Enrichment Unit 56 presents an interesting use of a very simple teacher-made manipulative that would allow the student to prove all the angle measurement theorems involving circles with one technique. A teacher can also present the same idea with other approaches, such as the one shown here. The student is simply requested to fill in the blanks (already filled in and encircled here) accompanying the following diagram.

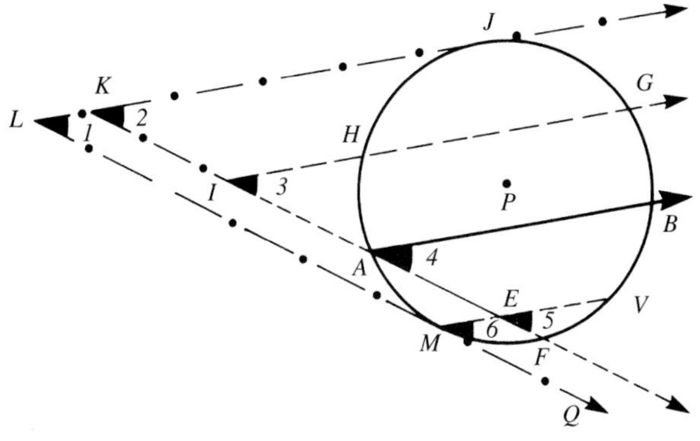

In the figure, consider all lines parallel that appear to be so. The answers to questions 2 through 8 are arcs.

1. Why are angles 1–6 congruent?

2. $m\angle BAF = \frac{1}{2} m\,\underline{\widehat{BF}}$

3. $m\widehat{BN} = m\,\underline{\widehat{AM}} = m\,\underline{\widehat{MF}}$

4. $\mathbf{m\angle NMQ} = m\angle BAF = \frac{1}{2}(m\widehat{BN} + m\,\underline{\widehat{NF}}) =$

   $\frac{1}{2}(m\widehat{MF} + m\,\underline{\widehat{NF}}) = \frac{1}{2}\mathbf{m}\,\underline{\widehat{NM}}$

5. $\mathbf{m\angle NEF} = m\angle BAF = \frac{1}{2}(m\widehat{BN} + m\,\underline{\widehat{NF}}) =$

   $\frac{1}{2}(\mathbf{m\widehat{AM} + m}\,\underline{\widehat{NF}})$

6. $\mathbf{m\angle GIF} = m\angle BAF = \frac{1}{2} m\,\underline{\widehat{BF}} =$

   $\frac{1}{2}(m\,\underline{\widehat{BF}} + m\widehat{BG} - m\widehat{BG}) = \frac{1}{2}(m\,\underline{\widehat{BF}}$

   $+ m\widehat{BG} - m\,\underline{\widehat{HA}}) = \frac{1}{2}(\mathbf{m\widehat{GBF} - m}\,\underline{\widehat{HA}})$

7. $\mathbf{m\angle JKF} = m\angle BAF = \frac{1}{2} m\,\underline{\widehat{BF}} =$

   $\frac{1}{2}(m\,\underline{\widehat{BF}} + m\widehat{JB} - m\widehat{JB}) = \frac{1}{2}(m\,\underline{\widehat{BF}}$

   $+ m\widehat{JB} - m\,\underline{\widehat{JA}}) = \frac{1}{2}(\mathbf{m\widehat{JBF} - m}\,\underline{\widehat{JA}})$

8. $\mathbf{m\angle JLM} = m\angle NMQ = \frac{1}{2} m\,\underline{\widehat{NM}} =$

   $\frac{1}{2}(m\,\underline{\widehat{NM}} + m\widehat{JN} - m\widehat{JN}) = \frac{1}{2}(m\,\underline{\widehat{NM}}$

   $+ m\widehat{JN} - m\,\underline{\widehat{JM}}) = \frac{1}{2}(\mathbf{m\widehat{JNM} - m}\,\underline{\widehat{JM}})$

9. Express verbally the bold-printed relationships in Exercises 4–8.

These exercises succinctly develop all the angle measurement theorems related to the circle that are generally taught in the high school geometry class. Students are led through a series of simple questions that, because of their structure, essentially prove the sought-after relationships. Discovery should be a natural result. We suggest interspersing discovery exercises with others, since their function satisfies only some of the purposes for assigning homework.

Summary

Teachers should be encouraged to constantly gather materials and ideas for enriching their teaching of mathematics. Regardless of the ability level of the students, appropriate enrichment activities can always be found. In some cases these enrichment activities may be harder to secure than in others, yet the process of searching for an appropriate topic can, in and of itself, prove to be of great benefit to the teacher.

Every teacher should make a genuine effort to enrich his or her instruction. Very often these motivating enrichment experiences go a long way toward developing a new appreciation for mathematics among the weaker or average students while being instrumental in encouraging further study in mathematics among the above-average and gifted students.

The Enrichment Units offered in this book should provide you with many ideas for enriching your teaching of mathematics. Another fine source of ideas is *A Bibliography of Recreational Mathematics*, Vols. 1–4, by W. L. Schaaf (Washington, DC: National Council of Teachers of Mathematics, 1970, 1973, 1978). With these tools at your disposal, you are ready to enrich your students' knowledge and appreciation of mathematics.

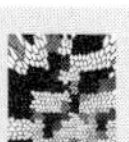

EXERCISES

1. Select a topic for enriching your instruction of each of the following:

   a. An average-ability eighth-grade mathematics class
   b. A gifted tenth-grade class
   c. A remedial ninth-grade class
   d. An average-ability eleventh-grade class
   e. A gifted seventh-grade class
   f. A gifted twelfth-grade class (currently studying calculus)

   Explain how you would treat each of the topics you listed. Specify how much material you would plan to cover.

2. For each of the following, select a grade level and ability level and provide an example of an enrichment topic that represents

   a. Expansion
   b. Digression

3. Suppose you are approached by the parents of one of your better-achieving students and asked to accelerate their son's mathematics instruction because they feel he is not being adequately challenged. Explain how you would deal with this request. Discuss your response to the parents and your actions before and after you give the response.

4. The parents of one of your deficient 9th-grade students have come to ask why you occasionally spend time with the class on "peripheral matters" (i.e., enrichment) instead of spending all your instructional time with remedial work. How would you answer these parents?

5. For a gifted class, prepare an outline for an enrichment unit for each of the following curriculum topics (specify whether it is an expansion or digression):

   a. Quadrilaterals (high school geometry course)
   b. Progressions (second year algebra course)
   c. Percentages (7th-grade mathematics class)
   d. Binomial theorem (11th- or 12-th-grade mathematics class)
   e. Angle measurement with a circle (high school geometry course)
   f. Systems of equations (first-year algebra course); also do this with a graphing calculator
   g. Quadratic equations (first-year algebra course)

6. Locate a secondary school mathematics textbook whose copyright date is earlier than 1950 and list the various types of enrichment activities included in the book. Repeat this activity with a textbook whose copyright date is later than 1980. Compare the two books with regard to their enrichment activities. How can you explain the differences in enrichment philosophies between the two books?

7. Choose a topic appropriate for the secondary school mathematics student that is not listed among the Enrichment Units in this book. Develop an enrichment activity based on your chosen topic in a style similar to that used in this book. This unit should be aimed at a gifted audience.

8. Choose a topic appropriate for the secondary school mathematics student that is not listed among the Enrichment Units in this book. Develop an enrichment activity based on your chosen topic in a style similar to that used in this book. This unit should be aimed at an average audience.

9. Choose a topic appropriate for the secondary school mathematics student that is not listed among the Enrichment Units in this book. Develop an enrichment activity based on your chosen topic in a style similar to that used in this book. This unit should be aimed at a lower ability audience.

Chapter 8

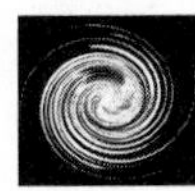

Extracurricular Activities in Mathematics

With the crowded mathematics curriculum at every level of the secondary school, teachers find extensive digressions from the sequential development of the mathematics course a hardship. Yet, a great benefit can be derived from a consideration of mathematics outside the regular curriculum. Teachers must therefore seek ways of providing students with mathematics that is extracurricular. Many extracurricular activities in mathematics can be conducted through the structure of a mathematics club, as well as in the regular classroom.

The Mathematics Club

Although the mathematics club structure can facilitate many of the activities to be discussed in this chapter, it is not necessary to form a club in order to conduct any of these activities. Forming a mathematics club requires substantial planning, ranging from a selection of participants (both a faculty sponsor and student members) to a determination of an organization and purpose. The germination of a mathematics club can come from an administrator or an interested teacher, as well as from a group of students interested in participating in such a club. Whatever the origin of the mathematics club, the teacher who is chosen as faculty sponsor should realize that a sizable investment of time, work, and effort will be required to make the venture successful. Naturally, the rewards for this investment usually make it all worthwhile. Club activities frequently allow the faculty sponsor to grow both mathematically and experientially. Because a mathematics club permits unlimited investigation of mathematical topics and applications beyond the scope of the secondary school curriculum, all involved can feel a sense of fulfillment that comes from a genuine appreciation of mathematics, its development, and its role in society.

Establishing a Mathematics Club

Once chosen, the faculty sponsor should begin to familiarize himself or herself with the task by discussing the problem of getting started with colleagues, administrators, and a select group of interested students. It is particularly helpful to seek out a mathematics club faculty sponsor in another school who may already have undergone similar experiences. Suggestions based on firsthand experiences and materials that have proved successful will be helpful to the new mathematics club sponsor, who would probably otherwise scramble for workable ideas. (See suggested readings for this chapter.)

After having received advice and suggestions from colleagues both in and outside school, and having gained the support of both the administration and a group of interested students, the teacher must tackle the job of recruiting. All paths of communication with the student body should be used. Announcements over the public address system, flyers sent to all homeroom sections, and student newspaper coverage of the new club should be included in the initial publicity. Especially important in the recruitment process is direct contact with mathematics classes that contain potential club members. This contact can be done by the class's teacher or by the faculty sponsor directly. The approach should be carefully planned so that the presentation about the club to these special classes is particularly attractive.

Part of the recruitment drive should involve inviting eligible students to an organizational meeting. This first meeting must have a carefully planned and well-thought-out agenda. Student input should be welcomed, yet the faculty sponsor might present the plans that were prepared in consultation with the administration and colleagues and have the group of interested students react. Although this prepared plan should be flexible and open for student suggestions, it is imperative there be one. For the faculty advisor to come to the first meeting unprepared, without some sort of plan, would be ill-advised. This first meeting might also be used for the selection of club officers, who would in turn form a steering committee. Together with the faculty sponsor, this committee would decide on time and frequency of meetings, membership eligibility, and, perhaps most important, the activities in which the club will engage. The rest of this chapter presents various extracurricular activities in mathematics that can be used with a mathematics club. However, a school may provide any of the activities without the structure of a mathematics club.

Mathematics Teams

Most regions of the country have mathematics leagues organized for the competition of local secondary schools. These competitions are usually organized on three levels: middle/junior high school students; senior high school students in grades 9, 10, and 11; and seniors in high school. The competition questions for each level are intended to be appropriately challenging yet within the scope of the student's knowledge of mathematics. Some mathematics leagues are organized so that schools compete directly against each other on a rotating basis; however, most leagues simply make an award to the team with the highest total score (e.g., number of correctly solved problems) at the end of the school year (or semester). Information about the mathematics leagues in your area can easily be obtained through local professional organizations or colleges.

It is likely that the school's mathematics team comprises students who are also members of the mathematics club. But recruiting should not by any means be limited to students in the mathematics club. There are likely to be some talented students in the school who, because of other commitments, were unable to join the mathematics club but might well join the mathematics team. In addition to obtaining teacher recommendations, the mathematics team coach should construct an entrance examination for all prospective candidates for the mathematics team. Such an examination should cover as wide a range of topics as possible, using the types of questions likely to come up at a mathematics team meet. In addition, the examination should include items in which a new topic (or concept) is introduced succinctly and then a question about this new topic asked. For such an examination for geometry students, one example might be to introduce Ptolemy's theorem and then ask a question that can be solved using that theorem.

EXAMPLE

Ptolemy's theorem: In an inscribed quadrilateral, the product of the lengths of the diagonals equals the sum of the products of the lengths of the opposite sides.

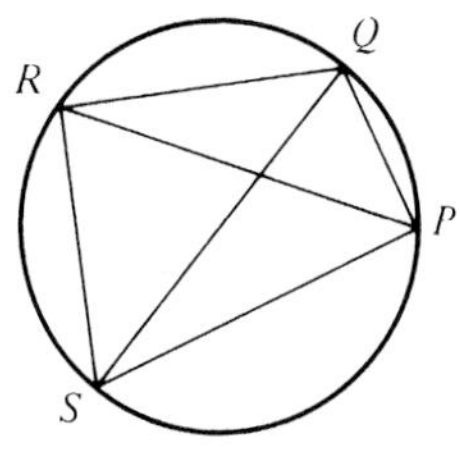

For the inscribed quadrilateral *PQRS*, Ptolemy's theorem gives us

$$(RP)(SQ) = (PQ)(RS) + (PS)(RQ).$$

Use Ptolemy's theorem to find the length of side $\overline{BC}$ of ΔABC, which is inscribed in a circle of radius of length 5. The lengths of $\overline{AB}$ and $\overline{AC}$ are 5 and 6, respectively.

The above-average mathematics student should correctly solve this problem with either answer: $3\sqrt{3} - 4$ or $3\sqrt{3} + 4$. The truly gifted mathematics student, however, will realize that there are *two* possible solutions, depending on whether $\angle A$ is acute or obtuse. A sample solution follows.

SOLUTION

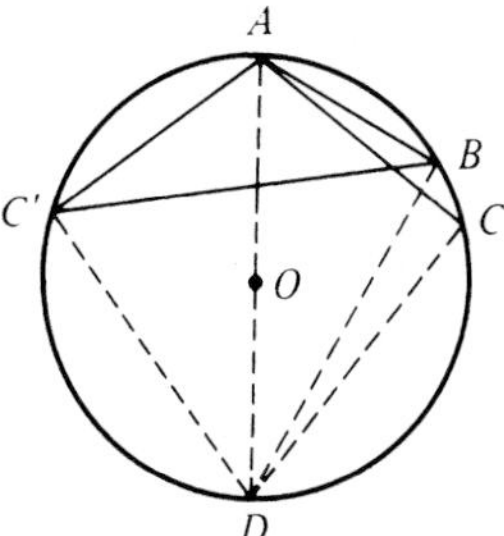

We notice that there are two possibilities to consider in this problem. Both ΔABC and $\Delta ABC'$ are inscribed in circle *O*, with $AB = 5$ and $AC = AC' = 6$. We are to find *BC* and *BC'*.

Draw diameter $\overline{AOD}$, which measures 10, and draw $\overline{DC}$, $\overline{DB}$, and $\overline{DC'}$. $m\angle AC'D = m\angle ACD = m\angle ABD = 90°$.

Consider the case in which $\angle A$ in ΔABC is acute. In right $\Delta ACD, DC = 8$, and in right $\Delta ABD, BD = 5\sqrt{3}$. By Ptolemy's theorem applied to quadrilateral *ABCD*,

$$(AC)(BD) = (AB)(DC) + (AD)(BC)$$

or

$$(6)(5\sqrt{3}) = (5)(8) + (10)(BC),$$

so

$$BC = 3\sqrt{3} - 4.$$

Now consider the case in which $\angle A$ is obtuse, as in $\Delta ABC'$. In right $\Delta AC'D, DC' = 8$. By Ptolemy's theorem applied to quadrilateral *ABDC'*,

$$(AC')(BD) + (AB)(DC') = (AD)(BC')$$

$$(6)(5\sqrt{3}) + (5)(8) = (10)(BC'), \text{ and}$$

$$BC' = 3\sqrt{3} + 4$$

In addition to testing a student's ability to use a newly learned fact, the preceding type of question permits the more able student to shine. The student will discover the ambiguity in the question posed and offer a complete solution. Each question on this entrance test should serve a clearly defined function.

Once the mathematics team members have been selected, a time must be set for them to be trained. Mathematics teams have been known to meet before the school day begins, during the lunch hour (students can eat their lunch while working on mathematics team activities), during the regular school day, or after the last period of the day. In some instances, the mathematics team might meet as a class. Some schools have chosen to give students course credit for a course on problem solving and special topics in mathematics that is not part of the secondary school curriculum. A course of this kind also serves to train members of a mathematics team. In addition to using the mathematics team materials listed at the end of this chapter, the mathematics team coach would be wise to try to obtain questions used at previous mathematics team meets. Knowing previous questions will give students an excellent idea as to what to expect at future mathematics team meets and how to prepare for them.

George Polya's classic book, *How to Solve It* (Princeton, NJ: Princeton University Press, 1945, 1973), is a good initial source for the mathematics team coach to use in preparing to train the mathematics team in problem-solving skills. Mathematics team training sessions provide an excellent opportunity to present topics normally not taught in the secondary school but useful for solving typical problems encountered at mathematics team meets. Another helpful source is A. Posamentier and S. Krulik's *Problem Solving Strategies for Efficient and Elegant Solutions* (Thousand Oaks, CA: Corwin, 1998).

The following list suggests some topics that might be useful to a mathematics team:

- Diophantine equations
- Means: arithmetic, geometric, and harmonic
- Modular arithmetic-algebra applications
- Divisibility tests
- Geometry theorems of Ceva, Menelaus, Ptolemy, Stewart, Heron, etc.
- Techniques in problem solving
- Various algebraic relationships
- Topics in number theory
- Sequences and series

Probability
Inequalities
Systems of equations
Topics from theory of equations
Maxima-minima problems in geometry and algebra

As an outgrowth of a discussion of these and many other appropriate mathematics topics, useful facts and relationships should be separately recorded by each student and kept available for ready reference. A student's collection of facts and relationships might include those listed at the end of this chapter.

Mathematics team coaching requires a total commitment from the faculty sponsor. In addition to preparing extensively and gathering previously used mathematics team questions (and other related materials), the faculty sponsor must be available for after-school mathematics team meets. This could likely involve traveling with the team to other schools. The work of the mathematics team coach requires much dedication, but the rewards are gratifying.

Mathematics Contests

Closely aligned with the activities of a mathematics team is the administration of various national, statewide, or local mathematics contests. These contests, including the American High School Mathematics Examination (AHSME) and the American Junior High School Mathematics Examination, which are sponsored chiefly by the Mathematical Association of America, are usually open to all students (not just those on the mathematics team). Extensive publicity in the school is required to attract as large a group for the contest as possible. Here students who may not be among the ten strongest mathematics students in the school can enter a contest for purely recreational reasons. Many of the questions on these mathematics contests are within reach of average mathematics students. (See the sample questions on page 215.) Naturally, these contests also contain challenging questions to help select the superior students. Often, schoolwide awards are given as well as regional, statewide, and sometimes national awards. As they are usually set up, the mathematics contests can offer entertainment and enrichment to a reasonably large portion of the school's population. These benefits are extended when the mathematics team coach reviews the contest problems with nonparticipating students after the contest has ended.

There are times when mathematics contests go beyond merely a test situation. A notable example is the American Regions Mathematics League (ARML). It involves an annual conference where teams of 15 students, representing winners of various city, county, and state competitions, meet to hear lectures on mathematics, compete against one another in yet another contest, and socialize.

The league continues to grow, currently representing states from most regions of the country. To facilitate matters, regional centers are used for these annual conferences.

High school mathematics contests generally go far toward promoting an interest in mathematics throughout the school. The National Council of Teachers of Mathematics as well as local mathematics teacher organizations are excellent sources of information about which mathematics leagues or which mathematics contests are available to your students.

Mathematics Projects

Consider assigning a term paper or doing a term project in your mathematics class. This activity has proved to be successful with groups of varying levels of ability. A mathematics project may take the form of a construction project such as curve stitching, special tool constructions, or construction of linkages. The term paper might involve an original investigation of some mathematics topic; it might report on an experiment that the student has conducted; it might be an exposition on some previously unfamiliar mathematics topic (this is best when not too broad in scope); or it might offer a discussion of a topic from the history of mathematics (e.g., involving the historical development of a topic or concept).

The topic for a mathematics project should be selected by the student, with the teacher serving as a facilitator by stimulating interest in various topics. Having selected a topic, the student should read as much about it as is available. Keeping accurate notes throughout this study period is essential for a successful project. Periodic conferences with the teacher will ensure that the student is kept properly on track. Careful notes taken during these sessions along with complete and accurate notes obtained from readings will make work on the written report simpler.

Listed below are some possible topics that students might use for a term paper (or project). This list is merely intended as a guide for generating additional topics.

Topics for Mathematics Projects

Advanced Euclidean Geometry
Algebraic Fallacies
Algebraic Models
Algebraic Recreations
Analog Computer
Ancient Number Systems and Algorithms
Arithmetic Fallacies
Arithmetic Recreations
Bases Other Than Ten
Binary Computer
Boolean Algebra
Brocard Points
Calculating Shortcuts
Cavalieri's Theorem
Checking Arithmetic Operations
Conic Sections
Continued Fractions
Cryptography
Crystallography
Curves of Constant Breadth

Cylindrical Projections
Desargues' Theorem
Determinants
Diophantine Equations
Divisibility of Numbers
Duality
Dynamic Symmetry
Elementary Number Theory Applications
The Euler Line
Extension of Euler's Formula to *N* Dimensions
Extension of Pappus's Theorem
Fermat's Last Theorem
Fibonacci Numbers
Fields
Finite Differences
Finite Geometry
The Five Regular Polyhedra
Flexagons
The Four-Color Problem
The Fourth Dimension
Fractals
Game Theory
Gaussian Primes
Geodesics
Geometric Dissections—Tangrams
Geometric Fallacies
Geometric Models
Geometric Stereograms
Geometric Transformations
Geometry of Bubbles and Liquid Film
Geometry of Catenary
Geometry Constructions (Euclid)
Gergonne's Problem
The Golden Section
Graphical Representation of Complex Roots of Quadratic and Cubic Equations
Groups
Higher Algebra
Higher Order Curves
Hyperbolic Functions
The Hyperbolic Paraboloid
Hypercomplex Numbers
Intuitive Geometric Recreations
Investigating the Cycloid
The Law of Growth
Linear Programming
Linkages
Lissajou's Figures
Lobachevskian Geometry
Logarithms of Negative and Complex Numbers
Logic
Magic Square Construction
Map Projections
Mascheroni's Constructions
Mathematics and Art
Mathematics and Music
Mathematics of Life Insurance
Matrices
Maximum-Minimum in Geometry
Means
Methods of Least Squares
The Metric System
Minimal Surfaces
Modulo Arithmetic in Algebra
Monte Carlo Method of Number Approximation
Multinomial Theorem
Napier's Rods
Networks
The Nine-Point Circle
Nomographs
The Number π, ϕ, or e
Number Theory Proofs
Paper Folding
Partial Fractions
Pascal's Theorem
Perfect Numbers
Polygonal Numbers
Prime Numbers
Probability
Problem Solving in Algebra
Projective Geometry
Proofs of Algebraic Theorems
Properties of Pascal's Triangle
Pythagorean Theorem—Triples
Regular Polygons
The Regular Seventeen-Sided Polygon
Relativity and Mathematics
Riemannian Geometry
Solving Cubics and Quartics
Special Factoring
Spherical Triangles
The Spiral
Statistics
Steiner Constructions
Tesselations
Theory of Braids
Theory of Equations
Theory of Perspectives

Three-Dimensional Curves
The Three Famous Problems of Antiquity
Topology
Unsolved Problems
Vectors

Sometime during the early stages of the project, the teacher should specifically indicate what the written product should include. The teacher should not fix the format and content so rigidly as to stifle creativity. The teacher might suggest individual conferences with students who find the suggested format inappropriate for their particular projects. Such features as a bibliography would probably be a part of all papers. Support of calculator and computer results should be encouraged, where appropriate.

The Mathematics Fair

In many regions of the country, regular (annual, semiannual, etc.) exhibitions of student mathematics projects are held. These range from schoolwide to national in scope. Some are locally sponsored; others may be sponsored by national organizations. Such information should be readily available from school administrators or local mathematics teacher organizations. The prospect of eventual exhibit at a mathematics fair could serve as additional motivation for students.

Naturally, when a student's project involves some physical model, such as a linkage or a geometric construction, the mere exhibition may be meaningful; however, when a student's project is a mathematical development or a study of some concept, then a presentation is necessary. Most mathematics fairs are organized to allow students to present their papers (orally) before a group of judges. In progressive stages, winners are selected, usually from each grade level entered. Community members are often attracted to such events.

The learning experience involved in the process of preparing a project or writing a paper, and then presenting or even defending it, is very valuable. Whether a student wins this fair competition is not as important as the recognition offered for his or her work.

Cooperation with a University

The proximity of a university could provide gifted youngsters with an opportunity to work alongside mathematicians. Here students could get firsthand experience of what mathematics is like beyond the instructional classroom. Students might become involved in the work the researcher is engaged in, or might pursue a parallel, yet somewhat lower level investigation under the tutelage of the mathematician. In either case, the enrichment can be quite productive. The student's end product might be worthy of submission to a mathematics fair or to a professional journal for publication. Affiliation with a local university can also provide gifted students with the opportunity to take some advanced mathematics courses. Care should be taken to select the appropriate instructors with whom to link students so that the experience becomes enriching rather than frustrating; the latter would clearly be counterproductive.

In the event that there is no university within reasonable proximity, a videoconference connection might be used to link students with working mathematicians. Such a connection might allow gifted students to engage in meaningful dialogue with research mathematicians and find out about their work. Further linkage might be through e-mail or other electronic connection.

The School Mathematics Magazine

A common activity for a mathematics club is the publication of a school mathematics magazine. A school mathematics journal could consist of some of the better student term papers (or projects). Student work (with some editorial refinements) could easily be disseminated by such a mathematics magazine. Typically such magazines are distributed (or sold) throughout the school and sent to other nearby schools, either to the students there or to the mathematics department head.

A project of this kind usually offers a productive activity for every member of the club. The more motivated mathematics students and the more advanced mathematics students might undertake writing the content of the prospective mathematics magazine, and the more artistic students might become involved in designing the layout, cover, and artwork. Others might be in charge of the business aspects of the project, such as publicity, circulation, or costs.

The role of the faculty sponsor is essentially that of a facilitator who defines the job and then allows students to adjust it to their needs and desires. As with any well-organized project, at least one person must be in charge of the entire project. Careful consideration of such things as organizational ability and leadership traits should be given before the student editor-in-chief is selected. The selection is most effective if it can come (at least in part) from the student group.

In addition to providing an outlet for exhibition of individual mathematics projects, a mathematics magazine will be a source of genuine pride on the part of all involved. Such an activity goes far in promoting an increased interest in mathematics while providing a good source for mathematics enrichment.

The Mathematics Assembly Program

Although less popular than a mathematics magazine, the mathematics assembly program may be an oral analog of the magazine. Students are provided an opportunity to exhibit some individual or group work to a larger audience. Most teachers' first reaction to the prospect of a mathematics assembly program is one of incredulity. The thought of presenting a program to a large heterogeneous group is overwhelming.

There are a variety of possibilities for such an assembly program. For example, a series of short skits could be presented to dramatize some of the major breakthroughs in the history of mathematics. These might also include some

Sample Mathematics Contest Questions

1. If $1 - \frac{4}{x} + \frac{4}{x^2} = 0$, then $\frac{2}{x}$ equals

   a. -1 b. 1 c. 2 d. -1 or 2 e. -1 or -2

2. If four times the reciprocal of the circumference of a circle equals the diameter of the circle, then the area of the circle is

   a. $\frac{1}{\pi^2}$ b. $\frac{1}{\pi}$ c. 1 d. π e. π^2

3. For all nonzero numbers x and y such that $x = \frac{1}{y}$, $\left(x - \frac{1}{x}\right)\left(y + \frac{1}{y}\right)$ equals

   a. $2x^2$ b. $2y^2$ c. $x^2 + y^2$ d. $x^2 - y^2$ e. $y^2 - x^2$

4. If $a = 1, b = 10, c = 100,$ and $d = 1000$, then $(a + b + c - d) + (a + b - c + d) + (a - b + c + d) + (-a + b + c + d)$ is equal to

   a. 1111 b. 2222 c. 3333
   d. 1212 e. 4242

5. Four boys bought a boat for \$60. The first boy paid one half of the sum of the amounts paid by the other boys; the second boy paid one third of the sum of the amounts paid by the other boys; and the third boy paid one fourth of the sum of the amounts paid by the other boys. How much did the fourth boy pay?

   a. \$10 b. \$12 c. \$13 d. \$14 e. \$15

6. The number of distinct pairs (x, y) of real numbers satisfying *both* of the equations

$$x = x^2 + y^2$$
$$y = 2xy$$

   is

   a. 0 b. 1 c. 2 d. 3 e. 4

7. Opposite sides of a regular hexagon are 12 inches apart. The length of each side, in inches, is

   a. 7.5 b. $6\sqrt{2}$ c. $5\sqrt{2}$ d. $\frac{9}{2}\sqrt{3}$ e. $4\sqrt{3}$

8. Al's age is 16 more than the sum of Bob's age and Carl's age, and the square of Al's age is 1632 more than the square of the sum of Bob's age and Carl's age. The sum of the ages of Al, Bob, and Carl is

   a. 64 b. 94 c. 96 d. 102 e. 140

9. How many pairs (m, n) of integers satisfy the equation $m + n = mn$?

   a. 1 b. 2 c. 3 d. 4 e. more than 4

10. Each of the three circles in the adjoining figure is externally tangent to the other two, and each side of the triangle is tangent to two of the circles. If each circle has radius 3, then the perimeter of the triangle is

    a. $36 + 9\sqrt{2}$ b. $36 + 6\sqrt{3}$

    c. $36 + 9\sqrt{3}$ d. $18 + 18\sqrt{3}$

    e. 45

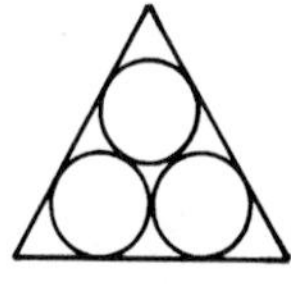

11. Three fair dice are tossed at random (i.e., all faces have the same probability of coming up). What is the probability that the three numbers turned up can be arranged to form an arithmetic progression with common difference one?

    a. $\frac{1}{6}$ b. $\frac{1}{9}$ c. $\frac{1}{27}$ d. $\frac{1}{54}$ e. $\frac{7}{36}$

12. If $y = (\log_2 3)(\log_3 4)\cdots(\log_n[n + 1])\cdots(\log_{31} 32)$, then

    a. $4 < y < 5$ b. $y = 5$ c. $5 < y < 6$

    d. $y = 6$ e. $6 < y < 7$

13. Let E be the point of intersection of the diagonals of convex quadrilateral $ABCD$, and let P, Q, R, and S be the centers of the circles circumscribing triangles ABE, BCE, CDE, and ADE, respectively. Then

    a. $PQRS$ is a parallelogram.
    b. $PQRS$ is a parallelogram if and only if $ABCD$ is a rhombus.
    c. $PQRS$ is a parallelogram if and only if $ABCD$ is a rectangle.
    d. $PQRS$ is a parallelogram if and only if $ABCD$ is a parallelogram.
    e. None of the above are true.

14. For how many paths consisting of a sequence of horizontal and/or vertical line segments, with each segment connecting a pair of adjacent letters in the adjoining diagram, is the word CONTEST spelled out as the path is traversed from beginning to end?

    a. 63 b. 128 c. 129
    d. 255 e. none of these

C
COC
CONOC
CONTNOC
CONTETNOC
CONTESETNOC
CONTESTSETNOC

light-hearted (yet instructive) skits, such as the story of young Gauss, described in Chapter 3 (page 68). A skit could be written dramatizing a useful application of a topic in secondary school mathematics. Here caution must be exercised so that topics selected are appropriate for the majority of the intended audience.

Successful mathematics assembly programs have been produced that involved having individual or small groups of students present short and highly stimulating topics to a general audience. For example, short arithmetic tricks are usually simple enough to generate interest among students of all abilities in the audience. The presenter may show the audience a method of multiplying 11 mentally. Multiplying 62 by 11 would involve simply adding $6 + 2$ and inserting this sum between the 6 and 2 to get 682. For a number like 75, the mental multiplication 75×11 would involve adding the tens digit of the sum $7 + 5$ to the 7 after inserting the units digit between the 7 and 5; that is, $75 \times 11 = 825$. For numbers of three or more digits, the rule involves adding every pair of digits starting from the right and each time successively inserting the units digit of the sum (carrying the tens digit) between the end digits. Thus, $3542 \times 11 = 3(3 + 5) \times (5 + 4)(4 + 2)2$, or 38,962.

Another exciting number "trick" might be the example on page 68 in Chapter 3. Here the whole audience can become actively involved. Simply have each student select his or her own three-digit number and follow the specified steps to attain 1089. The unusual result that everyone, regardless of the number they selected (within the guidelines), gets the same answer should certainly arouse student interest.

In part because of its visual nature, geometry offers many topics that might be appropriate for this type of mathematics assembly program. Cutting a very large Möbius strip first half the width from the edge and then one-third the width from the edge should produce some excitement in the audience. To avoid a lull in the presentation, it would be advisable to perforate (i.e., partially cut) the Möbius strip before the program.

Many other topological concepts can intrigue a general audience. Such topics might include removing a vest without removing a covering jacket, untying two people joined by ropes tied to their wrists without removing the ropes, and others. A perusal of the Enrichment Units in this book should enable you to come up with many additional ideas for a mathematics assembly program. Another fine source for such ideas is *Riddles in Mathematics* by E. P. Northrop (Princeton, NJ: Van Nostrand, 1944).

It is sometimes educational as well as entertaining for an audience to watch a mathematics quiz show on stage. Two teams might be selected to compete before a general audience. As long as the questions are presented clearly for all to hear and see, this experience might be stimulating to the audience, who would likely work along with the contestants on stage. Where possible, the questions selected for use should be within the realm of understanding of most students in the audience. A large screen should be used to present the questions to the audience.

The suggestions offered for a mathematics assembly program could also be used for a television production, either taped for viewing by individual classes or presented live through a closed circuit television system (if available) within a school or district. It is hoped that the ideas for possible programs presented will stimulate, and eventually generate, others that are appropriate to the intended audience.

Guest Speakers Program

Many areas throughout the country have mathematics speakers bureaus available to secondary schools. They are often sponsored by local universities or professional organizations. Generally, a listing of speakers, their addresses, and the topics on which they are prepared to speak is made available to all local schools. There is usually no cost to the host schools for this service. A customary activity for a mathematics club is to arrange the invitations for selected speakers and then to publicize each talk. Depending on the topic selected, the audience might be large or small, and it may be heterogeneous or homogeneous. It is probably most advisable to have students rather than a teacher select the speaker. Students will likely turn to the teacher for guidance and input. The teacher should be careful not to impose personal biases onto the speaker selection process, but merely provide guidance. The teacher might contact other secondary schools to find out which speakers were well received there and which were not. If properly planned, this activity could prove to be quite worthwhile.

Class Trips of Mathematical Significance

Large metropolitan areas offer many exciting examples of applications of mathematics. Teachers in these areas should occasionally avail themselves of these resources. For example, an engineering or research laboratory (such as Bell Laboratories or IBM Laboratory) might be of interest to students. Others may find a visit to a race track parimutuel installation interesting. There they can observe how betting odds are computed, a direct application of probability. There are occasionally special exhibits presented to motivate students toward further study in mathematics. These can also be used for an interesting mathematics class trip. A resourceful teacher will discover many other ideas for worthwhile mathematics class trips.

Proximity to a major metropolitan area is by no means necessary for a successful mathematics class trip. Every area has industry that relies heavily on mathematics. For example, if a road is being constructed, a class can benefit from observing engineers and surveyors preparing maps and other plans. Even a police helicopter automobile speed surveillance offers some interesting mathematics applications. In some localities a teacher's initiative and creativity will be more necessary than in others. This is part of the challenge of being a mathematics teacher!

Perhaps most important in preparing a successful class trip is careful planning. This refers to more than merely planning the logistics of the trip. Certainly the travel and other arrangements are necessary; however, perhaps even more important is planning a proper class preparation for the trip. The teacher should provide the class with the necessary mathematical and experiential background for a planned trip well before the departure dates. Background could entail presenting a topic that might otherwise not be taught, presenting a topic sooner than it otherwise would be reached, or perhaps embellishing a topic to make the trip more appropriate. Under certain circumstances, it may be possible to bring a representative from the place to be visited to the school, to motivate and prepare the students for the impending class trip. This extra dimension may help students get the most out of the planned trip. Planning a trip can be indispensable if it involves visiting a nearby museum with the purpose of seeking out only items of mathematical significance. These items can range from paintings and architecture to ancient tools. Whatever type of activity is involved, planning (including a preliminary visit by the teacher to the destination of the class trip) is an essential step in making a mathematics class trip a success.

Peer Teaching Program

A program of peer teaching can be conducted for all three levels of teaching: on-grade teaching, remediation, and enrichment. Perhaps it will be an activity that the mathematics club chooses to undertake or simply an activity initiated by a group of students along with a faculty advisor. Peer teaching can benefit the student doing the teaching as well as the student being taught. By teaching a concept or topic, one gains a much more comprehensive understanding of the topic. This understanding is, in part, the result of having to organize the presentation in an intelligible manner, which in turn causes the teacher to crystallize his or her thoughts on the topic. Although improved comprehension is usually not the primary reason for establishing a peer teaching program, it is an added benefit.

Before any peer teaching begins, time must be provided to train the students involved in teaching their peers. These students must be familiarized with basic teaching techniques and the resources available to them. It is natural to focus on the content when preparing peer teachers; however, a significant amount of time must be devoted to the actual teaching process.

Peer teaching can take various forms. It can be individualized tutoring, it can involve small groups of students, or it can supplement regular class instruction. Whichever format is used, substantial preparation must precede any peer teaching. Special skills are required for each type of instruction. If the peer teaching is to be for remedial purposes, then the peer teachers should be made aware of diagnostic procedures and trained to be sensitive to the needs of the slow learner. It is equally important for a peer teacher to know how to interest students considered average-ability learners. To ensure success with this activity, methods of instruction should be carefully developed.

When peer teaching is done by gifted students for the purpose of enriching others, a model can be established for involving a majority of the school population. For example, the faculty advisor may present enrichment topics to this select group of gifted peer teachers, or may set up a schedule of outside speakers to present various enrichment topics to these students. Once this has been done and the peer teachers feel reasonably comfortable with the new topic learned, they would convene under the guidance of a faculty member to set up a strategy for presenting this topic to various types of classes. The level of the intended audience should be considered carefully in the preparation of peer teaching. To the extent appropriate for varying ability levels, a majority of the students in the school can be offered enrichment in mathematics using this model.

Although we use the term *peer teaching* in the literal sense, the ideas presented here may easily be extended by having the "peer teachers" present material to younger students, either in the same school or in nearby lower schools. Under all circumstances, both content and methodology must be carefully planned before any peer teaching is attempted. Done properly, peer teaching can be rewarding for the peer teachers as well as for the students being taught.

The Computer

After students have demonstrated an acceptable degree of computer confidence and literacy, they should be encouraged to work with the computer during their unassigned school time or after classes have ended for the day. Students may find it fascinating to extend extracurricular explorations to two- and three-dimensional figures, real-world applications and modeling, random numbers, Mandelbrot's fractals, or whatever else they might reasonably choose.

The Bulletin Board

Every school should have at least one large bulletin board exclusively for mathematics and placed near the mathematics department office or near the mathematics classrooms. This bulletin board can tie together all the extracurricular activities described in this chapter. Both as an aid in providing these activities and as a means for publicity, the mathematics bulletin board can become indispensable in any secondary school. Often the bulletin board sets the tone for the mathematics department.

Some suggested uses for the mathematics bulletin board follow.

1. The bulletin board can be used to stimulate interest in a mathematical topic or process. Similarly, it can be used to motivate students for further study in mathematics by providing only enough material on a certain topic or concept to get students interested enough to do some individual research. Such motivation might well be in the form of a challenge as well as an open-ended question.
2. The results of mathematics team meets (including questions and model answers) can be exhibited on the bulletin board.
3. Mathematics contests (open to all students) can be publicized on the bulletin board.

4. The bulletin board can be the focus for an ongoing weekly intraschool mathematics contest, with a "Problem of the Week" posted weekly. Every week the preceding week's problem is shown along with a model solution and a list of successful solvers. Properly publicized by an enthusiastic teacher, this activity can set a very healthy mathematics atmosphere.
5. Mathematics club activities, including special events for nonmembers (e.g., guest speakers), can be publicized on the bulletin board.
6. Various appealing mathematics projects can be exhibited on the bulletin board. In addition, such events as mathematics fairs might also be publicized there.
7. The bulletin board also can be used to facilitate a peer teaching program by offering publicity and helping with the organization of the program.
8. Career guidance in mathematics, often sought after by stronger mathematics students, may well be given a place on the mathematics bulletin board.
9. The bulletin board may also be used to coordinate computer activities as well as display some more exceptional student programs, such as fractal art. Done attractively, this can help to extend the use of the computer to other students.
10. Seasonal displays as they relate to mathematics can be set up to entice students to investigate some unusual applications of mathematics (e.g., a spring display might relate phyllotaxis to the Fibonacci numbers).
11. The bulletin board can be used to post announcements by colleges and universities concerning special mathematics programs that are offered during the summer and academic year.

Summary

We have discussed many types of extracurricular activities in secondary school mathematics. Some of these activities are carried on outside of the mathematics class (such as clubs, teams, and contests); others can supplement the regular instruction (such as mathematics projects, guest speakers, and class trips).

It is highly unlikely that a single school will offer all these activities, yet an awareness of some options for extracurricular activities in mathematics is essential for designing an extracurricular program in mathematics suitable for a particular school. A good program of extracurricular activities in mathematics can go a long way toward strengthening the regular mathematics program in the school.

EXERCISES

1. Assume that you have volunteered to serve as faculty advisor to your school's mathematics club, which has been a department activity for some time. Your predecessor, who has just retired, was not very dynamic, and during his tenure the club membership declined sharply, and activities involving the club became few and far between. Explain the steps you would take to rejuvenate the club, increase its membership, and develop an attractive program of activities.
2. Assume that you have been coaching your school's mathematics team, which has been trained on a rather informal basis until now, mostly meeting during your spare time to work a few practice problems before each meet. Your supervisor advises you that next term the school is willing to make provision for scheduling the mathematics team as a formal class on your program. Formulate plans for improving the training program for members of the team and the topics you would plan to teach during the regularly scheduled class period, and justify your decisions.
3. In what type of mathematics class do you feel that a term paper or other project might be appropriately assigned as a requirement of the course? How would you respond to a student who feels that such a "chore" is a waste of time?
4. What would you do to encourage students to enter papers in a mathematics fair if they do not object to doing the research and writing the paper but do fear giving an oral presentation of their findings before a group of their peers and the judges?
5. Assume that you are the faculty advisor to the school's mathematics magazine. Address the following problems, and propose tentative solutions for each.
   a. Very few students are willing to expend the effort needed to write quality papers worthy of inclusion in the magazine.
   b. Too many articles are submitted for inclusion in the magazine. The student editorial staff fears rejecting any material submitted lest the authors be offended and never submit material again.
   c. The magazine sells poorly and you are unable to meet the expenses of its production.
   d. Conflict develops among the members of the student editorial board, and the editor-in-chief resigns 2 weeks before the due date of publication.
6. Plan a 40-minute mathematics assembly whose primary purpose is to fascinate a general audience of students and attract as many of them as possible to elect mathematics courses next term.

7. As faculty advisor to the mathematics club, you arrange for a speaker to be invited to address a meeting of the club. How would you deal with each of the following situations?
    a. The speaker's presentation is far over the heads of his audience and students begin to leave before the talk is completed.
    b. The speaker is boring, talks down to the students, discusses trivia to a great extent, and begins to lose his audience.
    c. The speaker's presentation degenerates into a sales pitch to have students apply for admission to the college at which the speaker is a faculty member.
    d. The speaker does not appear as scheduled.
8. The chapter discussed planning class trips and preparing students for the experiences they might have during the trip. What follow-up activities would be appropriate *after* the class has returned from a trip to make the trip a complete educational experience?
9. Assume that you are assigned to supervise a peer tutoring program operated by the mathematics department. Most of the tutors are members of the school's honor society and are in the highest mathematics classes in the department. The students being tutored often complain that their tutors are haughty, impatient with their slowness in learning, and sometimes confusing. Peer tutoring is a compulsory activity for honor society members in order to maintain their standing therein. How would you handle this situation?
10. As a professional assignment, your supervisor asks you to maintain the department bulletin board in an attractive manner. You find it cluttered with class honor rolls, announcements of coming activities, team scores, computer schedules, the "Problem of the Week," and many other items. What steps would you take to bring order out of a chaotic arrangement and develop a bulletin board of which the mathematics department can be proud?

Notes for the Mathematics Team

Triangle Properties

Stewart's Theorem:

$$pb^2 + qc^2 = a(d^2 + pq)$$

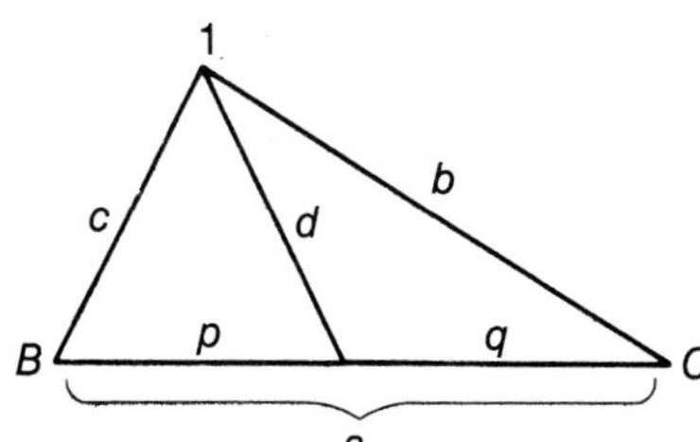

Angle Bisector Relationships:

1. $a : b = m : n$
2. $ab - mn = t_c^2$
3. $t_c = \dfrac{2\sqrt{abs(s - c)}}{a + b}$

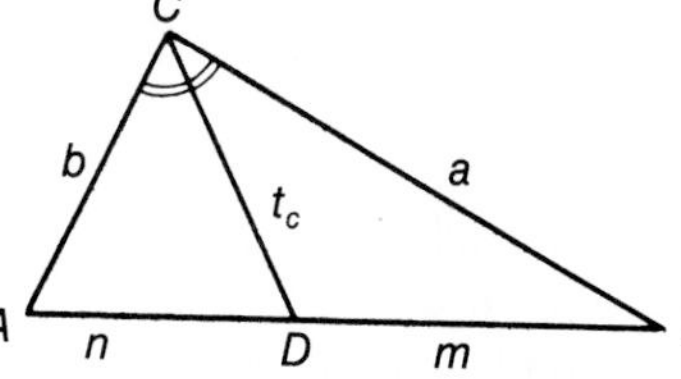

4. The point of intersection of the angle bisectors is the center of the inscribed circle of the triangle.

Triangle Median Relationships:

1. $m_a = \frac{1}{2}\sqrt{2b^2 + 2c^2 - a^2}$
2. $m_a^2 + m_b^2 + m_c^2 = \frac{3}{4}(a^2 + b^2 + c^2)$
3. $(a + b + c) > (m_a + m_b + m_c) > \frac{3}{4}(a + b + c)$
4. The medians of a triangle are concurrent at a point that trisects each median.
5. The median partitions a triangle into two triangles of equal area.
6. In a right triangle, the median to the hypotenuse
    a. divides the triangle into two isosceles triangles;
    b. is one-half the length of the hypotenuse.

Triangle Altitude Relationships:

1. $ah_a = bh_b = ch_c = 2\mathscr{A}$ (where $\mathscr{A}$ represents the area)
2. $a : \frac{1}{h_a} = b : \frac{1}{h_b} = c : \frac{1}{h_c} = 2\mathscr{A}$ or $h_a : h_b : h_c = \frac{1}{a} : \frac{1}{b} : \frac{1}{c} = bc : ac : ab$
3. $h_c = \frac{ab}{2R}$ (where R is the circumradius)

Area of a Triangle:

1. $\mathscr{A} = \frac{1}{2}ah_a$
2. $\mathscr{A} = \frac{1}{2}ab \sin C$
3. $\mathscr{A} = \frac{abc}{4R}$ (where R is the circumradius)
4. $\mathscr{A} = rs$ (where r is the inradius)
5. $\mathscr{A} = \sqrt{s(s - a)(s - b)(s - c)}$ (where s is the semiperimeter) (*Heron's formula*)
6. $\mathscr{A} = \dfrac{b^2 \sin A \sin C}{2 \sin(A + C)}$
7. For an equilateral triangle: $\mathscr{A} = \frac{S^2\sqrt{3}}{4} = \frac{h^2\sqrt{3}}{3}$ (where S is a side, h is the altitude)

8. The ratio of the areas of two triangles having an angle of equal measure equals the ratio of the products of the lengths of the pairs of sides including the congruent angles.

Inscribed and Circumscribed Circles of a Triangle:

1. $r = \frac{a}{s}\sqrt{\frac{(s-a)(s-b)(s-c)}{s}}$ (r is the inradius)

2. $R = \frac{abc}{4\mathcal{A}}$ (R is the circumradius)

3. $\frac{a}{\sin A} = \frac{b}{\sin B} = \frac{c}{\sin C} = 2R$

4. Radius of an *escribed circle*: $r_a = \sqrt{\frac{s(s-b)(s-c)}{s-a}}$

To Find the Measure of an Angle of a Triangle:

$$\cos A = \frac{b^2 + c^2 - a^2}{2bc} \quad \text{(law of cosines)}$$

Pythagorean Triples:

$a^2 + b^2 = c^2$, where $a = u^2 - v^2; b - 2uv; c = u^2 + v^2$; and $u > v$ for integers u and v.

Transversal Theorem:

1. In Figure 1, $\overline{AL}$, $\overline{BM}$, and $\overline{CN}$ are concurrent. Therefore, $AN \cdot BL \cdot CM = AM \cdot BN \cdot CL$. (Ceva's Theorem)

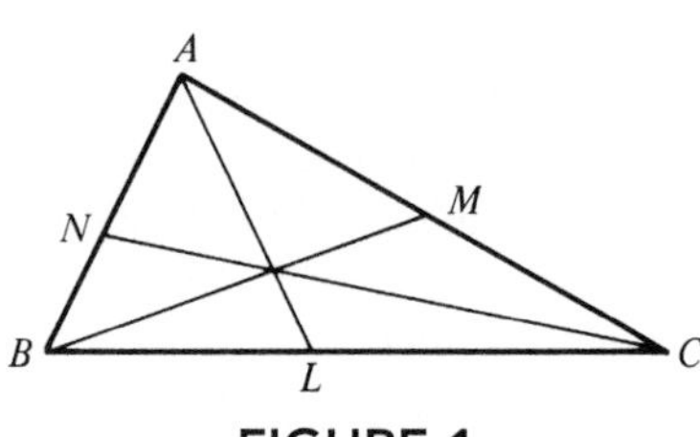

FIGURE 1

2. In Figure 2, points P, Q, and R are collinear. Therefore, $AP \cdot BR \cdot CQ = AQ \cdot BP \cdot CR$. (Menelaus's Theorem)

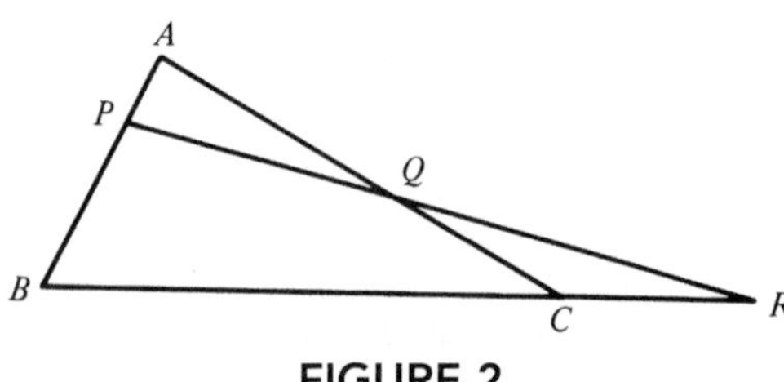

FIGURE 2

3. In Figure 3, lines a, b, and c are parallel. Therefore,

$$\frac{1}{a} + \frac{1}{b} = \frac{1}{c}; \frac{a}{x} = \frac{b}{y}.$$

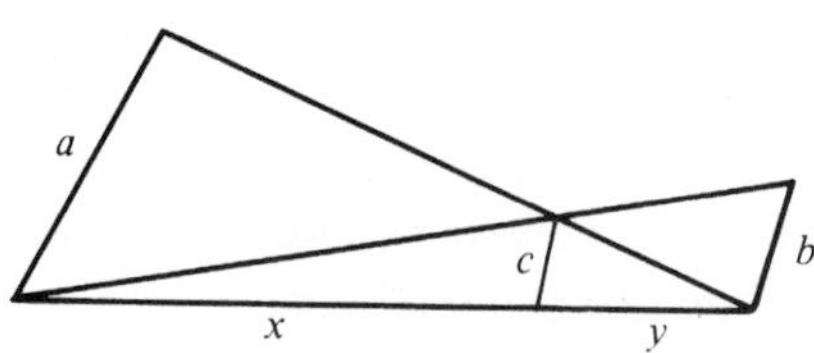

FIGURE 3

Properties of Polygons

1. The sum of the measures of the interior angles = $(n-2)\,180°$, where n = number of sides.
2. The sum of the measures of the exterior angles = 360°.
3. In an *equiangular polygon:*
   a. The measure of each interior angle = 180° − (measure of exterior angle).
   b. The measure of each interior angle $= \frac{(n-2)180°}{n}$.
   c. Each exterior angle has measure $= \frac{360°}{n}$.

Regular Polygons:

1. Triangle: $\mathcal{A} = \frac{S^2\sqrt{3}}{4} = \frac{h^2\sqrt{3}}{3} = \frac{3R^2\sqrt{3}}{4} = 3r^2\sqrt{3}$

2. Pentagon: $S = \sqrt{2r\sqrt{5} - 2\sqrt{5}} = \frac{1}{2}R\sqrt{10 - 2\sqrt{5}}$

3. Hexagon: $S = R$, and $\mathcal{A} = \frac{3}{2}R^2\sqrt{3} = 2r^2\sqrt{3}$
4. Octagon: $S = 2r(\sqrt{2} - 1) = R\sqrt{2 - \sqrt{2}}$
5. Decagon: $S = \frac{2}{5}r\sqrt{25 - 10\sqrt{5}} = \frac{1}{2}R(\sqrt{5} - 1)$
6. Dodecagon: $\mathcal{A} = 3R^2$
7. General: $\mathcal{A} = \frac{1}{2}ap = \frac{1}{2}rp$ (a = apothem; p = perimeter)

Areas of Quadrilaterals:

1. Rectangle: $\mathcal{A} = bh$
2. Square: $\mathcal{A} = S^2 = \frac{1}{2}d^2 = 2R^2 = 4r^2$
3. Parallelogram: $\mathcal{A} = bh = ab \sin C$
4. Rhombus: $\mathcal{A} = bh = \frac{1}{2}d_1d_2 = ab \sin C$
5. Trapezoid: $\mathcal{A} = \frac{1}{2}h(b_1 + b_2)$

Miscellaneous Triangle and Quadrilateral Theorems:

1. The sum of the lengths of the perpendiculars on the legs of an isosceles triangle from any point on the base is equal to the length of an altitude on one of the legs.

2. In an equilateral triangle, the sum of the lengths of the perpendiculars from any point to the three sides is equal to the length of an altitude.
3. In a circumscribed quadrilateral, the sum of the lengths of the opposite sides are equal.
4. In an inscribed quadrilateral, the sum of the products of the lengths of the opposite sides equals the product of the lengths of the diagonals (*Ptolemy's theorem*).
5. The area of a cyclic quadrilateral (i. e., an inscribed quadrilateral $= \sqrt{(s-a)(s-b)(s-c)(s-d)}$ (*Brahmagupta's formula*).
6. In any parallelogram, the sum of the squares of the lengths of the diagonals equals the sum of the squares of all the lengths of the sides.
7. In any triangle whose sides are 13, 14, 15, h_{14} divides side 14 into segments 5 and 9, and h_{14} is 12.
8. In any triangle, the square of the length of a side opposite an acute angle is equal to the sum of the squares of the lengths of the other two sides diminished by twice the product of the length of one of those sides and the length of the projection of the other side upon it.

(For ΔABC: $a^2 = b^2 + c^2 - 2cp$.)

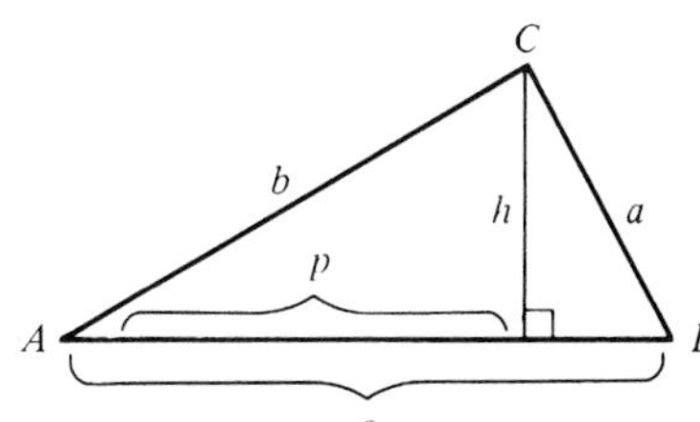

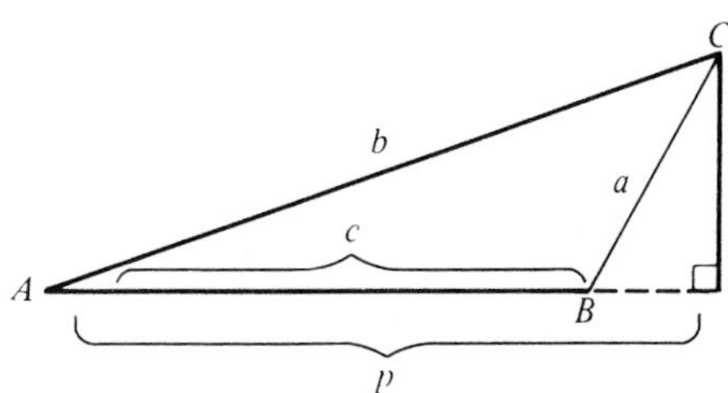

9. In any obtuse triangle, the square of the length of the side opposite the obtuse angle is equal to the sum of the squares of the lengths of the other two sides increased by twice the product of the length of one of these sides and the length of the projection of the other side upon it.

(For obtuse ΔABC: $a^2 = b^2 + c^2 + 2cp$.)

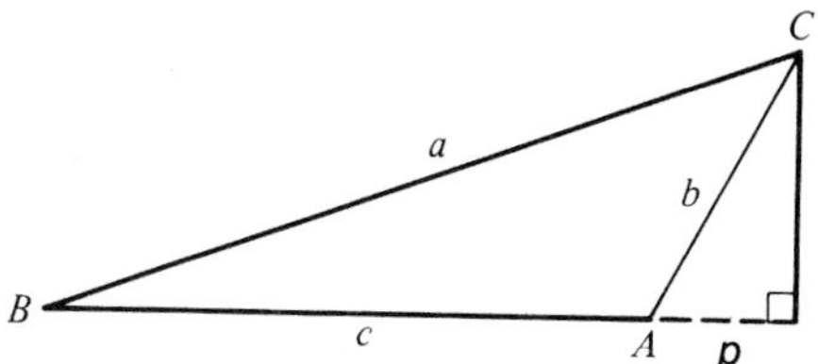

Miscellaneous Theorems on Perimeter and Area

1. Of all triangles having the same base and equal areas, the isosceles triangle has the minimum perimeter.
2. Of all triangles having the same base and equal perimeters, the triangle whose other two sides are congruent has the greatest area.
3. Of all polygons constructed with the same given sides in a given order, that which can be inscribed in a circle has the greatest area.
4. Of two regular polygons with equal perimeters, that which has the greatest number of sides has the greater area.
5. If similar polygons are constructed on the three sides of a right triangle, the sum of the areas of the polygons on the legs is equal to the area of the polygon on the hypotenuse. (This is an extension of the Pythagorean theorem.)

Pappus's Theorem

A *volume* that is generated by the motion of a plane section through space equals the product of the area of the plane section and the length of the path of the center of gravity of the plane section.

Some Number Theory Facts

1. Divisibility by 2: last digit of number is even.
2. Divisibility by 3: sum of the digits is divisible by 3.
3. Divisibility by 4: last two digits when considered as a number are divisible by 4 (e.g., 7812).
4. Divisibility by 5: last digit 5 or 0.
5. Divisibility by 6: rules for divisibility by 2 and 3.
6. Divisibility by 8: last three digits when considered as a number are divisible by 8 (e.g., 57256).
7. Divisibility by 9: sum of the digits is divisible by 9.
8. Divisibility by 10: last digit is 0.
9. Divisibility by 11: the difference of the sums of alternate digits is divisible by 11.
10. Divisibility by 12: rules for divisibility by 3 and 4.
11. *Fermat's theorem*: $N^{p-1} - 1 =$ multiple of p, where p is prime and N is prime relative to p (e.g., $3^{7-1} - 1$ is a multiple of 7).

Factoring

1. For odd e:
$$x^e + y^e = (x+y)(x^{e-1} - x^{e-2}y + x^{e-3}y^2 - \cdots + y^{e-1})$$
2. For all e:
$$x^e - y^e = (x-y)(x^{e-1} + x^{e-2}y + x^{e-3}y^2 + \cdots + y^{e-1})$$
3. For even e:
$$x^e + y^e = (x^{e/2} + y^{e/2})(x^{e/2} - y^{e/2})$$

Binomial Theorem

$$(a+b)^n = a^n + na^{n-1}b + \frac{n(n-1)}{1\cdot 2}a^{n-2}b^2 + \frac{n(n-1)(n-2)}{1\cdot 2\cdot 3}a^{n-3}b^3 + \cdots + b^n$$

Logarithms

1. $\log_a b = x$ means $a^x = b$
2. $(\log_a b)(\log_b c) = \log_a c$

Inequalities

1. $a + \frac{1}{a} \geq 2$
2. $\frac{a}{b} + \frac{b}{a} \geq 2$
3. $\frac{a+b}{2} \geq \frac{2ab}{a+b}$

Means

Arithmetic Mean (AM): $= \frac{a+b}{2}$

Geometric Mean (GM): $= \sqrt{ab}$

Harmonic Mean (HM): $= \frac{2ab}{a+b}$

1. $AM \geq GM \geq HM$
2. $(AM)(HM) = (GM)^2$

Enrichment Units for the Secondary School Classroom

A wide variety of mathematics topics are well suited as enrichment for secondary school mathematics courses. We can draw such topics from all branches of mathematics, and many of these clearly reinforce the NCTM standards. Numerical curiosities, algebraic investigations of number relationships, geometric phenomena not usually available to this audience, as well as many other topics generally not found in the secondary school or college curricula, are among the units found in this part of the book.

A very common topic viewed from a not-so-common viewpoint would certainly provide enrichment for the appropriate audience. The trick to providing students with enrichment activities is to present the material in a highly motivating and intelligible manner. This challenging objective will guide us through the units presented here. It should be remembered from the outset that enrichment activities are *not* limited only to gifted students. As you will see throughout this part of the book, many enrichment activities can be used successfully with students of average mathematical ability as well as in remedial classes, provided proper adjustments are made. Naturally these modifications in the presentation (both in content and in method of presentation) can be made only by the classroom teacher using the material. With this in mind, let us consider the format in which these enrichment units are presented.

Each enrichment unit treats a separate topic. With few exceptions, the topics can be considered in almost any order. Following a brief introduction, *Performance Objectives* for that unit are stated. Not only do these objectives succinctly foreshadow the content of the unit, but they provide a good indication of the scope of the material that follows. So you can determine better the suitability of the unit for your class, a *Preassessment* section is offered. In addition to assisting you to ascertain your students' readiness for the unit, this section often also serves as a source for motivation you may wish to use in presenting the topic to your class.

In the next section, *Teaching Strategies*, the enrichment topic is presented in a manner that you may use to introduce it to your class. Here the topic is carefully developed with an eye toward anticipating possible pitfalls and hurdles students may encounter along the way. The style is conversational throughout, making the reading more relaxed. Occasionally suggestions for extensions are offered so that the units do not appear to be terminal. Perhaps an underlying goal throughout these enrichment units is to allow them to serve as springboards for further investigation. Where appropriate, additional references are offered for further study.

One efficient way to ascertain whether the objectives for a particular unit have been met is to question the students on the topic presented. Sample questions are provided in the *Postassessment* section at the end of the unit. You are invited to augment these questions with some of your own where needed.

Since many of these enrichment units can be used in a variety of different mathematics classes and with students of different levels of mathematical ability, a cross-cataloguing chart is provided. The chart will enable you to select enrichment units according to subject, grade level, and student ability level. Naturally, you will need to make some modifications in the form to make the unit properly suit the intended audience. Many of these enrichment units very clearly support the NCTM standard of making connections, since they demonstrate how topics and concepts traditionally taught in one context can be used fruitfully in an entirely unexpected context.

On the whole, you ought to make every effort to inject enrichment activities into all your mathematics instruction, regardless of the students' mathematical ability. Such activities can be just as rewarding in a remedial class as in one comprised of gifted students. The benefit, although manifested differently, should be about the same for all classes.

The authors gratefully acknowledge the technical contributions to these enrichment units made by Dr. Peter Brouwer, SUNY–Potsdam.

Cross-Catalogue of Enrichment Units

To facilitate using the enrichment units found in this section, a cross-catalogue is provided. The units are listed in the order in which they are presented in this section (page numbers for each Unit are listed in the Table of Contents). The grade level, the ability level, and the branch of mathematics to which each unit is related are provided. These assessments are simply the opinion of the authors and some secondary school teachers. You may, however, try these units with audiences other than those specified.

You will notice that each ability level—Remedial, Average, or Gifted—has been partitioned into four grade level divisions: 7–8, 9, 10, 11–12.

For the remedial student, grades 7–8 are usually the junior high school low-level mathematics courses; at grades 9 and 10, a general mathematics or introductory algebra is assumed. At grades 11–12 there is usually a continuation of the earlier courses, but with a greater degree of sophistication.

The average student partition refers to the junior high school prealgebra program for grades 7–8, the elementary algebra course for grade 9, the high school geometry course for grade 10, and the second-year algebra (with trigonometry) course and beyond for grades 11–12.

Although very often the gifted student begins the study of elementary algebra in the eighth grade (or earlier), for the sake of simplicity we shall use the same course determination for the gifted students as for the average students (above). A greater ability in mathematics is assumed here, however.

The numbers 1 and 2 indicate the primary and secondary audiences for each unit. This implies that variations of these units can (and should) be used at all levels as you deem appropriate. Naturally, some modifications will have to be made. Some units may have to be "watered down" for weaker mathematics students, and for more gifted youngsters some units may serve as springboards for further investigation.

Ratings

1. Primary use (specifically intended for that audience)
2. Secondary use (may be used for that audience with some modifications)

Another important consideration when selecting an enrichment unit is the branch of mathematics to which it is related. For many units this is difficult to isolate, since these units relate to many branches of mathematics. Using the following code, the *Subject* column indicates the related branches of mathematics. Although very often the order could easily be changed with no loss of accuracy, every attempt has been made to list the branches of mathematics in descending order of relevance to each unit, as judged by a group of mathematics teachers.

Subject Code

1. Arithmetic
2. Number theory
3. Probability
4. Logic
5. Algebra
6. Geometry
7. Analytic geometry
8. Topology
9. Statistics
10. Problem solving
11. Applications
12. Mathematical curiosities

Technology Applications

The chart shows which technology applications might be used with specific enrichment units. However, the reader should make the final evaluation/decision.

ENRICHMENT UNIT TABLE

Unit	Unit Name	Subject Code	Scientific Calculator	Graphing Calculator or Graphing Software	Spreadsheet	Geometer's Sketchpad	Remedial Classes 7–8	9	10	11–12	Average Classes 7–8	9	10	11–12	Gifted Classes 7–8	9	10	11–12
1	Constructing Odd-Order Magic Squares	1,4,12					1	1	1	2	1	2						
2	Constructing Even-Order Magic Squares	1,12					1	1	1	2	1	2						
3	Introduction to Alphametics	1,4					2	2	1	1	1	1			1	2		
4	A Checkerboard Calculator	1,12					1	1	1	2	1	2			2	2		
5	The Game of Nim	4,1,12					2	1	1	1	1	2			2	2		
6	The Tower of Hanoi	4,1,12					2	1	1	1	1	2			2	2		
7	What Day of the Week Was It?	4,1,12					2	2	1	1	1	1			1	2		2
8	Palindromic Numbers	2,1,12					1	1	2	2	1	1		2	1	1		2
9	The Fascinating Number Nine	1,2,12					2	1	1	1	1	2			1	2		
10	Unusual Number Properties	1,2,12					2	1	1	1	1	2			1	2		
11	Enrichment with a Handheld Calculator	1,2,12					1	1	1	1	1	2			1	2		
12	Symmetric Multiplication	1,2,12					2	1	1	1	1	2		2	1	2		
13	Variations on a Theme—Multiplication	1,2,12					2	1	1	1	1	2		2	1	2		2
14	Ancient Egyptian Arithmetic	2,1						2	2	1	1	2		2	1	1		2
15	Napier's Rods	1,2,11					1	1	1	1	1	2		2	2			
16	Unit Pricing	1,11					1	1	1	1	1	2						
17	Successive Discounts and Increases	1,11,12					2	2	1	1	1	1		2	1	2		
18	Prime and Composite Factors of a Whole Number	1,2					1	1	1	2	2	2						
19	Prime Numeration System	2,1,12						2	1	1	2	1		2	1			

Unit	Unit Name	Subject Code	Scientific Calculator	Graphing Calculator or Graphing Software	Spreadsheet	Geometer's Sketchpad	Remedial Classes 7–8	9	10	11–12	Average Classes 7–8	9	10	11–12	Gifted Classes 7–8	9	10	11–12
20	Repeating Decimal Expansions	2,1	■							2	2	1		2	2			
21	Peculiarities of Perfect Repeating Decimals	2,1,12	■								1	1		2	1	2		
22	Patterns in Mathematics	4,5			■				2	2	1	1			2	2		
23	Googol and Goopolplex	1,12	■		■		2	1	1	2	1	2			2			
24	Mathematics of Life Insurance	3,9,5	■		■				2	2		2		1	2	1		2
25	Geometric Dissections	6,4,10				■			2	2	1	1	1		1	1	2	
26	The Klein Bottle	8										2	1	2	1	1	1	2
27	The Four-Color Map Problem	8,4									1	1	1	2	1	2		
28	Mathematics on a Bicycle	6,4,1			■			2	1	1	1	2	2		2			
29	Mathematics and Music	11,1										2	2	2	1	1		2
30	Mathematics in Nature	11,12,2	■		■			2	2	2	1	1	1	2	1	1	2	2
31	The Birthday Problem	3,12,11	■		■				2	2	2	1	2	1	1	1	1	1
32	The Structure of the Number System	1,5									2	1	2	1	1	1		
33	Excursions in Number Bases	2,1,5						2	2	2	1	1	2	2	1	2		2
34	Raising Interest	5,11	■		■							1		1	1	1		2
35	Reflexive, Symmetric, and Transitive Relations	4,2									1	1	1		1	1	2	
36	Bypassing an Inaccessible Region	6,10				■						2	1	1		1	1	
37	The Inaccessible Angle	6,10				■						2	1	1		1	1	
38	Triangle Constructions	6,10				■						2	1	1		1	1	1
39	The Criterion of Constructibility	6,5				■							1	1		1	1	1
40	Constructing Radical Lengths	6,5				■						2	1	1		1	1	2
41	Constructing a Pentagon	6,5				■						1	1	1		1	1	1
42	Investigating the Isoscles Triangle Fallacy	6,12				■							1	1		2	1	1

Unit	Unit Name	Subject Code	Scientific Calculator	Graphing Calculator or Graphing Software	Spreadsheet	Geometer's Sketchpad	Remedial Classes 7–8	9	10	11–12	Average Classes 7–8	9	10	11–12	Gifted Classes 7–8	9	10	11–12
43	The Equiangular Point	6											1	1		2	1	2
44	The Minimum-Distance Point of a Triangle	6											1	1		2	1	2
45	The Isosceles Triangle Revisited	6,10											1			2	1	2
46	Reflective Properties of the Plane	6,11										2	1	1		1	1	2
47	Finding the Length of a Cevian of a Triangle	6,5										2	1	1			1	
48	A Surprising Challenge	6,10											1	2		2	1	
49	Making Discoveries in Mathematics	6									2	1	1	1	1	1	2	
50	Tessellations	6,5									2	2	1	1	2	1	1	2
51	Introducing the Pythagorean Theorem	6,2,5										1	1	2		1	1	2
52	Trisection Revisited	6,5,12									2	1	1	1	2	1	1	2
53	Proving Lines Concurrent	6,10											2	2		2	1	2
54	Squares	6,10											1	2		1	1	2
55	Proving Points Collinear	6,10											2	2		2	1	1
56	Angle Measurement with a Circle	6											1			2	1	
57	Trisecting a Circle	6,12										1	1	2		1	1	2
58	Ptolemy's Theorem	6,10										2	1	1		1	1	2
59	Constructing π	6,1										2	1	1		1	1	2
60	The Arbelos	6,5										2	1	1		1	1	1
61	The Nine-Point Circle	6									2	2	1	2	2	1	1	2
62	The Euler Line	6										2	1	2	2	1	1	2
63	The Simson Line	6									2	2	1	2	2	1	1	2
64	The Butterfly Problem	6,10									2	2	1	2	2	1	1	1
65	Equicircles	6,5											1	2		2	1	1
66	The Inscribed Circle and the Right Triangle	6,5											2	2		2	1	1

Unit	Unit Name	Subject Code	Scientific Calculator	Graphing Calculator or Graphing Software	Spreadsheet	Geometer's Sketchpad	Remedial Classes 7–8	9	10	11–12	Average Classes 7–8	9	10	11–12	Gifted Classes 7–8	9	10	11–12
67	The Golden Rectangle	6,5,2										2	1	1		1	1	2
68	The Golden Triangle	6,5,2											1	1		1	1	1
69	Geometric Fallacies	6,5											1	1		1	1	2
70	Regular Polyhedra	6,5								2		2	2	1	2	1	1	1
71	An Introduction to Topology	8,4						2	2	1	1	1	1	2	1	1	1	2
72	Angles on a Clock	1,5					1	1	1	1	1	1	1	2	1	1	2	2
73	Averaging Rates—The Harmonic Mean	5,1							2	2	1	1	2	1	1	1	2	2
74	Howlers	1,5					1	1	1	1	1	1	1	1	1	1	1	1
75	Digit Problems Revisited	5,1					1	1	1	1	1	1	1	1	1	1	1	1
76	Algebraic Identities	5,6										1	1	2		1	2	
77	A Method for Factoring Trinomials of the Form $ax^2 + bx + c$	5										1	2	1		1		2
78	Solving Quadratic Equations	5,10										1	2	1		1		1
79	The Euclidean Algorithm	2,5										1		1		1		1
80	Prime Numbers	2,5										2		2		1		1
81	Algebraic Fallacies	5,12										1	2	1		1	2	1
82	Sum Derivations with Arrays	5,6,12								2	2	1	2	1	1	1		1
83	Pythagorean Triples	2,5,6										2	1	1	2	1	1	1
84	Divisibility	2,1,5					2	1	1	1	1	1	2	1	1	1	2	1
85	Fibonacci Sequence	5,2,12			See Unit 19				2	2	2	1	2	1	1	1	2	1
86	Diophantine Equations	5,2										2		1	2	1	2	1
87	Continued Fractions and Diophantine Equations	5,2										2		1	2	1	2	1
88	Simplifying Expressions Involving Infinity	5,2										2		1	2	1	2	1

Unit	Unit Name	Subject Code	Scientific Calculator	Graphing Calculator or Graphing Software	Spreadsheet	Geometer's Sketchpad	Remedial Classes 7–8	9	10	11–12	Average Classes 7–8	9	10	11–12	Gifted Classes 7–8	9	10	11–12
89	Continued Fraction Expansion of Irrational Numbers	5										2		1		1	2	1
90	The Farey Sequence	1,5						2	2	2	2	1	2	1	1	1	2	2
91	The Parabolic Envelope	6,7		■		■			2	2	2	2	1	1	1	1	1	1
92	Application of Congruence to Divisibility	2,5												2	2	1	2	1
93	Problem Solving—A Reverse Strategy	10,6,5				■						1	1	2	2	1	1	2
94	Decimals and Fractions in Other Bases	1,5										2	2	1	2	1	2	1
95	Polygonal Numbers	2,5			■					2		1	1	1	2	1	1	1
96	Networks	4,5,11,8							2	1	2	1	1	1	2	1	1	1
97	AngleTrisection—Possible or Impossible?	5,6,2											2	1		2	1	1
98	Comparing Means	5,2,6	■			■						1	1	1		1	1	1
99	Pascal's Pyramid	5			See Unit 119									1		2	1	1
100	The Multinomial Theorem	5,1,4	■									2		1		1	2	1
101	Algebraic Solution of Cubic Equations	5												2		1		1
102	Solving Cubic Equations	5										2		2		1		1
103	Calculating Sums of Finite Series	5			■							2		1		1		1
104	A General Formula for the Sum of Series of the Form $\sum_{t=1}^{n} t^r$	5	■											2		2		1
105	A Parabolic Calculator	7,5		■					2		2	2	1			1	1	1
106	Constructing Ellipses	6,5,12,7				■					2	2	1		1	1	1	
107	Constructing the Parabola	6,7,5				■			2	2	2	2	1	1	1	1	1	2

Unit	Unit Name	Subject Code	Scientific Calculator	Graphing Calculator or Graphing Software	Spreadsheet	Geometer's Sketchpad	Remedial Classes 7–8	9	10	11–12	Average Classes 7–8	9	10	11–12	Gifted Classes 7–8	9	10	11–12
108	Using Higher Plane Curves to Trisect an Angle	7,5,6											2	1		1	1	1
109	Constructing Hypocycloid and Epicycloid Circular Envelopes	6,5,7											2	1		1	1	1
110	The Harmonic Sequence	5,6										2	1	1		1	1	1
111	Transformations and Matrices	5,7												2		2	2	1
112	The Method of Differences	1,5												1		2	2	1
113	Probability Applied to Baseball	3,5,4								2		1	1	1	2	1	1	1
114	Introduction to Geometric Transformations	6,5											1	1		2	1	1
115	The Circle and the Cardioid	6,5,11										2	1	1		1	1	1
116	Complex-Number Applications	6,5,11											2	1		2	1	1
117	Hindu Arithmetic	2,1						2	2	1	1	2		2	1	1		2
118	Proving Numbers Irrational	5												1		1	2	1
119	How to Use a Computer Spreadsheet to Generate Solutions to Certain Mathematics Problems	1,2,10			****							2	1	1	1	1	2	2
120	The Three Worlds of Geometry	6														2	1	1
121	π Mix	5																1
122	Graphical Iteration	5															2	1
123	The Feigenbaum Plot	5															2	1
124	The Sierpinski Triangle	6													1		2	3
125	Fractals	6														1	1	1

Unit 1

 Constructing Odd-Order Magic Squares

This unit is intended for enrichment of students who have already mastered the fundamentals of elementary algebra. Carefully chosen parts of this unit may also prove effective in remedial classes, where students would appreciate some "recreational" mathematics.

PERFORMANCE OBJECTIVES

1. *Students will construct magic squares of any odd order required.*
2. *Students will discover properties of given odd-order magic squares.*
3. *Students will determine the sum of the elements of any row (or column, or diagonal) of any magic square, given only its order.*

PREASSESSMENT

Challenge students to form a 3×3 matrix with the numbers 1–9 so that the sum of the elements in each row, column, or diagonal is the same. Indicate to them that such a matrix is called a *magic square* (of order 3).

TEACHING STRATEGIES

After students have had enough time to be either successful with, or thoroughly frustrated by, the challenge (usually less than 15 minutes), you may begin to attack the problem with them. Have them realize the advantage of knowing beforehand the sum of each row (or column, or diagonal).

To develop a formula for the sum of the elements in any row, column, or diagonal of a magic square*, students must be familiar with the formula for the sum of an arithmetic series, $S = \frac{n}{2}(a_1 + a_n)$. If they are not familiar with this formula it can be very easily related to them by telling the story of young Carl Friedrich Gauss (1777–1855) who, at the age of 10, successfully responded to his teacher's challenge.

His teacher had a habit of providing rather lengthy chores for the students to complete (while he knew of a shortcut formula). One day this teacher told the class to add a series of numbers of the sort:
$1 + 2 + 3 + 4 + \cdots + 97 + 98 + 99 + 100$. As the teacher finished stating the problem, young Gauss submitted the answer. In amazement the teacher asked Gauss to explain his rapid solution. Gauss explained that rather than merely adding the 100 numbers in the order presented, he considered the following pairs $1 + 100 = 101$; $2 + 99 = 101$; $3 + 98 = 101$; $4 + 97 = 101; \ldots$; $50 + 51 = 101$. Since there were 50 pairs of numbers whose sum was 101, his answer was $50 \times 101 = 5{,}050$. In effect, he multiplied one-half the number of numbers to be added $\left(\frac{n}{2}\right)$ by the sum of the first and last numbers in the series $(a_1 + a_n)$ to obtain the sum of the entire series.

From this formula, the sum of natural numbers from 1 to n^2 (the numbers used in an $n \times n$ magic square) is $S = \frac{n^2}{2}(1 + n^2)$. However, if it is required that each row must have the same sum, then the sum is $\frac{S}{n}$. (From here on the expression "the sum of a row" will actually refer to "the sum of the numbers in a row.") Therefore the sum of any row is $\frac{n}{2}(n^2 + 1)$. You might want to have students consider why the sum of a diagonal is also $\frac{n}{2}(n^2 + 1)$.

Students are now ready to begin to systematically consider the original problem. Have them consider the following matrix of letters representing the numbers 1–9.

d_1	c_1	c_2	c_3	d_2
r_1	a	b	c	
r_2	d	e	f	
r_3	g	h	i	

Using the formula developed earlier, $S = \frac{n}{2} \times (n^2 + 1)$, we find that the sum of a row of a third order (3×3) magic square is $\frac{3}{2}(3^2 + 1) = 15$. Therefore $r_2 + c_2 + d_1 + d_2 = 4 \cdot 15 = 60$. However $r_2 + c_2 + d_1 + d_2 = (d + e + f) +$

*Unless stated otherwise, this unit will be concerned with magic squares of consecutive natural numbers beginning with 1.

$(b + e + h) + (a + e + i) + (c + e + g) = 3e + (a + b + c + d + e + f + g + h + i) = 3e + 45$ (since the sum of $1 + 2 + 3 + \cdots + 9 = \frac{9}{2}(1 + 9) = 45$). Therefore $3e + 45 = 60$ and $e = 5$. Thus it is established that the center position of a third order magic square must be occupied by 5.

Since the sum of each row, column, and diagonal in this magic square is 15, $a + i = g + c = b + h = d + f = 15 - 5 = 10$. (Note: Two numbers of an nth order magic square are said to be complementary if their sum is $n^2 + 1$; thus a and i are complementary.) Now lead your students through the following argument.

The number 1 cannot occupy a corner position. Suppose $a = 1$; then $i = 9$. However 2, 3, and 4 cannot be in the same row (or column) as 1, since there is no natural number less than 10 which would be large enough to occupy the third position of such a row (or column). This would leave only two positions (the nonshaded squares below) to accommodate these three numbers (2, 3, and 4). Since this cannot be the case, the numbers 1 and 9 may occupy only the middle positions of a row (or column).

1		
	5	
		9

The number 3 cannot be in the same row (or column) as 9, for the third number in such a row (or column) would then have to be 3, to obtain the required sum of 15. This is not possible because a number can be used only once in the magic square.

Now have students realize that neither 3 nor 7 may occupy corner positions. They should then use the above criteria to construct a magic square of order 3. Students should get any of the following magic squares.

2	7	6
9	5	1
4	3	8

4	3	8
9	5	1
2	7	6

8	1	6
3	5	7
4	9	2

6	1	8
7	5	3
2	9	4

2	9	4
7	5	3
6	1	8

4	9	2
3	5	7
8	1	6

8	3	4
1	5	9
6	7	2

6	7	2
1	5	9
8	3	4

Students might now want to extend this technique to constructing other odd-order magic squares. However, this scheme becomes somewhat tedious. Following is a rather mechanical method for constructing an odd-order magic square.

Begin by placing a 1 in the first position of the middle column. Continue by placing the next consecutive numbers successively in the cells of the (positive slope) diagonal. This, of course, is impossible since there are no cells "above" the square.

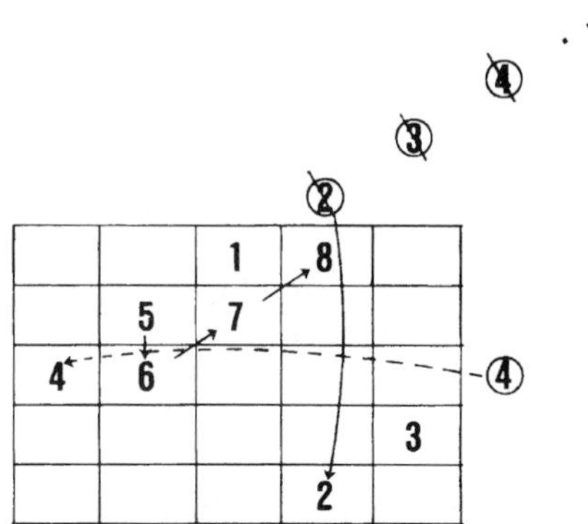

When a number must be placed in a position "above" the square, it should instead be placed in the last cell of the next column to the right. Then the next numbers are placed consecutively in this new (positive slope) diagonal. When (as in the figure above) a number falls outside the square to the right, it should be placed in the first (to the left) cell of the next row above the row whose last (to the right) cell was just filled (as illustrated). The process then continues by filling consecutively on the new cell until an already occupied cell is reached (as is the case with 6, above). Rather than placing a second number in the occupied cell, the number is placed below the previous number. The process continues until the last number is reached.

After enough practice students will begin to recognize certain patterns (e.g., the last number always occupies the middle position of the bottom row).

This is just one of many ways of constructing odd-order magic squares. More adept students should be urged to justify this rather mechanical technique.

POSTASSESSMENT

Have students do the following exercises:

1. Find the sum of a row of a magic square of order (a) 4; (b) 7; (c) 8.
2. Construct a magic square of order 11.
3. State some properties common to magic squares of odd order less than 13.

Unit 2

Constructing Even-Order Magic Squares

This topic can be used with a remedial class in high school as well as with a more advanced class at any secondary school grade level. In the former case, only magic squares of doubly-even order should be considered, while in the latter case, singly-even order magic squares may be included. When used with a remedial class, the development of doubly-even order magic squares may serve as motivation for drill of arithmetic fundamentals.

PERFORMANCE OBJECTIVES

1. *Students will construct magic squares of any even order required.*
2. *Students will discover properties of given even-order magic squares.*

PREASSESSMENT

Begin your introduction with a historical note. Mention the German artist (and mathematician) Albrecht Dürer (1471–1528), who did considerable work with mathematics related to his artwork. One of the more curious aspects of his work was the appearance of a magic square in an engraving of 1514 entitled "Melancholia" (Figure 1).

At the upper right hand corner of the engraving is the magic square (Figure 2). It is believed that this was one of the first appearances of magic squares in Western civilization. Of particular interest are the many unusual properties of this magic square. For example, the two center positions of the bottom row indicate the year the engraving was made, 1514. Offer your students some time to find other unusual properties (other than merely a constant sum of rows, columns, and diagonals).

FIGURE 1

TEACHING STRATEGIES

Students will probably enjoy discussing the many properties of this magic square, some of which are:

1. The four corner positions have a sum of 34.
2. The four corner 2×2 squares each has a sum of 34.
3. The center 2×2 square has a sum of 34.
4. The sum of the numbers in a diagonal equals the sum of those not in a diagonal.
5. The sum of the squares of the numbers in the diagonals (748) equals the sum of the squares of the numbers not in the diagonals.
6. The sum of the cubes of the numbers in the diagonals (9,248) equals the sum of the cubes of the numbers not in the diagonals.

FIGURE 2

7. The sum of the squares of the numbers in both diagonals equals the sum of the squares of the numbers in the first and third rows (or columns), which equals the sum of the squares of the numbers in the second and fourth rows (or columns).
8. Note the following symmetries:

$$2 + 8 + 9 + 15 = 3 + 5 + 12 + 14 = 34$$
$$2^2 + 8^2 + 9^2 + 15^2 = 3^2 + 5^2 + 12^2 + 14^2 = 374$$
$$2^3 + 8^3 + 9^3 + 15^3 = 3^3 + 5^3 + 12^3 + 14^3 = 4{,}624$$

9. The sum of each adjacent upper and lower pair of numbers vertically or horizontally produces an interesting symmetry.

vertically: 21 13 13 21
13 21 21 13

horizontally: 19 25
15 19
15 19
19 15

Consider first constructions of magic squares whose *order is a multiple of 4* (sometimes referred to as *doubly-even order*). Have students construct the square below with the diagonals as shown.

1	2	3	4
5	6	7	8
9	10	11	12
13	14	15	16

FIGURE 3

Then have them replace each number in a diagonal with its complement (i.e., that number which will give a sum of $n^2 + 1 = 16 + 1 = 17$). This will yield a 4×4 magic square (Figure 4). (Note: Dürer simply interchanged columns 2 and 3 to obtain his magic square.)

16	2	3	13
5	11	10	8
9	7	6	12
4	14	15	1

FIGURE 4

A similar process is used to construct larger doubly-even order magic squares. To construct an 8×8 magic square, divide the square into 4×4 magic squares (Figure 5) and then replace the numbers in the diagonals of each of the 4×4 squares with their complements.

The resulting magic square is shown as Figure 6. Now have students construct a magic square of order 12.

1	2	3	4	5	6	7	8
9	10	11	12	13	14	15	16
17	18	19	20	21	22	23	24
25	26	27	28	29	30	31	32
33	34	35	36	37	38	39	40
41	42	43	44	45	46	47	48
49	50	51	52	53	54	55	56
57	58	59	60	61	62	63	64

FIGURE 5

64	2	3	61	60	6	7	57
9	55	54	12	13	51	50	16
17	47	46	20	21	43	42	24
40	26	27	37	36	30	31	33
32	34	35	29	28	38	39	25
41	23	22	44	45	19	18	48
49	15	14	52	53	11	10	56
8	58	59	5	4	62	63	1

FIGURE 6

A different scheme is used to construct magic squares of singly-even order (i.e., those whose order is even but *not* a multiple of 4). Any singly-even order (say, of order n) magic square may be separated into quadrants (Figure 7). For convenience label them A, B, C, and D.

FIGURE 7

A	C
D	B

Students should now be instructed to construct four *odd-order* magic squares in the order A, B, C, and D (refer to the accompanying model "Constructing Odd-Order Magic Squares"). That is, square A will be an odd-order magic square using the first $\frac{n^2}{4}$ natural numbers; square B will be an odd-order magic square beginning with $\frac{n^2}{4} + 1$ and ending with $\frac{n^2}{2}$; square C will be an odd-order magic square beginning with $\frac{n^2}{2} + 1$ and ending with $\frac{3n^2}{4}$; square D will be an odd-order magic square beginning with $\frac{3n^2}{4} + 1$ and ending with n^2. (Figure 8 illustrates the case where $n = 6$.)

Have students notice the relation of the four magic squares of Figure 8 to the first magic square in the upper left position, A (Figure 9).

Now only some minor adjustments need be made to complete the construction of the magic squares. Let $n = 2(2m + 1)$. Take the numbers in the first m positions in

8	1	6	26	19	24
3	5	7	21	23	25
4	9	2	22	27	20
35	28	33	17	10	15
30	32	34	12	14	16
31	36	29	13	18	11

FIGURE 8

0 + 8	0 + 1	0 + 6	18 + 8	18 + 1	18 + 6
0 + 3	0 + 5	0 + 7	18 + 3	18 + 5	18 + 7
0 + 4	0 + 9	0 + 2	18 + 4	18 + 9	18 + 2
27 + 8	27 + 1	27 + 6	9 + 8	9 + 1	9 + 6
27 + 3	27 + 5	27 + 7	9 + 3	9 + 5	9 + 7
27 + 4	27 + 9	27 + 2	9 + 4	9 + 9	9 + 2

FIGURE 9

each row of A (except the middle row, where you skip the first position and take the next m positions) and interchange them with the numbers in the corresponding positions of square D. Then take the numbers in the last $m - 1$ positions of square C and interchange them with the number in the corresponding positions of square B. Notice that for $n = 6$ (Figure 10) $m - 1 = 0$, hence squares B and C remain unaltered.

35	1	6	26	19	24
3	32	7	21	23	25
31	9	2	22	27	20
8	28	33	17	10	15
30	5	34	12	14	16
4	36	29	13	18	11

FIGURE 10

17	24	1	8	15	67	74	51	58	65
23	5	7	14	16	73	55	57	64	66
4	6	13	20	22	54	56	63	70	72
10	12	19	21	3	60	62	69	71	53
11	18	25	2	9	61	68	75	52	59
92	99	76	83	90	42	49	26	33	40
98	80	82	89	91	48	30	32	39	41
79	81	88	95	97	29	31	38	45	47
85	87	94	96	78	35	37	44	46	28
86	93	100	77	84	36	43	50	27	34

FIGURE 11

Have students apply this technique to the construction of a magic square of order 10 ($n = 10$ and $m = 2$; see Figures 11 and Figure 12).

92	99	1	8	15	67	74	51	58	40
98	80	7	14	16	73	55	57	64	41
4	81	88	20	22	54	56	63	70	47
85	87	19	21	3	60	62	69	71	28
86	93	25	2	9	61	68	75	52	34
17	24	76	83	90	42	49	26	33	65
23	5	82	89	91	48	30	32	39	66
79	6	13	95	97	29	31	38	45	72
10	12	94	96	78	35	37	44	46	53
11	18	100	77	84	36	43	50	27	59

FIGURE 12

POSTASSESSMENT

As a formal postassessment, have students

1. construct a magic square of order (a) 12; (b) 16;
2. construct a magic square of order (a) 14; (b) 18;
3. find additional properties of magic squares of order (a) 8; (b) 12.

Unit 3

Introduction to Alphametics

This unit can be used to reinforce the concept of addition.

PERFORMANCE OBJECTIVE

Given alphametic problems, students will solve them in a systematic fashion.

PREASSESSMENT

Have students solve the following addition problems, either by simple addition in (a) and by filling in the missing digits in (b).

```
a.   562     b.    5 6 7 _
    3943          _ 8 _ 9
    8807        _ 3 _ 3 3
```

TEACHING STRATEGIES

The preceding problems should serve as a motivation for this lesson. Alphametics are mathematical puzzles that appear in several disguises. Sometimes the problem is associated with the restoration of digits in a computational problem; at other times, the problem is associated with decoding the complete arithmetical problem where letters of the alphabet represent all the digits. Basically, construction of this type of puzzle is not difficult, but the solution requires a thorough investigation of all elements. Every clue must be tested in all phases of the problem and carefully followed up. For example, suppose we were to eliminate certain digits in problem (a) above and supply the answer with some digits missing. Let us also assume that we do not know what these digits are. We may then be left with the following skeleton problem:

```
①②③④⑤
     _ 6 2
   3 9 4 _
   _ 8 _ 7
 _ 3 3 1 2
```

Have students analyze the problem. Lead them through the reconstruction as follows. From column five, 2 + _ + 7 = 12. Therefore the missing digit in the fifth column must be 3. In the fourth column, we have 1 + 6 + 4 + _ = 1, or 11 + _ = 1, therefore the digit must be zero. In the third column, we have 1 + _ + 9 + 8 = 23, and the missing digit must be 5. Now, from the second column, we have now 2 + 3 + _ = 13. This implies that the digit must be 8, and therefore, the digit to the left of 3 in the first column, bottom row must be 1. Thus, we have reconstructed the problem. Students should now be able to find the missing digits in the second problem of the preassessment (if they haven't already solved it). The completed solution is

```
 567④
 ⑦8⑤9
①3⑤33
```

Have students create their own problems and then interchange these with others in their class. So far, we have considered such problems that have exactly one solution. The following example will show a problem that has more than one solution.

```
  _ 8 7
  3 _ 1
+ 5 6 _
-------
_ 3 _ 0
```

In the units column 7 + 1 + _ = 10, the missing digit must be 2.

```
  _ 8 7
  3 _ 1
+ 5 6 2
-------
_ 3 _ 0
```

In the tens column, 1 + 8 + _ + 6 = _, or 15 + _ = _. An inspection must now be made of the hundreds column so that all possible outcomes are considered. In the hundreds column, we have _ + 3 + 5 = 13. Thus, if we assigned any of the digits 5, 6, 7, 8, or 9, for the value of the missing number (second row) in the tens column (second row position), we would have 15 + 5 = 20, or 15 + 6 = 21, or 15 + 7 = 22, or 15 + 8 = 23, or 15 + 9 = 24.

```
  3 8 7
  3 _ 1
+ 5 6 2
-------
1 3 _ 0
```

This will then make the digit in the hundreds column equal to 3, since a 2 is being carried. Hence, we have as possible solutions:

```
 387       387       387       387       387
 351       361       371       381       391
 562  or   562  or   562  or   562  or   562
1300      1310      1320      1330      1340
```

On the other hand, if we were to assign values for the missing digit in the second row of the tens column to be 0, 1, 2, 3, or 4, then the digit in the first row of the hundreds column would have to be a 4, since 1 is now being carried over from the tens column (rather than the 2 as before). These additional solutions would be acceptable:

```
 487       487       487       487       487
 301       311       321       331       341
 562  or   562  or   562  or   562  or   562
1350      1360      1370      1380      1390
```

Therefore, 10 different solutions result from having two missing digits in the same column.

In the second type of problem, where all digits are represented by letters (hence the name alphametics), the problem is quite different from the preceding ones. Here, the clues from the "puzzle" must be analyzed for all different possible values to be assigned to the letters. No general rule can be given for the solution of alphametic problems. What is required is an understanding of basic arithmetic, logical reasoning, and plenty of patience.

One fine example of this type is the following addition problem:

```
①②③④⑤
FORTY
  TEN
  TEN
-----
SIXTY
```

Since the first line and the fourth line have **T Y** repeated, this would imply that the sum of both the Es and the Ns in columns four and five must end in zero. If we let **N** = 0, then **E** must equal 5, and 1 is carried over to column three. We now have

```
F O R T Y
    T 5 0
    T 5 0
---------
S I X T Y
```

Since there are two spaces before each **T E N**, the 0 in **F O R T Y** must be 9, and with 2 carried over from the hundred's place (column three), the **I** must be one. And a 1 is carried to column one, making **F** + 1 = **S**. Ask the students why 2 and not 1 was carried over to the second column. The reason 2 must be carried from column three is that if a 1 were carried, the digits **I** and **N** would both be zero. We are now left with the following numbers 2, 3, 4, 6, 7, 8 unassigned.

```
F 9 R T Y
    T 5 0
    T 5 0
---------
S 1 X T Y
```

In the hundreds column, we have 2**T** + **R** + 1 (the 1 being carried over from column four), whose sum must be equal to or greater than 22; which implies T and R must be greater than 5. Therefore, F and S will be either 2, 3, or 4. Now X cannot be equal to 3, otherwise F and S would not be consecutive numbers. Then X equals 2 or 4, which is impossible if T is equal to or less than 7. Hence T must be 8, with R equal to 7 and X equal to 4. Then F = 2, S = 3, leaving Y = 6. Hence the solution to the problem is

```
 29,786
    850
    850
 ------
 31,486
```

POSTASSESSMENT

Have students solve the following alphametic problems.

1.

Problem	Answer
4 _ _ 3	4603
_ _ 1 4 _	99143
_ _ 3 7 4 6	103746

2.

Problem	Answer
5 _ 4 _	5349
_ 4 5 _ 8	24588
6 _ 2 5 9	64259
9 4 1 9 6	94196

3.

Problem	Answer
T R I E D	17,465
D R I V E	57,496
R I V E R	74,961

4.

Problem	Answer
S E N D	9,567
M O R E	1,085
M O N E Y	10,652

5.

Problem	Answer
A L L S	9,332
W E L L	8,433
T H A T	6,596
E N D S	4,072
S W E L L	28,433

For more on this topic and other related ideas, see *Math Wonders to Inspire Teachers and Students*, by Alfred S. Posamentier (Association for Supervision and Curriculum Development, 2003).

Unit 4

A Checkerboard Calculator

This enrichment unit will give students an easy, enjoyable method of operation with binary numerals.

PERFORMANCE OBJECTIVE

Students will be able to use a checkerboard calculator to do addition, subtraction, multiplication, and division with binary numerals.

PREASSESSMENT

Have students find:

a. $1100_2 + 110_2 =$ _ b. $12 + 6 =$ _
c. $111_2 \times 10_2 =$ _ d. $7 \times 2 =$ _

TEACHING STRATEGIES

John Napier, the 16th-century mathematician who developed logarithms and Napier's Bones (the calculating rods), also described in his work *Rabdologia* a method for calculating by moving counters across a chessboard. Besides being the world's first binary computer, it is also a valuable teaching aid. Although use of checkered boards was common in the Middle Ages and Renaissance period, by adopting a binary system and basing algorithms on old methods of multiplying by "doubling," Napier's Counting Board became much more efficient than any previous device.

Have students bring to school a standard chessboard or checkerboard. Begin by having students label rows and columns with the doubling series: 1, 2, 4, 8, 16, 32, 64, 128.

Now show how the board can be used for addition and subtraction. Every number is expressed by placing counters on a row. Each counter has the value of its column. For example, ask the students to add 89 + 41 + 52 + 14. The fourth row (89) will show 64 + 16 + 8 + 1 (Figure 1).

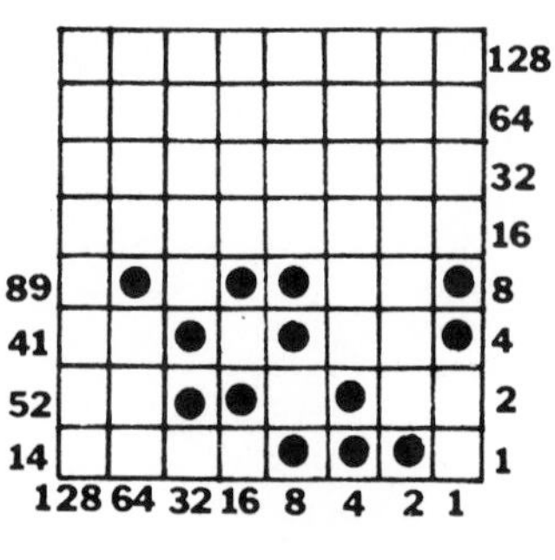

FIGURE 1

If the students think of each counter as a 1 and each empty space as a 0, 89 is represented in binary notation as 1011001_2.

The counters are positioned by starting at the left and putting a counter on the column of the largest number less than or equal to the number the student is representing. Place subsequent counters on the next largest number that when added to the previous number will not exceed the desired total, and so on.

To add, have students move all counters straight down (Figure 2).

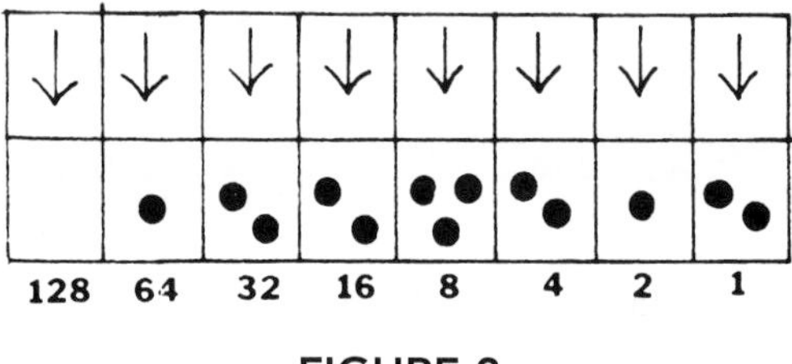

FIGURE 2

Adding the values of these counters will give the correct sum, but to use the board for binary notation, we must first "clear" the row of multiple counters on one cell. Have students start at the right, taking each cell in turn. Remove every PAIR of counters on a cell and replace them with a single counter on the next cell to the left. Assure students that this will not affect the sum as every two counters having value n are replaced by one counter having value $2n$. In our example, the final result is the binary number 11000100_2 (Figure 3).

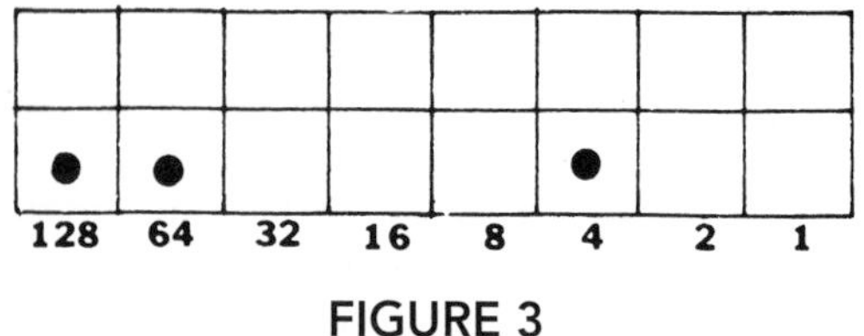

FIGURE 3

Subtraction is almost as simple. Suppose students want to take 83 from 108. Have them represent the larger number on the second row and the smaller number on the bottom row (Figure 4).

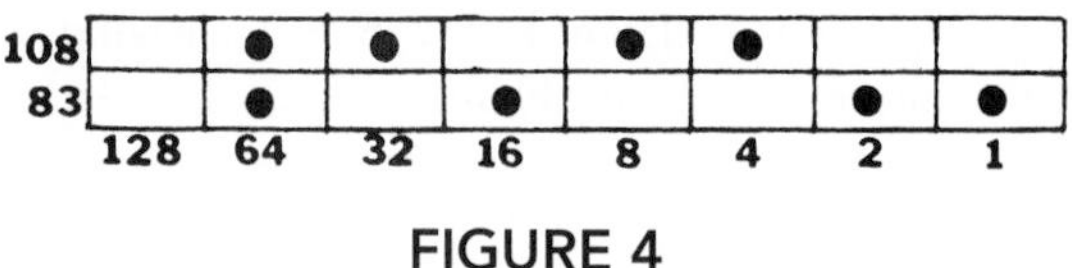

FIGURE 4

Students can now do subtraction in the usual manner, starting at the right and borrowing from cell to cell. Or instead, students can alter the entire second row until each counter on the bottom row has one or two counters above it, and no empty cell on the bottom row has more than one counter above it. This can be done by "doubling down" on the second row, removing a counter, and replacing it with two counters on the next cell to the right (Figure 5).

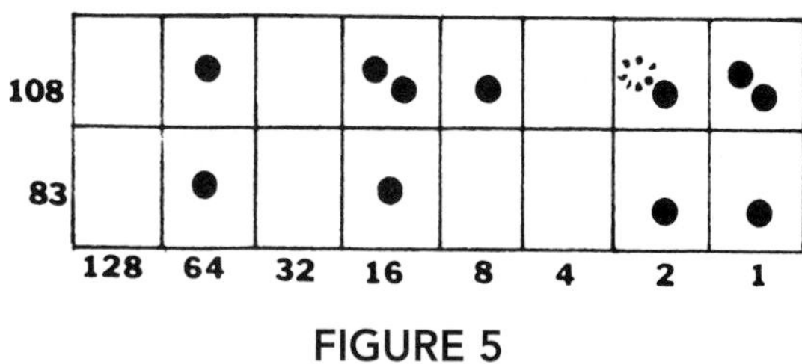

FIGURE 5

After this, "king" each counter in the bottom row by moving a counter on top of it from the cell directly above (Figure 6).

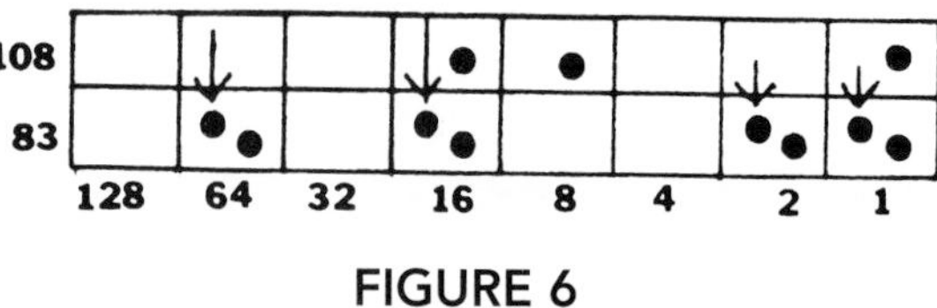

FIGURE 6

The top row now shows the difference of the two numbers in binary notation ($11001_2 = 25_{10}$).

Multiplication is also very simple. As an example use 19 × 13 = 247. Have students indicate one number, say 19, by marking below the board under the proper *columns* and the other number, 13, by marking the proper *rows*. Place a counter on every intersection of a marked column and marked row (Figure 7A). Every counter not on the extreme right-hand column is next moved diagonally up and to the right as a bishop in chess (Figure 7B).

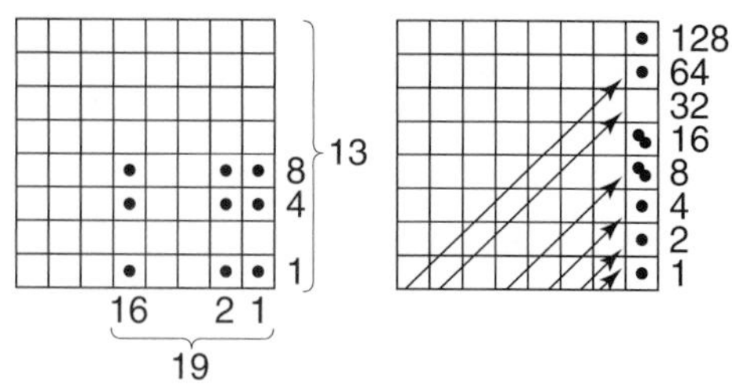

FIGURE 7A FIGURE 7B

Clear the column by having up as in addition, and the desired product is expressed in binary notation as 11110111_2 or 247_{10}, which students can quickly confirm.

Students will want to know how this works. Counters on the first row keep their values when moved to the right; counters on the second row double in value; counters on the third row quadruple in value; and so on. The procedure can be shown to be equivalent to multiplying with powers of the base 2. Nineteen is expressed in our example as $2^4 + 2^1 + 2^0$ and 13 as $2^3 + 2^2 + 2^0$. Multiplying the two trinomials gives us $2^7 + 2^6 + 2 \cdot 2^4 + 2 \cdot 2^3 + 2^2 + 2^1 + 2^0 = 247$. Moving the counters is equivalent to multiplying. We are, in effect, *multiplying* powers by *adding* exponents.

As an example of division, use $250 \div 13$. The procedure, as students may be expecting, is the reverse of multiplication. The divisor, in this case, 13, is marked at the bottom of the board and the dividend by counters on the column at the extreme right (Figure 8A). The dividend counters now move down and to the left, again like chess bishops, but in the opposite direction to multiplication. This procedure produces a pattern that has counters (one to a cell) only on marked columns, and each marked column must have its counters on the same rows. Only one such pattern can be formed. To do so it is necessary at times to double down on the right column; that is, remove single counters, replacing each with a pair of counters on the next lower cell. Have students start with the top counter and move it diagonally to the leftmost marked column. If the counter cannot proceed, have

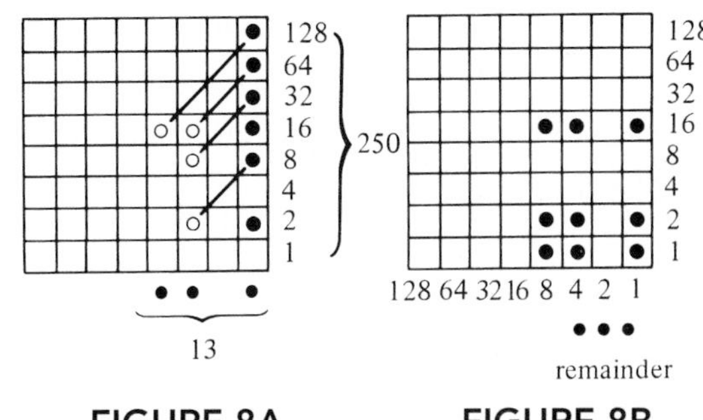

FIGURE 8A FIGURE 8B

students return it to the original cell, double down, and try again. Have them continue in this way, gradually filling in the pattern until the unique solution is achieved (Figure 8B).

After the final counter is in place, students should note that three counters are left over. This represents the remainder (3 or 11_2). The value of the right margin is now 10011_2 or 19_{10}, with $\frac{3}{13}$ left over.

POSTASSESSMENT

Have students solve the following problems by using the checkerboard methods:

a. $27 \cdot 64 =$ b. $194 - 63 =$
c. $54 + 43 =$ d. $361 \div 57 =$

Unit 5

The Game of Nim

This unit will present an application of the binary system through the playing of a simple game called Nim.

PERFORMANCE OBJECTIVE

Students will play the game of Nim using binary notation system strategy to win.

PREASSESSMENT

Have students represent in binary notation:

a. 14 b. 7 c. 13

TEACHING STRATEGIES

Nim, although sometimes played for money, can hardly be classified as a gambling game. This is because a player who knows the "secret" of the game can virtually always win.

The game of Nim may be played with sticks, pebbles, coins, or any other small objects. Describe the game to students as played with toothpicks. Have students arrange the toothpicks in three piles (other numbers of piles may be used, also) with any number of toothpicks in each pile. Have two students be players. The two players take turns making their moves. A move consists of taking away toothpicks according to certain rules. The rules are:

1. In each move a student may take away toothpicks from only one pile.
2. Each player may take any number of toothpicks, but must take at least one, and may take an entire pile at one time.
3. The player who takes away the last toothpick wins.

The "secret" of winning is quite simple, but practice is necessary to accurately perform mentally the arithmetic involved. Therefore, it is probably easier to start with a small number of toothpicks. The winning technique is based on choosing a move so that your opponent must draw from an *even set*.

First, it is necessary to learn how to identify an even set and an odd set. Suppose, for example, that the toothpicks are divided into three piles of (14), (7), and (13) toothpicks. Have students express each of these numbers in binary notation, and add the digits in each column in the same manner as when the decimal base is used. If at least one of the individual sums or digits is an odd number, the distribution is called an odd set. This example is an odd set because one sum is an odd number.

Fourteen	=	1 1 1 0	
Seven	=	1 1 1	
Thirteen	=	1 1 0 1	
		2 3 2 2	(odd set)

If the toothpicks are divided into the piles (9), (13) and (4) toothpicks, each individual sum is even and so it is considered an even set.

Nine	=	1 0 0 1	
Thirteen	=	1 1 0 1	
Four	=	1 0 0	
		2 2 0 2	(even set)

If a student draws from any even set, he necessarily must leave an odd set, for, considering the representation of the set in the binary scale, any draw will remove a one from at least one column, and the sum of the column will no longer be even.

On the other hand, if a player draws from an odd set, he can leave either an odd set or an even set. There are, however, usually only a few moves that can be made which will change an odd set into an even set. Therefore, a drawing at random from an odd set will very likely result in leaving an odd set.

Explain to the students that the object of the game is to try to force your opponent to draw from an even set, and his drawing will then leave an odd set. There are two winning end distributions that are even sets:

a. Two piles of two toothpicks each, designated symbolically (2), (2).
b. Four piles of one toothpick each, designated (1), (1), (1), (1).

If the student can leave an even set each time he plays, he is eventually able to force his opponent to draw from one of the above even sets, and the game is won. If at the start of the game the student has an even set before him, the best procedure is to draw a single toothpick from the largest pile leaving an odd set. If the opponent does not know the "secret" of the game, he or she will probably draw, leaving an odd set and you will then be able to force a win.

Have students follow moves in a sample game. Put toothpicks in piles of (7), (6), and (3) toothpicks each.

Seven	=	1 1 1	
Six	=	1 1 0	
Three	=	1 1	
		2 3 2	(odd set)

To leave an even set, the first student must draw two toothpicks from any one pile. Drawing from the first pile would give:

Five	=	1 0 1	
Six	=	1 1 0	
Three	=	1 1	
		2 2 2	(even set)

No matter how the second student moves, he is forced to leave an odd set. For instance, let him remove three toothpicks from the second pile.

Five	=	1 0 1	
Three	=	1 1	
Three	=	1 1	
		1 2 3	(odd set)

At this point the first student should draw all five toothpicks from the first pile.

Three	=	1 1	
Three	=	1 1	
		2 2	(even set)

Now, regardless of how the second student chooses the first will win. Students should now be permitted to play each other. This will provide reinforcement of the binary numeration system. After they have mastered the game as presented above, have them reverse the objective. (That is, let the loser be the player who must pick the last toothpick.)

POSTASSESSMENT

Have a student, who has been taught the strategy, play Nim against a student who only knows the rules. Use any (or all) of the following choices of piles of toothpicks:

a. (17), (15), (4); b. (18), (15), (4); c. (18), (15), (3)

The student who has been taught the strategy of the game should always win.

Unit 6

 The Tower of Hanoi

This unit provides students with an opportunity to construct and solve an ancient puzzle using the binary system of numeration. The puzzle, known as the Tower of Hanoi, was invented in 1883 by the French mathematician Edward Lucas.

PERFORMANCE OBJECTIVE

Each student will build and solve his own Tower of Hanoi puzzle using the binary system, and making use of knowledge required in this lesson.

PREASSESSMENT

Prior to this lesson students should be able to convert base 10 numerals to base 2 numerals. Administer the following quiz, instructing students to convert the given numerals (base 10) to base 2: (a) 4 (b) 8 (c) 16 (d) 60 (e) 125.

TEACHING STRATEGIES

Begin the lesson by relating the "history" of the puzzle to the class.

W. W. Rouse Ball, in his book *Mathematical Recreations and Essays*, relates an interesting legend of the origin of a puzzle called the Tower of Hanoi. In the great temple at Benares, beneath the dome that marks the center of the world, rests a brass plate in which are fixed three diamond needles, each a cubit high and as thick as the body of a bee. During creation, God placed 64 gold disks of diminishing size on one of these needles, the largest disk at the base resting on the brass plate. This is the tower of Bramah.

According to the legend the priests work day and night transferring the disks from one diamond needle to another according to the fixed laws of Bramah, which require that the priest on duty must *not* move *more than one disk at a time* and that he must place each disk on a needle so that *there is no smaller disk beneath it*. When the 64 disks have been transferred from the needle on which God placed them at creation to one of the other needles, tower, temple, and Brahmins alike will crumble into dust, and with a thunderclap the world will vanish.

The puzzle, which is sold commercially, can easily be made by each member of the class. Instruct students to cut out eight cardboard circles, each of different size. Have them punch three holes into a piece of thick cardboard so that the distance between the holes is greater than the outside radius of the largest disk. Next have them glue a dowel or pencil upright into each hole. In each disk, they should cut a hole at the center, wide enough for the dowel to fit through. Now they can place each disk on one of the dowels in order of size, with the largest one at the bottom. The arrangement of disks is called a *tower*.

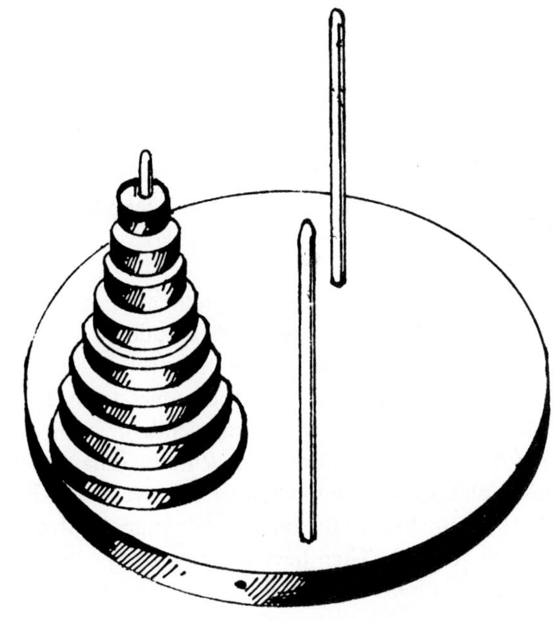

If you do not want to trouble yourself with cutting circles and gluing dowels into a board, you can make a simplified set by cutting eight squares of different sizes, and resting them on three plates instead of on dowels. In any case be sure to observe the rules:

At the start all the disks are placed on one post in order of size, the largest disk on the bottom. The puzzle involves shifting the disks, one at a time, from this post to another in such a way that a disk shall never rest on one smaller than itself. This should be done in the least possible number of moves. Remind students of the basic rules:

1. *Move only one disk at a time.*
2. *Never put a disk on top of a smaller disk.*

To familiarize students with the way the game works, demonstrate it first with only three disks. They should be able to transfer a tower of three disks in seven moves.

Now have them try it with four disks. To do this, seven moves are required to transfer the three top disks to one of the other two dowels. This frees the fourth disk which can then be moved to the vacant dowel. Seven more moves are now required to transfer the other three disks back on top of the fourth. Thus, the total number of moves required is 15.

When students consider the game with five disks they must move the top four disks twice, once to free the bottom disk, and once to get them back on the bottom disk, after the bottom disk has been moved. Thus, moving five disks takes 31 moves: six disks, 63 moves. Ask the class how many moves are required to transfer seven disks. Eight disks?

As students begin to comprehend the challenge of the puzzle, an interesting mathematical problem will emerge: *What is the minimum number of moves required to shift a specific number of disks from one post to another?* To solve this problem, suggest that students denote the number of disks by n, the least number of moves required by $2^n - 1$. Therefore, if there are eight disks, the least number of moves is $2^8 - 1 = 256 - 1 = 255$.

Have students consider the Brahmins with their 64 disks of gold. How many moves will it take them? $2^{64} - 1 = 18,$ 446, 744, 073, 709, 551, 615.

If the priests were to make one transfer every second and work 24 hours a day, 365 days a year, they would need more than *580 billion years* to perform the feat, assuming that they never made a mistake. How long would it take the priests to transfer half (or 32) of the disks? (4, 294, 967, 296 sec. = 136 years.)

Now have the class consider the problem of moving eight disks, the Tower of Hanoi. Suggest that students number the disks, one to eight according to size, from the smallest to the largest. Also, have them number the moves from 1 to 225 ($2^8 - 1 = 225$). As a class (or independent) project they should write the number of each move in the binary scale. To discover which disk to transfer at each move, and where to place it, they can refer to the binary scale numeral that corresponds to that move. Then have them count the digits from the right until the first unit digit is reached. The number of digits counted tells which disk to move. For example, if the first 1 from the right is the third digit, then the third disk is moved. Now its placement must be determined. If there are no other digits to the left of the first 1, then the disk is placed on the dowel that has no disks on it. If there *are* other digits to the left of the first 1, students should count digits from the right again until they reach the second 1. The number of digits counted this time identifies a larger disk that was previously moved. Students must decide whether to place the disk they are moving on top of this larger disk or on the "empty" dowel. To decide which strategy to take, they should count the number of zeros between the first 1 from the right and the second 1 from the right. If there are no zeros between them, or if there is an even number of zeros between them, they should put the disk that they are moving onto the disk that the second 1 refers to. If the number of zeros between them is odd, they put the disk on the empty dowel.

The numbers 1 to 15, written in the binary scale are presented here, along with the instructions for the first 15 moves.

1	Move disk 1.
10	Move disk 2.
11	Place disk 1 on disk 2.
100	Move disk 3.
101	Place disk 1 not on disk 3.
110	Place disk 2 on disk 3.
111	Place disk 1 on disk 2.
1000	Move disk 4.
1001	Place disk 1 on disk 4.
1010	Place disk 2 not on disk 4.
1011	Place disk 1 on disk 2.
1100	Place disk 3 on disk 4.
1101	Place disk 1 not on disk 3.
1110	Place disk 2 on disk 3.
1111	Place disk 1 on disk 2.

POSTASSESSMENT

To assess student progress have them complete the above table. Then have them make the first 25 moves on their model of the Tower of Hanoi.

Unit 7

 What Day of the Week Was It?

This topic may be used for enrichment in a recreational spirit, as well as an interesting application of mathematics. Students will also enjoy seeing the relationship between astronomy and mod 7. In addition, students will be surprised to see how many factors have to be considered in this seemingly simple problem.

PERFORMANCE OBJECTIVES

1. *Given any date, the student will determine the day of the week corresponding to this date.*
2. *Given any year, the student will determine the date of the Easter Sunday that year.*

PREASSESSMENT

The students must be familiar with the construction of the calendar.

Give the students a date in this year and ask them to indicate the day corresponding to this date. After they try this, ask them to do this for a date in the past. The students will be anxious to develop a rapid and accurate method for doing this.

TEACHING STRATEGIES

Start with a brief history of the calendar. The students will be most interested in knowing the development of the present day Gregorian Calendar and fascinated by how it was changed.

Discuss the relationship of the calendar to astronomy. Time can be measured only by observing the motions of bodies that move in unchanging cycles. The only motions of this nature are those of the celestial bodies. Hence we owe to astronomy the establishment of a secure basis for the measurement of time by determining the lengths of the day, the month, and the year. A year is defined as the interval of time between two passages of the earth through the same point in its orbit in relation to the sun. This is the solar year. It is approximately 365.242216 mean solar days. The length of the year is not commensurable with the length of the day; the history of the calendar is the history of the attempts to adjust these incommensurable units in such a way as to obtain a simple and practical system.

The calendar story goes back to Romulus, the legendary founder of Rome, who introduced a year of 300 days divided into 10 months. His successor, Numa, added 2 months. This calendar was used for the following six and a half centuries until Julius Caesar introduced the Julian Calendar. If the year were indeed 365.25 days, the introduction of an additional day to 365 days once every 4 years, making the fourth year a leap year, would completely compensate for the discrepancy. The Julian Calendar spread abroad with other features of Roman culture, and was generally used until 1582.

The difficulty with this method of reckoning was that 365.25 was not 365.242216, and although it may seem an insignificant quantity, in hundreds of years it accumulates to a discrepancy of a considerable number of days. The Julian Year was somewhat too long and by 1582 the accumulated error amounted to 10 days.

Pope Gregory XIII tried to compensate for the error. Because the Vernal Equinox occurred on March 11 in 1582, he ordered that 10 days be suppressed from the calendar dates in that year so that the Vernal Equinox would fall on March 21 as it should. When he proclaimed the calendar reform, he formulated the rules regarding the leap years. The Gregorian Calendar has years (based on approximately 365.2425 days) divisible by four as leap years, unless they are divisible by 100 and not 400. Thus 1700, 1800, 1900, 2100, ... are not leap years, but 2000 is.

In Great Britain and its colonies the change of the Julian to the Gregorian Calendar was not made until 1752. In September of that year, 11 days were omitted. The day after September 2 was September 14. It is interesting to see a copy of the calendar for Sept. 1752 taken from the almanac of Richard Saunders, Gent., published in London (Figure 1).

Mathematicians have pondered the question of the calendar and tried to develop ways of determining the days of any given date or holiday.

To develop a method for determining the day, the student should be aware that a calendar year (except for a leap year) is 52 weeks and one day long. If New Year's day in some year following a leap year occurs on a Sunday, the next New Year's will occur on Monday. The following New Year's day will occur on a Tuesday. The New Year's day of the leap year will occur on a Wednesday. Since there are 366 days in a leap year, the next New Year's day will occur on a Friday, and not on a

1752		September hath XIX Days this Year.				
		First Quarter, the 15th day at 2 afternoon. Full Moon, the 23rd day at 1 afternoon. Last Quarter, the 30th day at 2 afternoon.				
M D	W D	Saints' Days Terms, &c.	Moon South	Moon Sets	Full Sea at Lond.	Aspects and Weather
1	f	Day br. 3.35	3 A 27	8 A 29	5 A 1	□ ♃ ☿
2	g	London burn.	4 26	9 11	5 38	Lofty winds

According to an act of Parliament passed in the 24th year of his Majesty's reign and in the year of our Lord 1751, the Old Style ceases here and the New takes its place; and consequently the next Day, which in the old account would have been the 3d is now to be called the 14th; so that all the intermediate nominal days from the 2d to the 14th are omitted or rather annihilated this Year; and the Month contains no more than 19 days, as the title at the head expresses.

M D	W D	Saints' Days Terms, &c.	Moon South	Moon Sets	Full Sea at Lond.	Aspects and Weather
14	e	Clock slo. 5 m.	5 15	9 47	6 27	Holy Rood D.
15	f	Day 12 h. 30 m.	6 3	10 31	7 18	and hasty
16	g		6 57	11 23	8 16	showers
17	A	15 S. Aft. Trin.	7 37	12 19	9 7	
18	b		8 26	Morn.	10 22	More warm
19	c	Nat. V. Mary	9 12	1 22	11 21	and dry
20	d	Ember Week	9 59	2 24	Morn.	weather
21	e	St. Matthew	10 43	3 37	0 17	☌ ♀ ☿
22	f	Burchan	11 28	☾ rise	1 6	□ ♃ ♀
23	g	Equal D. & N.	Morn.	6 A 13	1 52	☌ ☉ ♂
24	A	16 S. Aft. Trin.	0 16	6 37	2 39	☌ ☉ ☿
25	b		1 5	7 39	3 14	
26	c	Day 11 h. 52 m.	1 57	8 39	3 48	Rain or hail
27	d	Ember Week	2 56	8 18	4 23	☌ ♂ ☿
28	e	Lambert bp.	3 47	9 3	5 6	now abouts
29	f	St. Michael	4 44	9 59	5 55	✱ ♄ ♀
30	g		5 43	11 2	6 58	

FIGURE 1

Thursday. The regular sequence is interrupted every 4 years (except during years where numbers are evenly divisible by 100 but not evenly divisible by 400).

First develop a method to find the weekday for dates in the same year.

Suppose February 4 falls on Monday. On what day of the week will September 15 fall? Assuming that this calendar year is not a leap year, one need only:

1. Find the number of days between Feb. 4 and Sept. 15. First find that Feb. 4 is the 35th day of the year and that Sept. 15 is the 258th day of the year. (The table in Figure 2 expedites this.) The difference of 258 and 35 is the number of days, namely, 223.
2. Since there are 7 days in a week, divide 223 by 7. [$\frac{223}{7} = 31 +$ remainder 6.]
3. The 6 indicates that the day on which Sept. 15 falls is the sixth day after Monday, thus Sunday. In the case of a leap year, one day must be added after February 28 to account for February 29.

A similar method for finding the weekday of the dates in the same year can be discussed as follows.

Because January has 31 days, the same date in the subsequent month will be 3 days after that day in January; the same date in March will also be 3 days later than in January; in April, it will be 6 days later than in January. We can then construct a table of Index Numbers for the months that will adjust all dates to the corresponding dates in January:

Jan.	0	Apr.	6	July	6	Oct.	0
Feb.	3	May	1	Aug.	2	Nov.	3
Mar.	3	June	4	Sept.	5	Dec.	5

DATE	1	2	3	4	5	6	7	8	9	10	11	12	13	14	15	16
JANUARY	1	2	3	4	5	6	7	8	9	10	11	12	13	14	15	16
FEBRUARY	32	33	34	35	36	37	38	39	40	41	42	43	44	45	46	47
MARCH	60	61	62	63	64	65	66	67	68	69	70	71	72	73	74	75
APRIL	91	92	93	94	95	96	97	98	99	100	101	102	103	104	105	106
MAY	121	122	123	124	125	126	127	128	129	130	131	132	133	134	135	136
JUNE	152	153	154	155	156	157	158	159	160	161	162	163	164	165	166	167
JULY	182	183	184	185	186	187	188	189	190	191	192	193	194	195	196	197
AUGUST	213	214	215	216	217	218	219	220	221	222	223	224	225	226	227	228
SEPTEMBER	244	245	246	247	248	249	250	251	252	253	254	255	256	257	258	259
OCTOBER	274	275	276	277	278	279	280	281	282	283	284	285	286	287	288	289
NOVEMBER	305	306	307	308	309	310	311	312	313	314	315	316	317	318	319	320
DECEMBER	335	336	337	338	339	340	341	342	343	344	345	346	347	348	349	350

FIGURE 2

DATE	17	18	19	20	21	22	23	24	25	26	27	28	29	30	31
JANUARY	17	18	19	20	21	22	23	24	25	26	27	28	29	30	31
FEBRUARY	48	49	50	51	52	53	54	55	56	57	58	59			
MARCH	76	77	78	79	80	81	82	83	84	85	86	87	88	89	90
APRIL	107	108	109	110	111	112	113	114	115	116	117	118	119	120	
MAY	137	138	139	140	141	142	143	144	145	146	147	148	149	150	151
JUNE	168	169	170	171	172	173	174	175	176	177	178	179	180	181	
JULY	198	199	200	201	202	203	204	205	206	207	208	209	210	211	212
AUGUST	229	230	231	232	233	234	235	236	237	238	239	240	241	242	243
SEPTEMBER	260	261	262	263	264	265	266	267	268	269	270	271	272	273	
OCTOBER	290	291	292	293	294	295	296	297	298	299	300	301	302	303	304
NOVEMBER	321	322	323	324	325	326	327	328	329	330	331	332	333	334	
DECEMBER	351	352	353	354	355	356	357	358	359	360	361	362	363	364	365

FIGURE 2 (Continued)

(The Index Numbers are actually giving you the days between the months divided by 7 to get the excess days as in the previous method.)

Now you need only add the date to the Index Number of the month, divide by 7 and the remainder will indicate the day of the week.

Example: Consider the year 1925. January 1 was on a Thursday. Find March 12.

To do this, add 12 + 3 = 15; divide 15/7 = 2 remainder 1. This indicates Thursday. In leap years an extra 1 has to be added for dates after February 29.

Students will now want to find the day for a date for any given year. Point out that first one need know what day January 1 of the Year 1 fell and also make adjustments for leap years.

The day of the week on which January 1 of Year 1 fell can be determined as follows. Using a known day and date, we find the number of days that have elapsed since January 1 of the Year 1. Thus, since January 1, 1952, was Wednesday, in terms of the value of the solar year, the number of days since January 1 is 1951 × 365.2425 = 712588.1175. Dividing by 7, we get 101,798 with a remainder of 2. The remainder indicates that 2 days should be counted from Wednesday. Since calculations refer to the past, the counting is done backwards, indicating that January 1 (in the Gregorian Calendar) fell on Monday.

One method for determining the day for any year suggests that dates in each century be treated separately. Knowing the weekday of the first day of that period, one could, in the same fashion as before, determine the excess days after that weekday (thus the day of the week that a given day would fall on for that century). For the years 1900–1999, the information needed is:

1. The Index Numbers of the months (see earlier discussion).
2. January 1 of 1900 was Monday.
3. The number of years (thus giving the number of days over the 52 week cycles) that have elapsed since the 1st day of the year 1900.
4. The number of leap years (i.e., additional days) that have occurred since the beginning of the century.

Knowing this, we can ascertain how many days in that Monday-week cycle we need count.

Examples:

1. *May 9, 1914.* Add 9 (days into the month), 1 (Index Number of the month), 14 (Number of years since the beginning of the century), and 3 (number of leap years in that century thus far). 9 + 1 + 14 + 3 = 27. Divide by 7, leaves 6, which is Saturday.
2. *Aug. 16, 1937.* Add 16 + 2 + 37 + 9 = 64. Divide by 7, leaves 1, which is Monday.

For the period, 1800–1899, the same procedure is followed except that January 1, 1800, was on Wednesday. For the period September 14, 1752, through 1799, the same procedure is followed except that the first day of that period would be Friday. For the period up to and including September 2, 1752, the same procedure is followed except that the whole year would be added and the number of the days would start with Friday.

Example: May 13, 1240.
Add 13 + 1 + 1240 + 10 = 1264/7, leaves 4, Monday.

There is another method for determining the day without having to consider separate periods.

Again we start by knowing the day of January 1 of the Year 1. We will not count the actual number of days that have elapsed since January 1 of Year 1, but count the number of excess days over weeks that have elapsed and to this number, add the number of days that have elapsed since January 1 of the given year. This total must be divided by 7, the remainder will indicate the number of days that must be counted for that week, thus the formula is, 1 (Monday) + the remainder of the division by 7 of (the number of years that have elapsed thus far + the number of days that have elapsed since January 1 of the given year + the number of leap years that have occurred since year 1) = the number of days of the week. The calculation of the number of leap years must take into account the fact that those years whose number ends with two zeros, which are not divisible by 400, are not leap years. Thus from the total number of leap years, a certain number of leap years must be subtracted.

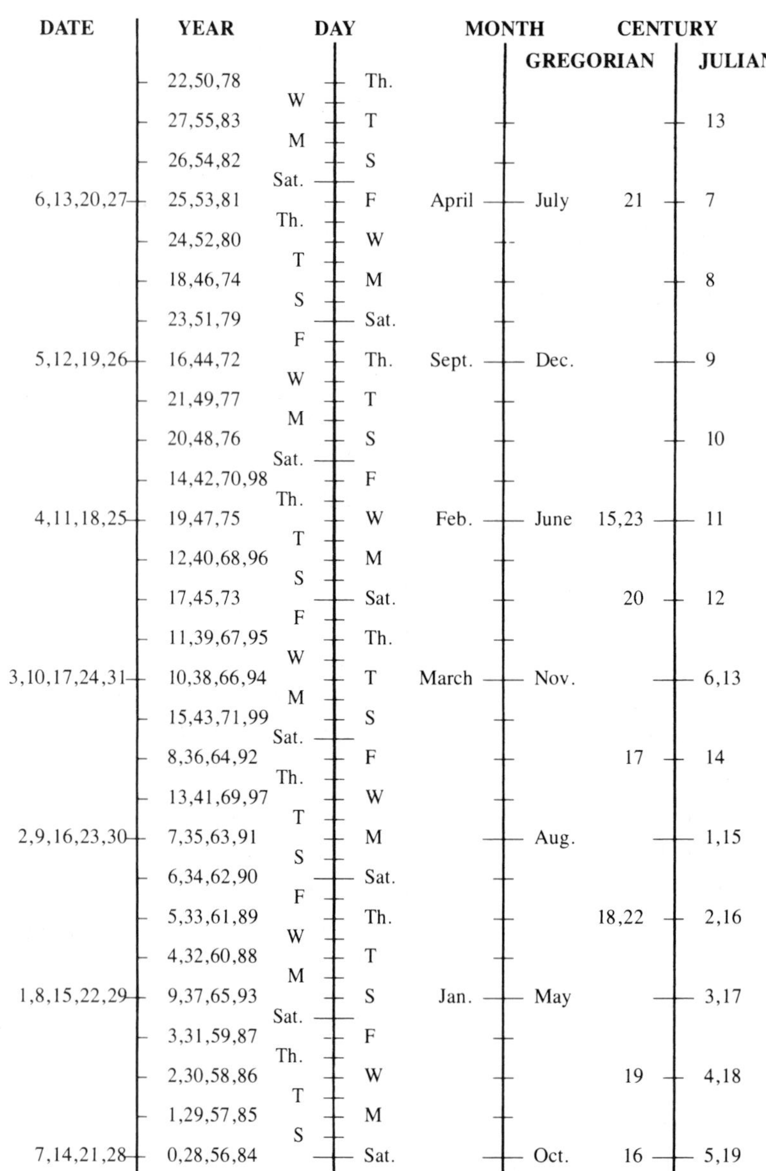

FIGURE 3 Perpetual Calendar

Example: Dec. 25, 1954. 1 + 1953 + 488 (leap years) −15 (century leap years 19 − 4) + 358 (number of days between January 1, 1954, and December 25, 1954) = 2785. Dividing by 7 gives remainder 6. Thus December 25, 1954, fell on the sixth day of the week, Saturday.

Many other tables and mechanisms have been devised to solve the problem of determining days. The following are two nomograms devised for this.

The first (see Figure 3) consists of four scales and is to be used as follows:

1. With a straightedge, join the point on the first scale indicating the date with the proper month on the third scale. Mark the point of intersection with the second scale.
2. Join this point on the second scale with the point on the fourth scale indicating the proper century. Mark the point of intersection with the third scale.
3. Join this point with the point indicating the appropriate year on the first scale. The point of intersection with the second scale gives the desired day of the week. (N.B. For the months of January and February use the year diminished by 1.)

The second arrangement (see Figure 4) consists of three concentric rings intersected by seven radii. The procedure is:

1. Locate the date and the month on the outer ring; if they are two points, draw a line between them; if they coincide, draw a tangent.
2. Locate the century on the intermediate ring. Through this point draw a line parallel to the line drawn, until it intersects the intermediate ring at another point. The point found will be a ring-radius intersection.
3. From the point just found, follow the radius to the inner ring, then locate the year. (If the month is January or

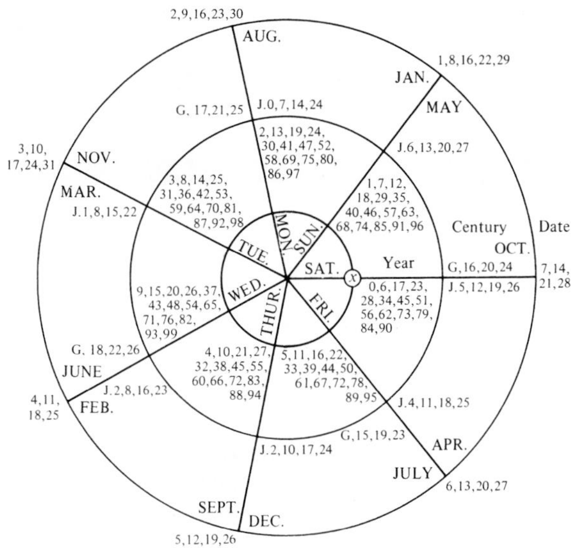

FIGURE 4 Perpetual Calender, Radius-Ring Type

February use the preceding year.) Draw a line between these two points on the inner ring. (If they coincide on Saturday, then Saturday is the weekday sought.)

4. Now find the point where the Saturday radius cuts the inner ring, and through this Saturday point draw a line parallel to the line just drawn. The line will meet the inner ring at some radius-ring intersection. The weekday on this latter radius is the weekday of the date with which we began.

The problem of a perpetual calendar occupied the attention of many mathematicians and many of them devoted considerable attention to calculating the date of Easter Sunday. All church holidays fall on a definite date. The ecclesiastical rule regarding Easter is, however, rather complicated. Easter must fall on the Sunday after the first full moon that occurs after the Vernal (Spring) Equinox. Easter Sunday, therefore, is a movable Feast that may fall as early as March 22 or as late as April 25. The following procedure to find Easter Sunday in any year from 1900–1999 is based on a method developed by Gauss.

1. Find the remainder when the year is divided by 4. Call this remainder a.
2. Find the remainder when the year is divided by 7. Call this remainder b.
3. Find the remainder when the year is divided by 19. Multiply this remainder by 19, add 24, and again find the remainder when the total is divided by 30. Call this remainder c.
4. Now add $2a + 4b + 6c + 3$. Divide this total by 7 and call the remainder d.

The sum of c and d will give the number of days after March 22 on which Easter Sunday will fall.

Example: Easter 1921

a. $\frac{21}{4}$ leaves 1

b. $\frac{21}{7}$ leaves 0

c. $\frac{21}{19}$ leaves 2; $[2(19) + 24]/30$ leaves 2

d. $[2 + 0 + 12 + 3]/7$ leaves 3
$2 + 3 = 5$ days after March 22 = March 27

(The method above gives the date accurately except for the years 1954 and 1981. These years it gives a date exactly 1 week late, the correct Easters being April 18 and 19, respectively.)

POSTASSESSMENT

1. Have the students determine the day of the week of their birth.
2. Have the students work out several given dates.

October 12, 1492	May 30, 1920	Christmas 1978
April 1, 1945	October 21, 1805	August 14, 1898
		July 4, 1776

3. Have the students find the dates of several Easter Sundays.

   1944, 1969, 1950, 1978, 1930, 1977, 1929

4. George Washington was born February 11, 1732. Why do we celebrate it February 22?

Unit 8

 Palindromic Numbers

This unit will define palindromic numbers and introduce some of their properties. The study of palindromic numbers is suited for any class: while it provides all students an approach for analyzing numbers and their relationships, certain aspects of this topic can be selected for the slow students (e.g., the reverse addition property) and more advanced properties can be investigated by the more adept students (e.g., modular palindromes).

PERFORMANCE OBJECTIVES

1. *Students will state and analyze properties of palindromic numbers.*
2. *Students will construct new palindromes from any specified integer.*

PREASSESSMENT

Have students analyze the expression "Madam I'm Adam" and the words "rotator" and "reviver" and point out their peculiarity (they spell the same backward and forward). Indicate to them that such an expression is called a palindrome and that in mathematics, numbers having the same property like 343 and 59695 are called palindromic numbers. Students can be asked to give their own examples of palindromic numbers and make a short list.

TEACHING STRATEGIES

After the students have compiled their lists, an analysis can be made of these numbers. Questions such as the following can be put to them to get a discussion going: Does a palindrome have an odd or even number of digits, or both? Are palindromic numbers prime, composite, or both? Is the square or cube of a palindromic number still a palindrome? Given a positive integer can a palindrome be constructed from some sort of operation on this integer? Students can attempt to answer these questions by testing their validity on the numbers from their lists or by seeking some new ones.

The students are ready at this point to study some of the following palindromic properties:

1. *Palindromic numbers contain both prime and composite numbers (e.g., 181 is a palindromic prime while 575 is a composite palindrome); however, a palindromic prime, with the exception of 11, must have an odd number of digits.*

   Proof of the latter: (by contradiction)

   Let p be a palindromic prime having an even number of digits. Let r be the sum of all digits in the even positions of the prime p and s be the sum of all the digits in the odd positions of the prime p. Since p is a palindrome with an even number of digits, the digits in odd positions duplicate the digits in even positions; therefore $s - r = 0$. But the test for divisibility by 11 states that a number is divisible by 11 if the difference between the sum of all digits in even positions and the sum of all digits in odd positions is 0 or a multiple of 11. Therefore, p has 11 as a factor and cannot be prime, a contradiction.
2. *All integers N, which yield palindromic squares, are not necessarily palindromes.* While there are infinitely many palindromes yielding palindromic squares (e.g., $22^2 = 484$ and $212^2 = 44944$), there exist some nonpalindromic integers whose squares are palindromes (e.g., $26^2 = 676$ and $836^2 = 698896$) as well as some palindromic integers yielding nonpalindromic squares (e.g., $131^2 = 17161$ and $232^2 = 53824$).

   Repunits, numbers consisting entirely of 1s (by notation, R_k where k is the number of 1s) are palindromic numbers and produce palindromic squares when $1 \leq k \leq 9 : R_2^2 = 121 : R_3^2 = 12321$ and in general $R_k^2 = 12\ldots k\ldots 21$, where $k = 9$. However, when $k > 9$ the carrying in addition would lose the palindromic product (e.g., $R_{10}^2 = 12\ldots 6790098\ldots 21$).

   Square numbers are much richer in palindromes than randomly chosen integers.
3. *In general, numbers that yield palindromic cubes (some of which are prime and some composite) are palindromic in themselves.* The numbers N that yield palindromic cubes are as follows:

   a. $N = 1,7,11$ $(1^3 = 1, 7^3 = 343, 11^3 = 1331)$

   b. $N = 10^k + 1$ has a palindromic cube consisting of $k - 1$ zeros between each consecutive pair of 1,3,3,1: e.g., when $k = 1$, $N = 11$ and $N^3 = 1331$; when $k = 2$, $N = 101$ and $N^3 = 1030301$; when $k = 3$, $N = 1001$ and $N^3 = 1003003001$, etc. Notice that when $k = 2m + 1$, $m > 0$, then N is divisible by 11 and hence is composite.

c. N consisting of 3 1s and any desired number (which must be even) of zeros is divisible by 3 and has palindromic cubes: e.g., $(111)^3 = 1367631$, $(10101)^3 = 1030607060301$.

d. $N =$ any palindromic arrangement of zeros and four 1's is a nonprime and has a palindromic cube, except when the same number of zeros appears in the three spaces between the 1's: e.g., $(11011)^3 = 1334996994331$, $(10100101)^3 = 1003033091390931903303001$, whereas $(1010101)^3$ is not a palindrome.

The only $N < 2.8 \times 10^{14}$ that is not a palindrome yet yields a palindromic cube is $2201^3 = 10662526601$.

4. *Given any integer N we can often reach a palindrome by adding the number to its reversal (the number obtained by reversing the digits) and continuing the process until the palindrome is achieved.* For example, if $N = 798$, then $798 + 897 = 1695$, $1695 + 5961 = 7656$, $7656 + 6567 = 14223$, $14223 + 32241 = 46464$ (a palindrome). Whereas some numbers can reach a palindrome in only two steps (e.g., 75 and 48), there are others that reach it in 6 steps like 97, and still others like 89 and 98 that reach a palindrome in 24 steps. However, certain numbers like 196 when carried out to over 1000 steps still do not achieve palindromes, so this rule cannot be taken to hold for all integers but certainly for most since these cases are very rare. The rule does not hold in base two; the smallest counterexample is 10110, which after 4 steps reaches the sum 10*11*01*00*, after 8 steps it is 10*111*01*000*, after 12 steps it is 10*1111*01*0000*. Every fourth step increases by one digit each of the two sequences underlined and it is seen that each of these increasing sums is not a palindrome. There are some generalities found in this process of reverse addition:

a. Different integers when subjected to this technique produce the same palindrome. For example, 554, 752, and 653 all produce the palindrome 11011 in 3 steps. In general, all integers in which the corresponding digit pairs symmetrical to the middle have the same sum will produce the same palindrome in the same number of steps. (In this case, all the digit pairs add up to 9.) There are however different integers that produce the same palindrome in different numbers of steps. For example, 99 reaches 79497 in 6 steps whereas 7299 reaches it in 2 steps.

b. Two-digit numbers can be categorized according to the total sum of the two digits to ascertain the number of steps needed to produce a palindrome. It is obvious that if the sum of the digits is 9, only 1 step is needed; if their digit sum is 10 (e.g., 64 and 73), 2 steps are needed. Similar analyses will lead the students to conclude that if their digit sum is 11, 12, 13, 14, 15, 16, 17, or 18, a palindrome results after 1, 2, 2, 3, 4, 6, 24, and 1 respectively. The students can be asked to perform an analysis of this type and put their results in table form.

This topic of palindromes can be investigated further by more adept students. Further investigation lies in the areas of multigrades with palindromic numbers as elements, special palindromic prime numbers such as primes with prime digits as elements, modular palindromes, and triangular and pentagonal numbers that are also palindromes.

POSTASSESSMENT

1. Do the following numbers yield palindromic cubes: (a) 1001001 (b) 1001001001 (c) 10100101 (d) 100101
2. Given the following two-digit numbers, indicate the number of steps required in reversal addition to reach a palindrome: (a) 56 (b) 26 (c) 91 (d) 96
3. Perform the reverse addition technique on these integers and find other integers that will yield the same palindrome as these: (a) 174 (b) 8699

Unit 9

 The Fascinating Number Nine

This unit is intended to offer a recreational presentation of the many interesting properties of the number 9. A long-range goal of presenting these amusing number topics is to motivate further student investigation and insight into the properties of numbers.

PERFORMANCE OBJECTIVES

1. *Students will demonstrate at least three properties of the number 9.*
2. *Students will provide an example of a short-cut calculation involving the number 9.*

PREASSESSMENT

Students should be familiar with the various field postulates and be reasonably adept with the operations of addition, subtraction, multiplication, and division. A knowledge of algebra is helpful but not essential.

TEACHING STRATEGIES

In presenting new ideas to a class it is always best to build on what they already know. For example, ask students to multiply 53×99. Unsuspecting students will perform the calculation in the usual way. After their work has been completed, suggest the following:

$$\begin{aligned} \text{Since} \qquad 99 &= 100 - 1 \\ 53 \times 99 &= 53\,(100 - 1) \\ &= 53\,(100) - 53(1) \\ &= 5300 - 53 \\ &= 5247 \end{aligned}$$

Now have them use this technique to multiply 42×999.

"Casting Out Nines" is a popular technique for checking calculations. For example, if students wish to check the addition $29 + 57 + 85 + 35 + 6 = 212$, they simply divide each number in the addition by 9 and retain only the remainder. Thus they have 2, 3, 4, 8, and 6, the sum of which is 23. (See below.)

$$\begin{array}{rcr} 29 & \rightarrow & 2 \\ 57 & \rightarrow & 3 \\ 85 & \rightarrow & 4 \\ 35 & \rightarrow & 8 \\ +\ 6 & \rightarrow & +6 \\ \hline 212 & & 23 \end{array}$$

The remainder of $212 \div 9$ is 5. If the remainder of $212 \div 9$ is the same as the remainder of $23 \div 9$, then 212 could be the correct answer. In this case, where 5 is the remainder of both divisions by 9, 212 *could* be the correct answer. Students cannot be sure from this checking method whether in fact this answer is correct since a rearrangement of the digits, to say 221, would also yield the same remainder when divided by 9.

Division by 9 is not necessary to find the remainder. All one has to do is add the digits of the number (to be divided by 9) and, if the result is not a single digit number, repeatedly add the digits until a single digit remains. In the above example the remainders are:

for 29: $2 + 9 = 11; 1 + 1 = 2$
for 57: $5 + 7 = 12; 1 + 2 = 3$
for 85: $8 + 5 = 13; 1 + 3 = 4$
for 35: $3 + 5 = 8$
for 6: 6
for the sum of $2 + 3 + 4 + 8 + 6 = 23; 2 + 3 = 5$
for 212: $2 + 1 + 2 = 5$

Students can use a similar procedure for other operations. For example, to check a multiplication operation: $239 \times 872 = 208{,}408$, they will find the remainders (when divided by 9) of each of the above numbers.

for 239: $2 + 3 + 9 = 14; 1 + 4 = 5$
for 872: $8 + 7 + 2 = 17; 1 + 7 = 8$
for the product $5 \times 8 = 40; 4 + 0 = 4$
for 208,408: $2 + 0 + 8 + 4 + 0 + 8 = 22; 2 + 2 = 4$

Stress to your classes that this is not a fool-proof check of a calculation, but simply one indication of possible correctness. Present this topic in a way that will have them begin to marvel at the interesting properties of the number 9.

Another unusual property of 9 occurs in the multiplication of 9 and any other number of 2 or more digits. Consider the example $65{,}437 \times 9$. An alternative to the usual algorithm is as follows:

1. Subtract the units digit of the multiplicand from 10. $\qquad 10 - 7 = \boxed{3}$
2. Subtract each of the remaining digits from 9 and add the rest to $\qquad 9 - 3 = 6 + 7 = 1\,\boxed{3}$

the preceding number of the multiplicand (at right). For any two-digit sums carry the tens digit to the next sum. $9 - 4 = 5 + 3 + 1 = \boxed{9}$

$9 - 5 = 4 + 4 = \boxed{8}$

$9 - 6 = 3 + 5 = \boxed{8}$

3. Subtract 1 from the left-most digit of the multiplicand. $6 - 1 = \boxed{5}$
4. Now list the results in reverse order to get the desired product. $\boxed{588{,}933}$

Although this method is somewhat cumbersome, it can set the groundwork for some rather interesting investigations into number theory.

To further intrigue your students with other fascinating properties of the number 9, have them multiply 12,345,679 by the first nine multiples of 9, and record their results:

$$\begin{aligned}
12345679 \times 9 &= 111{,}111{,}111\\
12345679 \times 18 &= 222{,}222{,}222\\
12345679 \times 27 &= 333{,}333{,}333\\
12345679 \times 36 &= 444{,}444{,}444\\
12345679 \times 45 &= 555{,}555{,}555\\
12345679 \times 54 &= 666{,}666{,}666\\
12345679 \times 63 &= 777{,}777{,}777\\
12345679 \times 72 &= 888{,}888{,}888\\
12345679 \times 81 &= 999{,}999{,}999
\end{aligned}$$

Students should realize that in the sequence of natural numbers (making up the above multiplicands) the number 8 was omitted. In other words, the number that is two less than the base, 10, is missing. Ask students how to extend this scheme to bases other than 10.

Now have them reverse the sequence of natural numbers including the 8, and multiply each by the first nine multiples of 9. The results will be astonishing:

$$\begin{aligned}
987654321 \times 9 &= 8\ 888\ 888\ 889\\
987654321 \times 18 &= 17\ 777\ 777\ 778\\
987654321 \times 27 &= 26\ 666\ 666\ 667\\
987654321 \times 36 &= 35\ 555\ 555\ 556\\
987654321 \times 45 &= 44\ 444\ 444\ 445\\
987654321 \times 54 &= 53\ 333\ 333\ 334\\
987654321 \times 63 &= 62\ 222\ 222\ 223\\
987654321 \times 72 &= 71\ 111\ 111\ 112\\
987654321 \times 81 &= 80\ 000\ 000\ 001
\end{aligned}$$

Some other interesting properties of the number 9 are exhibited below. Have students discover them by carefully guiding them to the desired result. Stronger students should be encouraged to investigate these relationships and discover *why* they "work."

1.
$$\begin{aligned}
9 \times 9 &= 81\\
99 \times 99 &= 9801\\
999 \times 999 &= 998001\\
9999 \times 9999 &= 99980001\\
99999 \times 99999 &= 9999800001\\
999999 \times 999999 &= 999998000001\\
9999999 \times 9999999 &= 99999980000001
\end{aligned}$$

2.
$$\begin{aligned}
999999 \times 2 &= 1999998\\
999999 \times 3 &= 2999997\\
999999 \times 4 &= 3999996\\
999999 \times 5 &= 4999995\\
999999 \times 6 &= 5999994\\
999999 \times 7 &= 6999993\\
999999 \times 8 &= 7999992\\
999999 \times 9 &= 8999991
\end{aligned}$$

3.
$$\begin{aligned}
1 \times 9 + 2 &= 11\\
12 \times 9 + 3 &= 111\\
123 \times 9 + 4 &= 1111\\
1234 \times 9 + 5 &= 11111\\
12345 \times 9 + 6 &= 111111\\
123456 \times 9 + 7 &= 1111111\\
1234567 \times 9 + 8 &= 11111111\\
12345678 \times 9 + 9 &= 111111111
\end{aligned}$$

4.
$$\begin{aligned}
9 \times 9 + 7 &= 88\\
98 \times 9 + 6 &= 888\\
987 \times 9 + 5 &= 8888\\
9876 \times 9 + 4 &= 88888\\
98765 \times 9 + 3 &= 888888\\
987654 \times 9 + 2 &= 8888888\\
9876543 \times 9 + 1 &= 88888888\\
98765432 \times 9 + 0 &= 888888888
\end{aligned}$$

An interesting way to conclude this unit would be to offer your students a seemingly harmless challenge. That is, ask them to find an eight-digit number in which no digit appears more than once, and which, when multiplied by 9, yields a nine-digit number in which no digit appears more than once. Most of their attempts will fail. For example, $76541238 \times 9 = 688{,}871{,}142$, which has repeated 8s and 1s. Here are several correct numbers:

$$\begin{aligned}
81274365 \times 9 &= 731469285\\
72645831 \times 9 &= 653812479\\
58132764 \times 9 &= 523194876\\
76125483 \times 9 &= 685129347
\end{aligned}$$

POSTASSESSMENT

Ask students to:

1. Demonstrate three unusual properties of 9.
2. Show a short cut for multiplying 547×99.
3. Explain now to "check" a multiplication calculation by "casting out nines."

Unit 10

 Unusual Number Properties

(Author's Note: This unit should be used after the unit entitled "Enrichment with a Handheld Calculator.")

The intention of this unit is to present a good supply of interesting number properties that can be best exhibited on a calculator.

PERFORMANCE OBJECTIVE

Students will investigate mathematical problems with the help of a hand calculator and then draw appropriate conclusions.

PREASSESSMENT

Students should be familiar with the basic functions of a calculator. The instrument required for this unit need only have the four basic operations.

TEACHING STRATEGIES

Perhaps one of the best ways to stimulate genuine excitement in mathematics is to demonstrate some short, simple and dramatic mathematical phenomena. The following are some examples that should provide you with ample material with which to motivate your students toward some independent investigations.

Example 1

When 37 is multiplied by each of the first nine multiples of 3 an interesting result occurs. Let students discover this using their calculators.

$$
\begin{aligned}
37 \times 3 &= 111\\
37 \times 6 &= 222\\
37 \times 9 &= 333\\
37 \times 12 &= 444\\
37 \times 15 &= 555\\
37 \times 18 &= 666\\
37 \times 21 &= 777\\
37 \times 24 &= 888\\
37 \times 27 &= 999
\end{aligned}
$$

Example 2

When 142,857 is multiplied by 2, 3, 4, 5, and 6, the products all use the same digits in the same order as in the original numbers, but each starting at a different point.

$$
\begin{aligned}
142{,}857 \times 2 &= 285{,}714\\
142{,}857 \times 3 &= 428{,}571\\
142{,}857 \times 4 &= 571{,}428\\
142{,}857 \times 5 &= 714{,}285\\
142{,}857 \times 6 &= 857{,}142
\end{aligned}
$$

When 142,857 is multiplied by 7, the product is 999,999. When 142,857 is multiplied by 8, the product is 1,142,856. If the millions digit is removed and added to the units digit (142,856 + 1) the original number is formed. Have students investigate the product 142,857 × 9. What other patterns can be found involving products of 142,857?

A similar pattern occurs with the following products of 76,923: 1, 10, 9, 12, 3, and 4; also 2, 5, 7, 11, 6, and 8. Ask students to inspect the sum of the digits of each of the products obtained. They should discover a truly fascinating result! Ask if they can find other such relationships.

Example 3

The number 1089 has many interesting properties. Have students consider the products of 1089 and each of the first nine natural numbers.

$$
\begin{aligned}
1089 \times 1 &= 1089\\
1089 \times 2 &= 2178\\
1089 \times 3 &= 3267\\
1089 \times 4 &= 4356\\
1089 \times 5 &= 5445\\
1089 \times 6 &= 6534\\
1089 \times 7 &= 7623\\
1089 \times 8 &= 8712\\
1089 \times 9 &= 9801
\end{aligned}
$$

Tell students to notice the symmetry of the first two and last two columns of the products. Each column lists consecutive integers. Encourage students not just to establish and explain this unusual occurrence, but also to build on it. What makes 1089 so unusual? What are the factors of 1089? Why does 1089 × 9 reverse the number 1089? Does a similar scheme work for other numbers? These questions and others should begin to set the tone for further investigation. Naturally students' calculators will be an indispensable tool in their work. The calculators will permit students to see patterns rapidly and without the sidetracking often caused by cumbersome calculations.

Example 4

Some other interesting number patterns for students to generate are given below. Be sure to encourage students to extend the patterns produced and to try to discover why they exist.

$$\begin{aligned}
1 \times 8 + 1 &= 9 \\
12 \times 8 + 2 &= 98 \\
123 \times 8 + 3 &= 987 \\
1{,}234 \times 8 + 4 &= 9{,}876 \\
12{,}345 \times 8 + 5 &= 98{,}765 \\
123{,}456 \times 8 + 6 &= 987{,}654 \\
1{,}234{,}567 \times 8 + 7 &= 9{,}876{,}543 \\
12{,}345{,}678 \times 8 + 8 &= 98{,}765{,}432 \\
123{,}456{,}789 \times 8 + 9 &= 987{,}654{,}321
\end{aligned}$$

$$\begin{aligned}
11 \times 11 &= 121 \\
111 \times 111 &= 12{,}321 \\
1{,}111 \times 1{,}111 &= 1{,}234{,}321 \\
11{,}111 \times 11{,}111 &= 123{,}454{,}321 \\
111{,}111 \times 111{,}111 &= 12{,}345{,}654{,}321 \\
1{,}111{,}111 \times 1{,}111{,}111 &= 1{,}234{,}567{,}654{,}321 \\
11{,}111{,}111 \times 11{,}111{,}111 &= 123{,}456{,}787{,}654{,}321 \\
111{,}111{,}111 \times 111{,}111{,}111 &= 12{,}345{,}678{,}987{,}654{,}321
\end{aligned}$$

Example 5

Have your students compute the divisions indicated by each of the following fractions. Tell them to record their results.

$$\begin{aligned}
\frac{1}{7} &= .\overline{142857} = \frac{142857}{999999} \\
\frac{2}{7} &= .\overline{285714} = \frac{285714}{999999} \\
\frac{3}{7} &= .\overline{428571} = \frac{428571}{999999} \\
\frac{4}{7} &= .\overline{571428} = \frac{571428}{999999} \\
\frac{5}{7} &= .\overline{714285} = \frac{714285}{999999} \\
\frac{6}{7} &= .\overline{857142} = \frac{857142}{999999}
\end{aligned}$$

Students will notice the similar order of the repeating part along with the different starting points. Point out that the product of $7 \times .142857 = .999999$ (which is *close* to $7 \times \frac{1}{7} = 1$). Remind students that this is not the same as $7 \times .\overline{142857}$.

Some students may want to inspect this product in a nondecimal form:

$$\begin{aligned}
7 \times 142{,}857 &= 999{,}999 \\
&= 999{,}000 + 999 \\
&= 1{,}000\,(142 + 857) + (142 + 857) \\
&= (142 + 857)(1000 + 1) \\
&= 1001\,(142 + 857) \\
&= 142{,}142 + 857{,}857
\end{aligned}$$

A better insight into an investigation of these fractions would come after students have already calculated the following quotients:

$$\begin{aligned}
\frac{1}{13} &= .\overline{076923} = \frac{076923}{999999} \\
\frac{3}{13} &= .\overline{230769} = \frac{230769}{999999} \\
\frac{4}{13} &= .\overline{307692} = \frac{307692}{999999} \\
\frac{9}{13} &= .\overline{692307} = \frac{692307}{999999} \\
\frac{10}{13} &= .\overline{769230} = \frac{769230}{999999} \\
\frac{12}{13} &= .\overline{923076} = \frac{923076}{999999}
\end{aligned}$$

Once these have been fully discussed, students may wish to consider the remaining proper fractions with a denominator of 13. They should discover similar patterns and relationships.

The positive impact of the above examples will be lost if students are not immediately guided to investigate and extend their discoveries. While the calculator is the guiding tool for discovering new relationships, students' logical conjectures will come from a deeper investigation of the properties of numbers.

POSTASSESSMENT

Have students complete the following exercises.

1. Multiply and add each of the following pairs of numbers:

   9,9
   24,3
   47,2
   497,2

   How do their sums compare with their products? (reverses)
2. Perform the indicated operations and justify the resulting patterns. Then extend the pattern and see if it holds true.

$$12321 = \frac{333 \times 333}{1 + 2 + 3 + 2 + 1} = \frac{110889}{9} = 12321$$

$$1234321 = \frac{4444 \times 4444}{1 + 2 + 3 + 4 + 3 + 2 + 1} = \frac{19749136}{16} = 1234321$$

Unit 11

 Enrichment with a Handheld Calculator

A recommended beginning-of-the-term small group activity suitable for any level, geared to make students feel comfortable with one another, with the teacher, with a new group, or with the entire class, is a quick review of the calculator's memory and square root keys. This could be followed by a speed and accuracy "contest" involving arithmetic operations.

Most calculators are equipped with memory keys that make possible a variety of challenging activities. These keys provide an efficient way to save intermediate results. They can also store a number that needs to be used several times during the course of an exercise.

> The [M+] key adds the number displayed to the contents of the memory and stores the sum in the memory. The number displayed is not changed.
>
> The [M−] key subtracts the number displayed from the contents of the memory and stores the difference in the memory. The number displayed is not changed.
>
> The [MR] key recalls the contents of the memory, which replaces the contents of the display.

EXAMPLE

Find the value of

$$5 \times 12 + 13 \times 16$$

SOLUTION

Press:

$5 \times 12 =$ [M+] $13 \times 16 = +$[MR] $=$

The display will read 268.

A longer range and more effective use of the calculator is as a problem-solving facilitator. Students who have difficulty solving problems are often faced with a double dilemma. They are unable to interpret the given problem into a solvable form, and they are unable to do the calculations necessary to compute an answer. Normally they cannot concentrate on problem solving until they can do the necessary calculations. However, by using the calculator, they can temporarily avoid the calculations pitfall and thereby concentrate on the key to successful problem solving: interpretation. When this aspect has been learned, a student can concentrate on mastering calculations as an essential ingredient in problem solving.

PERFORMANCE OBJECTIVE

Students will investigate mathematical problems with the help of a hand calculator and then draw appropriate conclusions.

PREASSESSMENT

Students should be familiar with the basic function of a calculator. The instrument required for this unit needs the four basic operations plus memory and square root keys.

For both practice and amusement, have students do the following on their calculators.

1. Compute:

$$2[60 - .243 + (12)(2400)] - 1.$$

To find what every man must pay, read your answer upside down.

2. Compute:

$$4590.5864 + (568.3)(.007) - 1379.26.$$

Then turn your calculator upside down and after reading your answer, look inside your shoe.

These two exercises should give your students a relaxed feeling about working with calculators. Now challenge your students to use the memory keys when finding the flaws in exercises such as these:

3. $15 \times 13 + 18 \times 32$
4. $-15 \times 13 + 226 - 81$
5. $(\frac{253}{11}) + (-23)$
6. $(335 - 281) \times (-81 + 37)$

TEACHING STRATEGIES

Begin the lesson with a simple but intriguing oddity. Have students consider the calendar for the month of May 1977. Tell them to make a square around *any* nine dates; one way to do so is shown in the figure below.

May 1977						
S	M	T	W	T	F	S
1	2	3	4	5	6	7
8	9	10	11	12	13	14
15	16	17	18	19	20	21
22	23	24	25	26	27	28
29	30	31				

Next, students should add 8 to the smallest number in the square and multiply it by 9. In the above example, we have $(11 + 8) \times 9 = 171$. Then students can use their calculators to multiply the sum of the numbers in the middle row (or column) by 3 and find the same result, 171. Have your students try this for other selections of 9 numbers. You should have them realize that the sum of the numbers in the middle row or column multiplied by 3 is in fact the sum of the 9 numbers. Students can verify this easily with their calculators.

From this point, you have an excellent opportunity to investigate properties of the arithmetic mean, as such study will shed more light on this cute "calendar trick." Students should realize that the *middle number* of the square of 9 numbers is in fact the arithmetic mean of the selected numbers. The use of the calculator will relieve them of burdensome computations and permit them to focus all their attention on the mathematical concepts being discovered.

For their next number investigation, have your students select any three-digit number, say 538. Then have them enter it twice into their calculators, without pressing any operation buttons. Their display should show 538538. Now have them divide by 7, then divide by 11, then divide by 13. Much to their surprise they will find their original number displayed. Immediately, student curiosity will arise. Ask them what single operation can be used to replace the 3 divisions. They should realize that a single division by $7 \times 11 \times 13 = 1001$ was actually performed. Since $538 \times 1001 = 538538$, the puzzle is essentially solved; yet students may wish to try this scheme on their calculators using other numbers. This should strengthen their knowledge about numbers, especially 1001, a rather significant number.

Students should now be motivated to try the following multiplications so that they can begin to appreciate (and predict) number patterns:

a. $3 \times 11 = 33$
$3 \times 111 = 333$
$3 \times 1111 = 3333$
$3 \times 11111 = 33333$

b. $4 \times 101 = 404$
$4 \times 10101 = 40404$
$4 \times 1010101 = 4040404$
$4 \times 101010101 = 404040404$

c. $5 \times 1001 = 5005$
$5 \times 110011 = 550055$
$5 \times 11100111 = 55500555$

d. $65 \times 101 = 6565$
$65 \times 10101 = 656565$
$65 \times 1010101 = 65656565$

e. $65 \times 1001 = 65065$
$65 \times 10001 = 650065$
$65 \times 100001 = 6500065$
$65 \times 1001001 = 65065065$

f. $7 \times 11 = 77$
$7 \times 11 \times 101 = 7777$
$7 \times 11 \times 10101 = 777777$
$7 \times 111 \times 1001 = 777777$

Now have students discover other ways of generating by multiplication: 777777, 7777777, and 77777777. At this point students ought to be interested enough to establish other number patterns from products.

Most of your students should now be ready to consider somewhat more sophisticated problems.

A *palindrome* is defined as "a word or verse reading the same backward or forward, e.g. *madam, I'm Adam*." In mathematics a number that reads the same in either direction is a palindrome. For example, have your students select any two-digit number and add to it the number whose digits are the reverse order of the original one. Now have them take the sum and add it to the number whose digits are in the reverse order. They should continue this process until a palindrome is formed. For example:

$75 + 57 = 132$
$132 + 231 = 363$, a *palindrome*

$79 + 97 = 176$
$176 + 671 = 847$
$847 + 748 = 1595$
$1595 + 5951 = 7546$
$7546 + 6457 = 14003$
$14003 + 30041 = 44044$, a *palindrome*

No matter which original two-digit number is selected, a palindrome will eventually be formed. Using a calculator the students will see various patterns arising, which should lead them to discover why this actually "works."

Encourage your students to carefully conjecture about other possible number relationships and then verify them using a calculator.

POSTASSESSMENT

Tell your students to use their calculators to verify the following phenomenon for six different numbers. Then they should try to prove it.

1. Select any three-digit number in which the hundreds digit and the units digit are unequal. Then write the number whose digits are in the reverse order from the select number. Now subtract the smaller of these two numbers from the larger. Take the difference, reverse its digits, and add the "new" number to the original difference. What number do you always end up with? Why?
2. Evaluate $\dfrac{23.4 \times 17.6}{50 \times 8}$ to the nearest tenth or even number.
3. Evaluate $\dfrac{2}{2 - 1}$ to the nearest hundredth.

Unit 12

 Symmetric Multiplication

This unit shows how some numbers, because of their symmetry, can be multiplied easily through the use of "form multiplication."

PERFORMANCE OBJECTIVE

Given a form multiplication example, students will perform the multiplication using the technique described in this unit.

PREASSESSMENT

Have students multiply each of the following by conventional means:

a. 66666 × 66666   b. 2222 × 2222   c. 333 × 777

TEACHING STRATEGIES

After students have completed the above computations, they will probably welcome a more novel approach to these problems. Have them consider the following rhombic form approach.

```
      66666
     ×66666
         36
       3636
     363636
   36363636
 3636363636
   36363636
     363636
       3636
         36
 4444355556
```

Students might wonder if this scheme works for other numbers of this type. Have them square 88888 first by the conventional method and then by rhombic form multiplication. To do the latter, students should replace the "36s" in the previous example with "64s." Soon students will wonder how to extend this multiplication technique to squaring a repeated-digit number where the square of a digit is a *one-digit* number.

In squaring a number such as 2222, students must write each partial product as 04.

```
     2222
   × 2222
       04
     0404
   040404
 04040404
   040404
     0404
       04
  4937284
```

At this juncture students may be convinced that this will be true for all numbers of this type. Have them consider squaring an n-digit number $uuu \ldots uuu$, where $u^2 = 10s + t$ (or written in base 10 as st). This multiplication would require an nth order rhombic form (i.e., one that increases the number of sts by one in each of the first n rows, and then decreases by one st in each of the remaining $n - 1$ rows). The case where $n = 5$ is shown below.

```
      uuuuu
     ×uuuuu
         st
       stst
     ststst
   stststst
 ststststst
   stststst
     ststst
       stst
         st
```

Students will be interested to notice that this multiplication technique can be further extended to finding the product

The next step in the method is:

$$\left[\frac{1}{2}\left(\frac{1}{2}a\right) - \frac{1}{2}\right] \cdot 4b = y$$

Then using the distributive property:

$$\left[\frac{1}{4}a \cdot 4b\right] - \left[\frac{1}{2} \cdot 4b\right] = y$$

Since $\frac{1}{4}a \cdot 4b = c$, then $c - 2b = y$

Therefore the new product, y, will be short of the correct answer, c, by $2b$ (which is the first desired number to be added since it is paired with an odd number, $\frac{1}{2}a$).

As the process continues, the "new products" will remain the same if ka (an entry in the first column) is even. If ka is odd and $ka \cdot mb = w$, the next product will decrease by mb (the number matches with the odd number). For example, $\left(\frac{1}{2}ka - \frac{1}{2}\right) \cdot 2mb = \left(\frac{1}{2}ka \cdot 2mb\right) - \left(\frac{1}{2} \cdot 2mb\right) = w - mb$

Finally when 1 appears in the first column:

$1 \cdot pb = Z$, with $pb = Z$
$Z = c -$ all deductions (numbers referred to above matched with odd $k$as)
c(desired result) $= Z +$ all deductions

A further consideration of the Russian Peasant Method for multiplication can be seen from the following illustration:

$$\begin{array}{rlrl}
{}^{*}\ 43 \cdot 92 = & (21 \cdot 2 + 1)(92) & = 21 \cdot 184 + 92 & = 3956 \\
{}^{*}\ 21 \cdot 184 = & (10 \cdot 2 + 1)(184) & = 10 \cdot 368 + 184 & = 3864 \\
10 \cdot 368 = & (5 \cdot 2 + 0)(368) & = 5 \cdot 736 + 0 & = 3680 \\
{}^{*}\ 5 \cdot 736 = & (2 \cdot 2 + 1)(736) & = 2 \cdot 1472 + 736 & = 3680 \\
2 \cdot 1472 = & (1 \cdot 2 + 0)(1472) & = 1 \cdot 2944 + 0 & = 2944 \\
{}^{*}\ 1 \cdot 2944 = & (0 \cdot 2 + 1)(2944) & = 0 + \underline{2944} & = 2944 \\
 & & 3956 &
\end{array}$$

Notice that summing only those numbers in the second column whose corresponding entries in the first column are odd, is justified by the above representation.

The teacher may wish to shed further light on this curiosity by presenting the binary nature of this multiplication.

$$\begin{aligned}
&(43)(92) \\
&= (1 \cdot 2^5 + 0 \cdot 2^4 + 1 \cdot 2^3 + 0 \cdot 2^2 + 1 \cdot 2^1 + 1 \cdot 2^0)(92) \\
&= 2^0 \cdot 92 + 2^1 \cdot 92 + 2^3 \cdot 92 + 2^5 \cdot 92 \\
&= 92 + 184 + 736 + 2944 \\
&= 3956
\end{aligned}$$

Other investigations should be encouraged by the students.

LATTICE MULTIPLICATION

Once again consider the multiplication $43 \cdot 92$. To perform this method, a 2 by 2 array is constructed and diagonals are drawn as shown.

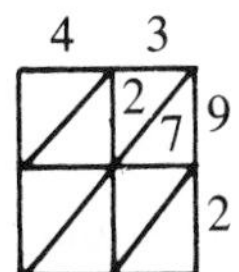

First multiply $3 \cdot 9 = 27$; the 2 is placed above the 7 as shown below.

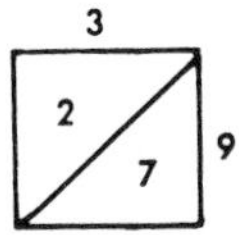

The next step is to multiply $4 \cdot 9 = 36$. Again, the 3 is placed above the 6 in the appropriate box.

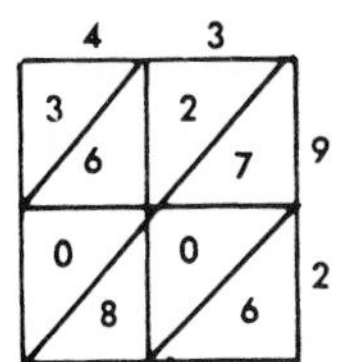

This process is continued, filling in the remainder of the square. Notice that $3 \cdot 2 = 6$ is recorded as 0/6.

Now that there are entries in all cells, add the numbers in the diagonal directions indicated, beginning at the lower right. The sums are circled.

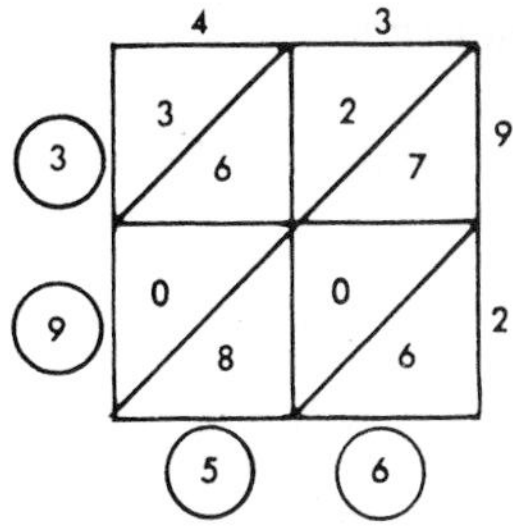

Notice that in the second addition, $8 + 0 + 7 = 15$, the 5 is recorded and the 1 is carried to the next diagonal addition. The correct answer (the product of $43 \cdot 92$) is then merely read from the circled numbers. That is, the answer is 3,956.

TRACHTENBERG SYSTEM

The Trachtenberg System is a method for high-speed multiplication, division, addition, subtraction, and square root. There are numerous rules for these operations. Concern here will only be focused on the multiplication of two 2-digit numbers.

Again, suppose the product of 43 and 92 is desired.

Step 1. Multiply the two units digits

$$[3 \cdot 2 = 6] \qquad \begin{array}{r} 43 \\ \times\ 92 \\ \hline 6 \end{array}$$

Step 2. Cross-multiply and add mentally

$$[(9 \cdot 3) + (2 \cdot 4) = 27 + 8 = 35]$$

Place the 5 as shown and carry the 3 (as an addend to the next step)

$$\begin{array}{r} 43 \\ \times\ 92 \\ \hline 56 \end{array}$$

Step 3 Multiply the two tens digits and then add any number carried over from the previous step.

$$[9 \cdot 4 = 36 \text{ and } 36 + 3 = 39]$$

$$\begin{array}{r} 43 \\ \times\ 92 \\ \hline 3956 \end{array}$$

The algebraic justification of this method is shown below: Consider the two 2-digit numbers ab and mn (written in place-value form)

$$\begin{aligned} &(10a + b) \cdot (10m + n) \\ &= 10a \cdot 10m + 10a \cdot n + 10b \cdot m + bn \\ &= \underbrace{100am}_{\text{Step 3}} + \underbrace{10an + 10bm}_{\text{Step 2}} + \underbrace{bn}_{\text{Step 1}} \end{aligned}$$

ANOTHER METHOD

A multiple of ten "squared" is an easy mental computation. This method of multiplication incorporates this idea. Have students consider the product of $m \cdot n$. They then choose x such that $x = 10p$ and $m < x < n$ with $x - m = a$ and $n - x = b$. Then $m \cdot n = (x - a)(x + b) = x^2 - ax + bx - ab$.

Consider the multiplication of $43 \cdot 92$.
Let $x = 60$.

$$\begin{aligned} \text{Then } 43 \cdot 92 &= (60 - 17)(60 + 32) \\ &= 3600 + (-17 \cdot 60 + 60 \cdot 32) + (-17 \cdot 32) \\ &= 3600 + (-1020 + 1920) + (-544) \\ &= 3600 + 900 - 544 \\ &= 3956 \end{aligned}$$

However, if the numbers are the same distance from the multiple of ten, the method is much faster. The middle term will be eliminated!

Suppose students wish to multiply $57 \cdot 63$. Then $57 \cdot 63 = (60 - 3)(60 + 3) = 60^2 - 3^2 = 3600 - 9 = 3591$.

Part of the skill in working with different multiplication methods involves selection of the most efficient method for the particular problem. This should be stressed with the class.

OTHER METHODS

Now that students have been exposed to several methods for multiplication, the teacher should suggest that students do research and explore other methods for multiplication. These could then be presented to the class.

POSTASSESSMENT

Multiply 52 by 76 using any four different methods.

Unit 14

Ancient Egyptian Arithmetic

The study of a number system and its arithmetic is valuable to students on many levels. A student on a high level can delve into the mechanics of the system through an intricate comparison between that system and our own, and perhaps go off on a suitable tangent from there, such as an inspection of bases and still other number systems. For other students it can serve as a reinforcement of basic arithmetic (multiplication and division) both of integers and of fractions since the students will want to check if this system really works. This unit introduces students to the ancient Egyptian numerical notation and to their system of multiplying and dividing.

PERFORMANCE OBJECTIVES

1. *Given a multiplication problem, students will find the answer using an Egyptian method.*
2. *Given a division problem, students will find the answer using an Egyptian method.*

3. *Given a nonunit fraction, students will obtain its unit fraction decomposition.*

PREASSESSMENT

Students should be familiar with addition and multiplication of fractions, as well as with the distributive property of real numbers. A knowledge of bases may also be useful.

TEACHING STRATEGIES

An example of a simple grouping system can be seen in the Egyptian hieroglyphics. This numeral system is based on the number 10. The symbols used when representing their numbers on stone, papyrus, wood and pottery were

for 1

for 10

for 10^2

for 10^3

for 10^4

Therefore, 13,521 would be represented as

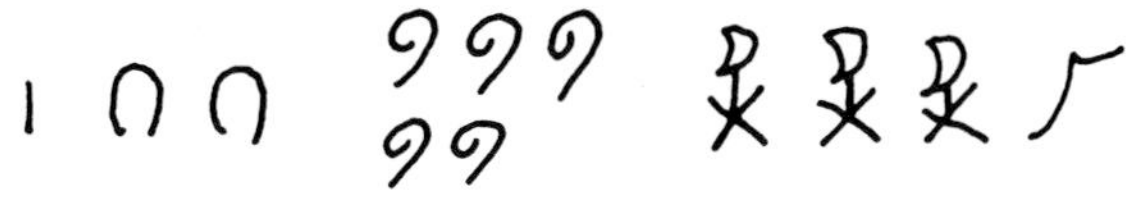

(Have students notice that the Egyptians wrote numbers from right to left.)

The Egyptians avoided a difficult multiplication or division method by using an easier (although at times longer) method. To multiply 14 by 27, they would have done the following:

1	27
* 2	54
* 4	108
* 8	216
16	432

To advance from any line to the next line, all the Egyptians had to do was double the number. Then, they picked out the numbers in the left-hand column that added up to 14 (the numbers with a *). By adding up the corresponding numbers in the right-hand column they arrived at the answer: $54 + 108 + 216 = 378$. This is an application of the distributive property of multiplication over addition, for what the Egyptians did is equivalent to

$$27(14) = 27(2 + 4 + 8) = 54 + 108 + 216 = 378.$$

Further justification for the method lies in the fact that any number can be expressed as the sum of powers of two. Investigate this process with your students to the extent you feel necessary.

The Egyptians performed division in a similar way. They viewed the problem $114 \div 6$ as 6 times whatever number equals 114.

1	6 *
2	12 *
4	24
8	48
16	96 *

Now since $114 = 6 + 12 + 96$, the Egyptians would have found that $114 = 6(1 + 2 + 16)$ or $6 \times 19 = 114$. The answer is 19.

While no problems could arise in the Egyptian method of multiplication, a slight one occurs with respect to their method of division. To call attention to this problem, ask your class to use the above method to solve $83 \div 16$.

1	16 *
2	32
4	64 *
8	128

Using $16 + 64 = 80$ the Egyptians were still missing 3. Since $1 \times 16 = 16$ they found that they needed fractions to complete this problem.

In the Egyptian number system, every fraction except $\frac{2}{3}$ was represented as the sum of "unit fractions," fractions whose numerators are 1. In this way, the Egyptians avoided some of the computational problems one encounters when working with fractions. Since their arithmetic was based on doubling, the only problem they had to deal with was how to change a fraction of the form $\frac{2}{n}$ to one of the form $\frac{1}{a} + \frac{1}{b} + \ldots$. They handled this problem with a table (found in the Rhind papyrus, dated approximately 1650 B.C.) which gives the decomposition of all fractions of the form $\frac{2}{n}$ for all odd n from 5 to 101. (Your class should be able to see why they considered only odd n.) A fraction such as $\frac{2}{37}$ was written as $\frac{1}{19} + \frac{1}{703}$ or, using the common notation for unit fractions, $\overline{19} + \overline{703}$ (This notation survives from the Egyptians who wrote a fraction such as $\frac{1}{4}$ as  and $\frac{1}{14}$ as  in hieroglyphics.) $\frac{2}{3}$ had its own symbol  and sometimes $\frac{1}{2}$ appeared as  .

The need now arises to consider a rule that can be used to decompose a fraction of the form $\frac{2}{pq}$ (where p or q may be 1). Have the class consider $\frac{2}{pq} = \frac{1}{\frac{p(p+q)}{2}} + \frac{1}{\frac{q(p+q)}{2}}$. They can add the fractions on the right side of the equation together to prove this is true. Also have them notice that since

pq is odd (since we only need a rule to decompose $\frac{2}{n}$ where n is odd) p and q are odd, so $p + q$ will be even, and therefore $\frac{p+q}{2}$ will be an integer.

Students can decompose $\frac{2}{15}$ at least two ways. If they set $p = 3$ and $q = 5$ they will have $\frac{2}{15} = \frac{1}{\frac{3(8)}{2}} + \frac{1}{\frac{5(8)}{2}} = \frac{1}{12} + \frac{1}{20}$, or $\overline{12} + \overline{20}$. If they let $p = 1$ and $q = 5$ they will have $\frac{2}{15} = \frac{1}{\frac{1(16)}{2}} + \frac{1}{\frac{15(16)}{2}} = \frac{1}{8} + \frac{1}{120}$ or $\overline{8} + \overline{120}$.

It seems the Egyptians had other ways to decompose fractions so as to make the new denominator less complicated. For instance, we could also view $\frac{2}{15}$ as $\frac{4}{30}$.

Then we have $\frac{4}{30} = \frac{3}{30} + \frac{1}{30} = \overline{10} + \overline{30}$. Have students check these conversions.

Now, have students reconsider the earlier division problem 83 ÷ 16.

1	16*
2	32
4	64*
8	128
$\overline{2}$	8
$\overline{4}$	4
$\overline{8}$	2*
$\overline{16}$	1*

By selecting a sum of 83 from the right column, they will arrive at the following answer: $1 + 4 + \overline{8} + \overline{16} = 5 + \overline{8} + \overline{16} = 5\frac{3}{16}$. Students should now be able to solve their arithmetic problems using methods developed by the ancient Egyptians.

POSTASSESSMENT

1. Have students write each of the following numbers in hieroglyphics.

   a. 5,280 b. 23,057 c. $\frac{2}{25}$ d. $\frac{2}{35}$

2. Have students change each of the following fractions into two different unit fraction decompositions.

   a. $\frac{2}{27}$ b. $\frac{2}{45}$ c. $\frac{2}{99}$

3. Have students solve the following problems using Egyptian methods.

   a. 30 × 41 b. 25 × 137 c. 132 ÷ 11 d. 101 ÷ 16

Unit 15

Napier's Rods

PERFORMANCE OBJECTIVES

1. *Students will construct a cardboard set of Napier's Rods.*
2. *Students will successfully perform multiplication examples using Napier's Rods.*

PREASSESSMENT

The only essential skill for this activity is the ability to do multiplication.

TEACHING STRATEGIES

Begin your presentation with a brief historical note about Napier's Rods. This multiplication "machine" was developed by John Napier (1550–1617), a Scotch mathematician, who was principally responsible for the development of logarithms. The device he developed consisted of flat wooden sticks with successive multiples of numbers 1–9 (see Figure 1).

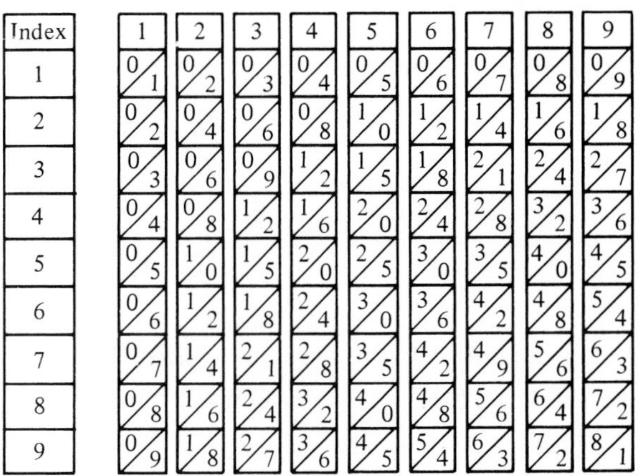

FIGURE 1

Each student should be given an opportunity to construct his own set of Napier's Rods. Perhaps the best way to explain how to use Napier's Rods is to illustrate with an example using this device.

Consider the multiplication 523 × 467. Have students select the rods for 5, 2, and 3, and line them up adjacent to the Index Rod (see Figure 2).

Students must then select the appropriate rows from the index corresponding to the digits in the multiplier. In a diagonal

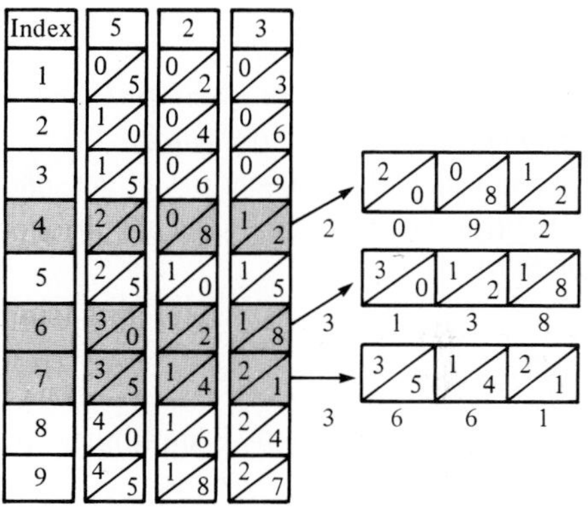

FIGURE 2

direction addition is done for each row (see Figure 2). The numbers thus obtained:

$$2092 = 4 \times 523$$
$$3138 = 6 \times 523$$
$$3661 = 7 \times 523$$

are added after considering the appropriate place values of the digits from which they were generated.

$$467 = 400 + 60 + 7$$
$$(467)(523) = (400)(523) + (60)(523) + (7)(523)$$
$$(467)(523) = \begin{array}{r} 209200 \\ 31380 \\ \underline{3661} \\ 244241 \end{array}$$

A careful discussion of this last step not only will insure a working knowledge of the computing "machine" by your students, but also should give them a thorough understanding as to *why* this technique "works."

1. 561 × 49
2. 308 × 275
3. 4932 × 7655

POSTASSESSMENT

Have students use a set of Napier's Rods (which they have constructed) to multiply each of the following:

1. 361 · 49
2. 308 · 275
3. 4932 · 7566

Unit 16

Unit Pricing

PERFORMANCE OBJECTIVES

1. *Students will determine which of two given fractions is greater using the technique described on this card.*
2. *Students will determine which of two quantities of the same product has the more favorable price, given the quantity and the price for that quantity.*

PREASSESSMENT

The only skill students need for this activity is multiplication of whole numbers.

TEACHING STRATEGIES

Ask your students if they would rather buy a 32 oz. jar of applesauce costing 30¢ or a 27 oz. jar costing 25¢. An organized thinker might translate the problem to one that asks which is larger, $\frac{30}{32}$ or $\frac{25}{27}$.

Students should realize that the fractions come from "price *per* ounce." The word *per* indicates division, so a fraction $\frac{\text{price}}{\text{ounces}}$ can be attained.

There are many ways in which two fractions can be compared, dividing the numerator by the denominator and comparing the resulting decimal, changing both fractions to equivalent fractions with the same denominator, and so on.

We shall now consider another method, which could easily be the most efficient method. Draw two arrows as indicated below. Then multiply as the arrows show, writing the product under the arrowheads.

$$\underset{810}{\downarrow}\ \frac{30}{32} \times \frac{25}{27}\ \underset{800}{\downarrow}$$

Simple inspection of these products indicates that 810 is the larger of the two; hence the fraction above the 810 (i.e., $\frac{30}{32}$) is the larger of the two fractions. Therefore, the unit price of the 27 ounce jar is lower and thus the better buy.

Before giving students problems involving comparison of unit prices, offer them some drill problems involving only comparison of fractions.

POSTASSESSMENT

Select the larger of each for the following pairs of fractions.

1. $\frac{5}{6}, \frac{7}{8}$
2. $\frac{8}{11}, \frac{17}{23}$
3. $\frac{7}{9}, \frac{4}{5}$
4. $\frac{13}{17}, \frac{19}{25}$
5. $\frac{11}{19}, \frac{5}{9}$
6. $\frac{7}{12}, \frac{18}{31}$
7. Which quantity has the lower unit price: a 7 oz. jar of mustard costing 11¢ or a 9 oz. jar of mustard costing 13¢?

Unit 17

 Successive Discounts and Increases

This unit provides students with a simple technique for expressing various successive discounts and/or increases as one equivalent discount or increase. They may be rather fascinated by the case of solution that this method brings to a usually complicated consumer situation.

PERFORMANCE OBJECTIVES

1. *Students will convert two or more successive discounts to one equivalent discount.*
2. *Students will convert two or more successive discounts and increases to one equivalent discount or increase.*

PREASSESSMENT

Use the following problem for diagnostic purposes as well as to motivate discussion.

> Ernie is deciding where to buy a shirt. Barry's Bargain Store offers the shirt at a 30% discount off the list price. Cheap Charlie's Store usually offers the same shirt at a 20% discount off the same list price. However, today Cheap Charlie's Store is offering the shirt at a 10% discount off the already discounted (20%) price. At which store will Ernie get a greater discount on the shirt today?

TEACHING STRATEGIES

Students may not immediately realize the difference in the discounts of the two stores mentioned in the problem above. Some students may feel that both stores offer the same discount. With your help they should begin to notice that, whereas Barry's Bargain Store offers a 30% discount off the original list price, Cheap Charlie's Store only offers a 20% discount off the original list price, while the 10% discount is taken off the lower, already discounted price. Hence, Ernie gets a greater discount with the 30% discount.

At this juncture your students may begin to wonder how large the actual difference is between the discounts offered by the two stores. You might then elicit from them that this quantitative comparison calls for finding a single discount equivalent to the two *successive discounts* of 20% and 10%.

Some students may suggest finding the required discounts by starting with a list price such as \$10.00. This would work well as 100 is the basis of percents. That is, a discount of 20% off \$10.00 yields a price of \$8.00. Then a 10% discount off \$8.00 yields a new price of \$7.20. Since \$7.20 may be obtained by a single discount of 28% off the original \$10.00, *successive discounts* of 20% and 10% are equivalent to a single discount of 28%. It is simple to compare this with the 30% discount from the original problem.

Students should consider a general method of converting any number of successive discounts to a single discount. Illustrate with two successive discounts percents of d_1 and d_2 operating on a price p.

Use the same procedure as before:

$p - \frac{pd_1}{100} = p\left(1 - \frac{d_1}{100}\right)$ represents the price after one discount has been computed; $\left[p\left(1 - \frac{d_1}{100}\right)\right] - \left[p\left(1 - \frac{d_1}{100}\right)\right]\left(\frac{d_2}{100}\right) = p\left(1 - \frac{d_1}{100}\right)\left(1 - \frac{d_2}{100}\right)$ represents the price after the second discount has been computed; $\left(1 - \frac{d_1}{100}\right)\left(1 - \frac{d_2}{100}\right)$ represents the percent that the new price is of the original price. Therefore $1 - \left(1 - \frac{d_1}{100}\right)\left(1 - \frac{d_2}{100}\right)$ represents the discount taken off the original price in order to obtain the new price.

Hence, successive discounts of $d_1\%$ and $d_2\%$ are equivalent to a single discount percent of $1 - \left(1 - \frac{d_1}{100}\right)\left(1 - \frac{d_2}{100}\right)$.

By translating this final algebraic expression into verbal form the students should be able to establish the following simple technique for converting two successive discounts to a single equivalent discount:

1. Change each of the successive discounts to decimal fractions.
2. Subtract each of these decimal fractions from the whole (i.e., 1.00).
3. Multiply the results of Step 2.
4. Subtract the results of Step 3 from the whole (i.e., 1.00).
5. Change the result of Step 4 to percent form.

Applying this to the successive discounts of 20% and 10% the students should show the following work:

1. 20% = .20 and 10% = .10
2. 1.00 − .20 = .80, and 1.00 − .10 = .90
3. (.80) (.90) = .72
4. 1.00 − .72 = .28
5. .28 = 28% (discount)

Students will notice that the rules above do not specify the number of successive discounts considered. This may prompt them to investigate the case where more than two successive discounts are to be converted to a single equivalent discount. Students should proceed in a manner similar to the one used above for two successive discounts. They should find that these same rules do in fact hold true in converting any number of successive discounts to a single equivalent discount.

A natural question to be expected at this juncture would probe the nature of *successive increases* or *successive decreases* and *increase*. An increase requires adding a percent of the price to the original price, while a discount requires subtracting a percent of the price from the original price. So the students could be expected to guess that the technique for converting successive increases or combinations of successive increases and discounts to a single increase or discount will be similar to the conversion technique used for successive discounts. Suggest they work out this technique.

Broadening the scope of this conversion technique to include increases as well as discounts will allow students to consider problems such as the following:

> When the entrance price to a basketball game was decreased by 25%, the attendance at the game increased by 35%. What was the effect of these changes on the daily receipts?

In solving this problem the student's work should resemble the following:

1. 25% = .25, and 35% = .35
2. 1.00 − .25 = .75 and 1.00 + .35 = 1.35
3. (.75) (1.35) = 1.0125
4. 1.0125 − 1.0000 = .0125
5. .0125 = 1.25% (increase)

You might wish to ask your students what they feel would be the net effect of a successive discount of 10% and increase of 10%. Students generally feel that these two changes counteract one another, leaving the original price unaltered. However they should be encouraged to apply the conversion technique. The net effect of these two changes is in fact a discount of 1%.

The following chart of successive discounts and increases of the same percent should lead students to making an intelligent conjecture about the "break even" point.

Successive Changes							
% Discount	20	15	10	5	1	.5	.1
% Increase	20	15	10	5	1	.5	.1
Equivalent % Discount Change	4	2.25	1	.25	.01	.0025	.0001

Students may want to discover what combinations of successive discount and increase will leave the original price unaltered. One possible approach would be to use the conversion technique for a successive discount of *d*% and increase of *i*%:

$$1 - \left(1 - \frac{d}{100}\right)\left(1 + \frac{i}{100}\right) = 0;\ 1 - \left(1 - \frac{d}{100} + \frac{i}{100} - \frac{di}{100^2}\right) = 0;\ 100d - 100i + di = 0;$$

$$d = \frac{100i}{100 + i} \quad \text{or} \quad i = \frac{100d}{100 - d}$$

The chart below lists possible values for *d* and *i*.

d	0	$9.0\overline{909}$	$16.66\overline{6}$	20	50	75	10	25
i	0	10	20	25	100	300	$11.11\overline{1}$	$33.33\overline{3}$

By now the students should have some insight into the topic of *successive percents*. The conversion technique introduced in this model is rather easy to remember as the basic steps merely call for subtraction (and/or addition), multiplication, and subtraction (and/or addition).

POSTASSESSMENT

Have students try to solve several problems such as the following.

1. Alice wants to buy a dress whose list price is \$20. One store, which generally discounts its dresses $12\frac{1}{2}$%, is offering an additional 20% on its already discounted price. A nearby store offers the same dress at a single 32% discount. Which store offers the lower price?
2. When the price of a magazine was decreased by 15% the sales increased by 20%. How were the receipts affected by these changes?

REFERENCES

Posamentier, Alfred S. *Students! Get Ready for the SAT I: Problem Solving Strategies and Practical Tests*. Thousand Oaks, CA: Corwin Press, 1996.

Posamentier, Alfred S., and S. Krulik. *Teachers! Prepare Your Students for the Mathematics for SAT I: Methods and Problem Solving Strategies*. Thousand Oaks, CA: Corwin, 1996.

Posamentier, Alfred S., and Charles T. Salkind. *Challenging Problems in Algebra*. New York: Dover, 1996.

Unit 18

Prime and Composite Factors of a Whole Number

This unit presents a different approach to the process of factoring a number. It allows students to find the complete set of all different factors of a composite whole number. At the same time, this unit helps students better understand the factorization process.

PERFORMANCE OBJECTIVES

1. *Students will determine the total number of factors, prime and composite, of a given composite whole number.*
2. *Students will determine each of the elements of the set of prime and composite factors of this number.*
3. *Students will find the sum of all the elements of this set.*

PREASSESSMENT

Students should be familiar with the basic rules of divisibility and able to find the prime factorization of a number.

TEACHING STRATEGIES

To find the set of prime and composite factors of the given number, you should first find the prime factorization of the number and then determine all possible products of these factors.

To find the prime factorization of the number, the "peeling" technique may be used. For example, to find the prime factorization of 3960, you should proceed as follows:

2)3960	3960 $= 2 \times 1980$
2)1980	$= 2 \times 2 \times 990$
2) 990	$= 2 \times 2 \times 2 \times 495$
3) 495	$= 2 \times 2 \times 2 \times 3 \times 165$
3) 165	$= 2 \times 2 \times 2 \times 3 \times 3 \times 55$
5) 55	$= 2 \times 2 \times 2 \times 3 \times 3 \times 5 \times 11$
11	

The prime factorization of 3960 is

$$2 \times 2 \times 2 \times 3 \times 3 \times 5 \times 11 = 2^3 \times 3^2 \times 5 \times 11$$

The total number of factors of a given number is determined by the product of the exponents (*each* increased by one) of the different factors in the prime factorization of the number expressed in exponential form.

Therefore, the total number of factors of 3960 will be given by the product:

$$(3 + 1)(2 + 1)(1 + 1)(1 + 1) = 4 \times 3 \times 2 \times 2 = 48$$

To find each of the 48 factors, prepare the following self-explanatory table:

1	2	2^2	2^3
1	3	3^2	
1	5		
1	11		

Now have students multiply each number in the first row by each number in the second row:

1×1	1×2	1×2^2	1×2^3
1×3	2×3	$2^2 \times 3$	$2^3 \times 3$
1×3^2	2×3^2	$2^2 \times 3^2$	$2^3 \times 3^2$

Then each resulting product would be multiplied by each number in the third row:

$1 \times 1 \times 1$	$1 \times 1 \times 2$	$1 \times 1 \times 2^2$	$1 \times 1 \times 2^3$
$1 \times 1 \times 3$	$1 \times 2 \times 3$	$1 \times 2^2 \times 3$	$1 \times 2^3 \times 3$
$1 \times 1 \times 3^2$	$1 \times 2 \times 3^2$	$1 \times 2^2 \times 3^2$	$1 \times 2^3 \times 3^2$
$1 \times 1 \times 5$	$1 \times 2 \times 5$	$1 \times 2^2 \times 5$	$1 \times 2^3 \times 5$
$1 \times 3 \times 5$	$2 \times 3 \times 5$	$2^2 \times 3 \times 5$	$2^3 \times 3 \times 5$
$1 \times 3^2 \times 5$	$2 \times 3^2 \times 5$	$2^2 \times 3^2 \times 5$	$2^3 \times 3^2 \times 5$

You should continue this same process until all rows are exhausted. In the case of our example, 3960, we finally have:

$1 \times 1 \times 1 \times 1$	$1 \times 1 \times 1 \times 2$	$1 \times 1 \times 1 \times 2^2$	$1 \times 1 \times 1 \times 2^3$
$1 \times 1 \times 1 \times 3$	$1 \times 1 \times 2 \times 3$	$1 \times 1 \times 2^2 \times 3$	$1 \times 1 \times 2^3 \times 3$
$1 \times 1 \times 1 \times 3^2$	$1 \times 1 \times 2 \times 3^2$	$1 \times 1 \times 2^2 \times 3^2$	$1 \times 1 \times 2^3 \times 3^2$
$1 \times 1 \times 1 \times 5$	$1 \times 1 \times 2 \times 5$	$1 \times 1 \times 2^2 \times 5$	$1 \times 1 \times 2^3 \times 5$
$1 \times 1 \times 3 \times 5$	$1 \times 2 \times 3 \times 5$	$1 \times 2^2 \times 3 \times 5$	$1 \times 2^3 \times 3 \times 5$
$1 \times 1 \times 3^2 \times 5$	$1 \times 2 \times 3^2 \times 5$	$1 \times 2^2 \times 3^2 \times 5$	$1 \times 2^3 \times 3^2 \times 5$
$1 \times 1 \times 1 \times 11$	$1 \times 1 \times 2 \times 11$	$1 \times 1 \times 2^2 \times 11$	$1 \times 1 \times 2^3 \times 11$

$1 \times 1 \times 3 \times 11$	$1 \times 2 \times 3 \times 11$	$1 \times 2^2 \times 3 \times 11$	$1 \times 2^3 \times 3 \times 11$
$1 \times 1 \times 3^2 \times 11$	$1 \times 2 \times 3^2 \times 11$	$1 \times 2^2 \times 3^2 \times 11$	$1 \times 2^3 \times 3^2 \times 11$
$1 \times 1 \times 5 \times 11$	$1 \times 2 \times 5 \times 11$	$1 \times 2^2 \times 5 \times 11$	$1 \times 2^3 \times 5 \times 11$
$1 \times 3 \times 5 \times 11$	$2 \times 3 \times 5 \times 11$	$2^2 \times 3 \times 5 \times 11$	$2^3 \times 3 \times 5 \times 11$
$1 \times 3^2 \times 5 \times 11$	$2 \times 3^2 \times 5 \times 11$	$2^2 \times 3^2 \times 5 \times 11$	$2^3 \times 3^2 \times 5 \times 11$

However, students can obtain the same results in a simpler and quicker way: Find the divisors of each of the factors in the number's prime factorization when written in exponential form. In our example:

$$\underset{a}{2^3\begin{cases} 2^1 = 2 \\ 2^2 = 4 \\ 2^3 = 8 \end{cases}} \quad \underset{b}{3^2\begin{cases} 3^1 = 3 \\ 3^2 = 9 \end{cases}} \quad \underset{c}{5^1\{5^1 = 5} \quad \underset{d}{11^1\{11^1 = 11}$$

Have students prepare a table in which the first row is formed by number one and the numbers in a (see below). Have pupils draw a line and multiply each number in b by each number above this line. Students will draw a new line and multiply the element in c by all the numbers above the second line. The process will continue until all divisors of each of the factors in the number's prime factorization are multiplied.

1	2	4	8	I
3	6	12	24	
9	18	36	72	II
5	10	20	40	
15	30	60	120	III
45	90	180	360	
11	22	44	88	
33	66	132	264	
99	198	396	792	
55	110	220	440	IV
165	330	660	1320	
495	990	1980	3960	

The table that contains the 48 factors we are looking for starts with number 1 and ends with our given number 3960.

Part 1 is formed by number I and the factors in a. Part II is constituted by the products of each of the numbers in b and each of the numbers in I. Part III is made up by the products obtained when multiplying each of the numbers of c by each of the numbers in I and II. And finally, part IV is formed by multiplying each number of d by each of the numbers in I, II, and III. The table has $4 \times 12 = 48$ factors. All of the factors of 3960 appear in this table: the prime as well as the composite factors of 3960.

To find the sum of the factors of a number N, let us represent the prime factorization of N by $a^{\alpha} \cdot b^{\beta} \cdot c^{\rho} \cdot d^{\theta}$, such that $N = a^{\alpha} \cdot b^{\beta} \cdot c^{\rho} \cdot d^{\theta}$. The sum of all the factors of N will be given by the formula

$$s = \frac{a^{\alpha+1}\ 1}{a-1} \cdot \frac{b^{\beta+1}\ 1}{b-1} \cdot \frac{c^{\rho+1}\ 1}{c-1} \cdot \frac{d^{\theta+1}\ 1}{d-1}.$$

In our example: $N = 3960$, $a = 2$, $b = 3$, $c = 5$, $d = 11$, $\alpha = 3$, $\beta = 2$, $\rho = 1$, $\theta = 1$ as $3960 = 2^3 \times 3^2 \times 5 \times 11$. Therefore:

$$\begin{aligned} s &= \frac{2^4 - 1}{2 - 1} \cdot \frac{3^3 - 1}{3 - 1} \cdot \frac{5^2 - 1}{5 - 1} \cdot \frac{11^2 - 1}{11 - 1} \\ &= \frac{15}{1} \cdot \frac{26}{2} \cdot \frac{24}{4} \cdot \frac{120}{10} \\ &= 15 \times 13 \times 6 \times 12 \\ &= 14{,}040 \end{aligned}$$

POSTASSESSMENT

1. Have students calculate the total number of factors and then find each of them (either prime or composite), for each of the following:
   a. 3600 b. 540 c. 1680 d. 25725
2. Find the sum of all the factors in each of the cases above.

Unit 19

Prime Numeration System

This unit will present an unusual way to express numbers. Consideration of this "strange" numeration system should strengthen student understanding of a place value system as well as appreciation of prime factorization.

PERFORMANCE OBJECTIVES

1. *Students will convert numbers from the prime numeration system into base-ten numerals.*
2. *Students will convert numbers from base-ten into the prime numeration system.*

PREASSESSMENT

Students should know what a prime number is. Students should also be able to factor a base-ten numeral into its prime factors.

TEACHING STRATEGIES

To familiarize students with the prime numeration system, have students consider the following problems:

a. $5 \cdot 4 = 9$, b. $12 \cdot 24 = 36$, c. $8 \div 2 = 6$.

Initially students will be quite puzzled. After further inspection those familiar with exponents will begin to conjecture along those lines. Yet, this system is probably quite different from any numeration system studied before.

In the prime numeration system, there is no base. The value of each place is a prime number. The first place (starting at the right) is the first prime, 2; the next place (to the left) is the next prime, 3. This continues with the consecutive prime numbers with each succeeding place (moving left) corresponding to the next consecutive prime. This can be shown by using a dash for each place and indicating its value below it.

$$\overline{29}\ \overline{23}\ \overline{19}\ \overline{17}\ \overline{13}\ \overline{11}\ \overline{7}\ \overline{5}\ \overline{3}\ \overline{2}$$

As with our base-ten system, this prime system continues indefinitely to the left.

To find the value of a number in base-ten, digits occupying each place are multiplied by their place value and then added. However, in this prime numeration system, the value of a number is obtained by taking each place value to the *power* of the number occupying that place and then *multiplying*. For example, the number 145_p (the subscript p will be used to indicate that the number is in the prime numeration system) equals $5^1 \cdot 3^4 \cdot 2^5 = 5 \cdot 81 \cdot 32 = 12960$. Notice the exponents of the prime numbers 5, 3, and 2 are 1, 4, and 5, respectively. Have students practice converting from the prime numeration system to base-ten numeration. When they begin to feel somewhat comfortable with this work, have them consider the representation of 0 and 1. Have students express 0_p and 10_p as a base-ten numeral. Indicate to the students that by definition $2^0 = 1$. Elicit from students that representation of zero will be impossible in the prime numeration system.

To convert a base-ten numeral into the prime numeration system, a review of prime factorization is necessary. Explain to students that any whole number greater than one can be expressed as the product of prime factors in precisely one way (The Fundamental Theorem of Arithmetic). For example, 420 can be factored as follows: $7^1 \cdot 5^1 \cdot 3^1 \cdot 2^2$. Therefore $420 = 1112_p$. Have students factor (a) 144, (b) 600, and (c) 1960 into their prime factors and represent their equivalents in the prime numeration system. Emphasize that exponents of the prime factors are the digits of the prime numeral.

When students have mastered this numeration system, challenge them with multiplication; $5_p \cdot 4_p$. $5_p \cdot 4_p$ may be rewritten as $2^5 \cdot 2^4 = 2^9 = 512$. Therefore, $5_p \cdot 4_p = 9_p$. Now have them consider $25_p \cdot 4_p = 3^2 \cdot 2^5 \cdot 2^4 = 3^2 \cdot 2^9 = 29_p$ (or 4608). Other related exercises should be presented (e.g., $8_p \div 2_p$). Indicate that the operations of addition and subtraction would require conversion to base-ten numeration before actually adding or subtracting. These problems allow students to practice working with exponents in a new and unusual way.

The prime numeration system can be implemented to review the greatest common divisor and least common multiple of two numbers.

Suppose students were required to find the greatest common divisor of 18,720 and 3,150. They should change these two base-ten numerals to the prime numeration system to get 100125_p and 1221_p. By listing the *smallest value of each place*

Prime System	Base-Ten
0_p	$2^0 = 1$
1_p	$2^1 = 2$
2_p	$2^2 = 4$
3_p	$2^3 = 8$
4_p	$2^4 = 16$
5_p	$2^5 = 32$
6_p	$2^6 = 64$
7_p	$2^7 = 128$
8_p	$2^8 = 256$
9_p	$2^9 = 512$
10_p	$3^1 \cdot 2^0 = 3$
11_p	$3^1 \cdot 2^1 = 6$
12_p	$3^1 \cdot 2^2 = 12$
13_p	$3^1 \cdot 2^3 = 24$
14_p	$3^1 \cdot 2^4 = 48$
15_p	$3^1 \cdot 2^5 = 96$
16_p	$3^1 \cdot 2^6 = 192$
17_p	$3^1 \cdot 2^7 = 384$
18_p	$3^1 \cdot 2^8 = 768$
19_p	$3^1 \cdot 2^9 = 1536$
20_p	$3^2 \cdot 2^0 = 9$
21_p	$3^2 \cdot 2^1 = 18$
22_p	$3^2 \cdot 2^2 = 36$
23_p	$3^2 \cdot 2^3 = 72$
24_p	$3^2 \cdot 2^4 = 144$
25_p	$3^2 \cdot 2^5 = 288$
26_p	$3^2 \cdot 2^6 = 576$
27_p	$3^2 \cdot 2^7 = 1152$
28_p	$3^2 \cdot 2^8 = 2304$
29_p	$3^2 \cdot 2^9 = 4608$

to form a new number, they will obtain 121_p. Which is the greatest common divisor of the two numbers.

Now suppose students were faced with the problem of finding the least common multiple of 18,720 and 3,150. Having changed these two base-ten numerals to the prime numeration system to get 100125_p and 1221_p, they must merely list the *largest value of each place* to get 101225_p, which is the least common multiple of the two numbers.

Students will enjoy applying the prime numeration system methods to other problems that require finding the greatest common divisor or the least common multiple of given numbers (more than two numbers may be considered at one time). The true value of these methods rests in the justification of these methods. Teachers should present these justifications as soon as students have mastered the techniques involved.

Now have students convert 0_p through 29_p into base-ten numerals and record their answers. Students will begin to see the base-ten numerals being generated in an unusual way.

Elicit from students other possible applications of the prime numeration system.

POSTASSESSMENT

Students should:

1. Express each of the following numbers in the base-ten numeration system.

   a. 31_p b. 24_p c. 15_p d. 41_p e. 221_p f. 1234_p

2. Express each of the following base-ten numerals as a product of primes, and then in the prime numeration system.

   a. 50 b. 100 c. 125 d. 400
   e. 1000 f. 260 g. *350*

3. Solve the following problems:

   a. $3_p \cdot 6_p$ b. $12_p \cdot 13_p$ c. $6_p \div 3_p$

Unit 20

 Repeating Decimal Expansions

The terms *never-ending* and *infinite* are often confusing to students. One of the first places they really come into contact with the concept is in the junior high school where they confront nonterminating decimal expansions. Students themselves realize the need for specific notation when they encounter the repeating decimals certain fractional forms produce. In this unit students discover the patterns and seemingly inconsistent arithmetic procedures that occur with repeating decimals.

PERFORMANCE OBJECTIVES

1. *Students will be able to determine which rational numbers will yield repeating decimal expansions and which will terminate.*
2. *Students will determine minimum length of a repeating cycle.*
3. *Students will be able to use decimal equivalents to find other repeating decimals.*
4. *Students will examine an alternate method to determine decimal expansions.*

PREASSESSMENT

Students should know how to change from the fractional form $\left(\frac{a}{b}\right)$ of a rational number to its decimal equivalent. They should be familiar with prime factorization.

Have students guess which of the following fractions would become repeating decimals: $\frac{1}{2}, \frac{1}{3}, \frac{1}{4}, \frac{1}{5}, \frac{1}{6}$. Have them work out these fraction-to-decimal conversions to check the accuracy of their guesses. Note also that a terminating decimal can be considered a repeating decimal with an infinite repetition of zeros.

TEACHING STRATEGIES

Begin by having students work with fractions of the form $\frac{1}{n}$. This will force them to focus their attention (and guesswork) on the denominator. If they have difficulty figuring out how to determine repeating decimals without actually performing the expansion, suggest they factor into primes each of the denominators to see if any patterns become apparent. They will quickly see that the decimal terminates if, and only if, the prime factors of the denominator are 2s and/or 5s. They can easily justify that when the numerator takes on a decimal point and a series of zeroes, it becomes a multiple of 10 (for division purposes only); since the only prime factors of 10 are 5 and 2, it is only division by these factors that will terminate the division process.

Challenge students to determine to how many decimal places they must proceed before a pattern becomes evident. In some cases, as in $\frac{1}{3}$, it will take two decimal places before the pattern is clear. In others, it will not be so simple. Ask students to find the repeating pattern of $\frac{1}{17}$. This decimal ex pansion has 16 places before any pattern establishes itself $\frac{1}{17} = .0588235294117647\overline{0588235294117647}$.

Some students may want to generalize and assume $\frac{1}{n}$ will have $(n - 1)$ repeating digits. However, $\frac{1}{3} = .\overline{3}$, one repeating digit, which quickly disproves their theory. However, by examining each of the expansions of $\frac{1}{n}$, students will see that each expansion has at most $(n - 1)$ repeating digits. They should realize that each of the expansion digits comes from the remainder after the division process of the previous step. For each of the remainders there are only $(n - 1)$ choices. (The remainder cannot equal zero because then the process would terminate; it cannot equal n because then it would have been divisible once again.) If the remainder is the same as any previous remainder, students have found the repeating digits; if not they must continue until a remainder repeats. This will have to happen in, at most, $(n - 1)$ steps. Therefore $\frac{1}{n}$, if repeating, will have at most $(n - 1)$ repeating digits.

Students will also find it interesting to note that the repeating expansion for a number such as $\frac{1}{7}$ also yields the expansions for $\frac{2}{7}, \frac{3}{7}, \frac{4}{7}, \frac{5}{7}$, and $\frac{6}{7}$. The fraction $\frac{2}{7}$ can be rewritten in terms of $\frac{1}{7}$. Thus,

$$\frac{2}{7} = 2 \times \frac{1}{7} = 2 \times .\overline{142857} = .\overline{285714}.$$

By adding different repeating decimals, students will be able to find new repeating decimals. For example,

$$\begin{array}{rcr} \frac{1}{3} & = & .\overline{333333} \\ +\frac{1}{7} & = & +\ .\overline{142857} \\ \hline \frac{10}{21} & = & .\overline{476190} \end{array}$$

To find the general repeating digits for $\frac{1}{n}$ when $n = 21$, have students divide $.\overline{476190}$ by the numerator, 10, to get $.\overline{047619}$.

In working with repeating decimals and in performing arithmetic operations, students may come upon the fact that $1 = .\overline{9}$. This is a difficult concept for a junior high school student to grasp. The following proof, which they can perform for themselves, should clarify the situation.

$$\begin{array}{rcl} \frac{1}{3} & = & .\overline{3} \\ + \\ \frac{2}{3} & = & .\overline{6} \\ \hline 1 & = & .\overline{9} \end{array}$$

Similarly, since

$$\frac{1}{9} \times 9 = .\overline{1} \times 9$$

$$\frac{9}{9} = .\overline{9}$$

$$1 = .\overline{9}$$

Students often concentrate and comprehend more thoroughly when they feel they are learning something new. The following method, which basically outlines the division process used to change from fractional to decimal form, gives students another means of finding the repeating decimal.

To find the decimal expansion of $\frac{3}{7}$, let $r_0 = \frac{3}{7}$, and multiply by 10 (comparable to bringing down the 0).

1. $\frac{3}{7} \times 10 = \frac{30}{7} = 4\frac{2}{7}$

Now let the 4 occupy the tenths place of the decimal and use $\frac{2}{7}$ as the new remainder, r_1. Repeat the process, using the fraction as the new remainder and retaining the whole as the decimal digit for the next place.

2. $\frac{2}{7} \times 10 = \frac{20}{7} = 2\frac{6}{7} \quad r_2 = \frac{6}{7}$

   hundredths place = 2

3. $\frac{6}{7} \times 10 = \frac{60}{7} = 8\frac{4}{7} \quad r_3 = \frac{4}{7}$

   thousandths place = 8

4. $\frac{4}{7} \times 10 = \frac{40}{7} = 5\frac{5}{7} \quad r_4 = \frac{5}{7}$

   ten thousandths place = 5

5. $\frac{5}{7} \times 10 = \frac{50}{7} = 7\frac{1}{7} \quad r_5 = \frac{1}{7}$

   hundred thousandths place = 7

6. $\frac{1}{7} \times 10 = \frac{10}{7} = 1\frac{3}{7} \quad r_6 = \frac{3}{7}$

   millionths place = 1

Tell students to repeat the process until the remainder is the same as the one with which they began. In this case $r_6 = r_0 = \frac{3}{7}$, and the decimal expansion is $\frac{3}{7} = .\overline{428571}$

A clear demonstration of this method is an excellent tool to help students better understand what is involved in the division process and why remainders are such a big factor in determining the length of the repetition.

POSTASSESSMENT

Have students do the following:

1. Determine which of the following will terminate, without actually finding their decimal expansions: $\frac{2}{9}, \frac{1}{8}, \frac{3}{13}, \frac{19}{20}$
2. Determine the maximum number of digits in the repeating cycle of each: $\frac{1}{37}, \frac{4}{9}, \frac{3}{7}$
3. Knowing that $\frac{1}{14} = .0\overline{714285}$, find the decimal expansion for $\frac{3}{14}$ without dividing.
4. Show that $.5 = .4\overline{9}$. (Hint: think about the fractions $\frac{1}{3}$ and $\frac{1}{6}$.)
5. Using the alternate method described, evaluate $\frac{2}{9}$ as a repeating decimal.

Unit 21

Peculiarities of Perfect Repeating Decimals

This unit can be used as an interesting sidelight to the subject of decimals and fractions by showing "magical" properties of a certain class of numbers. These numbers are reciprocals of prime numbers whose decimal equivalents repeat after no less than P − 1 places, where P is the prime number. Such numbers are said to have *perfect repetends*. In any repeating decimal, the sequence that repeats is called the repetend. It would be advisable to use this unit after the preceding one.

PERFORMANCE OBJECTIVES

1. *Students will test various examples of perfect repetends to verify specific principles.*
2. *Students will discover and reinforce important ideas about division, remainders, and decimal equivalents of fractions.*

PREASSESSMENT

Students should know that the decimal equivalents of some fractions have 0 remainders, while others have repeating periods of various lengths. They should begin by converting $\frac{1}{7}$ to a decimal.

TEACHING STRATEGIES

It should be noted that in converting $\frac{A}{P}$ to a decimal, the repetend can have no more than P − 1 places, because in dividing A by P there can be at most P − 1 different remainders, and as soon as a remainder appears for the second time, the same sequence will be repeated. Perfect repetends, as well as the sequence of P − 1 remainders that accompanies each one, have several interesting properties. Only the simplest of these will be discussed here, but a more thorough listing of the principles of repeating decimals appears in *Philosophy of Arithmetic* by Edward Brooks (Norwood Editions), pp. 460–485.

One of the simpler properties to explain is that multiples 1 to P − 1 of $\frac{1}{P}$ are cyclic variations of the repetend of $\frac{1}{P}$. After students find $\frac{1}{7} = .\overline{142857}$, students can multiply the decimal by 2, 3, 4, 5, or 6, and get answers of $.\overline{285714}$, $.\overline{428571}$, $.\overline{571428}$, $.\overline{714285}$, $.\overline{857142}$, which are also decimal equivalents of $\frac{2}{7}, \frac{3}{7}, \frac{4}{7}, \frac{5}{7}, \frac{6}{7}$, respectively. Once this is understood, an easy way to find the multiples of $\frac{1}{7}$ is to find the last place first. For example, $4 \times .\overline{142857}$ ends in 8, so it must be $.\overline{571428}$. Where the period is longer, or where any digit appears more than once in the repetend, it may be necessary to find the last two or three digits first. An explanation of this cyclic variation is that in dividing *P* into 1, at the point where the remainder is *A*, the same sequence will begin as occurs when dividing *P* into *A*. Remember also that every possible $A(1 < AP)$ occurs as a remainder. Incidentally, when the repetend of $\frac{1}{P}$ is multiplied by P the result is .999999. Some other perfect repetends are

$$\frac{1}{17} = .0588235294117647$$

$$\frac{1}{19} = .052631578947368421$$

$$\frac{1}{23} = .0434782608695652173913$$

The only others for $P < 100$ are $\frac{1}{29}, \frac{1}{47}, \frac{1}{59}, \frac{1}{61}, \frac{1}{97}$.

Another curiosity of these numbers is that if the repetend is divided into two equal shorter sequences, their sum is $.\overline{99999}$. A graphic illustration of this is shown below. The inner circle is the repetend of $\frac{1}{29}$, and the outer circle is the sequence of remainders occurring after each number on the inner circle. The figure has the following properties (as do similar figures for all perfect repetends):

1. Any two diametrically opposite terms of the repetend add up to 9.
2. Any two opposite remainders add up to 29.
3. To multiply the repetend by $a\,(1 < a < 29)$, find a in the circle of remainders and begin the new repetend with the decimal term following the one associated with a (clockwise).

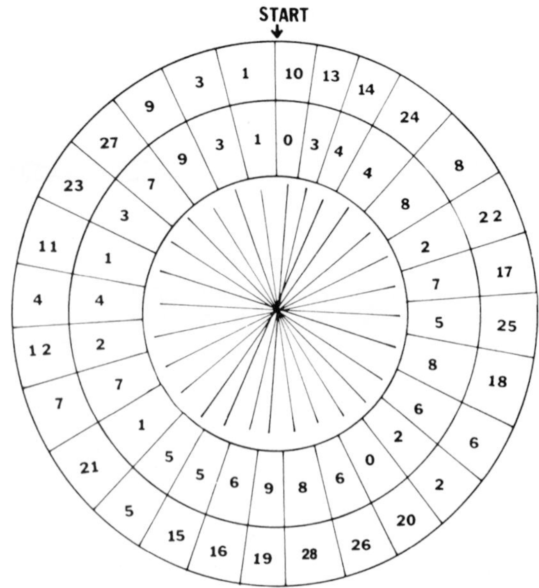

Some students may not have the patience to test out these generalizations on this figure, but of course a similar figure can be made for any of the perfect repetends. Students may construct their own figures, starting only with the information that $\frac{1}{17}$ is such a number.

Here is one alternative to plowing straight ahead with division when generating a repetend: after dividing 19 into 1 to five places, we get a remainder of 3. $\frac{1}{19} = .05263\frac{3}{19}$.* But from this we know that $\frac{3}{19} = 3\left(.05263\frac{3}{19}\right) = .15789\frac{9}{19}$. So $\frac{1}{19} = .0526315789\frac{9}{19}$. But because we know that $\frac{1}{19}$ is a perfect repetend, 9 = first + tenth digit = second + eleventh = third + twelfth, etc., and we have generated all 18 digits.

This leads into a special property of the repetend of $\frac{1}{97}$, $\frac{1}{97} = .01\frac{3}{97} = .0103\frac{9}{97} = .010309\frac{27}{97} = .01030927\frac{81}{97}$. Unfortunately, 243 has 3 places, so this neat pattern changes, but we can still add powers of three in the following way to generate the repetend:

```
.0103092781
        243
         729
         2187
           6561 etc.
```

Students should be encouraged to discover other patterns of repetends.

$*\ \frac{1}{19} = .05263 + \frac{3}{19} \times 10^{-5}$; i.e., $\frac{3}{19}$ represents the 6th decimal place.

POSTASSESSMENT

Have students generate any of the perfect repetends by using the rules shown here, then find multiples of the repetend. Explore with the class reasons why only primes have this peculiarity. For example, if $\frac{1}{14}$ had a perfect repetend, what happens to $\frac{2}{14}$ or $\frac{4}{14}$?

Unit 22

Patterns in Mathematics

This unit is designed for ninth-year students of mathematics. Parts of this unit could be used for enrichment of remedial classes in finding the patterns by observation alone.

PERFORMANCE OBJECTIVES

1. *Students will find patterns by observation.*
2. *Students will find formulas for the patterns by trial and error.*
3. *Students will find the formulas for the patterns by discovering the rules for finding the constant and the coefficients of x and x^2.*

PREASSESSMENT

Challenge students to find succeeding numbers in the following patterns and formulas for the patterns:

a)

x	y
0	1
1	3
2	5
3	7
4	?
5	?

b)

x	y
0	1
1	4
2	7
3	10
4	?
5	?

c)

x	y
0	1
1	5
2	9
3	13
4	?
5	?

d)

x	y
0	3
1	5
2	7
3	9
4	?
5	?

Most students will be able to find the patterns and the formulas by trial and error. Have students fill in missing numbers, formulas, and note the differences between the successive *y*s. The completed charts will look like this. D denotes difference between successive *y*s:

a)

x	y	D
0	1	
1	3	2
2	5	2
3	7	2
4	9	2
5	11	2

$y = 2x + 1$

b)

x	y	D
0	1	
1	4	3
2	7	3
3	10	3
4	13	3
5	16	3

$y = 3x + 1$

c)

x	y	D
0	1	
1	5	4
2	9	4
3	13	4
4	17	4
5	21	4

$y = 4x + 1$

d)

x	y	D
0	3	
1	5	2
2	7	2
3	9	2
4	11	2
5	13	2

$y = 2x + 3$

Have students notice constants in each case. Do they observe any pattern? Perhaps they will notice that the constant is the value of *y* when *x* is zero. Draw their attention to the difference between the successive *y*s. Do they observe anything? Yes, the difference between the *y*s is the coefficient of *x*. Do several patterns of this type until students can quickly find the patterns and the formulas for the patterns.

TEACHING STRATEGIES

Give your students the following exercise and have them find the pattern and the formula if they can.

How many rectangles in all?

Complete the table

x No. of small rectangles	y Total no. of rectangles
0	
1	
2	
3	
4	
5	
6	

By observation of the rectangles, many will be able to find the pattern and fill in the table. Have them record the first difference. They will notice that it is not constant. Have them record the second difference. They will notice it is constant. Have them summarize their findings in a table. Perhaps some will find the formula also.

x No. of small rectangles	y Total no. of rectangles	D_1	D_2
0	0		
1	1	1	
2	3	2	1
3	6	3	1
4	10	4	1
5	15	5	1
6	21	6	1

$$y = \frac{x^2}{2} + \frac{x}{2}$$

Have them do the same with the following pattern: What is the largest number of pieces you can make with *x* cuts?

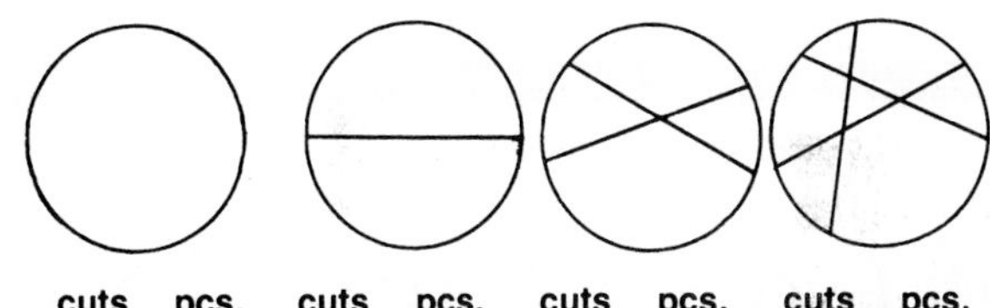

Have them fill out the following:

x No. of cuts	y No. of pcs.	D_1	D_2
0	1		
1	2	1	
2	4	2	1
3	7	3	1
4	11	4	1
5	16	5	1

Notice the first difference. It is not constant. Notice the second difference. It is constant. Perhaps someone will be able to come up with the formula

$$y = \frac{x^2}{2} + \frac{x}{2} + 1.$$

Are there any patterns one can see for the values of the constants or the coefficients in the two preceding problems? Yes, the constant is the value of *y* when *x* is zero.

Let us examine the formula $ax^2 + bx + c = y$ and find the values of *y* for various values of *x*.

x	y	D_1	D_2
0	c		
1	$a + b + c$	$a + b$	
2	$4a + 2b + c$	$3a + b$	$2a$
3	$9a + 3b + c$	$5a + b$	$2a$
4	$16a + 4b + c$	$7a + b$	$2a$

Let us examine the pattern. As we found in the formulas, y is the constant when x is zero. The first difference is $a + b$, the sum of the coefficients of x^2 and x. The second difference is $2a$, twice the value of the coefficient of x^2. The value of the first difference when $x = 1$ is $a + b$. Since we know the value of a (it is one-half of the second difference), we can find the value of b by subtracting a from the first difference $(a + b)$. So if we reexamine the earlier pattern, we can derive the formula.

The constant is the value of y when x is zero. Therefore the constant is 1. D_2 is $2a$. Since D_2 is 1, the value of a is $\frac{1}{2}$. D_1 is $a + b$. Since D_1 is 1, and a is $\frac{1}{2}$, the value of b is $\frac{1}{2}$. The formula therefore is

$$y = \frac{1}{2}x^2 + \frac{1}{2}x + 1.$$

POSTASSESSMENT

Finish the tables and find the formulas for the following patterns by finding the first and second differences:

x	y
0	3
1	6
2	13
3	24
4	
5	

x	y
0	0
1	5
2	14
3	27
4	
5	

x	y
0	0
1	13
2	34
3	63
4	
5	

x	y
0	2
1	3
2	6
3	11
4	
5	

Unit 23

Googol and Googolplex

This unit presents a discussion of large numbers. It introduces students to the finite world of large numbers and the ease of expressing large numbers using scientific notation.

PERFORMANCE OBJECTIVES

1. *Students will give examples of scientific notation as used in science and mathematics.*
2. *Given any number, students will convert it into scientific notation.*

PREASSESSMENT

Students should be able to solve the following problems:

1. Compute the following products. Find the solution without using a pencil.
   a. 10×63 b. $100 \times .05$ c. 1000×951.
2. Compute the following quotients.
   a. $470 \div 10$ b. $4{,}862 \div 1000$ c. $46{,}000 \div 1000$
3. What is the largest number you can think of?

TEACHING STRATEGIES

You might want to tell the old story of two children engaged in a violent argument in the street. The argument stems from the fact that each child is trying to state a larger number than the other. Finally, they realize each one can state a larger number than the other.

Numbers are fun to play with and many interesting things can be done with them. However, all too often we forget what a number really is. The students should be asked, how large is one million? Can we visualize the sum of the first billion natural numbers? Why should we care about numbers of great magnitude, we never use them—or do we?

At this point the teacher should state that scientists who use very large or very small numbers usually express these numbers in scientific notation. To learn how to use this system of numeration, we will recall some patterns in mathematics. It is up to the teacher at this point to introduce scientific notation. You may wish to refer to any standard textbook for an appropriate development.

1. When a number is expressed as the product of a power of 10 and a number that is less than ten but greater than or equal to one ($1 \leq n < 10$), the number is said to be written in scientific notation.
2. A science teacher may be able to suggest very large or very small numbers that students have used or read about in their science classes. These can then be converted into scientific notation.

A general discussion should ensue on when large numbers are used (for example, grains of sand on a beach, stars in the sky, or in economics or science). Current newspaper and magazine articles abound with references to millions and billions. How many people have seen a million of anything? Most people do not have a clear idea of the size of a million.

To earn a million dollars how long would you have to work at $100 a week? (almost 200 years). How many stars can you see with the naked eye on a clear night? No, not millions, but only about 3,500 (3.5×10^3 in scientific notation). A hundred sheets of paper make a stack about 5 millimetres thick or $\frac{1}{5}$ of an inch (25.4 millimetres equal an inch). A million sheets of paper would make a pile about 55 yards high, or roughly the height of a 12 story building. Suppose you are riding in a car at 65 mph. How long would it take you going constantly to travel one million miles? ($1\frac{3}{4}$ years).

Just how big is a billion? The 2006 federal budget called for more tax dollars than there were seconds since the birth of Christ. (Note: According to the ability of a particular class and allotted time all large numbers should be converted to scientific notation by the student.) Students should be led to the fact that it is virtually impossible for the human mind to comprehend the enormity of a billion. Remember how high a pile of a million sheets of paper would be—a hundred sheets of paper make a stack about 5 millimetres thick (about $\frac{1}{5}$ of an inch). A billion sheets of paper would make a pile 31 miles high.

A car traveling nonstop at 100 mph would take 1,140 years to travel a billion miles. If you earn $100 a week, you would have to work 192,307 years to earn a billion dollars. (Some of these illustrations may be calculated on an electronic calculator.)

You should pose the following problem.

> John did me a favor the other day and I asked him what reward he would like. John, being very wise said, "Give me one penny for the first day, two pennies for the second day, four pennies for the third day, and likewise for sixty-four days, doubling the number of pennies for each successive day." How much money would I have to pay John?

Making a table gives students an opportunity to see numbers growing and the magnitude they can reach.

Number of Days	Number of Pennies
1	1
2	2
3	4
4	8
5	16
etc.	etc.
64	9,223,372,036,854,775,808

Now the sum of all the numbers in the second column is the number of pennies needed to pay John:

18,446,744,073,709,551,615

It is read: Eighteen quintillion, four hundred forty-six quadrillion, seven hundred forty-four trillion, seventy-three billion, seven hundred nine million, five hundred fifty-one thousand, six hundred fifteen. Students should be able to see that even though it is an enormous number it is not infinite, but finite. Have them express it approximately in scientific notation.

The next question that may arise at this point concerns the largest number that can be expressed by three digits. In ordinary notation the answer is 999. What about 99^9? (Review of exponents reveals the fact that this means 99 multiplied by itself 8 times.) But if exponents are permitted, the answer is 9^{9^9}, that is, 9 with the exponent 9^9, or simply 9 with the exponent 387,420,489 (the product of 387,420,489 nines). If printed with 16 figures to an inch, it has been estimated, this huge number would fill 33 volumes of 800 pages each, printing 14,000 figures on a page. It has been estimated that this number is more than four million times as large as the number of electrons in the universe, but a *finite* number. (Ask students to find the largest three digit number that can be written with fours.)

Say the number of grains of sand at Coney Island is about 10^{20}. Students could be asked to devise a method for establishing this estimate. The number of electrons which pass through the filament of an ordinary light bulb in a minute equals the number of drops of water that flow over Niagara Falls in a hundred years. The reason for giving such examples of very large numbers to students is to emphasize that the elements of even very large sets can be counted.

Students may now ask what the largest number that has a name is. The term *googol* was coined to describe the figure 1 followed by a hundred zeros. Another term, *googolplex*, was invented for a still larger, but still finite, number consisting of a 1 followed by a googol of zeros. Thus, a googol times a googol would be a 1 with 200 zeros. Students who try to write a googolplex on the chalkboard or a sheet of paper will get some idea of the size of this very large but finite number (there would not be enough room to write it if you travelled to the farthest visible star, writing zeros all the way).

Astronomers find the light-year a very convenient unit of length in measuring great astronomical distances. The North Star is 47 light years away. What does this mean? Light travels at the rate of 186,000 miles per-second. In one year light travels 6,000,000,000,000 (6×10^{12}) miles. This tremendous distance is called a light year. The nearest star is 4.4 light-years away, and the farthest known star is 1.4×10^9 light years away. Have students consider this: It takes 47 light-years for light from Earth to reach the North Star. What would a person looking at the Earth from the North Star see today?

POSTASSESSMENT

Have students complete the following:

1. The distance of the planet Pluto from the earth is approximately 4,700,000,000,000 miles. Express this answer in scientific notation. (4.7×10^{12})
2. The circumference of the earth at the equator is approximately 25,000 miles. Express this in scientific notation. (2.5×10^4)

Unit 24

Mathematics of Life Insurance

This unit describes to students how insurance companies take into account probability and compound interest in calculating the net premium of life insurance.

PERFORMANCE OBJECTIVES

1. *Students will use a compound interest formula to compute the value of money left in a bank for a given period at a given rate.*
2. *Students will compute the present value of money that increases to a given amount when left in a bank for a given period at a given rate.*
3. *Students will use appropriate probabilities and interest rate to calculate the net premium a life insurance policyholder must pay.*

PREASSESSMENT

Use the following problem for diagnostic purposes as well as to motivate the lesson. Out of 200,000 men alive at age 40, 199,100 lived at age 41. What is the probability that an insured man of age 40 will live at least one year? What is the probability that he will die within one year?

TEACHING STRATEGIES

By posing the above problem, students become aware of the applicability of probability theory to life insurance. These companies must be able to measure the risks against which people are buying the life insurance. To decide on the premiums, a life insurance company must know how many people are expected to die in any group. They do this by collecting data about the number of people who died in the past from each age group. Since the data is collected from a large number of events, the law of large numbers applies. This law states that *with a large number of experiments, the ratio of the number of successes to the number of trials gets very close to the theoretical probability*.

Life insurance companies construct mortality tables based on past deaths in order to predict the number of people who will die in each age group. Below is a portion of the Commissioners 1958 Standard Ordinary Mortality Table. To construct this table a sample of ten million people was used. Their life span was recorded from birth till age 99. At each age level the table records the number of people alive at the start of the year and the number of deaths that occurred during the year. Then the following ratio is computed:

$$\frac{\text{Number of deaths during year}}{\text{Number of people alive at start of year}}$$

This ratio is then converted to deaths per 1000. The number of deaths per 1000 is called the *death rate*. This death rate, as students will see, is crucial in computing the premium that policyholders will pay.

Age	Number Living	Deaths Each Year	Deaths Per 1,000
0	10,000,000	70,800	7.08
1	9,929,200	17,475	1.76
2	9,911,725	15,066	1.52
3	9,896,659	14,449	1.46
4	9,882,210	13,835	1.40
10	9,805,870	11,865	1.21
11	9,794,005	12,047	1.23
12	9,781,958	12,325	1.26
13	9,769,633	12,896	1.32
18	9,698,230	16,390	1.69
25	9,575,636	18,481	1.93
30	9,480,358	20,193	2.13
42	9,173,375	38,253	4.17
43	9,135,122	41,382	4.53
44	9,093,740	44,741	4.92

FIGURE 1

After this introduction, the teacher should ask the class: What is the probability that an 18-year-old will die if out of 6,509 18-year-olds alive at the beginning of the year, 11 died? The probability is $\frac{11}{6509}$. However, life insurance companies prefer to transform this ratio into death rate per 1000. The teacher should have the class change $\frac{11}{6509}$ into $\frac{x}{1000}$ by setting up the following proportion:

$$\frac{x}{1000} = \frac{\text{Number of dying during the year}}{\text{Number alive at start of the year}}$$

x = death rate per 1000

The answer to the above problem is

$$\frac{11}{6509} = \frac{x}{1000} \text{ or } x = 1.69.$$

This means that 1.69 people out of the original 1000 will have died by the end of the 18th year. The insurance company uses this information to calculate the premium it will charge a group of 18-year-olds. Suppose there were 1000 people age 18 who insured themselves for $1000 each for one year. How much would the company have to pay out at the end of the year? If 1.69 people die, the company will pay out $1690 ($1.69 \times 1000 = 1690$). Thus, how much must the company charge each of the 1000 policyholders? (This does not take into account profit or operating expenses.) The $1690 divided evenly among 1000 people equals $1.69 per person.

In the previous discussion, students did not take into consideration the fact that money paid to the company earns interest during the year. So besides considering the death rate, the interest rate must also be taken into account when calculating the premium.

The teacher must now develop the concepts of compound interest. The teacher should ask the class how much money will be on deposit in a bank at the end of the year if one deposits $100 at 5 percent interest. The answer is $100 plus .05 (100) or 100×1.05 which is $105. If the $105 is kept in the bank another year, what will it amount to? $105 + .05(105) or $\$100 \times 1.05 \times 1.05$ or $\$100 \times (1.05)^2$ which amounts to $110.25. Have the students write the general formula using P = original principal, i = rate of interest per period, A = the amount of money at the end of the specified time and n = the number of years the principal is on deposit. The formula is $A = P(1 + i)^n$.

The teacher should now ask the students how much money they would have to deposit now in a bank whose rate of interest is 5 percent, if they wanted $100 accumulated in one year from now. In the previous example, the students saw that $100 grew to $105 in one year's time. This information is used to set up a proportion: $\frac{x}{100} = \frac{100}{105} = .9524, x = 100(.9524) = \$95.24$.

How much would have to be deposited now to accumulate $100 at the end of two years from now? $\frac{x}{100} = \frac{100}{110.25} = .9070, x = \$90.70$.

The students should now be able to derive a formula for calculating the present value from the formula for compound interest ($A = P(1 + i)^n$).

This formula is $P = \dfrac{A}{(1 + i)^n}$.

Your students will now return to the original problem of the life insurance company that has to pay out $1690 at the end of the year to the deceased 18-year-olds. What is the present value of $1690? In other words, how much must the insurance company collect at the beginning of the year so that it can pay out $1690 at the end of the year? By using the present value formula, the students computed that for every $1 the company has to pay, it must collect $.9524 at the beginning of the year. If the company has to pay $1690, then it has to collect $1609.56 in total from its 1000 18-year-olds ($1690 \times .9524 = \$1609.56$). Thus each policyholder must contribute a premium of $\frac{\$1609.56}{1000} = 1.60956$ or about $1.61.

You may now pose another problem. Suppose another group of 1000 people aged 25 bought policies for one year worth $1000 apiece (the death benefit is $1000). According to the mortality table their death rate is 1.93, or 1.93 out of 1000 25-year-olds die during their 25th year. What will the net premium be if the interest rate is 5 percent? Death rate per 1000 at age 25 = 1.93. Amount needed to pay claims = (1.93×1000) = $1930. Interest factor = $.9524. Present value of claims due in 1 year ($\$1930 \times .9524$) = $1838.13. Number of persons paying premium = 1000. Net premium $\frac{\$1838.13}{1000} = 1.83813$ of $1.84. This process may be continued for additional years of insurance.

POSTASSESSMENT

Calculate the net premium for a 2-year policy for a group of 1000 all age 30, with interest at 5 percent. Death rate at 30 is 2.13, death rate at 31 is 2.19.

Unit 25

 Geometric Dissections

Unlike Humpty Dumpty, dissected geometric figures can be put back together again. In fact, the primary purpose of dissections is to cut a plane rectilinear figure with straight lines in such a way that the resulting pieces can be reassembled into a desired figure. This unit will introduce the wide range of geometric dissections by emphasizing their mathematical as well as recreational value.

PERFORMANCE OBJECTIVES

1. *Students will see familiar polygonal area formulas in a concrete and interrelated manner.*
2. *Students will transform certain polygonal figures into other polygonal figures of equal area through dissections.*

PREASSESSMENT

Present your students with the following problem: Given an equilateral triangle, dissect the triangle into four pieces, which can be put together to form a rectangle. One possible solution: construct the perpendicular bisector from C to point D on side $\overline{AB}$; from D draw a line segment to the midpoint of $\overline{BC}$; bisect $\angle A$ extending the bisecting ray to point F on $\overline{CD}$. These four pieces will form a rectangle.

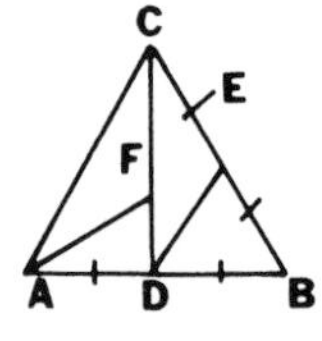

FIGURE 1

TEACHING STRATEGIES

Begin discussion of dissections by demonstrating the area equality between a rectangle and a parallelogram with the same base. The dissection proceeds as follows. Using heavy paper or cardboard, construct a rectangle ABCD. Make a straight cut from vertex A to a point E on side $\overline{DC}$. Remove ΔADE placing side $\overline{AD}$ along side $\overline{BC}$ to form parallelogram ABE′E.

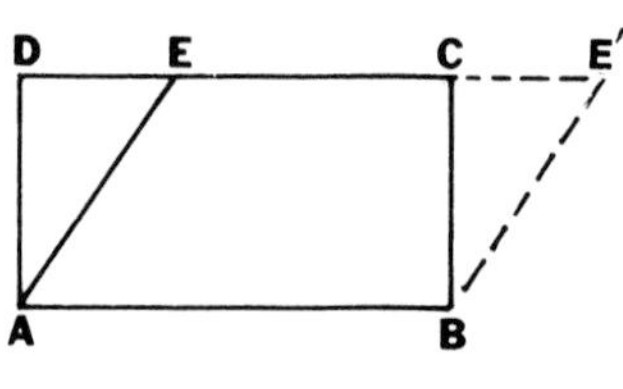

FIGURE 2

In a similar manner, you can also demonstrate that a parallelogram and a trapezoid with the same base have equal areas. Consider any trapezoid; find the midpoint E of side $\overline{BC}$, and through E draw a line parallel to $\overline{AD}$ which intersects $\overline{AB}$ at X and $\overrightarrow{DC}$ at Y. Since $\triangle CEY$ and $\triangle BEX$ are congruent, the areas of trapezoid ABCD and parallelogram AXYD are equal.

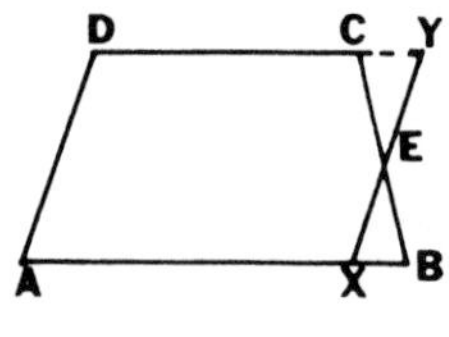

FIGURE 3

The range of possible transformations of polygons into other polygons by means of dissections is vast. Janos Bolyai, one of the founders of non-Euclidean geometry, was the first to suggest that given any two polygons with equal area, either figure could be dissected a finite number of times such that upon rearrangement it would be congruent to the other. However, we are concerned with specific transformations that require a minimum number of dissections.

For example, you could consider the problem of dissecting a given acute triangle to form a rectangle. In Figure 4,

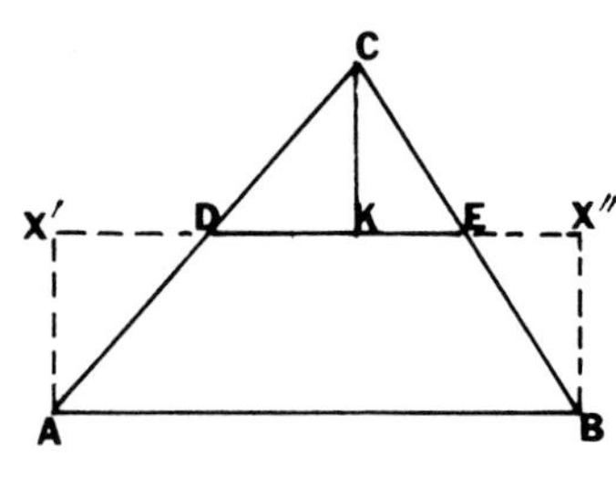

FIGURE 4

first find the midpoints of sides $\overline{AC}$ and $\overline{BC}$ and connect these points to form $\overline{DE}$. From C construct a perpendicular to $\overline{DE}$ at X. Take $\triangle DXC$ and place it so that X is now at X′ and $\angle DCX$ is adjacent to $\angle CAB$. Similarly move $\triangle EXC$ so that X is now at X″ and $\angle ECX$ is adjacent to $\angle CBA$.

To encourage students to begin solving dissection problems on their own, suggest that they carefully construct a 10 cm by 10 cm square as follows: Let $AL = BG = 7$, $CT_1 = 3.1$, $AR_1 = 2.9$, $DN = 4.2$; draw $\overline{AG}$ and $\overline{LN}$; on $\overline{LN}$ let $LS_1 = 1.6$; on $\overline{AG}$ locate points R, S, K, and T such that $AR = 2.4$, $RS = 3.3$, $SK = 2.4$ and $KT = 3.3$; draw $\overline{RR_1}$, $\overline{SS_1}$, $\overline{KB}$, and $\overline{TT_1}$.

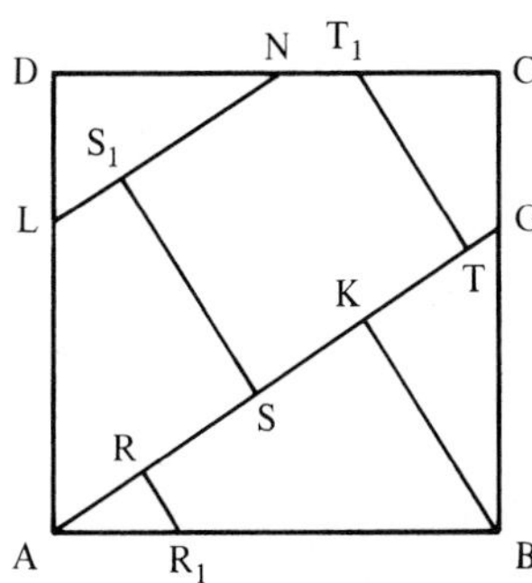

FIGURE 5

After cutting the student should have seven pieces. Using all of these pieces, students should attempt to form: (1) three squares of the same size, and (2) an isosceles trapezoid.

A beautiful dissection is possible with three regular hexagons. Leaving the first hexagon uncut, dissect the second and third as shown below in Figure 6. These 13 pieces can be combined to form a single hexagon.

This transformation can be considered in terms of rotations, and others in terms of reflections, translations, as well as rotations. You can then determine that a side of the larger hexagon is $\sqrt{3}$ times a side of the smaller hexagons. Since the area of the new hexagon is three times the area of each of the smaller hexagons, we have verified a significant relationship that holds between similar figures: the ratio of their areas is the square of the ratio between any two corresponding sides.

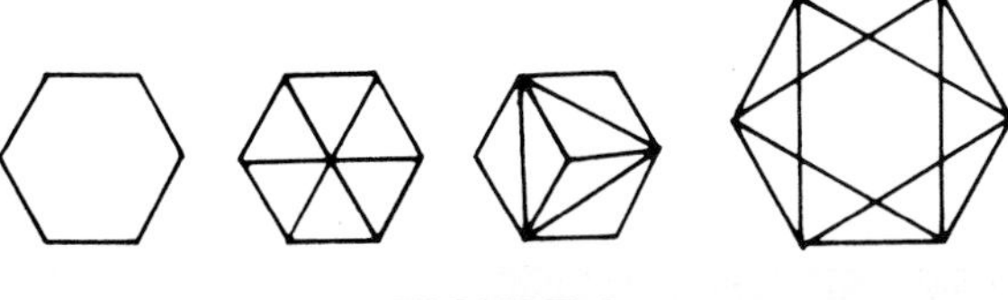

FIGURE 6

POSTASSESSMENT

Students should complete the following exercises.

1. Demonstrate by dissection that a rectangle can be divided into two congruent trapezoids that each have one-half the area of the rectangle.
2. With the pieces from the dissected 10 cm by 10 cm square, form (1) a rectangle, and (2) a parallelogram.
3. Dissect the regular dodecagon that appears below into a square (cut along indicated lines).

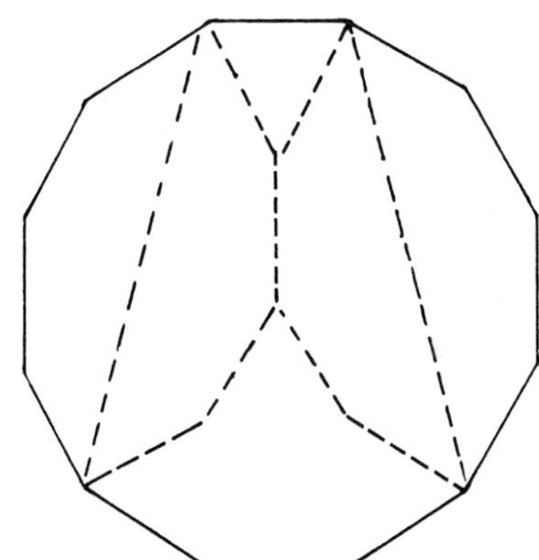

Unit 26

 The Klein Bottle

This unit will provide students with an insight into one of the very fascinating topics of topology, the Klein bottle. They will be surprised to see a solid figure whose inside cannot be distinguished from its outside.

PERFORMANCE OBJECTIVES

1. *Students will create a Klein bottle from a flat piece of paper.*
2. *Students will characterize a surface by certain topological properties.*
3. *Students will determine the Betti number of topological surfaces.*

TEACHING STRATEGIES

Before demonstrating how the above situation can be created, briefly discuss the one-sided topological figure, the Klein bottle. The Klein bottle was invented by Felix Klein, a German mathematician, in 1882. If we were to compare the Klein bottle to something realistic, we would use a flexible object, such as a cylinder with a hole cut through the surface. We would then stretch one end to make a wide base and the other end narrowed like the neck of a bottle. But we would have to bring these two-end circles together with their arrows running in opposite directions (see diagram below). Imagine the narrow end of the cylinder bent up, and plunged through the hole on the cylinder and joined to the wide base as in the figure below.

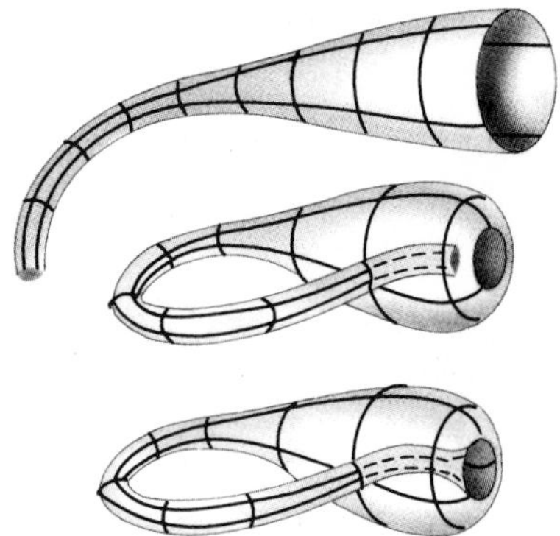

The hole on the surface of the cylinder should not be actually thought of as a hole but rather an intersection of surfaces covered by a continuation of the surface of the bottle.

Let us now return to the original problem. The situation can easily be visualized if we compare the sleeves of the jacket to the ends of the cylinder and one of the armholes to the hole in the cylinder. We have now created a figure that is topologically equivalent to the Klein bottle.

Once the students have a clear understanding as to what a Klein bottle appears to be, demonstrate how it can be created from a piece of paper. To construct a Klein bottle, what we are supposed to do with the flat piece of paper is to join the respective corners of the edges AB to A′B′, but we are also to join the remaining edges AB′ to A′B.

First create a cylinder by folding the sheet of paper in half and joining the open edges with a strip of tape. Cut a slot through the thickness of the paper nearest you about a quarter of the distance from the top. This will correspond to the "hole" in the surface of the cylinder. Fold the model in half and push the lower end through the slot. Join the edges as indicated by the arrows in the diagram. It is easily seen that this paper model is topologically identical to the Klein bottle created from the cylinder.

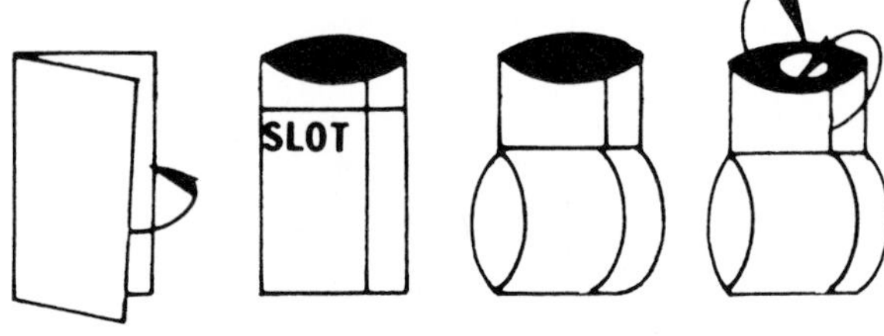

If we were now to examine the Klein bottle and try to distinguish the outside from the inside, and vice versa, we would find it impossible to do so. It would be evident that the surface is one-sided and edgeless, a notion very unusual to geometric figures.

Since it may be difficult to recognize a Klein bottle or any surface whose shape has been extremely distorted, it is necessary to be able to characterize each surface by simpler topological properties. Two of the properties have already been mentioned: number of edges and number of sides. A Klein bottle was found to be one-sided and have no edges. A third distinguishing feature of these surfaces is the *Betti number*. The Betti number is the maximum number of cross cuts (a simple cut with a pair of scissors that begins and ends on the edge) that can be made on a surface without dividing it into more than one piece. This means that a figure in the shape of a disk has a Betti number zero, since any cross cut will divide it into two pieces. On the other hand the lateral surface of a cylinder has a Betti number of one.

Ask students why it would be difficult to determine the Betti number of a doughnut shaped figure or a Klein bottle using the cross cut method. Most students should realize that the problem here is that both of these topological figures contain no edges. Therefore, an alternate method using a *loop-cut* (it starts at any point on the surface, and returns to it without crossing itself, avoiding the edge entirely) provides another way of determining the Betti number. When using the loop-cut to determine the Betti number, we count the number of edges and say that the Betti number equals the number of loop-cuts we can make in a surface without dividing it into more pieces than there were edges. A doughnut-shaped figure requires two loop-cuts: one horizontally and the other vertically so the Betti number is two. The Klein bottle also requires two loop-cuts as shown in the diagram below.

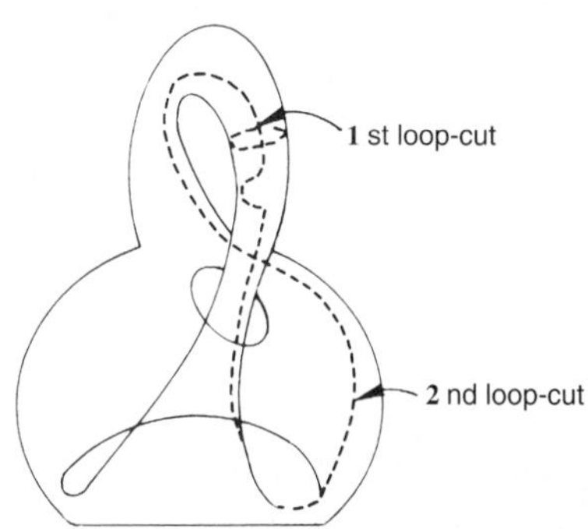

POSTASSESSMENT

1. Have students determine the Betti number of the following surfaces:
   a. a tube
   b. a punctured tube
   c. a punctured sphere
2. Have students determine which figures would be created if you cut a Klein bottle in half.

Unit 27

The Four-Color Map Problem

Topology is a branch of mathematics related to geometry. Figures discussed may appear on plane surfaces or on three-dimensional surfaces. The topologist studies those properties of a figure that remain *after* the figure has been distorted or stretched according to a set of rules. A piece of string with its ends connected may take on the shape of a circle, or a square. In going through this transformation, the order of the "points" along the string does not change. This retention of ordering has survived the distortion of shape, and is a property that attracts the interest of topologists.

PERFORMANCE OBJECTIVES

1. *Students will state the Four-Color Map Problem.*
2. *Given a geographical map on a plane surface, the student will show, by example, that four colors are sufficient to successfully color the entire map.*

PREASSESSMENT

Students should know the meaning of common boundaries and common vertices as applied to geographical maps on a plane surface.

TEACHING STRATEGIES

Begin by indicating that this problem was only recently solved with the extensive aid of computers. Previously it was considered one of the famous unsolved problems of mathematics.

Have students analyze this fictional, geographic map (Figure 1) of eight different countries, and list all countries that have a common boundary with country H and countries that share a common vertex with region H. A map will be considered correctly colored when each country is completely colored and two countries that share a common boundary have

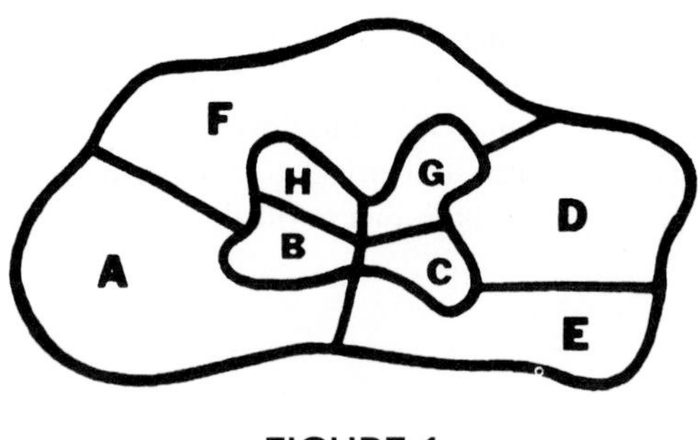

FIGURE 1

different colors. Two countries sharing a common vertex may also share the same color. Have students color in several maps according to the rules for coloring as stated above (*b*/blue; *r*/red; *y*/yellow; *g*/green).

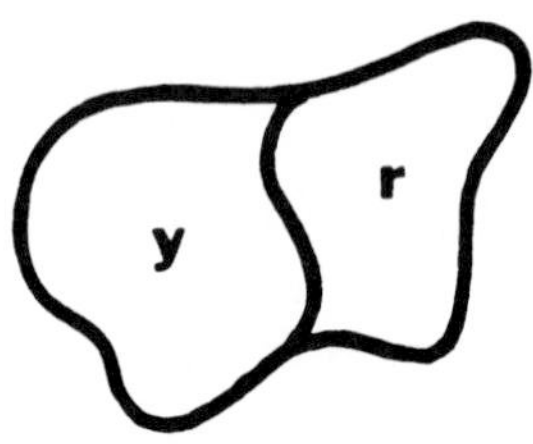

FIGURE 2

This map (Figure 2) consists of two regions with one common boundary and therefore requires two colors to color correctly.

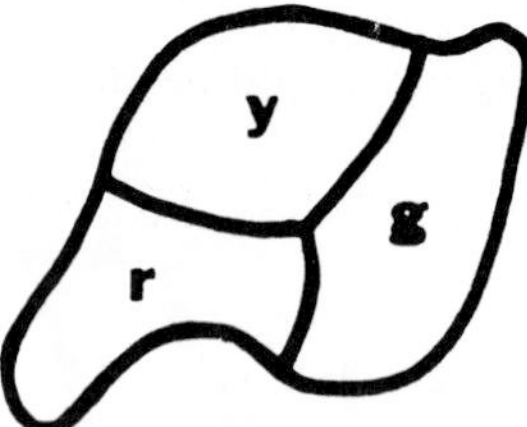

FIGURE 3

This map (Figure 3) consists of three different regions and the students should conclude that three different colors are required to color it correctly. It seems as though a map with two regions requires two colors and a map with three regions requires three colors.

Ask the students if they can devise a map that has three different countries that will require less than three colors to color it. As an example see Figure 4.

FIGURE 4

Since the innermost country and the outermost country share no common boundary, they may share the color red and still retain their separate identity.

It seems reasonable to conclude that if a three-country map can be colored with less than three colors, a four-region map can be colored with less than four colors. Have the students create such a map.

Figure 5 has four regions and requires only two colors for correct coloring. Figure 6 also consists of four regions and requires three colors for correct coloring.

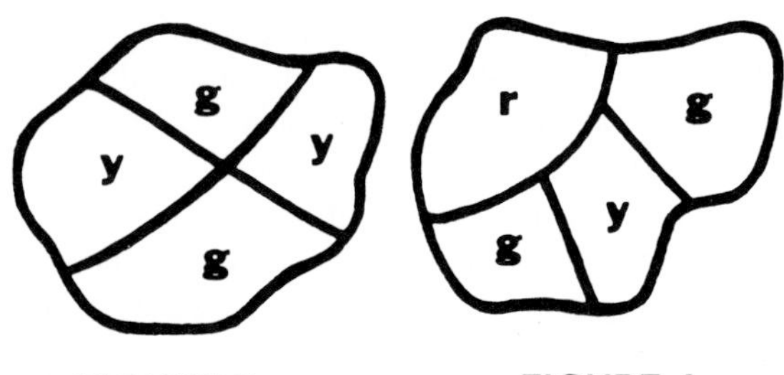

FIGURE 5 FIGURE 6

Challenge students to devise a map that consists of four countries and requires exactly four colors for correct coloring. Before undertaking such a task students should now realize that this map calls for each of the four countries to share a common boundary with the other three. Figure 7 is an example of this map.

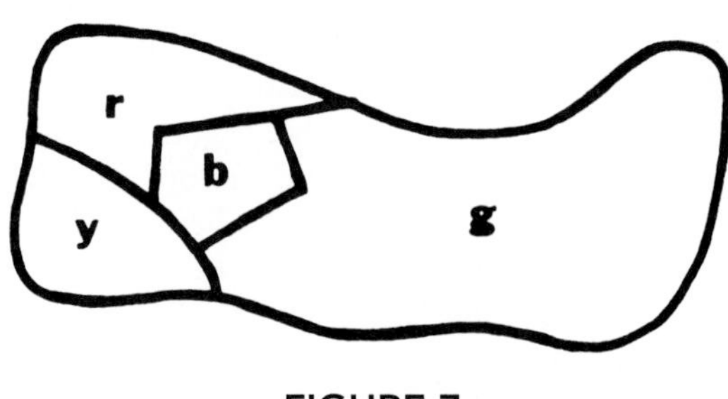

FIGURE 7

Ask students to take the next logical step in this series of map-coloring problems. They should come up with the idea of coloring maps involving five distinct regions. It will be possible to draw maps that have five regions and require two, three, or four colors to be colored correctly. The task of drawing a five-country map that *requires* five colors for correct coloring will be impossible. This curiosity can be generalized through further investigation and students should arrive at the idea that any map, on a plane surface, with any number of regions, can be successfully colored with four or fewer colors.

It is more satisfying to present the problem as a direct challenge in the following form: "Can you draw a geographic map, on a plane surface, with any number of regions, that requires five colors to be correctly colored?" This is the statement of the Four-Color Problem. Whereas the Three Famous Problems of antiquity have been proved to be impossible many years ago, this problem was only solved recently.

POSTASSESSMENT

1. In a paragraph, using diagrams, describe what is meant by The Four-Color Problem of Topology.
2. Using the colors *g*/green, *r*/red, *b*/blue, *y*/yellow, show that it is possible to correctly color each of the following maps with four or fewer colors.

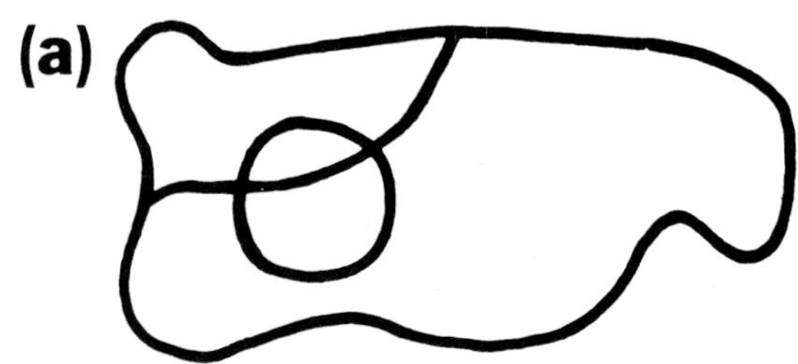

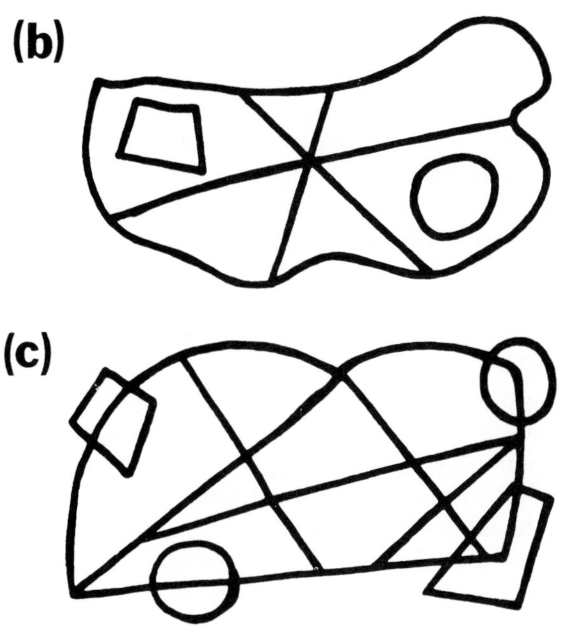

3. Draw a map that has an infinite number of regions but requires only two colors for correct coloring.

REFERENCE

Appel, K., and W. Haken. "The Solution of the Four-Color-Map Problem." *Scientific American* 237, no. 4 (December 1977): 108–121.

Unit 28

Mathematics on a Bicycle

With the many variations of gears on the traditional ten-speed bicycle, there are lots of applications of mathematics. These ought to help students better understand their bicycles while at the same time reinforce their mathematics.

PERFORMANCE OBJECTIVES

1. *Given the number of teeth (or sprockets) in the front and rear sprocket wheels, and diameter of the wheel, students will find gear ratios and distance traveled with each turn of the pedals. (New vocabulary will be developed.)*
2. *Students will be able to explain why pitch is important.*

PREASSESSMENT

Students should have the basic skills of algebra and be somewhat familiar with a bicycle.

TEACHING STRATEGIES

The adult bicycles that we shall consider have two wheels, front and rear cable brakes, gears—three, five, or ten—and are made of steel in its various alloys.

Let's examine first the differences in gearing between the three- and ten-speed bicycles, and in particular the mechanism of the ten-speed bicycle.

In a three-speed bicycle the gearing mechanism is located within the rear hub (or axle). It is a clutch type mechanism with pieces that interlock within the hub. It has constraints in that no ratio greater than the inside diameter of the rear hub can exist.

Cross section

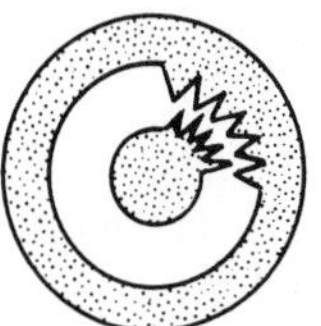

On a ten-speed bicycle the back wheel has five sprocket wheels called a cluster, with the largest sprocket wheel closest to the spokes and then the rest gradually getting smaller. The gearing (i.e., the connection of sprocket wheels by a chain) is obtained by moving the chain from one sprocket to the other by means of a derailleur.

Let's examine closely the basic setup.

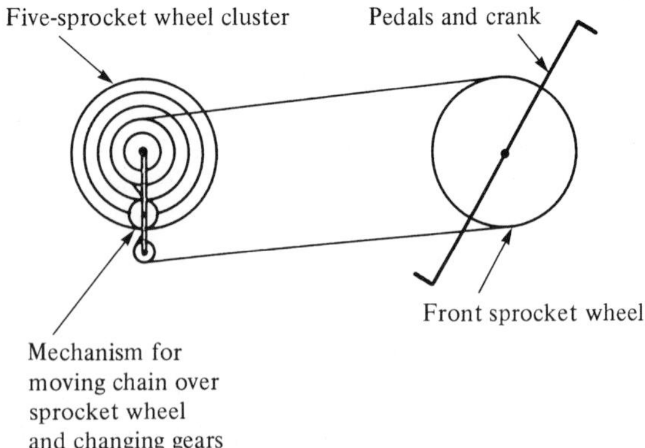

There exists a front and rear sprocket wheel with teeth set in gear by a connecting chain. The numbers of teeth on the front and rear sprocket wheels are important. Suppose the front sprocket wheel has 40 teeth and the rear sprocket wheel has 20 teeth; the ratio would then be $\frac{40}{20}$ or 2. This means that the rear sprocket wheel turns twice every time the front sprocket wheel turns once. But the rear sprocket wheel is attached to the bicycle wheel and a translation of energy again occurs depending on the diameter of the wheel. On a ten-speed bicycle the diameter of the wheel (including the tire) is 27 inches. This arrangement is shown in the diagram below.

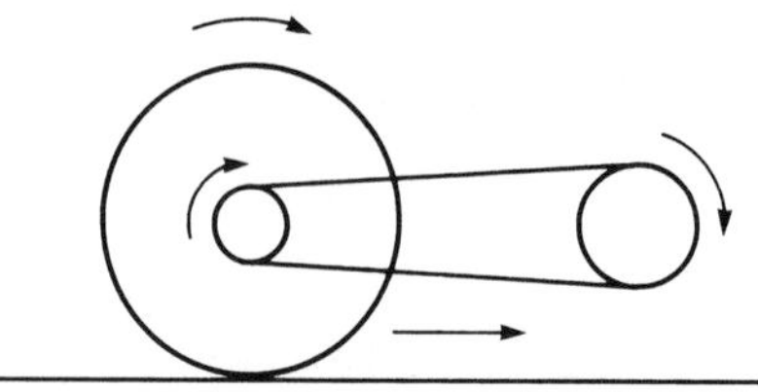

The relationship (when the bicycle wheel is included in the consideration) is: $\text{gear ratio} = \text{ratio} \times \text{diameter} = \frac{2}{1} = 27'' = 54$. The number generated here is usually between 36 and 108. It gives a comparison between gears and is useful for relating gear ratios to work performed.

For example, a rider using a sprocket wheel with 46 teeth in the front and a 16 tooth wheel in the rear along with a 27″ wheel gets a rear ratio of $77.625 \approx 78$. Another rider using a 50-tooth front sprocket wheel and 16-tooth sprocket wheel in the rear gets a gear ratio of $84.375 \approx 84$, which would be harder to pedal than a 78 gear ratio.

Where does this extra difficulty in pedaling benefit the rider? If one multiplies the gear ratio obtained in the formula above by π, one gets the distance traveled forward with each turn of the pedals. Students should recall that Circumference = $\pi \times$ *Diameter*.

For example, the rider with the 78 gear ratio goes approximately 245 inches forward for each turn of the pedals, the rider with the 84 gear ratio goes approximately 264 inches forward for each complete turn of the pedals. Hence the increase in work (increased difficulty in pedaling) is returned in greater distance per pedal revolution.

Now let us examine applications of various gearing ratio to the average rider.

Suppose Danny was riding comfortably on level ground in a 78 gear ratio and then he came to a rather steep hill. Should he switch to a higher or lower gear ratio?

Your reasoning should be as follows: If Danny switches to an 84 gear ratio, he will go 264 inches forward for each turn of the pedals. This requires a certain amount of work. To overcome the effects of gravity to get up the hill requires additional energy. So Danny would probably end up walking his bicycle. If Danny had switched to a lower gear, he would use less energy to turn the pedals and the additional energy required to climb the hill would make his gearing feel about the same as the 78 gear ratio. So the answer is to switch to a lower number gear ratio.

Danny will have to turn the pedal more revolutions to scale the hill; more than if he had chosen the 84 gear ratio and more than if he stayed in the 78 gear ratio. Remember, his gearing only feels like 78 because of the hill. This is the "trade-off" Danny made: more revolutions at a constant torque (angular force) instead of the same number of revolutions per distance with varying force.

The benefit of this trade-off is understood by comparing the human body to the engine. An engine works most effectively at a constant torque than a varying torque and compensates by changing gear ratios with changing speed and revolutions per minute.

A more concise description is given below. A car uses gears to overcome static friction and accelerate to operating speed while providing constant torque or less torque than overload to the engine. This is not similar to the bicycle because the human machine can overcome an increase in torque for the short period of time to accelerate the bicycle. When a bicycle is in motion, the only force needed to keep it in motion at constant speed on level ground is that required to overcome internal friction and wind resistance. This is the same for a car. Should a rider wish to accelerate quickly, he would want to turn the pedals as fast as possible. All machines (including the human machine) have optimum torque capacity for this. There are two things that can happen to prevent the machine from reaching its maximum possible speed. First, if the torque is too high, it prevents rapid spin. This corresponds to a car in third gear trying to pass without a downshift. The engine doesn't have the power for rapid acceleration and can only accelerate slowly. The same is true for a rider trying to accelerate quickly in the harder gears; he is without the necessary power. Second is spin-out. This corresponds to when your car reaches 30 m.p.h. in first gear and cannot turn any faster even though there exists power for greater distance with each turn. An example is a manual shift car accelerating from a light in first without shifting. This compares on a bicycle to the rider turning the pedals as fast as possible but not at maximum force.

If the rider reaches maximum spin at maximum torque, he will reach maximum speed.

At this point you might want to have your students try some applications.

Model Problem Max can turn a 68 gear ratio at 100 r.p.m. or a 72 gear ratio at 84 r.p.m. For maximum speed which should Max choose? (These are the very considerations bicycle racers use in determining which gear to use for the final sprint.) Assume these speeds are constant for the duration of the sprint.

Solution A 68 gear ratio times π = 214 inches per revolution (approximately). If Max spins 100 r.p.m., she is traveling at 21,400 inches/min. or 20.27 m.p.h.

A 72 gear ratio times π = 226 inches per revolution (approximately) at a rate of 84 r.p.m. would produce a speed of 18,984 inches/min. or 17.98 m.p.h. Therefore Max would be better off sprinting in the 68 gear ratio.

As mentioned earlier, these torque and spin performance items are given careful attention by racers. A racer will carefully select his or her back sprocket wheel cluster depending on the course. A relatively flat course would necessitate a 13–18 tooth range in the rear sprocket wheel cluster with a 47 tooth inner front sprocket wheel and 50 tooth outer front sprocket wheel.

This is where the ten speeds come from. When the chain is on the 47 tooth sprocket wheel, there are 5 different gear ratios as the rear derailleur moves the chain through the 5 rear sprocket wheels. When the chain is on the 50 tooth sprocket wheel, there are again 5 different gear ratios.

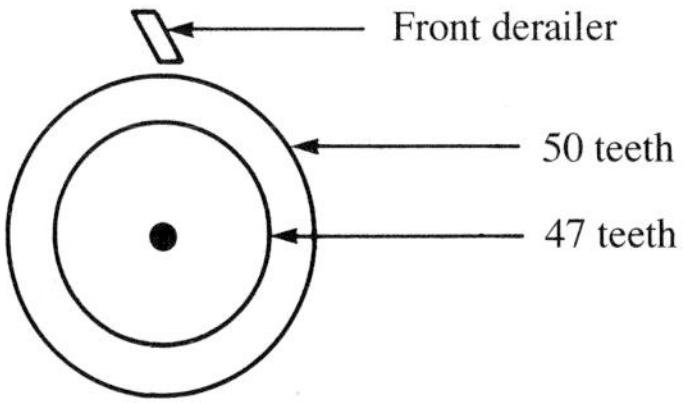

One other consideration a racer will make in selecting gears is inertia. You will notice that a 54 front sprocket wheel and 18-tooth rear sprocket wheel gives the same gear ratio as would a 48-tooth front sprocket wheel and a 16-tooth rear sprocket wheel; that is, $\frac{48}{16} = 3$. The rider will choose the $\frac{48}{16}$ because work is expended without return to accelerate through an angular acceleration a sprocket wheel of larger radius than a sprocket wheel of smaller radius due to inertia considerations. Since a 10″ radius sprocket wheel is the smallest to take the heavy shear forces, a 34-tooth sprocket wheel is the smallest available. We are currently using $\frac{1}{2}$ pitch (distance between teeth), an improvement over 1″ pitch to increase the number of ratios without letting sprocket wheels get too large. A well-made sprocket wheel would look like the diagram below, where most of the unnecessary mass is cut out.

Inertia = M × distance from the axle of rotation squared. The smaller the distance, the smaller the inertia.

Thus in selecting a ten-speed bicycle remember that with each difference in price goes a difference in thought toward design, performance, and work required for riding.

As a final example many inexpensive bicycles really only have 6 to 8 speeds because of duplication. Consider our previous example on inertia, where the choice was between a 48-tooth and 54-tooth front sprocket wheel. We saw duplication of the same gear ratio with a 16 and 18 rear sprocket wheel. This case occurs on many less expensive bicycles.

POSTASSESSMENT

1. Lisa approaches a hill that raises whatever gear ratio she is in by 10. Lisa cannot pedal anything harder than a 62 gear ratio. If her three-speed bicycle has 48, 58, and 78 gear ratio, which should she use?
2. How far forward with each revolution of the pedals will a 78 gear ratio move a bicycle whose wheel radius is 27″?
3. Josh can spin a 72 gear ratio 80 r.p.m. and a 96 gear ratio 48 r.p.m. Which gives a greater velocity?

Unit 29

 Mathematics and Music

Students who are acquainted with operations on fractions but whose knowledge of music theory is limited will find a correlation between these fields.

PERFORMANCE OBJECTIVES

1. *Students will demonstrate knowledge of certain formulas relating pitch of a note to properties of a string or an air column.*
2. *Students will know how to create Pythagoras' diatonic scale.*
3. *Students will show how Euclid proved that an octave is less than six whole tones.*

PREASSESSMENT

Obtain a stringed instrument such as a banjo, violin, or guitar. If these are unavailable, the science department can probably lend you a sonometer, which is a scientific instrument with strings used in experimentation.

Perform the following three demonstrations. In each case, have students determine whether the pitch becomes higher or lower.

1. Pluck a string, tighten it, then pluck it again.
2. Pluck a string. Then by pressing down on the middle of the string (fretting) cause only half the string to vibrate.
3. Using two strings of different diameters (thickness), pluck each one.

TEACHING STRATEGIES

Elicit from the students the following three facts:

1. As tension increases, pitch becomes higher.
2. As length decreases, pitch becomes higher.
3. As diameter decreases, pitch becomes higher.

At this point explain that the above is grounded in mathematical formulas. However, these formulas use frequency, which is the number of vibrations of the string per second, rather than pitch. Since the pitch of a tone gets higher whenever the frequency increases, it will not really alter the formulas. They are

$$\underset{\left(\begin{smallmatrix}\text{strings are}\\ \text{same type}\end{smallmatrix}\right)}{\frac{F_1^2}{F_2^2} = \frac{T_1}{T_2}}; \quad \underset{\left(\begin{smallmatrix}\text{tension}\\ \text{constant}\end{smallmatrix}\right)}{\frac{F_1}{F_2} = \frac{L_2}{L_1}}; \quad \underset{\left(\begin{smallmatrix}\text{length and}\\ \text{tension constant}\end{smallmatrix}\right)}{\frac{F_1}{F_2} = \sqrt{\frac{D_2}{D_1}}}$$

where F = frequency
T = tension
D = diameter of string

Have students try numerical examples: A string that vibrates at a frequency of 400 vps (vibrations per second) is 20 inches long. A second string of the same type is plucked in a similar manner. (The tension being the same as in the first case.) If its frequency is 800 vps, how long is it? Have them solve $\frac{400}{800} = \frac{L_2}{20}$, concluding that the length of the second string is 10 inches. Another example could be the effect on the tension if the frequency of a string doubles. Elicit that the tension quadruples. $\left(\frac{1^2}{2^2} = \frac{1}{4}\right)$

Music and mathematics are also related to the creation of a scale. Pythagoras, familiar to most students for his work with the right triangle, produced a scale that could make beautiful melodies, but limited the combination of tones possible and the use of harmony.

Pythagoras felt that those tones, which were particularly pleasing, or *consonant*, were related to the numbers 1, 2, 3 and 4. He took several strings of the same length, letting the note C be the fundamental tone. If the sonometer is used, the teacher can demonstrate the basics of what Pythagoras did. This means that the string vibrates as a whole (see Diagram 1). To obtain the note C an octave higher, the string must vibrate in two parts, i.e., have twice the frequency (see Diagram 2). One can also accomplish the same thing by dividing a string into two parts of the ratio 1:2 (see Diagram 3).

In Diagram 3, vibrating $\overline{AD}$ and $\overline{DB}$ separately will have the same effect of producing two notes an octave apart. Thus, if C corresponds to the number 1, then C an octave higher would correspond to the number $\frac{2}{1}$ or 2. Pythagoras also added notes F and G corresponding to $\frac{4}{3}$ and $\frac{3}{2}$, respectively.

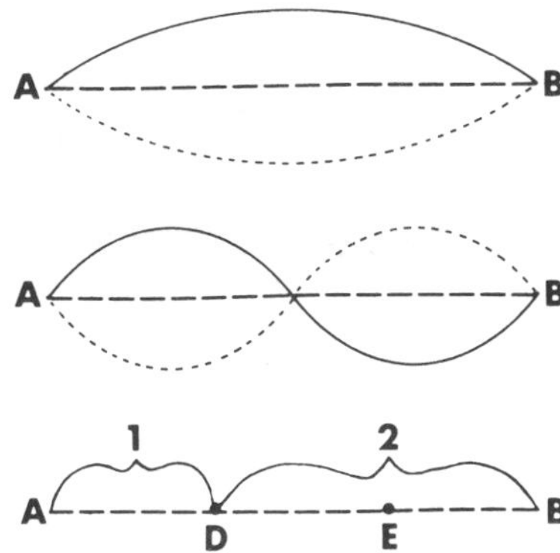

Ask the students how the string can be divided into the ratio 3:2. Elicit that the string can be divided into five parts to obtain the result.

This is one reason why this note can be called a perfect fifth.

To obtain a note corresponding to $\frac{4}{3}$ the string should be divided into seven parts as shown.

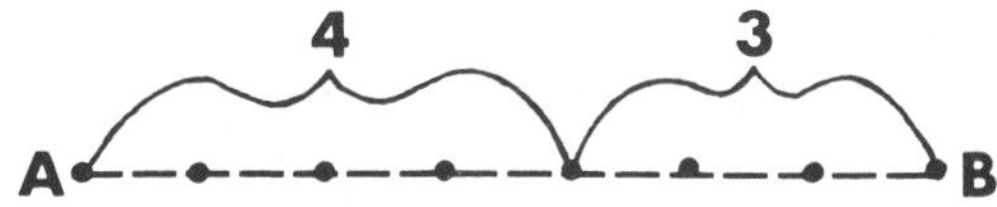

However, this note is called a fourth and not a seventh.

Pythagoras added to his scale $\frac{3}{2}G$ or $\frac{3}{2} \cdot \frac{3}{2} C = \frac{9}{4} C$.

Since C = 1 and the octave C = 2, $\frac{9}{4} C = 2\frac{1}{4} C$ would not fit between these notes.

Challenge the students to find a tone "basically" the same that would fit between C and its octave. Have them recall that doubling or halving a frequency only changes a tone by an octave. Thus, instead of $\frac{9}{4}$, Pythagoras used $\frac{1}{2}$ of $\frac{9}{4}$ or $\frac{9}{8}$. By adding the third harmonic of each successive tone (i.e., multiplying by $\frac{3}{2}$), students will be able to obtain tones whose relative frequencies are $1, \frac{3}{2}, \frac{9}{8}, \frac{27}{16}, \frac{81}{64}, \frac{243}{128}$. Of course, some additional "halving" was done when needed as in the case of $\frac{9}{8}$. Pythagoras' diatonic scale is thus obtained.

C	D	E	F	G	A	B	C	
1	$\frac{9}{8}$	$\frac{81}{64}$	$\frac{4}{3}$	$\frac{3}{2}$	$\frac{27}{16}$	$\frac{243}{128}$	2	(Relative Frequencies)

G, which occupies the fifth position, is considered a perfect fifth. This occurs whenever the ratio of the fifth to the first is $\frac{3}{2}$. Throughout the discussion, the fact that frequencies are in the same ratio as their lengths should be stressed.

Have students study the scale in its new form. Elicit that there is a constant ratio of $\frac{9}{8}$ between notes (except between E and F and between B and C where the ratio is $\frac{256}{243}$). It should also be noted that $\frac{9}{8}$ corresponds to a whole tone (W) while the other is called a semitone (S). Thus, the pattern obtained is as follows:

C		D		E		F		G		A		B		C
1		$\frac{9}{8}$		$\frac{81}{64}$		$\frac{4}{3}$		$\frac{3}{2}$		$\frac{27}{16}$		$\frac{243}{128}$		2
	V		V		V		V		V		V		V	
	W		W		S		W		W		W		S	

This is called a major scale.

However, there is some difficulty with harmony. When one sounds a tone on a musical instrument it not only vibrates in one piece making the fundamental tone, but also in parts creating tones called overtones. The overtones have 2, 3, 4, and 5 times the frequency of the fundamental. The fifth overtone corresponds to 5 or $\frac{5}{4}$ if it is to be placed between 1 and 2 (recall continuous halving like $\frac{1}{2} \cdot \frac{1}{2}$ creates a similar tone). The closest tone on the Pythagorean scale is E of frequency $\frac{81}{64}$. When a C is played and then followed by an E, the ear expects to hear the same E just heard as an overtone of C. However, to the individual the Pythagorean E can be quite disturbing. This disturbance is due to the fact that the two E's involved have only slightly different frequencies, one being $\frac{81}{64}$ and the other $\frac{5}{4}$ or $\frac{80}{64}$.

POSTASSESSMENT

1. If the tension is constant and the length is increased, how is a string's pitch affected?
2. How does string tightening affect pitch?
3. Suppose C corresponds to $\frac{4}{5}$ instead of 1 in Pythagoras' scale. Find the relative frequencies of the next 8 notes of this major scale.

Unit 30

Mathematics in Nature

PERFORMANCE OBJECTIVE

Students will identify and explain where mathematics is found in nature in at least one situation.

PREASSESSMENT

A famous sequence of numbers (*The Fibonacci Numbers*) was the direct result of a problem posed by Leonardo of Pisa in his book *Liber Abaci* (1202) regarding the regeneration of rabbits. A brief review of this problem indicates that the total number of pairs of rabbits existing each month determined the sequence: 1,1, 2,3,5,8,13,21,34,55,89, ...

Fibonacci numbers have many interesting properties and have been found to occur in nature.

TEACHING STRATEGIES

Have students divide each number in the Fibonacci sequence by its right hand partner to see what sequence develops. They will get a series of fractions:

$$\frac{1}{1}, \frac{1}{2}, \frac{2}{3}, \frac{3}{5}, \frac{5}{8}, \frac{8}{13}, \frac{13}{21}, \frac{21}{34}, \frac{34}{55}, \frac{55}{89}, \ldots$$

Ask students if they can determine a relationship between these numbers and the leaves of a plant (have a plant on hand). From the standpoint of Fibonacci numbers, one may observe two items: (1) the number of leaves it takes to go (rotating about the stem) from any given leaf to the next one similarly placed (i.e., above it and in the same direction) on the stem; and (2) the number of revolutions as one follows the leaves in going from one leaf to another one similarly placed. In both cases, these numbers turn out to be the Fibonacci numbers.

In the case of leaf arrangement, the following notation is used: $\frac{3}{8}$ means that it takes three revolutions and eight leaves to arrive at the next leaf similarly placed. In general, if we let r equal the number of revolutions, and s equal the number of leaves it takes to go from any given leaf to one similarly placed, then $\frac{r}{s}$ will be the *phyllotaxis* (the arrangement of leaves in plants). Have students look at Figure 1 and try to find the plant ratio. Draw a diagram on the board, and if possible, provide a live plant.

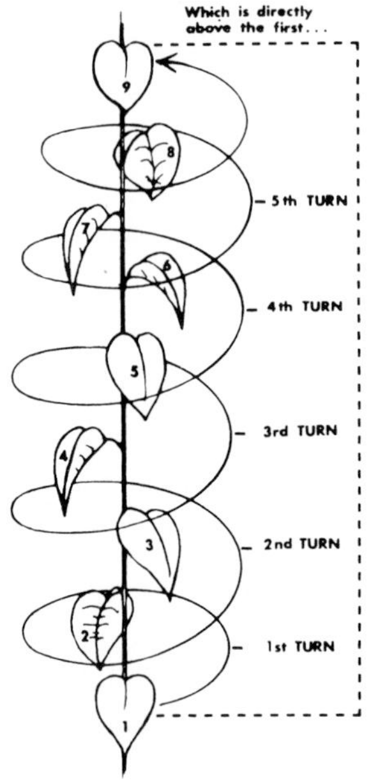

FIGURE 1

In this figure, the plant ratio is $\frac{5}{8}$.

The pine cone also presents a Fibonacci application. The bracts on the cone are considered to be modified leaves compressed into smaller space. Upon observation of the cone, one can notice two spirals, one to the left (clockwise) and the other to the right (counterclockwise). One spiral increases at a sharp angle, while the other spiral increases more gradually. Have students consider the steep spirals and count them as well as the spirals that increase gradually. Both numbers should be Fibonacci numbers. For example, a white pine cone has five clockwise spirals and eight counterclockwise spirals. Other pine cones may have different Fibonacci ratios. Later, have students examine the daisy to see where the Fibonacci ratios apply to it.

If we look closely at the ratios of consecutive Fibonacci numbers, we can approximate their decimal equivalents. Some are

1. $\frac{2}{3} = .666667$
2. $\frac{3}{5} = .600000$
3. $\frac{89}{144} = .618056$
4. $\frac{144}{233} = .618026$

Continuing in this manner, we approach what is known as the *golden ratio*. Point B in Figure 2 divides line $\overleftrightarrow{AC}$ into the golden ratio, $\frac{AB}{BC} = \frac{BC}{AC} \approx .618034$.

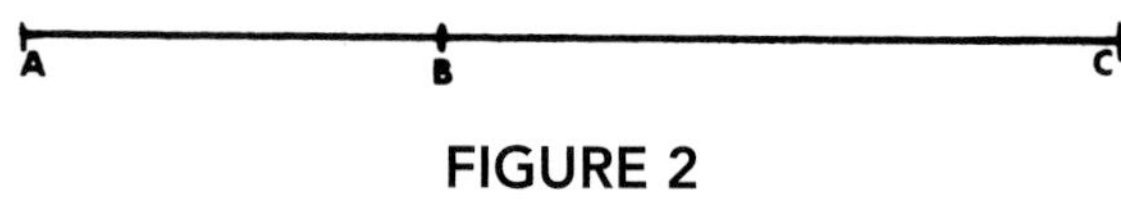

FIGURE 2

Now consider the series of golden rectangles (Figures 3a and 3b), those whose dimensions are chosen so that the ratio of $\frac{\text{width}}{\text{length}}$ is the golden ratio $\left(\text{i.e., } \frac{w}{1} = \frac{1}{w+1}\right)$.

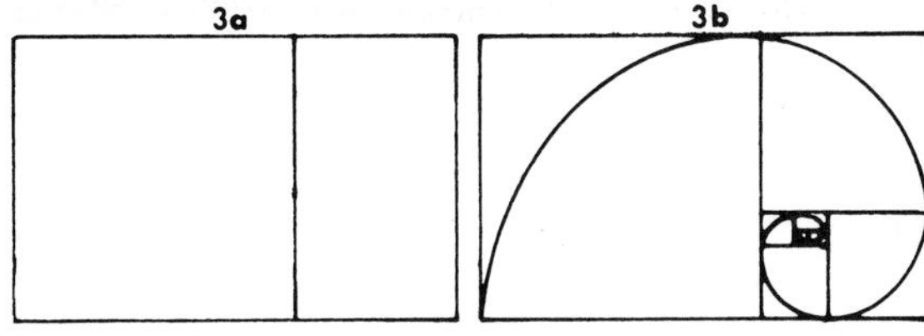

FIGURE 3

If the rectangle (Figure 3a) is divided by a line into a square and a golden rectangle, and if we keep partitioning each new golden rectangle in the same way, we can construct a logarithmic spiral in the successive squares (Figure 3b). This type of curve is frequently found in the arrangements of seeds in flowers or in the shapes of seashells and snails. Bring in illustrations to show these spirals (Figure 4).

FIGURE 4

For another example of mathematics in nature, students should consider the pineapple. Here there are three distinct spirals of hexagons: a group of *five* spirals winding gradually in one direction, a second group of *13* spirals winding more steeply in the same direction, and a third group of *eight* spirals winding in the opposite direction. Each group of spirals consists of a Fibonacci number. Each pair of spirals interacts to give Fibonacci numbers. Figure 5 shows a representation

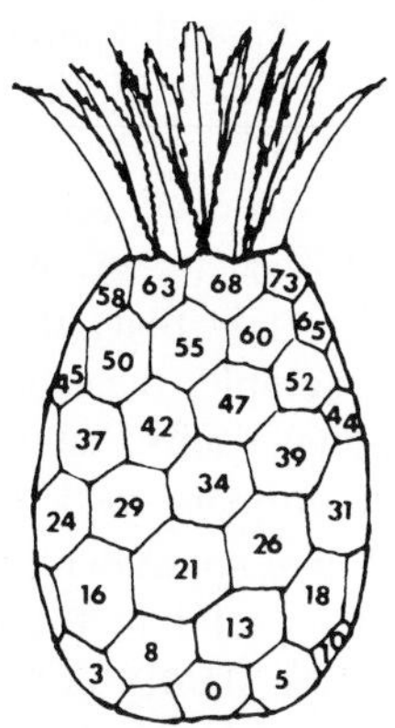

FIGURE 5

of the pineapple with the scales numbered in order. This order is determined by the distance (relative) each hexagon is from the bottom. That is, the lowest is numbered 0, the next higher one is numbered 1. Note hexagon 42 is slightly higher than hexagon 37.

See if students can note three distinct sets of spirals in Figure 5 that cross each other, starting at the bottom. One spiral is the 0,5,10, etc., sequence, which increases at a slight angle. The second spiral is the 0,13,26, etc., sequence, which increases at a steeper angle. The third spiral has the 0,8,16, etc., sequence, which lies in the opposite direction from the other two. Have students figure out the common difference between the numbers in each sequence. In this case, the differences are 5,8,13, all of which are Fibonacci numbers. Different pineapples may have different sequences.

In concluding this topic, consider briefly the regeneration of male bees. Male bees hatch from unfertilized eggs; female bees from fertilized eggs. The teacher should guide students in tracing the regeneration of the male bees. The following pattern develops:

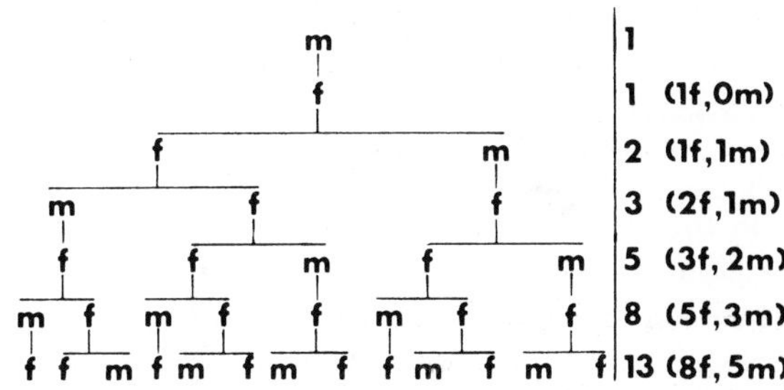

It should be obvious by now that this pattern is the Fibonacci sequence.

POSTASSESSMENT

1. Ask students to explain two distinct ways mathematics manifests itself in nature.
2. Have students find examples of Fibonacci numbers in nature (other than those presented in this unit) and have them explain the manner in which the sequence is used.

REFERENCES

Brother U. Alfred. *An Introduction to Fibonacci Discovery*. San Jose, CA: The Fibonacci Association, 1965.

Bicknell, M., and Verner E. Hoggatt, Jr. *A Primer for the Fibonacci Numbers*. San Jose, CA: The Fibonacci Association, 1972.

Dunlap, Richard A. *The Golden Ration and Fibonacci Numbers*. River Edge, NJ: World Scientific Publishing Co., 1997.

Posamentier, Alfred S., Ingmar Lehmann. *The Fabulous Fibonacci Numbers*. Amherst, NY: Prometheus Books, 2007.

Unit 31

 The Birthday Problem

Students are fascinated by problems that involve surprise or unpredictable outcomes. The "birthday problem" will engage them in the study of mathematical probability.

PERFORMANCE OBJECTIVE

In problems involving sequences of successive events, such as indications of birthdays, tossing of coins, drawing of cards, throwing of dice, students will calculate the probability that a specified outcome (a) occurs at least once, (b) fails to occur at all.

PREASSESSMENT

Ask the class what they think the probability is of two students in the class sharing the same birthday. The students will respond that the chances of this being true are remote. Surprise them by telling them that, in a class of 30 students, the probability of at least two students having the same birthday is approximately 0.68 (a probability of 1.00 indicates an absolute certainty). In a class of 35 students, this probability rises to about 0.80. Restate these probabilities in the language of "odds." Point out that the odds in favor of the desired outcome in the first instance are better than two to one and in the second about four to one. Copy and distribute a list of the 43 presidents of the United States, with the dates of their birth and death next to their names. Give students time to look for any dates the presidents had in common (two, Polk and Harding, were born on November 2; two, Fillmore and Taft, died on March 8; and three, Adams, Jefferson, and Monroe, died on July 4). Now take a class survey to determine if any students share the same birthday. If they do, this fact will reinforce the probability figures and will help convince them of the statistical plausibility. If they do not, indicate that no claim of absolute certainty was made.

TEACHING STRATEGIES

Review the following fundamental principles the students will need to know. Mathematical probabilities are stated as decimals between 0.00 and 1.00, and a probability of 0 (zero) means that a particular outcome is impossible, while a probability of 1 (one) means that a particular outcome is a certainty.

Each of the principles enumerated here may be illustrated by simple examples in the tossing of coins, the throwing of dice, the drawing of cards, etc. For example, the probability of throwing a total of 13 with a pair of ordinary dice is equal to zero, while the probability of throwing some number between 2 and 12 inclusive is equal to one. The probability of a desired outcome occurring can be calculated by forming a fraction whose numerator represents the number of "acceptable" or "successful" outcomes and whose denominator represents the sum of the "successful" outcomes and the "unsuccessful" outcomes or "failures." Symbolically, $P = \frac{S}{S+F}$ or $P = \frac{S}{T}$. P represents the probability of a particular event occurring, S the number of successful outcomes, F the number of failures, and T the total number of outcomes possible. Either form of this fraction may be converted to a decimal between zero and one, since the numerator may never exceed the denominator.

The students should also note that the probability of a desired outcome *failing* to occur would be equal to $\frac{F}{S+F}$. Since $\frac{S}{S+F} + \frac{F}{S+F} = \frac{S+F}{S+F} = 1$, it follows that $\frac{S}{S+F} = 1 - \frac{F}{S+F}$. The students should now state in words that the probability of a desired outcome *occurring* is equal numerically to 1.00 minus the probability of this outcome failing to occur. This statement enables them to complete the lesson.

Students should be familiar with a fundamental theorem of probability and it is presented here without proof: If the probability of an event is P_1, and if, after it has happened, the probability of a second event is P_2, then the probability that both events will happen is P_1P_2. Point out that this principle may be generalized to calculate the probability that a sequence of n events will occur, given that each preceding event has occurred, and that the result would be $P_1P_2P_3P_4 \ldots P_n$. For example, the students, by performing the following activities, will realize that the probability of drawing a spade from an ordinary deck of 52 cards is $\frac{13}{52}$ or 0.25 and the probability of *not* drawing a spade is $\frac{39}{52}$ or 0.75; where both probabilities refer to the drawing of a single card from the deck, they should note that $0.25 = 1.00 - 0.75$. The probability of tossing a head, followed by a tail, followed by another tail, where a "true" coin is tossed three times in succession, is $\frac{1}{2} \cdot \frac{1}{2} \cdot \frac{1}{2}$ or $\frac{1}{8}$, illustrating the use of the fundamental principle for dealing with successive events.

Back to the birthday problem. You might point out that it will be simpler to calculate the probability that *no* students in the class share the same birthday and then to subtract this result from 1.00, than to directly calculate the probability that at least two students in the class have the same birthday. Help the students to formulate the following representation of the probability that *no* students in the class share the same birthday:

$$\frac{365}{365} \cdot \frac{364}{365} \cdot \frac{363}{365} \cdot \frac{362}{365} \cdot \frac{361}{365} \cdot \frac{360}{365} \cdot \frac{359}{365} \cdot \frac{358}{365} \cdot \frac{357}{365} \cdot \frac{356}{365} \cdot \ldots .$$

There will be as many fractions in this product as there are students in the class. Note that this formulation is based on an ordinary year of 365 days. If any of your students has a February 29 birthday, use denominators of 366 and have the first fraction read $\frac{366}{366}$.

Explain that these fractions represent the probabilities that students questioned in sequence as to their birthdays would *not* name a day already mentioned by a preceding student. Point out the fundamental principle for calculating the probability of successive events—sequential questioning. They will be interested in learning how they can best perform the sequence of multiplications and divisions—the simplest approach is through the use of calculators.

The students will discover that the value of their product has decreased to about 0.32 when the number of factors has reached 30, and to about 0.20 when the number of factors has reached 35. Since these figures represent the probabilities that no students in the class shared the same birthday, they represent "failures," in the terminology of this problem. Using the principle of subtraction from 1.00, already mentioned, to arrive at the probabilities of "successes"—the probabilities that at least two students in the class share the same birthday—we arrive at 0.68 or 0.80 or some other high decimal, depending on the size of the class. When the number of people in a group reaches just 55, the probability of finding at least two with the same birthday reaches the astonishing value of 0.99!

POSTASSESSMENT

Students who have met the performance objective will be able to answer these or similar probabilities correctly:

1. Represent the probability that, given a group of 15 people, at least 2 share the same birthday.
2. If a coin is tossed into the air five times, what is the probability that (a) none of the tosses will turn up heads and (b) at least one of the tosses will turn up heads?
3. If a card is drawn from an ordinary deck of 52 cards, examined and replaced, and if this is repeated four times, what is the probability that (a) at least one of the cards drawn is a spade, and (b) none of the cards drawn is an ace?

Unit 32

The Structure of the Number System

PERFORMANCE OBJECTIVE

Given any number, the student will identify it as belonging to the set of natural numbers, integers, rational numbers, real numbers, or complex numbers. The student will also convert any decimal representing a rational number to its equivalent fractional form and vice versa.

PREASSESSMENT

Assess students' ability with the following pretest, assuring them, of course, that this is a trial test and they will not be graded on it.

1. Identify the following numbers as belonging to the set of natural numbers, integers, rational numbers, real numbers, or complex numbers (name the "smallest" possible set in each case): -3, $\frac{5}{3}$, 17, $\sqrt{2}$, 3.14, $\frac{22}{7}$, $\sqrt{-9}$, $.\overline{4}$, 0.2133333 . . . , 2.71828 . . . , 0.121121112 . . . , $.\overline{15}$, $.1\overline{5}$, $-\frac{1}{4}$, $-\sqrt{16}$, etc.
2. Convert each of the following fractions to decimals: $\frac{3}{8}$, $\frac{7}{5}$, $\frac{2}{3}$, $\frac{7}{9}$, $\frac{5}{11}$, $\frac{5}{12}$.
3. Convert each of the following decimals to fractions: 0.875, $.\overline{8}$, .272727 . . . , 0.8333333 . . . .

Students who do well on the pretest have already attained the performance objective. Give them a different assignment while you present this lesson to the rest of the class.

TEACHING STRATEGIES

Ask your students to solve a simple linear equation such as $3x + 5 = 11$. When the correct solution, $x = 2$, is offered, ask what kind of number this is. Students may use such terms as *whole number* or *positive number* in their responses. Explain that 2 is a *counting* number and that the set of counting numbers is known mathematically as the set of natural numbers. Elicit other illustrations of natural numbers and have the students describe the set by roster: $N = \{1, 2, 3, \ldots\}$. They should note that the elements of this set are ordered and infinite in number, and that the set possesses a first or smallest element, the number 1.

Proceed in a similar fashion to develop the concept of the set of integers. Modify the equation just explored by reversing the two constants: $3x + 11 = 5$. When they obtain $x = -2$ as the solution, the students will volunteer that this is a negative whole number or some other similar description. Introduce the term *integer* if it is not mentioned by the class. They will readily understand that this term is synonymous with the term *whole number* and that the natural numbers just studied are a subset of the set of integers. This can be illustrated by a Venn diagram that, at this stage of the lesson, consists of an inner circle labeled N to represent the set of natural numbers and an outer circle labeled I to represent the set of integers. This diagram will be built up as the lesson develops by the addition of three more circles, each completely encircling all of the preceding circles. Elicit several illustrations of integers and help your students to describe this set by roster: $I = \{\ldots, -3, -2, -1, 0, 1, 2, 3 \ldots\}$. They will note that this set is also an infinite one and that it is ordered, but that it possesses *no* first element.

Now offer the equation $2x + 1 = 6$. When the answer, $\frac{5}{2}$, is forthcoming, students will recognize that this number is *not* a member of the set of natural numbers or the set of integers since it is not a whole number but, rather, a fraction. Point out that such numbers are formed by setting up the ratio of two integers, $\frac{a}{b}$, where the denominator, b, is not equal to zero (ask your students why not!). The term *rational number* derives naturally from the word *ratio*. Add the third circle to your Venn diagram, completely enclosing the previous two circles. Label the new circle Q for quotient.

Elicit numerous illustrations of rational numbers, including proper and improper fractions, both positive and negative. Students should be aware that the set of rational numbers is infinite and ordered, but that no roster can be prepared for this set. You might explain that the rational numbers are "everywhere dense" and that an infinitude of rationals exists between any two rational numbers.

We are now ready to examine the decimals. Students will generally exhibit some uncertainty as to which of these represent rational numbers. We must consider terminating decimals, nonterminating but repeating decimals, and nonterminating and nonrepeating decimals. Your students can obtain some clues by converting a few fractions such as $\frac{1}{8}$, $\frac{5}{9}$, and $\frac{1}{6}$ to decimals by dividing their numerators by their denominators. They will observe that the result in every case is either a terminating decimal or a nonterminating but repeating decimal. Students can show easily that every terminating decimal represents a rational number by simply writing each one as a decimal fraction.

Next, introduce nonterminating decimals. Students who believe that $0.\overline{3}$ represents a rational number can be challenged to write it in fractional form. Some may recognize this decimal as being equal to $\frac{1}{3}$. If so, challenge them with the decimal $0.\overline{5}$, which they obtained earlier themselves by converting $\frac{5}{9}$ to a decimal, or with $0.16666\ldots$ which they also obtained themselves by converting $\frac{1}{6}$ to a decimal. Ask them whether they could convert these decimals to fractions if they did *not* know the answers! Or, challenge them with the decimal $0.\overline{13}$, for which it is unlikely that they will know the result. If they need your help to convert such decimals to fractions, two illustrations will make the technique clear.

$$
\begin{aligned}
N &= 0.131313\ldots \\
&\text{Multiply by 100:} \\
100N &= 13.131313\ldots \\
N &= 0.131313\ldots \\
\hline
99N &= 13 \text{ by subtraction} \\
N &= \frac{13}{99} \\
N &= .1666666\ldots \\
&\text{Multiply by 10:} \\
10N &= 1.666666\ldots \\
N &= 0.166666\ldots \\
\hline
9N &= 1.5 \text{ by subtraction} \\
90N &= 15 \\
N &= \frac{15}{90} = \frac{1}{6}
\end{aligned}
$$

Provide several illustrations for your students, including some with nonrepeating portions in the decimal before the repetand appears, as in the second example above. Help them to grasp the fact that such decimals represent rational numbers, even though their nonrepeating portions may be lengthy, as long as they are finite in length *and* they are followed by repetands of one or more digits.

Your students are now ready to consider the nonterminating, nonrepeating decimals. They are already familiar with some of these, notably $\pi = 3.14159\ldots$ and perhaps the square roots of some of the nonperfect squares. (Be certain they understand that such numbers as $\frac{22}{7}$ and 3.14 or 3.1416 are only *rational approximations* to the *irrational* number π.) Propose the equation $x^2 + 2 = 7$. Those who are familiar with the square root algorithm may be asked to work out $\sqrt{5}$ to a few decimal places to determine whether a pattern of repetition appears. They will discover, of course, that it does not, since $\sqrt{5} = 2.236\ldots$ and is irrational.

Students unfamiliar with the algorithm may refer to a table of square roots. They will discover that the only square roots that contain a repetand in their decimal representations are those of perfect squares. All other square roots are irrational numbers, since they are nonterminating, nonrepeating decimals. You may also wish to generalize this result to the nth roots of nonperfect nth powers.

Explain to your students that the set of the rational numbers together with the set of irrational numbers form the set of real numbers. Add a fourth circle to your Venn diagram, labeling it R, and have it completely enclose the three circles previously drawn. The students should realize that the sets of natural numbers, integers, and rational numbers are each proper subsets of the set of real numbers.

This development of the structure of the number system may be concluded with a brief treatment of the complex numbers. Ask your students to try to solve the equation $x^2 + 4 = 0$. Help them to see why answers such as $+2$ and -2 are incorrect. They should soon realize that no real number squared can equal -4, or any other negative number, for that matter. Explain that numbers that are not real are called "imaginary" and that the imaginary numbers and the real numbers together form the set known as the "complex numbers." You may wish to introduce the symbol $i = \sqrt{-1}$ so they can write a solution for their equation as $+2i$ and $-2i$. Complete the Venn diagram with the fifth and last circle, completely enclosing the other four circles, and showing the real numbers as a proper subset of the complex numbers, C.

POSTASSESSMENT

Give students a test similar to the pretest. Compare each student's pre-and posttest answers to measure progress.

Unit 33

Excursions in Number Bases

Students learn early in their school careers that the base used in our everyday number system (the "decimal system") is the number 10. Later, they discover that other numbers can serve as bases for number systems. For example, numbers written in base 2 (the "binary system") are used extensively in computer work. This lesson will explore a variety of problems involving numbers written in many different positive integral bases.

PERFORMANCE OBJECTIVE

Students will solve a variety of numerical and algebraic problems involving numbers expressed as numerals in any positive integral base b, $b \geq 2$.

PREASSESSMENT

How far you go in this lesson will depend somewhat on the algebraic background of the class. Question students or evaluate their previous work to determine how well they understand the idea of place value in writing numerals, the meaning of zero and negative exponents, and the techniques for solving quadratic and higher degree equations.

TEACHING STRATEGIES

Review briefly the fact that decimal numerals are written by using a system of place values. Point out, for example, that in the numeral 356 the digit *3* represents *300* rather than merely a *3*, the digit *5* represents *50* rather than merely a *5*, and the digit *6* is a units digit and really does represent a *6*. Briefly, $356 = 300 + 50 + 6 = 3(100) + 5(10) + 6 = 3(10)^2 + 5(10)^1 + 6(10)^0$. Likewise, $3{,}107 = 3(10)^3 + 1(10)^2 + 0(10)^1 + 7(10)^0$. Ask students for further illustrations. If necessary, review or teach at this point the meaning of the zero exponent and also of negative exponents, since these will be used later.

Explain that the use of the number 10 as a base is somewhat arbitrary, and students should note that other numbers can be used as bases. If the number 2 is used as a base, numbers are expressed as sums of powers of 2 rather than as sums of positive integral multiples of powers of 10, and the only digits used to represent numerals are 0 and 1. For example, the number 356 considered above is equal to $256 + 64 + 32 + 4 = 2^8 + 2^6 + 2^5 + 2^2 = 1(2)^8 + 0(2)^7 + 1(2)^6 + 1(2)^5 + 0(2)^4 + 0(2)^3 + 1(2)^2 + 0(2)^1 + 0(2)^0 = 101100100_{\text{two}}$, the subscript indicating the base. In base 3 (where the digits used to represent the numerals are 0, 1, and 2) $356 = 243 + 81 + 27 + 3 + 2(1) = 1(3)^5 + 1(3)^4 + 1(3)^3 + 0(3)^2 + 1(3)^1 + 2(3)^0 = 111012_{\text{three}}$. In base 5 (where the digits used are 0, 1, 2, 3, and 4) $356 = 2(125) + 4(25) + 1(5) + 1(1) = 2(5)^3 + 4(5)^2 + 1(5)^1 + 1(5)^0 = 2411_{\text{five}}$. Subscripts should be written in words rather than in numerals to avoid any possible confusion. The class should note that when numerals are in base b, the only digits available for such representations are those from zero to $b - 1$, and that if the value of b is greater than 10, new digits must be created to represent the numerals 10, 11, 12, etc. Remind the class that numerals such as 2411_{five} should be read "two, four, one, one, base 5." Provide practice in writing and reading whole numbers in the numerals of bases other than base 10, according to class needs.

Next consider numbers other than integers. Help your students to see that 12.2_{ten} means $1(10)^1 + 2(10)^0 + 2(10)^{-1}$, since $10^0 = 1$ and $10^{-1} = \frac{1}{10}$, and that this number can be represented in the numerals of other bases just as integers can. For example, in base 5 we have $12.2_{ten} = 2(5)^1 + 2(5)^0 + 1(5)^{-1}$, since $\frac{1}{5} = \frac{2}{10}$, so $12.2_{ten} = 22.1_{five}$. Illustrate further with such problems as the conversion of 7.5_{ten} to base 2: $7.5_{ten} = 1(2)^2 + 1(2)^1 + 1(2)^0 + 1(2)^{-1} = 111.1_{two}$. Decimal numerals whose decimal parts are $.5\left(\frac{1}{2}\right)$,$.25\left(\frac{1}{4}\right)$,$.75\left(\frac{3}{4}\right)$, $.125(\frac{1}{8})$, etc., can be easily converted to base 2 numerals. For example, $8.75_{ten} = 1(2)^3 + 1(2)^{-1} + 1(2)^{-2}$, since $.75 = \frac{3}{4} = \frac{1}{2} + \frac{1}{4} = \frac{1}{2^1} + \frac{1}{2^2} = 2^{-1} + 2^{-2}$, so $8.75_{ten} = 1000.11_{two}$. Numbers can also be converted from numeral representations in one base to equivalent numeral representations in another base, where neither base is equal to 10. For example, 12.2_{four} can be represented in base 6 numerals as follows: $12.2_{four} = 1(4)^1 + 2(4)^0 + 2(4)^{-1} = 4 + 2 + \frac{2}{4} = 6 + \frac{3}{6} = 1(6)^1 + 0(6)^0 + 3(6)^{-1} = 10.3_{six}$. In base 10, this is the numeral 6.5. Provide practice with these types of numerical problems according to the interests and abilities of your students.

The class is ready to consider algebraic problems next. Offer the following challenge: "In a certain base b, the number 52 is double the number 25. Find the value of b." The students should note that 52 (read "five, two") really represents the expression $5b + 2$, since $52_b = 5(b)^1 + 2(b)^0$. Accordingly, the problem states that $5b + 2 = 2(2b + 5)$. Solve for b to get $b = 8$. Checking shows that $52_{eight} = 5(8) + 2 = 42_{ten}$ and $25_{eight} = 2(8) + 5 = 21_{ten}$ and $42 = 2(21)$. The above equation is only a linear one, but the following problem requires the use of a quadratic equation: "In what base b is the number represented by 132 twice the number represented by 33?" You have $132b = 1(b)^2 + 3(b)^1 + 2(b)^0$ and $33_b = 3(b)^1 + 3(b)^0$, so our equation becomes $b^2 + 3b + 2 = 2(3b + 3)$ or $b^2 - 3b - 4 = 0$. Solve for b in the usual fashion to obtain $b = -1$, (which must be rejected since the domain of b is positive), and $b = 4$, the only acceptable solution. Check: $132_{four} = 1(4)^2 + 3(4)^1 + 2(4)^0 = 1(16) + 3(4) + 2 = 30_{ten}$ and $33_{four} = 3(4)^1 + 3(4)^0 = 3(4) + 3 = 15_{ten}$; and 30 is twice 15. Offer students similar problems. If they have studied the solution of equations of degree higher than two, by synthetic division (since all results will be integral), include numbers whose representations in the bases being used involve more than three digits. For example: "In what base b is the number represented by the numeral 1213 triple the number represented by the numeral 221?" You have $1(b)^3 + 2(b)^2 + 1(b)^1 + 3(b)^0 = 3[2(b)^2 + 2(b)^1 + 1(b)^0]$ or $b^3 + 2b^2 + b + 3 = 3(2b^2 + 2b + 1)$, which simplifies to $b^3 - 4b^2 - 5b = 0$. Since this equation can be factored without resorting to synthetic division, solve it as follows: $b(b - 5)(b + 1) = 0$ and $b = 0, 5, -1$. As before, the only acceptable solution is the positive one, $b = 5$. Ask the class to check this result.

A final interesting algebraic application of number base problems is suggested by the following: "In base 10, the numeral 121 represents a number that is a perfect square. Does the numeral represent a perfect square in any other positive integral base?" Help your students investigate this problem as follows: $121_b = 1(b)^2 + 2(b)^1 + 1(b)^0 = b^2 + 2b + 1 = (b + 1)^2$. Surprise! The numeral 121 represents a perfect square in *any* positive integral base $b \geq 3$, and is the square of one more than the base number! Are there any other such numerals? Students may discover others by squaring such expressions as $b + 2$ and $b + 3$ to obtain the numerals 144 and 169. These perfect squares in base 10 are also perfect squares in any positive integral base containing the digits used in them ($b \geq 5$ and $b \geq 10$, respectively). It's not necessary for the coefficient of b to equal 1. If you square $2b + 1$, for example, you obtain $4b^2 + 4b + 1 = 441_b$, which will be a perfect square in any positive integral base $b \geq 5$. Invite your students to try to square expressions such as $3b + 1$, $2b + 2$, $4b + 1$, etc., to obtain other perfect squares. Some may wish to continue this investigation into a search for perfect cubes, perfect fourth powers, etc. Help them to cube $b + 1$, for example, to obtain $b^3 + 3b^2 + 3b + 1$, indicating that the numeral 1331 is a perfect cube in any positive integral base $b \geq 4$ (in base 10, $1331 = 11^3$). As a matter of fact, 1331 is the cube of one more than the base number in each case! This study can be carried as far as the interest and ability of your class permits. Students familiar with the binomial theorem will find it convenient to use in expanding higher powers of such expressions as $b + 1$, $2b + 1$, etc.

POSTASSESSMENT

Students who have met the performance objective will be able to solve problems such as the following:

1. Represent the decimal numeral 78 as a numeral in base 5.
2. The number represented by the numeral 1000.1 in base 2 is represented by what numeral in base 8?
3. In a certain base b, the number represented by the numeral 54 is three times the number represented by the numeral 16. Find the value of b.
4. In a certain base b, the number represented by the numeral 231 is double the number represented by the numeral 113. Find the value of b.
5. In what bases would the numeral 100 represent a perfect square? In what bases would the numeral 1000 represent a perfect cube? Can you make a generalization of these results?

Unit 34

Raising Interest

Students are often confronted with advertisements by savings institutions offering attractive interest rates and frequent compounding of interest on deposits. Since most banks have a variety of programs, it's valuable for potential depositors to understand how interest is calculated under each of the available options.

PERFORMANCE OBJECTIVE

Students will use the formula for compound interest to calculate the return on investments at any rate of interest, for any period of time, and for any commonly used frequency of compounding, including instantaneous (continuous) compounding. They will also determine which of two or more alternatives gives the best return over the same time period.

PREASSESSMENT

This lesson requires the ability to apply the laws of logarithms, so question students to be certain they're familiar with these laws. You should also determine the extent to which they are familiar with limits, since the class's background will help you determine how deeply you treat the concept of instantaneous compounding.

TEACHING STRATEGIES

Propose the following interesting problem: "In the year 1626, Peter Minuit bought Manhattan Island for the Dutch West India Company from the Indians for trinkets costing 60 Dutch guilders, or about \$24. Suppose Indians had been able to invest this \$24 at that time at an annual interest rate of 6%, and suppose further that this same interest rate had continued in effect all these years. How much money could the present-day descendants of these Indians collect if (1) only simple interest were calculated, and (2) interest were compounded (a) annually, (b) quarterly and (c) continuously?" The answers to a, b, and c should surprise everyone!

Review briefly the formula for simple interest, studied in earlier lessons. The class will recall that simple interest is calculated by taking the product of the principle P, the annual interest rate r, and the time in years t. Accordingly, you have the formula $I = Prt$, and in the above problem $I = (24)(.06)(354) = \$509.76$ simple interest. Add this to the principal of \$24.00 to obtain the amount A of \$533.76 available at present. You have just used the formula for "amount," $A = P + Prt$.

With this relatively small sum in mind (for a return after 354 years!) turn to investigate the extent to which this return would have been improved if interest had been compounded annually instead of being calculated on only a simple basis. With a principle P, an annual rate of interest r, and a time $t = 1$, the amount A at the end of the first year is given by the formula $A_1 = P + Pr = P(1 + r)$. (The subscript indicates the year at the end of which interest is calculated.) Now $A_1 = P(1 + r)$ becomes the principle at the beginning of the second year, upon which interest will be credited during the second year. Therefore, $A_2 = P(1 + r) + P(1 + r)r = P(1 + r)(1 + r) = P(1 + r)^2$. Since the last expression represents the principle at the beginning of the third year, you have $A_3 = P(1 + r)^2 + P(1 + r)^2r = P(1 + r)^2(1 + r) = P(1 + r)^3$. By now, your students will see the emerging pattern and should be able to suggest the generalization for the amount after t years, $A_t = P(1 + r)^t$.

Now try this formula on the \$24 investment made in 1626! Assuming annual compounding at 6% per annum, you have $A_{354} = 24(1 + .06)^{354} = 21{,}801{,}558{,}740$. This means that the original \$24 is now worth almost \$22 billion! Most students are truly surprised by the huge difference between this figure and the figure \$533.76 obtained by computing simple interest.

Most banks now compound not annually, but quarterly, monthly, daily, or continuously, so next generalize the formula $A = P(1 + r)^t$ to take into account compounding at more frequent intervals. Help your students observe that if interest is compounded semi-annually, the *periodic rate* would be only *one-half* the annual rate, but the number of periods would be *twice* the number of years: so $A = P\left(1 + \frac{r}{2}\right)^{2t}$. Likewise, if interest is compounded quarterly $A = P\left(1 + \frac{r}{4}\right)^{2t}$. In general, if interest is compounded n times per year, you have $A = P\left(1 + \frac{r}{n}\right)^{nt}$. This formula may be used for any finite value of n. Letting $n = 4$ in the problem yields $A = 24\left(1 + \frac{.06}{4}\right)^{4(354)} = 24(1.015)^{1416} = 34{,}365{,}848{,}150$. The \$24 has now risen to about \$34 billion.

Students should note that changing the compounding from annually to quarterly increased the yield by about $12 billion.

Students may now ask whether the yield can be increased indefinitely by simply increasing the frequency of compounding. A complete treatment of this question requires a thorough development of the concept of limits, but an informal, intuitive approach will suffice here. Have students first explore the simpler problem of an investment of $1 at a nominal annual interest rate of 100% for a period of one year. This will give $A = 1\left(1 + \frac{1.00}{n}\right)^n = \left(1 + \frac{1.00}{n}\right)^n$. Ask the students to prepare a table of values for A for various common values of n, such as $n = 1$ (annual compounding), $n = 2$ (semiannual), $n = 4$ (quarterly), $n = 12$ (monthly). They should note that the amount A does *not* rise astronomically as n increases, but rather rises slowly from $2.00 ($n = 1$) to about $2.60 ($n = 12$). Explain that the amount A would approach, but not quite reach, the value $2.72. (The extent to which you may wish to discuss the fact that $\lim_{n\to\infty}\left(1 + \frac{1}{n}\right)n = e = 2.71828\ldots$ will depend on the backgrounds and abilities of your math students.)

Since investments generally don't draw 100% interest, you must next convert to a general interest rate or r. Setting $\frac{r}{n} = \frac{1}{k}$, you have $n = kr$, and $A = P\left(1 + \frac{r}{n}\right)^{nt}$ becomes $A = P\left(1 + \frac{1}{k}\right)^{krt} = P\left[\left(1 + \frac{1}{k}\right)^k\right]^{rt}$. Clearly, as n approaches infinity so does k, since r is finite, so the expression in brackets approaches the value e as a limit. You then have the formula $A = Pe^{rt}$ *for instantaneous compounding*, where r is the nominal annual rate of interest and t is the time in years.

Students might be interested in knowing that this formula is a special representation of the general "Law of Growth," which is usually written in the $N = N_0e^{rt}$ form, where N represents the final amount of a material whose initial amount was N_0. This law has applications in many other areas such as population growth (people, bacteria in a culture, etc.) and radioactive decay of elements (in which case it becomes the "Law of Decay," $N = N_0e^{-rt}$).

Completing the investment problem, using 2.72 as an approximation to e, you have $A = 24(2.72)^{.06(354)} =$ 40,780,708,190.

Students can see that the "ultimate" return on a $24 investment (at a nominal annual interest rate of 6% for 354 years) is about $41 billion.

Students may now apply the formulas developed. Banks currently offer interest rates ranging from 5% to as much as 12% (usually for time deposits of 2 years or more) and compounding is commonly done quarterly, monthly, daily, or continuously. Students can work problems with varying principles, periodic rates, frequencies of compounding and time periods, and compare yields. They'll probably be surprised by what they learn!

POSTASSESSMENT

Students who have met the performance objective will be able to answer questions such as these:

1. Banks offering 5% annual interest compounded quarterly claim that money doubles in 14 years. Is this claim accurate?
2. If you had $1,000 to invest for 2 years, would you get a greater return from a savings bank offering a 5% annual rate compounded quarterly or from a commercial bank offering a $4\frac{1}{2}$% annual rate compounded continuously?
3. Banks offering a 6% nominal annual rate compounded continuously on term savings of 2 years or longer claim that this rate is equivalent to an "effective annual rate" (the rate under annual compounding) of 6.27%. Prove that this is true, assuming a deposit of $500 (the usual minimum) for a period of 2 years.

Unit 35

Reflexive, Symmetric, and Transitive Relations

In this lesson students will have the opportunity to explore some properties of mathematical relations among numbers, geometric figures, sets, propositions, persons, places, and things.

PERFORMANCE OBJECTIVE

Students will identify a given relation as reflexive symmetric, transitive, or as an equivalence relation.

PREASSESSMENT

Ask students to describe what the mathematical term *relation* refers to. If you are not satisfied they understand the term, present some examples before beginning the lesson. You may wish to vary the relations you present students, according to their grade level and background in such areas as algebra, geometry, set theory, number theory, and logic.

TEACHING STRATEGIES

Begin with a consideration of a very simple relation such as "is equal to" for real numbers. From their previous math experience, students will recognize that any quantity a is equal to itself; that if a quantity a is equal to another quantity b, then b is also equal to a; and that if a quantity a is equal to another quantity b, and b is in turn equal to a third quantity c, then a is equal to c. Symbolically, we have $a = a$, $a = b \rightarrow b = a$, and $a = b$ and $b = c \rightarrow a = c$. The arrow is read "implies" as in ordinary symbolic logic. (Replace the arrow with the word if the class is unfamiliar with this notation.) Explain that when a quantity a has a given relation to itself (as in $a = a$) that relation is called *reflexive*. Further, when a quantity a has a given relation to another quantity b and this results in b having the same relation to a (as in $a = b \rightarrow b = a$) that relation is called *symmetric*. Add that when a quantity a has a given relation to another quantity b and b has the *same* relation to a third quantity c, and this results in a having that *same* relation to c (as in $a = b$ and $b = c \rightarrow a = c$) that relation is called *transitive*. A relation possessing all three of these properties is an *equivalence relation*.

Now invite students to examine some of the relations with which they are familiar from earlier work in mathematics. You've just established that "is equal to" is an equivalence relation. Follow up by considering the relations "is greater than" and "is less than" for real numbers. Your class will quickly discover that these relations are neither reflexive nor symmetric, but that they *are* transitive. An interesting variation is the relation "is not equal to" for real numbers. Although this relation is not reflexive, it *is* symmetric. Students may also think that this relation is transitive, but a simple counterexample will prove that it is not: $9 + 6 \neq 7 + 2$ and $7 + 2 \neq 11 + 4$, but $9 + 6 = 11 + 4$. So the relation "is not equal to" is not transitive.

Of course, none of the relations just considered is an equivalence relation. Have the class consider other relations, for example: "is a multiple of" (or "is divisible by") and "is a factor of" for integers. Both of these relations are reflexive and transitive, but neither is symmetric. Ask students to prove these facts algebraically. For the first relation, for example, they may write $a = kb$ and $b = mc$, where k and m are integers. Clearly, $a = 1a$ so a is divisible by a (reflexivity); $\frac{a}{b} = k$ since a is divisible by b but $\frac{b}{a} = \frac{1}{k}$, which is *not* an integer, so b is not divisible by a (no symmetry); $a = kb$ and $b = mc \rightarrow a = k(mc)$ or $\frac{a}{c} = km$, which *is* an integer, since the product of two integers is an integer (the set of integers being closed under multiplication), so a is divisible by c (transitivity).

Consider next some relations in geometry. First explore the relations "is congruent to" and "is similar to" for geometric figures. Students will have little difficulty recognizing that both of these are equivalence relations. Ask the class to examine each of these relations when it is negated. Each will then possess only the symmetric property.

The relations "is parallel to" and "is perpendicular to" are very interesting when applied to lines in a plane and to planes themselves. For example, for lines in a plane, "is parallel to" is symmetric *and* transitive but "is perpendicular to" is *only* symmetric. Ask your students why! They should recall such ideas from geometry as "lines parallel to the same line are parallel to each other" and "lines perpendicular to the same line are parallel to each other." These relations may also be negated as exercises.

Students who have some familiarity with set theory may explore the relations "is equal to" and "is equivalent to" as applied to sets. Since *equal* sets are sets containing identical elements, it's obvious that "is equal to" is an equivalence relation. *Equivalent* sets have the same number of elements (their elements can be placed into one-to-one correspondence with each other), but not necessarily identical ones. A little reflection reveals that "is equivalent to" is also an equivalence relation. Another interesting relation is "is the complement of" as applied to sets. The class should discover that this relation is symmetric, but that it is neither reflexive nor transitive. (If a is the complement of b and b is the complement of c, then a is *not* the complement of c, but rather $a = c$.)

An interesting relation from number theory is "is congruent to, modulo m" for integers. Students familiar with this concept should be able to prove easily that this is an equivalence relation, using simple algebra: $a = a(\text{mod } m)$ since $a - a = 0m$ (proving the reflexive property); $a \equiv b\ (\text{mod } m) \rightarrow b \equiv a\ (\text{mod } m)$ since $b - a = -(a - b) = -km$ (proving the symmetric property); $a \equiv b\ (\text{mod } m)$ and $b \equiv c\ (\text{mod } m) \rightarrow a \equiv c\ (\text{mod } m)$ since $a - c = (a - b) + (b - c) = km + pm = (k + p)m$ (proving the transitive property).

Students familiar with symbolic logic may be invited to consider the relation "implies" for propositions (e.g., as designated by p, q, r). The alert student will recognize that this relation is reflexive, $p \rightarrow p$ (since any proposition implies itself) and transitive, $(p \rightarrow q) \wedge (q \rightarrow r) \rightarrow (p \rightarrow r)$ (since this can be proved to be a tautology by using a truth table) but that it is *not* symmetric, $(p \rightarrow q) \rightarrow (q \rightarrow p)$ is *false* (since the truth of a proposition does *not* guarantee the truth of its converse).

Now broaden the concept of relations from strictly mathematical settings to involve relations between persons, places, and things. Your class should find this amusing as well as instructive. Suggest a relation such as "is the father of." A little reflection reveals that this relation is not reflexive, not symmetric, and not transitive! It is obvious that a cannot be his own father (not reflexive); that if a is the father of b, then b is the son or daughter and not the father of a (not symmetric); and that if a is the father of b and b is the father of c, then a is the grandfather of c, not the father (not transitive)! Many similar relations may be considered, including "is the mother of," "is the brother of" (caution: *only* transitive, *not* symmetric, since b may be the sister of a), "is the sister of," "is the sibling of" (this one *is* symmetric), "is the spouse of," "is the ancestor of," "is the descendent of," "is taller than," and "weighs more than." Any of these relations may be explored in the negative sense as well as in the positive one. With respect to places, students may consider relations such as "is north of," "is west of" (caution: transitivity here is *not* necessarily true if places may be selected from anywhere on the globe rather than from merely a small area or only one country), "is at a higher altitude than," "is exactly one mile from" (symmetric only), and "is less than one mile from" (reflexive *and* symmetric). Relations among things may include "is above," "is older than," "costs as much as" and "costs more than," among others.

POSTASSESSMENT

Students who have met the performance objective will be able to answer questions such as the following.

1. Identify each of the following relations as reflexive, symmetric, transitive, or an equivalence relation:
   a. "is supplementary to" for angles
   b. "is congruent to" for line segments
   c. "is a subset of" for sets
   d. "is a proper subset of" for sets
   e. "is equivalent to" for propositions
   f. "is wealthier than" for nations
   g. "is smaller than" for objects
   h. "is colder than" for places
2. Prove algebraically that the relation "is complementary to" for acute angles is symmetric but neither reflexive nor transitive.
3. Which of the following relations is reflexive and transitive but not symmetric?
   a. "is a positive integral power of" for real numbers
   b. "has the same area as" for triangles
   c. "is the converse of" for propositions
   d. "is younger than" for people

Unit 36

 Bypassing an Inaccessible Region

This unit will present the problem of constructing a straight line through an inaccessible region using only straightedge and compasses, and without using the tools in or over this inaccessible region. This activity will provide an opportunity for students to exhibit creativity.

PERFORMANCE OBJECTIVES

1. *Given a straight line segment with an endpoint on the boundary of an inaccessible region, students, using straightedge and compasses, will construct another straight line segment collinear with the given one and on the other side of the inaccessible region (an endpoint will be on the boundary of this region).*
2. *Given one point on either side of an inaccessible region, students, using only straightedge and compasses, will construct two collinear straight line segments, each having one given point as an endpoint and neither intersecting the inaccessible region.*

PREASSESSMENT

Students should be familiar with the basic geometric constructions using straightedge and compasses.

TEACHING STRATEGIES

To generate initial interest, begin this topic by developing a story about two countries that are separated by a mountain, and each of which wants to construct a straight road and tunnel through the mountain. Neither country can decide how to dig the tunnel, so they both decide to construct a road on one side of the mountain at the point where the anticipated tunnel (the continuation of a straight road on the other side of the mountain) will emerge from the mountain. Using only straightedge and compasses they seek to plot the path for this new road.

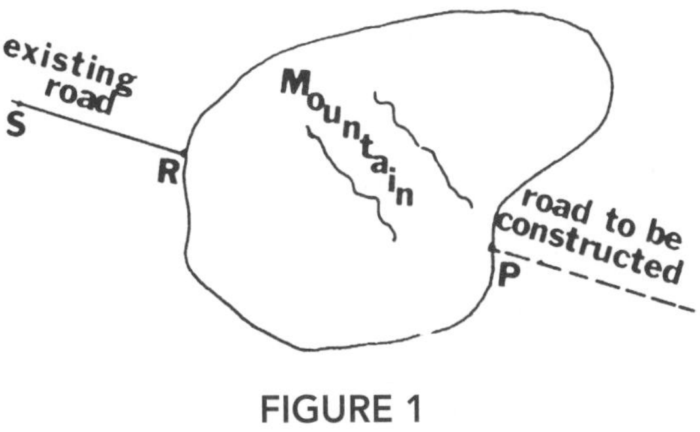

FIGURE 1

Once students understand the problem, have them draw a diagram (maps) of this situation.

Students must construct the collinear "continuation of $\overline{SR}$" at point P (using straightedge and compasses) and never touch or go over the inaccessible region.

There are various ways to construct the collinear continuation of $\overline{SR}$ at P. One method is to erect a perpendicular (line ℓ) to $\overline{SR}$ at a convenient point N of $\overline{SR}$. Then at a convenient point M of line ℓ a perpendicular (line k) to ℓ is constructed (see Figure 2).

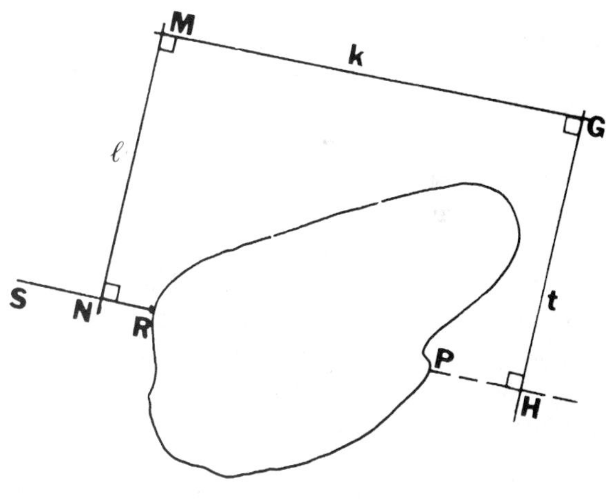

FIGURE 2

At a convenient point G of line k a perpendicular (line t) to line k is constructed. Point H is then obtained on line t, so that GH = MN. The line constructed perpendicular to line t at point H will be the required line through P and collinear with $\overline{SR}$. (Although P was collinear with $\overline{SR}$ it was virtually not needed for the construction.) The justification for this method is that a rectangle (minus part of a side) was actually constructed.

Another method for solving this problem involves replacing the above rectangle with an equilateral triangle, since angles of measure 60° are rather simple to construct. Figure 3 presents this method and ought to be rather self-explanatory.

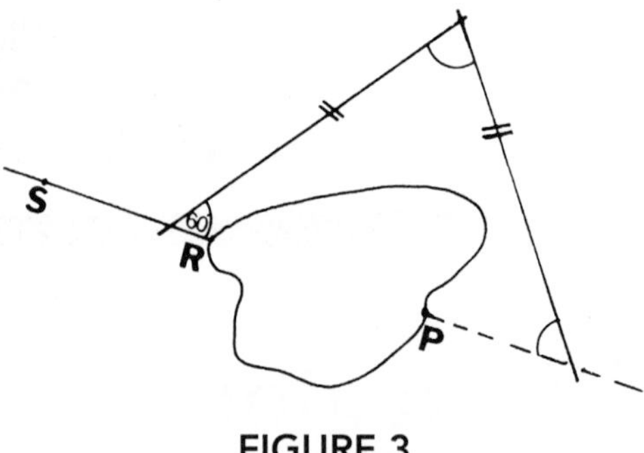

FIGURE 3

The problem of constructing a straight line "through" an inaccessible region, when only the two endpoints (at either side of the region) are given, is a much more challenging problem. Naturally an appropriate story can be built around this situation.

To construct two collinear straight line segments at each of two points (P and Q) situated at opposite sides of an inaccessible region, begin by drawing any convenient line segment from point P and construct a perpendicular line to it at a convenient point R. This perpendicular should not intersect the inaccessible region (see Figure 4).

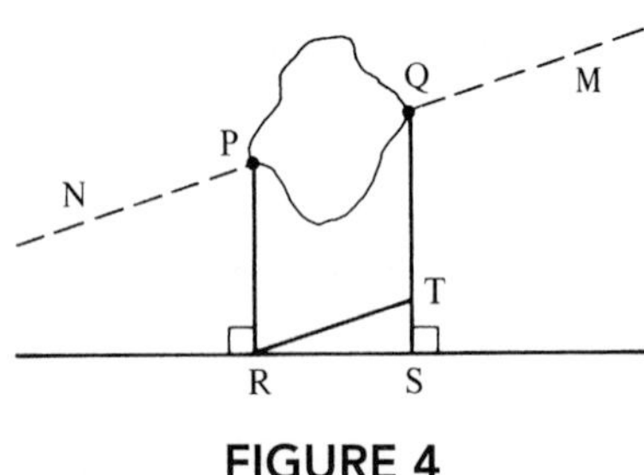

FIGURE 4

Now construct a perpendicular from Q, to this last line drawn, intersecting it at S. Locate T on $\overleftrightarrow{QS}$ so that PR = QS. Draw $\overline{RT}$.

At P construct ∠RPN ≅ ∠PRT, and at Q construct ∠TQM ≅ ∠QTR. This completes the required construction, since $\overline{NP}$ and $\overline{QM}$ are extensions of side $\overline{PQ}$ of "parallelogram" PRTQ, and therefore are collinear.

There are many other methods of solving this problem. Many involve constructing similar triangles in order to then construct the two required lines. However students select to approach this problem, they are apt to be led to a creative activity.

POSTASSESSMENT

1. Have students construct a "continuation" of $\overline{SP}$ on the other side of the inaccessible region (using only straightedge and compass and not touching or going over the inaccessible region).

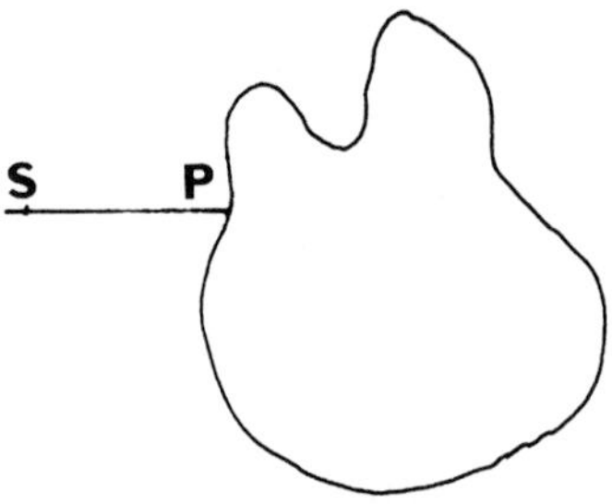

FIGURE 5

2. Have students construct two collinear segments at opposite ends (P and Q) of an inaccessible region (using only straightedge and compasses and not touching or going over the inaccessible region). These post-assessment items become more challenging if original methods are sought.

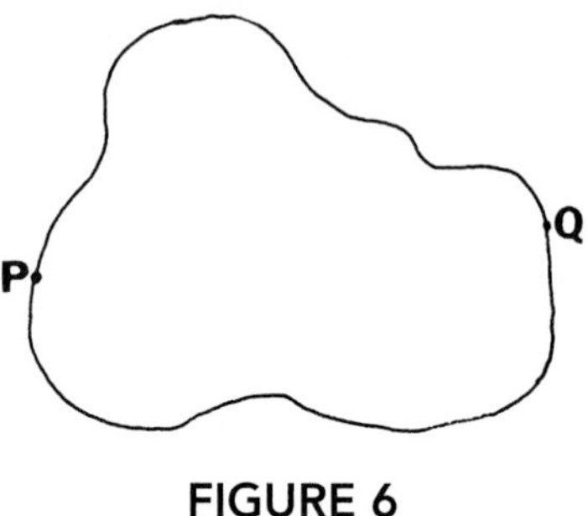

FIGURE 6

This decision depends on the ability level of the class.

Unit 37

 The Inaccessible Angle

Through a recreational application, this unit will provide the students the opportunity to use in novel ways various geometrical relationships they have learned. It also opens the door to a host of creative activities.

PERFORMANCE OBJECTIVE

Given an angle whose vertex is in an inaccessible region (hereafter referred to as an inaccessible angle), students will construct its angle bisector using straightedge and compasses.

PREASSESSMENT

Students should be familiar with the basic geometric constructions using straightedge and compasses.

See that students can properly bisect a given angle using only straightedge and compasses.

TEACHING STRATEGIES

After students have reviewed the basic geometric constructions present them with the following situation:

Problem Given an angle whose vertex is inaccessible (i.e., tell students that the vertex of the angle is in a region in which, and over which, a straightedge and compasses cannot be used), construct the angle bisector using only straightedge and compasses.

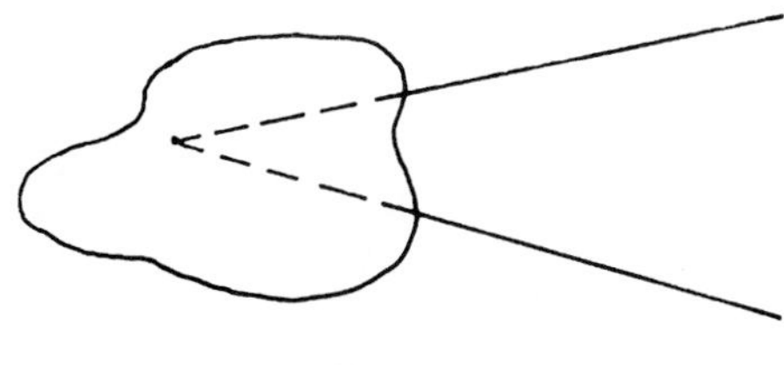

FIGURE 1

Most students' first attempts will probably be incorrect. However, careful consideration of students' responses should serve as a guide to a correct solution. Students will eventually present some rather strange (and creative) solutions. All should be given careful attention.

To best exhibit the true source of creativity that this problem provides, three different solutions are presented.

Solution 1
Draw any line ℓ intersecting the rays of the inaccessible angle at points A and B. Label the inaccessible vertex P.

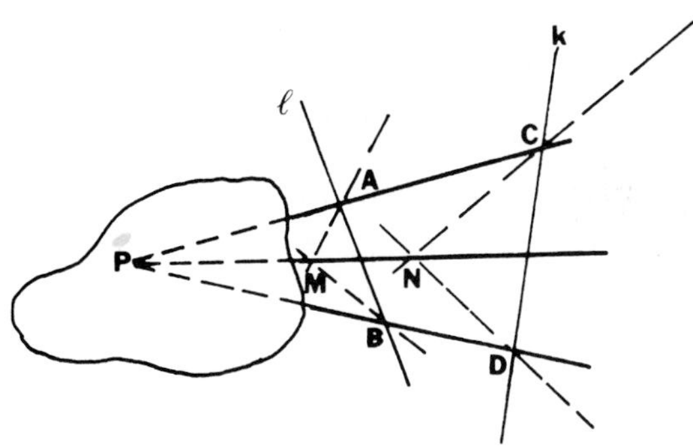

FIGURE 2

Construct the bisectors of $\angle PAB$ and $\angle PBA$, which then intersect at M. Remind students that since the angle bisectors of a triangle (here ΔAPB) are concurrent, the bisector of $\angle P$, which we are trying to construct, must contain point M.

In a similar way, draw any line k, intersecting the rays of the inaccessible angle at points C and D. Construct the bisectors of $\angle PCD$ and $\angle PDC$, which intersect at N. Once again students should realize that, since the bisectors of a triangle (in this case ΔCPD) are concurrent, the bisector of $\angle P$ must contain point N. Thus it has been established that the required line must contain points M and N, and therefore by drawing $\overleftrightarrow{MN}$ the construction is completed.

Solution 2

Begin this method by constructing a line parallel to one of the rays of the inaccessible angle (see Figure 3). This can be done in any one of various ways.

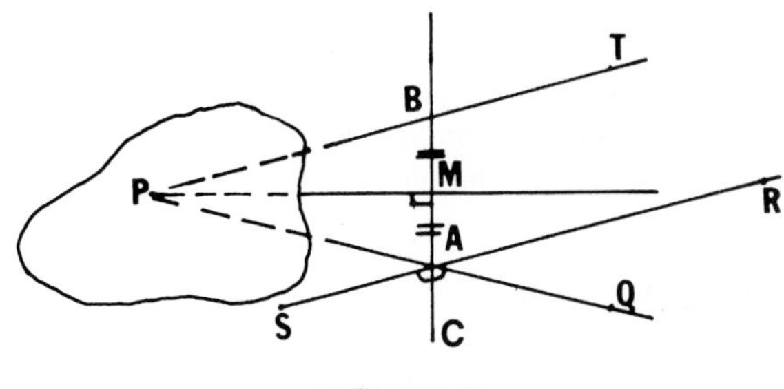

FIGURE 3

In Figure 3, $\overleftrightarrow{RS}$ is parallel to $\overrightarrow{PT}$ (a ray of the inaccessible ∠P), and intersects $\overrightarrow{PQ}$ at point A. Construct the bisector of ∠SAQ, which will intersect $\overrightarrow{PT}$ at B. Since $\overleftrightarrow{SR}//\overrightarrow{PT}$, ∠SAC ≅ ∠PBA. However ∠SAC ≅ ∠*CAQ* ≅ ∠*PAB*. Therefore ∠PBA ≅ ∠PAB, thereby making ΔPAB isosceles. Since the perpendicular bisector of the base of an isosceles triangle also bisects the vertex angle, the perpendicular bisector of $\overline{AB}$ is the required angle bisector of the inaccessible angle (∠P).

Solution 3

Start by constructing a line ($\overline{MN}$) parallel to one of the rays ($\overrightarrow{PT}$) of the inaccessible angle (∠P), and intersecting the other ray at point A (see Figure 4).

Then construct a line ($\overleftrightarrow{RS}$) parallel to the other ray ($\overrightarrow{PQ}$) of the inaccessible angle intersecting $\overrightarrow{PT}$ and $\overleftrightarrow{MN}$ at points B and C, respectively. With a pair of compasses, mark off a segment, $\overline{AD}$, on $\overrightarrow{AC}$ of the same length as $\overline{BC}$. Through D, construct $\overleftrightarrow{DE}//\overrightarrow{PQ}$, where E is on $\overrightarrow{PT}$. It can now be easily shown that ED = AD (since EBCD is a parallelogram and ED = BC. Since PEDA is a parallelogram with two adjacent sides congruent ($\overline{ED}$ ≡ $\overline{AD}$), it is a rhombus. Thus, the diagonal $\overline{PD}$ *is* the bisector of the inaccessible angle. $\overline{PD}$ can be constructed simply by bisecting ∠EDA or constructing the perpendicular bisector of $\overline{EA}$.

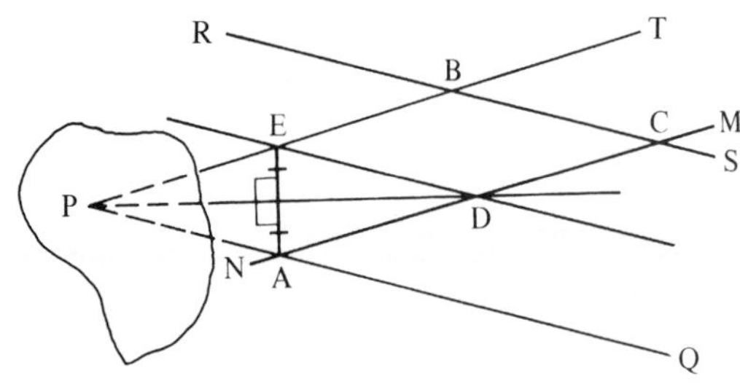

FIGURE 4

After presenting these solutions to your students, other solutions created by the students should follow directly. Free thinking should be encouraged to promote greater creativity.

POSTASSESSMENT

Present students with an inaccessible angle and ask them to bisect it.

Unit 38

Triangle Constructions

Often teachers will justify the basic triangle congruence postulates by showing that unique triangles can be constructed with such given data as the lengths of three sides of a triangle or perhaps the lengths of two sides and the measure of the included angle. This unit will extend this usually elementary discussion of triangle constructions to some rather interesting problems.

PERFORMANCE OBJECTIVE

Given the measures of three parts of a triangle (which determine a triangle) students will analyze and construct the required triangle with straightedge and compasses.

PREASSESSMENT

Students should be familiar with the basic geometric constructions normally taught in the high school geometry course.

TEACHING STRATEGIES

To begin to familiarize students with this topic have them construct the triangle, where the measures of two angles and the length of the included side are given.

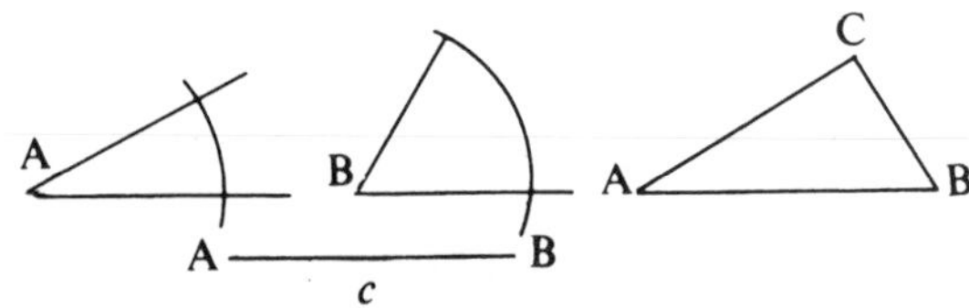

FIGURE 1

Students will draw a line and mark off the length of $\overline{AB}$ (sometimes referred to by *c*, the length of the side opposite ∠C). By constructing angles A and B at either end of $\overline{AB}$, they eventually find that they have constructed a *unique* △ABC.

Surely, if the students were given the measures of the three angles of a triangle, each student would probably construct a triangle of different size (although all should be the same shape). Yet if the students were given the lengths of the three sides of a triangle they would all construct triangles congruent to one another. At this point students should realize that certain data will determine a *unique* triangle while other data will not. A student is thus limited in investigating such cases where the measures of only sides and angles are provided. Students will want to consider other parts of triangles as well. Present the following problem:

> Construct a triangle given the lengths of two sides and the length of an altitude to one of these sides.

We shall write this problem as $[a, b, h_a]$, where h_a is the length of the altitude to side a.

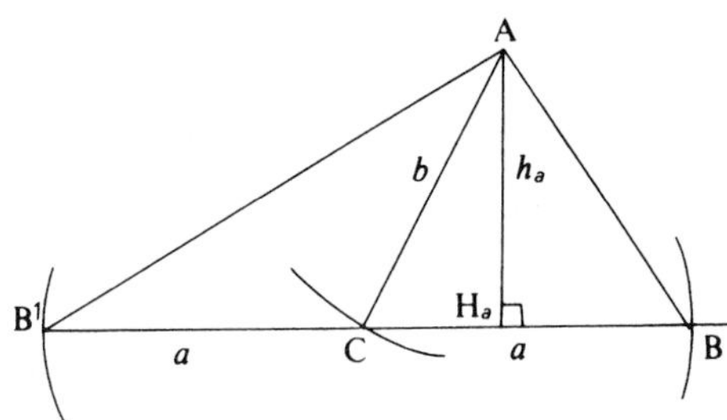

FIGURE 2

To do this construction, take the point H_a on any line and erect a perpendicular H_aA (using the usual straightedge and compasses method) of length h_a. With arc (A,b) (Note: This ordered pair symbol is merely a short way of referring to the circle with center A and radius b) intersect the base line at C, then with arc (C,a), intersect this base line again at B and B′. The *two* solutions are △ABC and △AB′C, each of which has the given $\{a,b,h_a\}$. Further inspection of this solution will indicate that $b > h_a$ was a necessary condition, and that if $b = h_a$ there would have only been *one* solution.

A much simpler problem is to construct a triangle given $\{a,b,h_c\}$. Here students begin in much the same way. On any line, erect at H_c a perpendicular length h_c. At C, the other extremity of h_c, draw (C,a) and (C,b). Their points of intersection with the original base line will determine points B and A, respectively. Once again a discussion of uniqueness should follow.

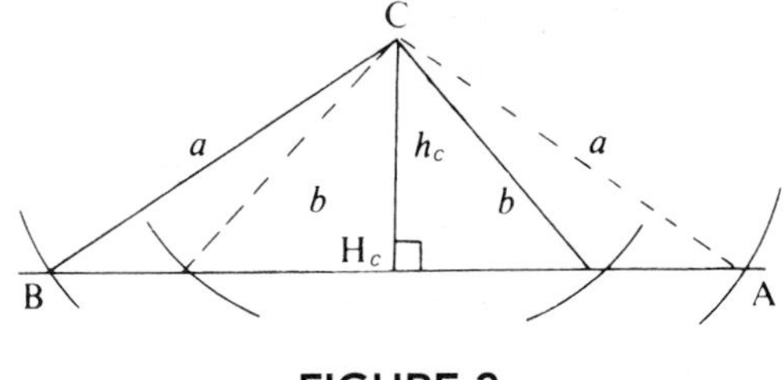

FIGURE 3

The figure above should help in this discussion.

Some triangle constructions require a good deal more analysis before actually beginning the construction. An example of such a problem is to construct the triangle given the lengths of its three medians $\{m_a,m_b,m_c\}$.

One approach for analyzing this problem is to consider the finished product, △ABC.

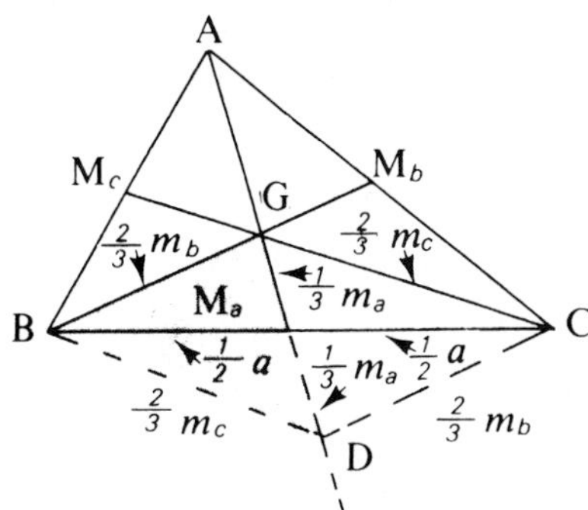

FIGURE 4

The objective here is to be able to construct one of the many triangles shown in the above figure by various elementary methods. By extending m_a (the median to side a), one third of its length to a point D and then drawing $\overline{BD}$ and $\overline{CD}$, we have created a triangle, △BGD, which is easily constructible. Since the medians of a triangle trisect each other, we know that $BG = \frac{2}{3}m_b$. Since $GM_a = DM_a = \frac{1}{3}m_a$ (by construction), and $BM_a = CM_a$, we may conclude that BGCD is a parallelogram. Therefore $BD = GC = \frac{2}{3}m_c$. It is then rather simple to construct △BGD, since its sides are each two thirds the length of one of the given medians (lengths easily obtained). After constructing △BGD, the students should be able to complete the required construction by (1) extending BG one half its length to point M_b, (2) extending $\overline{DG}$ its own length to A, and (3) extending $\overline{BM_a}$ its own length to C (where M_a is the midpoint of $\overline{DG}$). The required triangle is then obtained by drawing $\overline{AM_b}$ to intersect $\overline{BM_a}$ at point C, and drawing $\overline{AB}$.

Not only does this problem review for the students many important concepts from elementary geometry, but it also provides an excellent opportunity for students to practice "reverse" reasoning in analyzing the problem.

For additional practice have students construct △ABC given $\{a,h_b,m_c\}$.

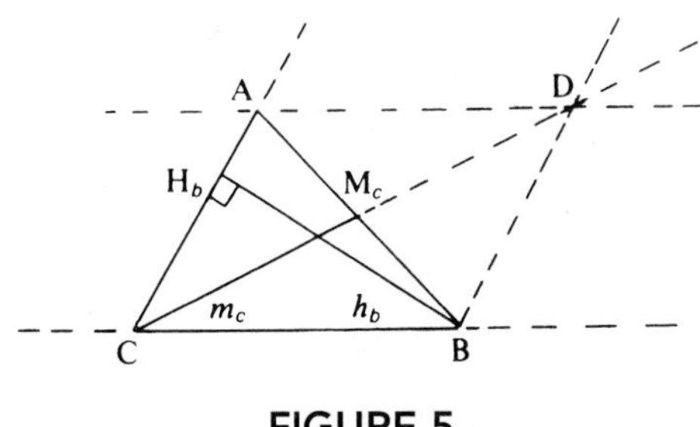

FIGURE 5

Once again have students first inspect the desired triangle. They should notice that $\triangle CBH_b$ can be easily constructed by erecting at H_c a perpendicular to $\overleftrightarrow{AC}$ of length h_b. At its extremity, B, draw (B, a) to intersect $\overleftrightarrow{AC}$ at C, to complete $\triangle CBH_b$. Further inspection of the above figure suggests that $\triangle CDB$ may also be constructed. Construct a line ($\overleftrightarrow{DB}$) parallel to $\overleftrightarrow{AC}$ and intersecting arc (C,$2m_c$) at D. To find A, construct a line ($\overleftrightarrow{AD}$) parallel to $\overleftrightarrow{CB}$ and intersecting $\overleftrightarrow{CH_b}$ at A. Since ADBC is a parallelogram, $\overleftrightarrow{CD}$ bisects $\overleftrightarrow{AB}$ at M_c, and $CM_c = \frac{1}{2}CD = m_c$. Thus the problem is analyzed in a rather reverse fashion, and then the required triangle is constructed.

When you consider the measures of other parts of a triangle such as angle bisectors, radius of the inscribed circle, radius of the circumscribed circle, and the semi-perimeter (as well as the measures of parts considered earlier in this unit), then there exist 179 possible triangle construction problems, where each consists of measures of three of these parts of a triangle. While some may be rather simple (e.g., $\{a,b,c\}$) others are somewhat more difficult (e.g., $\{h_a,h_b,h_c\}$).

This type of construction problem may very well serve as a springboard for a more careful study of this topic as well as various other geometric construction problems. A recently published book that contains much more on this topic (including the *complete* list of the 179 triangle constructions!) as well as a variety of other stimulating geometric construction topics (e.g., a review of the basic constructions, a variety of applications, and circle constructions) is Posamentier, A. S., *Advanced Euclidean Geometry: Excursions for Secondary Teachers and Students*. Emeryville, CA: Key College Publishing, 2002.

POSTASSESSMENT

Have students construct triangles given:

1. $\{a,b,m_a\}$
2. $\{a,h_b,t_c\}$
3. $\{a,h_b,h_c\}$
4. $\{h_a,m_a,t_a\}$
5. $\{h_a,h_b,h_c\}$

N.B. t_a is the length of the angle bisector of $\angle A$.

Unit 39

The Criterion of Constructibility

This unit will develop a criterion of constructibility for the Euclidean tools, straightedge and compasses.

PERFORMANCE OBJECTIVES

1. *Students will state the criterion of constructibility.*
2. *Students will represent algebraic expressions geometrically (in terms of given lengths).*

PREASSESSMENT

Ask students to represent geometrically AB + CD and AB − CD, given AB and CD.

TEACHING STRATEGIES

Most students should have been able to successfully do the above problem. Now let AB = a and CD = b.

A____a____B C____b____D

The next logical concern would be to represent the *product* of two given line segments. Here, however, a segment of unit length must be introduced.

To construct ab, two cases should be considered: (I) where $a > 1$ and $b > 1$, and (II) where $a < 1$ and $b < 1$.

In the first case (I), students would construct the figure below. Note $\overline{MN} // \overline{AB}$, and $\angle C$ is any convenient angle.

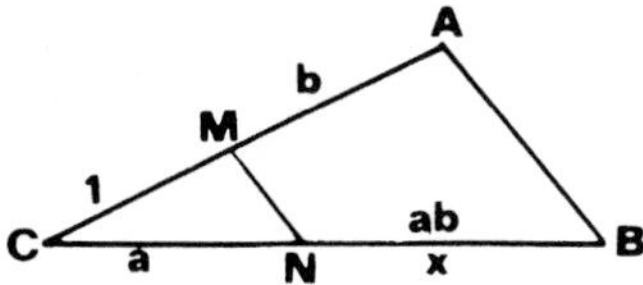

Since $\overline{MN} // \overline{AB}$, $\frac{x}{a} = \frac{b}{1}$, and $x = ab$; thus $\overline{NB}$ is the segment of desired length (i.e., ab). Note that $ab > a$, and $ab > b$, which is expected if $a > 1$ and $b > 1$.

In the second case (II), students would proceed in the same way as in case I, however since $a < 1$ and $b < 1$, it should be made clear that geometrically $ab < a$, and $ab < b$.

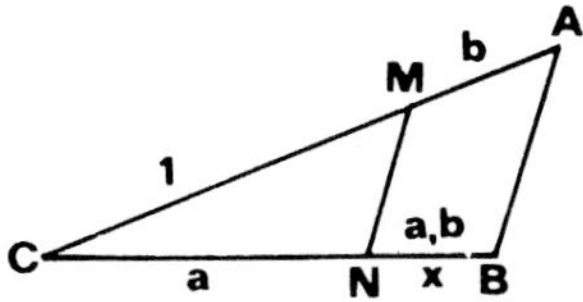

Students should now be challenged to discover a similar scheme for constructing a line segment that can represent the quotient of two given line segments, a and b. Again two cases should be considered:

Case I $a < b < 1$. Once again have students construct the figure above, where $\overline{MN} // \overline{AB}$.

In this case either $a < \frac{a}{b} < b < 1$ or $a < b < \frac{a}{b} < 1$. Students should be encouraged to verify this.

Case II $b < a \leq 1$. Proceed as above to construct the figure below.

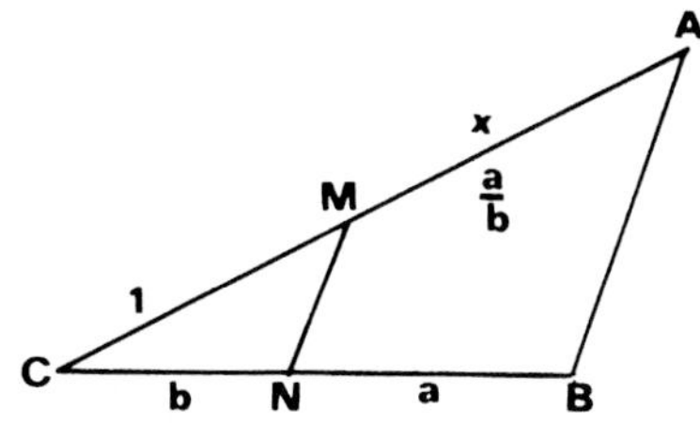

Here $b < a < \frac{a}{b}$.

Until now all segments considered were of positive length. Students will now become curious about using segments of negative length to represent products and quotients.

To consider segments of negative length, we must introduce number line axes, horizontal and oblique. To find ab, locate A on the horizontal axis so that OA $= a$, and locate B on the oblique axis so that OB $= b$. Draw the line through the 1 on the oblique axis and A. Through B draw a line parallel to the first line, intersecting the horizontal axis in a point C. Thus OC $= ab$.

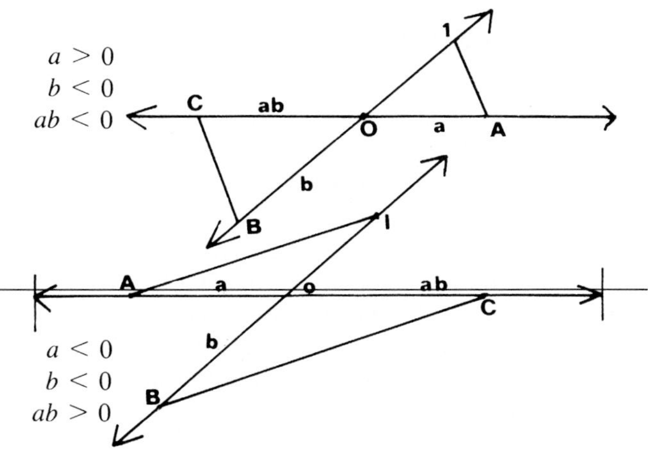

Students will notice that a and b were marked off on different axes and that in each case the product, ab, was appropriately less than or greater than zero.

As before, we shall find a quotient by considering division as the inverse of multiplication. To find $\frac{a}{b}$, we find x such that $bx = a.a > 0$, and $b > 0$, then $\frac{a}{b} > 0$.

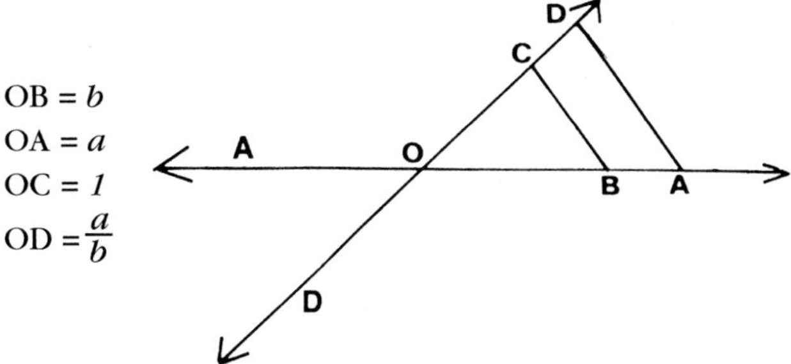

Similarly, when $a < 0$ and $b > 0$, it follows that $\frac{a}{b} < 0$.

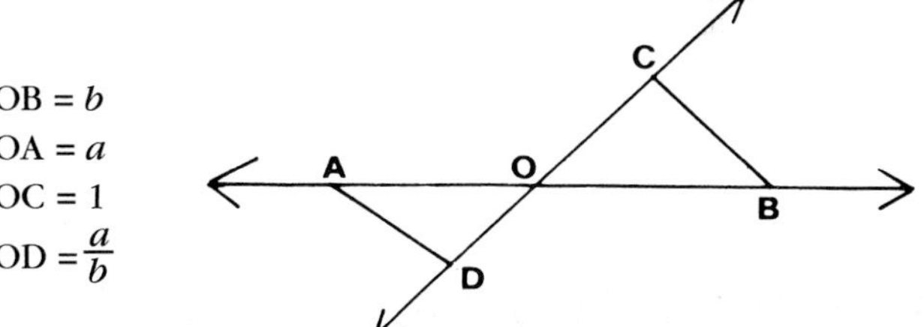

Have students consider division by zero. That is, where is B if $b = 0$? What happens to OD?

The only remaining operation for which a geometric representation is needed is square root extraction. Here students merely construct a semicircle on $1 + a$ (where $\sqrt{a}$ is sought). Then at the common endpoint, B, of segment 1 and a erect a perpendicular to intersect the semicircle at D. Thus BD $= \sqrt{a}$. Students should be able to apply mean proportional theorems to prove this.

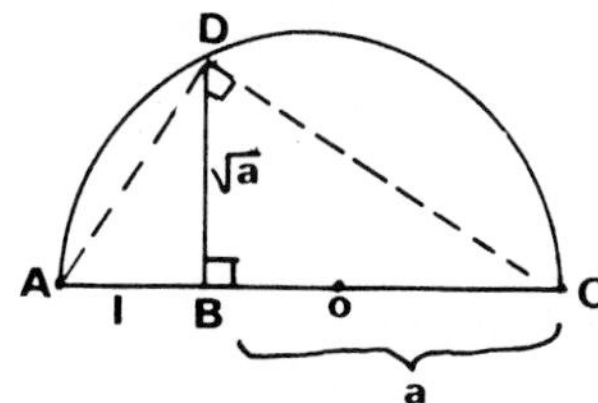

The solution to a construction problem may be expressed as a root of an equation. For example, consider the problem of duplication of a cube. We must find the edge of a cube whose volume is twice that of a given cube. That is, we must find x, when $x^3 = 2$.

If we can obtain the solution by a finite number of applications of the operations $+$, $-$, $\times$, $\div$, and $\sqrt{\ }$, using given segments and a unit length, then the construction is possible.

Conversely, if the construction is possible, then we can obtain it by a finite number of applications of addition, subtraction, multiplication, division, and extractions of square root, using the given segments and an arbitrary unit of length. We know that the straight lines and circles that we construct are determined either by given segments or those obtained from the intersections of two straight lines, a straight line and a circle, or two circles. To show the converse above, we must show that these intersections can be obtained from the coefficients of the equations by a finite number of applications of the operations of addition, subtraction, multiplication, division, and extraction of square root.

Two straight lines

$$y = mx + b$$
$$y = m'x + b' \qquad m \neq m'$$

have as their point of intersection the point (x, y) with

$$x = \frac{b - b'}{m - m'} \qquad y = \frac{mb' - m'b}{m - m'}$$

These relationships are obtained from the equations by applying the above operations. An equation for a circle with radius r and center (c,d) is $(x - c)^2 + (y - d)^2 = r^2$. To find the intersection of the circle with the line $y = mx + b$, we can substitute for y in the equation for the circle

$$(x - c)^2 + (mx + b - d)^2 = r^2$$

This forms a quadratic equation in x. Since the solution of the quadratic $ax^2 + bx + c = 0$ is

$$x = \frac{-b \pm \sqrt{b^2 - 4ac}}{2a}$$

we know that the quadratic $(x - c)^2 + (mx + b - d)^2 = r^2$ has a root that can be obtained from the known constants by applying the above five operations.

The intersection of two circles is the same as the intersection of one circle with the common chord. Thus, this case can be reduced to finding the intersection of a circle and a line.

Criterion of Constructibility A proposed geometric construction is possible with straightedge and compass alone if and only if the numbers that define algebraically the required geometric elements can be derived from those defining the given elements by a finite number of rational operations and extractions of square root.

POSTASSESSMENT

1. Restate and explain the Criterion of Constructibility.
2. Given lengths a, b, 1 construct a line segment of length $\sqrt{\frac{ab}{a + b}}$.

REFERENCE

Posamentier, A. S. *Advanced Euclidean Geometry: Excursions for Secondary Teachers and Students*. New York, NY: John Wiley Publishing, 2002.

Unit 40

 Constructing Radical Lengths

Often students ask how a line of length $\sqrt{2}$ can be constructed. This activity will address itself to this question as well as find the length of other radical segments.

PERFORMANCE OBJECTIVE

Students will construct a segment of a given radical length after being given a unit length.

PREASSESSMENT

Students should be able to apply the Pythagorean theorem and be familiar with the basics of geometric constructions with straightedge and compasses.

TEACHING STRATEGIES

Ask students to construct a triangle with one side of length $\sqrt{2}$ (be sure to tell them to select a convenient unit length). In all likelihood they will draw an isosceles right triangle with a leg of length 1. By the Pythagorean theorem they will find that the hypotenuse has length $\sqrt{2}$.

Now have them construct a right triangle using this hypotenuse and have the other leg be of unit length. This newly formed right triangle has a hypotenuse of length $\sqrt{3}$. Students should easily discover that fact using the Pythagorean theorem.

By repeating this process, students will generate, in sequence, radicals of integers, i.e., $\sqrt{2}$, $\sqrt{3}$, $\sqrt{4}$, $\sqrt{5}$, ... The figure, frequently referred to as a "radical spiral," shows this process.

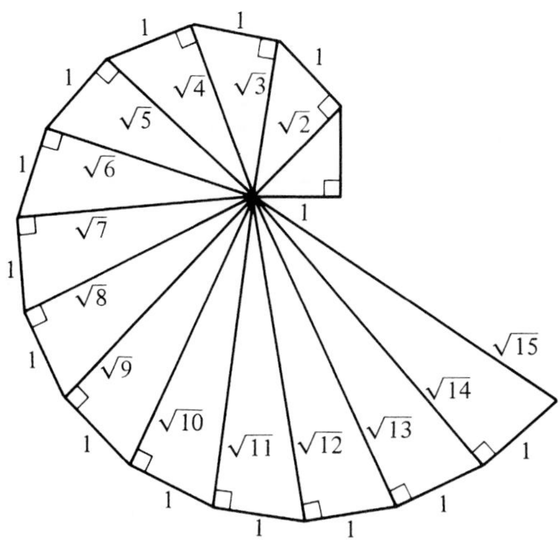

FIGURE 1

A student might ask if there is a more expedient method for constructing $\sqrt{15}$, rather than generating a radical spiral up to $\sqrt{15}$.

Lead students to recall one of the "mean proportional" theorems. In the figure below CD is the mean proportional between AD and BD.

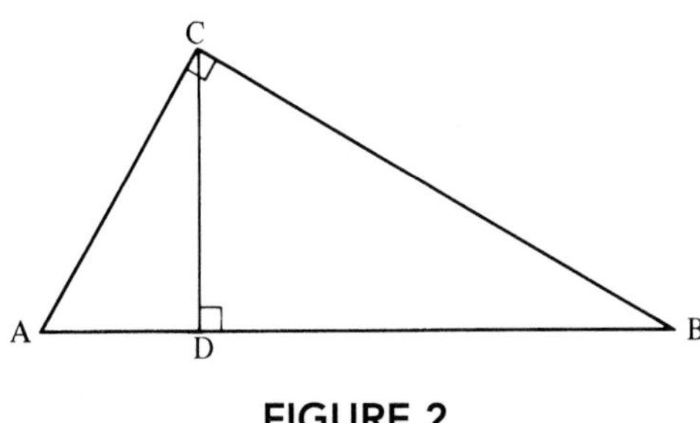

FIGURE 2

That is, $\frac{AD}{CD} = \frac{CD}{BD}$, or $(CD)^2 = (AD)(BD)$, which implies that $CD = \sqrt{(AD)(BD)}$.

This relationship will help them construct a segment of length $\sqrt{15}$ in one construction. All they need do is to construct the above figure and let AD = 1 and BD = 15; then $CD = \sqrt{(1)(15)} = \sqrt{15}$.

What they should do is draw a segment of length 16 and partition it into two segments of lengths 1 and 15. At the partitioning point have them erect a perpendicular to this segment. The intersection of the perpendicular and the semicircle having the segment of length 16 as diameter determines the other endpoint of the perpendicular segment of length $\sqrt{15}$ (see Figure 3).

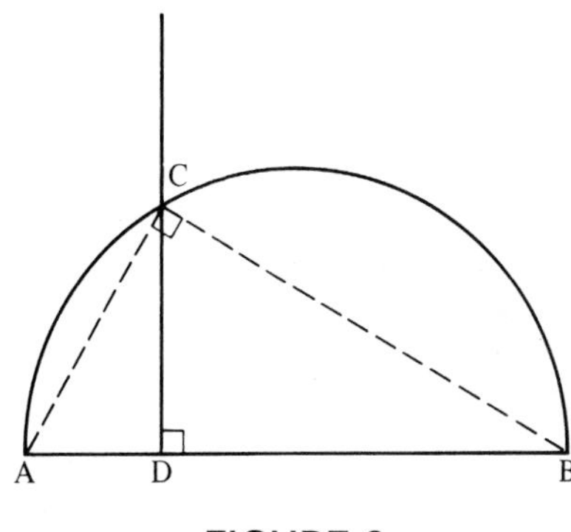

FIGURE 3

The dashed lines are merely needed to justify the construction.

POSTASSESSMENT

1. Construct a radical spiral up to $\sqrt{18}$.
2. Construct a segment of length $\sqrt{18}$ using a given unit length. Do *not* construct a radical spiral here.

Unit 41

 Constructing a Pentagon

PERFORMANCE OBJECTIVE

Students will construct a regular pentagon given the length of the radius of the circumscribed circle.

PREASSESSMENT

Students should be familiar with the properties of regular polygons.

TEACHING STRATEGIES

Begin your lesson by having the class consider a regular decagon whose radius is 1 (Figure 1).

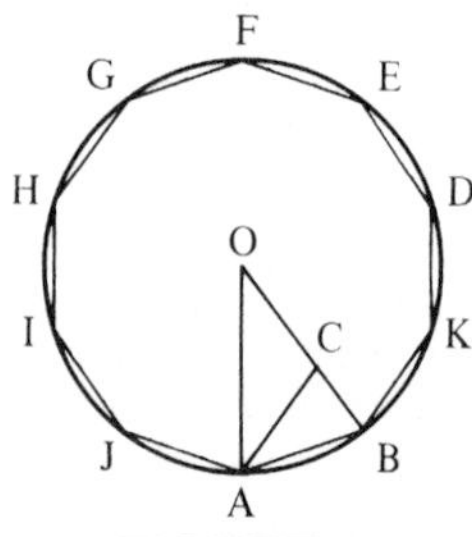

FIGURE 1

With center O, draw $\overline{OA}$ and $\overline{OB}$ to form isosceles ΔAOB. The class should easily see that $m\angle AOB = 36°$ (i.e., $\frac{360}{10} = 36$). Therefore $m\angle OAB = m\angle OBA = 72°$.

Isolate $\triangle AOB$ for clarity (Figure 2).

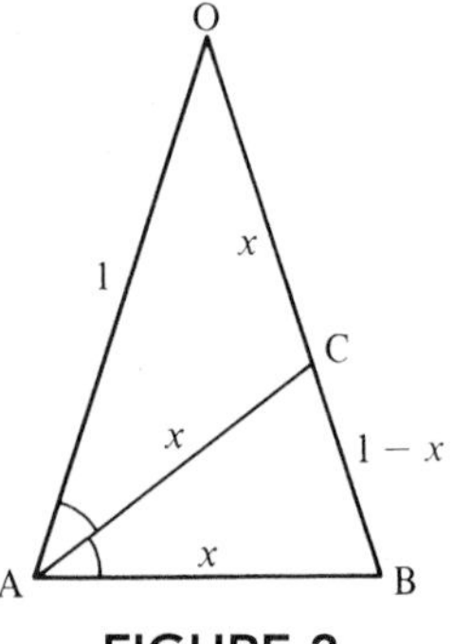

FIGURE 2

Draw angle bisector $\overline{AC}$. Therefore $m\angle OAC = 36°$, making $\triangle OCA$ isosceles. Similarly, $\triangle CAB$ is isosceles. Moreover, $\triangle AOB \sim \triangle BAC$. If we let $x = OC$, then $CB = 1 - x$; also $CA = x = AB$. From the similarity, students should obtain the proportion: $\frac{1}{x} = \frac{x}{1-x}$, which leads to the equation $x^2 + x - 1 = 0$. This equation has two roots, one of which has geometric significance: $x = \frac{\sqrt{5}-1}{2}$.

Now have students consider the construction of this value of x. At any point A of a line, erect a perpendicular of length $1 = OA$, and construct the unit circle (i.e., the circle with radius of length 1) tangent to that line at A. On the line make $AP = 2$ and then draw $\overline{OP}$. By using the Pythagorean theorem, students should establish that $OP = \sqrt{5}$ and $PQ = OP - OQ = \sqrt{5} - 1$. Finally the perpendicular bisector of $\overline{PQ}$ gives us $QR = QR = \frac{\sqrt{5}-1}{2} = x$.

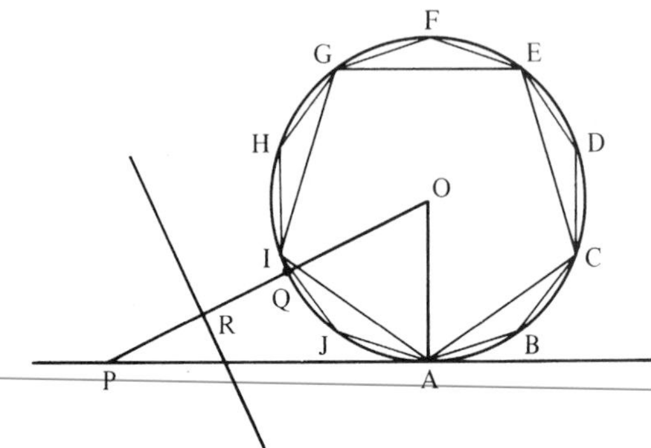

FIGURE 3

Students should now mark consecutive segments of x on the original unit circle. When done accurately, this value of x will give exactly 10 arcs on the circle. After students have constructed the decagon, they ought to realize that by joining the alternate vertices of the decagon, the desired pentagon is formed.

POSTASSESSMENT

Have students construct a regular pentagon given a specific unit length.

For an unusual method for constructing a (almost) regular pentagon, see *101+ Great Ideas for Introducing Key Concepts in Mathematics* by Alfred S. Posamentier and Herbert A. Hauptman (Corwin Press, 2006).

Unit 42

 Investigating the Isosceles Triangle Fallacy

This unit offers an opportunity to consider fully the Isosceles Triangle Fallacy. This fallacy can be used to reinforce the concept of betweenness.

PERFORMANCE OBJECTIVES

1. *Students will exhibit the Isosceles Triangle Fallacy.*
2. *Students will indicate the "error" in the Isosceles Triangle Fallacy and prove their conjecture.*

PREASSESSMENT

Students should be familiar with the various methods for proving triangles congruent, as well as angle measurement in a circle.

TEACHING STRATEGIES

Begin the discussion by challenging your students to drawn any *scalene* triangle on the chalkboard, which you will then prove isosceles.

To prove the scalene △ABC isosceles, draw the bisector of ∠C and the perpendicular bisector of $\overline{AB}$. From their point of intersection, G, draw perpendiculars to $\overline{AC}$ and $\overline{CB}$, meeting them at points D and F, respectively.

There are four possibilities for the above description for various scalene triangles. Figure 1, where $\overline{CG}$ and $\overline{GE}$ meet inside the triangle:

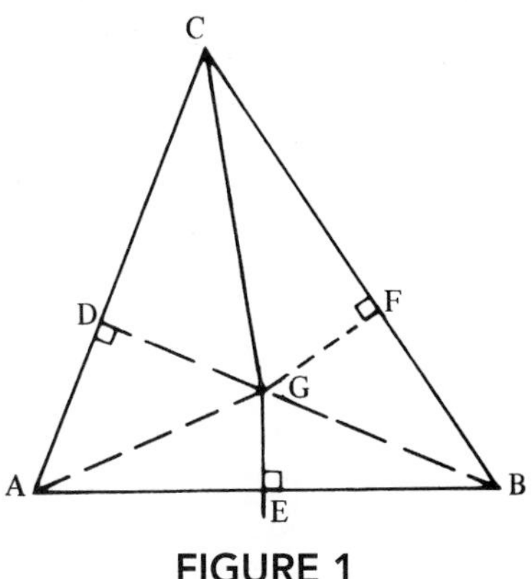

FIGURE 1

Figure 2, where $\overline{CG}$ and $\overline{GE}$ meet on $\overline{AB}$:

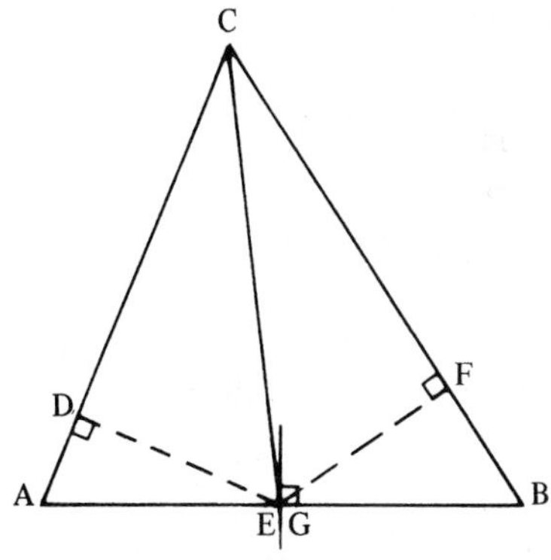

FIGURE 2

Figure 3, where $\overline{CG}$ and $\overline{GE}$ meet outside the triangle, but the perpendiculars $\overline{GD}$ and $\overline{GF}$ fall on $\overline{AC}$ and $\overline{CB}$:

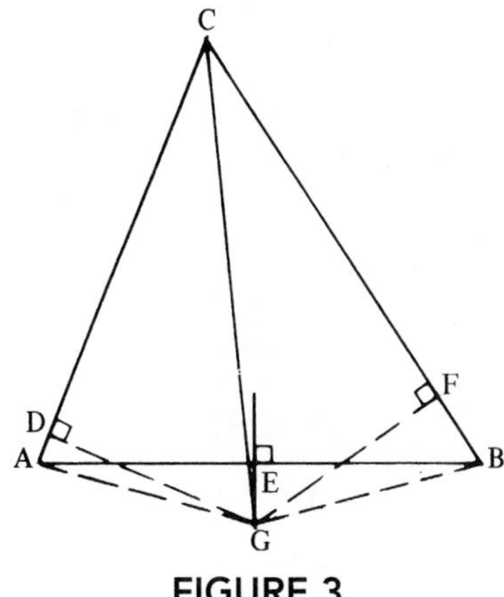

FIGURE 3

Figure 4, where $\overline{CG}$ and $\overline{GE}$ meet outside the triangle, but the perpendiculars $\overline{GD}$ and $\overline{GF}$ meet $\overline{CA}$ and $\overline{CG}$ outside the triangle:

The "proof" of the fallacy can be done with any of the above figures. Have students follow the "proof" on any (or all) of these figures.

Given:

ABC is scalene

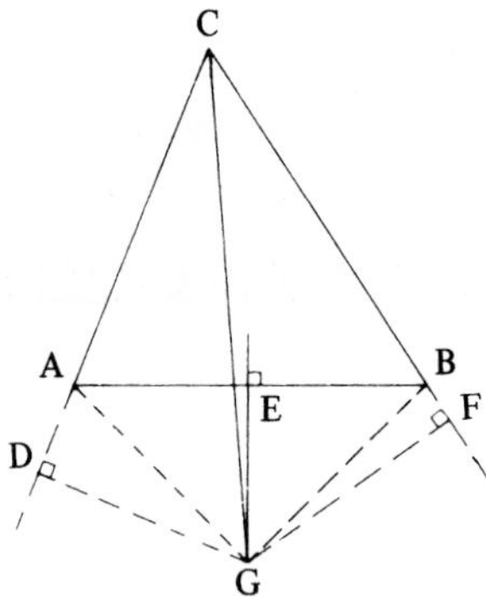

FIGURE 4

Prove:
AC = BC (or △ABC is isosceles)
"*Proof:*" Since ∠AGG ≅ ∠BCG and *rt* ∠CDG ≅ *rt* ∠CFG, △CDG ≅ △CFG (SAA). Therefore DG = FG and CD = CF. AG = BG (a point on the perpendicular bisector of a line segment is equidistant from the endpoints of the line segment) and ∠ADG and ∠BFG are right angles, △DAG ≅ △FBG (H.L.). Therefore DA = FB. It then follows that AC = BC (by addition in Figures 1, 2, and 3; and by subtraction in Figure 4).

At this point students will be quite disturbed. They will wonder where the error was committed that permitted this fallacy to occur. Some students will be clever enough to attack the figures. By rigorous construction students will find a subtle error in the figures:

a. The point G *must* be outside the triangle.
b. When perpendiculars meet the sides of the triangle, one will meet a side *between* the vertices, while the other will not.

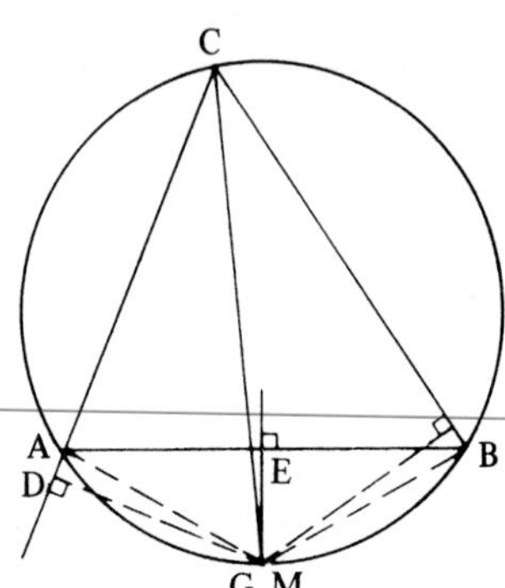

FIGURE 5

Some discussion of Euclid's neglect of the concept of betweenness should follow. However, the beauty of this particular fallacy is the powerful proof of items *a* and *b* (above), which indicate the *error* of the fallacy.

Begin by considering the circumcircle of △ABC. The bisector of ∠ACB must contain the midpoint, M, of $\overset{\frown}{AB}$ (since ∠ACM and ∠BCM are congruent inscribed angles). The perpendicular bisector of $\overline{AB}$ must bisect $\overset{\frown}{AB}$, and therefore pass through M. Thus, the bisector of ∠ACB and the perpendicular bisector of $\overline{AB}$ intersect *outside* the triangle at M (or G). This eliminates the possibilities of Figures 1 and 2.

Now have students consider inscribed quadrilateral ACBG. Since the opposite angles of an inscribed (or cyclic) quadrilateral are supplementary, $m\angle CAG + m\angle CBG = 180$. If ∠CAG and ∠CBG are right angles, then $\overline{CG}$ would be a diameter and △ABC would be isosceles. Therefore, since ΔABC is scalene, ∠CAG and ∠CBG are not right angles. In this case one must be acute and the other obtuse. Suppose ∠CBG is acute and ∠CAG is obtuse. Then in △CGB the altitude on $\overline{CB}$ must be *inside* the triangle, while in obtuse △CAG, the altitude on $\overline{AC}$ must be *outside the triangle. (This is usually readily accepted by students but can be easily proved.)* The fact that one and *only one* of the perpendiculars intersects a side of the triangle *between* the vertices destroys the fallacious "proof." It is important that the teacher stress the importance of the concept of betweenness in geometry.

POSTASSESSMENT

Have students:

1. "Prove" that any given scalene triangle is isosceles.
2. Indicate (and prove) where the "proof" in question 1 is fallacious.
3. Discuss the concept of betweenness in terms of its significance in geometry.

REFERENCES

Posamentier, A. S. *Advanced Euclidean Geometry.* New York, NY: John Wiley Publishing, 2002.

Posamentier, A. S. *Math Wonders to Inspire Teachers and Students.* Alexandria, VA: Association for Supervision and Curriculum Development, 2003.

Unit 43

 The Equiangular Point

This unit will develop interesting geometric relationships from an unusual geometric configuration. The topic is appropriate for any student who has mastered most of the high school geometry course.

PERFORMANCE OBJECTIVES

1. *Students will define the equiangular point of an acute triangle.*
2. *Students will locate the equiangular point of an acute triangle.*
3. *Students will state at least three properties of the figure used to locate the equiangular point of an acute triangle.*

PREASSESSMENT

Before attempting to present this unit to your classes, review with them angle measurement of a circle and the basic properties of congruence and similarity.

TEACHING STRATEGIES

Begin your presentation by challenging students with the following problem:

Given: Acute $\triangle ABC$.
$\triangle ACD$ and $\triangle ABF$ are equilateral.
Prove: DB = CF

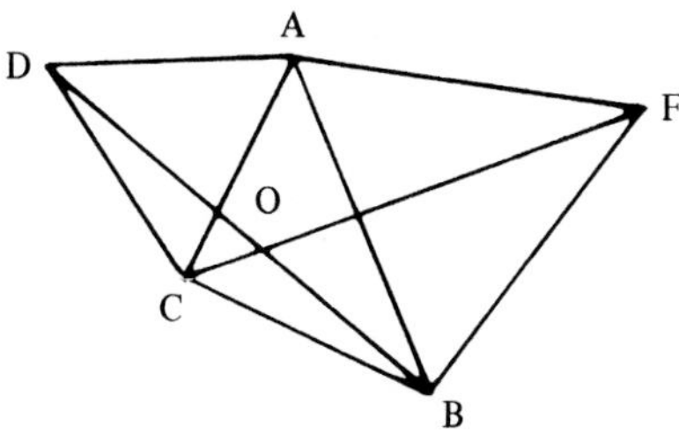

FIGURE 1

Although this problem uses only the most elementary concepts of the high school geometry course, students tend to find it somewhat challenging. What seems to be most perplexing is the selection of the proper pair of triangles to prove congruent. If, after a few minutes, students do not find these, tell them to name triangles that use the required segments $\overline{DB}$ and $\overline{CF}$ as sides. Soon they will realize that they must prove $\triangle CAF \cong \triangle DAB$.

Next arises the problem of *how* to prove these triangles congruent. Lead students to realize that overlapping triangles usually share a common element. Here the common element is $\angle CAB$. Since $\triangle ACD$ and $\triangle ABF$ are equilateral, $m\angle DAC = 60°$, $m\angle FAB = 60°$, and $m\angle DAB = m\angle FAC$ (addition). Since $\triangle ACD$ is equilateral, AD = AC, and since $\triangle ABF$ is equilateral, AB = AF. Therefore $\triangle CAF \cong \triangle DAB$ (S.A.S.), and thus DB = CF.

Once students have fully understood this proof, have them consider a third equilateral triangle, $\triangle BCE$, drawn on side $\overline{BC}$. Ask them to compare the length of $\overline{AE}$ to that of $\overline{DB}$ and $\overline{CF}$.

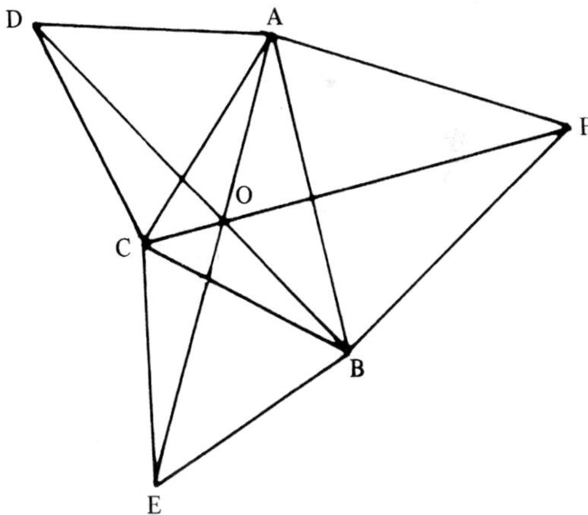

FIGURE 2

Most students will realize that all three segments have the same length. A proof of this is done in the same way as the previous one. That is, simply have them prove that $\triangle CAE \cong \triangle CDB$ to get AE = DB.

The fact that AE = DB = CF is quite astonishing when we bear in mind that $\triangle ABC$ was *any* acute triangle. A number of equally surprising results can now be established from this basis. Present each of these separately, but once each has been proved, carefully relate it to the previously established facts.

1. *The line segments $\overline{AE}$, $\overline{DB}$, and $\overline{CF}$ are concurrent.*

Proof: Consider the circumcircles of the three equilateral triangles, $\triangle ACD$, $\triangle ABF$, and $\triangle BCE$.

Let K, L, and M be the centers of these circles (see Figure 3).

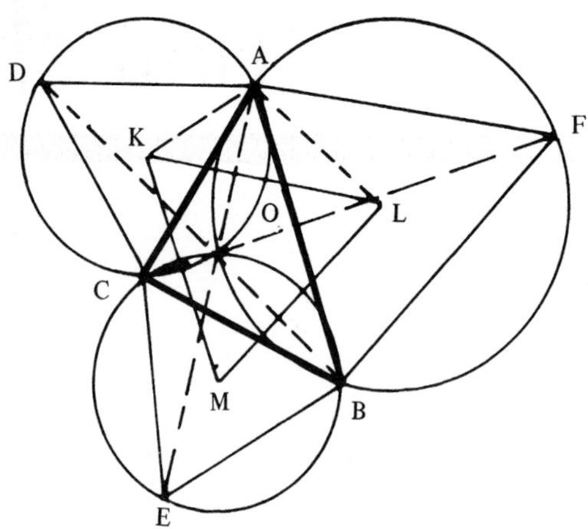

FIGURE 3

Circles K and L meet at points O and A. Since m$\widehat{ADC}$ = 240°, and we know that m∠AOC = $\frac{1}{2}$(m$\widehat{ADC}$), m∠AOC = 120°, Similarly, m∠AOB = $\frac{1}{2}$(m$\widehat{ADC}$) = 120°. Therefore m∠COB = 120°, since a complete revolution = 360°.

Since m$\widehat{CEB}$ = 240°, ∠COB is an inscribed angle and point O must lie on circle M. Therefore, we can see that the three circles are concurrent, intersecting at point O.

Now have students join point O with points A, B, C, D, E, and F. m∠DOA = m ∠AOF = m∠FOB = 60°, and therefore $\overleftrightarrow{DOB}$. Similarly $\overleftrightarrow{COF}$ and $\overleftrightarrow{AOE}$.

Thus it has been proved that $\overline{AE}$, $\overline{CF}$, and $\overline{DB}$ are concurrent, intersecting at point O (which is also the point of intersection of circles K, L, and M).

Now ask the class to determine the point in ΔABC at which the three sides subtend congruent angles. They should quickly recall that we just proved that m∠AOB = m∠AOC = m∠BOC = 120°. Thus, the point—called the *equiangular point* of a triangle—at which the sides of △ABC subtend congruent angles is point O.

2. *The circumcenters K, L, and M of the three equilateral triangles △ACD, △ABF, and △BCE, respectively, determine another equilateral triangle.*

Proof: Before beginning this proof, review briefly with students the relationship among the sides of a 30-60-90 triangle.

Have your students consider equilateral ΔDAC. AK is 2/3 of the altitude (or median), so we obtain the proportion AC:AK = $\sqrt{3}$:1.

Similarly, in equilateral △AFB, AF:AL = $\sqrt{3}$:1.

Therefore, AC:AK = AF:AL.

m∠KAC = m∠LAF = 30°, m∠CAL = m∠CAL (reflexive) and m∠KAL = m∠CAF (addition).

Therefore, △KAL ~ △CAF.

Thus, CF:KL = CA:AK = $\sqrt{3}$:1.

Similarly, we may prove DB:KM = $\sqrt{3}$:1, and AE:ML = $\sqrt{3}$:1. Therefore, DB:KM = AE:ML = CF:KL. But since DB = AE = CF, as proved earlier, we obtain KM = ML = KL. Therefore, △KML is equilateral.

As a concluding challenge to your class, ask them to discover other relationships in Figure 3.

POSTASSESSMENT

To test student comprehension of this lesson, give them the following exercises.

1. Define *the equiangular point* of an acute triangle.
2. Draw any acute triangle. Using straightedge and compasses, locate the equiangular point of the triangle.
3. State three properties found in Figure 3 above.

REFERENCE

Posamentier, A. S. *Advanced Euclidean Geometry*. New York, NY: John Wiley Publishing, 2002.

Unit 44

The Minimum-Distance Point of a Triangle

This unit will develop a search for the point in a triangle the sum of whose distances to the vertices is a minimum.

PERFORMANCE OBJECTIVES

1. *Students will prove that the sum of the distances to the sides of an equilateral triangle from an interior point is constant.*
2. *Students will locate the minimum distance point of a triangle with no angle of measure 120° or greater.*

PREASSESSMENT

Students should be familiar with basic concepts of geometric inequalities.

Ask students to find the position of a point of a quadrilateral, the sum of whose distances to the vertices is a minimum.

TEACHING STRATEGIES

Begin the discussion by having students consider the location of the point in the interior of a given quadrilateral, the sum of whose distances from the vertices is the smallest possible (from here on we shall refer to such a point as the *minimum-distance point*).

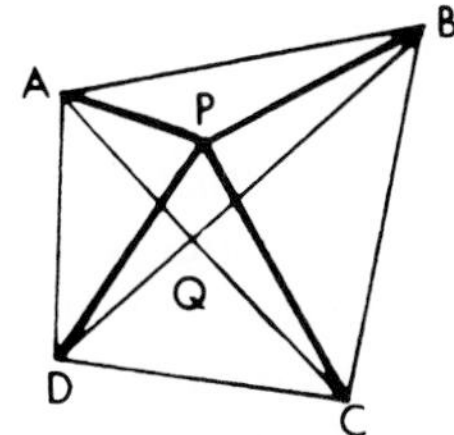

FIGURE 1

You can expect most students to guess that the point of intersection of the diagonals (point Q in Figure 1) would be this minimum-distance point. Although the conjecture is a clever one, try to elicit a justification (proof) for this point selection.

Let students select any point P (not at Q) in the interior of quadrilateral ABCD (Figure 1). PA + PC > QA + QC (since the sum of the lengths of two sides of a triangle is greater than the length of the third). Similarly, PB + PD > QB + QD. By addition, PA + PB + PC + PD > QA + *QB* + *QC* + *QD*, which shows that the sum of the distances from the point of intersection of the diagonals of a quadrilateral to the vertices is less than the sum of the distances from *any other* interior point of the quadrilateral to the vertices.

The next logical concern of students is usually, "What is the minimum-distance point in a triangle?" Before tackling this question, it is useful to first consider another interesting theorem that will later help students develop the minimum-distance point of a triangle.

Once again ask students to use their intuition and reason inductively. Have them construct a large equilateral triangle. Then have them select any interior point and carefully measure its distances from the three *sides* of the equilateral triangle. After students have recorded the sum of these three distances, ask them to repeat the procedure three times, each time with a different interior point. Accurate measurements should yield equal distance sums for each point selected. Consequently, students ought to be able to draw the following conclusion: *The sum of the distances from any point in the interior of an equilateral triangle to the sides of the triangle is constant.* Two proofs of this interesting finding are provided here.

Method I:

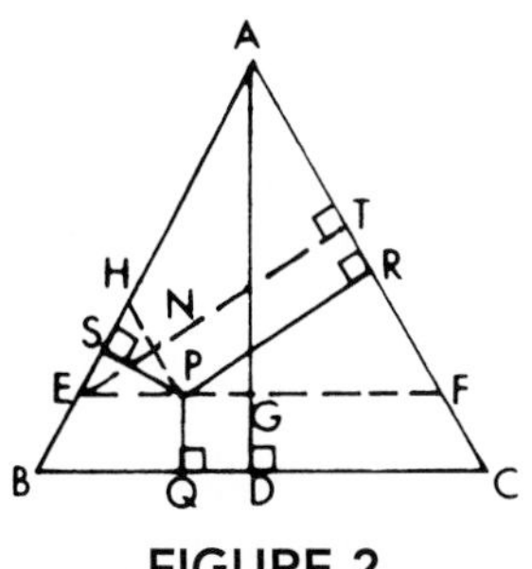

FIGURE 2

In equilateral $\triangle ABC$, $\overline{PR} \perp \overline{AC}$, $\overline{PQ} \perp \overline{BC}$, $\overline{PS} \perp \overline{AB}$, and $\overline{AD} \perp \overline{BC}$.

Draw a line through P parallel to $\overline{BC}$ meeting $\overline{AD}$, $\overline{AB}$, and $\overline{AC}$ at G, E, and F, respectively.
PQ = GD.
Draw $\overline{ET} \perp \overline{AC}$. Since $\triangle$AEF is equilateral, $\overline{AG} \cong \overline{ET}$ (all the altitudes of an equilateral triangle are congruent).
Draw $\overline{PH} // \overline{AC}$ meeting $\overline{ET}$ at N. $\overline{NT} \cong \overline{PR}$.
Since $\triangle$EHP is equilateral, altitudes $\overline{PS}$ and $\overline{EN}$ are congruent. Therefore, we have shown that PS + PR = ET = AG. Since PQ = GD, PS + PR + PQ = AG + GD = AD, a constant for the given triangle.
Method II:

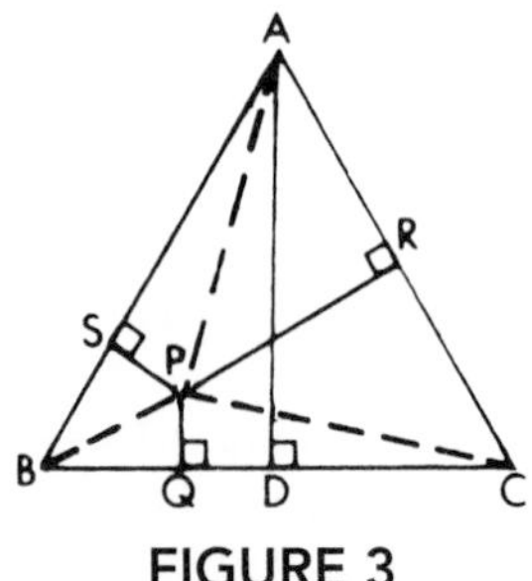

FIGURE 3

In equilateral $\triangle$ABC, $\overline{PR} \perp \overline{AC}$, $\overline{PQ} \perp \overline{BC}$, $\overline{PS} \perp \overline{AB}$, and $\overline{AD} \perp \overline{BC}$,
Draw $\overline{PA}$, $\overline{PB}$, and $\overline{PC}$.
The area of $\triangle$ABC

$$= \text{area of } \triangle APB + \text{area of } \triangle BPC + \text{area of } \triangle CPA$$
$$= \frac{1}{2}(AB)(PS) + \frac{1}{2}(BC)(PQ) + \frac{1}{2}(AC)(PR).$$

Since AB = BC = AC, the area of $\triangle ABC = \frac{1}{2}(BC)$ $[PS + PQ + PR]$. However, the area of $\triangle ABC = \frac{1}{2}(BC)(AD)$, therefore, PS + PQ + PR = AD, a constant for the given triangle.

Students are now ready to consider the original problem: to find the minimum-distance point of a triangle. We shall consider a scalene triangle with no angle having a measure greater than 120°.

Students, realizing the apparent need for symmetry in this problem, may suggest selecting the point at which the sides subtend congruent angles. If they are to accept this conjecture, they must prove it.

We shall therefore prove that *the point in the interior of a triangle (with no angle greater than 120°), at which the sides subtend congruent angles, is the minimum-distance point of the triangle.*

Proof:

In Figure 4, let M be the point in the interior of $\triangle$ABC, where $m\angle AMB = m\angle BMC = m\angle AMC = 120°$.

Draw lines through A, B, and C that are perpendicular to $\overline{AM}$, $\overline{BM}$, and $\overline{CM}$, respectively.

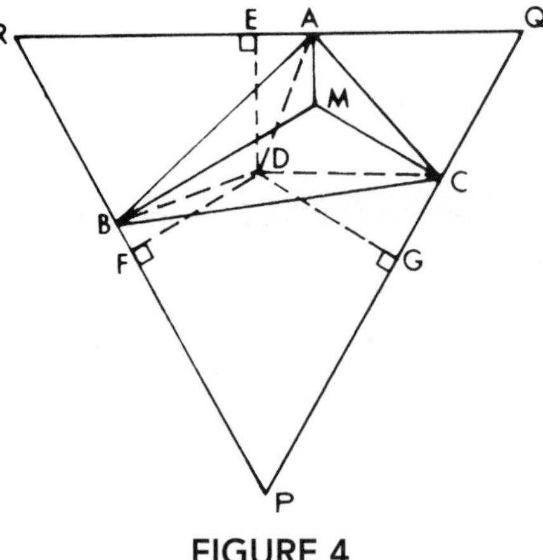

FIGURE 4

These lines meet to form equilateral $\triangle$PQR. (To prove $\triangle$PQR is equilateral, notice that each angle has measure 60°. This can be shown by considering, for example, quadrilateral AMBR. Since $m\angle RAM = m\angle RBM = 90°$, and $m\angle AMB = 120°$, it follows that $m\angle ARB = 60°$.)
Let D be *any other* point in the interior of ΔABC. We must show that the sum of the distances from M to the vertices is less than the sum of the distances from D to the vertices.
From the theorem we proved above, MA + MB + MC = DE + DF + DG (where $\overline{DE}$, $\overline{DF}$, and $\overline{DG}$ are the perpendiculars to $\overline{REQ}$, $\overline{RBP}$ and $\overline{QGP}$, respectively).
But DE + DF + DG < DA + DB + DC. (The shortest distance from an external point to a line is the length of the perpendicular segment from the point to the line.)

By substitution:

$$MA + MB + MC < DA + DB + DC.$$

Now having proved the theorem, students may wonder why we chose to restrict our discussion to triangles with angles of measure less than 120°. Let them try to construct the point M in an obtuse triangle with one angle of measure 150°. The reason for our restriction should become obvious.

POSTASSESSMENT

To test student comprehension of the above exercises, ask them to:

1. Prove that the sum of the distances to the sides of an equilateral triangle from an interior point is constant.
2. Locate the minimum-distance point of a triangle with no angle of measure greater than 120°.
3. Locate the minimum-distance point of a quadrilateral.

REFERENCE

Posamentier, A. S. *Advanced Euclidean Geometry*. New York, NY: John Wiley Publishing, 2002.

Unit 45

The Isosceles Triangle Revisited

Early in the high school geometry course, students perform many practice proofs using isosceles triangles. One such proof involves proving that the angle bisectors of the base angles of an isosceles triangle are congruent. Although this is a rather simple proof, its converse is exceedingly difficult—perhaps among the most difficult statements to prove in Euclidean geometry. This unit presents several methods by which students can prove the statement.

PERFORMANCE OBJECTIVE

Students will prove that if two angle bisectors of a triangle are congruent, then the triangle is isosceles.

PREASSESSMENT

Students should have had practice with geometric proofs, including indirect proofs.

TEACHING STRATEGIES

Begin your presentation by asking students to prove:

> The angle bisectors of the base angles of an isosceles triangle are congruent.

You may wish to start them uniformly:

Given: Isosceles $\triangle ABC$, with $AB = AC$, $\overline{BF}$ and $\overline{CE}$ are angle bisectors
Prove: $\overline{BF} \cong \overline{CE}$

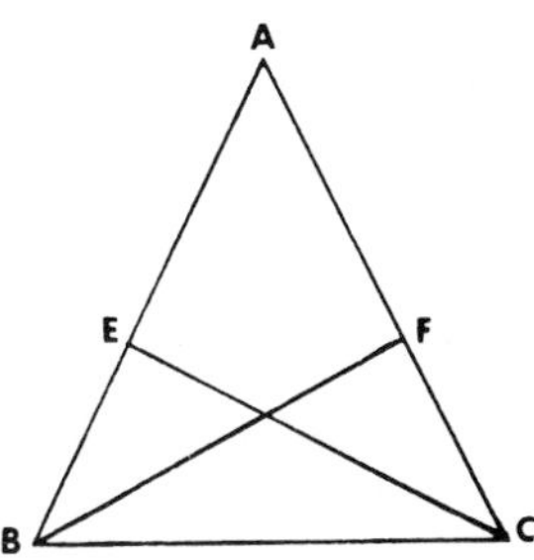

Proof: $m\angle FBC = \frac{1}{2} m\angle ABC$, and $m\angle ECB = \frac{1}{2} m\angle ACB$. Since $m\angle ABC = m\angle ACB$ (base angles of an isosceles triangle), $m\angle FBC = m\angle ECB$. Since $\overline{BC} \cong \overline{BC}$, $\triangle FBC \cong \triangle ECB$ (ASA). Therefore $\overline{BF} \cong \overline{CE}$.

When students have completed this proof, ask them to state the converse of the statement just proved:

> If two angle bisectors of a triangle are congruent, then the triangle is isosceles.

Challenge students to prove this new statement. It is highly unlikely that your students will be able to prove this statement in a short time, so you may wish to show them some of the following proofs. They will be quite astonished that the converse of a rather simply proved statement is so difficult to prove. Each of the following proofs is quite instructional and merits special attention.

Given: $\overline{AE}$ and $\overline{BD}$ are angle bisectors of $\triangle ABC$, $\overline{AE} \cong \overline{BD}$.
Prove: $\triangle ABC$ is isosceles.

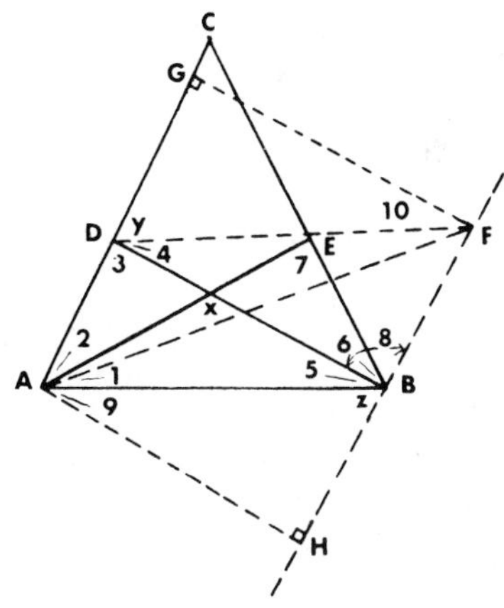

Proof: Draw $\angle DBF \cong \angle AEB$ so that $\overline{BF} \cong \overline{BE}$.
Draw $\overline{DF}$.
Also draw $\overline{FG} \perp \overline{AC}$ and $\overline{AH} \perp \overline{FH}$.
By hypothesis, $\overline{AE} \cong \overline{DB}, \overline{FB} \cong \overline{EB}$.
And $\angle 8 \cong \angle 7$.
Therefore $\triangle AEB \cong \triangle DBF$ (SAS) $DF = AB$ and $m\angle 1 = m\angle 4$.
$m\angle x = m\angle 2 + m\angle 3$ (exterior angles) of a triangle)
$m\angle x = m\angle 1 + m\angle 3$ (substitution)
$m\angle x = m\angle 4 + m\angle 3$ (substitution)
$m\angle x = m\angle 7 + m\angle 6$ (exterior angles of a triangle)

$m\angle x = m\angle 7 + m\angle 5$ (substitution)
$m\angle x = m\angle 8 + m\angle 5$ (substitution)
Therefore, $m\angle 4 + m\angle 3 = m\angle 8 + m\angle 5$ (transitivity).
Thus $m\angle z = m\angle y$.
Right △FDG ≅ right △ABH(SAA), DG = BH, and FG = AH.
Right △AFG ≅ right △FAH(HL) and AG = FH.
Therefore, GFHA is a parallelogram.
Also, $m\angle 9 = m\angle 10$ (from △ABH and △FDG).
$m\angle$DAB = $m\angle$DFB (subtraction)
$m\angle$DFB = $m\angle$EBA (from △DBF and △AEB)
Therefore, $m\angle$DAB = m△EBA (transitivity), and △ABC is isosceles.

The following proofs of this theorem are *indirect proofs* and may deserve special introduction.

Given: $\overline{BF}$ and $\overline{CE}$ are angle bisectors of △ABC. $\overline{BF} \cong \overline{CE}$
Prove: △ABC is isosceles.

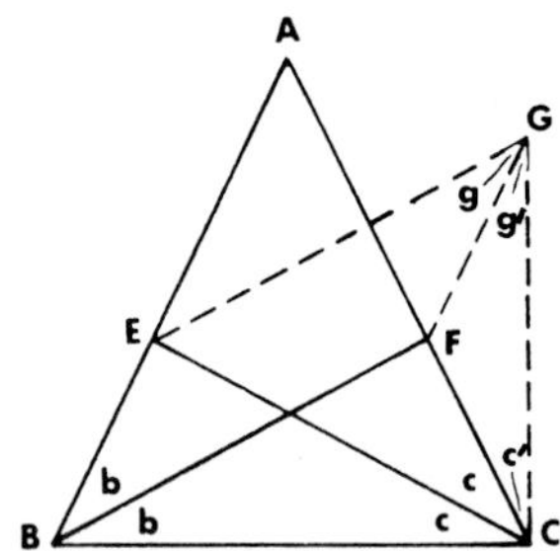

Indirect proof I:

Assume △ABC is *not* isosceles.
Let $m\angle$ABC > $m\angle$ACB
$\overline{BF} \cong \overline{CE}$ (hypothesis)
$\overline{BC} \cong \overline{BC}$
$m\angle$ABC > $m\angle$ACB (assumption)
$\overline{CF} > \overline{BE}$.
Through F, construct $\overline{GF}$ parallel to $\overline{EB}$.
Through E, construct $\overline{GE}$ parallel to $\overline{BF}$.
BFGE is a parallelogram.
$\overline{BF} \cong \overline{EG}$, $\overline{EG} \cong \overline{CE}$, △GEC is isosceles.
$m\angle(g + g') = m\angle(c + c')$
but $m\angle g = m\angle b$
$m\angle(b + g') = m\angle(c + c')$
Therefore, $m\angle g' < m\angle c'$, since $m\angle b > m\angle c$.
In △GFC, we have CF < GF
But GF = BE.
Thus CF < BE.

The assumption of the inequality of $m\angle$ABC and $m\angle$ACB leads to two contradictory results, CF < BE and CF > BE. Therefore △ABC is isosceles.

A second indirect proof follows:

Given: $\overline{BE}$ and $\overline{DC}$ are angle bisectors of △ABC. $\overline{BE} \cong \overline{DC}$
Prove: △ABC is isosceles.

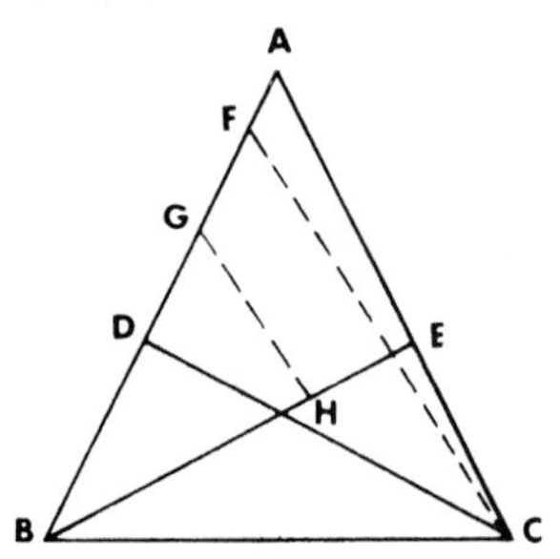

Indirect Proof II:

In △ABC, the bisectors of angles ABC and ACB have equal measures (i.e., BE = DC).
Assume that $m\angle$ABC < $m\angle$ACB; then $m\angle$ABE < $m\angle$ACD.
We then draw ∠FCD congruent to ∠ABE. Note that we may take F between B and A without loss of generality. In △FBC,FB > FC. (If the measures of two angles of a triangle are not equal, then the measures of the sides opposite these angles are also unequal, the side with the greater measure being opposite the angle with the greater measure.)
Choose a point G so that $\overline{BG} \cong \overline{FC}$.
Then draw $\overline{GH} // \overline{FC}$.
Therefore, ∠BGH ≅ ∠BFC (corresponding angles), and △BGH ≅ △CFD(ASA).
Then it follows that BH = DC.

Since BH < BE, this contradicts the hypothesis that the angle bisectors are equal. A similar argument will show that it is impossible to have $m\angle$ACB < $m\angle$ABC.

It then follows that $m\angle$ACB = $m\angle$ABC and that △ABC is isosceles.

POSTASSESSMENT

Have students prove that if two angle bisectors of a triangle are congruent then the triangle is isosceles.

REFERENCE

Posamentier, Alfred S., and Charles T. Salkind. *Challenging Problems in Geometry*. New York: Dover, 1996.

Unit 46

Reflective Properties of the Plane

PERFORMANCE OBJECTIVE

Given a line and two points on one side of a line, students will determine the shortest combined path from one point to the line and then to the second point.

PREASSESSMENT

Using the following illustration, ask students to locate the precise point on the cushion $\overline{PQ}$ of the "billiard table" that ball A must hit in order to then hit ball B (assume no "English" on the ball).

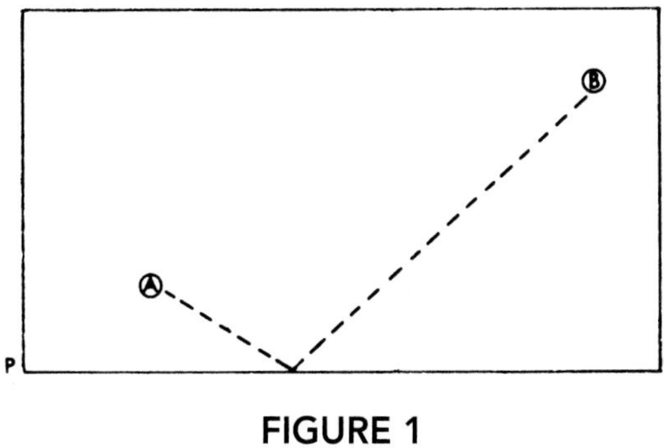

FIGURE 1

The disagreement as to where to hit the ball will develop enough interest to motivate the topic of the properties of reflection.

TEACHING STRATEGIES

Have the class try to prove the following property: "A ray of light will make equal angles with a mirror before and after reflecting off a mirror." (This theorem can be easily proved after considering the following proof.)

To find the *shortest path* from point A to line m then to point B in Figure 2, consider the perpendicular from A to line m (meeting line m at point C). Let D be the point on $\overrightarrow{AC}$ such that $\overline{AC} \cong \overline{CD}$. Point D is called the *reflected image* of point A in line m.

The point of intersection of $\overline{BD}$ and line m determines point P, the required point in the original problem. However, what must be shown now is that AP + PB is less than *any other* path from A to line m (say at point Q), and then to B.

Students might be more comfortable stating this as a "formal proof":

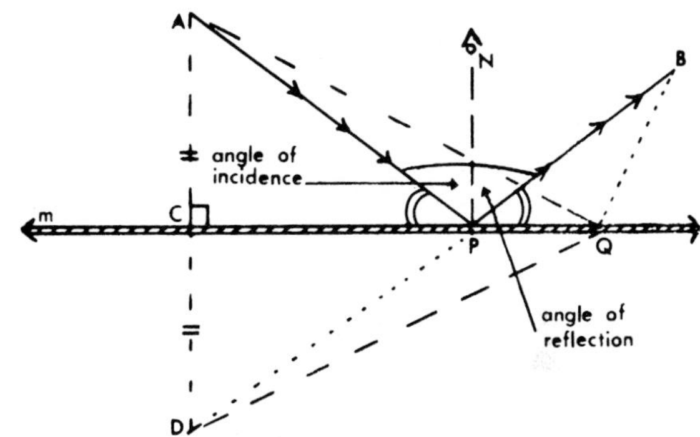

FIGURE 2

Given: Points A and B are on the same side of line m$\overleftrightarrow{ACD} \perp \overleftrightarrow{CPQ}$, where Q is any point on $\overleftrightarrow{CP}$ (other than P).
$\overleftrightarrow{DPB}$
$\overline{AC} \cong \overline{CD}$

Prove: AP + PB < AQ + QB

Outline of proof: Because line m is the perpendicular bisector of $\overline{ACD}$, $\overline{AP} \cong \overline{DP}$ and $\overline{AQ} \cong \overline{QD}$. In $\triangle$DQB, BD < BQ + QD (triangle inequality). Since BD = DP + PB, AP + PB < AQ + BQ.

You can now show the class that since $\angle$BPQ $\cong$ $\angle$CPD, and $\angle$APC $\cong$ $\angle$CPD, that $\angle$APC $\cong$ $\angle$BPQ. If $\overleftrightarrow{PN} \perp$ line m, then $\angle$APN, the angle of incidence, is congruent to $\angle$BPN, the angle of reflection.

Have students apply the properties of reflection to the billiard table problem. A billiard ball will rebound off a cushion as a ray of light "bounces" off a mirror. Thus if a ball is at position A (Figure 3) and the player desires to hit it off cushion

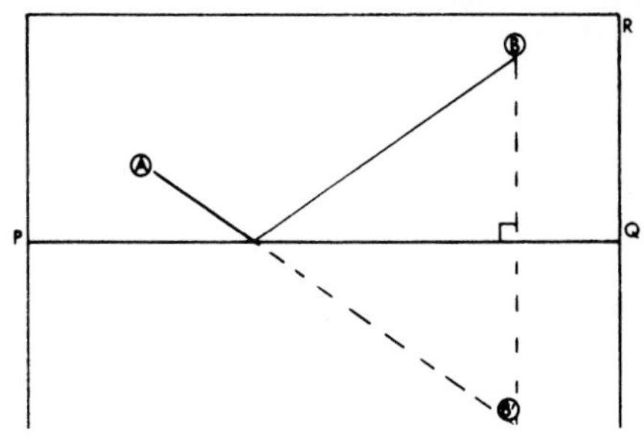

FIGURE 3

$\overline{PQ}$ to position B, he can aim his shot at the point on $\overline{PQ}$ where he would see B (if a mirror were placed along $\overline{PQ}$).

Now have students consider the problem of hitting two cushions ($\overline{PQ}$ then $\overline{QR}$) before hitting B.

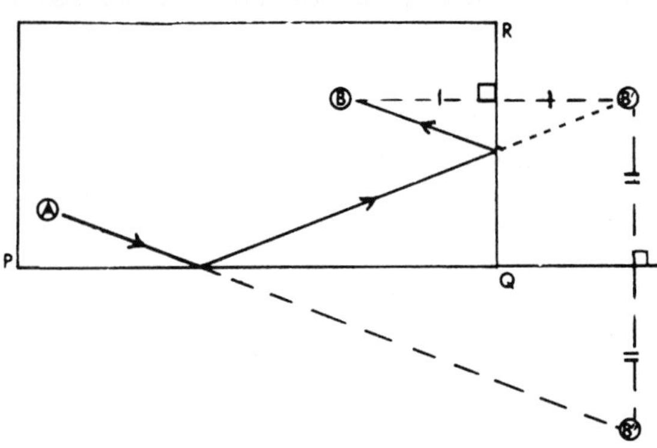

FIGURE 4

Consider the reflected image of B in $\overline{QR}$; call it B' (Figure 4). Now they merely have to consider the problem of where to hit the ball from A off cushion $\overleftrightarrow{PQ}$ so that it will roll toward B'. To do this, have them take the reflected image of B' in $\overleftrightarrow{PQ}$ then the intersection of the line connecting A and the reflected image of B' (call it B'') and $\overleftrightarrow{PQ}$ is the point to aim for to make this two-cushion shot. Students may envision this point as the reflection of the ball at B in the mirror placed along $\overleftrightarrow{PQ}$ that they would see as the reflection in the mirror placed along $\overline{QR}$.

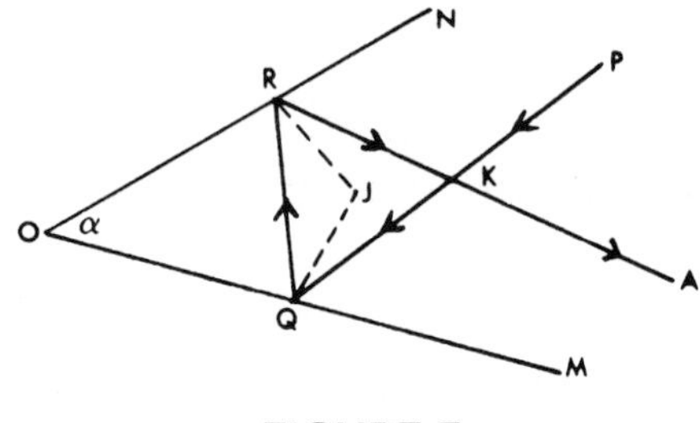

FIGURE 5

A motivated class may now wish to look beyond the double reflection to where the angle between the two planes is always fixed as a right angle.

Two mirrors with a fixed dihedral angle between them are called *angle mirrors*. Have the class prove that if an observer shines a light into the angle mirrors so that the ray reflects off one mirror, then the other, the final reflected ray will form an angle with the original ray, which is double the dihedral angle between the two mirrors. In other words:

Given: Mirrors OM and ON, let $\angle NOM = \alpha$ also a light ray originating at point P aimed at point Q reflecting off OM onto $\overrightarrow{ON}$ then to A.

Prove: $m\angle PKR = 2\alpha$ (Figure 5)

Outline of proof: Draw the normals (the perpendiculars) to the planes (the mirrors) at the points of incidence in each plane, i.e., $\overleftrightarrow{QJ} \perp \overleftrightarrow{OM}$, at point Q, and draw $\overleftrightarrow{RJ} \perp \overleftrightarrow{ON}$, at point R (the point of incidence in mirror $\overleftrightarrow{ON}$). Then, by the property of reflection, $\overleftrightarrow{QJ}$ and $\overleftrightarrow{RJ}$ bisect $\angle PQR$ and $\angle QRA$, respectively. Then $m\angle PKR = m\angle KQR + m\angle KRQ$ (exterior angle of a triangle theorem). Then $m\angle PKR = 2(m\angle JQR + m\angle QRJ)$ and $m\angle PKR = 2(180 - m\angle RJQ)$. But, both $\angle JRO$ and $\angle JQO$ are right angles, so $m\angle ROQ = 180 - m\angle RJQ$ (the sum of the measures of the interior angles of a quadrilateral is 360). By substituting, $m\angle PKR = 2(m\angle ROQ) = 2\alpha$.

One of the applications of angle mirrors is that when the dihedral angle is 45° the ray will be reflected 90°. Such a pair of mirrors is often called an "optical square," because it is used to determine perpendicular lines of sight.

To show how the optical square is used, station one student at each of the three points O, A, and B, so that the three points will define a triangle (Figure 6). Using the optical square they will be able to determine where the perpendicular from B to $\overleftrightarrow{AO}$. meets $\overleftrightarrow{AO}$. Have the student standing at O look at the student standing at A. Have another student, P, holding the optical square move along the line of sight from O to A until (at some point m) the student at O is able to see the student at B in the angle mirror. The point m is the foot of the altitude from B to $\overleftrightarrow{OA}$

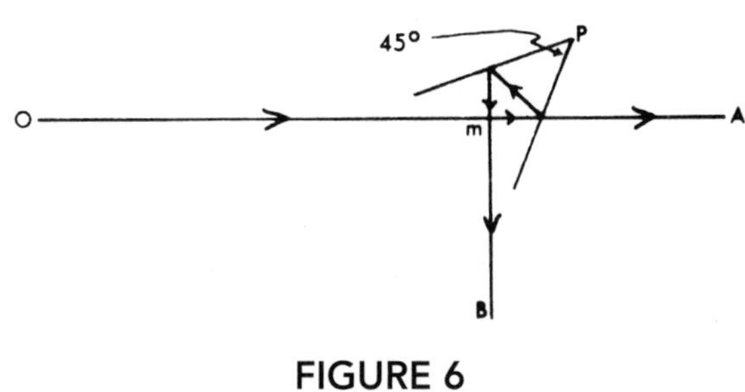

FIGURE 6

POSTASSESSMENT

Using the property of reflection, have students prove that the height of a flagpole is

$$x = \frac{h \cdot BC}{AB}$$

where x is the height of the flagpole and h is the height of an observer.

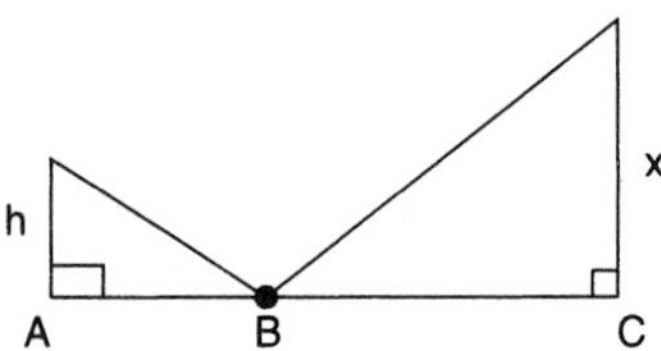

Unit 47

 Finding the Length of a Cevian of a Triangle

This unit presents a method for finding the length of *any* line segment joining a vertex of a triangle with any point on the opposite side. Such a line segment is called a cevian, after Giovanni Ceva who developed a theorem about the concurrency of such line segments. This technique is particularly useful to students since it fills a void in many curricula. Students are usually taught methods for finding the lengths of special cevians such as altitudes and some medians. However, by using Stewart's theorem (named after Matthew Stewart who published it in 1745), students will now be able to find the length of *any* cevian of a triangle.

PERFORMANCE OBJECTIVES

1. *Students will find the length of a specific cevian of a given triangle, all of whose side (and segment) lengths are known.*
2. *Students will use a special formula to find the length of an angle bisector of a triangle, given the lengths of its sides.*

PREASSESSMENT

Students should have mastered most of the standard high school geometry course. For review purposes, have students work the following problem:

> In a triangle whose sides have lengths 13, 14, and 15, what is the length of the altitude to the side of length 14?

TEACHING STRATEGIES

One of the major skills needed to develop Stewart's theorem is a working knowledge of the Pythagorean theorem. The problem stated above requires this skill.

After students have drawn the diagram required by this problem, they will immediately see two right triangles.
To this figure they will apply the Pythagorean theorem twice, once to △ACD and a second time to △ABD.

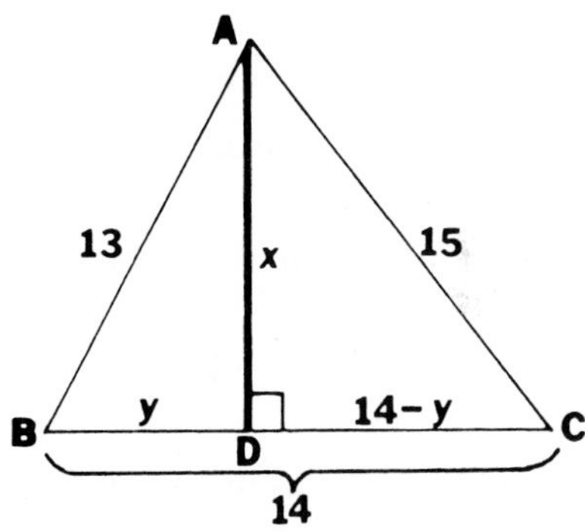

FIGURE 1

$$\begin{aligned} \text{For } \triangle ACD: &\quad x^2 + (14 - y)^2 = 225 \\ \text{For } \triangle ABD: &\quad x^2 + y^2 = 169 \\ \text{By subtraction: } &\quad (14 - y)^2 - y^2 = 56 \end{aligned}$$

$$196 - 28y + y^2 - y^2 = 56$$
$$y = 5$$
$$\text{and then } x = 12$$

Thus, students will see two right triangles with integral length sides: 5, 12, 13 and 9, 12, 15.

Now challenge your students to find the length of the angle bisector from vertex A of △ABC. After a short time, their frustration will be evident. At this juncture, have the class stop working and discuss with them Stewart's theorem:

Stewart's theorem:

In Figure 2, the theorem states that:

$$a^2n + b^2m = c\,(d^2 + mn)$$

By this theorem, d may be found if a, b, m, and n are known. The proof of this most useful theorem follows.

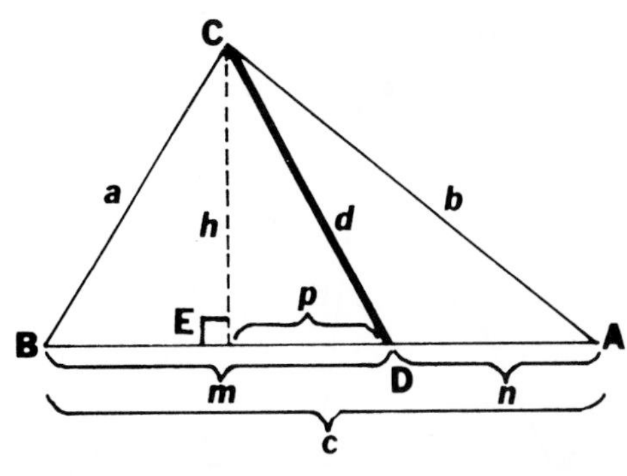

FIGURE 2

Proof:

In $\triangle ABC$, let BC $= a$, AC $= b$, AB $= c$, CD $= d$. Point D divides $\overline{AB}$ into two segments; BD $= m$ and DA $= n$. Draw the altitude CE $= h$ and let ED $= p$.

To proceed with the proof of Stewart's theorem, we first derive two necessary formulas. The first one is applicable to $\triangle CBD$. We apply the Pythagorean theorem to $\triangle CEB$ to obtain

$$(CB)^2 = (CE)^2 + (BE)^2.$$

$$\text{Since BE} = m - p,\ a^2 = h^2 + (m - p)^2. \qquad \text{(I)}$$

However, by applying the Pythagorean theorem to $\triangle CED$, we have $(CD)^2 = (CE)^2 + (ED)^2$, or $h^2 = d^2 - p^2$. Replacing h^2 in equation (I), we obtain

$$a^2 = d^2 - p^2 + (m - p)^2,$$

$$a^2 = d^2 - p^2 + m^2 - 2mp + p^2.$$

$$\text{Thus, } a^2 = d^2 + m^2 - 2mp. \qquad \text{(II)}$$

A similar argument is applicable to $\triangle CDA$. Applying the Pythagorean theorem to $\triangle CEA$, we find that

$$(CA)^2 = (CE)^2 + (EA)^2.$$

$$\text{Since EA} = (n + p),\ b^2 = h^2 + (n + p)^2. \qquad \text{(III)}$$

However, $h^2 = d^2 - p^2$, substitute for h^2 in (III) as follows:

$$b^2 = d^2 - p^2 + (n + p)^2,$$

$$b^2 = d^2 - p^2 + n^2 + 2np + p^2.$$

$$\text{Thus, } b^2 = d^2 + n^2 + 2np. \qquad \text{(IV)}$$

Equations (II) and (IV) give us the formulas we need. Now multiply equation (II) by n to get

$$a^2n = d^2n + m^2n - 2mnp, \qquad \text{(V)}$$

and multiply equation (IV) by m to get

$$b^2m = d^2m + n^2m + 2mnp. \qquad \text{(VI)}$$

Adding (V) and (VI), we have

$$a^2n + b^2m = d^2n + d^2m + m^2n + n^2m + 2mnp - 2mnp.$$

Therefore, $a^2n + b^2m = d^2(n + m) + mn(m + n)$.
Since $m + n = c$, we have $a^2n + b^2m = d^2c + mnc$, or

$$a^2n + b^2m = c\,(d^2 + mn).$$

Your students should now be ready to find the length of the median from vertex A of $\triangle ABC$, where AB $= 13$, BC $= 14$, and AC $= 15$. All they need do is apply Stewart's theorem as follows:

$$c^2n + b^2m = a(d^2 + mn)$$

However, since $\overline{AD}$ is a median $m = n$.

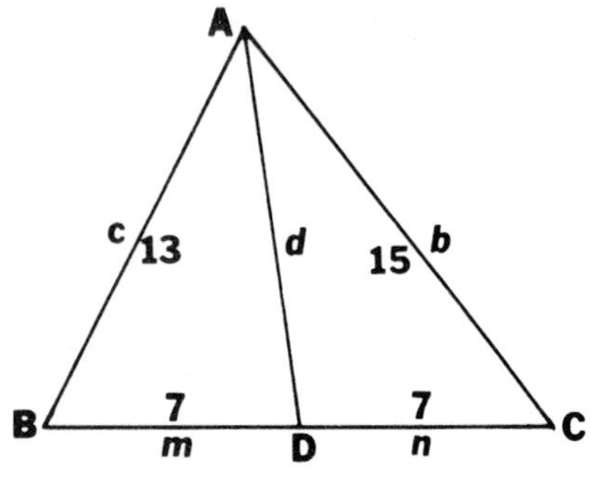

FIGURE 3

Substituting in the above formula:

$$13^2(7) + 15^2(7) = 14(d^2 + 49)$$

Therefore, $d = 2\sqrt{37}$.

To find the length of an angle bisector of a triangle, Stewart's theorem leads to a very concise relationship, which students will find easy to use.

Have students consider $\triangle ABC$ with angle bisector $\overline{AD}$.

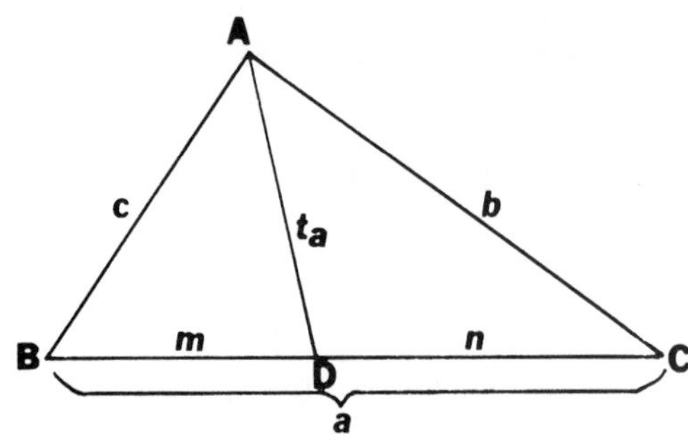

FIGURE 4

By Stewart's theorem we obtain the following relationship:

$$c^2n + b^2m = a(t_a^2 + mn), \text{ or}$$

$$t_a^2 + mn = \frac{c^2n + b^2m}{a}, \text{ or}$$

as illustrated by Figure 4.

But, $\frac{c}{b} = \frac{m}{n}$. (The bisector of an angle of a triangle divides the opposite side into segments whose measures are proportional to the measures of the other two sides of the triangle. The converse is also true.) Therefore, $cn = bm$.
Substituting in the above equation,

$$t_a^2 + mn = \frac{cbm + cbn}{m + n} = \frac{cb(m + n)}{m + n} = cb.$$

Hence, $t_a^2 = cb - mn$.

At this juncture, your students should be able to find the length of *any* cevian of a triangle. For reinforcement, present problems involving angle bisectors and medians before going on to other types of cevians.

POSTASSESSMENT

Have students complete the following exercises:

1. Find the length of an altitude drawn to the longest side of a triangle whose sides have lengths 10, 12, and 14.
2. Find the length of a median drawn to the longest side of a triangle whose sides have lengths 10, 12, and 14.
3. Find the length of an angle bisector drawn to the longest side of a triangle whose sides have lengths 10, 12, and 14.
4. In $\triangle PQR$, if PR $= 7$, PQ $= 8$, RS $= 4$, and SQ $= 5$, find PS when S is on $\overline{RQ}$.

REFERENCE

Posamentier, A. S. *Advanced Euclidean Geometry: Excursions for Secondary Teachers and Students*. New York, NY: John Wiley Publishing, 2002.

Unit 48

 A Surprising Challenge

This activity will alert geometry students to the fact that what may appear easy may actually be quite difficult.

PERFORMANCE OBJECTIVE

Given a geometric problem of the kind posed here, students will properly analyze it and solve it.

PREASSESSMENT

Students should be able to handle geometric proofs with relative ease before attempting this unit. The problem posed here is quite difficult to prove, yet easy to state. It ought to be within the reach of a slightly above-average student of high school geometry.

TEACHING STRATEGIES

The geometric problem you are about to pose to your students appears to be quite simple and certainly innocent.

Problem: $\triangle ABC$ is isosceles ($CA = CB$). $m\angle ABD = 60°$, $m\angle BAE = 50°$, and $m\angle C = 20°$. Find the measure of $\angle EDB$.

Students should be given a fair amount of time to grapple with this problem. Immediately, they will find the measures of most of the angles in the diagram. However, they will soon realize that this problem was not as simple as they first imagined, since they will be most likely unable to solve the problem. At this point you can begin your discussion of a solution of this problem.

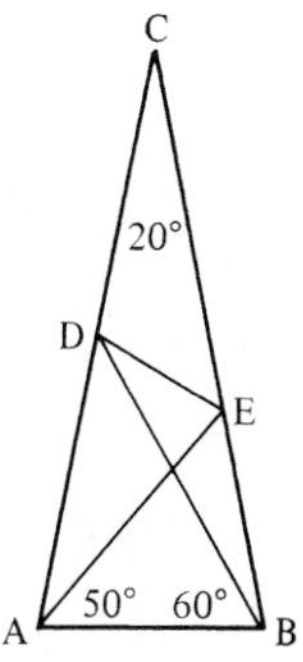

FIGURE 1

Students will be quick to realize that auxiliary lines are necessary in order to solve this problem. Suggest that they draw $\overline{DG} \parallel \overline{AB}$, where G is on $\overline{CB}$. Then draw $\overline{AG}$ intersecting $\overline{BD}$ at F. The last segment to be drawn is $\overline{EF}$ (see Figure 2).

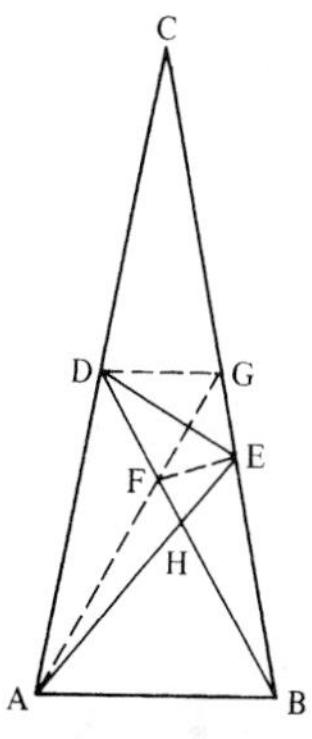

FIGURE 2

Students should be able to prove that $\angle ABD \cong \angle BAG$. Then $m\angle AGD = m\angle BAG = 60°$ (alternate interior angles of parallel lines). Thus $m\angle AFB$ must be 60° and ΔAFB is equilateral, and $AB = FB$.

Since $m\angle EAB = 50°$, and $m\angle ABE = 80°$, $m\angle AEB = 50°$ making $\triangle ABE$ isosceles and $AB = EB$. Therefore $FB = EB$ (transitivity), and $\triangle EFB$ is isosceles.

Since $m\angle EBF = 20°$, $m\angle BEF = m\angle BFE = 80°$. As $m\angle DFG = 60°$, $m\angle GFE = 40°$. $GE = EF$ (equal length sides of an isosceles triangle), and $DF = DG$ (sides of an equilateral triangle). Thus $DGEF$ is a kite, i.e., two isosceles triangles externally sharing a common base. $\overline{DE}$ bisects $\angle GDF$ (property of a kite), therefore $m\angle EDB = 30°$.

Another possible method of solution follows:

In isosceles $\triangle ABC$, $m\angle ACB = 20°$, $m\angle CAB = 80°$, $m\angle ABD = 60°$, and $m\angle EAB = 50°$.

Draw $\overline{BF}$ so that $m\angle ABF = 20°$; then draw $\overline{FE}$ (Figure 3). In $\triangle ABE$, $mAEB = 50°$ (sum of measures of the angles of a triangle is 180°) therefore $\triangle ABE$ is isosceles and $AB = EB$. (I)

Similarly, $\triangle FAB$ is isosceles, since $m\angle AFB = m\angle FAB = 80°$. Thus $AB = FB$. (II)

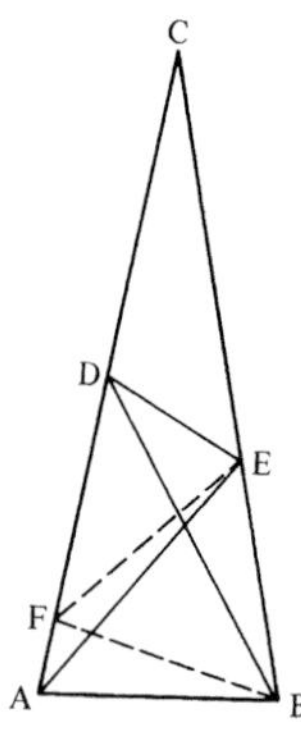

FIGURE 3

From (I) and (II), $EB = FB$. Since $m\angle FBE = 60°$, $\triangle FBE$ is equilateral and $EB = FB = FE$. (III)

Now, in $\triangle DFB$, $m\angle FDB = 40°$, and $m\angle FBD = m\angle ABD - m\angle ABF = 60° - 20° = 40°$.
Thus $\triangle DFB$ is isosceles and $FD = FB$. (IV)

It then follows from (III) and (IV) that $FE = FD$, making $\triangle FDE$ isosceles, and $m\angle FDE = m\angle FED$. Since $m\angle AFB = 80°$ and $m\angle EFB = 60°$, then $m\angle AFE$, the exterior angle of isosceles ΔFDE, equals 140°, by addition. It follows that $m\angle ADE = 70°$. Therefore, $m\angle EDB = m\angle ADE - m\angle FDB = 70° - 40° = 30°$.

There are various other methods for solving this problem. One source for seven solutions of this problem is *Challenging Problems in Geometry* by A. S. Posamentier and C. T. Salkind, pp. 149–54 (New York: Dover, 1996).

POSTASSESSMENT

Have students discover another solution for the above problem.

Unit 49

Making Discoveries in Mathematics

This activity is intended to permit the student to make discoveries based on observation, and then propose a conclusion.

PERFORMANCE OBJECTIVE

Faced with a mathematical pattern students will state their discoveries and propose a conclusion.

TEACHING STRATEGIES

This activity will be comprised of a series of mathematical mini-activities, each of which will require the student to discover a pattern or relationship and then state his or her conclusion.

1. Select any two consecutive square numbers (e.g., 4 and 9). Give one prime between these two numbers. Repeat this for 10 other pairs of consecutive square numbers. Now try to find a pair of consecutive square numbers that do *not* have a prime number between them. What conclusion can you draw from this experiment?
2. Select any even integer greater than 2. Now express this even integer as the sum of exactly two prime numbers. For example, $8 = 3 + 5$, and $18 = 7 + 11$. Repeat this for at least 25 even integers before you draw any conclusions.
3. Draw *any* triangle. Using a protractor carefully trisect each of the angles of the triangle. Locate the points of intersection of the adjacent angle trisectors as illustrated below.

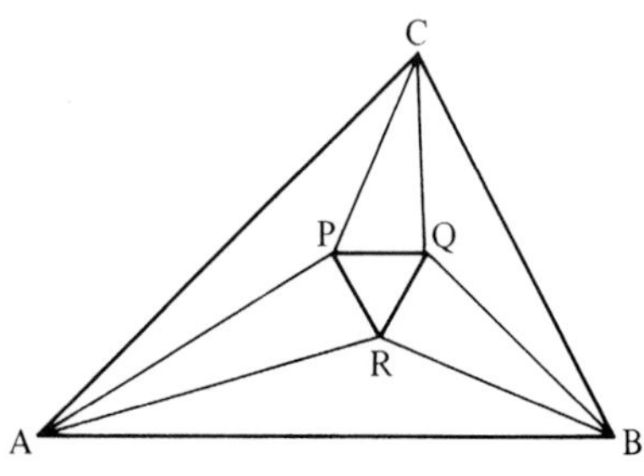

FIGURE 1

Join these three points and inspect the triangle formed. Repeat this construction for at least six different triangles before drawing any conclusion.

4. Draw *any* parallelogram. Construct an equilateral triangle externally on two adjacent sides as shown below. Then join the two remote vertices of the equilateral triangles to each other and to the farthest vertex of the parallelogram. What kind of triangle is formed? Before stating a conclusion repeat this experiment with at least six different parallelograms.

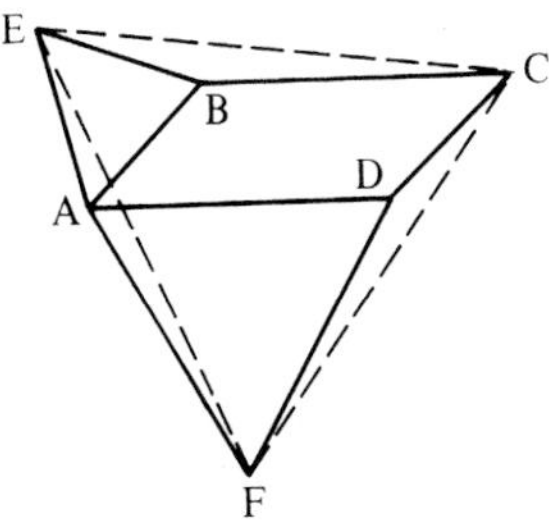

FIGURE 2

Students ought to be able to actually prove this last example. However, the other three examples should not be attempted; 1 and 2 have never been proved, and 3 is extremely difficult to prove.*

You might try to replicate these experiments with others similar to these. It is important for students to learn to trust their intuition in mathematics and be able to draw correct inductive conclusions.

POSTASSESSMENT

Ask students to find the sum of the first 1, 2, 3, 4, 5, 6, . . . 15 odd integers and list the 15 different sums. Then have the students state a logical conclusion.

*Two proofs of this theorem can be found in *Challenging Problems in Geometry* by A. S. Posamentier and C. T. Salkind (New York: Dover, 1996).

Unit 50

Tessellations

PERFORMANCE OBJECTIVES

1. *Given a regular polygon, each student will determine whether it will tessellate a plane.*
2. *Given a combination of various regular polygons, each student will determine whether they will tessellate a plane.*

PREASSESSMENT

Before beginning this lesson explain to students that when polygons are fitted together to cover a plane with no spaces between them and no overlapping, the pattern is called a *tessellation.* (Mention the pattern of tiles on bathroom floors as one of the more common tessellations.) A tessellation made up entirely of congruent regular polygons that meet so that no vertex of one polygon lies on a side of another is referred to as a regular tessellation. Explain further that a network of equilateral triangles, a checkerboard pattern of squares and a hexagonal pattern are the *only* tessellations of regular polygons that exist.

TEACHING STRATEGIES

To mathematically show why the previous three patterns are the only tessellations that fit the description, ask the class to suppose m regular polygons are required to fill the space around one point (where the vertex of the angles of the polygon is situated). If they assume that each regular polygon has n sides, each interior angle of the polygon is equal to $\frac{(n-2)180°}{n}$. Therefore $\frac{m(n-2)180°}{n} = 360°$ and $(m-2)(n-2) = 4$.

Considering the nature of the problem, both integers m and n are greater than 2. If $m = 3$, then $n = 6$. If $m > 3$, then $n < 6$ and since $n > 2$ only the values $n = 3$, $n = 4$, and $n = 5$ need be considered. If $n = 3$, then $m = 6$; if $n = 4$, then $m = 4$. If $n = 5$, m is nonintegral; therefore, the only solutions are $m = 3, n = 6$; $m = 4, n = 4$; $m = 6, n = 3$.Have students suggest more convenient ways of symbolizing these tessellations (6^3, 4^4, 3^6). Use the following diagrams to show that no other regular polygon has an interior angle that will divide 360° (see Figures 1 and 2).

Through further investigation, the range of tessellations may be expanded. Tessellations can also be formed by fitting together two or more kinds of regular polygons, vertex to vertex, in such a way that the same polygons, in the same cyclic order, surround each vertex. These are called *semiregular* tessellations in which there can be no fewer than three and no more than six polygons at any vertex.

Ask students to consider a ternary arrangement (three polygons share one point as vertex). Because the sum of the angles around any vertex must be 360°, a ternary arrangement of polygons of n_1, n_2, and n_3 sides, respectively, will be possible only if

$$\left(\frac{n_1 - 2}{n_1} + \frac{n_2 - 2}{n_2} + \frac{n_3 - 2}{n_3}\right) 180° = 360°.$$

From this we obtain

$$\left(\frac{n_1}{n_1} - \frac{2}{n_1} + \frac{n_2}{n_2} - \frac{2}{n_2} + \frac{n_3}{n_3} - \frac{2}{n_3}\right) 180° = 360°.$$

$$1 + 1 + 1 - 2\left(\frac{1}{n_1} + \frac{1}{n_2} + \frac{1}{n_3}\right) = 2.$$

Therefore, $\frac{1}{n_1} + \frac{1}{n_2} + \frac{1}{n_3} = \frac{1}{2}$.

In a similar way students can find the following conditions for other possible arrangements.

$$\frac{1}{n_1} + \frac{1}{n_2} + \frac{1}{n_3} + \frac{1}{n_4} = 1$$

$$\frac{1}{n_1} + \frac{1}{n_2} + \frac{1}{n_3} + \frac{1}{n_4} + \frac{1}{n_5} = \frac{3}{2}$$

$$\frac{1}{n_1} + \frac{1}{n_2} + \frac{1}{n_3} + \frac{1}{n_4} + \frac{1}{n_5} + \frac{1}{n_6} = 2$$

Following are the 17 possible integer solutions that need be considered (Table 1).

(Solutions 10, 14, and 17 have already been discussed. Solutions 1, 2, 3, 4, 6, and 9 each can be formed at a single vertex, but they cannot be extended to cover the whole plane.) They are made up of different combinations of triangles, squares, hexagons, octagons, and dodecagons.

Any of the remaining solutions can be used as the only type of arrangement in a design covering a whole plane except solution 11, which must be used in conjunction with others, e.g., 5 or 15.

Have the class consider what happens in solution 5. Here two dodecagons and a triangle meet at a vertex. The

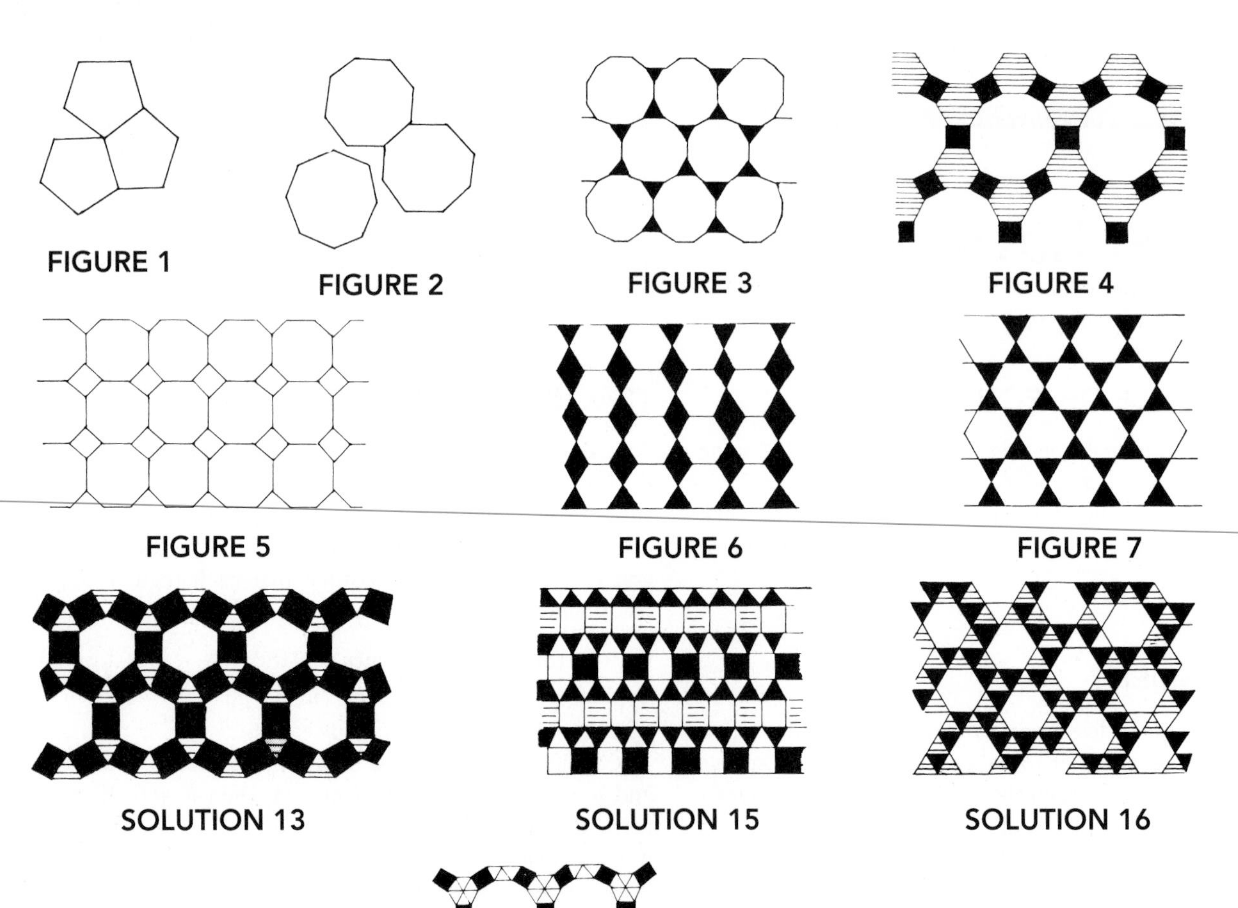

FIGURE 1

FIGURE 2

FIGURE 3

FIGURE 4

FIGURE 5

FIGURE 6

FIGURE 7

SOLUTION 13

SOLUTION 15

SOLUTION 16

SOLUTIONS 11 AND 17

TABLE 1

No.	n_1	n_2	n_3	n_4	n_5	n_6
1	3	7	42			
2	3	8	24			
3	3	9	18			
4	3	10	15			
5	3	12	12			
6	4	5	20			
7	4	6	12			
8	4	8	8			
9	5	5	10			
10	6	6	6			
11	3	3	4	12		
12	3	3	6	6		
13	3	4	4	6		
14	4	4	4	4		
15	3	3	3	4	4	
16	3	3	3	3	6	
17	3	3	3	3	3	3

extended figure can be formed by juxtaposing dodecagons as in Figure 3. The remaining spaces form the triangles.

Solution 7, composed of dodecagons, hexagons, and squares, one at each vertex, gives a more complicated pattern (Figure 4).

A juxtaposition of octagons (Figure 5) forms solution 8. The empty spaces provide the areas needed for the squares.

Two different patterns can be obtained from Solution 12 by the juxtaposition of hexagons. In one the hexagons have edges in common; in the other they have only vertices in common (Figures 6 and 7). The empty spaces form triangles or diamond shapes composed of pairs of triangles.

Call on individual students to determine and draw the patterns for the remaining solutions.

POSTASSESSMENT

1. Which of the following regular polygons will tessellate a plane: (a) a square; (b) a pentagon; (c) an octagon; (d) a hexagon.
2. Which of the following combinations of regular polygons will tessellate a plane: (a) an octagon and a square; (b) a pentagon and a decagon; (c) a hexagon and a triangle.

Unit 51

Introducing the Pythagorean Theorem

This unit is intended for students taking the regular geometry course.

PERFORMANCE OBJECTIVE

Given appropriate measures, the student will use the Pythagorean theorem to solve geometric problems.

In addition, it is expected that student appreciation for the Pythagorean theorem will increase.

PREASSESSMENT

Have your students answer the following question:

> Can a circular table top with a diameter of 9 feet fit through a rectangular door whose dimensions are 6 feet wide and 8 feet high?

TEACHING STRATEGIES

Students will immediately realize that the table top can possibly only fit through the door if it is tilted. Thereupon they will find a need for determining the length of the diagonal of this 6′ by 8′ rectangle. This is where you ought to introduce the Pythagorean theorem. There are over 360 proofs of the Pythagorean theorem available (see Elisha S. Loomis, *The Pythagorean Proposition*, National Council of Teachers of Mathematics, Washington, DC, 1968.) A teacher may select the proof that she feels would be most interesting and intelligible for her particular class. Some proofs rely heavily on algebra while others are purely geometric.

Once the Pythagorean theorem has been proved, the student is ready to apply his knowledge of the theorem to some problems. Surely, he can now find that the length of the diagonal of the door (of the original problem) is 10 feet, and hence conclude that the table top would certainly fit through. There are many other "practical" problems that may be used to offer further application of the Pythagorean theorem. For example, suppose your students wanted to find the diameter of a pipe. All they would have to do is place a carpenter's measuring square as shown in the figure. Then by measuring the length of x, the diameter would merely be 4.828 x. Students should of course be asked to analyze this. The broken lines in the diagram will help in the justification of this situation. Applying the Pythagorean theorem to the right triangle shown:

$$R^2 + R^2 = (R + x)^2, \text{ or } R = x(1 + \sqrt{2}).$$

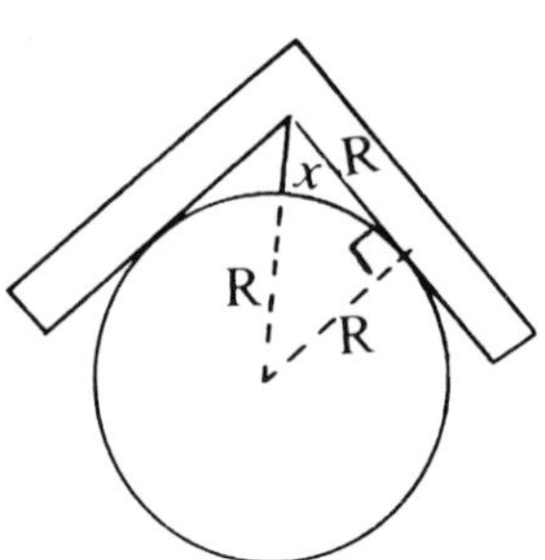

Another problem the students might solve is that of finding the original diameter of broken plate where only a segment of the circle remains. Once again the diagram below depicts the situation: The lengths AB and CD are measurable, and the broken lines are provided only for a discussion of the solution. Let AB $= x$, CD $= y$ and OB (the radius to be found) $=$ R. Thus OD $=$ R $- y$ and by the Pythagorean theorem (in $\triangle$ODB) $(R - y)^2 + \frac{x^2}{4} = R^2$, and then $R = \frac{y}{2} + \frac{x^2}{8y}$ so that the diameter (in terms of the measurable lengths x and y) is $y + \frac{x^2}{4y}$.

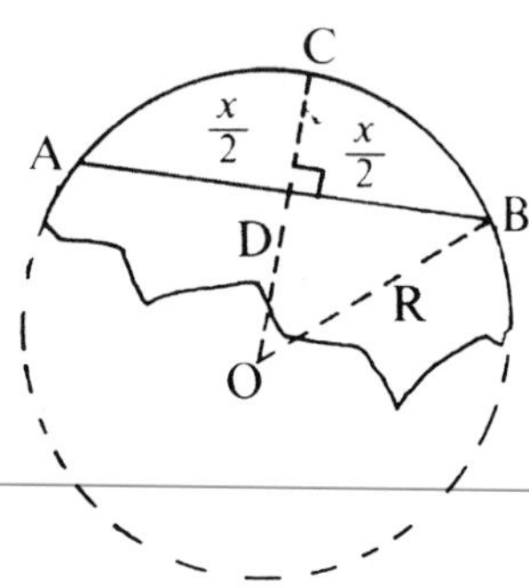

From a strictly geometric point of view, there are some rather interesting relationships which may be proved by applying the Pythagorean theorem. You may wish to present some of these to your class as further application of this theorem.

1. If E is any point on altitude $\overline{AD}$, then $(AC)^2 - (CE)^2 = (AB)^2 - (EB)^2$.

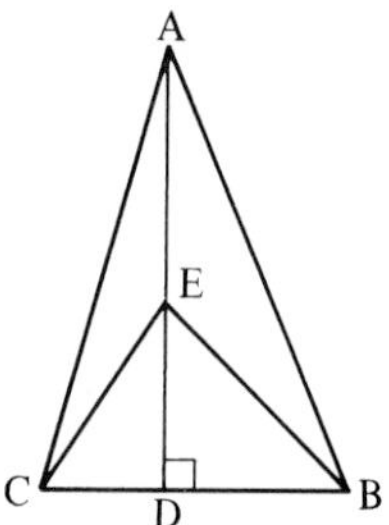

2. If medians $\overline{AD}$ and $\overline{BE}$ of $\triangle$ABC are perpendicular, then $AB = \sqrt{\frac{(AC)^2 + (BC)^2}{5}}$.
3. If from any point inside a triangle, perpendiculars are drawn to the sides of the triangle, the sum of the squares of the measures of every other segment of the sides so formed equals the sum of the squares of the remaining three segments. That is in $\triangle$ABC below:

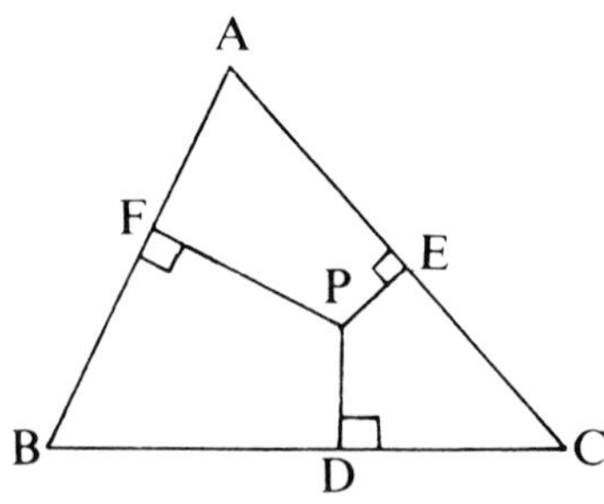

$$(BD)^2 + (CE)^2 + (AF)^2 = (DC)^2 + (EA)^2 + (FB)^2.$$

4. If $\overline{AD}$, $\overline{BE}$, and $\overline{CF}$ are medians of $\triangle$ABC,
   a. then $\frac{3}{4}[(AB)^2 + (BC)^2 + (CA)^2]$
   $= (AD)^2 + (BE)^2 + (CF)^2$.
   b. then $5(AB)^2 = 4(AE)^2 + (BE)^2$, if $m\angle C = 90$.

The complete solutions of these problems and many other more challenging problems can be found in *Challenging Problems in Geometry* by Alfred S. Posamentier and Charles T. Salkind (New York : Dover, 1996).

Once students have a fair command of this celebrated theorem, they are ready to consider a generalization of it.

To this juncture the students have considered the Pythagorean theorem as $a^2 + b^2 = c^2$, where a and b represented the *lengths* of the legs of a right triangle and c represented the *length* of its hypotenuse. However this statement could also be interpreted to mean the following: "The sum of the *areas* of the squares on the legs of a right triangle equals the *area* of the square on the hypotenuse." For the right triangle below $\mathcal{A}\, S_a + \mathcal{A}\, S_b = \mathcal{A}\, S_c$ ($\mathcal{A}$ represents "area of").

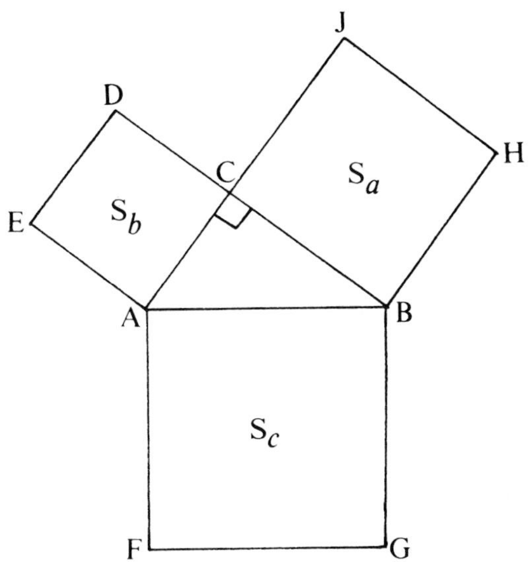

Now have students replace these squares with semicircles with diameters $\overline{BC}$, $\overline{AC}$, and $\overline{AB}$, or have them replace the squares with any similar polygons so that the corresponding sides are on the sides of $\triangle ABC$.

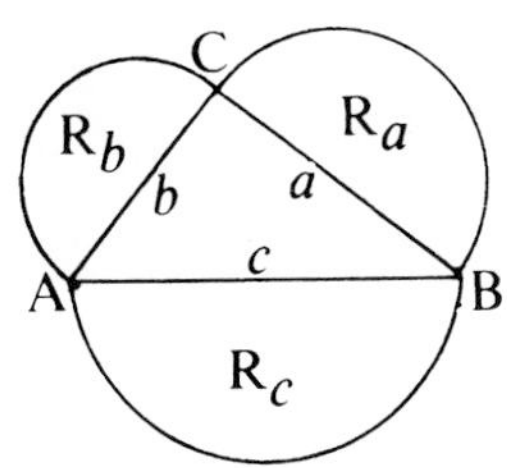

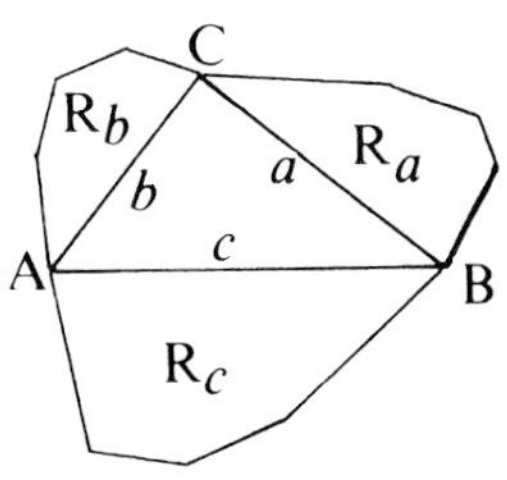

From a basic area relationship:

$$\frac{\mathcal{A}R_a}{\mathcal{A}R_c} = \frac{a^2}{c^2} \text{ and } \frac{R_b}{R_c} = \frac{b^2}{c^2}$$

$$\text{Then } \frac{\mathcal{A}R_a + \mathcal{A}R_b}{\mathcal{A}R_c} = \frac{a^2 + b^2}{c^2}$$

However, by the Pythagorean theorem: $a^2 + b^2 = c^2$ so that $\frac{\mathcal{A}R_a + \mathcal{A}R_b}{\mathcal{A}R_c} = 1$, and $\mathcal{A}R_a + \mathcal{A}R_b = \mathcal{A}R_c$.
The interesting significance of this extension of the Pythagorean theorem ought to be highlighted. Then have students pose other extensions.

Before leaving the geometric discussion of the Pythagorean theorem, you might wish to show students how the converse of this theorem can be used to determine whether an angle of a triangle is acute, right or obtuse, given the lengths of the sides of the triangle.

That is,

if $a^2 + b^2 = c^2, \angle C$ is a right angle;
if $a^2 + b^2 > c^2, \angle C$ is acute;
if $a^2 + b^2 < c^2, \angle C$ is obtuse.

These relationships should prove to be quite fascinating and useful to the students.

Having considered the Pythagorean theorem from a geometric standpoint, it should be interesting to consider this theorem from a number theoretic point of view. A *Pythagorean Triple*, written as (a, b, c), is a set of three positive integers a, b, and c, where $a^2 + b^2 = c^2$. For any Pythagorean Triple (a, b, c) and any positive integer k, (ka, kb, kc) is also a triple. Your students should be able to prove this.

A *Primitive Pythagorean Triple* is a Pythagorean Triple whose first two members are *relatively prime*, one even and the other odd. Introduce this: where $a^2 + b^2 = c^2$ (and m and n are natural numbers, and $m > n$), $a = m^2 - n^2$, $b = 2mn$ and $c = m^2 + n^2$. (For a development of these relationships, see W. Sierpinski, *Pythagorean Triangles*. New York: Yeshiva University Press, 1962.) After setting up a table such as the following, students will begin to conjecture about properties of m and n that generate specific types of Pythagorean Triples. Students will also begin to group different types of Pythagorean Triples.

m	n	$m^2 - n^2$	$2mn$	$m^2 + n^2$
2	1	3	4	5
3	2	5	12	13
4	1	15	8	17
4	3	7	24	25
5	4	9	40	41
3	1	8	6	10
5	2	21	20	29

Some questions to anticipate are: What must be true about m and n in order for (a, b, c) to be a Primitive Pythagorean Triple? Can c of this triple ever be even? Why must the even member of a Primitive Pythagorean Triple be divisible by 4? What must be true about m and n in order that the third member of a Primitive Pythagorean Triple exceed one of the other members by 1? Why is one side of a Primitive Pythagorean Triple always divisible by 5? And why is the product of the three members of any Pythagorean Triple divisible by 60?

In a short while students will begin to probe the parity of numbers and the relationships of Pythagorean Triples. This genuine interest brought about by a rather elementary and superficial introduction to a topic in number theory may be the beginning of a student's investigation into a heretofore unfamiliar field.

Thus a study of the Pythagorean theorem has a wide range of possibilities for interesting your students. *You* must take the initiative of introducing these variations on the theme. If this is properly done, your students will carry these endeavors further.

POSTASSESSMENT

1. Have students explain why the following "Proof Without Words" shows how some paper folding can prove the Pythagorean theorem.

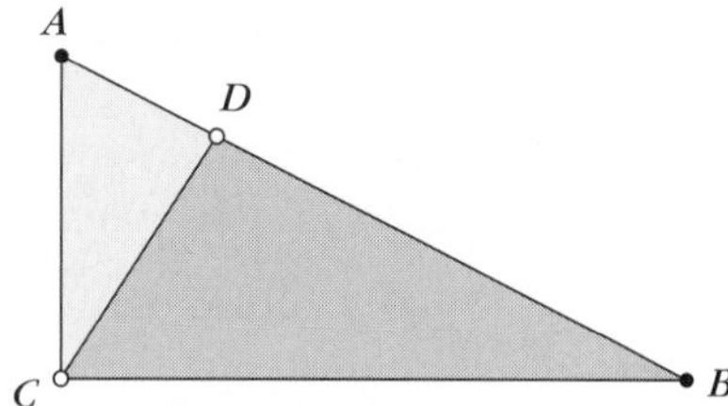

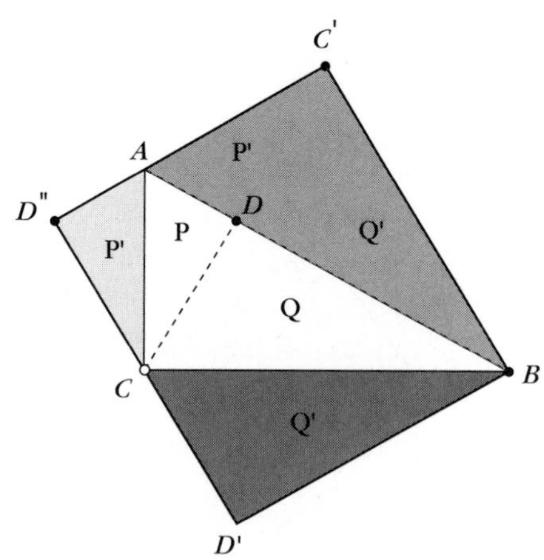

2. Have students show why one member of a primitive Pythagorean triple must always be even.
3. Have student show why the product of a primitive Pythagorean triple is always a multiple of 60.

REFERENCES

Posamentier, A. S. *Math Wonders To Inspire Teachers and Students.* Alexandria, VA: Association for Supervision and Curriculum Development, 2003.

Posamentier, A. S., J. H. Banks, and R. L. Bannister. *Geometry, Its Elements and Structure,* 2d ed. New York: McGraw-Hill, 1977.

Unit 52

Trisection Revisited

PERFORMANCE OBJECTIVES

1. *Students will trisect a given angle using any of the four methods presented.*
2. *Students will prove the four methods of trisection.*

PREASSESSMENT

Students should have a working knowledge of algebra. They should also have mastered constructions commonly taught in high school geometry and proofs of those constructions.

TEACHING STRATEGIES

After demonstrating and proving the following construction, discuss why it is not really a solution to the ancient problem of trisecting an angle using only Euclidean tools.

Given $\angle AOB_0$ with $m\angle AOB_0 = x$
Construct $\angle AOB_n$ such that $m\angle AOB_n = 2x/3$

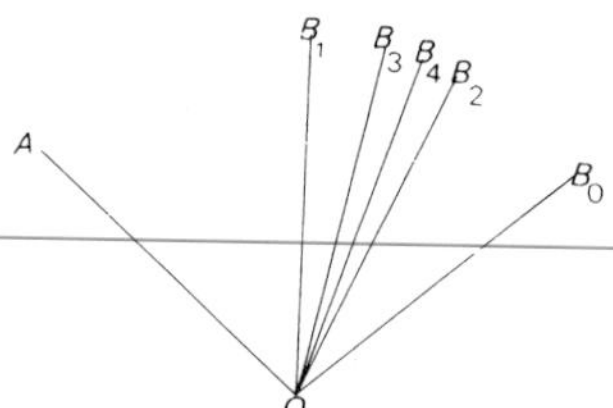

FIGURE 1

Construction and Proof

1. Construct $\overline{OB_1}$, the bisector of $\angle AOB_0$ then $m\angle AOB_1 = x - \frac{1}{2}x$.
2. Construct $\overline{OB_2}$, the bisector of $\angle B_1OB_0$ then $m\angle AOB_2 = x - \frac{1}{2}x + \frac{1}{4}x$.
3. Construct $\overline{OB_3}$, the bisector of $\angle B_1OB_2$ then $m\angle AOB_3 = x - \frac{1}{2}x + \frac{1}{4}x - \frac{1}{8}x$.

4. Construct $\overline{OB_4}$, the bisector of $\angle B_3OB_2$ then $m\angle AOB_4 = x - \frac{1}{2}x + \frac{1}{4}x - \frac{1}{8}x + \frac{1}{16}x.$

5. Continuing in this fashion we will reach $m\angle AOB_n = x - \frac{1}{2}x + \frac{1}{4}x - \frac{1}{8}x + \ldots \pm \left(\frac{1}{2}\right)^n x.$

   Then we multiply by $\left(\frac{1}{2}\right)$ to obtain $\left(\frac{1}{2}\right)m\angle AOB_n$ $= \frac{1}{2}x - \frac{1}{4}x + \frac{1}{8}x - \frac{1}{16}x + \ldots \pm \left(\frac{1}{2}\right)^{n+1} x.$

   Now we add the second equation to the first to get

$$\left(\frac{3}{2}\right)m\angle AOB_n = x \pm \left(\frac{1}{2}\right)^{n+1} x$$

$$m\angle AOB_n = \frac{2x}{3}\left[1 \pm \left(\frac{1}{2}\right)^{n+1}\right].$$

6. Now we observe that as n increases to infinity (which corresponds to carrying out an *infinite number* of construction operations) the term $\left(\frac{1}{2}\right)^{n+1}$ approaches zero. Then $m\angle AOB_n$ approaches $\frac{2x}{3}$.

The second construction adds to the Euclidean tools a strange looking device called a *tomahawk* (first published by Bergery in the third edition of *Geometrie Appliquee al' Industrie*, Metz, 1835).

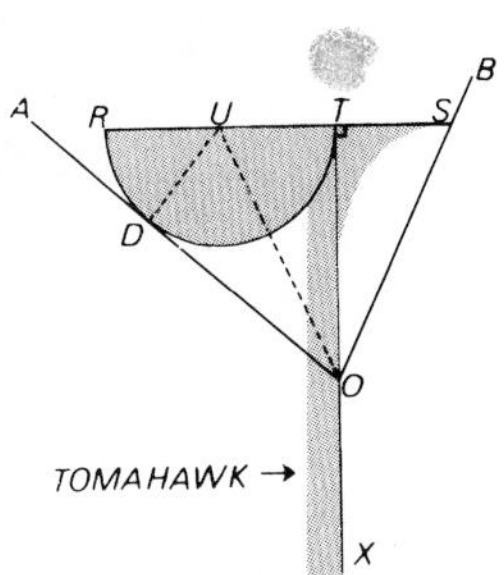

FIGURE 2

To construct a tomahawk, start with a line segment $\overline{RS}$ trisected at U and T. Draw a semicircle about U with radius $\overline{UT}$ and draw $\overline{TX}$ perpendicular to $\overline{RS}$. Complete the instrument as shown in the diagram.

To trisect any $\angle AOB$, simply place the implement on the angle so that S falls on $\overline{OB}$, $\overline{TX}$ passes through vertex O, and the semicircle is tangent to $\overline{AO}$ at some point, say D. Then, since we may easily show that $\triangle DOU \cong \triangle TOU \cong \triangle TOS$, we have $m\angle DOU = m\angle TOU = m\angle TOS = \frac{1}{3}m\angle AOB.$

The third construction is implied by a theorem given by Archimedes. In it we use a straightedge on which a line segment has been marked. This extension of Euclidean tools makes possible an *insertion principle trisection*.

To demonstrate the insertion principle to students, have them try the following problem using Euclidean tools.

Given $\overline{MN}$ with curves q and n (such that the smallest distance between q and n is $\leq$ MN) and point O not on q or n.

Construct a line through O that intersects q and n at M_1 and N_1, respectively, so that $M_1N_1 = MN$.

Except for certain special cases, this problem is impossible using only Euclidean tools. Now have students mark a line segment on their straightedges whose measure is equal to MN. It is now a simple matter to adjust the marked straightedge until it describes a line through O with the distance between the two intersections equal to MN.

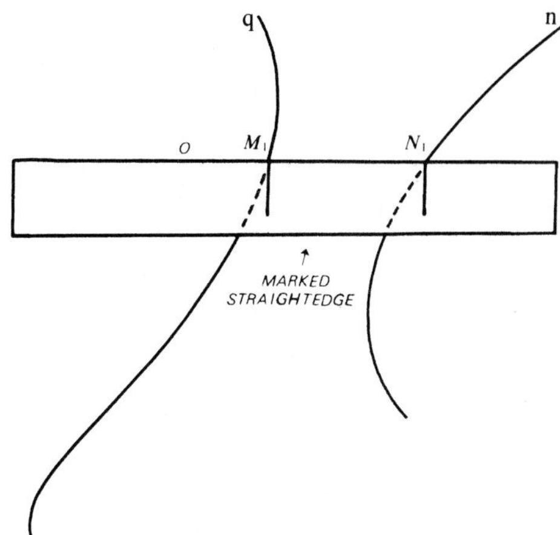

FIGURE 3

Now students are ready for the insertion principle trisection.

Given Circle O with central $\angle AOB$.

Construct $\angle ADB$ so that $m\angle ADB = \frac{1}{3}m\angle AOB$.

Construction

1. Draw $\overrightarrow{AO}$.
2. Mark AO on a straightedge.
3. Using the insertion principle draw $\overline{BD}$ such that D is on $\overrightarrow{AO}$ and $\overline{BD}$ intersects circle O at C with $\overline{AO} \cong \overline{CD}$. Then $m\angle ADB = \frac{1}{3}m\angle AOB$.

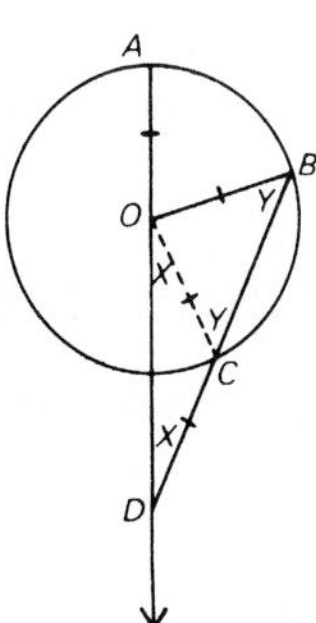

FIGURE 4

Proof

1. Draw $\overline{OC}$.
2. By construction $\overline{AO} \cong \overline{BO} \cong \overline{CO} \cong \overline{DC}$ (since the first three are radii of circle O and the last was constructed to be congruent to $\overline{AO}$).

3. $\triangle OCD$ and $\triangle BOC$ are isosceles.
4. Therefore $m\angle DOC = m\angle CDO = x$ and $m\angle OCB = m\angle OBC = y$.
5. Since $\angle OCB$ is the exterior angle of $\triangle OCD$, $m\angle OCB = m\angle DOC + m\angle CDO = 2x$ or $y = 2x$.
6. Similarly since $\angle AOB$ is the exterior angle of $\triangle OBD$, $m\angle AOB = m\angle ADB + m\angle OBD = x + 2x = 3x$.
7. Thus, $m\angle ADB = \frac{1}{3}m\angle AOB$.

Ceva's method of trisection (the last of this unit) utilizes a device that consists of four hinged straightedges. In the diagram of Ceva's linkage, points C, D, E, and O are pivots such that the figure CDEO is a rhombus. To trisect a given angle A′O′B′ one must first draw the circle about the vertex O′ with radius equal to the length of a side of the rhombus CDEO. Ceva's instrument is then placed on the angle so that O and O′ coincide. It is then adjusted until $\overrightarrow{DC}$ and $\overrightarrow{DE}$ go through the points where $\overline{OA'}$ and $\overline{OB'}$ intersect the circle, points A and B, respectively. Then

$$m\angle AOF = m\angle FOG = m\angle GOB = \left(\frac{1}{3}\right)m\angle AOB.$$

The proof uses the rhombus CDEO to obtain $m\angle ACG = m\angle COE = m\angle FEB = m\angle CDE = x$. Then

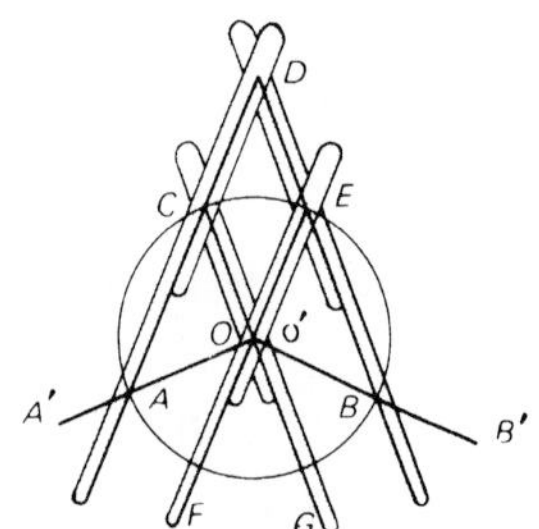

FIGURE 5

$m\angle FOG = x$. Noting that points C and E are on the circle, we have $\angle ACG$ and $\angle FEB$ inscribed in the circle. Then $m\angle ACG = x = \frac{1}{2}m\angle AOG$ and $m\angle FEB = x = \frac{1}{2}m\angle FOB$, which gives us $2x = m\angle AOG$ and $2x = m\angle FOB$. Clearly then $m\angle AOF = m\angle FOG = m\angle GOB = \frac{1}{3}m\angle AOB$.

POSTASSESSMENT

1. Prove the *tomahawk* trisection method valid.
2. Trisect any given arbitrary angle using any two of the methods presented in this unit.

Unit 53

Proving Lines Concurrent

This unit will present the student with a theorem that is quite useful in some cases when proving lines concurrent.

PERFORMANCE OBJECTIVE

Given appropriate problems, students will apply Ceva's theorem to prove lines concurrent.

PREASSESSMENT

Have students try to prove any of the following:

1. Prove that the medians of a triangle are concurrent.
2. Prove that the angle bisectors of a triangle are concurrent.
3. Prove that the altitudes of a triangle are concurrent.

TEACHING STRATEGIES

An above-average geometry student should, given enough time, be able to prove some of these theorems. The proofs they would normally attempt (synthetically) are among the more difficult in the high school geometry course. Challenging students with these rather difficult problems sets the stage for the introduction of a theorem, that will permit these problems to be done quite easily.

This theorem, first published in 1678 by the Italian mathematician Giovanni Ceva, is stated as follows:

> Three lines drawn from the vertices A, B, and C of $\triangle ABC$ meeting the opposite sides in points L, M, and N, respectively, are concurrent if and only if
>
> $$\frac{AN}{NB}\cdot\frac{BL}{LC}\cdot\frac{CM}{MA} = 1$$

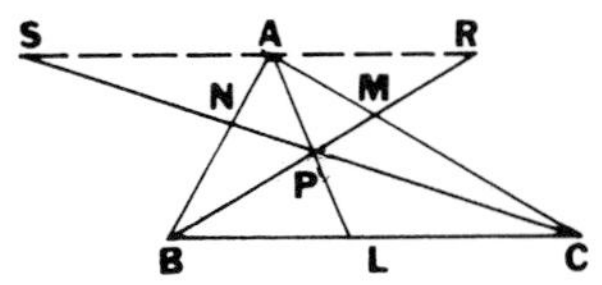

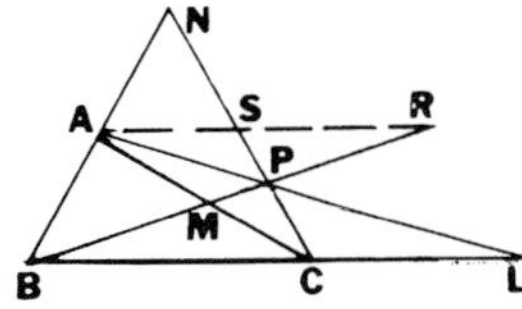

Note: There are two cases: The three lines meeting inside or outside the given triangle.

Before applying this theorem to the problems posed earlier, it might be wise to prove the theorem.

Given: $\triangle ABC$, with N on $\overleftrightarrow{AB}$, M on $\overleftrightarrow{AC}$, and L on $\overleftrightarrow{BC}$; also $\overleftrightarrow{AL}$, $\overleftrightarrow{BM}$, and $\overleftrightarrow{CN}$ are concurrent at P.

Prove: $\frac{AN}{NB} \cdot \frac{BL}{LC} \cdot \frac{CM}{MA} = 1$

Proof: Draw a line through A, parallel to $\overleftrightarrow{BC}$ meeting $\overleftrightarrow{CP}$ at S and $\overleftrightarrow{BP}$ at R.

$$\triangle AMR \sim \triangle CMB$$

$$\text{Therefore } \frac{AM}{MC} = \frac{AR}{CB} \qquad \text{(I)}$$

$$\triangle BNC \sim \triangle ANS$$

$$\text{Therefore } \frac{BN}{NA} = \frac{CB}{SA} \qquad \text{(II)}$$

$$\triangle CLP \sim \triangle SAP$$

$$\text{Therefore } \frac{CL}{SA} = \frac{LP}{AP} \qquad \text{(III)}$$

$$\triangle BLP \sim \triangle RAP$$

$$\text{Therefore } \frac{BL}{RA} = \frac{LP}{AP} \qquad \text{(IV)}$$

From (III) and (IV) we get $\frac{CL}{SA} = \frac{BL}{RA}$, or

$$\frac{CL}{BL} = \frac{SA}{RA} \qquad \text{(V)}$$

Now multiplying (I), (II), and (V) yields

$$\frac{AM}{MC} \cdot \frac{BN}{NA} \cdot \frac{CL}{BL} = \frac{AR}{CB} \cdot \frac{CB}{SA} \cdot \frac{SA}{RA} = 1.$$

Since Ceva's theorem is biconditional, it is necessary to prove the converse of the implication we have just proved.

Given: $\triangle ABC$ with N on $\overleftrightarrow{AB}$, M on $\overleftrightarrow{AC}$, and L on $\overleftrightarrow{BC}$; also

$$\frac{BL}{LC} \cdot \frac{CM}{MA} \cdot \frac{AN}{NB} = 1.$$

Prove: $\overleftrightarrow{AL}$, $\overleftrightarrow{BM}$, and $\overleftrightarrow{CN}$ are concurrent.

Proof: Let $\overleftrightarrow{BM}$ and $\overleftrightarrow{AL}$ meet at P. Let $\overleftrightarrow{CP}$ meet AB at N′. Since $\overleftrightarrow{AL}$, $\overleftrightarrow{BM}$, and $\overleftrightarrow{CN}$ are concurrent, by the part of Ceva's theorem we have already proved, we get:

$$\frac{BL}{LC} \cdot \frac{CM}{MA} \cdot \frac{AN'}{N'B} = 1.$$

However $\frac{BL}{LC} \cdot \frac{CM}{MA} \cdot \frac{AN}{NB} = 1$ (given).

Therefore $\frac{AN'}{N'B} = \frac{AN}{NB}$, so that N and N′ must coincide.

Thus the three lines are concurrent.

Students should now be ready to apply Ceva's theorem to the three problems posed earlier.

1. Prove that the medians of a triangle are concurrent.

   Proof: In $\triangle ABC$, $\overline{AL}$, $\overline{BM}$, and $\overline{CN}$ are medians (see figure below).

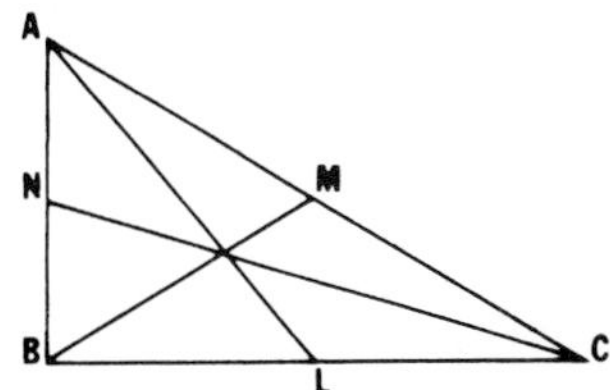

Therefore, AN = NB, BL = LC, and CM = MA. By multiplication (AN)(BL)(MC) = (NB)(LC)(MA), or $\frac{AN}{NB} \cdot \frac{BL}{LC} \cdot \frac{CM}{MA} = 1$.

Thus by Ceva's theorem $\overleftrightarrow{AL}$, $\overleftrightarrow{BM}$, and $\overleftrightarrow{CN}$ are concurrent.

2. Prove that the angle bisectors of a triangle are concurrent.

   Proof: In $\triangle ABC$, $\overline{AL}$, $\overline{BM}$, and $\overline{CN}$ are interior angle bisectors (see figure below).

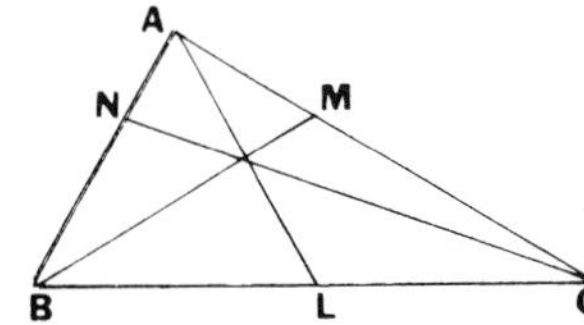

Since an angle bisector of a triangle partitions the opposite side into segments proportional to the two remaining sides of the triangle, it follows that

$$\frac{AN}{NB} = \frac{AC}{BC}, \frac{BL}{LC} = \frac{AB}{AC}, \text{ and } \frac{CM}{MA} = \frac{BC}{AB}.$$

Then by multiplying

$$\frac{AN}{NB} \cdot \frac{BL}{LC} \cdot \frac{CM}{MA} = \frac{AC}{BC} \cdot \frac{AB}{AC} \cdot \frac{BC}{AB} = 1.$$

Thus by Ceva's theorem the three angle bisectors are concurrent.

3. Prove that the altitudes of a triangle are concurrent.

   Proof: In $\triangle ABC$, $\overline{AL}$, $\overline{BM}$, and $\overline{CN}$ are altitudes (see figure below).

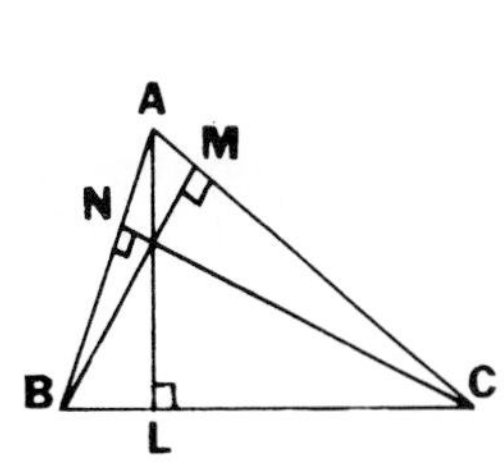

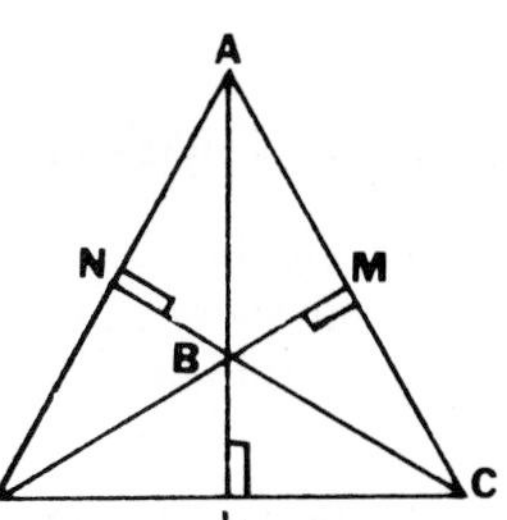

$$\triangle ANC \sim \triangle AMB, \text{ and } \frac{AN}{MA} = \frac{AC}{AB}$$

$$\triangle BLA \sim \triangle BNC, \text{ and } \frac{BL}{NB} = \frac{AB}{BC}$$

$$\triangle CMB \sim \triangle CLA, \text{ and } \frac{CM}{LC} = \frac{BC}{AC}$$

By multiplying these three fractions, we get

$$\frac{AN}{MA}\cdot\frac{BL}{NB}\cdot\frac{CM}{LC}=\frac{AC}{AB}\cdot\frac{AB}{BC}\cdot\frac{BC}{AC}=1.$$

Thus by Ceva's theorem the altitudes are concurrent.

These are some of the simpler applications of Ceva's theorem. One source for finding more applications of Ceva's theorem is *Challenging Problems in Geometry* by A. S. Posamentier and C. T. Salkind, (New York: Dover, 1996).

POSTASSESSMENT

1. Have students use Ceva's theorem to prove that when $\triangle ABC$ has points P, Q, and R on sides $\overline{AB}$, $\overline{AC}$, and $\overline{BC}$, respectively, and when $\frac{AQ}{QC}=\frac{BR}{RC}=2$, and $AP = PB$, it follows that $\overline{AR}$, $\overline{BQ}$, and $\overline{CP}$ are concurrent.

2. $\triangle ABC$ cuts a circle at points E, E′, D, D′, F, F′ (see figure below). Prove that if $\overline{AD}$, $\overline{BF}$, and $\overline{CE}$ are concurrent, then $\overline{AD'}$, $\overline{BF'}$, and $\overline{CE'}$ are also concurrent.

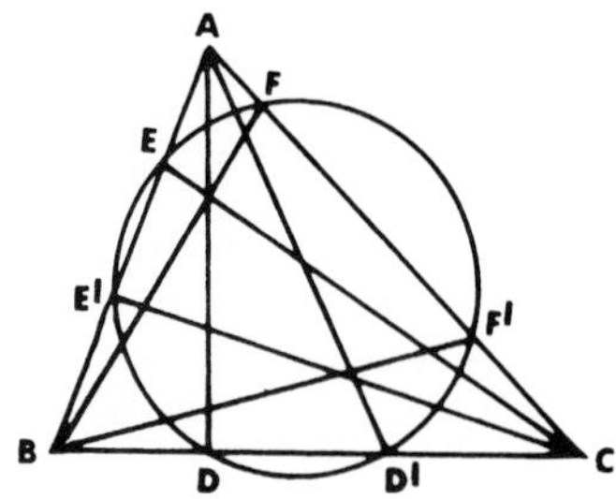

REFERENCE

Posamentier, A. S. *Advanced Euclidean Geometry: Excursions for Secondary Teachers and Students*. New York, NY: John Wiley Publishing, 2002. (Contains lots of applications of Ceva's theorem.)

Unit 54

Squares

This unit will strengthen students' skills at proving quadrilaterals to be squares in addition to revisiting the topic of concurrency.

PERFORMANCE OBJECTIVE

Students will explain a method for proving concurrency.

PREASSESSMENT

Students should be familiar with the various properties of a square and should have had some experience in proving quadrilaterals to be squares.

TEACHING STRATEGIES

Have students construct a square externally on each side of a given parallelogram (see figure below). Have them locate the center of each square by drawing the diagonals. Ask the class what figure they believe will result by joining the centers of consecutive squares. Natural curiosity should motivate them to try to prove that PQRS is a square.

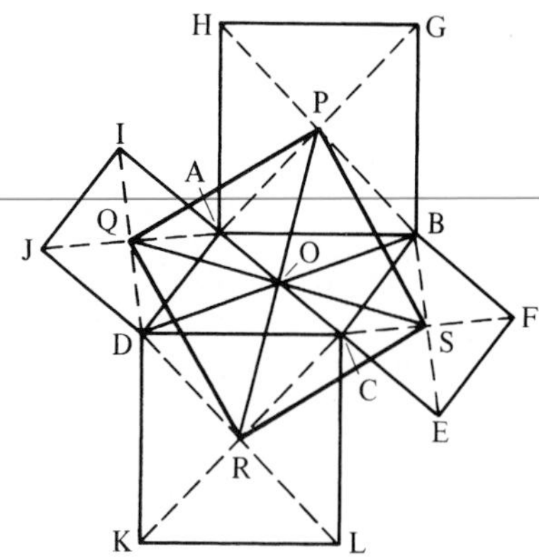

Proof:

ABCD is a parallelogram.

Points *P*, *Q*, *R*, and *S* are the centers of the four squares *ABGH*, *DAIJ*, *DCLK*, and *CBFE*, respectively. $PA = DR$ and $AQ = QD$ (each is one-half a diagonal).

$\angle ADC$ is supplementary to $\angle DAB$, and $\angle IAH$ is supplementary to $\angle DAB$ (since $\angle IAD$ and $\angle HAB$ are right angles). Therefore $\angle ADC \cong \angle IAH$.

Since m$\angle RDC$ = m$\angle QDA$ = m$\angle HAP$ = m$\angle QAI$ = 45°, $\angle RDQ \cong \angle QAP$. Thus $\triangle RDQ \cong \triangle PAQ$ (SAS) and $QR = QP$.

In a similar fashion, it may be proved that $QP = PS$ and $PS = RS$.

Therefore, $PQRS$ is a rhombus.

Since $\Delta RDQ \cong \Delta PAQ$, $\angle DQR \cong \angle AQP$; therefore, $PQR \cong \angle DQA$ (by addition).

Since $\angle DQA \cong$ right angle, $\angle PQR \cong$ right angle, and $PQRS$ is a square.

Careful drawing of the figure above should indicate that the diagonals of square $PQRS$ and the diagonals of parallelogram $ABCD$ are concurrent. This proof deserves special attention since it illustrates an all too often neglected skill: proving concurrency.

To prove that the diagonals of square $PQRS$ are concurrent with the diagonals of parallelogram $ABCD$, we must prove that a diagonal of the square and a diagonal of the parallelogram bisect each other. In other words, we prove that the diagonals of the square and the diagonals of the parallelogram all share the same midpoint, (i.e., point O).

$BAC \cong \angle ACD$, and m$\angle PAB$ = m$\angle RCD$ = 45, therefore $\angle PAC \cong \angle RCA$.

Since $\angle AOP \cong \angle COR$ and $AP = CR$, $\triangle AOP \cong \triangle COR$ (SAA).

Thus, $AO = CO$, and $PO = RO$.

Since $\overline{DB}$ passes through the midpoint of $\overline{AC}$, (diagonals bisect each other) and similarly, $\overline{QS}$ passes through the midpoint of $\overline{PR}$, and since $\overline{AC}$ and $\overline{PR}$ share the same midpoint (i.e., O), we have shown that $\overline{AC}$, $\overline{PR}$, $\overline{DB}$, and $\overline{QS}$ are concurrent (i.e., all pass through point O).

POSTASSESSMENT

Ask students to explain a method for proving lines concurrent. It is expected that they will explain the method used in this lesson.

Unit 55

Proving Points Collinear

This unit will present the student with a theorem that is quite useful in certain cases, when proving points collinear.

PERFORMANCE OBJECTIVE

Given appropriate problems students will apply Menelaus' theorem to prove points collinear.

PREASSESSMENT

Have students try to prove that the interior angle bisectors of two angles of a nonisosceles triangle and the exterior angle bisector of the third angle meet the opposite sides in three collinear points.

TEACHING STRATEGIES

The average student of high school geometry is not properly trained or equipped to prove points collinear. Thus, in most cases you will find the preassessment problem beyond student ability. However, this unit will provide you with sufficient student interest to introduce a theorem that will provide a simple solution.

This theorem, originally credited to Menelaus of Alexandria (about 100 a.d.) is particularly useful in proving points collinear. It states that

Points P, Q, and R on sides $\overline{AC}$, $\overline{AB}$, and $\overline{BC}$ of $\triangle ABC$ are collinear if and only if

$$\frac{AQ}{QB}\cdot\frac{BR}{RC}\cdot\frac{CP}{PA} = 1.$$

This is a two part (biconditional) proof.

Part I to prove $\frac{AQ}{QB}\cdot\frac{BR}{RC}\cdot\frac{CP}{PA} = 1$

Proof: Points P, Q, and R are collinear. Consider the line through C, parallel to $\overline{AB}$, and meeting $\overline{PQR}$ at D.

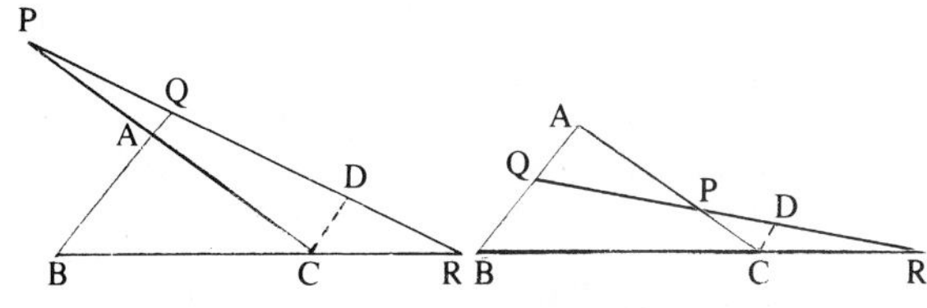

Since $\triangle DCR \sim \triangle QBR$, $\frac{DC}{QB} = \frac{RC}{BR}$ or $DC = \frac{(QB)(RC)}{BR}$. (a)

Similarly, since $\triangle PDC \sim \triangle PQA$, $\frac{DC}{AQ} = \frac{CP}{PA}$, or

$DC = \frac{(AQ)(CP)}{PA}$. (b)

From (a) and (b): $\frac{(QB)(RC)}{BR} = \frac{(AQ)(CP)}{PA}$.

Therefore $(QB)(RC)(PA) = (AQ)(CP)(BR)$, which indicates that $\frac{AQ}{QB} \cdot \frac{BR}{RC} \cdot \frac{CP}{PA} = 1$.

Part II involves proving the converse of the implication proved in Part I, since this theorem is biconditional.

Proof: In the figures above let the line through R and Q meet $\overleftrightarrow{AB}$ at P′. Then by the theorem just proved $\frac{AQ}{QB} \cdot \frac{BR}{RC} \cdot \frac{CP'}{P'A} = 1$.

However by hypothesis,

$\frac{AQ}{QB} \cdot \frac{BR}{RC} \cdot \frac{CP}{PA} = 1$.

Therefore $\frac{CP'}{P'A} = \frac{CP}{PA}$ and P and P' must coincide.

At this point students should be ready to apply Menelaus' theorem to the problem presented in the preassessment.

Given: $\triangle ABC$, where $\overline{BM}$ and $\overline{CN}$ are interior angle bisectors and $\overline{AL}$ bisects the exterior angle at A.

Prove: N, M, and L are collinear.

Have students recall the important proportionality theorem about the angle bisector of a triangle.

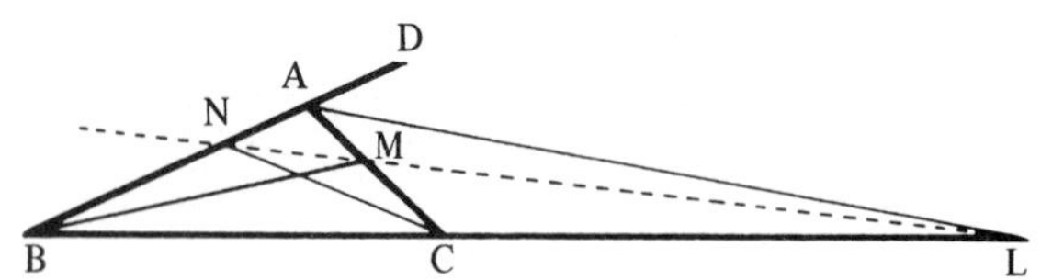

Proof: Since $\overline{BM}$ bisects $\angle ABC$, $\frac{AM}{MC} = \frac{AB}{BC}$.

Since $\overline{CN}$ bisects $\angle ACB$, $\frac{BN}{NA} = \frac{BC}{AC}$.

Since $\overline{AL}$ bisects the exterior angle at A, $\frac{CL}{BL} = \frac{AC}{AB}$.

Therefore by multiplication:

$$\frac{AM}{MC} \cdot \frac{BN}{NA} \cdot \frac{CL}{BL} = \frac{AB}{BC} \cdot \frac{BC}{AC} \cdot \frac{AC}{AB} = 1.$$

Thus, by Menelaus' theorem N, M, and L must be collinear.

To provide further practice applying this useful theorem, have students consider the following problem.

Prove that if tangents to the circumcircle of $\triangle ABC$, at A, B, and C, meet sides $\overleftrightarrow{BC}$, $\overleftrightarrow{AC}$, and $\overleftrightarrow{AB}$ at points P, Q, and R, respectively, then points P, Q, and R are collinear.

Proof: Since $m\angle BAC = \frac{1}{2} m\widehat{BC} = m\angle QBC$, $\triangle ABQ \sim \triangle BCQ$ and $\frac{AQ}{BQ} = \frac{BA}{BC}$, or $\frac{(AQ)^2}{(BQ)^2} = \frac{(BA)^2}{(BC)^2}$. (I)

However $(BQ)^2 = (AQ)(CQ)$. (II)

Substituting (II) into (I) yields $\frac{AQ}{CQ} = \frac{(BA)^2}{(BC)^2}$. (III)

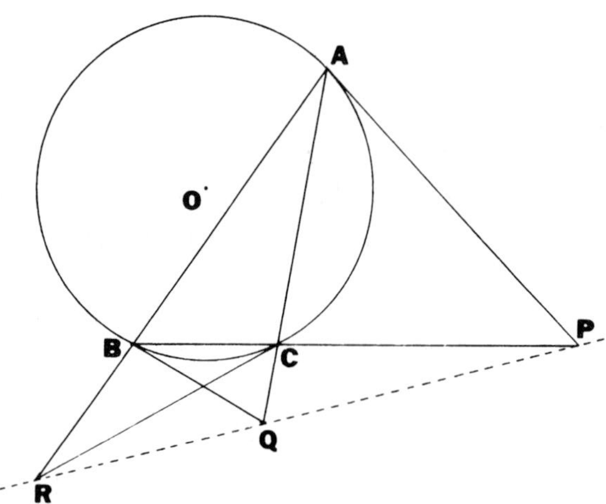

Similarly, $m\angle BCR = \frac{1}{2} m\widehat{BC} = m\angle BAC$; therefore $\triangle CRB \sim \triangle ARC$ and $\frac{CR}{AR} = \frac{BC}{AC}$, or $\frac{(CR)^2}{(AR)^2} = \frac{(BC)^2}{(AC)^2}$. (IV)

However, $(CR)^2 = (AR)(RB)$. (V)

Substituting (V) into (IV) yields

$\frac{RB}{AR} = \frac{(BC)^2}{(AC)^2}$. (VI)

Students should now be asked to use the same scheme to prove $\triangle CAP \sim \triangle ABP$ and in a similar manner obtain

$\frac{PC}{BP} = \frac{(AC)^2}{(BA)^2}$. (VII)

Now multiplying these proportions [i.e., (III), (VI), and (VII)] yields

$$\frac{AQ}{CQ} \cdot \frac{RB}{AR} \cdot \frac{PC}{BP} = \frac{(BA)^2}{(BC)^2} \cdot \frac{(BC)^2}{(AC)^2} \cdot \frac{(AC)^2}{(BA)^2} = 1.$$

Thus, by Menelaus' theorem, P, Q, and R are collinear.

POSTASSESSMENT

Have students use Menelaus' theorem to prove that the exterior angle bisectors of any nonisosceles triangle meet the opposite sides in three collinear points. The figure below should be useful.

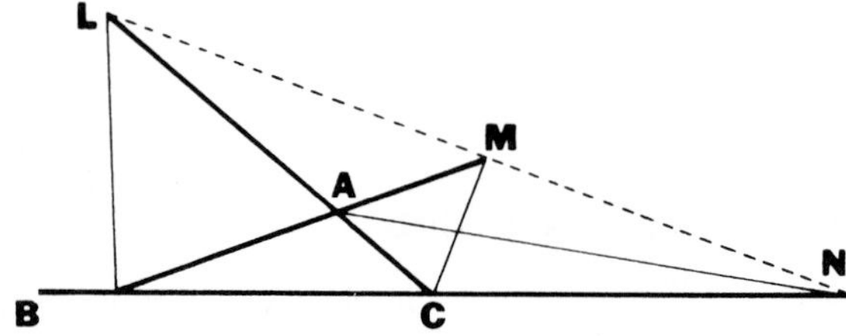

REFERENCES

Posamentier, A. S., and C. T. Salkind. *Challenging Problems in Geometry*. New York: Dover, 1996.

Posamentier, A. S. *Advanced Euclidean Geometry: Excursions for Secondary Teachers and Students*. New York, NY: John Wiley Publishing, 2002.

Unit 56

Angle Measurement with a Circle

This unit presents a rather unusual method for developing the theorems on angle measurement with a circle, normally considered in the tenth-grade geometry course.

PERFORMANCE OBJECTIVES

1. *Given appropriate materials, students will generate the various angle measurement theorems in the manner developed in this unit.*
2. *Given problems that require the use of the theorems discussed in this unit, students will be able to solve them successfully.*

PREASSESSMENT

Students should be familiar with an inscribed angle and the relationship of its measure to that of its intercepted arc.

TEACHING STRATEGIES

In addition to using the usual classroom materials, you should prepare the following:

1. A piece of cardboard with two dark colored pieces of string attached, forming an angle of convenient size.
2. A cardboard circle with an inscribed angle congruent to the "string angle."

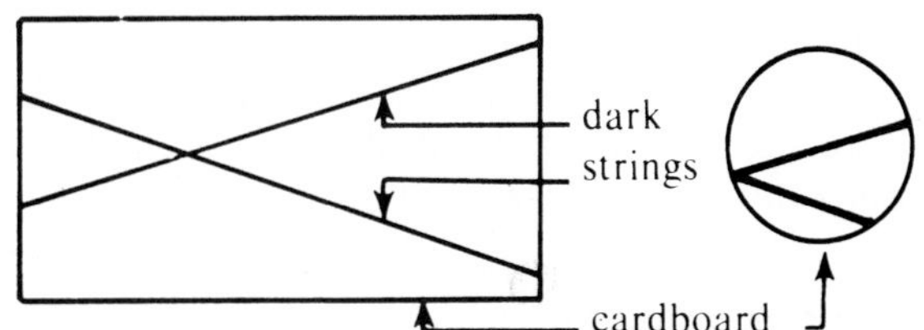

Naturally, it would be best if each student could prepare his or her own set of these materials in order to perform the following activities individually.

Refresh your students' memories about the relationship of an inscribed angle and its intercepted arc. Have them place the circle under the strings so that the two angles coincide:

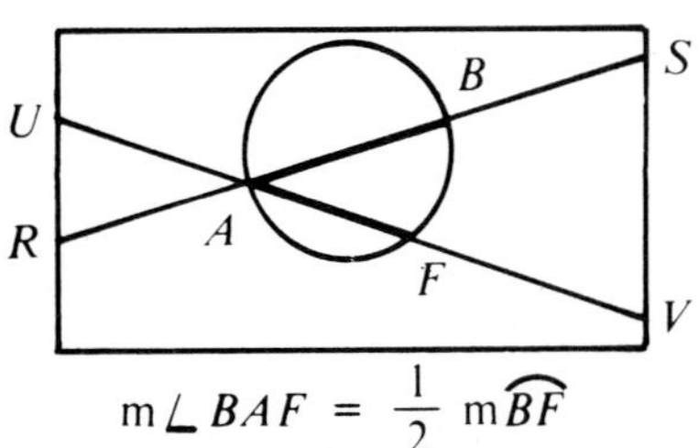

$$m\angle BAF = \frac{1}{2}\, m\widehat{BF}$$

Now have students slide the circle to the position illustrated below, where the rays of $\angle BAF$ are respectively parallel to the rays of the "string angle," $\angle NMQ$, and where the circle is tangent to $\overleftrightarrow{UQV}$ at M.

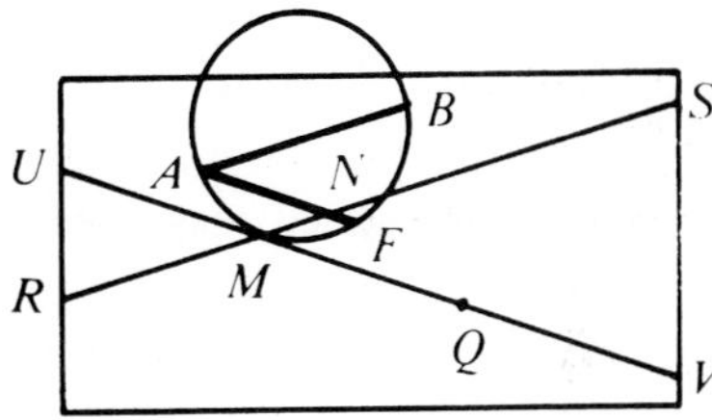

Students should realize that $m\widehat{FM} = m\widehat{AM}$, and $m\widehat{AM} = m\widehat{BN}$ (due to the parallel lines). Therefore $m\widehat{FM} = m\widehat{BN}$. Since $m\angle NMQ = m\angle BAF$, and $m\angle BAF = \frac{1}{2}\, m\widehat{BF} = \frac{1}{2}(m\widehat{BN} + m\widehat{NF}) = \frac{1}{2}(m\widehat{FM} + m\widehat{NF}) = \frac{1}{2}(m\widehat{MN}\ m\angle\ NMQ = \frac{1}{2}\, m\widehat{MN}$. This proves the theorem that *the measure of an angle formed by a tangent and a chord of a circle is one half the measure of its intercepted arc.*

Now have your students slide the circle to a position where the vertex of the string angle is on a $\overline{AF}$ and where $\overline{AB} // \overline{RS}$.

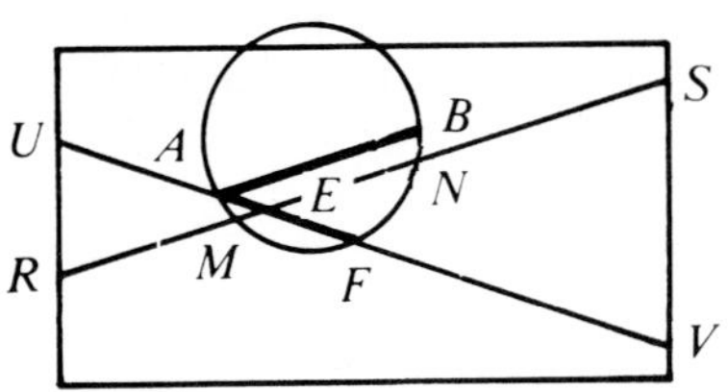

Once again because parallel lines exist here ($\overleftrightarrow{AB} // \overleftrightarrow{MN}$) = $m = \widehat{AM} = m\widehat{BN}$), and $m\angle BAF = m\angle NEF$. The students should now see that $m\angle BAF = \frac{1}{2}m\widehat{BF} = \frac{1}{2}(m\widehat{BN} + m\widehat{NF}) = \frac{1}{2}(m\widehat{AM} + m\widehat{NF})$. They may then conclude that $m\angle NEF = \frac{1}{2}(m\widehat{AM} + m\widehat{NF})$. This proves the theorem that *the measure of an angle formed by two chords intersecting in a point in the interior of a circle is one half the sum of the measures of the arcs intercepted by the angle and its vertical angle.*

To consider the next type of angle, have your students slide the circle to the position illustrated below, where the string angle now appears as an angle formed by two secants.

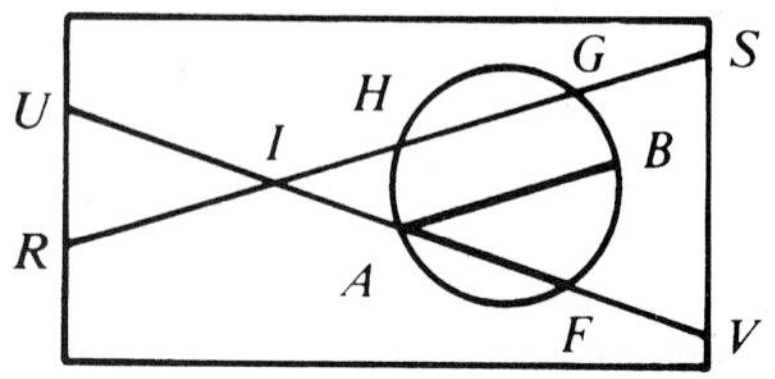

In this new position $\overline{AB} // \overleftrightarrow{GI}$ and $\overline{AF}$ is in $\overleftrightarrow{IF}$. Because $\overline{AB} // \overleftrightarrow{GI}$ $m\widehat{BG} = m\widehat{HA}$, and $m\angle BAF = m\angle GIF$. Have students once again follow the reasoning that $m\angle BAF = \frac{1}{2}m\widehat{BF} = \frac{1}{2}(m\widehat{BF} + m\widehat{BG} - m\widehat{BG} = \frac{1}{2}(m\widehat{BF} + m\widehat{BG} - m\widehat{HA} = \frac{1}{2}(m\widehat{GBF} - m\widehat{HA})$. They may then conclude that $m\angle GIF = \frac{1}{2}(m\widehat{GBF} - m\widehat{HA})$, which proves the theorem that *the measure of an angle formed by two secants intersecting in a point in the exterior of a circle is equal to one half the difference of the measures of the intercepted arcs.*

The next position of the circle will enable students to consider an angle formed by a tangent and a secant intersecting in the exterior of a circle. Have students slide the circle to the position as indicated in the following illustration.

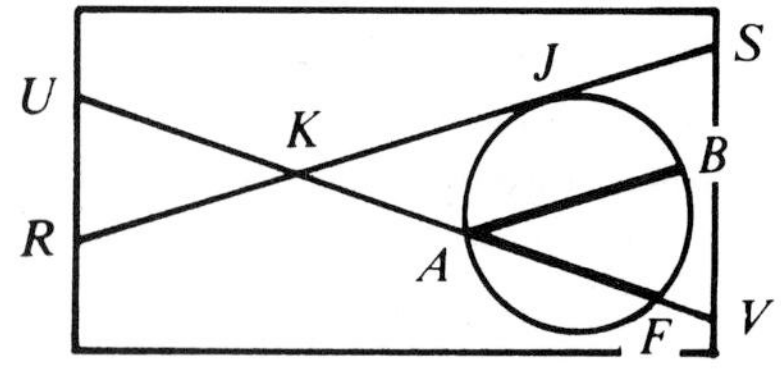

Here $\overline{AB} // \overleftrightarrow{KJS}, \overline{AF}$ is in $\overleftrightarrow{KV}$ and the circle is tangent to $\overline{KS}$ at J. Because $\overline{AB} // \overline{KJS}$, $m\widehat{JA} = m\widehat{JB}$ and $m\angle BAF = m\angle JKF$.

By now students should be able to produce the following without much difficulty: $m\angle BAF = \frac{1}{2}m\widehat{BF} = \frac{1}{2}(m\widehat{BF} + m\widehat{JB} - m\widehat{JB}) = \frac{1}{2}(m\widehat{BF} + m\widehat{JB} - m\widehat{JA} = \frac{1}{2}(m\widehat{JBF} - m\widehat{JA})$. They should then conclude that $m\angle JKF = \frac{1}{2}(m\widehat{JBF} - m\widehat{JA})$, which proves the theorem that *the measure of an angle formed by a secant and a tangent to a circle intersecting in a point exterior to the circle is equal to one half the difference of the measures of the intercepted arcs.*

The last type of angle to be considered is an angle formed by two tangents. To form this angle the circle should be positioned tangent to each of the two strings so that each string is parallel to one of the rays of the angle in the circle.

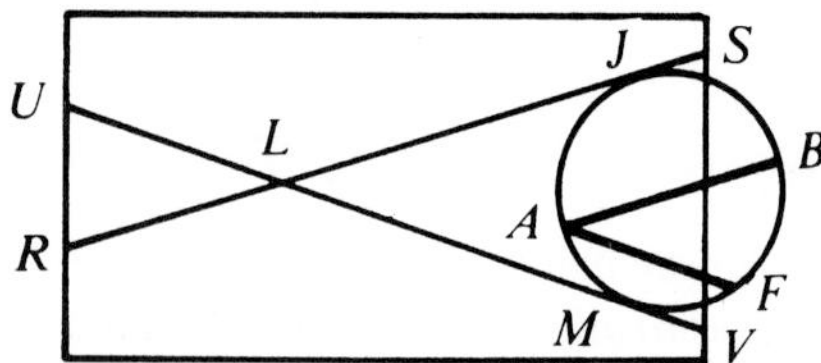

With the circle in the above position $\overline{AB} // \overleftrightarrow{LJS}$ and $\overline{AB} // \overleftrightarrow{LMV}$ Students should now be able to complete this proof independently. They should reason that $m\widehat{JB} = m\widehat{JA}$ and $m\widehat{MF} = m\widehat{MA}$; also $m\angle BAF = m\angle JLM$. Hence, $m\angle BAF = \frac{1}{2}m\widehat{BF} = \frac{1}{2}(m\widehat{BF} + m\widehat{JB} + m\widehat{MF} - m\widehat{JB} - m\widehat{MF}) = \frac{1}{2}(m\widehat{BF} + m\widehat{JB} + m\widehat{MF} - m\widehat{JA} - m\widehat{MA}) = \frac{1}{2}(m\widehat{JBM} - \frac{1}{2}m\widehat{JAM}$. Thus, $m\angle JLM = \frac{1}{2}(m\widehat{JBM} - m\widehat{JAM})$, which proves the theorem that *the measure of an angle formed by two tangents is equal to one half the difference of the measures of the intercepted arcs.*

To summarize this presentation, have students realize that (1) the measure of an angle whose vertex is *on* the circle is one half the measure of the intercepted arc, (2) the measure of an angle whose vertex is *inside* the circle is one half the *sum* of the measures of the intercepted arcs, and (3) the measure of an angle whose vertex is *outside* the circle is one half the *difference* of the measures of the intercepted arcs.

As an alternative method for using this technique with your classes, see *Geometry, Its Elements and Structure*, 2d ed., by A. S. Posamentier, J. H. Banks, and R. L. Bannister (McGraw-Hill, 1977), pp. 396–402.

POSTASSESSMENT

Have students redevelop some of the above theorems using methods presented in this unit.

Unit 57

Trisecting a Circle

To partition a circle into two regions of equal area is a rather simple matter. However, to partition a circle into *three* regions of equal area is a more interesting problem. In this unit students will investigate various methods of accomplishing this.

PERFORMANCE OBJECTIVE

Students will be able to partition a circle into three regions of equal area.

PREASSESSMENT

Students should be able to perform some simple geometric constructions using a straightedge and compass. They should also be familiar with the Pythagorean theorem and the formula for the area of a circle.

TEACHING STRATEGIES

Ask students to partition a circle into two regions of equal area. The obvious solution is for them merely to draw the diameter of the given circle. Now ask students to partition a circle into three regions of equal area (hereafter referred to as "trisecting a circle"). This, too, should cause no problem as students will realize that they must merely construct (using straightedge and compasses) three adjacent angles of measure 120°.

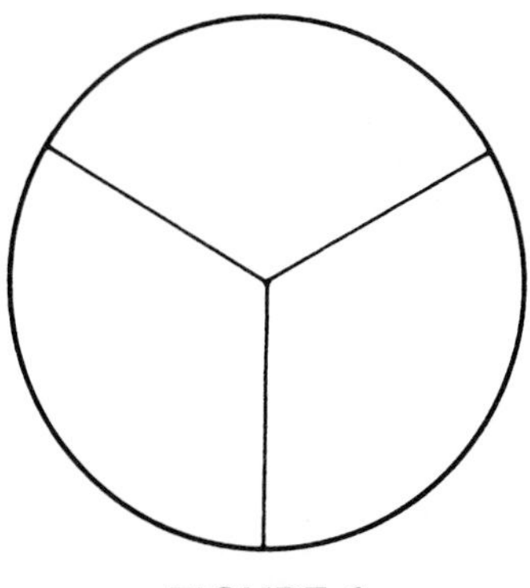

FIGURE 1

To construct this trisection they simply mark off six equal arcs along the circle with the compasses open to the radius of the circle. You may wish to justify this construction by referring to the inscribed hexagon, similarly constructed.

If you now ask students for another method of trisecting a circle, you will find them experimenting with another symmetry about the center. Ultimately this experimentation should lead to a consideration of two concentric circles, each concentric with the given circle. The problem then is to determine the lengths of the radii of the two circles.

Suppose students first find the radius, x, of a circle whose area is $\frac{1}{3}$ that of a given circle of radius r. Then $\pi x^2 = \frac{1}{3}\pi r^2$, which yields $x = \frac{r}{\sqrt{3}} = \frac{r\sqrt{3}}{3}$. In a similar way they can find the radius, y, of a circle whose area is $\frac{2}{3}$ that of a given circle of radius r. That is, $\pi y^2 = \frac{2}{3}\pi r^2$, which yields $y = \frac{r\sqrt{2}}{\sqrt{3}} = \frac{r\sqrt{6}}{3}$.

Now that the lengths have been established, the only problem remaining is to do the actual construction. Have students begin with a circle of radius r. To construct x, rewrite $x = \frac{r\sqrt{3}}{3}$ as $\frac{x}{\sqrt{3}} = \frac{r}{3}$. Then mark off the lengths r and 3 on a convenient line segment.

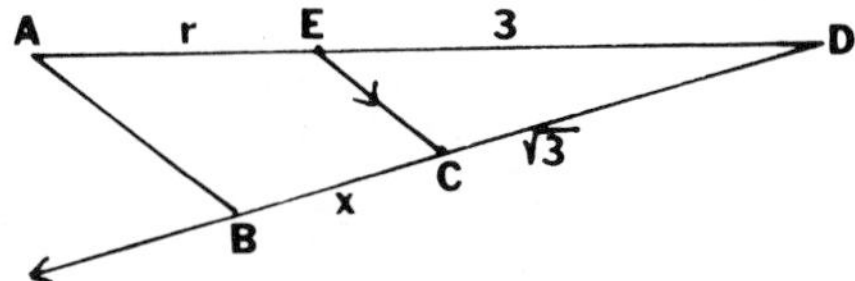

FIGURE 2

With any convenient angle, have students mark off a length $\sqrt{3}$ along this newly drawn ray. To construct a line segment of length $\sqrt{3}$, students may use any convenient method. For example, the radical spiral may be used (Figure 3).

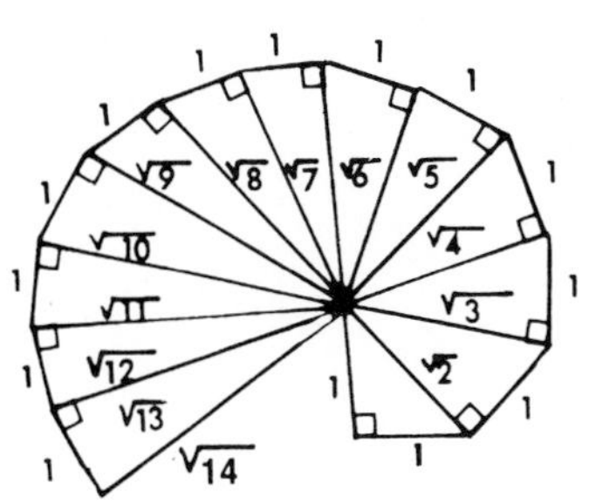

FIGURE 3

Another method for constructing a line segment of length $\sqrt{3}$ would involve setting up a diagram as shown in Figure 4.

Once this length ($\sqrt{3}$) has been marked off along $\overline{DCB}$ (see Figure 2), students can construct a line through A parallel to $\overline{EC}$ to meet $\overleftrightarrow{DC}$ at B. Using proportions, they can establish that $x = BC = \dfrac{r\sqrt{3}}{3}$.

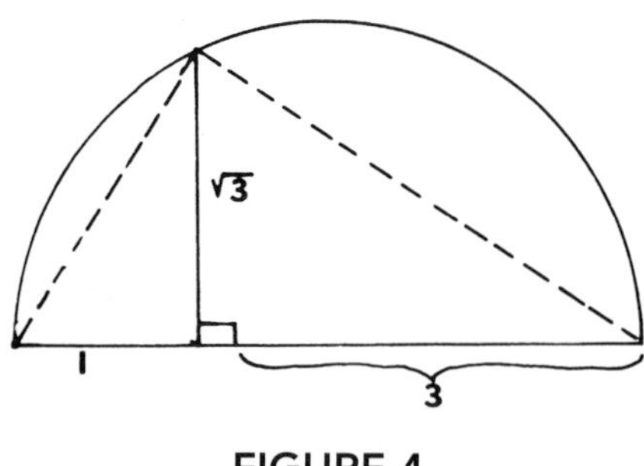

FIGURE 4

Thus, tell students to draw a circle of radius x concentric with the given circle. (Figure 5). The smaller circle has an area $\frac{1}{3}$ that of the large circle. To complete the trisection students should construct a circle, radius y, concentric with the given circle.

The area of the circle of radius y must be $\frac{2}{3}$ the area of the of circle radius r. Therefore, $\pi y^2 = \frac{2}{3}\pi r^2$, and $y = \dfrac{r\sqrt{2}}{\sqrt{3}} = \dfrac{r\sqrt{6}}{3}$. Have students construct y in a manner similar to the construction of x and then draw the circle concentric with the others (see the dotted-line circle in Figure 5).

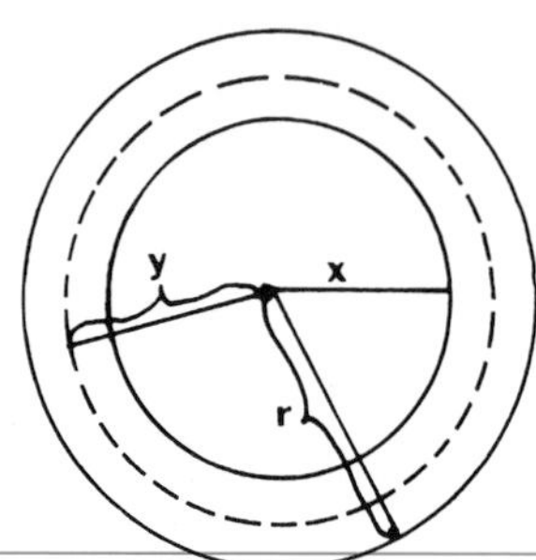

FIGURE 5

The resulting figure shows a trisected circle.

A more intriguing trisection of a circle involves a rather unusual partitioning.

In Figure 6 the diameter of the given circle is trisected at points C and D. Four semicircles are then drawn as shown in the figure. Each of the two shaded regions is $\frac{1}{3}$ the area of the given circle. Therefore the nonshaded region must also be $\frac{1}{3}$ the area of the circle and thus the circle is trisected.

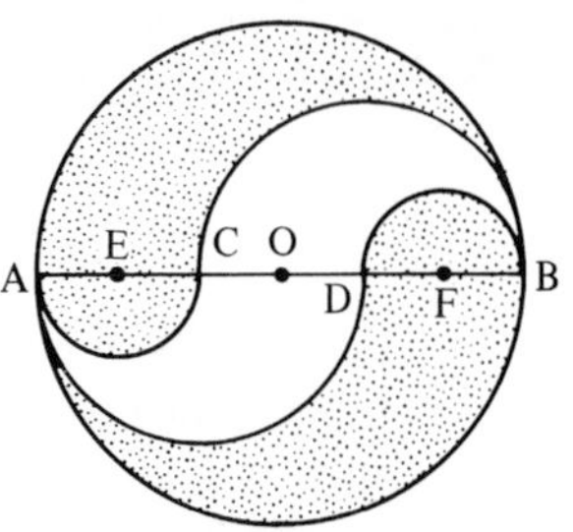

FIGURE 6

To prove this trisection valid, students need to show that one of the shaded regions has an area $\frac{1}{3}$ that of the original circle. The area of the "upper" shaded region = area semicircle AB − area semicircle BC + area semicircle AC. If AE $= r$, AO $= 3r$, and BD $= 2r$. Therefore the area of the "upper" shaded region $= \frac{1}{2}\pi(3r)^2 - \frac{1}{2}\pi(2r)^2 + \frac{1}{2}\pi r^2 = \dfrac{9\pi r^2}{2} - \dfrac{4\pi r^2}{2} + \dfrac{\pi r^2}{2} = 3\pi r^2$. However the area of the original circle to be trisected $= \pi(3r)^2 = 9\pi r^2$. Thus, the area of each shaded region is $\frac{1}{3}$ the area of the original circle, which is then trisected.

POSTASSESSMENT

Give students a circle and ask them to partition it into three regions of equal area.

REFERENCE

Posamentier, A. S., and I. Lehmann. *π: A Biography of the World's Most Mysterious Number*. Amherst, NY: Prometheus Books, 2004.

Unit 58

Ptolemy's Theorem

This unit will offer the student a very powerful theorem about cyclic (inscribed) quadrilaterals.

PERFORMANCE OBJECTIVE

Given appropriate problems, students will apply Ptolemy's theorem to successfully solve the problem.

PREASSESSMENT

Present students with an isosceles trapezoid with bases of length 6 and 8 and legs of length 5. Ask them to find the length of a diagonal of the trapezoid.

TEACHING STRATEGIES

Students who are familiar with the Pythagorean theorem should be able to solve this problem with two applications of this theorem. However, most students, after being shown this method, will certainly welcome a less tedious method of solution. This is when you introduce Ptolemy's theorem.

> *Ptolemy's theorem:* In a cyclic (inscribed) quadrilateral, the product of the lengths of the diagonals is equal to the sum of the products of the lengths of the pairs of opposite sides.

Before proving this theorem, be sure students understand the statement of the theorem and understand what a cyclic quadrilateral is. Some of the more popular theorems about cyclic quadrilaterals ought to be reviewed here. Examples of noncyclic quadrilaterals should also be given, so that students better appreciate cyclic quadrilaterals.

Proof: Consider quadrilateral ABCD inscribed in circle O. Draw a line through A to meet $\overrightarrow{CD}$ at P, so that $m\angle BAC = m\angle DAP$.

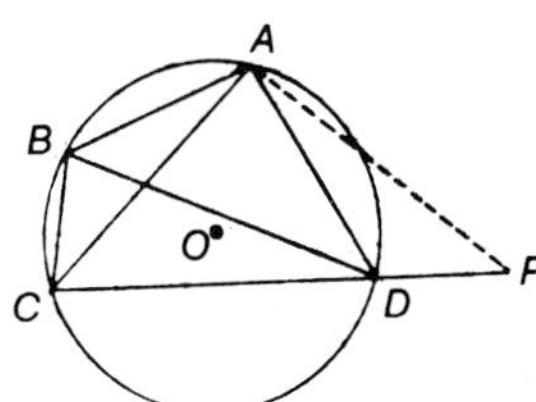

Since quadrilateral ABCD is cyclic, $\angle ABC$ is supplementary to $\angle ADC$. However, $\angle ADP$ is supplementary to $\angle ADC$. Therefore $m\angle ABC = m\angle ADP$. We can then prove $\triangle BAC \sim \triangle DAP$, and $\frac{AB}{AD} = \frac{BC}{DP}$, or $DP = \frac{(AD)(BC)}{AB}$. Since $m\angle BAC = m\angle DAP$, $m\angle BAD = m\angle CAP$. Since $\triangle BAC \sim \triangle DAP$, $\frac{AB}{AD} = \frac{AC}{AP}$. Therefore $\triangle ABD \sim \triangle ACP$, then $\frac{BP}{CP} = \frac{AB}{AC}$, or $CP = \frac{(AC)(BD)}{AB}$.

But, $CP = CD + DP$.

By substitution $\frac{(AC)(BD)}{AB} = CD + \frac{(AD)(BC)}{AB}$.

Now simplifying this expression gives us the desired result:

$$(AC)(BD) = (AB)(CD) + (AD)(BC)$$

which is Ptolemy's theorem.

Show students how Ptolemy's theorem may be used to solve the preassessment problem. Since an isosceles trapezoid is a cyclic quadrilateral, Ptolemy's theorem may be used to get $d^2 = (6)(8) + (5)(5) = 73$.

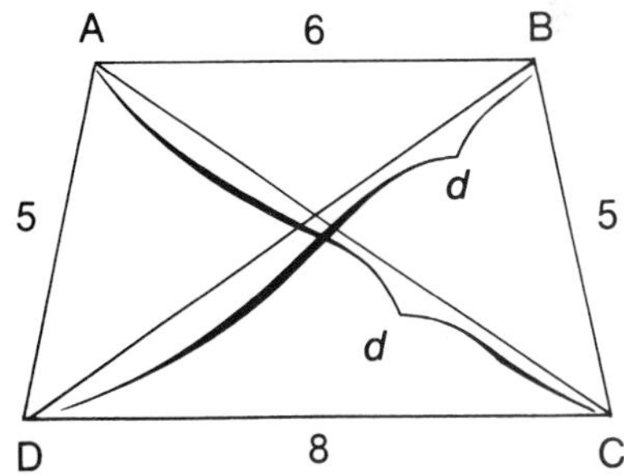

Therefore the length of a diagonal (d) is $\sqrt{73}$.

Students are often curious if a "new" theorem is consistent with theorems they learned earlier. Have students apply Ptolemy's theorem to a rectangle (which is clearly a cyclic quadrilateral). For rectangle ABCD, Ptolemy's theorem appears as $(AC)(BD) = (AD)(BC) + (AB)(DC)$.

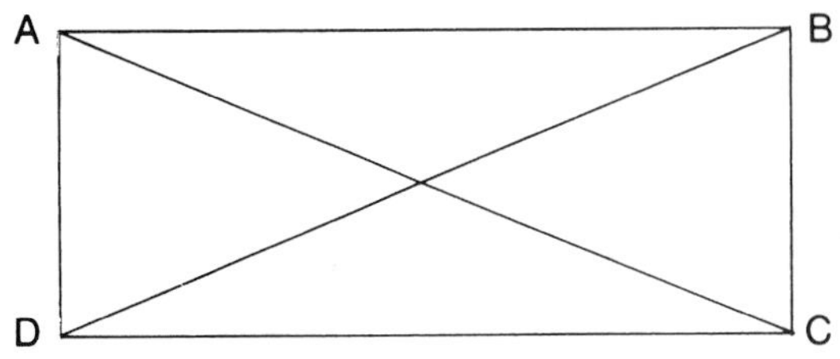

However, in the rectangle AB = DC, AD = BC, and AC = BD. Therefore by substitution $(AC)^2 = (AD)^2 + (DC)^2$, which is the Pythagorean theorem.

Now have students consider a rather simple application of this celebrated theorem.

Problem: If point P is on arc AB of the circumscribed circle of equilateral △ABC, and AP = 3 while BP = 4, find the length of $\overline{CP}$.

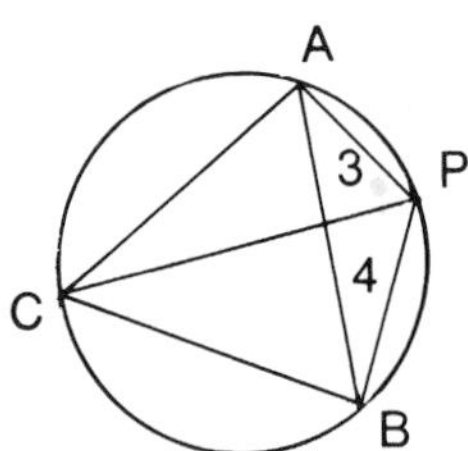

Solution: Let *t* represent the length of a side of equilateral △ABC. Since quadrilateral APBC is cyclic, we may apply Ptolemy's theorem, which yields

$$(CP)(t) = (AP)(t) + (BP)(t).$$
$$\text{Therefore } CP = AP + BP = 3 + 4 = 7.$$

Students should be encouraged to investigate similar problems where the equilateral triangle is replaced with other regular polygons.

Often problems appear to be easier than they actually are. The next problem seems to be easily solvable by simply using the Pythagorean theorem. However, in solution it becomes useful to employ Ptolemy's theorem.

Problem: On side $\overline{AB}$ of square ABCD, a right ΔABF, with hypotenuse $\overline{AB}$, is drawn externally to the square. If AF = 6 and BF = 8, find EF, where E is the point of intersection of the diagonals of the square.

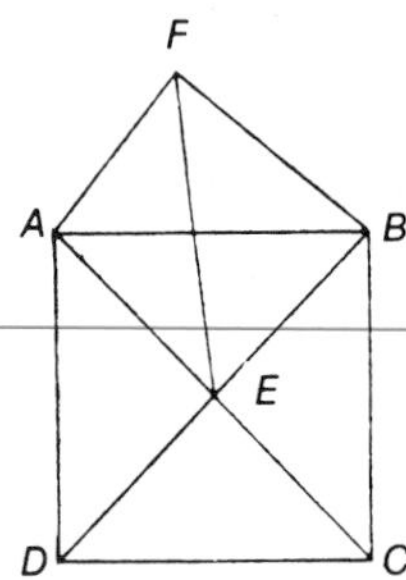

Solution: Applying the Pythagorean theorem to right ΔAFB, we get AB = 10, and to right △AEB, we get AE = *BE* = $5\sqrt{2}$. Since $m\angle AFB = m\angle AEB = 90$, quadrilateral AFBE is cyclic. Now we may apply Ptolemy's theorem to quadrilateral AFBE, to get (AB)(EF) = (AF)(BE) + (AE)(BF). Substituting the appropriate values gives us $(10)(EF) = (6)(5\sqrt{2}) + (5\sqrt{2})(8)$, or $EF = 7\sqrt{2}$.

Students should be encouraged to reconsider this problem with right △ABF drawn internally to the square. In that case $EF = \sqrt{2}$.

POSTASSESSMENT

Have students solve each of the following problems:

1. E is a point on side $\overline{AD}$ of rectangle ABCD, so that DE = 6, while DA = 8, and DC = 6. If $\overline{CE}$ extended meets the circumcircle of the rectangle at F, find the measure of chord $\overline{DF}$.

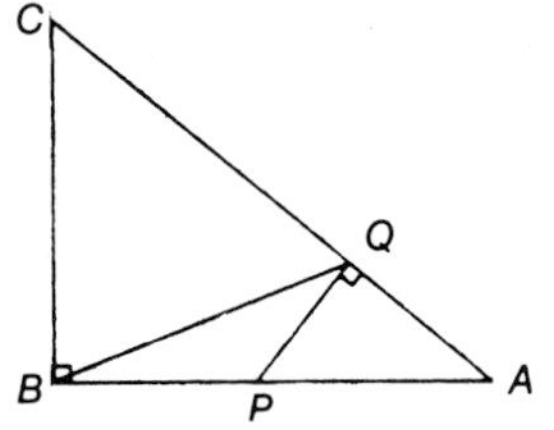

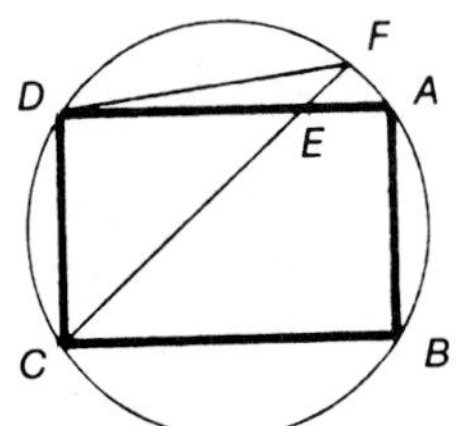

2. Point P on side $\overline{AB}$ of right △ABC is placed so that BP = PA = 2. Point Q is on hypotenuse $\overline{AC}$ so that $\overline{PQ}$ is perpendicular to $\overline{AC}$. If CB = 3, find the measure of $\overline{BQ}$, using Ptolemy's theorem.

REFERENCES

Posamentier, A. S. *Advanced Euclidean Geometry: Excursions for Secondary Teachers and Students.* New York, NY: John Wiley Publishing, 2002.

Posamentier, Alfred S., and Charles T. Salkind. *Challenging Problems in Geometry.* New York: Dover, 1996.

Unit 59

Constructing π

PERFORMANCE OBJECTIVES

1. *Students will demonstrate a clear knowledge of the π ratio and its relationship to the circle.*
2. *Students will construct π in more than one way.*

PREASSESSMENT

Before beginning a discussion of π, review with students the meaning of diameter and circumference. Have students measure the diameter and circumference of a 25-cent piece. Also ask them to obtain similar measurements of other circular objects. Stress the importance of accurate measurement.

TEACHING STRATEGIES

Begin the lesson by writing the following chart on the chalkboard:

Object	C	D	C + D	C − D	C·D	$\frac{C}{D}$

Record some of the measurements that the students obtained. They should all have found that the diameter of the quarter is *about* 2.4 mm long and that its circumference is *approximately* 7.8 mm. Have students then fill in the rest of the chart for the objects that they have measured. Ask them if any column seems to result in approximately the same value for each object measured and have them take the average of the numbers in that column. Their averages should be close to 3.14 (i.e., $\frac{C}{D} \approx 3.14$). Reemphasize that all the other columns produced varying results, whereas in the last column $\frac{C}{D}$ was the same regardless of the size of the object.

In 1737, this ratio was given the special name of "π" by Leonhard Euler, a famous Swiss mathematician. The exact value of π can never be determined; only approximations can be established. Here is the value of π correct to 50 decimal places:

$$\pi = 3.14159265358979323846264338327950288419716939937 51\ldots$$

Throughout the years, many attempts have been made to compute π, both algebraically and geometrically. This unit presents some of the geometric constructions involving π.

One of the first serious attempts to compute π to a certain degree of accuracy goes back to Archimedes, who tried to exactly determine π. His method was based on the fact that the perimeter of a regular polygon of n sides is smaller than the circumference of the circle circumscribed about it, while the perimeter of a similar polygon circumscribed about the circle is greater than the circle's circumference. By successively repeating this situation for larger values of n, the two perimeters will approach the circumference from both sides. Archimedes started with a regular hexagon and each time doubled the number of sides until he obtained a polygon of 96 sides. He was then able to determine that the ratio of the circumference of a circle to its diameter, or π, is less than $3\frac{10}{70}$ but greater than $3\frac{10}{71}$. We can write this in decimal notation as $3.14085 < \pi < 3.142857$. To aid in the students' understanding of this method, you might illustrate with a few diagrams. The following chart might also aid in explaining this concept, as the students will see that as the number of sides increases, π is more accurately approximated.

Number of sides	Perimeter of circumscribed polygon	Perimeter of inscribed polygon
4	4.0000000	2.8284271
8	3.3137085	3.0614675
16	3.1825979	3.1214452
32	3.1517249	3.1365485
64	3.1441184	3.1403312
128	3.1422236	3.1412773
256	3.1417504	3.1415138
512	3.1416321	3.1415729
1024	3.1416025	3.1415877
2048	3.1415951	3.1415914

Students will now see how they can actually construct a line segment whose length closely approximates π. This construction was developed in the mid 1800s and involves the ratio $\frac{355}{113}$ (which had been previously discovered by a Chinese astronomer in the fifth century). $\frac{355}{113} = 3 + \frac{16}{113} =$

3.1415929 . . . which is a correct approximation of π to six decimal places. The construction begins with a quadrant of unit radius. AO is $\frac{7}{8}$ of the radius, $\overline{AB}$ is drawn and a point C is marked off so that CB $= \frac{1}{2}$ of the radius. $\overline{CD}$ is drawn parallel to $\overline{AO}$ and $\overline{CE}$ is drawn parallel to $\overline{AD}$.

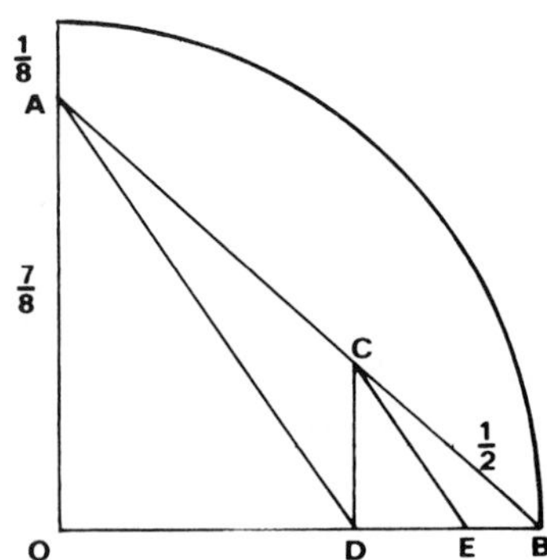

Have students find AB: $\left(\frac{7}{8}\right)^2 + 1^2 = (AB)^2 \therefore AB = \frac{\sqrt{113}}{8}$.

Using similar triangles, the following relationships can easily be seen. (Have students explain why $\triangle CDB \sim \triangle AOB$ and $\triangle CEB \sim \triangle ADB$.)

$$\frac{DB}{OB} = \frac{CB}{AB} \text{ and } \frac{EB}{DB} = \frac{CB}{AB}$$

Multiplying these expressions we obtain

$$\frac{EB}{OB} = \frac{CB^2}{AB^2} = \frac{\frac{1}{4}}{\frac{113}{64}} = \frac{16}{113}$$

but since OB = 1, we get

$$\frac{EB}{1} = \frac{16}{113} \text{ or } EB = \frac{16}{113} \text{ or } \approx .1415929204\ldots$$

Since $\frac{355}{113} = 3 + \frac{16}{113}$, a line segment can now be drawn that is 3 times the radius extended by the distance EB. This will give us a line segment that differs from π by less than a millionth of a unit.

A slightly more difficult geometric approximation of π was developed in 1685 by Father Adam Kochansky, a librarian to King John III of Poland. A circle of unit radius is drawn. Then draw a tangent segment $\overline{QR}$, equal in length to 3 times the radius. Draw a diameter perpendicular to $\overline{QR}$ at Q, the point of tangency. Now draw a line, d, tangent at the other end of the diameter such that the measure of central angle = 30°. Connect points and extend line segments to form the figure pictured in the figure below. The students are now ready to calculate the value of π. (It will be shown that if the length of the radius is 1, line c approximates π.)

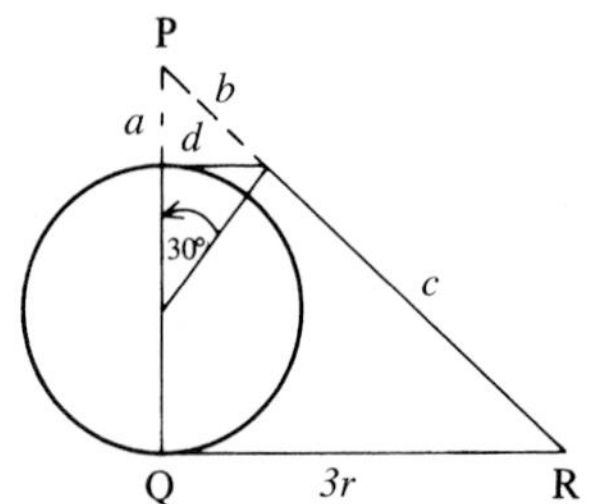

If $r = 1$, in $\triangle PQR$, $(a + 2)^2 + (3)^2 = (b + c)^2$. (1)

Also, using similar triangles, we have $\frac{a}{a + 2} = \frac{d}{3}$ (2)

and $\frac{b}{b + c} = \frac{d}{3}$. (3)

From equation (2) we obtain $3a = ad + 2d$ or $a = \frac{2d}{3 - d}$. But $\tan 30° = \frac{d}{1} = d = \frac{\sqrt{3}}{3}$.

Therefore $a = \dfrac{2\frac{\sqrt{3}}{3}}{3 - \frac{\sqrt{3}}{3}}$ or $a = \frac{2\sqrt{3}}{9 - \sqrt{3}}$. (4)

Similarly, from equation (3) we can obtain

$$b = \frac{cd}{3 - d} = \frac{c\sqrt{3}}{9 - \sqrt{3}}. \quad (5)$$

Substituting equations (4) and (5) into equation (1), we now have $\left(\frac{2\sqrt{3}}{9 - \sqrt{3}} + 2\right)^2 + 9 = \left(\frac{c\sqrt{3}}{9 - \sqrt{3}} + c\right)^2$.

Students should be able to solve this equation for c and obtain $c = \sqrt{\frac{40}{3} - 2\sqrt{3}}$.

Have students simplify this radical to obtain 3.141533 as an approximate value for c.

Throughout the lesson it should be emphasized that these are all *approximations* of the value π, since it is impossible to construct π with straightedge and compasses.

POSTASSESSMENT

1. Find the diameter of a circle whose circumference is 471 feet.
2. Construct a geometric approximation of π in more than one way.

REFERENCES

Posamentier, A. S., and I. Lehmann. *π A Biography of the World's Most Mysterious Number*. Amherst, NY: Prometheus Books, 2004.

Posamentier, A. S., and Gordon, Noam. "An Astounding Revelation on the History of π." *The Mathematics Teacher*, Vol. 77, No. 1, Jan. 1984. NCTM.

Unit 60

 The Arbelos

The region bounded by three semicircles in a manner resembling a shoemaker's knife has some rather interesting properties. This region, often called an arbelos, is the topic of this unit. Here the student will be introduced to this geometric figure with the intention of pursuing its properties further.

PERFORMANCE OBJECTIVES

1. *Students will identify the arbelos.*
2. *Students will solve problems involving the arbelos.*

PREASSESSMENT

This unit should be presented to students who have studied geometry (or arc currently enrolled in the last term of a geometry course). They should be able to compute lengths of arcs, areas of triangles, and areas of circles.

TEACHING STRATEGIES

Have students draw a semicircle with center O and diameter $\overline{AB}$. Let AB = 2R. Have them then mark off a point C, between A and B. Then have them let $\overline{AC}$ and $\overline{CB}$ be diameters of semicircles D and E, respectively (see Figure 1). Let $AC = 2r_1$ and $BC = 2r_2$. The shaded portion of the figure is known as the *Arbelos* or *Shoemaker's Knife*. It has some very interesting properties that were considered by Archimedes, the famous Greek mathematician.

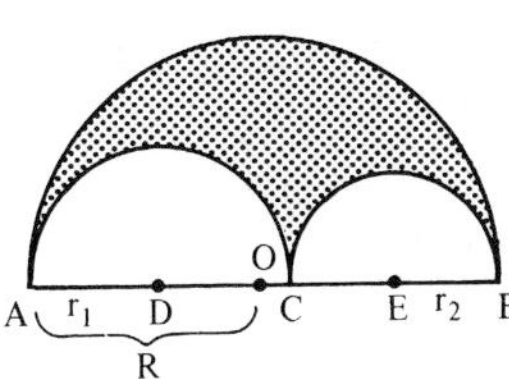

FIGURE 1

You should now direct student attention to the diagram. Try to elicit from your students the following property of the arbelos: that $\ell\widehat{AB} = \ell\widehat{AC} + \ell\widehat{CB}$. Once students understand this property, a proof should be established. In a circle, the length of an arc $= \frac{n}{360} \times 2\pi r$ (where n is the number of degrees of the arc and r is the length of the radius), we have

$$\ell\widehat{AB} = \frac{180}{360}\cdot 2\pi R = \pi R$$

$$\ell\widehat{AC} = \frac{1}{2}\cdot 2\pi r_1 = \pi r_1$$

$$\ell\widehat{CB} = \frac{1}{2}\cdot 2\pi r_2 = \pi r_2$$

Also $R = r_1 + r_2$, therefore multiplying by π we get $\pi R = \pi r_1 + \pi r_2$ or $\ell\widehat{AB} = \ell\widehat{AC} + \ell\widehat{CB}$. Have students consider the case where three semicircles (instead of two) are taken on $\overline{AB}$. Would a similar relationship hold true?

Students should now draw the perpendicular to $\overline{AB}$ at point C, which meets the circle at H. Also draw the common tangent to circles D and E and call the points of tangency F and G, respectively. Denote the point where these two segments intersect as S (see Figure 2). Since a line segment drawn perpendicular to a diameter is the geometric mean between the segments of the diameter, we have that $(HC)^2 = 2r_1 \cdot 2r_2 = 4r_1r_2$. Also FG = JE (have students

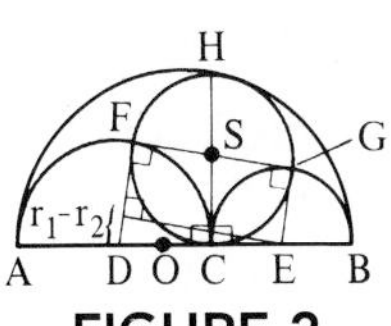

FIGURE 2

explain why from the diagram). Since $JD = r_1 - r_2$ and $DE = r_1 + r_2$, then $(JE)^2 = (r_1 + r_2)^2 - (r_1 - r_2)^2 = r_1^2 + 2r_1r_2 + r_2^2 - r_1^2 + 2r_1r_2 - r_2^2 = 4r_1r_2$. Therefore $(FG)^2 = 4r_1r_2$ or $(HC)^2 = (FG)^2 = 4r_1r_2$.

Ask your students if they can suggest another relationship that exists between $\overline{HC}$ and $\overline{FG}$. Once someone gives the response that $\overline{HC}$ and $\overline{FG}$ bisect each other at S, have the students try to prove it by themselves. $\overline{SC}$ is a common internal tangent to both circles, therefore, FS = SC and SC = SG, which gives us FS = SG. But since HC = FG (have students explain why), we also know that HS = SC. Also since $FS = SG = HS = SC$, the points F, H, G, C determine a circle with center S.

A very interesting property of the arbelos is one that involves this circle, which has $\overline{HC}$ and $\overline{FG}$ as diameters. Have students try to express the area of the arbelos in terms of r_1 and r_2. Area of the arbelos = Area of semicircle ABH − (Area of semicircle AFC + Area of semicircle CGB).

Since Area of a semicircle $= \frac{\pi r^2}{2}$, we have

$$\text{Area of the arbelos} = \frac{\pi R^2}{2} - \left(\frac{\pi r_1^2}{2} + \frac{\pi r_2^2}{2}\right) = \frac{\pi}{2}(R^2 - r_1^2 - r_2^2).$$

We know that $R = r_1 + r_2$ and substituting we get Area

$$\text{of the arbelos} = \frac{\pi}{2}((r_1 + r_2)^2 - r_1^2 - r_2^2)$$
$$= \frac{\pi}{2}(r_1^2 + 2r_1r_2 + r_2^2 - r_1^2 - r_2^2)$$
$$= \frac{\pi}{2}(2r_1r_2) = \pi r_1 r_2.$$

Have the students now find the area of circle S. The diameter $HC = 2\sqrt{r_1r_2}$, therefore the radius $= \sqrt{r_1r_2}$. The area of the circle then $= \pi(\sqrt{r_1r_2})^2 = \pi r_1 r_2$. It is now apparent that they have must proved that the area of the arbelos is equal to the area of circle S.

You may wish to introduce another interesting arbelos.

Let P and R be the midpoints of arcs $\overset{\frown}{AC}$ and $\overset{\frown}{CB}$ respectively. Let Q be the midpoint of the semicircle below $\overline{AB}$. Connect points P and R to C and to Q. A concave quadrilateral PQRC is formed (see Figure 3).

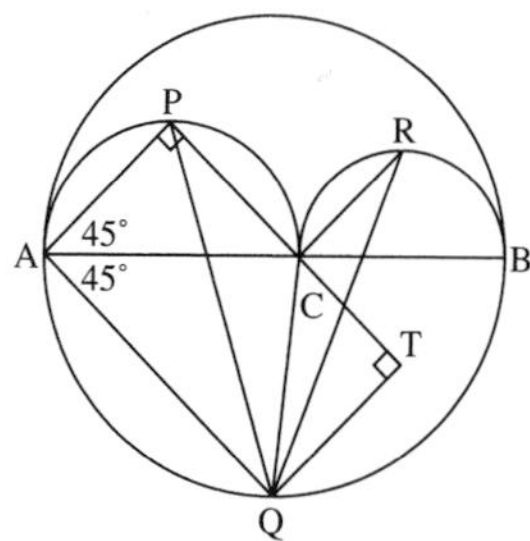

FIGURE 3

The area of this quadrilateral is equal to the sum of the squares of the radii, r_1 and r_2, of the two smaller semicircles.

A proof follows: The quadrilateral can be divided into two triangles by drawing $\overline{CQ}$. The area of $\triangle QCP$ can be shown to be equal to the area of right $\triangle APC$. The two triangles have a common base $\overline{CP}$, therefore their heights must be proved to be equal. To do this, draw $\overline{AP}$, $\overline{AQ}$ and draw $\overline{QT}$ perpendicular to $\overline{PC}$ extended (see Figure 3). Since Q is the midpoint of semicircle AB, $m\overset{\frown}{QB} = 90°$. Therefore $m\angle QAB = 45°$. Also since $\triangle APC$ is an isosceles right triangle, $m\angle PAB = 45°$, which gives us that $m\angle PAQ = 90°$. But since $m\angle APC = 90°$ and $m\angle PTQ$ is also quadrilateral APTQ is a rectangle and $AP = QT$.

Therefore, Area of $\triangle QCP = \dfrac{CP \cdot PA}{2}$.

Since in isosceles right triangle APC, $(CP)^2 + (PA)^2 = (2r_1)^2$ or $2(CP)^2 = (2r_1)^2$, therefore $(CP)^2 = 2r_1^2$ or $\dfrac{CP \cdot PA}{2} = r_1^2$.

We therefore have that area of $\Delta QCP = r_1^2$.

Similarly, it can be shown that area of $\triangle QCR = \dfrac{CR \cdot RB}{2} = r_2^2$.

Therefore, Area of the quadirlateral $= r_1^2 + r_2^2$.

POSTASSESSMENT

1. If $r_1 = 16$ and $r_2 = 4$, show that $\overset{\frown}{AB} = \overset{\frown}{AC} + \overset{\frown}{CB}$; find the radius of circle S; find the area of the arbelos.
2. Describe semicircle D below $\overline{AB}$ (Figure 4). Let $\overline{AN}$ be tangent to circle E. Show that the area of the shaded region is equal to the area of the circle, which has $\overline{AN}$ as its diameter.
3. Find the area of quadrilateral PQRC (Figure 3), if $r_1 = 8$ and $r_2 = 5$.

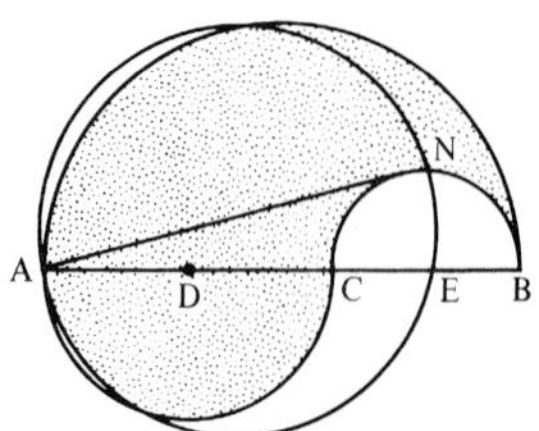

FIGURE 4

4. What is the relationship between the arbelos in Figure 3 and Fibonacci numbers.

REFERENCE

Gardner, Martin. "The Diverse Pleasures of Circles that Are Tangent to One Another." *Scientific American*, 240 (1), January, 1979.

Unit 61

The Nine-Point Circle

An often neglected concept in the high school geometry curriculum is that of establishing points concyclic (on the same circle). This unit presents one of the more famous sets of concyclic points.

PERFORMANCE OBJECTIVES

1. *Students will define and construct the nine-point circle.*
2. *Students will locate the center of the nine-point circle.*

PREASSESSMENT

Students should be aware of elementary methods of proving four points concyclic. For example, they should be aware of at least the following two theorems:

1. If one side of a quadrilateral subtends congruent angles at the two nonadjacent vertices, then the quadrilateral is cyclic (may be inscribed in a circle).
2. If a pair of opposite angles of a quadrilateral are supplementary, then the quadrilateral is cyclic.

TEACHING STRATEGIES

Present students with a $\triangle ABC$, with midpoints of its sides A', B', C' (see Figure 1). Draw altitude $\overline{CF}$. Ask students to

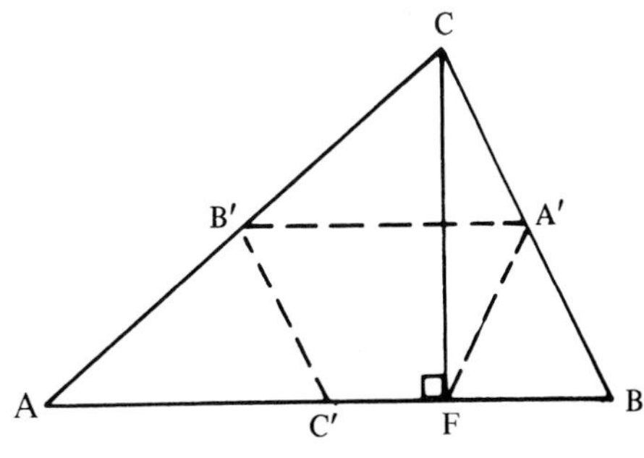

FIGURE 1

prove that quadrilateral $A'B'C'D'$ is an isosceles trapezoid. To do this they should realize that since $\overline{A'B'}$ is a segment joining the midpoints of two sides of a triangle, it is parallel to the third side of the triangle. Since $\overline{B'C'}$ joins the midpoints of $\overline{AC}$ and $\overline{AB}$, $B'C' = \frac{1}{2}(BC)$. Since the median to the hypotenuse of a right triangle is half the length of the hypotenuse, $A'F = \frac{1}{2}(BC)$. Therefore, $B'C' = A'F$, and trapezoid $A'B'C'F$ is isosceles.

Now have students prove that an isosceles trapezoid is always cyclic (using Theorem 2, above).

To avoid confusion redraw $\triangle ABC$ with altitude $\overline{AD}$ as shown below.

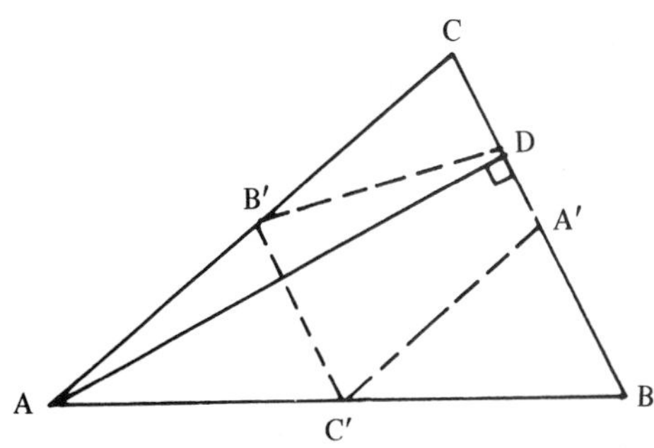

FIGURE 2

In the same way as for altitude $\overline{CF}$, have students independently prove that the points B', C', A', and D are concyclic. This should be done with the above proof as a guide.

Students should now be prepared to generalize a statement about the points B', C', A', and E, for altitude $\overline{BE}$. This will lead to the conclusion that the points D, F, and E each lie on the unique circle determined by points A', B', C'. Thus, students can summarize that the feet of the altitudes of a triangle are concyclic with the midpoints of the sides. So far they have established a "six-point circle."

By this time, students should have proved that the altitudes of a triangle are concurrent. This point is called the

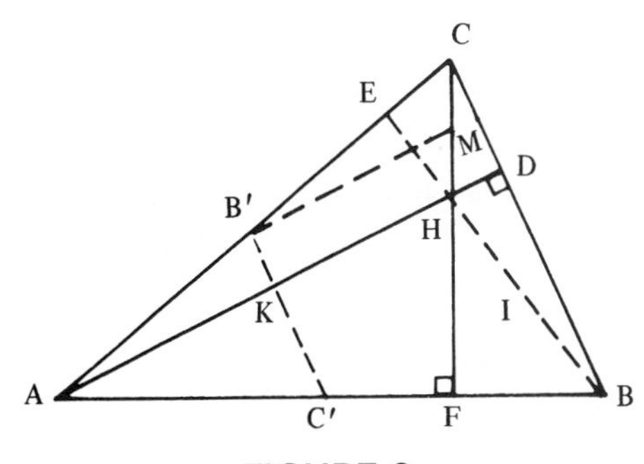

FIGURE 3

orthocenter. Have them consider the orthocenter, H, of $\triangle ABC$, and the midpoint M of $\overline{CH}$.

$\overline{B'M}$ is a segment joining the midpoints of two sides of $\angle ACH$. Therefore $\overline{B'M} \parallel \overline{AH}$. Similarly in $\angle ABC$, we have $\overline{B'C'} \parallel \overline{BC}$. Since altitude $\overline{AD} \perp \overline{BC}$, $\overline{B'M} \perp \overline{B'C'}$, or $m\angle MB'C' = 90°$. Remember that $m\angle AFC = 90°$. Therefore quadrilateral MB′C′F is cyclic, since its opposite angles are supplementary. This is the same circle established above, since three vertices (B′, C′, and F) are common with the six concyclic points, and three points determine a unique circle. Thus, a "seven-point circle" has been established.

To reinforce this proof, students should now prove that K and L (the midpoints of $\overline{AH}$ and $\overline{BH}$, respectively), also lie on this circle. To do this they merely need to repeat the above procedure for points K, C′, A′, D and for points L, C′, B′, E. A brief review of the entire proof thus far will reveal a *nine-point circle*.

Have students consider $\overline{MC'}$ in Figure 4. Since it subtends right angles at points B′ and F, it must be the diameter of the circle through B′, C′, F, and M. To locate the center N of this circle, simply tell students to find the midpoint of $\overline{MC'}$. This is the center of the nine-point circle.

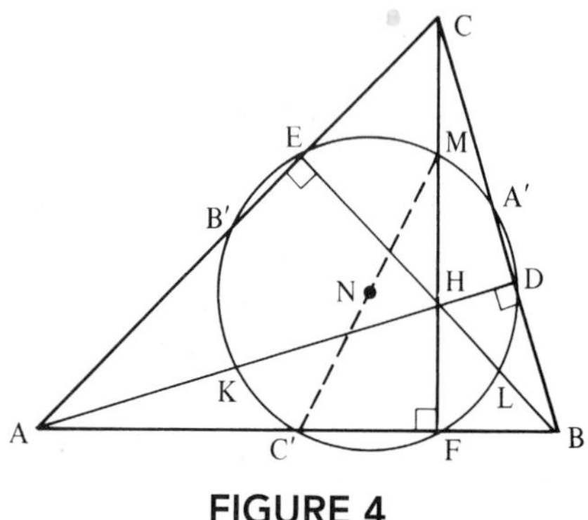

FIGURE 4

POSTASSESSMENT

To conclude the lesson ask students to do the following:

1. Define the nine-point circle.
2. Construct the nine-point circle using straightedge and compasses.
3. Locate the center of the nine-point circle.

Interesting relationships involving the nine-point circle can be found in the accompanying unit, The Euler Line.

Many other interesting relationships involving the nine point circle can be found in:

REFERENCE

Posamentier, A. S. *Advanced Euclidean Geometry: Excursions for Secondary Teachers and Students*. New York, NY: John Wiley Publishing, 2002.

Unit 62

 The Euler Line

This unit should be presented to students *after* they have studied the unit (61) on the nine-point circle. This unit uses some of the material developed there and relates it to other points of a triangle.

PERFORMANCE OBJECTIVES

1. *Students will locate the Euler line of a triangle.*
2. *Students will establish a relationship among the circumcenter, orthocenter, centroid, and the center of the nine-point circle of a triangle.*

PREASSESSMENT

Have students draw a scalene triangle and construct its nine-point circle as well as the circumcircle of the triangle.

TEACHING STRATEGIES

To facilitate the discussion, students should label their construction as in Figure 1.

Students should now draw $\overline{OH}$, the segment joining the orthocenter (the point of intersection of the altitudes) and the circumcenter (the point of intersection of the perpendicular bisectors of the sides of the triangle). This is the *Euler line*.

Have students locate the center of the nine-point circle by finding the midpoint of $\overline{MC'}$ (this was proved in *The Nine-Point Circle*). An accurate construction should place this point on the midpoint of the Euler line $\overline{OH}$. Student curiosity should now request a proof of this astonishing occurrence.

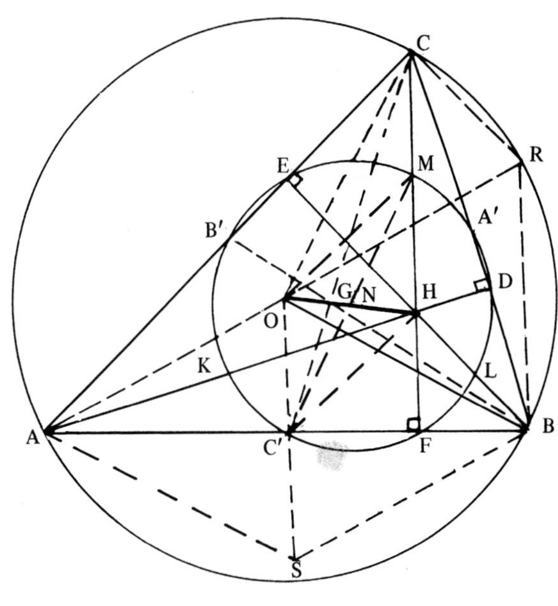

FIGURE 1

1. Draw $\overleftrightarrow{OA}$ to intersect circle O at R.
2. $\overline{OC'} \perp \overline{AB}$ (since O is on the perpendicular bisector of $\overline{AB}$ and C′ is the midpoint of $\overline{AB}$).
3. $m\angle ABR = 90°$ (an angle inscribed in a semicircle).
4. Therefore, $\overline{OC'} \parallel \overline{RB}$ (both are perpendicular to $\overline{AB}$).
5. Similarly, $\overline{RB} \parallel \overline{CF}$, and $\overline{RC} \parallel \overline{BE}$.
6. $\Delta AOC' \sim \Delta ARB$ (with a ratio of similitude of $\frac{1}{2}$).
7. Therefore $OC' = \frac{1}{2}(RB)$.
8. Quadrilateral RBHC is a parallelogram (both pairs of opposite sides are parallel).
9. Therefore, $RB = HC$, and $OC' = \frac{1}{2}(HC) = HM$.
10. Quadrilateral OC′HM is a parallelogram (one pair of sides is both congruent and parallel).
11. Therefore, since the diagonals of a parallelogram bisect each other, N (the midpoint of $\overline{MC'}$), is the midpoint of $\overline{OH}$.

So far we proved that the center of the nine-point circle bisects the Euler line. At this point we can easily prove that the radius of the nine-point circle is half the length of the radius of the circumcircle. Since $\overline{MN}$ is a line segment joining the midpoints of two sides of ΔCOH, it is half the length of the third side $\overline{OC}$. Thus the radius, $\overline{MN}$, of the nine-point circle is half the length of the radius, $\overline{OC}$, of the circumcircle.

In 1765, Leonhard Euler proved that the centroid of a triangle (the point of intersection of the medians) trisects the line segment joining the orthocenter and the circumcenter (the Euler line).

Since $\overline{OC'} \parallel \overline{CH}$, $\Delta OGC' \sim \Delta HGC$.

Earlier we proved that $OC' = \frac{1}{2}(HC)$.

Therefore, $OG = \frac{1}{2}(GH)$,

or $OG = \left(\frac{1}{3}\right)(OH)$.

The only thing remaining is to show that G is the centroid of the triangle.

Since $\overline{CC'}$ is a median and $\overline{GC'} = \frac{1}{2}(GC)$,

G must be the centroid since it appropriately trisects the median.

Thus G trisects $\overline{OH}$.

Ask students why the median $\overline{BB'}$ also trisects $\overline{OH}$ (because it contains G, the centroid).

To this point we have bisected and trisected the Euler line with significant triangle points. Before ending the discussion of the Euler line, an interesting vector application should be considered. Review the concept of a vector and a parallelogram of forces. We shall show that $\overrightarrow{OH}$ is the resultant of $\overrightarrow{OA}$, $\overrightarrow{OB}$, and $\overrightarrow{OC}$. This was first published by James Joseph Sylvester (1814–1897).

Consider the point S on $\overline{OC'}$,

where $OC' = SC'$.

Since $\overline{OC'S}$ is the perpendicular bisector of $\overline{AB}$, quadrilateral AOBS is a parallelogram (rhombus).

Therefore, vectors $\overrightarrow{OS} = \overrightarrow{OA} + \overrightarrow{OB}$, or $\overrightarrow{OC'} = \frac{1}{2}(\overrightarrow{OA} + \overrightarrow{OB})$.

Since $\Delta OGC' \sim \Delta HGC$, $CH = 2(OC')$.

Thus $\overrightarrow{CH} = \overrightarrow{OA} + \overrightarrow{OB}$.

Since $\overrightarrow{HO}$ is the resultant of $\overrightarrow{OC}$ and $\overrightarrow{CH}$, $\overrightarrow{HO} = \overrightarrow{OC} + \overrightarrow{CH}$.

Therefore, $\overrightarrow{HO} = \overrightarrow{OC} + \overrightarrow{OA} + \overrightarrow{OB}$. (Substitution)

POSTASSESSMENT

At the conclusion of this lesson ask students:

1. To construct the Euler line of a given scalene triangle, and
2. To state a relationship that exists among the circumcenter, orthocenter, centroid, and the center of the nine-point circle of a given scalene triangle.

REFERENCE

Posamentier, A. S. *Advanced Euclidean Geometry: Excursions for Secondary Teachers and Students.* New York, NY: John Wiley Publishing, 2002.

Unit 63

The Simson Line

One of the more famous sets of collinear points is known as the *Simson line*. Although this line was discovered by William Wallace in 1797, careless misquotes have, in time, attributed it to Robert Simson (1687–1768). This unit will present, prove, and apply the Simson theorem.

PERFORMANCE OBJECTIVES

1. *Students will construct the Simson line.*
2. *Students will prove that the three points that determine the Simson line are, in fact, collinear.*
3. *Students will apply the properties of the Simson line to given problems.*

PREASSESSMENT

When students are presented with this unit, they should be well into the high school geometry course, having already studied angle measurement with a circle. Students should also review cyclic quadrilaterals (quadrilaterals that may be inscribed in a circle) before beginning this unit.

TEACHING STRATEGIES

Have each student construct a triangle inscribed in a circle. Then, from any convenient point on the circle (but not at a vertex of the triangle), have students construct perpendicular segments to each of the three sides of the triangle. Now, ask the class what relationship seems to be true about the three feet of the perpendiculars. If the constructions were done accurately, everyone should notice that these three points determine the *Simson line*.

The obvious question should be quickly forthcoming: "Why are these three points collinear?" This is where you begin your proof.

Simson's theorem: The feet of the perpendiculars drawn from any point on the circumcircle of a given triangle to the sides of the triangle are collinear.

Given: $\triangle ABC$ is inscribed in circle O.
P is on circle O.
$\overleftrightarrow{PY} \perp \overleftrightarrow{AC}$ at Y, $\overleftrightarrow{PZ} \perp \overleftrightarrow{AB}$ at Z, and $\overleftrightarrow{PX} \perp \overleftrightarrow{BC}$ at X.

Prove: Points X, Y, and Z are collinear.

Proof:

1. $\angle PYA$ is supplementary to $\angle PZA$ (both are right angles).
2. Quadrilateral PZAY is cyclic (opposite angles are supplementary).
3. Draw $\overline{PA}$, $\overline{PB}$, and $\overline{PC}$.
4. $m\angle PYZ = m\angle PAZ$ (both are inscribed in the same arc).
5. $\angle PYC$ is supplementary to $\angle PXC$ (both are right angles).
6. Quadrilateral PXCY is cyclic (opposite angles are supplementary).
7. $m\angle PYX = m\angle PCB$ (both are inscribed in the same arc).
8. $m\angle PAZ$ ($m\angle P\overset{\frown}{A}B$) $= m\angle PCB$ (both are inscribed in the same arc of circle O).
9. $m\angle PYZ = m\angle PYX$ (transitivity with steps 4, 7, and 8).
10. Since both angles, $\angle PYZ$ and $\angle PYX$, share the same ray $\overrightarrow{YP}$, and have the same measure, their other rays $\overrightarrow{YZ}$ and $\overrightarrow{YX}$ must coincide. Therefore, points X, Y, and Z are collinear.

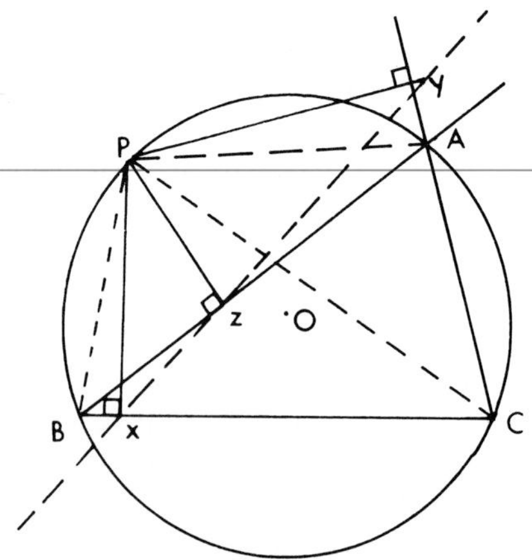

FIGURE 1

Present carefully to students this technique for proving collinearity. Although it is a somewhat unusual approach, it should prove quite useful to them in later work.

To strengthen the impact of the Simson line, show students a proof of the converse of the above theorem.

Given: $\triangle ABC$ is inscribed in circle O.
Points X, Y, and Z are collinear.
$\overleftrightarrow{PY} \perp \overleftrightarrow{AC}$ at Y, $\overleftrightarrow{PZ} \perp \overleftrightarrow{AB}$ at Z, and $\overleftrightarrow{PX} \perp \overleftrightarrow{BC}$ at X.

Prove: P is on the circumcircle of $\triangle ABC$.

Proof:

1. Draw PA, PB, and PC (see Figure 1).
2. $m\angle PZB = 90° = m\angle PXB$.
3. Quadrilateral PZXB is cyclic ($\overline{PB}$ subtends two congruent angles in the same half-plane).
4. $\angle PBX$ is supplementary to $\angle PZX$ (opposite angles of a cyclic quadrilateral).
5. $\angle PZX$ is supplementary to $\angle PZY$ (points X, Y, and Z are collinear).
6. Therefore, $m\angle PBX = m\angle PZY$ (both are supplementary to $\angle PZX$).
7. Quadrilateral PZAY is cyclic (opposite angles, $\angle PYA$ and $\angle PZA$, are supplementary).
8. $m\angle PZY = m\angle PAY$ (both are inscribed in the same arc of the circumcircle of quadrilateral PZAY).
9. Therefore, $m\angle PBX = m\angle PAY$ (transitivity of steps 6 and 8).
10. Thus, $\angle PBC$ is supplementary to $\angle PAC$ (since $\overleftrightarrow{YAC}$ is a line).
11. Quadrilateral PACB is cyclic (opposite angles are supplementary), and, therefore, P is on the circumcircle of $\triangle ABC$.

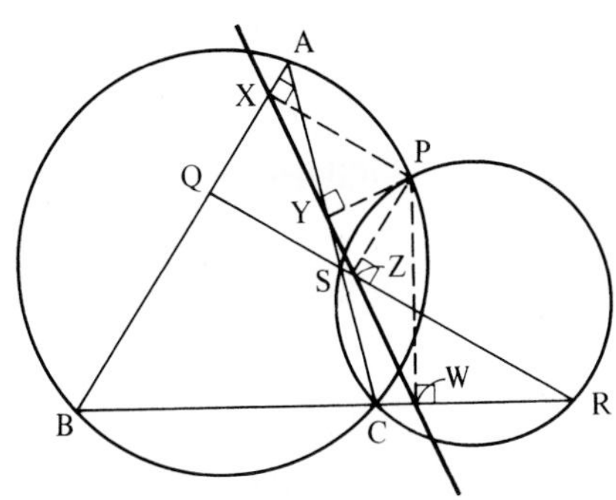

FIGURE 2

Students should now be ready to apply the Simson line to a geometric problem.

Sides $\overleftrightarrow{AB}$, $\overleftrightarrow{BC}$, and $\overleftrightarrow{CA}$ of ΔABC are cut by a transversal at points Q, R, and S, respectively. The circumcircles of $\triangle ABC$ and $\triangle SCR$ intersect at P. Prove that quadrilateral APSQ is cyclic.

Draw perpendiculars $\overline{PX}$, $\overline{PY}$, $\overline{PZ}$, and $\overline{PW}$ to $\overleftrightarrow{AB}$, $\overleftrightarrow{AC}$, $\overleftrightarrow{QR}$, and $\overleftrightarrow{BC}$, respectively, as in Figure 2. Since point P is on the circumcircle of $\triangle ABC$, points X, Y, and W are collinear (Simson's theorem). Similarly, since point P is on the circumcircle of $\triangle SCR$, points Y, Z, and W are collinear. It then follows that points X, Y, and Z are collinear. Thus, P must lie on the circumcircle of $\triangle AQS$ (converse of Simson's theorem), or quadrilateral APSQ is cyclic.

POSTASSESSMENT

Have students complete the following exercises.

1. Construct a Simson line of a given triangle.
2. How many Simson lines does a triangle have?
3. Prove Simson's theorem.
4. From a point P on the circumference of circle O, three chords are drawn meeting the circle in points A, B, and C. Prove that the three points of intersection of the three circles with $\overline{PA}$, $\overline{PB}$, and $\overline{PC}$ as diameters, are collinear.

REFERENCES

Posamentier, A. S. *Advanced Euclidean Geometry*. New York, NY: John Wiley Publishing, 2002.

Posamentier, A. S., and C. T. Salkind. *Challenging Problems in Geometry*. New York: Dover, 1996.

Unit 64

 The Butterfly Problem

One of the most intriguing geometric relationships involves a figure that resembles a butterfly. Most students will easily understand the problem and think it just as simple to prove. But this is where the problem begins to generate further interest since the proof is somewhat elusive. This unit will suggest ways of presenting the problem to your class and provide a number of different proofs of this celebrated theorem.

PERFORMANCE OBJECTIVES

1. *Students will state the Butterfly Problem.*
2. *Students will prove the Butterfly Problem valid.*

PREASSESSMENT

Students should have mastered most of the high school geometry course (especially the study of circles and similarity).

TEACHING STRATEGIES

Use a duplicating machine to prepare a sheet of paper for each student with a large circle containing a chord, $\overline{AB}$, (not the diameter), and its midpoint, M, clearly marked. Tell students to draw *any* two chords, $\overline{EF}$, and $\overline{CD}$, containing M. Now have them draw the chords $\overline{CE}$ and $\overline{FD}$ which intersect $\overline{AB}$ at points Q and P, respectively. Their diagrams should resemble Figure 1.

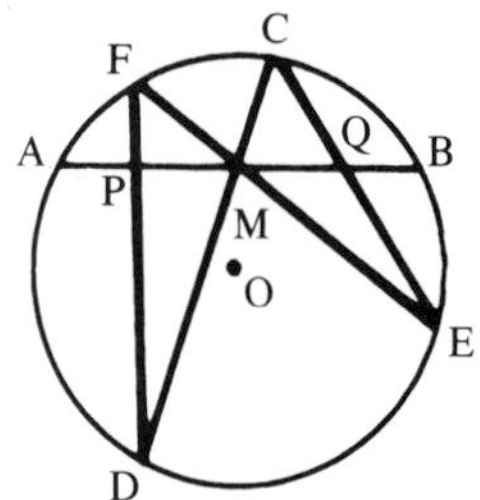

FIGURE 1

Ask your class to measure any segments that appear congruent in their diagrams, and to list the pairs. You should find that most students will have included on their lists the segments $\overline{AP} \cong \overline{BQ}$ and $\overline{MP} \cong \overline{MQ}$. Remind students that they all started their diagrams with *different* segments $\overline{CE}$ and $\overline{FD}$, and, although their diagrams resemble a butterfly in a circle, their art may differ substantially from their classmates'. This should dramatize the most astonishing result of this situation, that *everyone's* $\overline{MP} \cong \overline{MQ}$!

Students will now want to prove this remarkable result. Toward this end, a number of proofs of this celebrated theorem are presented here.

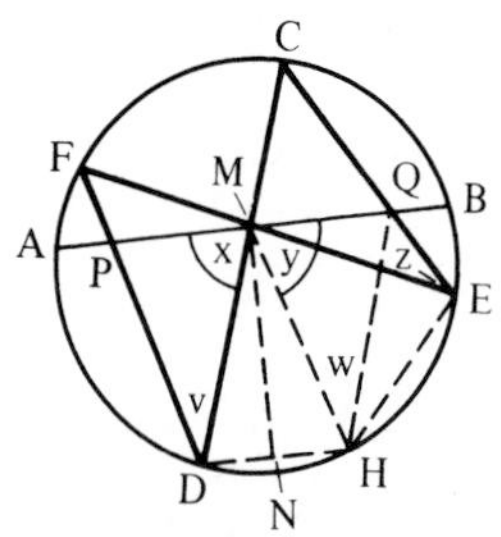

FIGURE 2

Proof I: With M the midpoint of $\overline{AB}$ and chords $\overline{FME}$ and $\overline{CMD}$ drawn, we now draw $\overline{DH} \parallel \overline{AB}$, $\overline{MN} \perp \overline{DH}$, and line segments $\overline{MH}$, $\overline{QH}$, and $\overline{EH}$. Since $\overline{MN} \perp \overline{DH}$ and $\overline{DH} \parallel \overline{AB}$, $\overline{MN} \perp \overline{AB}$.

$\overline{MN}$, the perpendicular bisector of $\overline{AB}$, must pass through the center of the circle. Therefore $\overline{MN}$ is the perpendicular bisector of $\overline{DH}$, since a line through the center of the circle and perpendicular to a chord, bisects it.

Thus MD = MH, and $\Delta MND \cong \Delta MNH$ (H.L.). $m\angle DMN = m\angle HMN$, so $m\angle x = m\angle y$ (they are the complements of congruent angles). Since $\overline{AB} \parallel \overline{DH}$, $m\overset{\frown}{AD} = m\overset{\frown}{BH}$, $m\angle x = \frac{1}{2}(m\overset{\frown}{AD} + m\overset{\frown}{CB})$ (angle formed by two chords) $m\angle x = \frac{1}{2}(m\overset{\frown}{BH} + m\overset{\frown}{CB})$ (substitution). Therefore, $m\angle y = \frac{1}{2}(m\overset{\frown}{BH} + m\overset{\frown}{CB})$. But $m\angle CEH = \frac{1}{2}(m\overset{\frown}{CAH})$ (inscribed angle). Thus, by addition, $m\angle y + m\angle CEH = \frac{1}{2}(m\overset{\frown}{BH} + m\overset{\frown}{CB} + m\overset{\frown}{CAH})$. Since $m\overset{\frown}{BH} + m\overset{\frown}{CB} + m\overset{\frown}{CAH} = 360°$, $m\angle y + m\overset{\frown}{CEH} = 180°$. It then follows that quadrilateral MQEH is inscriptable, that is, a circle may be circumscribed about it. Imagine a drawing of this circle. $\angle w$ and $\angle z$ are measured by the same arc, $\overset{\frown}{MQ}$ (inscribed angle), and thus $m\angle w = m\angle z$.

Now considering our original circle $m\angle v = m\angle z$, since they are measured by the same arc, $\overset{\frown}{FC}$ (inscribed angle).

Therefore, by transitivity, $m\angle v = m\angle w$, and $\triangle MPD \cong \triangle MQH$ (A.S.A.). Thus, MP = MQ.

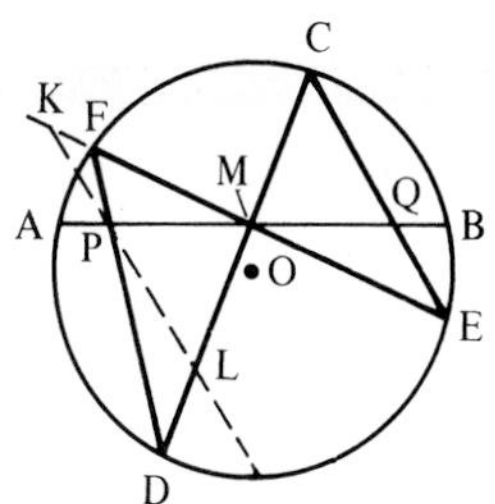

FIGURE 3

Proof II: Extend $\overline{EF}$ through F.
Draw $\overline{KPL} \parallel \overline{CE}$.
$m\angle PLC = m\angle ECL$ (alternate interior angles),
therefore, $\triangle PML \sim \triangle QMC$ (A.A.), and $\frac{PL}{CQ} = \frac{MP}{MQ}$
$m\angle K = m\angle E$ (alternate interior angles),
therefore, $\triangle KMP \sim \triangle EMQ$ (A.A.), and $\frac{KP}{QE} = \frac{MP}{MQ}$. By multiplication,

$$\frac{(PL)\,(KP)}{(CQ)\,(QE)} = \frac{(MP)^2}{(MQ)^2}. \qquad \text{(I)}$$

Since $m\angle D = m\angle E$ (inscribed angle), and $m\angle K = m\angle E$ (alternate interior angles), $m\angle D = m\angle K$. Also, $m\angle KPF = m\angle DPL$ (vertical angles). Therefore, $\triangle KFP \sim \triangle DLP$ (A.A.), and $\frac{PL}{DP} = \frac{FP}{KP}$; and so

$$(PL)\,(KP) = (DP)\,(FP). \qquad \text{(II)}$$

In equation (I), $\frac{(MP)^2}{(MQ)^2} = \frac{(PL)\,(KP)}{(CQ)\,(QE)}$;
we substitute from equation (II) to get

$$\frac{(MP)^2}{(MQ)^2} = \frac{(DP)\,(FP)}{(CQ)\,(QE)}.$$

Since (DP) (FP) = (AP) (PB), and (CQ) (QE) = (BQ) (QA) (product of segments lengths of intersecting chords),

$$\frac{(MP)^2}{(MQ)^2} = \frac{(AP)\,(PB)}{(BQ)\,(QA)}$$
$$= \frac{(MA - MP)\,(MA + MP)}{(MB - MQ)\,(MB + MQ)} = \frac{(MA)^2 - (MP)^2}{(MB)^2 - (MQ)^2}.$$

Then $(MP)^2(MB)^2 = (MQ)^2(MA)^2$.
But MB = MA. Therefore, $(MP)^2 = (MQ)^2$, or MP = MQ.

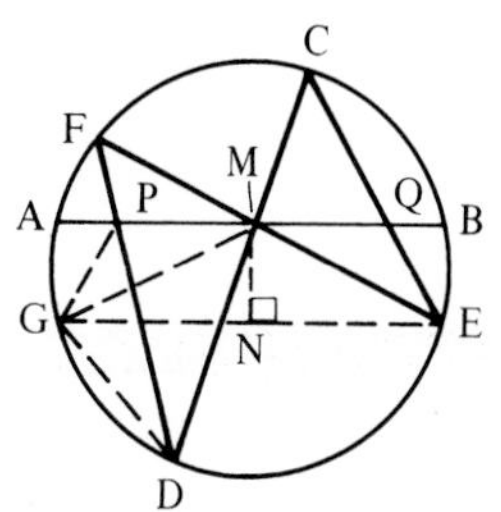

FIGURE 4

Proof III: Draw a line through E parallel to $\overline{AB}$ meeting the circle at G, and draw $\overline{MN} \perp \overline{GE}$. Then draw $\overline{PG}$, $\overline{MG}$, and $\overline{DG}$.

$m\angle GDP$ ($\angle GDF$) = $m\angle GEF$ (inscribed angles). (I)
$m\angle PMG = m\angle MGE$ (alternate interior angles). (II)

Since the perpendicular bisector of $\overline{AB}$ is also the perpendicular bisector of $\overline{GE}$,
then GM = ME, and $m\angle GEF = m\angle MGE$ (base angles). (III)

From (I), (II), and (III), $m\angle GDP = m\angle PMG$. (IV)

Therefore, points P, M, D, and G are concyclic. (A quadrilateral is cyclic if one side subtends congruent angles at the two opposite vertices.) Hence, $m\angle PGM = m\angle PDM$ (inscribed angles, in a new circle). (V)
However, $m\angle CEF = m\angle PDM(\angle FDM)$ (inscribed angles). (VI)

From (V) and (VI), $M\angle PGM = m\angle QEM(\angle CEF)$.
From (II), we know that $m\angle PMG = m\angle MGE$.
Thus, $m\angle QME = m\angle MEG$ (alternate interior angles), and $m\angle MGE = m\angle MEG$ (base angles).
Therefore, $m\angle PMG = m\angle QME$ and $\triangle PMG \cong \triangle QME$ (A.S.A.). It follows that PM = QM.

Although these proofs of the Butterfly Problem are not of the sort the average student is likely to discover independently, they do provide a very rich learning experience in a well-motivated setting.

POSTASSESSMENT

Ask students to:

1. State the Butterfly Problem.
2. Explain why the Butterfly Problem is true. (Students should either present one of the above proofs or one of their own.)

REFERENCE

Additional solutions can be found in:

Posamentier, A. S., and C. T. Salkind. *Challenging Problems in Geometry*. New York: Dover, 1996.

Unit 65

 Equicircles

Equicircles is a term used to refer to both the inscribed and escribed circles of a triangle. This unit will develop a number of fascinating relationships between these circles.

PERFORMANCE OBJECTIVES

1. *Students will define equicircles.*
2. *Students will state at least four properties involving equicircles.*
3. *Students will state and prove one property of equicircles.*

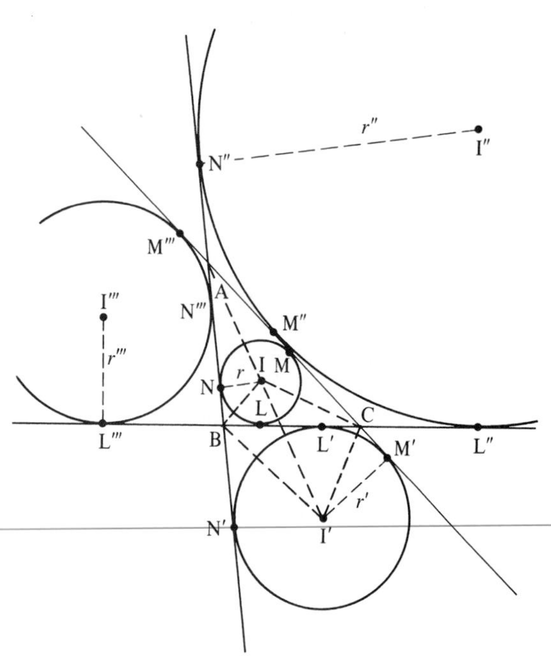

PREASSESSMENT

Students should have mastered the topic of circles in their high school geometry course.

Present the following figure to your students and ask them to find the length of $\overline{AN'}$, if the perimeter of $\triangle ABC = 16$. (Points M′, N′, and L′ are points of tangency.)

TEACHING STRATEGIES

Although the problem posed above is quite simple, its approach is rather unusual and therefore could cause your students some difficulty. The only theorem they need to recall is that two tangent segments from an external point to a circle are congruent. Applying this theorem to the above problem we get

$$BN' = BL' \text{and } CM' = CL'.$$

The perimeter of $\triangle ABC = AB + BC + AC$
$= AB + (BL' + CL') + AC$

which by substitution yields

$$AB + BN' + CM' + AC$$

or

$$AN' + AM'.$$

However, $AN' = AM'$ (they too are tangent segments from the same external point to the same circle).

Therefore $AN' = \frac{1}{2}(\text{perimeter of } \triangle ABC) = 8$. By summarizing this rather fascinating fact, students will be motivated toward pursuing further relationships in this figure.

Next, let s = semiperimeter of $\triangle ABC$

$$a = BC; b = AC; c = AB$$

With your guidance, students should now be able to establish the following relationship:

$$BN' = BL' = AN' - AB = s - c$$
$$CM' = CL' = AM' - AC = s - b$$

At this point you ought to indicate to students that these are just a few of the segments that will be expressed in terms of the lengths of the sides of $\triangle ABC$. Here the relationship of the two circles to the triangle should be defined. Students will recognize circle I as the *inscribed* circle of $\triangle ABC$. Most likely they are not familiar with circle I′. This circle, which is also tangent to the lines of the three sides of $\triangle ABC$, yet contains no interior points of the triangle, is called an *escribed* circle. A triangle has four equicircles, one inscribed and three escribed. The center of an escribed circle, called an *excenter*, is the point of intersection of two exterior angle bisectors and one interior angle bisector.

Students should again further familiarity with these circles by expressing other segments in terms of the lengths of the sides of $\triangle ABC$. Once again provide guidance where necessary.

$$\begin{aligned} AN + AM &= (AB - NB) + (AC - MC) \\ &= (AB - LB) + (AC - LC) \\ &= (AB + AC) - (LB + LC) \\ &= c + b - a \end{aligned}$$

Challenge your students to show that

$$c + b - a = 2(s - a).$$

Therefore $AN + AM = 2(s - a)$.
However $AN = AM$, thus $AN = s - a$.
Have your students conjecture how BN and CL can be expressed in terms of the lengths of the sides of $\triangle ABC$.

$$\begin{aligned} BN &= s - b \\ CL &= s - c \end{aligned}$$

We are now ready to apply some of these expressions to establish two interesting relationships. These are $BL = CL'$ and $LL' = b - c$, the difference between the lengths of the other two sides of $\triangle ABC$.

Since both BL and CL′ were shown to be equal to $s - b$, $BL = CL'$.
Consider LL′, which equals $BC - BL - CL'$.
By substitution $LL' = a - 2(s - b) = b - c$.

We can now prove rather easily that the length of the common external tangent segment of an inscribed and escribed circle of a triangle equals the length of the side contained in the line that intersects the tangent segment.
The proof proceeds as follows: $NN' = AN' - AN$
Earlier we showed that $AN' = s$, and $AN = s - a$.
By substitution, $NN' = s - (s - a) = a$.
The same argument holds true for MM′.

Another interesting theorem states that the length of the common external tangent segment of two escribed circles of a triangle equals the sum of the lengths of the two sides that intersect it.

To prove this theorem, have students recall that $BL'' = s$ and $CL''' = s$. This was proved when the *Preassessment* problem was solved. Therefore

$$\begin{aligned} L'''L'' &= BL'' + CL''' - BC \\ &= s + s - a \\ &= b + c \end{aligned}$$

We can also show that the length of each of the common internal tangent segments of two escribed circles of a triangle equals the length of the side opposite the vertex they determine. The proof is rather simple:

$$L'L'' = BL'' - BL' = BL'' - BN' = s - (s - c) = c$$

Encourage students to investigate the above figure and discover other relationships. A consideration of the radii of the equicircles will produce some interesting results. These radii are called *equiradii*.

A theorem states that the radius of the inscribed circle of a triangle equals the ratio of the area to the semiperimeter. That is

$$\mathcal{A}\triangle ABC = \mathcal{A}\triangle BCI + \mathcal{A}\triangle CAI + \mathcal{A}\triangle ABI$$

(note: $\mathcal{A}$ reads "area of")

$$\begin{aligned} \mathcal{A}\triangle ABC &= \frac{1}{2}ra + \frac{1}{2}rb + \frac{1}{2}rc \\ &= \frac{1}{2}r(a + b + c) = sr. \end{aligned}$$

$$\text{Therefore } r = \frac{\mathcal{A}\triangle ABC}{s}.$$

A natural extension of this theorem states that the radius of an escribed circle of a triangle equals the ratio of the area of the triangle to the difference between the semiperimeter and the length of the side to which the escribed circle is tangent.

To prove this have students consider

$$\begin{aligned} \mathcal{A}\triangle ABC &= \mathcal{A}\triangle ABI' + \mathcal{A}\triangle ACI' - \mathcal{A}\triangle BCI' \\ &= \frac{1}{2}r'c + \frac{1}{2}r'b - \frac{1}{2}r'a \\ &= \frac{1}{2}r'(c + b - a) \\ &= r'(s - a). \end{aligned}$$

$$\text{Therefore } r' = \frac{\mathcal{A}\triangle ABC}{s - a}.$$

In a similar manner students should show that

$$r'' = \frac{\mathcal{A}\triangle ABC}{s - b}$$

and

$$r''' = \frac{\mathcal{A}\triangle ABC}{s - c}.$$

To conclude this discussion, have students find the product of all the equiradii of a circle. All they need do is multiply the last few expressions:

$$rr'r''r''' = \frac{(\mathcal{A}\triangle ABC)^4}{s(s - a)(s - b)(s - c)}$$

However by Heron's formula

$$\mathcal{A}\triangle ABC = \sqrt{s(s - a)(s - b)(s - c)}.$$

Therefore: $rr'r''r''' = (\mathcal{A}\triangle ABC)^2$.

At this point ask students to summarize the various theorems and relationships developed in this unit.

POSTASSESSMENT

To conclude the lesson, have students complete the following exercises.

1. Define equicircles and equiradii.
2. State four properties of equicircles.
3. State and prove one property of equicircles.

REFERENCE

Posamentier, A. S. *Advanced Euclidean Geometry: Excursions for Secondary Teachers and Students.* New York, NY: John Wiley Publishing, 2002.

Unit 66

The Inscribed Circle and the Right Triangle

After having completed a unit on circles and a separate unit dealing with right triangles, students may enjoy seeing some relationships that integrate these units. This unit will deal with some interesting properties of the radius of an inscribed circle of a right triangle.

PERFORMANCE OBJECTIVES

1. *Given a right triangle with integral length sides, students will be able to show that the inradius is an integer.*
2. *Students will be able to explain how the altitude drawn to the hypotenuse of a right triangle is related to the inradii of the triangles formed.*
3. *Students will know and be able to derive a formula relating the inradius to the area and perimeter of a right triangle.*
4. *Given a particular integral inradius, students will be able to determine the number of right triangles with integral relatively prime sides having this given inradius.*
5. *Students will be able to give one possible triple of the lengths of sides of a right triangle when given a positive integral value of the inradius.*

PREASSESSMENT

Have students try the following problems:

1. Find the radius of a circle inscribed in a right triangle whose sides have lengths 3, 4, 5.
2. Repeat this problem for a triangle whose sides have lengths 5, 12, 13.

TEACHING STRATEGIES

After having completed the above problems either individually or as a class, students will want to consider the following question: "Given a right triangle of integral sides, will this guarantee that the radius of the inscribed circle is also an integer?" To prove that the answer is affirmative, consider the diagram below. Here, r is the inradius (i.e., the radius of the inscribed circle), and $\triangle ABC$ has a right angle at C and sides

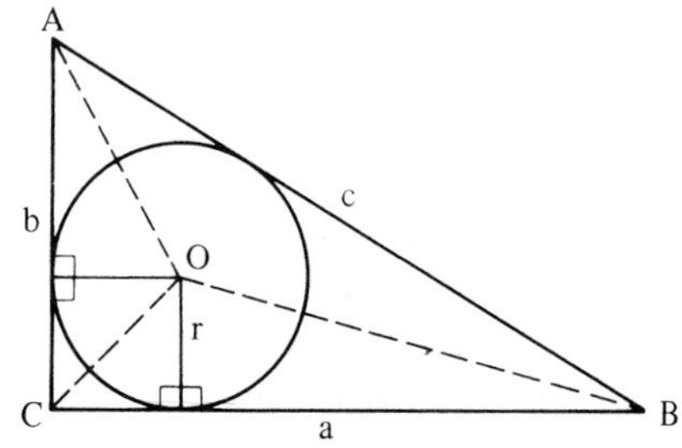

of lengths a, b, c. The proof involves finding a relationship between r, a, b, and c. If the center of the circle is joined to each of the three vertices, three triangles are formed. The area of one triangle is $\frac{1}{2}ra$, the second triangle's area is $\frac{1}{2}rb$, and the third's is $\frac{1}{2}rc$. The area of $\triangle ABC$ is $\frac{1}{2}ab$. Challenge the students to set up a relationship between r and a, b, c. By adding areas one gets $\frac{1}{2}ra + \frac{1}{2}rb + \frac{1}{2}rc = \frac{1}{2}ab$, which is the area of $\triangle ABC$. Thus, $r = \frac{ab}{a+b+c}$. But this only seems to make r rational for integral a, b, and c. At this point, remind students (or show them for the first time) how integral values of a, b, and c are obtained from a formula. That is, show them this generating formula for sides of right triangles.

$$\begin{aligned} a &= (m^2 - n^2) \\ b &= 2mn \\ c &= (m^2 + n^2), \end{aligned}$$

where $m > n$ and m and n are relatively prime positive integers of different parity.

Using $r(a + b + c) = ab$, substitute a, b, and c. Thus, $2r(m^2 + mn) = 2mn(m^2 - n^2)$ or $r = n(m - n)$.

Since m and n are integers, $m > n$, then r is also an integer. Therefore, *whenever a right triangle has integral sides it also has an integral inradius.*

As a result of the above, a concise formula can be established relating the inradius to the area and perimeter of a right triangle. Since $r = \frac{ab}{a + b + c}$, substitute p (perimeter) for $a + b + c$. Also note that the area of $\triangle ABC = \mathscr{A}\frac{ab}{2}$ or $2\mathscr{A}\triangle ABC = ab$ (where $\mathscr{A}$ represents "area of"). Thus $r = \frac{2\mathscr{A}\triangle}{p}$. For practice, have students find the inradius, given various values of $\mathscr{A}\triangle$ and p.

Students have probably worked for some time with right triangles whose altitude to the hypotenuse is drawn (see figure below). Now they can relate the inradius to this familiar diagram.

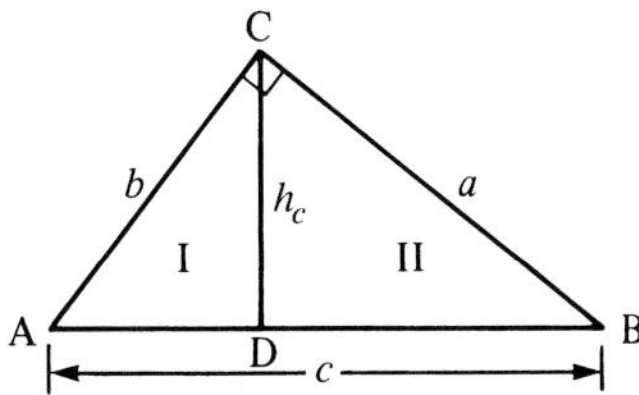

Let $\triangle ADC$ be called $\triangle$I with inradius r_{I}. Similarly, $\triangle DCB$ ($\triangle$II) has inradius r_{II} and $\triangle ABC$ ($\triangle$III) has inradius r_{III}. It can be shown that the sum of the inradii of $\triangle$I, $\triangle$II, and $\triangle$III equals the length of the altitude from C, which will be called h_c. Note that $\triangle ADC \sim \triangle DCB \sim \triangle ABC$. Since the corresponding inradii of the similar triangles are in the same ratio as any pair of corresponding sides, $\frac{r_{\text{I}}}{r_{\text{III}}} = \frac{b}{c}$ or $r_{\text{I}} = \frac{b}{c}r_{\text{III}}$.

In the same manner, $r_{\text{II}} = \frac{a}{c}r_{\text{III}}$. Therefore, $r_{\text{I}} + r_{\text{II}} + r_{\text{III}} = \frac{a + b + c}{c}r_{\text{III}}$. Recalling that $r = \frac{2\mathscr{A}\triangle\text{III}}{p}$, $\frac{a + b + c}{c}r_{\text{III}} = \left(\frac{a + b + c}{c}\right)\left(\frac{2\mathscr{A}\triangle\text{III}}{p}\right) = \frac{2\mathscr{A}\triangle\text{III}}{c}$. But $\mathscr{A}\triangle\text{III} = \frac{1}{2}h_c c$.

Thus $\frac{2\mathscr{A}\triangle\text{III}}{c} = h_c$ making $r_{\text{I}} + r_{\text{II}} + r_{\text{III}} = h_c$, which is what was to be proved.

One can also use the above to prove that the area of the inscribed circle in $\triangle$I plus the area of the inscribed circle in $\triangle$II equals the area of the inscribed circle in $\triangle$III. This can be seen by recalling that it has been shown that $r_{\text{I}} = \frac{b}{c}r_{\text{III}}$ and $r_{\text{II}} = \frac{a}{c}r_{\text{III}}$. Thus $r_{\text{I}}^2 + r_{\text{II}}^2 = \frac{b^2}{c^2}r_{\text{III}}^2 + \frac{a^2}{c^2}r_{\text{III}}^2 = \frac{a^2 + b^2}{c^2}r_{\text{III}}^2 = r_{\text{III}}^2$ (since $a^2 + b^2 = c^2$). Multiplying by π one gets $\pi r_{\text{I}}^2 + \pi r_{\text{II}}^2 = \pi r_{\text{III}}^2$, which is the theorem to be proved.

Another interesting relationship concerning the inradius is: "The number of primitive Pythagorean Triples is 2^{ℓ} where ℓ is the number of odd prime divisions of $r (\ell \geq 0)$, and r is the length of the corresponding inradius." The full meaning of this theorem should be clear to students before embarking on the proof. Show students that for every natural number r there exists at least one right triangle of sides $2r + 1$, $2r^2 + 2r$, and $2r^2 + 2r + 1$ where r is the inradius. Students should be able to check that this satisfies the Pythagorean theorem. As an example, have them try various values for r. For $r = 1$, one gets a triangle of side lengths 3, 4, and 5.

Getting back to proving the above theorem, let a, b, and c be sides of a right triangle with sides of integral length, where b is even, a, b, and c are relatively prime. The inradius of this triangle is the positive integer r. Recall that $r = \frac{ab}{a + b + c}r$ can also be written as $\frac{1}{2}(a + b - c)$ by noting that $\frac{ab}{a + b + c} = \frac{a + b - c}{2}$ is an identity. Students should be urged to verify this identity remembering that $a^2 + b^2 = c^2$. From the original generating formula, substitute for a, b, and c. Students should obtain $r = (m - n)n$. Since m and n are relatively prime, then $(m - n)$ and n are also relatively prime. (Note: $(m - n)$ is odd m and n are relatively prime and of opposite parity.) Thus, the inradius can be decomposed into a product of two positive integers that are relatively prime and where the factor $(m - n)$ is odd.

Now consider r as any positive integer where $r = xy$ is any decomposition of r into a product of two relatively prime positive integers where one is odd. Let $m = x + y, n = y$. Then m and n are also relatively prime. Also, since x is odd, if $n = y$ is odd, then $m = x + y$ is even. Similarly, if m is odd, n must be even. Thus, one of the numbers m and n is even.

Recall $m > n$. Letting $a = m^2 - n^2, b = 2mn, c = m^2 + c^2$ one obtains the type of triangle desired with inradius $r = (m - n)'nab$. Therefore, every decomposition of the number r into a product of two relatively prime numbers where one is odd will determine the type of triangle desired of inradius r. It can be shown that if $\ell \geq 0$ where

$$r = 2p_1^{x1}p_2^{x2}p_3^{x3} \cdot p_t^{x\ell} \quad \text{with } p_t$$

being an odd prime integer (i a positive integer), then the number of decompositions of r is 2^{ℓ}. Thus 2_{ℓ} must be the number of decompositions or r into two relatively prime factors where one is odd.

Thus, for every positive integer r, there exists as many distinct right triangles whose sides have lengths that are relatively prime integers with inradius r as there are distinct decompositions of r into a product of two relatively prime factors of which one is odd. The numbers of such triangles are 2_{ℓ}. This completes the proof.

Students desiring to look into the matter further might try to prove that if r is a positive even integer, then the total number of right triangles with integral length sides that are not necessarily relatively prime, having r as an inradius, is given by $(x + 1)(2x_1 + 1)(2x_2 + 1)\cdots(2x_{\ell} + 1)$ where x and ℓ are the numbers found by decomposing r into $2^1p_1^{x_1}p_2^{x_2} \cdot p_t^{x\ell}$, $x \geqq 0$, $\ell \geqq 0$ and $p_{\ell} =$ odd prime, $x_1 \geq 1$ and

$2 < p_1 < p_2 < \cdots < p_\ell$. Any positive integer can be so decomposed.

Other interesting relationships concerning the inradius might be researched by the students. For example, they might try to prove the formula (for any triangle) that the inradius r of $\triangle XYZ$ (sides x,y,z and $s = \frac{x + y + z}{2}$) is $r = \sqrt{\frac{(s - x)(s - y)(s - z)}{5}}$. Other investigations should prove to be challenging to the class.

POSTASSESSMENT

1. If a right triangle has sides of 5, 12, and 13, does this guarantee r will also be an integer? If so, which integer is it? If not, explain why.
2. If an altitude drawn to the hypotenuse of a right triangle creates three similar triangles of inradii 2, 3, and 4, find the length of this altitude.
3. Find the number of distinct right triangles whose sides have lengths that are relatively prime integers having 70 as its inradii.
4. If the inradius equals 3, find the lengths of the sides of one right triangle with this inradius.
5. $\triangle XYZ$ has an area of 6 and a perimeter of 12. Find the length of its inradius.

Unit 67

The Golden Rectangle

In this unit, the concept of the golden ratio will be introduced together with some of its elementary algebraic and geometric ramifications.

PERFORMANCE OBJECTIVES

1. *Students will construct a golden rectangle.*
2. *Students will state the golden ratio.*
3. *Students will demonstrate certain properties of the golden rectangle and the golden ratio.*

PREASSESSMENT

Some knowledge of geometry and intermediate algebra is necessary.

TEACHING STRATEGIES

Have your students draw a golden rectangle using the following construction. Given square ABCD, with each side one unit long, locate the midpoint, M, of $\overline{AD}$. Draw $\overline{MC}$. By the Pythagorean theorem, $MC = \frac{\sqrt{5}}{2}$. With center of compasses at M and radius $\overline{MC}$, have students describe an arc cutting $\overrightarrow{AD}$ at E. Then,

$$DE = ME - MD = \frac{\sqrt{5}}{2} - \frac{1}{2}, = \frac{\sqrt{5} - 1}{2}. \quad (1)$$

From this result, it follows that

$$AE = AD + DE = 1 + \frac{\sqrt{5} - 1}{2}, \text{ or } = \frac{\sqrt{5} + 1}{2} = 1.61803\cdots$$

By erecting a perpendicular at E to meet $\overrightarrow{BC}$ at F, rectangle ABFE is constructed, where the ratio of length to width is

$$\frac{AE}{AB} = \frac{\frac{\sqrt{5} + 1}{2}}{1} = \frac{\sqrt{5} + 1}{2}. \quad (2)$$

The ratio (2) is called the *golden ratio* or *golden section*, denoted by the Greek letter phi (ϕ), and a rectangle having such a ratio of length to width is called a *golden rectangle*. Note that the value of (2), $\phi = 1.61803\cdots$, is an irrational

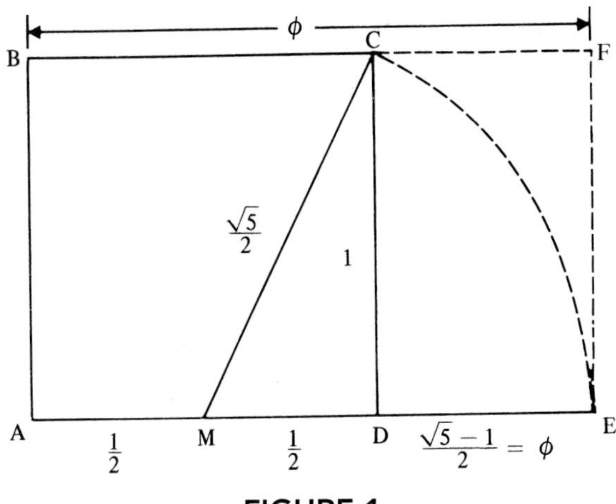

FIGURE 1

number approximately equal to $\frac{8}{5}$. A rectangle with such a ratio of length to width was thought by the ancient Greeks, and corroborated experimentally by the psychologist Fechner in 1876, to be the most pleasing and harmoniously balanced rectangle to the eye.

Have your students solve the equation $x^2 - x - 1 = 0$, solutions for which are

$$r_1 = \frac{\sqrt{5}+1}{2} \text{ and } r_2 = \frac{-\sqrt{5}+1}{2}. \tag{3}$$

From (2), $r_1 = \phi$, and r_2, when evaluated, is equal to $-1.61803\cdots$

A relation between ϕ and r_2 will become apparent if we first evaluate the reciprocal of ϕ, i.e., determine $\frac{1}{\phi}$. From (2),

$$\frac{1}{\phi} = \frac{1}{\frac{\sqrt{5}+1}{2}} = \frac{\sqrt{5}-1}{2} = 0.61803\cdots.$$

The ratio $\frac{\sqrt{5}-1}{2}$ is denoted by ϕ'. Thus, from (3), $r_2 = \frac{-\sqrt{5}+1}{2}$ is the additive inverse of ϕ' and is denoted by $-\phi'$. In summary, then,

$$\phi = \frac{\sqrt{5}+1}{2} = 1.61803\cdots, \tag{4}$$

$$-\phi = \frac{\sqrt{5}-1}{2} = -1.61803\cdots, \tag{5}$$

$$\frac{1}{\phi} = \phi' = \frac{\sqrt{5}+1}{2} = 0.61803\cdots, \tag{6}$$

$$-\phi' = \frac{\sqrt{5}+1}{2} = -0.61803\cdots. \tag{7}$$

Keep in mind that the ratio of width to length for a golden rectangle is ϕ', whereas the ratio of length to width is ϕ.

Thus, in Figure 1, $\frac{\text{DE}}{\text{DC}} = \phi'$, so that CDEF is a golden rectangle.

Some rather unique relationships can be derived from (4) − (7). For example, using (4) and (6),

$$\phi \cdot \phi' = 1, \tag{8}$$

and

$$\phi - \phi' = 1. \tag{9}$$

ϕ and ϕ' are the only two numbers in mathematics that bear the distinction of having both their products and differences equal to one!

$$\phi^2 = \left(\frac{\sqrt{5}+1}{2}\right)^2 = \frac{5+2\sqrt{5}+1}{4} = \frac{3+\sqrt{5}}{2}. \tag{10}$$

$$\text{But, } \phi + 1 = \frac{\sqrt{5}+1}{2} + 1 = \frac{3+\sqrt{5}}{2}. \tag{11}$$

Thus, from (10) and (11),

$$\phi^2 = \phi + 1. \tag{12}$$

Furthermore, by using (6) and (12),

$$(\phi')^2 + \phi = \frac{1}{\phi^2} + \phi = \frac{1}{\phi+1} + \phi = \frac{1+\phi^2+\phi}{\phi+1}$$

$$= \frac{\phi^2+\phi^2}{\phi^2} = \frac{2\phi^2}{\phi^2} = 2. \tag{13}$$

Again, using (6) and (12),

$$\phi^2 - \phi^1 = \phi + 1 - \frac{1}{\phi} = \frac{\phi^2+\phi-1}{\phi}$$

$$= \frac{\phi+1+\phi-1}{\phi} = 2. \tag{14}$$

Hence, from (13) and (14)

$$(\phi')^2 + \phi = \phi^2 - \phi' \tag{15}$$

Powers of ϕ: A fascinating occurrence of the Fibonacci series can be obtained if we derive powers of ϕ in terms of ϕ and take note of the coefficients and constants that arise.

For example, using (12),

$$\begin{aligned}\phi^3 &= \phi^2 \cdot \phi = (\phi+1)\phi = \phi^2 + \phi \\ &= \phi + 1 + \phi = 2\phi + 1,\end{aligned} \tag{16}$$

$$\begin{aligned}\phi^4 &= \phi^3 \cdot \phi = (2\phi+1)\phi = 2\phi^2 + \phi \\ &= 2(\phi+1) + \phi = 2\phi + 2\phi \\ &= 3\phi + 2,\end{aligned} \tag{17}$$

$$\begin{aligned}\text{and } \phi^5 &= \phi^4 \cdot \phi = (3\phi+2)\phi = 3\phi^2 + 2\phi \\ &= 3(\phi+1) + 2\phi = 3\phi + 3 + 2\phi \\ &= 5\phi + 3.\end{aligned} \tag{18}$$

Have students generate further powers of ϕ.

$$\begin{aligned}\phi^1 &= 1\phi + 0 \\ \phi^2 &= 1\phi + 1 \\ \phi^3 &= 2\phi + 1 \\ \phi^4 &= 3\phi + 2 \\ \phi^5 &= 5\phi + 3\end{aligned} \tag{19}$$

$$\phi^6 = 8\phi + 5$$
$$\phi^7 = 13\phi + 8$$
$$\phi^8 = 21\phi + 13$$
$$\vdots \quad \vdots \quad \vdots$$

Let us return to Figure 1. If, along $\overline{CD}$, the length DE $= \phi'$ is marked off, we obtain square DEGH, each side equal in length to ϕ'.

Thus, CH $= 1 - \phi'$ (remember that originally CD $= \frac{1}{\phi}$ one unit). But $1 - \phi' = 1 - \frac{1}{\phi} = \frac{\phi - 1}{\phi} = \frac{\phi}{\phi} = \frac{1}{\phi^2} = (\phi')^2 = \frac{1}{\phi^2}$. With CF (or GH) $= \phi' = \frac{1}{\phi}$, $\frac{CH''}{CF} = \frac{(\phi')^2}{\phi'} = \phi'$.

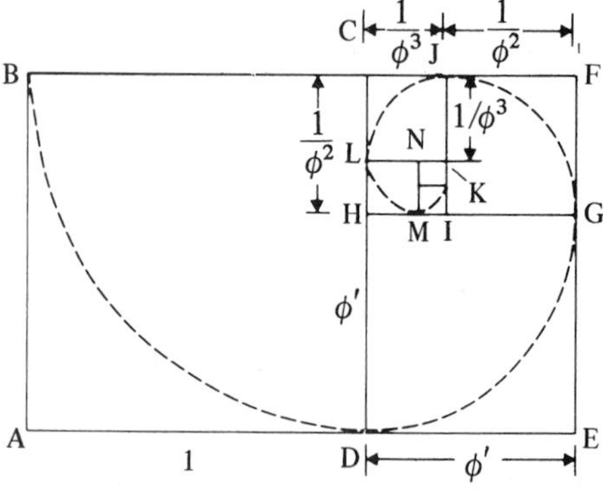

FIGURE 2

Thus, CFGH is also a golden rectangle.

In like fashion, a square, each of whose sides is $(\phi')^2$ units in length, can be partitioned along side CF of CFGH, whereby we obtain another golden rectangle CJIH. CJIH can similarly be partitioned to obtain square GJKL, leaving golden rectangle IKLH. This process of partitioning squares from golden rectangles to obtain another golden rectangle can be indefinitely continued in the manner suggested in Figure 2.

If points B,D,G,J,L,M are connected by a smooth curve (see Figure 2), a spiral-shaped curve will result. This is part of an equiangular spiral, a detailed discussion of which is not possible at this time.

POSTASSESSMENT

1. A line segment $\overline{AE}$ is said to be divided into *extreme and mean ratio* if a point D can be located on $\overline{AE}$ such that

$$\frac{AE}{AD} = \frac{AD}{DE}. \qquad (20)$$

In Figure 1, let AE $= x$ and AD $= 1$. Then, from (20), derive the quadratic equation that was used to determine the value of ϕ in (3).

REFERENCES

Posamentier, A. S. *Advanced Euclidean Geometry: Excursions for Secondary Teachers and Students*. New York, NY: John Wiley Publishing, 2002.

Posamentier, Alfred S., Ingmar Lehmann. *The Fabulous Fibonacci. Numbers*. Amherst, NY: Prometheus Books, 2007.

Dunlap, Richard A. *The Golden Ration and Fibonacci Numbers*. River Edge, NJ: World Scientific Publishing Co., 1997.

Livio, Mario. *The Golden Ratio*. New York: Broadway Books, 2002.

Walser, Hans. *The Golden Section*. Washington, DC: Mathematical Association of America, 2001.

Unit 68

The Golden Triangle

This unit will help to develop student understanding in areas of mathematics not usually dealt with.

PERFORMANCE OBJECTIVES

1. *Students will demonstrate understanding of various relationships among the pentagon, the pentagram, and the golden ratio.*
2. *Students will construct a golden triangle.*
3. *Students will demonstrate certain properties of the golden triangle with trigonometric functions.*

PREASSESSMENT

Some knowledge of geometry and intermediate algebra is necessary.

TEACHING STRATEGIES

Have your students construct a regular pentagon ABCDE by any method, after which they should draw pentagram ACEBD (see Figure 1). Let each side of the pentagon be ϕ units in length. Review with your students the various angle measures and isosceles triangles formed by the pentagram and pentagon. Particular note should be made of similar isosceles triangles BED and DEF, since they will be chosen, quite arbitrarily, from the many similar triangles in Figure 1, for the discussion that follows.

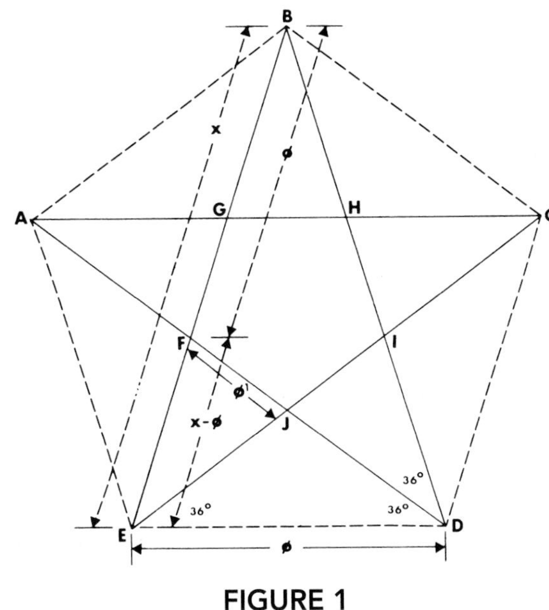

FIGURE 1

With $\overline{DF}$ the bisector of $\angle BDE$, triangles DEF and BDF are isosceles, so that

$$ED = DF = FB = \phi. \tag{1}$$

Let $BE = BD = x$. Then $FE = x - \phi$, and

$$\frac{BF}{FE} = \frac{BD}{ED}, \frac{\phi}{x-\phi} = \frac{x}{\phi}, \tag{2}$$

so that $x^2 - \phi x - \phi^2 = 0.$ (3)

The positive root of (3), from the quadratic formula, is

$$x = \phi\left(\frac{1+\sqrt{5}}{2}\right). \tag{4}$$

But by definition, $\dfrac{1+\sqrt{5}}{2} = \phi.$

Hence, from (4),

$$x = \phi \cdot \phi = \phi^2 = BE, \tag{5}$$

and $EF = x - \phi = \phi^2 - \phi = \phi + 1 - \phi = 1.$ (6)

Thus, in $\triangle BED$, the ratio of leg to base, using (5), is

$\dfrac{BE}{ED} = \dfrac{\phi^2}{\phi} = \phi,$

and in $\triangle DEF$, the ratio of leg to base is again ϕ,

since $\dfrac{DE}{EF} = \dfrac{\phi}{1} = \phi,$

so that in any 72°-72°-36° isosceles triangle (hereafter referred to as the golden triangle), the ratio of

$$\frac{\text{leg}}{\text{base}} = \phi. \tag{7}$$

This is the same ratio of length to width defined for the golden rectangle.

In isosceles $\triangle EFJ$, $FJ = \phi'$, since, using (6) and (7),

$$\frac{EF}{FJ} = \frac{1}{FJ} = \phi, \text{ implying that } FJ = \frac{1}{\phi} = \phi'. \tag{8}$$

Thus, regular pentagon FGHIJ has side length of ϕ'.

Returning to isosceles $\triangle DEF$, it is apparent that $\overline{EJ}$ is the bisector of $\angle DEF$. In Figure 2, let $\overline{FK}$ be the bisector of $\angle EFJ$. Then $FJ = FK = \dfrac{1}{\phi}$ and base $JK = \dfrac{1}{\phi^2}$. Moreover, $\overline{FK} \| \overline{BD}$, since $m\angle KFJ = m\angle JDB$.

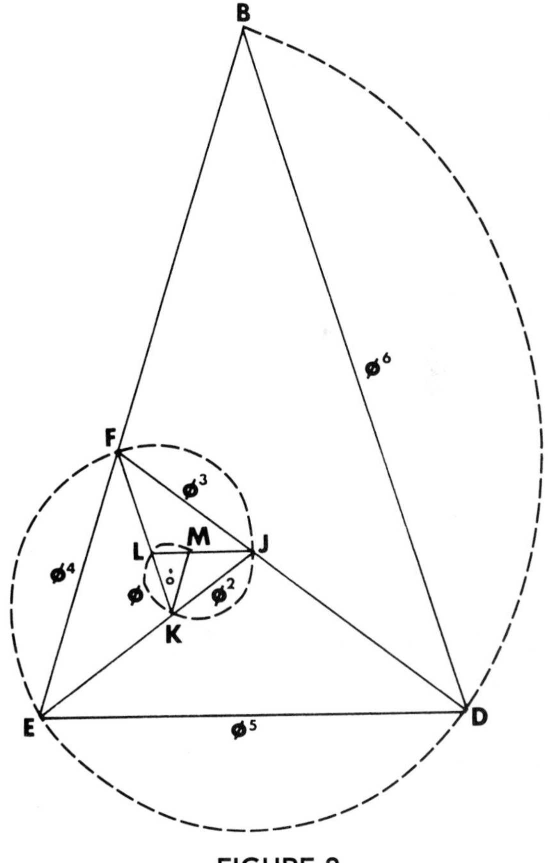

FIGURE 2

In like fashion, the bisector of $\angle FJK$ is parallel to $\overline{ED}$ and meets $\overline{FK}$ at L, forming another golden triangle, $\triangle JKL$. This process of bisecting a base angle of a golden triangle can be continued indefinitely to produce a series of smaller and smaller golden triangles, which converge to a limiting point, 0. This point, comparable to that obtained in the golden rectangle, is the pole of an equiangular spiral which passes through the vertices B,D,E,F,J,K,L, . . . of each of the golden triangles.

A number of additional properties of the golden triangle are worth mentioning:

1. In Figure 2, let ML be of unit length. Then, from (7),

$$\begin{aligned} LK &= \phi = 1\phi + 0 \\ KJ &= \phi^2 = 1\phi + 1 \\ JF &= \phi^3 = 2\phi + 1 \\ FE &= \phi^4 = 3\phi + 2 \\ ED &= \phi^5 = 5\phi + 3 \\ DB &= \phi^6 = 8\phi + 5 \end{aligned} \tag{9}$$

forming a Fibonacci series.

2. The bisector of the vertex angle of a golden triangle divides the bisectors of the base angles in the golden ratio (see Figure 1). Since the angle bisectors of a triangle are concurrent, the bisector of $\angle EBD$ must pass through J. However, from (6), EF = 1 = EJ = JD, and from (8), FJ = ϕ'.

   Hence, $\frac{JD}{FJ} = \frac{1}{\phi'} = \phi$.

3. The golden triangle can be used to represent certain trigonometric functions in terms of ϕ (see Figure 3). Let

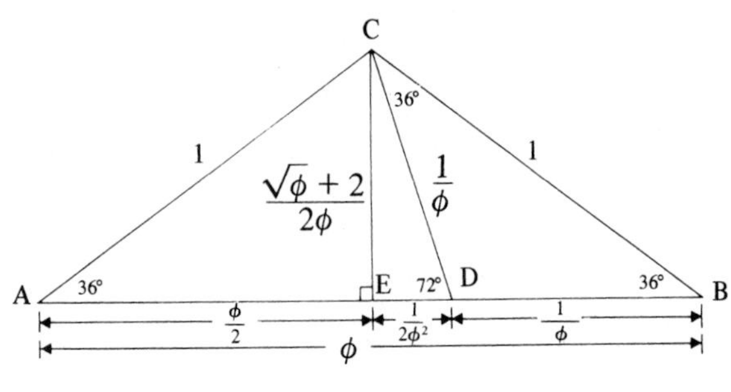

FIGURE 3

$\triangle ABC$ be a 36°-36°-108° isosceles triangle, with AC = CB = 1. Let one of the trisectors of angle C meet $\overline{AB}$ at D. Then $\triangle ACD$ is a golden triangle with $m\angle CDA = m\angle DCA = 72°$. Since AC = 1, then AD = 1, and from (7), CD $= \frac{1}{\phi}$. Furthermore, $\triangle BCD$ is isosceles with $m\angle BCD = m\angle DBC = 36°$. Thus CD $=$ DB $= \frac{1}{\phi}$, and

$$AB = AD + DB = 1 + \frac{1}{\phi} = \phi.$$

From C, drop a perpendicular to meet $\overline{AB}$ at E. This makes AE = EB $= \frac{\phi}{2}$. Immediately, in right

$$\triangle ACE \cos 36° = \frac{\phi}{2}, \text{ implying that} \tag{10}$$

$$\sin 54° = \frac{\phi}{2}. \tag{11}$$

Furthermore,

$$ED = AD - AE = 1 - \frac{\phi}{2} = \frac{2-\phi}{2} = \frac{1}{2\phi^2}. \tag{12}$$

Now in right $\triangle CED$,

$$\cos 72° = \frac{ED}{CD} = \frac{\frac{1}{2\phi^2}}{\frac{1}{\phi}} = \frac{1}{2\phi} = \sin 18°. \tag{13}$$

POSTASSESSMENT

1. Using the reciprocal trigonometric identities, determine values in terms of ϕ for tan, cot, sec, and csc for the angle measures indicated in (10), (11), and (13) above.
2. Using the half-angle formulas, determine trigonometric function values for 18° and 27° in terms of ϕ.

This unit should be used in conjunction with "The Golden Rectangle."

REFERENCES

Dunlap, Richard A. *The Golden Ration and Fibonacci Numbers*. River Edge, NJ: World Scientific Publishing Co., 1997.

Huntley, H. E. *The Divne Proportion*. New York: Dover, 1970.

Posamentier, Alfred S., Ingmar Lehmann. *The Fabulous Fibonacci Numbers*. Amherst, NY: Prometheus Books, 2007.

Walser, Hans. *The Golden Section*. Washington, DC: Mathematical Association of America, 2001.

Unit 69

 Geometric Fallacies

Geometry students studying proofs using auxillary sets often question the need for a rigorous reason for that set's existence. Often they don't appreciate the need for proving the existence and uniqueness of these sets. Students also develop a dependence on a diagram without analyzing its correctness. This unit introduces fallacious proofs to students in the hope that they can better grasp the need for such rigor.

PERFORMANCE OBJECTIVE

Given a geometric fallacy, students will determine where the fallacy occurs.

PREASSESSMENT

Students should be well acquainted with geometric proofs of both congruent and similar triangles.

Present your students with the following proof. They will recognize that it contains a fallacy. Ask them to try to determine where the error occurs.

Given: ABCD is a rectangle
$\overline{FA} \cong \overline{BA}$
R is the midpoint of $\overline{BC}$
N is the midpoint of $\overline{CF}$

To Prove: A right angle is equal in measure to an obtuse angle ($\angle CDA \cong \angle FAD$)

Draw $\overrightarrow{RL}$ perpendicular to $\overline{CB}$.

Draw $\overrightarrow{NM}$ perpendicular to $\overline{CF}$.

$\overrightarrow{RL}$ and $\overrightarrow{NM}$ intersect at point O. If they didn't intersect, $\overline{RL}$ and $\overline{NM}$ would be parallel and this would mean $\overline{CB}$ is parallel to $\overline{CF}$, which is impossible.

Draw $\overline{DO}$, $\overline{CO}$, $\overline{FO}$, and $\overline{AO}$.

Since $\overline{RO}$ is the perpendicular bisector of $\overline{CB}$ and $\overline{DA}$, $\overline{DO} \cong \overline{AO}$.

Since $\overline{NO}$ is the perpendicular bisector of $\overline{CF}$, $\overline{CO} \cong \overline{FO}$.
And, since $\overline{FA} \cong \overline{BA}$ and $\overline{BA} \cong \overline{CD}$, we have $\overline{FA} \cong \overline{CD}$.
$\therefore \triangle CDO \cong \triangle FAO$(SSS $\cong$ SSS), so $\angle ODC \cong \angle OAF$.
Since $\overline{OD} \cong \overline{OA}$, we have $\angle ODA \cong \angle OAD$.
Now, $m\angle ODC - m\angle ODA = m\angle OAF - m\angle OAD$ or $m\angle CDA = m\angle FAD$.

TEACHING STRATEGIES

When students have inspected the proof and have found nothing wrong with it, ask them to use rulers and compasses to reconstruct the diagram. The correct diagram looks like this:

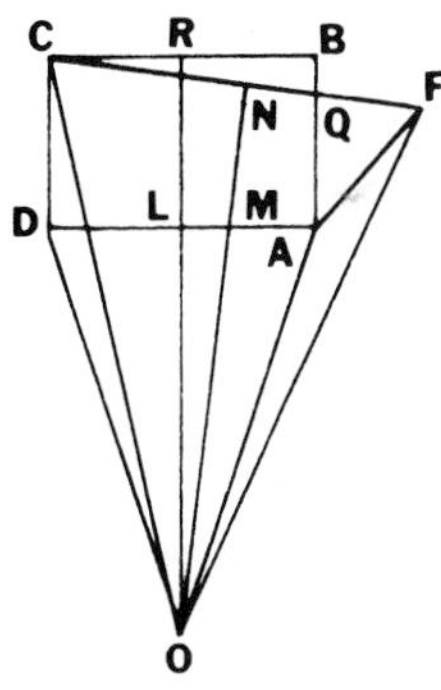

Although the triangles are congruent, our ability to subtract the specific angles no longer exists. Thus, the difficulty with this proof lies in its dependence on an incorrectly drawn diagram.

To show that $\angle OAF$ cannot be obtuse, we must show that when $\overline{OF}$ intersects $\overline{AB}$ and $\overline{AD}$, and point O is on the perpendicular bisector of $\overline{CF}$, then point O cannot be on the perpendicular bisector of $\overline{AD}$.

Suppose point O is the intersection of the two perpendicular bisectors (as in the original diagram). Since $\overline{CD} \,//\, \overline{AQ}$, $\angle DCF \cong \angle AQF$. In isosceles ΔABF, $\angle ABF \cong \angle AFB$. But $m\angle AFB > m\angle AFC$; by substitution $m\angle ABF > m\angle AFC$. Since $\angle AQF$ is an exterior angle of ΔBQF, $m\angle AQF > m\angle ABF$. Therefore $m\angle AQF > m\angle ABF > m\angle AFC$, or $m\angle AQF > m\angle AFC$. By substitution $m\angle DCF > m\angle AFC$. Since $\angle OCF \cong \angle OFC$ by subtraction we have $m\angle DCO > m\angle OFA$. Thus, $DO > OA$. This is a contradiction since $DO = AO$ if O is bisector of $\overline{DA}$

on the perpendicular. Therefore point O cannot be on the perpendicular bisector of $\overline{DA}$ for any point O such that $\angle$OAF is obtuse.

The above proof also holds true for the following diagram, which shows that $\angle$OAF cannot be acute.

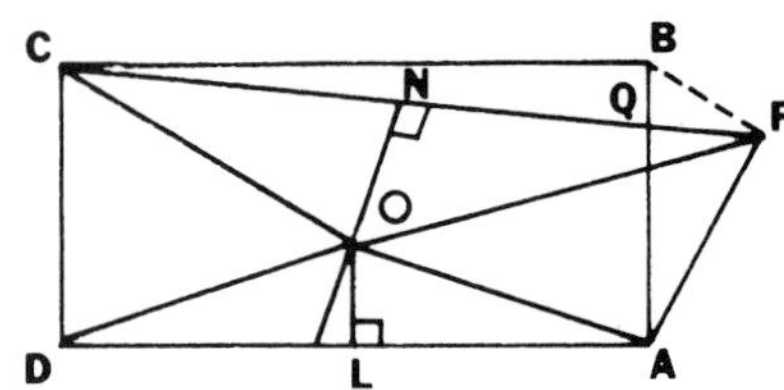

Now present your students with the following proof that any point in the interior of a circle is also on the circle.

Given: Circle O, with radius *r*
Let A be any point in the interior of the circle distinct from O.

Prove: A is on the circle

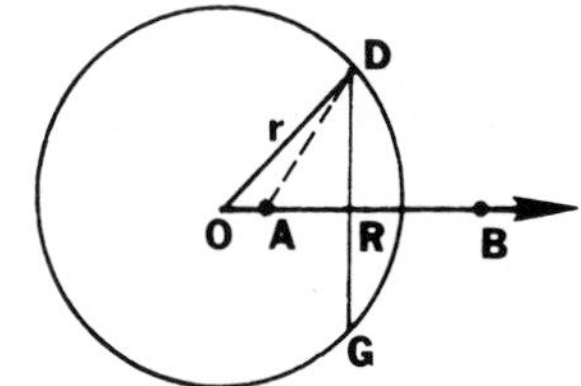

Let B be on the extension of $\overline{OA}$ through A such that $OA \cdot OB = r^2$. (Clearly OB is greater than *r* since OA is less than *r*.) Let the perpendicular bisector of $\overline{AB}$ meet the circle in points D and G, where R is the midpoint of $\overline{AB}$.

We now have OA = OR − RA and OB = OR + RB = OR + RA.

$\therefore r^2 = (OR - RA)(OR + RA)$
$r^2 = OR^2 - RA^2$
$r^2 = (r^2 - DR^2) - (AD^2 - DR^2)$ by the Pythagorean theorem
$r^2 = r^2 - AD^2$
$\therefore AD^2 = 0$
$\therefore$ A coincides with D, and lies on the circle.

The fallacy in this proof lies in the fact that we drew an auxillary line ($\overleftrightarrow{DRG}$) with *two* conditions—that $\overline{DRG}$ is the perpendicular bisector of $\overline{AB}$ and that it intersects the circle. Actually, all points on the perpendicular bisector of $\overline{AB}$ lie in the exterior of the circle and therefore cannot intersect the circle.

$$r^2 = OA\,(OB)$$
$$r^2 = OA\,(OA + AB)$$
$$r^2 = OA^2 + (OA)\,(AB)$$

Now, the proof assumes $OA + \dfrac{AB}{2} < r$

$$2(OA) + AB < 2r$$
$$4(OA)^2 + 4(OA)(AB) + AB^2 < 4r^2$$

Since $r^2 = OA^2 + (OA)(AB)$
we have $4r^2 + AB^2 < 4r^2$
$AB^2 < 0$,
which is impossible.

This proof points to the care we must take when drawing auxillary sets in using *one* condition only.

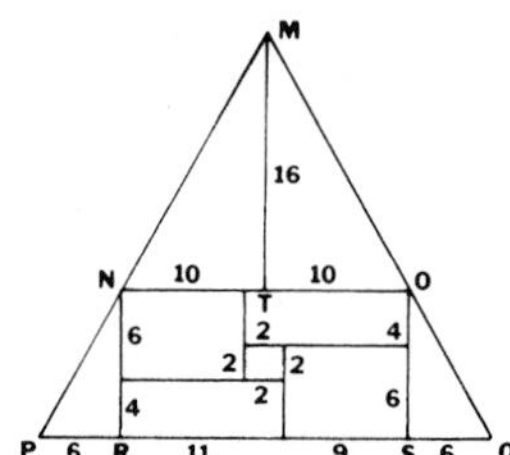

Here is a "triangle" consisting of four right triangles, four rectangles and a "hole."

1. Have your students calculate the area of the eight regions (not the hole) [416].
2. Now have them calculate the area of the entire figure. [Since PQ = 32 and height = 26, $\frac{1}{2}PQ \cdot h = 416$.] We are now faced with this problem: How did we arrive at the same area with and without the hole?

The fallacy occurs because of an error in 2. The figure is *not* a triangle, since points M, N, and P are not collinear.

If points M, N, and P were collinear,

since $\angle$RNO is a right angle, $\angle$PNR is the complement of $\angle$MNT
since $\angle$NRP is a right angle, $\angle$PNR is the complement of $\angle$RPN

$\therefore \angle MNT \cong \angle RPN$
$\therefore \Delta MNT \sim \Delta NPR$
But, this is not the case.

The same argument holds for points M, O, and Q. Therefore the figure is a pentagon; thus the formula we used in 2 is incorrect.

POSTASSESSMENT

Have students select a geometric fallacy from any of the following books and explain the "error" in the proof.

REFERENCES

Maxwell, E. A. *Fallacies in Mathematics.* Cambridge University Press, 1963.

Northrop, E. P. *Riddles in Mathematics.* D. Van Nostrand Co., 1944.

Posamentier, A. S. *Advanced Euclidean Geometry: Excursions for Secondary Teachers and Students.* New York, NY: John Wiley Publishing, 2002.

Posamentier, A. S., J. H. Banks, and R. L. Bannister. *Geometry, Its Elements and Structure*, 2d ed. McGraw-Hill, 1977, pp. 240–44, 270–71.

Unit 70

Regular Polyhedra

This unit will present a method that can be used to prove that there are not more than five regular polyhedra.

PERFORMANCE OBJECTIVE

Students will define a regular polyhedron, identify all regular polyhedra, and explain why no more than five regular polyhedra exist.

PREASSESSMENT

Display physical models of various polyhedra and have students count the number of vertices (V), the number of edges (E), and the number of faces (F) of each polyhedron. After tabulating their results, they should notice the relationship:

$$V + F = E + 2.$$

TEACHING STRATEGIES

Having empirically established Euler's theorem, $(V + F = E + 2)$, students may wish to apply it to reach other conclusions about polyhedra. Depending on class interest, proof of this theorem may be in order. One source for the proof is *Geometry, Its Elements and Structure* by A. S. Posamentier, J. H. Banks, and R. L. Bannister, pp. 574–576 (McGraw-Hill, 1977).

One interesting application of this theorem is the proof that more than five *regular* polyhedra cannot exist. You should begin by defining a regular polyhedron as *a solid figure bounded by portions of planes called faces, each of which is a regular polygon* (congruent sides and angles). The cube is a common example of a regular polyhedron.

To begin the proof that *there are only five regular polyhedra*, let s represent the number of sides of each face and let t represent the number of faces at each vertex.

Since there are t faces at each vertex, students should realize that there are also t edges at each vertex. Suppose in counting the number of edges (E) of a given polyhedron, the number of edges at each vertex were counted and then multiplied by the number of vertices (V). This would produce *twice* the number of edges (2E) of the polyhedron, as each edge was counted twice, once at each of the two vertices it joins. Hence:

$$tV = 2E, \text{ or } \frac{V}{\frac{1}{t}} = \frac{E}{\frac{1}{2}}$$

Similarly, in counting the number of edges of the polyhedron, the number of sides (s) of each face were counted and then multiplied by the number of faces (F) of the polyhedron. This would also produce *twice* the number of edges of the polyhedron, as each side (edge) counted belongs to two faces. Hence, $sF = 2E$, or $\frac{F}{\frac{1}{s}} = \frac{E}{\frac{1}{2}}$

$$\text{Therefore } \frac{V}{\frac{1}{t}} = \frac{E}{\frac{1}{2}} = \frac{F}{\frac{1}{s}}$$

Students should recall the following theorem on proportions:

$$\frac{a}{b} = \frac{c}{d} = \frac{e}{f} = \frac{a + c + e}{b + d + f}$$

Then have them apply it to the following:

$$\frac{V}{\frac{1}{t}} = \frac{-E}{-\frac{1}{2}} = \frac{F}{\frac{1}{s}} = \frac{V - E + F}{\frac{1}{t} - \frac{1}{2} + \frac{1}{s}}$$

However, by Euler's theorem $(V - E + F = 2)$,

$$\frac{V}{\frac{1}{t}} = \frac{E}{\frac{1}{2}} = \frac{F}{\frac{1}{s}} = \frac{2}{\frac{1}{t} - \frac{1}{2} + \frac{1}{s}}$$

Students may now solve for V, E, and F:

$$V = \frac{4s}{2s + 2t - st}$$

$$E = \frac{2st}{2s + 2t - st}$$

$$F = \frac{4t}{2s + 2t - st}$$

Students should be asked to inspect the nature of V, E, and F. Realizing that these numbers must be positive, elicit from students that the denominators must be positive (since s and t are positive, as well as the numerators). Thus,

$$2s + 2t - st > 0.$$

To enable factoring, add -4 to both members of the inequality to get

$$2s + 2t - st - 4 > -4.$$

Then multiply both sides by -1:

$$-2s - 2t + st + 4 < 4, \text{ or } (s - 2)(t - 2) < 4.$$

At this point have students place restrictions on s and t. They should be quick to state that no polygon may have less than three sides; hence $s \geq 3$. Also, they should realize that at each vertex of the polyhedron there must at least be three faces; hence $t \geq 3$.

These facts will indicate that $(s - 2)$ and $(t - 2)$ must be positive. Since their product must be less than four, students should be able to generate the following table:

(s – 2)(t – 2)	(s – 2)	(t – 2)	s	t	V	E	F	Name of Polyhedron
1	1	1	3	3	4	6	4	Tetrahedron
2	2	1	4	3	8	12	6	Hexahedron (cube)
2	1	2	3	4	6	12	8	Octahedron
3	3	1	5	3	20	30	12	Dodecahedron
3	1	3	3	5	12	30	20	Icosahedron

Since there are no other possible values for s and t the above table is complete, and hence there are only five regular polyhedra. More able students should be encouraged to investigate the existence of these five regular polyhedra. One source is Euclid's *Elements*, Book XIII.

Further inspection of the above table reveals an interesting symmetry between the hexahedron and the octahedron as well as the dodecahedron and the icosahedron. That is, if s and t are interchanged, these symmetries will be highlighted. Furthermore, this table indicates that the faces of these regular polyhedra are either equilateral triangles, squares, or regular pentagons (see column s). Students should also be encouraged to further verify Euler's theorem ($V + F = E + 2$) with the data in the above table.

The figure shows the five regular polyhedra as well as "patterns" that can be used to construct (by cutting them out and appropriately folding them) these polyhedra.

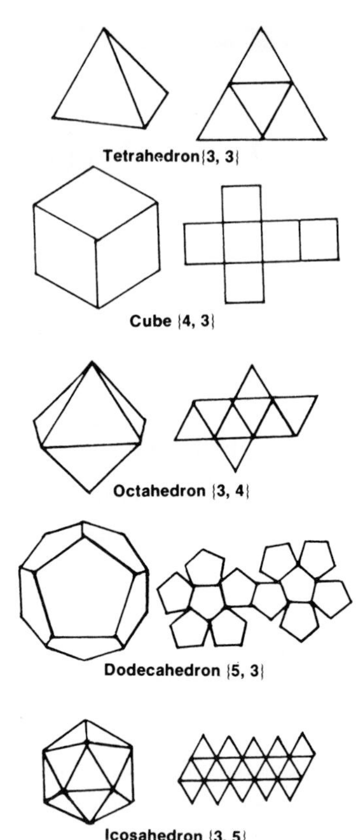

Although often referred to as the five Platonic Solids, it is believed that three (tetrahedron, hexahedron, and dodecahedron) of the five solids were due to Pythagoreans, and the remaining two solids (octahedron, and icosahedron) were due to the efforts of Theaetetus (414–369 B.C.). There is enough history about these solids to merit a brief report by one of the students.

POSTASSESSMENT

1. Have students define and identify regular polyhedra.
2. Have students explain why more than five regular polyhydra cannot exist.

Unit 71

An Introduction to Topology

A lesson on topology can be taught as an enrichment of geometry. This unit will present some basic concepts of topology and their applications.

PERFORMANCE OBJECTIVES

1. *Given two geometric drawings students will determine whether they are topologically equivalent.*
2. *Given a polyhedron or a plane figure students can show that* $V + F - E = 2$ *(space), and* $V + F - E = 1$ *(plane).*

PREASSESSMENT

A basic knowledge of seventh-grade geometry is desirable preceding this unit.

TEACHING STRATEGIES

Have students draw several closed curves. Then have them distinguish between those that are simple closed curves and those that are not. Some possible student responses may be the following.

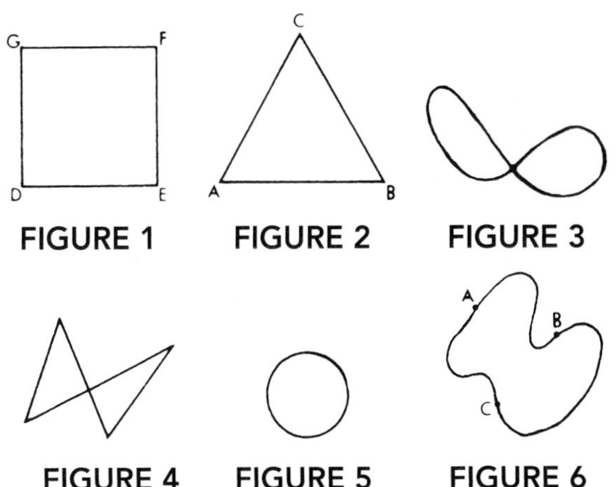

FIGURE 1 FIGURE 2 FIGURE 3

FIGURE 4 FIGURE 5 FIGURE 6

Ask students to redraw each of the figures without lifting their pencils off their paper. Students should realize that if Figure 1 were drawn on a rubber sheet they could twist and bend it into Figures 2, 5, and 6.

Suppose they now consider some geometric figures in space. Have them draw a cube.

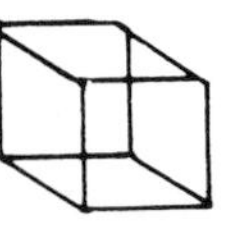

FIGURE 7

Ask students if this cube can be transformed into any of Figures 8, 9, or 10 by twisting or bending it.

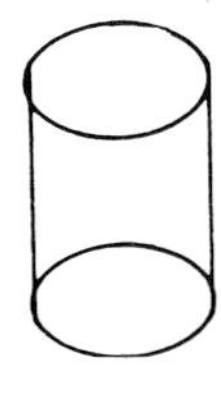

FIGURE 8

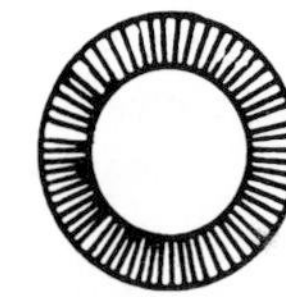

FIGURE 9

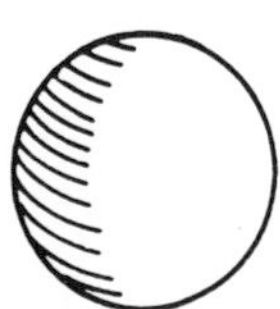

FIGURE 10

They should find that the only figure of these that the cube can be transformed into is a sphere.

Therefore, a cube is topologically equivalent to a sphere. Tell students that studying figures in this way leads to a branch of mathematics called *topology* or "rubber sheet geometry."

One of the more fascinating relationships in geometry is directly taken from topology. This relationship involves the vertices (V), edges (E), and faces (F) of a polyhedron or polygon (see Unit 70). It reads: $V + F - E = 2$ (in three-dimensional space) or $V + F - E = 1$ (in a plane). Have students consider a pentagon. A pentagon has five vertices, five edges, and one face; hence $V + F - E = 5 + 1 - 5 = 1$. Students may now wish to consider a three-space figure. The cube (Figure 7) has 8 vertices, 6 faces, and 12 edges. Therefore, $V + F - E = 8 - 12 + 6 = 2$. These relationships can be demonstrated to the class by using overhead projector transparencies or with physical models.

Suppose a plane were to cut all edges of one of the trihedral angles of a cube (a piece of clay in the form of a cube would be useful here). This plane would then separate one of the vertices from the cube. However, in the process, there would be added to the original polyhedron: 1 face, 3 vertices, and 3 edges. Thus, for this new polyhedron, V is increased by 2. F is increased by 1, and E is increased by 3; yet, V + F − E remains unchanged. More such experiments should be encouraged.

Figures are topologically equivalent if one can be made to coincide with the other by distortion, shrinking, stretching, or bending. If one face of a polyhedron is removed, the remaining figure is topologically equivalent to a region of a plane. This new figure (see Figure 11) will not have the same

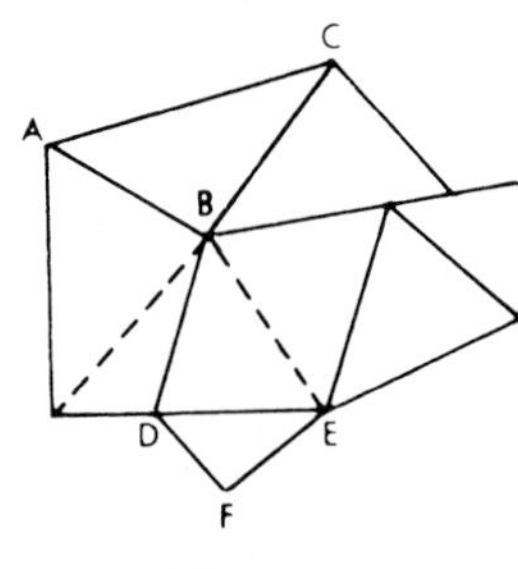

FIGURE 11

shape or size, but its *boundaries* are preserved. The edges will become sides of polygonal regions, and there will be the same number of edges and vertices in the plane figure as in the polyhedron. Each polygon that is not a triangle can be cut into triangles, or triangular regions, by drawing diagonals. Each time a diagonal is drawn, we increase the number of edges by one, but we also increase the number of faces by one. The value of V − E + F is preserved. Triangles on the outer edge of the region will have either one edge on the boundary of the region, as △ABC in Figure 11, or have two edges on the boundary, as △DEF. Triangles such as △ABC can be removed by removing the one boundary side (i.e., $\overline{AC}$). By doing this we decrease the number of faces by one and the number of edges by one. Still V − E + F is unchanged. Triangles such as DEF can be removed by removing two edges (i.e., $\overline{DF}$ and $\overline{EF}$). By doing this we decrease the number of edges by two, the number of faces by one, and the number of vertices by one. V − E + F is still preserved. We continue in this manner until we are left with one triangle. This triangle has three vertices, three edges, and one face. Hence, V − E + F = 1 in the plane. We conclude that when we replace the face we removed we have V − E + F = 2 for a polyhedron in space.

After students have had a chance to familiarize themselves with this theorem, they should be encouraged to test it empirically with student constructed polyhedra. Clay is a good medium for this activity. Students may want to record their results on a chart.

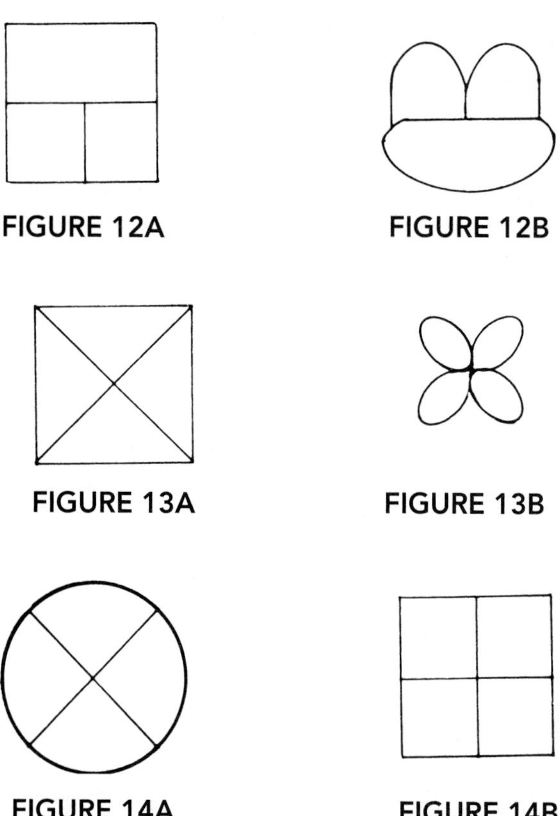

FIGURE 12A

FIGURE 12B

FIGURE 13A

FIGURE 13B

FIGURE 14A

FIGURE 14B

POSTASSESSMENT

1. Have students decide if any of Figures 12, 13, or 14 can be bent into the other figures.
2. Show that V + F − E = 2 holds for a tetrahedron and an octahedron.
3. Show that V + F − E = 1 holds for a hexagon and a dodecagon.

Unit 72

Angles on a Clock

This unit can be used in earlier junior high school grades as a recreational activity where some interesting relationships can be discovered, or it can be used as an enrichment application for beginning algebra students studying the topic of uniform motion.

PERFORMANCE OBJECTIVES

1. *Students will determine the precise time that the hands of a clock form a given angle.*
2. *Students will solve problems related to the positions of the hands on a clock.*

PREASSESSMENT

Ask students at what time (exactly) will the hands of a clock overlap after 4 o'clock.

TEACHING STRATEGIES

Your students' first reaction to the solution to this problem will be that the answer is simply 4:20. When you remind them that the hour hand moves uniformly, they will begin to estimate the answer to be between 4:21 and 4:22. They will realize that the hour hand moves through an interval between minute markers every 12 minutes. Therefore it will leave the interval 4:21–4:22 at 4:24. This however doesn't answer the original question about the exact time of this overlap.

In a beginning algebra class studying uniform motion problems, have students consider this problem in that light. The best way to have students begin to understand the movement of the hands of a clock is by having them consider the hands traveling independently around the clock at uniform speeds. The minute markings on the clock (from now on referred to as "markers") will serve to denote distance as well as time. An analogy should be drawn here to the uniform motion of automobiles (a popular and overused topic for verbal problems in an elementary algebra course). A problem involving a fast automobile overtaking a slower one would be appropriate.

Experience has shown that the analogy should be drawn between specific cases rather than mere generalizations. It might be helpful to have the class find the distance necessary for a car traveling at 60 m.p.h. to overtake a car with a head start of 20 miles and traveling at 5 m.p.h.

Now have the class consider 4 o'clock as the initial time on the clock. Our problem will be to determine exactly when the minute hand will overtake the hour hand after 4 o'clock. Consider the speed of the hour hand to be r, then the speed of the minute hand must be $12r$. We seek the distance, measured by the number of markers traveled, that the minute hand must travel to overtake the hour hand.

Let us refer to this distance as d markers. Hence the distance that the hour hand travels is $d - 20$ markers, since it has a 20-marker head start over the minute hand. For this to take place, the times required for the minute hand, $\frac{d}{12r}$, and for the hour hand, $\frac{d-20}{r}$, are the same. Therefore, $\frac{d}{12r} = \frac{d-20}{r}$, and $d = \frac{12}{11} \cdot 20 = 21\frac{9}{11}$. Thus the minute hand will overtake the hour hand at exactly $4{:}21\frac{9}{11}$.

Consider the expression $d = \frac{12}{11} \cdot 20$. The quantity 20 is the number of markers that the minute hand had to travel to get to the desired position, assuming the hour hand remained stationary. However, quite obviously, the hour hand does not remain stationary. Hence, we must multiply this quantity by $\frac{12}{11}$ as the minute hand must travel $\frac{12}{11}$ as far. Let us refer to this fraction $\left(\frac{12}{11}\right)$ as the correction factor. Have the class verify this correction factor both logically and algebraically.

To begin to familiarize the students with use of the correction factor, choose some short and simple problems. For example, you may ask them to find the exact time when the hands of a clock overlap between 7 and 8 o'clock. Here the students would first determine how far the minute hand would have to travel from the "12" position to the position of the hour hand, assuming again that the hour hand remains stationary. Then by multiplying the number of markers, 35, by the correction factor, $\frac{12}{11}$, they will obtain the exact time $\left(7{:}38\frac{2}{11}\right)$ that the hands will overlap.

To enhance students' understanding of this new procedure ask them to consider a person checking a wristwatch against an electric clock and noticing that the hands on the wristwatch overlap every 65 minutes (as measured by the electric clock). Ask the class if the wristwatch is fast, slow, or accurate.

You may wish to have them consider the problem in the following way. At 12 o'clock the hands of a clock overlap exactly. Using the previously described method we find that the hands will again overlap at exactly $1{:}05\frac{5}{11}$, and then again at exactly $2{:}10\frac{10}{11}$, and again at exactly $3{:}16\frac{4}{11}$, and so on. Each time there is an interval of $65\frac{5}{11}$ minutes between overlapping positions. Hence, the person's watch is inaccurate by $\frac{5}{11}$ of a minute. Have students now determine if the wristwatch is fast or slow.

There are many other interesting, and sometimes rather difficult, problems made simple by this correction factor. You may very easily pose your own problems. For example, you may ask your students to find the exact times when the hands of a clock will be perpendicular (or form a straight angle) between, say, 8 and 9 o'clock.

Again, you would have the students determine the number of markers that the minute hand would have to travel from the "12" position until it forms the desired angle with the stationary hour hand. Then have them multiply this number by the correction factor $\left(\frac{12}{11}\right)$ to obtain the exact actual time. That is, to find the exact time that the hands of a clock are *first* perpendicular between 8 and 9 o'clock, determine the desired position of the minute hand when the hour hand remains stationary (here, on the 25-minute marker). Then, multiply 25 by $\frac{12}{11}$ to get $8{:}27\frac{3}{11}$, the exact time when the hands are *first* perpendicular after 8 o'clock.

For students who have not yet studied algebra, you might justify the $\frac{12}{11}$ correction factor for the interval between overlaps in the following way:

> Think of the hands of a clock at noon. During the next 12 hours (i.e., until the hands reach the same position at midnight) the hour hand makes one revolution, the minute hand makes 12 revolutions, and the minute hand coincides with the hour hand 11 times (including midnight, but not noon, starting just after the hands separate at noon). Because each hand rotates at a uniform rate, the hands overlap each $\frac{12}{11}$ of an hour, or $65\frac{5}{11}$ minutes.

This can be extended to other situations.

Your students should derive a great sense of achievement and enjoyment as a result of employing this simple procedure to solve what usually appears to be a very difficult clock problem.

POSTASSESSMENT

1. At what time will the hands of a clock overlap after 2 o'clock?
2. At what time will the hands of a clock be perpendicular after 3 o'clock?
3. How would the "correction factor" change if our clock were a 24-hour cycle clock?
4. What would the "correction factor" be if we sought the exact time when the second hand and the minute hand were perpendicular after (*fill in a specified time*)?
5. What angle is determined by the hands of a clock at (*fill in a specified time*)?
6. What is the first time (exactly) when the second hand bisects the angle formed by the minute and hour hands of a clock after (*fill in a specified time*)?

Unit 73

Averaging Rates–The Harmonic Mean

This unit will present a shortcut method for determining the average of two or more rates (rates of speed, cost, production, etc.).

PERFORMANCE OBJECTIVES

1. *Given various rates for a common base, students will find the average of these rates.*
2. *Given a problem calling for the average of given rates, students will correctly apply the concept of a harmonic mean when applicable.*

PREASSESSMENT

Have students solve the following problem:

> Noreen drives from her home to work at the rate of 30 mph. Later she returns home from work over the same route at the rate of 60 mph. What is her average rate of speed for both trips?

TEACHING STRATEGIES

The preceding problem should serve as excellent motivation for this unit. Most students will probably incorrectly offer 45 mph as their answer to this problem. Their explanation will be that 45 is the average of 30 and 60. True! You must convince them that since the numbers 30 and 60 represent rates, they cannot be treated as simple quantities. Students will wonder what difference this should make.

The first task is to convince your students that their original answer, 45 mph, is incorrect. Have them realize that when Noreen drove from home to work she had to drive twice as much time than she did on her return trip. Hence, it would be incorrect to give both rates the same "weight." If this still does not convince your students, ask them that if their test scores throughout the semester were 90, 90, 90, 90, and 40, which of the following methods would they use to find their average:

$$\begin{array}{rl} & 90 \text{ (average of first four tests)} \\ + & 40 \text{ (their last test score)} \\ \hline & 130 \div 2 = 65 \end{array}$$

Or: $90 + 90 + 90 + 90 + 40 = 400;\ 400 \div 5 = 80.$

It would be expected that students would now suggest that the answer to the original problem could be obtained by: $\frac{30 + 30 + 60}{3} = 40$. This is perfectly correct; however, a simple solution as this would hardly be expected if one rate were not a multiple of the other. Most students would now welcome a more general method of solution. One such solution is based on the relationship: *Rate* × *Time* = *Distance*. Consider the following:

$$T_1 \text{ (time going to work)} = \frac{D}{30}$$

$$T_2 \text{ (time returning home)} = \frac{D}{60}$$

$$T \text{ (total time for both trips)} = T_1 + T_2 = \frac{D}{20}$$

$$R \text{ (rate for the entire trip)} = \frac{2D}{T} = \frac{2D}{\frac{D}{20}} = 40$$

R is actually the *average rate* for the entire trip, since problems of this nature deal with uniform motion.

Of particular interest are those problems where the rates to be averaged are for a common base (e.g., the same distance for various rates of speed). Have students consider the original problem in general terms, where the given rates of speed are R_1 and R_2 (instead of 30 and 60), each for a distance D. Therefore, $T_1 = \frac{D}{R_1}$ and $T_2 = \frac{D}{R_2}$, so that

$$T = T_1 + T_2 = D\left(\frac{1}{R_1} + \frac{1}{R_2}\right) = \frac{D(R_1 + R_2)}{R_1R_2}.$$

However, have students consider:

$$R = \frac{2D}{T} = \frac{2D}{D\left(\frac{1}{R_1} + \frac{1}{R_2}\right)} = \frac{2}{\frac{1}{R_1} + \frac{1}{R_2}} = \frac{2R_1R_2}{R_1 + R_2}. \quad (1)$$

They should notice that $\frac{2R_1R_2}{R_1 + R_2}$ is actually the reciprocal of the average of the reciprocals of R_1 and R_2. Such an average is called the *harmonic mean*.

Perhaps a word about the harmonic mean would be in order. A progression of numbers is said to be harmonic if any three consecutive members of the progression (a, b, and c) have the property that

$$\frac{a}{c} = \frac{a - b}{b - c}. \qquad (2)$$

This relationship may also be written as

$$a(b - c) = c(a - b). \qquad (3)$$

Dividing by abc we get

$$\frac{1}{c} - \frac{1}{b} = \frac{1}{b} - \frac{1}{a}. \qquad (4)$$

This relationship shows that the reciprocals of a harmonic progression are in an arithmetic progression, as with $\frac{1}{a}$, $\frac{1}{b}$, and $\frac{1}{c}$. When three terms are in an arithmetic progression, the middle term is their mean. Thus $\frac{1}{b}$ is the arithmetic mean between $\frac{1}{a}$ and $\frac{1}{c}$; b is the harmonic mean between a and c.

Expressing b in terms of a and c in equation (4):

$$\frac{2}{b} = \frac{1}{a} + \frac{1}{c}, \text{ and } b = \frac{2ac}{a + c} \qquad (5)$$

Have students compare (1) with (5)!

In a similar manner you may wish to have the class consider the harmonic mean of three numbers, r, s, and t:

$$\frac{3}{\frac{1}{r} + \frac{1}{s} + \frac{1}{t}} = \frac{3rst}{st + rt + rs}$$

Students may even wish to extend this to determine a "formula" for the harmonic mean of four numbers, k, m, n, and p:

$$\frac{4}{\frac{1}{k} + \frac{1}{m} + \frac{1}{n} + \frac{1}{p}} = \frac{4kmnp}{mnp + knp + kmp + kmn}.$$

Have students consider the following problem:

Lisa bought 2 dollars worth of each of three different kinds of pencils, priced at 2¢, 4¢, and 5¢ each, respectively. What is the average price paid per pencil?

The answer to this question is $3\frac{3}{19}$, the harmonic mean of 2, 4, and 5. Stress the point that this was possible since each rate acted on the same base, 2 dollars. Similar problems (see the Postassessment) may be posed and solved by the students at this time.

You may wish to consider a geometric illustration of the concept. Although the harmonic mean enjoys the most prominence geometrically in projective geometry, it might be more appropriate to give an illustration of the harmonic mean in synthetic geometry.

Have the students consider the length of the segment containing the point of intersection of the diagonals of a trapezoid and parallel to the bases, with its endpoints in the legs (see $\overline{EGF}$ below). The length of this segment, $\overline{EGF}$, is the harmonic mean between the lengths of the bases, $\overline{AD}$ and $\overline{BC}$. In the figure below, ABCD is a trapezoid, with $\overline{AD}//\overline{BC}$ and diagonals intersecting at G. Also $\overline{EGF}//\overline{BC}$, and $\overline{DEC}$ and $\overline{AFB}$.

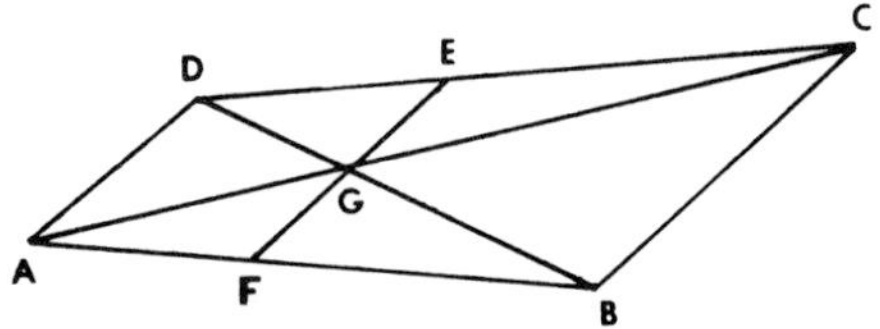

Since $\overline{GF} // \overline{BC}$, $\triangle AFG \sim \triangle ABC$, and $\frac{AF}{FG} = \frac{AB}{BC}$. Similarly, because $\overline{GF} // \overline{AD}$, $\triangle GBF \sim \triangle DBA$, and $\frac{BF}{FG} = \frac{AB}{AD}$. Therefore, $\frac{AF}{FG} + \frac{BF}{FG} = \frac{AB}{BC} + \frac{AB}{AD}$. Because $AF + BF = AB$, $\frac{AB}{FG} = \frac{AB}{BC} + \frac{AB}{AD}$, or $FG = \frac{(BC)(AD)}{BC + AD}$. In a similar manner it can be shown that $EG = \frac{(BC)(AD)}{BC + AD}$. Therefore, $EF = FG + EG = \frac{2(BC)(AD)}{BC + AD}$; hence, EF is the harmonic mean between BC and AD.

POSTASSESSMENT

1. If a jet flies from New York to Rome at 600 mph and back along the same route at 500 mph, what is the average rate of speed for the entire trip?
2. Alice buys 2 dollars worth of each of three kinds of nuts, priced at 40¢, 50¢, and 60¢ per pound, respectively. What is the average price Alice paid per pound of nuts?
3. In June, Willie got 30 hits for a batting average of .300; however, in May he got 30 hits for a batting average of .400. What is Willie's batting average for May and June?
4. Find the harmonic mean of 2, 3, 5, 6, 2, and 9.

REFERENCES

Posamentier, A.S., and S. Krulik. *Teachers! Prepare Your Students for the Mathematics for SAT 1: Methods and Problem Solving Strategies*. Thousand Oaks, CA: Corwin, 1996.

Posamentier, Alfred S., and Charles T. Salkind. *Challenging Problems in Algebra*. New York: Dover, 1996.

Posamentier, Alfred S., and Charles T. Salkind, *Challenging Problems in Geometry*. New York: Dover, 1996.

Posamentier, A. S. "The Harmonic Mean and Its Place Among Means" in *Readings for Enrichment in Secondary School Mathematics*. Edited by Max A. Sobel. Reston, VA: NCTM, 1988.

Unit 74

Howlers

In *Fallacies in Mathematics*, E. A. Maxwell refers to the following cancellations as *howlers:*

$$\frac{1\not{6}}{\not{6}4} = \frac{1}{4}$$
$$\frac{2\not{6}}{\not{6}5} = \frac{2}{5}$$

This unit will offer a method of presenting these howlers to elementary algebra students so students better understand number concepts.

PERFORMANCE OBJECTIVES

1. *Students will develop a howler not already presented in class.*
2. *Students will explain why there are only four howlers composed of two-digit fractions.*

PREASSESSMENT

Students should be able to reduce fractions to lowest terms. They should also be familiar with such concepts as factor and prime number, and be able to perform all operations on fractions.

TEACHING STRATEGIES

Begin your presentation by asking students to reduce to lowest terms the following fractions: $\frac{16}{64}, \frac{19}{95}, \frac{26}{65}, \frac{49}{98}$. After they have reduced to lowest terms each of the fractions in the usual manner, tell them that they did a lot of unnecessary work. Show them the following cancellations:

$$\frac{1\not{6}}{\not{6}4} = \frac{1}{4}$$
$$\frac{1\not{9}}{\not{9}5} = \frac{1}{5}$$
$$\frac{2\not{6}}{\not{6}5} = \frac{2}{5}$$
$$\frac{4\not{9}}{\not{9}8} = \frac{4}{8} = \frac{1}{2}$$

At this point your students will be somewhat amazed. Their first reaction is to ask if this can be done to any fraction composed of two-digit numbers. Challenge your students to find another fraction (comprised of two-digit numbers) where this type of cancellation will work. Students might cite $\frac{5\not{3}}{\not{3}5} = \frac{5}{5} = 1$ as an illustration of this type of cancellation. Indicate to them that although this will hold true for all multiples of eleven, it is trivial, and our concern will be only with proper fractions (i.e., whose value is less than one).

After they are thoroughly frustrated you may begin a discussion on why the four fractions above are the only ones (composed of two-digit numbers) where this type of cancellation will hold true.

Have students consider the fraction $\frac{10x + a}{10a + y}$.

The nature of the above four cancellations was such that when canceling the *a*s the fraction was equal to $\frac{x}{y}$. Therefore $\frac{10x + a}{10a + y} = \frac{x}{y}$.

This yields:

$$\begin{aligned} y\,(10x + a) &= x\,(10a + y) \\ \text{or } 10xy + ay &= 10ax + xy \\ 9xy + ay &= 10ax \\ \text{and } y &= \frac{10ax}{9x + a}. \end{aligned}$$

At this point have students inspect this relationship. They should realize that it is necessary that x, y, and a be integers, since they were digits in the numerator and denominator of a fraction. It is now their task to find the values of a and x for which y will also be integral.

To avoid a lot of algebraic manipulation you might have students set up a chart that will generate values of y from $y = \frac{10ax}{9x + a}$. Remind them that x, y, and a must be *single digit* integers. Below is a portion of the table they will construct. Notice that the cases where $x = a$ are excluded since $\frac{x}{a} = 1$.

The portion of the chart pictured above already generated two of the four integral values of y; that is, when $x = 1$, $a = 6$, then $y = 4$, and when $x = 2$, $a = 6$ and $y = 5$. These values yield the fractions $\frac{16}{64}$, and $\frac{26}{65}$, respectively. The

		x \ a	1	2	3	4	5	6	...	9
		1		$\frac{20}{11}$	$\frac{30}{12}$	$\frac{40}{13}$	$\frac{50}{14}$	$\frac{60}{15}=4$		
		2	$\frac{20}{19}$		$\frac{60}{21}$	$\frac{80}{22}$	$\frac{100}{23}$	$\frac{120}{24}=5$		
		3	$\frac{30}{28}$	$\frac{60}{29}$		$\frac{120}{31}$	$\frac{150}{32}$	$\frac{180}{33}$		
		:								
		.								
		9								

remaining two integral values of y will be obtained when $x = 1$, $a = 9$, then $y = 5$; and when $x = 4, a = 9$, then $y = 8$. These yield the fractions $\frac{19}{95}$ and $\frac{49}{98}$, respectively. This should convince students that there are only four such fractions composed of two-digit numbers.

Students may now wonder if there are fractions composed of numerators and denominators of more than two digits where this strange type of cancellation holds true. Have students try this type of cancellation with $\frac{4\not{9}\not{9}}{\not{9}\not{9}8}$. They should find that, in fact,

$$\frac{499}{998} = \frac{4}{8} = \frac{1}{2}.$$

Soon they will realize that

$$\frac{49}{98} = \frac{499}{998} = \frac{4999}{9998} = \frac{49999}{99998} = \cdots.$$
$$\frac{16}{64} = \frac{166}{664} = \frac{1666}{6664} = \frac{16666}{66664} = \frac{166666}{666664} = \cdots.$$
$$\frac{19}{95} = \frac{199}{995} = \frac{1999}{9995} = \frac{19999}{99995} = \frac{199999}{999995} = \cdots.$$
$$\frac{26}{65} = \frac{266}{665} = \frac{2666}{6665} = \frac{26666}{66665} = \frac{266666}{666665} = \cdots.$$

Students with higher ability may wish to justify these extensions of the original howlers.

Students who at this point have a further desire to seek out additional fractions that permit this strange cancellation should be shown the following fractions. They should verify the legitimacy of this strange cancellation and then set out to discover more such fractions.

$$\frac{3\not{3}2}{8\not{3}0} = \frac{32}{80} = \frac{2}{5}$$
$$\frac{3\not{8}5}{8\not{8}0} = \frac{35}{80} = \frac{7}{16}$$
$$\frac{1\not{3}8}{\not{3}45} = \frac{18}{45} = \frac{2}{5}$$
$$\frac{2\not{7}5}{\not{7}70} = \frac{25}{70} = \frac{5}{14}$$
$$\frac{1\not{6}\not{3}}{\not{3}2\not{6}} = \frac{1}{2}$$
$$\frac{2\not{0}3}{6\not{0}9} = \frac{1}{3}$$

POSTASSESSMENT

Have students:

1. Generate a "howler" not already presented in this discussion.
2. Explain why there are only four howlers, each composed of two-digit numbers.

Unit 75

 Digit Problems Revisited

Problems involving the digits of a number as presented in the elementary algebra course are usually very straightforward and somewhat dull. Often they serve merely as a source of drill for a previously taught skill. This unit shows how digit problems (perhaps somewhat "off the beaten path" in nature) can be used to improve a student's concept of numbers.

PERFORMANCE OBJECTIVES

1. *Students will solve problems involving the digits of a number.*
2. *Students will analyze a mathematical fact about the nature of certain numbers.*

PREASSESSMENT

Students should be able to solve simple linear equations as well as simple simultaneous equations.

TEACHING STRATEGIES

Begin your presentation by asking your students to select any three-digit number in which the hundreds digit and units digit are unequal. Then have them write the number whose digits are in the reverse order from the selected number. Now tell them to subtract these two numbers (the smaller number from the greater one). Once again tell them to take this difference, reverse its digits and add the "new" number to the *original difference*. They *all* should end up with 1,089.

For example, suppose a student selected the number 934. The number with the digits reversed is 439. The computation would appear as:

$$\begin{array}{rl} 934 & \\ \underline{439} & \\ 495 & \text{(difference)} \\ \underline{594} & \text{(reversed digits)} \\ 1089 & \text{(sum)} \end{array}$$

When students compare results they will be amazed to discover uniformity in their answers. At this point they should be quite eager to find out why they all came up with the same result.

Begin by letting them represent the original number by $100h + 10t + u$, where h, t, and u represent the hundreds, tens, and units digits, respectively. Let $h > u$, which would have to be true in one of the original numbers. In subtracting, $u - h < 0$; therefore take 1 from the tens place to make the units place $10 + u$ (of the minuend).

Since the tens digits of the two numbers to be subtracted are equal, and 1 was taken from the tens digit of the minuend, then the value of this digit is $10(t - 1)$. The hundreds digit of the minuend is $h - 1$, since 1 was taken away to enable subtraction in the tens place, making the value of the tens digit $10(t - 1) + 100 = 10(t + 9)$. Pictorially this appears as

$$\begin{array}{lll} 100\,(h-1) & +\,10\,(t+9) & +\,(u+10) \\ \underline{100\,u} & \underline{+\,10t} & \underline{+\,h} \\ 100\,(h-u-1) & +\,10\,(9) & +\,u-h+10. \end{array}$$

Reversing the digits of this difference yields

$$100(u - h + 10) + 10(9) + h - u - 1.$$

Adding the last two lines yields

$$100(9) + 10(18) + (10 - 1) = 1089.$$

Another problem involving the digits of a number and presenting a somewhat unusual twist follows:

> Seven times a certain two-digit number equals a three-digit number. When the digit 6 is written after the last digit of the three-digit number, the three-digit number is increased by 1,833. Find the two-digit number.

The major obstacle students encounter in the solution of this problem is how to indicate placing a 6 after a number. Let students represent the two-digit number by a. Therefore the three-digit number is $7a$. Now to place a 6 after a number is to multiply the number by 10 and add the 6. The required equation is then $70a + 6 = 7a + 1833$, and $a = 29$.

To further exhibit the usefulness of working algebraically with a digital expression of a number, you may find it exciting to show students why a number is divisible by 9 (or 3) if the sum of its digits is divisible by 9 (or 3). Have them consider any five-digit number, say, ab, cde, that is $10{,}000a + 1{,}000b + 100c + 10d + e$. Since this number may be rewritten as $(9{,}999 + 1)a + (999 + 1)b + (99 + 1)c + (9 + 1)d + e$, or $9{,}999a + 999b + 99c + 9d + a + b + c + d + e$, and the sum of the first four terms is divisible by 9 (or 3), the sum of the remaining terms must also be divisible by 9 (or 3). That is, for the number to be divisible by 9 (or 3), $a + b + c + d + e$ must be divisible by 9 (or 3).

Another digit problem with a rather nonroutine solution should now be presented. Students will find the following analysis a bit unusual.

> Find the two-digit number N such that when it is divided by 4 the remainder is zero, and such that all of its positive integral powers end in the same two digits as the original number, N.

Students will naturally want to begin solving this problem by letting $N = 10t + u$. Since $10t + u = 4m$ (i.e., a multiple of 4), u is even. Ask students which even digits have squares terminating with the same digit as the original digit. Once students establish that only 0 and 6 satisfy this property, therefore $u = 0$ or 6.

The case $u = 0$ implies that $t = 0$ so that $N = 00$, a trivial case, for if $t = 0$, N will terminate in 0 while its square will terminate in 00.

Now have students consider $u = 6$. Then $N = 10t + 6 = 4m$, or $5t + 3 = 2m$. This indicates that $t = 1,3,5,7$, or 9. But $N^2 = (10t + 6)^2 = 100t^2 + 120t + 36 = 100t^2 + 100d + 10e + 36$, where $120t = 100d + 10e$. Since the last two digits of N^2 are the same as those of N, $10e + 36 = 10t + 6$, and $t = e + 3$, so that $t \geq 3$. Also, $120t = 100d + 10(t - 3)$, whereby $11t = 10d - 3$, and $11t \leq 87$, or $t \leq 7$.

Have students try $t = 3$, $36^2 = 1296$ (reject) then try $t = 5$, $56^2 = 3136$ (reject). Finally try $t = 7$, then $76^2 = 5776$ (accept since $N = 76$).

There are many other problems involving the digits of numbers that you may wish to present to your class to advance the number theory introduction which this model provided.

POSTASSESSMENT

1. Show, using a digital representation of a number, that a given number is divisible by 8, if the last three digits (considered as a new number) are divisible by 8.
2. There are two numbers formed of the same two digits—one in reverse of the other. The difference between the squares of the two numbers is 7,128 and the sum of the number is 22 times the difference between the two digits. What are the two numbers?
3. By shifting the initial digit 6 of the positive integer N to the end, we obtain a number equal to $\frac{1}{4}$N. Find the smallest possible value of N that satisfies the conditions.

Unit 76

Algebraic Identities

This unit will present a geometric process for carrying out algebraic identities. With only the representation of a number by a length, and lacking sufficient algebraic notation, early Greeks devised the method of application of areas to prove these identities.

PERFORMANCE OBJECTIVE

Students will geometrically establish algebraic identities using the method of application of areas.

PREASSESSMENT

1. Have students expand $(a + b^2)$.
2. Have students expand $a(b + c)$.
3. Have students expand $(a - b)^2$.
4. Elicit for what values of a and b each of the above generated equalities are true.

TEACHING STRATEGIES

After students have considered the questions above, they should be reacquainted with the properties of an identity. Once students understand the concept of an identity, introduce the method of application of areas by illustrating geometrically the identity $(a + b)^2 = a^2 + 2ab + b^2$. To begin, have students draw a square of side length $(a + b)$. The square should then be partitioned into various squares and rectangles (see Figure 1). The lengths of the various sides are appropriately labeled.

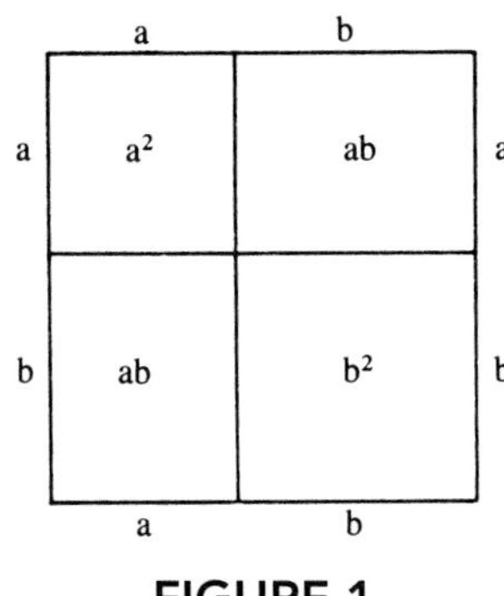

FIGURE 1

Students can easily determine the area of each region. Since the area of the large square equals the areas of the four quadrilaterals into which it was partitioned, students should get

$$(a + b)^2 = a^2 + ab + ab + b^2 = a^2 + 2ab + b^2.$$

A more rigorous proof can be found in Euclid's *Elements*, Proposition 4, Book II.

Next illustrate geometrically the identity $a(b + c) = ab + ac$. To begin, have students draw a rectangle whose adjacent sides are of lengths a and $(b + c)$. The rectangle should then be partitioned into various rectangles (see Figure 2). The lengths of these sides are also labeled.

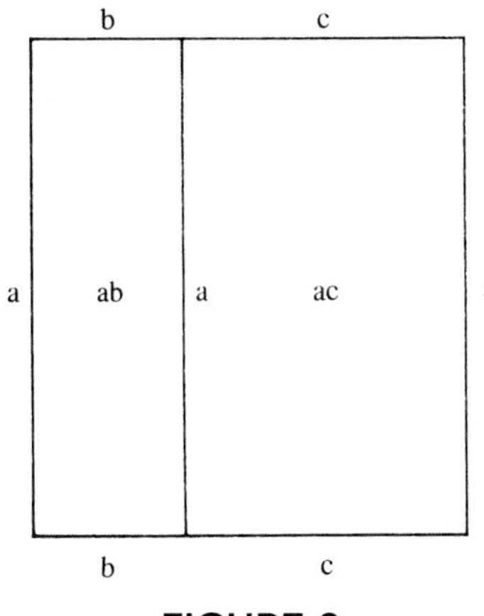

FIGURE 2

Students can easily determine the area of each partition. Elicit from students that since the area of the large rectangle equals the areas of the two quadrilaterals into which it was partitioned, the diagram illustrates $a(b + c) = ab + ac$.

Have students consider the following identity $(a + b) \times (c + d) = ac + ad + bc + bd$. Guide students to draw the appropriate rectangle with side lengths $(a + b)$ and $(c + d)$. The rectangle should be partitioned into various rectangles (see Figure 3). The lengths of sides and areas of regions have been labeled. As in the other cases, the area of the large rectangle equals the areas of the four quadrilaterals into which it was partitioned.

Figure 3 illustrates the identity $(a + b) \times (c + d) = ac + ad + bc + bd$. Explain to students that the method of

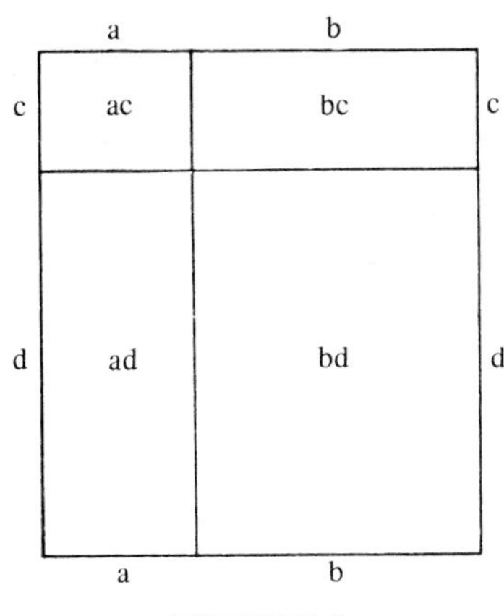

FIGURE 3

application of areas can be used to prove most algebraic identities. The difficulty will lie in their choice of dimensions for the quadrilateral and the partitions made.

After students feel comfortable using areas to represent algebraic identities, have them consider the Pythagorean relationship, $a^2 + b^2 = c^2$. Although this is not an identity, the application of areas is still appropriate. Have students draw a square of side length $(a + b)$. Show students how to partition this square into four congruent triangles and a square (see Figure 4). The lengths of the sides have been labeled.

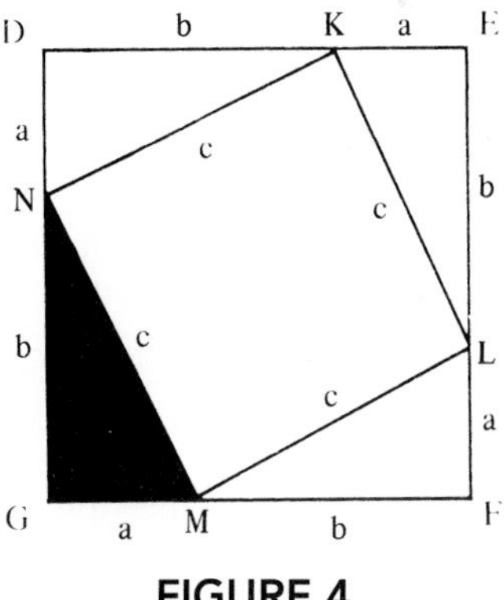

FIGURE 4

Figure 4 illustrates:

1. Area DEFG = 4 × (Area of △GNM) + Area KLMN.
2. Therefore, $(a + b)^2 = 4\left(\frac{1}{2}ab\right) + c^2$.
3. If we now substitute the identity for $(a + b)^2$, which was proven before, we obtain, $a^2 + 2ab + b^2 = 2ab + c^2$.

Elicit from students the remainder of the proof to conclude that $a^2 + b^2 = c^2$. Students should now be able to pose and solve geometrically their own identities.

POSTASSESSMENT

1. Have students indicate how to establish the following algebraic identities geometrically.
   a. $(a - b)^2 = a^2 - 2ab + b^2$
   b. $a^2 - b^2 = (a + b) \times (a - b)$
2. Have students determine other identities that can be proved using the method of application of areas.

REFERENCES

Posamentier, A. S., and H. A. Hauptman. *101 Great Ideas for Introducing Key Concepts in Mathematics*. Thousand Oaks, CA: Corwin, 2001.

Unit 77

A Method for Factoring Trinomials of the Form $ax^2 + bx + c$

This unit presents a rather unusual method for factoring, when possible, trinomials of the form $ax^2 + bx + c$, where a, b, and c are integers. This technique is especially helpful when the coefficient a of $ax^2 + bx + c$ is different from I, because in this case the usual method based on trial and error is rather tedious for most of the trinomials.

PERFORMANCE OBJECTIVES

1. *Given various trinomials of the form $ax^2 + bx + c$, students will analyze and factor them.*
2. *Students will be able to apply this technique to the solution of quadratic equations.*

PREASSESSMENT

Students should be familiar with multiplications and factorizations of binomials and with factorizations of perfect square trinomials.

TEACHING STRATEGIES

Begin this lesson by giving several examples of multiplications of binomials: $(x + 5)(x + 2)$, $(2x - 3)(x + 1)$, $(5x - 2)(3x - 7)$, etc. Have students notice the following properties of these multiplications:

a. They always yield trinomials of the form $ax^2 + bx + c$, where a, b, and c are integers.
b. The product of the first terms of the binomials is the first term of the trinomial.
c. It is impossible for a to obtain the value of zero from the product of any two binomials. Thus a is always different from zero in the trinomial of the form $ax^2 + bx + c$.

Once students have practiced these multiplications, have them consider the inverse operation. That is, given trinomials of the form $ax^2 + bx + c$, have students factor them as the product of two binomials. Ask for suggestions on how to factor different trinomials; for example: $x^2 + 5x + 6$, $2x^2 - 7x - 4$, and so on. Then have students consider the factorization of the general trinomial $ax^2 + bx + c$ in the following fashion:

$$ax^2 + bx + c = \frac{a(ax^2 + bx + c)}{a} = \frac{a^2x^2 + abx + ac}{a},$$

this being possible because a is always different from zero.

If $a^2x^2 + abx + ac$ can be factored, one factorization could be $(ax + y)(ax + z)$, where y and z are to be determined. Thus, we have

$$ax^2 + bx + c = \frac{a^2x^2 + abx + ac}{a} = \frac{(ax + y)(ax + z)}{a}$$
$$= \frac{a^2x^2 + a(y + z)x + yz}{a}.$$

If the second and fourth equalities are now compared, we notice that $y + z = b$ and $yz = ac$. Thus, to factor a trinomial of the form $ax^2 + bx + c$, it is only necessary to express it as the product $\frac{(ax + y)(ax + z)}{a}$, where y and z can be determined by noticing that their sum must be b and their product must be ac. Also have students notice that because $\frac{(ax + y)(ax + z)}{a} = \frac{a^2x^2 + abx + ac}{a}$, it follows that the numerator is a multiple of a, and therefore, it will always be possible to cancel the constant a.

Example 1

$$\text{Factor } 5x^2 + 8x + 3$$

We have $5x^2 + 8x + 3 = \dfrac{(5x + y)(5x + z)}{5}$, where $y + z = 8$ and $yz = (5)(3) = 15$. An analysis of the constant term 15 reveals that the possible pairs of numbers y and z whose product is 15 are 15 and 1, -15 and -1,5 and 3, and -5 and -3; but because their sum must be 8, the only possible combination of y and z is 5 and 3. Therefore,

$$\begin{aligned} 5x^2 + 8x + 3 &= \frac{(5x + 5)\,(5x + 3)}{5} \\ &= \frac{\cancel{5}(x + 1)\,(5x + 3)}{\cancel{5}} \\ &= (x + 1)\,(5x + 3). \end{aligned}$$

Example 2

$$\text{Factor } 6x^2 + 5x - 6$$

We have $(6x^2 + 5x - 6) = \dfrac{(6x + y)(6x + z)}{6}$, where $y + z = 5$ and $yz = (6)(-6) = -36$. An analysis of the product yz, that is, of -36 reveals that the possible pairs of numbers whose product is -36 are 36 and -1,-36 and 1, 18 and -2,-18 and 2, 12 and -3,-12 and 3, 9 and -4,-9 and 4, and 6 and -6. But because the algebraic sum of y and z must be $+5$, we have that the only possible combination is 9 and -4. Therefore,

$$\begin{aligned} 6x^2 + 5x - 6 &= \frac{(6x + 9)\,(6x - 4)}{6} \\ &= \frac{3(2x + 3)\,2(3x - 2)}{6} \\ &= (2x + 3)\,(3x - 2). \end{aligned}$$

If $a = 1$, we have the simpler form $x^2 + bx + c$. Thus, $x^2 + bx + c = \dfrac{(1x + y)(1x + z)}{1} = (x + y)(x + z)$, where $y + z = b$ and $yz = c$.

Example 3

$$\text{Factor } x^2 - 4x - 5$$

We have $x^2 - 4x - 5 = (x + y)(x + z)$, where $y + z$ is -4 and yz is -5. Thus, the possible pairs of numbers are 5 and -1, and -5 and 1; but because the algebraic sum is -4 the only possible combination is -5 and $+1$. Therefore, $x^2 - 4x - 5 = (x - 5)(x + 1)$. This technique is also applicable to the solution of quadratic equations, that is, equations of the form $ax^2 + bx + c = 0$.

Example 4

$$\text{Solve } 2x^2 - 7x - 4 = 0$$

We first factor $2x^2 - 7x - 4$. Thus, $2x^2 - 7x - 4 = \dfrac{(2x + y)(2x + z)}{2}$, where $y + z$ is -7 and yz is -8. Because the product is -8, we find that the possible pairs are 8 and -1, -8 and 1, 4 and -2, and -4 and 2. But because the algebraic sum is -7, the only possible combination is -8 and 1. Thus, $2x^2 - 7x - 4 = \dfrac{(2x - 8)(2x + 1)}{2} = (x - 4)(2x + 1)$. Therefore we have $2x^2 - 7x - 4 = (x - 4)(2x + 1) = 0$ and the roots of this quadratic equation will be 4 and $-\frac{1}{2}$. It is important for students to understand that there is no guarantee that "any" given trinomials can be factored; $x^2 - 5x - 7$ and $x^3 - 5x - 6$ *cannot* be factored.

POSTASSESSMENT

Have students complete the following exercises.

1. Factor the following trinomials:

a. $x^2 - 8x + 12$	b. $4x^2 + 4x - 3$
c. $x^2 + 10x + 25$	d. $3x^2 - 5x$
e. $2r^2 + 13r - 7$	f. $9m^2 - 1$

2. Solve the following quadratic equations:

   a. $x^2 - 3x - 4 = 0$ b. $6x^2 + x = 2$

REFERENCES

Posamentier, A. S., and H. A. Hauptman. *101 plus Great Ideas for Introducing Key Concepts in Mathematics*. Thousand Oaks, CA: Corwin, 2006.

Unit 78

Solving Quadratic Equations

This unit presents four new methods for solving quadratic equations.

PERFORMANCE OBJECTIVE

Students will solve a given quadratic equation in at least four different ways.

PREASSESSMENT

Students should be able to solve the equation:

$$x^2 - 7x + 12 = 0$$

TEACHING STRATEGIES

In all likelihood most of your students solved the above equation by the *Factoring* method. That is, to solve they performed the following operations:

$$x^2 - 7x + 12 = 0$$
$$(x - 3)(x - 4) = 0$$

$$x - 3 = 0 \quad\Big|\quad x - 4 = 0$$
$$x = 3 \quad\Big|\quad x = 4$$

This method cannot be used to solve all types of quadratic equations. If the trinomial $ax^2 + bx + c$ from the equation $ax^2 + bx + c = 0$ is not factorable, then this method cannot be used to solve the equation.

The rest of this lesson develops four new methods for solving quadratic equations.

Completing the Square

Consider the equation $ax^2 + bx + c = 0$, where a, b, and c are integers and $a \neq 0$.

$$ax^2 + bx + c = x^2 + \frac{b}{a}x + \frac{c}{a} = 0$$

Add the square of one-half the coefficient of x to both sides:

$$x^2 + \frac{b}{a}x + \left(\frac{b}{2a}\right)^2 = -\frac{c}{a} + \left(\frac{b}{2a}\right)^2$$

$$\left(x + \frac{b}{2a}\right)^2 = -\frac{c}{a} + \frac{b^2}{4a^2}$$

Take the square root of both sides:

$$x + \frac{b}{2a} = \pm\sqrt{\frac{b^2 - 4ac}{4a^2}}$$

$$x = \frac{-b \pm \sqrt{b^2 - 4ac}}{2a}$$

This is the quadratic formula.

Example: Solve $x^2 - 7x + 12 = 0$

$$x^2 - 7x + \left(\frac{-7}{2}\right)^2 = -12 + \left(\frac{-7}{2}\right)^2$$

$$\left(x - \frac{7}{2}\right)^2 = -12 + \frac{49}{4} = \frac{-48 + 49}{4} = \frac{1}{4}$$

$$x - \frac{7}{2} = \pm\sqrt{\frac{1}{4}} = \pm\frac{1}{2}$$

$$x = \frac{7}{2} \pm \frac{1}{2} \qquad x = 3, 4$$

Splitting the Difference

Let x_1 and x_2 be the roots of the given equation $ax^2 + bx + c = 0$. Then $x^2 + \frac{b}{a}x + \frac{c}{a} = 0$ or

$$(x - x_1)(x - x_2) = 0$$

We know that the sum of the roots $x_1 + x_2 = \frac{-b}{a}$ and that the product of the roots $x_1x_2 = \frac{c}{a}$.

Let $x_1 = \frac{-b}{2a} + \text{N}$, where N is some rational number and $x_2 = \frac{-b}{2a} - \text{N}$.

Then the product of the roots, $\frac{c}{a} = x_1x_2 = \left(-\frac{b}{2a} + \text{N}\right)\left(-\frac{b}{2a} - \text{N}\right)$.

In solving for N, we get

$$\text{N} = \pm\frac{\sqrt{b^2 - 4ac}}{2a}.$$

Therefore the roots are $x = \frac{-b}{2a} \pm \frac{\sqrt{b^2 - 4ac}}{2a}$.

Example: Solve $x^2 - 7x + 12 = 0$
Students will establish that the sum of the roots $x_1 + x_2 = 7$.
Therefore one root must be $\frac{7}{2} + N$ and the other must be $\frac{7}{2} - N$, where N is some rational number.
Because the product of the roots is 12, $x_1x_2 = \left(\frac{7}{2} + N\right)\left(\frac{7}{2} - N\right) = \frac{49}{4} - N^2 = 12.$

Therefore $N^2 = \frac{1}{4}$, and $N = \pm\frac{1}{2}$.

Thus the roots are $x_1 = \frac{7}{2} + N = \frac{7}{2} + \frac{1}{2} = 4$

$$x_2 = \frac{7}{2} - N = \frac{7}{2} - \frac{1}{2} = 3$$

Method of Simultaneous Equations

Rather than developing the general case first, we shall first solve the given equation $x^2 - 7x + 12 = 0$. This order should be easier to follow for this method.

Example: Solve $x^2 - 7x + 12 = 0$
Consider the sum and product of the roots $x_1 + x_2 = 7$ and $x_1x_2 = 12$.
Square the sum $(x_1 + x_2)^2 = 49$.
Multiply the product by -4: $-4x_1x_2 = -48$.
By addition $(x_1 + x_2)^2 - 4x_1x_2 = 49 - 48 = 1$.
However, the left side simplifies to $(x_1 - x_2)^2$.
Therefore $x_1 - x_2 = \pm\sqrt{1} = \pm 1$.
Remember that $x_1 + x_2 = 7$.
Now solving these equations simultaneously:

$$2x_1 = 8 \quad x_1 = 4 \quad x_2 = 3$$

The general case for $ax^2 + bx + c = 0$ follows: The square of the sum of the roots

$$(x_1 + x_2)^2 = x_1^2 + 2x_1x_2 + x_2^2 = \frac{b^2}{a^2}.$$

The product of the roots and -4 is

$$-4x_1x_2 = \frac{-4c}{a}.$$

As above, we add these last two equations:

$$x_1^2 - 2x_1x_2 + x_2^2 = \frac{b^2}{a^2} - \frac{4c}{a}$$

$$(x_1 - x_2)^2 = \frac{b^2 - 4ac}{a^2}$$

Therefore:

$$x_1 - x_2 = \pm\frac{\sqrt{b^2 - 4ac}}{a}.$$

Since $x_1 + x_2 = \frac{-b}{a}$

$$x_1 \text{ or } x_2 = \frac{1}{2}\left(\frac{-b}{a} \pm \frac{\sqrt{b^2 - 4ac}}{a}\right)$$

$$= \frac{-b \pm \sqrt{b^2 - 4ac}}{2a}$$

Method of Root Reduction

Again we start the discussion with the solution for a specific equation before considering the general form.

Example: Solve $x^2 - 7x + 12 = 0$
Let $r = x - n$, then $x = r + n$, and $x^2 = (r + n)^2 = r^2 + 2rn + n^2$.

We now substitute the appropriate values in the original equation.

$$(r^2 + 2rn + n^2) - 7(r + n) + 12 = 0$$

$$r^2 + r(2n - 7) + (n^2 - 7n + 12) = 0$$

If $2n - 7 = 0$, then the r term is annihilated.

This will happen when $n = \frac{7}{2}$.

We then have $r^2 + (n^2 - 7n + 12) = 0$ or by substituting

$$n = \frac{7}{2}: \quad r^2 + \left(\frac{49}{4} - 7\left(\frac{7}{2}\right) + 12\right) = 0$$

$$r^2 = \frac{49}{4} - 12 = \frac{1}{4}; \text{ and } r = \pm\frac{1}{2}$$

Thus the roots $(x = r + n)$ are

$$x_1 = +\frac{1}{2} + \frac{7}{2} = 4 \qquad x_2 = -\frac{1}{2} + \frac{7}{2} = 3$$

The general case proceeds in a similar manner. Consider the equation $ax^2 + bx + c = 0$. Let $r = x - n$, then $x = r + n$ and

$$x^2 = (r + n)^2 = r^2 + 2rn + n^2.$$

Now substitute these values into the original equation:

$$x^2 + \frac{bx}{a} + \frac{c}{a} = 0$$

$$(r^2 + 2rn + n^2) + \frac{b}{a}(r + n) + \frac{c}{a} = 0$$

$$\text{or} \quad r^2 + r\left(2n + \frac{b}{a}\right) + \left(n^2 + \frac{bn}{a} + \frac{c}{a}\right) = 0$$

To annihilate the r term we let

$$2n + \frac{b}{a} = 0, \text{ or } n = \frac{-b}{2a}.$$

This then gives us

$$r^2 + \left(n^2 + \frac{b}{a}n + \frac{c}{a}\right) = 0$$

$$\text{or} \quad r^2 = -\left(n^2 + \frac{b}{a}n + \frac{c}{a}\right).$$

However, because $n = \frac{-b}{2a}$

$$r^2 = -\left(\frac{b^2}{4a^2} - \frac{b^2}{2a^2} + \frac{c}{a}\right)$$

$$r^2 = \frac{b^2 - 4ac}{4a^2} \quad \text{and} \quad r = \pm\frac{\sqrt{b^2 - 4ac}}{2a}$$

Therefore, since $x = r + n$, $x = \frac{-b}{2a} \pm \frac{\sqrt{b^2 - 4ac}}{2a}$

or $x = \frac{-b \pm \sqrt{b^2 - 4ac}}{2a}$.

Although some of these methods for solving quadratic equations are not too practical, they do offer students a better understanding of many of the underlying concepts.

POSTASSESSMENT

Ask students to use at least four of the methods presented in this lesson to solve the following equations.

1. $x^2 - 11x + 30 = 0$
2. $x^2 + 3x - 28 = 0$
3. $6x^2 - x - 2 = 0$

Unit 79

The Euclidean Algorithm

This unit presents a method of introducing students to the Euclidean Algorithm for finding the greatest common divisor of two given integers.

PERFORMANCE OBJECTIVES

1. *Given any two integers, students will determine the greatest common divisor of the two integers, regardless of the magnitude of the two integers.*
2. *Having determined the greatest common divisor, the students will then be able to express the greatest common divisor in terms of the two integers.*

PREASSESSMENT

Ask students how they would weigh 12 ounces, 2 ounces, 3 ounces, 4 ounces, 1 ounce, and 11 ounces using only a set of two pan balance scales and some 5 and 7 ounce weights.

TEACHING STRATEGIES

Students should be able to suggest weighing the weights in the following manner:

1. **12 ounces:** Place one 5 oz. and one 7 oz. weight on the same pan, and the 12 ounces can be weighed on the other pan.
2. **2 ounces:** Place one 7 oz. weight on one pan and a 5 oz. weight on the other pan. Then the desired 2 oz. weight is that which must be placed on the pan containing the 5 oz. weight in order to balance the scales.
3. **3 ounces:** Place two 5 oz. weights on one pan and a 7 oz. weight on the other pan. The desired 3 oz. weight is that which must be added to the 7 oz. weight in order to balance the scales.
4. **4 ounces:** Place two 5 oz. weights on one pan and two 7 oz. weights on the other. The desired weight is that which must be added to the two 5 oz. weights in order to balance the scales.
5. **1 ounce:** Place three 5 oz. weights on one pan and two 7 oz. weights on the other. The desired weight is that which must be added to the two 7 oz. weights in order to balance the scales.
6. **11 ounces:** Place five 5 oz. weights on one pan and two 7 oz. weights on the other pan. The desired weight is that which must be added to the two 7 oz. weights in order to balance the scales.

Students should then be asked to weigh 1 ounce, 2 ounces, 3 ounces, and 4 ounces using other combinations of given weights. They should soon be able to discover that the smallest weight that can be weighed using any combination of given weights is equal to the *greatest common divisor* of the two weights:

The greatest common divisor of A and B will be referred to as either G.C.D. of A and B or (A,B).

To find (945, 219) we can use the *Euclidean Algorithm*. The Euclidean Algorithm is based on a lemma, which states:

Given Weights	G.C.D.	Minimum Weighable
2 and 3	1	1
2 and 4	2	2
3 and 9	3	3
8 and 20	4	4
15 and 25	5	5

A and B are integers where A does not equal zero. If B is divided by A a quotient Q and remainder R is obtained (B = QA + R), then (B,A) = (A,R). Using the following procedure, the G.C.D. of 945 and 219 can be found:

Divide 945 by 219: $945 = (4)(219) + 69$ (1)

Divide 219 by 69: $219 = (3)(69) + 12$ (2)

now continue this process

$69 = (5)(12) + 9$ (3)

$12 = (1)(9) + 3$ (4)

$9 = (3)(3) + 0$ . . . until R equals 0.

Therefore, the G.C.D. of 945 and 219 is 3, which was the last nonzero remainder in the successive divisions. This method may be used to find (A,B) where A and B are any two integers. Have students practice this algorithm with some exercise before continuing the lesson.

For stronger students in the class (or just for your interest), a proof of this algorithm is provided. The following is a statement and proof of the Euclidean Algorithm.

For given nonzero integers a and b, divide a by b to get remainder r_1: divide b by r_1 to get remainder r_2. This is continued so that when remainder r_k is divided by r_{k+1} the remainder r_{k+2} is obtained. Eventually there will be an r_n such that $r_{n+1} = 0$. It follows that $|r_n|$ is the greatest common divisor of a and b.

Proof: The division algorithm will determine integers $q_1, r_1, q_2, r_2, q_3, r_3, \cdots$, where

$$\begin{aligned} a &= q_1 b + r_1 \\ b &= q_2 r_1 + r_2 \\ r_1 &= q_3 r_2 + r_3 \\ &\vdots \end{aligned}$$

and where $0 \leq \cdots < r_3 < r_2 < r_1 < |b|$. There are only $|b|$ nonnegative integers less than $|b|$. Therefore there must be an $r_{n+1} = 0$ for $n + 1 \leq |b|$. If $r_1 = 0$ then $(a, b) = b$. If $r_1 \neq 0$ then

$$\begin{aligned} a &= q_1 b + r_1 \\ b &= q_2 r_1 + r_2 \\ r_1 &= q_3 r_2 + r_3 \\ &\vdots \\ r_{n-2} &= q_n r_{n-1} + r_n \\ r_{n-1} &= q_{n+1} r_n \end{aligned}$$

Let $d = (a,b)$. Since $d|a$, and $d|b$, then $d|r_1$. Similarly, since $d|b$ and $d|r_1$, then $d|r_2$. Again, since $d|r_1$ and $d|r_2$, then $d|r_3$. Continuing this reasoning eventually yields $d|r_{n-2}$, and $d|r_{n-1}$, then $d|r_n$.

Since $r_n \neq 0, r_n|r_{n-1}$. Also $r_n|r_n$; therefore $r_n|r_{n-2}$. Similarly, $r_n|r_{n-3}, r_n|r_{n-4}, \cdots r_n|r_2, r_n|r_1, r_n|b$, and $r_n|a$. Since $r_n|a$ and $r_n|b$, therefore $r_n|d$. Thus, $r_n|d$ and $d|r_n$, it follows that $r_n = d$, or $r_n = (a,b)$.

At this juncture it would be nice to be able to express the G.C.D. of two integers in terms of the two integers, that is, MA + NB = (A,B), where M and N are integers. In the earlier case of (945, 219),3 = M(219) + N(945). By working backwards ("up" the Euclidean Algorithm), we can accomplish the following:

From line (4) above: $3 = 12 - 9$

Substituting for 9 from line (3) above:

$$3 = 12 - (69 - 5 \cdot 12), \quad 3 = 6 \cdot 12 - 69$$

Substituting for 12 from line (2):

$$3 = 6(219 - 3 \cdot 69) - 69$$

Substituting for 69 from line (1):

$$\begin{aligned} 3 &= 6 \cdot 219 - 19(945 - 4 \cdot 219), \text{ or} \\ 3 &= 82(219) - 19(945). \end{aligned}$$

Earlier students have determined the minimum that can be weighed by a 945 oz. and a 219 oz. weight by finding (945, 219). Now they can also determine how many 945 oz. weights to place on one pan and how many 219 oz. to place on the other pan, by expressing (945, 219) in terms of 945 and 219. That is, they must place 82 219 oz. weights on one pan and 19 945 oz. weights on the other pan. The desired weight is that which must be added to the 19 945 oz. weights in order to balance the weights. This scheme may be used to develop an understanding of Diophantine Equations.

POSTASSESSMENT

Students should be able to compute the G.C.D. of the following pairs of integers and express the G.C.D. in terms of the two integers:

1. 12 and 18
2. 52 and 86
3. 865 and 312
4. 120 and 380

Unit 80

Prime Numbers

This unit will introduce students to fascinating facts concerning prime numbers.

PERFORMANCE OBJECTIVES

1. *Given a number, students will use Euler's ϕ function to find the number of positive integers less than the given number that are relatively prime to it.*
2. *Students will explain why it is not possible for a polynomial with integral coefficients to exist that will generate only primes.*

PREASSESSMENT

Ask students to identify which of the following are prime numbers:

(a) 11	(b) 27	(c) 51
(d) 47	(e) 91	(f) 1

TEACHING STRATEGIES

Mathematicians have spent years trying to find a general formula that would generate primes. There have been many attempts, but none have succeeded.

Have students test the expression $n^2 - n + 41$ by substituting various positive values for n. Make a chart on the chalkboard recording their findings. As they proceed they should begin to notice that as n ranges in value from 1 through 40, only prime numbers are being produced. (If they have not substituted $n = 40$, have them do so.) Then ask them to try $n = 41$. The value of $n^2 - n + 41$ is $(41)^2 - 41 + 41 = (41)^2$, which is not prime. A similar expression, $n^2 - 79n + 1601$, produces primes for all values of n up to 80. But for $n = 81$, we have $(81)^2 - 79 \cdot 81 + 1601 = 1763 = 41 \cdot 43$, which is not a prime. Students might now wonder if it is possible to have a polynomial in n with integral coefficients whose values would be primes for every positive integer n. Advise them not to try to find such an expression; Leonhard Euler (1707–1783) proved that none can exist. Euler showed that any proposed expression will produce at least one nonprime.

Euler's proof follows. First, assume that such an expression exists, being in the general form: $a + bx + cx^2 + dx^3 + \cdots$ (understanding that some of the coefficients may be zero). Let the value of this expression be s when $x = m$. Therefore: $s = a + bm + cm^2 + dm^3 + \ldots.$ Similarly, let t be the value of the expression when $x = m + ns$: $t = a + b(m + ns) + c(m + ns)^2 + d(m + ns)^3 \ldots.$ This may be transformed to

$$t = (a + bm + cm^2 + dm^3 + \ldots) + A,$$

where A represents the remaining terms all of which are multiples of s. But the expression within the parentheses is, by hypothesis, equal to s. This makes the whole expression a multiple of s, and the number produced is not a prime. Every such expression will produce at least one prime, but not necessarily more than one. Consequently, no expression can generate primes exclusively.

Although this last statement was recognized early in mathematical history, mathematicians continued to conjecture about forms of numbers that generated only primes.

Pierre de Fermat (1601–1665), who made many significant contributions to the study of number theory, conjectured that all numbers of the form $F_n = 2^{2^n} + 1$, where $n = 0, 1, 2, 3, 4, \ldots$ were prime numbers. Have students find F_n for $n = 0, 1, 2$. They will see that the first three numbers derived from this expression are 3, 5, and 17. For $n = 3$, students will find that $F_n = 257$; by telling them $F_4 = 65{,}537$, they should notice these numbers are increasing at a very rapid rate. For $n = 5$, $F_n = 4{,}294{,}967{,}297$, and Fermat could not find any factor of this number. Encouraged by his results, he expressed the opinion that all numbers of this form are probably also prime. Unfortunately he stopped too soon, for in 1732, Euler showed that $F_5 = 4{,}294{,}967{,}297 = 641 \times 6{,}700{,}417$ (not a prime!). It was not until 150 years later that the factors of F_6 were found: $18{,}446{,}744{,}073{,}709{,}551{,}617 = 247{,}177 \times 67{,}280{,}421{,}310{,}721$. As far as is now known, many more numbers of this form have been found but *none* of them have been prime. It seems that Fermat's conjecture has been completely turned around, and one now wonders if any primes beyond F_4 exist.

Euler also continued further into his study of primes. He began examining those integers that are *relatively prime* (two integers are relatively prime if they have no common positive factor except 1). Have students write down the number 12 and the positive integers less than 12. Tell them to cross out

12 itself and then all the integers that have a factor greater than 1 in common with 12.

1 ~~2~~ ~~3~~ ~~4~~ 5 ~~6~~ 7 ~~8~~ ~~9~~ ~~10~~ 11 ~~12~~

They will see that 1, 5, 7, 11 are the only integers remaining. Therefore, there are four positive integers less than 12 that are relatively prime to it. The number of such integers is denoted by $\phi(n)$ and is known as Euler's ϕ function. For $n = 1$, we have $\phi(n) = 1$. For $n > 1, \phi(n) =$ the number of positive integers less than n and relatively prime to it. Thus, as we just saw, $\phi(12) = 4$.

Let students now find values of $\phi(n)$ for $n = 1, 2, 3, 4, 5$. A chart, such as Figure 1 below, is convenient for this.

n	integers relatively prime to and less than n	ϕ(n)
1		1
2	1 2	1
3	1 2 3	2
4	1 2 3 4	2
5	1 2 3 4 5	4
6	1 2 3 4 5 6	2
7	prime	6
8	1 2 3 4 5 6 7 8	4
9	1 2 3 4 5 6 7 8 9	6
10	1 2 3 4 5 6 7 8 9 10	4
11	prime	10
12	1 2 3 4 5 6 7 8 9 10 11 12	4

FIGURE 1

Students should notice that when n is prime, it is not necessary to list all the numbers. Since a prime is relatively prime to all positive integers less than it, we therefore have $\phi(n) = n - 1$, for n a prime.

Have students continue to find $\phi(n)$ for $n = 6$ through 12. Looking down the ϕ (n) column, it does not seem that any particular pattern is emerging. We would like to, though, obtain an expression for the general term, so that $\phi(n)$ can be calculated for any number. We have already stated that if n is prime, then $\phi(n) = n - 1$. To discover an expression for $\phi(n)$ if n is not prime, we will look at a particular case. Let $n = 15$. Decomposing 15 into primes, we obtain $15 = 3 \cdot 5$. We can write this as $n = p \cdot q$, where $n = 15, p = 3$, and $q = 5$. Next, have students write down 15 and all positive integers less than 15. Have them cross out all integers having 3 (which is p) as a factor:

1 2 ~~3~~ 4 5 ~~6~~ 7 8 ~~9~~ 10 11 ~~12~~ 13 14 ~~15~~

They will see that there are 5 or $5 = \frac{15}{3} = \frac{n}{p}$ of these.

There are 10 numbers remaining or $10 = 15 - \frac{15}{3} = n - \frac{n}{p} = n\left(1 - \frac{1}{p}\right)$.

From these 10 integers, have students cross out those having 5 (which is q) as a factor:

1 2 4 ~~5~~ 7 8 ~~10~~ 11 13 14

There are only 2 of these or $2 = \frac{1}{5}(10) = \frac{1}{q}\left[n\left(1 - \frac{1}{p}\right)\right]$.

There are now 8 numbers left: $8 = 10 - \frac{1}{5}(10) = n\left(1 - \frac{1}{p}\right) - \frac{1}{q}\left[n\left(1 - \frac{1}{p}\right)\right]$. $n\left(1 - \frac{1}{p}\right)$ is a factor of both terms of the expression. We have therefore established a formula for the number of positive integers less than n and relatively prime to it:

$$\phi(n) = n\left(1 - \frac{1}{p}\right)\left(1 - \frac{1}{q}\right)$$

The number n, though, might have more than 2 factors in its prime decomposition, so let us now state a more general formula (given without proof). Let the number n be decomposed into its prime factors $p, q, r, \ldots, w$. Then $n = p^a \cdot q^b \cdot r^c \cdot \cdots w^h$, where $a, b, c, \ldots, h$ are positive integers (which may or may not be all 1s). Then $\phi(n) = n\left(1 - \frac{1}{p}\right)\left(1 - \frac{1}{q}\right)\left(1 - \frac{1}{r}\right)\cdots\left(1 - \frac{1}{w}\right)$. The teacher should also show the students that if n is a prime, the formula still holds since $\phi(n) = n - 1 = n\left(\frac{n-1}{n}\right) = n\left(1 - \frac{1}{n}\right)$. To see how the formula works, work together with students in finding the following: $\phi(21), \phi(43), \phi(78)$.

Solutions: $\phi(21) = \phi(7 \cdot 3) = 21\left(1 - \frac{1}{7}\right)\left(1 - \frac{1}{3}\right) = 21\left(\frac{6}{7}\right)\left(\frac{2}{3}\right) = 12$

$\phi(43) = 43 - 1$ (since 43 is a prime) $= 42$

$\phi(78) = \phi(2 \cdot 3 \cdot 13) = 78\left(1 - \frac{1}{2}\right)\left(1 - \frac{1}{3}\right)\left(1 - \frac{1}{13}\right) = 78\left(\frac{1}{2}\right)\left(\frac{2}{3}\right)\left(\frac{12}{13}\right) = 24$

At this point, some students might have noticed that every value of $\phi(n)$ is even. Justification of this may serve as a springboard for further investigation.

POSTASSESSMENT

1. Find each of the following:
   a. $\phi(13)$ b. $\phi(14)$ c. $\phi(48)$ d. $\phi(73)$ e. $\phi(100)$
2. Have students explain why there is no polynomial with integral coefficients that will generate only primes.

Unit 81

 Algebraic Fallacies

All too often students make errors in their mathematics work that are more subtle than an error in computation or some other careless act. To prevent errors that are the results of violations of mathematical definitions of concepts, it would be wise to exhibit such flaws beforehand. This is the main mission of this unit.

PERFORMANCE OBJECTIVE

Given an algebraic fallacy, students will analyze and determine where the fallacy occurs in the algebraic "proof."

PREASSESSMENT

Students should be familiar with the basic algebraic operations normally taught in the high school elementary algebra course.

TEACHING STRATEGY

When the theory behind mathematical operations is poorly understood, there exists the possibility that the operations will be applied in a formal and perhaps illogical way. Students, not aware of certain limitations on these operations, are likely to use them where they do not necessarily apply. Such improper reasoning leads to an absurd result called a fallacy. The following paradoxes will illustrate how such fallacies can arise in algebra when certain algebraic operations are performed without realizing the limitations on those operations.

Almost everyone who has been exposed to elementary algebra will come across, at one time or another, a proof that $2 = 1$ or $1 = 3$, etc. Such a "proof" is an example of a fallacy.

"Proof":

1. Let $a = b$
2. Multiply both sides by a: $a^2 = ab$
3. Subtract b^2 from both sides: $a^2 - b^2 = ab - b^2$
4. Factoring: $(a + b)(a - b) = b(a - b)$
5. Dividing both sides by $(a - b)$: $(a + b) = b$
6. Since $a = b$, then $2b = b$
7. Dividing both sides by b: $2 = 1$

Ask the students to analyze the "proof" and find out where the reasoning breaks down. Of course, the trouble is in the fifth step. Since $a = b$, then $a - b = 0$. Therefore, division by zero was performed, which is *not permissible*. It would be appropriate at this time to discuss what division means in terms of multiplication. To divide a by b implies that there exists a number y such that $b \cdot y = a$, or $y = \frac{a}{b}$. If $b = 0$, there are two possibilities, either $a \neq 0$ or $a = 0$. If $a \neq 0$, then $y = \frac{a}{0}$ or $0 \cdot y = a$. Ask your students if they can find a number that when multiplied by zero will equal a. Your students should conclude that there is no such number y. In the second case, where $a = 0$, $y = \frac{0}{0}$ or $0 \cdot y = 0$.

Here any number for y will satisfy the equation, hence any number multiplied by zero is zero. Therefore we have the "rule" that division by zero is not permissible. There are other fallacies based on division by zero. Have your students discover for themselves where and how the difficulty occurs in each of the following examples.

1. To "prove" that any two unequal numbers are equal. Assume that $x = y + z$, and x, y, z are positive numbers. This implies $x > y$. Multiply both sides by $x - y$. Then $x^2 - xy = xy + xz - y^2 - yz$. Subtract xz from both sides:

   $$x^2 - xy - xz = xy - y^2 - yz$$

   Factoring, we get $x(x - y - z) = y(x - y - z)$. Dividing both sides by $(x - y - z)$ yields $x = y$. Thus x, which was assumed to be greater than y, has been shown to equal y. The fallacy occurs in the division by $(x - y - z)$, which is equal to zero.
2. To "prove" that all positive whole numbers are equal. By doing long division, we have, for any value of x

$$\frac{x-1}{x-1} = 1$$
$$\frac{x^2-1}{x-1} = x + 1$$
$$\frac{x^3-1}{x-1} = x^2 + x + 1$$
$$\frac{x^4-1}{x-1} = x^3 + x^2 + x + 1$$
$$\vdots$$
$$\frac{x^n-1}{x-1} = x^{n-1} + x^{n-2} + \ldots + x^2 + x + 1$$

Letting $x = 1$ in all of these identities, the right side then assumes the values $1, 2, 3, 4, \ldots, n$. The left side members are all the same. Consequently, $1 = 2 = 3 = 4 = \ldots = n$. In this example, the left-hand side of each of the identities assumes the value $\frac{0}{0}$ when $x = 1$. This problem serves as evidence that $\frac{0}{0}$ can be any number.

Consider the following, and ask your students if they would agree with the following statement, "If two fractions are equal and have equal numerators, then they also have equal denominators." Let the students give illustrations using any fractions they choose. Then have them solve the following equation.

$$6 + \frac{8x - 40}{4 - x} = \frac{2x - 16}{12 - x} \qquad (1)$$

Add terms on the left-hand side, to get

$$\frac{6(4 - x) + 8x - 40}{4 - x} = \frac{2x - 16}{12 - x} \qquad (2)$$

Simplifying: $\frac{2x - 16}{4 - x} = \frac{2x - 16}{12 - x}$

Since the numerators are equal, this implies $4 - x = 12 - x$. Adding x to both sides, $4 = 12$. Again, as in some of the previous examples, the division by zero is disguised. Have students find the error. Point out that the axioms cannot be blindly applied to equations without considering the values of the variables for which the equations are true. Thus, equation (1) is not an identity true for all values of x, but it is satisfied only by $x = 8$. Have students solve $(12 - x)(2x - 16) = (4 - x) \times (2x - 16)$ to verify this. Thus $x = 8$, implies that the numerators are zero. You may also have the students prove the general case for $\frac{a}{b} = \frac{a}{c}$, to show that a cannot be zero.

Another class of fallacies includes those that neglect to consider that a quantity has two square roots of equal absolute value; however, one is positive and the other is negative. As an example, take the equation $16 - 48 = 64 - 96$. Adding 36 to both sides gives $16 - 48 + 36 = 64 - 96 + 36$. Each member of the equation is now a perfect square, so that $(4 - 6)^2 = (8 - 6)^2$. Taking the square root of both sides, we get $4 - 6 = 8 - 6$, which implies $4 = 8$. Ask the students where the fallacy occurs. The fallacy in this example lies in taking the improper square root. The correct answer should be $(4 - 6) = -(8 - 6)$.

The following fallacies are based on the failure to consider all the roots of a given example.

Have students solve the equation $x + 2\sqrt{x} = 3$ in the usual manner. The solutions are $x = 1$ and $x = 9$. The first solution satisfies the equation, while the second solution does not. Have students explain where the difficulty lies.

A similar equation is $x - a = \sqrt{x^2 + a^2}$. By squaring both sides and simplifying we get $-2ax = 0$, or $x = 0$. Substituting $x = 0$ in the original equation, we find that this value of x does not satisfy the equation. Have the students find the correct root of the given equation.

So far we have dealt with square roots of positive numbers. Ask the students what happens when we apply our usual rules to radicals containing imaginary numbers, in light of the following problem. The students have learned that $\sqrt{a} \cdot \sqrt{b} = \sqrt{ab}$, for example, $\sqrt{2} \cdot \sqrt{5} = \sqrt{2 \cdot 5} = \sqrt{10}$. But this gives then, $\sqrt{-1} \cdot \sqrt{-1} = \sqrt{(-1)(-1)} = \sqrt{1} = 1$. However $\sqrt{-1} \cdot \sqrt{-1} = \left(\sqrt{-1}\right)^2 = -1$. It therefore may be concluded that $1 = -1$, since both equal $\sqrt{-1} \times \sqrt{-1}$. Students should try to explain the error. They should realize that we cannot apply the ordinary rules for multiplication of radicals to imaginary numbers.

Another proof that can be used to show $-1 = +1$ is the following:

$$\sqrt{-1} = \sqrt{-1}$$
$$\sqrt{\frac{1}{-1}} = \sqrt{\frac{-1}{1}}$$
$$\frac{\sqrt{1}}{\sqrt{-1}} = \frac{\sqrt{-1}}{\sqrt{1}}$$
$$\sqrt{1} \cdot \sqrt{1} = \sqrt{-1} \cdot \sqrt{-1}$$
$$1 = -1$$

Have students replace i for $\sqrt{-1}$, and -1 for i^2 to see where the flaw occurs.

Before concluding the topic on algebraic fallacies, it would be appropriate to consider a fallacy involving simultaneous equations. The students, by now, should realize that in doing the preceding proofs a certain law or operation was violated. Consider an example where hidden flaws in equations can bring about ludicrous results. Have students solve the following pairs of equations by substituting for x in the first equation:

$2x + y = 8$ and $x = 2 - \frac{y}{2}$. The result will be $4 = 8$

Have students find the error. When students graph these two equations, they will find the two lines to be parallel and therefore have *no* points in common.

Further exhibition of such fallacies will prove a worthwhile activity due to the intrinsically dramatic message they carry.

POSTASSESSMENT

Have students determine where and how the fallacy occurs in the following examples.

1. a. $x = 4$
   b. $x^2 = 16$
   c. $x^2 - 4x = 16 - 4x$
   d. $x(x - 4) = 4(4 - x)$
   e. $x(x - 4) = -4(x - 4)$
   f. $x = -4$
2. a. $(y + 1)^2 = y^2 + 2y + 1$
   b. $(y + 1)^2 - (2y + 1) = y^2$
   c. $(y + 1)^2 - (2y + 1) - y(2y + 1)$
   $= y^2 - y(2y + 1)$
   d. $(y + 1)^2 - (y + 1)(2y + 1) + \frac{1}{4}(2y + 1)^2$
   $= y^2 - y(2y + 1) + \frac{1}{4}(2y + 1)^2$

e. $\left[(y + 1) - \frac{1}{2}(2y + 1)\right]^2 = \left[y - \frac{1}{2}(2y + 1)\right]^2$

f. $y + 1 - \frac{1}{2}(2y + 1) = y - \frac{1}{2}(2y + 1)$

g. $y + 1 = y$

Other fallacies/paradoxes can be found in: *Math Wonders to Inspire Teachers and Students* by Alfred S. Posamentier (Assc. for Supervision and Curriculum Development 2007)

Unit 82

Sum Derivations With Arrays

PERFORMANCE OBJECTIVES

1. *Students will derive the formula for the sum of the first* n *natural numbers, triangular numbers, square numbers, or pentagonal numbers.*
2. *Given any integral value of* n, *students will apply the proper formula to find the sum of the first* n *figurate numbers.*

PREASSESSMENT

Before beginning this lesson, be sure students are familiar with the meanings of *figurate numbers* and *formation of sequences of figurate numbers*. They should also have some knowledge of elementary algebra.

TEACHING STRATEGIES

To begin to familiarize students with this topic, have them construct dot arrays on graph paper to illustrate the first few terms in the sequences of various figurate numbers.

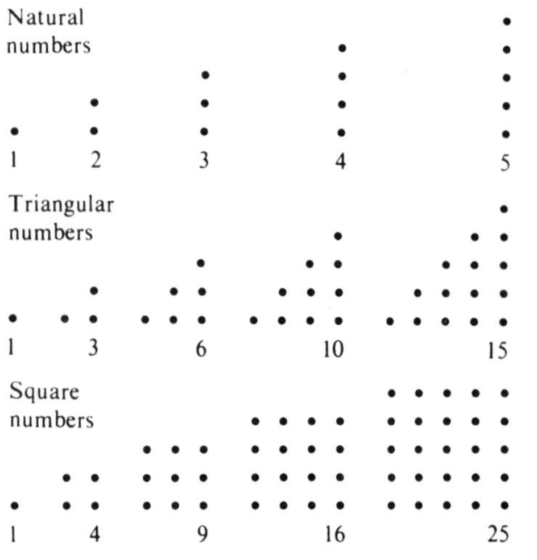

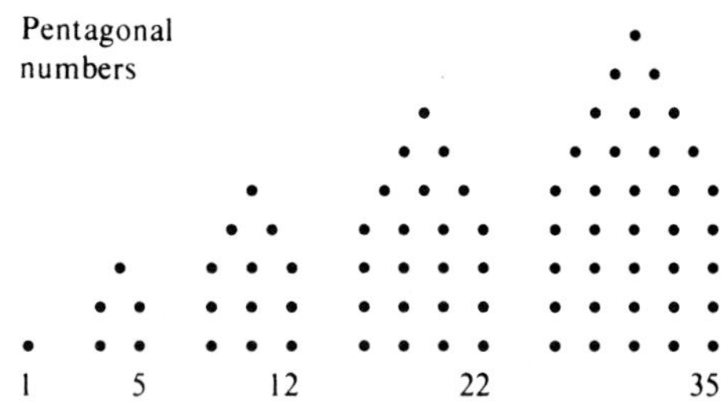

Discuss with the class the visual relationships. Most students will clearly see that we can represent the sum of the first *n* natural numbers as follows:

$$\begin{aligned} N_n &= \text{Sum of the first } n \text{ natural numbers} \\ &= 1 + 2 + 3 + \ldots + n \\ &= 1 + (1 + 1) + (1 + 1 + 1) + \ldots \\ &\quad + \underbrace{(1 + 1 + \ldots + 1)}_{n} \end{aligned}$$

N_n can also be represented as the sum of the numbers in an array:

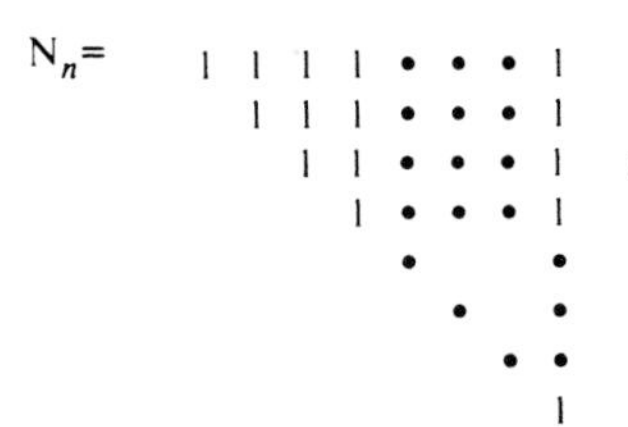

By switching the rows with the columns, N_n can be made to look slightly different:

N_n=

n

n

These two representations of N_n in array form can now be combined to produce an array for $2N_n$ as shown below:

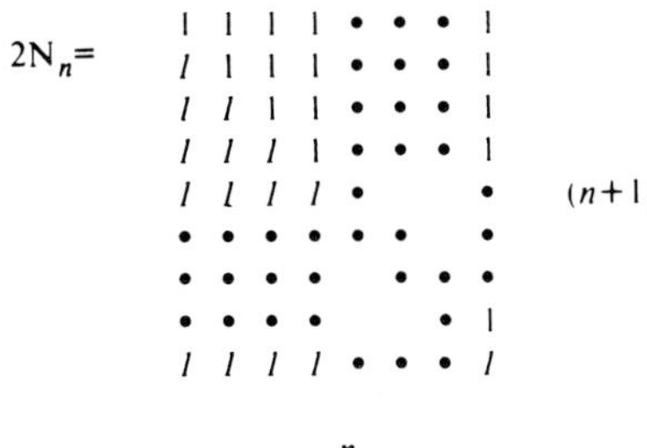

Students can distinctly see that $2N_n = n(n + 1)$ from an inspection of the array for $2N_n$. We therefore have

$$N_n = \frac{n(n+1)}{2}$$

This resulting formula for N_n can be applied whenever it is required to find the sum of the first n natural numbers.

Have students consider trying to derive a formula for the first n triangular numbers. Clearly, from the dot arrays presented earlier, the following can be established:

$$\begin{aligned} T_n &= \text{Sum of the first } n \text{ triangular numbers} \\ &= 1 + 3 + 6 + \ldots + N_n \\ &= 1 + (1+2) + (1+2+3) + \ldots + (1+2+3+ \ldots +n) \end{aligned}$$

T_n can now be represented as the sum of the numbers in an array:

```
T_n=
     1
     1 2
     1 2 3
 n   1 2 3 4
     • • • • •
     • • • •   •
     • • • •     •
     1 2 3 4 • • • n
           n
```

By applying the previously determined formula for N to each row of this array we obtain

$$T_n = \frac{1(1+1)}{2} + \frac{2(1+2)}{2} + \frac{3(1+3)}{2} + \frac{4(1+4)}{2} + \ldots + \frac{n(1+n)}{2}$$

Students should now see that

$$2T_n = 1(2) + 2(3) + 3(4) + 4(5) + \ldots + n(n+1),$$

which can be represented in a very convenient form as the sum of the numbers in an array:

```
2T_n=  2 3 4 5 • • • (n+1)
         3 4 5 • • • (n+1)
           4 5 • • • (n+1)
             5 • • • (n+1)   n
               •       •
                 •     •
                   •   •
                     (n+1)
```

The combination of the array for T_n and the array for $2T_n$ produces an array for $3T_n$, which is easy to sum up:

```
          (n+1)
3T_n=
   1 2 3 4 5 • • • (n+1)
   1 2 3 4 5 • • • (n+1)
   1 2 3 4 5 • • • (n+1)
   1 2 3 4 5 • • • (n+1)   n
   • • • • • • •       •
   • • • •     • •     •
   • • • •       • •   •
   1 2 3 4 • • • n (n+1)
```

Our formula for N_n directly yields

$$3T_n = n\frac{(n+1)(1 + [n+1])}{2}$$

$$T_n = \frac{n(n+1)(n+2)}{6}$$

Students are now ready to consider the sum of the first n square numbers.

$$\begin{aligned} S_n &= \text{Sum of the first } n \text{ square numbers} \\ &= 1^2 + 2^2 + 3^2 + 4^2 + \ldots + n. \end{aligned}$$

In array form this appears as

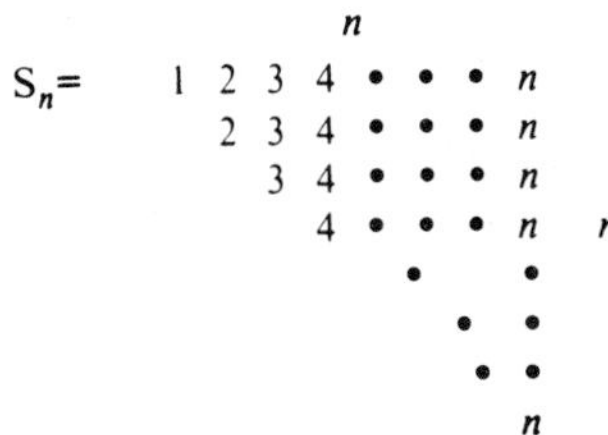

Combining the array for T_n with this array for S_n, we obtain an array for $S_n + T_n$:

```
                  n
          1 2 3 4 • • • n
S_n+T_n=  1 2 3 4 • • • n
          1 2 3 4 • • • n
          1 2 3 4 • • • n   (n+1)
          1 2 3 4 •     •
          • • • • • •   •
          • • • •   • • •
          • • • •     • n
          1 2 3 4 • • • n
```

Students should observe that each row of the array for $S_n + T_n$ is the sum of the first n natural numbers. In the present notation, this is N_n. Because the array has $(n + 1)$ rows, we clearly obtain

$$S_n + T_n = (n + 1)N_n.$$

Substituting the formulas previously derived for T_n and N_n is an exercise in elementary algebra which quickly yields

$$\boxed{S_n = \frac{n(n + 1)(2n + 1)}{6}}$$

POSTASSESSMENT

Have each student:

1. derive a formula for the sum of the first n pentagonal numbers using arrays.
2. apply the various formulas the class has derived to find the sum of the first n figurate numbers for several integral values of n.

Unit 83

Pythagorean Triples

While teaching the Pythagorean theorem at the secondary school level, teachers often suggest that students recognize (and memorize) certain common ordered sets of three numbers that can represent the lengths of the sides of a right triangle. Some of these ordered sets of three numbers, known as Pythagorean triples, are: (3, 4, 5), (5, 12, 13), (8, 15, 17), (7, 24, 25). The student is asked to discover these Pythagorean triples as they come up in selected exercises. How can one generate more triples without a trial and error method? This question, often asked by students, will be answered in this unit.

PERFORMANCE OBJECTIVES

1. *Students will generate six primitive Pythagorean triples using the formulas developed in this unit.*
2. *Students will state properties of various members of a primitive Pythagorean triple.*

PREASSESSMENT

Students should be familiar with the Pythagorean theorem. They should be able to recognize Pythagorean triples and distinguish between primitive Pythagorean triples and others.

TEACHING STRATEGIES

Ask your students to find the missing member of the following Pythagorean triples:

1. (3, 4, _____)
2. (7, _____, 25)
3. (11, _____, _____)

The first two triples can be easily determined using the Pythagorean theorem. However, this method will not work with the third triple. At this point you can offer your students a method for solving this problem.

Before beginning the development of the desired formulas, we must consider a few simple lemmas.

Lemma 1: When 8 divides the square of an odd number, the remainder is 1.

Proof: We can represent an odd number by $2k + 1$, where k is an integer.
$(2k + 1)^2 = 4k^2 + 4k + 1 = 4k(k + 1) + 1$
Since k and $k + 1$ are consecutive, one of them must be even. Therefore $4k(k + 1)$ must be divisible by 8.
Thus $(2k + 1)^2$, when divided by 8, leaves a remainder of 1.

The following lemmas follow directly.

Lemma 2: When 8 divides the sum of two odd square numbers, the remainder is 2.

Lemma 3: The sum of two odd square numbers cannot be a square number.

Proof: Since the sum of two odd square numbers, when divided by 8, leaves a remainder of 2, the sum is even but not divisible by 4. It therefore cannot be a square number.

We are now ready to begin our development of formulas for Pythagorean triples. Let us assume that (a, b, c) is a primitive Pythagorean triple. This implies that a and b are relatively prime. Therefore they cannot both be even. Can they both be odd?

If a and b are both odd, then by Lemma 3: $a^2 + b^2 \neq c^2$. This contradicts our assumption that (a, b, c) is a Pythagorean triple; therefore a and b cannot both be odd. Therefore one must be odd and one even.

Let us suppose that a is odd and b is even. This implies that c is also odd.

We can rewrite $a^2 + b^2 = c^2$ as

$$b^2 = c^2 - a^2$$
$$b^2 = (c + a) \cdot (c - a)$$

Since the sum and difference of two odd numbers is even,

$c + a = 2p$, and $c - a = 2q$ (p and q are natural numbers).

By solving for a and c we get

$$c = p + q, \text{ and } a = p - q.$$

We can now show that p and q must be relatively prime. Suppose p and q were not relatively prime; say $g > 1$ was a common factor. Then g would also be a common factor of a and c. Similarly g would also be a common factor of $c + a$ and $c - a$. This would make g^2 a factor of b^2, since $b^2 = (c + a) \cdot (c - a)$. It follows that g would then have to be a factor of b. Now if g is a factor of b and also a common factor of a and c, then a, b, and c are not relatively prime. This contradicts our assumption that (a, b, c) is a *primitive* Pythagorean triple. Thus p and q must be relatively prime.

Since b is even, we may represent b as

$$b = 2r.$$

But $b^2 = (c + a)(c - a)$.

Therefore $b^2 = (2p) \cdot (2q) = 4r^2$, or $pq = r^2$.

If the product of two relatively prime natural numbers (p and q) is the square of a natural number (r), then each of them must be the square of a natural number. Therefore we let

$$p = m^2 \quad \text{and} \quad q = n^2,$$

where m and n are natural numbers. Since they are factors of relatively prime numbers (p and q), they (m and n) are also relatively prime.

$$\text{Since } a = p - q \quad \text{and} \quad c = p + q$$
$$a = m^2 - n^2 \quad \text{and} \quad c = m^2 + n^2$$
$$\text{Also, since } b = 2r \quad \text{and} \quad b^2 = 4r^2 = 4pq = 4m^2n^2$$
$$b = 2mn$$

To summarize we now have formulas for generating Pythagorean triples:

$$a = m^2 - n^2 \qquad b = 2mn \qquad c = m^2 + n^2$$

The numbers m and n cannot both be even, since they are relatively prime. They cannot both be odd, for this would make $c = m^2 + n^2$ an even number, which we established earlier as impossible. Since this indicates that one must be even and the other odd, $b = 2mn$ must be divisible by 4. Therefore no Pythagorean triple can be composed of three prime numbers. This does *not* mean that the other members of the Pythagorean triple may not be prime.

Let us reverse the process for a moment. Consider relatively prime numbers m and n (where $m > n$) and where one is even and the other odd. We will now show that (a, b, c) is a primitive Pythagorean triple where $a = m^2 - n^2$, $b = 2mn$, and $c = m^2 + n^2$.

It is simple to verify algebraically that

$$(m^2 - n^2)^2 + (2mn)^2 = (m^2 + n^2)^2,$$

thereby making it a Pythagorean triple. What remains is to prove that (a, b, c) is a *primitive* Pythagorean triple.

Suppose a and b have a common factor $h > 1$. Since a is odd, h must also be odd. Because $a^2 + b^2 = c^2$, h would also be a factor of c. We also have h a factor of $m^2 - n^2$ and $m^2 + n^2$ as well as of their sum, $2m^2$, and their difference $2n^2$.

Since h is odd, it is a common factor of m^2 and n^2. However m and n (and as a result m^2 and n^2) are relatively prime. Therefore h cannot be a common factor of m and n. This contradiction establishes that a and b are relatively prime.

Having finally established a method for generating primitive Pythagorean triples, students should be eager to put it to use. The table below gives some of the smaller primitive Pythagorean triples.

PYTHAGOREAN TRIPLES

m	n	a	b	c
2	1	3	4	5
3	2	5	12	13
4	1	15	8	17
4	3	7	24	25
5	2	21	20	29
5	4	9	40	41
6	1	35	12	37
6	5	11	60	61
7	2	45	28	53
7	4	33	56	65
7	6	13	84	85

A fast inspection of the above table indicates that certain primitive Pythagorean triples (a, b, c) have $c = b + 1$. Have students discover the relationship between m and n for these triples.

They should notice that for these triples $m = n + 1$. To prove this will be true for other primitive Pythagorean triples (not in the table), let $m = n + 1$ and generate the Pythagorean triples.

$$a = m^2 - n^2 = (n + 1)^2 - n^2 = 2n + 1$$
$$b = 2mn = 2n(n + 1) = 2n^2 + 2n$$
$$c = m^2 + n^2 = (n + 1)^2 + n^2 = 2n^2 + 2n + 1$$

Clearly $c = b + 1$, which was to be shown!

A natural question to ask your students is to find all primitive Pythagorean triples that are consecutive natural numbers. In a method similar to that used above, they ought to find that the only triple satisfying that condition is (3, 4, 5).

Other investigations can be proposed for student consideration. In any case students should have a far better appreciation for Pythagorean triples and elementary number theory after completing this unit.

POSTASSESSMENT

1. Find six primitive Pythagorean triples that are not included in the above table.
2. Find a way to generate primitive Pythagorean triples of the form (a, b, c) where $b = a + 1$.
3. Prove that every primitive Pythagorean triple has one member that is divisible by 3.
4. Prove that every primitive Pythagorean triple has one member that is divisible by 5.
5. Prove that for every primitive Pythagorean triple the product of its members is a multiple of 60.
6. Find a Pythagorean triple (a, b, c) where $a^2 = b + 2$.

Unit 84

Divisibility

The unit will present methods for finding divisors without doing division.

PERFORMANCE OBJECTIVES

1. *Given any integer, students will determine its prime factors, without doing any division.*
2. *Students will produce rules for testing divisibility by all natural numbers less than 49, and some greater than 49.*

PREASSESSMENT

Have students indicate without doing any division which of the following numbers are divisible by 2, by 3, and by 5.

a. 792 b. 835 c. 356 d. 3890 e. 693 f. 743

TEACHING STRATEGIES

Students are probably aware that any even number is divisible by 2; hence of the above numbers, (a), (c), and (d) are divisible by 2. Many will also recognize that a number whose terminal digit (units digit) is either 5 or 0, is divisible by 5; hence, (b) and (d) are divisible by 5. At this point students will be eager to extend this rule to hold true for testing divisibility by 3. Of the above numbers, (c), (e), and (f) are the only numbers whose terminal digit is a multiple of 3; yet only one of these numbers, 693, is in fact divisible by 3. This should stir up sufficient curiosity so as to create a desire among the students to develop rules to test divisibility by numbers other than 2 and 5.

There are various ways to develop rules for testing divisibility by various numbers. They may be developed in order of magnitude of the numbers. This method may be appealing to some; however it detracts from the various patterns that students so often appreciate in the development of mathematics. In this unit we shall consider the rules in groups of related methods.

Divisibility by powers of 2: A given number is divisible by 2^1 (or $2^2, 2^3, \ldots 2^n$, respectively) if the last 1 (or 2, 3, ... n, respectively) digit(s) is (are) divisible by 2^1 (or $2^2, 2^3, \ldots 2^n$, respectively).

Proof: Consider the following n-digit number:

$$a_{n-1}a_{n-2}a_{n-3}\cdots a_2a_1a_0,$$

which can be written as

$$10^{n-1}a_{n-1} + 10^{n-2}a_{n-2} + \ldots + 10^2a_2 + 10^1a_1 + 10^0a_0.$$

Since all terms except the last are always divisible by 2, we must be assured of the divisibility of the last term when testing divisibility by 2. Similarly, since all the terms except the last two are always divisible by 2^2, we must merely determine if the last two digits (considered as a number) is divisible by 2^2. This scheme may easily be extended to the nth case.

Divisibility by powers of 5: A given number is divisible by 5^1 (or $5^2, 5^3, \ldots 5^n$, respectively) if the last 1 (or 2, 3, ... n, respectively) digit(s) is (are) divisible by 5^1 (or $5^2, 5^3, \ldots 5^n$, respectively).

Proof: The proof of these rules follows the same scheme as the proof for testing divisibility by powers of two, except the 2 is replaced by a 5.

Divisibility by 3 and 9: A given number is divisible by 3 (or 9) if the sum of the digits is divisible by 3 (or 9).

Proof: Consider the number $a_8a_7a_6a_5a_4a_3a_2a_1a_0$ (the general case $a_na_{n-1}\ldots a_3a_2a_1a_0$ is similar). This expression may be written as

$$a_8(9+1)^8 + a_7(9+1)^7 + \ldots + a_1(9+1) + a_0.$$

Using the expression $M_i(9)$ to mean a multiple of 9, for $i = 1, 2, 3, \ldots 7, 8$, we can rewrite the number as

$$a_8[M_8(9)+1] + a_7[M_7(9)+1] + \ldots + a_1[M_1(9)+1] + a_0.$$

(A mention of the binomial theorem may be helpful here.) The number equals $M(9) + a_8 + a_7 + a_6 + a_5 + a_4 + a_3 + a_2 + a_1 + a_0$, where M(9) is a multiple of 9. Thus the number is divisible by 9 (or 3) if the sum of the digits is divisible by 9 (or 3).

A rule for testing divisibility by 11 is proved in a manner similar to the proof for divisibility by 3 and 9.

Divisibility by 11: A given number is divisible by 11 if the difference of the two sums of alternate digits is divisible by 11.

Proof: Consider the number $a_8a_7a_6a_5a_4a_3a_2a_1a_0$ (using the general case is similar). This expression may be written as

$$a_8(11-1)^8 + a_7(11-1)^7 + \ldots + a_1(11-1) + a_0 = a_8[M_8(11)+1] + a_7[M_7(11)-1] + \ldots + a_1[M_1(11)-1] + a_0.$$

This expression then equals $M(11) + a_8 - a_7 + a_6 - a_5 + a_4 - a_3 + a_2 - a_1 + a_0$. Thus the number is divisible by 11 if $a_8 + a_6 + a_4 + a_2 + a_0 - (a_7 + a_5 + a_3 + a_1)$ is divisible by 11.

You would be wise to indicate the extensions in bases other than ten of each of the previously mentioned divisibility rules. Often students are able to make these generalizations on their own (especially with appropriate coaxing). The remainder of this unit will deal with rules for testing divisibility of primes ≥ 7 and composites.

Divisibility by 7: Delete the last digit from the given number, then subtract twice *this deleted digit from the remaining number. If the result is divisible by 7, the original number is divisible by 7. This process may be repeated if the result is too large for simple inspection of divisibility by 7.*

Proof: To justify the technique, consider the various possible terminal digits and the corresponding subtraction:

Terminal digit	Number subtracted from original	Terminal digit	Number subtracted from original
1	20 + 1 = 21 = 3·7	5	100 + 5 = 105 = 15·7
2	40 + 2 = 42 = 6·7	6	120 + 6 = 126 = 18·7
3	60 + 3 = 63 = 9·7	7	140 + 7 = 147 = 21·7
4	80 + 4 = 84 = 12·7	8	160 + 8 = 168 = 24·7
		9	180 + 9 = 189 = 27·7

In each case a multiple of 7 is being subtracted one or more times from the original number. Hence, if the remaining number is divisible by 7, then so is the original number.

Divisibility by 13: This is the same as the rule for testing divisibility by 7, except that the 7 is replaced by 13 and instead of subtracting twice *the deleted digit, we subtract* nine times *the deleted digit each time.*

Proof: Once again consider the various possible terminal digits and the corresponding subtraction:

Terminal digit	Number subtracted from original	Terminal digit	Number subtracted from original
1	90 + 1 = 91 = 7·13	5	450 + 5 = 455 = 35·13
2	180 + 2 = 182 = 14·13	6	540 + 6 = 546 = 42·13
3	270 + 3 = 273 = 21·13	7	630 + 7 = 637 = 49·13
4	360 + 4 = 364 = 28·13	8	720 + 8 = 728 = 56·13
		9	810 + 9 = 819 = 63·13

In each case a multiple of 13 is being subtracted one or more times from the original number. Hence, if the remaining number is divisible by 13, then the original number is divisible by 13.

Divisibility by 17: This is the same as the rule for testing divisibility by 7 except that the 7 is replaced by 17 and instead of subtracting twice *the deleted digit, we subtract* five times *the deleted digit each time.*

Proof: The proof for the rule for divisibility by 17 follows a similar pattern to those for 7 and 13.

The patterns developed in the preceding three divisibility rules (for 7, 13, and 17) should lead students to develop similar rules for testing divisibility by larger primes. The following chart presents the "multipliers" of the deleted digits for various primes.

To test divisibility by	7	11	13	17	19	23	29	31	37	41	43	47
Multiplier	2	1	9	5	17	16	26	3	11	4	30	14

To fill in the gaps in the set of integers, a consideration of divisibility of composites is necessary.

Divisibility by composites: A given number is divisible by a composite number if it is divisible by each of its relatively prime factors. The chart below offers illustrations of this rule. You or your students should complete the chart to 48.

To be divisible by	6	10	12	15	18	21	24	26	28
The number must be divisible by	2,3	2,5	3,4	3,5	2,9	3,7	3,8	2,13	4,7

At this juncture the student has not only a rather comprehensive list of rules for testing divisibility, but also an interesting insight into elementary number theory. Have students practice using these rules (to instill greater familiarity) and try to develop rules to test divisibility by other numbers in base ten and to generalize these rules to other bases. Unfortunately lack of space prevents a more detailed development here.

POSTASSESSMENT

Have students do these exercises.

1. State a rule for testing divisibility by
   a. 8 b. 18 c. 13 d. 23 e. 24 f. 42
2. Determine the prime factors of
   a. 280 b. 1001 c. 495 d. 315 e. 924

REFERENCES

Further references on this topic may be found in:

Posamentier, A. S., and S. Krulik. *Teachers! Prepare Your Students for the Mathematics for SAT 1: Methods and Problem Solving Strategies*. Thousand Oaks, CA: Corwin, 1996.

Posamentier, A. S., and C. T. Salkind. *Challenging Problems in Algebra*. New York: Dover, 1996.

Unit 85

Fibonacci Sequence

PERFORMANCE OBJECTIVES

Students will:

1. *define the Fibonacci Sequence.*
2. *find sums of various Fibonacci numbers.*
3. *find the sum of squares of the first Fibonacci numbers.*
4. *discover properties of Fibonacci numbers.*

PREASSESSMENT

Have students try to solve the following problem:

How many pairs of rabbits will be produced in a year, beginning with a single pair, if in one month each pair bears a new pair which becomes productive from the second month on?

TEACHING STRATEGIES

Italian mathematician Leonardo of Pisa (he was the son, figlio, of Bonaccio, hence the name Fibonacci) presented the above problem in his book *LIBER ABACI* published in 1202. Consider its solution with students. Begin by drawing a chart as pictured below.

let A = Adult pairs, B = Baby pairs

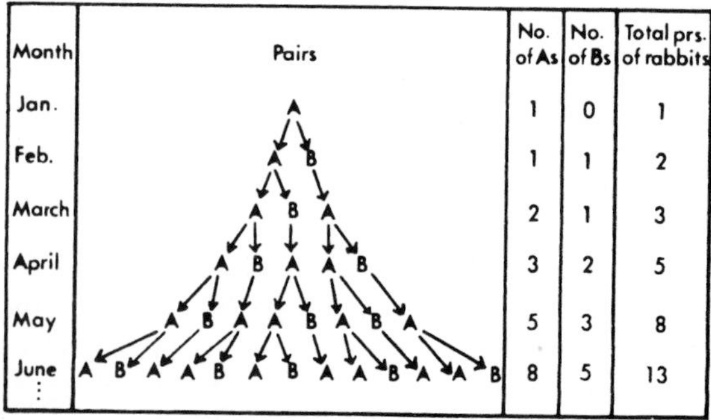

FIGURE 1

Start with first month and proceed to the next months explaining the procedure as you go along. Remind students that a baby pair must mature one month before becoming productive.

Continue the chart until the twelfth month where it will be discovered that 377 pairs of rabbits are produced in a year. Now focus students' attention on the third column (Number of As), the Fibonacci Sequence. Have them try to discover a rule for continuing this sequence. Tell students to notice that each term is the sum of the two preceding terms. This can be written as a general expression: $f_n = f_{n-1} + f_{n-2}$, where f_n stands for the nth Fibonacci number. For example, $f_3 = f_1 + f_2$; $f_4 = f_2 + f_3$; $f_7 = f_5 + f_6$. Also $f_1 = f_2 = 1$.

The Fibonacci Sequence has many interesting properties that students can observe by studying the relationships between the terms. It can be proved that the sum of the first n Fibonacci numbers,

$$f_1 + f_2 + \dots + f_n = f_{n+2} - 1 \qquad \text{(A)}$$

It has already been noted that the following relations hold: $f_1 = f_3 - f_2$ (since $f_3 = f_1 + f_2$)

$$f_2 = f_4 - f_3$$
$$f_3 = f_5 - f_4$$
$$\vdots$$
$$f_{n-1} = f_{n+1} - f_n$$
$$f_n = f_{n+2} - f_{n+1}$$

By *termwise* addition of all these equations it follows that $f_1 + f_2 + f_3 + \dots + f_n = f_{n+2} - f_2$, but we know that $f_2 = 1$. Therefore $f_1 + f_2 + f_3 + \dots + f_n = f_{n+2} - 1$.

In a similar manner we can find an expression for the sum of the first n Fibonacci numbers with odd indices:

$$f_1 + f_3 + f_5 + \dots + f_{2n-1} = f_{2n} \qquad \text{(B)}$$

To do this we write

$$\begin{aligned} f_1 &= f_2 \\ f_3 &= f_4 - f_2 \text{ (because } f_4 = f_2 + f_3) \\ f_5 &= f_6 - f_4 \\ f_7 &= f_8 - f_6 \\ f_{2n-3} &= f_{2n-2} - f_{2n-4} \\ f_{2n-1} &= f_{2n} - f_{2n-2}. \end{aligned}$$

Again by termwise addition, we obtain

$$f_1 + f_3 + f_5 + \ldots + f_{2n-1} = f_{2n}.$$

The sum of the first n Fibonacci numbers with even indices is $f_2 + f_4 + f_6 + \ldots + f_{2n} = f_{2n+1} - 1$ (C)

To prove this we subtract equation (B) from twice equation (A), that is, $f_1 + f_2 + f_3 + \ldots + f_{2n} = f_{2n+2} - 1$, to obtain $f_2 + f_4 + \ldots + f_{2n} = f_{2n+2} - 1 - f_{2n} = f_{2n+2} - f_{2n} - 1 = f_{2n+1} - 1$ (because $f_{2n+2} = f_{2n} + f_{2n+1}$ and $f_{2n+1} = f_{2n+2} - f_{2n}$), which is what we wanted to prove.

By yet another application of the process of termwise addition of equations we can derive a formula for the sum of the squares of the first n Fibonacci numbers. We must first note that for $k > 1$

$$f_k f_{k+1} - f_{k-1} f_k = f_k(f_{k+1} - f_{k-1}) = f_k \cdot f_k = f_k^2.$$

This gives us the following relations:

$$\begin{aligned} f_{1^2} &= f_1 f_2 - f_0 f_1 \text{ (where } f_0 = 0) \\ f_{2^2} &= f_2 f_3 - f_1 f_2 \\ f_{3^2} &= f_3 f_4 - f_2 f_3 \\ &\vdots \\ f_{n-1^2} &= f_{n-1} f_n - f_{n-2} f_{n-1} \\ f_{n^2} &= f_n f_{n+1} - f_{n-1} f_n \end{aligned}$$

By adding termwise we obtain

$$f_{1^2} + f_{2^2} + f_{3^2} + \ldots + f_{n^2} = f_n \cdot f_{n+1}.$$

The Fibonacci Sequence is also connected to a famous, ancient topic in mathematics. Examining the ratios of the first successive pairs of numbers in the sequence we obtain the following:

$$\begin{array}{ll} \frac{1}{1} = 1.0000 & \frac{2}{1} = 2.0000 \\ \frac{3}{2} = 1.5000 & \frac{5}{3} = 1.6667 \\ \frac{8}{5} = 1.6000 & \frac{13}{8} = 1.6250 \\ \frac{21}{13} = 1.6154 & \frac{34}{21} = 1.6190 \\ \frac{55}{34} = 1.6176 & \frac{89}{55} = 1.6182 \\ \frac{144}{89} = 1.6180 & \frac{233}{144} = 1.6181 \end{array}$$

The ratios $\frac{f_n}{f_{n-1}}$ $(n > 0)$ form a decreasing sequence for the odd values of n and an increasing sequence for the even values of n. Each ratio on the right-hand side is larger than each corresponding ratio on the left-hand side. The ratio approaches a limiting value between 1.6180 and 1.6181. It can be shown that this limit is $\frac{1 + \sqrt{5}}{2}$ or approximately 1.61803 to five decimal places.

The ratio was so important to the Greeks that they gave it a special name, the "golden ratio" or the "golden section." They did not express the relationship in decimal form but with a geometric construction in which two line segments are in the exact golden ratio, 1.61803... to 1.

The golden ratio yields the basic connection between the Fibonacci Sequence and geometry. Consider again the ratios of consecutive Fibonacci numbers. As we said earlier, the table of fractions above seems to be approaching the golden ratio. Let us investigate this notion further by considering the line segment $\overline{APB}$, with P partitioning $\overline{AB}$ so that $\frac{AB}{AP} = \frac{AP}{PB}$.

A———————•—B
P

Let $x = \frac{AB}{AP}$. Therefore $x = \frac{AB}{AP} = \frac{AP + PB}{AP} = 1 + \frac{PB}{AP} = 1 + \frac{AP}{AB} = 1 + \frac{1}{x}$. Thus $x = 1 + \frac{1}{x}$ or $x^2 - x - 1 = 0$.

The roots of this equation are

$$a = \frac{1 + \sqrt{5}}{2} \approx 1.6180339887, \text{ and}$$

$$b = \frac{1 - \sqrt{5}}{2} \approx -.6180339887.$$

Since we are concerned with lengths of line segments, we shall use only the positive root, a. As a and b are roots of the equation $x^2 - x - 1 = 0$, $a^2 = a + 1(1)$ and $b^2 = b + 1(2)$.

Multiplying (1) by a^n (where n is an integer) $a^{n+2} = a^{n+1} + a^n$. Multiplying (2) by b^n (where n is an integer) $b^{n+2} = b^{n+1} + b^n$. Subtracting equation (2) from equation (1):

$$a^{n+2} - b^{n+2} = (a^{n+1} - b^{n+1}) + (a^n - b^n)$$

Now dividing by $a - b = \sqrt{5}$ (nonzero!):

$$\frac{a^{n+2} - b^{n+2}}{a - b} = \frac{a^{n+1} - b^{n+1}}{a - b} + \frac{a^n - b^n}{a - b}.$$

If we now let $t_n = \frac{a^n - b^n}{a - b}$, then $t_{n+2} = t_{n+1} + t_n$ (same as the Fibonacci Sequence definition). All that remains to be shown to establish t_n as the nth Fibonacci number, f_n, is that $t_1 = 1$ and $t_2 = 1$:

$$t_1 = \frac{a^1 - b^1}{a - b} = 1$$

$$t_2 = \frac{a^2 - b^2}{a - b} = \frac{(a - b)(a + b)}{a - b} = \frac{(\sqrt{5})(1)}{(\sqrt{5})} = 1$$

Therefore $f_n = \frac{a^n - b^n}{a - b}$, where $a = \frac{1 + \sqrt{5}}{2}$, $b = \frac{1 - \sqrt{5}}{2}$, and $n = 1, 2, 3, \ldots$

POSTASSESSMENT

1. Find the sum of the first 9 Fibonacci numbers.
2. Find the sum of the first 5 Fibonacci numbers with odd indices.

REFERENCES

Bicknell, M., and Verner E. Hoggatt, Jr. *A Primer for the Fibonacci Numbers*. San Jose, California: The Fibonacci Association, 1972.

Brother, U. Alfred. *An Introduction to Fibonacci Discovery*. San Jose, Calif.: The Fabonacci Association, 1965.

Garland, T. H. *Fascinating Fibonaccis*. Palo Alto, CA: Dale Seymour Public, 1987.

Hoggatt, Verner E., Jr. *Fibonacci and Lucas Numbers*. Boston: Houghton Mifflin, 1969.

Posamentier, A. S. *Advanced Euclidean Geometry: Excursions for Secondary Teachers and Students*. New York, NY: John Wiley Publishing, 2002.

Posamentier, Alfred S., Iangmar Lehmann. *The Fabulous Fibonacci Numbers*. Amherst, NY: Prometheus Books, 2007.

Vorob'ev, N. N. *Fibonacci Numbers*. New York: Blaisdell Publishing, 1961.

Unit 86

Diophantine Equations

This unit may be presented to any class having mastered the fundamentals of elementary algebra.

PERFORMANCE OBJECTIVES

1. *Given an equation with two variables, students will find integral solutions (if they exist).*
2. *Given a verbal problem that calls for a solution of a Diophantine equation, students will determine (where applicable) the number of possible solutions.*

PREASSESSMENT

Have students solve the following problem: Suppose you are asked by your employer to go to the post office and buy 6-cent and 8-cent stamps. He gives you 5 dollars to spend. How many combinations of 6-cent and 8-cent stamps could you select from to make your purchase?

TEACHING STRATEGIES

Most students will promptly realize that there are two variables that must be determined, say x and y. Letting x represent the number of 8-cent stamps and y represent the number of 6-cent stamps, the equation: $8x + 6y = 500$ should follow. This should then be converted to $4x + 3y = 250$. At this juncture the student should realize that although this equation has an infinite number of solutions, it may or may not have an infinite number of *integral* solutions; moreover, it may or may not have an infinite number of *positive integral* solutions (as called for by the original problem). The first problem to consider is whether integral solutions, in fact, exist.

For this a useful theorem may be employed. It states that if the greatest common factor of a and b is also a factor of k, where a, b, and k are integers, then there exist an infinite number of integral solutions for x and y in $ax + by = k$. Equations of this type whose solutions must be integers are known as *Diophantine equations* in honor of the Greek mathematician Diophantus, who wrote about them.

Since the greatest common factor of 3 and 4 is 1, which is a factor of 250, there exist an infinite number of integral solutions to the equation $4x + 3y = 250$. The question now facing your students is how many (if any) *positive* integral solutions exist?

One possible method of solution is often referred to as Euler's method (Leonhard Euler, 1707–1783). To begin, students should solve for the variable with the coefficient of least absolute value; in this case, y. Thus $y = \frac{250 - 4x}{3}$. This is to be rewritten to separate the integral parts as

$$y = 83 + \frac{1}{3} - x - \frac{x}{3} = 83 - x + \frac{1 - x}{3}.$$

Now introduce another variable, say t; and let $t = \frac{1 - x}{3}$. Solving for x yields $x = 1 - 3t$. Since there is no fractional coefficient in this equation, the process does *not* have to be repeated as it otherwise would have to be (i.e., each time introducing new variables, as with t above). Now substituting for x in the above equation yields $y = \frac{250 - 4(1 - 3t)}{3} = 82 + 4t$. For various integral values of t, corresponding values for x and y will be generated. A table of values such as that below might prove useful.

t	...	−2	−1	0	1	2	...
x	...	7	4	1	−2	−5	...
y	...	74	78	82	86	90	...

Perhaps by generating a more extensive table, students will notice for what values of t positive integral values for x and y may be obtained. However, this procedure for determining the number of positive integral values of x and y is not very elegant. The students should be guided to the following inequalities to be solved simultaneously:

$$1 - 3t > 0 \quad \text{and} \quad 82 + 4t > 0.$$

$$\text{Thus} \quad t < \frac{1}{3} \quad \text{and} \quad t > -20\frac{1}{2},$$

or $-20\frac{1}{2} < t < \frac{1}{3}$. This indicates that there are 21 possible combinations of 6-cent and 8-cent stamps that can be purchased for 5 dollars.

Students might find it helpful to observe the solution to a more difficult Diophantine equation. The following is such an example:

Solve the Diophantine equation $5x - 8y = 39$.

1. Solve for x, since its coefficient has the lower absolute value of the two coefficients:

$$x = \frac{8y + 39}{5} = y + 7 + \frac{3y + 4}{5}.$$

2. Let $t = \dfrac{3y + 4}{5}$, then solve for y:

$$y = \frac{5t - 4}{3} = t - 1 + \frac{2t - 1}{3}.$$

3. Let $u = \dfrac{2t - 1}{3}$, then solve for t:

$$t = \frac{3u + 1}{2} = u + \frac{u + 1}{2}.$$

4. Let $v = \dfrac{u + 1}{2}$, then solve for u:

$$u = 2v - 1.$$

We may now reverse the process because the coefficient of v is an integer.

5. Now substituting in the reverse order:

$$t = \frac{3u + 1}{2}$$

$$\text{therefore: } t = \frac{3(2v - 1) + 1}{2} = 3v - 1.$$

$$\text{also: } y = \frac{5t - 4}{3}$$

$$\text{therefore: } y = \frac{5(3v - 1) - 4}{3} = \boxed{5v - 3 = y}$$

$$\text{Similarly: } x = \frac{8y + 39}{5}$$

$$\text{therefore: } x = \frac{8(5v - 3) + 39}{5} = \boxed{8v + 3 = x}$$

v	...	−2	−1	0	1	2	...
x	...	−13	−5	3	11	19	...
y	...	−13	−8	−3	2	7	...

The above table indicates how the various solutions of this Diophantine equation may be generated. Students should be urged to inspect the nature of the members of the solution set.

Another method of solving Diophantine equations is presented in Unit 87.

POSTASSESSMENT

Have students solve each of the following Diophantine equations and then determine the number of positive integral solutions (if any).

1. $2x + 11y = 35$
2. $7x - 3y = 23$
3. $3x - 18y = 40$
4. $4x - 17y = 53$

REFERENCE

Related works by the author include:

Posamentier, Alfred S., and Charles T. Salkind. *Challenging Problems in Algebra.* New York: Dover, 1996.

Unit 87

Continued Fractions and Diophantine Equations

This lesson should be considered after the accompanying unit, "Diophantine Equations" is presented. This unit describes another method of solving Diophantine equations.

PERFORMANCE OBJECTIVES

1. *Given an equation with two variables, students will find integral solutions (if they exist).*
2. *Given a verbal problem that calls for a solution of a Diophantine equation, students will determine (where applicable) the number of possible solutions.*
3. *Given an improper fraction, students will write an equivalent continued fraction.*

PREASSESSMENT

Students should have successfully mastered the concepts of the unit "Diophantine Equations."

TEACHING STRATEGIES

Before discussing this method of solution of Diophantine equations, an excursion into continued fractions would be appropriate. Every improper fraction (reduced to lowest terms) has an equivalent continued fraction. For example:

$$\frac{11}{7} = 1 + \frac{4}{7} = 1 + \frac{1}{\frac{7}{4}} = 1 + \frac{1}{1 + \frac{3}{4}}$$

$$= 1 + \frac{1}{1 + \frac{1}{\frac{4}{3}}} = 1 + \frac{1}{1 + \frac{1}{1 + \frac{1}{3}}}$$

The last expression is called a *simple continued fraction*, since all the numerators after the first term are 1. These are the only types of continued fractions we shall consider here.

Consider a general improper fraction (reduced to lowest terms) and its equivalent simple continued fraction:

$$\frac{r}{s} = a_1 + \cfrac{1}{a_2 + \cfrac{1}{a_3 + \cfrac{1}{a_4 + \cfrac{1}{a_5}}}}$$

We shall call $c_1 = a_1$ the first convergent;

$c_2 = a_1 + \dfrac{1}{a_2}$ the second convergent;

$c_3 = a_1 + \cfrac{1}{a_2 + \cfrac{1}{a_3}}$ the third convergent;

$c_4 = a_1 + \cfrac{1}{a_2 + \cfrac{1}{a_3 + \cfrac{1}{a_4}}}$ the fourth convergent;

$c_5 = a_1 + \cfrac{1}{a_2 + \cfrac{1}{a_3 + \cfrac{1}{a_4 + \cfrac{1}{a_5}}}}$ the last convergent.

For example, for the above continued fraction equivalent to: $\frac{11}{7}$,

$$c_1 = 1; c_2 = 2; c_3 = \frac{3}{2}; c_4 = \frac{11}{7}$$

It would be appropriate at this juncture to derive a method for finding the nth convergent of a general continued fraction.

Let $c_n = \dfrac{r_n}{s_n}$ (the nth convergent)

$c_1 = a_1$, therefore $r_1 = a_1$ and $s_1 = 1$.

$c_2 = a_1 + \dfrac{1}{a_2} = \dfrac{a_1a_2 + 1}{a_2}$

therefore $r_2 = a_1a_2 + 1$, and $s_2 = a_2$.

$$c_3 = a_1 + \cfrac{1}{a_2 + \cfrac{1}{a_3}} = a_1 + \cfrac{1}{\cfrac{a_2a_3 + 1}{a_3}}$$

$$= a_1 + \frac{a_3}{a_2a_3 + 1} = \frac{a_1a_2a_3 + a_1 + a_3}{a_2a_3 + 1}$$

$$= \frac{a_3(a_1a_2 + 1) + a_1}{a_3a_2 + 1}, \text{ because}$$

$a_1a_2 + 1 = r_2$; $a_1 = r_1$; $a_2 = s_2$; $1 = s_1$; we get

$$c_3 = \frac{a_3r_2 + r_1}{a_3s_2 + s_1}. \text{ Therefore, } r_3 = a_3r_2 + r_1,$$

and $s_3 = a_3s_2 + s_1$.

Similarly $c_4 = \dfrac{a_4r_3 + r_2}{a_4s_3 + s_2}$. Following this pattern

$$\boxed{c_n = \frac{a_nr_{n-1} + r_{n-2}}{a_ns_{n-1} + s_{n-2}} = \frac{r_n}{s_n}}$$

(This can be proved by mathematical induction.) Now consider the general case for $n = 2$:

$$c_2 = \frac{a_2r_1 + r_0}{a_2s_1 + s_0}. \text{ Earlier } c_2 \text{ was found to}$$

equal $\dfrac{a_1a_2 + 1}{a_2}$.

Equating corresponding parts yields

$$a_2r_1 + r_0 = a_1a_2 + 1.$$

Therefore, $r_1 = a_1$ and $r_0 = 1$

$$\text{also, } a_2s_1 + s_0 = a_2.$$

Therefore, $s_1 = 1$ and $s_0 = 0$.
In a similar way consider the general case for $n = 1$:

$$c_1 = \frac{a_1r_0 + r_{-1}}{a_1s_0 + s_{-1}} \quad \text{Earlier this was found}$$

equal to $\dfrac{a_1}{1}$.

Equating corresponding parts yields:

$$a_1r_0 + r_{-1} = a_1.$$

Therefore, $r_0 = 1$ and $r_{-1} = 0$

$$\text{also, } a_1s_0 + s_{-1} = 1.$$

Therefore, $s_0 = 0$ and $s_{-1} = 1$.

Have students convert $\dfrac{117}{41}$ to the equivalent continued

fraction, $2 + \cfrac{1}{1 + \cfrac{1}{5 + \cfrac{1}{1 + \cfrac{1}{5}}}}$

Now set up a table:

CONVERGENTS

n	-1	0	1	2	3	4	5
a_n			2	1	5	1	5
$c_n = \frac{r_n}{s_n}$	0	1	2	3	17	20	117
	1	0	1	1	6	7	41

The first two columns for r_n and s_n are constant. However, the other values vary with the particular fraction. The values of a_n are taken directly from the continued fractions. Each value of r_n and s_n is obtained from the general formula derived earlier. To check if this chart was constructed properly students should notice that the last convergent is in fact the original improper fraction.

An inspection of the various cross-products suggests $r_n \cdot s_{n-1} - r_{n-1} \cdot s_n = (-1)^n$.

With this background material learned, the students are now ready to apply their knowledge of continued fractions to solving Diophantine equations of the form $ax + by = k$, where the greatest common factor of a and b is a factor of k. First they should form an *improper* fraction using the two coefficients, say $\frac{a}{b}$. Then convert this fraction to a continued fraction: $\frac{a}{b} = \frac{r_n}{s_n}$

Using the previously discovered formula:

$$r_n \cdot s_{n-1} - r_{n-1} \cdot s_n = (-1)^n$$

and substituting $a \cdot s_{n-1} - b \cdot r_{n-1} = 1$
(or multiply by -1). Now multiplying by k:
$a(k \cdot s_{n-1}) - b(k \cdot r_{n-1}) = k$.

Thus, $x = k \cdot s_{n-1}$, and $y = -k \cdot r_{n-1}$ is a solution of the Diophantine equation.
For example, consider the Diophantine equation

$$41x - 117y = 3.$$

After setting up the above table, the $n - 1$ convergent is used. That is, $r_{n-1} = 20$ and $s_{n-1} = 7$. The above relationship

$$a(k \cdot s_{n-1}) - b(k \cdot r_{n-1}) = k$$

yields with appropriate substitution:

$$41(3 \cdot 20) - 117(3 \cdot 7) = 3.$$

Thus one solution of $41x - 117y = 3$ is $x = 60$ and $y = 21$.

To find the remaining solutions the following scheme is used.
Subtract $41(60) - 117(21) = 3$ from $41x - 117y = 3$ to obtain $41(x - 60) - 117(y - 21) = 0$.
Therefore, $41(x - 60) = 117(y - 21)$

$$\text{or} \quad \frac{x - 60}{117} = \frac{y - 21}{41} = t.$$

Thus, $t = \dfrac{x - 60}{117}$ and $\boxed{x = 117t + 60}$

Also $t = \dfrac{y - 21}{41}$ and $\boxed{y = 41t + 21}$

A table of solutions may then be constructed.

t	**...**	**−2**	**−1**	**0**	**1**	**2**	**...**
x	...	−174	−57	60	177	294	...
y	...	−61	−20	21	62	103	...

POSTASSESSMENT

Have students change each of the following improper fractions to equivalent continued fractions.

1. $\dfrac{37}{13}$ 2. $\dfrac{47}{23}$ 3. $\dfrac{173}{61}$

Have students solve each of the following Diophantine equations and then determine how many (if any) positive solutions exist.

4. $7x - 31y = 2$
5. $18x - 53y = 3$
6. $5x - 2y = 4$
7. $123x - 71y = 2$

Unit 88

Simplifying Expressions Involving Infinity

This unit presents simple algebraic methods (appropriate for elementary algebra students) to solve seemingly difficult problems involving infinity.

PERFORMANCE OBJECTIVE

Given an algebraic problem involving infinity, students will use a simple algebraic method to solve the problem.

PREASSESSMENT

Students should be able to work with radical equations and quadratic equations.

TEACHING STRATEGIES

Offer the following problem to your students for solution:

Find the value of x if

$$x^{x^{x^{x^{\cdot^{\cdot^{\cdot}}}}}} = 2.$$

Most students' first reaction will be one of bewilderment. Since they have probably never worked with an infinite expression they are somewhat overwhelmed. Students may try to substitute into the expression values for x_2 in order to estimate an answer to the problem. Before they are entirely frustrated, begin by explaining the infinite nature of the expression. Explain also that

$$3^{3^{3}} \neq 27^{3} = 19{,}683 \text{ but rather } 3^{3^{3}} = 3^{27} =$$

7,625,597,484,989. Now have your students inspect the original expression in the following way: if

$x^{x^{x^{\cdot^{\cdot^{\cdot}}}}} = 2$, then, since there are an infinite number of xs, one x less would not affect the expression. Therefore the exponent of the first x (lowest base) is 2.

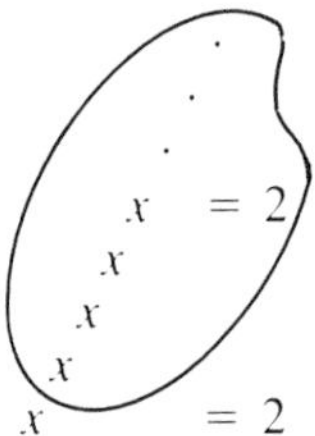

Thus, this expression simplifies to $x^2 = 2$, and $x = \sqrt{2}$. Students should be asked to consider the possibility of $x < 0$.

Students will naturally wonder if they could compose a similar problem by replacing 2 with, say, 5 or 7. Without elaborating, indicate to them that values to replace 2 may not be chosen at random, and that in fact these replacement values may not exceed e (i.e., the base of the natural system of logarithms, approximately 2.7182818284...).

To reinforce the scheme used in the solution of the above problem, have students consider the value of the nest of radicals

$$\sqrt{5+\sqrt{5+\sqrt{5+\sqrt{5+\sqrt{5+\ldots}}}}}$$

To find x, where

$x = \sqrt{5+\sqrt{5+\sqrt{5+\sqrt{5+\sqrt{5+\ldots}}}}}$ have students realize that nothing is lost by deleting the first 5 of this nest of radicals, since there are an infinite number of them. Thus

$$x = \sqrt{5+\underbrace{\sqrt{5+\sqrt{5+\sqrt{5+\sqrt{5+\ldots}}}}}_{=x}}$$

or $x = \sqrt{5+x}$, which is a simple radical equation. Students merely square both sides of the equation and solve the resulting quadratic equation:

$$x^2 = 5 + x$$
$$x^2 = x - 5 = 0$$
$$x = \frac{1 \pm \sqrt{21}}{2}$$

Since x is positive, $x = \dfrac{1+\sqrt{21}}{2} \approx 2.79$.

An alternative approach to evaluating a nest of radicals is to first square both sides of the original equation to get $x^2 = 5 + \sqrt{5+\sqrt{5+\sqrt{5+\sqrt{5+\ldots}}}}$ and then substitute x, so that $x^2 = 5 + x$. The rest is as in the previous method.

It is important that you stress inspecting the reasonability of the value of the nest of radicals. That is, should the value be positive or negative, real or imaginary, etc.

Another application of this method of evaluating expressions involving infinity is with continued fractions. Before introducing infinite continued fractions, you ought to refresh your students' memories about continued fractions. You may wish to have them write $\dfrac{13}{5}$ as a continued fraction:

$$\frac{13}{5} = 2 + \frac{3}{5} = 2 + \cfrac{1}{\frac{5}{3}} = 2 + \cfrac{1}{1+\frac{2}{3}}$$
$$= 2 + \cfrac{1}{1+\cfrac{1}{\frac{3}{2}}} = 2 + \cfrac{1}{1+\cfrac{1}{1+\frac{1}{2}}}$$

Further, you may also want to have them simplify the continued fraction $1 + \cfrac{1}{2+\cfrac{1}{3+\frac{1}{4}}}$

$$1 + \cfrac{1}{2+\cfrac{1}{3+\frac{1}{4}}} = 1 + \cfrac{1}{2+\cfrac{1}{\frac{13}{4}}} = 1 + \cfrac{1}{2+\frac{4}{13}}$$
$$= 1 + \cfrac{1}{\frac{30}{13}} = 1 + \frac{13}{30} = \frac{43}{13}$$

Now have students consider the infinite continued fraction $1 + \cfrac{1}{1+\cfrac{1}{1+\cfrac{1}{1+\cfrac{1}{1+\cdots}}}}$.

They will soon realize that the previous method of simplification will no longer work. At this point you would show them the following method:

Let $x = 1 + \cfrac{1}{1+\cfrac{1}{1+\cfrac{1}{1+\cdots}}}$.

Once again deleting the first "part" of the infinite continued fraction will not affect its value (because of the nature of infinity).

Therefore $x = 1 + \cfrac{1}{\underbrace{1+\cfrac{1}{1+\cfrac{1}{1+\cdots}}}_{=x}}$

or $x = 1 + \dfrac{1}{x}$, which yields $x^2 = x + 1$

$$x^2 - x - 1 = 0$$

and $x = \dfrac{1 \pm \sqrt{5}}{2}$; however, since $x > 0$, $x = \dfrac{1+\sqrt{5}}{2}$. Some of your students may recognize this value as that of the golden ratio.

More advanced students might wonder how a nonrepeating infinite expression is evaluated. For these students you may wish to present the following:

$$\text{Evaluate } \sqrt{1+2\sqrt{1+3\sqrt{1+4\sqrt{1+5\sqrt{1+\ldots}}}}}.$$

To evaluate this expression some preliminary work must first be done. Since

$(n+2)^2 = n^2 + 4n + 4 = 1 + (n+1)(n+3)$,

$n + 2 = \sqrt{1+(n+1)(n+3)}$.

$n(n+2) = n\sqrt{1+(n+1)(n+3)}$

Let $f(n) = n(n+2)$

then $f(n+1) = (n+1)(n+3)$.

Thus $f(n) = n\sqrt{1 + (n + 1)(n + 3)}$

$$f(n) = n\sqrt{1 + f(n + 1)}$$
$$f(n) = n\sqrt{1 + (n + 1)\sqrt{1 + f(n + 2)}}$$
$$f(n) = n\sqrt{1 + (n + 1)\sqrt{1 + (n + 2)\sqrt{1 + f(n + 3)}}},$$

and so on.

Now if $n = 1$, then $f(n) = 1(1 + 2) = 3$ and $3 =$

$$1\sqrt{1 + (1 + 1)\sqrt{1 + (1 + 2)\sqrt{1 + (1 + 3)\sqrt{1 + \ldots}}}}$$

$$= 1\sqrt{1 + 2\sqrt{1 + 3\sqrt{1 + 4\sqrt{1 + \ldots}}}}$$

As a result of presenting the methods considered in this unit, your students should have a more solid concept of infinite expressions.

POSTASSESSMENT

1. Simplify: $\sqrt{7 + \sqrt{7 + \sqrt{7 + \sqrt{7 + \ldots}}}}$
2. Simplify: $2 + \cfrac{1}{3 + \cfrac{1}{3 + \cfrac{1}{3 + \cfrac{1}{3 + \ldots}}}}$
3. Simplify: $1 + \cfrac{1}{2 + \cfrac{1}{1 + \cfrac{1}{2 + \cfrac{1}{1 + \cfrac{1}{2 + \ldots}}}}}$

Unit 89

Continued Fraction Expansion of Irrational Numbers

PERFORMANCE OBJECTIVES

1. *Given an irrational number, students will write an equivalent continued fraction.*
2. *Given an infinite expansion, students will get back to the irrational number.*

PREASSESSMENT

Students should be familiar with continued fractions.

TEACHING STRATEGIES

The procedure for expanding an irrational number is essentially the same as that used for rational numbers. Let x be the given irrational number. Find a_1, the greatest integer less than x, and express x in the form

$$x = a_1 + \frac{1}{x_2}, \quad 0 < \frac{1}{x_2} < 1,$$

where the number

$x_2 = \dfrac{1}{x - a_1} > 1$ is irrational: for, if an integer is subtracted from an irrational number, the difference and the reciprocal of the difference are irrational.

Find a_2, the largest integer less than x_2 and express x_2 in the form

$$x_2 = a_2 + \frac{1}{x_3}, \quad 0 < \frac{1}{x_3} < 1, \quad a_2 \geq 1,$$

where again the number

$$x_3 = \frac{1}{x_2 - a_2} > 1.$$

This calculation may be repeated indefinitely, producing in succession the equations

$$\begin{aligned}
x &= a_1 + \frac{1}{x_2}, x_2 > 1 \\
x_2 &= a_2 + \frac{1}{x_3}, x_3 > 1, a_2 \geq 1 \\
x_3 &= a_3 + \frac{1}{x_4}, x_4 > 1, a_3 \geq 1 \\
&\vdots \\
x_n &= a_n + \frac{1}{x_{n+1}}, x_{n+1} > 1, a_n \geq 1 \\
&\vdots
\end{aligned}$$

where $a_1, a_2, a_3, \ldots, a_n, \ldots$ are all integers and the numbers $x, x_2, x_3, \ldots$ are all irrational. This process cannot end because the only way this could happen would be for some integer a_n to be equal to x_n. This is impossible since each successive x_i is irrational.

Substituting x_2 from the second equation above into the first equation, then x_3 from the third into this result, and so on, produces the required infinite simple continued fraction

$$x = a_1 + \frac{1}{x_2} = a_1 + \cfrac{1}{a_2 + \cfrac{1}{x_3}} = a_1 + \cfrac{1}{a_2 + \cfrac{1}{a_3 + \cfrac{1}{x_4}}}$$

or sometimes written as $x = [a_1, a_2, a_3, a_4, \ldots]$, where the three dots indicate that the process is continued indefinitely.

Example 1
Expand $\sqrt{3}$ into an infinite simple continued fraction.
Solution: The largest integer less than $\sqrt{3}$ is 1. Therefore, $a_1 = 1$ and

$$\sqrt{3} = 1 + \frac{1}{x_2}.$$

Solving this equation for x_2, we get

$$x_2 = \frac{1}{\sqrt{3}-1}\cdot\frac{\sqrt{3}+1}{\sqrt{3}+1} = \frac{\sqrt{3}+1}{2}.$$

Therefore: $\sqrt{3} = a_1 + \frac{1}{x_2} = 1 + \cfrac{1}{\cfrac{\sqrt{3}+1}{2}}$

$x_2 = a_2 + \frac{1}{x_3}$ where $a_2 = 1$, since it is the largest integer less than $\frac{\sqrt{3}+1}{2}$.

Therefore:

$$x_3 = \cfrac{1}{\cfrac{\sqrt{3}+1}{2} - 1} = \frac{2}{\sqrt{3}-1}\cdot\frac{\sqrt{3}+1}{\sqrt{3}+1}$$
$$= \sqrt{3}+1$$
$$\sqrt{3} = 1 + \cfrac{1}{1 + \cfrac{1}{\sqrt{3}+1}}.$$

Continuing this process:

$x_3 = 2 + \frac{1}{x_4}$, $a_3 = 2$ since 2 is the largest integer less than $\sqrt{3}+1$.

$$x_4 = \frac{1}{\sqrt{3}-1}\cdot\frac{\sqrt{3}+1}{\sqrt{3}+1} = \frac{\sqrt{3}+1}{2}$$
$$\sqrt{3} = 1 + \cfrac{1}{1 + \cfrac{1}{2 + \cfrac{1}{\cfrac{\sqrt{3}+1}{2}}}}$$

Since $x_4 = \frac{\sqrt{3}+1}{2}$ is the same as $x_2 = \frac{\sqrt{3}+1}{2}$, x_3 will produce the same result as x_3, namely $\sqrt{3}+1$. All the following partial quotients will be 1,2,1,2 and the infinite expansion of $\sqrt{3}$ will be

$$\sqrt{3} = 1 + \cfrac{1}{1 + \cfrac{1}{2 + \cfrac{1}{1 + \cfrac{1}{2 + \ddots}}}} = [1,1,2,1,2,\cdots] = [1,\overline{1,2}].$$

The bar over the 1 and 2 indicates that the numbers 1 and 2 are repeated indefinitely.

Example 2
Find the infinite continued fraction expansion for

$$x = \frac{\sqrt{30}-2}{13}$$

Solution: Since $\sqrt{30}$ is between 5 and 6, the largest integer less than x is $a_1 = 0$. Then

$$x = \frac{\sqrt{30}-2}{13} = 0 + \frac{1}{x_2},$$

$$\text{where } x_2 = \frac{1}{x} = \frac{13}{\sqrt{30}-2}\cdot\frac{\sqrt{30}+2}{\sqrt{30}+2}$$
$$= \frac{\sqrt{30}+2}{2} > 1.$$

The largest integer less than x_2 is $a_2 = 3$, therefore,

$$x_2 = a_2 + \frac{1}{x_3} = 3 + \frac{1}{x_3}.$$

$$\text{Therefore } x_3 = \frac{1}{x_2 - 3} = \cfrac{1}{\cfrac{\sqrt{30}+2}{2} - 3}$$
$$= \frac{2}{\sqrt{30}-4}\cdot\frac{\sqrt{30}+4}{\sqrt{30}+4}$$
$$= \frac{2(\sqrt{30}+4)}{14} = \frac{\sqrt{30}+4}{7}.$$

The largest integer less than x_3 is $a_3 = 1$.

$$\text{Therefore } x_4 = \frac{1}{x_3 - 1} = \cfrac{1}{\cfrac{\sqrt{30}+4}{7} - 1}$$
$$= \frac{7}{\sqrt{30}-3}\cdot\frac{\sqrt{30}+3}{\sqrt{30}+3} = \frac{\sqrt{30}+3}{3}.$$

In a similar way we get $x_5 = \frac{\sqrt{30}+3}{7}$, $x_6 = \frac{\sqrt{30}+4}{2}$, and $x_7 = \frac{\sqrt{30}+4}{7} = x_3$.

Further investigation will show that the sequence 1,2,1,4 repeats. The required expansion is

$$x = 0 + \frac{1}{x_2} = 0 + \cfrac{1}{3 + \cfrac{1}{x_3}} = 0 + \cfrac{1}{3 + \cfrac{1}{1 + \cfrac{1}{x_4}}}$$

$$= 0 + \cfrac{1}{3 + \cfrac{1}{1 + \cfrac{1}{2 + \cfrac{1}{x_5}}}} = 0 + \cfrac{1}{3 + \cfrac{1}{1 + \cfrac{1}{2 + \cfrac{1}{1 + \cfrac{1}{x_6}}}}}$$

$$= 0 + \cfrac{1}{3 + \cfrac{1}{1 + \cfrac{1}{2 + \cfrac{1}{1 + \cfrac{1}{4 + \cfrac{1}{x_7}}}}}}$$

so finally we obtain

$$x = \frac{\sqrt{30}-2}{13} = [0,3,\overline{1,2,1,4}].$$

Students may prove that a given infinite continued fraction actually represents an irrational number. Consider showing that $[2,\overline{2,4}]$ represents $\sqrt{6}$. Begin by writing:

$$\text{Let } x = 2 + \cfrac{1}{2 + \cfrac{1}{4 + \cfrac{1}{2 + \cfrac{1}{4 + \ddots}}}}$$

$$\text{where } y = 2 + \cfrac{1}{4 + \cfrac{1}{2 + \cfrac{1}{4 + \ddots}}}$$

$$\text{Therefore } y = 2 + \cfrac{1}{4 + \cfrac{1}{y}} = 2 + \frac{y}{4y+1}.$$

Solving for y yields: $\frac{2+\sqrt{6}}{2}$.

However, $x = 2 + \frac{1}{y} = 2 + \frac{2}{2+\sqrt{6}}$.

Hence, $x = 2 + \sqrt{6} - 2 = \sqrt{6}$.

POSTASSESSMENT

Have students change each of the following into an infinite simple continued fraction.

1. $\sqrt{2}$ 2. $\sqrt{43}$ 3. $\frac{25+\sqrt{53}}{22}$

Have students show that the infinite continued fraction $[\overline{3,6}] = \sqrt{10}$.

Unit 90

The Farey Sequence

This unit presents a discussion of a rather unusual sequence of numbers. This topic can be presented to students at various levels. However, the emphasis will change with the various ability and maturity levels of the students.

PERFORMANCE OBJECTIVES

1. *Students will show that the fraction immediately before $\frac{1}{2}$ and its immediate successor of the Farey Sequence are complementary.*
2. *Students will establish the relationship between π and the number of terms in the Farey Sequence.*

PREASSESSMENT

Using the sequence of fractions below, have students find the sum of the two fractions:

a. fifth term to the left and third term to the right of $\frac{1}{2}$;

b. third term to the left and third term to the right of $\frac{1}{2}$;

c. second term to the left and second term to the right of $\frac{1}{2}$;

$$\frac{1}{7}, \frac{1}{6}, \frac{1}{5}, \frac{1}{4}, \frac{2}{7}, \frac{1}{3}, \frac{2}{5}, \frac{3}{7}, \frac{1}{2}, \frac{4}{7}, \frac{3}{5}, \frac{2}{3}, \frac{5}{7}, \frac{3}{4}.$$

Ask students to generalize their results.

TEACHING STRATEGIES

A review of the preassessment activity will indicate that the three sums students were asked to find all resulted in 1. That is,

$$\frac{1}{4} + \frac{3}{4} = 1; \frac{1}{3} + \frac{2}{3} = 1 \text{ and } \frac{2}{5} + \frac{3}{5} = 1.$$

We shall refer to a pair of fractions whose sum is 1 as *complementary*. Let us now inspect the given sequence.

If we list all proper common fractions in their lowest terms in order of magnitude up to some arbitrarily assigned limit-such as with denominators not exceeding 7—we have the 17 fractions

$$\frac{1}{7}, \frac{1}{6}, \frac{1}{5}, \frac{1}{4}, \frac{2}{7}, \frac{1}{3}, \frac{2}{5}, \frac{3}{7}, \frac{1}{2}, \frac{4}{7}, \frac{3}{5}, \frac{2}{3}, \frac{5}{7}, \frac{3}{4}, \frac{4}{5}, \frac{5}{6}, \frac{6}{7}.$$

This is called the Farey Sequence. The Farey Sequence F_n, of order n, is defined as the *ordered set consisting of 0, the irreducible proper fractions with denominators from $\frac{1}{2}$ to* n, *arranged in order of increasing magnitude, and $\frac{1}{1}$*. There are many characteristic properties of the Farey Sequence. One is the relationship students discovered earlier; fractions equidistant from $\frac{1}{2}$ are complementary; that is, their sum equals one. Another interesting relationship involves the number of terms in the Farey Sequence of order n and π.

Before beginning a development of this sequence, students should be given some background on the Farey Sequence. They should be told that Farey, in 1816, discovered the sequence while perusing lengthy tables of decimal quotients. Apparently the numerator of any fraction in the Farey Sequence is obtained by adding the numerators of the fractions on each side of it, and similarly for the denominators. Since the result must be in lowest terms, this holds true for triplet:

$$\frac{1}{3}, \frac{2}{5}, \frac{3}{7} \quad \text{where} \quad \frac{3+1}{3+7} = \frac{4}{10} = \frac{2}{5}.$$

Students will see that the sum of fractions equidistant from $\frac{1}{2}$ equals 1. This can be proved many ways.

Suppose that $\frac{\ell}{n}$ is a number of the series that is less than $\frac{1}{2}$ and such that ℓ and n are relatively prime. Comparing the corresponding number of the other side of $\frac{1}{2}$, we find $\frac{(n-\ell)}{n}$. Since this belongs to the Farey Sequence it is necessary that g.c.d. $(n-\ell, n) = 1$. Supposing that $(n-\ell)$ and n are not relatively prime, then $n - \ell = qd$ and $n = qd + \ell$. Also $n = rd$ and thus $rd = qd + \ell$. Therefore d divides ℓ and consequently d divides $(n-\ell)$ for d divides n. This however contradicts the fact that $\frac{(n - \ell)}{n}$ was in its lowest terms (which is the definition of terms in the Farey Sequence) and therefore g.c.d. $(n - \ell, n) = 1$.

Now to prove that $\frac{\ell}{n} + \frac{a}{b} = 1$. Let $\frac{\ell}{n}$ be the immediate predecessor of $\frac{1}{2}$. If there was another term immediately succeeding $\frac{1}{2}$ and belonging to F_n, then the fractions are arranged as follows:

$$\frac{\ell}{n}, \frac{1}{2}, \frac{a}{b} \quad \text{where} \quad \frac{1}{2} = \frac{\ell + a}{n + b}$$

(one of the properties of the sequence). To prove that $\frac{\ell}{n} + \frac{a}{b} = 1$, $\frac{a}{b}$ must be in lowest terms if it belongs to F_n. If two fractions whose sum is 1 are in lowest terms, then their denominators are equal. Thus if $\frac{\ell}{n} + \frac{a}{b} = 1$, b must equal n. Therefore $\frac{\ell + a}{n} = 1$ and $l + a = n$, or $a = n - \ell$. But $\frac{\ell}{n}$ was the immediate predecessor of $\frac{1}{2}$ and $\frac{a}{b} = \frac{n - \ell}{n}$. Thus the immediate predecessor of $\frac{1}{2}$ and its immediate successor are complementary because their sum equals 1.

Another very interesting property results between π and the sum of the terms in the Farey Sequence. The number of fractions of order n is obtained as follows. Since the fractions are all in lowest terms, it follows that for a given denominator b, the number of numerators is the number of integers less than, and prime to, b. Students should then see the number of fractions N, in the Farey Sequence is equal to $\phi(2) + \phi(3) + \phi(4) + \ldots + \phi(n)$, where $\phi(n)$ is the number of positive integers less than or equal to n that are relatively prime to n. If $n = 7$, we have $N = \phi(2) + \phi(2) + \phi(3) + \phi(4) + \phi(5) + \phi(6) + \phi(7) = 1 + 2 + 2 + 4 + 2 + 6$. The value of N increases rapidly as n increases and when $n = 100$, $N = 3043$. Thus there are many irreducible common fractions with numerators and denominators not exceeding 100.

There is a remarkable formula involving the ϕ function and π (the ratio of the circumference to the diameter of the circle).

The ϕ function refers to Euler's function. The sum of the Farey Sequence can be written by using a formula in terms of Euler's function ϕ. If $\frac{h}{k}$ is a term in the Farey Sequence, then g.c.d. $(h,k) = 1$. For any fixed number $k > 1$ the number of terms of the form $\frac{h}{k}$ is $\phi(k)$. It can be demonstrated that the sum $\phi(1) + \phi(2) + \ldots + \phi(n)$ is approximated by the expression $\frac{3n^2}{\pi^2}$, the approximation becoming more and more accurate as n increases. Except for the first term this sum represents the number of terms, N in a Farey Sequence of order n. Since we know the value of π to any desired degree of accuracy, this means we can find approximately the number of terms in a Farey Sequence without evaluating separately $\phi(1), \phi(2), \phi(3) \ldots . \phi(n)$. Thus for $n = 100$ we would have $N = \frac{3 \cdot 100^2}{\pi^2} = 3039.6355 \ldots$ whereas the true value is 3043.

Thus the number of terms of the Farey series approaches $\frac{3n^2}{\pi^2}$.

POSTASSESSMENT

1. Given $n = 200$, $n = 8$, find the number of terms in the Farey Sequence using the expression $\frac{3n^2}{\pi^2}$.
2. Have students find other properties of the Farey Sequence.

Unit 91

The Parabolic Envelope

This unit describes briefly the mechanical construction of the parabolic envelope and shows how students can use the envelope to derive a host of related curves.

PERFORMANCE OBJECTIVE

Using the envelope as a foundation, students will draw a variety of curves by different techniques without point by point plotting from an equation. In the process, they will be introduced to the visual concepts of an envelope, evolute and pedal to a given curve.

PREASSESSMENT

Students should have completed a basic geometry course and be familiar with the conic sections.

TEACHING STRATEGIES

Have your students construct tangents to a parabola in the following manner:

Draw an angle of any measure, and divide each side of the angle into the same number of equally-spaced intervals. In Figure 1, we have an angle, A, of measure 50°, divided on each side into 17 equally-spaced, numbered intervals. Starting, as we did, at the lower left of the angle, lines were drawn connecting points 1 to 17, 2 to 16, 3 to 15, and so on, terminating with 17-1, (where the notation "17-1" means the segment connecting point 17 to point 1, or conversely). The resulting array of lines are tangents, which *envelope* a parabola.

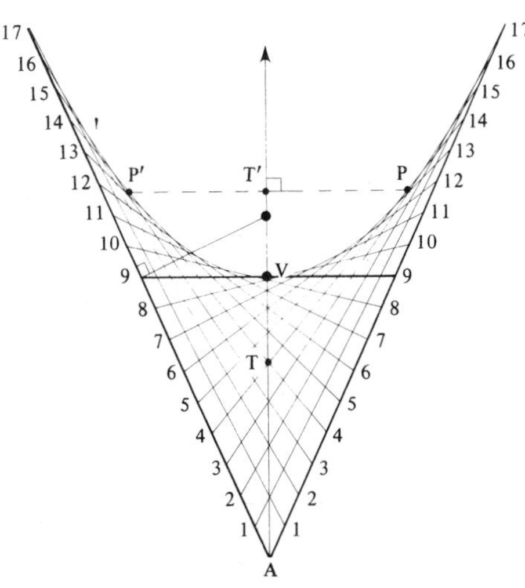

FIGURE 1

The midpoint, V, of the line 9-9, is the *vertex* of the parabola, and 9-9 is the tangent to the parabola at V. A line from A to V, extended beyond V, is the parabola's *axis of symmetry*, and is also included in Figure 1. Ask students why 9-9 is the tangent perpendicular to AV.

Erect a perpendicular to either side of the angle at point 9. We state without proof that the intersection of this perpendicular with the axis of symmetry determines the *focus*, F, of the parabola. More ambitious students may wish to prove this. At any rate, it would be meaningful to mention the reflective and locus properties of the focus.

Specific points of tangency on the parabola can be visually approximated directly from Figure 1. They can be more exactly located from the fact that a tangent to the parabola intersects the axis at a distance from the vertex equal to the ordinate of the point of tangency. As an example in Figure 1, tangent 14-4 intersects the axis at T. Locate a point T′ on the axis above V such that TV = VT′. Draw a line through T′ parallel to 9-9 so as to intersect the envelope at P and P′, then P and P′ are the points on the parabola where 14-4 and 4-14 are tangent. Other points on the parabola can be determined in the same manner.

Evolute to the Parabola

Having located all such points of tangency P and P′ on the parabola, use a right-angled triangle or carpenter's square to erect perpendiculars at each of these points. These perpendiculars to a curve at the point of tangency are called *normals*. The envelope of all such normals defines the *evolute* to the curve; that is, the normals are then tangents to the evolute of the given curve. Thus, the evolute to the parabola can be shown to be a one-cusped curve called a *semi-cubic parabola*. This is shown in Figure 2.

To realize an accurately drawn evolute, utilize the symmetry of the parabola about the axis. Hence, normals to P and P intersect at Q on the axis of symmetry.

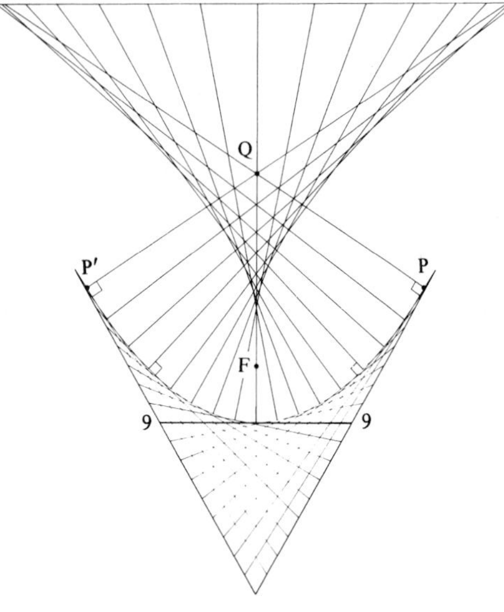

FIGURE 2

Pedal Curves to the Parabola

Figure 3 shows a given curve, C, and a fixed point, F, on or in the neighborhood of C. Dropping perpendiculars from F to each of the tangents to the curve, we find that the locus of the feet of the perpendiculars, P, defines the *pedal curve* to the given curve with respect to F. For a given curve, different choices of F will result in different pedal curves.

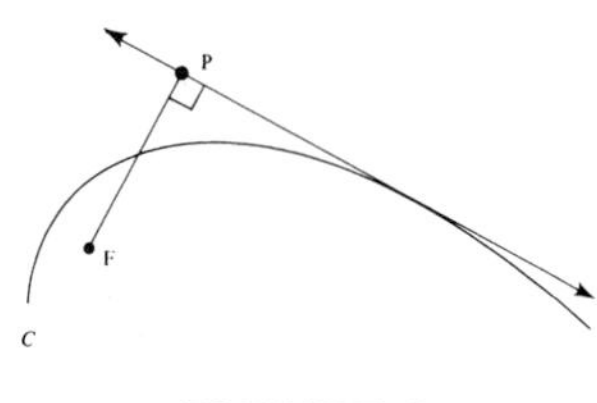

FIGURE 3

Now let the focus, F, of the parabola in Figure 1 be the fixed point for consideration. If perpendiculars are dropped to each of the tangents, students will note that the locus of the feet of these perpendiculars is the line 9-9. That is, the tangent to the vertex is the pedal curve to a parabola with respect to its focus. Conversely, it can be shown that a perpendicular erected to a tangent with 9-9 will pass through F. This latter fact justifies the technique used earlier to locate the parabola's focus. (Students should recall that to prove a locus, a biconditional statement must be proved.)

Next let V be the fixed point. From V, we drop perpendiculars to each of the tangents obtained in Figure 1. The locus of the feet is shown in Figure 4 as a curve having a cusp at V, and symmetric to the axis. We state without proof that the locus is the *cissoid of Diocles*. Locate F′ on the axis, below V, such that FV = VF′. Through F′ draw a line parallel to 9-9. This line is the parabola's *directrix*, and can be shown to be the asymptotic line that the cissoid approaches.

At this point you may wish to discuss the various properties of a parabola, such as its reflective properties. You may

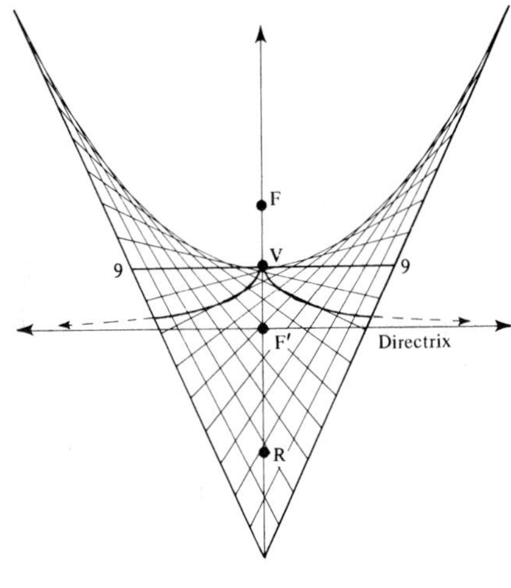

FIGURE 4

also define the parabola in terms of a locus, now that the focus and direction have been determined. Thus, a parabola is the locus of points equidistant from a point (the focus), and a line (the directrix), not containing the point. Folding waxed paper clearly demonstrates this locus. Draw a line and an external point on a piece of wax paper. Fold the wax paper repeatedly in such a manner that the point is superimposed on the line. The creases produced form a parabolic envelope.

POSTASSESSMENT

Have students draw two additional pedal curves to the parabola. Tell them to use the following as a guide:

a. Let F′ be the fixed point. The pedal curve will be seen to the *Right Strophoid*.
b. Locate R (Figure 4), the reflection of F through the directrix such that FF′ = F′R. Have R be the fixed point. The pedal curve is the *trisectrix of MacLaurin*.
c. The *contrapedal* to a given curve is the locus of the feet of the perpendiculars from a given fixed point to the normals to a given curve. In Figure 2, with F as fixed point, determine the locus of the contrapedal. From F, drop perpendiculars to each of the normals you drew to obtain the evolute. The locus of the contrapedal is a parabola whose turning point concurs with F.
d. Confirm by measurement that the contrapedal locus in (c) is identical to the locus of the midpoints of the segment of a normal from the point of tangency on the parabola to the point of intersection of the normal and the parabola's axis of symmetry.

REFERENCES

Lockwood, E. H. *A Book of Curves*. Cambridge University Press, 1961.

Posamentier, A. S., and H. A. Hauptman. *101 plus Great Ideas for Introducing Key Concepts in Mathematics*. Thousand Oaks, CA: Corwin, 2006.

Zwikker, C. *The Advanced Geometry of Plane Curves and their Applications*. New York: Dover Publications, 1963.

Unit 92

Application of Congruence to Divisibility

PERFORMANCE OBJECTIVES

1. *Given any integer, students will determine its prime factors without doing any division.*
2. *Students will produce rules for testing divisibility by natural numbers other than those presented in this unit.*

PREASSESSMENT

1. Have students find the prime factors of each of the following: (a) 144 (b) 840 (c) 360
2. Have students indicate, without doing any division, which of the following numbers are divisible by 2, 3, and 5: (a) 234 (b) 315

TEACHING STRATEGIES

Begin the lesson by introducing the concept of number congruences. Two numbers that have the same remainder when divided by 7 are said to be *congruent modulo 7*.

For example, 23 and 303 give the same remainder when divided by 7. Therefore, we say that 23 and 303 are congruent modulo 7. This statement can be represented by symbols as follows: $23 \equiv 303 \pmod 7$.

In general, two integers a and b are congruent modulo m (written as $a \equiv b \pmod m$) if they give the same nonnegative remainder when divided by the integer $m \neq 0$.

Because of this definition, we have the following double implication:

$$a \equiv b \pmod m \Leftrightarrow \begin{cases} a = mk + r \\ b = mk' + r \end{cases} \quad 0 \leq r < |m|$$

The symbol "$\equiv$" was first used in 1801 by Karl Friedrich Gauss (1777–1855), the famous German mathematician. It is suggested by its similarity with the ordinary equality. It has nothing to do with geometric congruence. The sign $\not\equiv$ means "is not congruent to."

Example 1

$$17 \equiv -4 \pmod 7$$
$$17 = 72 + 3$$

Because:

$$-4 = 7 \cdot (-1) + 3$$

In this example, we must use -1 as a quotient. If we use 0, the remainder would be negative against the definition of congruence.

Example 2

$a \equiv 0 \pmod a$. This is true because they both give the same remainder 0.

Another Definition of Congruences

Two numbers are congruent modulo m, *if and only if their difference is divisible by* m. We want to prove that $a \equiv b \pmod m \Leftrightarrow a - b = \overline{m}$ ($\overline{m}$ reads "a multiple of m").

Proof:

If $a \equiv b \pmod m \Leftrightarrow \begin{matrix} a = mk_1 + r \\ b = mk_2 + r \end{matrix}$

Subtracting: $a - b = m(k_1 - k_2)$ or $a - b = \overline{m}$

Therefore: $a \equiv b \pmod m \Rightarrow a - b = \overline{m}$

Conversely: if $a - b = \overline{m} \Rightarrow a = b + \overline{m}$

$\Rightarrow a = b + km$ (1)

But $b = mk' + r$ (2). Thus, from (1) and (2) we have

$$\begin{aligned} a = b + km &= (mk' + r) + km \\ &= m(k' + k) + r \\ &= mk'' + r \ (3) \end{aligned}$$

From (2) and (3) we then have

$$\begin{aligned} a &= mk'' + r \\ b &= mk' + r \text{ therefore: } a \equiv b \pmod m \end{aligned}$$

Thus, $a - b = \overline{m} \Rightarrow a \equiv b \pmod m$

Therefore, $a \equiv b \pmod m \Rightarrow a - b = \overline{m}$, *Q.E.D.* Students should now be ready to consider the following.

Some Elementary Properties of Congruences

If $a \equiv b \pmod m$ and $c \equiv d \pmod m$, then

(I) $a + c \equiv b + d \pmod m$
(II) $ac \equiv bd \pmod m$
(III) $ka \equiv kb \pmod m$ for every integer k.

These properties follow from the definition of congruences. We shall prove (II); the others can be proved by following the same method.

Since $a \equiv b \pmod m \Leftrightarrow a = b + \overline{m}$ (1)
and $c \equiv d \pmod m \Leftrightarrow c = d + \overline{m}$ (2)

Then, multiplying (1) and (2):

$$\begin{aligned} ac &= bd + b\overline{m} + d\overline{m} \\ &= bd + (b + d)\overline{m} \\ &= bd + \overline{m} \end{aligned}$$

Therefore, $ac \equiv bd \pmod{m}$.

Another interesting aspect of modular systems are *power residues*. The *power residues* of a number a with respect to another number m are *the remainders obtained when the successive powers $a^0, a^1, a^2, \ldots.$ of a are divided by m.*

Example 3

Find the power residues of 5 with respect to 3. Since:

$$\begin{aligned} 5^0{:}3 &= 1{:}3 = 0 \cdot 3 + 1 \text{ therefore } r_0 = 1. \\ 5^1{:}3 &= 5{:}3 = 1 \cdot 3 + 2 \text{ therefore } r_1 = 2. \\ 5^2{:}3 &= 25{:}3 = 8 \cdot 3 + 1 \text{ therefore } r_2 = 1. \\ 5^3{:}3 &= 125{:}3 = 41 \cdot 3 + 2 \text{ therefore } r_3 = 2. \end{aligned}$$

and so on.

Therefore, the power residues of 5 with respect to 3 will be: 1, 2, 1, 2, ... Have students consider why no number other than 1 or 2 appears in this sequence.

Example 4

Find the power residues of 10 modulo 2. Also indicate the different congruences. We have

$$\begin{aligned} 10^0{:}2 &= 1{:}2 = 0 \cdot 2 + 1 \text{ therefore } r_0 = 1. \\ 10^1{:}2 &= 10{:}2 = 5 \cdot 2 + 0 \text{ therefore } r_1 = 0. \\ 10^2{:}2 &= 100{:}2 = 50 \cdot 2 + 0 \text{ therefore } r_2 = 0. \end{aligned}$$

Therefore, the power residues are 1, 0, 0, ... Thus, the congruences will be

$$10^0 \equiv 1,\ 10^1 \equiv 0,\ 10^2 \equiv 0, \ldots, \pmod{2}.$$

Students should be able to justify the appearance of this sequence.

Once students have mastered the concept of power residues, they should be ready to consider various *properties of power residues.*

(I) The power residue of a^0, when divided by m, is always 1.

Proof: We have that $a^0 : m = 1 : m = 0 \cdot 1 + 1$, i.e., a remainder of 1. Hence, $a^0 \equiv 1 \pmod{m}$.

(II) If a power residue is zero, then the following power residues are also zero.

Proof: Let a^h give a zero power residue when divided by m. Then, $a^h \equiv 0 \pmod{m}$. If both sides are multiplied by a, we have $a \cdot a^h \equiv a \cdot 0 \pmod{m}$ or $a^{h+1} \equiv 0 \pmod{m}$. Therefore, $a^{h+1}, a^{h+2}, \ldots$ will give zero power residues also. This was evident in example 4 above.

Criteria for Divisibility

Have students consider any number $N = a_n a_{n-1} \ldots a_2 a_1 a_0$ written in base 10. Therefore: $N = a_0 10^0 + a_1 10^1 + a_2 10^2 + \ldots + a_n 10^n$. Let $r_0, r_1, \ldots, r_n$ be the power residues of 10 (mod m). Therefore, $10^0 \equiv 1$, $10^1 \equiv r_1, \ldots 10^n \equiv r_n \pmod{m}$. Have students multiply each congruence by $a_0, a_1, \ldots, a_n$, respectively, to get $a_0 10^0 \equiv a_0, a_1 10^1 \equiv a_1 r_1, \ldots, a_n 10^n \equiv a_n r_n \pmod{m}$. If they are added in order, we will get $a_0 10^0 + \ldots + a_n 10^n \equiv a_0 + a_1 r_1 + a_2 r_2 + \ldots + a_n r_n \pmod{m}$. Thus, $N \equiv a_0 + a_1 r_1 + a_2 r_2 + \ldots + a_n r_n$.

From this last congruence, N will be divisible by m if and only if $a_0 + a_1 r_1 + \ldots + a_n r_n$ is divisible by m. This statement can be used to find the different criteria for divisibility the following way:

Divisibility by 2 and 5

We have for any number N that

$$N \equiv a_0 + a_1 r_1 + \ldots + a_n r_n \pmod{m}.$$

If students consider $m = 2$ (or $m = 5$), they will have that $r_1 = 0$ because $10^1 \equiv 0 \pmod{2}$ (or mod 5). Therefore, $r_2 = 0, r_3 = 0, \ldots.$ Hence they will have $N \equiv a_0$ (mod 2 or 5). This means that: A number is divisible by 2 or 5, if and only if its last digit is divisible by 2 or 5.

Divisibility by 3 and 9

We have that

$$10^0 \equiv 1,\ 10^1 \equiv 1, \ldots \text{ (mod 3 or 9)}.$$

Since $N \equiv a_0 + a_1 r_1 + a_2 r_2 + \ldots + a_n r_n \pmod{m}$, thus, $N \equiv a_0 + a_1 + a_2 + \ldots + a_n$ (mod 3 or 9). Therefore, a given number is divisible by 3 or 9, if and only if the sum of its digits is divisible by 3 or 9.

Divisibility by 11

Since $10^0 \equiv 1, 10^1 \equiv -1, 10^2 \equiv 1, \ldots, \pmod{11}$. Hence, $N \equiv a_0 - a_1 + a_2 - \ldots + (-1)^n a_n \pmod{11}$. Therefore, a given number is divisible by 11 if and only if the difference of the two sums of the alternate digits is divisible by 11.

The previous method will lead students to develop similar rules for testing divisibility by other primes. It should be emphasized and justified that a number is divisible by a composite number if it is divisible by each of its *relative prime* factors.

Therefore, if we want to determine if a number is divisible by 6, we only have to test its divisibility by 2 and 3.

With sufficient discussion students should be able to establish a comprehensive list of rules for testing divisibility as well as develop insight into some elementary theory of congruences.

POSTASSESSMENT

Have students perform these exercises:

1. State a rule for testing divisibility by
   a. 4 and 25 b. 7 c. 13 d. 101
2. Determine the prime factors of:
   a. 1220 b. 315 c. 1001
3. Find the criteria for divisibility by 6 and 11 in base 7.

Unit 93

Problem Solving—A Reverse Strategy

Geometry teachers are frequently asked, "How did you know which approach to take in order to prove these two line segments parallel?" Generally, the teacher would like to think that experience prompted the proper conclusion. This would, of course, be of no value to the questioning student. He or she would like to learn a definite procedure to follow. The teacher would be wise to describe to the student a reverse strategy that would have the student begin with the desired conclusion and discover each preceding step in order.

PERFORMANCE OBJECTIVE

Given a problem situation that lends itself to a reverse strategy of solution, students will employ this strategy to successfully solve the problem.

PREASSESSMENT

Have students solve the following problem:

> If the sum of two numbers is 2, and the product of the same two numbers is 3, find the sum of the reciprocals of these numbers.

TEACHING STRATEGIES

A reverse strategy is certainty not new. It was considered by Pappus of Alexandria about 320 A.D. In Book VII of Pappus' *Collection* there is a rather complete description of the methods of "analysis" and "synthesis." T. L. Heath in his book, *A Manual of Greek Mathematics* (Oxford University Press, 1931, pp. 452–3) provides a translation of Pappus' definitions of these terms:

> *Analysis* takes that which is sought as if it were admitted and passes from it through its successive consequences to something which is admitted as the result of synthesis; for in analysis we assume that which is sought as if it were already done, and we inquire what it is from which this results, and again what is the antecedent cause of the latter, and so on, until, by so retracing our steps, we come upon something already known or belonging to the class of first principles, and such a method we call analysis as being solution backwards.
>
> But in *synthesis*, reversing the process, we take as already done that which was last arrived at in the analysis and, by arranging in their natural order as consequences what before were antecedents, and successively connecting them one with another, we arrive finally at the construction of that which was sought; and this we call *synthesis*.

Unfortunately, this method has not received its due emphasis in the mathematics classroom. This discussion will reinforce the value of reverse strategy in problem solving.

To better understand this technique for problem solving, a number of appropriate problems will be presented. Discussion of their solutions should help students attain a better grasp of this method.

Let us first consider the following simple problem from basic geometry.

Problem 1:

Given: $\overline{AB} \cong \overline{DC}$

$\overline{AB} \parallel \overline{DC}$

$\angle BAH \cong \angle DCG$

$\overline{BEGHFD}$

$\overline{GE} \cong \overline{HF}$

Prove: $\overline{AE} \parallel \overline{CF}$

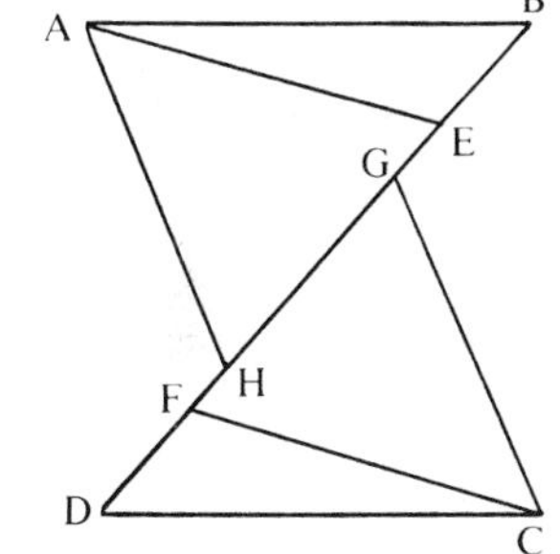

Solution: The first thoughts of a student trying to do this proof is to consider what information is given, and then what is to be proved. Having considered the given information, the poorly trained student will usually proceed blindly, proving segments, angles, and triangles congruent until (if ever) he or she reaches the desired conclusion.

On the other hand, a well-trained student, after considering the given information, will immediately look at the desired conclusion and begin working in reverse from that conclusion ("analysis"). First this student will ask what methods there are for proving lines parallel. This will for the most part lead to proving angles congruent. In this proof clever students will realize that if they were able to prove $\angle AED \cong \angle CFB$, they would then be able to prove $\overline{AE}$ parallel to $\overline{CF}$. But how can they prove $\angle AED \cong \angle CFB$? Because of the type of training they receive, most students will generally react to this question by trying to find a pair of congruent triangles that have $\angle AED$ and $\angle CFB$ as a pair of corresponding angles. Continuing this reverse approach, students must now locate such a pair of congruent triangles. It would be helpful if students could prove $\triangle AEH \cong \triangle CFG$, as these triangles have $\angle AED$ and $\angle CFB$ as a pair of corresponding angles. Can these triangles be proven congruent? Evidently not. All that students know about these triangles at this point is that $\overline{HE} \cong \overline{GF}$. Using this type of reasoning they soon will prove that $\triangle ABH \cong \triangle CDG$, which will help to prove $\triangle AEH \cong \triangle CFG$. Then, by retracing steps of reverse reasoning in the opposite order ("synthesis") students will easily attain the desired conclusion. It is clear that reverse strategy was instrumental in formulating a path to the desired conclusion.

The reverse approach to solving a problem becomes dramatically stronger, when the resulting solution becomes significantly more elegant. As an example, let us consider the following problem offered in the preassessment.

Problem 2: If the sum of two numbers is 2 and the product of these same two numbers is 3, find the sum of the reciprocals of these two numbers.

Solution: A first reaction after reading this problem would be to set up the equation $x + y = 2$, and $xy = 3$. A well-trained student of algebra would promptly set out to solve these equations simultaneously. She or he may solve the first equation for y to get $y = 2 - x$, and then substitute appropriately in the second equation so that $x(2 - x) = 3$ or $x^2 - 2x + 3 = 0$. As $x = 1 \pm \sqrt{-2}$ the two numbers are $1 + i\sqrt{2}$ and $1 - i\sqrt{2}$. Now the sum of their reciprocals is

$$\frac{1}{1 + i\sqrt{2}} + \frac{1}{1 - i\sqrt{2}} = \frac{(1 - i\sqrt{2}) + (1 + i\sqrt{2})}{(1 + i\sqrt{2})\cdot(1 - i\sqrt{2})} = \frac{2}{3}.$$

This solution is by no means elegant.

Had students used a reverse strategy ("analysis"), they would have first inspected the desired conclusion; that is, $\frac{1}{x} + \frac{1}{y}$.

The sum of these fractions is $\frac{x + y}{xy}$. The two original equations immediately reveal the numerator and the denominator of this fraction. This produces the answer, $\frac{2}{3}$, immediately. For this particular problem, a reverse strategy was superior to the more common, straightforward approach.

Problem 3: If the sum of two numbers is 2, and the product of the same two numbers is 3, find the sum of the squares of the reciprocals of these numbers.

Solution: To find the sum of the squares of the reciprocals (of the numbers described in the above problem) by a reverse approach, the student must first consider the conclusion, that is: $\left(\frac{1}{x}\right)^2 + \left(\frac{1}{y}\right)^2$ or $\frac{1}{x^2} + \frac{1}{y^2}$. Once again students would be required to add the fractions to get $\frac{x^2 + y^2}{x^2y^2}$. Therefore the denominator of the answer is $(xy)^2 = 9$. However, the numerator is not as simple to evaluate as it was earlier. Students must now find the value of $x^2 + y^2$. Once again students must look backward. can they somehow generate $x^2 + y^2$? Students will be quick to suggest that $(x + y)^2$ will yield $x^2 + y^2 + 2xy$, which in part produces $x^2 + y^2$. Besides, $(x + y)^2 = (2)^2 = 4$ and $2xy = 2 \cdot 3 = 6$. Hence $x^2 + y^2 = -2$. The problem is therefore solved, as $\frac{1}{x^2} + \frac{1}{y^2} = \frac{x^2 + y^2}{x^2y^2} = \frac{-2}{9}$.

A similar procedure can be employed to find the value of $\left(\frac{1}{x}\right)^3 + \left(\frac{1}{y}\right)^3$ from the original two equations, $x + y = 2$ and $xy = 3$. Once again beginning with the conclusion and working in reverse, $\frac{1}{x^3} + \frac{1}{y^3} = \frac{x^3 + y^3}{(xy)^3}$. Since students already know that $(xy)^3 = (3)^3 = 27$, they need only to find the value of $x^3 + y^3$. How can they generate $x^3 + y^3$?

From $(x + y)^3 = x^3 + y^3 + 3x^2y + 3xy^2$

we get
$$x^3 + y^3 = (x + y)^3 - 3xy\,(x + y)$$
$$x^3 + y^3 = (2)^3 - 3(3)(2)$$
$$x^3 + y^4 = -10$$

Therefore, $\frac{1}{x^3} + \frac{1}{y^3} = \frac{x^3 + y^3}{(xy)^3} = \frac{-10}{27}$.

This procedure may also be used to find the sum of higher powers of these reciprocals.

Another problem whose solution lends itself nicely to a reverse strategy ("analysis") involves geometric constructions.

Problem 4: Construct a triangle given the lengths, m_a and m_b, of two medians of a triangle and the length, c, of the side whose endpoints are each an endpoint of one of the medians.

Solution: Rather than immediately trying to perform the required construction, students would be wise to use a reverse strategy. They may assume construction and inspect the results.

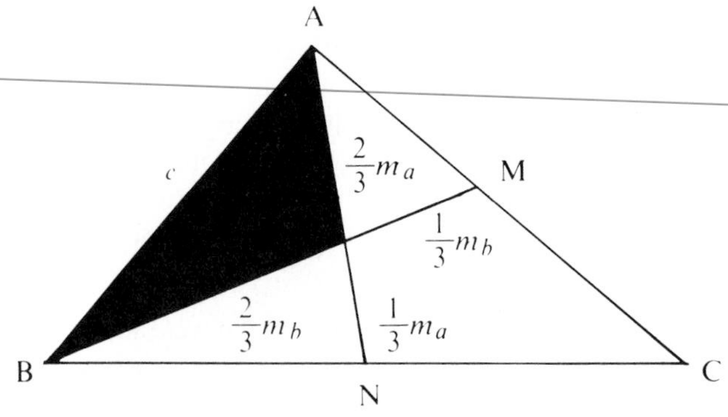

Students will soon realize that they would be able to construct the shaded triangle above as they can easily obtain the lengths of its sides $\left(c, \frac{2m_a}{3}, \frac{2m_b}{3}\right)$. Points M and N can then be located using the property of the centroid. Then point C will be determined by the intersection of $\overrightarrow{AM}$ and $\overrightarrow{BN}$. Having started from the conclusion and working in reverse, students have formulated a plan for constructing the required triangle, by merely retracing steps in the reverse direction ("synthesis").

Although there are many problems whose solutions can be significantly simplified by using a reverse strategy, there are also a great number of problems where a straightforward approach is best. It is natural for a student to approach a problem in a straightforward manner. Yet we as teachers must encourage our students to abandon the straightforward approach when a solution is not easily forthcoming, and attempt a reverse solution.

Some problems require only a partial reverse strategy. In such problems it is useful to begin with the conclusion and work backward until a path to the conclusion is established. Let us consider the following problems.

Problem 5: Find the solution of the following: $(x - y^2)^2 + (x - y - 2)^2 = 0$, where x and y are real numbers.

Solution: Students of algebra might naturally use a straightforward approach to solve this equation. After squaring each of the polynomials as indicated, confusion would mount. Students previously exposed to a reverse strategy would then try to analyze the solution set of the equation. The values of x and y must be such that the sum of the squares of the polynomials equals zero. How can the sum of two positive numbers equal zero? Students can answer this question by saying that $x - y^2 = 0$ and $x - y - 2 = 0$. Up to this point students used a reverse strategy ("analysis"). However, now they must proceed in a straightforward manner ("synthesis") solving the equations $x - y^2 = 0$ and $x - y - 2 = 0$ simultaneously.

In his book *How to Solve It,* George Polya discusses a backward method of problem solving that is similar to a reverse strategy discussed in this article. Polya emphasizes the importance of the role of a teacher in presenting such methods to students when he states that "there is some sort of psychological repugnance to this reverse order which may prevent a quite able student from understanding the method if it is not presented carefully."

It is the responsibility of the mathematics teacher to make a conscious effort to stress the importance, benefits, and possible limitations of a reverse strategy in problem solving.

POSTASSESSMENT

1. If $x + y = 2$ and $xy = 3$, find $\frac{1}{x^4} + \frac{1}{y^4}$.
2. Construct a triangle given the lengths of two sides and the length of an altitude to one of these sides.
3. Have students use analysis and synthesis to prove the following:

   In right $\triangle ABC$, $\overline{CF}$ is the median drawn to hypotenuse $\overline{AB}$, $\overline{CE}$ is the bisector of $\angle ACB$, and $\overline{CD}$ is the altitude to $\overline{AB}$.

   Prove that $\angle DCE \cong \angle ECF$.

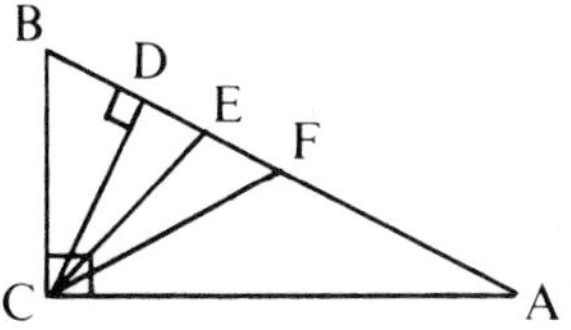

4. Evaluate $x^5 + \frac{1}{x^5}$, if $x^2 + \frac{1}{x^2} = 7$.

   (Answer: $\pm$ 123)

REFERENCES

Posamentier, A. S., and S. Krulik. *Problem-Solving Strategies of Efficient and Elegant Solutions: A Resource for the Mathematics Teacher*. Thousand Oaks, CA: Corwin, 2nd ed., 2008.

Polya, G. *How to Solve It*. Princeton, NJ: Princeton University Press, 1973.

Unit 94

 Decimals and Fractions in Other Bases

PERFORMANCE OBJECTIVE

Students will rationalize repeating decimals or repeating fractions in other bases.

PREASSESSMENT

Ask students to find the decimal number equivalent to $\frac{87}{99}\left(=\frac{87}{10^2 - 1}\right)$. Challenge students to represent a repeating decimal by a simple rational number.

TEACHING STRATEGIES

Decimal numbers are usually classified as repeating and nonrepeating. Repeating decimals are further partitioned into terminating and nonterminating decimals. Students are usually readily aware that a terminating decimal represents a particular rational number. But the nature of a nonterminating decimal is more intriguing. We begin this exploration by confining ourselves to nonterminating repeating decimals. Consider the repeating decimal: $.1212\overline{12}$. (The bar over the last two digits indicates the repeating digits.) What we want to do is to represent this decimal by an equivalent rational simple fraction. If we let $x = .12\overline{12}\ldots$ and then $100x = 12.12\overline{12}\ldots$ subtracting the former from the latter yields the equation: $100x - x = 12$, or $x = \frac{12}{100 - 1} = \frac{12}{99}$. We have now found a ratio representation for $.1212\ldots$. Some further exploration is in order now. Notice that $\frac{12}{99} + \frac{88}{99} = 1$. However, if we add the equivalent decimal representations

$$\begin{array}{r} .1212\overline{12} \\ +.8787\overline{87} \\ \hline .9999\overline{99} \end{array}$$

one would think that $.99999\overline{9} = 1$. Indeed, applying the above technique yields $x = .9999\overline{9}$ and $10x = 9.9999\overline{9}$; therefore, $10x - x = 9$, and $x = \frac{7}{10 - 1}$, $x = 1$.

This illustration leads us to an important theorem: any repeating decimal can be represented as a rational number (i.e., the *ratio* of two integers, the denominator not zero).

Proof: Let the repeating decimal be represented by $.a_1a_2\ldots a_n\ldots$ where a_i is a digit and n is an integer that represents the length of the repetition. As before, let

$$x = .a_1a_2\ldots a_n\ldots$$

and

$$10^nx = a_1a_2\ldots a_n.a_1a_2\ldots a_n\ldots.$$

Now

$$\begin{aligned} 10^nx - x &= a_1a_2\ldots a_n \\ x(10^n - 1) &= a_1a_2\ldots a_n \\ x &= \frac{a_1a_2\ldots a_n}{10^n - 1} \end{aligned}$$

The repeating decimal is now represented by a rational number.

Students will now want to consider repeating fractions in bases other than 10 (no longer called decimals!). Suppose we have in base 3 the repeating fraction: $.12\overline{12}$. Students should be guided to asking the following:

1. Can this repeating fraction be represented by a rational number in base 3?
2. In general can *any* repeating fraction in *any* given base be represented by a rational number?

Begin by using the approach applied earlier to repeating decimals. Let $x = .12\overline{12}$. Ask students how the ternary point may be shifted two places to the right (note the ternary point in base 3 is analogous to the decimal point in base 10). Now $3^2x = 12.12\overline{12}$. By subtracting x we get $3^2x - x = 12$, $x(3^2 - 1) = 12$, $x = \frac{12}{3^2 - 1} = \frac{12}{22}$. Thus the repeating fraction in base 3 can be represented by a rational number. Have students notice the analogous form in base 10.

Using these illustrations as models we shall prove that a repeating fraction in any base can be represented by a rational number in that base.

Proof: Consider any base B and any repeating fraction in that base: $.a_1a_2\ldots a_n\ldots$ where a_1 is a digit of the number and n is an integer that represents the length of the repetition $x = .a_1a_2\ldots a_n\ldots$

$$\begin{aligned} B^nx &= a_1a_2\ldots a_n.a_1a_2\ldots a_n\ldots \\ B^nx - x &= a_1a_2\ldots a_n \\ x &= \frac{a_1a_2\ldots a_n}{B^n - 1} \end{aligned}$$

This proves that any repeating fraction can be represented by a rational number.

POSTASSESSMENT

Have students do the following exercises:

1. If $x = \dfrac{123}{10^3 - 1}$, what is its decimal representation?
2. If $x = \dfrac{11256}{7^4 - 1}$, represent x as a rational fraction.
3. Rationalize the repeating fraction $x = .23\overline{23}$ when x is in base 10, 8, and 5.

Unit 95

Polygonal Numbers

This unit can be taught to a class that has a reasonably good command of the basic algebraic skills. Since most of the unit employs intuitive thinking, a good degree of this training should result. It would be helpful if the students were familiar with arithmetic sequences and the formula for the sum of its series. However, if students are not familiar with this topic, essentials can be developed in a reasonably short time.

PERFORMANCE OBJECTIVES

1. *Given the rank of any regular polygon, the student will find a number that corresponds to it.*
2. *The student will discover relations between two or more different polygonal numbers of given ranks.*

PREASSESSMENT

The ancient Babylonians discovered that some whole numbers can be broken down into patterns of units. This link between arithmetic and geometry was also of concern to the ancient Greeks. For example, the number 3 can be represented as three dots forming a triangle, as can be number 6.

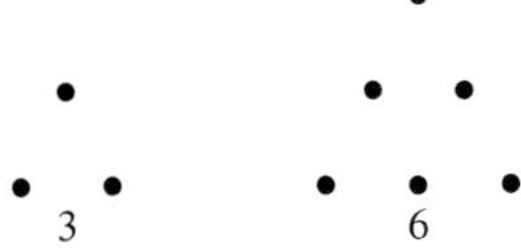

Which regular polygon do you think the number 4 represents? The number 9? After the students have had some time to find such polygons, ask them to provide the answers.

Numbers that can be related to geometric figures are called *figurate* or *polygonal* numbers.

TEACHING STRATEGIES

Tell the students that it would be very easy to find the number that corresponds to a given regular polygon if we could find a formula such that given any regular polygon and its rank we could obtain that number from it.

Begin by telling the students what the rank of a regular polygon indicates. For any regular polygon, the rank indicates, in order, the corresponding polygonal number. For example, for a triangle, rank $1 = 3$ (the first triangular number), rank $2 = 6$ (the second triangular number), rank $3 = 10$, etc.

Now draw five figures that will show how to get the first five ranks of the first five figurate numbers (triangular, square, pentagonal, hexagonal, heptagonal). To save time you may use an overhead projector instead, or you may distribute mimeographed sheets with the drawings. Make a corresponding table. Both the drawings and the table that follow indicate what might be shown to your students.

It should be clear to the student that making a figure to obtain every possible triangular, square, etc. number is a very tedious task. Instead we will study how consecutive polygonal

TABLE 1

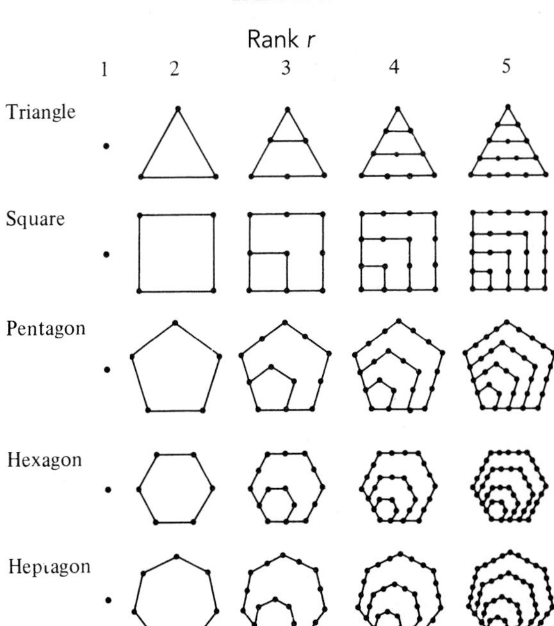

TABLE 2

Figure	No. sides N	1	2	Rank r 3	4	5
Triangular	3	1	3	6	10	15
Square	4	1	4	9	16	25
Pentagonal	5	1	5	12	22	35
Hexagonal	6	1	6	15	28	45
Heptagonal	7	1	7	18	34	55

numbers of a given polygon follow each other and, by looking at the sequence formed, try to obtain a formula for the *r*th rank of each given polygon.

If we look at the first row of figurate numbers corresponding to triangular numbers, and if we also look at their corresponding ranks (Table 1), we will notice that they can be written as

$$\begin{aligned}1 &= r\\ 3 &= (r-1)+r\\ 6 &= (r-2)+(r-1)+r\\ 10 &= (r-3)+(r-2)+(r-1)+r\\ 15 &= (r-4)+(r-3)+(r-2)+(r-1)+r\end{aligned}$$

If we look at the ranks we will also notice that their sequence forms an arithmetic sequence and that each triangular number of rank *r* is the sum of that arithmetic sequence 1,2,3,...,*r* from 1 to *r*. Thus we can conclude that the *r*th triangular number is given by $T_r = \dfrac{r(r+1)}{2}$.

Next, let's look at the square numbers:

$$\begin{aligned}1 &= r^2 = 1^2\\ 4 &= r^2 = 2^2\\ 9 &= r^2 = 3^2\\ 16 &= r^2 = 4^2\\ 25 &= r^2 = 5^2\end{aligned}$$

It is clear that each square number is the square of its corresponding rank. So the *r* square number is r^2.

The formula for the rth pentagonal number can be obtained if we write each number in the following way:

$$\begin{aligned}1 &= r^2+0 = 1+0\\ 5 &= r^2+1 = 2^2+1\\ 12 &= r^2+3 = 3^2+3\\ 22 &= r^2+6 = 4^2+6\\ 35 &= r^2+10 = 5^2+10\end{aligned}$$

If we study the second part of the sums 0,1,3,6,10, we will see that each of the numbers correspond to the sum of the arithmetic sequence $0,1,2,\ldots,(r-1)$, which is $\dfrac{(r-1)r}{2}$. So the rth pentagonal number is

$$r^2 + \frac{(r-1)r}{2} = \frac{2r^2+(r-1)r}{2} = \frac{(2r^2+r^2-r)}{2} = \frac{(3r^2-r)}{2} = \frac{r(3r-1)}{2}.$$

To find a formula for the rth hexagonal number, consider the first five as follows:

$$\begin{aligned}1 &= 1r\\ 6 &= 3r = 3(2)\\ 15 &= 5r = 5(3)\\ 28 &= 7r = 7(4)\\ 45 &= 9r = 9(5)\end{aligned}$$

An inspection of the coefficients of *r*: 1,3,5,7,9, would reveal that each corresponds to the sum of the corresponding rank and the rank immediately before it. That is, each coefficient is equal to $r + (r-1)$. Therefore, the rth hexagonal number is $[r+(r-1)]\,r = (2r-1)r$.

The rth heptagonal number is found as follows. Write the first seven heptagonal numbers in the following way:

$$\begin{aligned}1 &= 2r^2-1 = 2(1)^2-1\\ 7 &= 2r^2-1 = 2(2)^2-1\\ 18 &= 2r^2+0 = 2(3)^2+0\\ 34 &= 2r^2+2 = 2(4)^2+2\\ 55 &= 2r^2+5 = 2(5)^2+5\end{aligned}$$

It probably will be very difficult for the students to arrive at a formula for the second part *X* of each number $2r^2 + X$. Therefore after the students have looked at the numbers for a short time the teacher should immediately point out that each *X* is equal to the sum of the arithmetic sequence $-1,0,1,2,3,\ldots,(r-2)$ minus one, which is $\dfrac{(r-2)(r-1)}{2} - 1$. Students should test the formula on each of the given numbers above. So the rth heptagonal number is

$$\begin{aligned}2r^2 + \frac{(r-2)(r-1)}{2} - 1 &= 2r^2 + \frac{(r-2)(r-1)-2}{2}\\ &= 2r^2 + \frac{r^2-3r+2-2}{2} = \frac{r(5r-3)}{2}.\end{aligned}$$

Call attention to the fact that we now have a formula for the rth rank of each of the first five polygonal numbers. So we are now able to find any triangular, square, pentagonal, hexagonal, and heptagonal number. But, there are regular polygons of 8,9, . . .20,100, etc. sides, and we would also like to have a formula for the rth rank of each of them. It is our next task to find such formulas.

To do this let's write the formulas we have already found as follows:

No. sides	Rank = r
3	$\frac{r(r+1)}{2} = \frac{r^2+r}{2} = \frac{1r^2}{2} + \frac{r}{2}$
4	$r^2 = \frac{2r^2}{2} = \frac{2r^2}{2} + \frac{0}{2}$
5	$\frac{r(3r-1)}{2} = \frac{3r^2-r}{-2} = \frac{3r^2}{2} - \frac{r}{2}$
6	$r(2r-1) = \frac{4r^2-2r}{2} = \frac{4r^2}{2} - \frac{2r}{2}$
7	$\frac{r(5r-3)}{2} = \frac{5r^2-3r}{2} = \frac{5r^2}{2} - \frac{3r}{2}$
⋮	
N	

Let's now look at the last column. We will notice that the coefficients of the $\frac{r^2}{2}$ terms can be written as $(N-2)$. Also the coefficients of the $\frac{r}{2}$ terms can be written as $-(N-4)$. Therefore, the rth rank of a N-gonal number is

$$\frac{(N-2)r^2}{2} - \frac{(N-4)r}{2} = \frac{(N-2)r^2-(N-4)r}{2} =$$
$$\left(\frac{r}{2}\right)\left[(N-2)r-(N-4)\right] = \left(\frac{r}{2}\right)\left[(r-1)N-2(r-2)\right].$$

The completed table (including the first five ranks of the N-gonal number) looks like this:

No. sides	1	2	3	4	5	.....	r
3	1	3	6	10	15	.....	$\frac{r(r+1)}{2}$
4	1	4	9	16	25	.....	r^2
5	1	5	12	22	35	.....	$\frac{r(3r-1)}{2}$
6	1	6	15	28	15	.....	$r(2r-1)$
7	1	7	18	34	55	.....	$\frac{r(5r-3)}{2}$
⋮							
N	1	..... $\left(\frac{r}{2}\right)[(r-1)N-2(r-2)]$					

At this point it would be instructive for the students to work out some simple examples using the formula for the rth N-gonal number.

Example 1
Find the third octagonal number.

Solution: Let $N = 8$ and $r = 3$. Substitute these numbers in the formula $\frac{r}{2}[(r-1)N-2(r-2)]$

$$= \frac{3}{2}[(3-1)8-2(3-2)] = \frac{3}{2}(2)8-2(1)$$
$$= \frac{3}{2}[16-2] = \frac{3\times 14}{2} = 21$$

Example 2
To what regular polygon does the number 40 correspond if $r = 4$?

Solution: In this case we know the rank and the number, but we must find N. We substitute into and solve the following equation:

$$\left(\frac{r}{2}\right)[(r-1)N-2(r-2)] = 40$$
$$\left(\frac{4}{2}\right)[(4-1)N-2(4-2)] = 40$$
$$2[3N-2(2)] = 40, \quad \text{and} \quad N = 8.$$

So the figure is a regular octagon.

The following examples are a little more difficult for they call for applications of the formulas to find relationships between different types of polygonal numbers.

Example 3
Show that the rth pentagonal number is equal to r plus three times the $(r-1)^{\text{th}}$ triangular number.

Solution: To do this problem, we must first write the formula for the rth pentagonal number:

$$P_r = \frac{r(3r-1)}{2} = \frac{3r^2}{2} - \frac{r}{2}.$$

Rewrite $\frac{-r}{3}$ as $\frac{-3r}{2} + r$.

Now we have $\frac{3r^2}{2} - \frac{3r}{2} + r = \frac{3(r^2-r)}{2} + r$

$$\frac{3r(r-1)}{2} + r = 3T_{r-1} + r, \text{ where}$$

T_{r-1} is the $(r-1)^{\text{st}}$ triangular number.

Example 4
Show that any hexagonal number is equal to the sum of a pentagonal number of the same rank and a triangular number of the preceding rank.

Solution: $(\text{Hex})_r = r(2r-1) = 2r^2 - r$

$$= \frac{3r^2-r}{2} + \frac{r^2-r}{2}$$
$$= \frac{r(3r-1)}{2} + \frac{r(r-1)}{2} = P_r + T_{r-1}$$

POSTASSESSMENT

1. Draw a regular octagon corresponding to the third octagonal number of example 1 (study the drawings of the first five figurate numbers before doing this problem).
2. Find the first three dacagonal (10 sides) numbers.
3. Show that any heptagonal number is equal to the sum of a hexagonal number of the same rank and a triangular number of the previous rank (i.e., show $(\text{Hep})_r = (\text{Hex})_r + T_{r-1}$).
4. Show that any N-gonal number ($N \geq 5$) is equal to the sum of the $(N - 1)$-gonal number of the same rank and a triangular number of the previous rank. (Hint: Begin with the $(N - 1)$-gonal number of rank r and T_{r-1}. Carry out the addition.)
5. Show that the sum of any number of consecutive odd integers, starting with 1, is a perfect square (i.e., a square number).

Unit 96

Networks

This unit will serve as an introductory lesson in topology.

PERFORMANCE OBJECTIVE

Given a closed curve, students will determine if it is traversible or nontraversible.

PREASSESSMENT

Have students try to trace with a pencil each of the following configurations without missing any part and without going over any part twice.

Ask students to determine the number of arcs or line segments that have an endpoint at each of A, B, C, D, E.

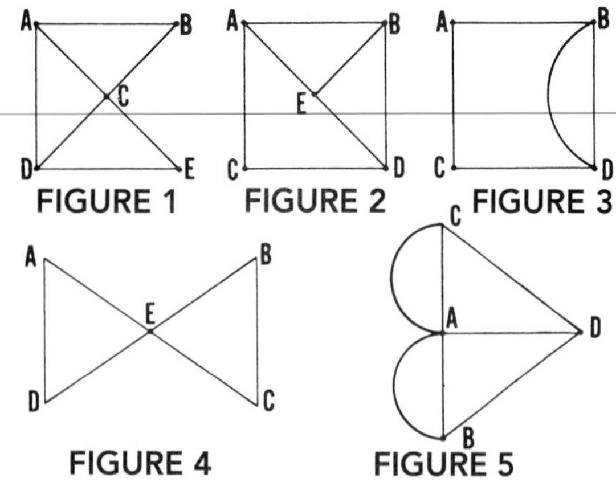

TEACHING STRATEGIES

Configurations such as Figures 1–5, which are made up of line segments and/or continuous arcs are called *networks*. The number of arcs or line segments that have an endpoint at a particular vertex, is called the *degree* of the vertex.

After trying to trace these networks without taking their pencils off the paper and without going over any line more than once, students should notice two direct outcomes. The networks can be traced (or *traversed*) if they have (1) all even degree vertices or (2) exactly two odd degree vertices. The proof of these two outcomes follows.

There are an even number of odd degree vertices in a connected network.

Proof: Let V_1 be the number of vertices of degree 1, let V_3 be the number of vertices of degree 3, and V_n the number of vertices of degree n. Also let $N = V_1 + V_3 + V_5 + \cdots + V_{2n-1}$. N is the number of odd degree vertices in a given connected network ("connected" meaning without loose ends). Since there are 3 arc endpoints at V_3, 5 at V_5, and n at V_n, the total number of arc endpoints in a connected network is $M = V_1 + 2V_2 + 3V_3 + 4V_4 + \cdots + 2n\,V_{2n}$.

$$\begin{aligned} M - N &= 2V_2 + 2V_3 + 4V_4 + 4V_5 + \cdots \\ &\quad + (2n - 2)V_{2n-1} + 2nV_{2n} \\ &= 2(V_2 + V_3 + 2V_4 + 2V_5 + \cdots \\ &\quad + 2(n - 1)V_{2n-1}2nV_{2n}) \end{aligned}$$

Since the difference of two even numbers is an even number, $M - (M - N) = N$ is an even number.

A connected network can be traversed only if it has at most two odd degree vertices.

Proof: On a continuous path the inside vertices must be passed through. That is, if a line "enters" the point another must "leave" the point. This accounts for the endpoints. The only vertices that do not conform to this rule are the beginning and endpoints in the traversing. These *two* points may be of odd order. By the previous theorem, it was established that there must be an even number of odd vertices; therefore there can only be *two* or *zero* vertices of odd order in order to traverse a network.

Have students now draw both traversable and nontraversible networks (using these two theorems). Network 1 in the Preassessment has five vertices. Vertices B,C,E are of even degree and vertices A and D are of odd degree. Since Figure 1 has exactly two odd degree vertices as well as three even degree vertices, it is traversable. If we start at A then go down to D, across to E, back up to A, across to B, and down to D we have chosen a desired route.

Network 2 has five vertices. Vertex C is the only even degree vertex. Vertices A,B,E, and D, are all of odd degree. Consequently, since the network has more than two odd vertices, it is not traversible.

Network 3 is traversible because it has two even vertices and exactly two odd degree vertices.

Network 4 has five even degree vertices and can be traversed.

Network 5 has four odd degree vertices and *cannot* be traversed.

To generate interest among your students, present them with the famous Königsberg Bridge Problem. In the eighteenth century the small Prussian city of Königsberg, located where the Pregel River formed two branches, was faced with a recreational dilemma: Could a person walk over each of the seven bridges exactly once in a continuous walk through the city? In 1735 the famous mathematician Leonhard Euler (1707–1783) proved that this walk could not be performed. Indicate to students that the ensuing discussion will tie in their earlier work with networks to the solution of the Königsberg Bridge Problem.

Tell pupils to indicate the island by A, the left bank of the river by B, the right one by C, and the area between the two arms of the upper course by D. If we start at Holzt and walk to Sohmede and then through Honig, through Hohe, through Kottel, through Grüne we will never cross Kramer. On the other hand if we start at Kramer and walk to Honig, through Hohe, through Kottel, through Sohmede, through Holzt we will never travel through Grüne.

The Königsberg Bridge Problem is the same problem as the one posed in Figure 5. Let's take a look at Figures 5 and 6 and note the similarity. There are seven bridges in Figure 6 and there are seven lines in Figure 5. In Figure 5 each vertex is of odd degree. In Figure 6 if we start at D we have three choices, we could go to Hohe, Honig, or Holzt. If in Figure 5 we start at D we have three line paths to choose from. In both figures if we are at C we have either three bridges we could go on or three lines. A similar situation exists for locations A and B in Figure 6 and vertices A and B in Figure 5. Emphasize that this network *cannot* be traversed.

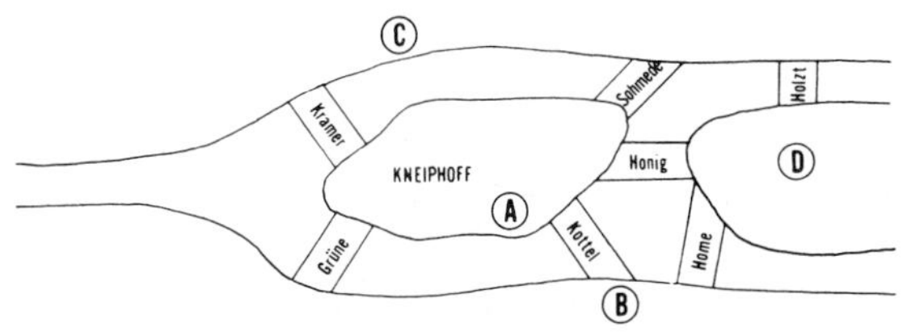

FIGURE 6

Another example of a problem where the consideration of the traversibility of a network is important is the Five Room House Problem. Have students consider the diagram of a five-room house.

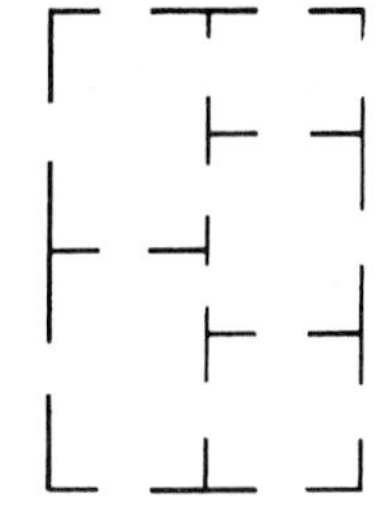

FIGURE 7A

Each room has a doorway to each adjacent room and a doorway leading outside the house. The problem is to have a person start either inside or outside the house and walk through each doorway *exactly once.*

Students should be encouraged to try various paths. They will realize that although the number of attempts is finite, there are far too many to make a trial-and-error solution practical. They should be guided to a network diagram analogous to this problem.

Figure 7b shows various possible paths joining the five rooms A, B, C, D, and E, and the outside F. The problem now reduces to merely determining if this network is traversible. There are *four vertices* of odd degree and two vertices of even degree. Because there are not *exactly* two or zero vertices of odd order, this network *cannot* be traversed; hence the Five Room House Problem does not have a solution path.

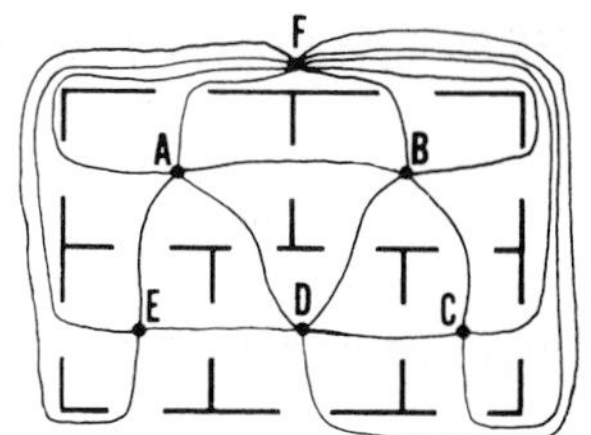

FIGURE 7B

Other problems of a similar nature may now be presented to the students.

POSTASSESSMENT

1. Have students find out if the following figures can be traced without removing their pencils from the paper and without going over any line twice (i.e., traversed).

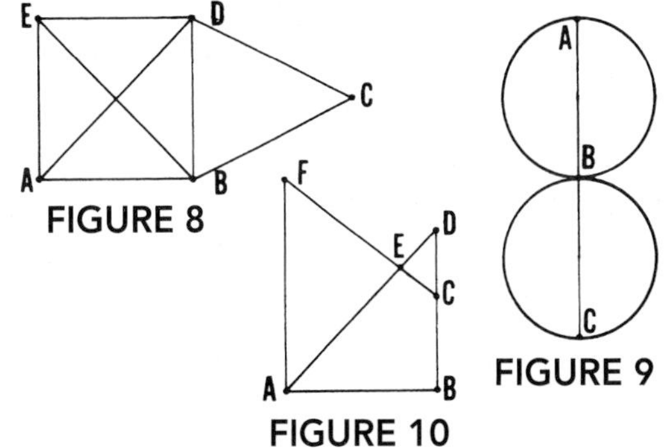

FIGURE 8

FIGURE 9

FIGURE 10

2. Have students draw a house floor plan and then determine if one can walk through each doorway exactly once.

REFERENCE

Posamentier, A. S., and W. Schulz (eds.). *The Art of Problem-Solving: A Resource for the Mathematics Teacher*. Thousand Oaks, CA: Corwin, 1996.

Unit 97

Angle Trisection—Possible or Impossible?

Of the Three Famous Problems of Antiquity, the one most instructive to a high school student is the angle trisection. This unit will present a discussion and proof that any angle cannot be trisected with only straightedge and compasses.

PERFORMANCE OBJECTIVE

Students will outline a proof that an angle of measure 120° cannot be trisected.

PREASSESSMENT

Students should be familiar with the basic geometric constructions.

TEACHING STRATEGIES

Ask students to trisect an angle of measure 90° using only straightedge and compasses. With little difficulty they ought to be able to construct an angle of measure 60° at the vertex of the given angle. This virtually completes the trisection. However, now ask students to trisect an angle of measure 120°. This will cause difficulty because it is impossible with straightedge and compasses. At this point, begin discussion of the impossibility of angle trisection using only straightedge and compasses.

With the aid of a unit length and an angle of measure A, it is possible to construct a line segment of length cos A (see Figure 1).

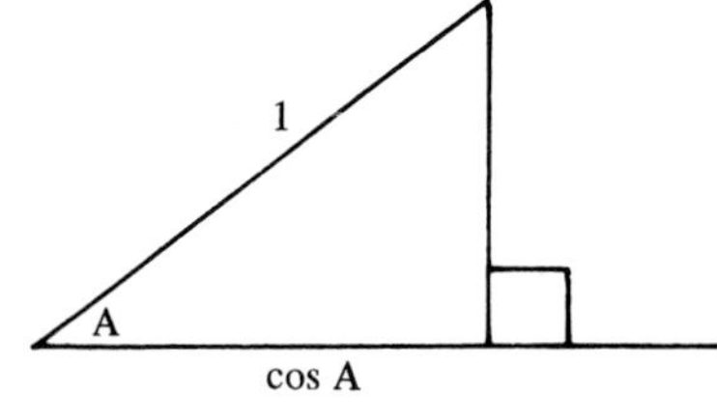

FIGURE 1

If we can trisect ∠A, then we can also construct the $\cos\frac{A}{3}$. If we can show that $\cos\frac{A}{3}$ cannot be constructed, then we have shown that ∠A cannot be trisected. Here we shall let $m\angle A = 120°$, and show ∠A cannot be trisected.

We shall first obtain an expression for cos A in terms of $\cos\frac{A}{3}$.

$$\cos 3y = \cos(2y + y) = \cos 2y \cos y - \sin 2y \sin y$$

But, $\cos 2y = 2\cos^2 y - 1$.
Substituting

$$\begin{aligned}\cos 3y &= \cos y\,(2\cos^2 y - 1) - \sin 2y \sin y\\ &= [2\cos^3 y - \cos y] - \sin 2y \sin y.\end{aligned}$$

But, $\sin 2y = 2\sin y \cos y$.
Therefore:

$$\begin{aligned}\cos 3y &= [2\cos^3 y - \cos y] - \sin y\,(2\sin y \cos y)\\ \cos 3y &= [2\cos^3 y - \cos y] - 2\sin^2 y \cos y\\ \cos 3y &= [2\cos^3 y - \cos y] - 2\cos y(1 - \cos^2 y)\\ \cos 3y &= [2\cos^3 y - \cos y] - 2\cos y + 2\cos^3 y\\ \cos 3y &= 4\cos^3 y - 3\cos y\end{aligned}$$

Let $3y = A$ to obtain

$$\cos A = 4\cos^3\frac{A}{3} - 3\cos\frac{A}{3}.$$

Multiply by 2 and replace $2\cos\frac{A}{3}$ with x to get

$$2\cos A = x^3 - 3x.$$

Because $\cos 120° = -\frac{1}{2}$, $x^3 - 3x + 1 = 0$.
Students should now recall that one of the criteria of constructibility indicates that constructible roots must be of the form $a + b\sqrt{c}$, where a and b are rational and c is constructible.

First, then, we must show that $x^3 - 3x + 1 = 0$ has no rational roots. To do this, we assume that there is a rational root, $\frac{p}{q}$, where p and q have no common factor greater than 1. Substituting for $\frac{p}{q}$, we have

$$\begin{aligned}\left(\frac{p}{q}\right)^3 - 3\left(\frac{p}{q}\right) + 1 &= 0\\ p^3 - 3pq^2 + q^3 &= 0\\ q^3 &= 3pq^2 - p^3\\ q^3 &= p(3q^2 - p^2).\end{aligned}$$

This means that q^3, and hence q, has the factor p.

Therefore p must equal ± 1. Also, solving for p^3

$$p^3 = 3pq^2 - q^3$$
$$p^3 = q^2(3p - q)$$

This means p and q must have a common factor, and hence $q = \pm 1$. We can conclude from this that the only rational root of $x^3 - 3x + 1 = 0$ is $r = \pm 1$. By substitution, we can show that neither $+1$ nor -1 is root.

Next, assume $x^3 - 3x + 1 = 0$ has a constructible root $a + b\sqrt{c}$. By substitution in the equation $x^3 - 3x + 1 = 0$, we can show that if $a + b\sqrt{c}$ is a root, then its conjugate, $a - b\sqrt{c}$, is also a root. The sum of the roots of the polynomial equation $x^n + a_1x^{n-1} + a_2x^{n-2} + \cdots + a_n = 0$ is

$$r_1 + r_2 + r_3 + \cdots + r_n = -a_1.$$

It follows from this that the sum of the roots $x^3 - 3x + 1 = 0$ is zero. If two roots are $a + b\sqrt{c}$ and $a - b\sqrt{c}$, with the third root r, we have

$$a + b\sqrt{c} + a - b\sqrt{c} + r = 0$$
$$r = -2a.$$

But a is rational and hence r is rational, and we have a contradiction. Hence the angle whose measure is 120° cannot be trisected. This essentially proves that any angle cannot be trisected with only straightedge and compasses.

POSTASSESSMENT

Have students write an outline of the proof presented in this unit as well as a discussion of its significance.

Unit 98

Comparing Means

This unit can be used as a major part of a lesson on statistics.

PERFORMANCE OBJECTIVES

1. *Students will compare magnitudes of three means for any two or more numbers.*
2. *Students will prove comparison relationships between means.*

PREASSESSMENT

After students have reviewed the arithmetic and geometric means, have students express h in terms of a and b, where a,h,b is a harmonic sequence.

TEACHING STRATEGIES

Begin by defining the three means (arithmetic, harmonic, and geometric) in the following way.

Suppose a,m,b are an arithmetic sequence. The middle term (m) is said to be the *arithmetic mean*. Since a,m,b have a common difference $m - a = b - m$, and

$$\boxed{m = \frac{a + b}{2} = \text{arithmetic mean (A.M.)}}$$

Now suppose a,h,b are a harmonic sequence. The middle term (h) is said to be the *harmonic mean*. Since a,h,b have reciprocals with a common difference, $\frac{1}{h} - \frac{1}{a} = \frac{1}{b} - \frac{1}{h}$ and

$$\boxed{h = \frac{2ab}{a + b} = \text{harmonic mean (H.M.)}}$$

Finally suppose a,g,b are a *geometric sequence*. Since a,g,b have a common ratio, $\frac{g}{a} = \frac{b}{g}$ and

$$\boxed{g = \sqrt{ab} = \text{geometric mean (G.M.)}}$$

Often a pictorial model crystallizes understanding, so a geometric interpretation is appropriate here. Consider the semicircle with diameter $\overline{AOPB}$ with $\overline{AO} \cong \overline{OB}$ and $\overline{PR} \perp \overline{APB}$. (R is on the semicircle.) Also $\overline{PS} \perp \overline{RSO}$. Let AP $= a$ and PB $= b$.

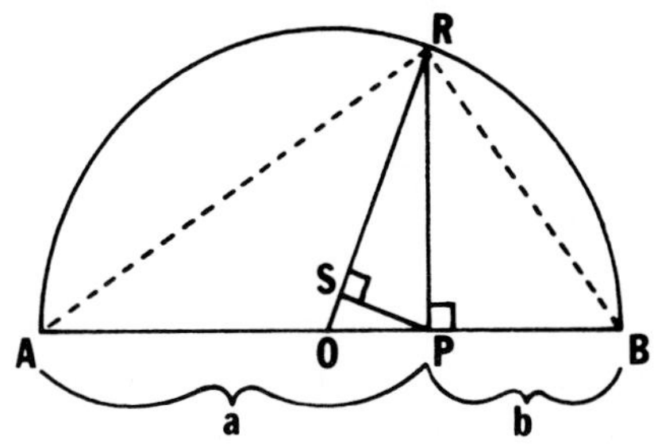

Since $RO = \frac{1}{2}AB = \frac{1}{2}(AP + PB) = \frac{1}{2}(a + b)$, RO is the *arithmetic mean* (A.M.) between a and b.

Consider right $\triangle ARB$. Since $\triangle BPR \sim \triangle RPA$, $\frac{PB}{PR} = \frac{PR}{AP}$ or $(PR)^2 = (AP) \cdot (PB) = ab$. Therefore $PR = \sqrt{ab}$. Thus PR is the *geometric mean* (G.M.) between a and b.

Because $\triangle RPO \sim \triangle RSP$, $\frac{RO}{PR} = \frac{PR}{RS}$. Therefore $RS = \frac{(PR)^2}{RO}$. But $(PR)^2 = ab$ and $RO = \frac{1}{2}AB = \frac{1}{2}(a + b)$. Thus $RS = \frac{ab}{\frac{1}{2}(a+b)} = \frac{2ab}{a+b}$, which is the *harmonic mean* (H.M.) between a and b.

This geometric interpretation lends itself quite well to a comparison of the magnitudes of these three means. Since the hypotenuse of a right triangle is its longest side, in $\triangle ROP$, RO > PR and in $\triangle RSP$, PR > RS. Therefore, RO > PR > RS. However, these triangles may degenerate, so RO ≥ PR ≥ RS, which implies that A.M. ≥ G.M. ≥ H.M.

The student is familiar with both arithmetic mean and geometric mean (sometimes called the mean proportional), but a brief introduction to the harmonic mean might be in order.

The *harmonic mean* between two numbers is the *reciprocal of the arithmetic mean between the reciprocals* of these two numbers. This is because a harmonic sequence is a sequence of reciprocals of members of an arithmetic sequence. For a and b,

$$\text{H.M.} = \frac{1}{\frac{\frac{1}{a} + \frac{1}{b}}{2}} = \frac{2ab}{a+b}$$

Example 1:
Find the harmonic mean of a,b, and c.
Solution: By the definition

$$\text{H.M.} = \frac{1}{\frac{\frac{1}{a} + \frac{1}{b} + \frac{1}{c}}{3}} = \frac{3abc}{ab + ac + bc}$$

Both the arithmetic mean and the geometric mean have popular applications in secondary school curriculum. The harmonic mean also has a very useful and often neglected application in elementary mathematics. The harmonic mean is the "average of rates." For example, suppose the average rate of speed for the trip to and from work is desired, when the rate of speed to work is 30 m.p.h. and returning (over the same route) is 60 m.p.h. The average speed is the harmonic mean between 30 and 60; that is,

$$\frac{(2)(30)(60)}{30 + 60} = 40.$$

To show that the average rate of speed of two (or more) speeds is in fact the harmonic mean of these speeds, consider rates of speed $r_1, r_2, r_3, \ldots, r_n$, each traveled for a time $t_1, t_2, t_3, \ldots, t_n$, respectively, and *each* over a distance d.

$$t_1 = \frac{d}{r_1}, t_2 = \frac{d}{r_2}, t_3 = \frac{d}{r_3}, \ldots t_n = \frac{d}{r_n}$$

The average speed (for the entire trip) is

$$\frac{\text{total distance}}{\text{total time}} = \frac{nd}{t_1 + t_2 + t_3 + \cdots + t_n}$$

$$= \frac{nd}{\frac{d}{r_1} + \frac{d}{r_2} + \cdots + \frac{d}{r_n}} = \frac{n}{\frac{1}{r_1} + \frac{1}{r_2} + \frac{1}{r_3} + \cdots + \frac{1}{r_n}},$$

which is the harmonic mean.

Example 2
If Lisa bought \$1.00 worth of each of three kinds of candy, 15¢, 25¢, and 40¢ per pound, what was her average price paid per pound?
Solution: Because the harmonic mean is the average of rates (taken over the same base), the average price per pound was

$$\frac{(3)(15)(25)(40)}{(15)(25) + (15)(40) + (25)(40)} = 22\frac{62}{79}\text{¢}.$$

To complete the discussion of a comparison of the magnitude of the three means, consider with the class a more general (algebraic) discussion.

In general terms,

$$\text{A.M.} = \frac{a_1 + a_2 + a_3 + \cdots + a_n}{n}$$

$$\text{G.M.} = \sqrt[n]{a_1 \cdot a_2 \cdot a_3 \cdot \ldots \cdot a_n}$$

$$\text{H.M.} = \frac{n}{\frac{1}{a_1} + \frac{1}{a_2} + \frac{1}{a_3} + \cdots + \frac{1}{a_n}}$$

Theorem 1: A.M. ≥ G.M.
Proof: Let $g = \sqrt[n]{a_1 \cdot a_2 \cdot a_3 \cdot \cdots \cdot a_n}$;

then $1 = \sqrt[n]{\frac{a_1}{g} \cdot \frac{a_2}{g} \cdot \frac{a_3}{g} \cdot \cdots \cdot \frac{a_n}{g}}$.

Therefore, $1 = \frac{a_1}{g} \cdot \frac{a_2}{g} \cdot \frac{a_3}{g} \cdot \cdots \cdot \frac{a_n}{g}$.

However, $\frac{a_1}{g} + \frac{a_2}{g} + \frac{a_3}{g} + \cdots + \frac{a_n}{g} \geq n$ since if the product of n positive numbers equals 1, their sum is *not* less than n. Therefore,

$$\frac{a_1 + a_2 + a_3 + \cdots + a_n}{n} \geq g.$$

Hence, $\frac{a_1 + a_2 + a_3 + \cdots + a_n}{n} \geq \sqrt[3]{a_1 \cdot a_2 \cdot a_3 \cdot \cdots \cdot a_n}$,

or A.M. ≥ G.M.

This proof for two numbers a and b ($a > b$) is rather cute:

Since $a - b > 0$, $(a - b)^2 > 0$, or $a^2 - 2ab + b^2 > 0$. By adding $4ab$ to both sides of the inequality

$$a^2 + 2ab + b^2 > 4ab.$$

Taking the positive square root yields

$$\frac{a+b}{2} > \sqrt{ab}.$$

Hence A.M. $>$ G.M. (Note: if $a = b$ then A.M. $=$ G.M.)

Theorem 2: G.M. $\geq$ H.M.
Proof: Since A.M. $\geq$ G.M. for $a_1^b, a_2^b, a_3^b \cdots, a_n^b$

$$\frac{a_1^b + a_2^b + a_3^b + \cdots + a_n^b}{n} \geq \sqrt[n]{a_1^b \cdot a_2^b \cdot a_3^b \cdots a_n^b}.$$

when $\frac{1}{b} < 0$, $\left[\sqrt[n]{a_1^b \cdot a_2^b \cdot a_3^b \ldots . a_n^b}\right]^{\frac{1}{b}} \geq$

$$\left[\frac{a_1^b + a_2^b + a_3^b + \cdots + a_n^b}{n}\right]^{\frac{1}{b}}$$

Take $b = -1$, then $\sqrt[n]{a_1 \cdot a_2 \cdot a_3 \ldots . a_n} \geq$

$$\left[\frac{a_1^{-1} + a_2^{-1} + a_3^{-1} + \cdots + a_n^{-1}}{n}\right]^{-1}$$

Hence, $\sqrt[n]{a_1 \cdot a_2 \cdot a_3 \cdots a_n} \geq$

$$\frac{n}{\frac{1}{a_1} + \frac{1}{a_2} + \frac{1}{a_3} + \cdots + \frac{1}{a_n}}, \text{ or G.M.} \geq \text{H.M.}$$

Once again for two numbers a and b ($a > b$) the proof becomes much simpler:

Because (from above) $a^2 + 2ab + b^2 > 4ab$, $ab\,(a + b)^2 > (4ab)\,(ab)$.

Therefore, $ab > \frac{4a^2b^2}{(a+b)^2}$, or $\sqrt{ab} > \frac{2ab}{a+b}$.

Hence, G.M. $>$ H.M. (Note if $a = b$ then G.M. $=$ H.M.)

POSTASSESSMENT

1. Find the A.M., G.M., and H.M. for each of the following:
   a. 20 and 60 b. 25 and 45 c. 3, 15, and 45
2. Arrange the G.M., H.M., and A.M. in ascending order of magnitude.
3. Show that for two given numbers the G.M. is the geometric mean between the A.M. and H.M.
4. Prove that the G.M. $>$ H.M. for a, b, and c.

REFERENCE

Posamentier, A. S., and H. A. Hauptman. *101 Plus Great Ideas for Introducing Key Concepts in Mathematics.* Thousand Oaks, CA: Corwin, 2006.

Unit 99

Pascal's Pyramid

The ability to expand and generalize is one of the most important facilities a teacher can help a student develop. In this unit, the familiar application of Pascal's triangle to determine the coefficients of a binomial expansion $(a + b)^n$ is expanded by the use of "Pascal's pyramid" to consider the coefficients of $(a + b + c)^n$.

PERFORMANCE OBJECTIVES

1. *Students will evaluate trinomial expansions $(a + b + c)^n$ of lower powers.*
2. *Students will discover important relationships between Pascal's triangle and Pascal's pyramid.*

PREASSESSMENT

If your students are familiar with Pascal's triangle, have them perform the following expansions:

a. $(a + b)^3$
b. $(a - b)^4$
c. $(x + 2y)^5$

Ask your students to test their algebraic multiplication (and patience) by evaluating

a. $(a + b + c)^3$
b. $(a + b + c)^4$

TEACHING STRATEGIES

Begin by reviewing Pascal's triangle. You might mention that this triangle is not Pascal's alone. In fact, the triangle was well known in China before 1300 and was also known to Omar Khayyam, author of the *Rubiyat*, almost 600 years before Pascal. Historical accuracy aside, each row of Pascal's (or Khayyam's or Ying Hui's) triangle yields the coefficients of $(a + b)^n$.

1	$(a + b)^0$
1 1	$(a + b)^1$
1 2 1	$(a + b)^2$
1 3 3 1	$(a + b)^3$
1 4 6 4 1	$(a + b)^4$
1 5 10 10 5 1	$(a + b)^5$

For example, to find $(a + b)^4$ use the coefficients in row 5 of the triangle: $a^4 + 4a^3b + 6a^2b^2 + 4ab^3 + b^4$.

Whereas a binomial expansion can be represented by a readily visible triangle, the trinomial expansion is represented by the more complex pyramid. The first expansion $(a + b + c)^0$ has the single coefficient 1. We can visualize this as the vertex of the pyramid. Each succeeding expansion is then represented by a triangular cross section of the pyramid with the coefficient 1 at each of the vertices.

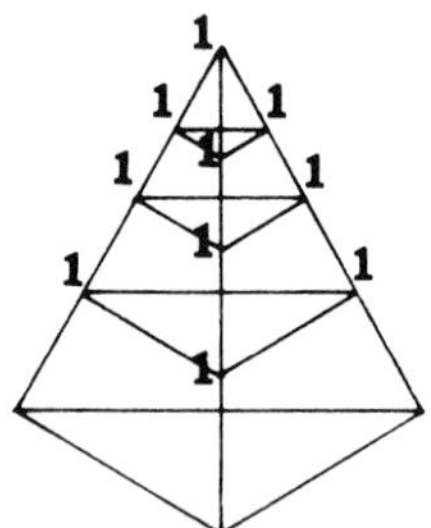

FIGURE 1

Therefore each of the lateral edges of the pyramid consists of a sequence of 1s. The second expansion $(a + b + c)^1$ has coefficients $1a + 1b + 1c$, which are represented by the first layer triangle with entries only at the vertices,

1
1 1.

There are two methods of generating the coefficients of higher powers by means of the pyramid. In the first, again consider each expansion as a triangular cross section of a pyramid. The numbers on the outer edge of each layer (the numbers between the vertices) are found by adding the two numbers that lie directly above. For example, $(a + b + c)^2$ has 1s at each vertex, and 2s between

1
2 2
1 2 1

To determine the terms in the interior of the triangle, add the three terms that lie above; for example, $(a + b + c)^3$ has the following coefficients:

1
3 3
3 6 3
1 3 3 1

or referring to the pyramid:

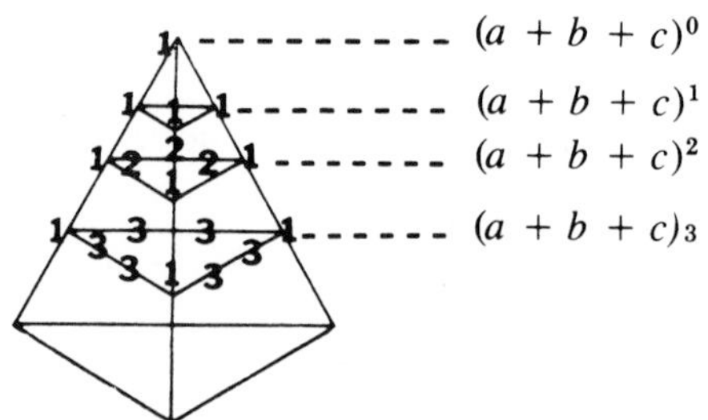

FIGURE 2

To assign these coefficients to the correct variables:

1. let the coefficient in the first row of the pyramid be "a" to the highest power of that expansion;
2. let the elements of the second row be the coefficients of the product of "a" to the second highest power and the other variables to the first power;
3. in the third row again decrease the power of "a" and arrange the other variables such that the sum of the exponents of each term equals the power the original expansion was raised to;
4. within each row the powers of "a" remain the same while the power of "b" decreases left to right and the power of "c" increases.

Specifically, consider $(a + b + c)^3$, which has a coefficient configuration:

1
3 3
3 6 3
1 3 3 1

The full expansion would then be $a^3 + 3a^2b + 3a^2c + 3ab^2 + 6abc + 3ac^2 + b^3 + 3b^2c + 3bc^2 + c^3$.

In working with these pyramids students may notice that the edge of each triangle corresponds exactly to a row of the Pascal triangle, i.e., the edge of $(a + b + c)^3$, 1 3 3 1, is the same as the fourth row in Pascal's triangle. This observation leads to the second method of deriving the pyramid.

Let the left edge of the trinomial expansion be represented by the corresponding row of Pascal's triangle. Then multiply each row of Pascal's triangle by the number on the left edge to generate the coefficients for the trinomial expansion. For example, the left edge of $(a + b + c)^4$ will be 1 4 6 4 1, corresponding to the fifth row of Pascal's triangle.

1	(1×1)
1 1	$(4 \times 1)(4 \times 1)$
1 2 1	$(6 \times 1)(6 \times 2)(6 \times 1)$
1 3 3 1	$(4 \times 1)(4 \times 3)(4 \times 3)(4 \times 1)$
1 4 6 4 1	$(1 \times 1)(1 \times 4)(1 \times 6)(1 \times 4)(1 \times 1)$

Multiplying these elements along the edge by the consecutive rows of the triangle yields $(a + b + c)^4$.

$$\begin{array}{ccccccccc} & & & & 1 & & & & \\ & & & 4 & & 4 & & & \\ & & 6 & & 12 & & 6 & & \\ & 4 & & 12 & & 12 & & 4 & \\ 1 & & 4 & & 6 & & 4 & & 1 \end{array}$$

This may at first appear to be a complicated procedure, but practice in its use will clear up initial confusion and introduce an intriguing and useful technique.

POSTASSESSMENT

1. Have the students compare the time required to expand $(a + b + c)^4$ algebraically versus the pyramid expansion.
2. Expand $(a + b + c)^5$, $(a + b + c)^6$.
3. Expand $(a + 2b + 3c)^3$, $(a + 4b + c)^4$.
4. Some students may be interested in constructing a working model of the pyramid, composed of detachable triangular sections with the appropriate coefficients noted on each surface.

Unit 100

The Multinomial Theorem

This unit should be used with a class that has already studied the Binomial Theorem.

PERFORMANCE OBJECTIVES

1. *Students will find the coefficient of any given term of a given multinomial expansion without actually expanding it.*
2. *Students will justify the existence of the coefficients of the multinomial expansion.*
3. *Students will successfully apply the Multinomial Theorem to a given trinomial.*

PREASSESSMENT

Have students expand $(a + b)^4$ by using the Binomial Theorem. Ask students to determine the number of different arrangements that can be formed from the letters AAABBBCC.

TEACHING STRATEGIES

Begin by reviewing student responses concerning the number of arrangements of AAABBBCC. They should realize that this problem differs from asking them to determine the number of arrangements of ABCDEFGH (where each symbol to be arranged is different from the rest). In the latter case the first place (of the eight places) can be filled in any one of eight ways, the second place can be filled in any one of seven ways, the third in six ways, the fourth in five ways, . . . , the eighth in only one way. Using the counting principle, the total number of ways is $8 \cdot 7 \cdot 6 \cdot 5 \cdot 4 \cdot 3 \cdot 2 \cdot 1 = 8!$ (read "8 factorial").

Having already studied the Binomial Theorem, students should be familiar with the basic concepts of *combinations*. That is, ${}_nC_r = \binom{n}{r} = \frac{nPr}{r!} = \frac{n!}{r!(n-r)!}$.

Students should now be ready to consider the original problem, finding the number of arrangements of AAABBBCC. They should be carefully led through the following development.

Let #(A) represent the "number of ways of selecting positions for the As." Because there are three As, from the 8 positions 3 must be selected. This can be done ${}_8C_3$ or $\binom{8}{3}$ ways. Hence $= \binom{8}{3} = \frac{8!}{3! \cdot 5!}$.

Similarly $\#(B) = \binom{5}{3} = \frac{5!}{3! \cdot 2!}$, because 3 positions for the three Bs must be selected from the remaining 5 positions. This leaves 2 positions to be selected for the two Cs. Since only 2 positions remain, there is only one way of selecting these 2 positions, that is $\binom{2}{2} = \frac{2!}{2! \cdot 0!} = 1$. Indicate that $0! = 1$ by definition. By using the counting principle. $\#(\text{A and B and C}) = \#(A) \cdot \#(B) \cdot \#(C) =$

$$\frac{8!}{3! \cdot 5!} \cdot \frac{5!}{3! \cdot 2!} \cdot \frac{2!}{2! \cdot 0!} = \frac{8!}{3! \cdot 3! \cdot 2!}.$$

This last expression is usually symbolized as $\binom{8}{3,3,2}$, which represents the number of ways of arranging 8 items consisting of repetitions of 3 items, 3 items, and 2 items.

To reinforce this technique, ask your students to determine the number of ways in which the letters of *Mississippi* can be arranged. Taking into consideration the repetitions (i.e., 1-M, 4-Is, 4-Ss, 2-Ps) students should obtain

$$\frac{11 \quad 10 \quad 9 \quad \not{8} \quad 7 \quad \not{6} \quad 5 \quad \not{4} \quad \not{3} \quad \not{2} \quad \not{1}}{1 \quad \not{4} \quad \not{3} \quad \not{2} \quad 1 \quad \not{4} \quad \not{3} \quad \not{2} \quad 1 \quad \not{2} \quad \not{1}} = 34{,}650.$$

Students should now be guided to generalizing this scheme for counting to n items that include n_1 items of one kind, n_2 items of another, n_3 items of a third kind, . . . , n_r items of a last kind. Clearly $n_1 + n_2 + n_3 + \ldots + n_r = n$. Applying the scheme from before, #(N_1) shall represent "the number of ways in which n_1 positions may be selected from the n positions available." Hence $\#(N_1) = \frac{n!}{n_1!(n-n_1)!}$. Similarly, $\#(N_2) = \frac{(n-n_1)!}{n_2!(n-n_1-n_2)!}$, since only $n - n_1$ places remained from which to select n_2 positions. Similarly, $\#(N_r) = \frac{(n-n_1-n_2-\ldots-n_{r-1})!}{n_r!(n-n_1-n_2-\ldots-n_r)!}$. Since $n_1 + n_2 + n_3 + \ldots + n_r = n$, $\#(N_r)\ldots 1, \frac{n_r!}{n_r!\cdot 0!} = 1$.

Using the counting principle for these r cases the numbers of ways of arranging these n items (with r items being repeated) is obtained:

$$\frac{n!}{n_1!(n-n_1)!}\cdot\frac{(n-n_1)!}{n_2!(n-n_1-n_2)!}\cdot\frac{(n-n_1-n_2)!}{n_3!(n-n_1-n_2-n_3)!}\ldots\cdot 1 = \frac{n!}{n_1!\cdot n_2!\cdot n_3!\ldots n_r!} = \binom{n}{n_1,n_2,n_3,\ldots,n_r},$$

which is a convenient symbol to use here.

Students should apply this general formula to the case where $r = 2$. They will get $\binom{n}{n_1 n_2} = \frac{n!}{n_1!\cdot n_2!} = \frac{n!}{n_1!(n-n_1)!}$, which is the familiar ${}_nC_{n_1}$ or $\binom{n}{n_1}$.

The students should now be ready to tackle the Multinomial Theorem. In the preassessment they were asked to expand $(a + b)^4$. They should note that certain terms appear more than once. For example, the term *aaab*, commonly written a^3b, appears $\binom{4}{3}$ times. This corresponds to the number of arrangements of *aaab*. For each such term the same argument holds.

Students should now consider the expansion of $(a + b + c)^4$. To actually compute this expansion, students may multiply a different combination of the members of each of the factors to obtain each term. For example, some of the 81 terms will appear as *aaaa*, *aaab*, *aabb*, *abac*, *abab*, *cbcb*,.... These are commonly written as $a^4, a^3b, a^2b^2, a^2bc, a^2b^2, b^2c^2$. In the above list a^2b^2 appeared twice; however, in the complete expansion (of 81 terms) it would appear $\binom{4}{2,2,0} = \frac{4!}{2!\ 2!\ 0!} = 6$ times. Thus if a student were asked to find the coefficient of the term a^3bc^2 in the expansion $(a + b + c)^6$, he would merely evaluate $\binom{6}{3,1,2} = \frac{6!}{3!\cdot 1!\cdot 2!} = 60$. Hence the entire expansion may be written as $(a+b+c)^4 = \sum_{n_1+n_2+n_3=4} \frac{4!}{n_1!\cdot n_2!\cdot n_3!}\cdot a^{n_1}\cdot b^{n_2}\cdot c^{n_3}$.

From here the general Multinomial Theorem follows easily:

$$(a_1 + a_2 + a_3 + \ldots + a_r)^n = \sum_{n_1+n_2+\ldots+n_r=n} \frac{n!}{n_1!\cdot n_2!\cdot\ldots\cdot n_r!}\cdot a_1^{n_1}\cdot a_2^{n_2}\cdot a_3^{n_3}\cdot\ldots\cdot a_r^{n_r}.$$

Although rather cumbersome, some students might wish to prove this theorem by mathematical induction.

Following are two applications of the Multinomial Theorem.

1. Expand and simplify: $(2x + y - z)^3$

$$\begin{aligned}
&= \binom{3}{3,0,0}(2x)^3(y)^0(-z)^0 + \binom{3}{0,3,0}(2x)^0(y)^3(-z)^0\\
&+ \binom{3}{0,0,3}(2x)^0(y)^0(-z)^3 + \binom{3}{2,1,0}(2x)^2(y)^1(-z)^0\\
&+ \binom{3}{2,0,1}(2x)^2(y)^0(-z)^1 + \binom{3}{1,1,1}(2x)^1(y)^1(-z)^1\\
&+ \binom{3}{0,2,1}(2x)^0(y)^2(-z)^1 + \binom{3}{0,1,2}(2x)^0(y)^1(-z)^2\\
&+ \binom{3}{1,2,0}(2x)^1(y)^2(-z)^0 + \binom{3}{1,0,2}(2x)^1(y)^0(-z)^2
\end{aligned}$$

$$(2x + y - z)^3 = 8x^3 + y^3 - z^3 + 12x^2y - 12x^2z + 6xy^2 + 6xz^2 - 12xyz - 3y^2z + 3yz^2.$$

2. Find the term in the expansion of $\left(2x^2 - y^3 + \frac{1}{2}z\right)^3$ that contains x^4 and z^4. The general term of the expansion is $\binom{7}{a,b,c}(2x^2)^a(-y^3)^b\left(\frac{1}{2}z\right)^c$, where $a + b + c = 7$. Thus the terms containing x^4 and z^4 have $a = 2$ and $c = 4$, $\therefore b = 1$. Substituting in the above gives

$$\binom{7}{2,1,4}(2x^2)^2(-y^3)^1\left(\frac{1}{2}z\right)^4 = \frac{7!}{2!1!4!}(4x^4)(-y^3)\times\left(\frac{1}{16}z^4\right) = \frac{-105}{4}x^4y^3z^4.$$

POSTASSESSMENT

1. Have students find the coefficient of a^2b^5d in the expansion of $(a + b - c - d)^8$.
2. Ask students to explain how the coefficients for any term of a multinomial expansion are derived.
3. Have students expand $(2x + y^2 - 3)^5$.

Unit 101

Algebraic Solution of Cubic Equations

People's interest in cubic equations can be traced back to the times of the early Babylonians about 1800–1600 B.C. However, the algebraic solution of third degree equations is a product of the Italian Renaissance.

The algebraic solution of cubic equations is thus associated with the names of the Italian mathematicians Scipione del Ferro, Nicolo de Brescia (called Tartaglia), Girolamo Cardan, and Rafael Bombelli.

PERFORMANCE OBJECTIVES

1. *Given some cubic equations, students will find their solutions.*
2. *Given a verbal problem that calls for a solution of a cubic equation, students will determine (where applicable) the real solutions to the problem.*

PREASSESSMENT

Students should have mastered operations with quadratic equations. They should also have a solid background in complex numbers and trigonometry.

TEACHING STRATEGIES

Review roots of complex numbers in the following fashion:

The nth root of a complex number z is obtained by taking the nth root of the absolute value r, and dividing the amplitude ϕ by n. This will give you the principal value of that root. The general formula to get all the roots of z is

$$\sqrt[n]{z} = \sqrt[n]{r}\left[\operatorname{Cos}\frac{\phi + 2k\pi}{n} + i \operatorname{Sin}\frac{\phi + 2k\pi}{n}\right].$$

For $k = 0$, this yields the principal value, and for $k = 1, 2, 3, \ldots, n - 1$, we get the rest of the roots.

Example 1

Find the cube roots of unity. We have that $1 = \operatorname{Cos} 0° + i \operatorname{Sin} 0°$, therefore, $\phi = 0°$ and $r = 1$. The general formula is then, $z = \operatorname{Cos}\frac{2k\pi}{3} + i\operatorname{Sin}\frac{2k\pi}{3}$, where $k = 0,1$, and 2.

If $k = 0$, $z_1 = \operatorname{Cos} 0 + i \operatorname{Sin} 0 = 1$ (Principal value)

If $k = 1$, $z_2 = \operatorname{Cos}\frac{2\pi}{3} + i\operatorname{Sin}\frac{2\pi}{3} = \operatorname{Cos} 120° + i \operatorname{Sin} 120°$

$$= -\operatorname{Cos} 60° + i \operatorname{Sin} 60° = -\frac{1}{2} + \frac{\sqrt{3}}{2}i$$

If $k = 2$, $z_3 = \operatorname{Cos}\frac{4\pi}{3} + i\operatorname{Sin}\frac{4\pi}{3} = \operatorname{Cos} 240° + i \operatorname{Sin} 240°$

$$= -\operatorname{Cos} 60° - i \operatorname{Sin} 60° = -\frac{1}{2} - \frac{\sqrt{3}}{2}i$$

Notice that each one of the complex roots of unity generates the other roots. To do so, we only have to take the second and third powers of those roots. For example,

if we take $\alpha = z_2 = -\frac{1}{2} + \frac{\sqrt{3}}{2}i$, we get

$$\alpha^2 = \left(-\frac{1}{2} + \frac{\sqrt{3}}{2}i\right)^2 = \left(-\frac{1}{2}\right)^2 + 2\left(-\frac{1}{2}\right)\left(\frac{\sqrt{3}}{2}i\right) + \left(\frac{\sqrt{3}}{2}i\right)^2$$

$$\alpha^2 = \frac{1}{4} - \frac{\sqrt{3}}{2}i + \frac{3}{4}i^2, \text{ but } i^2 = -1, \text{ thus,}$$

$$\alpha^2 = \frac{1}{4} - \frac{3}{4} - \frac{\sqrt{3}}{2}i = -\frac{1}{2} - \frac{\sqrt{3}}{2}i = z_3.$$

Similarly,

$$\alpha^3 = \alpha^2 \cdot \alpha = \left(-\frac{1}{2} - \frac{\sqrt{3}}{2}i\right)\left(-\frac{1}{2} + \frac{\sqrt{3}}{2}i\right)$$

$$\alpha^3 = \left(-\frac{1}{2}\right)^2 - \left(\frac{\sqrt{3}}{2}i\right)^2 = \frac{1}{4} - \frac{3}{4}i^2$$

$$= \frac{1}{4} + \frac{3}{4} = 1 = z_1.$$

Therefore, the three roots of unity are 1, α and α^2 where α can be either $z_2 = -\frac{1}{2} + \frac{\sqrt{3}}{2}i$ or $z_3 = -\frac{1}{2} - \frac{\sqrt{3}}{2}i$.

Example 2

Find the cubic roots of the real number a. We have that $a = a\ (\text{Cos } 0° + i \text{ Sin } 0°)$; therefore, $\sqrt[3]{a} = \sqrt[3]{r}\left(\text{Cos }\frac{2k\pi}{3} - i \text{ Sin }\frac{2k\pi}{3}\right)$, where $k = 0$, 1 or 2. But, $\text{Cos }\frac{2k\pi}{3} - i \text{ Sin }\frac{2k\pi}{3}$ where $k = 0$,1 or 2, will give the three roots of unity (see Example 1). Thus, if the real root of a is a', the three roots of a will be a', $a'\alpha$, and $a'\alpha^2$, where α can be either $-\frac{1}{2} + \frac{\sqrt{3}}{2}i$, or $-\frac{1}{2} - \frac{\sqrt{3}}{2}i$.

Let us now consider the general cubic equation:

$$ax^3 + bx^2 + cx + d = 0,$$

where a, b, c, and d are arbitrary complex numbers. This equation can be reduced to a simpler form without the second degree term, by making the transformation $x = y - \frac{b}{3a}$. Thus, we have

$$a\left(y - \frac{b}{3a}\right)^3 + b\left(y - \frac{b}{3a}\right)^2 + c\left(y - \frac{b}{3a}\right) + d = 0$$

$$a\left(y^3 - \frac{b}{a}y^2 + \frac{b^2}{3a^2}y - \frac{b}{27a^3}\right) + b\left(y^2 - \frac{2b}{3a}y + \frac{b^2}{9a^2}\right) c\left(y - \frac{b}{3a}\right) + d = 0, \text{ and we have}$$

$$ay^3 + \left(\frac{b^2}{3a} - \frac{2b^2}{3a} + c\right)y + \left(-\frac{b^3}{27a^2} + \frac{b^3}{9a^2} - \frac{bc}{3a} + d\right) = 0.$$

Now, if we make $\frac{b^2}{3a} - \frac{2b^2}{3a} + c = c'$ and $\frac{-b^3}{27a^2} + \frac{b^3}{9a^2} - \frac{bc}{3a} + d = d'$, the general equation will become

$$ay^3 + c'y + d' = 0.$$

To avoid fractions in the solution of this equation, we divide it by a, and write it in the following fashion:

$$y^3 + 3py + 2q = 0$$

This last equation is called the reduced cubic equation and, as we have shown, any cubic equation can be reduced to that form.

To solve the reduced equation, the following identity is considered:

$$(a + b)^3 - 3ab(a + b) - (a^3 + b^3) = 0$$

If this identity is compared with the reduced equation, we have that

$$a + b = y,\ ab = -p, \text{ and } a^3 + b^3 = -2q.$$

From these equations, we see that we only have to find the values of a and b to find y. This can be done by solving the system

$$\begin{matrix} ab = -p \\ a^3 + b^3 = -2q \end{matrix} \quad \text{or} \quad \begin{matrix} a^3b^3 = -p^3 \\ a^3 + b^3 = -2q \end{matrix}$$

From the second equation we have that $b^3 = -2q - a^3$, and substituting this value in the first equation, we have $-a^3\ (2q + a^3) = -p^3$, therefore, $a^6 + 2a^3q - p^3 = 0$.

If we make $a^3 = v$, we obtain the following quadratic equation: $v^2 + 2qv - p^3 = 0$.

The roots of this quadratic equation are

$$v_1 = -q + \sqrt{q^2 + p^3} \quad \text{and}$$
$$v_2 = -q - \sqrt{q^2 + p^3}.$$

Because of the symmetry of a and b in the system, we can take v_1 or v_2 to be a^3 or b^3 randomly.

So, $a^3 = -q + \sqrt{q^2 + p^3}$ and
$b^3 = -q - \sqrt{q^2 + p^3}$.

Therefore, $a = \sqrt[3]{-q + \sqrt{q^2 + p^3}}$ and

$$b = \sqrt[3]{-q - \sqrt{q^2 + p^3}}.$$

But $y = a + b$, thus,

$$y = \sqrt[3]{-q + \sqrt{q^2 + p^3}} + \sqrt[3]{-q - \sqrt{q^2 + p^3}},$$

which is called Cardan's formula for the cubic.

Since a^3 and b^3 have three roots each, it seems that the equation has nine roots. This is not the case, for since $ab = -p$, the cubic roots of a^3 and b^3 are to be taken in pairs so that their product (which is ab) is a rational number $-p$.

Now, we know that the cubic roots of a^3 are a (the principal value), $a\alpha$, and $a\alpha^2$, where α is one of the complex roots of unity. Similarly, the cubic roots of b^3 are b, $b\alpha$, and $b\alpha^2$.

However, if the product of a and b must be rational, we have that the only admissible solutions are (a, b), $(a\alpha, b\alpha^2)$, and $(a\alpha^2, b\alpha)$, because

$$ab = -p$$
$$a\alpha \cdot b\alpha^2 = ab\alpha^3 = ab = -p \text{ (because } \alpha^3 = 1)$$
$$a\alpha^2 \cdot b\alpha = ab\alpha^3 = ab = -p.$$

Therefore, the values of y are $a + b$, $a\alpha + b\alpha^2$, and $a\alpha^2 + b\alpha$.

But $x = y - \frac{b}{3a}$, and so the roots of the general cubic equation will be found once we know y.

Example 3

Solve the equation $x^3 + 3x^2 + 9x - 13 = 0$. First, we must reduce this equation to eliminate the second degree term. The transformation is $x = y - \frac{b}{3a}$. In this example, $a = 1$, $b = 3$, $c = 9$, and $d = -13$. Therefore, $x = y - \frac{3}{3(1)} = y - 1$.

Thus, substituting $y - 1$ for x in the equation, $(y - 1)^3 + 3(y - 1)^2 + 9(y - 1) - 13 = 0$, or $(y^3 - 3y^2 + 3y - 1) + 3(y^2 - 2y + 1) + 9(y - 1) - 13 = 0$. So, $y^3 - 6y - 20 = 0$ is the reduced equation.

Therefore,

$$3p = 6, p = 2, \text{ and } p^3 = 8$$
$$2q = -20, q = -10, \text{ and } q^2 = 100.$$

Thus, $\sqrt{q^2 + p^3} = \sqrt{108} = 6\sqrt{3}$, and,

$$a = \sqrt[3]{10 + 6\sqrt{3}} = \sqrt[3]{1 + 3\sqrt{3} + 9 + 3\sqrt{3}}$$
$$= \sqrt[3]{(1 + \sqrt{3})^3} = 1 + \sqrt{3}$$
$$b = \sqrt[3]{10 - 6\sqrt{3}} = \sqrt[3]{1 - 3\sqrt{3} + 9 - 3\sqrt{3}}$$
$$= \sqrt[3]{(1 - \sqrt{3})^3} = 1 - \sqrt{3}.$$

The solutions for the reduced equation are then

$$y_1 = a + b = (1 + \sqrt{3}) + (1 - \sqrt{3}) = 2$$
$$y_2 = a\alpha + b\alpha^2 = (1 + \sqrt{3})\left(-\frac{1}{2} + \frac{\sqrt{3}}{2}i\right)$$
$$+ (1 - \sqrt{3})\left(-\frac{1}{2} - \frac{\sqrt{3}}{2}i\right) = -1 + 3i$$
$$y_3 = a\alpha^2 + b\alpha = \left(1 + \sqrt{3}\right)\left(-\frac{1}{2} - \frac{\sqrt{3}}{2}i\right)$$
$$+ (1 - \sqrt{3})\left(-\frac{1}{2} + \frac{\sqrt{3}}{2}i\right)$$
$$= -1 - 3i.$$

But, $x = y - 1$. Therefore:

$$x_1 = y_1 - 1 = 2 - 1 = 1$$
$$x_2 = y_2 - 1 = -1 + 3i - 1 = -2 + 3i$$
$$x_3 = y_3 - 1 = -1 - 3i - 1 = -2 - 3i.$$

Thus, in this example, we have for solutions one real and two conjugate complex roots. In this first of two units, we have studied the general solution of the cubic. In a second, we will study the different cases, reducible and irreducible, in the solution of cubic equations using Cardan's formula.

POSTASSESSMENT

1. Find the roots of $x^3 + 6x^2 + 17x + 18 = 0$.
2. Solve $x^3 - 11x^2 + 35x - 25 = 0$.
3. Find the solution of $x^3 - 3x^2 + 3x - 1 = 0$.

Unit 102

Solving Cubic Equations

In the first of two units on cubic equations, we have studied the general solution of the cubic. In this second, we will study the different cases, reducible and irreducible, in the solution of cubic equations using Cardan's formula.

PERFORMANCE OBJECTIVES

1. *Given some cubic equations, students will analyze them to see the kind of solutions they are going to obtain when the equation is solved.*
2. *Students will solve given cubic equations.*

PREASSESSMENT

Students should have mastered operations with complex numbers and quadratic equations. They should also have a solid background in trigonometry.

TEACHING STRATEGIES

Review the content of the previous unit on cubic equations in the following fashion:

Given a general cubic equation $Ax^3 + Bx^2 + Cx + D = 0$, it is always possible to eliminate the second degree term by making the change of variables $x = y - \frac{B}{3A}$. This transformation will lead to an equation of the form $y^3 + 3py + 2q = 0$, which is called the reduced or normal cubic equation.

The solution of the reduced equation is given by the Cardan's formula $y = \sqrt[3]{-q + \sqrt{q^2 + p^3}} + \sqrt[3]{-q - \sqrt{q^2 + p^3}}$. If $a = \sqrt[3]{-q + \sqrt{q^2 + p^3}}$ and $b = \sqrt[3]{-q - \sqrt{q^2 + p^3}}$, the roots of the reduced equations are $y_1 = a + b$, $y_2 = a\alpha + b\alpha^2$, and $y_3 = y_3 = a\alpha^2 + b\alpha$, where $\alpha = -\frac{1}{2} + \frac{\sqrt{3}}{2}i$ and $\alpha^2 = \frac{1}{2} - \frac{\sqrt{3}}{2}i$ are cube roots of unity.

Once the values y_1, y_2, and y_3 are found, the solutions of the general cubic equation will be obtained by using the transformation $x = y - \frac{B}{3A}$.

From the Cardan's formula, it is obvious that the nature of the solutions will depend on the value of $q^2 + p^3$, which for this reason is called the discriminant of the cubic. This is so, because $q^2 + p^3$, being under a square root, will yield real or imaginary values according to the sign of the sum $q^2 + p^3$.

Before discussing the discriminant, it is useful to rewrite solutions of the reduced equation in the following fashion:

$$y_1 = a + b;\ y_2 = a\alpha + b\alpha^2 = a\left(-\frac{1}{2} + \frac{\sqrt{3}}{2}i\right) + b\left(-\frac{1}{2} - \frac{\sqrt{3}}{2}i\right);\ y_3 = a\alpha^2 + b\alpha = a\left(-\frac{1}{2} - \frac{\sqrt{3}}{2}i\right) + b\left(-\frac{1}{2} + \frac{\sqrt{3}}{2}i\right)$$

and simplifying:

$$y_1 = a + b;\ y_2 = -\frac{a+b}{2} + \frac{a-b}{2}\sqrt{3}i;$$

$$y_3 = -\frac{a+b}{2} - \frac{a-b}{2}\sqrt{3}i.$$

Let us now consider the discriminant $q^2 + p^3$.

1. If $q^2 + p^3 > 0$, a and b have each one real value, then we can suppose a and b will be real also. Consequently, $a + b$ and $a - b$ will be real also. Therefore, we have that if $a + b = m$ and $a - b = n$, the solutions of the reduced equation are

$$y_1 = a + b = m;\ y_2 = -\frac{m}{2} + \frac{n}{2}\sqrt{3}i;$$

$$y_3 = -\frac{m}{2} - \frac{n}{2}\sqrt{3}i.$$

Thus, if $q^2 + p^3 > 0$, we have one real root and two conjugate imaginary roots.

Example 1

Solve $x^3 - 6x^2 + 10x - 8 = 0$.

First, we must eliminate the square term. The transformation for this example is

$$x = y - \frac{B}{3A} = y - \frac{-6}{3} = y + 2.$$

Thus, substituting $y + 2$ for x in the equation

$$(y+2)^3 - 6(y+2)^2 + 10(y+2) - 8 = 0$$
$$y^3 + 6y^2 + 12y + 8 - 6y^2 - 24y - 24 + 10y + 20 - 8 = 0$$
$$y^3 - 2y - 4 = 0 \text{ (Reduced equation)}$$

Therefore:

$$3p = -2 \quad p = -\frac{2}{3} \quad \text{and} \quad p^3 = -\frac{8}{27}$$
$$2q = -4 \quad q = -2 \quad \text{and} \quad q^2 = 4$$

Thus, $q^2 + p^3 = 4 - \frac{8}{27} = \frac{100}{27} > 0$.

Therefore, we know that in the solution one root must be real and two conjugate imaginary.

The values for a and b are

$$a = \sqrt[3]{-q + \sqrt{q^2 + p^3}} = \sqrt[3]{2 + \sqrt{\frac{100}{27}}} = \sqrt[3]{2 + \frac{10}{3\sqrt{3}}}$$

$$b = \sqrt[3]{-q - \sqrt{q^2 + p^3}} = \sqrt[3]{2 - \sqrt{\frac{100}{27}}} = \sqrt[3]{2 - \frac{10}{3\sqrt{3}}}$$

and simplifying:

$$a = \sqrt[3]{\frac{6\sqrt{3} + 10}{3\sqrt{3}}} = \sqrt[3]{\frac{3\sqrt{3} + 9 + 3\sqrt{3} + 1}{\sqrt{27}}} = \sqrt[3]{\frac{(3-1)^3}{\sqrt{27}}}$$

$$b = \sqrt[3]{\frac{6\sqrt{3} - 10}{3\sqrt{3}}} = \sqrt[3]{\frac{3\sqrt{3} - 9 + 3\sqrt{3} - 1}{\sqrt{27}}} = \sqrt[3]{\frac{(\sqrt{3}-1)^3}{\sqrt{27}}}$$

$$a = \frac{\sqrt{3}+1}{\sqrt{3}} \text{ and } b = \frac{\sqrt{3}-1}{\sqrt{3}}.$$

The solutions for the reduced equation are then

$$y_1 = a + b = \frac{\sqrt{3}+1}{\sqrt{3}} + \frac{\sqrt{3}-1}{\sqrt{3}} = 2$$

$$y_2 = a\alpha + b\alpha^2 = \left(\frac{\sqrt{3}+1}{\sqrt{3}}\right)\left(-\frac{1}{2} + \frac{\sqrt{3}}{2}i\right) + \left(\frac{\sqrt{3}-1}{\sqrt{3}}\right)\left(\frac{1}{2} - \frac{\sqrt{3}}{2}i\right)$$

$$y_3 = a\alpha^2 + b\alpha = \left(\frac{\sqrt{3}+1}{\sqrt{3}}\right)\left(\frac{1}{2} - \frac{\sqrt{3}}{2}i\right) + \left(\frac{\sqrt{3}-1}{\sqrt{3}}\right)\left(-\frac{1}{2} + \frac{\sqrt{3}}{2}i\right)$$

and simplifying

$$y_1 = 2; y_2 = -1 + i; y_3 = -1 - i.$$

Therefore the solutions of the general equation are

$$x_1 = y_1 + 2 = 2 + 2 = 4$$
$$x_2 = y_2 + 2 = -1 + i + 2 = 1 + i$$
$$x_3 = y_3 + 2 = -1 - i + 2 = 1 - i.$$

2. If $q^2 + p^3 = 0$, a and b are equal; therefore if m represents the common real value of a and b, we have

$$y_1 = m + m = 2m$$
$$y_2 = -\frac{m+m}{2} + \frac{m-m}{2}\sqrt{3}i = -m$$
$$y_3 = -\frac{m+m}{2} - \frac{m-m}{2}\sqrt{3}i = -m.$$

Thus, in this case we have that all the roots are real and two are equal.

Example 2
Find the roots of $x^3 - 12x + 16 = 0$. In this example we already have the reduced equation, therefore:

$$3p = -12 \quad p = -4 \quad \text{and} \quad p^3 = -64$$
$$2q = 16 \quad q = 8 \quad \text{and} \quad q^2 = 64.$$

Thus, $q^2 + p^3 = 64 - 64 = 0$. This means that the solution will have three real roots, two of them equal. The values of a and b are

$$a = \sqrt[3]{-q + \sqrt{q^2 + p^3}} = \sqrt[3]{-8} = -2$$
$$b = \sqrt[3]{-q - \sqrt{q^2 + p^3}} = \sqrt[3]{-8} = -2.$$

Therefore the roots are

$$y_1 = a + b = -4$$
$$y_2 = a\alpha + b\alpha^2 = -2(\alpha + \alpha^2)$$
$$= -2\left(-\frac{1}{2} + \frac{\sqrt{3}}{2}i - \frac{1}{2} - \frac{\sqrt{3}}{2}i\right) = 2$$
$$y_3 = a\alpha^2 + b\alpha = -2(\alpha^2 + \alpha)$$
$$= -2\left(-\frac{1}{2} - \frac{\sqrt{3}}{2}i - \frac{1}{2} + \frac{\sqrt{3}}{2}i\right) = 2.$$

3. If $q^2 + p^3 < 0$, a and b will be complex numbers because of the square root of the discriminant, which is negative in this case. Therefore, if the values a and b are $a = \text{M} + \text{N}i$ and $b = \text{M} - \text{N}i$, the solutions of the reduced equation will be

$$y_1 = a + b = 2\text{M}$$
$$y_2 = -\frac{2\text{M}}{2} + \frac{2\text{N}i}{2}\sqrt{3}i = -\text{M} - \sqrt{3}\text{N}$$
$$y_3 = -\frac{2\text{M}}{2} - \frac{2\text{N}i}{2}\sqrt{3}i = -\text{M} + \sqrt{3}\text{N},$$

which are all real roots and unequal.

However, there is no general arithmetic or algebraic method of finding the exact value of the cubic root of complex numbers. Therefore, Cardan's formula is of little use in this case, which for this reason is called the irreducible case.

The solution of this case can be obtained with the use of trigonometry. Thus, when the Cardan's formula has the form $y = \sqrt[3]{u + vi} + \sqrt[3]{u - vi}$, we call $r = \sqrt{u^2 + v^2}$ and $\tan\Theta = \frac{v}{u}$; therefore, the cubic root of them will be

$$y = \sqrt[3]{r}\left[\text{Cos}\frac{\Theta + 2k\pi}{3} + i\,\text{Sin}\frac{\Theta + 2k\pi}{3}\right]$$
$$+ \sqrt[3]{r}\left[\text{Cos}\frac{\Theta + 2k\pi}{3} - i\,\text{Sin}\frac{\Theta + 2k\pi}{3}\right],$$

where $k = 0, 1$, and 2.

If we simplify this expression, we obtain $y = 2\sqrt[3]{r}\,\text{Cos}\frac{\Theta + 2k\pi}{3}$, where $k = 0, 1$, and 2. Therefore the three roots are

$$y_1 = 2\sqrt[3]{r}\,\text{Cos}\frac{\Theta}{3};\ y_2 = 2\sqrt[3]{r}\,\text{Cos}\frac{\Theta + 2\pi}{3};$$
$$y_3 = 2\sqrt[3]{r}\,\text{Cos}\frac{\Theta + 4\pi}{3}.$$

Example 3
Solve $x^3 - 6x - 4 = 0$.
From this equation, we have $3p = -6$ and $2q = -4$; therefore, $p^3 = -8$, $q^2 = 4$, $p^3 + q^2 = -4$ and $\sqrt{p^3 + q^2} = 2i$.

The solution then would be $y = \sqrt{2 + 2i} + \sqrt{2 - 2i}$, thus, $r = \sqrt{4 + 4} = \sqrt{8}$, $\tan\Theta = \frac{2}{2}$ or $\tan\Theta = 1$ and $\Theta = \frac{\pi}{4}$. Therefore, the roots of the equation are

$$x_1 = 2\sqrt[3]{r}\,\text{Cos}\frac{\Theta}{3} = 2\sqrt[3]{\sqrt{8}}\,\text{Cos}\frac{\pi}{12} = 2\sqrt{2}\,\text{Cos}\,15°$$
$$x_2 = 2\sqrt[3]{r}\,\text{Cos}\frac{\Theta + 2\pi}{3} = 2\sqrt{2}\,\text{Cos}\frac{\frac{\pi}{4} + 2\pi}{3}$$
$$= 2\sqrt{2}\,\text{Cos}\,135°$$
$$x_3 = 2\sqrt[3]{r}\,\text{Cos}\frac{\Theta + 14\pi}{3} = 2\sqrt{2}\,\text{Cos}\frac{\frac{\pi}{4} + 4\pi}{3} =$$
$$= 2\sqrt{2}\,\text{Cos}\,255°.$$

But,

$$\text{Sin}\frac{y}{2} = \sqrt{\frac{1 - \text{Cos}x}{2}} \quad \text{and} \quad \text{Cos}\frac{x}{2} = \sqrt{\frac{1 + \text{Cos}x}{2}}.$$

Therefore,

$$\text{Sin}\,15° = \sqrt{\frac{1 - \text{Cos}\,30°}{2}} = \sqrt{\frac{1 - \sqrt{3}/2}{2}}$$
$$= \frac{\sqrt{2 - \sqrt{3}}}{2}$$

and

$$\text{Cos } 15° = \sqrt{\frac{1 + \text{Cos } 30°}{2}} = \sqrt{\frac{1 + \sqrt{3}/2}{2}} = \frac{\sqrt{2 + \sqrt{3}}}{2}.$$

Thus, the roots are

$$x_1 = 2\sqrt{2}\frac{\sqrt{2 + \sqrt{3}}}{2} = \sqrt{4 + 2\sqrt{3}}$$
$$= \sqrt{1 + 2\sqrt{3} + 3} = 1 + \sqrt{3}$$
$$x_2 = 2\sqrt{2} \cos 135° = 2\sqrt{2}(-\cos 45°)$$
$$= 2\sqrt{2}\left(-\frac{\sqrt{2}}{3}\right) = -2$$

$$x_3 = 2\sqrt{2}(\sin 15°) = 2\sqrt{2}\left(\frac{\sqrt{2 - \sqrt{3}}}{2}\right)$$
$$= \sqrt{1 + 2\sqrt{3} + 3} = 1 - \sqrt{3}.$$

The reducible cases may also employ the aid of trigonometry.

POSTASSESSMENT

Analyze and then solve the following cubics:

1. $x^3 - 6x^2 + 11x - 6 = 0$
2. $x^3 - 5x^2 + 9x - 9 = 0$
3. $x^3 - 75x + 250 = 0$
4. $x^3 - 6x^2 + 3x + 10 = 0$

Unit 103

 Calculating Sums of Finite Series

Mathematical induction has become thoroughly entrenched in secondary school curricula. Many textbooks provide a variety of applications of this technique of proof. Most popular among these applications is proving that specific series have given formulas as sums. Although most students merely work the proof as required, some may question how the sum of a particular series was actually generated.

This unit will provide you with a response to students' requests for deriving formulas for certain series summations.

PERFORMANCE OBJECTIVES

1. *Given some finite series, students will find their sum.*
2. *Students will develop formulas for determining the sum of various finite series.*

PREASSESSMENT

Students should have mastered operations with algebraic expressions, functions, and concepts of finite sequence and series.

TEACHING STRATEGIES

Review concepts of sequences and series in the following fashion:

A *finite sequence* is a finite set of ordered elements or terms, each related to one or more of the preceding elements in some specifiable way.

Examples: 1. $1, 3, 5, 7, \ldots, 19$
2. $\sin x, \sin 2x, \sin 3x, \ldots, \sin 20x$
3. $2, 4, 6, 8, \ldots, 2n$

Let us now consider any finite sequence of elements $u_1, u_2, \ldots, u_n$. We can obtain the following partial sums:

$$s_1 = u_1$$
$$s_2 = u_1 + u_2$$
$$s_3 = u_1 + u_2 + u_3$$
$$\cdots\cdots\cdots\cdots\cdots$$
$$s_n = u_1 + u_2 + \ldots + u_n$$

We call this sum $u_1 + u_2 + \ldots + u_n$ a *finite series* of the elements of the sequence $u_1, u_2, \ldots, u_n$. s_n represents the total sum of these elements. For example, if we have the sequence 1, 2, 3, 4, the series is $1 + 2 + 3 + 4$, and the sum s_4 is 10.

This example is a simple one. However, if instead of considering four terms 1, 2, 3, and 4, we consider "n" terms $1, 2, 3, \ldots, n$, it will not be that simple to calculate their sum $s_n = 1 + 2 + 3 + \ldots + n$. Sometimes, there are easy ways to calculate the sum of a specific series, but we cannot apply that particular method to all the series.

For example, the previous series $1 + 2 + 3 + \ldots + n$, could be calculated by using the following artifice:

$$1 = 1 = \frac{1 \cdot 2}{2}$$

$$1 + 2 = 3 = \frac{2 \cdot 3}{2}$$

$$1 + 2 + 3 = 6 = \frac{3 \cdot 4}{2}$$

$$\cdots\cdots\cdots\cdots\cdots\cdots$$

$$1 + 2 + \ldots + n = \frac{n(n+1)}{2},$$

which is the total sum of the series.

This means that if we want to calculate the sum of the series $1 + 2 + 3 + \ldots + 10$, we will have $S_{10} = \frac{10(10+1)}{2} = \frac{10 \cdot 11}{2} = 55$.

We cannot apply this artifice to every series, therefore, we must find a more general method that permits us to calculate the sum of several series. This method is given by the following theorem:

Theorem: Let us consider a finite series $u_1 + u_2 + u_3 + \ldots + u_n$. If we can find a function $F(n)$ such that $u_n = F(n+1) - F(n)$, then $u_1 + u_2 + \ldots + u_n = F(n+1) - F(1)$.

Proof: We have by hypothesis that $u_n = F(n+1) - F(n)$; therefore, if we apply it for $n-1, n-2, \ldots, 3, 2, 1$, we will get the following relations:

$$\begin{aligned} u_n &= F(n+1) - F(n) \\ u_{n-1} &= F(n) - F(n-1) \\ u_{n-2} &= F(n-1) - F(n-2) \\ &\vdots \\ u_2 &= F(3) - F(2) \\ u_1 &= F(2) - F(1) \end{aligned}$$

If we now add these relations, we will get: $u_1 + u_2 + u_3 + \ldots + u_n = F(n+1) - F(1)$, which proves the theorem.

Before having students embark on applications, have them consider the following examples:

1. Find the sum of the series $1 + 2 + 3 + \ldots + n$. Because $u_n = n$, we consider $F(n) = An^2 + Bn + C$. (A polynomial one degree higher than u_n should be used.) Therefore, $F(n+1) = A(n+1)^2 + B(n+1) + C$. According to the theorem above, we must have

$$\begin{aligned} u_n &= F(n+1) - F(n) \\ n &= [A(n+1)^2 + B(n+1) + C] \\ &\quad - [An^2 + Bn + C] \\ n &= 2An + (A + B). \end{aligned}$$

Therefore, by equating coefficients of powers of n, we get $2A = 1$, and $A + B = 0$. By solving these simultaneously, we get $A = \frac{1}{2}$ and $B = -\frac{1}{2}$.

Therefore, $F(n) = \frac{1}{2}n^2 - \frac{1}{2}n + C$, $F(n+1) = \frac{1}{2}(n+1)^2 - \frac{1}{2}(n+1) + C$, and $F(1) = C$.

Thus, $1 + 2 + 3 + \ldots + n = F(n+1) - F(1) = \frac{1}{2}(n+1)^2 - \frac{1}{2}(n+1) = \frac{1}{2}n(n+1)$.

2. Find the sum of the series $1^2 + 2^2 + 3^2 + \ldots + n^2$. Since $u_n = n^2$, we consider $F(n) = An^3 + Bn^2 + Cn + D$ [One degree higher than u_n, since the highest power of $F(n)$ will be annihilated in $F(n+1) - F(n)$.] Thus $F(n+1) = A(n+1)^3 + B(n+1)^2 + C(n+1) + D$.

$$\begin{aligned} \text{Now, } u_n = n^2 &= F(n+1) - F(n) \\ n^2 &= [A(n+1)^3 + B(n+1)^2 + C(n+1) + D] \\ &\quad - [An^3 + Bn^2 + Cn + D] \\ n^2 &= 3An^2 + (3A + 2B)n + (A + B + C). \end{aligned}$$

By equating coefficients of powers of n, we get $3A = 1$; $3A + 2B = 0$; and $A + B + C = 0$ and solving simultaneously:

$$A = \frac{1}{3};\ B = -\frac{1}{2};\ C = \frac{1}{6}.$$

$$\text{Thus, } F(n) = \frac{1}{3}n^3 - \frac{1}{2}n^2 + \frac{1}{6}n + D$$

$$F(n+1) = \frac{1}{3}(n+1)^3 - \frac{1}{2}(n+1)^2 + \frac{1}{6}(n+1) + D$$

$$F(1) = \frac{1}{3} - \frac{1}{2} + \frac{1}{6} + D = D$$

$$\begin{aligned} \text{Hence, } 1^2 + 2^2 + 3^2 + \ldots + n^2 &= F(n+1) - F(1) \\ &= \frac{1}{3}(n+1)^3 - \frac{1}{2}(n+1)^2 + \frac{1}{6}(n+1) \\ &= \frac{n(n+1)(2n+1)}{6}. \end{aligned}$$

3. Find the sum of the series $1^3 + 3^3 + 5^3 + \ldots + (2n-1)^3$. Since u_n is the third degree, $F(n) = An^4 + Bn^3 + Cn^2 + Dn + E$ and $F(n+1) = A(n+1)^4 + B(n+1)^3 + C(n+1)^2 + D(n+1) + E$.
Thus, $u_n = (2n-1)^3 = F(n+1) - F(n)$;
or $8n^3 - 12n^2 + 8n^3 - 12n^2 + 6n - 1 = 4An^3 + (6A + 3B)n^2 + 4A(4A + 3B + 2C)n + (A + B + C + D)$.
Equating coefficients:

$4A = 8$, and $A = 2$; $6A + 3B = -12$, and $B = -8$;
$4A + 3B + 2C = 6$; and $C = 11$;
$A + B + C + D = -1$, and $D = -6$.

Therefore, $F(n) = 2n^4 - 8n^3 + 11n^2 - 6n + E$;

$F(n+1) = 2(n+1)^4 - 8(n+1)^3 + 11(n+1)^2 - 6(n+1) + E$;

and $F(1) = -1 + E$.

Thus,

$1^3 + 3^3 + 5^3 + \ldots + (2n-1)^3 = F(n+1) - F(1) = 2(n+1)^4 - 8(n+1)^3 + 11(n+1)^2 - 6(n+1) + E - 1 + E) = 2n^4 - n^2 = n^2(2n^2 - 1)$.

4. Find the sum of the series $\frac{1}{2} + \frac{1}{4} + \ldots + \frac{1}{2^n}$. Let us consider $F(n) = \frac{A}{2^n}$ and therefore, $F(n+1) = \frac{A}{2^{n+1}}$. Hence, $u_n = F(n+1) - F(n)$. Thus, $\frac{1}{2^n} = \frac{A}{2^{n+1}} - \frac{A}{2^n}$, therefore $A = -2$. Hence, $F(n+1) = -\frac{1}{2^n}$; and $F(1) = -1$. Therefore,

$$\frac{1}{2} + \frac{1}{4} + \ldots + \frac{1}{2^n} = F(n+1) - F(1) = -\frac{1}{2^n} + 1 = 1 - \frac{1}{2^n}.$$

After sufficient practice, students should be able to fine $F(n)$ more easily.

POSTASSESSMENT

1. Find the sum of the series $1 + 8 + 27 + \ldots + n^3$.
2. Find the sum of the series $\frac{1}{5} + \frac{1}{25} + \frac{1}{125} + \ldots + \frac{1}{5^n}$.
3. Find the formula for the sum of a finite arithmetic progression.

Unit 104

A General Formula for the Sum of Series of the Form $\sum_{t=1}^{n} t^r$

The calculation of the sum of convergent series is an important topic. There is not, however, a general formula to calculate the sum of any given convergent series.

This unit will provide you with a general formula to calculate the sum of the series of the specific type $\sum_{t=1}^{n} t^r$.

PERFORMANCE OBJECTIVES

1. *Given some finite series of the form* $\sum_{t=1}^{n} t^r$, *students will find their sum.*
2. *Students will demonstrate an understanding of the technique used to find general formulas for certain specific series.*

PREASSESSMENT

Students should know the Binomial Theorem and have a fair knowledge of series and elementary linear algebra.

TEACHING STRATEGIES

Review the concept of series and the Binomial Theorem in the following fashion:

A series is a sum of the elements of a given sequence. For example, if we have the sequence of elements $u_1, u_2, \ldots, u_n$, the series is $u_1 + u_2 + \ldots + u_n$. This series can also be represented by the symbol $\sum_{r=1}^{n} u_r$. Thus, the symbol $\sum_{n=1}^{n} k^2$ means $1^2 + 2^2 + \ldots + n^2$.

Another example of series is the one represented by $\sum_{m=0}^{k} \binom{k}{m} a^{k-m} b^m$, where a and b are arbitrary real numbers, k is any positive integer, and $\binom{k}{m} = \frac{k!}{m!(k-m)!}$. This series can be proved to be equal to $(a+b)^k$, and this fact is known as the *Binomial Theorem.*

There is also a less known but important theorem from the theory of series whose proof we are going to give in this unit. We are going to use this theorem and the Binomial Theorem in the development of our discussion.

Lemma: Let us consider a finite series $\sum_{r=1}^{n} u_r$. If we can find a function $f(n)$ such that $u_n = f(n+1) - f(n)$, then $\sum_{r=1}^{n} u_r = f(n+1) - f(1)$.

Proof: We have by hypothesis that $u_n = f(n+1) - f(n)$; therefore, if we apply it for $n-1, n-2, \ldots, 3, 2, 1$, we will get the following relations:

$$\begin{aligned} u_n &= f(n+1) - f(n) \\ u_{n-1} &= f(n) - f(n-1) \\ u_{n-2} &= f(n-1) - f(n-2) \\ &\cdots\cdots\cdots\cdots\cdots\cdots \\ u_2 &= f(3) - f(2) \\ u_1 &= f(2) - f(1) \end{aligned}$$

If we now add these relations, we will get $\sum_{r=1}^{n} u_r$ equal to $f(n+1) - f(1)$, which proves the theorem.

Let $\sum_{t=1}^{n} t^r$ be the series whose sum we want. To apply the previous Lemma to this series, we may consider the arbitrary function $f(n) = \sum_{k=0}^{r+1} b_k n^k$, where b is any real number and n is any positive integer. Thus, $f(n+1) = \sum_{k=0}^{r+1} b_k (n+1)^k$. If we now impose the condition of the hypothesis of the Lemma to this function for the series $\sum_{t=1}^{n} t^r$, we have

$$u_n = f(n+1) - f(n)$$

or

$$n^r = \sum_{k=0}^{r+1} b_k (n+1)^k - \sum_{k=0}^{r+1} b_k n^k$$

$$n^r = \sum_{k=0}^{r+1} b_k [(n+1)^k - n^k].$$

But according to the Binomial Theorem,

$$(n+1)^k = \sum_{m=0}^{k} \binom{k}{m} n^{k-m} \text{ and thus,}$$

$$(n+1)^k - n^k = \sum_{m=1}^{k} \binom{k}{m} n^{k-m}.$$

Therefore in (I) we have

$$n^r = \sum_{k=0}^{r+1} b_k \left[\sum_{m=1}^{k} \binom{k}{m} n^{k-m} \right].$$

This equation leads to the following system of equations:

$$\begin{aligned} &\binom{r+1}{1} b_{r+1} &&= 0 \\ &\binom{r+1}{2} b_{r+1} + \binom{r}{1} b_r &&= 0 \\ &\binom{r+1}{3} b_{r+1} + \binom{r}{2} b_r + \binom{r-1}{1} b_{r-1} \ldots\ldots\ldots\ldots &&= 0 \\ &\ldots\ldots\ldots\ldots\ldots\ldots\ldots\ldots\ldots\ldots\ldots\ldots &&= 0 \\ &\binom{r+1}{m} b_{r+1} + \binom{r}{m-1} b_r + \binom{r-1}{m-2} b_{r-1} + \ldots\ldots\ldots &&= 0 \\ &\ldots\ldots\ldots\ldots\ldots\ldots\ldots\ldots\ldots\ldots\ldots\ldots &&= 0 \\ &\binom{r+1}{r+1} b_{r+1} + \binom{r}{r} b_r + \ldots\ldots + \binom{1}{1} b_1 \ldots\ldots\ldots &&= 0 \end{aligned}$$

This system of equations can be expressed in matrix form as follows:

$$\begin{bmatrix} \binom{r+1}{1} & 0 & 0 & 0 & \cdots & 0 \\ \binom{r+1}{2} & \binom{r}{1} & 0 & 0 & \cdots & 0 \\ \binom{r+1}{3} & \binom{r}{2} & \binom{r-1}{2} & 0 & \cdots & 0 \\ \cdot & \cdot & \cdot & \cdot & \cdots & \cdot \\ \cdot & \cdot & \cdot & \cdot & \cdots & \cdot \\ \cdot & \cdot & \cdot & \cdot & \cdots & \cdot \\ \binom{r+1}{m} & \binom{r}{m-1} & \binom{r-1}{m-2} & 0 & \cdots & 0 \\ \cdot & \cdot & \cdot & \cdot & \cdots & \cdot \\ \cdot & \cdot & \cdot & \cdot & \cdots & \cdot \\ \cdot & \cdot & \cdot & \cdot & \cdots & \cdot \\ \binom{r+1}{r+1} & \binom{r}{r} & \binom{r-1}{r-1} & \binom{r-2}{r-2} & \cdots & 1 \end{bmatrix} \begin{bmatrix} b_{r+1} \\ b_r \\ b_{r-1} \\ \cdot \\ \cdot \\ \cdot \\ b_m \\ \cdot \\ \cdot \\ \cdot \\ b_1 \end{bmatrix} = \begin{bmatrix} 1 \\ 0 \\ 0 \\ \cdot \\ \cdot \\ \cdot \\ 0 \\ \cdot \\ \cdot \\ \cdot \\ 0 \end{bmatrix}$$

If we call these three matrices A, X, and B, respectively, we have that AX = B. But A is a diagonal matrix, thus, det $A = \prod_{s=1}^{r+1} \binom{s}{1} = 0$ and therefore A^{-1} exists. (Det A is the determinant of A, which for a simple case is $\begin{vmatrix} a_1 & b_1 \\ a_2 & b_2 \end{vmatrix} = a_1 b_2 - a_2 b_1$. The Π represents "product," in the way the $\sum$ represents "sum.") Thus we have $X = A^{-1}B$. If a_{ij} represents any element of A^{-1}, that implies that A^{-1}, that implies that

$$X = A^{-1}B = \begin{pmatrix} a_{11} \\ a_{21} \\ \vdots \\ a_{r+1,1} \end{pmatrix} \text{ because B is a column vector.}$$

Thus,

$$\begin{pmatrix} b_{r+1} \\ b_r \\ \vdots \\ b_1 \end{pmatrix} = \begin{pmatrix} a_{11} \\ a_{21} \\ \vdots \\ a_{r+1,1} \end{pmatrix}$$

But this means that $b_{r+2-i} = a_{i,1}$ for all $i \in \{1,2,3,\ldots,r+1\}$. Therefore for the function $f(n) = \sum_{k=0}^{r+1} b_k n^k$ we have $f(n+1) = \sum_{k=0}^{r+1} b_k (n+1)^k$ and $f(1) = \sum_{k=0}^{r+1} b_k$ where $b_{r+2-i} = a_{i,1}$ for all $i \in \{1,2,3,\ldots,r+1\}$.

Thus, by the previous Lemma,

$$\sum_{t=1}^{n} t^r = \sum_{k=0}^{r+1} b_k (n+1)^k - \sum_{k=0}^{r+1} b_k \text{ or}$$

$$\sum_{t=1}^{n} t^r = \sum_{k=0}^{r+1} b_k [(n+1)^k - 1] \qquad \text{(II)}$$

But by the Binomial Theorem we have that

$$(n+1)^k - 1 = \binom{k}{0} n^k + \binom{k}{1} n^{k-1} + \ldots + \binom{k}{k-1} n.$$

Thus, in (II)

$$\sum_{t=1}^{n} t^r = \sum_{k=0}^{r+1} b_k \left[\binom{k}{0} n^k + \binom{k}{1} n^{k-1} + \ldots + \binom{k}{k-1} n \right]$$

or

$$\sum_{t=1}^{n} t^r = n\sum_{k=0}^{r+1}\left[b_k\binom{k}{0}n^{k-1} + b_k\binom{k}{1}n^{k-2} + \ldots + b_k\binom{k}{k-1}\right].$$

And if we call $b_k\binom{k}{j} = c_j$, we have $\sum_{t=1}^{n} t^r = n\sum_{j=0}^{r} c_j n^j$, because when $k = 0$, $b_0\binom{0}{j} = c_j = c_0$, which implies that $j = 0$, and when $k = r + 1$, $b_{r+1}\binom{r+1}{j} = c_j$, which implies that $j = r$. Thus:

Theorem: The general formula for series of the form $\sum_{t=1}^{n} t^r$ is $n\sum_{j=0}^{r} c_j n^j$, where $c_j = b_k\binom{k}{j}$ for all $j \in \{0, 1, 3, \ldots, r\}$ and $b_{r+2-i} = a_{i,1}$ for all $i \in \{1, 2, 3, \ldots, r + 1\}$.

Example 1

Find $\sum_{t=1}^{n} t^2$.

In this example $r = 2$, therefore we have

$$\begin{pmatrix}\binom{3}{1} & 0 & 0\\ \binom{3}{2} & \binom{2}{1} & 0\\ \binom{3}{3} & \binom{2}{2} & \binom{1}{1}\end{pmatrix}\begin{pmatrix}b_3\\ b_2\\ b_1\end{pmatrix} = \begin{pmatrix}1\\ 0\\ 0\end{pmatrix}$$

Thus, $A = \begin{pmatrix}3 & 0 & 0\\ 3 & 2 & 0\\ 1 & 1 & 1\end{pmatrix}$ and A^{-1} is

$$A^{-1} = \frac{(\text{Adj. A})'}{\text{Det. A}} = \frac{\begin{pmatrix}2 & -3 & 1\\ 0 & 3 & -3\\ 0 & 0 & 6\end{pmatrix}'}{\begin{vmatrix}3 & 0 & 0\\ 3 & 2 & 0\\ 1 & 1 & 1\end{vmatrix}} \text{ or}$$

$$A^{-1} = \frac{\begin{pmatrix}2 & 0 & 0\\ -3 & 3 & 0\\ 1 & -3 & 6\end{pmatrix}}{6}.$$

Therefore,

$$X = \frac{1}{6}\begin{pmatrix}2 & 0 & 0\\ -3 & 3 & 0\\ 1 & -3 & 6\end{pmatrix}\begin{pmatrix}1\\ 0\\ 0\end{pmatrix} = \frac{1}{6}\begin{pmatrix}2\\ -3\\ 1\end{pmatrix}$$

and $\begin{pmatrix}b_3\\ b_2\\ b_1\end{pmatrix} = \frac{1}{6}\begin{pmatrix}2\\ -3\\ 1\end{pmatrix}$ implies that $\begin{cases} b_3 = \frac{1}{6}(2)\\ b_2 = \frac{1}{6}(-3).\\ b_1 = \frac{1}{6}(1)\end{cases}$

Thus,

$$f(n) = \frac{1}{6}[2n^3 - 3n^2 + n + b_0]$$

$$f(n + 1) = \frac{1}{6}[2(n + 1)^3 - 3(n + 1)^2 + (n + 1) + b_0]$$

and,

$$f(1) = \frac{1}{6}(b_0).$$

Hence, the sum of the series will be

$$\begin{aligned} k^2 &= f(n + 1) - f(1)\\ &= \frac{1}{6}[2(n + 1)^3 - 3(n + 1)^2 + (n + 1)]\\ &= \frac{1}{6}n(n + 1)(2n + 1). \end{aligned}$$

Example 2

Find the sum of $1 + 2 + 3 + \ldots + n$.

In this example the series is $\sum_{k=1}^{n} k$ and $r = 1$. Thus, the equation will be

$$\begin{pmatrix}\binom{2}{1} & 0\\ \binom{2}{2} & \binom{1}{1}\end{pmatrix} \cdot \begin{pmatrix}b_0\\ b_1\end{pmatrix} = \begin{pmatrix}1\\ 0\end{pmatrix}. \text{ Then, } A = \begin{pmatrix}2 & 0\\ 1 & 1\end{pmatrix}.$$

The inverse of A will then be $A^{-1} = \left(\frac{\begin{matrix}1 & 0\\ -1 & 2\end{matrix}}{2}\right)$, and

$$X = \frac{1}{2}\begin{pmatrix}1 & 0\\ -1 & 2\end{pmatrix}\begin{pmatrix}1\\ 0\end{pmatrix} = \frac{1}{2}\begin{pmatrix}1\\ -1\end{pmatrix}.$$

This implies that $b_0 = \frac{1}{2}(1)$ and $b_1 = \frac{1}{2}(-1)$.

Then

$$f(n) = \frac{1}{2}(n^2 - n + a_2)$$

$$f(n + 1) = \frac{1}{2}[(n + 1) - (n + 1) + a_2]$$

$$\text{and } f(1) = \frac{1}{2}(a_2).$$

$$\begin{aligned} \text{Then, } \sum_{k=1}^{n} k &= f(n + 1) - f(1)\\ &= \frac{1}{2}[(n + 1)^2 - (n + 1)] = \frac{1}{2}n(n + 1). \end{aligned}$$

POSTASSESSMENT

1. Find the sum of $1^3 + 2^3 + \ldots + n^3$.
2. Find the sum of $\sum_{k=1}^{n} k^5$.
3. What are the changes in the general theorem if, in $\sum_{t=1}^{n} t^r$, t is an even number?

Unit 105

 A Parabolic Calculator

After having taught the properties of the parabola to an eleventh grade mathematics class, the teacher might want to discuss some applications of the parabola. The teacher may discuss the reflective properties of a parabolic surface such as a searchlight or the mirror in a telescope. The light source at the focus of a parabolic reflecting surface (Figure 1) reflects its rays off the surface in *parallel paths*. It may be noted that the angle of incidence, ∠FTP, equals the angle of reflection, ∠FTQ.

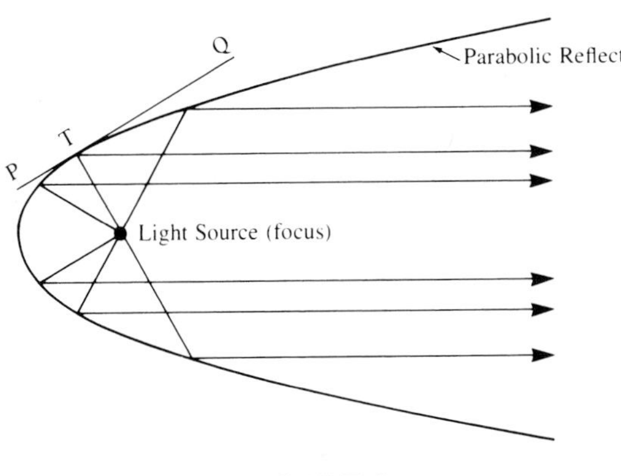

FIGURE 1

The same principle is used in telephone (Figure 2) (or radar unit). However here the rays are generated from external sources and reflected off the mirror (or radar screen) to the focus, which may consists of a camera or other sensing device.

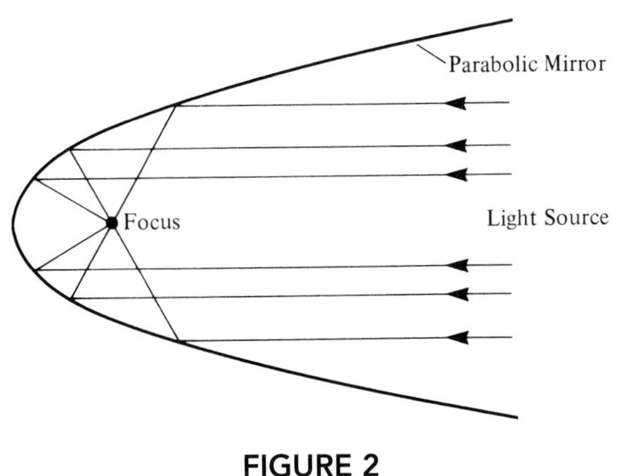

FIGURE 2

Other applications such as parabolic path of a thrown object may be considered. However, a rather unusual application of the parabola involves its properties on the Cartesian plane. This unit will present a method of using a parabola on the Cartesian plane as a calculating device for performing multiplication and division. The only supplies students will need are graph paper and a straightedge.

PERFORMANCE OBJECTIVES

1. *Students will draw an appropriate parabola and perform a given multiplication with it.*
2. *Students will draw an appropriate parabola and perform a given division with it.*
3. *Students will justify (analytically) why the multiplication method presented in this unit "works."*

PREASSESSMENT

Before presenting this unit to the class the teacher should be sure that students are able to graph a parabola and are able to find the equation of a line, given two points on the line.

TEACHING STRATEGIES

On a large sheet of graph paper (preferably one with small squares) have students draw coordinate axes and graph the parabola $y = x^2$. This must be done very accurately. Once this has been completed students are ready to perform some calculations. For example, suppose they wish to multiply 3×5. They would simply draw the line joining the point on the parabola whose abscissa is 3 with the point whose abscissa is -5. The point product of 3 and 5 is the ordinate of the point where this line intersects the y-axis (Figure 3, AB).

For further practice have students multiply 2.5×3.5. Here they must draw the line containing the points (2.5, 6.25) and (-3.5, 12.25). (These are the points on parabola $y = x^2$, whose abscissas are 2.5 and -3.5.) The ordinate of the point where this line (Figure 3, $\overleftrightarrow{CD}$) intersects the Y-axis is the product of 2.5 and 3.5, that is, 8.75. Naturally the size of the graph will determine the degree of accuracy that can be obtained. Students should realize that the points on the parabola whose abscissas were -2.5 and 3.5 could just as

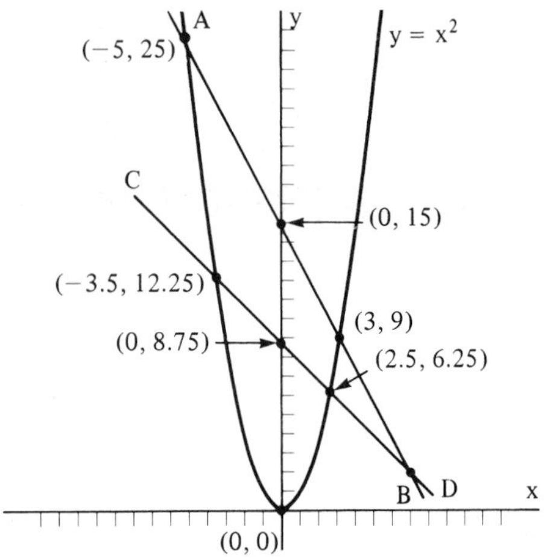

FIGURE 3

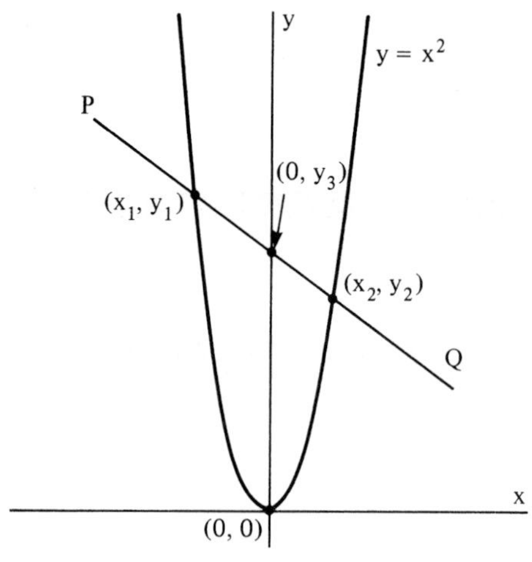

FIGURE 4

well have been used in place of the points whose abscissas were 2.5 and −3.5 in the past example.

At this point the teacher may ask students how this same scheme can be used to do division. Students, noting that division is the inverse operation of multiplication, should suggest that $\overleftrightarrow{CD}$ could have been used to divide the following: $8.75 \div 3.5$. The other point of intersection that $\overleftrightarrow{CD}$ makes with the parabola, point (2.5, 6.25) yields the answer 2.5.

The teacher would be wise to offer students a variety of drill exercises to better familiarize them with this technique. Students can use a straightedge (without drawing a line) to read the answers from the graph.

After sufficient drill, students may become curious about the reason why this technique of calculation actually "works." To prove that it does work, have the class consider the following general case (Figure 4).

Let $\overleftrightarrow{PQ}$ intersect the parabola $y = x^2$ at points (x_1, y_1) and (x_2, y_2), and intersect the y-axis at $(0, y_3)$. This proof must conclude that $y_3 = |x_1x_2|$.

Proof:

The slope of $\overleftrightarrow{PQ} = \dfrac{y_2 - y_1}{x_2 - x_1} = \dfrac{x_2^2 - x_1^2}{x_2 - x_1} = x_1 + x_2$ (since $y_2 = x_2^2$, and $y_1 = x_1^2$).

The slope of $\overleftrightarrow{PQ}$ expressed with any point (x,y) is $\dfrac{y - y_1}{x - x_1}$.

Therefore $\dfrac{y - y_1}{x - x_1} = x_1 + x_2$ is the equation of $\overleftrightarrow{PQ}$.

At the point $(0, y_3)\dfrac{y_3 - y_1}{0 - x_1} = x_1 + x_2$ and $y_3 = -x_1^2 - x_1x_2 + y_1$.

But $y_1 = x_1^2$, thus $y_3 = -x_1x_2$, but this is positive, so $y_3 = |x_1x_2|$.

With a knowledge of this proof students may wish to experiment with other parabolas in an attempt to replace $y = x^2$ with a more "convenient" parabola.

This scheme also provides the student with a host of further investigations. For example, it may be used to "construct" a line of length $\sqrt{a}$. The student need only construct a line parallel to the x-axis and intersecting the y-axis at $(0,a)$. The segment of that line that is between the y-axis and the parabola has length $\sqrt{a}$. Further student investigations should be encouraged.

POSTASSESSMENT

1. Have students draw the parabola $y = x^2$ and then use it to do the following exercises:
   a. 4×5
   b. 4.5×5.5
   c. $4 \div 2.5$
   d. $1.5 \div .5$
2. Have students show how $y = \frac{1}{2}x^2$ may be used to perform multiplication and division operations.

Unit 106

Constructing Ellipses

This unit provides a means of constructing ellipses using a straightedge and a compass.

PERFORMANCE OBJECTIVES

1. *Students will plot points on an ellipse without the use of an equation.*
2. *The relation of the circle to the ellipse will be used by students in the constructions of ellipses.*

PREASSESSMENT

Students should have completed tenth year mathematics and be familiar with fundamental trigonometric identities. Knowledge of analytic geometry is helpful, but not necessary. Ask students to construct an ellipse using any method (i.e., analytically or with special tools).

TEACHING STRATEGIES

After inspecting student attempts to construct an ellipse, have them consider the accuracy of their work. Some students may have attempted a freehand drawing, while others may have plotted an appropriate curve on a piece of graph paper. This should lead comfortably to Method I.

Method I: Point-by-Point Construction

One of the definitions of an ellipse is: *the locus of a point, P, which moves such that the sum of its distances from two given fixed points. F and F′, is a constant*. From Figure 1, the definitions just given implies that PF + PF′ = a constant. (1)

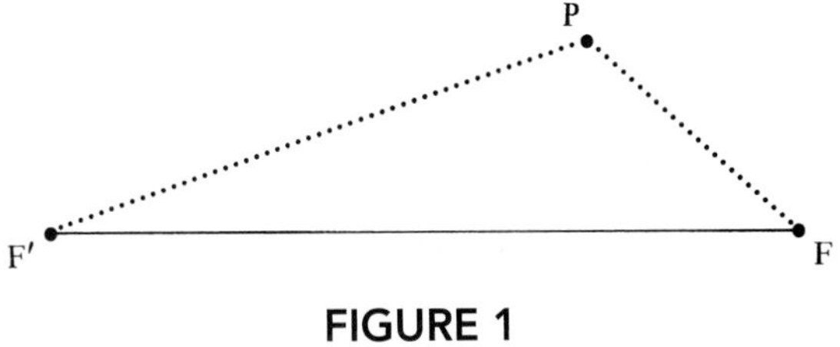

FIGURE 1

Customarily, this constant is given the value 2a, and it is not too difficult to derive from this definition the equation of the ellipse:

$$\frac{x^2}{a^2} + \frac{y^2}{b^2} = 1 \qquad (2)$$

Indeed, the popular thumbtack and string-loop construction is directly based on this definition (where a string-loop is held taut between two thumbtacks and a pencil that changes position).

Procedure: Place an $8\frac{1}{2}'' \times 11''$ sheet in the horizontal position and center on it a 4″ horizontal line whose endpoints F and F′ are the ellipse's foci (see Figure 2). Let the constant in (1) equal 6″. Thus, PF + PF′ = 6″. (3)

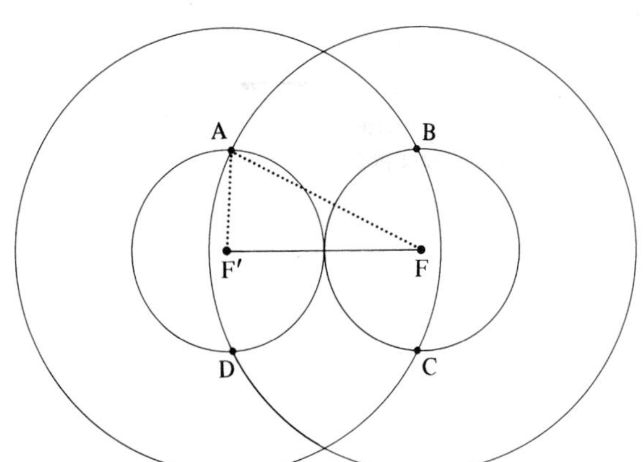

FIGURE 2

With F as center, draw a circle of 4″ radius. Do likewise with F′ as center. Next, again use F and F′ as centers for circles of 2″ radius. Note that these four circles intersect in four points A, B, C, and D, which lie on the ellipse. For, if point A is arbitrarily chosen, by construction FA = 2″ and F′A = 4″; hence FA + F′A = 6″, satisfying (3).

A rather accurate construction can be made by using increments of $\frac{1}{2}''$ for the radii of each circle centered on F and F′, starting with $9\frac{1}{2}''$ and $2\frac{1}{2}''$ radii. The next set of four points on the ellipse would be obtained by drawing two circles of 5″ and 1″ radius, both on F and F′. These two pairs of circles would be followed by another two pairs of radii 9″ and 3″, and so on, as indicated in Figure 3. Indeed, additional ellipses can then be sketched from Figure 3.

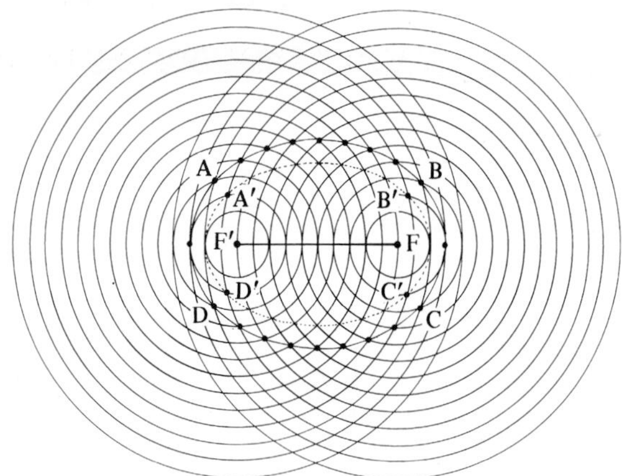

FIGURE 3

Assume that PF + PF′ = 5″. (4)

Then, one need only mark the intersections of those circles centered on F and F′, the sum of whose radii is 5. For example, in constructing (3) by using the suggested $\frac{1}{4}''$ increment, it was necessary at some point to use a radius of $3\frac{1}{2}''$ centered on F and F′ and another radius of $1\frac{1}{2}''$ again centered on F and F′. The intersection of these four circles, A′, B′, C′, and D′, provide four points on *another* ellipse such that, using A′ arbitrarily, FA′ + $\overline{F'A'}$ = 5″.

Figure 3 thus shows the two ellipses sketched, both of which have F and F′ as their foci. Other ellipses can be sketched in a similar manner from the same figure.

Method II: Tangent Construction

Centered on an $8\frac{1}{2}''$ by 11″ sheet of paper, have students draw a circle of radius 3″. Locate a point F in the interior of the circle $2\frac{1}{4}''$ from the center (see Figure 4).

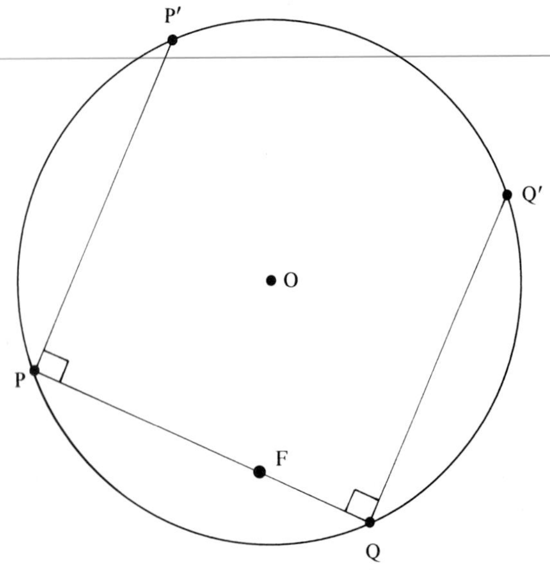

FIGURE 4

Through F draw a chord to intersect the circle at P and Q. Using a right triangle template or carpenter's T-square, erect perpendiculars at P and Q to meet the circle at P′ and Q′, respectively. Then $\overleftrightarrow{PP'}$ and $\overleftrightarrow{QQ'}$ are each tangents to an ellipse having F as one of its foci. Continue this procedure for many such chords $\overline{PQ}$, obtaining a diagram similar to that shown in Figure 5.

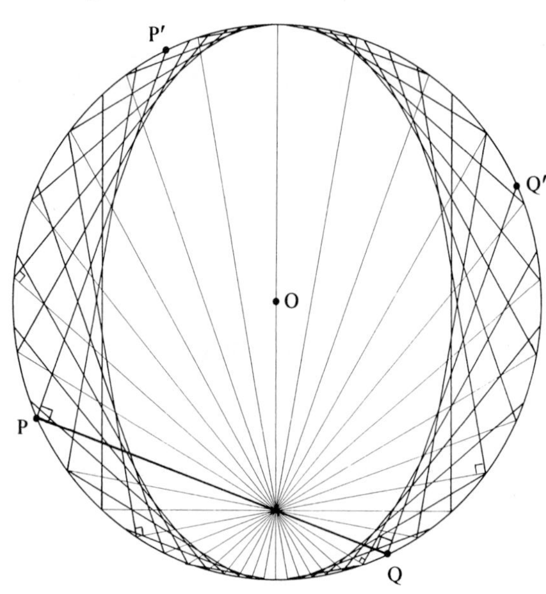

FIGURE 5

The proof of this construction is based on the converse of the following theorem: *The locus of the intersection of the tangent to an ellipse with the perpendicular on it from either focus is a circle.* A proof of this theorem can be found in Bowser's *An Elementary Treatise on Analytic Geometry*, pages 139–140.

Varying the position of F will change the size and shape of the ellipse. Furthermore, the second focus, F′, is located on $\overleftrightarrow{FO}$ extended through O its own distance.

POSTASSESSMENT

1. Have students draw Figure 3 on a larger scale, such as FF′ = 6″. Coloring in the numerous regions formed by the intersections of the circles may prove quite satisfying.
2. Have students draw a circle of radius r, with O as center. They then locate a fixed point, F, inside the circle, and draw $\overline{OF}$. Clearly, $r >$ OF. Then have them draw an arbitrary radius OQ. Connect FQ, and construct its midpoint, M. At M, they should erect a perpendicular to intersect $\overline{OQ}$ at P. Then P lies on an ellipse with F as one of its foci. Moreover, $\overleftrightarrow{MP}$ extended through P is a tangent to the same ellipse. Have students complete this construction and justify it.

REFERENCE

Posamentier, A. S., and H. A. Hauptman. *101 Plus Great Ideas for Introducing Key Concepts in Mathematics*. Thousand Oaks, CA: Corwin, 2006.

Unit 107

Constructing the Parabola

PERFORMANCE OBJECTIVE

With straightedge and compasses, students will construct a parabola without using an equation.

PREASSESSMENT

Ask students to construct the parabola $y = x^2$ on a sheet of graph paper. When this has been done, have them draw any other parabola on a sheet of "blank" paper.

TEACHING STRATEGIES

In all likelihood students will be unable to draw a parabola without use of graph paper. At this point the teacher may define the parabola in terms of locus. That is, it is the locus of points equidistant from a fixed point and a fixed line. Perhaps students will find this a useful hint in deriving a method of construction of a parabola. After considering students' suggestions, have them consider the following methods.

Method I: Point-by-Point Construction

Toward the left of an $8\frac{1}{2}$-by-11-inch sheet of paper held horizontally, lightly draw about 15 vertical parallel lines each spaced $\frac{1}{2}$ inch apart (see Figure 1). Each line segment should be 8 inches long. Draw the common perpendicular bisector of these lines. Label your drawing as shown in Figure 1,

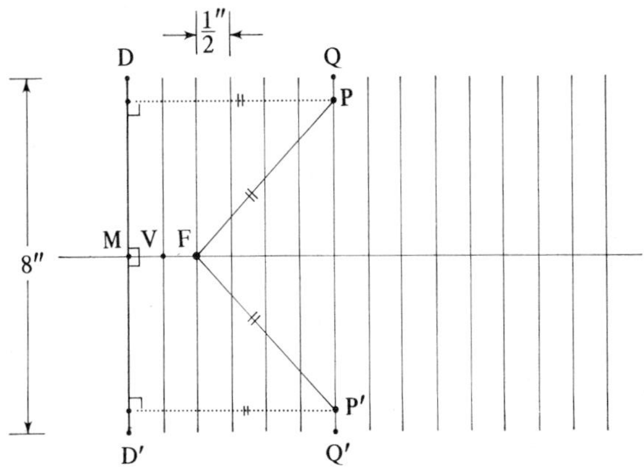

FIGURE 1

being sure to place F at the intersection of the third parallel line and the perpendicular bisector. Let $\overleftrightarrow{QQ'}$ be any arbitrary parallel line, say the sixth one from $\overleftrightarrow{DD'}$. By construction, $\overleftrightarrow{QQ'}$ is $(6 \cdot \frac{1}{2}) = 3''$ from $\overleftrightarrow{DD'}$. Maintaining this distance, using F as center, swing an arc with your compasses cutting $\overleftrightarrow{QQ'}$ above and below the perpendicular bisector at P and P′. Then P and P′ are on the parabola with F as the *focus* of the parabola. Repeat this procedure for the other parallel lines, joining all the points so determined (see Figure 2).

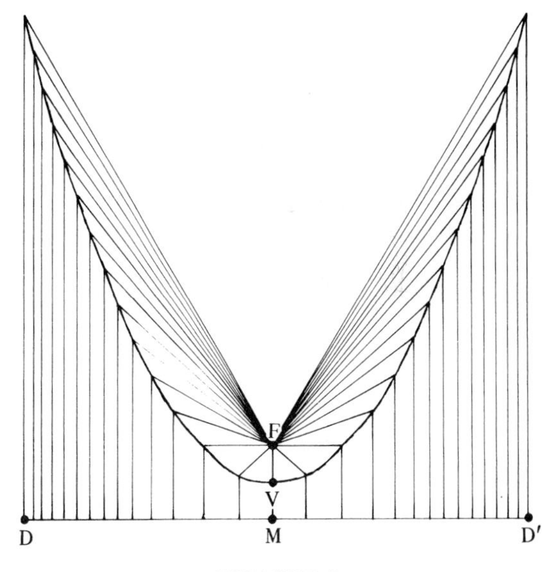

FIGURE 2

Discussion: By construction, the perpendicular distance of either P or P′ from $\overleftrightarrow{DD'}$ is equal to FP or FP′. The definition of a parabola is based on such an equivalence of distance of a varying point from a fixed line and a fixed point. A parabola is the locus of points each of whose distances from a fixed point equals its distance from a fixed line. The line $\overleftrightarrow{DD'}$ is referred to as the *directrix*, and its perpendicular bisector is the *axis* of the parabola. If M is the intersection of the axis and the directrix $\overleftrightarrow{DD'}$, by letting $FM = 2p$, it is not difficult, using the distance formula and the above definition, to show that the parabola's equation is $y^2 = 4px$. (1)
The midpoint, V, of $\overline{MF}$ is the parabola's *vertex* and is often referred to as the parabola's turning point.

Method II: Point-by-Point Construction

Draw a rectangle ABCD (see Figure 3), letting V and G be the midpoints of $\overline{AD}$ and $\overline{BC}$, respectively. Divide $\overline{AB}$ and $\overline{BG}$ into the same *number* of equal parts. Starting from B, let the successive points of equal division be 1, 2, 3, . . . on $\overline{AB}$ and $a, b, c\ldots$ on $\overline{BG}$. Draw $\overline{aa'}$ perpendicular to $\overline{BG}$. Note that $a', b', c', \ldots$ are points on $\overline{AV}$. Draw $\overline{V1}$, meeting $\overline{aa'}$ at P. Similarly, draw $\overline{bb'}$ perpendicular to $\overline{BG}$ and draw $\overline{V2}$, meeting $\overline{bb'}$ at P′. Continue this for the other points. Then P and P′, and other points so obtained are on a parabola with V as its vertex and $\overline{VG}$ as its axis.

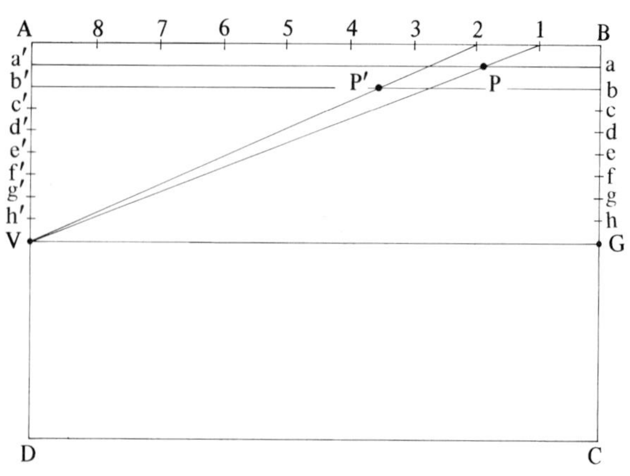

FIGURE 3

Proof: From Figure 3, let $\overleftrightarrow{AD}$ be the y-axis and $\overleftrightarrow{VG}$ the x-axis (see Figure 4). Let b on $\overline{BG}$ now be called Q, b' on $\overline{AV}$ to be labeled Q′. Similarly, let point 2 in Figure 3 be called T. Draw $\overline{VT}$ and $\overline{QQ'}$, meeting at P′. Let VQ′ = GQ = y, Q′P′ = x, VG = h, AV = a.

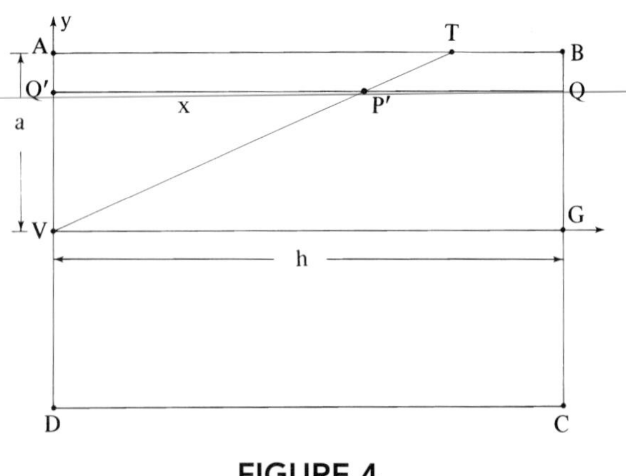

FIGURE 4

By construction (i.e., points T and Q were selected with this property),

$$\frac{AT}{AB} = \frac{GQ}{GB}, \text{ or } \frac{AT}{h} = \frac{y}{a}. \tag{2}$$

From similar triangles VQ′P′ and VAT, $\frac{x}{y} = \frac{AT}{AV} = \frac{AT}{a}$, or

$$AT = \frac{ax}{y}. \tag{3}$$

Substituting this value of AT in (2), $\frac{\frac{ax}{y}}{h} = \frac{y}{a}$, or

$$\frac{a^2x}{y} = hy. \tag{4}$$

Solving (4) for y^2 yields $y^2 = \frac{a^2x}{h}$, (5)

Which is of the same form as (1) in which $4p = \frac{a^2}{h}$. (6)

Because p is the distance from the vertex to the focus, solving (6) for p will locate the focus in terms of a and h of the original rectangle.

Method III: Envelope Construction

Near the bottom edge of a vertically held $8\frac{1}{2}$-by-11-inch sheet of paper, draw a horizontal line the full width of the paper (see Figure 5). Label this line $\overleftrightarrow{AA'}$. Draw the perpendicular

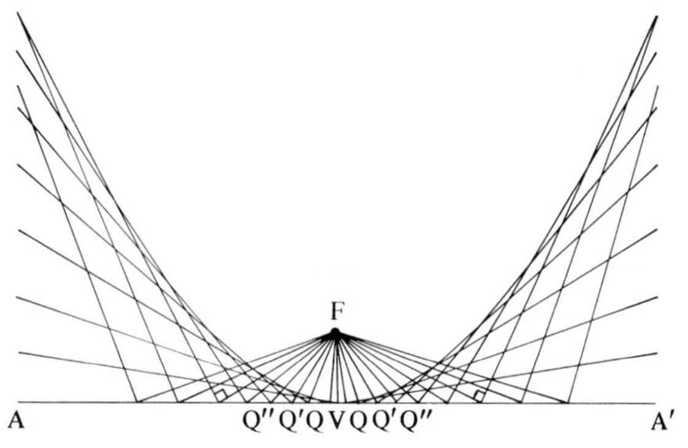

FIGURE 5

bisector of $\overline{AA'}$, with midpoint V. Locate F on the perpendicular bisector, one inch above V. On $\overline{AA'}$, on either side of V, mark off points Q, Q′, Q″, . . . , gradually increasing, by a very small increment, the successive distances from V to Q, Q to Q′, Q′ to Q″, ... Place a right triangle template or carpenter's T-square such that a leg passes through F and the vertex of the right angle is concurrent with any of the points Q, Q′, Q″, ... Construct a right angle with one ray $\overrightarrow{FQ}$ and drawing an extended line to the edge of the paper with the other ray of the right angle. Repeat this procedure for other points Q′, Q″, ... The resulting diagram should be similar to Figure 5, and the shape "enveloped" by all these lines is a parabola.

POSTASSESSMENT

Have your students draw an angle of any measure, making both sides equal in length. Starting from the vertex, have them measure off equally spaced intervals along each side, labeling the intervals on each side 1, 2, 3, 4, ..., 10, with the vertex labeled 0. Then ask them to connect point 10 on one side with point 1 on the other side. See that they do likewise for points 9 and 2, 8 and 3, and so forth, always being sure that the sum of the numbers joined is 11. The resulting appearance will be somewhat similar to Figure 5. Students will have drawn an envelope to a parabola. Have students attempt to justify this construction, as well as that for Figure 5.

REFERENCE

Posamentier, A. S., and H. A. Hauptman. *101 Plus Great Ideas for Introducing Key Concepts in Mathematics*. Thousand Oaks, CA: Corwin, 2006.

Unit 108

Using Higher Plane Curves to Trisect an Angle

This unit will introduce two higher plane algebraic curves, showing analytically and visually (experimentally) how the trisection is done.

PERFORMANCE OBJECTIVES

1. *Given a certain locus condition, students will learn how to sketch a curve directly from the locus without using an equation.*
2. *Given a polar equation, students will plot the curve on polar coordinate paper.*
3. *Given one of the curves discussed in this unit, students will trisect any angle.*

PREASSESSMENT

Students should have done some work with polar coordinates.

TEACHING STRATEGIES

The trisection of an angle can be considered a consequence of the following locus problem: Given $\triangle OAP$ with fixed base $\overline{OA}$ and variable vertex P, find the locus of points P such that $m\angle OPA = 2m\angle POA$ (see Figure 1). Let O be the pole of a polar coordinate system and $\overleftrightarrow{OA}$ the initial line, with A having coordinate (2a,0).

Let $m\angle AOP = \theta$ and $OP = r$. Then by hypothesis, $m\angle APO = 2\theta$, from which it follows $m\angle OAP = \pi - 3\theta$ (π radians $= 180°$). Extend $\overline{OA}$ through A a distance of a units, thereby locating point B. Then $m\angle BAP = 3\theta$. By the law of sines,

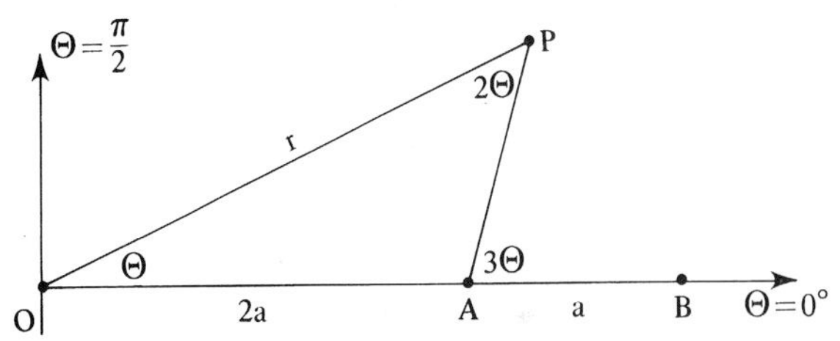

FIGURE 1

$$\frac{r}{\sin(\pi - 3\theta)} = \frac{2a}{\sin 2\theta} \quad (1)$$

from which it follows $r = \dfrac{2a \cdot \sin(\pi - 3\theta)}{\sin 2\theta}$ (2)

Since $\sin(\pi - 3\theta) = \sin 3\theta$ and $\sin 2\theta = 2\sin\theta\cos\theta$, the appropriate substitutions for equation (2) yield

$$r = \frac{a \cdot \sin 3\theta}{\sin\theta\cos\theta}. \quad (3)$$

With $\sin 3\theta = 3\sin\theta - 4\sin^3\theta = \sin\theta(3 - 4\sin^2\theta)$,

$$\text{(3) yields } r = \frac{3a - 4a \cdot \sin^2\theta}{\cos\theta}. \quad (4)$$

Letting $\sin^2\theta = 1 - \cos^2\theta$ in (4),

$r = \dfrac{-a + 4a \cdot \cos^2\theta}{\cos\theta}$, which can easily be simplified, by

letting $\dfrac{1}{\cos\theta} = \sec\theta$, to $r = a(4\cos\theta - \sec\theta)$ (5)

the required polar equation for the *Trisectrix of Maclaurin*.

By placing P on the other side of $\overleftrightarrow{OA}$ (Figure 1) a similar derivation will yield

$$r = a(4\cos\theta - \sec\theta). \qquad (6)$$

Since $\cos(-\theta) = \cos\theta$ and $\sec(-\theta) = \sec\theta$, it follows that (5) is symmetric with respect to $\overleftrightarrow{OA}$. Thus, as confirmed by (6), for all points of the locus above $\overleftrightarrow{OA}$, there are corresponding points below it as well. (These corresponding points are reflections in $\overleftrightarrow{OA}$.)

To sketch the locus, assigning values to θ in (5) and (6) will, of course, furnish points of the Trisectrix. Have students make an exact copy of △AOP on polar coordinate graph paper, so that O is at the origin and $\overleftrightarrow{OA}$ is on the horizontal axis (at $\theta = 0$ radians). Then students should plot various points of the curve and draw the curve.

Students may now use the original diagram (on regular paper). A novel approach to curve sketching would be to plot points and draw lines directly from the given locus condition. One need only assign various values to θ and a corresponding 3θ value to ∠BAP. With $\overleftrightarrow{OB}$ a fixed base for each of these angles, the intersection of the second side of each angle will yield point P. Figure 2 shows such a construction for values of $0° \leq \theta \leq 55°$ in 5° intervals.

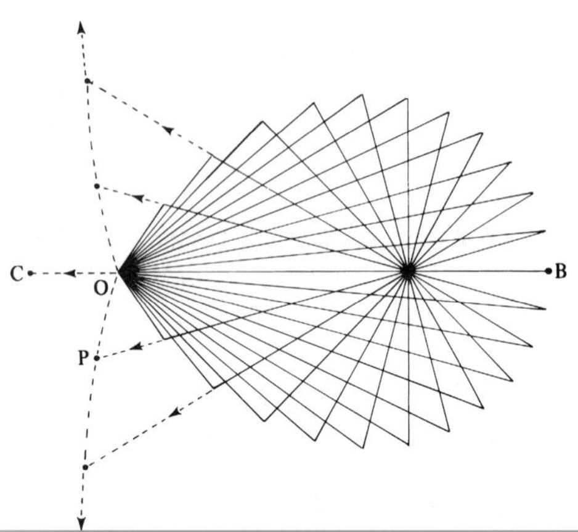

FIGURE 2

For $\theta = 0°$ and 60°, there is no triangle, merely $\overline{OB}$. For $\theta > 60°$, consider some arbitrary point C such that $\overleftrightarrow{COA}$. Let the measure of reflex $m\angle BAP = 195°$, thus placing P below $\overleftrightarrow{COA}$. Then $m\angle COP = 65°$, preserving the trisection property. Note that for $|\theta| \angle 60°$, there will be two asymptotic branches above and below $\overleftrightarrow{OB}$.

Conversely, given (5), it is a bit more difficult to show that for any point P on the Trisectrix, $m\angle BOP = \frac{1}{3}m\angle BAP$. The proof rests on showing that $m\angle OPA = 2\theta$, from which it follows that $m\angle BAP = 3\theta$.

Equation (5) for the Trisectrix of Maclaurin can also be obtained from the following locus problem (see Figure 3):

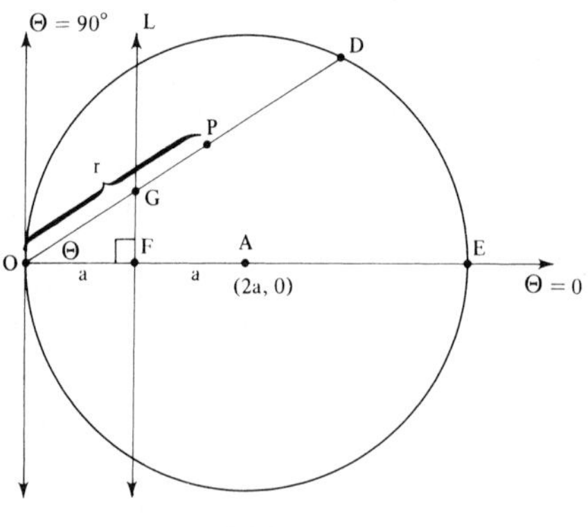

FIGURE 3

Given O, the pole of a polar coordinate system and E $(4a,0)$. At A $(2a,0)$ as center, draw a circle of radius $2a$. Through F $(a,0)$ draw a line L perpendicular to $\overleftrightarrow{OE}$. Locate an arbitrary point D on the "upper" semicircle's circumference and draw $\overleftrightarrow{OD}$, intersecting L at G. Arbitrarily locate P on $\overleftrightarrow{OD}$. As D varies along the semicircle, find the locus of P on $\overleftrightarrow{OD}$ such that OP = GD. The resulting polar equation will be identical to (5). (*Hints for solution:* Let $m\angle AOD = \theta$, $OP = r = GD$. Draw $\overleftrightarrow{DE}$, forming right triangle ODE. Express OD in terms of a and $\cos\theta$, and express OG in terms of a and $\sec\theta$.)

The student now has a method for trisecting an angle (using an additional tool, a curve). Once students have grasped the above, they may consider another curve, the Limacon of Pascal, which also can be used to trisect an angle. However, the following construction for the Limacon should be attempted first.

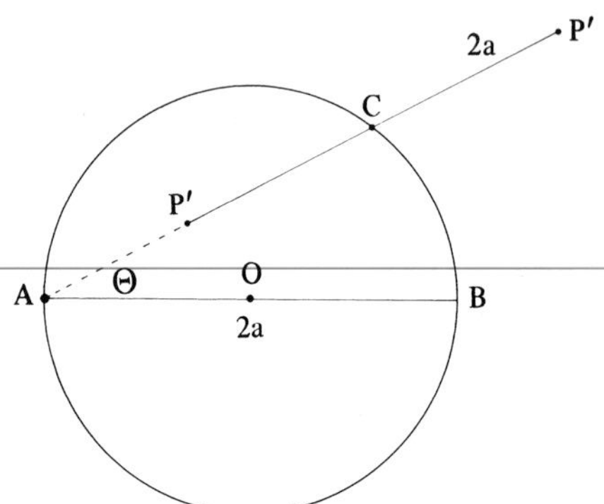

FIGURE 4

Draw a circle of diameter AB = $2a$, center O. Locate an arbitrary point C, distinct from A or B, on the circle's circumference. Place the edge of a ruler at C in such a way that the ruler's midpoint rests on C and that the same edge passes through A. Locate two points P and P′ at a distance of a units on either side of C. Repeat this for different positions of C. P and P′ are then points on the Limacon.

For a visual effect analogous to Figure 2, divide the circle's circumference into 18 evenly spaced arcs. Repeat the procedure in the preceding paragraph for each of these 18 points, thereby yielding 36 points on the Limacon's circumference. Be sure to draw a line to connect all corresponding points P and P′, taking note of the loop that occurs *inside* the Limacon. A suggested diameter for the base circle O is 3″, making $P'C = CP = 1\frac{1}{2}''$.

Figure 5 shows the base circle O, the Limacon's inner loop, as well as a few other points and lines used for the following trisection: Let $\angle BAT$ be congruent to the angle to be trisected, making $AT = a$. Draw $\overline{TO}$, intersecting the loop at P′, and then draw $\overline{AP'}$. We now show that $m\angle BAT = 3$ times $m\angle BAP'$.

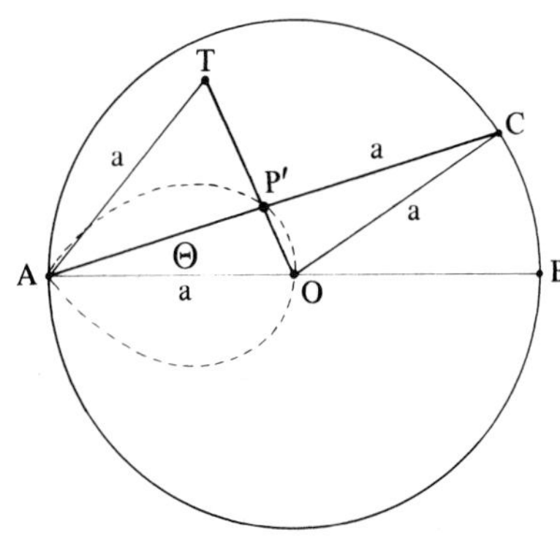

FIGURE 5

Extend $\overline{AP'}$ to intersect the circle at C. Because P′ is a point on the Limacon, $CP' = a$, from the above construction. Draw $\overline{OC}$ and let $m\angle OAP' = \theta$. Immediately, $OA = OC$, $m\angle C = \theta$, therefore $m\angle AOC = \pi - 2\theta$. Since $\triangle OCP'$ is isosceles, each of its base angles has measure $\frac{\pi}{2} - \frac{1}{2}\theta$. $m\angle AP'O = \frac{\pi}{2} + \frac{1}{2}\theta$, and it follows that $m\angle AOP' = \frac{\pi}{2} - \frac{3}{2}\theta$.

However, $\triangle ATO$ is also isosceles, hence $m\angle T = \frac{\pi}{2} - \frac{3}{2}\theta$, from which it follows that $m\angle BAT = 3\theta$, which was to be proved.

POSTASSESSMENT

Construct the Limacon of Figure 4 by locating P and P′ a distance of $2a$ units on either side of C.

Unit 109

 Constructing Hypocycloid and Epicycloid Circular Envelopes

In this unit, two elementary cycloidal curves will be related to each other. Students will then create a circular envelope that will simultaneously encompass both curves.

PERFORMANCE OBJECTIVES

1. *Students will define hypocycloid and epicycloid.*
2. *Students will construct a hypocycloid and an epicycloid.*
3. *Students will generalize these constructions to other hypocycloids and epicycloids.*

PREASSESSMENT

Tenth year mathematics is necessary. A minimal knowledge of polar coordinates is helpful.

TEACHING STRATEGIES

Initiate the introduction of hypocycloid and epicycloid curves by rolling varying sized circular discs about the interior and exterior circumference, respectively, of a fixed circular disc of constant radius. If possible, let the radius of the fixed circle be some integral multiple of the radius of the rolling circle. Have your students speculate on the loci obtained by a fixed point on the circumference of the varying sized rolling circles. For the interior rotations, it will be necessary for the fixed circle to be hollowed out. A Spirograph Kit, if available, is an excellent motivational source.

This unit analyzes the case when the interior and exterior rolling circles each have radius $b = \frac{a}{3}$, as shown in Figure 1 (next column). O is the center of the fixed circle, radius a,

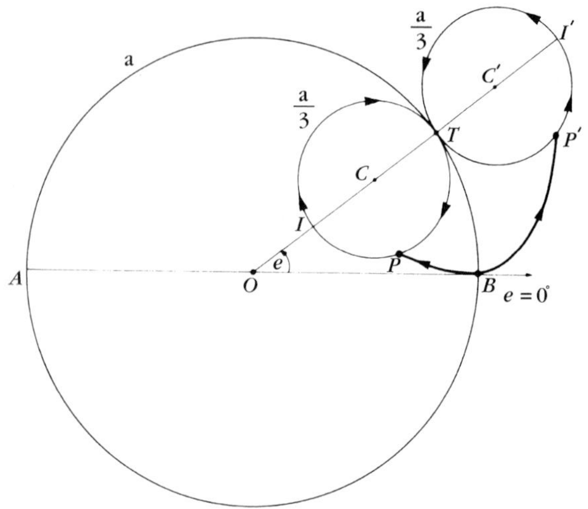

FIGURE 1

and is also the pole of a polar coordinate system. C and C' are the centers, respectively, of the interior and exterior rolling circles. We will assume that both rotating circles are continuously in tangential contact with each other at T. Therefore, $\overleftrightarrow{OT}$, making an angle of measure θ with the initial line, intersects circles C and C' at I, T, and I', and contains the centers, C and C'. It is understood that initially each circle was tangent to the fixed circle at B; furthermore, P and P' are respectively fixed points on the circumference of circles C and C'. At the instant both circles began their circuits, P and P' were coincident with B. The partial loci from B to P and P' are shown in Figure 1.

In Figure 2, we show the complete loci swept out by each fixed point. The locus of P is a *hypocycloid of three cusps*, often called the *deltoid*; whereas the locus of P' is an *epicycloids of three cusps*. Each circle requires three complete rotations before returning to point B. The fixed circle is then a circumcircle for the deltoid and an incircle for the three-cusped epicycloid.

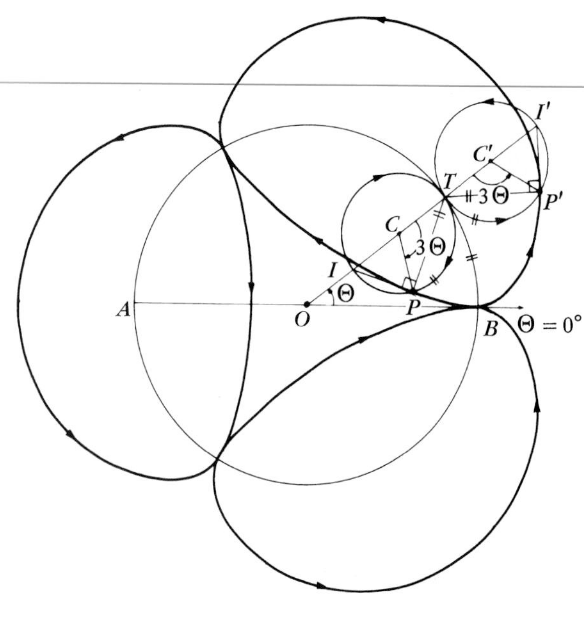

FIGURE 2

The following lines are drawn in each circle: $\overline{IP}$, $\overline{CP}$, and $\overline{TP}$ for circle C; $\overline{TP'}$, $\overline{C'P'}$, and $\overline{I'P'}$ for circle C'. Have your students explain why length $\widehat{TP}$ = length $\widehat{TB}$ = length $\widehat{TP'}$. (1) Then show that

$$m\angle TCP = 3\theta = m\angle TC'P'. \tag{2}$$

Since the radii of circles C and C' are equal, $\triangle TPC \cong \triangle TP'C'$(SAS); and corresponding sides,

$$TP = TP'. \tag{3}$$

Observe that $m\angle TPI = 9° = m\angle TP'I'$. Furthermore, we state without proof that $\overline{PI}$ and $\overline{P'I'}$ are, respectively, tangents to the deltoid at P and the epicycloids at P'. Further details can be found in reference (2).

The above equation (3) implies that a circle centered at T, with radius $TP = TP'$, will be tangent to each curve at P and P'. Certainly, as T varies, there is a corresponding change in the length of $\overline{TP'}$ (or $\overline{TP}$). We show in Figure 3 the final

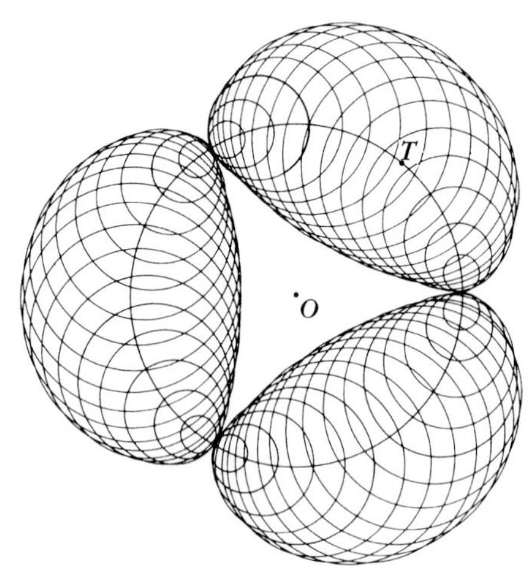

FIGURE 3

result obtained when circles are drawn for 60 equally spaced positions of T along the fixed circle. We utilize symmetry properties of each curve to minimize the work required to determine the varying lengths of $\overline{TP}$: since each curve repeats itself every 120°, and $\overline{OI'}$ divides the curve symmetrically at $m\angle\theta = 60$, it is only necessary to obtain those lengths of $\overline{TP}$ between $0° \leq \theta \leq 60°$, in intervals of measure 6. These lengths were obtained by making an accurate drawing of the required ten positions of either rolling circle.

POSTASSESSMENT

1. Figure 4 (below) shows the results obtained when $b = \frac{a}{4}$. Justify the occurrence of a four-cusped hypocycloid and a four-cusped epicycloid.
2. Generalize for $b = \frac{a}{n}$, $n = 5, 6, \ldots$

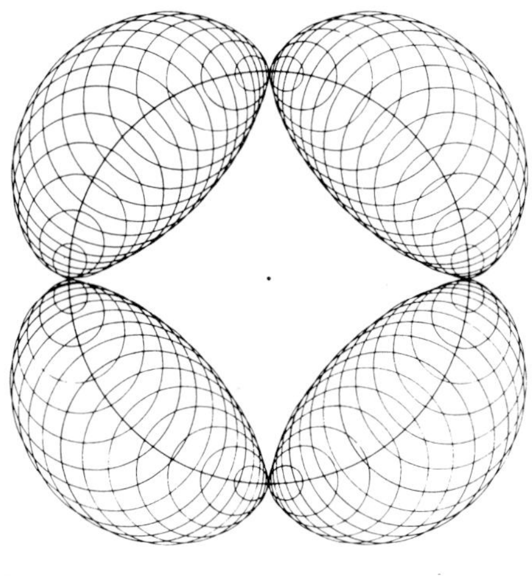

FIGURE 4

3. Make a drawing for the case $b = \frac{a}{2}$ (the *nephroid*). Visually show that the locus of a fixed point on the interior rolling circle is a diameter of the fixed circle.
4. Repeat for $b = a$, the *cardioid*. Show that all the circles centered on T pass through a fixed point; i.e., one of the loci degenerates to a point.

REFERENCES

Beard, Robert S. *Patterns in Space*. Creative Publications, 1973.

Lockwood, E. H. *A Book of Curves*. Cambridge University Press, 1961.

Unit 110

The Harmonic Sequence

This unit is best presented to a class after arithmetic and geometric sequences have been mastered.

PERFORMANCE OBJECTIVES

1. *Students will define harmonic sequence.*
2. *Students will illustrate a harmonic sequence geometrically.*
3. *Students will solve simple problems with harmonic sequences.*

PREASSESSMENT

Ask students to find the fourth term of the sequence:

$1\frac{1}{3}, 1\frac{11}{17}, 2\frac{2}{13}$.

TEACHING STRATEGIES

A natural response on the part of your students is to try to find the fourth term of the above sequence by trying to find a common difference, and when that fails, a common ratio. In a short time your students will feel frustrated. This will offer you a good opportunity to motivate your students toward a "new" type of sequence. Ask students to write each term in improper fraction form and then write its reciprocal. This will yield: $\frac{3}{4}, \frac{17}{28}, \frac{13}{28}$ or $\frac{21}{28}, \frac{17}{28}, \frac{13}{28}$. Further inspection of this new sequence will indicate it to be an arithmetic sequence with a common difference of $\frac{-4}{28}$. Students will now easily obtain the required fourth term, $\frac{1}{\frac{9}{28}} = \frac{28}{9} = 3\frac{1}{9}$.

Students should now be motivated to learn more about the harmonic sequence.

Consider three or more terms in an arithmetic sequence; for example, $a_1, a_2, a_3 \ldots, a_n$. The sequence of reciprocals of these terms, $\frac{1}{a_1}, \frac{1}{a_2}, \frac{1}{a_3}, \ldots, \frac{1}{a_n}$ is called a harmonic sequence. The term *harmonic* comes from a property of musical sounds. If a set of strings of uniform tension whose lengths are proportional to $1, \frac{1}{2}, \frac{1}{3}, \frac{1}{4}, \frac{1}{5}, \frac{1}{6}$ are sounded together, the effect is said to be "harmonious" to the ear. This sequence is harmonic, as the reciprocals of the terms from an arithmetic sequence, 1, 2, 3, 4, 5, 6.

There is no general formula for the sum of the terms in a harmonic series. Problems dealing with a harmonic sequence are generally considered in terms of the related arithmetic sequence.

Two theorems would be useful to consider:
Theorem 1: If a constant is added to (or subtracted from) each term in an arithmetic sequence, then the new sequence is also arithmetic (with the same common difference).
Theorem 2: If each term in an arithmetic sequence is multiplied (or divided) by a constant, the resulting sequence is also arithmetic (but with a different common difference).

The proofs of these theorems are left as exercises.

The proofs of these theorems are simple and straightforward and do not merit special consideration here. However, the following example will help students gain facility in work with harmonic sequences.

Example

If a, b, c forms a harmonic sequence, prove that $\frac{a}{b+c}$, $\frac{b}{c+a}$, $\frac{c}{a+b}$ also forms a harmonic sequence.

Solution: Since $\frac{1}{a}, \frac{1}{b}, \frac{1}{c}$, forms an arithmetic sequence, $\frac{a+b+c}{a}, \frac{a+b+c}{b}, \frac{a+b+c}{c}$ also forms an arithmetic sequence. This may be written as $1+\frac{b+c}{a}, 1+\frac{a+c}{b}, 1+\frac{a+b}{c}$. Therefore $\frac{b+c}{a}, \frac{a+c}{b}, \frac{a+b}{c}$, forms an arithmetic sequence. Thus $\frac{a}{b+c}, \frac{b}{a+c}, \frac{c}{a+b}$ forms a harmonic sequence.

Perhaps one of the more interesting aspects of any sequence is to establish a geometric model of the sequence.

One geometric interpretation of a harmonic sequence can be taken from the intersection points of the interior and exterior angle bisectors of a triangle with the side of the triangle.

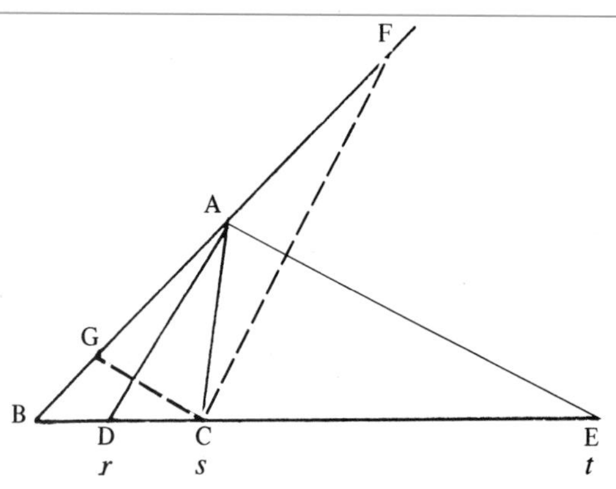

FIGURE 1

Consider $\triangle ABC$, where $\overline{AD}$ bisects $\angle BAC$ and $\overline{AE}$ bisects $\angle CAF$ and B, D, C, and E are collinear (see Figure 1). It can easily be proved that for exterior angle bisector $\overline{AE}$, $\frac{BE}{CE} = \frac{AB}{AC}$ (i.e., draw $\overline{GC} // \overline{AE}$; AG = AC; also $\frac{BE}{CE} = \frac{AB}{AG} = \frac{AB}{AC}$).
Similarly for interior angle bisector $\overline{AD}$,

$$\frac{BD}{CD} = \frac{AB}{AC}$$

(The proof is done by drawing $\overline{CF} // \overline{AD}$; AF = AC; $\frac{BD}{CD} = \frac{AB}{AF} = \frac{AB}{AC}$.)

Therefore $\frac{BE}{CE} = \frac{BD}{CD}$ or $\frac{CD}{CE} = \frac{BD}{BE}$. It is then said that the points B and C separate the points D and E harmonically.

Now suppose $\overleftrightarrow{BDCE}$ is a number line with B as the zero point, point D at coordinate r, point C at coordinate s, and point E at coordinate t. Therefore BD = r, BC = s, and BE = t. We shall show that r, s, t forms a harmonic sequence.

Since $\frac{CD}{CE} = \frac{BD}{BE}, \frac{BC-BD}{BE-BC} = \frac{BD}{BE}$, or $\frac{s-r}{t-s} = \frac{r}{t}$. Therefore $t(s-r) = r(t-s)$ and $ts - tr = rt - rs$. Dividing each term by rst, we get $\frac{1}{r} - \frac{1}{s} = \frac{1}{s} - \frac{1}{t}$, which indicates that $\frac{1}{t}, \frac{1}{s}, \frac{1}{r}$ forms an arithmetic sequence. Thus, r, s, t forms a harmonic sequence.

Students should now have reasonably good insight into a harmonic sequence.

POSTASSESSMENT

1. Set up and equation with the terms of the harmonic sequence a, b, c. (Use the definition.)
2. Find the 26th term of the sequence:

$$2\frac{1}{2}, 1\frac{12}{13}, 1\frac{9}{16}, 1\frac{6}{19} \ldots$$

3. Prove that if a^2, b^2, c^2 forms an arithmetic sequence, then $(b+c), (c+a), (a+b)$ forms a harmonic sequence.

Unit 111

Transformations and Matrices

This unit will algebraically formalize a discussion of geometric transformations by use of matrices.

PERFORMANCE OBJECTIVES

1. *Given a particular geometric transformation, students will name the 2 × 2 matrix that effects that transformation.*
2. *Given certain 2 × 2 matrices, students will, at a glance, none the transformation each matrix effects.*

PREASSESSMENT

1. On a Cartesian plane, graph △ABC with vertices at A(2,2), B(4,2), C(2,6). Write the coordinates of A′, B′, C′ that result when △ABC undergoes each of the following transformations:
   a. Translation by −5 units in the x direction and 2 units in the y direction.
   b. Reflection across the x-axis.
   c. Rotation of 90° about the origin.
   d. Enlargement scale factor 2 with center at (2,2).
2. Given an equilateral triangle as shown with each vertex the same distance from the origin, list geometric transformations that leave the position of the triangle unchanged, assuming the vertices are indistinguishable.

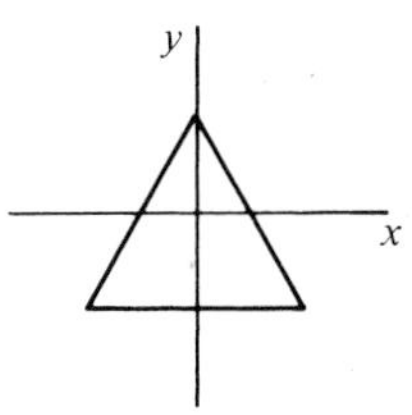

FIGURE 1

TEACHING STRATEGIES

The teacher should first make students aware of a matrix array of numbers. Tell the students that a matrix of size $a \times b$ has a rows and b columns enclosed in brackets. When $a = b$ the matrix is said to be *square*. The class should see that adding matrices involves adding the numbers is corresponding positions in each matrix, for example $\begin{bmatrix} a \\ b \end{bmatrix} + \begin{bmatrix} c \\ d \end{bmatrix} = \begin{bmatrix} a + c \\ b + d \end{bmatrix}$, and the students must see that matrices must be of the same size (dimension) to be added.

When showing students how to multiply matrices, you should use the following general form. Note carefully the column-row relationship between the two matrix factors in the product.

$$\begin{bmatrix} a\,b \\ c\,d \end{bmatrix} \cdot \begin{bmatrix} x \\ y \end{bmatrix} = \begin{bmatrix} ax + by \\ cx + dy \end{bmatrix}$$

Students may now describe the position of a point either by its coordinate (x, y) or by a 2 × 1 matrix, called a *position vector*, $\begin{bmatrix} x \\ y \end{bmatrix}$, which represents the vector from the origin to the point.

You may find it effective to use the phrase "is mapped onto" when describing the effect of a transformation. The symbol for this phrase using matrices is "$\longrightarrow$."

Translations provide a simple introduction into the use of matrices.

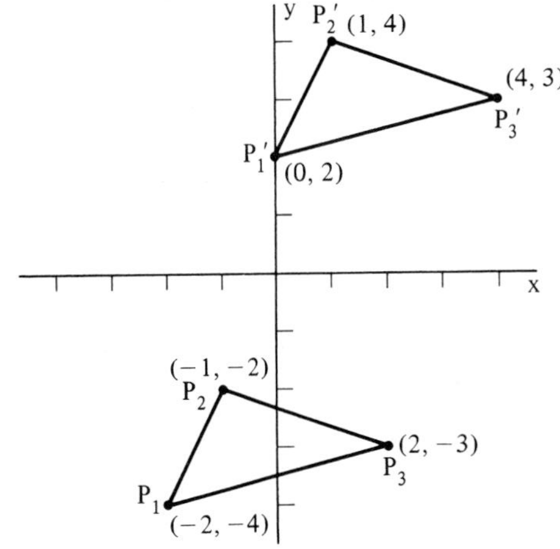

A translation of the triangle $P_1P_2P_3$ to $P_1'P_2'P_3'$ can be generalized in matrix form

$$\begin{bmatrix} x \\ y \end{bmatrix} \longrightarrow \begin{bmatrix} x \\ y \end{bmatrix} + \begin{bmatrix} 2 \\ 6 \end{bmatrix}$$

$\begin{bmatrix} 2 \\ 6 \end{bmatrix}$ represents here a "translation vector," meaning it translates (x, y) 2 units in the x direction and 6 units in the y directions. Students should readily see that by matrix addition each point P_1, P_2, P_3 is mapped onto P_1', P_2', P_3' respectively. That is, $P_1\begin{bmatrix} -2 \\ -4 \end{bmatrix} + \begin{bmatrix} 2 \\ 6 \end{bmatrix} = P'_1\begin{bmatrix} 0 \\ 2 \end{bmatrix}$, $P_2\begin{bmatrix} -1 \\ -2 \end{bmatrix} + \begin{bmatrix} 2 \\ 6 \end{bmatrix} = P'_2\begin{bmatrix} 1 \\ 4 \end{bmatrix}$, $P_3\begin{bmatrix} 2 \\ -3 \end{bmatrix} + \begin{bmatrix} 2 \\ 6 \end{bmatrix} = P'_3\begin{bmatrix} 4 \\ 3 \end{bmatrix}$ Matrix addition of 2×1 position vectors can therefore describe any translation in the two-dimensional plane. Students should be given several examples and exercises where a particular point (x_1, y_1) is translated into any other point $(x_2, y_2)$by a suitable choice of 2×1 matrix $\begin{bmatrix} x \\ y \end{bmatrix}$ such that

$$\begin{bmatrix} x_1 \\ y_1 \end{bmatrix} + \begin{bmatrix} x \\ y \end{bmatrix} = \begin{bmatrix} x_2 \\ y_2 \end{bmatrix}.$$

Rotations, *reflections*, and *enlargements* are more interesting, and to describe them algebraically requires 2×2 matrices. Students should first be given two or three example of the type $\begin{bmatrix} 2 & 3 \\ -1 & 2 \end{bmatrix} \cdot \begin{bmatrix} 3 \\ 2 \end{bmatrix} = \begin{bmatrix} 12 \\ 1 \end{bmatrix}$ for two reasons. For one, they may need practice in matrix multiplication, a skill they must master before embarking on the rest of this topic, and second, and most important in this strategy, is that students begin to think of the matrix $\begin{bmatrix} 2 & 3 \\ -1 & 2 \end{bmatrix}$ (or any 2×2 matrix) as a transformation of the point P(3,2) onto the point P′(12, 1). Each example of this type should be accompanied by an illustration, as in Figure 2.

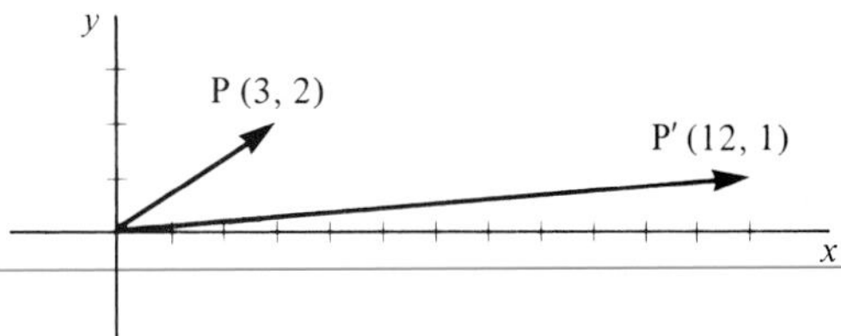

FIGURE 2

When the students are familiar with the notion that any 2×2 matrix represents a transformation, the teacher should be ready to show them that some 2×2 matrices represent special transformations with which they are familiar. For example, the teacher may give them the matrix and point, respectively (which follow):

1. $\begin{bmatrix} -1 & 0 \\ 0 & 1 \end{bmatrix} \cdot \overset{P_1}{\begin{bmatrix} 2 \\ 3 \end{bmatrix}} = \overset{P'_1}{\begin{bmatrix} -2 \\ 3 \end{bmatrix}}$

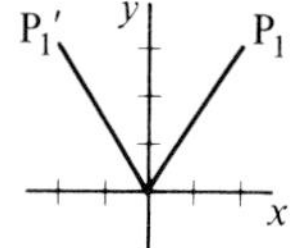

and

2. $\begin{bmatrix} 0 & -1 \\ 1 & 0 \end{bmatrix} \cdot \overset{P_2}{\begin{bmatrix} 3 \\ 1 \end{bmatrix}} = \overset{P'_3}{\begin{bmatrix} -1 \\ 3 \end{bmatrix}}$

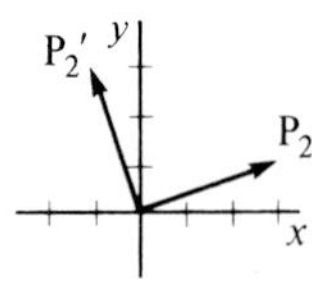

and

3. $\begin{bmatrix} 3 & 0 \\ 0 & 3 \end{bmatrix} \cdot \overset{P_3}{\begin{bmatrix} -2 \\ -1 \end{bmatrix}} = \overset{P'_3}{\begin{bmatrix} -6 \\ -3 \end{bmatrix}}$

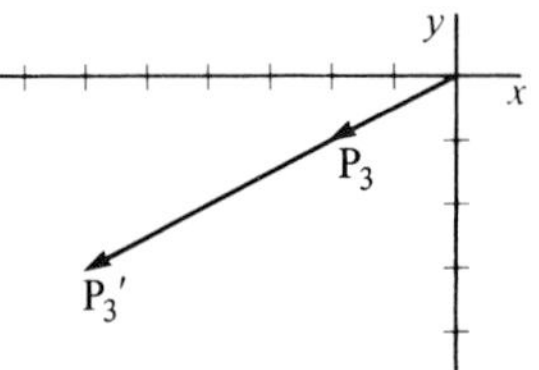

Students may have recognized the transformations in these examples as (1) a reflection (across the y axis), (2) a positive rotation of 90°, and (3) an enlargement, scale factor 3. To emphasize the point that it was not merely by chance that the matrices accomplished these transformations, ask the students to take the general point $\begin{bmatrix} x \\ y \end{bmatrix}$ and multiply it by each of the matrices. The students' answers will be, respectively, $\begin{bmatrix} -x \\ y \end{bmatrix}$, $\begin{bmatrix} -y \\ x \end{bmatrix}$, $\begin{bmatrix} 3x \\ 3y \end{bmatrix}$. Students will therefore see (the second case may require some insight) that the matrices $\begin{bmatrix} -1 & 0 \\ 0 & 1 \end{bmatrix}$, $\begin{bmatrix} 0 & -1 \\ 1 & 0 \end{bmatrix}$, and $\begin{bmatrix} 3 & 0 \\ 0 & 3 \end{bmatrix}$ do indeed accomplish, in the general case, the transformations they recognized in the particular examples.

To achieve performance objectives, whereby matrices provide a handy tool in transformational work, show what 2×2 matrices do to the unit vectors $i\begin{bmatrix} 1 \\ 0 \end{bmatrix}$ and $j\begin{bmatrix} 0 \\ 1 \end{bmatrix}$.

Choose any 2×2 matrix, as in the previous example, $\begin{bmatrix} 2 & 3 \\ -1 & 2 \end{bmatrix}$, and ask your students to multiply the unit vectors i and j by this matrix.

$$\begin{bmatrix} 2 & 3 \\ -1 & 2 \end{bmatrix} \cdot \begin{bmatrix} 1 \\ 0 \end{bmatrix} = \begin{bmatrix} 2 \\ -1 \end{bmatrix},$$

$$\begin{bmatrix} 2 & 3 \\ -1 & 2 \end{bmatrix} \cdot \begin{bmatrix} 0 \\ 1 \end{bmatrix} = \begin{bmatrix} 3 \\ 2 \end{bmatrix}$$

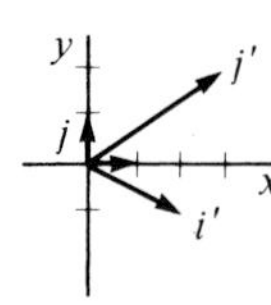

Use another example:

$$\begin{bmatrix} -1 & 0 \\ 0 & -1 \end{bmatrix} \cdot \begin{bmatrix} 1 \\ 0 \end{bmatrix} = \begin{bmatrix} -1 \\ 0 \end{bmatrix},$$

$$\begin{bmatrix} -1 & 0 \\ 0 & -1 \end{bmatrix} \cdot \begin{bmatrix} 0 \\ 1 \end{bmatrix} = \begin{bmatrix} 0 \\ -1 \end{bmatrix},$$

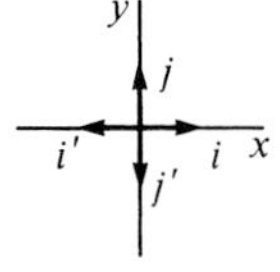

Continue with more examples until it is obvious to the students that

In any 2×2 matrix $\begin{bmatrix} a & b \\ c & d \end{bmatrix}$, multiplying by $\begin{bmatrix} 1 \\ 0 \end{bmatrix}$ gives the first column $\begin{bmatrix} a \\ c \end{bmatrix}$ and multiplying by $\begin{bmatrix} 0 \\ 1 \end{bmatrix}$ gives the second column $\begin{bmatrix} b \\ d \end{bmatrix}$. In other words, the matrix maps the base vectors $\begin{bmatrix} 1 \\ 0 \end{bmatrix}$ and $\begin{bmatrix} 0 \\ 1 \end{bmatrix}$ onto $\begin{bmatrix} a \\ c \end{bmatrix}$ and $\begin{bmatrix} b \\ d \end{bmatrix}$, respectively.

When this conclusion is reached and appreciated by each student, the class then holds the key to reaching the performance objectives. Check whether the class can answer each of the following two types of problems:

1. Which transformation is performed by applying the matrix $\begin{bmatrix} 2 & 0 \\ 0 & 2 \end{bmatrix}$ to the unit vectors?

   Show them that $\begin{bmatrix} 2 & 0 \\ 0 & 2 \end{bmatrix} \cdot \begin{bmatrix} 1 \\ 0 \end{bmatrix} = \begin{bmatrix} 2 \\ 0 \end{bmatrix}$

   and so $\begin{bmatrix} 1 \\ 0 \end{bmatrix}$ has been mapped onto $\begin{bmatrix} 2 \\ 0 \end{bmatrix}$, and $\begin{bmatrix} 2 & 0 \\ 0 & 2 \end{bmatrix} \cdot \begin{bmatrix} 0 \\ 1 \end{bmatrix} = \begin{bmatrix} 0 \\ 2 \end{bmatrix}$ and so $\begin{bmatrix} 0 \\ 1 \end{bmatrix}$ has been mapped onto $\begin{bmatrix} 0 \\ 2 \end{bmatrix}$.

   Conclude that $\begin{bmatrix} 2 & 0 \\ 0 & 2 \end{bmatrix}$ is therefore an enlargement, scale factor 2.

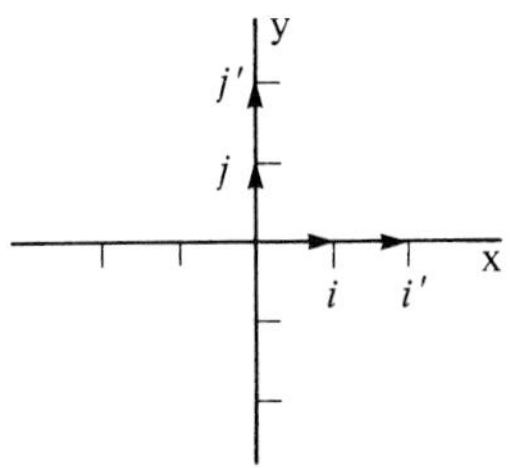

2. Which matrix effects the transformation: rotation by 180°, centered at the origin? Ask the students to draw the effect of 180 rotation the base vectors.

   Check with them that $\begin{bmatrix} 1 \\ 0 \end{bmatrix} \rightarrow \begin{bmatrix} -1 \\ 0 \end{bmatrix}$ and $\begin{bmatrix} 0 \\ 1 \end{bmatrix} \rightarrow \begin{bmatrix} 0 \\ -1 \end{bmatrix}$. Ask them what 2×2 matrix will give the results $\begin{bmatrix} a & d \\ c & d \end{bmatrix} \cdot \begin{bmatrix} 1 \\ 0 \end{bmatrix} = \begin{bmatrix} -1 \\ 0 \end{bmatrix}$ and $\begin{bmatrix} a & b \\ c & d \end{bmatrix} \cdot \begin{bmatrix} 0 \\ 1 \end{bmatrix} = \begin{bmatrix} 0 \\ -1 \end{bmatrix}$. They should by now know that $\begin{bmatrix} -1 \\ 0 \end{bmatrix}$ gives the first column of the 2×2 matrix and $\begin{bmatrix} 0 \\ -1 \end{bmatrix}$ gives the second column.

Therefore the desired matrix is $\begin{bmatrix} -1 & 0 \\ 0 & -1 \end{bmatrix}$. Numerous examples and exercises should follow, such as those found in the postassessment.

Depending on his or her aims, the teacher may want to go on at this point to discuss inverse transformations (i.e., ones that reverse the effect of the original transformation) and transformations followed in the same problem by other transformations. The teacher should be aware here too of the value of using matrices, for the inverse of a matrix represents the inverse of a transformation, and multiplying two 2×2 matrices represents the effect of one transformation followed by another.

POSTASSESSMENT

1. What transformation does the matrix
   a. $\begin{bmatrix} 0 & 1 \\ -1 & 0 \end{bmatrix}$
   b. $\begin{bmatrix} 2 & 0 \\ 0 & -2 \end{bmatrix}$
   c. $\begin{bmatrix} 0 & -1 \\ -1 & 0 \end{bmatrix}$ represent?
2. Find the matrix of each of the following transformations:
   a. Reflection across the line $y = x$.
   b. Enlargement with center at the origin, scale factor $\frac{1}{2}$.
   c. Rotation by $-90°$.

Unit 112

 The Method of Differences

Many students familiar with arithmetic and geometric progressions will welcome the opportunity to extend their knowledge of sequences and series to a much broader class of simple function.

PERFORMANCE OBJECTIVES

1. *Given sufficient terms of a sequences whose* nth *term is a rational, integral function of* n, *students will form an array consisting of the successive order of differences.*
2. *Given such an array, students will then use the method to differences to find expressions for the* nth *term and the sum of the first* n *terms.*

PREASSESSMENT

Students should be acquainted with the Binomial Theorem for positive, integral exponents as it is ordinarily taught in high schools.

TEACHING STRATEGIES

Begin the lesson by challenging the class to find the general term of the sequence 2, 12, 36, 80, 150, 252.... After initial efforts of most students to find the familiar arithmetic and geometric progressions have proved unsuccessful, hint that sequences of this sort might be generated by single polynomials, e.g., n^2 (1, 4, 9, ...) or n^3 (1, 8, 27, ...). One student or another may shortly recognize that the nth term is given by $n^3 + n^2$.

Elicit that an infinite number of such sequences could be produced by using familiar polynomial functions. Then explain that a simple method exists for finding both the general term and the sum of these sequences. It is called the Method of Differences, and although it is not generally taught to high school students, it is nonetheless well within their grasp.

Have the class form the "difference between successive terms" of the above sequence, and then continue the process as shown below.

$$\begin{array}{ccccccc} 2 & 12 & 36 & 80 & 150 & 252\ldots \\ & 10 & 24 & 44 & 70 & 102\ldots \\ & & 14 & 20 & 26 & 32\ldots \\ & & & 6 & 6 & 6\ldots \end{array} \qquad (1)$$

Observe that we reach a line of differences in which all terms are equal. To test whether this occurrence is merely accidental, have the students form sequences from polynomials such as $n^3 + 5n$, $2n^3 + 3$, and so forth, and then repeat the process of taking successive differences. A consensus will soon emerge that an eventual line of equal terms is indeed characteristic of such sequences. The formal proof of this proposition (although simple) is not necessary at this time. Sufficient motivation will have been produced to examine the general case shown below.

Given sequence:	$U_1, U_2, U_3, U_4, U_5, U_6, \ldots$	
1st order of difference:	$\Delta U_1, \Delta U_2, \Delta U_3, \Delta U_4, \Delta U_5, \ldots$	(2)
2nd order of difference:	$\Delta_2 U_1, \Delta_2 U_2, \Delta_2 U_3, \Delta_2 U_4, \ldots$	
3rd order of difference:	$\Delta_3 U_1, \Delta_3 U_2, \Delta_3 U_3, \ldots$	
	....	

The notation will be self-evidence to all who have written out several previous arrays. Thus: $\Delta U_3 = U_4 - U_3$, $\Delta_2 U_3 = \Delta U_4 - \Delta U_3$. etc. If the delta symbol, Δ, appears too forbidding for some, if can simply be replaced by the letter D.

From the method of forming each entry in (2) it can be seen that any term is equal to the sum of the term immediately preceding it added to the term below it on the left.

Using nothing more than this simple observation, we will now express each term of the given sequence as a function of the descending terms making up the left-hand boundary.

Thus: $\boxed{U_2 = U_1 + \Delta U_1}$ (3)

Also, $U_3 = U_2 + \Delta U_2$ with $\Delta U_2 = \Delta U_1 + \Delta_2 U_1$.
$U_3 = (U_1 + \Delta U_1) + (\Delta U_1 + \Delta_2 U_1)$

$\boxed{U_3 = U_1 + 2\Delta U_1 + \Delta_2 U_1}$ (4)

By referring to (2) students should be able to follow the reasoning that leads to an expression for U_4 in terms of U_1.
$U_4 = U_3 + \Delta U_3$; however, $\Delta U_3 = \Delta U_2 + \Delta_2 U_2$.
But, $\Delta U_2 = \Delta U_1 + \Delta_2 U_1$, and $\Delta_2 U_2 + \Delta_2 U_1 + \Delta_3 U_1$.
Therefore, $\Delta U_3 = \Delta U_1 + 2\Delta_2 U_1 + \Delta_3 U_1$

Now, using (3) and (4):
$U_4 = (U_1 + 2\Delta U_1 + \Delta_2 U_1) + (\Delta U_1 + 2\Delta_2 U_1 + \Delta_3 U_1)$

$$\boxed{U_4 + U_1 + 3\Delta U_1 + 3\Delta_2 U_1 + \Delta_3 U_1} \quad (5)$$

Calling attention to the boxed expressions for U_2, U_3, U_4 the teacher can elicit the fact that the numerical coefficients involved are those of the Binomial Theorem. Note, however, that the coefficients used for the *fourth* term (1, 3, 3, 1) are those found in a binomial expansion for the exponent *three*. If this remains true generally, we shall be able to write

$$\boxed{Un = U_1 + (n-1)\Delta U_1 + \frac{(n-1)(n-2)}{1 \cdot 2}\Delta_2 U_1 + \dots + {}_{n-1}C_r \Delta_r U_1 + \dots + \Delta_{n-1} U_1} \quad (6)$$

If desired, the formal proof of (6) can be easily obtained by mathematical induction once the identity ${}_nC_r + {}_nC_{r-1} = {}_{n+1}C_r$ is established.

Some teachers may wish to rewrite (6) so as to resemble the notation typically used in treating arithmetic progressions. To do this, let the first term of the sequence be "a" and the first terms of each successive order of difference are $d_1, d_2, d_3 \dots$. Then the nth term will be:

$$\ell = a + (n-1)d_1 + \frac{(n-1)(n-2)}{1 \cdot 2} d_2 + \dots \quad (7)$$

Finding the Sum of the First *n* Terms

Examine the following array, in which $U_1, U_2 \dots$ are again the terms of the given sequence we wish to sum.

$$\begin{array}{ccccc} S_1 & S_2 & S_3 & S_4 & S_5 \dots \\ & U_1 & U_2 & U_3 & U_4 \dots \\ & & \Delta U_1 & \Delta U_2 & \Delta U_3 \dots \end{array} \quad (8)$$

Observe that the S-terms are formed by relations such as

$$S_2 = 0 + U_1 = U_1$$
$$S_3 = S_2 + U_2 = U_1 + U_2$$
$$S_4 = S_3 + U_3 = U_1 + U_2 + U_3$$
$$S_5 = S_4 + U_4 = U_1 + U_2 + U_3 + U_4$$

Thus, if we can find an expression for S_{n+1} we will have also found the sum of the first n terms. To find S_{n+1} one simply applies the previously determined equation (6) to the above array (8). Before doing so, students should carefully compare (8) with (2). Then it should become evident that the proper application of equation (6) yields

$$S_{n+1} = 0 + nU_1 + \frac{n(n-1)}{1 \cdot 2}\Delta U_1 + \dots + \Delta_n U_n \quad \text{or}$$

$$\boxed{U_1 + U_2 + \dots U_n = n\,U_1 + \frac{n(n-1)}{1 \cdot 2}\Delta U_1 + \dots + \Delta_n U_n} \quad (9)$$

As an illustration, let us sum the first n squares of the integers.

$$\begin{array}{l} 1,\ 4,\ 9,\ 16,\ 25\ \dots \\ \quad 3,\ 5,\ 7,\ 9\ \dots \\ \qquad 2,\ 2,\ 2\ \dots \end{array}$$

$$\text{Sum of } n^2 = n \cdot 1 + \frac{n(n-1)}{1 \cdot 2} \cdot 3 + \frac{n(n-1)(n-2)}{1 \cdot 2 \cdot 3} \cdot 2$$
$$= \frac{6n + 9n(n-1) + 2n(n-1)(n-2)}{(6)}$$
$$= \frac{n}{6}(n+1)(2n+1)$$

Students may readily confirm the validity of this expression. Again, as before, the teacher may elect to rewrite (9) in terms of $a, d_1, d_2, \dots$ and so forth.

POSTASSESSMENT

Have students find the nth term and the sum of n terms for

1. 2, 5, 10, 17, 26 . . .
2. 1, 8, 27, 64, 125 . . .
3. 12, 40, 90, 168, 280, 432 . . .

Have students create sequences of their own from simple polynomials, and then challenge their classmates to discover the general term.

Unit 113

 Probability Applied to Baseball

Each year the first months of school coincide with the last months of major league baseball. The playing of the World Series in October normally provides a source of distraction. For mathematics teachers, however, this event can be harnessed to provide useful motivation for a host of probability applications that have high intrinsic academic value.

PERFORMANCE OBJECTIVES

1. *Given odds for opposing World Series teams, students will calculate the expected number of games to be played.*
2. *Given the batting average of any hitter, students will estimate the probability of his attaining any given number of hits during a game.*

PREASSESSMENT

Previous study of permutations and probability is not necessary if some introductory discussion is provided. The topic is thus suitable for younger senior high school students (who have not yet learned the Binomial Theorem). Older students need even less preparation.

TEACHING STRATEGIES

The lesson should begin with an informal, spirited discussion of which team is likely to win the World Series. Newspaper clippings of the "odds" should be brought in. This leads directly to the question of how many games will be required for a decision.

Length of Series

If the outcome of a World Series is designated by a sequence of letters representing the winning team (NAANAA means National League won the first and fourth games while losing the rest), challenge the class to find the total number of possible outcomes.

Discuss the solution in terms of "permutations of objects that are not all different." Observe that separate cases of four, five, six, or seven objects must be considered. Elicit that a constraint in the problem is that the winning team must always win the last game. The results can be tabulated as

As to the probabilities that the series will actually last four, five, six, or seven games, these clearly depend on the relative strengths of the teams. Most students will recognize intuitively that the prospects for a long series increase when the teams are closely matched, and vice versa.

TABLE 1

No. of Games Played	4	5	6	7
No. of Sequences	2	8	20	40

If newspapers "odds" are available, these should be translated into the probability of As winning (p) and Ns winning ($q = 1 - p$). If the odds are $m{:}n$ then $p = \frac{m}{(m + n)}$.

After a brief discussion reviewing the principle that governs the probability of independent events (perhaps illustrated by coin throws), it should become clear that the probability of an American League sweep is $\text{P(A in 4)} = p \cdot p \cdot p \cdot p = p^4$. Similarly $\text{P(N in 4)} = q^4$ and the overall probability of a four-game series is simply $p^4 + q^4$.

It is rewarding for students to find their intuitions confirmed, so it will be illuminating to substitute the various values for p and q that result from different odds, as shown by Table 2 below.

TABLE 2

If odds favoring A are	1:1	2:1	3:1
P (4-game series)	.13	.21	.32

Students should be encouraged to extend this table of values.

Before calculating the likelihood of a five-game series, recall work done at the outset to determine the number of possible five-game sequences. There were eight such sequences (NAAAA, ANAAA, AANAA, AAANA, ANNNN, and so forth) and the probability associated with *each* of the first four is given by $q \cdot p \cdot p \cdot p \cdot p = p \cdot q \cdot p \cdot p \cdot p = p \cdot p \cdot q \cdot p \cdot p = p \cdot p \cdot p \cdot q \cdot p = p^4q$.

Since these outcomes are mutually exclusive, the probability of $\text{P(A in 5)} = 4p^4q$. In identical fashion $\text{P(N in 5)} =$

$4pq^4$ and the overall chance for a five-game series is $4p^4q + 4pq^4 = 4pq(p^3 + q^3)$.

Similarly, by falling back on the work done on permutations at the start of the lesson, it is simple to show that P(six-game series) $= 10p^2q^2(p^2 + q^2)$ and P(seven-game series) $= 20p^3q^3(p + q) = 20p^3q^3[p + q = 1]$.

As more complete information is derived, Table 2 can be extended to five, six, and seven games for various initial odds.

At this point, students may be introduced to (or reminded of) the important concept of Mathematical Expectation, E(X). With probabilities available for each outcome, E(X) for the length of the series can be calculated.

TABLE 3
ODDS 1:1

X – no. of Games	4	5	6	7
P(X)	.13	.24	.31	.31

$$E(X) = \sum X_i P(X_i) = 5.75$$

$$\left[\sum \text{ notation can be avoided}\right]$$

Batting Probabilities

Most students who follow baseball believe they have a clear understanding of the meaning of "batting average," and its implications for a hitter going into a game. Challenge the class to estimate the chances of a player getting at least one hit in four times at bat if his season-long batting average has been .250. Some may feel there is a virtual certainty of a hit since $.250 = \frac{1}{4}$.

Begin the analysis, as before, by using a sequence of letters to denote the hitter's performance (NHNN means a hit the second time up). Again, calculate the total number of possible sequences, which will be seen to be 16. Weaker students would be advised to write out each of these permutations.

Select the simplest case of NNNN. From previous work, the probability of this outcomes should be evident to the class as P(hitless) $= \frac{3}{4}\cdot\frac{3}{4}\cdot\frac{3}{4}\cdot\frac{3}{4} = \frac{(3)^4}{(4)} = \frac{81}{256} = 0.32$. (Recall: P(H) $= \frac{1}{4}$ and P(N) $= \frac{3}{4}$.) Since all other sequences involve at *least* one hit, their combined probability is $1 - .32 = 0.68$. Thus there is only a 68 percent chance that the batter will achieve at least one hit in four times. Although this result is not startling, it may definitely entail some readjustment in the thinking of some students.

In a similar manner, probabilities can be calculated for the cases of one hit (four possible sequences), two hits (six possible sequences), and so on.

The above topics represent examples of Binomial Experiments and Bernouilli Trials. Discuss with the class the definition of a Bernouilli Trial and the criteria for a Binomial Experiment, using illustrations from dice tossing, coin throwing, and so forth. Elicit their estimation of whether these concepts might be usefully applied to other real-life events such as gamete unions in genetics, the success of medical procedures such as surgery, and finally, the success of a batsman in baseball.

There are inherent limitations in attempting to treat baseball performances as Bernouilli Trials, especially in a unique situation like a World Series. Nonetheless, there is value in having students acquire a sense of "first-order approximations." At the same time, their insight into the applications of mathematics can be deepened by confronting a topic with which they feel familiar and are competent to evaluate.

POSTASSESSMENT

Have students

1. extend Table 2 for P(five-game series), P(6), P(7) for the odds shown, as well as other realistic odds.
2. reconstruct Table 3 for odds of 2:1, 3:1 and then calculate E(X) for these cases.

Unit 114

Introduction to Geometric Transformations

Beginning with an introduction to the three basic rigid motion transformations, this unit will show how a group can be developed, where the elements are transformations.

PERFORMANCE OBJECTIVES

1. *Students will define translation, rotation, and reflection.*

2. *Students will identify the appropriate transformation from a diagram showing a change of position.*
3. *Students will test the group postulates for a given set of transformations under composition.*

PREASSESSMENT

This unit should be presented when students have mastered the basics of geometry. They should be familiar with the concept of group, but do not need to have had any exposure to transformations prior to this unit. A knowledge of functions is also helpful for this unit.

TEACHING STRATEGIES

The first part of this unit will concern itself with a brief introduction to the three basic rigid motion transformations: translations, rotations, and reflections.

Students should recall that a one-to-one and onto function is a congruence. That is, $\overline{AB} \xrightarrow[\text{onto}]{\text{1-1}} \overline{CD}$ implies that $\overline{AB} \cong \overline{CD}$.

Translations

Consider $T{:}\alpha \xrightarrow[\text{onto}]{\text{1-1}} \alpha$, that is, a mapping of the entire plane onto itself in the direction of a given vector v.

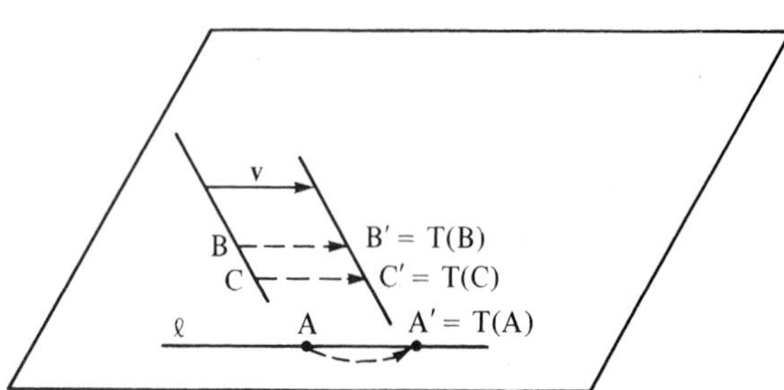

In the figure above each point in the plane is taken to a new point in the plane in the direction and distance of the translation vector v. here T(B) = B′,B′ is the image of B under the translation. Points along line ℓ, which is parallel to **v**, are mapped onto other points of ℓ. To insure a good understanding of this type of transformation ask your students the following questions:

1. Which lines are mapped onto themselves? (those parallel to the translation vector)
2. Which points are mapped onto themselves? (none)
3. Which vector determines the inverse of T? (the negative of v)

Rotations

Consider $R{:}\alpha \xrightarrow[\text{onto}]{\text{1-1}} \alpha$, that is a mapping of the entire plane onto itself as determined by a rotation of any angle about a point. We shall agree to consider only counterclockwise rotations unless specified otherwise.

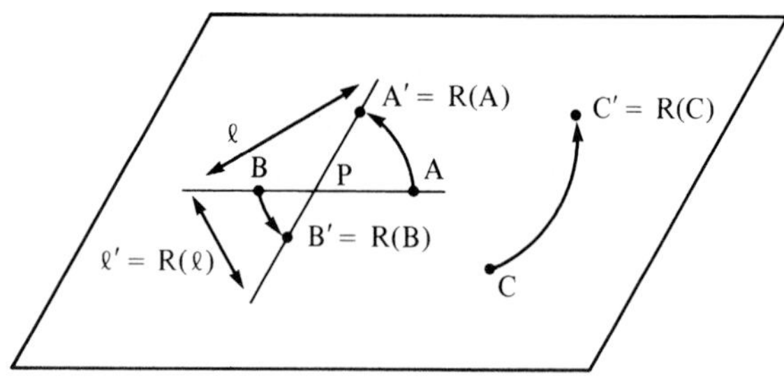

In the figure above R represents a rotation of 90° about P. The following questions should help your students understand this transformation:

1. Are any points mapped upon themselves by a rotation R? (yes, P)
2. Are any lines mapped upon themselves by a rotation R? (No, unless the rotation is 180°, written R_{180}, then any line through the center of rotation (P) is mapped upon itself.)
3. If ℓ is in the plane, how are ℓ and $\ell' = R_{90}(\ell)$ related? (perpendicular)
4. What is the inverse of R_{90}? (either R_{270}, or R_{630}, etc., or R_{-90})
5. What is the inverse of R_{180}? (R_{180})
6. If R_aR_b means a rotation of $b°$ followed by a rotation of $a°$, describe R_a^2, R_b^3, R_a^4 (R_{2a}, R_{3b}, R_{4a}).
7. Simplify $R_{200} \cdot R_{180}$. ($R_{380} = R_{380-360} = R_{20}$)
8. Simplify $R_{90} \cdot R_{270}$. ($R_{360} = R_0$)
9. Simplify R_{120}^4. ($R_{480} = R_{480-360} = R_{120}$)

Reflections

Consider $M_\ell{:}\ \alpha \xrightarrow[\text{onto}]{\text{1-1}} \alpha$, a mapping of the entire plane onto itself as determined by a reflection in a point or a line.

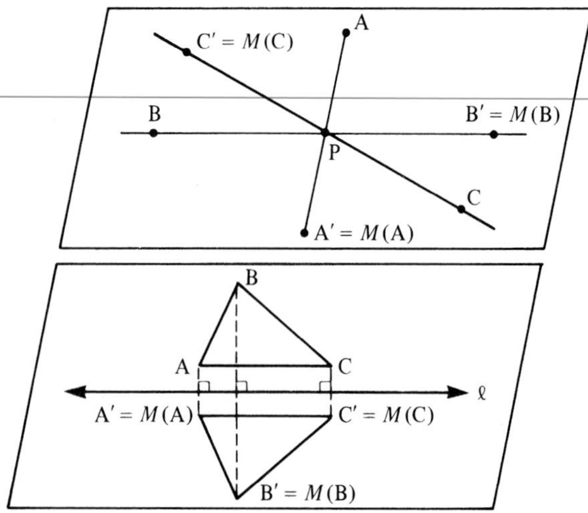

To find the reflection of a point A in a given point P, simply locate the point A′ on ray $\overrightarrow{AP}$ (on the opposite side of P as is A) so that A′P = AP. In the top figure above, A′ is the image (or reflection) of A.

To find the reflection of a point A in a given line ℓ, locate the point A′ on the line perpendicular to ℓ and containing A, at the same distance from ℓ as A, but on the opposite side. In the bottom figure above, the points of a triangle (and hence the triangle itself) are reflected in ℓ.

Once again some questions for your students:

1. What is the inverse of M_ℓ? (M_ℓ)
2. How does an image differ from its pre-image? (different orientation, or "mirror image")
3. How does the reflection of a line in a given point change the line's orientation? (changes the order of points on the line from given to the reverse of that)
4. Describe each of the following:
   (a) $M_\ell(m)$, where $\ell // m$.
   ($m' // \ell$ on the opposite side of ℓ as is m)
   (b) $M_\ell(n)$, where $\ell \perp n$. (n' is the same line as n)
   (c) $M_\ell(k)$, where ℓ is oblique to k.
   (k' forms the same angle with ℓ as does k at the same point as k but on the opposite side of ℓ)

Groups

To discuss a group of transformations, it would be helpful to review the definition of a group.

1. A set with one operation.
2. Associative property must hold true.
3. An identity element must exist.
4. Every element must have an inverse.

To consider the elements as the three types of transformations would be confusing. We shall therefore show that (I) any translation is the product of two reflections, and (II) any rotation is the product of two reflections. This will enable us to work exclusively with reflections. The word *product* as it was used above refers to the "composition" of transformations; that is, one transformation performed after the other.

I. To show that any translation T_v is equivalent to the composition of two reflections consider the figure below.

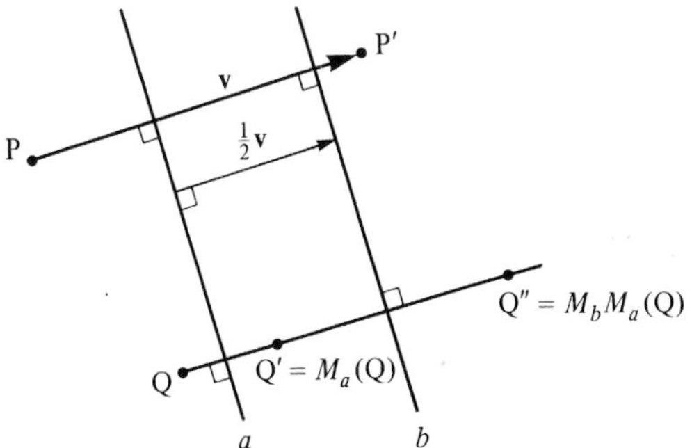

At either end of any vector $\frac{1}{2}$v consider the lines perpendicular to v. By reflecting any point Q in line a and then in line b, Q^n is obtained, which is $T_v(Q)$. That is, $M_a(Q) = Q'$ and $M_b(M_a(Q)) = Q'' = M_b M_a(Q)$.

II. To show that any rotation R_θ is equivalent to the composition of two reflections consider the figure below.

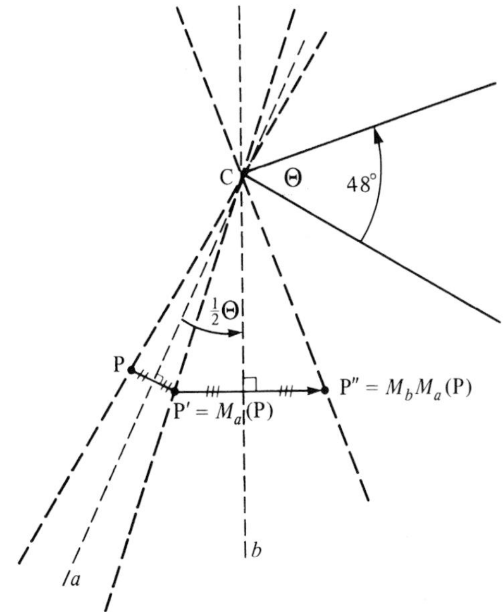

Through the center of rotation, C, draw two lines forming an angle of measure $\frac{1}{2}\Theta$. Select any point P and reflect it through line a and then reflect that image through line b.

For convenience we shall use line a before line b. Using the two pairs of congruent triangles in the figure above, we can easily prove that $M_b M_a(P) = P''$ is in fact equal to $R_\Theta(P)$.

Now that we can replace translations and rotations with combinations of reflections, ask your students to verify that a group of transformations is at hand. They must demonstrate *all* four properties listed above.

POSTASSESSMENT

1. Define translation, rotation, and reflection.
2. Describe each of the following as a single transformation.
3. Show that reflections form a group under the operation of composition.

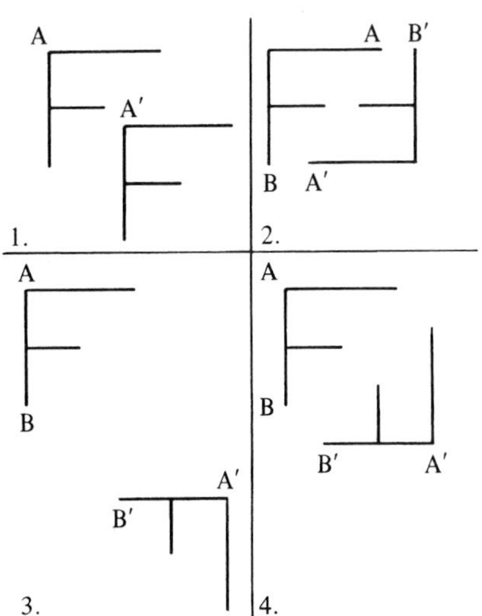

Unit 115

 The Circle and the Cardioid

PERFORMANCE OBJECTIVES

1. *Given a circle, students will be able to draw a cardioid without using an equation.*
2. *Students will be able, by experimentation, to generate curves other than the cardioid.*

PREASSESSMENT

Introduce students to the cardioid by having them set up a table of values for $r = 2a(1 + \cos\theta)$. Then have students locate the corresponding points on a polar coordinate graph. After they have constructed this curve, which was first referred to as a *cardioid* (heart-shaped) by de Castillon in 1741, students should be enticed to consider some rather unusual methods for constructing this curve.

TEACHING STRATEGIES

Method I. Ask the students to draw a base circle, O, of diameter 3 inches, centered evenly on an $8\frac{1}{2}$-by-11-inch sheet. With a protractor, divide the circumference into 36 equally spaced points (see Figure 1). Through any of these 36 points. T, construct a tangent, t, to the circle. This need not necessarily be constructed in the classical way using straightedge and compasses, but rather with a right triangle template, or a carpenter's T-square, in which one leg of the triangle passes through the center of the circle. Drawing a tangent to a circle in this manner is based on the fact that the tangent to a circle is perpendicular to the radius at the point of tangency. From a *fixed* point, A, on the circle's circumference (where A is one of the 36 points), drop a perpendicular to meet t at P. Now construct tangents to all the remaining points (except through A), to each tangent repeating the preceding step of dropping a perpendicular from A to t. The resulting figure will appear as shown in Figure 2; the locus of all such points P is a

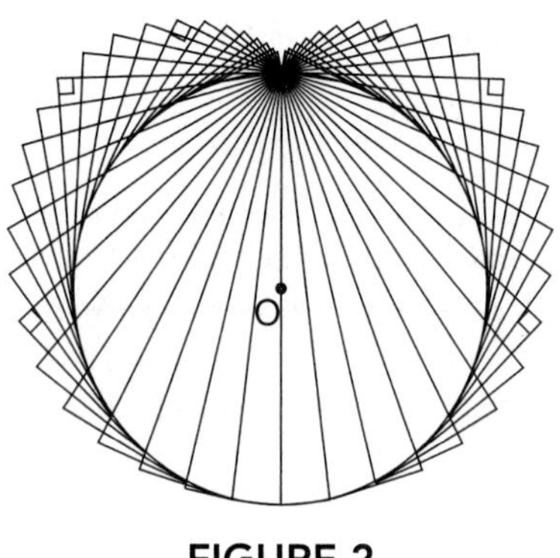

FIGURE 2

cardioid. Point A is then the cardioid's *cusp*. In Figure 2, certain construction lines from Figure 1 were eliminated so as to enhance the final drawing. Also, 48 points were used along the base circle in Figure 2 for a more compact appearing effect. Finally, note that the orientation of the cardioid in Figure 2 differs from that in Figure 1 by a 90° clockwise rotation of the cardioid about A.

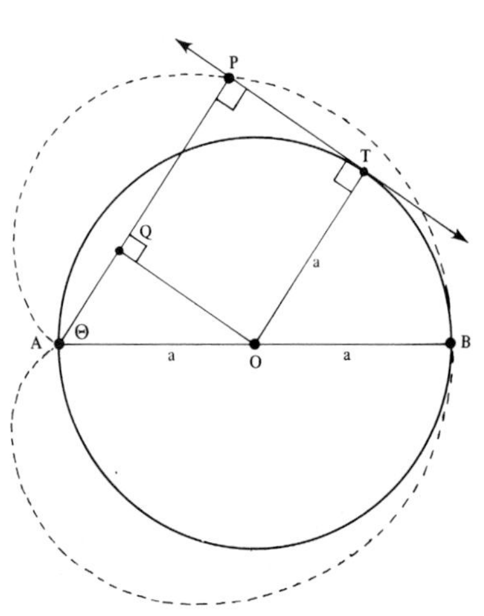

FIGURE 1

Proof: In Figure 1, let A be the fixed point on the circle O. Let A also be the pole, and diameter $\overline{AB}$ the initial line, of a polar coordinate system. Draw $\overline{OT}$. Thus, $\overline{AP} // \overline{OT}$. From O, drop a perpendicular to meet $\overline{AP}$ at Q.

Then $\overline{OQ} // \overleftrightarrow{TP}$ and OTPQ is a rectangle. Let $OT = OP = a$, $r = AP$ and $m\angle BAP = \theta$. Then, from figure 1, $r = AQ + QP$. (1)

In right $\triangle AQO$, $\cos\theta = \dfrac{AQ}{a}$, so that

$$AQ = a \cdot \cos\theta. \tag{2}$$

With QP = a, and using (2), (1) becomes

$$r = a \cdot \cos\theta + a, \text{ or}$$
$$r = a(1 + \cos\theta), \qquad (3)$$

which is the polar equation of a cardioid.

The procedure given above is an example of how a *pedal* curve to a given curve is generated (i.e., the cardioid is referred to as the *pedal* to circle O with respect to A). All pedal curves are obtained in this manner: Some arbitrary fixed point is chosen, often on the curve itself, and from that point perpendiculars are dropped to various tangents to the particular curve. The locus of the intersection of the perpendiculars to each tangent from a fixed point defines the pedal curve. Though the tangent to a circle can easily be constructed, and hence a pedal curve drawn, further pedal constructions of a visual nature can prove challenging.

Method II. As in Method I, draw a base circle of diameter 3 inches, except that the circle should be placed about one inch left of center on a vertically held $8\frac{1}{2}$-by-11-inch sheet (see Figure 3). Divide the circle into 18 equally spaced points.

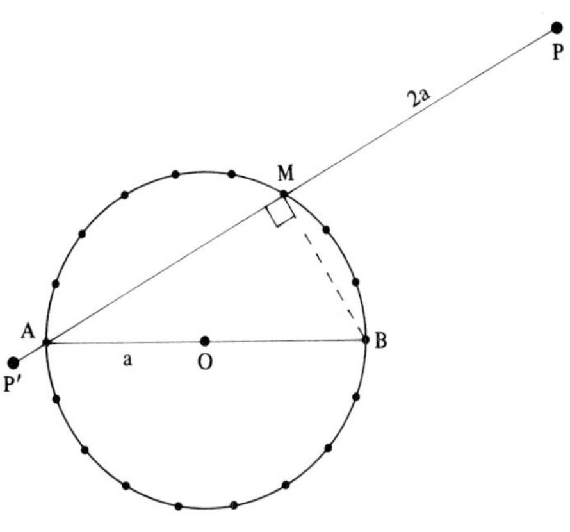

FIGURE 3

Label the diameter AB = 2a, with A once again a fixed point. Let M be one of these 18 points, distinct from A. Place the edge of a marked straightedge on M, being sure that the straightedge also passes through A. Locate two points of $\overleftrightarrow{AM}$, P and P′, on either side of M, at a distance of 2a units from M. Thus M is the midpoint of $\overline{PP'}$. Continue for all such points M, as M is allowed to move to each of the remaining points (of the originally selected 18 points) around the circumference. The locus of all such points P and P′ is a cardioid (see Figure 4).

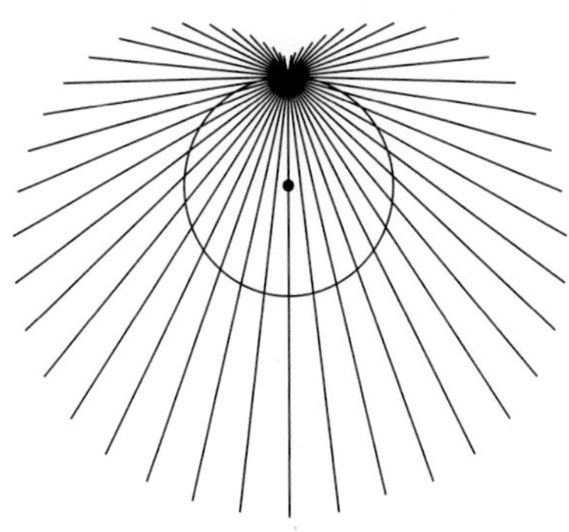

FIGURE 4

Proof: In Figure 3, draw $\overline{MB}$, let AP = r, and let m∠BAM = θ. Since △AMB is a right triangle,

$$AM = 2a \cdot \cos\theta. \qquad (4)$$

But r = AM + MP, (5)

and by construction, MP = $2a$. Substituting this, as well as (4), into (5), we get

$$r = 2a \cdot \cos\theta + 2a,$$
$$\text{or} \quad r = 2a(1 + \cos\theta), \qquad (6)$$

a form identical with (3) except for the constant $2a$. For $\theta + 180°$, we obtain P′, so that $r = AP'$. Since $\cos(\theta + 180°) = -\cos\theta$, we would have obtained

$$r = 2a(1 - \cos\theta) \qquad (7)$$

had we repeated the above steps.

The cardioid construction given here is an example of a *conchoid* curve. Using this technique with an ellipse, the choice of a fixed point could be an extremity of the major or minor axis. Varying the length of the line on either side of M to equal the major or minor axis creates several interesting combinations of conchoid curves for the ellipse.

Method III. The cardioid can also be generated as the locus of a point, P, on the circumference of a rolling circle which rolls, without slipping on a fixed circle of equal diameter.

Proof: Let the fixed circle, C_1, of a radius a, be centered at the pole of a polar coordinate system. Let O be the intersection of circle C_1 with the initial line. Circle C_2, whose initial position was externally tangent to circle C_1 at O, has now rolled to the position shown in Figure 5, carrying with it fixed point P. The locus of P is desired.

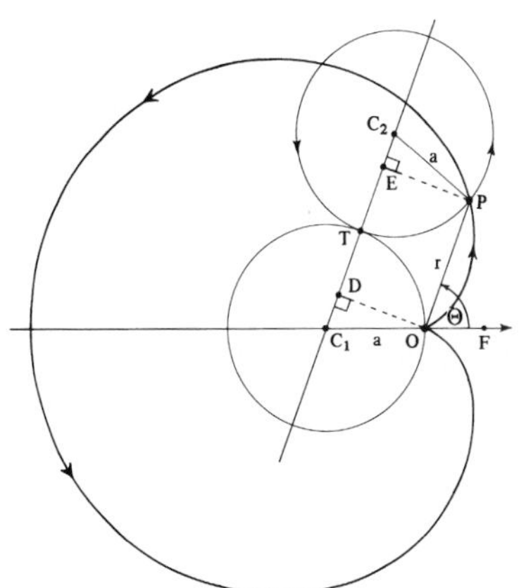

FIGURE 5

Circle C_2 is now tangent to circle C_1 at T. A line joining C_1 to C_2 will pass through T. Because $\overset{\frown}{PT} \cong \overset{\frown}{OT}$, m∠$OC_1T$ = m∠PC_2T. If $C_2P = a$ is drawn, as well as $\overline{OP}$, we obtain isosceles trapezoid OC_1C_2P, and hence m∠POF = θ.

Drop perpendiculars from O and P to $\overleftrightarrow{C_1C_2}$, meeting $\overleftrightarrow{C_1C_2}$, at D and E, respectively. Immediately, $\triangle ODC_1 \cong \triangle PEC_2$, from which it follows that $C_1D = EC_2$ and $DE = OP$. In triangles ODC_1 and PEC_2,

$$C_1D = a \cdot \cos\theta, \tag{8}$$

and $C_2E = a \cdot \cos\theta$. (9)

Now $C_1C_2 = 2a = C_1D + DE + C_2E$. (10)

Substituting (8) and (9) into (10), and remembering that $DE = OP = r$,

$$2a = a \cdot \cos\theta + r + a \cdot \cos\theta, \tag{11}$$

which yields, upon simplification,

$$r = 2a(1 - \cos\theta). \tag{12}$$

This is identical with (7).

The concept of a circle rolling smoothly on the circumference of another, fixed circle has been well studied. The locus of a point on the circumference of the rolling circle gives rise to a curve called an *epicycloid*, of which the cardioid is a special case. Changing the ratio of the fixed circle results in a variety of well-known higher plane curves.

POSTASSESSMENT

Refer to Method I for drawing the following two variations, and in so doing, possibly obtain equations similar to (3):

1. choose the fixed point A *outside* the circle at a distance of $2a$ units from O;
2. choose A *inside* the circle, at a distance of $\frac{a}{2}$ units from O.

Unit 116

Complex-Number Applications

The number system we presently use has taken a long time to develop. It proceeded according to the necessity of the time. To early humans, counting numbers was sufficient to meet their needs. Simple fractions, such as the unit fractions employed by the Egyptians followed. Although the early Greeks did not recognize irrational numbers, their necessity in geometric problems brought about their acceptance. Negative numbers, too, were used when their physical application became apparent, such as their use in temperature. Complex numbers, however, are studied because the real number system is not algebraically complete without them. Their application to the physical world is not explored by most mathematics students. This unit introduces students to some physical applications of complex numbers.

PERFORMANCE OBJECTIVE

Students will be able to solve some physics problems involving complex numbers and vector quantities.

PREASSESSMENT

Students should be familiar with operations with complex numbers and vector analysis. A knowledge of basic physics is also recommended.

TEACHING STRATEGIES

In algebra, a complex plane is defined by two rectangular coordinate axes in which the real parts of the complex numbers are plotted along the horizontal axis and the imaginary parts are plotted along the vertical axis. This complex plane can be developed if we take an approach in which i is treated as the "sign of perpendicularity" as an operator functioning to rotate a vector through an angle of 90°.

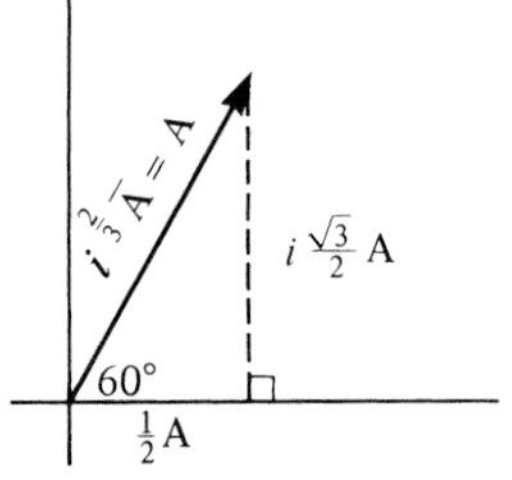

FIGURE 1

To develop this idea we begin with any vector quantity, A, which is represented by a vector ⟶ whose length indicates the magnitude and whose arrow tip indicates sense. (To distinguish between vector and scalar quantities, a bar is placed over the symbol to indicate a vector quantity, $\overline{A}$, while a symbol without a bar indicates a scalar quantity, A). Now, if $\overline{A}$ is operated upon by -1 (multiplied by -1), we have $-\overline{A}$ whose graphical representation is $\longleftarrow$. Thus, operating upon the vector $\overline{A}$ by -1 rotates it through 180° in the positive sense. Now, since $i^2 = -1$, i must represent rotating the vector through an angle of 90°, since two applications of 90° will result in a rotation of 180°. Therefore, operating upon a vector by i^3 rotates the vector through 270°, and so on. Similarly we can consider using as operators higher roots of -1, which will rotate the vector through a smaller angle. So $\sqrt[3]{-1} = (i^2)^{\frac{1}{3}} = i^{\frac{2}{3}}$ will rotate a vector through an angle of 60° since three applications of this operator is equivalent to operating by -1. We can show this in a vector diagram. Given a vector $\overline{A}$, with magnitude A, we operate upon it by $i^{\frac{2}{3}}$, i.e., we rotate the vector through 60°. This, of course, does not change its magnitude, A. Therefore, the real component is $A\cos 60° = \frac{1}{2}A$ and the imaginary component is $A\sin 60° = \sqrt{\frac{3}{2}}A$. So $\sqrt[3]{-1}\,\overline{A} = i^{\frac{2}{3}}\overline{A} = A\cos 60° + iA\sin 60°$, which indicates the position of the vector. In this way $\sqrt[n]{-1}\,\overline{A} = i^{\frac{2}{n}}\overline{A} = A\,\mathrm{Cos}\,\frac{\pi}{n} + i\,A\,\mathrm{Sin}\,\frac{\pi}{n}$. To generalize, to rotate a vector A through the angle Θ we use the operator $\cos\Theta + i\sin\Theta$.

Now, if we are given a vector $\overline{A}_1 = a + bi$, we can graph it on the complex plane. The position of the vector is given by

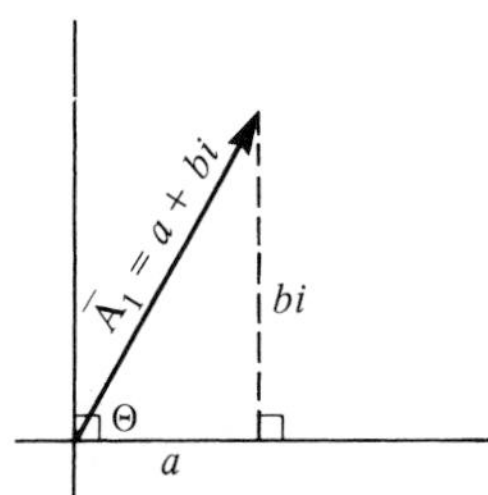

FIGURE 2

$\Theta_1 = \arctan\frac{b}{a}$. Its magnitude is $A_1 = \sqrt{a^2 + b^2}$. Vector $\overline{A}_1$ is pictured in Figure 2. Similarly vector $\overline{A}_2 = -a - bi$ has magnitude $A_2 = \sqrt{(-a)^2 + (-b)^2}$, the same as that of vector A_1. Its position is given by $\Theta_2 = \arctan\frac{-b}{-a}$ and is located in the third quadrant as pictured in Figure 3.

Now, we can explore a physical interpretation of these operators. In physics books $\sqrt{-1}$ is represented by the letter j and electrical current by the letter I. Since this unit is written for mathematics students, we used i to represent $\sqrt{-1}$ and, for the sake of clarity, we will use the letter J to represent the electrical current.

In the study of alternating currents, we have for the current the vector $\overline{J} = j_1 + ij_2$. The voltage $\overline{E}$ of this frequency

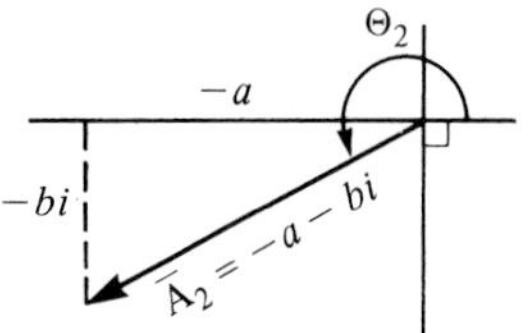

FIGURE 3

can be represented by $E = \epsilon_1 + \epsilon_2 i$. The impedance (effective resistance of the current) of the circuit, *not* a vector, can be represented by $Z = r \pm ix$, where r is the ohmic resistance and x is the reactance. The angle between $\overline{E}$ and $\overline{J}$ is the phase angle (the angle by which the current lags behind the electromotive force, emf) and is represented by $\phi = \arctan\frac{r}{x}$.

We can obtain mathematically the product of two impedances, but it has no physical meaning. The product of the voltage and the current, although it has no physical meaning, is referred to as apparent power. If, however, we take the product of the current and the impedance $Z\overline{J} = (r + ix)(j_1 + ij_2) = (rj_1 + xj_2) + i(rj_2 + xj_1)$, we have a voltage of the same frequency as the current, *the actual voltage*, i.e., $Z\overline{J} = \overline{E}$. This is Ohm's law in the complex form (Ohm's law states that for direct currents the voltage is equal to the product of the resistance and the current). So, in direct currents one deals with scalar quantities, whereas in alternating current circuits the quantities are vectors expressable as complex numbers obeying the laws of vector algebra. In the following diagrams for Ohm's law, the first diagram (Figure 4) has $\overline{J}$ on the real axis, the second diagram (Figure 5) does not.

Let us now try some problems.

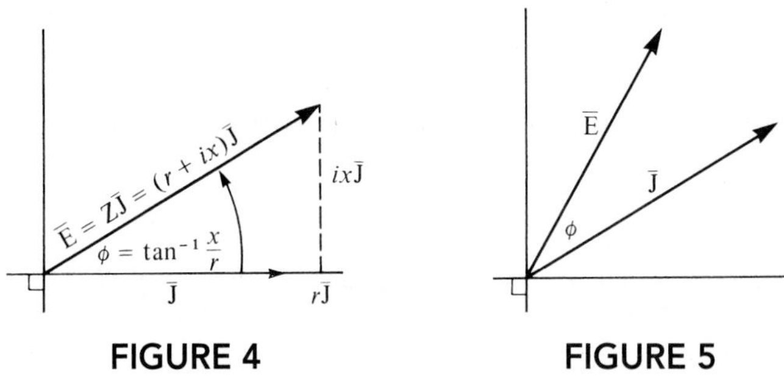

FIGURE 4 FIGURE 5

Example 1

Let $r = 5$ ohms, $x = 4$ ohms and the current J is 20 amperes. Take J on the real axis.

Given this information we have the impedance, $Z = 5 + 4i$. The inductive circuit is $\overline{E} = \overline{J}Z = 20(5 + 4i) = 100 + 80i$. Therefore $E = \sqrt{100^2 + 80^2} = 128$ volts. The angle $\overline{E}$ makes with the real axis is $\Theta = \arctan\frac{80}{100} = 38°40'$, which also happens to be the phase angle for this problem. The vector diagram is shown in Figure 6.

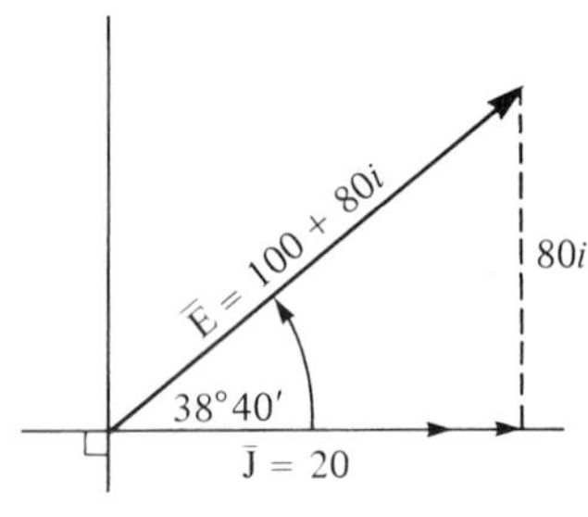

FIGURE 6

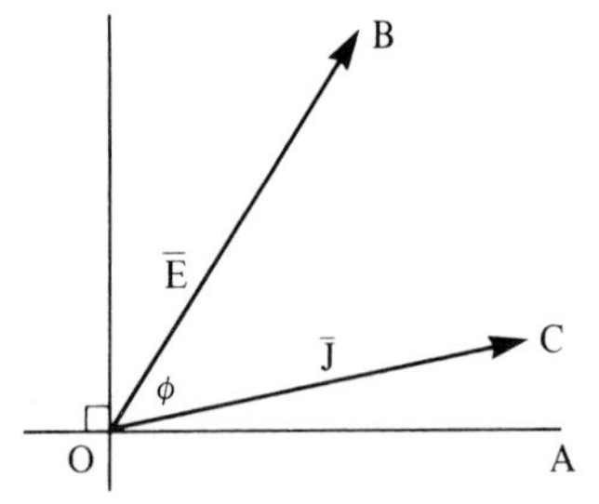

FIGURE 7

Example 2

Let us change the above example slightly by letting the angle that the current vector $\bar{J}$ makes with the real axis be 30°. We will let the remaining data be as before.

We still have $Z = 5 + 4i$. We now have $\bar{J} = 20 (\cos 30° + i \sin 30°) = 20 (.866 + .5i) = 17.32 + 10i$

$\bar{E} = \bar{J}Z = (17.32 + 10i) \cdot (5 + 4i) = 46.6 + 119.28i$

$E = \sqrt{(46.6)^2 + (119.28)^2} = 128$ volts, just as before. The angle E makes with the real axis is $\theta = \arctan \frac{119.28}{46.6} = 68°40'$.

The phase angle ϕ remains the same, $\phi = \arctan \frac{4}{5} = 38°40'$.

The vector diagram for this problem is:

Students should now be able to solve similar physics problems involving complex numbers.

POSTASSESSMENT

1. Let $r = 3$ ohms and $x = 4$ ohms. Take $\bar{J}$ on the real axis, $J = 3$. Find the impedance Z, the complex expression for $\bar{E}$ and the magnitude of E. What is Θ, the angle $\bar{E}$ makes with the real axis? What is ϕ, the phase angle? Draw a vector diagram for this problem.
2. Use the data for the above problem, letting $\bar{J}$ make an angle of 20° with the real axis. Recalculate all quantities, both the complex expressions and the magnitudes. Draw the vector diagram.
3. Let $\bar{E} = 4 + 14i$ and $\bar{J} = 2 + 3i$. Find the complex expression for Z and its magnitude. What is the phase angle? Draw a vector diagram.

REFERENCE

Suydam, Vernon A. *Electricity and Electromagnetism*. New York: D. Van Nostrand Company, 1940.

Unit 117

Hindu Arithmetic

The mathematics curriculum may be enriched for students on many levels by the study of a number system and its arithmetic. An investigation into the mechanics of the system, its contribution to our own system, and other suitable tangents may be entered upon by a student on a high level. For other students it can serve as practice in basic skills with integers, as students check the answers they obtain in working out problems. This unit introduces students to the ancient Hindu numerical notation and system of adding, subtracting, multiplying, and dividing (circa 900, India).

PERFORMANCE OBJECTIVES

1. *Given an addition problem, students will find the answer using a Hindu method.*
2. *Given a subtraction problem, students will find the answer using a Hindu method.*
3. *Given a multiplication problem, students will find the answer using a Hindu method.*
4. *Given a division problem, students will find the answer using a Hindu method.*

PREASSESSMENT

Students need only be familiar with the basic operations of integers, i.e., addition, subtraction, multiplication, and division.

TEACHING STRATEGIES

The symbols of the nine numerals used in Hindu reckoning in ascending order are १, २, ३, ४, ५, ६, ७, ८, ९, ०. This system included a symbol for zero, ०. This, then, was a positional system, as in our own, as opposed to a grouping system such as that used by the ancient Egyptians. Therefore, similar to our modern system, 5639 would be represented as ५६३९.

At this point we can discuss the importance of the Hindu symbol for zero. A comparison with the Egyptian numeral system might be instructive (see Unit 14 on Ancient Egyptian Arithmetic). The historical importance of zero could be investigated. Without a zero numbers were cumbersome, and intricate computations were difficult. In the Hindu system, record keeping and other computations necessary for commerce, astronomical computations, and mathematical tables were advanced, for with the existence of a placeholder numbers are easier to write and read, and can be manipulated with greater ease.

Hindu computation was generally written upon surfaces where corrections and erasures were easily done. For our purposes, instead of erasing numbers we will cross out numbers so that the methods discussed will be more easily followed.

Hindu addition, though set up vertically as in our method, was done from left to right. Consider the problem: 6537 + 886. The addition begins on the left with 8 being added to the 5. The 1 of this 13 is added to the numeral on the left, 6, changing it to 7, and the 5 is now changed to a 3. This process continues, from left to right. Thus, the solution would look like this:

7 4 2
7 ~~3~~ ~~1~~ 3
~~6~~ ~~5~~ ~~3~~ ~~7~~
8 8 6

The result is 7423.

Subtraction was also done from left to right, the larger number being placed above the smaller one. To subtract 886 from 6537, we being by subtracting 8 from 5. Since this is not possible, we subtract the 8 from 65, leaving 57. We put the 5 in place of the 6, and the 7 in place of the 5. We continue this process by subtracting 8 from 3 using the described method. The solution of the entire problem would look like this:

6
5 ~~7~~ 5 1
~~6~~ ~~5~~ ~~3~~ ~~7~~
8 8 6

The result is 5651.

To multiply as the Hindus did, we begin by placing the units' digit of the multiplier under the highest place of position of the multiplicand. To multiply 537 by 24 we begin this way:

5 3 7
2 4

We multiply 2 by 5 and place the resulting 0 above the 2, and the 1 to the left. We now multiply 4 by the 5, placing the resulting 0 in place of the 5 above the 4, and adding the 2 to the 0 we now have 2 in the next place:

2 0
1 ~~0~~ ~~5~~ 3 7
2 4

Now that we have finished with the 5, we shift the multiplier one place to the right, the 4 now being below the 3, indicating 3 is the number we are now concerned with.

2 0
1 ~~0~~ ~~5~~ 3 7
2 4

We multiply as before, first the 2 by the 3, then the 4, and when finished shift again to the right. When we have done the entire problem it will look like this:

8
~~7~~ 8
6 6
2 ~~0~~ ~~2~~ 8
1 ~~0~~ ~~5~~ ~~3~~ ~~7~~
~~2~~ ~~4~~
~~2~~ ~~4~~
2 4

The answer is 12,888.

It can be seen that crossing out, instead of erasing, requires space. As division is the most complex of the basic operations, the problem will be done step by step, instead of crossing out, substituting new results for the old numbers.

To divide, we place the divisor below the dividend, aligning them on the left. Thus, we begin the problem 5832 ÷ 253 as $\begin{matrix}5 & 8 & 3 & 2\\ 2 & 5 & 3 & \end{matrix}$. As 253 is below 583, we seek a number to multiply 253 by so that the product will be as close as possible to 583 without exceeding it. The number we seek here is 2, and it is placed thus:

2
5 8 3 2
2 5 3

We now multiply 253 by 2 (as the Hindus did) and subtract the result from 583 (as the Hindus did). This gives us 77, which we put in the place of 583. So we now have

2
7 7 2
2 5 3

The divisor is shifted to the right to get

$$\begin{array}{ccc} & 2 & \\ 7 & 7 & 2 \\ 2 & 5 & 3 \end{array}$$

The process continues as above until we reach the results

$$\begin{array}{c} 23 \\ 13 \\ 253 \end{array}$$

which shows the quotient to be 23 and the remainder 13.

Investigate these processes with your students to the extent you feel necessary. You will find instructive the similarity of these algorithms to ours.

POSTASSESSMENT

1. Have students write the following numbers using Hindu numerals:
   (a) 5342 (b) 230796
2. Have students solve the following problems using Hindu methods:
   (a) $3567 + 984$ (b) $8734 - 6849$
   (c) 596×37 (d) $65478 \div 283$

REFERENCES

Eves, Howard. *An Introduction to the History of Mathematics*, 4th ed. New York: Holt, Rinehart and Winston, 1976.

Waerden, B. L. van der. *Science Awakening*. New York: John Wiley & Sons, 1963.

Unit 118

Proving Numbers Irrational

When high school students are introduced to irrational numbers, they are usually asked to accept the fact that certain numbers like $\sqrt{2}$, sin 10°, and so on are irrational. Many students wonder, however, how it could be proved that a given number is irrational. This unit presents a method to prove the irrationality of certain algebraic numbers.

PERFORMANCE OBJECTIVES

1. *Given certain algebraic numbers students will be able to prove their irrationality.*
2. *Students will find some specific patterns that will determine in advance whether a given algebraic number is irrational.*

PREASSESSMENT

Students should be familiar with the concepts of irrational numbers and algebraic numbers. They should also have a general background in algebraic equations, radicals, trigonometry, and logarithms.

TEACHING STRATEGIES

Begin the lesson by asking students to give examples of irrational numbers. Ask them how they are sure these numbers are irrational. Then have them define irrational numbers. Students will be curious enough at this point to want to investigate the following theorem.

Theorem: Consider any polynomial equation with the integer coefficients $a_nx^n + a_{n-1}x^{n-1} + \ldots + a_1x + a_0 = 0$. If this equation has a rational root $\frac{p}{q}$, where $\frac{p}{q}$ is in its lowest terms, then p is a divisor of a_0 and q is a divisor of a_n.

Proof: Let $\frac{p}{q}$ be a root of the given equation. Then it satisfies the equation and we have

$$a_n\left(\frac{p}{q}\right)^n + a_{n-1}\left(\frac{p}{q}\right)^{n-1} + \ldots + a_1\left(\frac{p}{q}\right) + a_0 = 0 \quad \text{(I)}$$

We now multiply (I) by q^n to obtain

$$a_np^n + a_{n-1}p^{n-1}q + \ldots + a_1pq^{n-1} + a_0q^n = 0.$$

This equation can be rewritten as

$$a_np^n = -a_{n-1}p^{n-1}q - \ldots - a_1pq^{n-1} - a_0q^n$$

or

$$a_np^n = q(-a_{n-1}p^{n-1} - \ldots - a_1pq^{n-2} - a_0q^{n-1}).$$

This shows that q is a divisor of a_np^n. But if $\frac{p}{q}$ is in its lowest terms, then p and q are relatively prime and therefore q is a divisor of a_n. Likewise, if we rewrite equation (I) as

$$a_0q^n = p(-a_1q^{n-1} - \ldots - a_{n-1}p^{n-2}q - a_np^{n-1})$$

we see that p is a divisor of a_0q^n. Again, because p and q are relatively prime, we have that p is a divisor of a_0.
This completes the proof of the theorem.

Example 1
Prove that $\sqrt{5}$ is irrational.

$\sqrt{5}$ is a root of $x^2 - 5 = 0$. Then according to the notation used for the theorem, $a_2 = 1$ and $a_0 = -5$. Now any rational root, $\frac{p}{q}$, of this equation will have to be of such a nature that p will have to divide -5, and q will have to divide 1. This is so because of the previous theorem. But the only divisors of 1 are $+1$ and -1. Thus q must be either $+1$ or -1, and the rational root of the equation must be an integer. This integer p, according to the theorem must divide -5, and the only divisors of -5 are -1 1, 5, and -5. However, none of these is a root of the equation $x^2 - 5 = 0$, that is $(1)^2 - 5 = 0$; $(-1)^2 - 5 = 0(5)^2 - 5 = 0$; and $(-5)^2 - 5 = 0$, are *all false*. Hence $x^2 - 5 = 0$ has no rational root, and $\sqrt{5}$ is therefore an irrational number.

Example 2
Prove that $\sqrt[3]{2}$ is irrational.

$\sqrt[3]{2}$ is a root of $x^3 - 2 = 0$. Then p must divide -2, and q must divide 1. Thus, if this equation has a rational root, this root must be an integer and a divisor of -2. Now the only divisors of -2 are: 2, -2, 1, and -1. But none of these is a root of the equation $x^3 - 2 = 0$, because $(2)^2 - 2 = 0$, $(-2)^2 - 2 = 0$, $(1)^2 - 2 = 0$, and $(-1)^2 - 2 = 0$ are all false. Hence, $\sqrt[3]{2}$ is irrational.

Example 3
Prove that $\sqrt{2} + \sqrt{3}$ is irrational.

If we write $x = \sqrt{2} + \sqrt{3}$, we have that $x - \sqrt{2} = \sqrt{3}$. Now, square both sides and obtain $x^2 - 1 = 2x\sqrt{2}$. Squaring again gives us $x^4 - 2x^2 + 1 = 8x^2$ or $x^4 - 10x^2 + 1 = 0$.

This equation has been so constructed that $\sqrt{2} + \sqrt{3}$ is a root. But the only possible rational roots of this equation are those integers that are divisors of 1, that is, -1 and 1. But none of these is root of the equation because $(1)^4 - 10(1)^2 + 1 = 0$ and $(-1)^4 - 10(-1)^2 + 1 = 0$ are both false. Hence this equation has no rational roots and consequently $\sqrt{2} + \sqrt{3}$ is irrational.

Example 4
Prove the sin 10° is irrational.

We have the identity $\sin 3\theta = 3\sin\theta - 4\sin^3\theta$. Now if we replace θ by 10°, and notice that

$$\sin 30° = \frac{1}{2}, \text{ we get}$$

$$\frac{1}{2} = 3 \sin 10° - 4 \sin^3 10°.$$

If we now make $\sin 10° = x$, we obtain

$$\frac{1}{2} = 3x - 4x^3 \text{ or}$$

$$8x^3 - 6x + 1 = 0.$$

According to the theorem, p must be a divisor or 1, and q must be a divisor of 8, thus the only possible rational roots are $\pm\frac{1}{8}$, $\pm\frac{1}{4}$, $\pm\frac{1}{2}$, and ±1. But none of these eight possibilities is a root of the equation, as can be seen by substitution into the equation obtained. Therefore, this equation has no rational roots, and since sin 10° is a root of the equation, it must be irrational.

Students should now be able to prove irrational those numbers that occur most frequently in high school text books and that students are *told* are irrational. It is important to have students understand why a mathematical concept is true after they have comfortably worked with the concept. All too often students accept the irrationality of a number without question. This unit provides a method that should bring some true understanding to the average high school mathematics student. In addition to the problems posed in the *Postassessment*, students should be encouraged to use the technique presented here when the need arises.

POSTASSESSMENT

Those students who have mastered the technique learned through the previous examples, should be able to complete the following exercises:

1. Prove that $\sqrt{2}$ is irrational.
2. Prove that $\sqrt[3]{6}$ is irrational.
3. Prove that $\sqrt[3]{3} + \sqrt{11}$ is irrational.
4. Prove that Cos 20° is irrational.
5. Prove that a number of the form $\sqrt[n]{m}$, where n and m are natural numbers, is either irrational or an integer.

Unit 119

How to Use a Computer Spreadsheet to Generate Solutions to Certain Mathematics Problems

This unit presents some simple examples of how spreadsheets, such as Microsoft Excel, Clarisworks, or Lotus, can be used to generate solutions to certain mathematics problems. A computer with an appropriate spreadsheet must be available and pupils should be familiar with its operation. Secondary school students of any grade should find this challenging as well as fascinating.

PERFORMANCE OBJECTIVES

1. *Students will generate a Fibonacci sequence on a spreadsheet.*
2. *Students will create a Pascal triangle on a spreadsheet.*
3. *Students will list other mathematical problems appropriate for spreadsheet solution.*

PREASSESSMENT

Students need to review Enrichment Units 85 (Fibonacci sequence) and 99 (Pascal's pyramid—especially the first part, which discusses the Pascal triangle). Students should also be familiar with basic operations on a microcomputer and electronic spreadsheets.

TEACHING STRATEGIES

An electronic spreadsheet is an array that appears on the screen of a microcomputer. Most spreadsheets have built-in mathematical functions so that elements in the ith row, j^{th} column can be easily accessed for any given i or j. For example, show students how to use the functions that determine how maximum value, minimum value, average value, median, mode, standard deviation, and so on, for a set of numbers listed on a spreadsheet. Point out that many other mathematical applications may be found for spreadsheets in addition to those already built into the program.

One interesting application is to generate a Fibonacci sequence as well as a sequence of ratios of successive pairs of numbers. Pay special attention to the formula used to generate a Fibonacci sequence as it is listed in Enrichment Unit 85: $f(n) = f(n-1) + f(n-2)$.

One way this formula can be translated to "spreadsheet language" is, "For a given row, the number in the nth column is equal to the sum of the numbers in the two previous columns."

Together with the students, use "relative referencing" to develop the formula that a given cell's contents should equal the sum of the entries of the two columns to its left in the same row. Thus, if the initial numbers 1, 1 are entered in cells A1 and B1, then cell C1 will contain the formula

$$= \text{SUM}(\text{A1}, \text{B1})$$

or

$$= \text{A1} + \text{B1}.$$

This technique, in conjunction with the spreadsheet's feature for copying and updating a formula (fill handle in Excel) may be used to write as many terms as will fit onto one row. Then point and click to continue the formula onto the next row.

A second sequence of ratios of successive pairs of terms, as indicated in the enrichment unit, may be generated as follows. If the initial numbers 1, 1 are entered in cells A1 and B1, then cell B2 will contain the formula

$$= \frac{\text{C1}}{\text{B1}}.$$

The following sample was produced on the IBM-compatible computer using Microsoft Excel.

	A	B	C	D	E	F	G	H	I
1	1	1	2	3	5	8	13	21	34
2		2.000	1.500	1.667	1.600	1.625	1.615	1.619	
3									

Now suggest a second application that might be of interest: the Pascal triangle. After some discussion of Enrichment

Unit 99, especially the rule for generating the triangle, suggest that the triangle be written as follows:

1	1				
1	2	1			
1	3	3	1		
1	4	6	4	1	
1	5	10	10	5	1

Ask pupils to suggest an appropriate spreadsheet formula that would generate this triangle. Point out that the first and last entry of each row is 1 and that each of the other entries is the sum of the number in the row above and the number in that same row but one column to its left.

POSTASSESSMENT

Ask the class to prepare a list of mathematical topics that might be appropriate for development via a spreadsheet, and solve some of them. You might suggest topics taken from the enrichment units in this book.

The following could prove to be challenging:

Magic squares
Palindromic numbers
The Sieve of Eratosthenes
Solving a quadratic equation
Continued fractions

Unit 120

The Three Worlds of Geometry

The inquisitive nature of humans causes them to probe deeply into that which troubles them. This unit presents the startling results achieved after 20 centuries of probing into a seemingly minor problem.

Many people throughout history were responsible for the geometry we know today. One man, however, stands above all others. That man is *Euclid*, the brilliant Greek mathematician of antiquity who developed and wrote the first geometry text, the *Elements*, ca. 300 B.C. The significance of this treatise was that it showed the capability of the human mind to arrive at nontrivial conclusions by reasoning power alone—a power that no other creature possesses.

In the *Elements*, Euclid developed geometry as a postulational system based on five postulates:

1. A straight line may be drawn from any point to any other point.
2. A line segment may be extended any length along a straight line.
3. A circle may be drawn from any center at any distance from that center.
4. All right angles are congruent to one another.
5. If a straight line intersects two other straight lines, and makes the sum of the interior angles on the same side less than two right angles, the straight lines, if extended indefinitely, will meet on that side on which are the angles whose sum is less than two right angles.

It was the length and relative complexity of this fifth postulate that led to its intensive investigation and analysis by scholars throughout the ages. Some of the fruits of these investigations are presented in this unit.

PERFORMANCE OBJECTIVES

1. *Students will define the* Saccheri quadrilateral *and use it in formal proofs.*
2. *Students will compare and contrast the existence of parallel lines in the models of Euclid, Riemann, and Bolyai-Lobachevsky.*
3. *Students will learn how to prove that the sum of the measures of the angles of a triangle may be more than, less than, or equal to* 180°.

PREASSESSMENT

Students should be familiar with the traditional high school geometry course, especially the theorems related to parallel and perpendicular lines, the exterior angle of a triangle, geometric inequalities, and direct and indirect proofs.

TEACHING STRATEGIES

In the early part of the 19th century Playfair's postulate was shown to be a simpler, logical equivalent to Euclid's fifth postulate: *Through a point not on a given line, one and only one line can be drawn parallel to the given line. (When speaking of parallels in this unit, we use Euclid's definition: Parallel lines are straight lines that, being in the same plane and being extended indefinitely in both directions, do not meet one another in either direction.)*

An analysis of Euclid's fifth postulate yields three possible variations. We call them "worlds" and now compare them:

Euclid's postulate: Through a point not on a given line, one and only one line can be drawn parallel to the given line (Figure 1).

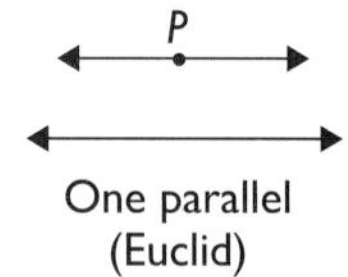

FIGURE 1

Riemann's postulate [in honor of Bernhard Riemann, German mathematician (1826–1866)]: Two straight lines always intersect one another (Figure 2).

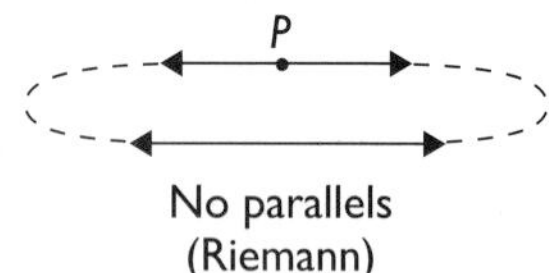

FIGURE 2

Bolyai & Lobachevsky's postulate: In honor of mathematicians Janos Bolyai (1802–1860), Hungarian, and Nikolai Lobachevsky (1793–1856), Russian: Through a point not on a given line, more than one line can be drawn not intersecting the given line (Figure 3).

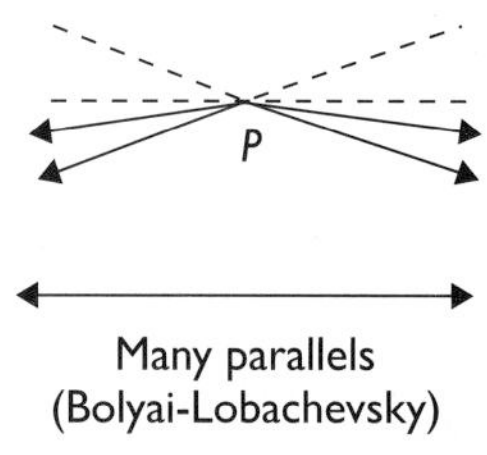

FIGURE 3

The Three Worlds

The teaching unit that you will present to your students will include some historical background about Euclid's fifth postulate. Girolamo Saccheri (1667–1733), an Italian monk-mathematician, devised this quadrilateral to help him in his attempt to prove that Euclid's fifth postulate was in reality a theorem based on the other four postulates and thus not independent of them. He failed, but during the course of his efforts, he developed *other* perfectly consistent postulational systems and thus, without realizing it, other types of geometries—forerunners of what we now call non-Euclidean geometry.

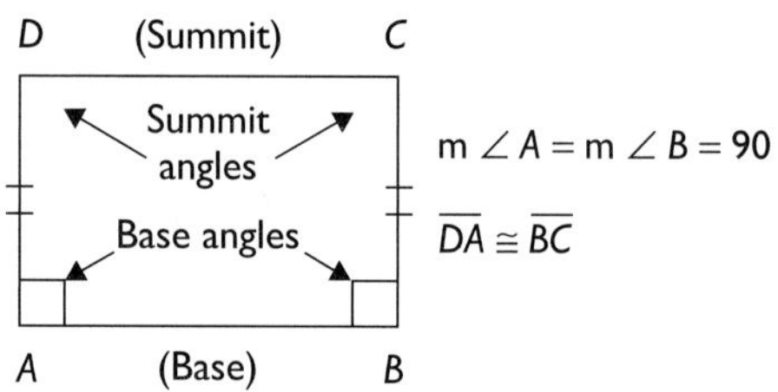

Now have the students use the following outline to complete the proof that the summit angles of a Saccherei quadrilateral are congruent.

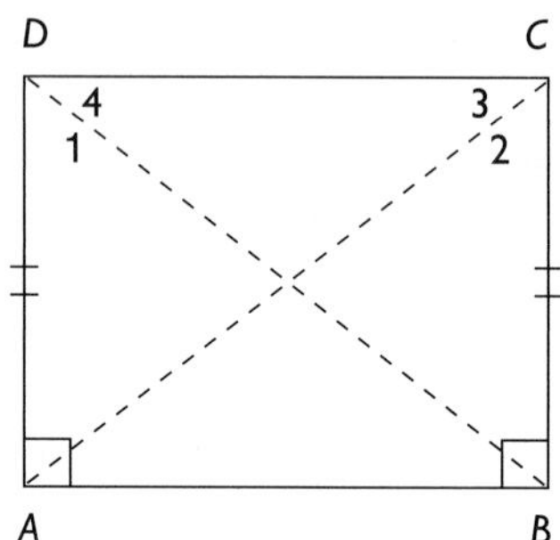

Given: Saccheri quadrilateral *ABCD*
Prove: $\angle D \cong \angle C$

1. Draw $\overline{BD}$ and $\overline{AC}$
2. Prove $\triangle ABD \cong \triangle ABC$
3. $\therefore \angle 1 \cong \angle 2$, and $\overline{BD} \cong AC$
4. Now prove $\triangle DCA \cong \triangle DCB$
5. $\therefore \angle 4 \cong \angle 3$
6. $\therefore \angle D \cong \angle C$

Next have the students show, using only the reasons with which they are familiar from high school geometry, that in the world of Euclid, the summit angles of a Saccheri quadrilateral are *right*. However, they can also now show that the summit angles of a Saccheri quardilateral are *obtuse* in the world of Riemann (where all lines meet)—*still using the same geometry they have been using all along.*

Given: Saccheri quardrilateral *ABCD*
Prove: $\angle 1$ and $\angle D$ are obtuse

1. Extend $\overline{AB}$ and $\overline{DC}$ until they meet at point P. (Why can this be done? Remember that this is the world where all lines meet.)
2. $m\angle 2 = 90$.
3. $m\angle 1 > m\angle 2$. (Recall a theorem about the exterior angle of a triangle.)
4. $\therefore \angle 1$ is obtuse.
5. But $\angle 1 \cong \angle D$.
6. $\therefore$ Both $\angle 1$ and $\angle D$ are obtuse.

At this point there can hardly be any doubt about the size of the summit angles of a Saccheri quadrilateral in the Bolyai-Lobachevsky world. Clearly they must be acute.

Next, show pupils how to develop a proof about the sum of the measures of the angles of a triangle as summarized in this chart:

Kind of world	Sum of the measure of the angles of a triangle
Riemann (no parallels)	Is more than 180°
Euclid (one parallel)	Is equal to 180°
Bolyai-Lobachevsky (many parallels)	Is less than 180°

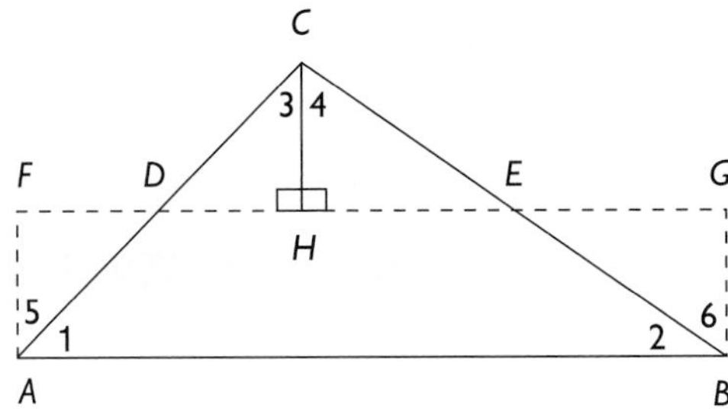

Given: $\triangle ABC$

1. Let D be the midpoint of $\overline{AC}$, and let E be the midpoint of $\overline{BC}$.
2. Draw $\overline{DE}$.
3. Draw $\overline{CH} \perp \overline{DE}$.
4. Mark off $\overline{DF} \cong \overline{DH}$ and $\overline{EG} \cong \overline{HE}$.
5. Draw $\overline{FA}$ and $\overline{BG}$.
6. $\triangle FDA \cong \triangle CDH$ and $\triangle CHE \cong \triangle BGE$.
7. Show that $FGBA$ is a Saccheri quadrilateral with base $\overline{FG}$.
8. $\angle 5 \cong \angle 3$ and $\angle 6 \cong \angle 4$.
   The sum of the measure of the angles of $\triangle ABC$
9. $= m\angle 1 + m\angle 2 + (m\angle 3 + m\angle 4)$.
10. $= m\angle 1 + m\angle 2 + (m\angle 5 + m\angle 6)$.
11. $= m\angle 1 + m\angle 5 + (m\angle 2 + m\angle 6)$.
12. $= m\angle FAB + m\angle GBA$.
13. = the sum of the measures of the summit angles of Saccheri quadrilatral $FGBA$.

Your students will not appreciate why Saccheri felt he failed in what he had set out to do. He did, after all, prove theorems that appeared to arrive at contradictory conclusions. Instead, he turned out to be one of the unsung heroes of mathematics.

POSTASSESSMENT

Show how residents of all three worlds can complete the following proofs.

1.

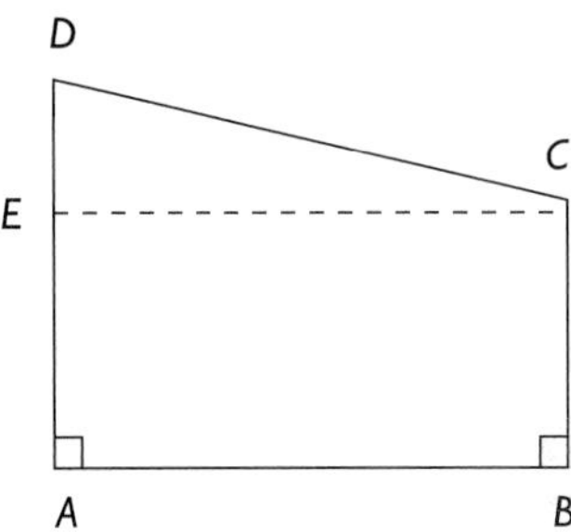

Given: $\overline{DA} \perp \overline{AB}$; $\overline{CB} \perp \overline{AB}$; $DA > CB$
Prove: $m\angle BCD > m\angle D$

2. The converse of (1) can also be proved by residents of each of the worlds. Show how this can be done by continuing the outlined proof.

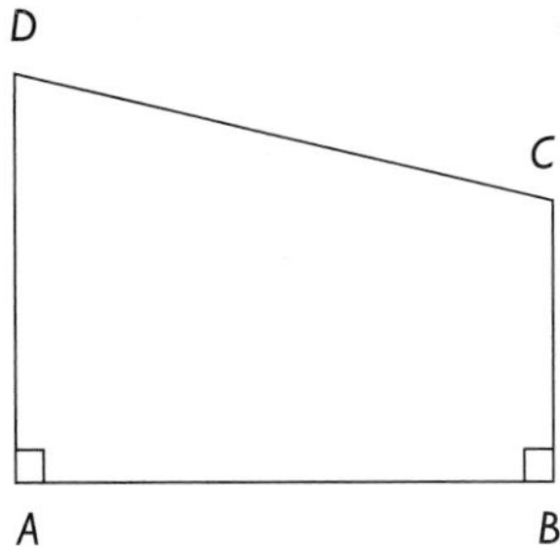

Given: $\overline{DA} \perp \overline{AB}$;$\overline{CB} \perp \overline{AB}$; $m\angle C > m\angle D$
Prove: $BDA > CD$
Hint: Use *reductio ad absurdum*.

3. Complete the proof that the line joining the midpoints of the base and summit of a Saccheri quadrilateral (the *midline*) is perpendicular to both of them.

Given: Saccheri quadrilateral $ABCD$; M and N are midpoints ($\overline{MN}$ is midline)
Prove: $\overline{MN} \perp \overline{AB}$ and $\overline{DC}$

1. Draw $\overline{DM}$ and $\overline{MC}$.
2. Prove $\triangle AMD \cong \triangle BMC$ and $\triangle DNM \cong \triangle CNM$.
3. To be completed by student.

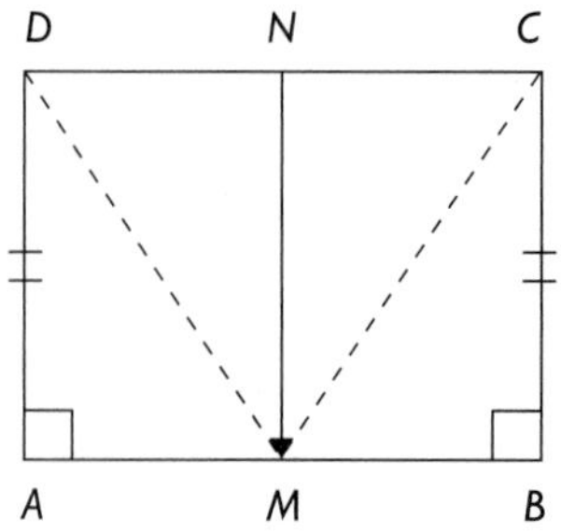

4. Only residents of Riemann's world (where the summit angles of a Saccheri quadrilateral are obtuse) can now prove this statement: The measure of the summit of a Saccheri quadrilateral is less than the measure of its base. An outline of the proof follows:

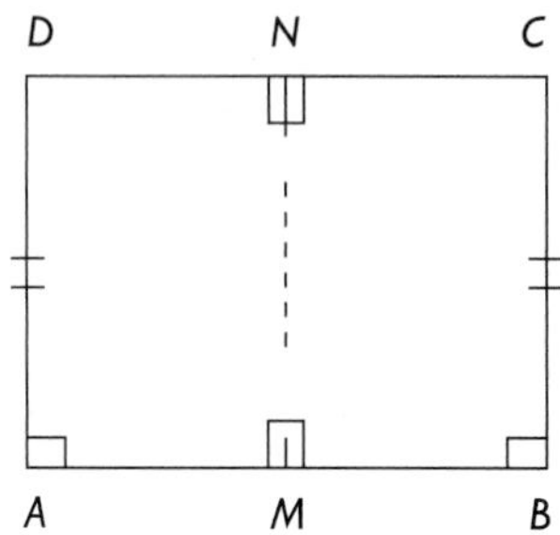

WORLD OF RIEMANN

Given: Saccheri quadrilateral ABCD

Prove: $DC < AB$

1. Draw the midline $\overline{MN}$.
2. $m\angle BMN = m\angle MNC = 90$.
3. $\angle C$ is obtuse. (Why?)
4. In quadrilateral $MNCB$ (with base $\overline{MN}$), $m\angle C > m\angle B$. (Why?)
5. $\therefore NC < MB$. (Why?)
6. $\therefore DC < AB$. (Why?)

5. Show how residents of the world of Bolyai-Lobachevsky (where the summit angles of a Saccheri quadrilateral are acute) can prove that the measure of the summit of a Saccheri quadrilateral is greater than the measure of the base.
6. Show how resident of the world of Euclid (where the summit angles of a Saccheri quadrilateral are right) can prove that the measure of the summit of a Saccheri quadrilateral is equal to the measure of the base.

REFERENCE

Wolfe, Harold E. *Introduction of Non-Euclidean Geometry*. New York: Dryden Press, 1945.

Unit 121

πie Mix

Leonhard Euler (1707–1783), a Swiss mathematician, startled the mathematical world when he discovered an expression that combined into a single formula theretofore seemingly unrelated numbers such as π, i, e, and 1. This unit demonstrates that formula and indicates how he might have developed it.

PERFORMANCE OBJECTIVES

1. *Students will learn that* e^x, $\sin x$, *and* $\cos x$ *may be represented by means of a power series.*
2. *Students will see the consequences of probing into a previously uncharted course in mathematics.*
3. *Students will use Euler's formula to derive two trigonometric identities.*

PREASSESSMENT

Students should be able to evaluate powers of the imaginary number i. They should be familiar with factorial notation. Students must also be familiar with the natural logarithm base, e, and trigonometric identities for sine and cosine of the sum of two angles.

TEACHING STRATEGIES

Tell students that for any real x, it can be proved in calculus that certain functions, under given conditions, may be represented as infinite series of powers. For example,

$$\sin x = x - \frac{x^3}{3!} + \frac{x^5}{5!} - \frac{x^7}{7!} + \frac{x^9}{9!} - \frac{x^{11}}{11!} + \ldots$$

$$\cos x = 1 - \frac{x^2}{2!} + \frac{x^4}{4!} - \frac{x^6}{6!} + \frac{x^8}{8!} - \frac{x^{10}}{10!} + \cdots$$

$$\text{and } e^x = 1 + x + \frac{x^2}{2!} + \frac{x^3}{3!} + \frac{x^4}{4!} + \frac{x^5}{5!} + \frac{x^6}{6!} + \cdots$$

Euler took a bold step when he questioned the hypothesis that x must be real, because if we substitute for x the imaginary number $i\theta$, where θ is real and $i = \sqrt{-1}$, an interesting thing happens:

$$e^{i\theta} = 1 + i\theta + \frac{(i\theta)^2}{2!} + \frac{(i\theta)^3}{3!} + \frac{(i\theta)^4}{4!} + \frac{(i\theta)^5}{5!} + \frac{(i\theta)^6}{6!} + \cdots$$

Recalling that $i^2 = -1$, $i^3 = -i$, and $i^4 = 1$, we can simplify the terms of the series until we get

$$\begin{aligned} e^{i\theta} &= 1 + i\theta - \frac{(\theta)^2}{2!} - i\frac{(\theta)^3}{3!} + \frac{(\theta)^4}{4!} + \frac{(\theta)^5}{5!} - \frac{(\theta)^6}{6!} - \cdots \\ &= \left[1 - \frac{(\theta)^2}{2!} + \frac{(\theta)^4}{4!} - \frac{(\theta)^6}{6!} + \cdots\right] \\ &\quad + i\left[\theta - \frac{(\theta)^3}{3!} + \frac{(\theta)^5}{5!} - \cdots\right] \\ &= \cos\theta + i\sin\theta. \end{aligned}$$

Recalling again that $\cos 2\pi = 1$, and $\sin 2\pi = 0$, we may conclude that $e^{2\pi i} = 1$. It is *this* formula that caused a stir. We now turn to an unanticipated result.

Letting $\theta = x + y$ gives us

$$e^{i(x+y)} = \cos(x + y) + i\sin(x + y). \qquad (1)$$

But also,

$$\begin{aligned} e^{i(x+y)} &= e^{ix}e^{iy} \\ &= (\cos x + i\sin x)(\cos y + i\sin y) \\ &= (\cos x\cos y - \sin x\sin y) \\ &\quad + i(\sin x\cos y + \cos x\sin y). \qquad (2) \end{aligned}$$

Equating the *real* and *imaginary* parts of (1) and (2), we get

$$\cos(x + y) = \cos x\cos y - \sin x\sin y$$

and $$\sin(x + y) = \sin x\cos y - \cos x\sin y.$$

These are easily recognized as familiar trigonometric formulas.

POSTASSESSMENT

1. Use the Maclaurin series approach to derive formulas for $\cos(x - y)$ and $\sin(x - y)$.
2. Show that $e^{\pi i} + 1 = 0$.
3. Show how $e^{i\theta}$ may represent an operator that rotates a complex number counterclockwise through an angle θ along a unit circle.
4. Show the connection between Euler's formula and DeMoivre's theorem for finding powers and roots of a complex number.

Unit 122

Graphical Iteration

This unit focuses on chaos theory and its connection to the secondary school curriculum. It offers an opportunity for students to explore a current area of interest in mathematics through the powers of the graphing calculator and the computer.

PERFORMANCE OBJECTIVES

1. *Given a graphing calculator or computer, students will exhibit graphical iteration under a quadratic.*
2. *Students will investigate the iterative behavior under the parabola $f(x) = ax(1 - x)$ for different values of a from 1 to 4 with various initial iterates in the interval from 0 through 1.*

PREASSESSMENT

Students should be familiar with the role the coefficient a plays in the shape of the quadratic $f(x) = ax(1 - x)$ and recognize the x-intercepts of the function. They should also have an initial understanding of the nature of iteration, where the output, $f(x_0)$, for the initial iterate, x_0, becomes the new next iterate, x_1.

TEACHING STRATEGIES

Begin with a discussion of the characteristics of the familiar general parabola, $f(x) = ax^2 + bx + c$, and then the specific quadratics, $f(x) = ax(1 - x)$. Illustrate how the reflecting

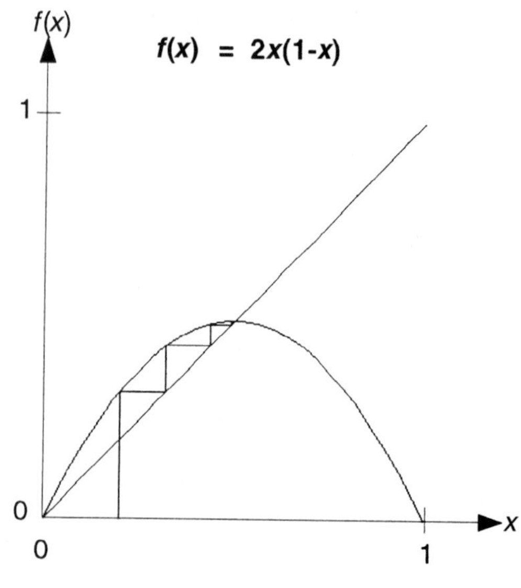
f(x)
f(x) = 2x(1-x)
1
0
0
1
x

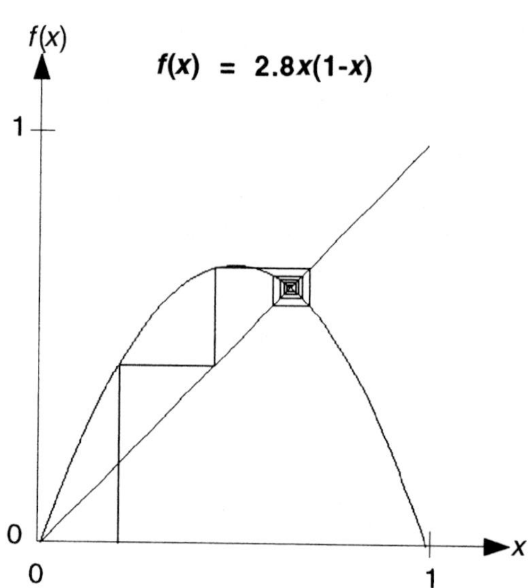
f(x)
f(x) = 2.8x(1-x)
1
0
0
1
x

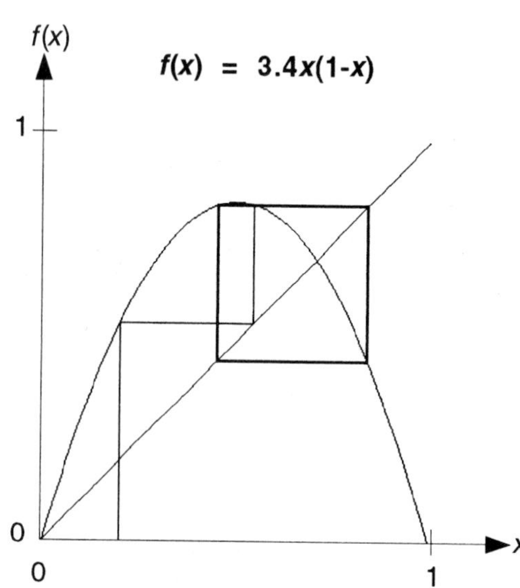
f(x)
f(x) = 3.4x(1-x)
1
0
0
1
x

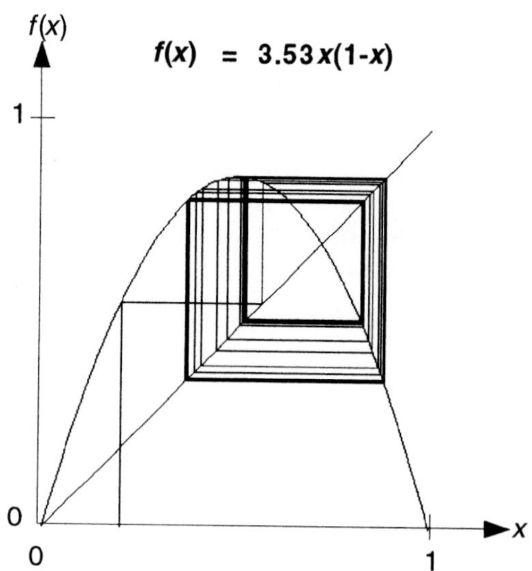
f(x)
f(x) = 3.53x(1-x)
1
0
0
1
x

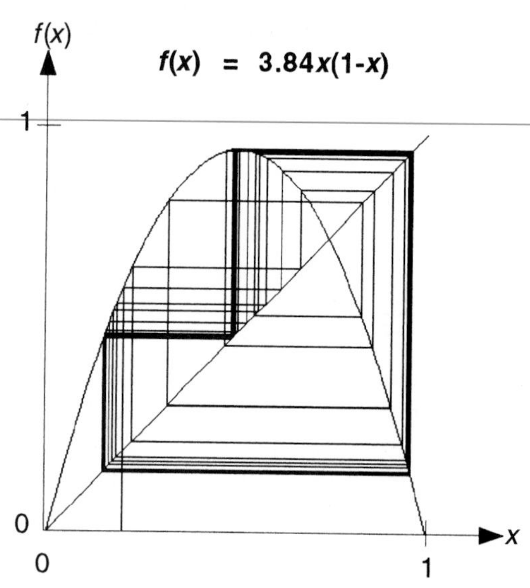
f(x)
f(x) = 3.84x(1-x)
1
0
0
1
x

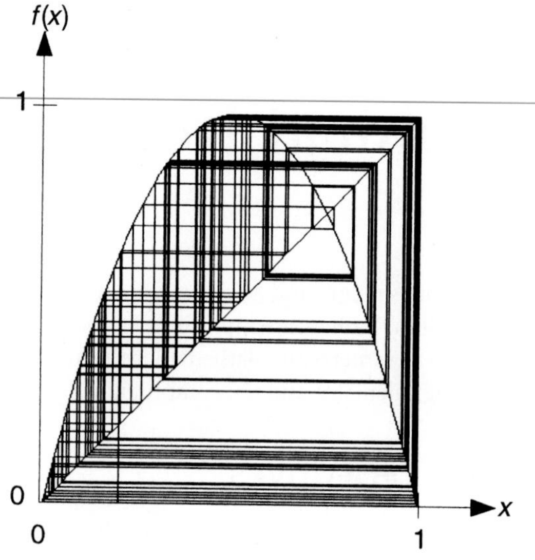
f(x)
1
0
0
1
x

line can geometrically transform an input x_i and its output $f(x_i)$ into a new input x_{i+1}. As various values of the coefficient a are used, note how the quadratic intersects the diagonal, reflecting line, $f(x) = x$, in different places as the coefficient a increases from 1 through 4.

As one explores the different iteration characteristics, various behaviors become apparent. Have students explore and discover that the starting value of the initial iterate does not affect the long-term behavior of the iteration, even though the early values will differ. For simplicity, the graphs shown here all start with the initial iterate 0.2.

A brief summary of the illustrated iteration behaviors is given here:

For $a = 2$, the iterates staircase into the intersection point $x = 0.5$.
For $a = 2.8$, the iterates ultimately spiral into the fixed point, $x = 0.643$.
For $a = 3.4$, a period-2 behavior appears between $x = 0.452$ and 0.842.
For $a = 3.53$, a period-4 behavior begins to develop, eventually moving among $x = 0.369$, 0.822, 0.517, and 0.881.
For $a = 3.84$, surprising period-3 behavior appears to emerge around $x = 0.149$, 0.488, and 0.959.
For $a = 4$, pure chaotic behavior appears.

There are many levels of explanation and interpretation associated with what we call chaotic behavior. It is often characterized by three separate but connected ideas: mixing, sensitivity, and periodicity.

For *mixing*, in every interval, however small, there exists a point that, through iteration, will reach and mix through all such intervals between 0 and 1.
For *sensitivity*, very small differences in iterates may lead to dramatically different behaviors after only a small number of successive iterations.
For *periodicity*, buried within the apparent chaotic behavior, certain points do not mix but visit repeatedly only a small number of locations.

Students should be encouraged to explore these properties as their own level of interest motivates them.

What governs this rather strange, changing iteration behavior under this rather simple quadratic? And where do the transitions from fixed point, to period-2, to period-4, to chaotic behavior occur? Are there any surprises in between, such as a period-3 behavior momentarily appearing after signs of chaos have already emerged? Some directions toward answering these questions can be found in the Feigenbaum plot described briefly in the next unit.

The purpose of this activity is one of motivation, having students utilize technology to explore iteration behavior. The underlying mathematical analysis comes later, along with more exploration of related issues, such as the iteration behavior when $a > 4$.

POSTASSESSMENT

With their graphing calculators or computers, students should be able to meaningfully perform these skills:

1. Recognize the different iteration behaviors that emerge for various values of a in the interval from 1 through 4 for $f(x) = ax(1 - x)$.
2. Find the specific values for fixed point and periodic iteration behavior.

REFERENCE

Peitgen, H., H. Jurgens, D. Saupe, E. Maletsky, T. Perciante, and L. Yunker. *Fractals for the Classroom: Strategic Activities, Volume Two*. New York: Springer-Verlag, 1992.

Thanks to Dr. Evan Maletsky.

Unit 123

The Feigenbaum Plot

This unit shows how the Feigenbaum plot details the bifurcation points in the changing iteration behavior under the quadratic $f(x) = ax(1 - x)$. Specific values of the coefficient a are plotted against the corresponding attractors of the fixed and periodic points. Regions of chaotic behavior are readily visible.

PERFORMANCE OBJECTIVES

1. *Students will read specific attractor values in the interval from 0 to 1 for x for various values of the coefficient a from 1 to 4.*
2. *Students can match the information in this unit against the data collected in unit 122 and explore again those iterations, this time with greater insight into the structure of the differing behaviors.*

PREASSESSMENT

Students should be familiar with the general iteration behavior of the quadratic $f(x) = ax(1 - x)$ as it moves from predictable, fixed-point behavior at $a = 1$ to totally unpredictable, chaotic behavior at $a = 4$ for x iterates between 0 and 1.

TEACHING STRATEGIES

Students expect to find the variable x on the horizontal axis as it was in the last unit on graphical iteration. Thus, the orientation of the Feigenbaum plot may cause some initial concern. The horizontal axis shows the parameter a ranging from 1 to 4, with the corresponding x-values of the attractions on the vertical axis and ranging from 0 to 1.

The spiral moves in to the fixed-point attractor of $x = 0.643$ when $a = 2.8$. This value of x can now be read directly from the Feigenbaum plot, as shown. Likewise, we can read the period-2 attractors of $x = 0.452$ and 0.842 when $a = 3.4$.

The Feigenbaum plot clearly shows the bifurcation points where the period is doubled from 1 to 2, from 2 to 4, from 4 to 8, and so on. Students should explore these regions again using unit 122, but they should not be discouraged if precise separation points cannot be found. Remember, the parameter a is a real number, not restricted by the finite arithmetic of the graphing calculator or computer.

Students will quickly discover where the period-3 window briefly appears in one of the gaps buried in surrounding chaotic behavior. The values of the period-3 attractors, $x = 0.149$, 0.488, and 0.959, are supported here for $a = 3.84$.

This plot is named after American physicist Mitchell Feigenbaum, who developed it while working at the Los Alamos Laboratory in the 1970s. Underlying this work is his discovery that the ratios of distances between successive bifurcation points converges, surprisingly, to a constant that now bears his name. This universal Feigenbaum constant is

$$\delta = 4.669202\ldots$$

and it appears in many different iteration situations in mathematics and science.

POSTASSESSMENT

Students should be able to explain

1. period-doubling bifurcation as seen in the Feigenbaum plot.
2. the connection between the Feigenbaum plot and the iteration behavior for the quadratic $f(x) = ax(1 - x)$.

REFERENCES

Gleick, J. *Chaos: Making a New Science.* New York: Penguin Books, 1987.

Peitgen, H., H. Jurgens, D. Saupe, E. Maletsky, T. Perciante, and L. Yunker. *Fractals for the Classroom: Strategic Activities, Volume Two.* New York: Springer-Verlag, 1992.

Thanks to Dr. Evan Maletsky.

Feigenbaum Plot

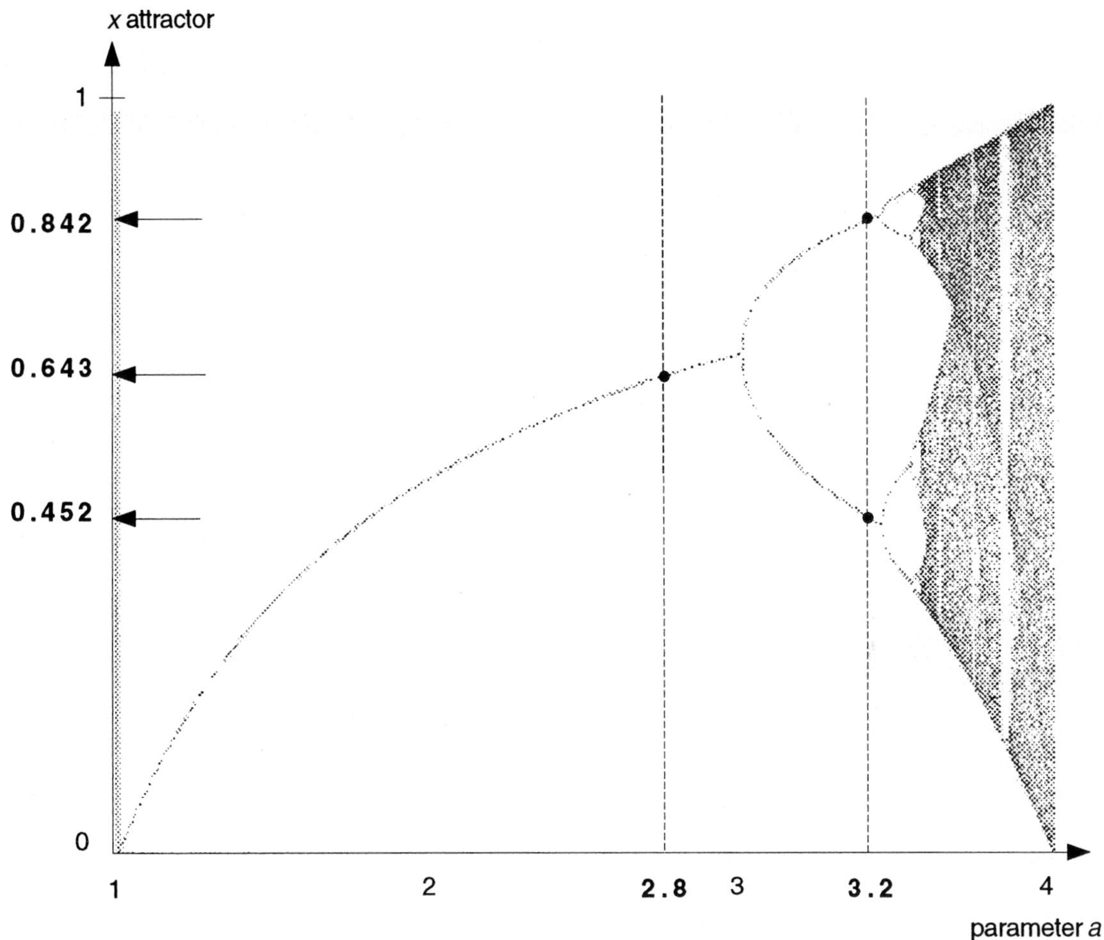

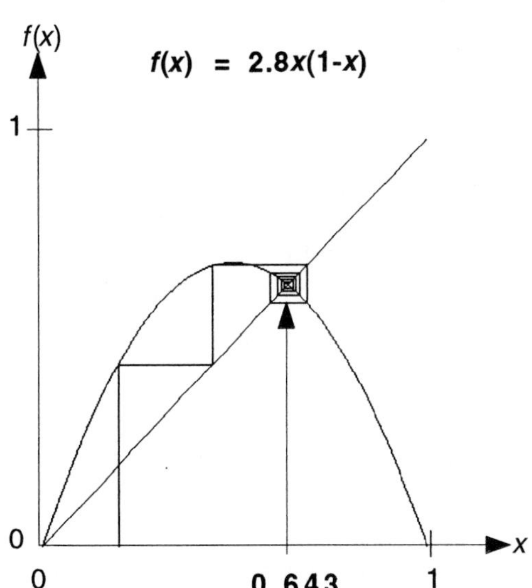

Fixed-point attractor at $x = 0.643$ when $a = 2.8$.

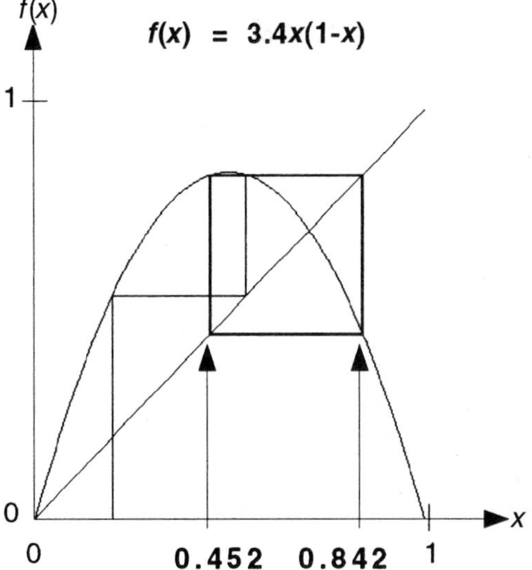

Period-2 attractors at $x = 0.452$ and 0.842 when $a = 3.4$.

Unit 124

 The Sierpinski Triangle

Now that the age of technology is upon us, iteration has taken on a new level of importance in mathematical thinking. This unit reflects how that attention can be directed into the school curriculum through geometry. A simple geometric process, repeated over and over, can transform a plain triangular region into an elegant, abstract fractal structure, the Sierpinski triangle.

PERFORMANCE OBJECTIVES

1. *Students will exercise geometric iteration, first seeing and then visualizing the geometric changes in successive stages of the structure, and then be able to express these changes in both numeric and algebraic form.*
2. *Students will be able to define and illustrate self-similarity.*

PREASSESSMENT

Students should have experience with scaling and similarity and with pattern recognition in various forms, and they should be familiar with the general notions of iteration and recursive thinking.

TEACHING STRATEGIES

In the late 1800s and early 1900s, mathematicians sought to create new kinds of geometric structures that possessed unique properties. Many of their results are recognized and classified today as fractals. One such creation from that period was the Sierpinski triangle, named after Polish mathematician Waclaw Sierpinski.

Have each student start with a triangular piece of paper. Connect the midpoints of the sides of the triangle to form four similar triangles at half linear size. Cut them apart. Keep the three corner triangles, and remove the middle one. Think of this as state 1. Apply the same algorithm again on each of the three new, smaller triangles to get stage 2. Then apply the algorithm again on the nine still smaller triangles to get stage 3. Imagine the iteration process continued through stage 4.

Each stage contains three times as many triangular parts as the preceding stage. It is thus apparent, from this approach, that each successive stage requires three times as many applications of the algorithm. There are always more and more applications on smaller and smaller parts. As far as the cutting goes, the triangular pieces soon get too small in size and too large in number. Is there another view of the process where the iteration rule remains exactly the same throughout and is always applied exactly once in going from one stage to the next? The answer is *yes*.

Have your students think globally of the whole structure at each stage, not of the ever-increasing number of smaller and smaller parts. Here is one possible scenario:

Take any stage of the figure to the copy machine.
Set the machine at 50%, reducing linear dimensions to half.
Make three copies at this half size.
Use them to build the next stage of the structure.

Let this be the iteration algorithm. Have your students actually build the first several stages this way, repeating the exact same process over and over again. Then have them imagine the iteration continuing, and let them visualize how the figure changes, becoming more and more delicate with increasing complexity at each successive stage.

Viewing the building process through these rules, the notion of self-similarity becomes very apparent. Successive structures contain more and more copies of the original stage-0 structure at more and more different scales. But it is only the limit figure that truly exhibits self similarity. Finite stages contain copies *essentially* like the whole, but only the limit figure contains *exact* copies of the whole at all scales!

The Sierpinski triangle is that limit figure. It is an abstract, infinitely complex fractal structure, where all the small triangular regions have reduced themselves to points. Students need to know that it can only be seen in the mind. What the eye sees, at its best, is only some limited finite stage in the development of the Sierpinski triangle.

Within this geometric iteration process, however, lie many mathematical connections. The following table shows how this building process can be related to number patterns, perimeter and area, exponents, geometric series, and limits, to name a few. Indeed, fractals, and the Sierpinski triangle in particular, offer one of the most powerful examples of the kind of mathematical connections referred to in the *Curriculum and Evaluation Standard of School Mathematics* of the National Council of Teachers of Mathematics.

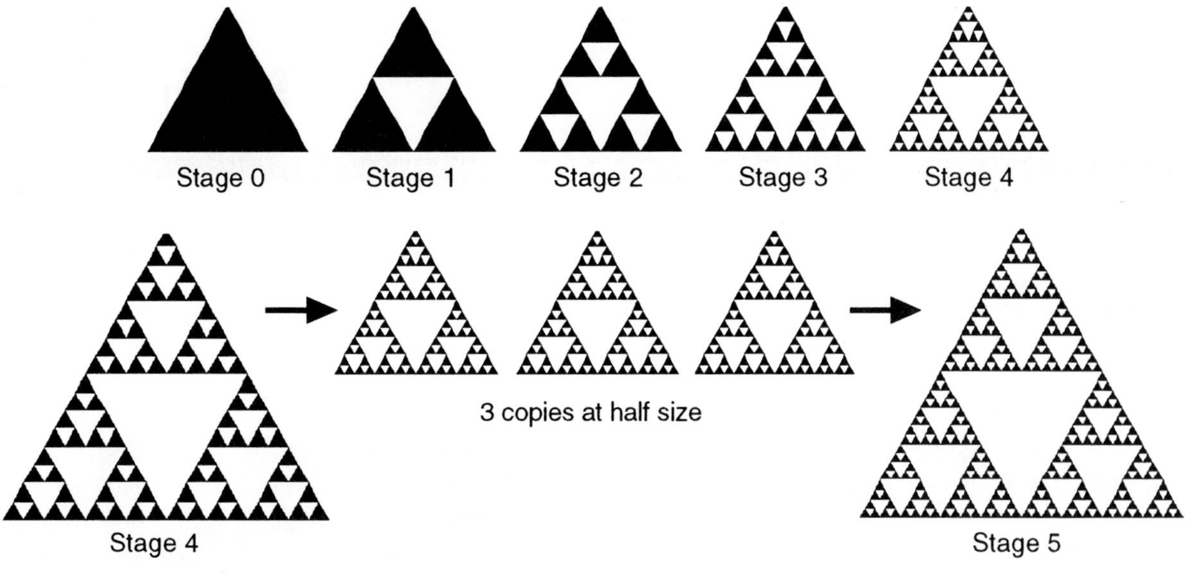

Stage	0	1	2	3	4	n
Number of triangles	1	3	9	27	81	3^n
Area	1	$\frac{3}{4}$	$\frac{9}{16}$	$\frac{27}{64}$	$\frac{81}{256}$	$\left(\frac{3}{4}\right)^n$
Perimeter	1	$\frac{3}{2}$	$\frac{9}{4}$	$\frac{27}{8}$	$\frac{81}{16}$	$\left(\frac{3}{2}\right)^n$

The perimeter and area at stage 0 are defined to be 1 unit and 1 square unit, respectively. This allows the student to focus on the constant multiplier in both sequences and to make the direct connection to geometric sequences. At a different level, the student might be asked to compute the changing perimeter and area starting with an equilateral triangle measuring 4 inches on each side.

Note that the areas in the table refer to those of the shaded triangular regions remaining at each and every stage. The students should see these as converging to 0. In that sense, the limiting area of the Sierpinski triangle is 0! On the other hand, the perimeters in the table refer to the distances around each and every triangular piece at each stage. Here, the students should see these as diverging. In that sense, the limiting perimeter is infinite! Put together, these two different behaviors for the area and perimeter of the same figure give yet another glimpse of the uniqueness of this structure.

POSTASSESSMENT

Students should be able to explain

1. a building algorithm that, when iterated, generates the Sierpinski triangle.
2. the nature of self-similarity as found in the Sierpinski triangle.
3. how the perimeter and area change as successive stages are generated.

REFERENCE

Peitgen, H., H. Jurgens, D. Saupe, E. Maletsky, T. Perciante, and L. Yunker. *Fractals for the Classroom: Strategic Activities, Volume One*. New York: Springer-Verlag, 1991.

Thanks to Dr. Evan Maletsky.

Unit 125

 Fractals

It was not quite 25 years ago that Benoit Mandelbrot coined the word *fractal*. At that time, it would have been hard to believe that this topic would move so fast and reach so many in such a short time. Nor would one likely have foreseen their being attracted, connected, and embedded in the curriculum of school mathematics so quickly. But technology, plus an urge to infuse our teaching with new ideas, has made that possible. Today, there are many software packages on the market that can put the dynamics and aesthetics of fractals directly before your students. It is quite another matter for students to see what mathematics underlies these fascinating structures. Much of that can be done in your classroom with assorted hands-on activities and experiences.

This activity expands and extends the iterative geometric generation of the Sierpinski triangle into a whole family of fractal structures.

PERFORMANCE OBJECTIVES

1. *Students will generate successive stages of various fractals based on an adaptation of the building code for the Sierpinski triangle.*
2. *Students will recognize self-similarity in fractals of this type, and find from that what their building codes are.*

PREASSESSMENT

Students should have experience with scaling, similarity, self-similarity, and the geometric transformations of rotations and reflections.

TEACHING STRATEGIES

Consider modifying the building blocks of the Sierpinski triangle to be centered around squares instead of triangles. For many students, this first step may be the hardest of all to take. How can the Sierpinski triangle emerge from a process that involves only squares?

Every finite stage of this developing fractal consists of small square regions: the higher the stage, the smaller the squares. But in the limit, each of these small squares approaches a point. Whether squares or triangles, in the limit, both approach points. The fact is, the limit figure, generated

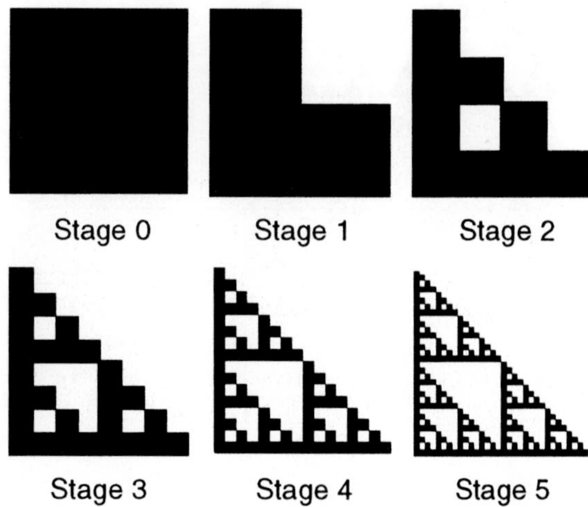

from squares or from triangles, is the same fractal structure, the Sierpinski triangle. Both sequences of figures, although always different, are approaching the same attractor.

Here is a model of the building code. Iterated over and over, the Sierpinski triangle emerges.

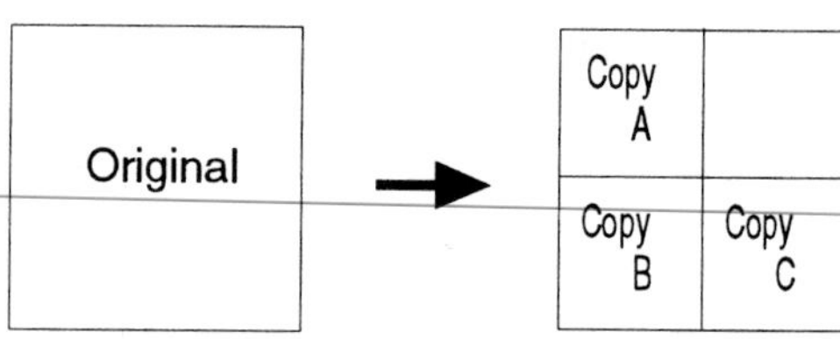

BUILDING CODE

Reduce to $\frac{1}{2}$ size.
Make 3 copies.
Rebuild.

Once this idea is established, incorporate the transformations of a square into the process, and a whole family of Sierpinski-like fractals can be constructed. The result will be that each of your students can explore her or his own personal fractal.

With this code, cell A is rotated 270° and cell B is rotated 180°, each clockwise. Students will quickly see that a very different structure begins to emerge.

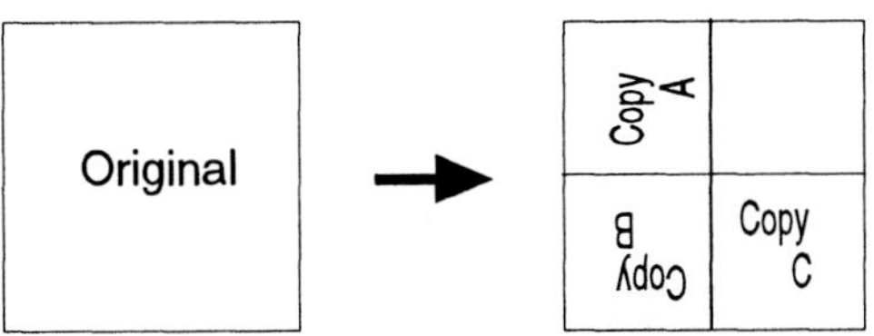

BUILDING CODE

Reduce to $\frac{1}{2}$ size.
Make 3 copies.
Rebuild, rotating copies
A and B as shown.

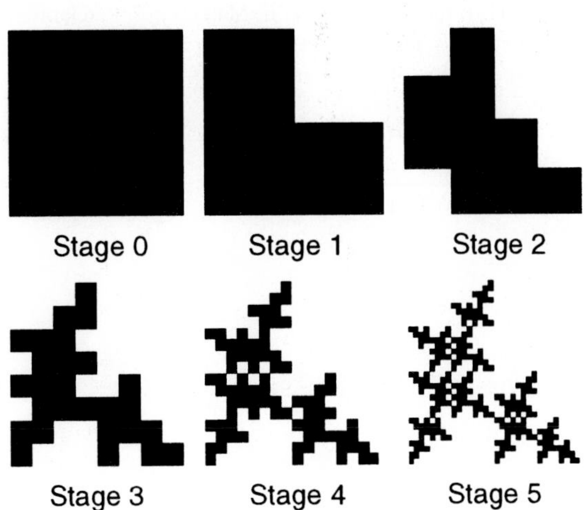

Encourage students to make up their own codes and create the first few stages of the corresponding fractal. Finely ruled graph paper can be used, or you can supply grids of this type for students to use.

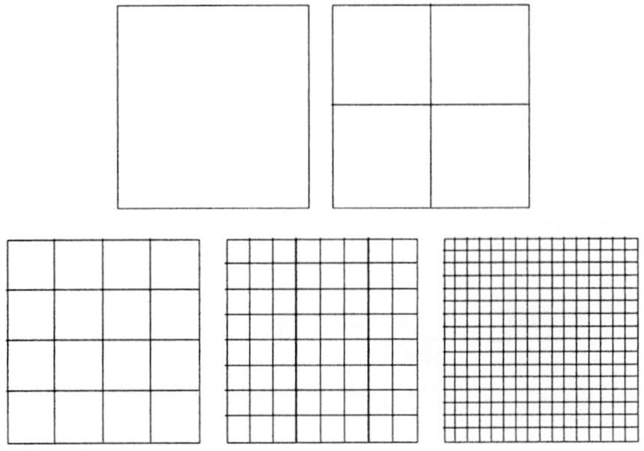

Software packages such as ClarisWorks contain draw programs that can be used very effectively in generating these structures by this process. Their snap-on grids enable accurate constructions.

One word of caution. Whether drawing by hand or using a computer to create the graphics, remember that it is the whole figure at each stage that is reduced, replicated, and rebuilt through the geometric transformations. Students who apply the process incorrectly to more and more smaller and smaller parts at each successive stage are not likely to create

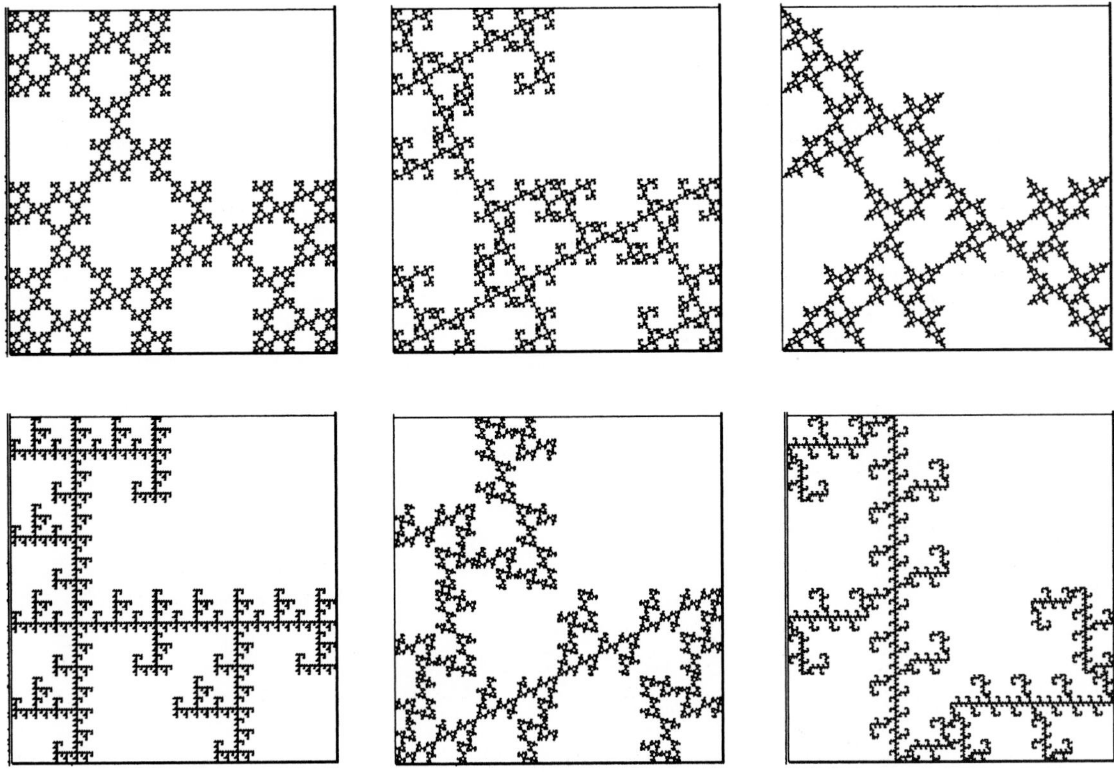

correct figures. At each and every stage, make just three reduced copies of the whole before you rebuild.

A second part of this activity is to have students look at the detailed stages of others and see if they can spot the building codes that were used. This can be a very powerful and challenging visual experience for some. Recall, there are eight possible transformations of the square:

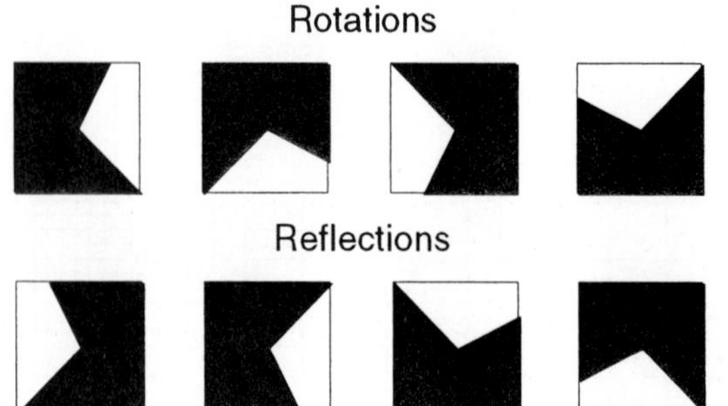

Start with structures that involve only rotations first. For many students, they are the easier ones to see. Save the reflections for later, when your students have had more practice. See if your students can write out the building codes used to create these fractals. Only rotations were used.

POSTASSESSMENT

Students should be able to

1. follow a given building algorithm through several successive stages of development.
2. use self-similarity to identify the building code from a constructed fractal of this type.

REFERENCE

Peitgen, H., H. Jurgens, D. Saupe, E. Maletsky, T. Perciante, and L. Yunker. *Fractals for the Classroom: Strategic Activities, Volume Three*. New York: Springer-Verlag, 1997.

Thanks to Dr. Evan Maletsky.

Appendix

Additional Exercises

1. Select one of the topics from the unit plan on radicals and write a lesson plan for it. What type of lesson plan did you write? Why did you choose that particular type for your topic?
2. a. What are the key features found in most lessons?
   b. What types of lessons lend themselves to the exploration technique?
   c. *True or false:* Every lesson can be exploratory. Discuss.
3. Select a topic from first-year algebra and develop a small group lesson for it.
4. a. Find a section in a first-year high school algebra textbook to teach as a mathematics-through-reading lesson. Write a list of ten questions you plan to ask the class after they read the section.
   b. Do the same in a geometry text.
   c. Do the same in a second-year algebra text.
   d. Do the same in an eighth-grade mathematics text.
5. Write a lesson plan for the day before a long vacation, featuring mathematics puzzles and games.
6. Write a lesson plan for the first day of any mathematics class.
7. Select a topic from an advanced mathematics course and prepare a lesson on it.
8. Write a drill lesson plan for each of the following:
   a. fractional and negative exponents
   b. simple trigonometry (sin, cos, tan)
   c. the distance and midpoint formulas in coordinate geometry
   d. the LCM and GCD in the eighth grade
9. Prepare a series of review lessons for the topic "percent" in a core course.

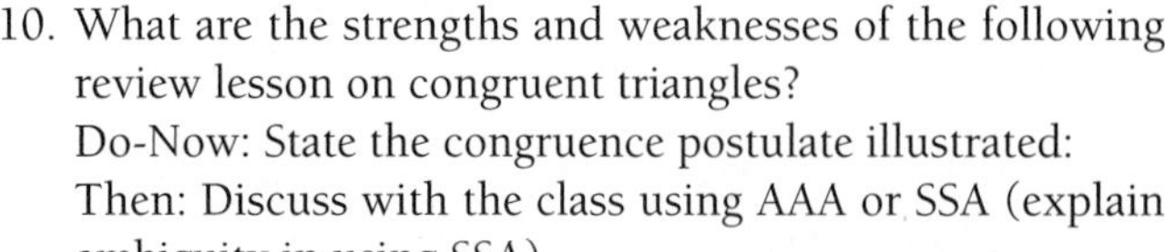

10. What are the strengths and weaknesses of the following review lesson on congruent triangles?
    Do-Now: State the congruence postulate illustrated:
    Then: Discuss with the class using AAA or SSA (explain ambiguity in using SSA).

(1)

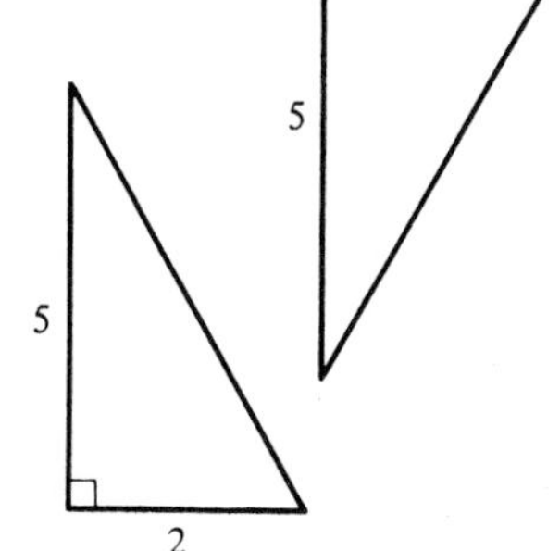

(2)

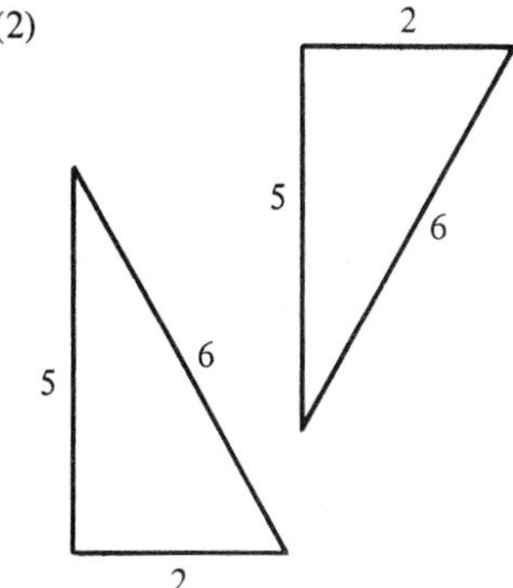

(3)

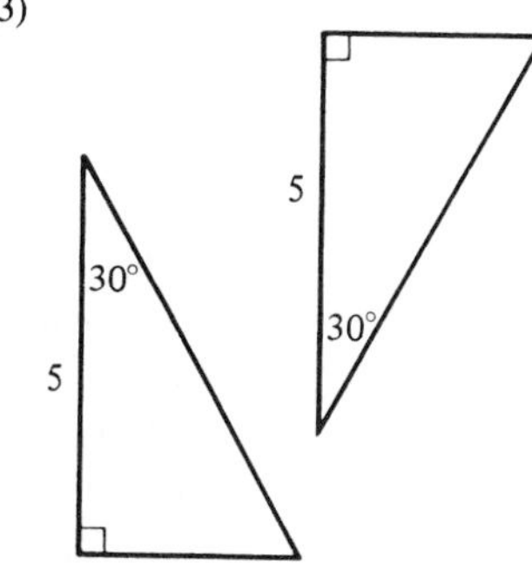

Then: Do the following proofs:

Given: $\overline{BD} \perp \overline{AC}$

$\overline{AD} \cong \overline{DC}$

Prove: $\Delta ABD \cong \Delta CBD$

B

A D C

Given: $\angle ADB \cong \angle CDB$
$\angle ABD \cong \angle CBD$
Prove: $\Delta ABD \cong \Delta CBD$

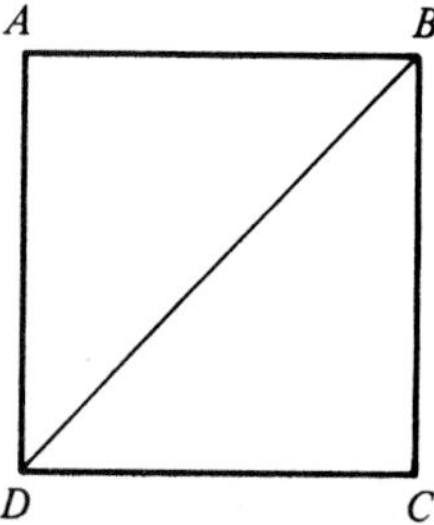

Given: $\overline{AB} \cong \overline{AD}$
$\overline{BC} \cong \overline{CD}$
Prove: $\Delta ABC \cong \Delta ADC$

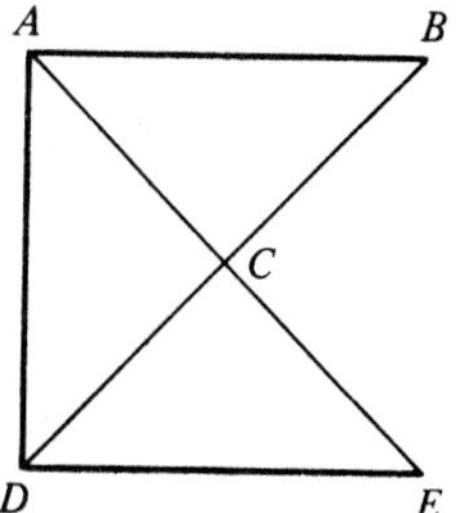

11. Prepare a calculator lesson on each of the following:
   a. The first lesson on systems of equations for a first-year algebra class
   b. The first lesson on trigonometric curves
   c. The first lesson on the law of sines
   d. The first lesson on addition and subtraction of signed numbers in a middle school class
   e. The first lesson on changing fractions to decimals in a high school core class
12. Develop a series of eight 10-minute presentations on any of the following topics to be made to a class that does individualized work for most of the period:
   a. sequences
   b. history of mathematics
   c. patterns in mathematics
   d. recreational mathematics
13. How would you differentiate between a formal lesson plan you might discuss in a college methods course and a plan you might write for a secondary school class you are teaching?
14. Suppose you are asked to develop a long-range unit on truth tables for an eighth-grade middle school mathematics class. Such concepts as negation, conjunction, disjunction, and truth values are to be included. Indicate each of the following:
   a. What steps you would take to set up such a unit
   b. The topics you would include
   c. How many lessons this unit would require
15. Select one topic from the truth-table unit you prepared for Exercise 14 and write a review lesson for it.
16. Prepare a lesson for a seventh-grade mathematics class that develops the mean, median, and mode in one period. Allow sufficient time for practice exercises.
17. Find four mathematics teachers who are willing to cooperate with you on a small research project. Two teachers should be very experienced and two should be relatively inexperienced. Ask each to write a lesson plan on a topic in secondary school mathematics. If possible, have them all work on the same lesson and then observe each teaching that lesson, having the lesson plan in hand. Write a critique of both the lesson and the lesson plan. (Promise each of the subjects that you will not share your critique with anyone and that it will be destroyed after use with this project.)
18. For each of the following topics write a homework assignment for an average-ability class. You may use any appropriate mathematics textbook to assist you. Try to make a provision for both ends of the ability spectrum in this class.
   a. The first lesson on the quadratic formula
   b. The last lesson before a test on special parallelograms
   c. The first lesson on multiplying signed numbers
   d. The first lesson on the law of sines
   e. A lesson on the greatest common factor (eighth grade)
   f. The first lesson on the Pythagorean theorem (high school geometry)
   g. The first lesson on metric measures (seventh grade)
19. Suppose you are teaching a mathematics class at the high school level. The principal asks the faculty to assign a short-term project to each class. Describe the project you would have your students do in each of the following courses. Then discuss how you would handle this project with the class. Include in your discussion the amount of class time you would devote to it, credit allotted, penalties for failure to do a creditable job or failure to do it at all, and uses to which student research would be put (follow-up activities).
   a. Elementary algebra
   b. Second year algebra
   c. Trigonometry
   d. Geometry
20. React to the following student reasons for not doing homework:
   a. "I did not have time last night, since I had too much homework in my other subjects."
   b. "I work after school and do not have much time to do homework."
   c. "I have to do various housework chores and care for my younger brothers and sisters after school and have no time for my homework."
   d. "I didn't understand the homework."
   e. "I forgot to copy my homework assignment yesterday."
   f. "I lost my (1) assignment pad, (2) textbook, (3) completed homework."
   g. "I didn't do my homework."
   h. "I left my homework at home."
   i. "I did the wrong assignment and threw it away this morning when a classmate told me I did the wrong work."
   j. "I forgot I had homework last night."
21. Select a unit of study in the secondary school curriculum and prepare a review homework assignment.
22. Prepare three different discovery homework assign-

ments. You may choose any three topics from the secondary school mathematics curriculum.

23. Indicate the topics that would be useful to review through "spiraling" in a homework assignment in each of the following areas:
    a. A first lesson in factoring polynomials
    b. A lesson on the area of a trapezoid
    c. A lesson on the reduction formulas (the general angle) in trigonometry
    d. A lesson on solving third- and fourth-degree equations having rational and irrational roots
    e. An introductory lesson on irrational numbers in elementary algebra
24. Prepare one enrichment problem for inclusion in a homework assignment on each of the following topics:
    a. Multiplication and division of monomials in elementary algebra
    b. Operations with complex numbers in second-year algebra
    c. Proving triangles congruent in plane geometry
25. Select any topic from secondary school mathematics and show how the homework assigned to prepare the class for a unit test differs from the homework assigned elsewhere in the unit.
26. React to the following student complaints:
    a. "You give too much homework."
    b. "The homework is too hard."
    c. "My other teachers don't give homework on weekends."
    d. "You collected my homework assignment three times this week and you didn't collect Jay's homework even once!"
    e. "I do my homework in a hardcover (bound) notebook and having to tear it out to hand it in is messing up my whole notebook!"
    f. "You didn't go over the problems in class that I didn't understand."
    g. "You don't *look* at the homework I hand in. All you do is place a check mark on it."
27. Develop a questionnaire to be administered to at least 12 mathematics teachers that asks the following questions:
    a. How frequently are students required to do homework?
    b. What type of assignments are required? What kind of questions are asked? How long are the assignments?
    c. Are assignments made on a daily, weekly, or monthly basis?
    d. How are assignments checked by the teacher or by other students?
    e. How are assignments reviewed for quality and completeness?
    f. What is the required format for these assignments?
    g. Does the respondent ever assign research projects or term papers in the mathematics class?

    After you collect the completed questionnaires, analyze the responses to see if there is agreement among the respondents on any of the issues or if there is total disagreement on some of the issues raised in the questionnaire. What can you conclude from this analysis?
28. Comment on the following note by a teacher to the dean of discipline:

    > I found Frank cheating on a test, so I tore up his paper. He cursed at me and threatened to "get me," then he ran out of the room in the middle of the period. I think he should be suspended from school.

29. A student receives his report card indicating 23 days' absence in his mathematics class, resulting in a failing mark, since a school rule mandates failure for pupils absent over 21 days. The student vehemently denies being absent that many days and claims that no other teacher recorded that many absences. How would you handle the situation?
30. A school guidance counselor informs you that three girls want to drop your class because there is too much noise in the room and they can't concentrate. What would be your reaction?
31. A note from the assistant principal summons you to her office to explain why your attendance records are often submitted late and why students from your homeroom class are often found wandering the hallways. What are some explanations that might be tenable?
32. A supervisor admonishes a teacher for regularly coming to class a little late. The teacher's response is:

    > The homework assignment and do-now are always up on the board (from my earlier class) before the period begins, the class knows which row is to put the homework up on the back chalkboard, and I have an excellent student monitor taking attendance, so it makes no difference whether or not I come in one or two minutes late.

    What is your reaction?
33. One of your students asks permission to leave the room. For some reason, you refuse his request. He insists he "must go" and, after an ensuing verbal battle, gets up and walks out. How would you handle the situation upon his return?
34. Several different teachers occasionally found one of their students repeatedly doing work for another subject during mathematics class, despite warnings not to do so. Following are the ways the situation was handled by the various teachers. What are your reactions to each of these "solutions"?
    a. The material was confiscated and destroyed.
    b. The situation was discussed with the teacher of the other subject.
    c. The parent was notified.
    d. The dean was notified.
    e. The student was sent out of the room.
35. A teacher has a preparation period immediately preceding his two consecutive first year algebra classes. Therefore, he always constructs and duplicates the tests and quizzes for these classes during this period. He feels that

this increases the security of these exams. What are some arguments for and against this procedure?

36. Comment on the following treatment for a discipline problem: If a student persists in disturbing your class, send her out of the room and into a nearby mathematics class functioning on a much lower level (with the other teacher's permission, of course).
37. Suppose a student in a ninth-grade mathematics class is constantly inattentive and intentionally disturbs other students nearby. Frequent requests to curb this disruptive activity go unheeded. Explain some steps you may take to seek relief for this situation. Justify your responses.
38. Ask a mathematics department supervisor to discuss classroom management during a portion of a department conference at which you serve as recorder. Following this conference, write a report to summarize the conference highlights, and contrast the different styles of classroom management as voiced by the teachers at the conference.
39. Arrange to have a videotape made of a mathematics lesson you would teach. Invite several teachers, both experienced and inexperienced, to view the videotape and comment on your classroom management techniques. Summarize the comments rendered during this videotape viewing.
40. A teacher notices that in some of the cooperative learning groups in her class the brightest student is doing all the work. What are some techniques that she can use to keep this from happening?
41. You receive a phone call from an angry parent of one of the brightest students in your class. The parent complains that his child is being held back by having to help the weaker students in his group. How would you respond to this parent?
42. The teacher notices that one of the lower-ability students is not participating in her group. How should the teacher handle this situation?
43. Design a cooperative learning exploration lesson that will enable students to make a conjecture regarding the relationship of the three angles of a triangle.
44. A teacher realizes that many of the cooperative groups in his class are not functioning effectively, so he decides to change the group formations at the end of the unit. What procedures can he use to rearrange the groups in the best possible manner?
45. Describe three student characteristics that a teacher should consider when forming heterogeneous groups.
46. What conflict management skills are needed by members of an effective cooperative learning group?
47. A student reports that her group is operating very well; there are no conflicts or disagreements. How would you handle this situation?
48. Describe some ways that a teacher can monitor the progress of cooperative learning groups.
49. Design a lesson that will enable members of cooperative learning groups to discover that the sum of the roots of an equation of the form $ax^2 + bx + c = 0$ is $-b/a$ and that the product of the roots is c/a. Assume that students can solve such a quadratic equation by factoring or by formula.
50. Here is a poorly stated performance objective:

    The student must be able to understand the law of cosines.

    Indicate whether the following test questions are appropriate for testing whether the objective has been attained or not.

    a. Derive the formula for the law of cosines, for an acute or obtuse triangle.
    b. Given a triangle ABC and the measures of a, b, and $\angle C$, solve for c to the nearest tenth.
51. Suppose a supervisor comes to your class and asks to see the performance objectives your students were expected to attain during the past week. She then randomly selects pupils to test them according to the objectives.
    a. Is this a fair way to measure your effectiveness?
    b. Would you choose low-level objectives from now on to ensure a better chance of demonstrating student success?
    c. Do you think that knowing your supervisor will do this periodically will make you a more effective teacher? Justify your response!
52. Write a list of 12 verbs that are too vague and unclear to be used in a performance objective statement. Write another 12 verbs that are unambiguous and that may be used to state performance objectives clearly.
53. Following are four performance objectives (not necessarily good ones). Write two questions that would test each objective to determine whether or not it had been attained. Also state whether each objective is well formulated.
    a. The pupils will state the domain and range of a function given the graph of the function.
    b. The pupils will understand how to solve a quadratic equation by "completing the square."
    c. The student will define *parallelogram, rectangle, square, rhombus*.
    d. The student will appreciate "indirect reasoning" in geometry.

References

Chapter 1

References

Barnett, Rosalind C., and Caryl Rivers. "The Persistence of Gender Myths in Math." *Education Week* 24, no. 7(2004): 39.

National Council of Teachers of Mathematics (NCTM). *Curriculum and Evaluation Standards for School Mathematics.* Reston, VA: NCTM, 1989.

National Council of Teachers of Mathematics (NCTM). *Professional Standards for Teaching Mathematics.* Reston, VA: NCTM, 1991.

National Council of Teachers of Mathematics (NCTM). *Assessment Standards for School Mathematics.* Reston, VA: NCTM, 1995.

National Council of Teachers of Mathematics (NCTM). *Making a Living, Making a Life.* Reston, VA: NCTM, 1997.

National Council of Teachers of Mathematics (NCTM). *Principles and Standards for School Mathematics.* Reston, VA: NCTM, 2000.

National Council of Teachers of Mathematics. *NCTM News Bulletin* 37, no. 9 (2001).

U. S. Department of Education. *Before It's Too Late: A Report to the Nation of Mathematics and Science Teaching for the 21st Century.* Washington, DC: U.S. Printing Office, 2000.

Suggested Readings

ARC Center at COMAP, Inc. *New Resources for School Mathematics*, Lexington, MA: COMAP, Inc., 2001.

Blair, Timothy. *New Teacher's Performance-Based Guide to Culturally Diverse Classrooms.* Boston, MA: Pearson Education, 2003.

Cozzens, Margaret B. *Learning From TIMSS-R About U.S. Mathematics Achievement.* The Mathematical Association of America (MAA), May/June, 2001.

The Ford Foundation. *Solving the Math Problem.* April, 1999.

Hoff, David. "Adding It All Up." *Education Week* 22, no. 23 (2003): 28–31.

International Association for the Evaluation of Educational Achievement (IEA). *Gender Differences in Achievement,* IEA's Third International Mathematics and Science Study (TIMSS), 2000.

International Association for the Evaluation of Educational Achievement (IEA). TIMSS 1999—*International Mathematics Report*, 1999.

Nasir, Na'ilah Suad, and Paul Cobb. "Diversity, Equity, and Mathematical Learning" [Special Issue]. *Mathematical Thinking and Learning: An International Journal* 4, no. 2 (2002): 3.

National Assessment of Educational Progress. Retrieved October 25, 2004, from http://nces.ed.gov/nationsreportcard/

National Center for Educational Statistics (NCES). *Pursuing Excellence: A Study of U.S. Twelfth Grade Mathematics and Science Achievement in International Context.* U.S. Department of Education (TIMSS), 1998.

National Commission on Mathematics and Science Teaching for the 21st Century. The Glenn Commission Report. *Before It's Too Late.* Jessup, MD: Education Publications Center, 2000.

National Council of Teachers of Mathematics (NCTM). *Changing School Mathematics.* Reston, VA: NCTM, 1981.

National Council of Teachers of Mathematics. *Learning Mathematics for a New Century: 2000 Yearbook of the National Council of Teachers of Mathematics.* Edited by Maurice J. Burke and Frances R. Curcio. Reston, VA: National Council of Teachers of Mathematics, 2000.

No Child Left Behind. Retrieved October 25, 2004, from http://www.ed.gov/nclb/landing.jhtml?src=pb

North Central Regional Educational Library. *Active, Meaningful Mathematics Learning: A Guidebook*, 1991.

Office of Education and Research. *Exemplary and Promising Mathematics Programs Report.* Department of Education. Retrieved from http://www.enc.org/professional/federalresources/exemplary/promising/?1s=bc

Rodriquez, Alberto, and Richard Kitchen. *Preparing Mathematics and Science Teachers for Diverse Classrooms.* Mahwah, NJ: Lawrence Erlbaum Associates, 2005.

Secada, Walter. *Changing the Faces of Mathematics: Perspectives on Multiculturalism and Gender Equity.* Reston, VA: National Council of Teachers of Mathematics, 2000.

Senk, Sharon, and Denisse Thompson. *Standards-Based School Mathematics Curricula: What Are They? What Do Students Learn?* Mahwah, NJ: Lawrence Erlbaum Associates, 2003.

Trends in International Mathematics and Science Study. Retrieved on October 25, 2004, from http://nces.ed.gov/timss/

For more:

The NRC report is at www.nap.edu/books/0309069955/html. The NCTM Web site is http://www.nctm.org

For an opposing view:

Schmidt, William H., Curtis C. McKnight, Senta A. Raizen, *A Splintered Vision: An Investigation of U.S. Science and Mathematics Education*. Boston: Kluwar Academic Publishers, 1997. (The Executive Summary of this publication is available at the following Web site: ustimss.msu.edu/splintrd.htm)

http://nces.ed.gov/nationsreportcard/mathematics/results/

Chapter 2

References

Growes, D. Mathematics. In G. Cawelti (ed.), *Handbook of Research on Improving Student Achievement* (pp. 160–178). Arlington, VA: Educational Research Service, 2004.

National Council of Teachers of Mathematics. *Principles and Standards for School Mathematics*. Reston, VA: NCTM, 2000.

Protheroe, N., E. Shellard, and J. Turner. *A Practical Guide to School Improvement: Meeting the Challenges of NCLB*. Arlington, VA: Educational Research Service, 2003.

Romberg, T. Problematic Features of the School Mathematics Curriculum. In P. W. Jackson (ed.), *Handbook of Research on Curriculum* (pp. 749–787). New York: Macmillan, 1992.

Suggested Readings

Artzt, Alice F., and Claire M. Newman. *How to Use Cooperative Learning in the Mathematics Class*. Reston, VA: National Council of Teachers of Mathematics, 1997.

———. "Implementing the Standards. Cooperative Learning." *Mathematics Teacher* 83, no. 6 (Sept. 1990): 448–452.

Boaler, Joy, and Cathy Humbhreys. *Connecting Mathematical Ideas: Middle School Video Cases*. Portsmith, NH: Heinemann, 2005.

Brown, Cheryl L. "Whole Concept Mathematics: A Whole Language Application." *Educational Horizons* 69, no. 3 (Spring, 1991): 159–163.

Burrill, Gail, John C. Burrill, Pamela Coffield, Gretchen Davis, Jan de Lange, Diane Resnick, and Murray Siegel. *Curriculum and Evaluation Standards for School Mathematics: Data Analysis and Statistics Across the Curriculum, Addenda Series, Grades 9–12*. Reston, VA: NCTM, 1992.

Carter, John, and Dorothy Carter. *The Write Equation: Writing in the Mathematics Classroom*. Palo Alto, CA: Dale Seymour Publications, 1994.

Clark, H. Clifford, and Marvin N. Nelson. "Improving Mathematics Evaluation through Cooperative Learning Strategies." *Middle School Journal* 24, no. 3 (Jan. 1993): 15–18.

Committee on Mathematical Sciences in the Year 2000. *EVERYBODY COUNTS: A Report to the Nation on the Future of Mathematical Education*. NRC, Washington, DC: National Academic Press, 1989.

Cooney, Thomas J., ed. *Teaching and Learning Mathematics in the 1990's: 1990 Yearbook*. Reston, VA: NCTM, 1990.

Cox, Arthur F. *Curriculum and Evaluation Standards for School Mathematics: Geometry from Multiple Perspectives, Addenda Series, Grades 9–12*. Reston, VA: NCTM, 1992.

Erickson, Tim, ed. *Get It Together: Math Problems for Groups Grades 4 to 12*. Berkeley, CA: EQUALS, 1989.

Frazer, Don. *Sports Math*. Palo Alto, CA: Dale Seymour Publications.

Froelich, Gary W. *Curriculum and Evaluation Standards for School Mathematics Addenda Series, Grades 9–12*. Reston, VA: NCTM, 1991.

Gregory, Gayle. *Differentiated Instructional Strategies in Practice*, 2nd ed. Thousand Oaks: Corwin Press, 2008.

Grouws, Douglas A., ed. *Handbook of Research on Mathematics Teaching and Learning*. New York, NY: Macmillan Publishing Company, 1992.

Grouws, Douglas, Thomas Cooney, and Douglas Jones, eds. *Perspectives on Research on Effective Mathematics Teaching, Vol. 1*. Reston, VA: NCTM, 1988.

Halpern, Diane F. *Enhancing Thinking Skills in Science and Mathematics*. Hillsdale, NJ: Lawrence Erlbaum Associates, 1992.

Higbee, Jeanne L., and Patricia L. Dwinell, eds. "Sharing Teaching Ideas." *Mathematics Teacher* 83, no. 9 (Dec. 1990): 721–724.

Johanning, Debra, and Teri Keusch. "Teaching to Develop Students as Learners." In Rheta N. Rubenstein and George W. Bright (eds.), *Perspectives on the Teaching of Mathematics: Sixty-Sixth Yearbook* (pp. 107–116). Reston, VA: National Council of Teachers of Mathematics, 2004.

Jones, Alanna. *Team Building Activities for Any Group*. Richland, WA: Rec Room Publishing, 1999.

Jones, Joan, C. Promoting Equity in Mathematics Education through Effective, Culturally Responsive Teaching. In Rheta N. Rubenstein and George W. Bright (eds.), *Perspectives on the Teaching of Mathematics: Sixty-Sixth Yearbook* (pp. 141–150). Reston, VA: National Council of Teachers of Mathematics, 2004.

Kagan, Spencer. *Cooperative Learning*. San Clemente, CA: Resources for Teachers, Inc., 1992.

Kastner, Bernice, ed. *Space Mathematics*. Washington, DC: U.S. Government Printing Office.

Keeler, Carolyn M., and others. "Cooperative Learning in Statistics." *Teaching Statistics* 16, no. 3 (Fall 1994): 81–84.

Kulm, Gerald. *Mathematics Assessment: What Works in the Classroom*. Washington, DC: MAA, 1994.

Leikin, Roza, and Orit Zaslavsky. "Facilitating Student Interactions in Mathematics in a Cooperative Learning Setting." *Journal for Research in Mathematics Education* 28, no. 3 (May 1997): 331–354.

Lesh, Richard, and Susan J. Lamon. *Assessment of Authentic Performance in School Mathematics.* Washington, DC: American Association for the Advancement of Science, 1992.

Mathematical Sciences Education Board. *Counting on You: Actions Supporting Mathematical Teaching Standards.* NRC, Washington, DC: National Academy Press, 1991.

Milgram, Roberta M., ed. *Teaching Gifted and Talented Learners in Regular Classrooms.* Springfield, IL: Charles C. Thomas, 1989.

National Council of Teachers of Mathematics. *Professional Standards for Teaching Mathematics.* Reston, VA: NCTM, 1991.

———. *Principles and Standards for School Mathematics.* Reston, VA: NCTM, 2000.

———. *Curriculum and Evaluation Standards for School Mathematics—Addenda Series.* Reston, VA: NCTM, 1991–1992.

———. *Teaching and Learning Mathematics in the 1990's.* NCTM 1990 Yearbook. Reston, VA: NCTM, 1990.

———. *Discrete Mathematics Across the Curriculum: K–12.* NCTM 1991 Yearbook. Reston, VA: NCTM, 1991.

Owens, Douglas T., ed. *Research Ideas for the Classroom: Volume II: Middle Grades Mathematics.* New York, NY: Macmillan Publishing Company, 1993.

Peitgen, Heinz Otto, Evan Maletsky, Hartmut Jurgens, Terry Perciante, Dietmar Saupe, and Lee Yunker. *Fractals for the Classroom: Strategic Activities Volumes One and Two.* New York: Springer Verlag/NCTM, 1991.

Perl, Teri. *Women and Numbers: Lives of Women Mathematicians Plus Discovery Activities.* San Carlos, CA: Wide World Publishing/Tetra House, 1993.

Posamentier, Alfred S., Hope Hartman, and Constanze Kaiser. *Tips for the Mathematics Teacher: Research-Based Strategies to Help Students Learn.* Thousand Oaks, CA: Corwin Press, 1998.

Quinn, Robert J. "Modeling Statistics Lessons with Preservice and Inservice Teachers." *Clearing House* 69, no. 4 (Mar.–Apr. 1996): 246–248.

Roueche, Suzanne D., ed. "Innovation Abstracts, Volume XV, 1993." *Innovation Abstracts* 15, no. 1–30 (Jan.–Dec. 1993).

Rubinstein, Gary. *Reluctant Disciplinarian.* Fort Collins, CO: Cottonwood Press, 1999.

Rubenstein, Rheta N., and Denisse R. Thompson. "Learning Mathematical Symbolism: Challenges and Instructional Strategies." *Mathematics Teacher* 94, no. 4 (April 2001): 265–271.

Slavin, Robert E., and others. "Cooperative Learning Models for the 3 R's. *Educational Leadership* 47, no. 4 (Dec.–Jan. 1989, 1990): 22–28.

Smith, M., and M. Stein. "Selecting and Creating Mathematical Tasks: From Research to Practice." *Mathematics Teaching in the Middle School* 3 (1998): 344–350.

Smith, Margaret. "Beyond Presenting Good Problems: How a Japanese Teacher Implements Mathematical Tasks." In Rheta N. Rubenstein and George W. Bright, (eds.), *Perspectives on the Teaching of Mathematics: Sixty-Sixth Yearbook* (pp. 96–106). Reston, VA: National Council of Teachers of Mathematics, 2004.

Spikell, Mark A. *Teaching Mathematics with Manipulatives: A Resource of Activities for the K–12 Teacher.* Needham Heights, MA: Allyn and Bacon, 1993.

Steen, Lynn A., ed. *Heeding the Call for Change: Suggestions for Curricular Action.* Washington, DC: MAA, 1992.

———. *On the Shoulders of GIANTS: New Approaches to Numeracy.* NRC. Washington, DC: National Academy Press, 1990.

Stein, Mary K., and Suzanne Lane. "Instructional Tasks and the Development of Student Capacity to Think and Reason: An Analysis of the Relationship between Teaching and Learning in a Reform Mathematics Project." *Educational Research and Evaluation* 2 (January 1996): 50–80.

Stein, Mary Kay, and Margaret Smith. "Mathematical Tasks as a Framework for Reflection: From Research to Practice." *Mathematics Teaching in the Middle School* 3, no. 4 (1998): 268–273.

Stenmark, Jean Kerr, ed. *Mathematics Assessment: Myths, Models, Good Questions, and Practical Suggestions.* Reston, VA: NCTM, 1991.

Stewart, Ian. *Nature's Numbers: The Unreal Reality of Mathematics.* New York: Basic Books, 1995.

Sutton, Gail Oberholtzer. "Cooperative Learning Works in Mathematics." *Mathematics Teacher* 85, no. 1 (Jan. 1992): 63–66.

Sved, Martha. *Journey Into Geometries.* Washington, DC: MAA, 1991.

Tietze, Martha. "A Core Curriculum in Geometry." *Mathematics Teacher* 85, no. 4 (Apr. 1992): 300–303.

———. "Sharing Teaching Ideas." *Mathematics Teacher* 83, no. 9 (Dec. 1990): 721–724.

Tomlinson, Carol Ann. *How to Differentiate Instruction in Mixed-Ability Classrooms.* Alexandria, VA: ASCD, 2001.

Ward, Cherry D. "Under Construction: On Becoming a Constructivist in View of the Standards." *Mathematics Teacher* 94, no. 2 (Feb. 2001): 94–96.

Welchman-Tischler, Rosamond. *Teaching with Manipulatives: Middle School Investigations.* White Plains, NY: Cuisenaire, 1996.

Wong, Harry K., and Rosemary T. Wong. *The First Days of School: How To Be an Effective Teacher.* Mountain View, CA: Harry K. Wong Publications, Inc., 1991.

Zaslovsky, Claudia. *Fear of Math: How to Get Over It & Get On With Your Life.* Palo Alto, CA: Dale Seymour Publications, 1996.

Chapter 3

Suggested Readings

Motivation

Ames, Carole, and Russell Ames, eds. *Research on Motivation.* San Diego, CA: Academic Press, 1989.

Carr, Martha. *Motivation in Mathematics.* Hampton Press, 1995.

Henson, Kenneth T. *Secondary Teaching Methods.* Lexington, MA: D.C. Heath, 1981, 165–167.

Johnson, David R. *Motivation Counts: Teaching Techniques That Work.* Dale Seymour Publications, 1997.

LaConte, R. T. *Homework as a Learning Experience.* Washington, DC: National Education Association, 1986.

McEntire, Arnold, and Anita Narvarte Kitchens. "A New Focus for Educational Improvement Through Cognitive and Other Structuring of Subconscious Personal Axioms." *Education* 105, no. 2 (Winter 1984).

Orlich, Donald C., et al. *Teaching Strategies: A Guide to Better Instruction.* Lexington, MA: D. C. Heath, 1985, chap. 6.

Sobel, M. A., and E. M. Maletsky. *Teaching Mathematics, A Sourcebook of Aids, Activities, and Strategies,* 2d ed. Englewood Cliffs, NJ: Prentice-Hall, 1988.

Stipek, Deborah J. *Motivation to Learn: From Theory to Practice.* Englewood Cliffs, NJ: Prentice-Hall, 1988.

Weinert, Franz, and Rainer Kluwe, eds. *Metacognition, Motivation, and Understanding.* Hillsdale, NJ: Lawrence Erlbaum Associates, 1987.

Wlodkowski, R. J. *Motivation.* Washington, DC: National Education Association, 1986.

Questioning

Cangelosi, James S. "Increasing Student Engagement During Questioning Strategy Sessions." *Mathematics Teacher* 77 (1984): 470.

Costa, Arthur. "Teacher Behaviors That Enable Student Thinking." In *Developing Minds: A Resource Book for Teaching Thinking.* Arthur Costa, ed. Alexandria, VA: Association for Supervision and Curriculum Development, 1985, 125–137.

Fey, James T. *Patterns of Verbal Communication in Mathematics Classes.* New York: Teachers College Press, 1970.

Gavelek, James, and Taffy Raphael. "Metacognition, Instruction, and the Role of Questioning Activities." Chap. 3 of *Instructional Practices.* Vol. 2 of *Metacognition, Cognition, and Human Performance.* D. L. Forrest-Pressley, G. E. MacKinnon, and T. Gary Waller, eds. Orlando, FL: Academic Press, 1985.

Henderson, Kenneth B. "Anent the Discovery Method." *Mathematics Teacher* 50 (1970): 287.

Interactive Mathematics Program. *Introduction and Implementation Strategies for the Interactive Mathematics Program.* Berkeley, CA: Key Curriculum Press, 1998.

Kilpatrick, Jeremy. "Inquiry in the Mathematics Classroom." *Academic Connections.* New York: The College Board, Summer 1987.

Orlich, Donald C., et al. *Teaching Strategies: A Guide to Better Instruction.* Lexington, MA: D. C. Heath & Co., 1985, pp. 161–200.

Redfield, Doris, and Elaine Rousseau. "A Meta-analysis of Experimental Research on Teacher Questioning Behavior." *Review of Educational Research* 51, no. 2 (1981): 237–245.

Rowe, Mary Budd. "Teaching Science as a Continuous Inquiry: A Basic." New York: McGraw Hill, 1978.

Swing, Susan, and Penelope Peterson. "Elaborative and Integrative Thought Problems in Mathematics Learning." *Journal of Educational Psychology* 80, no. 1 (1988): 54–66.

Walsh, Debbie. "Socrates in the Classroom." *American Educator* (Summer 1985): 20–25.

Wilen, W. W. *Questioning Skills for Teachers.* Washington, DC: National Education Association, 1987.

———. *Questions, Questioning Techniques, and Effective Teaching.* Washington, DC: National Education Association, 1987.

Wolf, Dennis Palmer. "The Art of Questioning." *Academic Connections.* New York: The College Board, Winter 1987.

Wong, Bernice. "Self-Questioning Instructional Research: A Review." *Review of Educational Research* 55, no. 2 (Summer 1985): 227–268.

Effective Strategies

Bauer, Madeline J., and Joseph P. Fagan. "MATHCOUNTS." In *Developing Mathematically Promising Students.* Linda Sheffield, ed. Reston, VA: National Council of Teachers of Mathematics, 1999, 297–302.

Bennett, Albert B., Jr., and Eugene Maier. "A Visual Approach to Solving Mixture Problems." *Mathematics Teacher* 89, no. 2 (February 1996): 108–111.

Bezuszka, Stanley. *Tessellations: The Geometry of Patterns.* Creative Publications, 1977.

Bidwell, James K. "Humanizing Your Classroom with History of Mathematics." *Mathematics Teacher* 86, no. 6 (September 1993): 461–464.

Blank, Rolf K., Doreen Langesen, Marty Bush, Suzanne Sardina, Ellen Pechman, and David Goldstein. *Mathematics and Science Content Standards and Curriculum Frameworks.* Washington, DC:Council of Chief State School Officers, 1997.

Boles, Martha, and Rochelle Newman. *Universal Patterns.* Pythagorean Press, 1990.

Brandon, Paul R., Barbara J. Newton, and Ormrod W. Hammond. "Children's Mathematics Achievement in Hawaii: Sex Differences Favoring Girls." *American Educational Research Journal* 24, no. 3 (Fall 1987): 437–461.

Britton, Jill, and Dale Seymour. *Introduction to Tessalations.* Palo Alto, CA: Dale Seymour Publications, 1989.

Brookhart, Clint. *Go Figure! Using Math to Answer Everyday Imponderables*. Lincolnwood, IL: Contemporary Publishing Group, 1998.

Coxeter, H. S. M. *Introduction to Geometry*, 2nd ed. New York: John Wiley & Sons, 1969.

Crowley, Mary L. "Student Mathematics Portfolio: More Than a Display Case." *Mathematics Teacher* 86, no. 7 (October 1993): 544–547.

Davis, Robert, Elizabeth Jocksuch, and Curtis McKnight. "Cognitive Processes in Learning Algebra." *Journal of Children's Mathematical Behavior* 2, no. 1 (Spring 1978).

Dossey, John A., ed. *Confronting the Core Curriculum: Considering Change in the Undergraduate Mathematics Major*. Washington, DC: Mathematical Association of America, 1998.

Driscoll, Mark. *Fostering Geometric Thinking: A Guide for Teachers, Grades 5–10*. Portsmith, NH: Heinemann, 2007.

Educational Psychologist 23, no. 2 (Spring 1988).

Ellis, Arthur K. "Planning for Mathematics Instruction." *Teaching Mathematics in Grades K–8*, 2d ed. Thomas R. Post, ed. Boston: Allyn & Bacon, 1992.

Geometry Center Hyperbolic Geometry Exhibit Welcome Page: www.math.ubc.ca/~robles/hyperbolic/index.html

Greenberg, Marvin Jay. *Euclidean and Non-Euclidean Geometries*. New York: W. H. Freeman, 1993.

Gurkewitz, Rona, and Bennett Arnstein. *3-D Geometric Origami*. New York: Dover Publications, 1995.

Lefrancois, Guy R. *Psychology for Teaching*, 8th ed. Belmont, CA: Wadsworth, 1994.

Leinhardt, Gaea, and Ralph T. Putnam. "The Skill of Learning from Classroom Lessons." *American Educational Research Journal* 24, no. 4 (Winter 1987): 557–587.

Mathematical Sciences Education Board—National Research Council. *High School Mathematics at Work: Essays of Examples for the Education of All Students*. Washington, DC: National Academy Press, 1998.

Mitchell, Julia H., Evelyn F. Hawkins, Pamela M. Jakwerth, Frances B. Stancavage, and John A. Dossey. *Student Work and Teacher Practices in Mathematics*. Washington, DC: National Center for Education Statistics, 1999.

Mu Alpha Theta. www.mualphatheta.org

Owens, Douglas T. *Research Ideas for the Classroom: Middle Grades Mathematics*. New York: Macmillan, 1993.

Piez, Cynthia, and Mary H. Voxman. "Multiple Representations: Using Efficient Perspectives to Form a Clearer Picture." *Mathematics Teacher* 90, no. 2 (February 1997): 164–166.

Reed, Stephan K., and Michael Ettinger. "Usefulness of Tables for Solving Word Problems." *Cognition and Instruction* 4, no. 1 (1987): 43–59.

Riley, Mary S., and James G. Greeno. "Developmental Analysis of Understanding Language about Quantities and of Solving Problems." *Cognition and Instruction* 5, no. 1 (1988): 49–101.

Schattschneider, Doris. *Visions of Symmetry: Notebooks, Periodic Drawings & Related Works of M. C. Escher*. W. H. Freeman, 1990.

Sprenger, Marilee. *How to Teacher So Students Remember*. Alexandria VA: Association for Supervision and Curriculum Development, 2005.

Sommers, Kay, John Dilendik, and Betty Smolansky. "Class Activities with Student-Generated Data." *Mathematics Teacher* 89, no. 2 (February 1996): 105–107.

Stigler, James W., and James Hiebert. *The Teaching Gap*. New York, NY: The Free Press, 1999.

Swing, Susan R., Karen C. Stoiber, and Penelope L. Peterson. "Thinking Skills Versus Learning Time: Effects of Alternative Classroom-Based Interventions on Students' Mathematics Problem Solving." *Cognition and Instruction* 5, no. 2 (1988): 123–191.

Takahira, Sayuri, Patrick Gonzales, Mary Frase, and Laura H. Salganik. *Pursuing Excellence: A Study of Twelfth-Grade Mathematics and Science Achievement in International Context*. Washington, DC: National Center for Education Statistics, 1998.

Venters, Diana, and Elaine Krajernke Ellison. *Mathematical Quilts*. Key Curriculum Press, 1999.

Zhu, Xinming, and Herbert A. Simon. "Learning Mathematics from Examples and By Doing." *Cognition and Instruction* 4, no. 3 (1987): 137–166.

Literacy

Azzolino, Aggie. "Writing As a Tool for Teaching Mathematics: The Silent Revolution." *1990 Yearbook*, Reston, VA: National Council of Teachers of Mathematics, 1990.

Barnes, Julia A. "Creative Writing in Trigonometry." *Mathematics Teacher* 92 (September 1999):498–503.

Barton, M., and C. Heidema. *Teaching Reading in Mathematics*, 2nd ed. Alexandria, VA: ASCD, 2002.

Becker, Jerry P., and Shigeru Shimada. *The Open-Ended Approach: A New Proposal for Teaching Mathematics*. Reston, VA: National Council of Teachers of Mathematics, 1997.

Blair, T. *New Teacher's Performance-Based Guide to Culturally Diverse Classrooms*. Boston: Allyn and Bacon, 2003.

Countryman, Joan. "Writing to Learn Mathematics." In *Functions*. Princeton, NJ: Woodrow Wilson National Fellowship Foundation, 1985.

Davison, David M., and Daniel L. Pearce. "Using Writing Activities to Reinforce Mathematics Instruction." *Arithmetic Teacher* 36 (1988): 42–45.

Dougherty, Barbara J. "The Write Way: A Look at Journal Writing in First Year Algebra." *Mathematics Teacher* 89 (October 1996): 556–560.

Edwards, L. *Reading and Writing in the Mathematics Classroom*. New York: Glencoe, 2002.

Elliot, Portia C., ed. *Communication in Mathematics, K–12 and Beyond. 1996 Yearbook*. Reston, VA: National Council of Teachers of Mathematics, 1996.

Elliot, Wanda Leigh. "Writing a Necessary Tool for Writing." *Mathematics Teacher* 89 (February 1996): 92–94.

Evans, Christine Sobray. "Writing to Learn Math." *Language Arts* 61 (December 1984): 828–835.

Fuentes, P. "Reading Comprehension in Mathematics." *The Clearing House* 72, no. 2 (1998): 81–88.

Goldberg, Dorothy. "Integrating Writing into the Mathematics Curriculum." *The Two-Year College Mathematics Journal* 14 (November 1983): 421–424.

Havens, Lynn. "Writing to Enhance Learning in General Mathematics." *Mathematics Teacher* 82 (October 1989).

Hurwitz, Marsha. "Student-Authored Manuals as Semester Projects." *Mathematics Teacher* 83 (December 1990): 701–703.

Keith, Sandra. "Exploratory Writing and Learning Mathematics Classroom." *Mathematics Teacher* 81 (December 1988): 714–719.

Le Gere, Adele. "Collaboration and Writing in the Mathematics Classroom." *Mathematics Teacher* 84 (March 1991): 166–171.

Macintosh, Margaret E. "No Time for Writing in Your Class?" *Mathematics Teacher* 84 (September 1991): 423–433.

McIntosh, Margaret, and Roni Draper. "Using Learning Logs in Mathematics: Writing to Learn." *Mathematics Teacher* 94, no. 7 (2001): 554–557.

Mett, Coreen L. "Writing as a Learning Device in Calculus." *Mathematics Teacher* (October 1987): 534–537.

Miller, L. Diane. "Writing to Learn Mathematics." *Mathematics Teacher* 84 (October 1991): 516–521.

Nahrgang, Cynthia L., and Bruce T. Peterson. "Using Writing to Learn Mathematics." *Mathematics Teacher* 79 (September 1986): 461–465.

Powell, Arthur B. "Capturing, Examining and Responding to Mathematical Thinking Through Writing." *Clearing House* 71, no. 1 (September–October 1997): 21–25.

Pugalee, David. "Using Communication to Develop Students' Mathematical Literacy." *Teaching Mathematics in the Middle School* 6, no. 5 (2001): 297–299.

———. "Promoting Mathematical Learning Through Writing." *Mathematics in School*, no. 1 (Jan. 1998): 20–22.

Pugalee, David K. "Connecting Writing to the Mathematics Curriculum." *Mathematics Teacher* 90 (April 1997): 308–310.

Reehm, S. P., and S. A. Long. "Reading in the Mathematics Classroom." *Middle School Journal* 27, no. 5 (1996): 35–41.

Robinson, Donita. "Student Portfolios in Mathematics." *Mathematics Teacher* 91 (April 1998): 318–325.

Schmidt, Don. "Writing in Math Class." In *Roots in the Sawdust: Writing to Learn Across the Disciplines*. Anne Ruggles Gere, ed. Urbana, IL: National Council of Teachers of English, 1985, 104–116.

Self, Judy. "The Picture of Writing to Learn." In *Plain Talk About Learning and Writing Across the Curriculum*. Richmond, VA: Virginia Department of Education, 1987.

Socha, Susan C. "Math Class Logs." *Mathematics Teacher* 82 (October 1989): 511–513.

Thiessen, Diane. *Exploring Mathematics Through Literature*. Reston, VA: NCTM, 2003.

Williams, Nancy B., and Brian D. Wynne. "Journal Writing in the Mathematics Classroom: A Beginner's Approach." *Mathematics Teacher* 93 (February 2000): 132–135.

Chapter 4

Suggested Readings

Sources for Problems

Abraham, R. M. *Winter Nights Entertainments*. London: Constable, 1932. Reprinted as *Easy-to-do Entertainments and Diversions with Coins, Cards, String, Paper and Matches*. New York: Dover, 1961.

Ainley, Stephen. *Mathematical Puzzles*. London: Bell, 1977.

Andreescu, T., and Z. Feng. *Mathematical Olympiads: Problems and Solutions from Around the World*. Washington, DC: Mathematical Association of America, 2000.

Alcuin (attrib.). *Propositiones Alcuini doctoris Caroli Magni Imperatoris ad acuendos juvenes*. Translated and annotated by John Hadley and David Singmaster as "Problems to Sharpen the Young." *Mathematical Gazette* 76, no. 475 (March 1992): 102–126.

Alexanderson, Gerald L., Leonard F. Klosinski, and Loren C. Larson. *The William Lowell Putnam Mathematical Competition—Problems and Solutions: 1965–1984*. Washington, DC: Mathematical Association of America, 1985.

Allen, Liz. *Brainsharpeners*. London: Hodder & Stoughton, New English Library, 1991.

ApSimon, H. *Mathematical Byways*. New York: Oxford University Press, 1984.

———. *More Mathematical Byways in Ayling, Beeling and Ceiling*. New York: Oxford University Press, 1990.

Aref, M. N., and W. Wernick. *Problems and Solutions in Euclidean Geometry*. New York: Dover, 1986.

Artino, R. A., A. N. Galione, and N. Shell. *The Contest Problem Book IV*. Washington, DC: Mathematical Association of America, 1982.

Barbeau, E., M. Klamkin, and W. Moser. *1001 Problems in High School Mathematics*. Montreal: Canadian Mathematical Congress, 1976, 1978, 1980, 1985.

———. *Five Hundred Mathematical Challenges*. Washington, DC: Mathematical Association of America, 1995.

Barr, Stephen. *A Miscellany of Puzzles*. New York: Crowell, 1965.

———. *Second Miscellany of Puzzles*. New York: Macmillan, 1969. Reissued as *Mathematical Brain Benders*. New York: Dover, 1982.

Barry, D. T., and J. R. Lux. *The Philips Academy Prize Examination in Mathematics*. Palo Alto, CA: Dale Seymour Publications, 1984.

Bates, N. B., and S. M. Smith. *101 Puzzle Problems*. Concord, MA: Bates Publishing Co., 1980.

Berloquin, Pierre. *100 Numerical Games*. New York: Scribner's, 1976.

———. *100 Geometric Games*. New York: Scribner's, 1976. Reprinted as *Geometric Games*. London: Unwin, 1980.

———. *100 Games of Logic*. New York: Scribner's, 1977. Reprinted as *Games of Logic*. London: Unwin, 1980.

———. *The Garden of the Sphinx*. New York: Scribner's, 1985.

Berzsenyi, G., and S. B. Maurer. *The Contest Problem Book V*. Washington, DC: Mathematical Association of America, 1997.

Birtwistle, Claude. *Mathematical Puzzles and Perplexities*. London: Allen & Unwin, 1971.

Brandes, Louis Grant. *The Math Wizard*. Rev. ed. Portland, ME: J. Weston Walch, 1975.

Bridgman, George. *Lake Wobegon Math Problems*. Rev. and enlarged ed. Minneapolis: George Bridgman, 1981.

Brousseau, Brother Alfred. A. *Saint Mary's College Mathematics Contest Problems*. Palo Alto, CA: Creative Publications, 1972.

Bryant, S. J., G. E. Graham, and K. G. Wiley. *Nonroutine Problems in Algebra, Geometry, and Trigonometry*. New York: McGraw-Hill, 1965.

Bryant, Victor, and Raymond Postill. *The Sunday Times Book of Brain Teasers—Book 1*. London: Unwin, 1980. Reprinted with *Book 1* omitted from title. New York: St. Martin's Press, 1982.

———. *The Sunday Times Book of Brain Teasers—Book 2*. Englewood Cliffs, NJ: Prentice-Hall, 1983.

Burkill, J. C., and H. M. Kundy. *Mathematical Scholarship Problems*. London: Cambridge University Press, 1961.

Butts, T. *Problem Solving in Mathematics*. Glenview, IL: Scott, Foresman, 1973.

CEMREL. *Elements of Mathematics. Problem Book* (Vols. 1 and 2). St. Louis, MO: CEMREL, 1975.

Charosh, M. *Mathematical Challenges*. Washington, DC: National Council of Teachers of Mathematics, 1965.

Clarke, Barry R. *Puzzles for Pleasure*. Cambridge: Cambridge University Press, 1994.

Clarke, Barry R., Rex Gooch, Angela Newing, and David Singmaster. *The Daily Telegraph Book of Brain Twisters No 1*. London: Pan, 1993.

Conrad, S. R., and D. Flegler. *Math Contests for High School, Volumes 1 and 2*. Tenafly, NJ: Math League Press, 1992, 1995.

———. *Math Contests Grades 7 and 8; Volumes 1 and 2*. Tenafly, NJ: Math League Press, 1992, 1994.

———. *Math Contests Grades 4, 5, and 6; Volumes 1 and 2*. Tenafly, NJ: Math League Press, 1994.

Crux Mathematicorum, Ottawa, ON: Canadian Mathematical Society.

Dorofeev, G., M. Potapov, and N. Rozov. *Elementary Mathematics, Selected Topics and Problem Solving*. Moscow: Mir Publishers, 1973.

Dorrie, H. *100 Great Problems of Elementary Mathematics*. New York: Dover, 1965.

Dowlen, N., S. Powers, and H. Florence. *College of Charleston Mathematics Contest Books*. Palo Alto, CA: Dale Seymour Publications, 1987.

Dudney, H. E. *Modern Puzzles*. Pearson, 1926; new edition, [1936].

———. *Puzzles and Curious Problems*. London: Nelson, [1932]; revised by J. Travers, [1936?].

———. *A Puzzle Mine*. J. Travers, ed. London: Nelson, [1941].

———. *The Canterbury Puzzles*. New York: Dover Publications, 1958.

———. *536 Puzzles and Curious Problems*. Edited by Martin Gardner from *Modern Puzzles and Puzzles and Curious Problems*. Contains almost all of both books. New York: Scribner's, 1967.

———. *Amusements in Mathematics*. New York: Dover Publications, 1970.

Dunn, A. *Mathematical Bafflers*. New York: McGraw-Hill, 1964.

Dunn, A. F. *Second Book of Mathematical Bafflers*. New York: Dover Publications, 1983.

Dynkin, Eugene B., and V. A. Uspenskii. *Multicolor Problems*. Heath, 1963.

Edwards, J. D., D. J. King, and P. J. O'Halloran. *All the Best from the Australian Mathematics Competition*. Melbourne, Australia: Ruskin Press, 1986.

Emmet, Eric Revell. *Brain Puzzler's Delight*, Buchanan, NY: Emerson Books; reprint New York: Sterling, 1993.

———. *Mind Tickling Brain Teasers*. Buchanan, NY: Emerson Books, 1976.

———. *The Puffin Book of Brain Teasers*. London: Puffin, 1976.

———. *A Diversity of Puzzles*. New York: Barnes & Noble, 1977.

———. *Puzzles for Pleasure*. Buchanan, NY: Emerson Books, 1977.

———. *The Great Detective Puzzle Book*. New York: Barnes & Noble, 1979.

———. *The Island of Imperfection Puzzle Book*. New York: Barnes & Noble, 1980.

———. *The Penguin Book of Brain Teasers*. Compiled by David Hall and Alan Summers from Emmet's posthumous notes. New York: Viking, 1984.

Emmet, Eric Revell, and Donald B. Eperson. *Patterns in Mathematics*. Oxford: Blackwell, 1988.

Engel, Arthur. *Problem Solving Strategies*. New York: Springer-Verlag, 1998.

Filipiak, A. S. *Mathematical Puzzles*. New York: Bell Publishing, 1942.

Fisher, L., and B. Kennedy. *Brother Alfred Brousseau Problem Solving and Mathematics Competition, Introductory Division*. Palo Alto, CA: Dale Seymour Publications, 1984.

Fisher, L., and W. Medigovich. *Brother Alfred Brousseau Problem Solving and Mathematics Competition, Senior Division*. Palo Alto, CA: Dale Seymour Publications, 1984.

Fleener, F. O. *Mathematics Contests: A Guide for Involving Students and Schools*. Reston, VA: National Council of Teachers of Mathematics, 1990.

Friedland, Aaron J. *Puzzles in Math and Logic*. New York: Dover, 1970.

Frohlichstein, Jack. *Mathematical Fun, Games and Puzzles*. New York: Dover, 1962.

Fujimura, Kobon. *The Tokyo Puzzles*. Martin Gardner, ed. New York: Scribner's, 1978.

Gamow, George, and Marvin Stern. *Puzzle-Math*. London: Macmillan, 1958.

Gardner, Martin. *Arrow Book of Brain Teasers*. New York: Scholastic, 1959.

———. *The Scientific American Book of Mathematical Puzzles and Diversions*. New York: Simon & Schuster, 1959. Rev., with new afterword and references, as *Hexaflexagons and Other Mathematical Diversions*. Chicago: University of Chicago Press, 1988.

———. *The Second Scientific American Book of Mathematical Puzzles and Diversions*. New York: Simon & Schuster, 1961.

———. *Martin Gardner's New Mathematical Diversions from Scientific American*. New York: Simon & Schuster, 1966; Chicago: University of Chicago Press, 1983; Washington, DC: Mathematical Association of America, 1995.

———. *The Numerology of Dr. Matrix*. New York: Simon & Schuster, 1967.

———. *Perplexing Puzzles and Tantalizing Teasers*. New York: Simon & Schuster, 1969.

———. *The Unexpected Hanging and Other Mathematical Diversions*. New York: Simon & Schuster, 1969. Rev. ed. Chicago: University of Chicago Press, 1991.

———. *Martin Gardner's Sixth Book of Mathematical Games from Scientific American*. San Francisco: Freeman, 1971; Chicago: University of Chicago Press, 1983.

———. *Mathematical Carnival*. New York: Knopf, 1975. Rev. ed. Washington, DC: Mathematical Association of America, 1989.

———. *The Incredible Dr. Matrix*. New York: Scribner's, 1976. [Contains all of *The Numerology of Dr. Matrix*.]

———. *Mathematical Magic Show*. New York: Knopf, 1977. Rev. ed. Washington, DC: Mathematical Association of America, 1990.

———. *More Perplexing Puzzles and Tantalizing Teasers*. New York: Pocket Books, Archway, 1977.

———. *Aha! Insight*. New York: Scientific American & Freeman, 1978.

———. *Mathematical Circus*. New York: Knopf, 1979. Rev. ed. Washington, DC: Mathematical Association of America, 1992.

———. *Science Fiction Puzzle Tales*. New York: C. N. Potter, 1981.

———. *Aha! Gotcha*. New York: Freeman, 1982.

———. *Wheels, Life and Other Mathematical Amusements*. New York: Freeman, 1983.

———. *The Magic Numbers of Dr. Matrix*. Buffalo, NY: Prometheus, 1985. [Contains all of *The Incredible Dr. Matrix*.]

———. *Entertaining Mathematical Puzzles*. New York: Dover, 1986.

———. *Knotted Doughnuts and Other Mathematical Entertainments*. New York: Freeman, 1986.

———. *Puzzles from Other Worlds*. New York: Random House, Vintage, 1986.

———. *Riddles of the Sphinx*. Washington, DC: Mathematical Association of America, New Mathematical Library, 1987.

———. *Time Travel and Other Mathematical Bewilderments*. New York: Freeman, 1988.

———. *Penrose Tiles to Trapdoor Ciphers*. New York: Freeman, 1989.

———. *Fractal Music, Hypercards and More*. New York: Freeman, 1992.

———. *My Best Mathematical and Logical Puzzles*. New York: Dover, 1994.

Garvin, A. D. *Discovery Problems for Better Students*. Portland, ME: Weston Walch, 1975.

Gleason, Andrew M., Robert E. Greenwood, and Leroy M. Kelly. *The William Lowell Putnam Mathematical Competitions. Problems and Solutions: 1938–1964*. Washington, DC: Mathematical Association of America, 1980.

Gould, Peter. *Senior Challenge '85–'91*. Mathematical Education on Merseyside, University of Liverpool, 1992.

Gould, Peter and Ian Porteous. *Senior Challenge '80–'84*. Mathematical Education on Merseyside, University of Liverpool, 1984.

Graham, L. A. *Ingenious Mathematical Problems and Methods*. New York: Dover, 1959.

———. *The Surprise Attack in Mathematical Problems*. New York: Dover, 1968.

Greitzer, S. L. *International Mathematical Olympiads 1959–1977*. Washington, DC: Mathematical Association of America, 1978.

Haber, Philip. *Mathematical Puzzles and Pastimes*. Mount Vernon, NY: Peter Pauper, 1957.

Halmos, Paul R. *Problems for Mathematicians Young and Old*. Dolciani Mathematical Expositions #12. Washington, DC: Mathematical Association of America, 1991.

Higgins, A. M. *Geometry Problems*. Portland, ME: J. Weston Walch, 1971.

Hill, T. J. *Mathematical Challenges II—Plus Six*. Washington, DC: National Council of Teachers of Mathematics, 1974.

Honsberger, R. *Mathematical Morsels*. Washington, DC: Mathematical Association of America, 1978.

———. *From Erdös to Kiev: Problems of Olympiad Caliber.* Washington, DC: Mathematical Association of America, 1996.

Honsberger, R. *In Polya's Footsteps: Miscellaneous Problems and Essays.* Washington, D.C.: Mathematical Association of America, 1997.

Holton, Derek. *Problem Solving Series.* Leicester, UK: Mathematical Association, 1988–1990. 1. *How To; 2. Combinatorics 1; 3. Graph Theory; 4. Number Theory; 5. Geometry 1; 6. Proof; 7. Geometry 2; 8. IMO Problems 1; 9. Combinatorics 2; 10. Geometry 2; 11. Number Theory 2; 12. Inequalities; 13. Combinatorics 3; 14. IMO Problems 2; 15. Creating Problems.*

Hunter, James Alston Hope. *Figures for Fun.* London: Phoenix House, 1957; 2nd ed., London: Dent Aldine, 1972.

———. *Fun with Figures.* New York: Dover, 1965.

———. *Mathematical Brain Teasers.* As *Hunter's Math Brain Teasers.* New York: Bantam, 1965; corrected and enlarged. New York: Dover, 1976.

———. *More Fun with Figures.* New York: Dover, 1966.

———. *Challenging Mathematical Teasers.* New York: Dover Publications, 1979.

———. *Entertaining Mathematical Teasers and How to Solve Them.* New York: Dover, 1983.

Kahan, Steven. *Have Some Sums to Solve: The Compleat Alphametics Book.* Farmingdale, NY: Baywood Publishing Co., 1978.

———. *At Last!! Encoded Totals Second Addition: The Long Awaited Sequel to "Have Some Sums to Solve."* Farmingdale, NY: Baywood Publishing Co., 1994.

———. *Take a Look at a Good Book: The Third Collection of Additive Alphametics for the Connoisseur.* Farmingdale, NY: Baywood Publishing Co., 1996.

Kendall, P. M. H., and G. M. Thomas. *Mathematical Puzzles for the Connoisseur.* London: Griffin, 1962; New York: Apollo edition (Crowell), 1962.

King, Tom. *The Best 100 Puzzles Solved and Answered.* London: Foulsham, [1927].

Kinnaird, [William] Clark, ed. *Encyclopedia of Puzzles and Pastimes.* New York: Grosset & Dunlap, 1946.

Klamkin, M. S. *International Mathematical Olympiads, 1979–1985.* Washington, DC: Mathematical Association of America, 1986.

Konhauser, Joseph D. E., Dan Velleman, and Stan Wagon. *Which Way did the Bicycle Go?* Washington, DC: Mathematical Association of America, 1996.

Kordemsky, Boris A. *The Moscow Puzzles.* Martin Gardner, ed. New York: Scribner's, 1972.

Krechmer, V. A. *A Problem Book in Algebra.* Translated by V. Shiffer. Moscow: Mir Publishers, 1974.

Krulik, S., and J. A. Rudnick. *Problem Solving: A Handbook for Teachers.* Boston: Allyn and Bacon, 1980.

———. *The New Sourcebook for Teaching Reasoning and Problem Solving in Junior and Senior High Schools.* Boston: Allyn and Bacon, 1996.

Kürschak, Jozsef. *Hungarian Problem Book I & II.* Based on the Eötvös Competitions, 1894–1905 and 1906–1928. Translated by Elvira Rapaport. New Mathematical Library, Washington, DC: Mathematical Association of America, 1963.

Kutepov, A., and A. Rubanov. *Problems in Geometry.* Translated by O. Meshkov. Moscow: Mir Publisher, 1975.

———. *Problem Book: Algebra and Elementary Function.* Translated by L. Levant. Moscow: Mir Publisher, 1978.

Larson, L. C. *Problem Solving Through Problems.* New York: Springer-Verlag, 1983.

Lenchner, G. *Creative Problem Solving in School Mathematics.* Boston: Houghton Mifflin Co., 1983.

———. *Math Olympiad Contest Problems for Elementary and Middle Schools.* East Meadow, NY: Glenwood Publications, 1997.

Loyd, Samuel. *Sam Loyd's Cyclopedia of 5,000 Puzzles, Tricks and Conundrums.* New York: Bigelow, 1914; New York: Lamb Publishing, 1914: New York: Corwin, 1976.

———. *Sam Loyd's Tricks and Puzzles,* Vol. 1. New York: Experimenter Publishing Co, 1927.

———. *Sam Loyd and His Puzzles.* New York: Barse & Co., 1928.

———. *Mathematical Puzzles of Sam Loyd,* Vol. 1. New York: Dover, 1959.

———. *Mathematical Puzzles of Sam Loyd,* Vol. 2. New York: Dover, 1960.

Luckács, C., and E. Tarján. *Mathematical Games.* New York: Walker, 1968.

Moser, W., and E. Barbeau. *The Canadian Mathematics Olympiads 1969, 1975.* Montreal: Canadian Mathematical Congress, 1976.

Morris, Ivan. *The Riverside Puzzles.* New York: Walker & Co., 1969.

———. *The Lonely Monk and Other Puzzles.* Boston: Little, Brown & Co., 1970.

———. *Foul Play and Other Puzzles of All Kinds.* New York: Random House, Vintage, 1972.

Moscovich, Ivan. *Super-Games.* London: Hutchinson, 1984.

———. *Fiendishly Difficult Math Puzzles.* New York: Sterling, 1991.

———. *Fiendishly Difficult Visual Perception Puzzles.* New York: Sterling, 1991.

Moser, William O. J., and Edward J. Barbeau. *The First Ten Canadian Mathematics Olympiads (1969–1978).* Montreal: Canadian Mathematical Society, 1978.

Mosteller, F. *Fifty Challenging Problems in Probability.* New York: Dover, 1965.

Mott-Smith, G. *Mathematical Puzzles for Beginners and Enthusiasts.* New York: Dover, 1954.

Newton, D. E. *One Hundred Quickies for Math Classes.* Portland, ME: J. Weston Walch, 1972.

Phillips, H., S. T. Shovelton, and G. S. Marshal. *Caliban's Problem Book*. New York: Dover, 1961.

Phillips, Hubert. *The Week-End Problems Book*. London: Nonesuch, 1932.

———. *The Playtime Omnibus*. London: Faber & Faber, 1933.

———. *The Sphinx Problem Book*. London: Faber, 1934.

———. *Brush Up Your Wits*. London: Dent, 1936.

———. *Question Time*. London: Dent, 1937; New York: Farrar & Rinehart, 1938.

———. *Ask Me Another*. London: Ptarmigan, 1945.

———. *Hubert Phillips's Heptameron*. London: Eyre & Spottiswoode, 1945.

———. *Something to Think About*. London: Ptarmigan, 1945; [with additional Foreword, one problem omitted and 11 problems added] London: Max Parrish, 1958.

———. *Playtime*. London: Ptarmigan, 1947.

———. *The Hubert Phillips Annual 1951*. London: Hamish Hamilton, 1950.

———. *Problems Omnibus*, vol. 1. London: Arco, 1960.

———. *My Best Puzzles in Logic and Reasoning*. New York: Dover, 1961.

———. *My Best Puzzles in Mathematics*. New York: Dover, 1961.

———. *Problems Omnibus*, vol. 2. London: Arco, 1962.

Polya, G., and J. Kilpatrick, *The Stanford Mathematics Book*. New York: Teachers College Press, 1974.

Posamentier, A. S. *Advanced Euclidean Geometry: Excursions for Secondary Teachers and Students*. New York, NY: John Wiley Publishing, 2002.

———. *Students! Get Ready for the Mathematics for SAT I: Problem-Solving Strategies and Practice Tests*. Thousand Oaks, CA: Corwin Press, 1996.

———. *Teachers! Prepare Your Students for the Mathematics for SAT I: Methods and Problem-Solving Strategies*. Thousand Oaks, CA: Corwin Press, 1996.

Posamentier, A. S., and C. T. Salkind. *Challenging Problems in Algebra*. Rev. ed. New York: Dover, 1996.

———. *Challenging Problems in Geometry*. Rev. ed. New York: Dover, 1996.

Posamentier, A. S., and G. Sheridan. *Math Motivators: Pre-Algebra, Algebra, and Geometry*. Menlo Park, CA: Addison-Wesley, 1984.

Posamentier, A. S., and S. Krulik. *Problem Solving Strategies for Efficient and Elegant Solutions: A Resource for the Mathematics Teacher*. Thousand Oaks, CA: Corwin Press, 2nd ed., 2008.

Posamentier, A. S., and W. Schulz, ed. *The Art of Problem Solving: A Resource for the Mathematics Teacher*. Thousand Oaks, CA: Corwin Press, 1996.

Posamentier, A. S., and W. Wernick. *Advanced Geometric Constructions*. Palo Alto, CA: Dale Seymour Publications, 1988.

Ransom, W. R. *One Hundred Mathematical Curiosities*. Portland, ME: J. Weston Walch, 1955.

Rapaport, E. *Hungarian Problem Book*, vol. 1 and 2. New York: Random House, 1963.

Reis, C. M., and S. Z. Ditor, eds. *The Canadian Mathematics Olympiads (1979–1985)*. Ottawa: Canadian Mathematical Society, 1988.

Ruderman, H. D. NYSML-ARML *Contests 1973–1982*. Norman, OK: Mu Alpha Theta, 1983.

Salkind, C. T. *The Contest Problem Book*. New York: Random House, 1961.

———. *The MAA Problem Book II*. New York: Random House, 1966.

Salkind, C. T., and J. M. Earl. *The MAA Problem Book III*. New York: Random House, 1973.

Saul, M. A., G. W. Kessler, S. Krilov, and L. Zimmerman. *The New York City Contest Problem Book*. Palo Alto, CA: Dale Seymour Publications, 1986.

Schneider, L. J. *The Contest Problem Book VI*. Washington, DC: Mathematical Association of America, 2000.

Shklarsky, D. O., N. N. Chentzov, and I. M. Yaglom. *The USSR Olympiad Problem Book*. San Francisco: W. H. Freeman, 1962.

———. *Selected Problems and Theorems in Elementary Mathematics*. Translated by V. M. Volosov and I. G. Volsova. Moscow: Mir Publisher, 1979.

Shortz, Will. *Will Shortz's Best Brain Busters*. New York: Random House, Times Books, 1991.

———. *Will Shortz's Best Brain Twisters*. New York: Random House, Times Books, 1991.

———. *Brain Twisters from the First World Puzzle Championships*. New York: Random House, Times Books, 1993.

Sierpinski, Waclaw. *A Selection of Problems in the Theory of Numbers*. London: Pergamon/Macmillan,1964.

———. *250 Problems in Elementary Number Theory*. New York: American Elsevier, 1970.

Sitomer, H. *The New Mathlete Problems Book*. Valley Stream, NY: Nassau County Interscholastic Mathematics League, 1974.

Snape, Charles, and Heather Scott. *How Puzzling*. Cambridge: Cambridge University Press, 1991.

Soifer, Alexander. *Mathematics as Problem Solving*. Colorado Springs: Center for Excellence in Mathematics Education, 1987.

Sole, Tim. *The Ticket to Heaven and Other Superior Puzzles*. London: Penguin, 1988.

Steinhaus, H. *One Hundred Problems in Elementary Mathematics*. New York: Pergamon Press, 1963.

Straszewicz, S. *Mathematical Problems and Puzzles from the Polish Mathematical Olympiads*. Translated by J. Smsliska. New York: Pergamon Press, 1965.

Vakil, Ravi. *A Mathematical Mosaic: Patterns and Problem Solving*. Burlington, ON: Brendan Kelly Publishing Co., 1996.

Vout, Colin, and Gordon Gray. *Challenging Puzzles*. Cambridge: Cambridge University Press, 1993.

Wall, H. S. *Creative Mathematics*. Austin: University of Texas Press, 1963.

Wells, D. *Can You Solve These?* Norfolk, England: Stradbroke, 1982.

Wells, David G. *Recreations in Logic*. New York: Dover, 1979.

Trigg, C. W. *Mathematical Quickies*. New York: McGraw-Hill, 1967.

Ulam, S. M. *Problems in Modern Mathematics*. New York: John Wiley, 1960.

Williams, W. Tom, and G. H. Savage. *The Penguin Problems Book*. London: Penguin, 1940.

———. *The Strand Problems Book*. London: Newnes.

———. *The Second Penguin Problems Book*. London: Penguin, 1944.

———. *The Third Penguin Problems Book*. London: Penguin, 1946.

Yaglom, A. M., and I. M. Yaglom. *Challenging Mathematical Problems with Elementary Solutions*, vol. 1 and 2. San Francisco: Holden-Day, 1964, 1967.

Readings On Problem Solving

Ackoff, Russell L. *The Art of Problem Solving*. New York: Wiley, 1978.

Adams, James L. *Conceptual Blockbusting*. San Francisco: Freeman, 1974.

Adler, Irving. *Mathematics and Mental Growth*. London: Dobson, 1970.

Averbach, Bonnie, and Orin Chein. *Mathematics: Problem Solving Through Recreational Mathematics*. San Francisco: Freeman, 1980.

Andre, Thomas. "Problem Solving and Education," Ch. 7 in *Cognitive Classroom Learning*. Gary Phye and Thomas Andre, eds. Orlando, FL: Academic Press, 1986.

Arnold, William R. "Students Can Pose and Solve Original Problems." *The Mathematics Teacher* 64 (1971): 325.

Bransford, John D., and Barry S. Stein. *The Ideal Problem Solver*. New York: W. H. Freeman, 1984.

Brown, Stephen I., and Marion I. Walter. *The Art of Problem Posing*. Hillsdale, NJ: Lawrence Erlbaum Assoc., 1983.

Butts, T. "In Praise of Trial and Error." *The Mathematics Teacher* 78 (1985): 167.

Charles, R., and F. Lester. *Teaching Problem Solving: What, Why, and How*. Palo Alto, CA: Dale Seymour Publications, 1982.

Chipman, Susan, Judith Segal, and Robert Glaser. *Thinking and Learning Skills Volume 2: Research and Open Questions*. Hillsdale, NJ: Erlbaum, 1985.

Cofman, Judita. *What to Solve? Problems and Suggestions for Young Mathematicians*. Oxford: Oxford University Press, 1990.

———. *Numbers and Shapes Revisited: More Problems for Young Mathematicians*. Oxford: Oxford University Press, 1995.

Costa, Art. "Mediating the Metacognitive." *Educational Leadership* (Nov. 1984): 57–62.

Curcio, Frances, ed. *Teaching and Learning, A Problem Solving Focus*. Reston, VA: NCTM, 1987.

Davis, Robert, Elizabeth Jockusch, and Curtis McKnight. "Cognitive Processes in Learning Algebra." *Journal of Children's Mathematical Behavior* 2, no. 1 (Spring 1978).

Derry, Sharon J., and Debra A. Murphy. "Designing Systems That Train Learning Ability: From Theory to Practice." *Review of Educational Research* 56, no. 1 (Spring 1986): 1–39.

Emmet, Eric Revell. *Learning to Think*. Verplanck, NY: Emerson Books, 1981.

Fisher, Richard B. *Brain Games*. London: Fontana, 1981.

Fixx, James F. *Solve It!* New York: Doubleday, 1978.

Frederiksen, Norman. "Implications of Cognitive Theory for Instruction on Problem Solving." *Review of Educational Research* 54, no. 3 (Fall 1984): 363–407.

Gardner, Martin. *Aha! Insight*. New York: Scientific American & Freeman, 1978.

———. *Aha! Gotcha*. San Francisco: Freeman, 1982.

Gordon, William J. J. *Synectics—The Development of Creative Capacity*. New York: Harper & Row, 1961.

Hadamard, Jacques. *The Psychology of Invention in the Mathematical Field*. New York: Dover, 1954.

Heiman, M., R. Narode, J. Slomianko, and J. Lochhead. *Thinking Skills: Mathematics, Teaching*. Washington, DC: National Education Association, 1987.

Honsberger, Ross. *Ingenuity in Mathematics*. Washington, DC: Mathematical Association of America, New Mathematical Library, 1970.

———. *Mathematical Gems*, Vol. 1. Dolciani Mathematical Expositions #1. Washington, DC: Mathematical Association of America, 1973.

———. *Mathematical Gems*, Vol. 2. Dolciani Mathematical Expositions #2. Washington, DC: Mathematical Association of America, 1976.

———. *Mathematical Morsels*. Dolciani Mathematical Expositions #3. Washington, DC: Mathematical Association of America, 1978.

———. *Mathematical Plums*. Dolciani Mathematical Expositions #4. Washington, DC: Mathematical Association of America, 1979.

———. *Mathematical Gems III*. Dolciani Mathematical Expositions #9. Washington, DC: Mathematical Association of America, 1985.

———. *More Mathematical Morsels*. Dolciani Mathematical Expositions #10. Washington, DC: Mathematical Association of America, 1991.

Hough, Julia S., ed. *Problem Solving*. Newsletter, vol. 1–5. Philadelphia, PA: Franklin Institute Press, 1984.

Hughes, Barnabas. *Thinking Through Problems*. Palo Alto, CA: Creative Publications, 1975.

Jensen, R. J. "Stuck? Don't Give Up! Subgoal-Generation Strategies in Problem Solving." *The Mathematics Teacher* 80 (1987): 614.

Karmos, Joseph, and Ann Karmos. "Strategies for Active Involvement in Problem Solving." In *Thinking Skills Instruction: Concepts and Techniques*. Marcia Heiman and Joshua Slomianko, eds. Washington, DC: National Education Association, 1987, 99–110.

Kluwe Rainer. "Executive Decisions and Regulation of Problem Solving Behavior." Chap. 2 in *Metacognition, Motivation and Understanding*. Franz Weinert and Rainer Kluwe, eds. Hillsdale, NJ: Lawrence Erlbaum Associates, 1987.

Krantz, Steven G. *Techniques of Problems Solving*. Providence, RI: American Mathematical Society, 1997.

Krulik, S., ed. *Problem Solving in School Mathematics, 1980 Yearbook*. Reston, VA: National Council of Teachers of Mathematics, 1980.

Krulik, S., and J. Rudnick. *Problem Solving: A Handbook for Teachers*, 2nd ed. Boston: Allyn and Bacon, 1987.

———. *Problem Solving: A Handbook for Senior High School Teachers*. Boston: Allyn and Bacon, 1989.

———. *Reasoning and Problem Solving: A Handbook for Elementary School Teachers*. Boston: Allyn and Bacon, 1993.

———. *The New Sourcebook for Teaching Reasoning and Problem Solving in Elementary Schools*. Boston: Allyn and Bacon, 1995.

———. *The New Sourcebook for Teaching Reasoning and Problem Solving in Secondary Schools*. Boston: Allyn and Bacon, 1996.

Mason, John. *Learning and Doing Mathematics*. Milton Keynes, UK: Open University Press, 1978, 1984.

Mason, John, with Leone Burton and Kaye Stacey. *Thinking Mathematically*. Reading, MA: Addison-Wesley, 1985.

McKim, Robert H. *Thinking Visually: A Strategy Manual for Problem Solving*. Palo Alto, CA: Dale Seymour, 1980.

Moses, Stanley. *The Art of Problem-Solving*. London: Transworld, 1974.

Mottershead, Lorraine. *Sources of Mathematical Discovery*. Oxford: Blackwell, 1978.

———. *Investigations in Mathematics*. Oxford: Blackwell, 1985.

Noller, Ruth B., Ruth E. Heintz, and David A. Blaeuer. *Creative Problem Solving in Mathematics*. D. O. K. Publishers, 1978.

Mayer, Richard. "Mathematics." Chap. 5 in *Cognition and Instruction*. Ronna Dillon and Robert Sternberg, eds. Orlando, FL: Academic Press, 1986.

Mayer, Richard, J. Larkin, and J. Kadane. "A Cognitive Analysis of Mathematical Problem Solving Ability." In *Advances in the Psychology of Human Intelligence*, Vol. 2. R. Sternberg, ed. Hillsdale, NJ: Erlbaum, 231–273.

Nickerson, Raymond. "Thoughts on Teaching Thinking." *Educational Leadership* (Oct. 1981): 21–24.

Nickerson, Raymond, David Perkins, and Edward Smith. *The Teaching of Thinking*. Hillsdale, NJ: Lawrence Erlbaum Associates, 1985.

Polya, G. *How To Solve It*. Princeton, NJ: Princeton University Press, 1945.

———. *Introduction and Analogy in Mathematics*. Princeton, NJ: Princeton University Press, 1954.

———. *Patterns of Plausible Inference*. Princeton, NJ: Princeton University Press, 1954.

———. *Mathematical Discovery*. 2 vols. New York: Wiley, 1962, and 1965; combined ed. with foreword by Peter Hilton, bibliography extended by Gerald Alexanderson, and index extended by Jean Pedersen, New York: Wiley, 1981.

Posamentier, A. S. *Teachers! Prepare Your Students for the Mathematics for SAT I: Methods and Problem-Solving Strategies*. Thousand Oaks, CA: Corwin Press, 1996.

Posamentier, A. S., and S. Krulik. *Problem Solving Strategies for Efficient and Elegant Solutions: A Resource for the Mathematics Teacher*. Thousand Oaks, CA: Corwin Press, 2008.

Posamentier, Alfred S., and Wolfgang Schulz, eds. *The Art of Problem Solving: A Resource for the Mathematics Teacher*. Thousand Oaks, CA: Corwin Press, 1996.

Reeves, C. A. *Problem Solving Techniques Helpful in Mathematics and Science*. Reston, VA: National Council of Teachers of Mathematics, 1987.

Schoenfeld, A. H. *Problem Solving in the Mathematics Curriculum*. Washington, DC: Mathematical Association of America, 1983.

———. *Mathematical Problem Solving*. Orlando, FL: Academic Press, 1985.

Segal, Judith, Susan Chipman, and Robert Glaser, eds. *Thinking and Learning Skills, Volume I: Relating Instruction to Research*. Hillsdale, NJ: Lawrence Erlbaum Associates, 1985.

Silver, E. A., ed. *Teaching and Learning Mathematical Problem Solving*. Hillsdale, NJ: Lawrence Erlbaum Associates, 1985.

Simon, Martin A. "The Teacher's Role in Increasing Student Understanding of Mathematics." *Educational Leadership* 43, no. 7 (April 1986): 40–43.

Skemp, Richard R. *The Psychology of Learning Mathematics*. Baltimore: Penguin Books, 1971.

Smullyan, Raymond. *What Is the Name of This Book?* Englewood Cliffs, NJ: Prentice-Hall, 1978.

Soifer, Alexander. *Mathematics As Problem Solving*. Colorado Springs: Center for Excellence in Mathematics Education, 1987.

Special issue—"Gifted Students." *The Mathematics Teacher* 76 (1983).

Topoly, William. "An Introduction to Solving Problems." *The Mathematics Teacher* 58 (1965): 48.

Troutman, Andrea, and Betty P. Lichtenberg. "Problem Solving in the General Mathematics Classroom." *The Mathematics Teacher* 67 (1974): 590.

Walter, Marion I., and Stephen I. Brown. "Problem Posing and Problem Solving." *The Mathematics Teacher* 70 (1977): 4.

Whirl, Robert J. "Problem Solving—Solution or Technique?" *The Mathematics Teacher* 66 (1973): 551.

Winckelgren, W. A. *How To Solve Problems*. San Francisco: W. H. Freeman, 1974.

Chapter 5

Reference

Masalski, William J. *How to Use the Spreadsheet as a Tool in the Secondary School Mathematics Classroom*, 2nd ed. Reston, VA: National Council of Teachers of Mathematics, 1999.

Suggested Readings

Alfred, Brother U. "Exploring Fibonacci Numbers." *Fibonacci Quarterly* 1 (Feb. 1963): 57–63.

Ameis, Jerry A. *Mathematics on the Internet,* 2nd ed. Columbus, OH: Merrill/Prentice Hall, 2002.

Bennett, Dan. *Exploring Geometry with The Geometer's Sketchpad*. Berkeley, CA: Key Curriculum Press, 1993.

Bethel, Sandra Callis, and Nicholas B. Miller. "From an E to an A in First-Year Algebra with the Help of a Graphing Calculator." *Mathematics Teacher* 91 (Feb. 1998): 118–119.

Billings, K., and D. Moursand. *Problem Solving with Calculators*. Salem, OR: Math Learning Center, University of Oregon, 1978.

Bitter, G. G., and J. L. Mikesell. *Activities Handbook for Teaching with the Hand-held Calculator*. Boston: Allyn and Bacon, 1980.

Bolt, B. *Mathematics Meets Technology*. New York: Cambridge University Press, 1991.

Bramble, W. J., and E. Mason. *Computers in Schools*. New York: McGraw-Hill, 1985.

Charischak, Ihor. "A Look at Technology's Role in Professional Development of Mathematics Teachers at the Middle School Level." *School Science and Mathematics* 100 (Nov. 2000): 349–354.

Chin, W. G., R. A. Dean, and T. N. Tracewell. *Arithmetic and Calculators*. San Francisco: W. H. Freeman, 1978.

Coburn, T. G. *How to Teach Mathematics Using a Calculator*. Reston, VA: National Council of Teachers of Mathematics, 1987.

Coburn, T. G., et al. *Practical Guide to Computers in Education*. Menlo Park, CA: Addison-Wesley, 1982.

Collis, B. *Computers, Curriculum, and Whole Class Instruction*. Belmont, CA: Wadsworth, 1988.

Demana, Franklin, and Bert K. Waits. "Enhancing Mathematics Teaching and Learning through Technology." In *Teaching and Learning Mathematics in the 1990s*. 1990 Yearbook of the National Council of Teachers of Mathematics. Edited by Thomas J. Cooney and Christian R. Hirsch. Reston, VA: The Council, 1990: 212–222.

De Villiers, Michael D. *Rethinking Proof with The Geometer's Sketchpad*. Berkley, CA: Key Curriculum Press, 1999.

Denney, Louise S. "A Better Way to Graph Piecewise Functions." *Mathematics Teacher* 91 (Oct. 1998): 628–629.

Dion, Gloria. "Reader Reflections: Fibonacci Revisited." *Mathematics Teacher* 81 (Mar. 1988): 162, 164.

Dudley, Underwood. *Elementary Number Theory*. New York: W. H. Freeman, 1978.

Elgarten, G., and A. S. Posamentier. *Using Computers: Programming and Problem Solving*. Menlo Park, CA: Addison-Wesley, 1984.

Elgarten, G., A. S. Posamentier, and S. Moresh. *Using Computers in Mathematics*, 2nd ed. Menlo Park, CA: Addison-Wesley, 1986.

Frost, Percival. *Curve Tracing*. New York: Chelsea, 1960.

Gardner, Martin. "Mathematical Games: The Multiple Fascinations of the Fibonacci Sequence." *Scientific American* 220 (Mar. 1969): 116–120.

Giamati, Claudia. "Square This: Using Scripts to Explore Complex Constructions." *Mathematics Teacher* 93 (Apr. 2000): 329–333.

Gleick, James. *Chaos: Making a New Science*. New York: Viking Press, 1987.

Goldberg, Samuel. *Introduction to Difference Equations*. New York: Dover Publications, 1986.

Goolsby, Ronnie C., and Thomas W. Polaski. "Extraneous Solutions and Graphing Calculators." *Mathematics Teacher* 90 (Dec. 1997): 718–720.

Hall, H. S., and S. R. Knight. *Higher Algebra*. London: Macmillan, 1960.

Heid, M. Kathleen. "Uses of Technology in Prealgebra and Beginning Algebra." *Mathematics Teacher* 83 (Mar. 1990): 194–198.

———."Computer Algebra Systems in Secondary Mathematics Classes: The Time to Act is Now!" *Mathematics Teacher* 95, no. 9 (Dec. 2002): 662–667.

———."The Technological Revolution and the Reform of School Mathematics." *American Journal of Education* 106 (Nov. 1997): 5–61.

Hembree, Ray. "Model for Meta-Analysis of Research in Education, with a Demonstration in Mathematics Education: Effects of Hand-held Calculators." *Dissertation Abstracts International* 45A (Apr. 1985): 3087.

Johnson, Luella H. "A Look at Parabolas with a Graphing Calculator." *Mathematics Teacher* 90 (Apr. 1997): 278–282.

Jones, Graham A. "Mathematical Modeling in a Feast of Rabbits." *Mathematics Teacher* 86 (Dec. 1993): 770–773.

Kastner, B. *Space Mathematics: A Resource for Secondary School Teachers*. Washington, DC: NASA, 1985.

Kelman, P. et al. *Computers in Teaching Mathematics*. Menlo Park, CA: Addison-Wesley, 1983.

Kenelly, J. W. *The Use of Calculators in the Standardized Testing of Mathematics*. New York: College Entrance Examination Board, 1989.

Kieren, T. E. "Computer Programming for the Mathematics Laboratory." *Mathematics Teacher* 66 (1973): 9.

Klein, Raymond J., and Ilene Hamilton. "Using Technology to Introduce Radian Measure." *Mathematics Teacher* 90 (Feb. 1997): 168–172.

Lawrence, J. Dennis. *A Catalog of Special Plane Curves*. New York: Dover Publications, 1972.

LeBlanc, John F., Donald R. Kerr, Jr., and Maynard Thompson. *Number Theory*. Reading, MA: Addison-Wesley Publishing Co., 1976.

Lee, Mary Ann. "Enhancing Discourse on Equations." *Mathematics Teacher* 93 (Dec. 2000): 755–756.

Linn, Andrew. "Reader Reflections: 'Generalized' Formula." *Mathematics Teacher* 81 (Oct. 1988): 514, 516.

Lockwood, E. H. *A Book of Curves*. Cambridge: Cambridge University Press, 1961.

Lund, Charles, and Edwin Andersen. *Graphing Calculator Activities: Emploring Topics in Algebra I and II*. Parsippany, NJ: Dale Seymour Publications, 1998.

Maor, Eli. "The Pocket Calculator as a Teaching Aid." *Mathematics Teacher* 69 (1976): 471.

McGehee, Jean J. "Interactive Technology and Classic Geometry Problems." *Mathematics Teacher* 91 (Mar. 1998): 204–208.

National Council of Teachers of Mathematics, Commission on Standards for School Mathematics. *Curriculum and Evaluation Standards for School Mathematics*. Reston, VA: The Council, 1989.

Olmstead, Eugene A. "Exploring the Locus Definitions of the Conic Sections." *Mathematics Teacher* 91 (May 1998): 428–434.

Olson, Alton T. "Difference Equations." *Mathematics Teacher* 81 (Oct. 1988): 540–544.

Patterson, Walter M., III. "Reader Reflections: The *n*th Fibonacci Number." *Mathematics Teacher* 80 (Oct. 1987): 512.

Persinger, Sharon E. "Using the Graphing Calculator and the Rational Roots Theorem to Factor Polynomials." *New York State Mathematics Teachers' Journal* 49, (1999): 32–38.

Polya, G. *How to Solve It*. Princeton, NJ: Princeton University Press, 1945.

Prielipp, Robert W., and Norbert J. Kuenzi. "Sums of Consecutive Positive Integers." *Mathematics Teacher* 68 (January 1975): 18–21.

Purdy, David C. "Using the Geometer's Sketchpad to Visualize Maximum-Volume Problems." *Mathematics Teacher* 93 (Mar. 2000): 224–228.

Scher, Daniel. *Exploring Conic Sections with The Geometer's Sketchpad*. Berkeley, CA: Key Curriculum Press, 1993.

Schielack, Vincent P., Jr. "The Fibonacci Sequence and the Golden Ratio." *Mathematics Teacher* 80 (May 1987): 357–358.

Selitto, George L. "Using Graphing Technology to Investigate Exponential Population Growth." *New York State Mathematics Teachers' Journal* 50 (no. 1): 44–47.

Shilgalis, Tom. "Exploring a Parabolic Paradox with the Graphing Calculator." *Mathematics Teacher* 90 (Sept. 1997): 488–493.

Sisitsky, Jeremiah David. "Reader Reflections: Connecting Fibonacci and Lucas Sequences." *Mathematics Teacher* 86 (Dec. 1993): 718–719.

Sloyer, Clifford W. *Fantastiks of Mathematics*. Providence, RI: Janson Publications, 1986.

Spence, Lawrence E. *Finite Mathematics*. New York: Harper & Row, 1981.

Stick, Marvin E. "Calculus Reform and Graphing Calculators: A University View." *Mathematics Teacher* 90 (May 1997): 356–363.

Suydam, M. N. *Using Calculators in Pre-College Ed.: Third State-of-Art Review*. Columbus, OH: Calculator Information Center, 1980.

Suydam, Marilyn N. *The Use of Calculators in Pre-College Education*. Columbus, OH: Calculator Information Center, 1982. (ERIC Document Reproduction Service No. ED 220 273).

Tiffany, Patrice, and Charles, Stolze. "Using Technology to Teach Calculus." *New York State Mathematics Teachers' Journal* 48, no. 2 (1998): 75–80.

Touval, Ayana. "Investigating a Definite Integral—From Graphing Calculators to Rigorous Proof." *Mathematics Teacher* 90 (Mar. 1997): 230–232.

Troputman, A. P., and J. A. White. *The Micro Goes to School*. Pacific Grove, CA: Brooks/Cole, 1988.

Vonder Embse, Charles. "Using a Graphing Utility as a Catalyst for Connections." *Mathematics Teacher* 90 (Jan. 1997): 50–56.

Waits, Bert, and Frank Demana. "Calculators in Mathematics Teaching and Learning: Past, Present and Future." In *Learning Mathematics for a New Century*, 2000 Yearbook of the National Council of Teachers of Mathematics. Maurice J. Burke and Frances R. Curcio, eds. Reston, VA: The Council, 2000.

Weeks, Audrey. "Graphing Functions with the Geometer's Sketchpad." *Mathematics Teacher* 93 (Nov. 2000): 722–723.

Worth, J. "Let's Bring Calculators Out of the Closet." *Elements: A Journal for Elementary Educators* 17 (1985): 18–21.

Yates, Robert C. *A Handbook of Curves and Their Properties*, 1952. Reprint. Reston, VA: National Council of Teachers of Mathematics, 1974.

Yerushalmy, Michal, and Shoshana Gilead. "Solving Equations in a Technological Environment." *Mathematics Teacher* 90 (Feb. 1997): 156–162.

Chapter 6

Suggested Readings

"Assessing Justification and Proof in Geometry Classes Taught Using Dynamic Software." *Mathematics Teacher* (Jan. 1998): 76–82.

Assessment Standards for School Mathematics. Reston, VA: National Council of Teachers of Mathematics, 1995.

Battista, Michael T. "The Mathematical Miseducation of America's Youth: Ignoring Research and Scientific Study in Education." *Phi Delta Kappan* 80 (Feb. 1999): 424–433.

Blank, Rolf K., and Linda Dager Wilson. *Understanding NAEP and TIMSS Results: Three Types of Analyses Useful to Educators*. Reston, VA: Educational Research Service, 2001.

Bush, William. *Mathematics Assessment: Cases and Discussion Questions for Grades 6–12*. Reston, VA: NCTM, 2000.

The Concord Consortium. *Balanced Assessment*. Retrieved October 16, 2004, from http://balancedassessment.concord.org/

Croker, Linda, and James Algina. *Introduction to Classical and Modern Test Theory*. New York: Holt, Rinehart, & Winston, 1986.

Darling-Hammond, L., and B. Falk. "Using Standards and Assessments to Support Student Learning." *Phi Delta Kappa* (Nov. 1997): 190–199.

Eisenhower National Clearinghouse for Mathematics and Science Education. *Assessment that informs practice*. Washington, DC: U.S. Department of Education, 2000.

———Assessment. Retrieved October 16, 2004, from http://www.enc.org/topics/assessment/

"Focusing on Worthwhile Mathematical Tasks in Professional Development: Using a Task from the National Assessment of Educational Progress." *Mathematics Teacher* (Feb. 1998): 156–161.

Greer, Anja S., Helen L. Compton, Alice B. Foster, Jo Ann Mosier, Lew Romagnano, and Carmen Rubino. *Mathematics Assessment: A Practical Handbook for Grades 9–12*. Assessment Standards for School Mathematics Addenda Series. Edited by William S. Bush and Jean Kerr Stenmark. Reston, VA: National Council of Teachers of Mathematics, 1999.

"Implementing the Assessment Standards for School Mathematics." *Mathematics Teacher* 94, no. 1 (Jan. 2000): 31–37.

Kitchen, Richard, April Cherrington, Joanne Gates, Judith Hitchings, Maria Majka, Michael Merk, and George Trubow. "Supporting Reform through Performance Assessment." *Mathematics Teaching in the Middle School* 8, no.1 (2002): 24–30.

Kulm, Gerald. *Mathematics Assessment: What Works in the Classroom*. Washington, DC: MAA, 1994.

Mathematics Assessment Resource Center. http://www.nott.ac.uk/education/MARS/

Office of Educational Research and Improvement (OERI). *Facilitating Systemic Change in Mathematics and Science Education: A Toolkit for Professional Developers*. North Central Regional Educational Laboratory. U.S. Department of Education, 2001.

———. *Improving Classroom Assessment: A Toolkit for Professional Developers*. North Central Regional Educational Laboratory. U.S. Department of Education, 2001.

Parke, Carol S. *Using Assessment to Improve Middle-Grades Mathematics Teaching and Learning Suggested Activities Using QUASAR Tasks, Scoring Criteria, and Students' Work*. Reston, VA: NCTM, 2003.

Principles and Standards for School Mathematics. Reston, VA: National Council of Teachers of Mathematics, 2000.

Rubrics: North Central Regional Educational Laboratory (1998). http://www.ncrel.org/sdrs/areas/issues/methods/instrctn/in51k59.htm

Silver, Edward, and Patricia Kenny. *Results from the Seventh Mathematics Assessment of the National Assessment for Educational Progress*. Reston, VA: NCTM, 2000.

"Students Generating Test Items: A Teaching and Assessment Strategy." *Mathematics Teacher* (Mar. 1998): 198–202.

"Student Portfolios in Mathematics." *Mathematics Teacher* (Apr. 1998): 318–325.

"Student Self-Assessment and Self-Evaluation." *Mathematics Teacher* (Oct. 1996): 548–554.

Thompson, Denisse R., and Sharon L. Senk. "Implementing the *Assessment Standards for School Mathematics:* Using Rubrics in High School Mathematics Courses." *Mathematics Teacher* 91 (Dec. 1998): 786–793.

Webb, Norman, ed. *Assessment in the Mathematics Classroom—1993 Yearbook*. Reston, VA: National Council of Mathematics, 1993.

Chapter 7

Suggested Readings

Babbage, Charles. *On the Principles and Development of the Calculator*. P. Morrison and E. Morrison, eds. New York: Dover 1961.

Berggren, L., J. Borwein, and P. Borwein. *Pi: A Source Book*. New York: Springer 1997.

Billings, K., and D. Moursand. *Problem Solving with Calculators*. Salem, OR: Math Learning Center, University of Oregon, 1978.

Bitter, G. G., and J. L. Mikesell. *Activities Handbook for Teaching with the Hand-Held Calculator*. Boston: Allyn and Bacon, 1980.

Bolt, B. *Mathematics Meets Technology*. New York: Cambridge University Press, 1991.

Bramble, W. J., and E. Mason. *Computers in Schools*. McGraw-Hill, 1985.

Chin, W. G., R. A. Dean, and T. N. Tracewell. *Arithmetic and Calculators*. San Francisco: W. H. Freeman, 1978.

Chrystal, G. *Algebra and Elementary Textbook*, 2 vols. New York: Chelsea, 1964.

Coburn, T. G. *How to Teach Mathematics Using a Calculator*. Reston, VA: NCTM, 1987.

Coburn, T. C., et al. *Practical Guide to Computers in Education*. Menlo Park, CA: Addison-Wesley, 1982.

Collis, B. *Computers, Curriculum, and Whole Class Instruction*. Belmont, CA: Wadsworth, 1988.

Court, N. A. *College Geometry*. New York: Barnes & Noble, 1952.

Coxeter, H. S. M. *Introduction to New Geometry*. New York: Wiley, 1969.

Day, R. P. "Solution Revolution." *Mathematics Teacher* 86, no. 1 (Jan. 1993): 15–22.

Devlin, Keith. *All the Math That's Fit to Print*. Washington, DC: Mathematical Association of America, 1994.

Dolan, D., ed. *Mathematics Teacher Resource Handbook: A Practical Guide for K–12 Mathematics Curriculum*. Millwood, NY: Kraus International Publications, 1993.

Dudley, Underwood. *A Budget of Trisections*. New York: Springer, 1987.

Easterday, K. E., L. L. Henry, and F. M. Simpson. *Activities for Junior High School and Middle School Mathematics*. Reston, VA: NCTM, 1981.

Eastaway, R., and J. Wyndham. *Why Do Buses Come in Three's? The Hidden Mathematics of Everyday Life*. New York: John Wiley, 1998.

Elgarten, G., and A. S. Posamentier. *Using Computers: Programming and Problem Solving*. Menlo Park, CA: Addison-Wesley, 1984.

Elgarten, G., A. S. Posamentier, and S. Moresh. *Using Computers in Mathematics*, 2nd ed. Menlo Park, CA: Addison-Wesley, 1986.

Farrell, M. A. *Imaginative Ideas for the Teacher of Mathematics, Grades K–12*. Reston, VA: NCTM, 1988.

Farrell, M. A., ed. *Imaginative Ideas for the Teacher of Mathematics, Grades K–12. Ranucci's Reservoir*. Reston, VA: NCTM, 1988.

Fleron, Julian F. "Quotations for Every Mathematics Class." *Mathematics Teacher* 91 (1998): 548–553.

Foletta, Gina M., and David B. Leep. "Isoperimetric Quadrilaterals: Mathematical Reasoning with Technology." *Mathematics Teacher* 93 (2000): 144–147.

French, Francis G. "The Divisibility of $x^n - y^n$ by $x - y$: A Constructive Example." *Mathematics Teacher* 91 (1998): 342–345.

Gleick, James. *Chaos, Making a New Science*. Viking Press, 1987.

Glidden, Peter L. "Beyond the Golden Ratio: A Calculator-Based Investigation." *Mathematics Teacher* 94 (2001): 138–144.

Gorini, Catherine A., ed. *Geometry at Work: A Collection of Papers Showing Applications of Geometry*. Washington, DC: Mathematical Association of America, 2000.

Hall, H. S., and S. R. Knight. *Higher Algebra*. London: Macmillan, 1960.

Ippolito, Dennis. "The Mathematics of the Spirograph." *Mathematics Teacher* 92 (1999): 354–357.

Kastner, B. *Space Mathematics: A Resource for Secondary School Teachers*. Washington, DC: NASA, 1985.

Kenelly, J. W. *The Use of Calculators in the Standardized Testing of Mathematics*. New York: College Entrance Examination Board, 1989.

Kieren, T. E. "Computer Programming for the Mathematics Laboratory." *Mathematics Teacher* 66 (1973): 9.

Klein M. F. "Mathematics as Current Events." *Mathematics Teacher* 86, no. 2 (Feb. 1993).

Lockwood, E. H. *A Book of Curves*. London: Cambridge University Press, 1971.

Loomis, E. S. *The Pythagorean Proposition*. Reston, VA: NCTM, 1968.

Maor, Eli. "The Pocket Calculator as a Teaching Aid." *Mathematics Teacher* 69 (1976): 471.

Markowsky, George. "Misconceptions About the Golden Ratio." *The College Mathematics Journal* 23 (Jan. 1992): 2–19.

Martin, George E. *Geometric Constructions*. New York: Springer, 1998.

Mathematics Enrichment Program Grades 3–12. Richmond, VA: Department of Mathematics, 1986.

Mathematics Teacher 71 (May 1978). Special Issue: Computers and Calculators.

Mathematics Teacher 74 (Nov. 1981). Special Issue: Microcomputers.

Morgan, Frank. *The Math Chat Book*. Washington, DC: Mathematical Association of America, 2000.

Mottershead, L. *A Source Book of Mathematical Discovery*. Palo Alto, CA: Dale Seymour Publications, 1977.

National Aeronautics and Space Administration. *Space Mathematics, A Resource for Teachers*. Washington, DC: NASA, 1972.

National Council of Teachers of Mathematics. *Calculators: Readings from Arithmetic and Mathematics Teacher* Bruce C. Burt. Reston, VA: NCTM, 1979.

———. *Enrichment Mathematics for the Grades*. Twenty-seventh Yearbook, 1963.

———. *Enrichment Mathematics for High School*. Twenty-eighth Yearbook, 1963.

———. *Topics in Mathematics for Elementary School Teachers*. Twenty-ninth Yearbook, 1964.

———. *Historical Topics for the Mathematics Classroom*. Thirty-first Yearbook, 1969.

———. *Geometry in the Mathematics Curriculum*. Thirty-sixth Yearbook, 1973.

———. *Applications in School Mathematics*. 1979 Yearbook.

———. *Problem Solving in School Mathematics*. 1980 Yearbook.

———. *Teaching Statistics and Probability*. 1981 Yearbook.

———. *Computers in Mathematics Education*. 1984 Yearbook.

———. *Secondary School Mathematics Curriculum*. 1985 Yearbook.

———. *Estimation and Mental Computation*. 1986 Yearbook.

———. *Learning and Teaching Geometry, K–12*. 1987 Yearbook.

———. *The Ideas of Algebra, K–12*. 1988 Yearbook.

———. *Calculators in Mathematics Education*. 1992 Yearbook.

———. *Connecting Mathematics Across the Curriculum*. 1995 Yearbook.

———. *Communication in Mathematics, K–12 and Beyond*. 1996 Yearbook.

———. *Developing Mathematical Reasoning in Grades K–12*. 1999 Yearbook.

Nord, G., D. Jabon, and John Nord. "The Mathematics of the Global Positioning System." *Mathematics Teacher* 90 (1997): 455–460.

Olson, Alton T. *Mathematics Through Paper Folding*. Reston, VA: NCTM, 1975.

Paulos, John Allen. *A Mathematician Reads the Newspaper*. New York: Basic Books, 1995.

Peterson, Ivars. *The Mathematical Tourist: Snapshots of Modern Mathematics*. New York: W. H. Freeman, 1988.

Posamentier, A. S. *Advanced Euclidian Geometry: Excursions for Secondary Teachers and Students*. New York, NY: John Wiley Publishing, 2002.

———. *Making Algebra Come Alive*. Thousand Oaks, CA: Corwin, 2000.

———. *Making Geometry Come Alive*. Thousand Oaks, CA: Corwin, 2000.

———. *Making Pre-Algebra Come Alive*. Thousand Oaks, CA: Corwin, 2000.

Posamentier, A. S., and H. Hauptman. *101 Plus Great Ideas for Introducing Key Concepts in Mathematics: A Resource for Secondary School Teachers*. Thousand Oaks, CA: Corwin, 2006.

Posamentier, A. S., and Noam Gordon. "An Astounding Revelation on the History of π." *Mathematics Teacher* 77 (1984): 52.

Posamentier, Alfred S., and Ingmar Lehman. "π A Biography of the World's Most Mysterious Number." Amherst, NY: Prometheus Books, 2004.

Posamentier, A. S., and S. Krulik. *Problem Solving Strategies for Efficient and Elegant Solutions: A Resource for the Mathematics Teacher*. Thousand Oaks, CA: Corwin Press, 2nd ed., 2008.

Posamentier, Alfred S., and Ingmar Lehmann. *The Fabulous Fibaconni Numbers*. Amherst, NY: Prometheus Books, 2007

Posamentier, A. S., and W. Schulz. *The Art of Problem Solving: A Resource for the Mathematics Teacher*. Thousand Oaks, CA: Corwin Press, 1996.

Posamentier, A. S., and W. Wernick. *Advanced Geometric Constructions*. Menlo Park, CA: Dale Seymour Publications, 1988.

Row, T. Sundara. *Geometric Exercises in Paper Folding*. New York: Dover, 1966.

Runion, G. E. *The Golden Section and Related Curiosa*. Glenview, IL: Scott Foresman, 1972.

Salem, L., F. Testard, and C. Salem. *The Most Beautiful Mathematical Formulas*. New York: Wiley, 1992.

Schaaf, W. L. *A Bibliography of Recreational Mathematics*, Vols. 1–4. Washington, DC: [National Council of Teachers of Mathematics], 1970, 1973, 1978.

Schimmel, Judith. "A New Spin on Volumes of Solid of Revolution." *Mathematics Teacher* 90 (1997): 715–717.

Sloyer, C. *Fan-Tas-Tiks of Mathematiks*. Providence, RI: Janson Publications, 1986.

Sobel, M. A., and E. M. Maletsky. *Teaching Mathematics: A Source Book of Aids, Activities and Strategies*. Englewood Cliffs, NJ: Prentice Hall, 1988.

Suydam, M. N. *Using Calculators in Pre-College Ed.: Third State-of-Art Review*. Columbus, OH: Calculator Information Center, 1980.

Troputman, A. P., and J. A. White. *The Micro Goes to School*. Pacific Grove, CA: Brooks/Cole, 1988.

Turner, S., and M. Land. *Tools for Schools*. Belmont, CA: Wadsworth, 1988.

Williams, D. E. "One Point of View: Remember the Calculator?" *Arithmetic Teacher* 30 (March 1983): 4.

Woo, Peter Y. "Straightedge Constructions, Given a Parabola." *The College Mathematics Journal* 31 (2000): 362–372.

Worth, J. "Let's Bring Calculators Out of the Closet." *Elements: A Journal for Elementary Educators* 17 (1985): 18–21.

Bibliography for the History of Mathematics

Aaboe, Asger. *Episodes from the Early History of Mathematics*. New York: Random House, 1964.

Babbage, Charles. *On the Principles and Development of the Calculator*. P. Morrison and E. Morrison, eds. New York: Dover, 1961.

Ball, W. W. Rouse. *A Short Account of the History of Mathematics*, 4th ed. New York: Dover, 1960.

Beckmann, Petr. *A History of Pi*. New York: St. Martin's Press, 1971.

Bell, Eric Temple. *Men of Mathematics*, 6th paperback ed. New York: Simon & Schuster, 1937.

———. *Mathematics: Queen and Servant of Science*. Washington, DC: Mathematical Association of America, 1987.

Boyer, Carl B. *The History of the Calculus and Its Conceptual Development*. New York: Dover, 1959.

———. *A History of Mathematics*. New York: Wiley, 1968.

Bunt, Lucas N. H., Philip S. Jones, and Jack D. Bedient. *The Historical Roots of Elementary Mathematics*. Englewood Cliffs, NJ: Prentice Hall, 1976.

Burton, David M. *The History of Mathematics, An Introduction.* Boston, MA: Allyn and Bacon, 1985.

Cajori, Florian. *A History of Mathematical Notations.* 2 vols. LaSalle, IL: Open Court, 1928.

———. *A History of Mathematics.* New York: Chelsea, 1985.

Campbell, Douglas M., and John C. Higgins, eds. *Mathematics: People, Problems, Results.* 3 vols. Belmont, CA: Wadsworth, 1984.

Cardano, Girolamo. *Ars Magna, or the Rules of Algebra.* Translated by T. R. Witmer. New York: Dover, 1993.

Eves, Howard W. *In Mathematical Circles.* 2 vols. Boston, MA: Prindle, Weber, Schmidt, 1969.

———. *Mathematical Circles Revisited.* Boston, MA: Prindle, Weber, Schmidt, 1971.

———. *Great Moments in Mathematics Before 1650.* Washington, DC: Mathematical Association of America, 1980.

———. *Great Moments in Mathematics After 1650.* Washington, DC: Mathematical Association of America, 1981.

———. *An Introduction to the History of Mathematics*, 5th ed. New York: W. B Saunders College Publishing, 1983.

Fauvel, J., and J. Gray, eds. *A History of Mathematics: A Reader.* Milton Keynes, UK: Open University, 1987.

Gittleman, Arthur. *History of Mathematics.* Columbus, OH: Charles E. Merrill, 1975.

Gray, Shirley B., and C. Edward Sandifer. "The Sumario Compendioso: The New World's First Mathematics Book." *Mathematics Teacher* 94 (2001): 98–103.

Heath, Thomas. *History of Greek Mathematics.* 2 vols. New York: Dover, 1981.

Herz-Fischler, Roger. *A Mathematical History of the Golden Number.* New York: Dover, 1998.

Hoffmann, Joseph E. *The History of Mathematics to 1800.* Totowa, NJ: Littlefield, Adams & Co., 1967.

Kaplan, Robert. *The Nothing That Is: A Natural History of Zero.* New York: Oxford University Press, 1999.

Karpinski, Louis C. *The History of Arithmetic.* New York: Rand McNally, 1925.

Kelley, Loretta. "A Mathematical History Tour." *Mathematics Teacher* 93 (2000): 14–17.

Martzloff, Jean-Claude. *A History of Chinese Mathematics.* New York: Springer, 1997.

Mathematics Teacher 98 (Nov. 2000) entire issue.

National Council of Teachers of Mathematics. *Historical Topics for the Mathematical Classroom.* Thirty-first Yearbook. Reston, VA: NCTM, 1969.

Newman, James Roy, ed. *The World of Mathematics.* 4 vols. New York: Simon & Schuster, 1956; paperback, 1962.

Posamentier, A. S., and Noam Gordon. "An Astounding Revelation on the History of π." *Mathematics Teacher* 77 (1984): 52.

Posamentier, Alfred S., and Ingmar Lehman. "π A Biography of the World's Most Mysterious Number." Amherst, NY: Prometheus Books, 2004.

Posamentier, Alfred S., and Ingmar Lehmann. *The Fabulous Fibacconi Numbers.* Amherst, NY: Prometheus Books, 2007.

Perl, Teri. *Math Equals: Biographies of Women Mathematicians and Related Activities.* Menlo Park, CA: Addison-Wesley, 1978.

Sanford, Vera. *A Short History of Mathematics.* Boston: Houghton Mifflin, 1958.

Smith, David E. *History of Mathematics.* 2 vols. New York: Dover, 1953.

Struik, Dirk J. *A Concise History of Mathematics*, 3rd ed. New York: Dover, 1967.

Turnbull, Herbert W. *The Great Mathematicians.* New York: New York University Press, 1961.

van der Waerden, B. L. *Science Awakening.* New York: Wiley, 1963.

New Mathematics Library

Mathematical Association of America, New Mathematics Library, on topics designed to enrich the mathematics curriculum. These can be ordered from the Mathematical Association of America, 1529 Eighteenth Street, N.W., Washington, DC 20036. A list of the first 42 titles follows:

1. *Numbers: Rational and Irrational* by Ivan Niven.
2. *What Is Calculus About?* by W. W. Sawyer.
3. *An Introduction to Inequalities* by E. F. Beckenbach and R. Bellman.
4. *Geometric Inequalities* by N. D. Kazarinoff.
5. *The Contest Problem Book I.* Annual High School Mathematics Examinations 1950–1960. Compiled and with solutions by Charles T. Salkind.
6. *The Lore of Large Numbers* by P. J. Davis.
7. *Uses of Infinity* by Leo Zippin.
8. *Geometric Transformations I* by I. M. Yaglom, translated by A. Shields.
9. *Continued Fractions* by Carl D. Olds.
10. *Graphs and Their Uses* by Oystein Ore.
11. *Hungarian Problem Books I and II.* Based on the Eötvös.
12. Competitions 1894–1905 and 1906–1928, translated by E. Rapaport.
13. *Episodes from the Early History of Mathematics* by A. Aaboe.
14. *Groups and Their Graphs* by I. Grossman and W. Magnus.
15. *The Mathematics of Choice* by Ivan Niven.
16. *From Pythagoras to Einstein* by K. O. Friedrichs.
17. *The Contest Problems Book II.* Annual High School Mathematics Examinations 1961–1965. Compiled and with solutions by Charles T. Salkind.
18. *First Concepts of Topology* by W. G. Chinn and N. E. Steenrod.
19. *Geometry Revisited* by H. S. M. Coxeter and S. L. Greitzer.

20. *Invitation to Number Theory* by Oystein Ore.
21. *Geometric Transformations II* by I. M. Yaglom, translated by A. Shields.
22. *Elementary Cryptanalysis: A Mathematical Approach* by A. Sinkov.
23. *Ingenuity in Mathematics* by Ross Honsberger.
24. *Geometric Transformations III* by I. M. Yaglom, translated by A. Schenitzer.
25. *The Contest Problem Book III*. Annual High School Mathematics Examinations 1966–1972. Compiled and with solutions by C. T. Salkind and J. M. Earl.
26. *Mathematical Methods in Science* by George Polya.
27. *International Mathematical Olympiads 1959–1977*. Compiled and with solutions by S. L. Greitzer.
28. *The Mathematics of Games and Gambling* by Edward W. Packel.
29. *The Contest Problem Book IV*. Annual High School Mathematics Examinations 1973–1982. Compiled and with solutions by R. A. Artino, A. M. Gaglione, and N. Shell.
30. *The Role of Mathematics in Science* by M. M. Schiffer and L. Bowden.
31. *International Mathematical Olympiads 1979–1985*. Compiled and with solutions by Murray S. Klamkin.
32. *Riddles of the Sphinx* by Martin Gardner.
33. *USA Math Olympiads 1972–1986* by Murray S. Klamkin.
34. *Graphs and Their Uses* by Oystein Ore.
35. *Exploring Math with Your Computer* by Arthur Engel.
36. *Game Theory and Strategy* by Philip Straffin.
37. *Episodes in Nineteenth and Twentieth Century Euclidean Geometry* by Ross Honsberger.
38. *The Contest Problem Book V*. American High School Mathematics Examinations and American Invitational Mathematics Examinations 1983–1988. Compiled and augmented by George Berzsenyi and Stephen B. Maurer.
39. *Over and Over Again* by Gengzhe Chang and Thomas W. Sederberg.
40. *The Contest Problem Book VI*. American High School Mathematics Examinations 1989–1994. Compiled and augmented by Leo J. Schneider.
41. The Geometry of Numbers by C. D. Olds, Anneli Lax, and Giuliana Davidoff.
42. *Hungarian Problem Book III*. Based on the Eötvös. Competitions 1929–1943, translated by Andy Liu.

Other titles in preparation.
There are many additional ideas in the Enrichment Units in the second part of this book.

Chapter 8

Suggested Readings

Altshiller-Court, Nathan A. *College Geometry*. New York: Barnes & Noble, 1952.

Barnett, I. A. *Elements of Number Theory*. Boston: Prindle, Weber & Schmidt, 1972.

Berggren, L., J. Borwein, and P. Borwein. *Pi: A Source Book*. New York: Springer, 1997.

Bruckheimer, Maxim, and Rina Hirshkowitz. "Mathematics Projects in Junior High School." *Mathematics Teacher* 70 (1977): 573.

Chrystal, G. *Textbook of Algebra*. 2 vols. New York: Chelsea, 1964.

Courant, Richard, and Herbert Robbins. *What Is Mathematics?* New York: Oxford University Press, 1941.

Coxeter, H. S. M., and S. L. Greitzer. *Geometry Revisited*. New York: Random House, 1967.

Davis, David R. *Modern College Geometry*. Reading, MA: Addison-Wesley, 1949.

Dudley, Underwood. *A Budget of Trisections*. New York: Springer, 1987.

Elgarten, Gerald H. "A Mathematics Intramurals Contest." *Mathematics Teacher* 69 (1976): 477.

Farmer, David W., and Theodore B. Sanford. *Knots and Surfaces: A Guide to Discovering Mathematics*. Providence, RI: American Mathematical Society, 1996.

Gorini, Catherine A., ed. *Geometry at Work: A Collection of Papers Showing Applications of Geometry*. Washington, DC: Mathematical Association of America, 2000.

Hall, H. S., and S. R. Knight. *Higher Algebra*. London: Macmillan, 1960.

Holmes, Joseph E. "Enrichment or Acceleration?" *Mathematics Teacher* 63 (1970): 471.

House, Peggy A. *Interactions of Science and Mathematics*. Columbus, OH: ERIC Clearing House for Science, Mathematics, and Enviromental Education, 1980.

Ippolito, Dennis. "The Mathematics of the Spirograph." *Mathematics Teacher* 92 (1999): 354–357.

James, Robert C., and Glenn James, eds. *Mathematics Dictionary*, 4th ed. New York: Van Nostrand Reinhold, 1976.

Johnson, Roger A. *Modern Geometry*. Boston: Houghton Mifflin, 1929.

Jones, Mary H. "Mathcounts: A New Junior High School Mathematics Competition." *Mathematics Teacher* 76 (1983): 482.

Karush, William. *The Crescent Dictionary of Mathematics*. New York: Macmillan, 1962.

Leonard, William A. *No Upper Limit; The Challenge of the Teacher of Secondary Mathematics*. Fresno, CA: Creative Teaching Assoc., 1977.

Lichtenberg, Betty K. "Some Excellent Sources of Material for Mathematics Clubs." *Mathematics Teacher* 74 (1981): 284.

Martin, George E. *Geometric Constructions*. New York: Springer, 1998.

Morgan, F., E. R. Melnick, and R. Nicholson. "The Soap-Bubble-Geometry Contest." *Mathematics Teacher* 90 (1997): 746–750.

Morgan, Frank. *The Math Chat Book*. Washington, DC: Mathematical Association of America, 2000.

Newman, James R. *The World of Mathematics*. 4 vols. New York: Simon & Schuster, 1956.

Olds, C. D. *Continued Fractions*. New York: Random House, 1963.

Posamentier, Alfred S. *Advanced Euclidean Geometry: Excursions for Secondary Students and Teachers*. New York, NY: John Wiley Publishing, 2002.

———. *Making Algebra Come Alive*. Thousand Oaks, CA: Corwin, 2000.

———. *Making Geometry Come Alive*. Thousand Oaks, CA: Corwin, 2000.

———. *Making Pre-Algebra Come Alive*. Thousand Oaks, CA: Corwin, 2000.

———. "Math Wonders." Alexandria, Virginia: ASCD, 2003.

Sadovskii, L. E. and A. L. Sadovskii. Translated by S. Makar-Limanov. *Mathematics and Sports*. Providence, RI: American Mathematical Society, 1996.

Schaaf, William L., ed., *A Bibliography of Recreational Mathematics*. 4 vols. Washington, DC: National Council of Teachers of Mathematics, 1978.

Smith, David E., ed. *Source Book in Mathematics*. New York: McGraw-Hill, 1929.

Wright, Frank. "Motivating Students with Projects and Teaching Aids." *Mathematics Teacher* 58 (1965): 47.

Resources for Extracurricular Activities

History of Mathematics

Ball, W. W. Rouse. *A Short Account of the History of Mathematics*. New York: Dover, 1960.

Bell, E. T. *Men of Mathematics*. New York: Simon & Schuster, 1937.

———. *Mathematics, Queen and Servant of Science*. Washington, DC: Mathematical Association of America, 1979.

Boyer, Carl B. *A History of Mathematics*. New York: Wiley, 1968.

Bunt, Lucas N. H., Philip S. Jones, and Jack D. Bedient. *The Historical Roots of Elementary Mathematics*. Englewood Cliffs, NJ: Prentice Hall, 1976.

Cajori, Florian. *A History of Mathematic Notations*. 2 vols. LaSalle, IL: Open Court, 1928.

Campbell, Douglas M., and John C. Higgins, eds. *Mathematics: People, Problems, Results*. Belmont, CA: Wadsworth, 1984.

Eves, Howard. *An Introduction to the History of Mathematics*, 4th ed. New York: Holt, Rinehart & Winston, 1976.

Gray, Shirley B., and C. Edward Sandifer. "The Sumario Compendioso: The New World's First Mathematics Book." *Mathematics Teacher* 94 (2001): 98–103.

Hamburger, Peter, and Raymond E. Pippert. "Venn Said It Couldn't Be Done." *Mathematics Magazine* 73 (2000): 105–110.

Heath, Thomas L. *Greek Mathematics*. New York: Dover, 1963.

Kaplan, Robert. *The Nothing That Is: A Natural History of Zero*. New York: Oxford University Press, 1999.

Kelley, Loretta. "A Mathematical History Tour." *Mathematics Teacher* 93 (2000): 14–17.

Mathematics Teacher 98 (November 2000) entire issue.

Norwood, Rick. "A Star to Guide Us." *Mathematics Teacher* 92 (1999): 100–101.

Posamentier, Alfred S., and Noam Gordon. "An Astounding Revelation on the History of π." *Mathematics Teacher* 77 (1984): 52.

Posamentier, Alfred S., and Ingmar Lehman. "π A Biography of the World's Most Mysterious Number." Amherst, NY: Prometheus Books, 2004.

Resnikoff, H. L., and R. O. Wells, Jr. *Mathematics in Civilization*. New York: Dover, 1984.

Smith, David E. *A Source Book in Mathematics*. New York: McGraw-Hill, 1929.

———. *History of Mathematics*. 2 vols. New York: Dover, 1953.

van der Waerden, B. L. *Science Awakening*. New York: Wiley, 1963.

Mathematical Recreations

Ball, W. W. Rouse, and H. S. M. Coxeter. *Mathematical Recreations and Essays*. New York: Macmillan, 1960.

Barbeau, Edward J. *Mathematical Fallacies, Flaws, and Flimflam*. Washington, DC: Mathematical Association of America, 2000.

Bay, J. M., R. E. Reys, K. Simms, and P. M. Taylor. "Bingo Games: Turning Student Intuitions into Investigations in Probability and Number Sense." *Mathematics Teacher* 93 (2000): 200–206.

Beasley, John D. *The Mathematics of Games*. New York: Oxford University Press, 1989.

Benson, William, and Oswald Jacoby. *New Recreations with Magic Squares*. New York: Dover, 1976.

Caldwell, J. H. *Topics in Recreational Mathematics*. London: Cambridge University Press, 1966.

Cipra, Barry. *Misteaks ... and How to Find Them Before the Teacher Does*. San Diego, CA: Academic Press, 1989.

Cundy, H. Martyn, and A. P. Rollett. *Mathematical Models*. New York: Oxford University Press, 1961.

Gardner, Martin. *New Mathematical Diversions*. Washington, DC: Mathematical Association of America, 1995.

Honsberger, Ross. *Mathematical Morsels*. Washington, DC: Mathematics Association of America, 1978.

Kahan, Steven. *Take a Look at a Good Book: The Third Collection of Additive Alphametics for the Connoisseur*. Amityville, NY: Baywood Publ. Co., 1996.

Kraitchik, Maurice. *Mathematical Recreations*. New York: Dover, 1942.

Madachy, Joseph. *Mathematics on Vacation*. New York: Charles Scribner's Sons, 1966.

Nelsen, Roger B. *Proofs Without Words II: More Exercises in Visual Thinking*. Washington, DC: Mathematical Association of America, 2000.

Northrop, Eugene. *Riddles in Mathematics*. Princeton, NJ: Nostrand, 1944.

Ogilvy, C. Stanley. *Through the Mathescope*. New York: Oxford University Press, 1956.

Posamentier, Alfred S. *Advanced Euclidean Geometry: Excursions for Secondary Teachers and Students*. New York, NY: John Wiley Publishing, 2002.

———. *Advanced Geometric Constructions*. White Plains, NY: Dale Seymour Publications, 1988.

———. *Making Algebra Come Alive*. Thousand Oaks, CA: Corwin, 2000.

———. *Making Geometry Come Alive*. Thousand Oaks, CA: Corwin, 2000.

———. *Making Pre-Algebra Come Alive*. Thousand Oaks, CA: Corwin, 2000.

———. "Math Wonders." Alexandria, Virginia: ASCD, 2003.

Schuh, Fred. *The Master Book of Mathematical Recreations*. New York: Dover, 1968.

Stevenson, Frederick W. *Exploratory Problems in Mathematics*. Reston, VA: National Council of Teachers of Mathematics, 1992.

Mathematics Clubs

Carnahan, Walter H., ed. *Mathematics Clubs in High Schools*. Washington, DC: National Council of Teachers of Mathematics, 1958.

Gruver, Howell L. *School Mathematics Contests: A Report*. Washington, DC: National Council of Teachers of Mathematics, 1968.

Hess, Adrien L. *Mathematics Projects Handbook*. Washington, DC: National Council of Teachers of Mathematics, 1977.

Morgan, F., E. R. Melnick, and R. Nicholson. "The Soap-Bubble-Geometry Contest." *Mathematics Teacher* 90 (1997): 746–750.

Mu Alpha Theta. *Handbook for Sponsors*. Norman, OK: University of Oklahoma, 1970.

Ransom, William R. *Thirty Projects for Mathematical Clubs and Exhibitions*. Portland, ME: J. Weston Walch, Publisher, 1961.

Teppo, Anne R., and Ted Hodgson. "Dinosaurs, Dinosaur Eggs, and Probability." *Mathematics Teacher* 94 (2001): 86–92.

Problem Solving

Andreescu, Titu, and Zuming Feng. *Mathematical Olympiads 1998–1999*. Washington, DC: Mathematical Association of America, 2000.

Artino, R. A., A. M. Gaglione, and Shell. *The Contest Problem Book IV*. Washington, DC: Mathematical Association of America, 1982.

Berzsenyi, G., and S. B. Maurer. *The Contest Problem Book V*. Washington, DC: Mathematical Association of America, 1997.

Conference Board of Mathematical Sciences. *The Role of Axiomatics and Problem Solving in Mathematics*. Boston: Ginn, 1966.

Gardiner, Tony. *Mathematical Challenge*. Cambridge, UK: Cambridge University Press, 1996.

———. *More Mathematical Challenges*. Cambridge, UK: Cambridge University Press, 1997.

Hayes, John R. *The Complete Problem Solver*, 2d ed. Hillsdale, NJ: Lawrence Erlbaum, 1989.

Holton, Derek. *Let's Solve Some Math Problems*. Waterloo, ON: Waterloo Mathematics Foundation, University of Waterloo, 1993.

Honsberger, Ross. *From Erdös to Kiev, Problems of Olympiad Caliber*. Washington, DC: Mathematical Association of America, 1996.

Hudgins, Bryce B. *Problem Solving in the Classroom*. New York: Macmillan, 1966.

Krantz, Steven G. *Techniques of Problem Solving*. Providence, RI: American Mathematical Society, 1997.

Krulik, Stephen, and Jesse A. Rudnick. *Problem Solving, A Handbook for Teachers*. Boston: Allyn and Bacon, 1980.

Polya, George. *How to Solve It*. Princeton, NJ: Princeton University Press, 1945.

———. *Mathematics and Plausible Reasoning*. 2 vols. Princeton, NJ: Princeton University Press, 1954.

———. *Mathematical Discovery*. 2 vols. New York: John Wiley, 1962.

Posamentier, Alfred S. *Students! Get Ready for the Mathematics for SAT I: Problem-Solving Strategies and Practical Tests*. Thousand Oaks, CA: Corwin Press, 1996.

Posamentier, Alfred S., and Stephen Krulik. *Problem-Solving Strategies for Efficient and Elegant Solutions: A Resource for the Mathematics Teacher*. Thousand Oaks, CA: Corwin Press, 2nd ed., 2008.

———. *Teachers! Prepare Your Students for the Mathematics for SAT I: Methods and Problem-Solving Strategies*. Thousand Oaks, CA: Corwin Press, 1996.

Posamentier, Alfred S., and Wolfgang Schulz. *The Art of Problem Solving: A Resource for the Mathematics Teacher*. Thousand Oaks, CA: Corwin Press, 1996.

Schneider, Leo J. *The Contest Problem Book VI*. Washington, DC: Mathematical Association of America, 2000.

Whimbey, Arthur, and Jack Lochhead. *Problem Solving and Comprehension, A Short Course in Analytical Reasoning*. 2d ed. Philadelphia: Franklin Institute Press, 1980.

Wickelgren, Wayne A. *How to Solve Problems*. San Francisco: W. H. Freeman, 1974.

Sources for Mathematics Team Problems

Aref, M. N., and William Wernick. *Problems and Solutions in Euclidean Geometry*. New York: Dover, 1968.

Barbeau, E., M. Klamkin, and W. Moser. *1001 Problems in High School Mathematics*. Montreal, PQ: Canadian Mathematics Congress, 1978.

———. *Five Hundred Mathematical Challenges*. Washington, DC: Mathematical Association of America, 1995.

Barry, Donald T., and J. Richard Lux. *The Philips Academy Prize Examinations in Mathematics*. Palo Alto, CA: Dale Seymour Publications, 1984.

Brousseau, Brother Alfred, ed. *Mathematics Contest Problems*. Palo Alto, CA: Creative Publications, 1972.

Bryant, Steven J., George E. Graham, and Kenneth G. Wiley. *Nonroutine Problems in Algebra, Geometry, and Trigonometry*. New York: McGraw-Hill, 1965.

Butts, Thomas. *Problem Solving in Mathematics*. Glenview, IL: Scott, Foresman, 1973.

Charosh, Mannis, ed. *Mathematical Challenges*. Washington, DC: National Council of Teachers of Mathematics, 1965.

Comprehensive School Mathematics Program. *E. M. Problem Book*. 2 vols. St. Louis: CEMREL, 1975.

Dowlen, Mary, Sandra Powers, and Hope Florence. *College of Charleston Mathematics Contest Book*. Palo Alto, CA: Dale Seymour Publications, 1987.

Dunn, Angela, ed. *Mathematical Bafflers*. New York: McGraw-Hill, 1964.

———. *Second Book of Mathematical Bafflers*. New York: Dover, 1983.

Edwards, Josephine D., Declan J. King, and Peter J. O'Halloran. *All the Best From the Australian Mathematics Competition*. Canberra, Australia: The Australian Mathematics Competition, 1986.

Engel, Arthur. *Problem-Solving Strategies*. New York: Springer, 1998.

Fisher, Lyle, and Bill Kennedy. *Brother Alfred Brousseau Problem-Solving and Mathematics Competition*. Introductory Division. Palo Alto, CA: Dale Seymour Publications, 1984.

Fisher, Lyle, and William Medigovich. *Brother Alfred Brousseau Problem-Solving and Mathematics Competition*. Palo Alto, CA: Dale Seymour Publications, 1984.

Gardiner, A. *The Mathematical Olympiad Handbook: An Introduction to Problem Solving*. New York: Oxford University Press, 1997.

Greitzer, Samuel L. *International Mathematical Olympiads*. Washington, DC: Mathematical Association of America, 1978.

Hill, Thomas J., ed. *Mathematical Challenges II—Plus Six*. Washington, DC: National Council of Teachers of Mathematics, 1974.

Honsberger, Ross. *In Polya's Footsteps; Miscellaneous Problems and Essays*. Washington, DC: Mathematical Association of America, 1997.

Polya, George, and Jeremy Kilpatrick. *The Stanford Mathematics Book*. New York: Teachers College Press, 1974.

Posamentier, Alfred S., and Charles T. Salkind. *Challenging Problems in Algebra*. New York: Dover, 1970, 1988, 1996.

———. *Challenging Problems in Geometry*. New York: Dover, 1970, 1988, 1996.

Rapaport, Elvira, trans. *Hungarian Problem Book*. 2 vols. New York: Random House, 1963.

Salkind, Charles T., ed. *The Contest Problem Book*. New York: Random House, 1961.

———. *The MAA Problem Book II*. New York: Random House, 1966.

Salkind, Charles T., and James M. Earl, eds. *The MAA Problem Book III*. New York: Random House, 1973.

Saul, Mark E., G. W. Kessler, Sheila Krilov, and Lawrence Zimmerman. *The New York City Contest Problem Book*. Palo Alto, CA: Dale Seymour Publications, 1986.

Shklarsky, D. O., N. N. Chentzov, and I. M. Yaglom. *The U.S.S.R. Olympiad Problem Book*. San Francisco: W. H. Freeman, 1962.

Sitomer, Harry. *The New Mathlete Problem Book*. Nassau County, NY: Interscholastic Mathematics League, 1974.

Steinhaus, Hugo. *One Hundred Problems in Elementary Mathematics*. New York: Pergamon Press, 1963.

Straszewicz, S. *Mathematical Problems and Puzzles from the Polish Mathematical Olympiads*. New York: Pergamon Press, 1965.

Trigg, Charles W. *Mathematical Quickies*. New York: McGraw-Hill, 1967.

Index